THAILAND
HANDBOOK

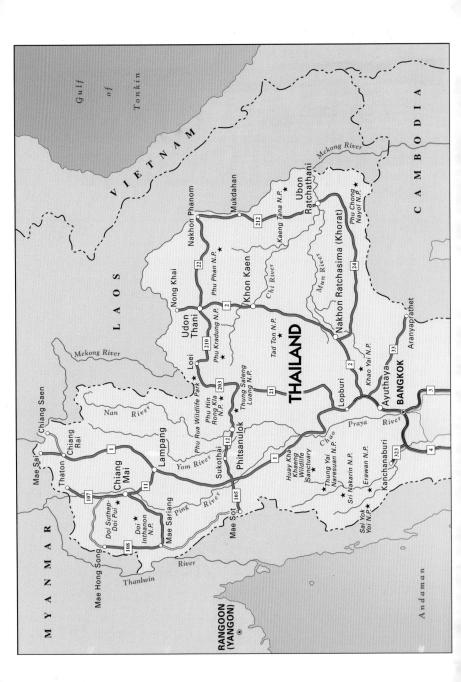

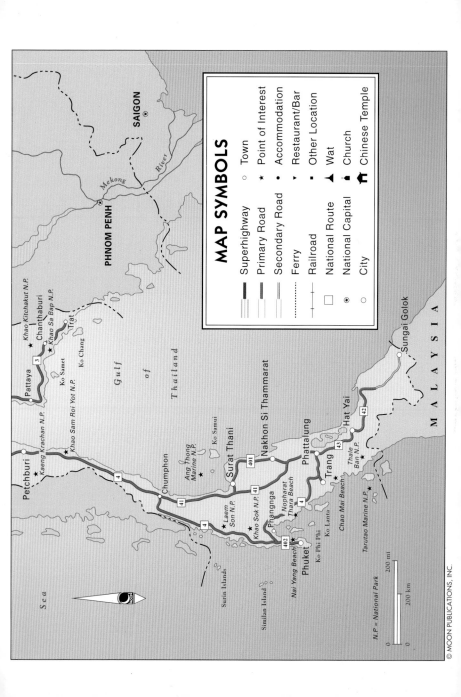

MAP SYMBOLS

Superhighway | ○ Town
Primary Road | ★ Point of Interest
Secondary Road | • Accommodation
Ferry | ▼ Restaurant/Bar
Railroad | ■ Other Location
National Route | ◢ Wat
⊛ National Capital | ♠ Church
○ City | ⌘ Chinese Temple

SAIGON ⊛

Mekong River

PHNOM PENH ⊛

Khao Kitchakut N.P.
Chanthaburi ★
Khao Sa Bap N.P.
Trat
Pattaya
Khao Sam Roi Yot N.P.
Ko Samet
Ko Chang
Petchburi
Kaeng Krachan N.P.

Gulf
of
Thailand

Chumphon
Ang Thong Marine N.P.
Ko Samui
Laem Son N.P.
Khao Sok N.P.
Surat Thani
Nakhon Si Thammarat
Phangnga
Nopharat Thara Beach
Phattalung
Ko Phi Phi
Ko Lanta
Trang
Chao Mai Beach
Hat Yai
Thale Ban N.P.
Nai Yang Beach
Phuket
Tarutao Marine N.P.
Sungai Golok

Surin Islands
Similan Island

Sea

MALAYSIA

N.P. = National Park

0   200 mi
0   200 km

© MOON PUBLICATIONS, INC.

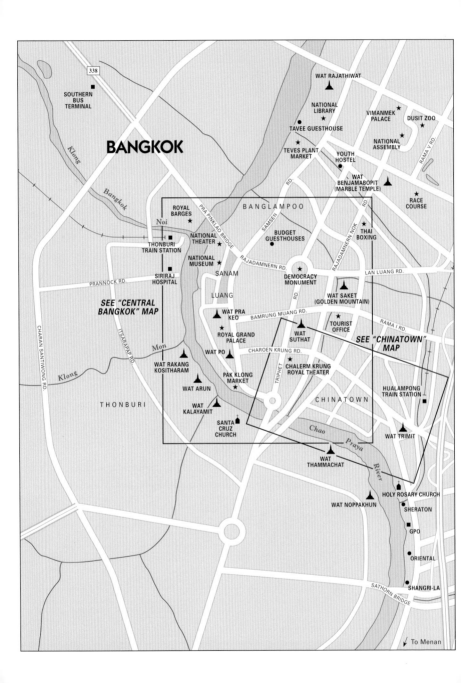

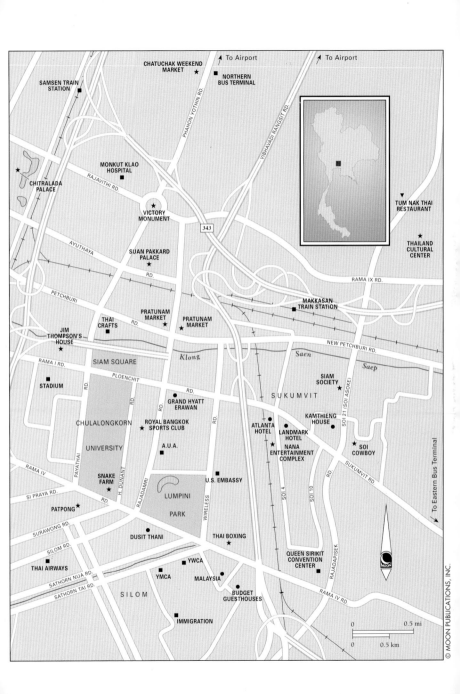

To Airport

To Airport

CHATUCHAK WEEKEND
MARKET

NORTHERN
BUS TERMINAL

SAMSEN TRAIN
STATION

PHAHON YOTHIN RD.

VIBHAVADI RANGSIT RD.

TUM NAK THAI
RESTAURANT

CHITRALADA
PALACE

MONKUT KLAO
HOSPITAL

RAJAVITHI RD.

VICTORY
MONUMENT

343

THAILAND
CULTURAL
CENTER

AYUTHAYA

SUAN PAKKARD
PALACE

RD.

RAMA IX RD.

PETCHBURI

PRATUNAM
MARKET

RD.

PRATUNAM
MARKET

MAKKASAN
TRAIN STATION

THAI
CRAFTS

NEW PETCHBURI RD.

JIM
THOMPSON'S
HOUSE

Klong

Saen

Saep

RAMA I RD.

SIAM SQUARE

PLOENCHIT

SIAM
SOCIETY

STADIUM

RD.

RD.

RD.

GRAND HYATT
ERAWAN

SUKUMVIT

CHULALONGKORN

ROYAL BANGKOK
SPORTS CLUB

ATLANTA
HOTEL

KAMTHIENG
HOUSE

SOI 21 (SOI ASOKE)

UNIVERSITY

A.U.A.

LANDMARK
HOTEL

NANA
ENTERTAINMENT
COMPLEX

SOI
COWBOY

PAYATHAI

RAMA IV

SNAKE
FARM

H. DUNANT

RAJADAMRI

U.S. EMBASSY

SUKUMVIT RD.

SI PRAYA RD.

RD.

LUMPINI

SOI 4

SOI 10

RD.

PATPONG

WIRELESS

PARK

SURAWONG RD.

DUSIT THANI

THAI BOXING

QUEEN SIRIKIT
CONVENTION
CENTER

RAJADAPISEK

SILOM RD.

YWCA

THAI AIRWAYS

SATHORN NUA RD.

YMCA

MALAYSIA

SATHORN TAI RD.

SILOM

BUDGET
GUESTHOUSES

RAMA IV RD.

IMMIGRATION

0   0.5 mi

0   0.5 km

To Eastern Bus Terminal

MOON

© MOON PUBLICATIONS, INC.

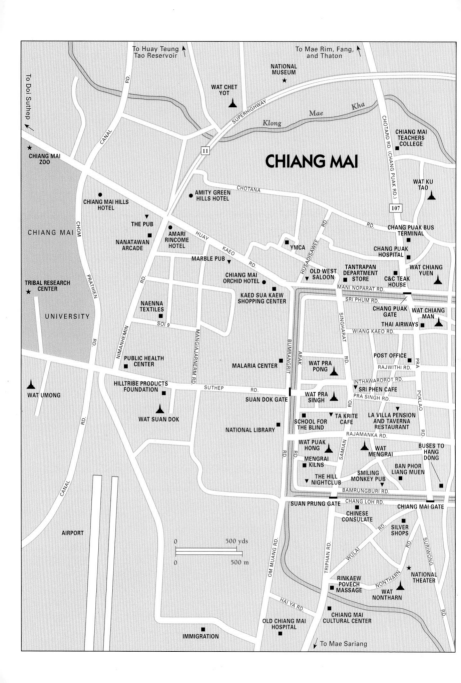

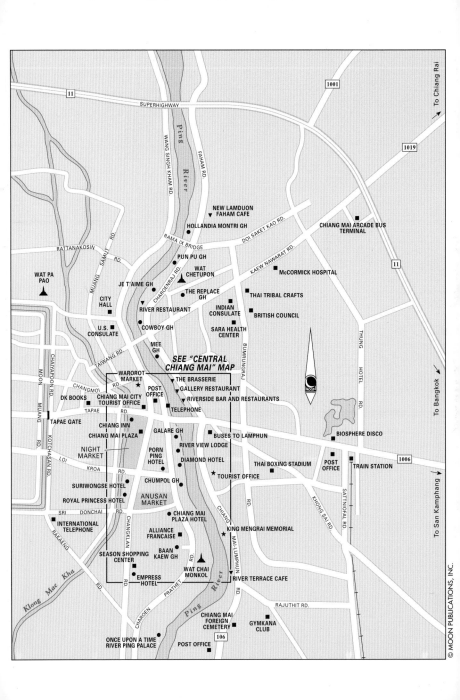

THAILAND
HANDBOOK

THIRD EDITION

CARL PARKES

MOON
TRAVEL
HANDBOOKS

THAILAND HANDBOOK
THIRD EDITION

Published by
Avalon Travel Publishing
5855 Beaudry St.
Emeryville, CA 94608, USA

Printed by
Colorcraft Ltd.

ISBN: 1-56691-173-7
ISSN: 1085-2638

Editors: Gina Wilson Birtcil, Elizabeth Larson, Jeannie Trizzino
Production & Design: Karen McKinley, David Hurst
Cartography: Brian Bardwell, Allen Leech, Mike Morgenfeld
Index: Gina Wilson Birtcil

Front cover photo: Lisu traditional headdress. © Image Bank, Pete Turner Inc.
Front cover photo background image courtesy SuperStock, Inc.

All photos by Carl Parkes unless otherwise noted.
All illustrations by Bob Race unless otherwise noted.

Distributed in the United States and Canada by Publishers Group West

Printed in China

Please send all comments,
corrections, additions,
amendments, and critiques to:

**THAILAND HANDBOOK
MOON TRAVEL HANDBOOKS
5855 Beaudry Street
Emeryville, CA 94608, USA
e-mail: travel@moon.com
www.moon.com**

Printing History
1st edition—1992
3rd edition—January 2000
5 4 3 2 1 0

Dedicated to Joe Biz,
the people of Thailand,
and all my friends in San Francisco

CONTENTS

BANGKOK . . . . 195~294

ABBREVIATIONS

a/c—air-conditioned
ASEAN—Association of Southeast Asian Nations
B—*baht*
B.E.—Buddhist Era
BCP—Myanmar Communist Party
BKS—Borisat Khon Song or Bor Kor Sor (bus company in Thailand)
d—double occupancy
GH—guesthouse
GPO—General Post Office
Hwy.—Highway
km—kilometer
KMT—Kuomintang National Army
KNU—Karen National Union
kph—kilometers per hour
NAUI—National Association of Underwater Instructors
PADI—Professional Association of Dive Instructors
pp—per person
s—single occupancy
TAT—Tourist Authority of Thailand

MAP SYMBOLS

- — — — INTERNATIONAL BORDER
- ·· —— ·· — PROVINCE BORDER
- —————— MAIN ROAD
- ———— OTHER ROAD
- — — — CART PATH, ROUGH ROAD (MAY BE PAVED IN PART)
- · — · — · PATH, TRAIL
- — ⊐⊏ — BORDER CROSSING
- BOAT ROUTE, FERRY ROUTE
- +++++++ RAILROAD
- ———— BRIDGE

- ★ RUINS. ATTRACTIONS
- ● ACCOMMODATIONS
- ■ SIGHT, POINT OF NOTE
- ○ CITY
- ○ TOWN, VILLAGE
- ▲ MOUNTAIN
- ② NUMBERED ROAD
- ✈ INTERNATIONAL AIRPORT
- ✈ SMALL AIRPORT, AIRSTRIP

GH = GUESTHOUSE

- WAT
- CHURCH, CATHEDRAL
- TEMPLE, PAGODA
- STUPA
- MOSQUE
- WATER
- WATERFALL

ACKNOWLEDGMENTS

Writers write alone, but survive only with generous doses of help and encouragement from friends, family, and associates. Top marks at Moon Publications go to the editing team of Jeannie Trizzino, Elizabeth Larson, and Gina Wilson Birtcil, art director David Hurst, and map makers Mike Morgenfeld, Allen Leech, Brian Bardwell all of whom labored well beyond the call of duty. Gratitude is also given to founder Bill Dalton, publisher Bill Newlin, and other Moonbeams who helped realize the book.

I am also indebted to the people of Thailand, who took me into their homes and left me with memories to last a lifetime.

Contributions from Readers

I would also like to thank the many readers who wrote to me about their travel adventures:

United States: Chris Baker (Oakland), Susan Brown (NY), Burt Blackburn (Alexandria,), Thom Burns (Ocean Park), W. S. Butterfield (Savannah), Alan Cartledge (AZ), Robert Chiang (San Antonio), Frank Cotter (Mounds View), Pat Crowley (San Diego), Stephen Downes (Marion), Mike Ellis (Niles), Rhys Evans (Grover City), Kathleen Flynn (Los Angeles), Jean Fournier (San Leandro), Leigh Fox (Guam), Leslie Freeman (Boise), Steve Gilman (Norcross), Lester Hamersly (Index), Stefan Hammond (San Francisco), Dr. Martin Hane (Chicago), Celeste Holmes (Oakland), Harry Hunter (Olympia), Terry Nakazono (Gardena), Martin Offenberger (La Habra), Irene Malone (San Pablo), Angelo Mercure (San Diego), Dan Moody (Studio City), Ms. Jan Morris (Louisville), James Patterson (Santa Cruz), Mark Peters (Muscatine), John Pierkarski (Huntington Beach), Michael Newman (LA), Roger Post (San Diego), Anna Redding (Atlanta), Rachel Rinaldo (Wilton), William Ring (San Diego), Yancey Rousek (Los Angeles), Claudia Siegel (Hackensack), Steve Stawarz (San Jose), Jefferson Swycaffer (San Diego), Michael Triff (Atlanta), Ray VarnBuhler (Wilseyville), Murray Westgate (Las Vegas), Chantal Yang (Cambridge), George Young (League City).

Australia: Gary Deering, Greg Duffy (Burleigh Wates), Martin Ellison (Darlinghurst), Cas Liber (Elizabeth Bay), Kevin Mulrain (Sydney), Morgana Oliver (Wodonga), Catherine Spence (Mona Vale), Keith Stephans (Noose), Amy Thomas (Bellevue Heights).

Austria: Herber Walland (Graz).

Belgium: Guy Crouna (Tieuen).

Canada: Michael Buckley (Vancouver), Bob Cadloff (Montreal), Melvin Green (Toronto), Pat and Tom Jorgrinson (Webb), Bruce Moore (Ganges), Lenny Morgan (Richmond), Bob Olajos (Peterborough), Scott Pegg (Vancouver), Laura White (Toronto), Tanya Whiteside (Ottawa).

China: Philip Drury.

England: Alan Cummings, Amanda Dixon (Cheam), Tim Eyre (Nottingham), H. L. Freeman (London), Linda Grace (Oxford), Mark Gregory (Leeds), David Host (Bulkington), John Maidment (Southbourne), Anthony Maude (Canterbury), C. Miller (London), Peter Moorhouse (Seathwaite), Anna Oldman (High Wycombe), Tina Ottman (Cambridge), Tim Prentice (Kent), Nick Slade (Flackwell Health), Lois Tadd (Chesham), David Veale (Fishbourne).

Germany: Christiane Moll (Berlin), Marcus Muller (Tubingen), Ralf Neugebauer (Lubeck), Wolfgang and Mosgit (Brey), Hans Zagorski (Gunterleben).

Japan: Bruce Swenson.

Netherlands: Vander Bel-Kampschuur (Eindhoven), Maarten Camps (Ryswyh), Claantie van der Grinten (Ryswyh), E. Cornelissen (Castricum), Rick Dubbeldam (Sas Van Gert), Jan Valkenbury (Heerlen), Michel van Dam (Den Haag), Erik van Velzen (Zoetermeer), Herbert Walland.

New Zealand: Gordon Boshell (Aro Valley), Barry Wells (Wellington).

Spain: Sevvy (Madrid).

Sweden: Stefan Samuelsson (Lomma).

Switzerland: Rolf Huber (Uitikon-Waldegg), Katharina Hug (Enalinpes).

Thailand: Jamie Donahoe who helped with my Bangkok restaurant reviews and Gary Hacker for setting me straight about Pattaya.

A Personal Note

Finally, I would like to extend my deepest gratitude and sincerest love to all my friends in San Francisco and throughout the world:

Terra and radio king Nickola, Norton (ready for another courier flight?), Dean (Wolfman) Bowden, Eric Dibbern and Sue, Roy T. Maloney, John Kaeuper, Jimbo & Kelly, Linda & Geek (now in Geneva), sexy El & handsome Dave, Vince "Dude," never-forgotten Lee & Pam, Ab Fab-Seinfeld Brucie, beam-me-up Scotty (Scotch!) & Juiceteen, lovely Rita & Eric, Dara & Roger (cool kids), amazing Amos, Zenbullet Stefan, Joel, Cuba Chris, Russian Vera, Peachy, sweet Cathy, Deke (Vegas?), Rich & Rens, Dave "Art Seen" Howard, Hai "Baby," tattoo Jerome (sans Harley), Ed Samarin, Chris & Ben, Juggler Ray (Key West), Joe C. and wife (Baja), Nancy Chandler, Kim Kacere, Michael, Rita & Eric (Santa Barbara), Susan T., Karen C. (thanks for the visit), Larsen (you still owe me $40), Zimme da Giant, Guru Das, Joe & Divine Dyan, Terri "The Terror," Stephanie (love all three), Hugh Linton (you started it all), Donna, Hazel & Rick, Richard (North Beach '75), Dianne (Aspen '76), Nam Chu (R.I.P.), Doctor Bob & German Ralph, Homeless Jim, June, Sheila, party Marty, Bill Bodewes (Amsterdam), Gary Flynn (Down Under), Michael Buckley (Vancouver), Joe & Nancy (Japan), David Stanley (Canada), Marael (Boots fan!), Joe Biz (R.I.P.) & Bob Nilsen (Chico), Rachel (Singapore), Nicole (Paris), Escola Nova de Samba, Lulu and the Atomics, sister Claud, fab Stan, cool Kev & (cooler) Heath, Mom & Dad.

REQUEST FOR COMMENTS

Travel books are collaborations between authors and readers. While every effort has been made to keep this book accurate and timely, travel conditions change quickly in a region as dynamic as Thailand. Please let us know about price hikes, new guesthouses, closed restaurants, transportation tips, and anything else that may prove useful to the next traveler. Your information will be checked in the field and then carefully interwoven into the next edition of this book. Moon Publications and the author deeply appreciate all suggestions sent in by our readers.

A Reader Profile questionnaire in the back of this book will help us find out who you are and your impressions about this guide. All correspondents will be acknowledged and the best letters will receive a new copy of any requested guide to Southeast Asia.

You may e-mail the author directly at cparkes@moon.com or send your Reader Profile and travel suggestions via snailmail to:

Carl Parkes
Thailand Handbook
Avalon Travel Publishing
5855 Beaudry Street
Emeryville, CA 94608
USA

INTRODUCTION

Bangkok and the Golden Triangle, Kanchanaburi and the River Kwai, Khun Sa and the king of Siam—these are images to fire the imagination. In a world gone increasingly dull, Thailand remains a land of magic and mystery, adventure and romance, a far-flung destination still strange and exciting in a Westernized world.

Thailand's romantic image began with the writers and adventurers who recorded their early journeys of discovery and voyages of inner exploration. Tales of intrigue by Marco Polo were followed by the stories of Conrad, Verne, Hesse, Maugham, Gurdjieff, Malraux, Fleming, Ginsberg, and Watts. Today, a new generation of writers—Theroux, Iyer, and Krich—continue to explore and interpret the brave new world of modern Southeast Asia.

Southeast Asia's image as an Eastern paradise has also been supported by Hollywood films such as The King and I, and by sobriquets bestowed by creative copywriters and the national tourist office—Land of Smiles, Treasures of a Kingdom, Amazing Thailand. While the hyperbole may be excessive, Thailand unquestionably deserves its accolade as one of the world's premier destinations, a region that richly rewards the discriminating visitor.

A World of Choices

Travelers heading off to Southeast Asia often ask this writer for a specific recommendation on "the best country" in the area. After 20 years of wandering the region, I've learned that each country offers unique strengths appealing to different types of travelers. Singapore may no longer be the exotic land of Conrad and Kipling, but the island state features the best food and most comfortable travel conditions in all of Southeast Asia. The Philippines may lack remarkable cuisine, and travel conditions are often rugged, but the archipelago offers outstanding beaches, superb diving, and the friendliest people in Asia. Myanmar remains controlled by one of the world's most repressive regimes, and internal transport is nothing short of an ordeal, but the isolated nation is a miraculous place for adventurous travelers. And then there is Indonesia, a bewildering expanse of islands far too expansive to

SIGHTSEEING HIGHLIGHTS

Where to go and what to see are often difficult decisions since few are familiar with the history, geography, or tourist attractions of Thailand. Sadly, few people contemplating a visit to the region could even name the major destinations in this exotic corner of the world. Despite the amazing number of possibilities, travel destinations familiar to the general public are largely limited to Bangkok, Chiang Mai, Pattaya, Phuket, and Ko Samui. A fine beginning, but there's far more to Thailand than just this short list.

But to make the most informed decision on where to go and what to see, you'll need to pour over maps to become familiar with the geography and conduct an organized reading campaign of travel guidebooks and historical works. To fire up your imagination, delve into some armchair travelogues.

Most visitors begin their tour in the capital city of Bangkok. Despite its stifling heat and unbearable traffic, Bangkok ranks as the most fascinating city in Southeast Asia. To properly explore the temples, museums, shopping centers, and restaurants would take months, if not years.

Within a 200-km radius of Bangkok are several well-developed beach resorts, the world's tallest Buddhist monument, the bridge on the River Kwai, and the splendid ruins of Ayuthaya. Several historic cities in central Thailand once served as ancient capitals. Chiang Mai, in the north, serves as both the cultural and artistic center of Thailand, as well as a convenient base for trekking into the mountains and touring the infamous Golden Triangle. Northeastern Thailand offers outstanding Khmer monuments, plus the rare opportunity to explore off the beaten track. South Thailand is a wonderland of pristine beaches and well-developed resort islands such as Ko Samui and Phuket.

The following sketches of the eight main regions of Thailand will provide a quick glimpse of the national highlights. Further descriptions are provided at the beginning of each regional chapter under "Sightseeing Highlights."

Bangkok

Thailand's rich and kaleidoscopic tapestry of tourist attractions is enough to keep most travelers busy for years, though a single region can be explored well in several weeks. Visitors generally fly into Bangkok, a chaotic and unnerving metropolis of immense traffic jams and modern high-rises. Appalled by the over-crowding, overdevelopment and pollution, many travelers make the mistake of pausing only long enough to buy a plane ticket before moving on.

While Bangkok is certainly an urban planner's nightmare, it is also home to dozens of dazzling Buddhist temples, outstanding restaurants, superb shopping, and one of the liveliest nightlife scenes in the world. You'll be surprised at the vitality and friendliness of many of its eight million residents . . . if you survive the heat and congestion.

East Coast

This area features historical monuments, beaches, and natural wonders—all within a 200-km radius of Bangkok.

Pattaya: Thailand's eastern seaboard boasts several highly developed beach resorts; Pattaya is the most famous. One of the largest resorts in Asia, this low-powered Riviera of the East annually attracts over a million pleasure-seekers to its breathtaking range of water sports, restaurants, and legendary nightlife. Lively, chaotic, exciting, polluted, highly commercialized, and tacky, Pattaya in the past catered almost exclusively to military personnel or single businessmen who filled the bars and nightclubs. Today the resort appeals primarily to families, with attractions such as zoos, botanical gardens, and water parks. Although the beaches are inferior to those of Phuket or Ko Samui, the proximity to Bangkok makes Pattaya convenient for visitors with limited time.

Ko Samet: To escape the high-rise development of Pattaya, many travelers continue eastward to this kris-shaped island south of Rayong. The beaches here are fairly good (no comparison with those further south); facilities are limited to simple bungalows and midlevel hotels.

Ko Chang: On the border of Cambodia lies the newest island resort in Thailand, with excellent beaches, magnificent topography, and dozens of untouched islands nearby. Ko Chang is rapidly developing into another Ko Samui; go now before the hotels arrive.

West of Bangkok

A quick and relaxing journey into Thai countryside can be made just west of Bangkok.

Nakhon Pathom: Often visited on a day-trip from Bangkok or as a stop en route to Kanchanaburi, this small town one hour west of Bangkok is home to the world's tallest Buddhist monument.

Damnern Saduak: Thailand's most authentic floating market, two hours south of Bangkok, Damnern Saduak is much less commercialized than the capital's artificial floating bazaar. You can join a tour or explore it yourself with an early start.

Kanchanaburi: This beautiful and relaxing region, three hours west of Bangkok, offers inexpensive floating guesthouses, refreshing waterfalls, hiking, national parks, and cool caves filled with Buddhas. Highly recommended for history buffs, nature lovers, and anyone annoyed with Bangkok's traffic jams. The bridge over the River Kwai is located here.

Three Pagodas Pass: The only legal land connection with Myanmar is subject to political skirmishes but offers some historical interest and lovely landscapes.

North of Bangkok

Historical sites north of Bangkok can be visited on day-trips, but the vast number of monuments and lengthy travel times demand a tour of several days.

Ayuthaya: For over 400 years the riverine-island town of Ayuthaya, two hours north of Bangkok, served as the second royal capital of Thailand. Though largely destroyed by the Burmese in 1767, many of the restored architectural ruins provide eloquent testimony to the splendor of Thailand's most powerful empire. Ayuthaya and Sukothai are Thailand's largest and most impressive archaeological sites.

Lopburi: Although nothing special, Lopburi features some modest Khmer ruins and an old summer capital for Ayuthayan kings. It also makes a convenient stopover en route to the northeast.

Central Thailand

Thai history started in the flat plains of central Thailand which now provide the broadest spectrum of historic architecture in the country.

Sukothai: In 1238 the Thai people proclaimed their independence from Khmer suzerainty and founded Sukothai, the first truly independent Thai capital. For over a century the Sukothai kingdom ruled the region and created a golden age of Thai arts which left behind a treasure trove of outstanding temples, *stupas,* and elegant Buddhas. Most of the ruins have been restored and are surrounded by manicured gardens and refreshing pools. A brief visit to *both* Ayuthaya and Sukothai is highly recommended for visitors interested in Thai architecture or history.

Si Satchanalai: A satellite town of Sukothai with architecture dating from the 13th and 14th centuries. Easily visited on a side trip from Sukothai.

Mae Sot: This small but intriguing town on the Burmese border offers visitors an ethnic flavor in an unspoiled region; travelers can take back roads to reach the north.

Northern Thailand

Chiang Mai: With its wealth of cultural and historical attractions, superb shopping, great food, friendly people, and delightful weather, Chiang Mai deservedly ranks as one of Thailand's leading tourist destinations. Unlike many Asian cities, which have lost their charm and character to unmanaged growth, Chiang Mai city still offers a few hidden neighborhoods of lovely teak homes and tree-shaded roads. Chiang Mai also serves as a convenient base for trekking into the countryside, touring the infamous Golden Triangle area, and visiting the historic towns of Lamphun and Lampang.

Hilltribes: Living in the remote highlands near the Thai-Myanmar-Laos borders are shifting agriculturalists who cling to ancient lifestyles despite encroaching Westernization and assimilation efforts by the Thai government. An organized trek of 5-10 days is a unique and memorable experience.

Mae Hong Son: The Shangri-la atmosphere of this small village, tucked away near the Burmese border, attracts increasing numbers of tourists and travelers who seek a destination somewhat off the beaten track. Mae Hong Son has changed dramatically in recent years due to the construction of new hotels and an aggressive recognition campaign conducted by the national tourist office, yet most of the region remains an untouched landscape of spectacular mountains with a pace of life from an earlier century.

Pai: A beautiful, isolated village with all the charms but none of the modern problems of Chiang Mai and Mae Hong Son. An excellent spot for trekking, river rafting, and simply lazing around. Highly recommended.

The Golden Triangle: For over two decades, travelers have headed from Chiang Mai up to the town of Thaton, boated down the Kok River to Chiang Rai, and continued up to Chiang Saen—the heart of the so-called Golden Triangle. Today, opium production has largely shifted to Laos and Myanmar, and tour buses are a greater threat to your safety than gun runners or drug warlords—don't expect a Wild West atmosphere.

continues on next page

SIGHTSEEING HIGHLIGHTS
(continued)

Chiang Saen: Chiang Saen, a sleepy town on the banks of the mighty Mekong, offers the visitor a handful of historic temples that predate the foundation of Chiang Mai, and a superb atmosphere where there's little to do but gaze across the river to Laos.

Northeastern Thailand
The sprawling plateau bordered by Laos and Cambodia is Thailand's forgotten destination. Known locally as the Issan, the dry and rugged northeast is home to a boisterous people with a distinctive culture, several worthwhile national parks, and the most impressive array of Khmer temples outside of Cambodia.

Khao Yai National Park: Thailand's most popular park, four hours northeast of Bangkok, Khao Yai boasts a dozen hiking trails, refreshing waterfalls, and protected wildlife from elephants to hornbills. Khao Yai is conveniently located en route from Bangkok to the Khmer monuments of the northeast.

Korat: Nakon Ratchasima (often called Korat) chiefly serves as the gateway to the Khmer temples and national parks of the northeast.

Khmer Monuments: Once under the suzerainty of various Khmer empires, the strategically situated northeast remains dotted with fantastic Cambodian temples erected to honor their gods and kings. Visitors with limited time will find Korat a convenient spot from which to explore the nearby monuments at Phimai and Phanom Rung. Travelers with extra time can follow the string of Cambodian temples which continue east to Buriram and Surin.

Ban Chiang: Ban Chiang, an important historical site and home to one of the earliest Bronze Age civilizations, will appeal to archaeologists and anyone intrigued by the origins of the Eastern world.

Nong Khai: Romantically situated on the Mekong River some 20 km from Vientiane, Nong Khai is one of the most relaxing towns in the northeast. The opening of the trans-Mekong bridge has brought additional traffic to the region, though Nong Khai remains in a surreal state, safely removed from the deeply grooved tourist trail.

West of Nong Khai: Some of Thailand's most rugged and beautiful scenery can be enjoyed on the road from Nong Khai to Chiang Khan, a cowboy town nestled on the banks of the muddy Mekong. All towns along the winding two-lane road have inexpensive guesthouses and decent cafes geared to the independent traveler—a great journey for motorcyclists and bicyclists.

Phu Kradung National Park: Phu Kradung, a forested plateau rising between 1,200 and 1,500 meters near the town of Loei, is a mysterious, moody spot popular with hikers, campers, and nature lovers. A great change from a steady diet of tropical beaches and urban sightseeing.

Ubon Ratchathani: Ubon is a major commercial center famed for its candle festival at the beginning of Buddhist rains retreat. The traditional and largely uncommercialized festivals of the northeast are considered a prime reason to visit the region. Ubon is also known for its boat rides down the Mekong past rugged landscapes, and for a meditation temple geared exclusively to Western practitioners of meditation.

Surin: Visitors flock here each November to attend the heavily promoted and enormously popular "Elephant Roundup," one of the few opportunities you'll ever have to watch elephant polo or participate in a tug-of-war with a pachyderm. Surin and Buriram also serve as convenient bases from which to explore nearby Cambodian temples.

Southern Thailand
The tropical beaches of Southern Thailand are among the finest in Southeast Asia and a major reason the country enjoys such enduring popularity with Western visitors. Blessed with crystalline sands and iridescent waters, southern Thai beach resorts come in various stages of development—rustic, midlevel, and luxury.

Hua Hin: Hua Hin, the first major beach resort south of Bangkok, is chiefly patronized by European families seeking a moderately priced sun-and-fun destination, without the tawdriness of Pattaya or

explore properly in any time frame—but where else can you find such an amazing diversity of cultures, religions, peoples, and histories?

All these factors make the selection of Southeast Asia's top destination a difficult call.

And yet, this travel writer always recommends first-time visitors head directly to Thailand. No other country offers such an outstanding array of attractions in such a compact package. Do you dream of crystalline beaches and brilliant is-the advanced development of Phuket. Safe, clean, and conveniently located near Bangkok, Hua Hin has recently lost some of its idyllic charm: misguided hotel construction has overwhelmed the intimate beach destination.

Prachuap Khiri Khan: Need to escape the crowds? Head for Prachuap Khiri Khan, a wonderful seaside resort barely touched by mass tourism or wholesale Westernization. Magnificently hemmed in by limestone mountains and situated near some great beaches, Prachuap is a delightful place; little to do but wander around and smile at the locals.

Ko Samui: This Penang-sized island, with superb beaches and lush coconut palms, was popularized in the early 1970s by hippie travelers who quietly praised their tranquil, virgin hideaway. By the mid-1980s, commercial developers were constructing international-standard hotels, restaurants, nightclubs, and a small airport to handle the daily flights from Bangkok. Ko Samui today is a middle-market destination, where the main beaches have succumbed to luxury hotels and the backpackers are forced to find more remote locales. Despite the change of clientele, Ko Samui remains a spectacularly beautiful island with dozens of remote, idyllic coves.

Ko Phangan: Those budget travelers who abandoned Ko Samui largely moved to this adjacent island, a few hours north by public boat from Ko Samui or the mainland town of Surat Thani. Ko Phangan beaches are smaller and less impressive than those on Ko Samui, but the island more than compensates with its mellow atmosphere, rock-bottom prices, and sense of isolation from advancing tourist hordes.

Phuket: Situated on the western side of peninsular Thailand and brimming with magnificent coves and powdery white beaches, Phuket claims place as Southeast Asia's largest and most popular beach resort—the Waikiki of Thailand. Although more commercialized than Ko Samui, and to some a lost paradise, Phuket has plenty to offer most visitors: an outstanding selection of hotels in all price ranges, excellent seaside restaurants, every imaginable water sport, and nightclubs that rage full-tilt until

sunrise. Travelers with adequate funds who can't decide between lively Phuket, mellow Ko Samui, or escapist Ko Phangan should visit all three.

Ko Phi Phi: This exquisite little island, located between Phuket and Krabi, is the first of an archipelago that stretches to the borders of Malaysia. Ko Phi Phi is small and stunning but packed during the winter tourist months Nov.-March. Travelers will find more remote and untouched islands to the south near Trang and Satun.

Krabi: Krabi is an extremely popular town chiefly serving as the launching point to nearby beaches and islands. Though often overrun with tourists and travelers, Krabi offers good accommodations, excellent transportation, and diverse diversions, from nightlife to organized sports.

Pranang: This tiny peninsula near Krabi attracts a more upscale crowd these days. Fortunately for Pranang, the wall of limestone mountains separating the peninsula from the mainland has stalled road construction and kept the tropical wonderland relatively free of major hotel construction.

Ko Lanta: Ko Lanta will almost certainly be the next major island resort south of Phuket. The nearly deserted beaches are good but the island is hard to reach and accommodations rudimentary. You'll find better sand near the southern end.

Trang: Trang is a clean and unspoiled town—an excellent region to find peace and calm. Divers will discover some of the best waters in Thailand.

Hat Yai: Southern Thailand's most important commercial center is a great place for shopping, food, and nightlife; easy access to the nearby beaches and the mellow seaside town of Songkla.

Narathiwat: A wonderful escape off the tourist trail, Narathiwat, a small and sleepy fishing village, lacks great sites but compensates with its charm and character.

Ko Tarutao: This string of islands west of Satun was sensibly granted national park status by the Thai government. Visitors enjoy attractive beaches, thick jungle, and simple villages inhabited by Muslim fishermen and itinerant sea gypsies. A modern ferry now connects Satun with Langkawi Island in Malaysia.

lands? Thailand offers world-class resorts with five-star amenities as well as remote islands untouched by the forces of modern tourism. Culture fans can seek out authentic festivals, tour archaeological parks, or visit 20 superb

museums scattered around the country.

Thailand is exotic. Thai religious architecture is almost unbelievable—a riotous fantasy of color, shapes, and mythological creatures that often appear inspired by Disney. Outdoor enthusiasts can enjoy hilltribe trekking in the north, river rafting in the Golden Triangle, and scuba diving over pristine coral in the remote south. Thailand guarantees superb shopping—the best in Asia—world-renowned cuisine, notorious nightlife, and all types of environments, from national parks to remote jungles.

Most important, Thailand is home to the Thais, wonderful people who have graciously preserved their traditions while accepting the conveniences of modern life.

Thailand remains one of the few nations in Asia where modernization has failed to triumph over local traditions. Many feel this strength is due to the fact that Thailand was never colonized by Western powers, but this author believes credit should be given to Buddhism, the world religion that teaches compassion and forgiveness rather than judgmental approaches to life. Buddhism, independence, and perhaps the tropical heat have given the Thais an extraordinary sense of serenity and a lack of the psychological tension so common to Western life.

The happy result is a wacky, wild, and wonderful society that can be neatly summarized by three common Thai phrases: *"chai yen"* ("cool heart"), *"mai pen rai"* ("what will be, will be"), and *"sanuk"* ("life is a pleasure"). This approach to life means the Thais maintain a cool heart, refuse to worry about the future, and always live for pleasure. No wonder Thailand is my top choice in Asia.

Brave New World

The visitor should arrive in Thailand with open eyes, leaving false expectations back home. Thailand today hardly resembles the world described by writers of earlier generations; this is no place for sentimental colonialism or quaint longing for unspoiled paradise forever lost. Modern Thailand is a highly developed nation, where the average citizen prefers Hollywood and holograms over meditation and mantras.

Western influences pervade even the remotest corners of the country. Ko Samui, once an unknown and untouched destination privy to a select group of world travelers, now ranks as a favorite stop for package tourists from Europe and

NAME GAME

The official name of the country formally known in English as Burma has been changed to the Union of Myanmar (MEE-an-ma). The current government (SLORC) says the change is intended to better reflect the country's ethnic diversity and provide Romanized spellings more phonetically in tune with local pronunciations. However, prodemocracy opposition groups claim it's yet another historical distortion by the military junta.

The name change has been adopted by most members of the international press, and the country's official UN designation is Myanmar. Yet some publications still use the older terminology as a sign of nonrecognition of the Burmese government. However, there is historical and linguistic support for the use of the "new" terms, which are gaining acceptance worldwide. Therefore, in this book we use the name Myanmar, as well as Yangon (Rangoon), Bagan (Pagan), etc.

Australia. Other destinations are overwhelmed with tourists and marred by schlock shops, sacrificing their souls for economic reward.

Still, travelers who venture off the beaten track will find destinations where nobody speaks a word of English and young schoolgirls run from the sight of a gangly Westerner. Even as you read this paragraph, somewhere in Thailand an adventurous backpacker sits on a deserted beach on an untouched island, smiling at the villagers and believing himself or herself the luckiest person in the world.

To see the real Thailand—the Thailand that lies beneath the Western veneer—you must travel with wide eyes and an open mind. Avoid spending money simply to isolate yourself against what appears to be an alien culture. Treat residents and other travelers as you would have them treat you, and resist measuring people by your standards or cultural values. Keep a cool heart, an optimistic attitude, and an openness to chance encounters. Believe in *chai yen, mai pen rai,* and *sanuk.* And have a great adventure.

THE LAND

GEOGRAPHICAL REGIONS

Thailand, a melange of subtropical and temperate zones situated between 5° and 21° north of the equator, offers the visitor a diverse and varied topography encompassing fertile alluvial plains, rugged mountains, rough savannah, tropical rainforests, and a sandy, irregular coastline facing the Andaman Sea to the west and Gulf of Thailand to the east.

The country is set in the center of mainland Southeast Asia, bordered by Myanmar to the west, Laos in the north, Cambodia to the east, and Malaysia down south. The insular kingdom stretches over 1,800 km from north to south, and contains a total land mass of 513,115 square kilometers—roughly equivalent to the size of France or slightly smaller than Texas.

Thailand's shape somewhat resembles an elephant's head, with the trunk forming the southern peninsula and Bangkok sited in the elephant's mouth. The capital lies approximately 14° north of the equator, roughly in line with Manila, Madras, and Khartoum.

Some national boundaries are defined by natural features, such as the long and winding Mekong River which demarcates much of the border with Laos. Other borders are ill-defined lines established in modern times by treaties with the British and French. Subsequent reinterpretations of these arrangements caused many 20th century territorial disputes, most notably the controversy over the exact location of Preah Vihar. In 1962 the famed Khmer temple was awarded by an International Court of Justice to Cambodia, though the temple steps were judged to be in Thailand.

Landforms and drainage divide the country into six natural regions. Each differs from the others in population, resources, natural features, historical background, ethnic and linguistic groups, and the level of social and economic development.

Thailand has its own system of land measurement. The basic units are the *wa* (four square km) and the *rai* (400 square *wa*, 1,600 square meters, or 0.16 hectares). One square kilometer equals 625 *rai*.

Bangkok and Vicinity

Much of Thailand's political and economic development occurred in the flat patchwork of emerald-green paddies around the capital city of Bangkok. Now the contemporary core of modern Thailand, the alluvial plains and highly developed irrigation systems which surround the city have long served as the rice bowl of Asia; this was the homeland of the region's earliest settlers.

Although many ricefields have been lost to urban encroachment and industrial estates, annual floods and rich soils still allow the region to support the most densely populated area of Thailand. Bangkok and vicinity encompass only 1.5% of the nation's total land mass but over 15% of the total population.

The most important geographical characteristic of lower and central Thailand is the Menam or

SIZE OF THAILAND VERSUS U. S. A.

PACIFIC OCEAN

SEATTLE

SAN FRANCISCO

LOS ANGELES

0   150 mi
0   150 km

© MOON PUBLICATIONS, INC.

AVERAGE HUMIDITY–BANGKOK

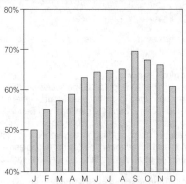

MAXIMUM TEMPERATURE–BANGKOK

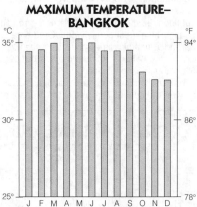

RAINFALL–BANGKOK

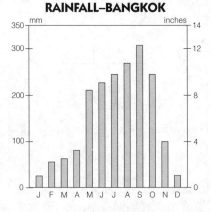

Chao Praya River, the Nile of Siam. This Mississippi-like stretch of water, together with its tributaries, drains an estimated one-third of the nation. The dual moniker itself demonstrates its importance. Menam means "mother of waters" or "river," while Chao Praya is an aristocratic title signifying female nobility. Thus the full term translates to "Noble lady, mother of waters." Most Thais simply say "Menam."

The annual flooding of the lower Menam delta is both a blessing and a curse. Each year during the June–Nov. monsoon season, heavy rains inundate the alluvial lowlands that stretch from the mouth of the Menam to the historic town of Lopburi, 130 km north. Farmers are thankful for the soaking but Bangkok residents must once again suffer through another season of flooded streets. The floods are due to the low-lying nature of Bangkok and nearby towns; the capital is only two meters above sea level. The river is still tidal at Ayuthaya, 95 km inland yet just four meters above sea level.

East Coast

The southeastern coastal regions of Trat, Chanthaburi, Rayong, and Chonburi are often placed in the same geographical group as the northeast, despite their completely unique charms. Somewhat isolated from mainstream travel, this stretch of superb beaches and remote islands also includes the land wedged between the Gulf of Thailand and the Phnom Damrek mountain range to the north.

To the west stretch the flattened summits of the Banthat range, outliers of the Cardomoms, which form the untamed frontier with Cambodia. Smugglers, Khmer army commanders, and independent miners live here, working the pits that supply Thailand with most of its rubies and sapphires.

The region nearest Bangkok has been transformed into new cities and industrial parks designed to take advantage of cheaper land and better roads to the shipping centers near Bangkok. Beyond these bedroom communities and huge shipping facilities lie the beach resort towns of Pattaya and Rayong. The coastline continues southeast to Trat, which serves as the launching point for boats to Ko Chang, a peaceful island graced with fine beaches and towering mountains.

Central Plains

The central plains between Bangkok and northern Thailand are an immensely fertile region; here arose the original Siamese empire, Sukothai, in the 13th and 14th centuries. The cultural heartland of the Siamese people also serves as the national "rice bowl," thanks to the annual flooding of the Chao Praya and alluvial lowlands, construction of dams, and sheer size and complexity of its hydroponic engineering. The central plains are the principal reason Thailand has remained the world's top exporter of rice for more than two decades.

As with the region around Bangkok, the true life force of the central plains is the Chao Praya River, which measures a modest 365 km. Three longer rivers in the upper regions empty into the Chao Praya: the Nan (627 km), Ping (590 km), and Pasak (513 km). Together they support over a third of the population of Thailand.

Northern Thailand

The northern regions of Thailand are dominated by the Yunnan massif, which continues north into China, and the central cordilleras, marking the western boundary with Myanmar and continuing south to form the backbone of the Malay Peninsula. This mountainous region, inhabited by seminomadic hilltribes who cultivate opium as their cash crop, is actually a continuation of the Himalayan mountain system that stretches from Tibet to the Andaman Sea.

All but five of Thailand's mountains above 1,700 meters are located in the Chiang Mai and Chiang Rai regions. The tallest, Doi Inthanon (2,590 meters), lies 50 km southwest of Chiang Mai. It is followed by Doi Chiang Dao at 2,182 meters, and Doi Pha Hom Pok at 2,298 meters. Northern Thailand is geographically the most impressive region in the country, with breathtaking landscapes, rolling hills, and hidden valleys reminiscent of a forgotten Shangri-la. This once isolated land also boasts an impressive range of cascading rivers, deep caves, and plunging waterfalls.

Northern Thailand also includes the kingdom's "second city" of Chiang Mai. Once an independent empire called Lanna, Chiang Mai now serves as the cultural capital for the northern regions. It also functions as an important handicraft center where the traveler will find an out-

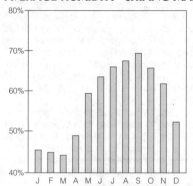

AVERAGE HUMIDITY–CHIANG MAI

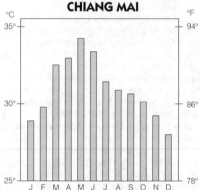

MAXIMUM TEMPERATURE–CHIANG MAI

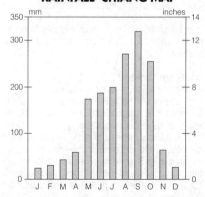

RAINFALL–CHIANG MAI

standing selection of traditional products such as textiles, silverwork, and wooden figurines.

A few other geographical features should be noted. Much of the northern boundary with Laos is defined by the legendary Mekong River, which flows over 4,000 km from the heart of Tibet to its alluvial fan in the South China Sea. Travelers can now enjoy all types of river journeys on the Mekong, including boat rides north all the way to China.

Another famous geographical region is the so-called "Golden Triangle" at the intersection of Thailand, Laos, and Myanmar. Once a region of opium smugglers and renegade Chinese armies, the triangle is now a popular tourist destination complete with hotels, restaurants, and a fascinating opium museum.

Northeastern Thailand

Northeastern Thailand, more commonly called the Issan, is a remarkable region situated over an almost horizontal bed of Triassic sandstone that rests uncomfortably on a floor of granite and sedimentary rocks. The Issan is geographically unfavored, beset with such myriad ecological problems as poor soils and a dire scarcity of rainfall. Few Westerners explore the region, despite its rich traditions, superb handicrafts, magnificent array of Khmer temples, and friendly and polite people.

The Korat Plateau is composed of a depressed but gently tilting plate ringed by mountains to the west and south, and hemmed to the north and east by the Mekong. Cursedly situated in the rain shadow of the Indochina Cordillera, the Issan suffers from interminable dry seasons only briefly relieved by violent monsoons. The territory is chiefly drained by the Mun River, which ultimately enters the Mekong and then journeys to the sea.

Southern Thailand

Finally, there's the heterogeneous topography of tropical jungle, mangrove swamps, and sandy beaches that stretch from Bangkok 1,150 km south to the Malaysian border.

This narrow peninsular region—distinctive in climate, terrain, and resources—has long been isolated from Siamese culture due to its mountainous spines and thick stands of impenetrable forest. Major mountain chains include the

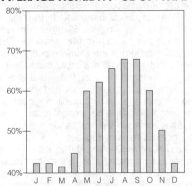

AVERAGE HUMIDITY–UDON THANI

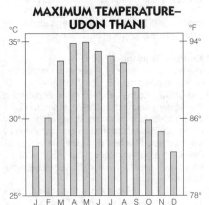

MAXIMUM TEMPERATURE– UDON THANI

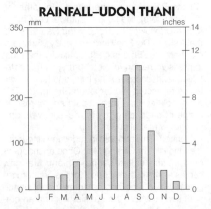

RAINFALL–UDON THANI

AVERAGE HUMIDITY–KO SAMUI

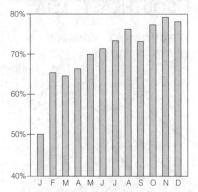

MAXIMUM TEMPERATURE– KO SAMUI

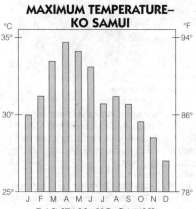

RAINFALL–KO SAMUI

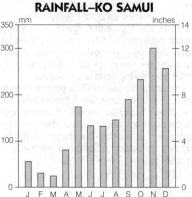

western Tenasserim, its eastern branches emerging from the sea to form the Mergui archipelago and the resort island of Phuket, and the eastern Sri Thammarat range, with peaks that include the traveler destinations of Ko Samui and Ko Phangan.

Coastlines on the west side of the peninsula are often craggy cliffs that plunge dramatically into the sea. Those on the east coast slope gently towards the huge bays, placid lagoons, and magnificent islands of Ko Samui and Ko Tao. South of Phuket, the western coastline breaks into a fantastic series of limestone karsts that emerge abruptly from the turquoise waters. Surrealistic to the extreme, this hauntingly beautiful landscape was featured in the James Bond film, *The Man with the Golden Gun.*

Travelers often continue south of Ko Samui and Phuket to visit the tropical beaches and islands of Ko Phi Phi, Krabi, Trang, and Tarutao National Marine Park near the Malaysia border.

CLIMATE

Thailand lies in a tropical zone and shares the same weather patterns as most Southeast Asian countries situated north of the equator. Although there's little you can do about the weather after arrival, an understanding of the elements can help you choose beforehand the season best suited to your personality.

Monsoons, not latitude, determine the seasons in Thailand. Monsoons are seasonal winds that change direction during the year as a result of differences in temperature and pressure between land and sea. Derived from the Arabic word *mansim,* monsoons are the life source for farms across the country.

Regional Variations
The climate of Thailand varies widely from region to region. Rainfall patterns and temperature levels described apply only to the central plains, including Bangkok, the north, and the northeast. These insular regions are subjected only to the summer monsoon, which brings three distinct seasons: dry (Dec.-Feb.), hot (March-June), and rainy (June-Dec.). Variations within seasons and between years can alter these monthly guidelines.

MONSOON PATTERNS IN SOUTHEAST ASIA

NORTHEAST MONSOON

THAILAND

0   300 mi
0   300 km

SOUTHWEST MONSOON

THAILAND

0   300 mi
0   300 km

<----- = AREAS SOMEWHAT SHELTERED

◄───── = AREAS OF WORST EFFECTS OF MONSOON

© MOON PUBLICATIONS, INC.

The exception to the "one monsoon, three seasons" rule is the peninsular world of southern Thailand, especially the southeast coast, which experiences both summer and winter monsoons. Winter rains—uncommon in the north—are caused by winds from the northeast passing over the gulf and thereby accumulating humidity. As a result of alternating monsoons, which also dictate temperatures, southern Thailand has just two seasons: wet and dry.

The climate here is similar to that of the region's peninsular neighbor, Malaysia, which experiences few variations between seasons. Year round, the area is warm and humid, with rain falling at any time but heaviest during the summer months and during the so-called "dry season" months of December and January.

There can be significant differences in rainfall levels between the west and east coasts depending on the strength of the storm. Travelers on Ko Samui surprised by sudden showers might find drier conditions across the peninsula on Phuket.

The Dry Season (December-February)

The dry and cooler season begins in the early winter as temperatures start to drop and the land begins to cool faster than the sea. The high-pressure zone which gradually builds over mainland Southeast Asia forces winds to blow from the land to the sea, from the northeast to the southwest. This northeastern monsoon brings pleasant, dry, and somewhat cooler weather.

Temperatures drop to tolerable levels in Bangkok and the central plains, but can approach freezing in the far northern provinces. Sweaters and jackets sold by sidewalk vendors are often necessary for mountain trekking or motorcycle touring north of Chiang Rai.

Thailand's dry season is a popular time to tour the kingdom, especially for those intolerant of heat and humidity. The chief disadvantages are the sheer number of tourists who arrive during the winter months, the scarcity of rooms, and the high-season prices demanded by some proprietors.

The Hot Season (March-June)

The hot season begins to build in March, blazes through April and May, and keeps sizzling brains until the arrival of the summer monsoons. Temperatures during the peak months of April and May often reach 35-40°C and barely drop during the evening. Conditions are worsened by the debilitating humidity, which hovers over 80% night and day.

Few visitors can tolerate this hellish season—especially in Bangkok—without air-conditioned rooms and plenty of cold showers.

The Wet Season (June-November)

The wet season begins when warm, humid air masses flow northeastward from the Indian Ocean and move toward the large low pressure zone over mainland Asia. As the winds blow over the cooler sea and on to the warmer land surfaces, humidity levels soar. This southwestern monsoon brings the rainy season, which continues until the winds reverse direction in the early winter.

The amount of rainfall varies with topography and the region's alignment with the approaching storm. Towns in the extreme northeast receive minimal rainfall, while the southwest coastal resorts of Phuket and Krabi are deluged Aug.-November.

Some travelers feel the rainy season is the best time to visit Thailand. Although the monsoons last five or six months, rainfall is sporadic and intermittent, not continuous. Most days are crisp and perfectly clear. The downpours that arrive in the late afternoon or early evening are heavy but relatively brief. Monsoons mean the kingdom is green, vibrant, and alive: nature at its most beautiful. Rather than view brown landscapes and harvested fields, you'll gaze across brilliant green paddies to glistening mountains covered with exuberant vegetation.

The rainy season also insures there will be fewer tourists, lower prices, and plentiful rooms. And what's wrong with rain? Seasoned travelers agree the violent but brief rains of summer provide the real drama of Asia, an opportunity to witness nature in all her uncontrolled fury.

FLORA

Much of Thailand's unique natural heritage is due to the unique shape of the country, an elongated land mass stretching over 1,800 km from north to south, spanning a melange of subtropical and temperate zones. The combination of these climatic zones and great topographic variety—alluvial plains, mountains, mangrove swamps, deserts—has provided Thailand with potential habitats for an astounding variety of flora and fauna.

The Forests

Thailand's pattern of vegetation has been determined by several factors. As with other tropical countries, the kingdom's stable climate combined with high temperatures and great humidity encourages the growth of immense forests.

The type of forest depends on variations in temperature and rainfall levels. At one end of the spectrum are forests with high rainfall and high average temperatures, and without pronounced cold or dry spells. These are the equatorial evergreen rainforests (the classic rainforest), which include subcategories such as evergreen montane forest, swamp forest, and lowland rainforest. Trees in each keep their leaves throughout the year. The world rainforest zone, which is confined to a narrow belt around the equator, includes large expanses of Brazil; portions of equatorial West Africa, Indonesia and Malaysia; and all of southern Thailand.

The second type of forest occurs somewhat north or south of the equator. The climate gradually becomes more seasonal, with pronounced cold and dry spells. These tropical semi-deciduous forests receive less rain, feature varying temperatures, and experience a marked dry season during which the trees lose their leaves. These seasonal forests are not as rich in species as the warmer, wetter equatorial forests in southern Thailand. Semi-deciduous forests (also called monsoonal or tropical-moist forests) grow in central, northern, and northeastern Thailand.

Thailand also has overlapping regions where both equatorial evergreen rainforests and tropical semi-deciduous forests grow.

Finding a Forest

Good luck. Aerial photos and satellite imagery have established that in 1961, 54% of Thailand was covered in some type of forest. By 1988, extensive logging and urban development had reduced this figure to 28%. Current estimates put the total much lower. Though the government has initiated conservation measures, such as a logging ban and various reforestation schemes, time is running out for anyone who wants to see a tree in Thailand.

The best place to experience the indigenous forests that once covered most of Thailand is in one of the nation's 77 national parks. Most forests outside the national parks have been cleared by logging consortiums or the general population.

Visitors generally find the rainforests of southern Thailand more enjoyable and varied than the semi-deciduous forests in the north. An excellent choice is Kaeng Krachan National Park, about three hours southwest of Bangkok, on the border with Myanmar. This remote, 3,000-square-km park offers one of the least disturbed forests in the kingdom, composed of 70% rainforest and 20% deciduous trees, 10% nondeciduous.

Khao Sam Roi Yot National Park near Hua Hin offers the widest range of scenery and activities. The chief draws are the isolated stocks of indigenous rainforest, dozens of deep caves, a good beach, vast wetlands recently converted into prawn farms, and limestone cliffs with panoramic views. This park is a personal favorite.

Rainforest Flora

Tropical rainforests harbor a complexity of flora and fauna which far outstrips the ecosystems of the temperate zones. Rainforests cover less than two percent of the globe, yet contain 40-50% of all types of living things—as many as five million species of plants and animals. A typical four-square-km patch of rainforest contains up to 1,500 species of flowering plants, 750 species of trees, 400 species of birds, and insects so abundant no one can accurately calculate their numbers.

Perhaps the most impressive of the giant rainforest trees is the yang *(Dipterocarpus alatus),* its great bare trunk rising to a height of almost 50 meters. The yang yields not only timber, but oil, as does the perfumed sandalwood tree. Rainforests also contain multitudes of fruit-bearing trees, of which the most famous is the durian, producing a football-sized fruit that "tastes like heaven, but smells like hell."

Other Flora

Thailand features other flora, which generally grow outside the rainforest. Perhaps the most common are the palms, of which four species carry particular commercial importance. The coconut palm,

fan palm

THAILAND'S FABULOUS ORCHIDS

*M*ost visitors to Thailand assume the orchid is the official flower of the kingdom after receiving an orchid on Thai Airways and discovering the amazing number of orchids sold throughout Bangkok. However, for reasons unclear to almost everyone in Thailand, the national flower is actually *Cassia fistula*—the golden shower tree, which is neither native to the country nor popular among local agronomists.

Despite this lack of official honorarium, orchids rank among the most important agricultural products in the nation. The resourceful Thais are now Southeast Asia's leading orchid growers, exporting an estimated US$100 million worth of flowers to the Japanese, who buy half; the Europeans, who account for a quarter of sales; and the Americans, who pick up 15-20%. An important offshoot of the orchid industry is the production of clones for international plant breeders.

Orchid culture is a relatively recent development. Despite the ideal growing climate for the most popularly traded genus of tropical orchid, *Dendrobium,* Thai horticulturists paid little attention to the flower until the late 1950s. No one dared compete with Singapore, the industry leader since the hybridization programs of the celebrated Botanical Gardens were launched in the 1920s.

Thailand's orchid business finally bloomed in the mid-1980s as farms multiplied in the central plains, and local growers discovered their drier climate superior to that of Singapore. Soon, Thailand surpassed Singapore as Asia's leading exporter of the sensual flower.

Their secret weapon proved to be *Dendrobium,* now the world's most popular genus of orchid. *Dendrobium* and its hybrids produce flowers within a single year, three times faster than other genuses. They also produce up to 30 orchid sprays a year, while other types render fewer than three sprays annually. Furthermore, the cut sprays live for a month with proper watering, and live plants continue to blossom for most of the year. These advantages, plus Thailand's ideal climate for cultivation of *Dendrobium,* make Thailand the current largest exporter of tropical Orchidacae in Asia.

The amazing growth of the orchid industry would have been even more dramatic if not for a shortage of air freight space on flights to Western nations. Thai Airways routinely ships over 3,500 kg

of blooms on each of its four weekly flights to Scandinavia alone, yet this is only 70% of total demand. There's no shortage of orchids, as Thailand boasts an estimated 1,000 wild and cultivated species grown by a half dozen firms such as the Bangkok Flower Center and Siam Flower Center, and by smaller companies in the Mae Rim District near Chiang Mai.

The orchid business runs on a hair-raising schedule. Nurseries cut the flower sprays in the early morning, pack them in cardboard boxes with moisturizing agents, and send them to Bangkok International Airport for immediate export. By the next morning, Thai orchids are attracting admiration in the flower markets of Copenhagen, Tokyo, and New York.

Orchid cultivators must also keep pace with current trends. Six years ago, the mainstay variety was the hardy, purple Madame Pompadour *Dendrobium,* which slowly declined in fashion and went into a price slump. But despite higher production costs, orchids still cost just 2-3B in Bangkok, the same price as in the previous decade. To increase their profit margins, growers are switching to more expensive species such as the *Mokkara, Alanda,* and *Vanda,* the second-most common variety in Thai gardens. Another rising favorite is *Cattleya,* an orchid from South America which has more registered hybrids than any other Orchidaceae genus. One lovely *Cattleya* variety—pure white with an accent of gold—is named after Queen Sirikit.

The latest and greatest profit angle to Thailand's orchid mania is the cloning of plants—everything from orchids to strawberries to eucalyptus trees—into thousands of perfectly identical plantlets, returned to the customer for replanting. Cloning surpasses seed reproduction, as guaranteed uniformity insures the perfect production of the most prolific, disease-resistant, attractive plants. Cloning also halves the time needed for maturation.

Thailand has the knack. Although tissue culture laboratories exist in Japan, Europe, and America, Thailand leads the world in cost-efficient cloning due to cheap labor, skilled technicians, and the Thai temperament for repetitive work. Prices remain far below those charged by tissue cutters in Taiwan and Japan. Plus, experts have discovered the secrets of working with new, highly profitable plants such as asparagus, decorative ferns, and exotic fruits.

covering over 48,000 hectares of the country—including the entire island of Ko Samui—is used for thatching, home construction, mattress stuffing, clothing, and many of your favorite Thai dishes, including *tom gai kai.* The ubiquitous areca palm produces the mildly narcotic betel nut, still popular with older folks. Oil palms, raised on plantations in the deep south, yield commercial oils used for cooking and in food processing. Not surprisingly, the sugar palm produces sugar.

Mangrove swamps are an important part of the Thai ecosystem. Thailand's longest stretch of mangroves and intertidal mudflats are found along the west coast of the peninsula, near Phuket and Krabi. These swamps not only protect the coast from erosion, but also provide ideal living conditions for several plants with great commercial value. The most highly prized are the impenetrable pandanus, its narrow leaves used for plaiting, and the nipa palm, which produces materials used in basketmaking and wickerwork. Some say the succulent, cactuslike fruit of the nipa is a genuine delicacy.

Ficus is a large genus that comprises over 800 species of trees and plants found throughout Asia. Some are valuable, some are sacred. Among those with commercial value are the rubber and fig trees. For the Thais, however, the most important member of the *Ficus* family is unquestionably *Ficus religiosa,* its name aptly reflecting its reputation. Buddhists honor this tree—also called a bodhi, banyan, or pipal—for its role in the life of Buddha. It was beneath the spreading branches of the *Ficus* in 596 B.C. that an Indian prince named Siddhartha achieved the enlightenment *(bodhi)* that brought him Buddhahood. A wonderful old *Ficus* grows on the grounds of Wat Benjamabophit, the Marble Temple of Bangkok.

FAUNA

Thailand's lush tropical forests and verdant grasslands have long been cradles for an assortment of wildlife, the enormous diversity surprising visitors accustomed to the faunal monoculture of more temperate climates. This diversity is due to the country's geographical location, which straddles several zoological zones. The northern portion is home to indigenous animal life typically of Indo-Chinese origins, while western borderlands feature fauna from the Indian subcontinent. South of the Isthmus of Kra—a geographical dividing line midway down the southern peninsula—animal life is generally of the Sundaic variety, that is, from Malaysia, Borneo, Sumatra, and Java.

Despite the grievous environmental problems, Thailand still provides a home for some 282 species of mammals, 916 birds, 298 reptiles, 107 amphibians, and thousands of species of insects and tropical fish. But years of deforestation and decimation by illegal hunting render it difficult for the average visitor to actually see any wildlife except, perhaps, in the nation's 77 national parks.

Recommended reading for animal lovers and ornithologists includes *Mammals of Thailand* (1988) by Boonsong Lekagul and Jeff McNeely, *A Guide to the Birds of Thailand* (1991) by Lekagul and Philip Round, *Thailand, The Kingdom Beneath the Sea* (1990) by Ashley Boyd and Collin Piprell, and *Field Guide to the Butterflies of Thailand* (1988) by Lekagul. These books are available in most large bookstores in Bangkok.

Mammals

Thailand's most famous mammal is certainly the Asian elephant, which until 1916 was the emblem of Siam and a source of national pride. Elephants survive across the country in much better shape than the two types of indigenous bears—the Asiatic black bear and the Malayan bear—that have been largely destroyed by hunters and poachers.

Other endangered mammals are the magnificent tiger, which once roamed the rainforests, and the leopards and black panthers once common to the jungles of the Malay Peninsula. Other feline species surviving to some degree include the "golden cat" *(Profelis temmincki)* found from northern Thailand to the Malaysian border; the "fishing cat" *(Prionailurus viverrinus)* sometimes encountered in the swamp forests; the "jungle cat" *(Felis chaus),* a close relative of the lynx; and the beautifully marked ocelot *(Prionalurus bengalensis).*

Among the more curious of Siamese mammals are the barking deer *(Muntiacus muntjak),* with a bark louder than a dog's; and the tapir, a shy, nocturnal animal with enormous eyes.

But you'll more likely encounter one of the nu-

THE SIAMESE CAT

*M*ention the word Siam and the average Westerner will conjure up the king of Siam, Siamese twins, and Siamese cats. In fact, it seems most people are more familiar with things Siamese than with anything Thai. Siam was the name of Thailand prior to 1942.

Long before Patpong and Phuket, Siamese twins and Siamese cats made the country known to the Western hemisphere. The world first noticed Siam in 1829 when an English trader named Robert Hunter brought the famous twins, Chang and Eng, to Europe and America for a series of exhibitions. Chang and Eng eventually settled in the United States, where they married two American sisters and left behind large families. They died in 1874.

About 10 years later, the world learned about another Asian curiosity: the Siamese cat. The story begins in 1884 when a pair of cats, Phu and Mia, were presented by King Chulalongkorn to Owen Gould, the British consul general in Bangkok. Gould took the cats to England the following year, where they were exhibited at the Crystal Palace, familiarizing European audiences to the distant Asian kingdom. Siamese cats were imported to America in 1895 and quickly aroused great interest among cat lovers. The breed soon enjoyed great popularity in the West, eventually surpassing other favorites such as the Persian, Abyssinian, and Manx.

In their native land, Siamese cats were legendary temple guardians and companions of Buddhist priests. Some say they were venerated as sacred creatures—repositories for the transmigrating souls of royal families. Others believe the cat was brought from Egypt by ancient traders, who also imported Egyptian deifications of the royal cat.

The first official reference to the Siamese breed occurred in a poem discovered in 1830, but dating back to the days of Ayuthaya or early Rattanakosin. The nicely illustrated manuscript describes 17 types of cats regarded as auspicious and six cats considered nothing but bad luck. This Samut Thai book is now displayed in the Rattanakosin Room of the National Museum.

Siamese cats are known for their air of aloofness, inscrutable brilliant blue eyes, regal bearing, and sharply contrasting colors. Owners claim Siamese cats make delightful pets, being fastidiously clean, extremely intelligent, and affectionate.

Weird trivia: All Siamese cats are born pure white, but display their variegated coloration within the first month. Study a Siamese cat and you'll notice the special movements of the Siamese classical dancer—graceful, ethereal, and detached. Their claws are not retractable, so they make quite a racket scampering across polished teak floors. Yet these same claws make them great mousers.

More weird trivia: All Siamese cats are born Buddhist and never convert to Christianity, no matter what they tell their American owners. Siamese cats make excellent watchdogs due to their growl, like an angry dog. They are passionately attached to their chosen companion, exhibit signs of jealousy, impatience, and boredom, detest silly games, and become household tyrants if they are spoiled or coddled.

Siamese cats, like the Thai people, firmly believe in the national credos of *mai pen rai* (no worry) and *sanuk* (life is pleasure).

---

merous species of monkeys which abound in Thailand, especially the white-pawed gibbon, with its mournful whoops trailing off in anguished sobs, and the endangered pileated gibbon, distinguished by its white beard. Another curious fellow is the crab-eating macaque, which lives in mangrove swamps and has developed the speciality of catching and cracking crabs. These talented primates are commonly trained to climb trees and pick coconuts; they also perform in miniature theaters, portraying a character called "Lakhon Ling."

Birds

Thailand has an amazing diversity of birdlife, its 900 species twice the number found in Europe.

The abundance is due to the country's location over three zoological zones, the varied nature of habitats, and the annual migration of wintering migrant birds from the northern latitudes. Although hunting and poaching have reduced bird populations, visitors will still find a wide range of birds in the country's national parks.

Among the indigenous species still extant are the world's smallest bird of prey, the collared falconet, which can take dragonflies in mid-flight; the white-throated kingfisher, which utters a staccato laugh; and the white-crested laughing thrush, known for its demonic laugh alternating with humorous chuckles. Listen for the large-tailed nightjar, whose distinctive call sounds like metallic twangs; the harsh croaking of the Indian roller; the high-pitched trilling of the green-tailed sunbird; and the five-note descending call of the red-headed trogon. Other species include the white-eyed river martin, the argus pheasant, the Chinese egret of marshes and swamps, and the white-rumped shama.

Perhaps the most famous but least graceful of all Thai birds is the great hornbill. This yellow-billed inhabitant of the rainforest is a real beauty, though it sounds like an airborne steam engine in flight, and its treetop landings are usually accomplished with a crashing thump. How could such a beautiful bird be such a klutz? Another important bird, especially to certain local economies, is the edible-nest swiflet, which builds the bird nest so prized by Chinese gourmands. Travelers can learn more about swiflets and their mucous creations in the limestone caves near Ko Phi Phi in southern Thailand.

Reptiles

Thailand has a good selection of those least loved and most feared members of the animal world—reptiles.

The most common are the 100-plus species of snakes; an estimated 30 of these are considered poisonous. Siam's venomous snakes are either the very deadly front-fanged variety or the less venomous back-fanged species. The latter includes whip snakes, water snakes, and cat snakes, but it is the front-fanged creatures who cause the most alarm. These beasties include Chinese cobras, monocled cobras, banded kraits, Russell's vipers, and, most significantly, king cobras, which grow to over six meters in length. The king cobra is feared for its aggressive nature and very powerful neurotoxin, which kills in under 30 minutes flat; some say cobras can kill elephants. Cobras and other types of poisonous snakes, fortunately, are rarely encountered by tourists, except at the Red Cross Farm in Bangkok.

Thailand's largest and most famous nonpoisonous snake is the reticulated python, which lives all over the country, including inside the thatched roofs of the cheap bungalows on Ko Samui. Listen carefully at night: did you hear something stir just above your bed? Pythons grow to enormous lengths—sometimes over 10 meters—are good swimmers, and survive on a diet of chickens, ducks, cats, dogs, and the occasional tourist. Most pythons say Westerners taste something like chicken.

You'll more likely encounter, or at least hear, the ubiquitous gecko, a small lizard who scampers across walls and issues a distinctive cry: geko-geko. Thais welcome this harmless creature into their homes, since geckos eat insects and are believed to bring good luck. Many people also enjoy betting on the number of clicks issued by the gecko, seven being the most common number.

There's a fairly large colony of monitor lizards slithering around the back roads of Phuket and other hot islands in the south. Another popular lizard, the beautifully marked Liolepis belliana, is probably doomed since rural people value its tasty flesh.

Finally, a limited number of leatherback turtles, Pacific ridleys, and hawksbills migrate to southern beaches during the egg-laying season from the end of November to late February. Visitors can see these behemoths at Phuket's Nai Yang National Park and in Tarutao National Marine Park near the Malaysian border.

ENVIRONMENTAL ISSUES

Thailand's lush tropical environment and enormous diversity of wildlife have come under tremendous pressure in the last few decades. Fueled by almost a decade of double-digit growth and an expanding population hungry for new land and greater economic opportunity, Thailand now faces the same dilemma as the rest of the developing world: how to balance the need for development against the cost of environmental deterioration. Thailand, as elsewhere in Asia, faces a collision between the imperatives of economic growth and the luxury of environmental protection.

The problems are serious:

* Thailand's forests have been almost completely decimated by commercial logging, dam construction, and population pressures.
* The loss of rainforest habitats and the illegal trade in endangered animals have reduced indigenous wildlife to rock-bottom levels. Of the nation's 282 species of mammals, over 40 are now endangered.
* Air pollution in Bangkok is among the worst in Asia. Carbon monoxide levels are 50% above standard; lead is double the standard.
* Thailand's Chao Praya River is nearly dead south of Bangkok, due to a lack of oxygen caused by coliform bacteria, human waste, and the dumping of pesticides and other industrial pollutants.
* Thailand's mangrove swamps face destruction from tin mining and the encroachment of prawn farms, which have denuded much of the east coast of the peninsula.
* Coral beds are disappearing at a frightening rate due to tourism, beachfront pollution, and illegal poaching by divers and unscrupulous local traders.
* Other habitats are under pressure. Full-blown disasters such as flooding caused by deforestation and fatal spills of toxic waste generally elicit an immediate response from the government. Less subtle but perhaps more serious are problems with soil erosion, the loss of watershed areas and fishing zones, and the destruction of farmland due to industrial expansion.

END OF THE RAINFORESTS

With a tropical climate covering four topographic zones, and a vast range of habitats from grasslands to rainforests, Thailand should be a wonderland for the naturalist and lover of the great outdoors. Unfortunately, this isn't the case.

For eons, Thailand was covered with the same impenetrable jungle which spread across all of Southeast Asia. At the beginning of the century, however, logging firms began to shave the hills, while the construction of new roads and railways helped open ancient forests to human habitation and commerce.

The destruction of the forests accelerated after WW II. According to the Royal Forestry Department, almost 70% of Thailand was covered by forest in 1950. Aerial photos showed this figure had fallen by 1988 to just 28%. Even that figure is disputed by environmentalists, since

AND ON THE EIGHTH DAY, WE BULLDOZED IT.

satellite information cannot distinguish forest from plantations and fruit orchards. Forestry officials concede forest cover is perhaps around 10%, and that virgin forest only accounts for half that amount. Conservationist Dr. Boonsong Lekagul, who for three decades has publicly campaigned for preservation of the remaining forests, agrees with international estimates that by the end of the century Thailand's remaining ground cover will be almost completely destroyed.

What happened? Government-licensed logging consortiums did a spectacular job, so spectacular that by 1967 the country—once a major exporter of timber—began importing wood from neighboring countries. These logging companies, often under the tacit control of government and military leaders, refused to follow scientific logging procedures such as felling only mature trees and implementing reforestation schemes to ensure a prosperous future.

Reforestation programs, in many ways, proved misguided and poorly administered. The Thai National Forest Policy of 1985 aimed to boost the country's forest cover towards 40% by encouraging private sector planting of commercial tree plantations. Unfortunately, most firms elected to plant fast-growing species such as eucalyptus, a tree which provides short-term economic gains but drains the soil of valuable nutrients at a terrible rate. The eucalyptus also leaves a monoculture environment utterly disastrous to wildlife; the leaves are inedible for most animals.

The other major factor in Thailand's pell-mell deforestation was the exploding national population, which skyrocketed from eight million in 1910 to over 60 million in 1994. Growth of this nature dramatically increased the demand for cleared land for agriculture, habitation, and industrial development, a problem exacerbated by the slash-and-burn agricultural practices of the northern hilltribes. The problem reappeared dramatically in late 1994, after forestry officials reported that land-hungry villagers had surreptitiously poisoned over 100,000 trees to free up much-needed land.

Timber Problems

The government made efforts over the last decade to protect rapidly disappearing forests, though legislation passed in Bangkok was often compromised by rampant corruption among forestry officers, logging companies, and local officials. Many of the largest logging companies were controlled by politically influential people with deep pockets, who had little trouble logging protected forests, even in national parks.

Timber firms and their financial backers devised countless ways to circumvent the rules. Some were rather ingenious. The Royal Forestry Department would classify ancient virgin forest as "degraded" land, thereby opening the area for commercial development and reforestation with eucalyptus. Another trick conducted by corrupt forestry officials was to remove plots of protected land by falsely declaring the forest cover already destroyed. A loophole popular with loggers was to encourage villagers to trespass on and lay claim to national forest reserves. After land ownership was granted, the operators would buy the land from the squatters, neatly taking advantage of a law designed to help the landless peasant. A final scam was to mix legally cut logs with illegitimately felled trees from nearby forests. Loggers also took advantage of timber deals with the Burmese regime. After all, who can tell a Thai tree from a Burmese one?

Despite new legislation and stronger enforcement, many of these tricks remain common in the Thai forestry industry.

LAST CHANCE FOR WILDLIFE

On Saturday, 1 September 1990, Seub Nakhasanthien, director of the Huay Kha Khaeng Wildlife Sanctuary, took his own life. His suicide was a last desperate cry to the world, intended to focus attention on the plight of his country's dwindling forests and its dying wildlife, hopelessly threatened by corrupt officials, loggers, and poachers. Seub, a conservationist despondent over his inability to protect Thailand's endangered species, now symbolizes his nation's attempt to protect its last remaining wildlife.

Thailand's fauna are the direct casualties of rainforest destruction and insatiable poaching. Without a haven and relentlessly hunted, Thailand's wildlife has declined to unsustainable levels over the last two decades. Endangered species include the pileated gibbon, the clouded leopard, the Malayan tapir, and the tiger. Threatened species include the hog-nosed bat, the Irrawaddy dolphin, the gaur, and the Asian tapir. Extinct species include the Javan and Sumatran rhinoceros, the kouprey, and Shomburgk's deer.

The endangered list includes more than mammals. Ecologists estimate up to 90% of the bird population has been sacrificed or is severely threatened. There are almost 200 endangered winged species, including the giant ibis, the Chinese egret, and the white-winged wood duck. All birds are considered fair game by hunters, while the more exotic species are hunted by collectors for the international bird market. Today in Thailand, aside from in some national parks, few visitors see or even hear a bird of any type.

As for other animals, the International Union for the Conservation of Nature and Natural Resources cites almost 40 endangered species of reptiles and dozens of endangered sealife species, such as the hawksbill turtle and the saltwater crocodile. Thailand has become a place where crocodiles only survive in tourist parks, waiting to be killed for their skins.

No Place to Hide

Thailand's loss of wildlife has been caused by destruction of habitat, overhunting, and weak enforcement of existing legislation designed to protect rare species. Another problem is the poaching and exporting of rare animals for the international trade. Endangered species command big prices on the wildlife market, an irresistible temptation to the poor and desperate. Penalties for illegal hunting and poaching remain absurdly low. Forestry Department efforts to stem destruction are hampered by low wages and a lack of manpower.

Thailand's weak enforcement of wildlife protection laws once made it a major trading center for endangered species, though the situation has improved considerably in recent years and much of this trade mas moved over to Cambodia and Laos. Thailand was once condemned by the World Wildlife Fund as "perhaps the worst in the world for the illegal trade of endangered animals." Thailand has signed the Convention on International Trade in Endangered Species (CITES), but illegal animals continue to be smuggled in from Cambodia, Laos, and Myanmar.

Smuggled animals are exported to Eastern European countries, which are not signatories to CITES. Unscrupulous dealers then quarantine the animals before reshipping them to buyers in Western countries with new certificates of origin that state Bred In Captivity. Some animals, such as barking deer, pangolin, and civet, never leave Thailand, but end up on the menus of restaurants serving so-called "jungle food." The most gruesome trend is to sever a gibbon's head while the animal is still alive, thereby obtaining an expression of terror that fetches top dollar.

Thai authorities are under pressure to end the international trade in endangered animals and to crush the embarrassing animal black market which takes place most weekends at Chatuchak Market in Bangkok. Today, the leopard skins, gibbons, endangered birds, and rare turtles are discreetly kept out of the sight until an interested client arrives. Raids are conducted periodically to placate international animal protection groups, but Thailand's notorious trade will probably remain a festering problem for the foreseeable future.

Tiger Steaks in Bangkok?

The most recent incident to outrage the Western world was a proposal in early 1995 to legalize the farming and slaughter of tigers for Chinese folk medicines. Apparently, the director of the Si Racha Farm intends to take advantage of a Thai loophole allowing the sale of Asian cats and cat parts on the domestic market. The proposal has been endorsed by a leading advisor to the Thai Royal Forestry Department, who insists tigers could be farmed as easily as pigs, and complains Westerners are far too sentimental about animals.

Protests were lodged by Leonie Vejjajiva of Thailand's Wildlife Foundation, who believes tigers and other Asian cats should not end up as tiger steaks and penis soups. Ethnic Chinese in Thailand and around the world believe tiger potions can cure everything from arthritis to impotence, despite the lack of scientific evidence to support such a view. Leonie also fears a legal market for tiger medicine would put a bounty on the head of all remaining wild tigers, a financial incentive which would destroy the last of the world's 5,000 wild tigers.

ELEPHANT EXTINCTION?

several years ago, an elephant working a tourist show near Chiang Mai became annoyed with an obnoxious onlooker, picked him up with his trunk, and hurled him into a nearby lake. Given the species' current status within the Siamese kingdom, it is difficult to blame the elephant for its temperamental outburst. The elephant may soon become extinct in Southeast Asia. It defies the imagination, but animal experts warn that unless drastic measures are quickly implemented, Thailand's population of wild elephants may be a distant memory in less than two decades.

Elephants have long been popular figures in the art and mythology of Southeast Asia, figuring prominently in the iconography of both Hindu and Buddhist tales. Pachyderms have served as central characters in the birth of the Buddha and in a previous life of the Buddha as recorded in the Jataka tales, as well as in the life of the Hindu god of learning and knowledge, potbellied Ganesha. Thai folklore includes legends of white elephants, flying elephants, magic elephants, and multiheaded elephants.

Recent traditions are equally profound. Thai people have long believed that national prosperity and royal strength were tied to the possession of sacred elephants—most importantly, the rare white elephant. Thai history abounds with battles fought on the backs of elephants, such as the final combat between Queen Suriyothai and a Burmese general, and the defeat of an invading Burmese crown prince by King Naresuan the Great.

The legendary military prowess of pachyderms almost brought them to America. In 1862, King Mongkut (Rama IV) discovered that elephants were unknown in the United States. Mongkut offered to send a shipload to President Abraham Lincoln to aid the Civil War fight. Lincoln declined, explaining American latitudes did not "favor the multiplication of the elephant."

What a fool! If Lincoln had had greater vision, perhaps America would now have herds of elephants thundering across the plains of Texas or gallumphing down the boulevards of New York. And American mythology would honor the memory of Ernest Elephant rather than Buffalo Bill.

In any event, elephants proved such an auspicious symbol, Thailand's favorite beast appeared on the national flag until 1917 and still serves as the central figure on the Royal Thai Navy insignia. Even today, the royal decoration most highly valued in Thailand remains the "Most Exalted Order of the White Elephant." And could it be coincidence that the shape of Thailand eerily resembles an elephant's head, with ears flapping toward Cambodia and sinewy trunk dangling into Malaysia?

Pachyderms now face an uncertain future. The main problems are overpopulation, lack of sufficient breeding space, and reduced land cover and food supplies. Another complication is deforestation. The destruction of the rainforests and the nationwide logging ban in 1989 put elephants on the unemployment rolls. Some were moved to Myanmar and Laos where the logging industry was enjoying an unexpected boom. Those left behind had fewer logs to move and found themselves downwardly mobile. Many giant tuskers were simply abandoned or herded into towns, where they were forced to perform silly shows for Western tourists and Thais. The mahouts' chief money churner soon became charging Thai citizens 20B to duck under the elephant's tusk for good luck.

The Royal Forestry Department estimated the 1984 elephant population to be around 20,000 animals. Recent figures by the same authorities cite 3,000 domestic and 2,000 wild, a drop of 75% in only 10 years. Domestic elephants work for a living by shifting illegal timber, doing logging shows for tourists, or enduring the good-luck routine; wild elephants are those creatures that miraculously escape poachers and game wardens working inside Thailand's national parks. Wild elephants also have avoided the golf courses located in and around national parks.

Little help is forthcoming for the elephants. Naturalists and preservation groups despair at stopping government officials from illegally allocating protected conservation areas to commercial developers. Consequently, the demise of grasslands and forests, which once provided pachyderms their daily 120 kg of food and the privacy to copulate, is another dilemma.

What will save the Thai elephant? Education and concern among Thai and Western people are perhaps the last chance for the sacred animal of Thailand. Without dramatic efforts by the government, it appears Thailand will have more golf courses than elephants within two decades.

A TURN IN THE ROAD

A major obstacle has been the attitude that environmental protection is inimical to economic growth, and that environmental destruction is simply a necessary component of economic success. The underlying problem is one of economic evaluation. Man-made assets and economic growth can easily be measured in monetary terms but natural resource assets are not so easily valued; their loss entails no debit charge against current income or future production. National prosperity appears unaffected as a country exhausts its mineral resources, cuts down its forests, pollutes its aquifers, and hunts its wildlife to extinction.

But the winds of opinion are shifting in Thailand, as elsewhere in Asia. Today, the government and public are embracing the idea that wanton environmental degradation is not only unhealthy and unaesthetic, but exacts an unacceptable economic cost.

The first major government environmental initiative occurred in January 1989, when Prime Minister Chatichai Choonhavan banned all commercial logging after a disastrous series of floods killed hundreds in southern Thailand. Although the exact cause of the floods could be debated, many felt illegal logging and the resultant lack of ground cover around Nakhon Si Thammarat were primarily to blame.

In March 1994 the government announced an ambitious plan to replenish the country's forests by tapping the environmental consciousness of major Bangkok companies. The three-year project is strongly supported by the king, a wise inducement since few companies can resist any program endorsed by the hugely respected monarch and his queen.

In June 1994 the government enacted new environmental legislation, under the umbrella of the National Environment Act, to tackle seven major targets, including water and air pollution, hazardous waste, and soil destruction.

But the most important change has been in the understanding and perception of the Thai public. The loss of their natural heritage has spurred ordinary Thais to increasingly strident calls for stronger protection of their forests, seas, and mountains. A surprising number of Thais now lend their support to environmental groups opposing illegal logging, dam construction, forest encroachment, and the export of endangered wildlife.

The problems of population pressures, equitable distribution of land, illegal logging, and the intransigence of the government continue to work against the environment. But the alternatives have become so grim serious efforts are finally underway to reverse the apocalyptic trends of recent years.

ENVIRONMENTAL ORGANIZATIONS

Western Organizations

Rainforest Action Network (RAN): RAN and the **World Rainforest Movement** are a worldwide network of concerned citizens who hope to crystallize concern and devise campaigns to stem the destruction of tropical rainforests. Membership includes a monthly newsletter which covers battles to protect the forests and a quarterly report drawn from its worldwide affiliates. Membership costs US$35/year. 450 Sansome St., Suite 700, San Francisco, CA 94111, tel. (415) 398-4404.

World Wildlife Fund: The world's largest organization dedicated to the preservation of tropical forests and indigenous wildlife. The group also works with local residents to help improve living standards, and publishes studies on the effects of international tourism and ecotourism movements. 1250 24th St. NW, Washington, D.C. 20037, tel. (202) 293-4800.

Nature Conservancy: An international agency which protects habitats through acquisition and purchase of rainforest land, a "debt-for-nature" swap which raises money for local environmental organizations. 1815 North Lynn St., Arlington, VA 22209, tel. (703) 841-5300.

Rainforest Alliance: A small nonprofit organization dedicated to saving the forests with public-awareness programs, research into the timber industry, and publication of a quarterly newsletter. Membership costs US$30/year. 295 Madison Ave., Suite 1804, New York, NY 10017, tel. (212) 599-5060.

Thai Organizations

Wildlife Fund Thailand: Under the royal patronage of the queen and an associate office of the World Wildlife Fund, WFT is a highly respected nonprofit organization dedicated to wildlife conservation and the wise use of natural resources. 251/88090 Phahonyothin Rd., Bangkhen, Bangkok 10220, tel. (02) 258-9134, fax (662) 258-9403.

The Siam Society: A popular organization dedicated to the study and preservation of Thai historical sites, arts and crafts, and natural environment. Excellent monthly tours to national parks led by naturalists and ecologists. Visit the office for more information: 131 Soi Asoke, Sukumvit Rd., Bangkok 10110.

Royal Forestry Department: Thailand's government agency charged with protecting the environment is now receiving better funding and increased authority to prosecute environmental criminals. Phahonyothin Rd., Bangkok 10900.

Project for Ecological Recovery: A private organization operated by both Thai citizens and concerned Western residents. 77/3 Soi Nomjit, Naret Rd., Bangkok 10500.

THE NATIONAL PARKS

Thailand's 77 national parks and 33 wildlife sanctuaries offer the opportunity to relax near waterfalls and lakes, enjoy nature walks, dive over coral reefs, and search for wildlife in some of the nation's last remaining stands of indigenous forest. The national parks system was established by the government in 1962 to help preserve the environment and safeguard rapidly diminishing forest cover. Today, the parks system covers over 11% of the nation's land area, one of the highest ratios of protected land in the world. A further 24 parks are slated for gazetting by the year 2000.

Reservations
Bungalows in the more popular parks—Khao Yai near Bangkok, Erawan near Kanchanaburi, Doi Inthanon near Chiang Mai—are often filled on weekends and holidays, making reservations imperative. Smaller parks located away from urban areas are rarely filled and visitors can usually arrive without reservations to find an available

ENVIRONMENTAL AWARENESS

*T*he preservation of rainforests and wildlife is often a complicated task, but visitors to Thailand can help by supporting the following organizations: World Wildlife Fund, Rainforest Action Network, and Friends of the Earth. Most importantly, be conscientious as you travel through Thailand; tourism is the world's biggest industry and thus the discriminating traveler has powerful leverage against the despoliation of the environment.

First, think before buying tropical hardwood products such as teak, rosewood, and mahogany furniture, or any items made from coral or endangered animals. Seemingly innocuous products made from hides, shells, and feathers on sale in public markets throughout Thailand are often illegal, species-threatening souvenirs. Regulations are complex, but prohibited products include crocodile hides, pangolin (anteater) leather, most wild bird feathers, and all ivory products.

One of the most obvious ecological problems is the piles of discarded plastic bottles polluting many of the country's beaches and rivers. Visitors should drink from glass bottles whenever possible and be sure to deposit plastic containers in legitimate collection bins. Plastic water bottles are not recyclable, but glass containers include a refundable 4B deposit. While recycling and trash collection are not the highest priorities in much of Thailand, Western travelers should set a positive example by monitoring their disposal of waste products.

Patronizing so-called jungle restaurants only encourages the poaching of endangered species. While it may seem exotic to feast on barbecued pangolin or bear, you may be wise to take down the name and address of the restaurant and report your findings to the Tourism Authority of Thailand, the Wildlife Fund Thailand, and the Thai Forestry Department. Restaurants serving endangered animals are against the law, though lax enforcement allows many of these places to stay open.

MODERN CHALLENGES

*T*hough acreage within the park system is surprisingly high, problems remain with park management. Illegal logging continues to reduce the land cover, while hunters and wildlife poachers operate with impunity. Many of the parks have been settled by agriculturalists, who refuse to surrender their homelands for the sake of wildlife conservation. Moreover, Forestry Department staff members are underpaid, demoralized, and given little training or direction. Many make deals with poachers and land thieves to supplement their meager incomes.

Unchecked tourism has ruined many popular destinations for Thai citizens and visitors alike. Two glaring examples are the islands of Ko Samet on the eastern seaboard and Ko Phi Phi near Phuket in southern Thailand. Although both are designated national parks and, according to national law, should never be developed with commercial enterprises, both islands are largely overrun with hotels, guesthouses, restaurants, dive shops, and nightclubs.

The Forestry Department periodically makes threatening noises about crackdowns, but little has been done to preserve these fragile ecosystems. Nobody stopped the mafia-like group that turned one national park into 80% shrimp ponds, destroying one of the last virgin mangrove swamps. Nobody complained when the Dusit Rayavadee hotel group constructed a luxury hotel in the middle of Had Nopparat National Park in Krabi Province. And, of course, nobody would dream of installing adequate sewage systems, providing clean water for visitors, or hauling away the trash threatening to bury Ko Samet and Ko Phi Phi under the refuse of modern civilization.

Another challenge is the Tourism Authority of Thailand's desire to assume control over significant chunks of the country's national parks. After eyeing the parks for several years, the TAT submitted proposals in 1994 to take legal ownership of some of the parks currently run by the Royal Forestry Department. The TAT announced plans to construct hotels and restaurants in conjunction with the private sector. Environmentalists are appalled by the idea, complaining the TAT has already ruined their beaches. Why must it take the parks? Some feel the failure of the Royal Forestry Department to protect the parks is reason enough to shift management to the tourism industry, but others fear the situation will go from bad to worse. Disposition of the parks remains under discussion.

bungalow or camp site. Bookings from Bangkok must be paid in advance.

Few parks have telephones and few rangers speak much English. For these reasons, peak season reservations for popular parks must be made in advance at the National Parks Division of the Royal Forestry Department, Paholyothin Rd., Bangkhen, Bangkok 10900, tel. (02) 579-4842. It's possible to make reservations by mail, and you can also reserve in person by visiting the parks office near Kasetsart University in north Bangkok. The reservation office is located at the back southwest corner of the compound. Reach the university by mail at Paholyothin Rd., Bangkhen, Bangkok, 10900.

Accommodations and Meals

Most parks provide a choice of bungalows or tents. Bungalows are usually large and rustic lodges that sleep 5-10 people and cost 500-1,500B per night—great for large groups, but problematic for solos or couples. Facilities generally include several screened rooms, electric-ity, running water, and beds with thin mattresses. Visitors should bring along a sleeping bag or warm blanket, and basic supplies such as rain gear, insect repellent, and a flashlight.

Most parks also feature a common camping area, where tent camping is allowed for a small fee (5B for Thais, 15-30B for foreigners). A few of the larger parks rent tents at low rates. Tents and other camping equipment are sold throughout Bangkok and at open-air markets in Chiang Mai.

Food is usually available at open-air cafes or larger restaurants operated by the Royal Forestry Department, but it's a good idea to bring along some extra food and a few bottles of Mekong.

When to Visit

The best time to visit parks is during the week. Avoid the weekends, when hundreds of teenagers might show up, spending their entire visit dancing around portable boomboxes.

Each season provides its own attractions. The cool season, Nov.-Feb., is a good time to visit parks in the lower elevations and the steamy parks in the deep south. This is also the best season for high-mountain wildflowers and migratory birds arriving from northern latitudes. Wildlife lovers should visit during April and May, when animals descend from the hills in search of water. Even the rainy season, June-Nov., has its advantages. Waterfalls, virtually nonexistent during the March-June hot season, roar to life during the monsoon months.

Activities and Tours

Thailand's parks, administered by the National Parks Division of the Royal Forestry Department, are often transversed by hiking trails originating from the main lodge. Trail systems are often poorly signposted and maps provided by the rangers are uniformly sketchy. Visitors intending to conduct longer treks or overnight excursions should hire a guide or park ranger for 200-300B per day. Park rangers sometimes offer evening wildlife sighting expeditions.

Several organizations in Bangkok sponsor inexpensive trips to wildlife sanctuaries and nature preserves, often led by experts in the field. Upcoming tours are advertised in the Bangkok Post—a great way to meet local expatriates and get the inside scoop on environmental conditions. Contact the Wildlife Fund Thailand at (02) 521-3435, the Natural History section of the Siam Society at (02) 258-3491, or the Bangkok Bird Club at (02) 374-6610.

The National Parks of Thailand (1991), by Denis Gray and Collin Piprell, provides an excellent survey of 30 national parks and wildlife sanctuaries.

HISTORY

Alone among the nations of Southeast Asia, Thailand has never fallen under colonial domination or experienced a divisive civil war—historical elements that give the Thai people their unique sense of independence and cultural identity.

PRE-HISTORY

Early Peoples

Prior to the arrival of the present inhabitants, Thailand was home to several Pleistocene cultures (600,000-130,000 B.C.) who left behind stone implements, pebble tools, and other artifacts from Lampang in the north to Krabi in the south. Later-period Hoabinhian (120,000-3,000 B.C.) tools and farming implements have been discovered near Mae Hong Son and Kanchanaburi.

Thailand apparently served as a land bridge between Asia and Australia through which successive racial groups filtered down from China and Tibet. These Proto-Malays encountered the Pleistocene and Hoabinhian-era inhabitants, who were forced south or absorbed by the new arrivals. Few of these peoples survive aside from isolated highland tribal groups such as the Malaysian Dayak and Sakai, Indonesian Batak, and various groups in the Philippines.

Archaeological Discoveries

Most major discoveries of artifacts from prehistoric Thailand have taken place in modern times. The first significant event occurred during WW II when a Dutch prisoner of war, working on the bridge over the River Kwai, stumbled across a collection of Hoabinhian tombs containing Neolithic pottery and human remains. The tombs lay untouched until Dutch archaeologists returned after the war to excavate the burial sites. The site and remains can now be viewed in situ near Kanchanaburi, two hours west of Bangkok.

The Kanchanaburi findings were subsequently surpassed by the work of an American archaeologist named Chester Gorman, a near legendary figure in Thai archaeology and prehistory. In 1972, Gorman discovered tools and seeds in Spirit Cave near Soppong in Mae Hong Son Province that were subsequently carbon-dated back to 10,000 B.C., and pottery and polished knives from 6,000-6,800 B.C.

Thailand's most spectacular discoveries occurred in 1974 near Ban Chiang in northeastern Thailand. Archaeologists from the University of Pennsylvania under the direction of Chester Gorman found sophisticated pottery and tools that made world headlines and set off a major controversy.

HISTORICAL BOUNDARIES OF MAINLAND SOUTHEAST ASIA

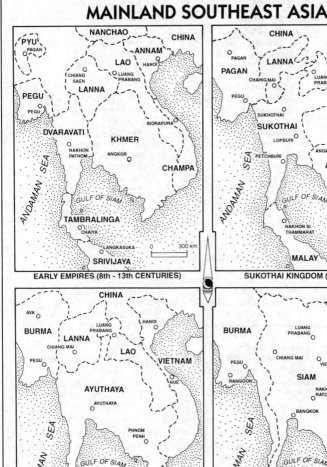

EARLY EMPIRES (8th - 13th CENTURIES)

PYU
PAGAN
NANCHAO
CHINA
ANNAM
LAO
HANOI
CHIANG SAEN
LUANG PRABANG
LANNA
PEGU
PEGU
INDRAPURA
DVARAVATI
NAKHON PATHOM
KHMER
ANGKOR
CHAMPA
ANDAMAN SEA
GULF OF SIAM
TAMBRALINGA
CHAIYA
LANGKASUKA
SRIVIJAYA
0   300 km

SUKOTHAI KINGDOM (1220 - 1378)

CHINA
PAGAN
LANNA
ANNAM
HANOI
CHAING MAI
LUANG PRABANG
PEGU
SUKHOTHAI
LAO
SUKOTHAI
LOPBURI
PETCHBURI
ANGKOR
ANGKOR
ANDAMAN SEA
GULF OF SIAM
NAKHON SI THAMMARAT
MALAY
0   300 km

AYUTHAYA KINGDOM (1378 - 1767)

CHINA
AVA
BURMA
LANNA
LUANG PRABANG
HANOI
CHIANG MAI
LAO
VIETNAM
PEGU
AYUTHAYA
HUE
AYUTHAYA
PHNOM PENH
ANDAMAN SEA
GULF OF SIAM
NAKHON SI THAMMARAT
PATTANI
MALACCA
0   300 km

SIAM AT RAMA I (1809 - 1824)

CHINA
BURMA
LUANG PRABANG
HANOI
CHIANG MAI
VIENTIANE
VIETNAM
SIAM
PEGU
RANGOON
NAKHON RATCHASIMA
HUE
BANGKOK
PHNOM PENH
SAIGON
ANDAMAN SEA
GULF OF SIAM
NAKHON SI THAMMARAT
PENANG
MALAY
0   300 km

THAILAND IN WORLD HISTORY~A TIME LINE

DATES	THAI HISTORY	WORLD HISTORY
3500 B.C.	Hoabinhian culture	Mesopotamian civilization
2000 B.C.	Ban Chiang bronzes	Egyptian pyramids
651 B.C.	Tai Empire begins at Nanchao	Life of Buddha
240 B.C.	Buddhist missionaries arrive	Great Wall of China
200 B.C.	Final Ban Chiang pottery	Hannibal crosses Alps
A.D. 0-300	Hinduization of Indochina	Roman Empire
500-600	Mons (Dvaravati) arrive	Mohammed
661	Mons establish Haripunjaya	Bagan (Myanmar) founded
600-800	Srivijayan Empire at Ligor	Muslims invade Spain
900-1200	Khmers control Siam	Normans conquer England
1238	Tais establish Sukothai	King Louis IX of France
1253	Kublai Khan sacks Nanchao	Chartres Cathedral completed
1283	Thai script invented	Marco Polo in China
1297	Lanna Kingdom founded	Spectacles invented
1350	Ayuthaya Kingdom founded	Hundred Years War begins
1378	Sukothai falls to Ayuthaya	Chaucer writing in Europe
1475	Buddhist Council Chiang Mai	The Gutenberg Bible
1516	Portuguese Embassy in Ayuthaya	Cortez confronts Aztec empire
1680	Siamese diplomats visit France	*Paradise Lost,* Milton
1767	Burmese destroy Ayuthaya	American Revolution
1768-82	Taksin makes Thonburi capital	"The Rights of Man," Paine
1782	Chakri Dynasty established	French Revolution
1844	Thailand's first newspaper	Famine in Ireland
1862	King Mongkut hires governess	U.S. Civil War
1876	Oriental Hotel opens	Bell invents telephone
1887	Joseph Conrad visits Bangkok	Japan defeats China
1908	Bangkok has 300 cars	Freud interprets dreams
1913	Thai citizens take surnames	World War I
1932	End of absolute monarchy	Hitler rises to power
1939	Siam renamed Thailand	World War II
1946	Bhumibol Adulyadej (Rama IX)	Philippines gains independence
1950	Students overthrow government	Nixon bombs Cambodia
1992	Democratic elections	Collapse of communism
1993	Thailand bans Madonna	Michael Jackson performs in Bangkok

Gorman's findings seemed to challenge the orthodox teaching that civilization—as defined by the introduction of agriculture, pottery, and metalworking—and the Bronze Age had originated in Mesopotamia or China, and then diffused around the world. Many of the Ban Chiang objects appeared to predate or be contemporaneous with artifacts from earlier civilizations, thereby challenging traditional beliefs about the origins of bronze, a major technological innovation in the evolution of mankind.

Initial carbon tests dated Ban Chiang's oldest spearheads at 3,500-3,000 B.C., older than Mesopotamian bronzes from 3,000 B.C. and Chinese bronzes from 2,000 B.C. Could bronze metallurgy—so hugely important that it names an entire era—have originated in Thailand and spread to China and the Middle East?

Subsequent retesting of the bronzes indicated dates between 2,500-2,000 B.C., contemporaneous with Chinese artifacts but somewhat later than those found in the Middle East. Ban Chiang remains an important puzzle piece in the origins of the Bronze Age.

Nanchao and the Tai Peoples

The origins and early histories of the Tai people largely remain a matter of speculation. This is due primarily to the lack of a written language until the 13th century, and to the scarcity of early historical records apart from a few descriptions by Chinese travelers. Other records were lost over the centuries to heat and humidity, and during warfare between the Thais, Burmese, and Vietnamese; the most tragic example was the 1767 destruction of Ayuthaya by the Burmese.

Determining the origins of Asian nations is never simple but few places are as controversial as Thailand. The debate centers on whether Thailand received its culture from outside sources such as China—the receptacle theory—or whether the Thais constitute a prototypical race that has inhabited the region since the late Neolithic age.

The most widely held theory is that the Tais are descended from people from Mongolia and Northern China, and that these early Tai speakers slowly migrated southward into mainland Southeast Asia.

Chinese historical records confirm an independent kingdom established by the Tais in 651 B.C. near Nanchao in Yunnan Province. The people were described by the Chinese as closely related kin with a degree of sophistication in Chinese-based arts and crafts.

Nanchao was hardly a peaceful place. According to Chinese chroniclers, Nanchao waged near continual warfare against Chinese warlords in the north, early Burmese empires such as the Pyu, and Vietnamese states near Tonkin. This political turmoil perhaps forced many Tais to migrate south into Thailand.

In 1253 the Mongol army under the command of Kublai Khan attacked and destroyed Nanchao, unleashing a migratory flood as Tais fled in all directions. Those who moved to upper Myanmar became Shans, Assam Tais are now called Ahom Thais, Mekong Tais are Lao, and Tais who occupied Vietnam formed several groups such as Black Tai, Red Tai, and White Tai. Despite centuries of assimilation, these widely dispersed groups continue to speak closely related languages and share common legends and traditions—a legacy of their origins in Yunnan.

This theory is questioned by scientists who argue the Tais are a prototypical race that originated in Thailand and then diffused their culture throughout Southeast Asia, introducing rice culture, pottery, and metallurgy to the Chinese. After bringing their skills to the Chinese, these peoples established the Tai empire at Nanchao, returning to Thailand following the Mongol invasion. Proponents of this theory are supported by the discoveries at Ban Chiang, Kanchanaburi, and Spirit Cave.

DVARAVATI (MON) PERIOD

Historians divide modern Thai history into four general periods: the Dvaravati or Mon (6th-13th

---

THAI OR TAI?

*T*hai is a political term referring to any citizen of Thailand, whether that person is of Tai, Chinese, Indian, or Western descent. If you've got a Thai passport, you are legally a "Thai."

On the other hand, Tai is a cultural and linguistic term which denotes a broad spectrum of peoples who migrated into Thailand over the last several millennia. Contemporary Tais spread over much of Southeast Asia but are known by regional names such as Tai, Lao, Shan, Lu, and Chuang. Tais speak a monosyllabic and tonal language with some degree of mutual intelligibility among the regional groups. In most cases, Tais have adapted to local conditions and assumed many of the conventions of the indigenous population. For example, the Tais who settled in the lower Chao Praya valley converted to the Theravada Buddhism favored by the Mons, while the Tais in Cambodia adopted Hinduism, the prominent religion of the Chams. An estimated 80 million Tais live throughout Southeast Asia, a cultural group comparable in number to the French or Germans.

Some Thais are not Tai—Hindus in Bangkok, Malay Muslims in the south—while many Tais are not Thai—Cambodians, Shans, and Chuangs in southern China.

centuries), Sukothai (1238-1350), Ayuthaya (1350-1767), and Bangkok or Rattanakosin (1767-present). Major influences include Srivijaya in Sumatra or Malaysia, Khmers in Cambodia, and Lanna in the north.

The Mons and Dvaravati Culture

As the Thai peoples slowly migrated from southern China into northern and central Thailand, they joined the people who populated many of the important river basins within the region. Most prominent among these groups were the Dvaravati, a Buddhist culture associated with the Mon people. Named by George Coedes, a French art historian who discovered the word Dvaravati on coins excavated near Nakhon Pathom, Dvaravati is actually a Sanskrit word denoting the city of Krishna in the Indian opus Mahabharata. The Dvaravati empire remains an enigma aside from the fact that it occupied an area of western and central Thailand and, most importantly, introduced Theravada Buddhism to the population.

Some scientists theorize the Mons originated in India, migrating across Myanmar sometime early in the Christian era to settle the lower Chao Praya basin. Mons failed to create major military powers or a centralized administration, forming casual associations of villages that maintained ties through marriage and trade. The more prominent bases of Mon culture were the northern empire of Haripunchai (present-day Lamphun) and around Nakon Pathom, considered the primary center of pre-Tai Mon culture.

The Mons brought with them the culture of Theravada Buddhism and thereby passed to Thailand its dominant religion. According to Indian records, Buddhism was introduced in the 3rd century by priests sent from King Asoka, a Buddhist ruler who dispatched missionaries throughout most of Asia.

The Dvaravati Empire at Nakhon Pathom disappeared sometime in the early 11th century after the Khmers established military outposts at Lopburi and Sukothai. Haripunchai in northern Thailand survived as an independent Mon-based entity until conquest by King Mengrai of Chiang Mai in 1281. Mons have largely disappeared in Thailand, though a sizable community still exists in Myanmar.

The Indianization of Thailand

One of the most profound shifts in Southeast Asian history effected during the Dvaravati Period was the introduction of Indian culture, religion, and political thought to the indigenous populations. Hinduism, Theravada Buddhism, the divinity of rulers, and Hindu art styles arrived in the region from Indian traders, who paused along the sea routes on their way to the trading centers of China. Other Hindu centers were established by Indian traders who passed along a variety of land routes from Three Pagodas Pass in Western Thailand to trading entrepots in Vietnam and southern China. Hindu political forms, religious traditions, and artistic styles soon dominated the region from the deep south to the remote corners of the northeast.

Hindu Brahmins and scholars were invited by local rulers to serve as advisers and astrologers, since Hinduism supported the concept of ruler as god-king—a notion carried to the extreme in the Khmer Empire at Angkor. Hindu art styles introduced in the early Christian era are seen in the Haripunchai temples near Lamphun, while Gupta and pre-Pala sculpture have been discovered in the south near Surat Thani and in the vicinity of Nakhon Pathom.

The Srivijaya Empire

Another influential empire was Srivijaya, a powerful yet mysterious Hindu civilization centered at Palembang in southern Sumatra. Little is known of Srivijaya, except that the empire controlled Ligor (now Nakhon Si Thammarat) in the 2nd century A.D. and later absorbed the Hindu empire at Chaiya.

Srivijaya dominated mercantile trade throughout Southeast Asia from the 3rd to 13th centuries, controlling the Straits of Malacca and enjoying the military cooperation of the Sailendra Empire on Java. Historians believe Srivijaya originated as a Hindu empire but embraced Mahayana Buddhism prior to its dissolution in the 13th century.

Srivijayan statuary uncovered near Chaiya and around Ligor indicate superb control and a stylistic melding of Indian, Javanese, Mon, and Khmer influences. The most significant discoveries include several 8th-century statues of Avalokitesvara, a principal bodhisattva, uncovered near Chaiya; and architectural ruins near Chaiya including Wat Pra Boromthat and Wat Keo.

CAMBODIAN EMPIRES

Early Cambodian Empires, A.D. 100-802

The Indian-influenced kingdoms of Cambodia made a strong impact on early Thai culture, religion, and political structure. Strategically located on the trade routes between China and India, the empires of the Khmers dominated the political landscape of Southeast Asia to an extent far greater than suggested by the country's present-day size or political influence.

Funan: Cambodian historical records begin with the rise of the Funan Empire in the 1st century A.D. Centered along the lower reaches of the Mekong and Tonle Sap Rivers, and prosperous due to its location on the east-west trade route between China and India, Funan eventually extended its political power south to the Malay Peninsula and east across most of present-day Vietnam. According to court records, Funan maintained trade and diplomatic relations with the early Mon civilizations of central Thailand.

Funan was among the earliest Asian kingdoms to embrace Hindu culture, a framework which profoundly shapes the history, art, and political landscapes of not only Cambodia but all of Southeast Asia. Although populated by an indigenous population plus immigrants from Indonesia and southern China, Funan absorbed most of its knowledge of religion and political organization from Indian merchants and theologians who arrived in the early millennium. By the 5th century, Funan society employed an Indian-based script, worshipped a pantheon of Hindu gods and Mahayana deities, and favored art styles inspired by the Gupta movement of India. Eventually, these Hindu elements merged with original designs to create the first truly original Cambodian empire.

Chenla: By the 6th century the empire of Funan had been slowly displaced by the rising power of Chenla, a Hindu-based dynasty originally located near Stung Treng in northern Cambodia and in southern Laos near Wat Phu. Diplomatic marriages subsequently gave rise to Chenla strongholds at Kampong Thom in the center of Cambodia and Angkor Borei at Takeo.

Chenla survived as a united dynasty until the 7th century, when disputes between feuding families led to the creation of "Land Chenla" near the Tonle Sap and "Water Chenla" on the lower Mekong. The Water Chenla Empire is chiefly remembered for its use of hydraulic techniques for cultivation, a sophisticated system later exploited in the complex and highly successful systems of Angkor. Chenla is also noted for the architectural inventions subsequently embraced by the Khmer builders of Angkor.

The rise of Srivijaya in southern Sumatra—and new trade routes favoring Indonesian over Cambodian entrepots—eventually made Chenla a vassal state of the Javanese Sailendra dynasty. Chenlan rulers who spent time at the Sailendra court returned home highly impressed by Hindu court rituals, political institutions, and artistic traditions. One of these leaders was a young king named Jayavarman II, who returned home around 800 and established the empire of Angkor. Thus, Hindu traditions passed from Java to Cambodia and then to Thailand via trade, diplomatic exchanges, and Mon and Tai soldiers who served as mercenaries in the Chenla armies. Chenla influence eventually reached the early Thai communities of Sukothai, Lopburi, and Ayuthaya.

The Khmers, 802-1431

Cambodia's most famous empire was that of the Khmers, founded in 802 by King Jayavarman II at his capital of Angkor just north of Tonle Sap. Renowned for its brilliant achievements in art and architecture, Angkor was also an immensely powerful nation which, between the 9th and 13th centuries, controlled most of Southeast Asia from China to Malaysia.

During this period of occupation, Khmer architects constructed Hindu-based temples across the breadth of Thailand, from the Cambodian border to Three Pagodas Pass. The largest concentration of temples was erected along a royal road connecting Angkor with Khmer military outposts at Lopburi and Sukothai. Thailand remained under Khmer suzerainty until 1238, when a pair of Thai princes from Sukothai revolted and founded the first independent Thai kingdom.

King Jayavarman, creator of the Khmer Empire, was not only an empire builder but a social innovator who made Hinduism the state religion, then crowned himself the reincarnation of Shiva. Jayavarman's concept of a god-king—perhaps a combination of Saivite concepts of divinity and older Megalithic beliefs—set the

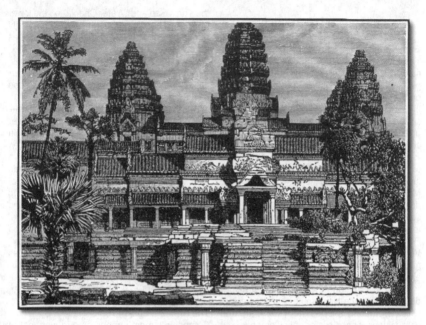

Angkor Wat (Cambodia)

style for succeeding rulers who, at times, considered themselves the earthly representatives of Shiva, Vishnu, and ultimately, the Buddha.

Centuries prior to the Thai achievements at Sukothai, Angkor functioned as an immense technological colossus from which central Cambodia derived its agricultural prosperity. By creating an elaborate and highly sophisticated system of lakes, channels, and irrigation canals radiating from Tonle Sap, the Khmer Empire became one of the wealthiest and most powerful empires on the face of the earth. With their vast resources and tens of thousands of slaves, Khmer kings embarked on a 400-year building spree which left the world with splendid baroque palaces, towering monuments, royal mausoleums, vast lakes, magnificent highways, and hundreds of immense temples bursting with diamonds, rubies, and gold. Many of the engineering marvels at Sukothai and Ayuthaya were adopted from Khmer prototypes at Angkor.

But Hindu-Khmer civilization eventually went into decline. The introduction of Mahayana Bud-dhism, which undermined the prestige of the king, combined with the extravagance of the throne, which bankrupted the elaborate irrigation system, finally led to the 13th-century decline and fall of the Angkor civilization. Thailand conquered Angkor and ended the Khmer reign in 1431.

A final note about the Khmer impact on Thailand. Linguists believe the Khmers called the Thai people "Syams" in reference to their darker skin color. This term later mutated into Siam, the country's name until WW II.

THE LANNA KINGDOM

Concurrent with the creation of Sukothai in 1238, several independent kingdoms dominated northern Thailand near the Mekong River. Most notable was Lanna (1259-1558), which ruled most of northern Thailand for almost three centuries, a remarkable run given the short life spans of most Thai kingdoms.

King Mengrai, 1259-1317

Mengrai, founder of Lanna, was born in 1239 in Chiang Saen on the banks of the Mekong River. According to historical records, Mengrai came from a royal Tai family which governed a large part of the Mekong district in the 13th century. In 1259 Mengrai succeeded his father as ruler over a small Tai-dominated principality. Disturbed at the petty fighting between Tai fiefdoms and determined to unite the warring factions, Mengrai conquered his neighbors in quick fashion. He then placed his own men in control of the Tai townships of Chiang Kham, Chiang Chang, and Phayao. In 1262 Mengrai transferred his capital from Chiang Saen to Chiang Rai. In addition to his military skills, Mengrai possessed a crafty diplomacy; he formed political alliances with the Tai rulers of Sukothai, Ayuthaya, and Nakhon Si Thammarat, plus the Burmese kings of Bago, Bagan, and Ava.

In 1281 Mengrai raised an enormous army and conquered Haripunchai (present-day Lamphun), the final surviving Mon outpost in Thailand. Nine years later a group of Ceylonese Buddhists reached Chiang Rai and presented Mengrai with two holy relics of the Buddha. Determined to consolidate his empire and enshrine the relics in lavish fashion, Mengrai moved his capital from Chiang Rai to Chiang Mai. The exact location was chosen after consultations with King Ngam Muang of Phayao and King Ramkamheng of Sukothai. Religious inspiration also played a role in the selection of Chiang Mai, which remains today the source of northern Thai culture.

In the space of just over two decades, Mengrai united all of northern Thailand into a kingdom now known as Lanna—the "Land of a Million Ricefields." Mengrai's most serious challenge came from Chinese Mongols who repeatedly attacked the empire from the north. To meet the challenge, in 1282 Mengrai formed a military alliance with the kings of Phayao and Sukothai, a strategic move which allowed him to defeat the Mongols in 1301.

Mengrai sought to integrate the varied racial groups living within his kingdom. He was particularly respectful of Mon culture and the people's devotion to Buddhism, a peaceful religion he promoted as a unifying element within his realm. In 60 years of rule, Mengrai not only fash-

ioned northern Thailand into a coherent kingdom and held his ground against Mongol pressure, he also introduced a legal framework of humane laws. Compromise and consultation were the keys to Mengrai—attributes still highly respected by contemporary Thais.

King Ku Na, 1355-1385

After Mengrai's death in 1317, the Lanna Empire slid into chaos under a series of weakened rulers. Momentum returned during the reign of Ku Na, an enlightened king and Buddhist devotee. Ku Na invited a monk from Sukothai named Sumana to establish the Sinhalese order of Buddhism in Chiang Mai. Sumana brought along powerful talismans; their engraved designs gave birth to the artistic style now closely associated with Lanna.

Sumana's version of Buddhism served as the leading intellectual and cultural force in northern Thailand during the next three centuries. Monasteries founded by Sumana and Buddhist texts created under his guidance helped unify the population under a single religion, molding northern Tais into a cultural group distinct from those in the remainder of Thailand.

King Tilok, 1441-1487

Lanna's final noteworthy ruler was King Tilokaracha, remembered as a successful warrior and builder of great monuments. During his decade-long struggle to secure the crown, Tilok waged battle against his exiled father as well as minor palace official Sam Dek Yoi who had placed Tilok on the throne, the governor of Fang, and the emergent empire of Ayuthaya. In 1443, Tilok defeated the independent kingdom of Nan, incorporating it into Lanna. The next three decades he spent fighting Ayuthaya on battlefields from Phrae to Phitsanulok.

Weary from near-constant warfare, Tilok devoted his final decade to the promotion of Buddhism and the construction of enormous monuments. His building frenzy peaked between 1475 and 1478, when he erected the enormous Maha Chedi Luang inside the city walls and funded a series of smaller temples outside the walled perimeter. By the time of his death in 1487, Tilok had unified his kingdom within carefully defined borders, leaving Lanna in its strongest position since the days of Mengrai.

Subsequent rulers were unable to protect the kingdom against foreign aggression. Weakened by internal dissension and royal conflict, Lanna fell to the Burmese in 1558. The Mengrai dynasty finally collapsed after a remarkable run of almost three centuries.

SUKOTHAI, 1238-1360

The brief but brilliant kingdom of Sukothai marks the true beginning of the Thai nation and to this day remains a source of great pride to the Thai people. While Sukothai's preeminence lasted less than 150 years, it gave rise to uniquely personified forms of architecture, sculpture, and governance. Under the leadership of King Ramkamheng (1278-1318), revered today as the father of modern Thailand, Sukothai fused Khmer and Mon political traditions into a dynamic kingdom that stretched from Laos to Malaysia. Military power and economic prosperity fueled the development of such highly refined artistic achievements as the world-renowned Sawankalok celadon and supremely sensitive Buddhist images. Even today Sukothai is considered one of the most remarkable empires in the long history of Southeast Asia.

Origins
Thailand's first national empire, Sukothai arose from the collapse of Khmer hegemony and the threat posed by the Mongol armies of Kublai Khan.

By the mid-13th century, Khan had successfully mounted campaigns against the Chinese and conquered the quasi-independent Tai kingdom of Nanchao in Yunnan Province. Heady with success, he then set out to conquer the emergent powers of present-day Thailand. Threatened with serious military challenge, Thai principalities consolidated their power and prepared for what appeared to be a final conflagration.

Another factor in the creation of Sukothai was the decline of the Khmer Empire after the death of King Jayavarman VII in 1220. As the Cambodian empire weakened, regional Thai rulers, long under the thumb of Khmer domination, revolted and established their own power bases. The most significant event occurred around 1240 when a pair of disgruntled princes from two small

Thai principalities gathered an army and marched on the main Khmer outpost at Sukothai. The Khmers resisted but were quickly defeated by Thai forces led by Prince Indraditya—the first sovereign of an independent Thai nation.

Although loosely functioning as a kingdom, Sukothai remained a rather insignificant outpost until 1278, when it was attacked by the ruler of Mae Sot. Threatened with certain defeat, Sukothai was saved through the efforts of Rama, the 19-year-old son of Indraditya. Rama rallied his troops and then, according to legend, killed the king of Mae Sot during a hand-to-hand battle on elephantback. For his bravery, Rama was accorded the title of Ramkamheng—Rama the Bold.

King Ramkamheng, 1278-1318
Ramkamheng established the first independent Thai nation through a combination of diplomatic skills and statesmanship, rather than military prowess. At the time of his ascension in 1278, Sukothai consisted of little more than the city itself and a few neighboring communities. By the end of his 40-year reign, Ramkamheng had increased his territorial holdings tenfold to include Luang Prabang in the north, the Mon homelands near Bangkok, and the peninsula south to Nakhon Si Thammarat. These gains were all accomplished through diplomatic relations and family intermarriages, rather than military conquest.

Ramkamheng today is honored as a capable administrator who brought peace to a divided land, an astute legislator who encouraged free trade and open borders, and a talented statesman who willingly absorbed many of the best elements from the Khmers, Mons, Indians, and Chinese. Ramkamheng also invented the Thai script, fusing the Mon and Khmer alphabets with Thai tonal inflections—an achievement denoted in a stele dated 1292 describing the idyllic conditions of his kingdom. Finally, Ramkamheng codified traditional laws into written canon, abolished slavery, and unified his nation under the umbrella of Buddhism. Small wonder the Thais have such great respect for Rama the Bold.

Many of his enlightened concepts sprang from Ramkamheng's desire to rule as a *dhammaraja,* a benign king who sustains legitimacy by governing under Buddhist precepts. In sharp contrast to the messianic god-king images of Khmer rulers, Ramkamheng promoted a benevolent and paternalistic system of monarchy. It is this philosophical concept of royal power that continues to be admired within contemporary Thai society.

Ramkamheng was additionally a major art patron, inviting Chinese potters to teach their glazing secrets and Sinhalese sculptors to work with court-sponsored artisans. Dozens of temples dedicated to the new state religion were constructed during Rama's reign. Ramkamheng provided a climate in which artistic traditions borrowed from Hindu Khmers, Chinese craftspeople, and Sinhalese Buddhists were fused into a unique style still considered the pinnacle of Thai artistic development.

The Final Kings, 1318-1438

Sukothai declined after the death of Ramkamheng in 1318; his successors appeared more involved with religious matters than with the maintenance of the empire. Three kings followed Ramkamheng but all failed to repulse Burmese attacks and retard the rise of Ayuthaya to the south.

The first king to follow Ramkamheng, his son Lo Thai (1318-47), favored the construction of Buddhist monuments over the control of tributary states. At the end of his reign, the Sukothai Empire had nearly shrunk back to its original size. Lo Thai left his mark in a series of temples designed to house sacred relics from Sri Lanka. He also established and supported the religious outpost of Kamphang Phet, 80 km southwest of Sukothai. Kamphang Phet served a dual role as military garrison and forest retreat for a large community of monks. The old city just north of the modern town remains an important repository of Thai religious architecture.

Lo Thai's son, Li Thai (1347-68), also favored religious pursuits over military matters; tributary states continued to deteriorate as more and more aligned themselves with Ayuthaya. Li Thai's reign, however, was the apogee of Sukothai's artistic and architectural legacy. Under his rule, Theravada Buddhism was promoted through active trade links with Sri Lanka and *chedi* construction was sharply accelerated. The most important architectural development of his reign was the introduction

of Sri Lankan-derived bell-shaped *chedis* capped with distinctive lotus bud finials. This period also saw the perfection of the sculpted Buddha images so admired throughout the world, including the famed "Walking Buddha" widely considered among the great achievements in Asian art.

Despite his significant artistic achievements, Li Thai was the final ruler of an independent Sukothai Kingdom. Suzerainty was granted to Ayuthaya in 1360. Descendants of Li Thai continued to serve as regional governors until Sukothai was completely abandoned in 1438.

AYUTHAYA, 1350-1767

By the end of the 14th century, several small but well-organized principalities ruled over much of what is now Thailand—most notably the Lanna and Sukothai Kingdoms. Other Southeast Asian powers—the Burmese at Bagan, the Khmers at Angkor, and the Mongol Chinese—were in steep decline. Conditions were ideal for the rise of Ayuthaya as the leading power in Southeast Asia.

Origins

The Kingdom of Ayuthaya was established in 1350 by King U Thong of Suphanburi, a principality which dominated the western side of the Chao Praya River basin. Suphanburi was predominantly a Siamese and Theravada Buddhist state which competed with Lopburi, the old Angkorian cultural and administrative center, for control of central Thailand after the decline of Sukothai. According to legend, U Thong moved his capital from Suphanburi to Ayuthaya to escape an outbreak of smallpox and occupy a more strategic location at the confluence of the Chao Praya, Lopburi, and Pasak Rivers. Military defense against the Burmese was a major factor in the choice of Ayuthaya.

The strategy proved successful. Within a few years, U Thong (renamed King Ramathibodi I) had united the whole of central Siam, from Sukothai in the north to the Malay Peninsula in the south. For the next 417 years, Ayuthaya served as the heart and soul of the Thai state— the religious, cultural, and commercial capital of modern Siam.

King Ramathibodi I, 1350-1369

Ramathibodi proved himself an ambitious and visionary leader. In 1360, the founder of Ayuthaya declared Theravada Buddhism the official religion of his kingdom and invited members of the Buddhist monastic order from Sri Lanka to establish new religious centers. Theravada Buddhism was eminently amenable to royal patronage and quickly become closely associated with other empires throughout the region. Ramathibodi also organized a legal code (the Dharmashastra) based on Hindu concepts but adapted to Thai customs and composed in Pali, the language of Buddhist scripture. During his administration, Ayuthayan court life fused Hindu rituals with Buddhist patronage, a potent combination that exists to this day.

Ramathibodi, however, was no Ramkamheng. Rather than accept the paternal and benign style of Sukothai rulers, he adopted Khmer cultural traditions and elevated the royal house to the status of absolute monarchs, "Lords of Life," who served as near god-kings. Paternal kingship ended at Ayuthaya; monarchs preferred to remain remote deities hidden behind walls of taboos and sumptuous rituals. As *devaraja* (divine kings), the rulers of Ayuthaya were venerated as earthly incarnations of Shiva and, as such, the objects of politico-religious cults officiated over by corps of royal Brahmans. Equality, fraternity, and the rights of the common people were subordinate to the supremacy of the crown.

In the final years of his reign, Ramathibodi seized Angkor and most of present-day Cambodia. Efforts to control his domestic territories were frustrated by persistent rebellions in Sukothai and the need for repeated military campaigns against the Lanna Kingdom of Chiang Mai. Ramathibodi died in 1369.

King Ramasuen, 1369-1395

The question of succession remained a vexing problem, as control of the throne continually shifted between the royal houses of Suphanburi and Lopburi. Ramathibodi was replaced by his son Ramasuen, who arrived from Lopburi to assume the crown. In 1370 Boromraja I, Ramasuen's uncle and ruler of Suphanburi, seized the throne and held power for 18 years, whereupon Ramasuen returned.

Ramasuen proved himself a highly creative social engineer. He established a political and social hierarchy which divided the citizens and royal court into tightly controlled and carefully defined classes. This arrangement was refined by King Boromatrailokat (1448-88), who decreed that royal ranks degenerate to common status within five generations. It was a clever solution to the problem of the burgeoning ranks of royalty created from the countless concubines and multiple wives of the king.

On a social level, Ramasuen required each citizen of Ayuthaya to register as a servant with the local mayor or warlord. All were expected to work up to six months each year in service to the state. Quite onerous by modern standards, this corvée labor system nevertheless guaranteed abundant manpower for public projects and insured a large standing army ready to wage almost continual warfare against the Khmers, Burmese, and northern Thais. The only citizens who stood outside this forced labor system were the Chinese, who, by the late 16th century, controlled most of Ayuthaya's internal and international trade.

Naresuan the Great, 1590-1605

Western contact with Siam began in 1511 when Ayuthaya received a diplomatic mission from the Portuguese. Encouraged by their annexation of the Muslim trading entrepôt of Malacca, the Portuguese were anxious to expand their commercial contacts within Southeast Asia. Five years later, the two nations concluded a treaty granting the Portuguese permission to conduct trade in exchange for Portuguese arms, ammunition, and warfare training. Portuguese mercenaries later fought in battles against Chiang Mai and helped Ayuthaya defeat other regional powers.

Western prowess in the arts of warfare did not stop relentless Burmese campaigns against Ayuthaya. In 1549, Bago raised an enormous army and marched on the Siamese capital. During a particularly spirited attack, the wife of the king, Queen Suriyothai, disguised herself as a warrior, mounted an elephant, and challenged the Bago ruler to a duel. According to Thai mythology, Suriyothai saved her husband's life and kingdom but died in the battle. Her sacrifice is commemorated by a *chedi* that still stands in Ayuthaya.

PHAULKON THE GREEK

*A*mong the more noteworthy and controversial *farangs* (foreigners) in Siamese history was Constantine Phaulkon, a Greek adventurer who rose to great power in the court of King Narai and served as the second most powerful figure in the land, the prime minister. In the end, however, political power and court intrigues led to his gruesome execution and the expulsion of most Westerners from Siam.

Phaulkon, son of a Greek innkeeper, began his colorful career as a cabin attendant with the East India Company at the age of 12. After quitting his British employers, Phaulkon sailed to Ayuthaya in 1678 and within two years became completely fluent in the Thai language. A talented linguist, accountant, and crafty diplomat, Phaulkon rose rapidly within royal service by acting as official translator and advising the Siamese court on its financial investments. He also promoted free trade by favoring private traders over the European companies that previously dominated local markets.

Phaulkon quickly became the favorite advisor of King Narai, who sought to make his kingdom known throughout the Western world. To this end, Narai sent diplomatic missions to China, India, and many European capitals. Under the influence of Phaulkon, Narai actively cultivated the French in an effort to counter the pervasive influence of the Dutch. The British were largely ignored, as they appeared uninterested in Siamese affairs. Narai also befriended French Jesuit missionaries who were allowed to preach Christianity and maintain a seminary in the capital.

During the height of his career, Phaulkon wielded tremendous political power within the Siamese court. He also amassed tremendous wealth, as shown by his private stone residence in Lopburi, the secondary capital and summer retreat for the Narai entourage. Phaulkon spent his days advising Narai on financial and political matters, while evenings revolved around socializing on a grand scale. According to Western chroniclers, his dinner table was set each night for 40 visitors who consumed vast quantities of wine imported solely for the needs of Phaulkon.

Despite his extravagant lifestyle, Phaulkon's brilliant financial acumen and linguistic skills earned him the position of prime minister and principal advisor to King Narai—an exalted position never since equaled by any foreigner in the Thai government.

Phaulkon's downfall was his attempted conversion of King Narai to Christianity, an ill-advised venture in a country as devoutly Buddhist as Thailand. Although not a deeply religious man, Phaulkon accepted Roman Catholicism in 1683 in order to marry a Japanese/Portuguese woman of that faith. Supported by the Jesuit community in Ayuthaya and the French court in Paris, Phaulkon initiated a series of philosophical discussions between the Siamese king and visiting Christian scholars. The Siamese court was aghast, bewildered, and terrified at the scene. Narai's most powerful minister was an alcoholic Greek sailor married to a Japanese Christian. The king was surrounded by French priests promoting the idea of Christianity and Dutch traders economically dominating the country.

Phaulkon's misguided support for royal conversion eventually ignited fires of revolt. In March 1688, King Narai fell ill and appeared near death. The struggle over succession was eventually settled in a firm fashion by a military leader named Phra Phetracha. Phetracha quickly moved to consolidate absolute control. Within a month he murdered several claimants to the crown, including Narai's adopted son and two of Narai's brothers.

Phetracha then turned his unbridled fury against Phaulkon and other Western elements. On 5 June 1688, Phetracha ordered the arrest and trial of Constantine Phaulkon on charges of treason. Phaulkon was tortured for several days and executed in a dirt field just outside Lopburi. Phetracha then forced the French out of Siam and initiated a period of isolation lasting almost 150 years.

Burmese forces finally triumphed in 1569, sacking the city and taking most of the royal court and citizenry back to Bago as hostages. The Siamese diaspora was reversed in 1584 after young prince Naresuan was repatriated from Bago to Ayuthaya. Naresuan quickly declared the independence of his country and initiated a six-year campaign of resistance against Burmese occupation forces. During his most celebrated battle, Naresuan challenged and defeated the Burmese crown prince in a battle conducted on elephantback.

After his father's death in 1590, Naresuan assumed power and continued to defend Ayuthaya against incursions from Burmese and Khmer forces. His military triumphs earned him the moniker "Naresuan the Great."

King Narai and the West, 1656-1688

Western contact with Siam dramatically increased during the reign of King Ekatosarot until, by the early 17th century, Ayuthaya was regarded by Western powers as a useful trading site and stopover point on the long voyages to China and Japan. Each Western nation competed vigorously to establish trading connections with the Thai crown. The initial Dutch contract signed in 1605 was followed by agreements with the English in 1612, the Danes in 1621, and the French in 1662. Commercial links were also maintained by Japanese traders who comprised a sizable community until their retreat to Cambodia in 1628.

European influence reached its zenith during the reign of King Narai (1656-1688). During his tenure, Ayuthaya was regarded as the strongest military power and grandest city in all of Southeast Asia. Western visitors described the realm as a splendid metropolis with a population larger than those of contemporary London or Paris. Within the city walls stood glorious palaces, hundreds of resplendent temples, and entire communities for military leaders, scholars, and artisans. Europeans described an awe-inspiring walled city some 10 km in circumference interlaced with more than 50 km of interconnecting canals. Many of these waterways were flanked by monumental Buddha images and exquisitely executed and richly embellished *objets d'art*. Outside the walled enclosure existed vast foreign settlements, factories, and warehouses de-

signed to serve the Western trade community. Visitors were amazed by the grandeur and opulence of this most splendid and cosmopolitan of all Asian cities.

Ayuthaya was also the major military and economic powerhouse within Southeast Asia. After the submission of Sukothai and containment of Lanna, Ayuthaya ruled over an empire that stretched from Laos and Malaysia to Angkor and Myanmar. Economic success was insured by the large contingent of foreign traders who positioned the city as the hub of international trade between China and the West. Ayuthaya shone as the brightest star in the East.

The Fall of Ayuthaya, 1763-1767

After the death of Narai and execution of Phaulkon, Ayuthaya entered a period of self-imposed isolation for almost 100 years. The French were forced from Siam, though British and Dutch traders continued to maintain small posts. Missionaries imprisoned during the palace coup were released and given permission to proselytize, despite their noted lack of earlier success in converting the population.

Ayuthaya during this period created its own golden age of arts and architecture, primarily under the 1733-58 reign of King Boromakot. Royal patronage during his rule was funneled into the construction of temples and artistic support rather than territorial expansion or trading disputes. Ayuthaya developed into a sophisticated and culturally refined empire, its citizens valuing elegance, beauty, and the arts.

But artistic development extracted a high price. Ayuthaya gradually declined, neglecting the military threat from Myanmar.

The political nemesis of Siam, Myanmar was by the mid-18th century poised for yet another attack on the Siamese capital. Initial forays were led by King Alaungpaya, a powerful leader and magnetic personality who single-handedly restored the Kingdom of Ava and recaptured the Mon Kingdom of Bago. Alaungpaya next set his sights on Ayuthaya. His attack of April 1760 might have leveled the city had not a Burmese cannon burst outside the city walls. The explosion killed Alaungpaya and sparked a hasty Burmese retreat.

The final siege began in 1763. Burmese forces initially besieged Chiang Mai and Lamphun; both cities fell within six months. Burmese troops then quickly conquered Chiang Rai, Nan, and Luang Prabang. Massing for the final assault on Ayuthaya, the main Burmese force departed Chiang Mai and headed south through easily captured Thai outposts at Sawankhalok, Sukothai, Phitsanulok, and Nakhon Sawan. Another Burmese expedition concurrently left Bago, marching across Three Pagodas Pass into Siamese territory. The southern flank took Kanchanaburi, Ratchburi, and Petchburi. Siam was now largely in Burmese hands. In February 1766 the two Burmese expeditions joined forces just outside the walls of Ayuthaya.

A terrible war ensued. Thai citizens over the next year valiantly resisted superior Burmese forces despite the famines, epidemics, and horrible fires that consumed most of the city. Conditions grew so grim that the king of Ayuthaya offered to surrender his empire in exchange for his life. The Burmese, however, demanded unconditional surrender.

Finally, on 7 April 1767, Ayuthaya fell to the Burmese. Retaliation was swift and completely horrific. In an unprecedented orgy of vandalism, murder, and destruction, most of the population was killed and the entire city was burned to the ground. The royal family and over 100,000 Siamese captives were marched back to Myanmar and sold as slaves. Mass slaughter and wholesale slavery reduced the population to under 10,000 people in a city which once held over one million.

The Burmese did more than simply kill the population. With complete disregard for their common religion, Burmese forces destroyed the artistic and literary heritage of Ayuthaya by pulling down many of the magnificent Buddhist temples and melting down most of the golden Buddha images—a savage act which still profoundly shocks the Thais. Ayuthaya was almost completely obliterated in the holocaust.

RATTANAKOSIN

General Taksin, 1767-1782

The destruction of Ayuthaya was devastating but, as is typical in Thai history, not a permanent setback. Shortly before the fall of Ayuthaya, an ambitious half-Chinese provincial governor from Tak in western Thailand quietly fled southeast to Chanthaburi with an expedition of some 500 soldiers. Taksin soon rallied his soldiers and returned to fight the Burmese.

Taksin marched into a fortuitous situation. Most of the Burmese troops stationed at Ayuthaya had been called away to resist Chinese aggression along the northern Burmese border. Remarkably, within seven months Taksin had defeated a dispirited Burmese garrison, recaptured the ruined Ayuthaya, and reestablished the Thai kingdom.

Taksin soon realized that Ayuthaya was finished as a viable capital, as it lay dangerously exposed to Burmese military threats and distant from international trade routes. After a propitious dream, Taksin transferred his capital to Thonburi, a small town on the banks of the Chao Praya River just opposite present-day Bangkok.

Although blessed with a brilliant tactical mind and financial support from the Chinese mercantile community, Taksin proved himself a rather inept ruler. Consumed with administrative matters in Thonburi, Taksin turned command of his army over to two brothers—Chao Phraya Chakri and Chao Phraya Sarasih—who in turn liberated Chiang Mai from Burmese domination and brought most of Cambodia and Laos under Thai suzerainty. During the Laotian campaign, Chao Phraya Chakri captured the famed Emerald Buddha, returning it to Thonburi in 1779. Now installed in Wat Pra Keo, the jadeite image remains the single most venerated statue in modern Thailand.

Taksin, in the meantime, was going mad. French missionaries reported he imagined himself a living reincarnation of the Buddha, spending his days in silent meditation attempting to fly. Monks who refused to acknowledge his divinity were flogged and sentenced to menial labor. Plagued with paranoia and delusions of grandeur, Taksin imprisoned and tortured his wife, his sons, his heir apparent, and many high officials. The situation deteriorated until his ministers and generals staged a revolt, forcing Taksin to abdicate the throne. This solution to unpopular rule—the military coup—remains a cornerstone of contemporary Thai politics.

Taksin was executed in the manner prescribed for royalty: placed in a velvet sack and gently beaten to death with a sandalwood club.

THE CHAKRI DYNASTY

King Ramathibodi—Rama I, 1782-1809

The popular Chao Phraya Chakri, on expedition in Cambodia, was recalled to Thonburi and crowned King Rama, first ruler of the Chakri dynasty which continues to the present day. Fearful of attack by Burmese forces, Rama I transferred his capital from Thonburi across the river to present-day Bangkok. He then attempted to re-create the former magnificence of Ayutthaya with the construction of the royal palaces, temples, and even canals which characterized the former capital. Rama I, formally known during his reign as Ramathibodi, also enshrined in his royal temple the Emerald Buddha captured from the Laotians and removed to Siam. The city continues to be called Bangkok by Western mapmakers, though Rama I renamed it a multisyllabled Sanskrit moniker abbreviated as Krung Thep, or "City of Angels."

Rama I spent much of his reign consolidating his empire, devising a new code of civil law which served the state for the next century, and issuing a series of ecclesiastical verdicts intended to restore discipline to the monkhood. He also oversaw the brilliant defeat of the Burmese during their 1785 invasion, in which some 70,000 Thai soldiers defended Bangkok against 100,000 Burmese. This encounter marked the final attempt by the Burmese to conquer their Siamese neighbors.

Rama I is also credited with setting to verse the complete Siamese version of the Indian epic Ramayana (called the Ramakien in Thailand), thereby recasting the classic Indian tome into a form still used to the present day. By the end of his reign, Rama I had created a new empire significantly more powerful and complex than had previously existed in Ayutthaya.

Phra Phutthalaetia—Rama II, 1809-1824

After the death of Rama I, his 41-year-old son, Prince Phutthalaetia, ascended to the throne, becoming the second king in the Chakri dynasty. Peace and prosperity within Siam allowed him to concentrate on the arts and literature. His chief accomplishment appears to have been penning the famous Thai verse play the Inao, adapted from a Javanese legend, and a version of the Ramakien frequently staged in the Royal Palace. Rama II also funded construction of Wat Arun (the Temple of Dawn) in Thonburi and is said to have personally carved the massive doors at Wat Suthat.

Rama II reestablished formal relations with the West, allowing the Portuguese to open an embassy and trading post a few blocks south of his royal palace.

King Phra Nangklao—Rama III, 1824-1851

The chief shortcoming of Rama II and the Thai crown in general was the failure to clearly define royal succession. In the event of an undesignated *uparaja* (heir), royal selection was left to a council of senior officials, princes, and Buddhist prelates. At the time of Rama II's death, Prince Mongkut—the king's eldest son by the queen—-had just entered the priesthood at the age of 20 and was not considered ready to assume the crown. After a series of debates, palace nobles asked Prince Chesda, the son of a consort, to claim the throne as Rama III. He ruled under the assumed title of Phra Nangklao.

Rama III was a devout Buddhist who renovated Wat Po and supported the monastic studies of Prince Mongkut, who wisely remained out of royal politics. Phra Nangklao was also a political and social conservative who distrusted the West and resisted trade and diplomatic advances from both Joseph Balestier on behalf of the United States and Sir James Brooke from Britain. The king correctly understood that the primary threat to Siamese independence came not from Myanmar or Cambodia but from the rising forces of the West.

On a more liberal note, Rama III did invite Baptists to establish a mission in Bangkok. The Baptists went on to introduce the smallpox vaccine and printing presses to Siam.

King Mongkut—Rama IV, 1851-1868

Thailand's modern phase began with the reign of King Mongkut. Mongkut served as Rama IV while the rest of Southeast Asia was methodically carved up and annexed by France (Indochina), Britain (Myanmar and Malaya), and Holland (Indonesia).

Prior to his accession to the throne on the death of his half- brother, Mongkut lived for 27 years as a monk in Buddhist temples around

THE KING AND I ~ REALITY OR RACISM?

*K*ing Mongkut, unfortunately, is largely known to the Western world as theautocratic despot who sang and danced his way through the film *The King and I*.

Starring Yul Brynner as the monarch and Deborah Kerr as his governess, the Rodgers and Hammerstein film is based on Margaret Landon's 1943 best-seller *Anna and the King of Siam* which was, in turn, based on the writings of one Anna Leonowens. Her two fanciful novels—*The English Governess at the Court of Siam* (1870) and *Romance of the Harem* (1873)—described her experiences as an English teacher in the court of King Mongkut.

Born in India in 1831, Anna married a clerk who took her to Penang, where he died in 1859. Unsure of her future, Anna moved to Singapore and then to Bangkok in 1862, where she broke with most of her family, including a grandnephew, Boris Karloff of *Frankenstein* fame. In Bangkok, she hooked up with American Protestant missionaries such as Dr. Dan Bradley, who reinforced her Christian prejudices during her employment as the English instructor to the king's children.

Her five years of service in the court made little impact on the king—his only written reference to Leonowens was an appendix to a shopping list. After completing her contract, Leonowens moved to the U.S., where she wrote her memoirs and made a living giving lectures about life in the Siamese court.

The Western world largely believed the story of Anna Leonowens until an English scholar wrote a biography of her family in the early 1970s. Dr. Bristowe discovered Anna had lied about her age, her birthplace, and the background of her husband, who was a clerk rather than a military officer. Worse yet, her memoirs were filled with glaring errors regarding Thai history, Buddhism, and activities within the royal court. Leonowens essentially plagiarized old books on Myanmar and invented all sorts of wild tales to help boost book sales. She neither spoke Thai nor had access to workings of the inner court. In the end, she portrayed King Mongkut as some sort of primitive despot and herself as the Victorian Christian who single-handedly modernized the backward nation.

Nothing could be farther from the truth. King Mongkut is universally regarded as an enlightened ruler whose imaginative diplomacy secured Thailand's sovereignty against Western colonialists. He also modernized his nation by reforming the legal system and encouraging contact with the West, leading the way by employing English teachers for his sons.

Leonowens, on the other hand, was a puritanical widow of low social standing whose colorful fabrications caused a great deal of embarrassment to the Thai government. After all, no group of people enjoy having others laugh at one of its most respected leaders.

Today, both the book and the film are banned in Thailand.

Bangkok. His religious tenure proved excellent preparation for the crown. During his monastic life, Mongkut studied English, Latin, Pali, Sanskrit, and Khmer; pursued Western history, geography, and mathematics; founded the Thammayut (Dhammakaiya) sect of Buddhism which stressed strict adherence to Theravada Buddhist ideals; and elevated Wat Bowonivet in Bangkok (where he served as chief abbot) to a major center of Buddhist thought and Western studies. He also came to understand that Siam could only survive as an independent nation by rapid modernization and close cooperation with Western powers.

Mongkut initiated diplomatic relations with most European powers and the United States. Trade treaties were signed with Britain in 1855, France in 1856, and Denmark and Holland in 1862. By negotiating these diplomatic and trade agreements, Mongkut cleverly played one colonial power against another, making Siam a neutral buffer zone between the competing nations.

Mongkut brought his country into the modern era by introducing political and social reforms. One of his early edicts allowed his subjects to gaze upon his face. He also used royal commands to attempt to improve the conditions of slaves and women. Mongkut continued to Westernize his nation by supporting the work of Christian missionaries and hiring European tutors—most notably Anna Leonowens—for his sons.

Mongkut helped popularize modern science. In 1868 he correctly predicted a solar eclipse from his royal palace in Petchburi, then went south to observe it. Tragically, he contracted malaria during the observation and died three weeks later in Bangkok. Chulalongkorn, his senior son, claimed the throne.

King Chulalongkorn—Rama V, 1868-1910

Mongkut's son, Chulalongkorn, ascended the throne at the age of 15 and reigned over Siam for 42 years. He continued Mongkut's policies of transforming Thailand from a medieval kingdom into a modern and progressive nation. Chulalongkorn abolished slavery in 1905, as well as ceremonial prostration before the king. He constructed the first railways, strengthened the national infrastructure through public projects, and adopted European concepts of government, education, and justice.

In 1886 he opened the first hospital in Siam and in 1892 established the first post and telegraph office. He also constructed a national library, museum, and important religious sites, such as the Marble Temple in Bangkok. His two visits to Europe helped introduce Siam to the outside world.

Chulalongkorn nevertheless clung to some autocratic customs, including polygyny on a grand scale, keeping a grand total of 92 wives who bore him some 77 children. Opium was strictly regulated but remained a lucrative government monopoly. He also continued to appoint men of royal descent to high administrative posts, a practice that offended some of the European-educated elite. At the same time he hired a grand total of 549 foreign advisers, the largest number British.

His greatest political success was to successfully balance the territorial ambitions of the

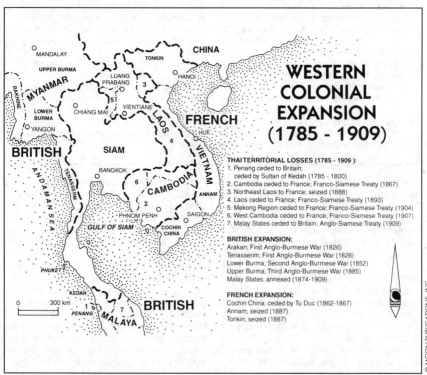

WESTERN COLONIAL EXPANSION (1785 - 1909)

THAI TERRITORIAL LOSSES (1785 - 1909):
1. Penang ceded to Britain;
   ceded by Sultan of Kedah (1785 - 1800)
2. Cambodia ceded to France; Franco-Siamese Treaty (1867)
3. Northeast Laos to France; seized (1888)
4. Laos ceded to France; Franco-Siamese Treaty (1893)
5. Mekong Region ceded to France; Franco-Siamese Treaty (1904)
6. West Cambodia ceded to France; Franco-Siamese Treaty (1907)
7. Malay States ceded to Britain; Anglo-Siamese Treaty (1909)

BRITISH EXPANSION:
Arakan; First Anglo-Burmese War (1826)
Tenasserim; First Anglo-Burmese War (1826)
Lower Burma; Second Anglo-Burmese War (1852)
Upper Burma; Third Anglo-Burmese War (1885)
Malay States; annexed (1874-1909)

FRENCH EXPANSION:
Cochin China; ceded by Tu Duc (1862-1867)
Annam; seized (1887)
Tonkin; seized (1887)

© MOON PUBLICATIONS, INC.

British and French. By the latter half of the 19th century, France controlled Indochina and England laid claim to Myanmar and Malaya. The final question appeared to be whether France or Great Britain would seize Siam.

The French approached from the east. In 1863 the French signed an agreement with the Cambodian king which effectively made his country a colonial protectorate. Alarmed, Chulalongkorn modernized his army and prepared to meet the French challenge. Siam resisted until 1893, when a French blockade of Bangkok forced Chulalongkorn to cede Laos and western Cambodia to the French.

The British approached from the south. In 1909 the four Thai-controlled Malayan states of Kelantan, Trengganu, Kedah, and Perlis were given to the British in exchange for diplomatic recognition of Siamese territorial rights. Chulalongkorn's skillful diplomacy and large but strategic land concessions allowed Thailand to remain the only nation in Southeast Asia never colonized by the West.

Chulalongkorn, the most honored of all past kings, is the only ruler recognized each year by a national holiday, on 23 October.

King Vajiravudh—Rama VI, 1910-1925

The death of Chulalongkorn in 1910 left Thailand with neatly defined borders on all sides and a centralized government dominated by royalty and a Western-educated bureaucracy. It also saw the rise of a new bourgeois intelligentsia unhappy with its lack of power within the royalist government.

Vajiravudh was a flamboyant, Oxford-educated prince who continued his father's process of modernization. Among his notable edicts was the 1913 law commanding all Thais to adopt surnames (Thais previously used only first names) and his 1921 introduction of compulsory universal education. He also reformed the calendar along Western lines and established the first national university, which he named after his father. Vajiravudh wisely sent an expeditionary force to France in June 1918 to participate in the final battles of WW II. Goodwill generated by this gesture allowed the Thais to renegotiate many of the unequal treaties previously signed with Western powers.

Vajiravudh made a few blunders. His extravagance almost bankrupted the government and

he left behind only one heir, a daughter born one day before his death in 1925. More ominously, Vajiravudh antagonized the military by creating a nationwide paramilitary corps recruited exclusively from the civil service. In 1912 a group of young army lieutenants—angered with their downgrading—plotted a military coup to overthrow his government. The revolt was quickly crushed but military leaders remained disenchanted with absolute monarchy.

THE END OF ABSOLUTE MONARCHY

King Prajadhipok—Rama VII, 1925-1935

Prajadhipok, Chulalongkorn's 76th child and final son, reigned as Siam's last absolute monarch. His was also the shortest and most controversial rule in the history of the Chakri dynasty.

Prajadhipok claimed the throne under difficult circumstances. As a military officer educated at Eton, he never expected to be crowned king and was never properly trained in civil and administrative matters. Early reforms improved the economic situation created by his predecessor, but the worldwide depression of the early 1930s forced Prajadhipok to cut salaries, raise taxes, and alienate many of his bureaucrats and military leaders. Prajadhipok understood political reform was inevitable but received little support from his government. Despite his efforts, his proposals for a democratic constitution were rejected by advisors who feared loss of status and position.

The pressure cooker finally blew in 1932 when a bloodless coup d'etat instigated by French-educated Thai intellectuals and supported by the military toppled the absolute monarchy. The coup leaders included a number of nationalists who remained major figures for the next three decades. Pridi Panomyong, one of the country's leading intellectuals, was a young leftist lawyer trained in France who served as the leader of the government's civilian faction. Phibul Songkram was an ambitious junior army officer who used his ministerial powers to assert the superior efficiency of the military over the civilian bureaucracy headed by Pridi. The third player was an old-line military officer named Phraya Phanon, who, as the first prime minister, maintained a precarious balance between the Pridi and Phibul factions in the new government.

After the coup, King Prajadhipok served in a minor role until deteriorating relationships with the new rulers forced him to flee to England. Prajadhipok formally abdicated on 2 March 1935. The National Assembly in Bangkok then invited Ananda Mahidol, the 10-year-old son of Prince Mahidol of Songkla and nephew to Prajadhipok, to ascend to the throne. A regency council was appointed to serve while Mahidol continued his studies in Switzerland.

RISE OF THE MILITARY

Phibul and the Nationalist Regime, 1938-1944

Relations in the 1930s between the civilian cabinet led by Pridi and the military forces headed by Field Marshal Phibul continued to deteriorate to the point of insurrection. Faced with a military threat he could no longer contain, Prime Minister Phanon retired in late 1938 to be replaced by Phibul.

The Phibul regime sold nationalism to the public by changing the name of the country, initiating a series of anti-Chinese measures to reassert Thai hegemony, and stirring up old animosities against the French, who still occupied former Thai territories. Thailand had never forgiven the French for their blockade of 1893 and the subsequent loss of Siamese control over portions of Laos and Cambodia. Sensing an opportunity to avenge the French seizure and reclaim lost lands, Phibul cultivated closer relations with Japan, praising that country as the only Asian nation to successfully challenge the West.

On 8 December 1941 Japanese forces invaded Thailand at nine points, chiefly along the southern peninsula to support the invasion of Malaya and Singapore. Facing certain defeat, Prime Minister Phibul quickly signed an agreement which guaranteed continued Thai independence in exchange for unimpeded Japanese passage through Thailand toward British-held Myanmar.

Thailand then formed a military alliance with Japan and issued a declaration of war against the United States and Great Britain. Pridi resigned in protest but accepted a position as chief regent for the absent Prince Mahidol. Whether a cynical move or sensible acceptance of a de facto situation, Thailand's alliance with Japan allowed the Thais to remain sovereign and relatively unscathed throughout the war.

Fortunately, the Thai ambassador in Washington, Seni Pramoj, refused to deliver the declaration of war to the American government. Seni simply filed the document away in his desk and never brought up the event in political discussion. It proved a wise move, since America never formally declared war on Thailand and continued to regard the Thai people as supporters of Allied efforts. Seni later worked with the American Office of Strategic Services, a precursor to the Central Intelligence Agency, and helped establish the Free Thai movement coordinated by Pridi back in Bangkok.

As the war dragged on, relations between Japan and Thailand deteriorated. By mid-1944 political winds and the tides of warfare were shifting against the Japanese and Prime Minister Phibul. The prime minister had become closely associated with General Tojo, who was disgraced in Tokyo. Authoritarian rule and military dictatorships were losing favor around the world. Sensing the imminent defeat of Japan, the National Assembly demanded the resignation of Phibul and the reintroduction of civilian rule.

Following the fall of Japan, Thailand lost its territories reclaimed under Japanese occupation but, thanks to American pressure against the wishes of Britain and France, was never punished for its alliance with the island nation. Phibul went into internal exile in June 1944, replaced by the first predominantly civilian government since the 1932 coup.

King Ananda Mahidol—Rama VIII, 1935-1946

After the bloodless coup of 1932 and the abdication of Vajiravudh in 1935, the Thai crown passed to Ananda Mahidol, a 10-year-old prince born in Germany. The son of Prince Mahidol of Songkhla and grandson of Chulalongkorn, Mahidol occasionally visited Thailand but largely remained in Europe away from the ongoing power struggles between military and civilian factions.

Ananda returned from his studies in Switzerland to occupy the throne as Rama VIII in December 1945. The following month saw the first openly democratic elections in almost a decade. Pridi was elected prime minister, the head of a civilian government.

FAREWELL SIAM

The name change of a nation is always a curious affair. Visitors to Thailand often wonder what happened to that wonderfully romantic name Siam. As with Myanmar, Sri Lanka (Ceylon), and Irian Jaya (New Guinea), the truth lies in political intrigue.

After Prime Minister Phanon retired in 1938 and Field Marshall Phibul took over in 1939, Phibul renamed Siam Thailand, or, more properly, Muang Thai—"Land of the Thai." The official line was that Siam was not a Thai word but a creation of foreign powers and therefore unacceptable to a free and independent nation. It was also argued that 23 million Thai-speaking citizens needed to be reflected in the nation's name.

Some criticized the new English name as being a bastardized conjunction—Thai being a local word and "land" being English—but the nomenclature served to unite the nation in the face of approaching war. A greater loss, perhaps, was the disappearance of the word Siam, which carried such vivid and exotic overtones.

There were other reasons for the change. Phibul was a right-wing, ultranationalist military leader who supported many of the xenophobic politics and nationalistic policies being advocated at the time in Germany and Italy. Among his chief concerns was the domination of the Thai economy by the Chinese, who had long comprised a sizable portion of the population. The Chinese had migrated to Siam in large numbers since the early 18th century and, with a flair for business, soon dominated many of the major industries, including the opium trade and tax collection, both despised occupations. Unlike earlier immigrants, Chinese arrivals in the 20th century resisted assimilation into Thai society by supporting a separate structure of social halls and Chinese-language schools. Legislation enacted after the turn of the century was often intended to force the integration of the Chinese into Thai society. To a large degree these laws were successful, as many Chinese changed their names to Thai derivatives and started to speak only Thai in public. But their domination of the economy remained an obvious source of resentment among less fortunate Thais.

In 1939, Phibul introduced his "Thailand for the Thai" economic plan, which levied heavy taxes on Chinese-owned businesses while offering state subsidies to Thai-owned enterprises. Chinese opium addicts were deported from the country, Chinese immigration was restricted, and numerous occupations previously held by Chinese were reserved for Thais. Phibul used another weapon to show the world that the country was controlled by the Thais and not the Chinese: Muang Thai or Thailand—Land of the Thais.

The jubilant mood that followed was shattered on 9 June 1946 when King Ananda was found dead in his bedroom at the royal palace—shot in the head under mysterious circumstances. Murder, conspiracy, or suicide? An official announcement that afternoon said the king had accidentally shot himself while examining his Colt .45 automatic, but a subsequent government commission that included American and British doctors concluded the king had probably been murdered or committed suicide.

The government bungled the investigation. Two years after his death, three of the king's bodyguards were arrested and charged with complicity in his murder. The three attendants responsible for the king's safety spent the next six years in a long, messy trial that resulted in their acquittal, retrial, guilty verdict, and 1954 execution.

Public opinion, however, held Prime Minister Pridi morally responsible for the murder, due to his long promotion of antiroyalist sentiments. Pridi resigned as prime minister in August 1946 and left the country on an extended vacation. The civilian government remained haunted by the unexplained death of Ananda and plagued with economic problems and persistent levels of bureaucratic corruption.

King Bhumibol Adulyadej— Rama IX (1946-present)

After the mysterious death of Ananda Mahidol, Prince Bhumibol took the throne at the tender age of 19. He continues to lead the country as the nation's longest serving head of state. A profile of this remarkable leader is included in the Government section below.

Phibul Power, 1947-1957

Except for the short civilian rule of Pridi and a three-year hiatus in the mid-1970s, Thailand since the coup of 1932 has been ruled by an alliance of military commanders and their approved civilian politicians.

The resignation of Pridi in 1946 opened the door for the return the following year of Phibul Songkram as prime minister, a post he kept until 1957. Pridi attempted political comebacks in 1949 and 1951 but both failed; he fled to China and finally to France, where he died in 1983. Pridi ended up a tragic figure: the father of Thai constitutionalism, forever linked to the mysterious death of a monarch.

Phibul ruled during an era of tumultuous political change: China fell to Mao in 1949, French forces lost to the Vietnamese at Dien Bien Phu in 1954, and both Cambodia and Laos chafed under growing insurgency movements. Blessed with strong support from the army and from the middle and upper Thai classes who feared the communist threat, Phibul established a military dictatorship that pursued an extreme anticommunist stance. Phibul's regime refused to recognize the People's Republic of China, supported the United Nation's anticommunist actions in Korea, and cooperated with French and American military efforts in Indochina. In return, Thailand received strong financial support from the American imperialist running dogs, who regarded the country as their chief bulwark against the red menace.

On a national level, Chinese residents within Thailand—often assumed to be sympathetic to communist causes—became the targets of government strictures. Chinese schools and family associations were closed or tightly monitored while military support was thrown against Chinese communist insurgents in southern Thailand and northern Malaya.

General Sarit and Military Rule, 1957-1973

Phibul's grip on power slowly declined into the mid-1950s as pressure mounted from General Sarit Thanarat, commander of the Bangkok garrison and rising favorite within the military clique. After an extended tour of the United States and Britain, Phibul attempted to establish a popular constituency among Thais by announcing a series of democratic reforms. Anti-Chinese campaigns were halted, the press was permitted to criticize the government, and democratic elections were announced for 1957.

The elections gave Phibul a narrow victory, but also pounded the final nail in his coffin. So corrupt and venal was the election—even by generous Thai standards—that General Sarit overthrew Phibul in a bloodless coup in September of that year. Phibul fled the country and the military recaptured control of Thailand. The political landscape had hardly changed from 1932. Phibul traveled around the United States, then visited India, where he donned the robes of a Buddhist monk. His last days were spent in Japan, where he died in 1964.

General Sarit

General Sarit responded harshly to Phibul's democratic reforms. He closed down the weekly dance at Lumpini Park, arrested men with long hair or tight pants, and made the twist an illegal dance form. Political parties were outlawed, Parliament dissolved, the constitution suspended, critics jailed, and dozens of newspapers closed. For the next 16 years, constitutionalism and parliamentary politics were considered illegitimate.

On the other hand, Sarit enjoyed great success in his efforts to achieve political stability and maintain economic growth through his promotion of five-year plans. The benefits filtered down to his military commanders, who became fabulously wealthy as they gradually took over control of major financial, industrial, commercial, and foreign enterprises. Sarit furthered the anticommunist stance of his predecessors by inviting the Americans to establish military bases throughout Thailand.

Sarit died of cirrhosis in 1963. It was soon discovered Sarit had left behind a fortune approaching US$150 million, and that, in addition to his wife, he'd kept more than 50 mistresses living in high style, perhaps on improper profits from the state lottery.

Sarit was replaced by his chief deputy, General Thanom Kittikachorn, who served as prime minister for almost a decade. A conservative ideologue, Thanom nevertheless encouraged democratic reforms and approved a new constitution in 1968. Martial law, however, remained in effect.

THE VIETNAM WAR AND DOMESTIC INSURGENCY

The War to the East

As the war in Vietnam intensified, Thai relations with the American government grew closer. By 1968 over 45,000 American military personnel were stationed on Thai soil, primarily in the northeast. From here U.S. planes conducted bombing raids over North Vietnam and Laos; Thailand received a staggering amount of financial aid from the American government.

The effects of the American presence extended through almost every aspect of Thai life. The economy was pumped up as hundreds of thousands of Thais became dependent on American dollars for their livelihoods. The construction industry and transportation infrastructure grew phenomenally to support the war effort. The American presence also created turbulent cultural change, as Thai society became exposed to Western ideas, cultures, values, music, fashions, and moral standards.

The Vietnam War also unleashed a massive outpouring of political sentiment from both the right and the left. Buddhist monks took political stands while large numbers of young Thais found new appeal in leftist movements like socialism and communism. There was a resurgence in the old Communist Party of Thailand. Largely funded by the Chinese and trained by communist cadres from Laos and Cambodia, the insurgency movement began a series of organized rebellions against the Bangkok administration. These demonstrations first broke in the northeast, spread to the north around Chiang Rai, and finally flared up in southern Thailand, where Muslim dissidents demanded a separate nation independent of Buddhist overlords. By the early 1970s, the Thai government faced serious security threats from both internal insurgencies and the conflicts raging in neighboring states.

The October 1973 Revolution

The constitution of 1968 and general elections in 1969 allowed General Thanom Kittikachorn to democratically reclaim his role as national leader. However, the three-year experiment with democracy ended in failure as governments and cabinets rose and fell sporadically. Finally, Thanom executed a coup against his own government and returned military rule to Thailand.

Dissatisfaction with the dictatorial regime continued to mount in the universities and among rival military cliques. The Thai public was also disenchanted with the prime minister, who attempted to create a political dynasty through his son Narong and blatantly promoted the large-scale aggrandizement of his family.

As with all revolutions, the events of 1973 were instigated by those with the least to lose and most to gain—in this instance the students. The democratic elections of 1969 had heightened expectations of the burgeoning middle classes and university students about democracy and power sharing within the government.

Despite a history of noninterference in the political landscape, Thai citizens now demanded an end to the military dictatorship, the promulgation of a new constitution, and the return to a true parliamentary democracy.

The government appeared unconcerned until June 1973, when military censors discovered an underground student newspaper whose editorials were sharply critical of the ruling junta. Nine students from Ramkamheng University were expelled as a result of government pressure. Upset with the government crackdown, an engineering student from Chulalongkorn University called a rally at Democracy Monument in Bangkok to demand the re-enrollment of the students. The rally was attended by tens of thousands of students from Thammasat, Chulalongkorn, and Ramkamheng Universities demanding government assurances concerning their freedoms of speech and rights of free assembly. The military responded by ordering the universities shut. The tactic backfired, leaving the city clogged with over 50,000 angry students. On 21 June, the student demonstrators were joined by labor unionists, environmental activists, and anti-Vietnam War agitators in an intimidating show of solidarity. The government wisely instructed the rector at Ramkamheng to re-enroll the expelled students.

The situation worsened in October after government enforcers arrested 11 student leaders on trumped-up charges of conspiracy to overthrow the government in a communist plot. Outraged students at Thammasat University once again staged a sit-in protest and demanded the promulgation of a democratic constitution. Within a few days the protest had swelled to over 70,000 people. The crowd marched to Democracy Monument, where they joined enormous numbers of ordinary citizens. The situation had become explosive.

On 13 October 1973, King Bhumibol met for an hour with Prime Minister Thanom and his cabinet in an attempt to diffuse the situation. The king met with student leaders who appeared satisfied with his assurances regarding their constitutional freedoms and government reforms. The students agreed to announce the settlement and disperse the crowd from Democracy Monument and Chitralada Palace, the residence of the royal family. But miscommunication between student leaders left enormous numbers of demonstrators milling around both locations, unsure of the next act. As dawn approached, the king's message of reconciliation was finally announced and the crowd began to peacefully disperse. But the police unwisely attempted to control the crowd flow by blocking the southern route to Rajavithi Road. Cornered and overwhelmed by the enormous crowd, the police soon found themselves being pelted with stones and Molotov cocktails.

The frightened police panicked and responded with a barrage of tear gas and gunfire. Within moments, a full-scale riot had erupted from Chitralada Palace to Democracy Monument as protesters smashed windows, seized buses, and set ablaze police stations. The military was called in, and Bangkok soon witnessed the horrifying spectacle of tanks rolling down Rajadamnern Avenue and helicopters firing down into Thammasat University. An estimated 350 people died in the gunfire; several thousands were evacuated to hospitals.

Thanom and other high-ranking officials took the advice of King Bhumibol and went into exile. King Bhumibol took the extraordinary step of going on television to announce the appointment of the rector of Thammasat University as head of the new government. For the first time in modern history, the constitutional monarch of Thailand had openly involved himself in the transition of political power. The two-day revolution also served notice to the military regime that the Thai public would take serious measures in its pursuit of democratic reforms.

Experiment in Democracy

Under the royal edict of 14 October 1973, an interim government was installed under the direction of Professor Sanya Dharmasakti of Thammasat University. A constitutional convention held that December drafted a new democratic constitution ratified in October 1974. General elections in January 1975 were won by a coalition of 17 parties headed by one Kukrit Pramoj. The coalition was dominated by leftist and socialist parties such as Kukrit's Social Action Party.

Kukrit's chaotic and unstable administration finally faced and lost a vote of confidence from Parliament. Kukrit's downfall was also blamed on his unpopular alignment with leftist causes, a disastrous policy considering the recent triumphs of communism in Vietnam and Cambodia.

Parliamentary elections in April 1976 saw the return of Seni Pramoj, the leader of the Democrat Party and elder brother of Kukrit. Seni faced a series of struggles against the radical students in Bangkok, the growing communist insurgency movement in the countryside, and widespread dissatisfaction over the lack of public order and economic reform.

Thailand's experiment with democracy ended in October 1976 when military forces staged a coup d'etat and retook control of the government. The events began with student protests over the return of disgraced ex-Prime Minister Thanom to Thailand in the guise of a monk. Once again, Thammasat University was invaded by the Bangkok police and various paramilitary groups such as the "New Force" Nawaphon, the extremely violent Red Gaurs, and the enormously popular Village Scouts. Newspapers reports claimed students were publicly lynched, burned alive, and beheaded, and had their eyes gouged out. The bloody assault left hundreds dead and injured in an orgy of violence only comparable with the massacre of 1973.

Three years of unfettered but cacophonous democracy had left the Thai people with an overwhelming desire for the peace, stability, and social order insured by strong military rule.

Return to Military Rule, 1976-1980

Thailand returned to authoritarian rule in 1976 with the installation of Thanin Kraivichien as prime minister. Though a civilian lawyer and former high court justice, he proved more repressive than any of his military predecessors. Press censorship was reimposed, labor unions banned, and student dissidents purged from the universities. Thanin even ordered the public burning of such books as Thomas More's *Utopia* and the novels of George Orwell.

In response, many liberal students and their professors fled to the countryside, where they took up arms and joined communist movements headed by Chinese elements, including members of the Chinese Communist Party from mainland China. Despite their idealistic hopes, most of these Thai dissidents soon became disillusioned with their Marxist mentors and returned to

Bangkok after a few years of hiding amid the hills of central Thailand.

Thanin was dismissed by the military in October 1977. His replacement, General Kriangsak Chomanand, encouraged the return of political exiles and stemmed the excesses of the right-wing paramilitary organizations responsible for the October 1976 massacre.

MODERN TIMES

Prime Minister Prem Tinsulanonda, 1980-1988

Kriangsak's power base weakened with time, until he was finally forced from power in February 1980. His replacement, General Prem Tinsulanonda, commander of the army, quickly won support by appointing a civilian majority to his cabinet and bringing aboard respected civilian advisors to help manage the economy. Prem had long enjoyed a reputation for incorruptibility, as he was not the product of the traditional client-patron system that had long dominated regional politics.

Prem proved a great surprise. Soon after his installation as prime minister, he retired from active military service to serve in a purely civilian role. Confident that military rank was no longer necessary to rule the country, Prem nevertheless guarded against future military intervention by retaining the defense ministry portfolio and keeping a tight control of the military budget. This clever balancing act allowed him to keep his position after military leaders dominated the parliamentary elections of 1983.

Among his more noteworthy accomplishments were the final dismantling of the Communist Party of Thailand and the introduction of democratic reforms that laid the groundwork for the following administration. The renewed sense of political stability allowed Prem to relax restrictions against the press and continue his development of a "controlled democracy," dubbed "Premocracy" by his detractors. He also enjoyed great support from the monarchy, a relationship that helped him survive the two coups mounted by the military during his administration. Prem was also known for his handsome looks, enigmatic smile, and uncanny ability to play both sides of every political issue.

Prem's strongest challenge came from a group of disgruntled military leaders known as the "Young Turks." This coterie of military officers—predominantly graduates from the class of 1960 at Chulachomklao Military Academy—declared their independence from the commander of the Bangkok army post by independently mounting a coup in 1981. The "April Fool's Coup" quickly failed, but the Young Turks scored with the Thai public with their images of patriotic zeal, unwavering support for the crown, and philosophical alliance with disenfranchised farmers. Also known as Class 7, the Young Turks continue to exert a powerful influence in modern Thai politics.

Prem's popularity with the public and the royal crown saved him from a second poorly organized coup in September 1985. The morning spectacle resulted in the death of two American journalists and, by all accounts, did little to enhance the reputation of the Thai military. For the first time in modern Thai politics, coups d'etats were declared by both civilian and military leaders to be an unacceptable way to change the government. Democratic succession was back in vogue.

Prem refused renomination and voluntarily retired in 1988 in an attempt, he said, to allow the Thai people to choose their prime minister from elected representatives. Prem had enjoyed a long and relatively peaceful tenure—an unprecedented era of political stability and economic prosperity. History will remember Prem for his economic savvy and his unparalleled eight years of leadership, Thailand's longest civilian administration.

Prime Minister Chatichai Choonhavan, 1988-1991

Prem was followed by Chatichai Choonhavan, a former general and deputy prime minister whose Chart Thai (Thai Nation) Party won the largest number of seats in the July 1988 parliamentary elections. Chatichai vowed to continue democratic reforms and promote Thailand as the economic tiger within the region, as well as smoke fewer cigars and curtail his nightlife activity in local discos. He also declared Indochina would be "turned from a battlefield into a marketplace," a statement which signaled his intentions to manage the country as "Thailand Inc."

Chatichai's flamboyant and often humorous personality presented a welcome contrast to the rigid and ceremonial style of his predecessor. He also scored points with the public for his nationwide ban on commercial logging, a mandate made soon after unchecked logging in the south contributed to a serious flood disaster.

As his term progressed, the military appeared to partially relinquish its traditional grip on political and social life. Many said military coups were, once again, an outdated concept unacceptable to both the public and the royal family. After 16 successful and attempted coups following the end of absolute monarchy in 1932, Thailand had managed without them since 1985. A stable democracy, it was argued, had made the antics of generals irrelevant.

Chatichai, however, faced serious challenges. The public euphoria over Thailand's apparent transition from strongman rule under military control to a democratic society was still tempered by accusations of widespread corruption. Most observers agreed that far too many civilian and military leaders continued to line their pockets at public expense. More ominously, the military began to seriously distrust Chatichai after he downgraded their political role by making independent cabinet appointments, and after he took control of foreign policy, a portfolio traditionally the domain of the military. The Thai generals had assumed Chatichai would be a malleable prime minister. They were wrong.

The situation peaked on 23 February 1991, when military chiefs staged a bloodless coup, dissolved the government, imposed martial law, and abolished the 1978 constitution. Once again, the generals were in control. The official reasons for the coup, cited by the National Peacekeeping Council, were corruption by members of the administration, political appointees who abused their power, the decline of the government into a "parliamentary dictatorship," the distortion of an assassination plot in 1982, and, perhaps most telling, undermining of the military.

The Horrors of 1992

In the early hours of 18 May 1992, a senior Thai military officer received instructions from the Supreme Command headquarters under Prime Minister Suchinda Kraprayoon to open fire on thousands of protesters gathered near Democracy Monument in Bangkok. During the next four days of violence, scores of lives were lost in a shocking barrage which severely shook the Thai people, military, and monarchy, and once again altered the world's perception of Thai society.

The seeds of the turmoil dated from the 1991 seizure of power and promises of fresh elections and constitutional reforms by General Suchinda. Instead, Suchinda imposed a constitution that appointed him prime minister and created a powerful senate filled with military personnel. His move prompted a hunger strike in May 1992 led by Chamlong Srimuang, the charismatic former governor of Bangkok.

On the evening of 17 May, police and military units set up roadblocks near Democracy Monument to control a crowd estimated at over 200,000. At 0400 the following morning, army paratroopers arrested Chamlong and attacked demonstrators with machine guns and armored vehicles. The military then stormed the Royal Hotel and hauled away over 1,000 demonstrators in full view of the international press. Scores died in the attack while hundreds simply disappeared from sight. It was the worst violence since student demonstrators toppled the government in 1973.

Thailand's revered monarch, King Bhumibol Adulyadej, then summoned Suchinda and Chamlong to Chitralada Palace where he demanded an end to the violence. After only six weeks on the job, Suchinda resigned on 24 May and constitutional amendments were quickly passed. On 11 June, King Adulyadej appointed a respected former prime minister, Anand Panyarachun, to take up the post as prime minister until fall elections.

Prime Minister Anand Panyarachun, 1992

Anand was brought in to resolve the political crisis which had brought Thailand to its knees. A former ambassador to the United States and successful businessman, Anand certainly proved himself a bold politician during his brief three-month tenure as caretaker prime minister.

Soon after his appointment, Anand announced fresh elections for the House would be held on 13 September, and he would not stand for reelection or reappointment. He then proceeded to demote the nation's supreme military commander, Kaset Rojananil, and the army commander, Isarapong Noonpackdee, to largely powerless positions

within the military hierarchy. Both generals had been widely held responsible for ordering troops to open fire on pro-democracy demonstrators. Anand also abolished internal security laws the military had used to justify intervention against demonstrators.

He then set out to reduce the economic power of the military elite by reducing their role within the 60-odd state-controlled industries, including Thai International Airlines, Telephone Authority of Thailand, and the State Railways. The military elite also served on the boards of directors of government-approved monopolies controlling trucking and cigarettes. Other fields of military interest included lucrative logging, construction, and gambling ventures. The military's influence was staggering: a 1991 survey revealed that 36% of the directorships of the 16 largely non-bank state enterprises were held by military officers. All these businesses were routinely squeezed for kickbacks and exorbitant commissions for the issuance of procurement contracts, a practice that angered both the Thai public and honest government bureaucrats. Anand forced many of the generals associated with these scandal-racked state enterprises to resign from their lucrative board positions.

Anand served only three months, but earned a great deal of praise by presiding over an administration widely regarded as the cleanest and most efficient in decades. Chuan Leekpai, a politician opposed to military interference in politics, was named Thailand's 20th prime minister in September 1992.

Prime Minister Chuan Leekpai, 1992-1995

Elections held in September 1992 pitted the so-called "angel" parties—the five political groups that openly sided with pro-democracy demonstrators in May—against the four "devil" parties that supported the military regime of General Suchinda. Despite widespread vote-buying, the Democrat Party led by Chuan Leekpai won the largest number of seats in the House of Representatives. Thailand's oldest political party then formed a coalition with the four other angelic parties to ensure a majority in the House of Representatives. The victory, however, was considered tenuous, as candidates of the devil parties won sizable shares of seats and most of their leaders were reelected to their former positions.

Chuan Leekpai was the first nonmilitary Thai to serve as prime minister and the first in this aristocratic country to come from humble origins. He was born in Trang Province of a schoolteacher father and a mother who sold vegetables in the market. He worked his way through school tapping rubber trees. In 1962 he received his law degree from Bangkok's prestigious Thammasat University and practiced law until 1969, when he was elected to parliament as the representative from Trang. Chuan was reelected nine times, and held a variety of cabinet posts, from minister of justice to head of national education. As leader of the reformist Democrat Party, Chuan was invited to become prime minister after his party claimed victory in September.

Chuan's most significant appointment was Wimol Songwanich as army commander. Wimol, a highly regarded military strategist, immediately announced the military would withdraw from politics and support freely elected and democratic forms of government.

Despite military support and public admiration, Chuan's administration quickly faced serious problems. Chuan was assailed almost from the start by his political allies and coalition partners, who railed against his lack of direction, indecisive nature, love of conciliation, and inability to maintain cohesion among the five governing political parties.

His initial challenge came from former general Chavalit Yongchaiyut, leader of the New Aspiration Party, the second largest member of the ruling coalition. Chuan also had problems with former Bangkok governor Chamlong Srimuang and his Palang Dharma Party, which lost ground to the Democrats in the September election. The other major coalition partner, the Social Action Party, proved so nettlesome it was expelled from the ruling partnership after threatening to jump ship. In a bizarre but disturbingly common move, the Social Action Party hopped the ideological fence and joined forces with the opposition.

Chuan was also attacked by Chatichai Choonhavan, the former prime minister deposed in the military coup of 1991. Prior to his fall, Chatichai had founded and led the Chart Thai Party, another party media-dubbed "satanic" for its support of the military junta. Perhaps to avoid demonic associations or simply to keep the dollars rolling, Chatichai abandoned his party prior to the September 1992 elections, forming the Chart Pattana Party. He won parliamentary position and soon found himself the de facto leader of the opposition—those evil parties he'd once tried so hard to avoid. Back in the saddle, Chatichai raised hell. First, he embarrassed Chuan by pursuing his own diplomatic and economic initiatives on Indochina trade. He was, after all, the fellow who dreamed up the catchy phrase about "turning battlefields into marketplaces." He then proceeded to fight the constitutional reforms proposed by the Chuan administration, such as a democratically elected prime minister and a reduced military role within the Senate.

In May 1995, the government of Chuan Leekpai collapsed in the midst of a scandal over a government land-reform program. The controversy stemmed from the discovery that several wealthy families on Phuket had benefitted from a government program intended to redistribute land to poor farmers. Deputy Prime Minister Chamlong Srimuang announced the Palang Dharma Party's withdrawal from the five-party coalition government. Chuan then moved to dissolve Parliament, scheduling new elections for July 1995.

Despite the byzantine political twists of Thai politics, Chuan will probably be remembered as Thailand's first honest and freely appointed prime minister, a man not dominated by the military graduates of the highly politicized Chulachomklao Royal Military Academy.

Prime Minister Banharn Silpa-archa, 1995-1997

The July 1995 elections witnessed the rise of Banharn Silpa-archa as the new prime minister and leader of the resurgent Chart Thai Party. Banharn, a Chinese billionaire from Suphanburi, presided over a hopelessly disorganized government, which collapsed in 1997 after a series of economic crisis threatened to throw Thailand into complete bankruptcy. Another prime minister was appointed, but he only lasted a short 11 months.

The Return of Leekpai, 1997-present

After the collapse of two short-lived and completely corrupt governments, new national elections saw the return of Chuan Leekpai to the position of prime minister during a period of economic collapse unparalleled in Thailand's history. For more information about recent economic conditions, look below under Economy.

Leekpai successfully led the country out of its economic turmoil by accepting International Monetary Fund aid and carefully following the requirements of the bail-out package. By the end of 1998, Thailand had reversed its fortunes, as ailing banks were either dissolved or propped up, and a measure of confidence finally returned to the country.

Chuan also was credited with replacing the sense of bumbling ineptitude and venality of previous governments with one of competence, confidence, and rectitude. He remained courteous, precise, and calm when many others panicked and made counterproductive statements. He appointed ministers who, for the most part—especially in the finance and economic sectors—seemed to know their jobs. Chuan also started to reform the finance sector by shaking up the Bank of Thailand, appointing a new governor, and closing down 56 mismanaged finance companies. Along with these dramatic moves, Chuan pushed ahead with downsizing the government by forcing a reduction in the bloated military, especially the number of generals.

GOVERNMENT

Thailand is a constitutional monarchy with a bicameral legislature consisting of a conservative 270-member Senate appointed by the prime minister to screen legislation, and a 360-member House of Representatives freely elected by the people. The House is currently dominated by several liberal-leaning parties that form shifting coalitions to maintain power against a similar number of pro-military parties. Most current Senate members are hangovers from the last military government; more than half are active or retired military officers.

The prime minister is chosen for a four-year term by the political party that holds the largest number of seats in the House of Representatives. The prime minister then selects a cabinet of 20 ministers drawn from the members of his victorious coalition. He also retains the right to dissolve Parliament and schedule new elections.

Thailand today features a compromise government largely elected by the public and staffed by civilians and professional bureaucrats, but still silently dominated by the military and pro-military sympathizers.

Although the idea of a freely elected, democratic government is now supported by the military, Thailand has witnessed 22 prime ministers, 54 governments, and 18 military coups since the abolition of absolute monarchy in 1932.

Party or Personality?
Thailand's byzantine political landscape can be partially understood by looking at several deeply ingrained traditions favoring personality and patronage over political platforms.

First, most Thais are not committed to any particular political ideology, but rather rally around those leaders who can provide them with patronage, such as new roads, government jobs, or money for votes. This attitude perpetuates a system where leaders accumulate power as individuals rather than through their political affiliations.

Secondly, political parties in Thailand are formulated quite differently than in Western democratic governments. Thai political parties are simply groups of people who register as a legal entity in order to acquire power, prestige, and profit. Party ideology is considered so unimportant that registered parties are often sold to individuals seeking ready-made legal entities. As you might expect, none of this inspires much confidence in the average Thai citizen. Recent constitutional changes may work to reduce this problem, though most analysts expect these changes to take many years.

Another problem associated with this lack of ideological commitment is that politicians often change parties as easily as they change clothing. One day you're in bed with the military, the next you're waving the flag of democracy. Party-hopping still carries little of the negative connotations found in most Western societies.

Since most political parties are dominated by regional individuals rather than universally recognized leaders, Thailand has failed to produce national political parties in the true sense of the word. Regional factionalism and the pursuit of self interest remain vexing problems in contemporary Thailand.

Finally, most political parties remain dominated by old-timers and veteran politicians whose prime is long past. This gerontocracy of the elders often discourages younger members of the

GEOGRAPHICAL AND ADMINISTRATIVE DIVISIONS OF THAILAND

Thailand is divided into eight administrative divisions and 76 provinces or *changwat,* including three new provinces created in early 1994. Provinces are subdivided into 648 districts *(amphoe),* 61 subdistricts *(king amphoe),* 6,000 communes *(tambon),* and over 50,000 villages *(muban)* which range in size from 50-200 families.

Larger urban designations include towns *(muang)* with populations of 10,000-50,000, and cities *(nakhon)* with over 50,000 inhabitants.

The following charts summarize the eight administrative regions and the 10 most populous provinces in Thailand:

THE EIGHT ADMINISTRATIVE REGIONS OF THAILAND

REGION	PROVINCES	AREA %	POP. %	CBD %	CARS %	PHONES %
1. Bangkok	---	0.3	9.6	61.7	70.7	56.8
2. Bangkok Vicinity	6	1.2	5.4	8.3	5.7	9.7
3. Central	6	3.2	4.9	2.6	2.4	2.6
4. Eastern	8	7.1	6.5	5.3	3.8	4.9
5. Western	6	8.4	5.9	3.5	2.3	3.0
6. Northeastern	19	32.9	34.7	5.7	4.4	7.7
7. Northern	17	33.1	20.2	7.0	6.5	8.5
8. Southern	14	13.8	12.8	5.9	4.1	6.9

Note: CBD are Commercial Bank Deposits.

THE 10 MOST POPULOUS PROVINCES IN THAILAND

PROVINCE	POP.	POP./ SQ. KM	AREA	AREA/ RANK	GPP	GPP/ RANK	GPP PER CAPITA
1. Bangkok	5,562	3,554	1,560	66/76	628,033	1/76	105,357
2. Nakhon Ratchasima	2,467	120	20,492	1/76	34,146	6/76	14,745
3. Ubon Ratchathani	1,945	103	18,900	4/76	20,690	18/76	11,145
4. Udon Thani	1,846	118	15,588	6/76	20,999	16/76	11,913
5. Khon Kaen	1,662	153	10,883	16/76	25,512	11/76	15,585
6. Chiang Mai	1,530	76	20,107	2/76	33,480	7/76	24,727
7. Nakhon Si Thammarat	1,477	149	9,942	19/76	25,068	12/76	16,859
8. Buri Ram	1,417	139	10,231	18/76	14,914	26/76	10,692
9. Surin	1,341	165	8,124	25/76	12,506	34/76	10,013
10. Si Sa Ket	1,335	151	8,840	22/76	12,007	36/76	9,418

Note: AREA is measured in square km; POP is population in units of 1,000; POP./SQ. KM indicates population density; GPP is Gross Provincial Product in millions of *baht;* GPP PER CAPITA is in *baht.*

public from considering political careers. All this adds up to a political landscape quite hostile to the growth of a real democracy.

A New Constitution
In response to the problems cited above, a new constitution was instituted in October 1997. This new document didn't offer mere cosmetic touch-ups to the old constitution; instead, it was radical surgery, designed to eliminate corruption and vote buying. New constitutional provisions include an independent election commission to oversee polls and an ombudsman to keep an eye on government officials. Voting has been made compulsory to minimize the problem of people being paid to cast ballots.

Under the new constitution, parties now must win at least five percent of the national vote, thus lessening small, divisive regional groups that often functioned as personal fiefdoms. Another rule mandates that all MPs must quit Parliament before they can be ministers, a move designed to prevent (or at least minimize) conflicts of interest.

Another goal of the new constitution is to attract quality professionals to politics. All parliamentary candidates must now have a university degree, a move that will quickly force the resignation of old-timers and bring in young blood.

Regional Administration
The political organization of Thailand reflects the people's love of order and dictated hierarchy. For administrative purposes, Thailand is divided into eight administrative divisions subdivided into 76 provinces *(changwat);* three new provinces were created in early 1994. Provinces are subdivided into 648 districts *(amphoe),* 61 subdistricts *(king amphoe),* 6,000 communes *(tambon),* and over 50,000 villages *(muban)* ranging in size from 50-200 families. Larger urban designations include *muang,* with populations of 10,000-50,000 citizens, and *nakhon,* defined as cities with over 50,000 inhabitants.

Local governments are supervised by the Ministry of the Interior, which appoints provincial governors to four-year terms. The only exception is Bangkok, which elects both its governor and provincial assembly. Assisting the governor in a consultative capacity are the members of the provincial board, who actually report to their superiors in Bangkok. The Interior Ministry also appoints district officers *(nai amphoe)* who stand on the lowest rung of the federal government hierarchy. As outsiders appointed from Bangkok, district officers are usually respected rather than liked by the local population.

Below district officer level are layers of regional leaders generally elected by popular vote but approved by the provincial governor. Communes are administered by a headman called *kamnan,* villages by *phuyaibun,* while small cities *(muang)* and large cities *(nakhon)* are administered by elected mayors.

THE MONARCHY

From the days of the Sukothai era, Thailand has been a monarchic state ruled by a king and his entourage. This continues to a remarkable degree today, despite the revolution of 1932, which ended absolute monarchy and curtailed the designated powers of the king. You will be amazed at the deep love and admiration the Thai people feel for their king, who remains among the most powerful royal figures on the planet.

Early Kings
Thai royal prestige dates back to the Sukothai Empire, when King Ramkamheng served as both warrior-ruler and father-figure to his devoted subjects. Ramkamheng and subsequent kings were regarded as incarnations of gods or bodhisattvas, protecting Buddhism and the national interest by supplicating the heavens. To a large degree, the early kings of Sukothai and Ayuthaya adopted the ancient Indian concept of ruler as god-king, then modified the system to emphasize the Buddhist traditions of accessibility and paternalism. Although Ayuthayan kings grew increasingly obsessed with power and ritual, the Thai monarchy continued to serve as *the* source of national divine inspiration and the centerpiece of religious and social consciousness.

Little has changed today. Under the present constitution, the king of Thailand is recognized as the head of state, upholder of religion, and chief of the Royal Thai Armed Forces. Despite these auspicious titles, the monarch is titular and possesses no constitutional power. And yet the man who holds the position is unquestionably the most powerful person in the kingdom.

The importance of the monarchy cannot be overstated. The king of Thailand enjoys a measure of national respect and power unequaled elsewhere in the world. He is a symbol of unification who stabilizes the country during military coups and revolutions, a living example of Buddhist compassion for the Thai people, and the chief linchpin in the three national pillars of nation, religion, and monarchy. Today, most Thais consider their king a semi-divine being, the living embodiment of their national consciousness.

King Bhumibol Adulyadej

The present king, Bhumibol Adulyadej, was born on 5 December 1927 in Cambridge, Massachusetts, where his father was studying medicine at Harvard University. Bhumibol's birth was an inauspicious event, hardly noted by the Siamese press; the American-born Thai was considered a highly unlikely candidate to ever reach the throne.

According to Siamese laws of royal succession, on the day of his birth, Bhumibol was outranked by the reigning King Prajadhipok (his uncle), Bhumibol's father (Prince Mahidol of Songkhla), and his elder brother, Prince Ananda. But fate intervened in a remarkable way. Prince Mahidol died abruptly in 1929 and Prajadhipok abdicated without a designated heir (he only had one daughter) in 1935. Prince Ananda briefly served as King Rama VIII until his mysterious death in 1946. Prince Bhumibol then became king of Thailand at the age of 19.

The young king finished his education at Lausanne University in Switzerland before returning to Thailand to claim the throne as Rama IX. Prior to this homecoming, Bhumibol lost an eye in a car accident, but also was introduced to Mom Rajawongse Sirikit, the beautiful daughter of the Thai ambassador to France. Bhumibol married Sirikit in April 1950, one week prior to his coronation. He then took his full, royal name: Phrabaat Somdet Boramintara Maha Phumipol Phonadunyadet.

The young king vowed to prove himself a worthy successor to his predecessors and "rule with dharma for the benefit and happiness of the Siamese people." His early years were more noted for his love of the arts, music, and the so-

MAJOR KINGS OF THAILAND

EMPIRE	DATE OF REIGN
THE KHMERS	
Suryavarman II	1113-1150
Jayavarman VII	1181-1220
Indravarman II	1220-1243
LANNA EMPIRE	
Mengrai	1259-1317
Ku Na	1355-1385
Tilok	1441-1487
SUKOTHAI KINGDOM	
Intraditya	1238-1270
Ban Muang	1270-1275
Ramkamheng	1278-1318
Lo Thai	1318-1347
Li Thai	1347-1368
AYUTHAYA	
Ramathibodi (U Thong)	1350-1369
Ramasuen	1369-1370
Boromraja I	1370-1388
Boromraja II	1424-1448
Boromtrailokat	1448-1488
Ramathibodi II	1491-1529
Naresuan	1590-1605
Prasat Thong	1630-1656
Narai	1656-1688
Borommakat	1733-1758
Ekatat	1758-1767
CHAKRI DYNASTY	
General Taksin (Pre-Chakri)	1767-1782
Ramatibodhi (Rama I)	1782-1809
Phutthalaetia (Rama II)	1809-1824
Nangklao (Rama III)	1824-1851
Mongkut (Rama IV)	1851-1868
Chulalongkorn (Rama V)	1868-1910
Vajiravudh (Rama VI)	1910-1925
Prajadhipok (Rama VII)	1925-1935
Ananda Mahidol (Rama VIII)	1935-1946
Bhumibol Adulyadej (Rama IX)	1946-present

A QUESTION OF SUCCESSION

King Bhumibol and Queen Sirikit have four children, Princess Ubol Ratana (born 1951), Crown Prince Vajiralongkorn (1952), Princess Mahachakri Sirindhorn (1955), and Princess Chulabhorn (1957).

The nation now faces one of the more controversial quagmires of modern Thai politics—the question of royal succession. Thailand's rules of succession are taken from a royal decree issued by King Tilok (1448-88), who sought to standardize succession when most kings were in polygamous relationships and produced hundreds of potential heirs. Tilok established the tradition still observed today that the king's senior son was first in line for the throne, followed by his brother, known as the *uparaja,* and then by other male offspring of the king.

According to these traditions, Crown Prince Vajiralongkorn, the sole son of Bhumibol, should claim the throne upon the death or abdication of his father. However, the situation changed dramatically in 1981, after new laws approved by the Thai Parliament made it theoretically possible for any member of the royal family to take the throne. Although Vajiralongkorn was officially designated crown prince and heir to the throne when he turned 20 years of age in 1972, in the event of illness, death, or voluntary declination, the throne might pass to one of his sisters.

The next ruler probably won't be the eldest daughter, Princess Ubol Ratana (Ubolrat), who attended M.I.T. in Massachusetts where she fell in love with and married an American student, Peter Jensen. The newlyweds moved to Los Angeles, where the princess studied statistics and public health at U.C.L.A. Because she married a foreigner, Ubolrat lost her title and royal allowance and later found work as a marketing assistant with a computer company in Los Angeles—quite a change from royal life in Bangkok.

Today Ubolrat and Peter reside in Los Angeles, where Peter works in the mining industry and Ubolrat raises their three children. Ubolrat appears satisfied to be uninvolved with the political and social intrigues of the royal family. She is also on good terms with her family, who had her reinstated as princess a few years ago.

The next ruler probably won't be Princess Chulabhorn, third eldest daughter of the king and queen.

Even though she's four steps down from the throne, Chulabhorn lacks the command of government affairs and social issues so vital for national leadership. Chulabhorn married a Thai commoner in 1982.

Could the next king be a queen? If public popularity held sway, the next monarch would probably be Bhumibol's second daughter, Princess Sirindhorn, a woman of many accomplishments, including academic distinction—she's a lecturer at two of Thailand's most prestigious universities and recipient of a string of degrees in sociology, the humanities, history, and education. Sirindhorn also presides over the Red Cross and, much like her beloved father, works incessantly to help the poor of Thailand.

Sirindhorn was elevated in 1981 to the rank of *Maha Chakri,* a title virtually equivalent to crown princess. Despite Princess Sirindhorn's popularity, the next monarch will most likely be Crown Prince Vajiralongkorn. He attended school at London's prestigious Royal College of Defense Studies and currently holds the rank of major general in the Royal Guards Regiment, military credentials being important in the political structure of Thailand. Vajiralongkorn has one daughter by his first wife, Princess Somsawali, and five younger children by his unofficial consort (or second wife), Yuwatida Surasawadee. The 1993 divorce of Vajiralongkorn and Somsawali ended an unhappy relationship similar to that of Britain's Prince Charles and Princess Diana, although Vajiralongkorn certainly received better treatment from the press than his British counterpart. Vajiralongkorn then married Surasawadee.

The crown prince is heir apparent, but Sirindhorn continues to be a popular candidate among the Thai people, who consider her a righteous choice for the throne. The question of royal succession is one of the favorite topics among the Thais, who constantly whisper the latest rumors circulating about the royal family. Negative publicity about the king, queen, or children is forbidden in Thai publications, but speculation comes up almost daily in most conversations.

Visitors may want to discuss the issue with a Thai, but remember most Thais are reluctant to discuss royal matters with a foreigner and deeply resent criticisms given by outsiders.

cial whirl of Bangkok society. Perhaps his deepest love was the world of jazz, where he proved himself a talented jazz saxophonist at formal university graduations, state functions, and even impromptu jam sessions held in the inner sanctums of the Royal Palace.

During his jazz period, the king led all-star late-night sessions with such luminaries as bandleader Les Brown and singer Patti Page. In 1960, the king played with the Benny Goodman band in New York; Goodman offered the king a job in his orchestra. Lionel Hampton, jazz's greatest vibest, called him the "coolest king in the land." Bhumibol's jazz compositions include "Hungry Man's Blues," "Blue Night," "Falling Rain" and the alma mater theme song for Chulalongkorn University. His compositional career peaked with the release of his three-movement "Manohra Ballet," a complex piece based on a classical Thai story accompanied by a variety of blues moods, Thai musical themes, and improvised melodies inspired by Coltrane and Monk. The work itself, previewed in Vienna during a state visit, earned Bhumibol the first admission of any Asian citizen to the Viennese Institute of Music and Art.

Bhumibol also has proved himself a talented artist, often using members of the royal family in his small- to medium-sized oils. A rare retrospective of his paintings in 1987 to honor his 60th birthday revealed his evolutionary style from portrait realism to semi-abstracts filled with bold colors and original design.

The king also has a great fondness for yachting. Despite the automobile accident which blinded him in one eye, Bhumibol's deft handling and intriguing boat designs won him the Gold Medal at the Southeast Asian Games in 1967. Bhumibol in this respect is similar to other national leaders who love the sea: King Constantine of Greece, King Olaf of Norway, and the duke of Edinburgh.

Bhumibol's interests changed with time, from jazz and sailing to more serious matters of social and political justice. In what is now the longest reign of any Thai king, Bhumibol has earned immense popularity as the working monarch who guides and unifies the nation as head of state and protector of national traditions. He also works ceaselessly to promote rural development, oversee construction of new roads to help the poor

farmers of the northeast, and encourage the opium growers of the north to experiment with alternative cash crops. The king is aided in his humanitarian efforts by his wife, Queen Sirikit, who oversees a foundation to preserve traditional arts and crafts.

Bhumibol is a wealthy man, with major financial interests in the Siam Cement Corporation and the many large banks managed by the Crown Property Bureau. This organization is the second-largest asset holder and fourth-largest investor in the country, with widely varied financial interests that include the Dusit Thani and Siam Intercontinental Hotels, offshore mining, and Honda car assembly.

In July 1988, Bhumibol became Thailand's longest reigning monarch after 42 eventful years on the throne. In 1996, His Majesty's 50 years of leadership were honored with nationwide festivals and celebrations, while in 1999 the King presided over the final year of the Amazing Thailand tourism campaign.

Respect for Royalty

Portraits of the king, queen, and royal family are seen everywhere in Thailand. All foreign visitors are warned to behave respectfully toward the royal family: an acceptable caveat since there is little doubt the Thai monarchy has earned this honor. When the royal anthem is played publicly each evening or prior to the screening of a film, everyone—including Westerners—is expected to stand at attention.

Never openly criticize the royal family, since the crime of lese majesty carries heavy penalties of up to seven years in prison—for both Thais and Westerners. For example, several years ago, the king was publicly criticized by a Thai intellectual and social critic, Sulak Sivaraksa, who casually joked about the king's passion for yachting. Sulak received a royal pardon for this first offense, but was forced to flee the country in 1991 after he further criticized the king.

HUMAN RIGHTS

Violations of human rights are not confined to any particular country or political system, but are found throughout the world. Jailing of political dissidents, torture of those who speak out for

A NEW POLITICAL MODEL

*T*hai politics over the last decade have been extraordinarily turbulent, moving from the first fully elected democratic government to a military coup, then from a technocratic government to a semi-elected military regime to the democratic government of Chuan Leekpai. Is the present civilian government just another periodic break from military rule, or has the military elite really given up the reins of power? Every change in government since the end of the absolute monarchy in 1932—that's 20 prime ministers, 52 governments, and 18 military coups—has students of Thai politics posing these questions.

The classic theory about the nature of modern Thai politics was proposed by Fred Riggs in his 1966 book, *Thailand: The Modernization of a Bureaucratic Polity*. Riggs argued the rotation of power between sections of the bureaucracy—the civil servants and military—effectively kept civilian politicians, businesspeople, and the Thai public out of the picture. Democracy was impossible because of an unspoken agreement between the bureaucrats and the military. The deal: Government bureaucrats would ignore most military excesses in exchange for managerial power and relative social peace.

Meanwhile, the average Thai citizen continued to follow a political culture inherited from the Sukothai Empire of the 13th century. Riggs suggested that Thais have traditionally sought out charismatic, paternalistic strongmen to lead the country, and have placed little value on democratic elections or a systematic method to replace leadership.

The Riggs model of the Thai political scene was widely accepted within the academic community until the events of the late 1980s. Although cultural mores and power-sharing agreements continued, major change was suggested by the rise of nonbureaucratic institutions within the government, and by the ability of businesspeople to affect government policy. For the first time in modern history, organized business associations appeared to be significant players in the conduct of government. The election of Chatichai Choonhavan, and his appointment of businesspeople, not military leaders, to his cabinet, seemed to support new political models proposed by Thai academics Likhit Dhiravegin and Anek Laothamatas.

The military coup that forced Choonhavan from office was seen by many as proof that the military elite will never relinquish power in Thailand, and that democratic governments will forever remain as only an occasional blip on the political landscape. Others theorize that the rise of a sizable middle class and independent business community will keep the generals under control. But if the past is an indication, the game shall, at least for now, remain the same.

---

human freedoms, press censorship, intimidation of the judiciary, persecution of labor movements, and manipulation of religion and nationalism to control the population are common problems under most forms of government—whether democratically elected or holding power by force of arms.

The Asian Perspective

Most Asian governments share a vision of human rights quite different from those of Western nations. In Asia, economic growth and social stability are more important than individual freedoms and Western protections must take a back seat to the pressing needs of society, state, and nation. Asian governments insist the West does not speak for the world when it comes to human rights, and that the civil policies of Asian countries should not be dictated by Western nations.

This viewpoint, reiterated at human rights conferences from Asia to Europe, was reflected a few years ago in the Bangkok Declaration, a measure approved by Asian governments shortly before the start of a United Nations Human Rights Conference in Vienna. The Bangkok Declaration—condemned in the West as retrogressive and reprehensible—insisted Asian nations are entitled to complete noninterference from the West in their internal affairs. That is, the United States government has no moral right to interfere with the human rights policies of the Burmese government, Portugal cannot fool around with Timor, and the U.N. should not criticize repression in, say, Cambodia. The Bangkok Declaration stated that Asian governments have the freedom to pursue, without worldwide criticism or interference, whatever political and social paths they choose.

The only conference participant to voice opposition was Japan, which stated criticism of human rights violations does not necessarily constitute interference in national internal affairs. Japan quickly found itself under attack from its Asian neighbors for being too Western in its ideology.

What's really going on here? Everyone knows that emerging nations defend their national sovereignty against foreign interference, but what are the underlying reasons for the insistence on complete noninterference?

Some trace the problem to linking human rights with the Western concept of "entitlements," such as universal access to education, work, rest, national health care, and scientific pursuits; rights that extend beyond the basic civil rights of life, liberty, and the pursuit of happiness. Entitlements of these types put unwanted pressures on foreign governments to perform to Western ideals.

Asian governments also point out that the explosion of individual liberties in the West has undermined legal authority and made Western societies among the least controlled and most dangerous in the world.

But Western governments fear the noninterference issue often is used as a smokescreen to deflect international scrutiny from human rights abuses, provide continued economic gains to elitist classes, and keep morally corrupt governments in absolute control. Many Asian human rights activists and some government officials also agree to these motivations for the noninterference clause. One Malaysian group suggested that government appeals to "cultural relativism" and "situational uniqueness" are simply efforts to justify deviation from international norms. A Filipino government official stated the emphasis on noninterference was just a political ploy by certain ruling elites to preserve existing methods of rule.

These criticisms largely do not apply to Thailand, which is considered by most Western observers to be one of the few Asian nations with constructive policies. A noteworthy example was the Thai government's admission of a group of Nobel Peace laureates to protest human rights violations in Myanmar, a bold move regarded as evidence of official maturity on human rights issues. Others, such as human rights lawyer

Thongbai Thongpao, insist the Thai government uses such means as lese majesty charges to prosecute those who criticize the political elite. But the general consensus is that the Thai government pursues one of the more enlightened human rights agendas in Southeast Asia.

Thailand
Unlike many other countries in the region, the citizens of Thailand enjoy a wide range of civil and political liberties. According to the U.S. Senate *Report on Human Rights,* autonomous political parties, gatherings, and associations are allowed, and freedom from arbitrary detention or search is generally safeguarded, aside from some rarely enforced restrictive laws. Although it practices some self-censorship, particularly in regard to the monarchy, Thailand's press is among the freest in Asia—certainly when compared to those of Singapore, Malaysia, and Indonesia.

Human rights activists are able to bring issues to the attention of the government and to lobby for corrective action without fear of official reprisals. Political killings are rare, although the government admits that police execution of habitual criminals without due process occasionally occurs, largely in southern Thailand. A number of journalists have died violently in the last decade, though generally not from exposing corruption or illegal activity, but because of participation in illicit behavior like blackmail or extortion.

The Thai government has stated its opposition to the use of cruel, inhuman, or degrading punishment. Problems with the Muslims in southern Thailand are ongoing, but the government has demonstrated great restraint dealing with radicals demanding autonomy or complete separation from the Thai state.

Thailand's criminal and civil codes follow Western models, and the rights of suspects are similar to those in European and North American countries. Arrest warrants are required and specific charges must be brought within a limited period of time. Reports of arbitrary arrest are infrequent. A small number of Muslim separatists have been detained without trial, though most are released after court proceedings and do not report serious mistreatment. Summary exile and compulsory labor are not practiced.

The Thai constitution grants citizens the presumption of innocence as well as access to the courts to seek redress, though suspects can be denied the right to legal counsel during the pretrial or investigative periods. Trials are conducted by judges rather than juries and alleged plotters in military coups are tried in civilian courts rather than the military court system. Royal amnesties are periodically granted, such as the pardons granted by the king in 1995-96 to mark his 50 years on the throne. There have been allegations, however, of both government and private influence being brought to bear on cases involving elected officials dealing narcotics.

Human Rights Organizations

Travelers visiting other Southeast Asian countries can obtain detailed information from the following organizations.

Amnesty International: An independent worldwide movement working for the release of all prisoners of conscience, fair and prompt trials for political prisoners, and an end to torture and execution. Amnesty has protested the torture of Burmese political dissidents, examined violations of political and religious liberties in Indonesia, and investigated the murder of civilians in the Philippines. Publications include country overviews and annual reports summarizing conditions in over 135 countries. 322 8th Ave., New York, NY 10001, tel. (212) 807-8400.

Asia Watch: A widely respected nonprofit organization that promotes the legal and moral obligation of the U.S. government to demand worldwide human rights. Asia Watch and its affiliate organizations—Human Rights Watch, Africa Rights Watch, etc.—sponsor missions abroad

to document abuses and expose discrepancies between Asian propaganda and actual practices. Membership US$40/year. 36 West 44th St., New York, NY 10036, tel. (202) 371-6592.

United States Senate Report on Human Rights: The *Annual Report on Human Rights* covers in great detail the issues of individual liberties (torture, arbitrary arrest, and denial of fair trial), civil liberties (freedom of speech, press, and religion), and political rights (fair and open elections, international supervision of human rights violations). The libraries in larger cities subscribe to and maintain copies available to the public.

Tribal Rights

The survival of cultural minorities is the focus of the following groups.

Survival International: The human rights of threatened tribal peoples from Myanmar to Borneo are monitored by this English organization, which publishes informative booklets banned in most Southeast Asian nations. Survival International digs deep into the issues of the Penans in Malaysia and the endangered minorities of Thailand. 310 Edgware Rd., London W2 1DY, tel. (01) 723-5535.

Cultural Survival: The economic, social, and cultural rights of indigenous peoples and ethnic minorities throughout the world are supported by this small, underfunded American organization. A subscription to the authoritative *Cultural Survival Quarterly* is included with the US$25 annual contribution. 11 Divinity Ave., Cambridge, MA 02138, tel. (617) 495-2562.

papaya (malaga)

ECONOMY

Economic Meltdown

After several decades of near phenomenal growth, Thailand hit the wall several years ago and today remains in a state of slow economic recovery.

The crisis began in January 1997, when a medium-sized Thai property firm defaulted on US$80 million worth of convertible Eurobonds. From that relative matchstick roared a consuming conflagration as attention turned to the overbuilt state of the Bangkok property market, overextended property developers and finance houses, and how much private foreign debt was actually due to be paid in 1997.

The crisis emerged slowly at first, as speculators began hammering the *baht* in February. The Bank of Thailand initially beat them back, but the attacks kept coming until they peaked in May.

The following month saw the resignation of the Thai finance minister, a key cabinet member who had staunchly argued against the devaluation of the *baht*. In June, the Thai central bank suspended operations of 16 cash-strapped finance companies as Thai Prime Minster Chavalit

---

THAILAND: FAST FACTS

GEOGRAPHY

Land Area: 513,115 sq. km
Number of Provinces: 76
Largest Province: Nakhon Ratchasima
Wettest Province: Trat (187 rainy days)
Highest Province: Chiang Mai (312 m)
Length of Coastline: 2,614 km
Highest Mountain: Doi Inthanon (2,298 m)
Longest River: Moon River (673 km)
Largest Island: Phuket (543 sq. km)
Rainforest Cover: 10-22%
Deforestation Rate: 2.5%

POPULATION

Population: 60,206,000
Population Estimate 2010: 71 million
Population Density: 120 per sq. km
Population Growth Rate: 1.65%
Rural Population: 77%
Urban Population: 22%
Rural Growth Rate: 1.1%
Urban Growth Rate: 4.6%

INCOME

National Average Income: US$1,736
Bangkok Average Income: US$4,214
Rural Average Income: US$547
Minimum Income Bangkok: 150B

Minimum Income National: 110B
Population in Poverty: 31%

THAI SOCIETY

Average Life Expectancy: 63 years
Leading Cause of Death: Heart Disease
Second Cause of Death: Accidents
Homicides: 4,768
Suicides: 3,801
Transport Deaths: 8,566

EDUCATION

Student Population: 12,249,146
Students Grades 1-6: 6,954,000
Students Grades 7-9: 1,415,000
Students Grades 10-12: 478,000
Students University: 194,983
Students PHD Programs: 137
Average Years of School: 3.8 years

BANGKOK VERSUS THAILAND

Land: 0.3%
Population: 11.2%
Gross Provincial Product: 35.4%
Commercial Bank Deposits: 61.7%
Passenger Cars: 70.7%
Telephones: 56.8%
Physicians: 67.2%

Yonchaiyudh assured the nation in a televised address that there would be no devaluation of the *baht*. Two days later, the Bank of Thailand announced a managed float of the *baht* and called on the International Monetary Fund for "technical assistance." The announcement effectively devalued the *baht* by 20% as it fell to a record low of 28.80 *baht* to the U.S. dollar.

What started as merely a bad exchange rate dream turned into a full-blown nightmare in the summer of 1997. Many Southeast Asian economies had pegged their currencies to the U.S. dollar, but the links started to fray once it became clear that high current-account shortfalls, inflation, and asset bubbles left many economies out of sync with America's economic fundamentals. Further, Asian financial institutions had borrowed massively from overseas lenders in order to take advantage of relatively low rates. As local currencies fell, foreign obligations swelled. The borrowers bought dollars, seeking to hedge against further devaluation, but the move only fulfilled their worst fears.

Meanwhile, most of the borrowed money had been misdirected into unsaleable property or uneconomic factories through cronyism, corruption, or plain bad business. The crisis also was fueled by Bangkok politicians, many with links to bad financial institutions.

In August 1997, the IMF approved a US$17 billion bailout package for Thailand. In November, Chavalit resigned as prime minister after intense public pressure and just 11 months in office. The opposition Democrat Party then formed a new coalition government, and Parliament soon asked Chuan Leekpai to return to his post. The *baht* fell to a record low of 44 per dollar in early December.

Along with the collapse of the *baht*, Leekpai also had to deal with the IMF bailout package, which required a hefty budget surplus in the forthcoming annual economic report. This meant that the government's revenues would have to exceed its expenditures by a significant amount—60 billion *baht*, to be precise. This led to huge cuts in government expenditures, an increase in the value-added tax (VAT) from seven to 10%, and stiff new taxes on luxury items.

Prime Minster Chuan Leekpai, unlike Suharto in Indonesia, bit the bullet and made the adjustments required by the IMF. By the end of January 1998, it was apparent that Thailand had turned the corner on the economic crisis and that its economy would eventually recover from the devastation of the previous year.

Leekpai made a very successful trip to the United States in March 1998, where he was praised for his reforms by American businessmen, the U.S. media, and President Clinton. He was able to renegotiate the purchase of jet warplanes and find American investors for several new electric power projects. The Peace Corps cancelled their plans to leave Thailand and the U.S. government agreed to finance rural health programs in Thailand.

The situation remains in flux, though early 1999 signals show a slow but steady recovery of the Thai economy. The *baht* has recovered from an all-time low of 58 per dollar and now stands at under 40 to the U.S. dollar.

Export Explosion

Agriculture, the traditional source of income for most Thais, still accounts for about 22% of the nation's exports, and continues to provide employment for over two-thirds of the population. Thailand ranks first in the world in the production of rice, tapioca, canned tuna, and natural rubber; second in prawns and sugar; and among the top five in coconuts and frozen chicken.

But the export product mix has shifted sharply over the past decade. Although Thailand remains the world's fifth largest exporter of agricultural products, manufactured products such as clothing, machinery, and jewelry now lead the field. Today, manufactured goods account for 67% of Thailand's exports, a significant figure when compared to the 1960 figure of just 2.4%. Thailand's most important exports are textiles and shoes (17% of total exports), electronics and machinery (15%), seafood (5.9%), and precious stones (4.8%). The chief recipients of these exports are the United States (22.4%), Japan (17%), Singapore (9%), and Hong Kong (4.6%).

ECONOMIC CHALLENGES

Thailand also faces serious economic problems in income distribution, infrastructure development, the debt required to service growth, shortcomings of the national education system, labor demands for higher wages, and a heavy assault against the environment.

Thailand's Hidden Poverty

Visitors to Bangkok often assume Thailand is a newly industrialized country filled with construction cranes, gleaming Mercedes, and well-dressed entrepreneurs. But few tourists explore the impoverished villages of the northeast or deep south, where millions of peasants suffer from poor diet, harsh climate, and the vagaries of petty bureaucrats. Explorers who venture into the more remote locales will discover the dark side of the Thai economic miracle: the vast economic discrepancy between the urban rich and the rural poor.

According to a study by the Thailand Research Development Institute, the wealthiest 40% of the population receive 77% of the national income; the poorest 60% account for only 23%. Another study by the World Bank indicated the incidence of poverty in Thailand is as high as in Indonesia, even though Thailand's average GNP per capita is 2.5 times higher. Perhaps most discouraging is the finding that the income gap is *widening*. Few are starving, but the rural poor often suffer from unrelieved and persistent malnutrition.

The truth about the Thai economic miracle is that development within the kingdom has been geographically unbalanced. Bangkok wages are relatively high, with an average income approaching US$3,000. But rural income is stagnant or falling due to declining agricultural prices, the lack of natural outlets to world trade, widespread landlessness, poor soil, harsh climate, lack of water and power, and the reluctance of the central government to spend large sums of money on these remote regions.

This persistent dichotomy is not only an economic problem, but a source of social and political instability as well. The concentration of wealth in Bangkok draws millions of workers from the farms to the city, straining public facilities and social services to the breaking limit. Bangkok may become the first city in the world to experience complete and total gridlock across its entire infrastructure—from transportation and shipping to telecommunications and energy supplies.

The yawning gap between urban rich and rural poor also encourages political dissension.

Most of the revolutionary movements within the kingdom have originated in the poorest sections of the country, then spread to the urban areas where intellectuals and students have taken up the cause. Another contributing factor is that rural residents often distrust the military troops who occupy their region. While many military troops perform useful social services, others arrive only to run lucrative logging and mining operations, industries which devastate the forests, watersheds, and soils of the hapless farmer.

What is to be done? The Thai government is trying to address these problems with plans to transfer several state industries to remote regions, and encourage rural investment with tax reductions and capital gains exclusions. Another idea is to allow manufacturers in the impoverished regions to pay their employees 20% under the national minimum wage.

So far success has been limited, since many international and domestic firms are wary of transport costs to Bangkok, the resistance of trained staff to leave the capital, and the lack of quality schools for the children of educated workers. Any solution will require creative thinking and a serious commitment on the part of the Thai government. But they must find a solution before the sprawling capital finds itself crammed with over 20 million citizens competing for economic survival.

Education for the Masses?

Another vexing problem is the shortcomings of the national education system. Thailand has the lowest secondary-school enrollment ratio of any country in ASEAN. Only 35% of children aged 12-17 are in school; the others work the farms or factories, helping their parents put rice on the table. Few impoverished farmers can afford the US$100 per year for tuition, books, transportation, and uniforms. For many poor Thais, the only choices are working their children or sending them to Buddhist temple-schools where pupils receive free, if inferior, education.

Serious consequences loom. Recent studies by the Thailand Development Research Institute report that, by the year 2000, 80% of the workforce will be citizens who completed only primary school—an ominous cloud over Thailand's ability to sustain the double-digit economic growth of recent years, and to keep pace with economic rivals elsewhere in Asia. Thailand's lack of educated workers also will handicap the economy as it attempts to shift from unskilled labor to high-technology industries requiring more skilled employees.

Low school enrollment rates also complicate the government's efforts to narrow the widening gap between rich and poor. Recent studies show the prohibitive cost of secondary school means only 14% of rural family children attend school, against 96% from middle and upper class families. Thailand is a country where the rich get richer and the poor get poorer. Many economists believe Thailand's educational shortcomings surpass the widening income gap and infrastructural gridlock as the most formidable barrier to long-term development.

The government responded in 1990 with a program to provide free books, tuition, and uniforms to qualified students in a limited number of villages. Early results are encouraging, but it remains to be seen whether the politicians in Bangkok are willing to invest in the nation's primary national asset. The government recently extended compulsory education from six to nine years, though this will be a Herculean task without adequate funding and a much larger number of qualified teachers.

Infrastructure—What Infrastructure?

Bangkok's infamous traffic situation is now approaching the point of complete gridlock. Everybody saw the transportation nightmare coming, but nothing was done about it. What happened?

Most observers blame the government for its failure to provide an environment conducive to the completion of several huge mass transit schemes—skytrains, elevated highways, undergrounds. All were to be funded and operated by private enterprise under a "build-operate-transfer" contract with the government. The delays became legendary. Some projects languished on the planning boards for over 20 years. Others were approved but left in interminable limbo while government officials squabbled over "revenue-sharing arrangements."

These "revenue-sharing arrangements"—kickbacks and bribes—doomed many of these projects. To date, only one transportation scheme has been completed, the 32-km Bangkok Expressway, which finally opened in late 1994 after

In congested Bangkok autos inch along at 5-7 km per hour (3-5 miles per hour) while scooters and mopeds brazenly zip by.

a long and embarrassing series of delays. The semi-comical fiasco was blamed on contract disputes and the government's last-minute alteration of the planned toll fee to an unrealistically low amount. The huge financial losses suffered by the Japanese construction company scared off many potential investors. With the government unable to pay for these horrendously expensive projects, Bangkok must continue to live with the world's worst traffic mess.

The transportation nightmare isn't limited to Bangkok; it now extends to every corner of the kingdom. Chiang Mai, once a charming town ideal for bicycle touring and leisurely walks, now suffers from traffic problems approaching those of Bangkok. The government's failure to construct a national highway system forces armies of thundering trucks and public buses to transverse the country on extraordinarily dangerous two-lane roads. Thousands of citizens needlessly die each year on the hopelessly inadequate road

TOURISM PROFILE

DOMINANT REGIONS

Northeast Asia: Japan, Taiwan, and Hong Kong
Southeast Asia: Malaysia and Singapore
Europe: Germany and Great Britain
North America: United States

TOP 10 ARRIVALS BY COUNTRY

Malaysia: 808,443 visitors
Japan: 559,501
Taiwan: 453,864
Hong Kong: 341,442
Singapore: 320,064
Germany: 257,031
United States: 248,441
Australia: 202,527
United Kingdom: 197,608
South Korea: 179,543

ESTIMATED VISITOR PROFILE

Northeast Asia: 30%
Europe: 27%
Southeast Asia: 21%
North America: 8%

LENGTH OF STAY/DAILY EXPENDITURES

7.09 days: US$120 per day

REVENUE RANK/AVERAGE STAY

Japan: 1st, 5.1 days
Malaysia: 3rd, 3.77 days
Germany: 4th, 13.92 days
U.S.: 6th, 7.68 days
Australia: 8th, 7.19 days
U.K.: 9th, 10.13 days
France: 10th, 11.16 days
Israel: 24th, 14.31 days

WHO VISITS THAILAND?

Independent Travelers: 55%
Organized Tours: 45%
Holiday: 88%
Business: 12%
Males: 65%
Females: 35%

system. The standard advice for surviving travel in Thailand is to take the trains; they still run on single-line tracks constructed over 60 years ago.

Need more horror stories? Bangkok's Klong Toey Port has been jammed with shipping traffic for several decades, yet little has been done to relieve the bottleneck that forces many freighters to wait a week for an available berth. The new deepwater port at Laem Chabang south of Bangkok will help relieve maritime congestion, though traffic on the nearby highway is already approaching gridlock. Bangkok to Pattaya once took about two hours by public bus; today it's a half-day nightmare.

Thailand's infrastructure mess also extends to power utilities and the national telephone system. The Telephone Authority of Thailand recently granted a concession to a private firm, TelecomAsia, to install and operate two million phone lines in Bangkok. This may improve the phone shortage in a few years, assuming TelecomAsia doesn't run into problems with government bureaucrats or military leaders seeking financial benefits for "handling" the project. Finally, the pace of industrial expansion has outstripped electrical supply to the point where several regions now face the prospect of crippling power outages.

The solution seems obvious. What Thailand desperately needs is a massive infusion of cash for the construction of new roads, mass transit systems, improved rail lines, more shipping facilities, and upgraded telecommunication networks. But the government, which has operated at a persistent deficit for many years, is reluctant to raise taxes or increase the national debt to pay for these projects. At present, the gap is filled by foreign money in the form of direct investments in businesses and the stock exchange.

The general feeling is that if the Thai government continues to make steady efforts to resolve its infrastructure bottlenecks, foreign investors will continue to pour funds into the Thai economy.

Tourism

In a country as pleasurable as Thailand, it is not surprising that tourism has become the leading source of foreign exchange, topping US$5 billion in 1995. Tourism now accounts for 5.4% of the national gross domestic product, a rate higher than that of any other Southeast Asian nation except Singapore. The number of tourists coming to Thailand has steadily and, in some cases, spectacularly grown—from one million in 1976 to almost 10 million in 1998.

The first year the Tourism Authority of Thailand recorded visitor arrivals was 1960, when 81,000 tourists came for an average visit of just three days. The numbers slowly increased until 1981, when TAT statistics showed some two million visitors who stayed an average of five days.

Tourism really began to take off during the Thai government's Sixth Economic Plan (1987-91), which promoted 1987 as "Visit Thailand Year." The marketing concept increased tourism income by 34% in 1987 and 58% in 1988. By 1991, revenue from tourism totaled two-thirds of the income from agricultural exports and almost as much revenue as textile exports.

Visitor arrivals remained steady in 1991, despite the Persian Gulf War and a minor military coup. Although the industry suffered from the political turmoil of May 1992, arrivals recovered

TOURIST OR TRAVELER?

ourist offices, resort owners, and visitors alike often debate the relative merit of conventional tourists, who tend to patronize high-cost accommodations and activities, versus independent travelers, who are usually on a more moderate budget. Who spends the most money? Who puts more money into local economies? Which group causes the least cultural and environmental damage? Some very interesting answers were provided in the 1994 *Quarterly Review* from the Thailand Development Research Institute (TDRI).

The survey showed Thailand attracts visitors chiefly for its warmth, friendliness, moderate cost of accommodations, and interesting nightlife. Thailand ranked fourth in cuisine after France, Italy, and Hong Kong (tough competition); second after Australia in overall appeal; but was rated the second-worst polluted country after India. Press reports about the deteriorated conditions of Pattaya Beach apparently made an impact.

But the most revealing section of the survey discussed the concept of "tourist" versus "traveler." Tourism in Thailand is often criticized as aiming for quantity rather than quality. The TAT, in fact, desires to attract only quality visitors to the kingdom—an equation often calculated by multiplying the number of days by average daily expenditures.

Everyone wants quality, but no one can agree on what constitutes the ideal visitor. As you might expect, representatives from the Thai Hotel Association assert that quality tourists are the big spenders—those who stay in international chain hotels, ride in chauffeur-driven limousines, and dine at expensive restaurants.

Others argue that true quality tourists are those who most affect income distribution. Under this socioeconomic definition, the ideal visitor stays in locally owned hotels or guesthouses, eats at local foodstalls, and rides around town in a *tuk tuk*.

Academic studies conducted by TDRI and several travel specialists conclude that money from big spenders tends to leak outside the country through franchise royalties and remitted dividends to end up on the New York Stock Exchange. TDRI states income generated from budget-to-moderate travelers penetrates into the most needy segments of the Thai population: the guesthouse owners, café managers, and young kids who sell durians in the marketplace.

But who spends the most? The *Quarterly Report* of TDRI states that although daily expenditures of typical guesthouse visitors are below those of hotel patrons, they ultimately spend more due to their longer stays in the country. Plus, they do more to help the average Thai by patronizing local guesthouses and cafes.

Finally, the report concludes that independent travelers generally cause less cultural and environmental damage than the tourist who stays in international hotels and meets only bellhops and bartenders. Guesthouses, local cafes, and public transportation cause far less environmental damage than the big, international hotels which chew up natural resources and require enormous amounts of energy for air-conditioned rooms, heated swimming pools, and the like. Finally, on a social level, TDRI felt genuine contact with ordinary people is more worthwhile and rewarding than brief superficial encounters with hotel employees and restaurant wine stewards.

in 1993 and rose slightly the following year.

In 1993 TAT announced plans to target Thailand as the center for tourism to Indochina, and sought to encourage visitors to tour the poorer and less developed provinces. Thailand and China agreed to conduct a feasibility study on a road from Thailand's Chiang Rai Province to Yunnan in China via Myanmar, the final link in a overland route from Europe to Singapore. In May, a Chinese vessel carrying 40 passengers sailed down the Mekong River from Yunnan to Chiang Rai.

In 1994 the government opened a bridge from Nong Khai to Laos and announced plans to construct another bridge crossing to Laos from Ubon Ratchathani. That same year, Thailand hosted over six million visitors and announced a goal of seven million visitors by 1996.

The 50th anniversary of King Bhumibol's coronation in 1996 was a banner year for visitors to the kingdom. Among the scheduled Golden Jubilee celebrations were five major travel industry events, festivals honoring the 700th anniversary of the founding of Chiang Mai, and a dramatic October procession of 35 wooden royal barges down the Chao Praya River in Bangkok. The tourist office's latest campaign, Amazing Thailand, ran two years—1998 and 1999.

An unusual sidelight to Thailand tourism is that the largest growth in travelers has been among the Thais themselves, who now often outnumber Western tourists in many of the most popular destinations. An estimated 40 million Thais take a vacation each year, certainly proving the nation has a burgeoning middle class with discretionary income.

THE PEOPLE

THE THAIS

Thailand is one of the most racially homogeneous countries in Southeast Asia—almost 80% of the country's 60 million inhabitants are Thai, speak a dialect of the Thai language, read a unified Thai script, and follow the Buddhist faith. The remainder of the population is comprised of ethnic Chinese (8-12%), Malay (4-6%), and minority groups (3-5%) such as Vietnamese, Cambodians, Burmese, and various hill peoples.

Thais are similar in physique and complexion to peoples of most neighboring countries, including Indonesia and the Philippines, and are roughly categorized as Deutero-Malay. As a racially tolerant people, they have assimilated large numbers of Chinese, Burmese, Mons, and Khmers to a degree that precludes any typical Thai physiognomy or physique. The degree of Chinese blood distinguishes Thais the most; genetic traces from other Southeast Asian peoples is significant.

Thais speak a dialect of Tai (Thai), the common language of those living in a remarkably diverse region that ranges from southern China to northern Borneo and from central Myanmar to the east coast of Vietnam. Their particular version, Siamese Tai, is an isolative and tonal language related to Lao and Shan, and is derived primarily from Sinitic sources or the Kadai language, related to Indonesian.

The so-called "Core Thai" majority can be divided into four regional groups: central Thai (36%), northeastern Thai (32%), northern Thai (8%), and southern Thai (8%).

Central Thais

This political, social, and culturally dominant group lives in the Chao Praya River basin and makes up the largest segment of the population.

Although their numbers barely exceed those of the Thai-Lao in the northeast, central Thais control the government, the military, the taxation system, and most forms of national development, a concentration of power resented by distant residents. These residents feel neglected in terms of economic development and controlled in matters of regional sovereignty—most notably the insistence of the central government that the central Thai dialect ("standard Thai") be taught in all public schools. Other unpopular programs include news broadcasts in standard Thai over public radio systems and political appointees from Bangkok assigned to positions removed from their area of origin.

Regional stereotypes are fading, but central Thais have long characterized northern and northeastern Thais as semi-barbaric country bumpkins, while the latter consider speakers of the central dialect to be untrustworthy, exploitative carpetbaggers. At the same time, northern groups often feel inferior to the central Thais, who represent (and control) national progress, prestige, wealth, and power.

Northeastern Thais

Perhaps the most neglected and under-represented group in Thailand is the northeastern Thai (Thai-Lao) of the Issan region.

The term Lao is of Siamese origin and refers to Tai speakers in the northeast who were distinguished by their preference for glutinous rice, particular styles of Buddhist architecture, religious script, and political alignment with the old kingdom of Lan Xiang in Luang Prabang. When the French extended their political control to the banks of the Mekong in the late 19th century, they used the Siamese term, changed to Laos, to name the protectorate they created.

The traditional Lao area encompasses modern Laos and most of the Korat Plateau (the Issan), which was settled by migrations of ethnic Lao across the Mekong from Lan Xiang—"Land of Million Elephants." The region was ruled by semi-autonomous Lao princes until the early 20th century when Siamese kings began to exercise control through administrators assigned from Bangkok. During this period, the impoverished peasants chafed under the rule of self-aggrandizing bureaucrats who imposed onerous taxes to support the rapidly expanding court, bureaucracy, and military in Bangkok.

Development programs and economic assistance began in the mid-1960s to quiet peasant revolts and, more importantly, to counter the rising threat of communism. Since the end of the Vietnam War, the Thai government has worked to improve relations with the Issan residents by constructing highways, building electrical generation plants, and initiating rural improvement schemes that have failed or succeeded to varying degrees.

Today, most Issan residents accept the benefits of Thai citizenship but remain proud of their Laotian ethnicity.

Northern Thais

The origin of the Thai people remains a subject of contentious debate among academics who divide themselves into three schools of thought based on different forms of research. Archaeologists argue that the Thais are an autochthonous race that originated in Thailand, a theory that carries strong nationalistic appeal to Thai academics. Linguistics, who study the similarities between languages, believe the Thais migrated north from Indonesia, or perhaps from as far away as Polynesia. The final group, historians, cite records that indicate the Thais originated near Nanchao in southern China, but migrated south in increasingly large numbers after the Mongol invasion in the 12th century.

Whatever their origins, the Thais moved into lands already inhabited by various races of peoples, such as the Lawa (Lua) from the north and the relatively sophisticated Mons and Khmers, who had settled in the central regions. These peoples either were absorbed into the new communities or found refuge in the more remote valleys and mountains.

The academic community may disagree on the origins of the Thai people, but few dispute the fact that the first major Thai empire was the Lanna Kingdom in northern Thailand, founded in the early 13th century well before the rise of Sukothai. This historical precedent remains a source of great pride to the northern Thai, a culturally distinct people who call themselves *Khon Muang,* People of the Region.

The people are also quite proud of their language, which is closely related to the Tai dialects of the Shan and Tai Lue. Although known as northern Thai in English and *phasa neua* (northern language) by the central Thais, northerners themselves prefer the term *Kham Muang,* or Language of the Region.

Other northern dialects include those of the Mons near Lamphun, Lawa, Thin, and Khamu, and the tribal languages of the Karen, Hmong, Akha, Lahu, and Lisu.

As elsewhere in Thailand, regional dialects are fading away due to modernization and the government's insistence that only standard (central) Thai be used in public schools, radio, and perhaps most significantly, television.

Southern Thais

Stretching from Bangkok to the borders of Malaysia is the land of the Thai *Pak Tai* or *Chao Pak Thai,* the southern Thais who inhabit a world far removed from the remainder of the country.

As you journey deeper into the south, the people take on a physiognomy distinctly different from that of northern peoples—darker, with larger eyes and rounder faces. The mixed Malay-Thai characteristics give way to pure Malays, who dominate the deep south, near the Malaysian border.

The culture, climate, religion, and language also change as you move south through a region influenced by a variety of Asian powers. Among the major civilizations that contributed to southern culture were the Indians (3rd-5th centuries), Buddhist Mons (5th-8th centuries), Malay-Indonesians and Srivijayans (8th-10th centuries), and Khmers (11th-13th centuries). All left behind something that can be detected in the architecture, food, performing arts, and other cultural mileposts.

Southern Thais speak a hotter and more abbreviated language that often clips off the ends of words and shortens idiomatic phrases into curiously compressed snippets. Even the residents of Bangkok have difficulty understanding the patter of the Thai *Pak Tai,* who continue to maintain their uniqueness despite ongoing government efforts to homogenize the distinctions.

THAI SOCIETY

Thai society is often described as a world of polite behavior, tolerance, and eternal pacifism—characteristics that complement their good-natured approach to life. To a large degree, this assessment rings true. Thais certainly smile more than most other peoples, and there are few outward signs of the anxieties and neurotic behavior that plague many Western societies. This lack of psychological tension insures that Westerners remember Thailand chiefly for the genuinely warm and friendly peo-

RESPONSIBLE TOURISM

*T*ourism, some say, broadens the mind, enriches our lives, spreads prosperity dissolves political barriers, and promotes international peace. While concurring with most of these sentiments, others feel mass tourism often destroys what it seeks to discover; it disrupts the economy by funneling dollars into international travel consortiums rather than local enterprise, exploits the people who find themselves ever more dependent on the tourist dollar, and reinforces cultural stereotypes rather than encouraging authentic dialogue between peoples. Responsible tourism is a movement that attempts to address both the virtues and vices of mass tourism by making each traveler more sensitive to these issues. The fundamental tenet is travel should benefit *both* the traveler and the host country, and travelers should travel softly and thoughtfully, with great awareness of their impact on the people and the environment.

Spearheading this movement is the Center for Responsible Tourism (2 Kensington Rd., San Anselmo, CA 94960), a Christian group that holds annual conferences on the impact of mass tourism, publishes a thought-provoking newsletter, and offers workshops on how to lead a responsible tour. Visitors are encouraged to seek out low-impact and locally based travel experiences by patronizing cafes, guesthouses, and pensions owned by indigenous people. Their guidelines:

1. Travel in a spirit of humility, with a genuine desire to meet and talk with the local people.
2. Sensitize yourself to the feelings of your hosts.
3. Cultivate the habit of listening and observing, rather than merely hearing and seeing.
4. Realize that other people's concepts of time and thought patterns may be dramatically different—not inferior—to your own.
5. Seek out the richness of foreign cultures, not just the escapist lures of tourist posters.
6. Respect and understand local customs.
7. Ask questions and keep a sense of humor.
8. Understand your role as a guest in the country; do not expect special privileges.
9. Spend wisely and bargain with compassion.
10. Fulfill any obligations or promises you make to local people.
11. Reflect on your daily experiences; seek to deepen your understanding of the people, the culture, and the environment.

ple, rather than the glittering temples or lovely beaches.

Thailand's happy state of affairs often is credited to the major religion, Buddhism, and the traditional value system, which places great importance on the sanctity of family, friends, and social harmony. Credit also must be given to their belief that life is to be enjoyed without restraint, provided the individual's activities do not impinge on the rights of another person. Thais generally refuse to be fanatical about productivity, deadlines, and goals.

Thais also detest conflict and will go to great pains to avoid confrontation and preserve harmony between individuals. The attitude of *jai yen* (cool heart) is strongly favored over *jai rohn* (hot heart). Criticism—a definite sign of a hot heart—may be valued as an honest characteristic in the West, but Thais consider direct criticism a personal attack that ruins face and may demand serious retribution in the future.

The above attitudes can be summarized by the popular, and perhaps most important, phrase *mai pen rai,* which means "never mind."

Names

Thais have personal first names such as Porn ("Blessings"), Boon ("Good Deeds"), Sri or Siri ("Glory"), Som ("Fulfillment"), or Arun ("Dawn"). Since Thais normally address each other by their first name rather than their family name, don't be surprised if they call you "Mr. John" or "Miss Judy." The prefix Khun is the ubiquitous title which substitutes for Mr. or Mrs. Affectionate nicknames such as Frog, Rat, Pig, Fat, or Shrimp are more popular than first names.

Buddhist Values

Buddhism—the most important element in Thai society—teaches a system of beliefs quite different from those of the West. Buddhist theology is based on doctrines of causality unlike those of Christianity.

Buddhism sees life as endless suffering (illness, disappointment, decrepitude, decay, and death) caused by desire, attachment, and the craving for ego satisfaction. Salvation occurs when the individual achieves nirvana and frees the self from the endless cycles of reincarnation.

Buddhism considers life a series of predetermined events dictated by the karma accumulated in a previous life. It assigns no sense of moral shame to the actions of an individual, but rather regulates life through nonjudgmental precepts such as karma and reincarnation. Buddhists are concerned about the cycles of reincarnation rather than an impending day of judgment or an eternity in heaven or hell.

Furthermore, the very basis of Buddhism leaves many questions about the nature of existence unanswered and refuses to synthesize the contradictory, opposed, and complementary experiences of life. The big picture is left as it is: contradictory, opposed, and complementary. In this sense, Buddhism parallels existentialist philosophy, which sees life as a series of random and impermanent events without easily defined meanings, and the individual as responsible for determining morality and values.

These fundamental aspects of Buddhism—free choice, predetermination, sin, punishment, heaven, hell, reincarnation—give the Thais their unique outlook on life. One fundamental is that Thais subjugate their egos to a remarkable degree, since ego gratification is considered mankind's chief source of pain and suffering. Yet equally important are their beliefs in predetermination and reluctance to judge individuals on the basis of sin or guilt.

The results are obvious as you travel around the country. Thais disregard with ease many of the commonplace aggravations that infuriate Western visitors, such as delayed buses, vague answers, and incompetent waiters. They also disregard—or at least tolerate—evildoers such as pickpockets and prostitutes; individuals assume sole responsibility for the consequences of their karma.

Agrarian Values

The Thai agrarian system of values starts with the family, then moves upward through households, neighborhoods, villages, and extended communities, until the pyramid forms the extended family of Thailand. This explains their respect for parents and other people in positions of authority, their need for social harmony, and their dedication to community and nation. Perhaps the most important result of this devotion to family, community, and nation—rather than to the individual—is the sense of emotional security it provides, a feeling of belonging beyond the comprehension of most Westerners.

Codes of behavior for relating to community members are instilled from earliest childhood. Respect for elders is taught through a complex system of titles, which are imbued with overtones of rank to indicate the amount of deference due each position. Social relationships are not egalitarian, as in the West, but rather hierarchically ordered. Children are taught the importance of moral goodness *(bunkhun),* gratefulness *(katanju),* reciprocity *(kaan tob thaen),* respect *(nap thay),* and inhibition *(krengjai)*—the ability to never impose upon the peace of other individuals.

Once learned, these systems of interaction remain viable as the child matures and moves into the hierarchies of school, office, and government. Many later move to Bangkok and assume the lifestyles of jaded youth *(way ruan),* but most continue to follow the values of an earlier era.

Emotional security allows most Thais to interact with fellow citizens and foreign visitors on a surprisingly warm basis. For example, Thais often address complete strangers with surprisingly familiar terms, such as "aunt" for female mango sellers and "younger brother" for waiters in a cafe. Westerners also will be greeted on intimate levels, provided they appear friendly and *taam sabai*—comfortable with their environment.

Social Hierarchy

Thai society differs from Western societies in many ways, including social hierarchy, attitudes toward authority, emotional expression, and concepts of time and work.

Perhaps the fundamental difference is the stratification of Thai society into carefully defined levels, a social hierarchy alien to Western societies that place great value on the ideals of equality and egalitarianism.

Thai society has traditionally given top status to the king, who enjoys the titles The Lord of the Land *(phra kha paedin)* and The Lord of Life *(phra kha chiwit).* Just below the king are the royal princes and members of the royal court, followed by government officials deemed important enough to receive honorific titles. The middle classes are judged according to their wealth and access to political power, while the remainder of the population is ranked by other factors such as age, social connections, lineal descent, earnings, and education.

This traditional system, in place since the Sukothai era, changed after the fall of the absolute monarchy when military leaders, the bureaucratic elite, and Chinese entrepreneurs gained power and weakened the strength of hereditary royalty.

On a more common level, Thais consider the search for social ranking an important element of all social interaction. Social conduct can only occur after status has been determined, often through direct questions such as "How much do you earn?" and "How old are you?" Westerners unaccustomed to such inquiries should consider them a form of flattery or simple curiosity rather than an invasion of privacy.

Even the Thai language includes dozens of forms of personal and impersonal pronouns depending on the social status of the speaker and listener.

Authority

In contrast to most Westerners' natural distrust of authority—especially absolute authority—Thais respect their rulers, whether royalty, military captains, or community leaders. This respect is derived from the client-patron relationship that requires superiors to provide protection and leadership in exchange for the services and respect of subordinates.

Beneath the Smile

As noted above, Thailand is often described as a nation of easygoing, carefree, and gracious people who lack visible signs of anger and aggression. Another viewpoint was offered in the mid-19th century by Anna Leonowens (of *The King and I* fame), who wrote that "in common with most of the Asiatic races, the Siamese are apt to be indolent, improvident, greedy, intemperate, servile, cruel, vain, inquisitive, superstitious, and cowardly."

The truth is that Thai society is more complicated, enigmatic, and ambiguous than either of these viewpoints.

Thai citizens do value smooth interaction and the avoidance of overt conflict. Polite smiles and polite speech accompanied by genuine kindness and interest in others help maintain the social harmony so highly valued by Thais. Yet this image of pleasantness hides certain psychological pressures held within by the individual and society—pressures created by the elevation of importance and high status over self-expression and communication.

Thailand is, in fact, a very violent country, as shown by the lurid crime stories in Thai newspapers such as the *Bangkok Post*. Goons, gangsters, and godfathers pack guns to prove their machismo and protect themselves against drive-by assassins. Thailand's per capita prison population is high, and petty crime and violence appear highly endemic.

Government statistics list the leading causes of death as homicide, suicide, accidents, poisoning, heart disease, and hypertension. Over the last decade, suicide rates have risen from 5.4 to 6.8 per 100,000 citizens, and a disproportionate percentage of the population appears to suffer from neurotic behavior. American Express cites Thailand as having one of the highest ratios of fraudulent to legitimate cards of all its worldwide markets, second only to that in the United States. The number of prostitutes is estimated at one percent of the population, yet AIDS cases per capita rank among the highest in the world. Statistics released from the Office of Narcotics Control Board suggest amphetamine and other substance abuse (glue and paint sniffing, marijuana, opium, heroin) are serious problems in 40% of Thailand's 70,000 communities.

Murder is commonplace in the land of smiles. According to figures provided by the Police Research and Planning Division, Thailand's murder rate hovers around 8.5 victims per 100,000—about the same as the rate in the United States, the so-called murder capital of the world. Although remarkably high, present figures seem insignificant compared to those of the previous decade, when murder rates were double or even triple that level. And death comes cheap according to the *Far Eastern Economic Review*, which states gunmen can be hired for as little as US$1,000 per murder.

Perhaps the most ominous aspect of societal decline is the disappearance of traditional and religious values, as typified by the incidents following the Air Lauda crash in the early 1990s. This event was described by the *Bangkok Post* as a "shocking occurrence that mirrored the uglier aspects of the society which we are part of—from naked greed to social breakdown and our own hypocrisy." While relatives mourned the victims of the crash, local villagers looted the dead without any sense of shame, remorse, or fear of the law. Fingers of the dead were chopped off for rings; corpses were stripped for gold necklaces and Rolex watches.

International coverage of the looting raised many questions about the famous kindness and generosity of Thai villagers and about the very nature of Thai society. Observers agreed the incident went deeper than simple greed: the looting of Air Lauda mirrored the breakdown of social order, the pervasiveness of theft and corruption, and the loss of traditional values without the development of a new code of civil ethics and responsibilities.

Blame for the shocking incident was placed on a variety of factors. Many political scientists emphasized that the public views law enforcement officials as "thieves in uniforms," and that this attitude breeds a sense of lawlessness that in turn justifies abuse, corruption, and exploitation on all levels. Thai society can no longer rely on morality for personal restraint, and respect or fear of the law is dissipating.

The public has called for greater emphasis on education and religion to solve the problems of moral erosion. Many social scientists disagree that these institutions can reform Thai society, pointing out that the educational system continues to promote submissiveness and ethnocentricity, and the moral influence of Buddhism has declined due to widespread malpractice among the clergy.

THE CHINESE

Thailand's largest and most important minority group is the Chinese. Early immigrants included the Hokkiens, who arrived during the late 18th century to serve as compradores and tax collectors for the Thai royalty, and the near-destitute Teochews, who became the leading merchants in early Bangkok. Later arrivals included thousands of economic refugees fleeing massive crop failures and widespread starvation in 20th-century China.

As elsewhere in Southeast Asia, Chinese immigrants worked hard, educated their children, and today completely dominate the trade and

Chinese calligrapher

finance sectors of the local economy. Estimates show that 60% of Thailand's largest companies is controlled by Sino-Thais (Thai nationals of Chinese descent), and a handful of extremely wealthy Sino-Thai families control almost 100% of Thai banks.

But unlike other countries in Southeast Asia, in Thailand the massive concentration of wealth in Chinese hands has not brought widespread racial conflicts or discriminatory legislation. Racial harmony could be attributed to widespread intermarriage. According to legend, King Mongkut (himself of Chinese lineage) encouraged Chinese immigration and intermarriage with Thai women—social intercourse he hoped would give future generations the traditional Chinese qualities of industry and thrift.

As a result, it is now difficult, if not impossible, to distinguish ethnic Thais from Sino-Thais; perhaps 50% of Bangkok's population is ethnically Chinese. Sino-Thais have Thai surnames and speak Thai rather than Chinese. Consequently, the Thai government has rarely been motivated to pass discriminatory laws but has let the Chinese help build the economic miracle of modern Thailand.

THE HILLTRIBES

Inhabiting the hills of northern Thailand are thousands of hilltribe peoples who struggle to maintain their traditional lifestyles against poverty,

overpopulation, and the pressures of encroaching civilization. Most of these semi-nomadic tribes are of Tibetan-Burmese or Tibetan-Chinese origin, having migrated across the border from southern China via Myanmar less than 100 years ago. Today they wander from camp to camp employing slash-and-burn farming techniques to cultivate rice, vegetables, and their most famous crop, opium.

Swidden agriculture typically begins in January when secondary or tertiary forests are cut down and left to dry before being burned in March or April. Rice is planted in the fertilizing ash after monsoon rains break in June. Rice stalks are cut four months later with small hand sickles, then threshed and winnowed to remove the chaff. Opium and maize are planted in October and harvested during a 10-week period from December to January. Although one of the world's oldest agricultural techniques, slash-and-burn farming is extremely destructive since it robs the soil of important nutrients and leaves the fields abandoned to useless shrubs such as *lalang*. It also perpetuates tribal migrations, making it impossible to divide the region into neatly defined ethnic districts.

Thailand's hilltribes are sometimes described as peaceful people living in idyllic harmony with nature—something of a forgotten Shangri-la—but nothing could be further from the truth. Most are extremely poor and live in dirty wooden shacks without running water, adequate sanitation, medical facilities, or educational opportunities for their children. Illiteracy, disease, opium addiction, and deforestation are other problems. Uncontrolled erosion and soil depletion have reduced crop yields while land, once plentiful and rich, has become scarce due to tribal overpopulation and the arrival of land-hungry lowlanders. Royal aid projects provide help and encourage alternative cash crops to opium, but official political influence of the tribes remains minimal since tribespeople are stateless wanderers, not Thai citizens.

More information on hilltribes can be found in the Northern Thailand chapter.

CONDUCT AND CUSTOMS FOR THE TRAVELER

Asian Bureaucracy

Dealing with immigration officials, ticket clerks, and tourist officers is much smoother if you dress properly and keep your emotions under control. You must never lose your cool no matter how slow, mismanaged, or disorganized the situation. Yelling and table pounding will only screw up things for you—in fact, Thai paper pushers *enjoy* slowing up for the obnoxious foreigner.

Smile, be polite, try humor, then firmly ask for help and suggestions. Stubborn bureaucrats can suddenly become extraordinarily helpful to the tourist who keeps his or her cool and knows how to play the game.

Begging

Travelers can be shameless pushovers. Faced with children on the streets of Chiang Mai or poor villagers in the far northeast, most of us succumb to their pleas for a handful of *baht.* We all feel genuine satisfaction in giving to those in need, but Thailand has enough sympathy milkers to last a lifetime.

The problem is most pronounced in outlying regions—such as northern hilltribe villages—which have been spoiled by well-meaning Westerners who senselessly dole out handfuls of candy and coins. You will meet genuine cases of need, kids who simply want to meet the funny-looking *farang,* and pesky urchins who affix themselves to your shoes until you cough up a Bic pen or a souvenir coin.

Better than money or candy, one of the more useful items you may want to offer is photographs of your home and family. Or bring along inexpensive yet educationally weird props, such as a Frisbee, magnifying glass, kaleidoscope, set of colored pencils, map of the world, or inflatable globe. Rather than giving these items away, use them as openings for conversation and communication. As presents you could give postcards of your hometown, ballpoint pens for schoolchildren, tops, colored pencils, silvery holograms, and other inexpensive yet fascinating toys.

Observe Asian traditions when giving presents. Gifts intended for children should first be

*Hilltribe children
in the Golden Triangle*

presented to their parents or older sibling, who will then make the presentation to the child. This gesture of respect reinforces the belief that family members are the source of real values and not the wealthy tourist.

Royalty

Thais hold the royal family in great reverence. All visitors are expected to show respect to all royal images, including national anthems preceding movies and royal portraits on Thai currency. While some Thais may tactfully criticize their government or local politicians, Thai royalty is beyond reproach and never openly criticized.

Buddha Images

Thais are a deeply religious people who consider all Buddhist images extremely sacred—no matter what their age or condition. Sacrilegious acts are punishable by imprisonment—even when committed by foreign visitors. Many years ago, two Mormon missionaries posed for photographs on top of a Buddha image in Sukothai. The developing lab in Bangkok turned the negatives over to a Bangkok newspaper, which published the offending photographs on the front page. Public outrage was so strong the foreigners were arrested and jailed.

Sports Illustrated was refused permission in 1988 to use religious shrines as backdrops for its annual swimsuit issue. On the island of Phuket in 1989, Kara Young, an international model, was arrested with photographer Sante d'Razzion of the French *Vogue* magazine for posing beside a religious monument. Kara and Sante were charged with desecration of a religious monument, even though the two had been invited to Thailand by the TAT and assured fashion photography was allowed at the monument. Both were booked in Phuket and briefly confined to their hotels before being allowed to leave the country.

And in 1995, deputy minister Pramote Sukhum lodged a government complaint against the French firm Le Clerc for its portrayal of Buddha on the label of a liquor bottle.

Monks

Monks must be treated with respect. Monks cannot touch or be touched by females, or accept anything from the hand of a woman. Rear seats in buses are reserved for monks; other passengers should vacate these seats when necessary. Never stand over seated monks since they should always remain at the highest elevation.

Temple Dress

All Buddhist temples in Thailand have very strict dress codes. Shorts are not acceptable attire in Buddhist temples; men should wear long pants and clean short-sleeved shirts. Women are best covered in either pants or long skirts, and shoulders should not be exposed. Leather sandals are better than shoes since footwear must be constantly removed. Rubber flip-flops are considered proper only in the bathroom, not in religious shrines. Buddhist temples are *extremely* sacred places; please dress appropriately.

Modest Dress

A clean and conservative appearance is absolutely necessary when dealing with border officials, customs clerks, local police, and bureaucrats. A great deal of ill feeling has been generated by travelers who dress immodestly. When in doubt, look at the locals and dress as they do.

Shorts are considered improper and low-class attire in Thailand, only acceptable for schoolchildren, street beggars, and common laborers—not wealthy tourists! Except at beach resorts, you should never wear skimpy shorts, halter tops, low-cut blouses, or anything else that will offend the locals. Long slacks and collared shirts are recommended for men in urban environments. Women should keep well covered. Swimwear is only acceptable on the beach.

Emotions

Face is very important in Thailand. Candor and emotional honesty—qualities highly prized in Western society—are considered embarrassing and counterproductive in the East. Never lose your temper or raise your voice no matter how frustrating or desperate the situation. Only patience, humor, and *chai yen* (cool heart) bring results in Thailand.

Personal Space

Thais believe the head—the most sacred part of the body—is inhabited by the *kwan,* the spiritual force of life. Never pat a Thai on the head even in the friendliest of circumstances. Standing over

MEDITATION IN THAILAND

*I*ncreasing numbers of travelers are investigating Buddhism and *vipassana* (insight) or *samatha* (calmness) meditation during their visits to Thailand.

Students of Buddhism cite several reasons to study in Thailand. Many feel Thai centers offer a superior atmosphere and purer level of instruction than Western locales. Thailand welcomes visitors who arrive with a genuine desire to study and practice the teachings of Buddha. Western novices are highly respected within Thai society, as are all Thai monks, earning great merit for their devotions to the dharma.

Another reason to study meditation in Thailand is the affordability. Month-long meditation retreats in the U.S. and Europe can be prohibitively expensive, but Thais believe Buddhism is a priceless gift that must be offered in the proper spirit. As a result, meditation retreats are free, aside from small donations to cover basic expenses such as rooms and meals.

Students of meditation need not worry about language difficulties. Today, almost a dozen temples and monasteries are supervised by Western monks who teach meditation practices in English. Other temples use Thai language as the medium of instruction, but have Western monks who conduct additional classes in English. A listing of temples offering courses in English or maintaining a sizable community of Western monks follows.

Finally, Thai meditation centers provide the opportunity to break the bonds of Western conditioning and enter the spiritual realm of Southeast Asia.

Most visitors interested in learning about Buddhist meditation arrive with the standard two-month visa, extendible for another 30 days. Students intending to study more than three months might consider obtaining a three-month nonimmigrant visa from a Thai consulate. These visas can be extended up to 12 months, but only with great difficulty. Note most temples have limited residential space and prefer that prospective students write in advance regarding meditation retreats.

The best resource on locations of meditation *wats* is *A Guide to Buddhist Monasteries and Meditation Centres in Thailand* researched and written by Bill Weir, *vipassana* devotee and author extraordinaire of Moon handbooks to Arizona and Utah. Bill spent seven months of travel updating the original 1970s guide written by Jack Kornfield. An updated edition released in 1995 includes new information on visas, travel conditions, health, language, forms of instruction, accommodations and quality of meals in each monastery; daily meditation schedules; and ordination procedures.

Bill's handy 100-page guide (US$8) is available from the World Fellowship of Buddhists, 33 Sukumvit Rd., Bangkok 10110. In the U.S., contact Insight Meditation West (Spirit Rock) at P.O. Box 909, Woodacre, CA 94973, tel. (415) 488-0170.

Another useful source of printed information is the small Mahamakut Bookstore on Pra Sumen Road, just across from Wat Bowonivet. The English-language section includes books published by the Pali Text Society, the Buddhist Publication Society, and Mahmakut Rajavidyalaya Press.

Bangkok

Bangkok is a fine spot to conduct some initial research, though noise and pollution make this a difficult place for serious meditation.

World Fellowship of Buddhists: English-language meditation classes for Western visitors are held on the first Sunday of every month, 1400-1730 in their headquarters on Sukumvit Road. Their small bookstore sells English literature on Buddhism and Weir's guide to meditation temples in Thailand. Located at 33 Sukumvit Rd. (between Soi 1 and Soi 3), Bangkok 10110, Thailand, tel. (02) 251-1188.

Wat Mahathat: The International Buddhist Meditation Centre (I.B.M.C.) in the Dhamma Vicaya Hall to the rear of Wat Mahathat is an excellent information source on Buddhism and meditation retreats. Founded by a former Thai monk and his English wife, along with scholars from adjacent Mahachulalongkorn Buddhist University, the center sponsors weekly lectures on Thai Buddhism and weekend meditation retreats to nearby temples. Their weekend at Buddha Monton in Nakhon Pathom costs 500B for food, accommodations, and transportation from Wat Mahathat. Upcoming English-language lectures are listed in the *Bangkok Post*. The center also publishes a list of meditation *wats* that welcome guests. For further information contact Vorasak and Helen Jandamit, c/o The International Buddhist Meditation Centre, 26/9 Chompol Lane, Lardprao Lane 15, Bangkok 10900, Thailand, tel. (02) 511-0439.

continues on next page

MEDITATION IN THAILAND
(continued)

Northern Thailand

Two monasteries near Chiang Mai are open for visitors.

Wat Ram Poeng: Twenty six-day *vipassana* courses are given by Thai monks with English interpretation provided. It's a popular but tough place to study the intensive *vipassana* based on the Four Foundations of Mindfulness. Students begin practice at 0400 and are encouraged to meditate up to 20 hours a day. The Mahasi Sayadaw system includes walking, bowing, and sitting, with four hours of reclining in the evening. Wat Ram Poeng has about 60 monks and 40-60 laypeople of whom half are foreigners. The popularity of this *wat* means reservations are necessary, preferably in person. Wat Ram Poeng (also called Wat Tapotaram or Northern Insight Meditation Center) is located four km west of Chiang Mai near Wat Umong. For more information contact Wat Ram Poeng, Tambon Suthep, Amphoe Muang, Chiang Mai 50000, Thailand, tel. (053) 278-620.

Wat Umong: *Anapanasati* meditation techniques and dharma talks are given by a German native named Phra Santitthito (Phra Santi) each Sunday 1500–1800 in the Chinese pavilion near the pond. Phra Santi, a resident of Wat U Mong for over 20 years, speaks English, German, and Thai. Travelers who wish to study meditation must write in advance to reserve one of the few *kutis* allotted to novices. Wat Umong is five km west of Chiang Mai at the end of a long and winding road. Write Wat Umong, Tambon Suthep, Amphoe Muang, Chiang Mai 5000, Thailand, tel. (053) 277-248.

Northeastern Thailand

Ubon Ratchathani (Ubon for short) has one *wat* that welcomes Western students, Wat Pah Nanachat, and several other monasteries, such as Wat Nong Pah Pong, suitable only for students fluent in Thai.

Wat Pah Nanachat: Students seriously interested in Buddhism and *vipassana* meditation will find the "International Forest Monastery" among the best in the country.

Wat Pah Nanachat was founded in 1975 by Achaan Cha, one of the most influential monks of Thai Buddhism and the man credited with spreading Theravada Buddhism to the West. Achaan Cha was a disciple of the famous Achaan Man (1870-1949) who is credited as the inspiration for over 40 forest monasteries located throughout the northeast. After wandering the countryside as an ordained *bhikku*, Achaan Cha established the monastery of Wat Nong Pah Pong near Ubon in 1954. Wat Pah Nanachat was founded 21 years later specifically for the instruction of Western disciples. Achaan Cha's Western abbots eventually moved on to establish almost 100 monasteries in Thailand, England, Australia, and America. Achaan Cha died in early 1992 after a long illness.

The book *A Still Forest Pool,* by Achaan Cha and translated by Jack Kornfield, provides a useful introduction to the meditation theories of Achaan Cha. Kornfield also authored *Living Buddhist Masters,* a useful guide describing the life and teachings of 12 prominent meditation masters from Thailand and Myanmar.

Wat Pah Nanachat provides excellent training and a rare opportunity to experience the monastic life of the forest tradition. The monastery primarily serves as a training center for non-Thai nationals

someone—especially someone older, wiser, or more enlightened than yourself—is also considered rude behavior since it implies social superiority. As a sign of courtesy, lower your head as you pass a group of people. When in doubt, watch other Thais.

Conversely, the feet are considered the lowest and dirtiest part of the body. The worst possible insult to a Thai is to point your unholy foot at his or her sacred head. Keep your feet under control; fold them underneath you when sitting down; don't point them toward another person, and never place them on a coffee table.

The left hand is also unclean and should not be used to eat, receive gifts, or shake hands. Aggressive stances such as crossed arms or waving your arms are also considered boorish.

A Graceful Welcome

Thailand's traditional form of greeting is the *wai,* a prayerlike gesture accompanied with a slight bow. Social status is indicated by the height of your *wai* and depth of your bow: infe-

preparing to take ordination, though a limited number of *kutis* are reserved for laypeople. English is the language of instruction. The staff includes a Canadian abbot named Ajahn Pasanno and an English vice-abbot named Ajahn Jayasaro, plus about 20 other Western monks and novices.

Wat Pah Nanachat is located 12 km southwest of Ubon Ratchathani. Take a taxi, *tuk tuk,* or bus heading toward Si Saket and ask to be dropped off at the signpost for the monastery. Space is limited and reservations are strongly recommended. Write Wat Pah Nanachat, Ban Bung Wai, Amphoe Warin, Ubon Ratchathani 34310, Thailand.

Southern Thailand

Wat Suan Mok is perhaps the most popular meditation retreat for first-term visitors, though Wat Kow Tham on Ko Phangan is also an excellent place for novices.

Wat Suan Mok: Wat Suan Mok was established by Pra Achaan Buddhadasa Bhikku (Phutthathat), a progressive and eclectic teacher who ranks among the most famous and controversial monks in Thailand. Buddhadasa's teachings and 16-stage meditation system combine traditional Buddhist beliefs with influences from Islamic Sufism and Japanese Zen. As a critic of superstitious beliefs, materialism, and militarism, Buddhadasa provoked major re-examinations of the religion followed by 95% of the Thai population. Buddhadasa died in July 1993 at age 87 from stroke complications.

Ten-day meditation intensives are held on the first day of each month in the International Dhamma Heritage Center, about two km east of Suan Mok. English is the medium of instruction. Abbots teach the *anapanasati* (mindfulness with breathing) style of meditation rather than the *vipassana* form favored by most Theravada Buddhists. Although the Heritage Center holds over 100 students, the overwhelming popularity of the retreats often fills the hall to capacity. Visitors should arrive one or two days in advance to ensure a spot. Mail reservations are not accepted and late arrivals will be turned away. Visitors accepted into the 10-day program are expected to stay for the entire duration and follow all instructions and daily schedules. Day visitors are only welcome after the 10th of each month. The daily fees of US$2 cover food and accommodations.

Wat Suan Mok is 53 km north of Surat Thani near the town of Chaiya. From Bangkok, take any southbound rapid train to Chaiya and continue to the monastery by *songtao.* Amphoe Chaiya, Surat Thani 84110, Thailand.

Wat Kow Tham: The "Mountain Cave Monastery" on the island of Ko Phangan near Ko Samui teaches *vipassana* techniques with concentrations on breathing and compassion as the basis of mental development. Ten-day retreats are given each month, generally beginning around the middle of the month. Many students come to this monastery after completing the 10-day course at Wat Suan Mok. Total capacity for each retreat is about 40 students. Reservations by mail are difficult due to erratic delivery, so it's best to show up a few days in advance and reserve your space. Visitors are welcome to practice meditation between retreats.

Accommodations are either simple dormitories or shared rooms. A daily fee of US$4 covers room, food, and instruction. The monastery is at the southeastern corner of Ko Phangan. From Surat Thani, take a direct ferry to Tong Sala on Ko Phangan and continue four km southeast to the junction for the monastery; then it's another one km up a steep road. Ko Phangan, Surat Thani 84280, Thailand.

riors initiate the *wai,* while superiors return the *wai* with just a smile. Under no circumstances should you *wai* waiters or waitresses, children, or clerks—this only makes you look ridiculous! Save your respect for royalty, monks, and immigration officials.

LANGUAGE

The Thai language is tonal (like Chinese) and quite difficult for most Westerners to learn. In most cases, this is not a major problem for Western visitors; many younger Thais speak some English and, with each passing year, the level of proficiency within the country improves. Communication may still present problems in the smaller towns and remote regions of the kingdom, though visitors traveling only to the major destinations will have few problems.

And yet, anyone who wishes to make true personal contact in Thailand should make an effort to learn a minimal amount of the language. By starting with a small core of basic words and phrases, almost anyone can make simple conversation and open up doors that would otherwise be closed.

Start with the basic greetings and then learn the numbering system to help with bargaining. Another important aspect is to learn directions when you can't find your hotel or the train station. Determined visitors can be up and running within a few weeks. Spend two months working on the language and you'll be amazed at how well you communicate with most Thais.

Once you've mastered a simple vocabulary, you'll find that prices drop quickly and that ordinary Thais will treat you with greater respect. The rewards are worth the effort. To learn more about the Thai language see the **Thai Language Appendix.**

RELIGION

BUDDHISM

Theravada Buddhism, the state religion of Thailand, is practiced by 90% of the population. Modern worldwide Buddhism is divided into the Theravada school adopted in Sri Lanka, Thailand, and Myanmar, and the Mahayana version favored in China and Japan. Thais further subdivide Theravada into the less rigorous Mahanikaya order (the majority group) and the stricter Thammayut order followed by less than 10% of the population.

Thailand's Buddhist *sangha* (monastic community) is currently headed by Somdej Pra Yanasangworm, the same monk who supervised the young King Bhumibol during his 15-day residency at Wat Bowornives in Bangkok.

The Life of Siddhartha Gautama
Buddhism began in southern Nepal with the teachings of its founder, Siddhartha Gautama (563-483 B.C.), a wealthy aristocrat who rejected his princely upbringing after encounters with an aged man, a sick man, a corpse, and finally an ascetic. Shocked and disillusioned, Siddhartha renounced his royal life and began a 45-year quest for truth. After self-mortification and temptation failed, he solved the riddle of existence while meditating beneath the sacred

amulet

bodhi tree at Bodgaya, India. The Buddha then set in motion the Wheel of Life (his teachings) and organized his *sangha* (community), comprised of *bhikkus* (monks). These pilgrims codified existing Buddhist doctrine and dialogues onto palm leaf to form a three-part compendium of works called the Tripitaka (Three Baskets of Wisdom).

Buddha's greatest achievement was to reform a calcifying Hinduism by reinterpreting traditional Hindu doctrines such as karma, reincarnation, and nirvana into a dynamic movement which promised salvation through personal effort rather than Brahmanic magic. He envisioned a middle path lying between the extremes of ascetic self-denial and worldly self-indulgence as the most practical way to achieve freedom from the endless cycle of death and rebirth.

After his death, some 500 disciples gathered to recite his teachings and form the Theravada branch of Buddhism to help maintain the purity of original traditions. The early Christian era saw the rise of Mahayana Buddhism, a school which promised a tangible paradise through the worship of supernatural intermediaries called bodhisattvas. Buddhism spread rapidly throughout India and was carried to Southeast Asia by the missionaries of Indian King Asoka (272-232 B.C.). The final irony is that Buddhism, as a major force, eventually died out in its country of origin.

Monkhood

To gain heavenly merit, improve their karma through correct living, and bring honor to their parents, many young Thai men elect to become monks for periods of a few days to several months. Initiates take vows of poverty and are allowed few possessions: three yellow robes, an alms bowl, and a strainer to filter any living creature from the water. Final daily meals are eaten before noon, while the remainder of the day is spent meditating and studying Buddhist scriptures.

Although instructed to remain unemotional and detached about worldly concerns, many are surprisingly friendly to Westerners and quite anxious to practice their English. The Golden Mount in Bangkok is an excellent place to meet Buddhist monks.

Brahma

Modern Beliefs

Somdej, head of the Buddhist order and one of the most powerful individuals in the country, currently faces several thorny challenges: the declining interest in Buddhism among the young, the corrupting influence of *phi* propitiation (see "Spirit Propitiation" following), and widespread decadence within the Buddhist *sangha*. Today in Thailand, it's not uncommon for monks to predict lottery outcomes, practice faith healing, distribute phallic symbols, sell magical charms, and charge hefty fees for ceremonial services. The country's monastic image was further damaged after it was revealed that several monasteries were selling bogus royal decorations.

Rebellion against conventional Buddhism is symbolized by Pra Bodhirak, an unorthodox but immensely popular and charismatic rebel who preaches his iconoclastic viewpoints from the Santi Asoke ("Peace, No Sorrow") headquarters on the eastern outskirts of Bangkok. Defrocked and under heavy legal pressures from the government, Bodhirak insists that Thai Buddhism has been badly corrupted by the deca-

dent practices and superstitious beliefs mentioned above. His message of nonmaterialism and religious purity has hit home. His popularity has soared; even the current governor of Bangkok supports Bodhirak's platforms of religious reform.

Spirit Propitiation

One festering problem for modern Buddhism is that Thailand has never completely replaced older religious traditions such as Hinduism and spiritualism. Hindu ceremonies still play an important role in Thai society, largely because ceremonies for life passages such as birth, death, and marriage were never prescribed by the Buddha. Brahmanic astrologers also prepare the national calendar and preside over annual rice-planting ceremonies.

But more important are the powers of astrology, the occult, and wandering supernatural spirits called *phis,* homeless and unhappy apparitions who can cause great harm to the living unless appeased with frequent offerings. *Phis* are propitiated (not worshipped) for dozens of reasons: to influence the future, grant wishes, guarantee the success of a financial venture, ensure that a school exam is passed, restore health to a sick family member, or cause a win in the biweekly lottery.

Believed to exist in all shapes and sizes, some *phis* enjoy a permanent existence unbounded by the law of karma, while others are reincarnations of dead human beings who have returned to haunt the living. People who died violently or whose funeral rites were improperly performed are especially dangerous, since witches can force them to consume the internal organs of the living. Others can make you remove your clothes in public!

Although these practices are not in accordance with the teachings of the Buddha, *phi* homage doesn't necessarily conflict with the reverence Thais feel for Buddhist philosophy. The average Thai is a Buddhist who was married according to Hindu rituals but makes frequent offerings to placate animist spirits.

ICONOGRAPHY OF THE BUDDHA IMAGE

Visitors to the National Museum and temples of Thailand are often confused by the variety of Buddhas they find. The following descriptions will define the basic symbolism and describe the delicate balancing act between religious symbolism and the artist's urge to create new forms.

First-time visitors often consider Buddhist images monotonous look-alikes created with little imagination or originality, not an unfair judgment since Buddhist sculptors have traditionally been copyists who depicted Buddha images exactly as described in Pali religious texts. Creativity was also stifled by the sculptor's desire to exactly reproduce earlier images which had demonstrated magical powers. According to legend, an authorized Buddha image carved during Sakyamuni's lifetime absorbed his magical potency; sculptors believed that exact likenesses of the original would share these magical powers and provide the pious with supernatural protection.

The image's comprehensible and undisturbing symbolism is conveyed in dozens of ways: feet must be engraved with 108 auspicious signs; toes and fingers should be of equal length; hands should resemble the opening of lotus buds; arms should extend all the way to the knees; the magical spot between the eyes and protuberance from the forehead must represent enlightenment.

Despite these religious straitjackets, Thai artists successfully created a half dozen unique styles which stand today as some of Asia's most refined art.

Mudras of the Buddha

Buddhist images throughout Thailand share common body positions (seated, standing, walking, and

calling the earth to witness

reclining) and hand gestures (mudras) which symbolically represent important events in the life of Buddha. Standing images depict Sakyamuni taming evil forces and bestowing blessings. Walking figures illustrate the Buddha returning to earth after preaching to his mother and deities in heaven. Reclining images embody the Buddha at the exact moment of nirvana—not sleeping, as visitors often assume. Sitting Buddhas represent various stories: meditating, witnessing divinity, or setting in motion the "Wheel of the Law." Understanding the following mudras will prove invaluable when examining Buddha images throughout the country.

Calling the Earth to Witness Mudra

Seated in either a full- or half-lotus position, the Buddha is shown reaching forward to touch the ground with his right hand. This immensely popular mudra symbolizes the Buddha's victory over the demons of Mara and testifies to his enlightenment.

reclining

TERRA MUZICK/2

Dispelling Fear Mudra

Either the left, right, or both hands are held at shoulder level with the palms turned outward. Rendered in both walking and standing Buddhas, this mudra evolved from a legend in which the Buddha raised his hand to subdue a rampaging elephant intent on his destruction. Also called the "Triumph over Evil" or "Giving of Protection" mudra.

Meditation Mudra

With one hand resting on the other and both legs crossed in a lotus position, this classic attitude represents the final meditation and enlightenment under the bodhi tree. Eyes are closed and breath is held to concentrate on the truth.

meditation

Adoration Mudra

Generally performed by bodhisattvas or lesser angels giving homage to the Buddha, this hand gesture is formed by joining both hands together vertically at the level of the breast—exactly like the Buddhist *wai*.

Dispensing Favors Mudra

Almost identical to the position of "Dispelling Fear" except the palm is completely exposed, open, and empty, this mudra symbolizes the Buddha's vows of assistance and gifts of truth.

Turning the Wheel of the Law Mudra

Both hands are held before the chest with the thumb and forefinger of the right hand forming a circle. Representing the position that set in motion the wheel of the Buddhist law, this indestructible wheel also symbolizes karma, samsara, and the reality of nirvana.

dispelling fear

turning the Wheel of Law

Spirit Houses

One of the most powerful forms of *phis* is the guardian spirits called *chao phis,* of which the guardian spirit of the house (*chao thi* or *pra phum* in Khmer) is the most important. Some Thais believe every plot of land harbors a spirit who must be provided with a small doll-like house. This curious spirit home, located on the exterior lawn where no shadow will ever fall, is furnished with a replica of the residing spirit holding a double-edged sword and a big book which lists deeds of the occupants. Other figurines include slaves, elephants, and sensuous dancing girls—all to keep the ghost happy! After proper installation of the spirit house by a Brahman priest at the auspicious place and time, human occupants make daily offerings of flowers, joss sticks, and food to placate the touchy spirit.

Thais also honor eight other household spirits, including one troublesome fellow who resides at the door's threshold. That's why it is proper behavior to step *over* rather than *on* the threshold. In recent years it has become popular to erect extremely elaborate shrines dedicated to the four-faced Hindu god, Lord Brahma. Thailand's most famous Brahman image is displayed at the Hyatt Grand Erawan Hotel

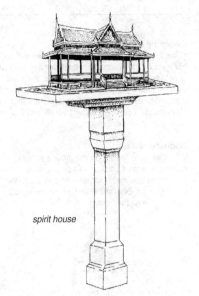

spirit house

KAREN McKINLEY

shrine in Bangkok, although in the strictest sense this is not a spirit house but in a category all its own.

ARTS AND ARCHITECTURE

THE MONS (5th-12th CENTURIES)

Thailand's earliest sculptural and architectural records were left by the Mons, a mysterious race who formed the loosely knit Dvaravati Kingdoms of lower Thailand and Myanmar. Archaeologists surmise that Nakhon Pathom served as the Mon capital until the westward push of the Khmers in the 8th century drove them north to Haripunchai, modern-day Lamphun. The Mons dominated northern Thailand until the arrival of the Thais in the 13th century.

Architecture

Except for the early temples of Bagan—heavy structures built by the Burmese but based on Mon designs—little Mon architecture has survived the ravages of time, weather, and heavy-

handed renovation. Thailand's premier Mon monument is Wat Kukut in Lamphun.

Sculpture

Mon Buddhist sculpture, often characterized as immobile and excessively solid, was perhaps influenced by Hindu Gupta art and the Ajanta cave temples. Mon Buddha images were either cast of bronze using the lost-wax method, or carved of limestone in a standing position or a seated one on a throne in the so-called European manner. Whether cast or carved, all are quite remarkable in their depiction of Mon physiognomy: strong square jaws, flat noses, thick lips. Outstanding Mon sculpture can be seen in the museums of Bangkok and Ayuthaya, and at Nakhon Pathom, where a hall adjacent to the golden *chedi* houses an immense seated Buddha.

KHMER STYLE (7th-14th CENTURIES)

Between the fall of the Mon Empire and the rise of Sukothai much of central and eastern Thailand was ruled from Khmer military outposts at Pimai, Lopburi, Sukothai, and Kanchanaburi. Khmer art is sometimes called the Lopburi style, after the town where much of the best art was produced. It stands in sharp contrast to other Thai styles, inspired by Hinduism rather than Buddhism, and funded by Khmer kings who considered themselves warrior gods and reincarnations of Shiva rather than benign Buddhist rulers. Cambodian art exudes energy and power, the mysterious and militaristic counterpart to gentle Thai art.

Architecture

By translating into stone the great myths of Hindu cosmology, Khmer architecture also created new motifs such as the *prang,* a bulbous, phallus-shaped tower which symbolizes the Hindu-Buddhist paradise of Mt. Meru. Well-preserved Khmer architecture can be seen in Sukothai, Lopburi, and Kanchanaburi, but the finest examples are scattered across the northeastern plains near Korat.

Sculpture

Khmer sculpture is typified by a seated, meditating Buddha who smiles enigmatically beneath the protective hood of the seven-headed *naga.* Other popular icons, either carved in stone or cast in bronze, include Hindu gods, bodhisattvas, and mythical *garudas.* The Lopburi style, by far the most famous of the various Khmer schools, developed a unique variation by fusing older Buddhist and Mon styles with Cambodian stylizations: thick upturned lips, elaborate headdresses, and enigmatic faces set with puzzling expressions of serenity and mystery.

THAI ART PERIODS AND STYLES

PERIOD	CENTURIES	LOCATIONS	STYLES AND INFLUENCES
Mon (Dvaravati)	6th-11th	Central (U-Thong)	Gupta-Indian
		West (Nakhon Pathom)	Greco-Roman
Haripunjaya	7th-13th	North (Lamphun)	Mon-Gupta-Indian
Khmer	7th-14th	Central (Lopburi)	Khmer-Mon
		Northeast (Phimai, Phanom Rung)	Khmer
Srivijaya	8th-13th	South (Chaiya)	Indian (3rd-5th C.)
		Sating Phra	Mon (5th-13th C.)
		Nakhon Si Thammarat	Khmer (11th-13th C.)
Lopburi	10th-13th	Central (Lopburi)	Khmer-Pala-Tai
Chiang Saen	10th-12th	North (Chiang Saen)	Tai-Lao
Lanna	11th-16th	North (Lampang)	Tai-Shan-Burmese-Lao
U-Thong	13th-15th	West (Suphanburi)	Mon-Khmer-Pala
Sukothai	13th-15th	Central (Sukothai)	Tai-Mon-Khmer
Ayuthaya			
A Period	1350-1488	Central (Ayuthaya)	Sukothai-Khmer
B Period	1488-1630	Central (Ayuthaya)	Sukothai-Ayuthaya
C Period	1630-1767	Central (Ayuthaya)	Ayuthaya-Baroque
Bangkok	1767-Present	Bangkok	Ayuthaya-Rattanakosin

STYLES OF NORTHERN THAILAND (10th-16th CENTURIES)

Haripunchai
Located in the sleepy town of Lamphun just south of Chiang Mai, the kingdom of Haripunchai served as the last bastion of Mon power until conquered by King Mengrai in 1292. Reconstruction and remodeling have erased the distinctive Mon characteristics of most Dvaravati temples, with the notable exception of the square *chedi* of Wat Kukut in Lamphun. Haripunchai Buddhas with Mon triple-curve eyebrows and thick lips are displayed in Bangkok and Lamphun museums.

Chiang Saen
Situated on the western banks of the Mekong just across from Laos, this small and practically deserted town served as the first capital of the Lanna Kingdom. Chiang Saen architecture is chiefly represented by the 7th-century Wat Pra That Chom Kitti and Wat Pasak constructed by King Mengrai's grandson from 1325 to 1335. Early Chiang Saen Buddha images with large hair curls and prominent eyes were influenced by the Pala school of northern India. Later Chiang Saen sculptures display a distinctive Thai style firmly rooted in the Sukothai tradition.

Chiang Mai (Lanna)
Both the Haripunchai and Chiang Saen schools are sometimes lumped together with art of the powerful Lanna Kingdom which flourished in northern Thailand between the 13th and 16th centuries. Lanna was established by King Mengrai, an ambitious Thai who conquered Chiang Saen and Haripunchai before establishing new capitals at Fang, Chiang Rai, and, finally, Chiang Mai. Mengrai's successor, King Tiloka, proved himself an energetic patron of religion and the arts.

Chiang Mai continued to produce robust art until the Burmese conquered northern Thailand in the 16th century. Most temples in Chiang Mai have been extensively restored and little of the original flavor has survived. Two important exceptions are Chedi Chet Yot, built in 1455 to celebrate Buddha's 2,000th anniversary, and Chedi Si Liem, built around 1300 by King Men-

grai; both are considered masterpieces of Lanna architecture. Lanna sculpture can be seen in the museums at Bangkok and Chiang Mai.

SUKOTHAI (13th-15th CENTURIES)

Reasons for the migration of the Thai (Tai) people into Siam are somewhat hazy. Some historians believe the Mongol invasion of Kublai Khan forced the Thai south from Yunnan into the fertile rice-growing plains of central Thailand. More likely, they slowly wandered down over the centuries or had possibly lived in the region since the early Bronze Age. The Thais remained an unorganized and subjugated race until the 13th century, when a pair of Thai princes revolted against Khmer rule and established the kingdom of Sukothai in central Thailand. This brief but brilliant period is now considered the Golden Age of Thai art.

Architecture
Sukothai architecture, initially little more than pre-existing Khmer buildings embellished by Thai artists, matured during the reign of King Ramkamheng into a dazzling array of architectural styles: octagonal-based Mon monuments, Sri Lankan *chedis* supported by stucco elephants, bulbous Khmer *prangs* surmounted by Hindu symbols, soaring temples capped with distinctive lotus-bud finials. One hundred years of inspired construction left behind one of Southeast Asia's architectural wonders, surpassed only by Bagan and Angkor Wat in Cambodia. Other impressive monuments in the same style can be seen in nearby Si Satchanalai and Kamphang Phet.

Sculpture
Although the architecture of central Thailand is justifiably famous, Sukothai's creative genius is best epitomized by the bronze statuary of enigmatic walking Buddhas, unquestionably some of the finest sculpture ever created in Southeast Asia. Conceived with an asexual and highly stylized body, hand raised in the gesture of teaching, arms like the trunk of an elephant, hair like the stingers of scorpions, this walking Buddha somehow transcends religious anthropomorphism to capture the transcendent state of Buddhist nir-

vana. Sukothai sculptors also devised a Buddha footprint with 108 auspicious signs, and were the first artists to portray Buddha in the four positions of standing, walking, sitting, and reclining.

AYUTHAYA (14th-18th CENTURIES)

Central Thailand, from the decline of Sukothai to the rise of Bangkok, was ruled by a powerful empire in Ayuthaya. Founded in 1350 by a U Thong prince who recognized the military importance of its location on the Lopburi River, Ayuthaya prospered from its enlightened trade policies, financed endless military campaigns, and by the 18th century boasted a population of over one million. European visitors of the age described it as one of the world's most impressive cities.

Architecture
If Sukothai was the Golden Age of Thai sculpture, then Ayuthaya was the Golden Age of Thai architecture. It was a period of great constructions; King Ramathibodi alone erected over 400 monuments based on Khmer and Sri Lankan prototypes. Important architectural developments included towering *chedis* crowned by slim spires, the evolution of Khmer-influenced *prangs,* and the overlapping roofs which characterize much of modern Thai architecture. Although Ayuthaya was almost completely destroyed by the Burmese in 1767, much of its former grandeur was reconstructed in 1980 by the government agency responsible for architectural preservation.

Sculpture
Ayuthayan sculpture, on the other hand, became stereotypical and lost the spirituality that characterized the sculpture of Sukothai. Although the sculpture is often dismissed as indelicate, monotonous, and overly preoccupied with intricate detail, many Westerners appreciate the uncompromising expressions and remote authority of Ayuthayan bronzes. The Bangkok National Museum displays several outstanding pieces.

Painting
Ayuthayan classical painting reflects a relatively high level of expertise despite its two-dimensionality and lack of Western perspective. Very little has survived, most tragically destroyed by

the Burmese or lost to inferior application techniques which left the murals vulnerable to Thailand's wet climate. For this reason, the finest examples are found outside Ayuthaya in Petchburi, Uttaradit, and Bangkok.

BANGKOK STYLE (18th CENTURY-PRESENT)

After Ayuthaya was destroyed in 1767, the Thais moved downriver and established a capital at Thonburi, a small customs port directly across from the present city of Bangkok. The seat of government was moved to modern Bangkok for reasons of military defense.

Architecture
A building program, designed to re-create as much as possible the brilliance of Ayuthaya, was soon set in motion by the Chakri kings. Early monasteries and palaces, constructed by Rama I and modeled on earlier prototypes, featured typical Ayuthayan structures such as *chedis, prangs,* and *viharns.* Temples constructed during the reign of Rama III were often embellished with Chinese touches, while Rama V fused such Thai features as multileveled roofs with Western neoclassical styles then popular in Europe. While this particular marriage wasn't successful, Bangkok-Period architecture is often a delightful combination of grand proportions, rich decorations, and blinding colors—all the elements Westerners associate with the exotic East.

Sculpture
While Bangkok-Period architecture was a major triumph, the sculpture of the period was generally uninspired, lifeless, and slavishly obedient to Ayuthaya models. Creative traditions withered after Rama I shipped more than 1,200 bronze images from Ayuthaya to Bangkok. When Bangkok sculptors finally returned to the task of casting images, both competency and creativity had been lost. Rattanakosin sculpture in the National Museum in Bangkok graphically demonstrates its dismal state.

Painting
Sculpture may have sharply declined in creativity and sensitivity during the Bangkok Period,

but classical Thai painting enjoyed its own Golden Age. Scenes taken from the Ramakien, Jataka Tales, and Traiphum which decorate the inner walls of temples and royal residences often follow a standard arrangement: panels between the windows depict scenes of the Buddha's life; walls behind the Buddha altar relate the punishments of hell (surprisingly similar to the demonic paintings of Hieronymus Bosch); walls above the main entrance portray Buddha in battle with the evil goddess Mara.

TEMPLE ARCHITECTURE

Thailand has over 30,000 Buddhist temples which share, to a large degree, common types of structures. The following descriptions will help you sort through the dazzling yet bewildering array of buildings found throughout the country.

Wat

An entire religious complex is known as a *wat*. This term does not properly translate to "temple," since temple implies a singular place dedicated to the worship of a god while *wats* are multiple buildings dedicated to the veneration, not worship, of the Buddha. *Wats* serve as religious institutions, schools, community meeting halls, hospitals, entertainment venues, and homes for the aged and abandoned. Some even serve as drug rehabilitation centers.

The title of a *wat* often explains much about its history and function. Some are named after the kings who constructed them, such as Ayuthaya's Wat Pra Ram, named for King Ramathibodi. Others use the word Rat, Raja, or Racha to indicate Thai royalty either constructed or restored the building. Others are named for their Buddha images, such as Wat Pra Keo in Bangkok, which holds the Keo or Emerald Buddha. *Pra,* the term which often precedes important Buddha images, means "honorable." Thailand's most important *wats* are called Wat Mahathat, a term that indicates they hold a great *(maha)* relic *(that)* of the Buddha. Wat Mahathats are found in Bangkok, Chiang Rai, Sukothai, Ayuthaya, Phitsanulok, Petchburi, Nakhon Si Thammarat, Yasothon, and Chai Nat.

chedi

Bot

Bots, the most important and sacred structure in the religious compound, are assembly halls where monks meet to perform ceremonies and ordinations, meditate, deliver sermons to laypeople, and recite the *patimokkha* (disciplinary rules).

On the exterior, ground plans vary from quadrilateral *cellas* with single doors to elaborate cruciform designs with multiple entrances. All are identified by *bai semas,* eight boundary stones defining the consecrated ground and helping to ward off evil spirits. *Bai semas* are often protected by small tabernacles richly decorated with spires and runic symbols. You'll find *bot* window shutters and doors carved and decorated with gold leaf and mirrored tiles, or engraved with mother-of-pearl designs. But the most arresting sights are the multitier roofs covered with brilliant glazed tiles. Roof extremities end with *chofas,* graceful curls which represent either *nagas* or mythological *garudas*. Wriggling down the edges of the bargeboards are more *nagas* that act as heavenly staircases between earthly existence and Buddhist nirvana. Some of the

TERRA MUZICK

best artwork is found in the triangular pediments: images of Vishnu riding Garuda or Indra riding elephant-headed Erawan.

In the interior, stunning murals often follow identical arrangements. Paintings behind the primary Buddha image depict scenes from the *Traiphum,* the Buddhist cosmological order of heaven, earth, and hell. Take a close look at the punishments of the damned—they might remind you of the Hieronymus Bosch painting of Dante's Inferno. Less interesting side walls are decorated with incidents from the life or earlier incarnations of the Buddha. The most spectacular murals, always located on the front wall above the main entrance, depict either the Buddha's enlightenment or his temptation by Mara. Shoes must be removed before entering all *bots* in Thailand.

Viharn

Secondary assembly halls where laypeople pay homage to the principal Buddha image are *viharns,* architecturally identical to *bots* except for the lack of consecrated boundary stones. Larger *viharns* are surrounded by magnificently decorated cloisters filled with rows of gilded Buddha images.

prasat

Chedi

Chedi is the Thai term for the Indian stupa. In ancient times, these dome-shaped monuments held such relics of the Buddha as pieces of bone or hair. Later prototypes were erected over the remains of kings or saints, and today anybody with sufficient *baht* can order a *chedi* constructed for his or her ashes. A *chedi* consists of a three-tiered base representing heaven, hell, and earth, with a bulbous stupa on top. The small pavilion *(harmika)* near the summit symbolizes the Buddha's seat of meditation. Above is a multitiered and highly stylized umbrella ringed with moldings representing the 33 Buddhist heavens. The pinnacle is often capped with crystals and precious jewels. The world's largest *chedi* stands in Nakhon Pathom, one hour west of Bangkok.

Prang

These towering spires, among Thailand's most distinctive and exciting monumental structures, trace their architectural heritage to the corner towers of Cambodian temples. Although the phallic-shaped structures rest on square bases like *chedis,* many have achieved a more elegant and slender outline than Kampuchean prototypes. Lower tiers are often ringed by a frieze of demons who appear to be, depending on your perspective, either dancing or supporting the tower. Summits are typically crowned by the Hindu thunderbolt, symbol of Shiva and a religious holdover from ancient traditions. Thailand's most famous *prang* is Wat Arun, just across the river from the Grand Palace in Bangkok.

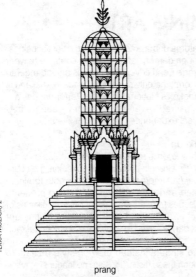

TERRA MUZICK/2

prang

sema

Mondop
These square, pyramidal-roofed structures enshrine highly venerated objects such as palm-leaf Tripitakas (Buddhist bibles) or footprints of the Buddha. Thailand's most famous example is the *mondop* of the Temple of the Buddha's Footprint at Saraburi.

Prasat
Elegant buildings with ground plans in the form of a Greek cross, *prasats* may either serve religious or royal functions. Those designed for secular or royal purposes are capped with familiar multiple rooflines; religious *prasats* are crowned with *prangs.* Thailand's most famous *prasat* is at Bang Pa In, one hour north of Bangkok.

Other Structures
A *sala* is an open-walled structure used by pilgrims to escape the heat and by monks as a casual dining room. *Salas* also serve as overnight shelters for pilgrims during temple festivals.

A bell or drum tower that summons monks to services and meals is called **ho rakang. Ho trai,** an elevated, graceful library, houses Buddhist canonical texts. The *ho trai* is built on stilts to prevent rats and white ants from devouring the precious manuscripts.

The **kutis** are the monks' quarters, often the simplest yet most attractive buildings in the *wat* complex. Older *kutis* frequently dangle on the verge of collapse; those in Petchburi are most evocative.

The **Kanbarien** Hall hosts religious instruction.

THE PERFORMING ARTS

DANCE AND DRAMA

Khon
The glory of Thai classic theater is the *khon,* a stunning spectacle of warriors, demons, and monkeys in brilliant costumes who perform acrobatics and highly stylized movements. *Khon* has its roots in court-sponsored ballets which thrived under royal patronage until the military revolution of 1932 ended Thailand's absolute monarchy.

Accompanied by the surrealistic sounds of the Thai *pipat* orchestra, the *khon* typically takes its storyline from either the Javanese *Inao* legend or the Indian Ramayana, called the Ramakien ("Glory of Rama") in Thailand. Actors and actresses never speak, but rather mime narration provided by professional troubadours and choruses. Originally a masked drama, modern *khon*

features unmasked heroes and celestial beings, though demons and monkeys continue to wear bizarre head coverings. *Khon* is an endangered art form; the only remaining venue in Thailand is Bangkok's National Theater. Performances are sponsored several times yearly—superb theatrical experiences not to be missed.

Lakhon
While *khon* is male-oriented and relies on virtuosity in strength and muscular exertion, the courtly *lakhon* impresses its audience with feminine grace and elegant fluidity. *Lakhon* presents episodes from the Ramakien, *Manora* folktales of southern Thailand, and *Lakhon Jatri* itinerant folk dances used to exorcise evil spirits. *Lakhon* is traditionally accompanied by a chorus and lead singers instead of *khon*-style recitation, though these distinctions are no longer strictly followed.

The costumes of elaborately embroidered cloth and glittering ornaments surpass the brilliance of the *khon*. Actresses are unencumbered by masks, allowing them to combine singing and dialogue with dance. Highly refined body gestures display a complex encyclopedia of movements while emotion is conveyed by demure dartings of the eyes and highly stylized, very specific movements of the hands. The dance itself lacks the dramatic leaps and whirling pirouettes of Western ballet but a great deal of dramatic tension and sensuality are achieved by the movement of the upper torso. *Khon* and *lakhon* are often combined into grand shows for the benefit of both visitors and Thais.

Likay

If *khon* and *lakhon* are classical art, then *likay* is slapstick comedy performed for the masses. The obvious lack of deep artistic talent is made up for with unabashed exuberance and a strong sense of earthiness. A form of people's theater performed at most provincial fairs, *likay* relies heavily on predictable plots, outrageous double entendres, and lowball comedy. Performers interact directly with the audience, which responds with raucous laughter at the political sarcasm and sexual innuendo. Costumes worn by the untalented but enthusiastic actors run from gaudy jewelry to heavy makeup. It is ironic that television, the universal destroyer of traditional theater, has helped keep *likay* alive by broadcasting daily performances of soap-opera sophistication.

OTHER PERFORMING ARTS

Thai Puppetry

In addition to *khon* and *lakhon*, the *nang,* or shadow play, enjoyed great popularity in the royal court during the reign of King Mongkut. Thai puppetry is today occasionally performed at dinner-dance shows in three versions.

The **nang yai** form of puppetry uses larger-than-life leather puppets painted with vegetable dyes for daytime performances and left translucent for nighttime shows. Oxhide figures are manipulated in front of the screen by puppeteers and illuminated by candles that cast eerie colored

shadows. Examples of this vanished art are displayed in the *wayang* room of the National Museum. Performances are held rarely on special occasions.

Nang talung, closely related to the *wayang kulit* of Indonesia, uses smaller and more maneuverable puppets. It is still popular in southern Thailand, where performances are occasionally staged during temple festivals.

Hun krabok, a vanished art, uses rod puppets similar to Chinese stick puppets. *Hun krabok* puppets are still created by the famous Thai painter Chakrabhand Posayahrit.

Sword Fighting—*Krabi Krabong*

Originally devised by warriors to practice combat techniques, sword fighting is only performed today as entertainment for dinner-dance shows. A complete cycle begins with sharpened swords, then moves through fighting with poles, knives, and finally hand-to-hand combat. Real swords give the fighters deadly potential in this skillful and exciting sport.

MOVIES FILMED IN THAILAND

*M*ore than 100 films and documentaries were shot in Thailand over the last few decades, primarily Vietnam War pictures which substituted Thailand topography for Vietnam's.

Over the years, Thailand has seen the likes of Sylvester Stallone in *Rambo III*, Jean Claude Van Damme in *Kick Boxer*, erotic classics such as *Emmanuelle in Bangkok* and Private Video's *Private Goes to Bali* (actually filmed in Thailand), as well as lighter fare starring Mel Gibson, Michael J. Fox, and Disney's *Dumbo Drop*. Recent efforts include the James Bond flick, *Tomorrow Never Dies,* and Leonardo DiCaprio in *The Beach*.

Films highlighting Thailand's landscape include:

Chang (1927): Although filmmakers Ernest Schoedsack and Merian Cooper will be forever associated with their 1933 classic *King Kong,* the inventive pair accomplished some of their greatest work with their depiction of Siamese peasant life near Nan. Filmed on location, *Chang* ("Elephant") established a cinematic blueprint for *King Kong,* complete with roaming jungle cats and marauding herds of elephants.

Anna and the King of Siam (1946): The original film account of King Mongkut (Rex Harrison) and his nanny (Irene Dunne) wasn't filmed in Thailand but the staging is reasonably authentic, except for the Balinese *gong kebayar* gamelan style of music which didn't exist until the 20th century.

The King and I (1956): Though Yul Brynner and Deborah Kerr never left the Hollywood soundstage, the costumes and set designs look quite accurate, except for the Japanese lantern in the garden. Based on the fictional life of a former governess, *The King and I* was immediately banned in Thailand due to Brynner's unfavorable portrayal of King Mongkut, one of the nation's most honored and accomplished rulers.

Around the World in 80 Days (1956): The classic story of Phileas Fogg and company includes a shot of David Niven as he watches the royal barges on the Chao Praya in Bangkok.

The Ugly American (1963): After a visit to Southeast Asia in 1958, Marlon Brando agreed to star in this film based on the controversial William Lederer novel about diplomatic intrigue and anti-American sentiments in the mythical country of Sarkhan. Brando, ever the political idealist, portrayed a quaintly simplistic American ambassador who struggles against the rising tide of communism. The well-intended film included extensive footage of Bangkok, the Thai countryside, and historic temples, but the complex political issues and obscurity of the region doomed it to commercial failure.

The Man with the Golden Gun (1973): Many of the brilliant chase scenes in this James Bond flick were filmed in Phangnga Bay, near Phuket in southern Thailand. Soon afterward, one of the towering limestone pinnacles was dubbed "James Bond Rock" by local tour promoters, a clever marketing ploy still used some 25 years after the film's release. The film also includes a wild car chase down an almost rural Sukumvit Road in Bangkok, an impossible feat today given the bone-crushing traffic.

Emmanuelle in Bangkok (1976): A French softcore romp largely staged in Bangkok with endless, mindless, jerky, poorly focused shots of Thai kids playing in the Bangkok *klongs.*

The Deer Hunter (1978): Most of the hair-raising river scenes in this Vietnam War classic were filmed on the River Kwai near the town of Kanchanaburi. The bar scenes might also look familiar since most were shot inside the Mississippi Queen on Patpong Road in Bangkok. *Deer Hunter* won a slew of Academy Awards and started the mania for Vietnam-era films.

Uncommon Valor (1983): Gene Hackman, Robert Stack, and Patrick Swayze (in one of his early roles) tell about Vietnam Vets who return to rescue imprisoned comrades held captive on some dusty hill in Thailand.

The Killing Fields (1984): This production, based on Sydney Schanberg's *The Life and Death of Dith Pran,* won several Academy Awards for its powerful depiction of the Cambodian holocaust. Most of the exterior scenes were shot in Thailand, including footage of Hua Hin's Railway Hotel, which doubled as the correspondent's hotel in war-torn Phnom Penh. Bangkok, Patpong Road, and Bang Tao Beach on Phuket were also used as backdrops. Finally, the elegant old Government House in Phuket town served as a replica of the French Embassy in Phnom Penh.

Volunteers (1985): This comedy-adventure flick about the American Peace Corps was filmed in Bangkok and around Mae Hong Son. Despite the leading roles of Tom Hanks and John Candy, *Volunteers* was quickly relegated to video rentals.

Platoon (1987): This film garnered Oliver Stone an Academy Award for Best Director of the Year, and Willem Dafoe a nomination for Best Supporting Actor. Street scenes of old Saigon were re-created by constructing fiberglass replicas of old blue-and-yellow Renault taxis. Chinese-Thai extras were hired to ensure a Vietnamese look.

Swimming to Cambodia (1987): Spalding Gray, San Francisco's famed but now hated monologist (he prefers New York), used his experiences as an actor in the filming of *The Killing Fields* to explore the social and political undercurrents of contemporary Southeast Asia. Jonathan Demme directed.

Good Morning Vietnam (1987): Hollywood's first Vietnam War comedy starred Robin Williams as a zany disc jockey who entertains troops via the American Forces Radio Service. The atmosphere of old Saigon was successfully re-created by production designers who arrived months in advance to scout locations and work on elaborate transformations, such as turning a small food store into the Minh Ngoc GI Bar, complete with American flags and flashing jukebox. Most of the Saigon street scenes were filmed along Rajadamnern Avenue. Director Barry Levinson sensibly used Bangkok's notorious Patpong Road as the substitute for Saigon's equally notorious brothel district along Tu Do Street.

Rambo III (1988): This film begins with our hero, played by Sylvester Stallone, meditating about the truths of life in a Thai monastery; he quickly decides to chuck the robes and do battle with the Soviets in Central Asia. The opening scenes were filmed in Bangkok and the meditation sessions at Wat Buddhaphat, a hillside temple about one hour southeast of Chiang Mai, near the weaving village of Pasang.

Air America (1990): This *M*A*S*H* rehash centers around a pair of wild and crazy U.S. pilots—played by Mel Gibson and Robert Downey, Jr.—working for Air America, the secret airline operated by the CIA out of Laos during the Vietnam War. *Air America* was largely filmed around Mae Hong Son in northern Thailand, including a dramatic scene of an elephant being airlifted over the Burmese-style temples around Chang Khom Lake.

Casualties of War (1991): The war drama, directed by Brian De Palma and starring Michael J. Fox and Sean Penn, was filmed in Kanchanaburi and on the island of Phuket.

The Good Woman of Bangkok (1991): Loosely based on Bertolt Brecht's *The Good Woman of Szechuan,* this documentary features a 25-year-old prostitute named Aoi, who made the confessional in exchange for enough cash to quit her job and buy a farm in her old village. Any traveler foolish enough to fall for a Thai prostitute should see this film.

Heaven and Earth (1993): Oliver Stone's final Vietnam War film approaches the conflict from the viewpoint of a Vietnamese woman who sympathizes with the communist cause but loves an American GI. The film was shot in Vietnam and around Phangnga Bay near Phuket in southern Thailand.

Street Fighter (1994): Jean Claude Van Damme makes his first appearance in Thailand in this hokey film, based on a video game, which is plagued with cheesy effects and costumes cloned from Nazi and sci-fi films.

Men of War (1994): Starring Swedish-born Dolph Lundgren, this film about hardened mercenaries and innocent natives was mostly filmed on Ao Nang Beach and in Khao Phanom Bencha National Park near Krabi. The "Cavern of the Dead" was created inside the caves of Suan Si Nakawan National Park near Phangnga; the boxing scenes were staged in Bangkok.

Day of Reckoning (1994): A flash-in-the-pan dirge with rogue travel guide Fred Dyer touring around Bangkok with a brief visit to the phallic shrine in the back yard of the Hilton International.

Operation Dumbo Drop (1995): This Walt Disney film about elephants and their mahouts was filmed over a two-month period in Mae Hong Son, Kanchanaburi, Chiang Mai, and Lopburi. Although the film starred Ray Liotta and Danny Glover, the real star was Pathet Thai, an elephant born in Thailand, raised in the United States, and returned to Thailand to assume the lead role as Dumbo.

The Quest (1995): Roger Moore, star of the 1973 James Bond film, returns to Thailand to play a villain opposite Jean Claude Van Damme. The Belgian kickboxer apparently was an old Thailand fan, as he married Darry Lapier at the Bangkok Regent Hotel in 1994.

Mortal Kombat (1995): This flick and its 1997 follow-up were largely filmed in Bangkok and on the beaches near Krabi.

Cutthroat Island (1995): A big budget Hollywood blockbuster which did even worse in box office receipts than *The Quest* and *Mortal Kombat* despite the drawing power of Hollywood stars Matthew Modine and Geena Davis. Geena pouts while the

continues on next page

MOVIES FILMED IN THAILAND
(continued)

area around Krabi substitutes for the Caribbean, including some great shots of the ship inside Maya Bay on Ko Phi Phi—the same wonderful location where Leonardo DiCaprio wandered aimlessly in *The Beach.*

Street Fighter II (1996): Jean Claude Van Damme returns to Bangkok to wage war on an Asian despot.

The Phantom (1996): Billy Zane (the evil husband in *Titanic*) as the Man in Purple Tights and Treat Williams as Xander Drax can't rescue the early half of this film shot in Thailand, though the latter half in New York features some nifty costumes from the 1930s.

Mortal Kombat II (1997): The Japanese robot action craze returned to Thailand with several scenes filmed in Ayuthaya, the ancient capital. After its release, some Thais protested the apparent sacrilegious desecration of the 600-year-old temples of Ayuthaya. Actually, the problem was that the plywood and styrofoam sets back in Hollywood were so realistic that it appeared on screen that Ayuthaya was going up in smoke.

Tomorrow Never Dies (1997): James Bond (Pierce Brosnan) and Michelle Yeoh tear up the streets of Bangkok, including some clips of the soaring Baiyoke Tower (tallest building in town) and a motorcycle chase which almost ended the career of Ms. Yeoh. Although these scenes supposedly took place in Vietnam, sharp-eyed viewers will find a significant amount of Thai script and a Thai flag waving from a mast in the harbor. Other goofs include the impossibility of helicopters hovering in place with their rotors tilted forward (a cool effect, but beyond the laws of physics) and the fact that Bond's car is actually a BMW 740i V8 and not a 750i V12.

Return to Paradise (1998): This highly acclaimed but largely ignored film revolves around two friends who must choose whether to help a third friend who was arrested in Malaysia for drug possession, starring Joaquin Phoenix and Anne Heche. The drug connection banned filming in Malaysia but areas around Krabi in southern Thailand substituted for the Malaysian prison.

Brokedown Palace (1999): Claire Danes and Kate Beckinsale are arrested for drug smuggling while vacationing in Thailand.

The Beach (1999): The biggest film to be lensed in Thailand since the 1973 James Bond flick, *The Man with the Golden Gun,* starred Leonardo DiCaprio and was directed by Danny Boyle *(Trainspotting).* *The Beach* caused a national uproar after the Fox production company asked to use Maya Bay on Ko Phi Phi as a central film set, planting over 100 coconut trees to enhance the atmosphere of the film, apparently an environmental assault on the pristine atmosphere of southern Thailand (cough, cough). Despite the protests, the film was completed in mid-1999 with additional scenes filmed at the On On Hotel in Phuket Town and at a waterfall in Khao Yai National Park. The film was based on an award-winning novel by British author Alex Garland and tells the story of a young backpacker who discovers an Edenic beach and takes up residence, only to ruin the island paradise. Beautiful Maya Bay was featured on the cover of the second edition of *Thailand Handbook.*

Fawn Lep

Women from the north of Thailand perform classical movements while wearing long artificial fingernails.

Ram Wong

This slow and graceful dance cleverly fuses traditional *lakhon* hand movements with Western dance steps. It is performed at most informal gatherings and is *very* popular after a few shots of Mekong whiskey. Westerners who try the *ram wong* always appear incredibly clumsy, although their comical efforts are appreciated by the gracious Thais.

TRADITIONAL MUSIC

Thai Orchestra

Backing up the *khon, lakhon,* and *likay* is the music of the *pipat,* Thailand's strange but captivating orchestra. Most Westerners find the surrealistic flavor of Thai music difficult to appreciate, as it seems to lack harmony or melody. Traditional Thai music, based on a five-tone diatonic scale with neither major nor minor keys, is more closely related to medieval Christian music or the abstract compositions of Ravel than to conventional Western compositions.

Similar to Javanese and Balinese *gamelan,* the Thai percussive orchestra is composed of 5-15 instruments such as drums, xylophones, gongs, metallophones, woodwinds, strings, and flutes. Musical passages indicate specific actions and emotions—marching, weeping, anger—immediately recognized by the dancers. Thai music is abstract, highly syncopated, and emotionally charged, but delightfully moving after repeated listening.

THAI CINEMA

The film industry of Thailand currently produces 100-150 titles per year, shown in about 1,000 cinemas nationwide. As elsewhere in Asia, most of the films are melodramas, gangster thrillers, love fantasies, ghastly ghost stories, or slapstick comedies set to absurdly simple plots with minimal production values. Creative films are rarely funded, due to the iron grip of regional producers and upcountry distributors who generate most of their profits from the unsophisticated audiences in the provinces. Aspiring directors with unconventional tastes cannot afford to ignore the distributors, who virtually dictate the content of their movies.

The Thai film industry is also hampered by a lack of government incentives to help promote quality productions, a hefty entertainment tax which consumes 35% of ticket prices, and paltry production budgets of just US$300,000 per film.

Western films released in Thailand are equally pedestrian, due to a public preference for potboilers and to high import taxes that increase the financial risk of showing sophisticated fare. As a result, Bangkok's 100-plus theaters screen either turgid Thai melodramas or predictable American films starring Sylvester Stallone, Claude Van Damme, or Arnold Schwarzenegger. Godard and Truffaut don't stand a chance in Thailand.

Despite all these obstacles, a handful of Thai directors have somehow managed to defy the odds and obtain funding for quality films, often about important social issues. A few directors and their films are described below.

Vichit Kounavudh

The doyen of Thai film directors is Vichit Kounavudh, who, over the last 30 years, has produced a steady series of realistic yet financially successful films and semi-documentaries. His most famous films include the 1954 production of *Phaleesau,* which documented the economic struggles of the northern hilltribes; his 1960 film *Sai Luead Sai Rak,* which earned him his first Thai Oscar; the 1979 feature *Khon Phoo Khao* ("Mountain People"), again examining hilltribe conditions; and his 1982 masterpiece *Look Esarn* ("Son of the Northeast"), about the lives of poor farmers trapped in a parched land.

New Film Directors

Thailand also has a younger generation of directors who produce films of great sensitivity. The first of these, Surasee Phathum, succeeded in turning a rather poor novel about an idealistic teacher fighting government corruption into a great film entitled *Kroo Ban Nork ("Country Teachers").* Surasee's triumph was followed in 1983 by director Cherd Songsri, whose *Phuan Phaeng* broke all attendance records in Bangkok. The film, set amid rural poverty, described a tragic love triangle.

Yuthana Mukdasnid

The same year also marked the emergence of director Yuthana Mukdasnid with his award-winning musical comedy, *Nguen Nguen Nguen ("Money Money Money").*

The following year, 1984, Yuthana lensed his highly acclaimed *Nampoo ("Fountain"),* a brilliant effort which broke all previous attendance records in Bangkok. Based on a true story penned by well-known novelist Suwanne Sukhontha, the film realistically depicted drug addiction among the slum dwellers of Bangkok. *Nampoo* also launched the acting careers of singer-extraordinaire Patrawadi Sritrairat and a 21-year-old named Amphorn Lamphun, who won the Best Actor Award from the Thai Film Academy for his convincing portrayal of a drug addict.

Prince Chatri Chalerm Yukol (Tan Mui)

Thailand's hottest director is Prince Chatri Chalerm Yukol, the great-grandson of King Chulalongkorn and the only Thai director whose films are currently distributed in the West. Despite his royal lineage, millions of Thai movie aficionados know him simply by his nickname, Tan Mui.

Tan Mui was born in northeastern Thailand during the Japanese occupation of Bangkok during WW II, and educated at the University of California in Los Angeles. He originally studied to be a geologist, but filmmaking was in his blood. Literally. His father had assisted American director Merian Cooper during the 1927 filming of *Chang,* while his uncle established Asawin Pictures as one of Thailand's first film production companies. His mother, Mom Ubol, worked as a film director with family-owned Pronmitr Productions.

During his undergraduate days at UCLA, Tan Mui studied film and worked as an intern under director Merian Cooper. He assumed control of Pronmitr Productions upon his return to Thailand in the 1960s.

Since then Tan Mui has produced more than 30 films dealing with controversial subjects and social realism. His first film, *Dr. Karn,* concerned political corruption during the authoritarian regime of Generals Kittikchorn and Praphat. Another film, *The Angel,* broke ground with its realistic portrayal of the lives of prostitutes and quickly garnered favorable reviews in *Newsweek* and *Box Office*—rare acknowledgement by the international press. In 1979 he released Tongpoon Koakpho *("The Citizen")* about an ordinary taxi driver and the impoverished farmers in the northwest. Other films include *The Gunman,* which examines the role of corruption within Thai police departments, and *The Violent Breed,* an urban epic that questions the impact of Western culture on Thai society.

Critical acclaim has earned Tan Mui over 30 Thai Oscars, a dozen Asian awards, and international awards for his 1990 film, *The Elephant Keeper.* His 1993 film, *Salween,* proved one of the biggest successes in the history of Thai cinema, while his 1995 release, *Sida,* bravely focuses on child prostitution and the spread of AIDS.

The Elephant Keeper

Tan Mui's 1990 film, set in the doomed tropical forests of Thailand, remains one of the few Thai films ever accepted for screening at international film festivals. A tragic tale of greed and survival, *Khon Liang Chang ("The Elephant Keeper")* conveys the complexities of the logging issue through the eyes of a desperate elephant keeper in a terrible dilemma: the end of the rainforests means the end of elephants and their mahouts. The film also records the beauty of the rainforests and emphasizes the inherent conflicts between rainforest preservation and economic growth.

Tan Mui's timing was quite remarkable, for it was during filming in the forests of Tak, Phrae, and Lampang, that the Thai government formally announced a nationwide ban on logging in a last-ditch effort to save the rainforests.

Salween

Tan Mui's biggest commercial success came in 1993 with the release of his 140-minute epic about life and death along the Thanlwin River. The film tells the story of a young policeman assigned to a remote outpost near the Burmese border, where he confronts political conflicts between Burmese troops and Karen refugees, and intractable problems with unscrupulous Thai logging firms. *Salween,* a milestone in modern Thai cinema, features brilliant camera work, excellent acting, and the spectacular scenery of the Thanlwin River on the border between Thailand and Myanmar.

ON THE ROAD
PLANNING YOUR TRIP

Before you leave for Thailand, you'll need to do a few things:

- Learn something about Thailand's history, people, and culture
- Figure out your personal interests and motivations for travel
- Pick your preferred destinations and activities
- Estimate your time and total expenditures
- Plan an itinerary and travel route
- Obtain necessary documents
- Check your health and safety needs
- Purchase an airline ticket
- Pack your bag
- Grab a taxi
- Head for the airport!

TRAVEL WITH A THEME

The first question for most visitors is where to go in a limited amount of time. Far too many travelers find themselves wandering around the country, unsure of their direction or personal motivations. To form an overall strategy, conduct a research campaign prior to departure and then concentrate on those places that satisfy your need for adventure, change, and personal gratification. Find what most appeals to your personality.

Remember that travel can be a craft done well or poorly, conscientiously or with a general disregard for detail. Like most things, travel is only satisfying when done properly and with a sense of purpose. Imagine Thailand as a colossal gallery that can only be explored with great attention to detail and a refined sense of selectivity. Mash too many experiences together and you'll end up with an unsatisfying mess. Find a few themes and follow them. It doesn't really matter what they are—just don't spread yourself too thin.

Advance Preparation
A well thought out trip begins with a logical travel itinerary followed with flexibility and a sense of spontaneity. What kind of traveler are you? What

are your interests? Examine your needs and conduct your background research *before* you get on the plane.

A good way to quickly obtain an overview of Thailand is to carefully read the "Sightseeing Highlights" in the Introduction and at the beginning of each regional chapter. These opinionated summaries, based on years of travel by the author, may help you decide which destinations and activities hold the strongest appeal.

Consider themes. If you enjoy history and museums, focus on places like Bangkok, Chiang Mai, Ayuthaya, and Sukothai, where museums and archaeology are major strengths. Music, dance, and performing arts aficionados should concentrate on areas where traditional theater and festivals still survive: Bangkok, Chiang Mai, northeastern Thailand. Shopping is best in the handful of towns that specialize in local crafts, such as Chiang Mai and the silk-weaving villages of the northeast.

The list is almost endless—educational tours, study programs, cultural minorities, adventure travel, restaurants, nightlife—but research and planning are essential for any successful and rewarding journey.

The following tips on travel themes and the author's top picks are designed to help you ferret out those venues worth special consideration. Your nominations for inclusion in the next edition of this book are highly appreciated. Please fill out the Reader's Profile in the back of this book and send it to Moon Publications. I'll tabulate the results and report back in the next edition.

In Search of History

While an endless procession of decaying old temples or ruined cities may not appeal to everyone, most visitors enjoy viewing a limited number of the more impressive monuments and historical sites. Although each country in Southeast Asia offers a selection of architectural gems, Thailand is richer than most in antiquity and artistic merit.

The problem is most often in proper selection, as dozens of archaeological sites and historical venues are spread across the breadth of Thailand. Visitors with limited time should concentrate on Bangkok, Ayuthaya, Sukothai, Chiang Mai, and the Khmer monuments in the northeast. Travelers with a stronger interest in history

and archaeology could expand the list to include Si Satchanalai, Kamphang Phet, Chiang Saen, and a few sites in southern Thailand, such as Petchburi and Chaiya near Surat Thani. The personal favorites of the author are listed under "Top Picks for Thailand."

The Performing Arts

Travelers who enjoy dance and drama will be thrilled with Thailand's extraordinarily rich bounty of performing arts: traditional dance at the National Theater in Bangkok, religious rituals at Buddhist shrines and memorials, dance performances from the northern hilltribes, itinerant theater companies in the northeast, Muslim religious ceremonies in the south.

The theater and dramas of Thailand are both great entertainment and a window of insight into the histories, cultures, and value systems of the people. Performances can be driven by tourism, or can be authentic spectacles intended only for the local population. Tourist performances are sometimes dismissed as contrived artificialities, but many are worth attending for their accessibility, reasonable prices, and superb levels of skill demonstrated by the nation's finest dancers, musicians, and actors.

To really understand Thailand's performing arts, you must search out local festivals and authentic shows. Tourist performances are acceptable for an introduction, but it's those sweating crowds, old women cracking peanuts, and kids running up and down the center aisle that make authentic theater so much more memorable than anything staged in the tourist venues.

The difficulty lies in finding the authentic experience. Outside of a handful of towns with strong theatrical traditions, you'll need to search English-language magazines and newspapers such as the *Bangkok Post,* inquire at local tourist offices for unpublished tips, and ask everyone from taxi drivers to waitresses for their personal advice on upcoming events. Your best odds of finding authentic performances is to wander by a Buddhist temple during a major religious festival, where you'll find classical dramas wedged between such modern alternatives as rock 'n' roll bands, reruns of old Hollywood films, and slapstick comedy laced with political satire and sexual innuendo.

TOP PICKS FOR THAILAND

CITY	HIGHLIGHTS
HISTORY AND ARCHITECTURE	
Bangkok	Superb Temples: Wat Pra Keo, Wat Po, Wat Suthat, Marble Temple
Ayuthaya	Thailand's Second Capital: restored ruins, near Bangkok
Sukothai	Thailand's First Capital: historic temples, palaces, museum
Si Satchanalai	Sukothai-Period Empire: lonely, moody, deserted
Chiang Mai	Lanna Kingdom: northern-style temples, teak architecture
Lampang	Burmese Temples: Wat Prathat Lampang Luang
Northeast	Khmer Monuments: Phimai, Phanom Rung, Prasat Pra Viharn
Ban Chiang	Archaeology: Paleolithic site, Bronze-age tools, pottery
Kanchanaburi	WW II: bridge over River Kwai, war cemeteries, memorials
Petchburi	Architecture: Mon, Khmer, Ayuthaya, Bangkok styles
PERFORMING ARTS VENUES	
Bangkok	National Theater: Ramayana, historical dramas, puppets
Bangkok	Cultural Center: Thailand's best arts center
Bangkok	Erawan Shrine: free dance, music, religious fervor
Chiang Mai	Night Market: nightly dance-drama performances
Chiang Mai	Khan Toke Restaurants: traditional dinner-dance shows
Northeast	Festivals: Thailand's most traditional and authentic festivals
ART AND HANDICRAFT CENTERS	
Bangkok	Shopping Centers: clothing, silk, brassware, gems
Chiang Mai	Handicrafts: Thailand's best handicrafts, artwork, antiques
Chanthaburi	Gems: precious stone capital of Thailand
Northeast	Traditional Crafts: silk, weaving, pottery, musical instruments
ENTERTAINMENT AND NIGHTLIFE	
Bangkok	Patpong: nightlife, night market, live shows
Bangkok	Soi Cowboy: low-key alternative, friendly vibes, British cafés
Bangkok	Nana Complex: nightclubs, cabarets, live shows
Pattaya	Beach Road: transvestite revues, discos, live bands
Chiang Mai	Nightclubs: intimate venues, jazz, country, rock
Phuket	Patong Beach: nightclubs, discos, cabarets, cafés, all-nighters
Ko Samui	Chaweng Beach: clubs, reggae, rap, rock, trance, world
BEACHES AND ISLANDS	
Ko Samui	Chaweng: sandy beach, budget to luxury hotels
Ko Samui	Lamai: good beach, nightlife, great sunrises
Phuket	Patong: water sports, parasailing, scuba, beach scene
Phuket	Bang Tao Bay: superb sand, no hotels, completely deserted
Ko Phangan	Hat Rin: small beach, freak scene, full-moon parties
Ko Tao	Chalok Ban Kao Bay: remote, good diving, uncrowded
Pranang	Railey West: incredible natural setting, superb sunsets
Ko Phi Phi	Tongsai Bay: Thailand's most beautiful, avoid high season
Ko Lanta	West Coast Beaches: remote, decent sand, blazing hot, cheap
Ko Chang	Klong Prao Bay: crystalline sand and waters, remote, cheap

Arts and Handicrafts

While shopping for handicrafts might seem an artificial theme for travel, visitors who understand the markets and enjoy bargaining will find Thailand to be Asia's greatest emporium. Thailand is superior to Hong Kong, Singapore, or Indonesia for arts, handicrafts, and antiques, as well as more mundane consumer items like clothing and shoes.

Each region of Thailand produces something unique. The trick is to understand the specialties of each region and purchase items directly from the artisan rather than from a department store in Bangkok. Unlike Western countries where distribution networks efficiently spread products across dozens of markets, in Thailand high-quality handicrafts at the lowest prices tend to be sold primarily near the manufacturing source. Of course, handicrafts from Chiang Mai are available in Bangkok, but the villages where such items originate generally offer the best selection at the lowest prices.

Shopping directly from the producer has several other advantages. You'll be able to watch craftspeople in action and gain a greater appreciation for their talents. You can request custom jobs and negotiate prices directly with the artisan. Most importantly, the money you spend goes directly to the artist rather than to the middlemen or wholesaler—responsible tourism in action.

Beaches—Relaxation and Escape

History and culture, architecture and archaeology, arts and shopping may be rewarding themes for travel, but beaches and warm water are unquestionably the most popular reasons to visit Thailand. And what a great place for escape—stunning sands, crystal-clear waters, waving palms, and glorious sunsets every night of the year.

Thailand is far more exotic and remote, and less commercialized, than anyplace in the Americas. Contrary to popular opinion, Thailand is surprisingly affordable since higher airfares can be more than offset by the lower costs of food and accommodations. The country certainly has luxurious resorts with first-class facilities, but it also offers isolated escapes where lodging and food hardly break US$10 per day. Spend US$20 a day and you'll enjoy clean and comfortable

bungalows, barbecued fish dinners prepared by gracious hosts, and unforgettable sunsets from private beaches uncluttered with high-rise hotels and mega-resorts.

The only problem might be selecting the perfect beach to fit your personality. It helps to understand the evolution of beach resorts everywhere in Southeast Asia.

All of Thailand's leading beaches and resort islands—Phuket, Ko Samui, Pattaya—began as deserted beaches favored by independent travelers who lived in simple grass shacks and survived on little more than sunshine and boiled fish. Discovering the financial incentives of tourism, local villagers soon constructed guesthouses and cafes. Increasing numbers of travelers quietly tiptoed down, hoping nobody else would discover their secret paradises. But the era of the information superhighway means travelers everywhere are connected to the same global network. And so the word leaks out, the trickle becomes a flood, and land speculators and hotel operators commence the deluge. What was once an idyllic stretch of sand with grass

SUGGESTED ITINERARIES

Depending on the length of your stay, it's suggested that you devote the time listed to the following destinations:

	2 WEEKS	1 MONTH	2 MONTHS	3 MONTHS
Bangkok	3 days	3 days	1 week	2 weeks
Chiang Mai & North	4 days	1 week	3 weeks	3 weeks
Sukothai-Ayuthaya	2 days	2 days	3 days	1 week
Kanchanaburi	---	2 days	4 days	1 week
East Coast	---	3 days	4 days	1 week
Northeast	---	4 days	1 week	2 weeks
Ko Samui	5 days	1 week	1 week	1 week
Phuket	---	---	3 days	1 week

shacks and cheap grass becomes an international clone of Waikiki or Mazatlán.

Although this sounds discouraging—and it's hard to deny that the hippie trails of the 1960s have surrendered to mass tourism in the 1990s—all is not lost. Even today, as you read these words, somewhere in Thailand adventurous backpackers are sitting on a deserted tropical beach, welcomed into the homes of villagers and exchanging smiles with friendly children. Paradises still exist in Thailand.

What's the perfect resort? Opinions differ, but for this author it begins with a long and wide stretch of thick, clean, powder-white sand. Water should be warm, clear, and aquamarine blue, the ocean floor flat and sandy. The wind should blow with enough velocity for windsurfing and sailing but not so hard as to ruin sunbathing. Behind the beach should stand a forest of palm trees interspersed with hiking trails and isolated villages. Beaches fitting this description are relatively plentiful in Thailand.

However, facilities that harmonize with the environment are often lacking. Imagine a major resort developed without any sort of zoning, government controls, or centralized planning. Tragically, many of Thailand's most promising beach resorts have not transformed themselves into tropical paradises but into travelers' ghettos of dilapidated guesthouses or touristy nightmares of faceless high-rises and noisy bars.

Perfect resorts are neither backpacking slums nor Asian Waikikis. They are locally developed, owned, and operated, so profits return to the people rather than to the New York Stock Exchange. Guesthouses are clean, spacious, and constructed from natural materials such as bamboo or palm fronds. Restaurants serve local fare—fish and vegetables—rather than pseudo-French or American fast food. Nightlife includes traditional entertainment and folk music along with the inevitable discos and video bars. Traffic and noise are minimized by limiting local traffic to service vehicles only. Cars and motorcycles are kept well away from the beach and residential areas. Best of all, some remote islands in Thailand use lanterns and candles rather than electricity—a wonderful idea still fashionable at far-flung destinations.

The author's favorite beaches and islands are listed in the Top Picks chart. Thailand still has dozens of remote beaches and rarely visited islands blessed with crystalline sand, sparkling waters, and a complete absence of Western visitors, but hidden paradises are best left to the adventurous traveler willing to wander off the beaten track to make personal discoveries. Consider this guidebook your guide, not a crutch or traveler's bible that stifles your spirit of independence.

Nightlife Pursuits

Thailand also offers the hedonist a world-famous variety of nightlife and sports opportunities—activities geared to all classes of visitors, from backpackers and newlyweds to families with children. Bangkok, the entertainment capital of

Asia, features cozy cafes and British-style pubs for quiet evenings, raging discos for the trendy set, and formal nightclubs with live jazz, cabaret revues, traditional dance-dramas, strip clubs, massage parlors, and even transvestite follies.

ALLOCATING YOUR TIME

Thailand is a large country which requires a minimum of a month for proper exploration. Visitors on shorter schedules should consider an organized tour or limit themselves to a few destinations such as Bangkok, Chiang Mai, and an island in the south. Visitors with more time can add other places, such as Ayuthaya and Sukothai for historical ruins, the northeast for Khmer monuments and traditional culture, and the remote beaches and islands in the deep south.

The "Suggested Itineraries" chart might help you plan your vacation, but be prepared for serendipity—Thailand is a place where the firmest of plans quickly go astray.

FIGURING THE COST

Everybody needs to estimate expenditures, whether traveling for two weeks or two years.

The basic rule is that time and money are inversely related. Short-term travelers must spend substantially more for guaranteed hotel reservations and air connections. Long-term travelers willing to use local transportation, stay in budget hotels, and eat at streetstalls can travel as cheaply in Thailand as anywhere in the world.

Expenses vary widely, but there are a few guidelines. Budget travelers should figure on about US$500-800 per month for land costs such as accommodations, meals, local transportation, and shopping. Shoestring types who laze on beaches and survive on fried rice can escape for US$250-400 per month.

Midlevel travelers who need better hotels with private bath and clean sheets will probably spend US$800-1200 per month. This level of travel includes a mix of fan-cooled rooms and a/c hotels, budget cafes and better restaurants, buses and trains supplemented with taxis and rental cars, and occasional splurges such as first-class restaurants and extravagant shopping sprees.

SAMPLE PRICES IN THAILAND

The following list will help you gauge local prices. The current exchange rate is 25B *(baht)* = US$1.

ACCOMMODATIONS

Camping (National Park): 5-10B
Budget Guesthouse: 50-150B
Budget Hotel: 150-300B
Moderate Hotel: US$25-60
Luxury Hotel: US$100-150
Super-luxury Hotel: US$150-500

FOOD

Fried Rice: 8-15B
Rice Dish With Meat: 15-30B
Budget Cafe: 40-60B
Moderate Restaurant: 100-250B
Luxury Restaurant: US$10+
Thai Beer (pint): 30-40B
Thai Beer (liter): 60-80B
Mekong Whiskey (pint): 40-60B
Thai Cigarettes: 15-20B
Coke: 5-8B
Fruit: 20-25B

TRANSPORTATION

Taxi from Bangkok Airport to City Center: 300B
Local Taxi: 100-200B
Bangkok to Chiang Mai by air: US$70
Bangkok to Phuket by air: US$85
Bus from Bangkok-Chiang Mai: 250-350B
Bus from Bangkok-Phuket: 300-400B

SUPPLIES AND SERVICES

Soap: 5-7B
Band-Aid: 1B
Rubber Sandals: 20-40B
Music Cassette: 20-40B
Batteries: 25-30B
Haircut: 20-30B
Shirt: 80-150B
Shorts: 35-60B
Movie Ticket: 10-25B
Film (36 exposures): 100-125B
Film Processing (36 slides): 50-80B

Travelers who demand a/c rooms every night and shudder at the thought of eating from street-stalls should allow US$1,500-2,000 per month. Anyone spending over US$2,000 per month is probably missing the best parts of travel—meeting the people and gaining true insight into this wonderful country.

Total costs can be figured by considering costs in four basic categories: airfare, accommodations, local transportation, and food.

Airfare
Airfare depletes a big chunk of everybody's budget, but you'll be surprised at how many kilometers can be covered per dollar with some planning and careful shopping. Roundtrip airfare from the United States or Europe should average US$800-1100. Except for a few short connections, there is little need for internal air flights.

Independent travelers should buy a one-way ticket to Bangkok and onward tickets from travel agencies along the way. Discount agencies in Thailand offer some of the world's lowest prices, due to fierce competition and the unwillingness of local agents to follow fares suggested by international airline consortiums.

Accommodations
While transportation costs are rather fixed, sleeping expenses can be carefully controlled. Accommodations are incredibly cheap all over Thailand: simple rooms under 100B can be found in almost every town in every province. Spend a few dollars more, and you can stay in simple but spotlessly clean rooms including clean sheets and a private bathroom with fresh towels. Visitors on shorter vacations will find the nation's upscale hotels and resorts among the finest in the world. All this makes Thailand a real jewel for travelers of all budgets.

The best news is the *baht* devaluation of 1997-98 has made Thailand about 30-40% cheaper than before the economic crisis. This applies to local train fares, buses, and all guesthouses and hotels which quote their rates in local currency.

On the other hand, luxury hotels have recently started quoting their room prices in U.S. dollars rather than *baht,* which means that a large gap now exists between the midlevel and luxury accommodation levels. Anyone who wishes to do Thailand in style, but not break the bank, should seek out quality hotels that still quote rooms prices in local *baht!*

Local Transportation
Trains, buses, taxis, and other forms of internal transportation are ridiculously cheap by Western standards. For example, a 36-hour train ride from Hat Yai to Bangkok costs under US$20 in second class, an overnight bus from Bangkok to Chiang Mai is US$12-15, a taxi from the Bangkok airport to most hotels runs US$8-10.

Food
In Thailand finding excellent meals at bargain prices involves the same process as anywhere else in the world. Avoid those places signposted "We Speak English" or displaying credit card stickers. Search out cafes filled with local customers, not groups of tourists. Don't be shy about streetstalls and simple cafes; these often provide the tastiest food at rock-bottom prices. By carefully patronizing a selection of local cafes and quality streetstalls, it's surprisingly easy to enjoy three outstanding meals for under US$10 a day.

WHAT TO BRING

Overpacking is perhaps the most serious mistake made by first-time travelers. Experienced vagabonders know that heavy, bulky luggage absolutely guarantees a hellish vacation. Travel light and you'll be free to choose your style of travel. With a single carry-on pack weighing less than 10 kg you can board the plane assured your bags won't be pilfered, damaged, or lost by baggage handlers. You're first off the plane and cheerfully skip the long wait at the baggage carousel. You grab the first bus and get the best room at the hotel.

Choosing Your Bag
First consideration should be given to your bag. The best modern invention for world travel is the convertible backpack/shoulder bag with zip-away shoulder straps. Huge suitcases that withstand gorilla attacks and truck collisions are more appropriate for group tours and those moving permanently to a new country.

Serious trekking packs with external frames work best for backpackers mainly interested in hiking and camping. Your bag should have an internal-frame, single-cell, lockable compartment without outside pockets to tempt thieves. A light, soft, and functional bag should fit under an airplane seat and measure no more than 18 by 21 by 13 inches.

Impossible, you say? It's done every day by thousands of experienced travelers who know they are the most liberated people on the road.

Baggage Allowances

Regulations on baggage vary with the airline, the route, and the class of your ticket; ask in advance. In general, international flights from the United States permit two bags of legal size weighing no more than 70 pounds to be checked. A third piece may be brought onto the plane if it fits into the overhead compartment or under the seat.

Baggage limits between international destinations outside the United States are often determined not by piece but by weight—40 kg for first class, 30 kg second class, and 20 kg economy. Flights between foreign cities that connect with transpacific flights to the United States are determined by piece, not by weight.

Special Needs for Female Travelers

Women travelers should bring along yeast infection medicine and an ample supply of tampons as these items can be difficult to find in Thailand.

Packing Tips

An important consideration is what to pack. Rule of thumb: total weight should never exceed 10 kg (22 pounds). Avoid bag bondage by laying out everything you think you need, then cut the pile in half. To truly appreciate the importance of traveling light, pack up and take a practice stroll around your neighborhood carrying your bag(s) on the hottest day of the year.

Take the absolute minimum and do some shopping on the road. The reasons are obvious: Asia is a giant shopping bazaar filled with everything from toothpaste to light cotton clothing, prices are much lower than back home, and local products are perfectly suited for the weather.

Minimize by bringing only two sets of garments: wash one, wear one. A spartan wardrobe means freedom and flexibility, plus it's great fun to purchase a new wardrobe when the old clothing no longer comes clean. Give some serious thought to what you *don't* need. Sleeping bags, parkas, bedding, and foul-weather gear are com-

BRING THE KIDS!

*T*raveling with children in Thailand may be slower, more expensive, riskier, and harder work than going childless, but it can also be the most rewarding travel experience of your life. Cultural barriers such as race and language seem to disappear in the presence of children, who help us remember the essential goodness and unity of humankind. Children speak a universal language that reduces personal barriers and helps us see the world through fresh, new eyes.

Best of all, children are treated like divine creatures throughout Southeast Asia. Adored and honored for their sheer rareness, Western children often become the center of all social events. Finding a baby-sitter is no problem; though keeping track of your children as they are passed around the crowd can sometimes be alarming.

On the road, accept the fact that children need more time to recover from jet lag, and tired children are grumpy children. Itineraries are subject to change no matter how ambitious your plans, and children are often more impressed with flying kites than with some solid-gold Buddha.

Detailed preparation and packing lists are essential, as are reading topical bedtime stories to prepare your children for their upcoming adventure. More useful ideas are given in *Travel with Children* from Lonely Planet (tel. 800-275-8555) and *Traveling with Children and Enjoying It* from Globe Pequot Press (tel. 800-243-0495). *Family Travel Times* (tel. 212-206-0688) is a monthly newsletter with travel tips. *Family Travel Guides* (tel. 510-527-5849) has a catalog with over 200 books and articles on family travel. How about a tour? **Rascals in Paradise** (tel. 800-872-7225) specializes in adventurous vacations for families.

pletely unnecessary in Thailand. Many travelers buy an umbrella when it rains and a sweater when it gets chilly.

It's a good idea to pack everything into individual plastic bags. Put underwear and socks in one bag, shirts in another, medical and sewing supplies into a third. Place the larger bags with pants and shirts at the bottom of your pack and smaller packages with books and socks at the top. Plastic compartmentalization keeps your bag neat and organized, and possibly even dry when the longtail boat capsizes in northern Thailand!

Here's a list of suggested items to include in your gear:

• two pairs of long pants—one casual, one formal
• one stylish pair of shorts
• two short-sleeved shirts with pockets
• five pairs of underwear and socks
• modest bathing suit
• one pair of comfortable walking shoes
• sandals or rubber thongs
• mini towel
• mini umbrella
• medical kit
• insect repellent
• International Drivers License
• photocopies of essential documents
• spare passport photos
• sunglasses
• plastic Ziploc freezer bags
• sewing kit
• two small padlocks
• alarm clock or alarm wristwatch
• Swiss Army knife
• good Thai dictionary
• *Thailand Handbook*

SPORTS AND RECREATION

Before you depart for Thailand, consider an organized tour with an adventure travel company or a conventional tour operator, a sensible strategy for visitors with limited time who enjoy the convenience of arranged travel.

Trekking

The rainforests of the south and mountains of the north often surprise hikers expecting the crowds and commercialization of Nepal. Despite rising popularity with outdoor enthusiasts, Thailand remains virgin territory for hikers willing to escape the trodden path.

Trekking comes in all forms for all types of travelers. Easy one-day hikes across rolling hills are plentiful in almost all the national parks and wildlife preserves. Moderately difficult hikes lasting several days are popular in the tribal areas of the north near Chiang Mai and Mae Hong Son. Extremely challenging treks lasting several weeks rarely happen in Thailand.

In most cases, guides can be hired in local villages and from national park headquarters. Longer journeys through remote regions and across international borders require professional assistance from trekking organizations located in larger towns.

See the Northern Thailand chapter for information on hilltribe trekking near Chiang Mai.

Caving

Thailand surprises spelunkers, who'll find extensive regions of limestone karsts and ancient hills cut with dozens of tunnel systems.

The most popular site for cave exploration is near the Golden Triangle in Mae Hong Son Province, where an expatriate offers advice to cave enthusiasts from his lodge at Soppong. John Spies, owner of Cave Lodge, has explored and mapped the vast expanses of Tham Nam Lang and calls the system the largest in Southeast Asia. The mountainous region also features some dozen other caves more than a kilometer in length, the largest sinkhole in the country, and remote caves where archaeological excavations during the 1960s uncovered evidence of human habitation dating back some 15,000 years.

In the south, the seashore regions near Phuket, Krabi, and Trang are walled in by enormous limestone karsts riddled with hundreds of caves, both small and large. Southern Thailand is generally more popular with climbers and canoe enthusiasts, but there's enough subter-

SPORTS AT SANAM LUANG

*A*lthough the huge public ground in front of the Grand Palace is used for royal cremations and the annual ploughing ceremony, you'll more likely come across traditional Thai sports such as kite flying and *takraw* here.

Kite Fighting: Thailand is one of the few countries in the world where a children's sport has developed into a form of combat. Kite fighting began after an Ayuthayan governor quelled a local rebellion by flying massive kites over the besieged city and using jars of explosives to bomb it into submission. Less violent competitions, such as the coveted King's Cup in April, are held today between two different types of kites with gender-inspired characteristics. Male kites *(chulas)* are sturdy three-meter star-shaped fighting vessels fixed with bamboo barbs on reinforced strings. Female kites *(pakpao)*, on the other hand, are one-meter kites set with long tails and loops of string. The male kite attempts to snag the female and drag her into his territory, while the female uses her superior speed and maneuverability to avoid the male and force him to the ground.

Takraw: One of Thailand's most popular sports, *takraw* comes in several versions. Circle *takraw* involves bouncing a light ball about the size of a grapefruit made of braided rattan, the object being to keep the ball in motion as long as possible without using the hands. Points are awarded for employing the least-accessible body parts such as knees, hips, and shoulders. Basket *takraw* players attempt to kick the rattan ball through a ring elevated 6-10 meters above the ground. Net *takraw*—unquestionably the most exciting version—is played almost exactly like volleyball without hands. Overhead serves and foot spikes in this variation require an amazing degree of dexterity and acrobatic skill.

Fish Fighting: Though formally banned by the Thai government, pairs of male Siamese fighting fish *(Betta splendens regan)* still do combat in the side streets for the benefit of gamblers. Captured in swamps and raised in freshwater tanks, when placed in common tanks these pugnacious fish transform themselves into vividly colored fighting creatures complete with quivering gills and flashing tails. Also popular is insect fighting, which pitches enormous horned male beetles against each other for the charms of a female attendant. The battle ends when the weaker beetle dies on its back.

ranean passages to keep any spelunker busy for weeks or months.

Rock-Climbing

Thailand may not have any soaring mountains to compare with those of Nepal or India, but the limestone walls in the south near Phuket and Krabi now attract rock-climbers from around the world. Not only do the walls provide a challenge for the best of rock-climbers, the scenery around the limestone karsts is spectacular—emerald waters, waving palm trees, crystalline beaches.

For the best resource, try the bilingual guidebook *Thailand Rock Climbing* by Dominique Potard and Francois Burnier. The US$30 guide can be ordered from Editions VAMOS, Boite Postale 3, 74400 Argentiere, France, fax (33) 50-54-05-28.

Sport climbing expeditions are organized by Jim Williams, Professional Mountain Guides, P.O. Box 4166, Jackson, WY 83001, tel. (307) 733-8812, fax (307) 733-1580. Jim also handles diving, elephant trekking, jungle explorations, and winter tanning.

WATER ADVENTURES

River Journeys

What could be more romantic than slowly drifting down a muddy river past simple villages and golden temples, imagining yourself a Conrad or Kipling? Such fantasies are still possible in Thailand, especially along the Mekong River and smaller tributaries in the north.

Several large and luxurious boats sail from Bangkok to Ayuthaya, and sail on shorter excursions to enjoy Bangkok temples at sunset. The smaller canals that lace Bangkok and Thonburi can be explored on longtail boats, which also serve as taxis for local residents. See the Bangkok chapter for more information.

Northern Thailand offers the largest number of rivers with organized boating adventures. A longtime favorite is the bamboo boat ride from Thaton, north of Chiang Mai, down the Kok River to Chiang Mai, but smaller rivers such as the Pai, midway between Chiang Mai and Mae Hong Son, are newer venues for whitewater rafting.

In early 1994, the governments of Thailand, Myanmar, Laos, and China signed agreements that allow boats and ships of various sizes to navigate portions of the Mekong River. Shorter excursions include day rides between Mae Sot and Chiang Saen, and from Nong Khai upriver to the town of Chiang Khong.

More adventurous types might consider a river journey from Nong Khai up to Vientiane in Laos, a two-day cruise with an overnight in a small village. The most ambitious tour is the five-day, 320-km journey from Nong Khai all the way to Sipsongbanna at the Chinese border—real adventure in a region that has been closed to foreigners for over five decades.

Sea Canoes

Since 1989, "Caveman" John Gray has organized sea canoe explorations of the coves and caves of Phangnga Bay near Phuket in southern Thailand. Participants paddle through tidal lagoons on sea canoe kayaks designed to reach even the most remote sites. Packages range from three-hour coastal departures to one-week expeditions including all camping supplies, food, and professional guide service.

For more information and reservations contact **Sea Canoe Thailand,** 100 Pine St., Suite 2715, San Francisco, CA 94111, tel. (800) 822-8438, fax (415) 391-2888. The contact in Thailand is at P.O. Box 276, Phuket 83000, tel./fax (076) 212-172.

Windsurfing

Windsurfing is a growing sport in several tourist regions. Winds blow strongest on the Gulf of Thailand side Feb.-April, while beach resorts on the west coast near Phuket get the best winds from Sept.-December.

Pattaya and Jomtien Beaches near Bangkok are convenient places to get started; both beaches have a good selection of modern windsurfing boards for rent. Windsurfers are also for rent on Ko Samet and to a limited degree on Ko Chang near the Cambodian border.

Phuket, the sports capital of Thailand, features several beaches with board rentals and excellent conditions during the windy and rainy seasons. You can rent boards on Ko Lanta but most are in poor condition.

Ko Samui is another popular island for windsurfing, scuba diving, and other forms of water sports. Windsurfers in good condition can be rented from shops on Chaweng and Lamai beaches, while the nearby islands of Ko Phangan and Ko Tao have a few boards for rent.

SCUBA DIVING

Scuba, one of the world's fastest-growing sports, is quickly gaining popularity in Thailand, where tropical waters host outstanding coral reefs and colorful marine life. Experienced divers can explore underwater wrecks and coral canyons, while beginners can earn PADI and NAUI certification from accredited dive schools.

Thailand has achieved a world-class reputation among scuba divers for its warm waters, which provide perfect conditions for coral growth and make wetsuits unnecessary for most divers.

Dive Seasons

The northeast and southwest monsoons dictate dive seasons. Ideal dive conditions can be found somewhere in the country 12 months a year.

During the summer monsoons from June to November, winds from the southwest lash Andaman Sea islands such as Phuket, the Similans, and the Surins. Islands on the other side of the peninsula—Ko Samui, Ko Phangan, Ko Tao—are protected from the elements. The milder northeast monsoons Nov.-May bring light rains to Ko Samui and Ko Phangan, but perfect conditions to Phuket and other Andaman locations. East coast spots such as Pattaya, Ko Samet, and Ko Chang are unaffected by monsoons and are open year-round.

Even during the height of the rainy season, Phuket enjoys intermittent days of sunny weather, when the seas are moderate and the underwater visibility ranges from good to excellent. On these days, dive operators assess the conditions and then set out on day-long excursions or longer dives on live-aboard cruise ships.

Dive Associations

Dive associations and clubs in Thailand exist to provide services for their members but also welcome foreign divers wishing to meet local dive enthusiasts.

Siam Diving Club: Popular club which caters primarily to Thai nationals, plus a few foreigners. 44/1 Soi 21, Sukumvit Rd., Bangkok, tel. (02) 258-3663.

SCUBA DIVING IN THAILAND

DIVE SITE	DIVE SEASON	DEPTHS	VISIBILITY	ATTRACTIONS
Pattaya	All year	18-30 m	6-10 m	Ko Lan, Ko Pai, Ko Rin
Ko Samet	Nov.-June	18-30 m	10-20 m	Ko Coral, shipwrecks
Ko Chang	Nov.-June	18-30 m	10-25 m	Ko Wai, Ko Kradat
Ko Samui	March-Oct.	15-40 m	10-25 m	Ko Tao, Angthong Park
Phuket	Nov.-April	30-45 m	10-25 m	Ko Racha, Shark Point
Similans	Dec.-April	25-90 m	35-40 m	Ko Huyong, Elephant Rock
Surin Islands	Dec.-April	25-70 m	20-40 m	HQ Bay, Turtle Ledge
Ko Phi Phi	Jan.-March	25-40 m	15-30 m	Phi Phi Don, Ko Bida Nok
Trang	Jan.-May	20-45 m	20-40 m	Emerald Cave, shipwrecks
Ko Tarutao	Dec.-May	15-35 m	15-35 m	Ko Khai, Ko Ngam

Thailand Sub Aqua Club: Thailand's largest organization for Western expatriates and Thai nationals. P.O. Box 11-1196, Bangkok 10110, tel. (02) 256-0170, ext. 298. The group is about 50% expatriates and 50% Thai citizens. Visitors are invited to join weekly dive trips and can obtain PADI certification all year.

Dive Locations
Dive centers are located on the east coast from Pattaya to the Cambodia border, and in the south on both sides of the peninsula.

Pattaya: Pattaya, about two hours southeast of Bangkok, was the first international sea resort in Thailand and remains very popular due to its proximity to the capital. Underwater coral beds are not considered as spectacular as those in the Andaman Sea or around Ko Samui, but the area can still be recommended for its excellent dive shops, variety of shipwrecks, and reliable weather which remains pleasant year-round.

Ko Chang: Ko Chang Marine National Park, adjacent to the Cambodian border, encompasses the second largest island in the country as well as over a dozen smaller islands with superb dive conditions. Skin and scuba diving equipment can now be rented in Ko Chang; private boats take divers from Ko Chang south to Ko Mak and Ko Kut.

Chumphon: Chumphon, about 500 km south of Bangkok, marks the beginning of the fringing reefs of southern Thailand. Some half dozen islands can be recommended, though Chumphon is largely visited by Thai divers rather than foreigners.

Ko Tao: This small island, four hours north of Ko Samui, is generally regarded as having the best diving in the Gulf of Thailand—better than in Ko Samui and Ko Phangan. Divers can explore the exceptionally clear waters year-round with dive excursions organized by dive shops on Ko Samui.

Phuket: Phuket is Thailand's largest island, and the dive center for the islands and reefs in the Andaman Sea. Over a dozen professional dive shops on the island rent equipment, offer courses for PADI and NAUI certification, and organize day-trips to nearby sites and longer excursions to the Similan and Surin Islands. Some trips go even further afield to the Myanmar Banks.

Ko Phi Phi: The geological landforms of the Andaman Sea come in two basic types: the granite outcroppings of the northern islands such as the Similans, and the limestone karsts of southern islands such as Ko Phi Phi, two hours south of Phuket. Divers rate the best southern islands to be Ko Phi Phi Don and Ko Bida Nok, about one km south of Ko Phi Phi Le.

Similan Islands: The nine islands of the Similans, 100 km north of Phuket, enjoy a reputation as some of the best dive destinations in Southeast Asia for their variety, superb bottom topography, and rich abundance of reef fish.

You can reach the Similans by fast boat from Phuket or much quicker through Thai Dive company in Thai Muang on the coast just opposite the Similans.

Surin Islands: The Surin Islands, 150 km north of Phuket, form the final archipelago before you enter the waters of Myanmar. Divers here report some of the best corals in the country as well as large numbers of sailfish and other reef life.

Myanmar Banks: Some 200 km northwest of Phuket or 150 km west of Rayong lie the so-called Myanmar Banks, submerged coral banks in the waters of Myanmar. This frontier area first opened to divers in 1991 and remains limited to a few visits each month by live-aboard cruises originating in Phuket. These 7- to 10-day cruises also include stops in the Similan and Surin Islands.

Trang: The islands lying off Trang Province—Ko Rok Nok, Hin Daeng, and Hin Muang—are rarely dived since Phuket dive shops generally conduct trips to the north, and the sole dive shop in Trang closed a few years ago. Your best bet is to visit one of the small dive shops on Ko Lanta and inquire about an upcoming dive excursion.

American Dive Companies

Dives can be arranged in advance with the following operators:

See and Sea Travel Service: America's largest and most respected dive operator leads groups to the Philippines, Indonesia, and Thailand. The owner, Carl Roessler, strongly urges all divers to try his live-aboard dive cruises rather than the typical land-based dive. 50 Francisco St., Suite 205, San Francisco, CA 94133, tel. (415) 434-3400 or (800) 348-9778.

Tropical Adventures: A dive wholesaler representing over 35 fully outfitted live-aboard boats located throughout the world, including the 147-foot *Island Explorer* in Indonesia and the 51-foot *Wanderlust* in Thailand. 111 2nd St. N, Seattle, WA 98109, tel. (206) 441-3483 or (800) 247-3483, fax (206) 441-5431.

FESTIVALS

The Thais are fun-loving people whose love of *sanuk* brings celebrations and festivals almost every week of the year. Whether a colorful parade filled with costumed participants, or a solemn procession to honor Buddha, all provide great entertainment for both participants and spectators alike.

The following festivals, described in greater detail under each chapter, are worth planning into your itinerary—despite the time or additional expense required.

The Lunar Calendar

Festival dating is an inexact science in Thailand since nature has provided the world with two obvious time markers—the sun and the moon. Festivals can be based on the familiar solar-based Gregorian calendar of 12 months and 365 days, or on the lunar-based calendar of 13 moons with 28 days each.

The disparity between the two systems makes dating difficult. Thai national holidays are set by Western calendars and fall on fixed dates, but festivals connected with Buddhism or agricultural cycles are generally dated by the lunar calendar and change from year to year.

To complicate matters further, Thais use a different lunar calendar than the Chinese; the Thai lunar new year (Songkram) takes place in November while the Chinese lunar new year generally occurs in February. And both systems use a solar calendar for solstice-oriented festivals but make adjustments by adding a lunar month once every three solar years.

Approximate dates are given below, but details should be checked with the tourist office and their *Major Events & Festivals* calendar, or in the entertainment section of the *Bangkok Post.*

National Holidays

Thailand has 13 official holidays celebrated nationwide, including the birthdays of Queen Sirikit and King Bhumibol, the founding of the Chakri dynasty (1782), Bhumibol's coronation (1950), and the reign of King Chulalongkorn.

National holidays also include the three major Buddhist events, plus New Year's Day, Labor

Day, Constitution Day, and Songkram (the Thai New Year).

National holidays are as follows:

1 January—New Years Day
February—Makha Puja
6 April—Chakri Day
13 April—Songkram
1 May—Labor Day
5 May—Coronation Day
May—Visakha Puja
July—Asanha Puja
12 August—Queen's Birthday
23 October—Chulalongkorn Day
5 December—King's Birthday
10 December—Constitution Day

Buddhist Festivals
Most Thai celebrations are religious, designed to honor the teachings of the Buddha. Most are lunar-based holidays held on the day or evening of the full moon.

girl marches in a parade

The three most important Buddhist events are public holidays celebrated nationwide in all temples. Makha Puja, third lunar month, February, marks the major sermon of the Buddha; Visakha Puja, sixth lunar month, May, commemorates the birth, death, and enlightenment of the Buddha; and Asanha Puja, eighth lunar month, August or September, honors the Buddha's first sermon.

Two other important Buddhist events (not national holidays) are Khao Phansa, the time for young boys to enter the monkhood at the beginning of the rainy season; and That Kathin, the end of the rainy season when laypeople present new robes to senior members of the *sangha.*

Many smaller regional festivals are only celebrated in a single town or province.

Brahmanic Festivals
Brahmanic ceremonies honor the elemental spirits of Hinduism still deeply ingrained within Thai society. These are often centered around ancient rites performed by white-robed priests, such as the Royal Ploughing Ceremony held at Sanam Luang in Bangkok.

Brahmanic festivals also include Loy Krathong (Festival of Lights), a thanksgiving ceremony associated with animist Hindu traditions, and rocket festivals that feature elements of pre-Buddhist tradition.

Nature Festivals
Rural festivals are often determined by the vagaries of nature and the annual cycles of rainfall and drought.

Pre-monsoon festivals designed to ensure bountiful rainfall and plentiful crops, such as the ploughing ceremony in Bangkok and rocket festivals in the north, are held in May and June before the onset of the monsoons. Post-monsoon harvest festivals take place during the cool season from November to February. Temple fairs neatly coincide with a period of low farm activity.

Agricultural festivals are often based on fruit and vegetable harvests, depending on the region and maturity cycle of the fruit. Many of these fairs are highlighted by the selection of a beauty queen, who then serves as Miss Rambutan, Miss Banana, or Lychee Queen. Curiously, Thailand lacks a durian festival, though Ko Samui would be the perfect location.

Popular fruit fairs include:

March—Chachonengsao—Mango Festival
April—Damnern Saduak—Grape Fair
May—Chiang Rai—Lychee Fair
May—Rayong—Fruit Festival
June—Chanthaburi—Fruit Festival
August—Surat Thani—Rambutan Fair
August—Lamphun—Longan Fair
September—Kamphang Phet—Banana Fair
September—Uttaradit—Langsat Fair

Regional Festivals

Almost every large town in Thailand has a festival unique to the region. Some are based on an historical event such as a military victory (the Don Chedi Fair in Suphanburi) or the foundation date of the city. Others honor an important product or craft (Borsang Umbrella Fair), a regional hobby (Chana Dove Festival), a famous resident (Rayong Suthorn Phu Day), or a sporting event (Phuket King's Cup Regatta). Chinese events include the traditional (Chinese New Year in Nakhon Sawan) and the modern (Phuket Vegetarian Festival).

The newest wrinkle seems to be festivals created solely to draw Thai and *farang* tourists, and localized events elevated to national status through the promotional efforts of the TAT. Examples include River Kwai Week and the Surin Elephant Roundup, respectively.

January

The year begins with the three-day hangover of New Year's Day; nobody on earth celebrates the new year like the Thais.

Mae Salong Cherry Blossom Festival: The Chinese settlement, Ban Santi Khiri, north of Chiang Rai, sponsors a floral parade attended by beau-

ty queens, local minority groups, and young Chinese marchers decked out in red costumes. Events also include traditional tea harvest dances and a *khao tok* hilltribe dinner. Mid-January.

Borsang Umbrella Festival: Borsang honors the town's main handicraft—hand-painted umbrellas—with painting competitions, exhibitions, and the crowning of Miss Borsang. Late January.

Don Chedi Memorial Fair: In 1592, Prince (later king) Naresuan defeated the prince of Myanmar on an elephantback duel that saved Ayuthaya from Burmese occupation. The actual battle site was lost until 1913 when Prince Damrong rediscovered the ancient *chedi* marking the site of the battle, now reenacted during the week-long festivities held just outside Suphanburi, two hours west of Bangkok. Late January.

REGIONAL FESTIVALS

MONTH	TOWN	EVENT
January	Suphanburi	Don Chedi Fair
January	Borsang	Umbrella Festival
February	Chainat	Giant Straw Birds
February	Petchburi	Historical Fair
February	Chiang Mai	Flower Festival
February	Pattani	Chao Mae Lim Fair
February	Nakhon Sawan	Chinese New Year
March	Yala	Singing Dove Festival
March	Korat	Suranari Heroine Week
April	Pattaya	Pattaya Fair
April	Buriram	Prasat Phanom Rung
May	Yasothon	Rocket Festival
June	Rayong	Suthorn Phu Day
July	Ubon Ratchathani	Candle Festival
September	Sakhon Nakhon	Wax Castles
September	Narathiwat	Narathiwat Fair
September	Phichit	Boat Races
October	Nan	Lanna Boat Races
October	Ayuthaya	Swan Boat Races
October	Phuket	Vegetarian Festival
November	Phimai	Historical Fair
November	Surin	Elephant Roundup
November	Kanchanaburi	River Kwai Week
December	Khon Kaen	Silk Fair
December	Phuket	King's Cup Regatta

Nakhon Phanom Prathat Phanom Festival: A week-long fair that honors the talismanic symbol of Issan Buddhism at the most sacred *stupa* in the northeast. Nakhon Phanom. Late January.

King Mengrai Festival: The founder of the Lanna Kingdom is honored with a week-long fair sponsored by the Mae Fah Luang Foundation and several private corporations. Highlights include a procession of young men and women dressed in traditional Lanna-style costumes, Shan and Burmese contingents, and a theatrical light-and-sound show based on a legendary Lanna warrior. Chiang Rai. Late January.

February

February is highlighted by Buddhist ceremonies, historical light-and-sound presentations, giant straw birds, orchids, beauty queens, and Chinese New Year.

Makha Puja: The Buddhist "All Saints Day" celebrates the spontaneous gathering of 1,250 disciples at Bodhgaya, India, when Buddha outlined his principal doctrines. The event is now honored with the release of fish and caged birds, sermons, and the burning of incense. After sunset, monks lead a lovely candle-lit procession of pilgrims on a triple circumambulation of Buddhist temples throughout the kingdom. Full moon of the third lunar month.

Hae Pha Khun That: Nakhon Si Thammarat—the "City of Monks"—is the religious capital of the south and therefore an important center for Buddhist festivals. During Hae Pha Khun That, pilgrims arrive from all over Thailand to pay homage to the relics of the Buddha enshrined at Wat Mahathat, and walk around the temple carrying a sacred yellow cloth over 300 meters long. Full moon of the third lunar month.

Petchburi Historical Fair: Petchburi, a small but historical town south of Bangkok, promotes its heritage with a *son et lumière* (sound-and-light) presentation over its 19th-century hillside complex, Khao Wang, and nearby temples from the Ayuthaya to Rattanakosin periods. Early February.

Chiang Mai Flower Festival: Temperate and tropical flowers—including fabulous orchids—are celebrated with elaborate floral processions, marching bands, and floats adorned with the pride of Chiang Mai: beautiful women. Early February.

Chainat Giant Straw Birds: A unique event during which villagers construct hundreds of huge, colorful birds with dry rice stalks left over from the harvest. The surprisingly realistic birds adorn trucks near city hall and are then moved to Chainat Bird Park eight km from town center. Early February.

Lampang Luang Wiang Lakhon: The northern town of Lampang parades five Buddha images through the streets and presents a *son et lumière* show at nearby Wat Prathat Lampang, one of the most impressive Buddhist sanctuaries in the country. Early February.

Hae Pha Khun That: During this three-day event, the people of Nakhon Si Thammarat honor the enshrined relics of the Buddha with religious ceremonies and a merit-making procession in which a *phra bot*—a cloth painting of the Buddha's life story—is circumambulated around the principal shrine. Mid-February.

Pattani Lim Ko Nieo Fair: A local heroine, believed to possess potent magic powers, is revered with a procession of her image and acts of penance performed by entranced devotees—fire walking and self-mutilation. The story of Lim Ko Nieo involves Chinese immigrants, Islam, a curse, suicide, and the doomed plans for a mosque. Pattani. Mid-February.

Chinese New Year: The most important social, moral, and personal festival of the Thai-Chinese is also a time for spiritual renewal, family reunions, and social harmony. The old are honored with mandarin oranges while the young receive red envelopes filled with lucky money. All debts are settled and salaried workers receive year-end bonuses. Miniature peach trees symbolizing good luck are exchanged as everyone calls out, *"Gung hay fah choi,"* or "Good luck making money." Clothes are purchased, houses are cleaned, and calligraphers paint messages of good luck on red banners. A special salad of raw fish and 20 vegetables is prepared, while the image of the Kitchen God (a deity who reports everyone's activities to the Jade Emperor) is courted with special candies, sweet wine, hell money, and perhaps a dab of sticky opium to seal his lips against speaking evil. After the bribe, he's taken outside and burned.

Chinese New Year is a fairly restrained event in most of Thailand except for towns with large Chinese populations, most notably Nakhon Sawan. Late February-early March.

March

Buddha, doves, and female heroines are March highlights.

Wat Pra Buddhapat Fair: Buddhist devotees make an annual pilgrimage to the Temple of the Holy Footprint in Saraburi. The temple houses the most famous footprint in the kingdom and is one of only six royal temples in the country honored with the rank *Raja Vorama Viharn*. The massive footprint, identified by its 108 auspicious marks, is enshrined under a *mondop* constructed during the reign of King Rama I. Early March.

Singing Dove Festival: Dove aficionados from Thailand and many other countries in Southeast Asia flock to Yala for the annual Singing Dove Contest attended by hundreds of breeding clubs and several thousand birds. The cooing competition is judged on three distinct pitches and a combination event during which Java Mountain doves, zebra doves, and Malayan doves are ranked on pitch, melody, and volume. Mid-March.

Thao Suranari Fair: This festival honors the national heroine (a.k.a. Khun Ying Mo), who rallied residents to resist Lao forces attacking from Vientiane during the reign of King Rama III. Homage ceremonies and a victory procession are held at her memorial in Nakhon Ratchasima (Khorat) in northeastern Thailand. Late March.

April

The hottest month of the year is the time for beach escapes and water festivals.

Pattaya Festival: Thailand's original beach resort hosts a week-long run of beauty queens, floral floats, fireworks, cultural and not-so-cultural dance, kite competitions, car races, and revelry from the prostitutes in this Baghdad-by-the-Bay. Early April.

Chonburi Fair: The booming business town one hour south of Bangkok sponsors a 10-day fair which includes an opening-day parade, exhibitions of handicrafts, pop concerts, *likay* (folk dance) shows, beauty contests, and open-air movies. Early April.

Chakri Day: A national holiday to commemorate the reign of Rama I, the founder of the Chakri dynasty, and the only day of the year it's possible to visit the sealed chapel within Wat Pra Keo. 6 April.

Songkran: Thailand's New Year is celebrated nationwide as the sun moves into Aries; Buddha images are purified with holy water, and young people honor their parents by pouring perfumed water over their hands.

Songkran ("move" or "change") is actually a time when *sanuk*-crazed Thais convert a religious ritual into a wild-and-crazy water-throwing festival involving white powder, water pistols, and buckets of freezing liquids. The more creative folks hire fire department trucks and cruise the streets searching for innocent tourists—the prime targets and hopeless victims who should leave their cameras, dignity, and inhibitions in their hotel rooms. 13-15 April.

Pra Pradang Songkran Festival: The Mon community in Samut Prakan, south of Bangkok, sponsors a Mon Songkran festival with parades, beauty queens, and nonstop deluges of water. Tours can be booked through the Siam Society. 13-15 April.

Poy Sang Long: Young men are ordained as novice monks during the spring school holidays throughout Thailand, but the most spectacular rituals are those celebrated by the Shans in Mae Hong Son. The Sang Long ("Jeweled Novice") dress in royal robes to symbolize Siddhartha's original status and the luxurious lifestyle he later rejected. After a procession through town, the novices are ordained at Wat Chong Kham, then don yellow robes for the next four to six weeks. Late April.

Si Satchanalai: Another spectacular ordination ceremony is the event at Si Satchanalai, near Sukothai, where novices are paraded through the streets on the backs of huge elephants. The ritual is taken from the Jataka scriptures, which portray the elephant as an important vehicle in the Buddha's search for enlightenment. Among the more unusual elements is the adornment of novices in resplendent floral headdresses *(chadas)* and the donning of brightly colored tunics and scarves rather than the traditional white robes. Late April.

Prasat Phanom Rung Fair: After restoration was completed in the late 1980s, an annual festival was started to honor the Khmer monument and attract visitors to one of the most impressive Cambodian *prasats* in the country. The weekend fair includes religious rites, a Khmer parade, and exhibitions of Issan dance. Late April.

May

Visaka Puja and pre-harvest festivals are May highlights.

Visaka Puja: This most sacred of all Buddhist holidays commemorates the birth, death, and enlightenment of Buddha with merit-making ceremonies identical to those of Maha Puja. During the day, temples are decorated with lanterns and lights, while at night the grounds come alive with the serene beauty of candlelight processions. Full moon of the sixth lunar month.

Coronation Day: King Bhumibol's ascension to the throne is commemorated with a private ceremony in the royal chapel. 5 May.

Royal Ploughing Ceremony: A colorful pageant of Hindu origins, which marks the beginning of the rice-planting season and seeks to ensure a bumper crop for the coming year. Staged on the Sanam Luang field in Bangkok and observed by the king and queen, the ceremony begins as a richly decorated plough is slowly pulled by buffaloes. Brahman priests and government ministers scatter rice seeds across the grounds. The Brahmans predict the upcoming season by interpreting the fall of the seeds, a highly prized commodity by farmers who eagerly gather the blowing kernels. Early May; the exact date is determined by Brahmanic priests.

Rocket Festival: Another ceremony designed to improve the harvest is the rocket festival *(bun bang fai),* which asks the gods for plentiful rains through rocket launches, dance processions, musical performances, beauty pageants, and ribald revelry that lampoons political figures. The phallic-shaped rockets *(bang jut),* which can measure up to five meters in length and hold up to 500 kg of gunpowder, are judged on their height and air time. Only about a third actually leave their launch pads; the rest either explode or spin into erratic trajectories that nose-dive into the crowds. Another category of rockets, *bnag eh,* are much larger missiles, up to 20 meters, that are never fired but are extravagantly decorated for a beauty contest.

Rocket festivals are a specialty of the northeast; each locality sets its own date of merry-making. The most famous site is Yasothon, though nearby Phanom Phrai is less crowded and the festival almost as spectacular. Second week in May.

Lychee Fair: This three-day fair features agricultural displays, handicraft demonstrations, and the selection of the sweetest Miss Lychee. Chiang Rai. Late May.

Intakin Festival: To invoke blessings for Chiang Mai and its inhabitants, this week-long festival is held at Wat Chedi Luang. Other animist rituals are held at Tapae Gate. Chiang Mai. Late May.

June

The beginning of the rainy season slows down the festival cycle as farmers wait out the rains and young men serve as novice priests.

Phi Ta Khon: Monsters, ghosts, and ghouls haunt the streets of Loei and the nearby town of Dan Sai in an annual festival designed to invoke the rains and honor two young lovers trapped in a cave near a highly venerated Buddha image. The deceased couple—Chao Por Kuan and Chao Mae Nang Tiam—are now regarded as the guardian spirits of the image, and are believed to lead the parade attended by hundreds of villagers decked out as dead spirits hidden behind masks and carrying phallic-shaped swords. Mid-June.

Suthorn Phu Day: The town of Rayong honors the literary works of Thailand's most famous poet, Suthorn Phu (1787-1855), with puppet shows and readings of his greatest works. 26 June.

July

Several major events occur at the beginning of the Buddhist Lent, the annual three-month rains retreat. It's an auspicious time for young Thai males to enter the Buddhist priesthood for a period of prayers, meditation, and religious studies.

Asalha Puja: Asalha Puja commemorates Buddha's first sermon to his five disciples and marks the beginning of the annual rains' retreat. Full moon of the eighth lunar month.

Khao Phansa: The day after Asalha Puja marks the first day of the novice retreat; a popular time for ordination ceremonies across the country. First day of the waning moon of the eighth lunar month.

Candle Festival: Ubon Ratchathani celebrates Khao Phansa with a procession of over 5,000 participants and up to 100 elaborately decorated floats that carry huge candles carved as three-headed elephants, garudas, and Buddhist deities. According to Buddhist belief, the candlelight symbolizes Buddhist sermons, which illuminate the mind toward enlightenment.

The smiling young women on the floats are judged and the finest beauty is honored as Miss Candlelight during the evening fair, an excellent opportunity to watch Issan dance, listen to excellent *kaen* flute music, and taste classic northeastern dishes. Full moon of the eighth lunar month.

August
Longan Fair: Lamphun celebrates the popular fruit with a Miss Longan Beauty Contest, agricultural displays, and a small parade. Early August.

Queen's Birthday: Municipal buildings are illuminated with colored lights during this national holiday that honors Her Majesty Queen Sirikit. 12 August.

September
Phichit Boat Races: Longtail boat races are held at several places in Thailand such as Phichit, Nan, Phimai, and Nakhon Phanom, starting in September. Championship races are held toward the end of the year. The boats are shaped like the mythological *naga* serpent embellished with sculpted heads, religious centerpieces, and feathery tails, and powered by crews decked out in historical costumes. Early September.

Narathiwat Fair: The small Muslim fishing village of Narathiwat sponsors a week-long fair with *kaoloe* boat races, singing dove competitions, *silat* martial arts contests, and other events judged by the Royal Family, who reside nearby at Taksin Palace. Third week in September.

Tambon Duan Sip: A 15-day festival held to placate dead relatives condemned to hell but granted a brief visit back home to haunt the living. These unhappy and potentially dangerous spirits are kept amused with merit-making ceremonies in the temples and nightly performances of shadow puppets, traditional dance, and modern Thai pop. Nakhon Si Thammarat. Full moon of the 10th lunar month.

October
The festival schedule picks up after the end of the rainy season.

Tod Kathin: The end of "Buddhist Lent" and the rainy season is marked by Wan Ok Phansa, celebrated with an increasing number of boat races around the country and the presentation of new robes to senior members of the *sangha*. Tod Kathin lasts until the next full moon, but each temple may only celebrate a single day of receiving gifts. The period also marks the return of Lord Buddha to the earth after teaching his doctrines in the heavens. Full moon of the 11th lunar month.

Sakhon Nakhon Wax Candle Festival: Ubon Ratchathani celebrates the beginning of Buddhist Lent with a candle parade, while Sakhon Nakhon marks the end of the period with a similar procession of beautifully embellished beeswax floats, often in the form of miniature Buddhist temples. Boat races are held two days later. Full moon of the 11th lunar month.

Chak Pra Festival: Chak Pra is a southern Thai specialty that centers around a ritualistic parading of Buddha images to raise funds for temple renovation, and evening performances of *nang talung* and *lakhon*. Chak Pra, meaning "pull a sacred image," is held in Songkhla, Nakhon Si Thammarat, and Surat Thani where the principal Buddha image is floated down the river on a raft decorated with *nagas,* then paraded to the temple for public veneration. Full moon of the 11th lunar month.

Phuket Vegetarian Festival: Phuket's renowned *Ngan Kin Jih*—a Taoist festival that marks the start of a month-long period of purification—begins with vegetarian offerings to the gods and a ritualistic cleaning of the five major Chinese temples on the island. During altarside rituals held around the clock, gods and spirits are invited to take possession of volunteers, who then use their newly acquired supernatural powers to perform bizarre acts of atonement for past transgressions that also help prevent bad luck in the future. Cheeks are pierced with needles and knives, ladders of razor-sharp blades are climbed, and burning coals are walked upon without any visible signs of pain or physical damage.

The festival culminates with an elaborate parade of Chinese deities and temple mediums who honor the Nine Emperor Gods with similar acts of self-mortification. Taoist priests chant from the Sutras and pour symbolic libations of tea that purify the heavens and suffuse the earth with a bright, clear light. The vegetarian festival is held during the first nine days of the Chinese ninth lunar month, generally in early October.

Chulalongkorn Day: Thailand's beloved King Rama V is honored with a national holiday during which wreaths are laid at his equestrian statue in the Royal Plaza near the old National Assembly. 23 October.

November
November marks the beginning of the cool season and a season of low farm activity, when rural Thais have extra time for village festivals and temple fairs.

Loy Kratong: Loy ("to float") Kratong ("a leaf cup")—the most charming festival in Thailand—honors both Buddhist traditions and the ancient water spirit of Mae Kong Ka, the Mother Waters of the Ganges River. Loy Kratong perhaps dates back to Hindu India, but the present form was developed by the Thais at Sukothai to honor the rains which had watered the earth and to wash away the sins of the previous year.

Loy Kratong begins with a full-day parade of beauty queens, floral floats, and hundreds of participants dressed in historical costumes. As the sun falls, pilgrims launch thousands of tiny banana-leaf boats, each carrying a single candle, onto the rivers and lakes throughout the kingdom—a wonderful, delicate illusion enhanced by the light of the full moon.

Loy Kratong is celebrated in both Sukothai and Chiang Mai, though Sukothai provides a superior venue due to smaller crowds and a more authentic setting among towering *chedis* and brightly illuminated temples. Full moon in the 12th lunar month.

Chiang Mai Yi Peng: Loy Kratong is known as Yi Peng in Chiang Mai. This major blow-out features massive parades, huge water floats, and the release of thousands of hot-air paper lanterns into the sky. Yi Peng takes place a few days after the Sukothai Loy Kratong; serious festival fanatics can attend both events.

Wat Saket Fair: Bangkok's most spectacular temple fair features folk drama, foodstalls, pop concerts, and candlelight processions around the Golden Mountain. Mid-November.

Surin Elephant Roundup: This internationally famous and heavily promoted event brings over 100 elephants to Surin for staged hunts, rodeo games, and elephant polo—a tug-of-war between a lone elephant and dozens of hopelessly outpachydermed men. Although the event is completely commercialized, it's also a rare opportunity to admire the gentle beasts and learn about one of Thailand's most endangered animals. Third Saturday in November.

Pra Pathom Chedi Fair: Folk dramas, beauty pageants, and a parade take place at Pra Pathom Chedi, the world's tallest Buddhist monument. Nakhon Pathom. Late November.

Phimai Historical Fair: A relatively new festival designed to honor Khmer culture and attract both Thai and *farang* visitors to the premier Cambodian momument near Nakhon Ratchasima. The TAT and Fine Arts Department-sponsored event includes a procession of the *nak prok* Buddha image, *chak nak duk dam ban* folk dances, and a *son et lumière* shown across the backdrop of the Phimai sanctuary. Late November.

River Kwai Historical Week: Another newly created festival that relates the grim history of this world-famous bridge. Festivities include a light-and-sound show complete with booming cannons and voice-over narration. The week-long event includes historical exhibitions, cultural performances, and rides across the bridge on vintage WW II steam engines. Late November.

Ayuthaya Swan Boat Races: An international event which attracts local and foreign crews to the championships of the fall racing season. Late November.

Sunflower Fair: The three-day festival celebrates Mexican sunflowers blooming amid the hills west of Chiang Mai during the cooler winter months. Oxcarts are decorated with the flowers, traditional folk shows presented, and, of course, Miss Sunflower is crowned. Mae Hong Son. Late November.

December
King's Birthday: The birthday of King Adulyadej Bhumibol is celebrated with a grand parade and citywide decorations of flags, royal portraits, and brilliantly colored lights along Rajadamnern Klang Avenue. 5 December.

King's Cup Regatta: Inaugurated in 1987, the King's Cup Regatta has quickly become one of Southeast Asia's blue-ribbon sailing classics, attracting almost 100 entrants from all over the world including North America, Australia, and Europe. The regatta brings international exposure to local waters and Thailand's booming business in yacht construction and charters—now almost as easy as renting a moped from the corner grocery store. Mid- to late December.

Christmas: Thais may not be Christians, but the habit of exchanging gifts and putting up decorated trees around the end of December is almost as popular in the Buddhist kingdom as in the Land of the Rising Sun. A curious twist is the tree decorations produced by dozens of companies around the country: velvet house lizards, red-hot chili peppers, and sequinned *nagas* known for their devotion to Lord Buddha rather than Lord Jesus. 25 December.

Chiang Mai Winter Fair: Held at the Municipal Stadium, this fair features cultural shows, agricultural displays, and the Miss Chiang Mai Beauty Contest. Late December.

ACCOMMODATIONS

Reservations?

Most travelers worry about finding proper accommodations their first night in Bangkok, especially those with late-night arrivals at the somewhat remote airport. Relating the current situation is difficult; although Bangkok is presently overstocked with hotel rooms, gluts often turn into droughts within a few years.

Reservations are highly recommended during the high tourist season from early December to late February, but are generally unnecessary during other times of the year. A hotel reservation desk at the Bangkok airport will check on hotel vacancies and make your reservations at good quality hotels.

The best way to make reservations is to contact your travel agent or a student travel agent. You can make reservations directly by sending a fax to the hotel in Bangkok, stating the date and time of your arrival (they may provide complimentary transportation from the airport) and length of stay, and inquiring about confirmation details such as credit card numbers and deposits. International phone calls are not recommended due to the language barrier.

Another excellent way to make a reservation is to use the hotel website on the Internet. Most mid-range and luxury hotels now have websites where you can check photos of the rooms and make an instant reservation—often at an "Internet discount rate."

For toll-free numbers of popular hotel companies, check the chart, "International Hotel Chains."

Reservations on Phuket and Ko Samui

Both of these tropical islands have been extremely busy in recent years, following the decline of tourism in Malaysia and Indonesia. Both islands now run at near-record capacity around the year; hotel reservations are highly recommended.

Once again, use Alta Vista or another search engine to find the URL of your preferred hotel and make your reservation via the Internet.

Guesthouses

Budget travelers who can accept simple rooms and common baths can sleep for under 100B everywhere, except possibly Bangkok and upscale tourist resorts such as Phuket and Pattaya.

The guesthouse phenomenon began about two decades ago as young backpackers crossed Thailand on the Kathmandu-to-Bali trail. Intrigued by these curiously dressed foreigners, and recognizing the potential for a small profit, enterprising Thai families opened up extra rooms and put up hand-painted signs marked "homestay" or "guesthouse." Coconut farmers on undiscovered islands such as Phuket and Ko Samui erected simple wooden A-frames and called them "bungalows."

Today, guesthouses specifically geared toward Western travelers and charging 50-100B for a basic room with shared bath can be found in all major tourist centers, on most beaches, and in some of the strangest nooks and crannies of the nation. The few towns that lack guesthouses need only wait until some bright soul opens up his or her home or English-language school to a Western backpacker.

Guesthouses range from simple beach shacks to three-story concrete warehouses with small swimming pools. The only unifying elements are

INTERNATIONAL HOTEL CHAIN TOLL-FREE NUMBERS

Accor Group . . . . (800) 221-4542
Ammanresorts . . . . (800) 447-7462
ANA Hotels . . . . (800) ANA-HOTELS
Best Western . . . . (800) 528-1234
Choice Hotels. . . . . (800) 4-CHOICE
Club Med . . . . (800) CLUB-MED
Conrad Hotels/Hilton . . . . (800) HILTONS
Dusit Hotels . . . . (800) 44-UTELL
Four Seasons . . . . (800) 332-3442
Golden Tulips . . . . (800) 344-1212
Holiday Inn . . . . (800) HOLIDAY
Hyatt International . . . . (800) 327-0200
Insignia Resorts . . . . (800) 467-4464
Intercontinental . . . . (800) 327-0200
ITT Sheraton . . . . (800) 334-8484
Mandarin Oriental . . . . (800) 526-6566
Marriott Hotels . . . . (800) 228-9290
Meridien Hotels . . . . (800) 543-4300
New Otani . . . . (800) 421-8797
Nikko Hotels . . . . (800) NIKKO-US
Omni Hotels . . . . (800) THE-OMNI
Pan Pacific. . . . . (800) 538-4040
Peninsula . . . . (800) 462-7899
Radisson Hotels. . . . . (800) 777-7800
Regent Hotels. . . . . (800) 545-4000
Renaissance Hotels . . . . (800) 228-9898
Shangri-La . . . . (800) 942-5050
Sterling Hotels . . . . (800) 637-7200
Westin Hotels . . . . (800) 228-3000

low prices and the Western clientele. Guest-houses in larger towns and cities may be packed together in a curious variation on those much-maligned "tourist ghettos"—the "backpackers' ghetto." Although some travelers resent the pseudo-hip mentality that permeates these scenes, many regard them as convenient spots to relax for a few days and hang out with other budget travelers.

Though towns without great appeal or significant sights may lack authentic guesthouses, budget Thai hotels with acceptable rooms will invariably be found around the train and bus stations. Note that many travelers feel the most memorable guesthouses are those situated in small and remote villages, well off the tourist trail and rarely visited by curious *farangs*.

Hotels

Budget: An excellent compromise between low-end guesthouses and expensive resorts are budget hotels specifically geared to Thai tourists and Thai businesspeople. These hotels are found in most towns and are perfectly adequate for travelers uncomfortable with shoestring accommodations but unwilling to spend copious amounts of cash. Hotels with fan-cooled rooms cost US$5-15, while a/c rooms are US$10-25, depending on the location and time of year. Each room will generally be furnished with a double bed fitted with clean sheets, decent furniture including a chair and writing table, and a private bathroom stocked with fresh towels and a small bar of soap.

Moderate: Hotel rooms in the US$25-50 range usually include a queen- or king-sized bed, individually controlled a/c, color TV, telephone, around-the-clock room service, small pool, restaurant, cocktail lounge, and other services such as a travel agency and car rental outlet. These hotels are located in all larger towns and most smaller places frequented by tourists or upscale Thai businesspeople.

Hotels priced US$50-100 could be ranked as either moderate or luxury depending on the location. For example, Bangkok hotels priced US$50-100 are ranked as moderately priced hotels when their rates are compared to average hotel rack rates in the capital. Similarly priced hotels in smaller towns would probably be of better quality and so placed in the luxury category. Your money goes farther, of course, outside of Bangkok.

Luxury: Thailand's premier hotels and beach resorts are ranked among the finest in the world for their superb architecture, wonderful ambience, and unrivaled level of service. The "Best Hotels of the World" listed in *Travel & Leisure* and recommended by readers of *Condé Nast Traveler* consistently include the Oriental and Shangri-La in Bangkok, the Amandari on Phuket, and the Baan Na Taling and Tongsai Bay Resort on Ko Samui. Room rates in luxury hotels can range US$100-500.

As noted above, many luxury hotels and a handful of mid-range properties are now quoting their room rates in U.S. dollars rather than local Thai *baht.* This has effectively killed off any savings you might find after the *baht* devaluation of 1997-98, so you'll save serious money by moving down a few notches and staying at an upper middle level hotel rather than at the absolutely top level.

Single and Double Rooms
Single rooms mean just one bed, while double rooms have two beds. Very few hotels in Thailand make this distinction or charge a different rate for either room. Even luxury hotels, which once charged slightly higher rates for double rooms, have dropped the practice. They now charge an identical rate whether you want a single or double room—whether you have two people per room or your entire family.

Just ask at the front desk for a room with two beds and, in most cases, they will take care of you at no extra charge.

FOOD AND DRINK

The cuisine of Thailand is unquestionably one of the highlights of a visit to the East. Twenty years ago, Thai food was largely unknown outside the country except to a handful of Westerners returning from the land of *sanuk* and *tom kha kai.*

Today, Thai cooking has emerged from relative obscurity to become one of the most popular and highly regarded culinary forms in the world. The dramatic proliferation of Siamese restaurants in every corner of the planet has made Thai food such an international favorite it now threatens to replace Chinese as the world's leading Asian cuisine.

CULINARY TRADITIONS

Whether your meal is an elaborate banquet enjoyed in a formal setting or a simple assortment of dishes served in a small cafe, a few mouthfuls make it evident that this is a singular creation of strong originality. Thai chefs have invented a style of cooking both varied and pleasurable—an aesthetic melange of finely crafted flavors.

Chinese Influence
Thai cuisine has been most strongly influenced by China; peoples migrated down from Yunnan to populate much of present-day Thailand. The Chinese migration continued until the end of the 19th century, when half the population of Bangkok was estimated to be of Chinese descent. These newcomers brought not only their languages and technologies, but also their culinary traditions and native eating habits. Many of these Chinese immigrants opened cafes and restaurants, introducing their culinary skills to the indigenous population. The result is that Thai

dishes today have much in common with the popular Chinese styles.

The connections are often quite obvious. For example, the ensemble of dishes in an average Thai meal typically follows the Chinese emphasis on the five primary flavors—bitter, salty, sour, hot, and sweet. The Chinese consider these five flavors essential to balance the life forces of *yin* and *yang*.

The widespread popularity of stir-fry cooking and the use of such ingredients as fish, rice, soy, ginger, duck, and noodles are also evidence of Chinese influence. The Thais also incorporate the culinary traditions of the provinces of Szechuan and Hunan.

Curries from India
Thai food has also been influenced by Indian cuisine, though the effects are more subtle and difficult to trace than those of China. Some dishes, such as *gaeng mussaman,* may have come directly from Muslim immigrants and Arab traders working the routes of ancient Southeast Asia. Other Indian dishes were perhaps learned from Hindu traders and Buddhist monks moving along the Silk Road that connected Tibet to Beijing.

Indian curries probably dominated the culinary styles of the Mons, the mysterious race of people who migrated from the Indian subcontinent to the lower Menan Valley several centuries before the foundation of Sukothai. Mons also brought their faith in Buddhism.

Foods from Other Lands
As trading patterns expanded between the Middle East and the Spice Islands of Eastern Indonesia, Muslim merchants carried to the Siamese entrepots the fabled spices of the East

Indies—nutmeg, cloves, and mace. These highly prized and wildly profitable spices were soon incorporated by the Thais into their local medicines and regional cuisines. Indonesia also contributed the spicy peanut sauces now used in the preparation of many Thai favorites, such as tiny skewers of barbecued meats called *satay*.

From the south of India and the coastlines of Malaysia came the rich creams of the coconut, a smooth and soothing ingredient now familiar to lovers of *tom kha kai* (coconut chicken soup) and *kaeng pet* (coconut curry).

Other foreign foods have met with varying degrees of success. Tomatoes, imported by European traders, now form an important element in the Thai diet, as does the tapioca successfully transplanted from Central America. The Siamese took an immediate liking to the coffee bean from Ethiopia, which arrived via Java sometime in the early 18th century. Coffee sweetened with condensed milk remains a favorite all over Thailand.

Not all foreign foods were so warmly welcomed. Potatoes, shipped in the 16th century from America to Asia, were soundly rejected by the Siamese as nothing but miserable little *man farang* (foreign roots).

BASIC INGREDIENTS

Thai cuisine combines coconut milk, lemongrass, tamarind, ginger, coriander, basil, and peanuts with the ubiquitous and intimidating chili. Describing Thai cuisine can be a challenge since a surprising amount of individuality is found in the creative use of curries, coconut creams, and fresh vegetables, but enough commonality exists to provide a few core themes.

Rice

The central ingredient to most meals is a plate of steamed or boiled rice *(khao)*. Rice is so elemental to the diet that the words "Have you eaten?" *("Kin khao?"),* literally mean "Have you eaten rice?"

Long-Grained Rice: Thai rice comes in several varieties and grades that vary from region to region. Common long-grained rice is a translucent variety grown in several grades, the finest being jasmine-fragrant rice *(khao hawn mali).*

Long-grained rice is generally boiled and steamed in an electric rice cooker and served as either *khao suay* (cooked rice) or *khao plao* (steamed rice). Unpolished rice and amber-colored red rice *(khao daeng)* are other popular varieties.

Sticky Rice: Sticky or glutinous rice *(khao niaow)* is a short-grained variety favored by the people in the northeast and parts of the north. Opaque rather than translucent like long-grained varieties, sticky rice must be soaked in cold water for several hours to soften the kernels prior to being steamed. Boiled sticky rice simply turns into a glutinous mess.

Chefs in the northeast often use woven bamboo baskets *(huad)* over a deep pan of boiling water to steam the rice. Another cooking method is to mix the rice with coconut milk and then shove the ingredients into bamboo tubes. The tubes are slowly roasted over a low open fire for several hours, then split open to reveal a tasty rice cake flavored with hints of banana, coconut, and wood smoke. These rice cakes often accompany spicy meat dishes and are consumed in the form of small rolled balls dipped into various sauces.

Coconut Milk

The coconut tree *(maprao)* is woven into the everyday fabric of life in Thailand. Every part of the palm—leaf, trunk, husk, nut—is used to produce a range of products, from rope and mats to clothing and roof thatching. The Thais use coconut milk *(nam katee)* as the basic ingredient in curries; in meat, vegetable, and fish dishes; and in sweets, desserts, and beverages.

Contrary to popular belief, the coconut milk used for cooking is not the watery liquid found inside the shell, but is created by pressing and filtering the extracts of coconut meat after it is soaked in boiling milk or water.

Chili Sauces

Chili sauces *(nam prik)* are hot and pungent pepper sauces made from fresh chilies, salt, sugar, vinegar, and any number of optional ingredients such as fermented fish, wild beetles, fruits, or vegetables.

Variations of *nam prik* come in reds and yellows and are bottled under various brand names, the most famous being the *Si Racha* sauce cre-

THE DREADED CHILI

*T*he Thai love affair with the fiery chili *(prik)* has given rise to the apparently indestructible myth that all Thai food is unbearably hot and spicy. While some dishes will instantly wreak havoc on the taste buds of *farangs,* the truth is many Thai recipes are not spicy and many Thais themselves cannot tolerate and tend to avoid the more aggressive dishes.

The origins of the chili pepper are almost as surprising as their effect on the uninitiated. In the year that every American schoolchild knows so well, a Portuguese captain on one of Christopher's ships discovered in the Caribbean some elongated little fruits in attractive hues of red and green. The pint-sized pepper traveled back to Europe and on to Thailand in the early 16th century with Portuguese merchants visiting the Siamese trading kingdom of Ayuthaya. For the spice-loving Siamese, the discovery of something more pungent than their beloved black pepper was taken with great enthusiasm.

Today, Thai cooking employs over 40 varieties of chilies, which are green when immature but change to yellow, orange, and red as they ripen. The hottest parts are the seeds and internal membranes, which can be removed, though this defeats the purpose of cooking with *Capsicum annum.* Bite unexpectedly into some varieties and you're launched on a breathtaking roller-coaster ride unrivaled by any other spice known to the human race.

As a general rule, chilies vary in pungency in inverse proportion to their size. Practical jokers sometimes urge newcomers to start with the smaller varieties and work their way up to the larger peppers. Novices should note the intensity of fire increases as the chili becomes smaller. For example, the large green-and-yellow *prik yuak* are as mild as green bell peppers in the West, while *prik num* and *prik chi fa,* middle-sized varieties from the north, are also relatively harmless. The thermometer rises sharply when the chilies start to resemble finger-sized torpedoes.

It is the tiny *prik kee noo* that packs a wallop so terrifying even experienced Thais treat the deceptive missile with deference and respect. Descriptively translated as "rat shit peppers" on account of their shape, these innocent-looking projectiles are guaranteed to clear your sinuses and have been know to make grown men cry.

Travelers who wish to avoid these experiences can push the suckers aside or order food as *mai phet* ("not hot") or *phet nit noy* ("a little hot"). Another tip—remember even the hottest of chilies loses much of its fierce flavor when safely cocooned in a mouthful of rice. In other words, the antidote for an overdose of chili is to eat more rice to remove the slippery oil, not panic and dive for a glass of water or beer. Finally, when sweat breaks out on your forehead and drips into your eyes, resist the sudden urge to wipe your eyes with the back of your hand. There are few experiences in life more painful than an eyeful of chili oil.

---

ated in a fishing village near Pattaya. Fresh chili sauces are commonly served in cafes and restaurants as spicy condiments used for dipping.

Although offensive to the uninitiated, chili sauce connoisseurs consider the finer versions somewhat akin to the fine Camemberts and well-aged Munsters of Europe, and the Thai equivalent of the classic aioli sauce from southern France.

Some brands such as *nam prik sri racha* are sweet and mild, while others are fiery concoctions made with whole chili seeds and body fragments. The most popular version is *nam prik kapi,* a thick and highly pungent paste made from *nam* (any liquid), *prik* (pepper or chili), and *kapi* (shrimp paste).

Another variation sure to excite the palate is *nam prik maeng da,* a highly prized dish made from the pounded carcasses of male *maeng da* beetles. The insect provides an exceptionally perfumed flavor.

Other versions include *nam prik nam po* made from pounded water crabs and guava leaves, *nam prik lohn thar* thickened with heavy coconut creams, and *nam prik plah rah* laced with fermented snakehead fish.

Other Ingredients

The following ingredients and spices are used to create the wide variety of popular Thai dishes.

Basil *(bai):* The three most common varieties are *bai horapa,* a sweet basil that resembles the

Western variety; *bai mangluk,* known as lemon basil; and *bai krapao,* a reddish-purple plant also known as holy basil.

Coriander, cilantro, or Chinese parsley *(pak chi):* A standard herb used for thousands of years in Asia, the Middle East, Europe, and the Americas. The leaves, roots, and seeds are each used in different dishes for a unique flavor. The seeds are used in curry pastes, the leaves as garnishes, the roots and stems to flavor everything from meatballs to pork pastes.

Eggplant *(makheua):* Thai aubergines range from a long and purple variety called the *makheua yao* to a round and hard variety known as *makheua khun,* with a crunchy texture but little flavor.

Galangal *(ka, laos):* A member of the ginger family and sometimes called "Siamese ginger," this strange-looking rhizome is considered a spice, digestive stimulant, remedy for stomachache, and mild aphrodisiac.

Kaffir lime *(makrut):* One of the most distinctive flavors of Thailand, this little-known member of the citrus family was once used in tonic medications, to drive away evil spirits, and to produce traditional hair shampoos. Today, the grated dark green rind adds an aromatic zest to curry pastes, while the leaves are incorporated into gravies that demand a strong lemon aroma.

Lemongrass *(takrai):* One of the most common and distinctive herbs used in Thai food, *takrai* is the primary ingredient for the lemony tang of most curry pastes, salads, and soups. Related to citronella, *takrai* is more aromatic than the lemon fruit despite the fact that only the lower portions of the stalk and bulb are used in Thai cooking.

Palm sugar *(nam taan peuk):* A coarse, brown, sticky sugar made from the boiled sap of the palmyra palm *(Borassus flabellifer).* Palm sugar's caramel flavor is less cloyingly sweet than that of cane sugars; buy it canned or in markets in the form of massive brown cakes.

Shrimp paste *(kapi):* What's that smell? If it isn't durian or a rotting pile of fish, it's probably the decomposed residue of pounded shrimp left to dry in the sun. The pungent mixture—a byproduct of the production of fish sauce *(nam pla)*—can be freshly packed into vacuum-sealed jars and refrigerated or compressed into slabs and sold in local markets. Both forms have a salty, anchovylike flavor that dissipates when cooked with other ingredients. *Kapi* is rich in vitamin B and is the main source of protein in most Southeast Asian countries.

Tamarind *(mak kam):* The brownish pods of the feathery tamarind tree provide the sour and bitter flavor to many soups, beverages, curries, and fish dishes. Thais also eat the green fruit unripened with a touch of sugar, salt, and dried chili flakes.

COMMON DISHES

Soups

Soup is an essential component in almost every meal in Thailand. Breakfast will start with a bland and thickened rice soup accompanied by a few simple side dishes. Lunch will often be a hearty bowl of *kuay teow* from a sidewalk vendor or open-fronted kitchen. Dinner will generally include a lighter soup, either delicate or hot and spicy, to complement the principal dishes of curries and rice plates.

The hot-and-sour broth *tom yam kung* is prepared with fragrant lemongrass, kaffir lime leaves to make it sour, chilies for the heat, fresh and lightly blanched straw mushrooms, fish sauce as a substitute for salt, fresh coriander for the garnish, and large tiger shrimp. The broth is Thailand's classic dish. There are many variations on this dish. When prepared with chicken, it's called *tom yam kai.* Vegetarian versions can be made with whole mushrooms and fresh tomatoes.

Another delicious soup is *tom kha kai*—a rich chicken and coconut-milk soup flavored with lemongrass, lime leaves, galangal, and shallots. This essential element of Thai cuisine is served throughout the country.

Khao tom (thick rice soup) can be served with fish *(khao tom pla),* pork *(khao tom mu),* or prawns *(khao tom kung).* Other noteworthy soups include *kaeng chut,* a mild flavored soup with vegetables and pork; and *kaeng liang,* a spicy soup with shrimp, vegetables, basil, and pepper.

Rice Dishes

The central ingredient in most Thai meals is a plate of steamed or boiled rice. The most common variety is the translucent long-grained type grown in several grades. Sticky or glutinous rice is an opaque, short-grained variety favored in the north and northeast. Brown, unpolished rice and varieties of red rice are occasionally used in special dishes. Popular rice dishes include:

khao daeng—red rice
khao hawn mali—jasmine rice
khao kaeng—rice with curry
khao man kai—steamed rice with marinated Hainan-style chicken
khao mu daeng—rice with Chinese-style red pork
khao na kai—steamed rice with sliced chicken
khao na pet—steamed rice with roast duck
khao pat—fried rice
khao pat kai—fried rice with chicken
khao pat kung—fried rice with shrimp
khao pat mu—fried rice with pork

Noodle Dishes

In Thailand, consuming noodles is a near-religious experience that defines the soul of the nation and the Thai way of life. For more information on the types of noodles, refer to "The Noodle Vendor" below. Some good noodle dishes to try are *bah mee haeng:* wheat noodles with meat and vegetable served dry without broth or meat gravy; *bah mee nam:* wheat noodles in broth with vegetables and meat; *bah mee ratna:* wheat noodles in meat gravy; and *kuay teow:* Chinese-style noodle soup—a lunchtime favorite from street vendors and open-air kitchens.

Kuay teow haeng is rice noodles served dry without any type of liquid soup or meat gravy. The classic *kuay teow pat thai* consists of rice vermicelli fried with small shrimp, bean sprouts, and fish sauce.

More noodle possibilities include: *kuay teow ratna,* rice noodles in a meat gravy of pork, broccoli, and oyster sauce; *mee krob,* rice vermicelli noodles fried and flavored with meats and vegetables in a tangy sweet-and-sour sauce; *pat si yii,* fried thin noodles with soy sauce; *pat thai,* thin rice noodles fried with tofu, vegetables, egg, and peanuts.

Curry Dishes

Curries are considered native to India, Pakistan, Sri Lanka, and other neighboring countries. Curries are created by cooking meats, fish, and vegetables in a combination of herbs and spices known as curry pastes to create stewlike dishes.

In Thailand, the word *kaeng* (liquid) is used to define curries. Coconut milk is often incorporated into a curry paste; this mixture is called *krung kaeng* (city of liquids). The most common are *krung kaeng ped* (red curry) which takes its color from fiery peppers, and *krung kaeng keo wan* (green curry) made from green chilies and often incorporated into poultry dishes. *Krung kaeng som* is an orange curry generally used in soups, while *krung kaeng kari* is yellow and often used for chicken and beef curries.

Among the most popular dishes in the country is *kaeng pet.* This spicy curry is made from sweet coconut milk and flavored with lemongrass, chilies, and shrimp paste. It is served with either pork, chicken, beef, fish, or prawns.

A milder version of a Muslim curry from India, *kaeng mussaman* is laced with beef, potato, onion, coconut milk, and peanut. The Thai name is a corruption of the word "Muslim." True to its foreign origins, this curry uses many spices absent from the Thai culinary repertoire, such as cinnamon, nutmeg, and other sweet spices.

Kaeng wan is a green curry thickened with coconut milk, eggplant, sweet basil, and lime leaves. Green curries have an innocent appearance but can often be extremely hot; be careful.

Kaeng kari, a yellow curry laced with turmeric, is a milder version of Indian curry. *Kaeng baa,* however, is Thailand's hottest curry—for veteran fire-eaters only.

Salads

Thai salads *(yam)* often consist of edible leaves and succulent flowers native to the country, in combination with distinctive mints and fish sauces. Toppings include crushed peanuts, dried chilies, garlic flakes, chopped coriander leaves, dried shrimp, and flakes of unsweetened coconut. Salads are often garnished with lime wedges and pickled garlic cloves carved into flowers.

Som tam, a shredded salad from northeastern Thailand, contains shredded raw papaya, diced long beans, dried shrimp, and toasted peanuts, all pounded in a mortar together with palm sugar, lemon juice, fish sauce, and hot chilies. Many,

many travelers survive solely on *som tam, tom kha kai, kuay teow* and *pat thai,* washed down with icy bottles of Singha beer.

Larb ped, a salad of ground duck, is served on a bed of lettuce with spice and acidic lemon to balance the richer flavors of the meat. Other meat salads include *yam kung,* prawn salad made with fish sauce, lime juice, finely chopped garlic, chili powder, minced lemongrass, red onion, coriander leaves, lettuce, and mint leaves; *yam nang mu,* pork skin salad; *yam neua,* a combination of grilled strips of beef with fresh coriander, mint, basil, spring onion, garlic, shallots, lime juice, fish sauce, chilies, and sugar; and *yam pla muk,* squid salad sautéed with onions, chilies, lemongrass, and mint leaves. *Yam pla muk* has great acid balance and is generally served with lettuce to help cut the biting heat.

More good salads to try are *yam tang kwa,* cucumber salad; *yam het,* mushroom salad; *yam mamuang,* green mango salad; and *yam wun sen,* cellophane noodle salad.

SIDEWALK SNACKS AND DESSERTS

*M*any of the most popular foods in Thailand fall into a category called *kap klaem* (drinking foods), intended for consumption when people gather for a glass of Mekong whiskey or a few rounds of Singha beer. Similar to *tapas* in Spain or *pupus* in Hawaii, these snacks are actually miniature meals in themselves that often provide some of the most convenient and tasty dining in the country.

These snacks and other sweets can be purchased from *mae khar harb rey,* a traveling woman who sells her goods from baskets levered on strong sticks *(mai khan)* balanced between her shoulders. She typically wears the *ngorb,* a broad-brimmed hat made from palm leaves, and a sarong of colorful cotton. Inside her two swinging baskets rest a wondrous collection of tiny pots, crockery, and cutlery used to serve her assortment of condiments and snacks. The following treats are offered by *mae khar harb rey,* as well as sidewalk vendors and small cafes:

kai sam yang: a plate of fried chicken with peanuts, chopped ginger, and fiery peppers; often consumed with beer and various forms of *yam*

satay: barbecued skewers of meat served with peanut sauce and cucumbers in vinegar and sugar

sang kaya: custard made from coconut milk, sugar, and eggs

chow kway: black-grass pudding shredded and mixed with a sugar syrup over ice

boh bok: green-grass drink made from crushed vines and sugar water. Bitter.

roti sai mai: small flat pancakes with strands of green or pink spun sugar wrapped inside

kanom buang: batter poured on a hot griddle, then folded over and filled with shredded coconut, egg yolk, and green onions

tong krob: golden yellow balls made from egg yolks and rice flour, then dusted with sugar

kao glab pat maw: thin crepe filled with fried shrimp, pork, peanuts, sugar, coconut, and even fish sauce. Delicious.

thua thawt: fried peanuts

What would you like to try today?

THE STREET DINING EXPERIENCE

Dining choices in Thailand range from five-star restaurants in air-conditioned hotels to simple cafes and common foodstalls perched on the side of the road.

First-time visitors often dismiss hawker food as unclean and assume any meal served on a rickety aluminum table must be inferior to a meal in a first-class restaurant. Nothing could be further from the truth. The unpretentious fare served from foodstalls and sidewalk cafes often provides stiff competition for many of the kingdom's finest restaurants.

Consider street food and simple cafes first for local dining. Large congregations of stalls in a single location ensure a greater array of food than could possibly be created by a single restaurant. Also, since sidewalk merchants have no rent or other forms of overhead, prices can be kept extremely low. A filling and delicious meal generally costs under US$2, a minuscule sum that includes a free cooking lesson and smiles from the chef. Finally, sidewalk dining allows you to meet people and acquire insight into traditional Thai lifestyles.

Will You Die?

Many Westerners are dissuaded by horror stories about the dangers of consuming meals from sidewalk cafes and movable vendors. Do not believe all these tales.

Thais are extremely fastidious about food preparation, and few diners suffer from anything more serious than the heartburn of chili or the pains of overindulgence. So abandon your fears of sanitary imperfection, pull up a chair, and ignore the mess. That succulent duck or noodle concoction may prove to be one of the best meals of your entire vacation.

Finding the Best

Your only challenge might be selecting the best cafe or foodstall. You'll always have choices, since sidewalk cafes and roving food vendors can be found on busy street corners, tucked away in narrow alleys, perched on river banks, blocking sidewalks and bus stops, spilling from markets, clogging bus aisles, and even bobbing down canals on rickety canoes.

Thailand is a nation obsessed with food. At all hours, in all locations, Thais search out undiscovered foodstalls and cafes with superb dishes. They're constantly sifting through the duds to uncover the gems.

A good strategy is to patronize only those foodstalls packed with Thais and to avoid vendors shunned by the general public. Another telltale sign is squadrons of Mercedes parked in alleys near simple foodstalls and cubbyhole cafes. However, though these signs of wealth often indicate the locations of cafes and foodstalls with excellent fare, they may also signal the presence of brothels and gambling dens.

THE NOODLE VENDOR

Eating off the streets may not be advisable in some Asian countries, but sitting down for a bowl of noodles (kuay teow) in Thailand is not only safe but a culinary delight.

To say kuay teow is merely a "bowl of noodles" seriously understates its marvelous qualities and place in Thai society. It would be like describing a Rolls Royce as just a car or Pablo Picasso as only a painter. Noodles are holy institutions, a way of life, and the fuel that drives the engines of the kingdom.

No dish excites the emotions of Thais with greater intensity than a bowl of noodles. Conversations at parties often stop when somebody mentions they discovered the perfect bowl of noodles served by an unknown vendor in a remote corner of town. People positively glow when the discussion turns to what comprises the perfect form of kuay teow. Thais attending lavish parties have been known to abandon buffets of smoked salmon and caviar to travel absurd distances for the seductive creations of some new noodle vendor.

Many noodle vendors are celebrated for their broths; the ingredients are shared only with family members. After all, fortunes are won or lost with the rise and fall of reputations. Several years ago, a rumor circulated around Bangkok that a particular chef was dosing his soup with aphrodisiacs, whose miraculous effects were hailed by hundreds of devoted customers. The imaginative chef apparently made a fast fortune but was driven into bankruptcy after newspaper exposure of his fraudulent ingredients. Mai pen rai.

Types of Noodles

Noodle stalls display several types of noodles and their optional condiments.

The most common form are **rice noodles** *(sen)*, made by soaking plain rice in water for several hours and then molding the mixture into flat pancakes. The square discs of dough are cut into either thin noodles *(sen lek)*, thick noodles *(sen yai)*, or very thin vermicelli *(sen mee)* also called rice-stick noodles.

All three sizes are consumed fresh but can also be sun-dried and later resoaked prior to preparation. Rice vermicelli when fried directly from the package makes the famous *mee krob*, a noodle dish flavored with meats and vegetables in a tangy sweet-and-sour sauce.

Wheat noodles *(bah mee)*, the second type, are those made from fresh wheat flour and moistened with eggs. Also called "yellow" or "egg" noodles, *bah mee* is popular in the north.

Finally, **mung bean noodles** are those made from mung beans *(wun sen)* into the familiar "cellophane" or "glass noodles." These noodles are formed from a puree of mung beans and water, which is strained to produce a clear liquid. The liquid is then dried into sheets or extruded to form "bean thread" noodles. *Wun sen* can be served fresh or sun-dried for storage.

How to Order

Many Westerners have trouble ordering *kuay teow*, since vendor signs are usually labeled only in Thai and most vendors speak little English. And yet customers must give the chef specific instructions on their choice of noodle, additional ingredients, and style of preparation. The specific types of noodles *(sen lek, sen yai, sen mee, bah mee)* are described above. Additional ingredients include chicken *(gai)*, pork *(mu)*, meatballs *(luchin)*, duck *(pet)*, prawns *(kung)*, or fish *(pla)*. Noodles can be prepared in broth as soup *(nam)* or in dried form without broth *(haeng)*.

Sometimes the name of a dish will indicate its contents; other times it will refer to a famous style from a particular location in Thailand, such as *kuay teow rad nar,* a popular dish of stir-fried noodles combined with pork, broccoli, and oyster sauce, or *kuay teow pat thai,* the classic dish of rice vermicelli with small shrimp, bean sprouts, and fish sauce. Regional variations include *sen mee Krung Thep,* the noodle style of Bangkok, and *mee krob,* a noodle dish of Chinese origins.

Travelers who don't speak any Thai can simply point to the case and indicate their choices, but it's much more fun to attempt some Thai and work on your communication skills.

Examples of noodle combinations include: noodle soup, wide noodles, pork, broth: *kuay teow, sen yai, mu, nam;* noodle soup, egg noodles, chicken, no broth: *kuay teow, bah mee, gai, haeng;* noodle soup, thin noodles, meatballs, broth: *kuay teow, sen yek, luchin, nam.*

OTHER DINING VENUES

Cafes

Moving up a notch from streetstalls are small cafes almost as economical as dining on the sidewalk. Noodle shops *(raan kuay teow)* will serve the same dishes as the noodle vendor with somewhat better furnishings and better hygiene. The common curry-and-rice cafes *(raan khao kaeng)* generally prepare familiar noodle dishes plus rice plates accompanied by a choice of curries *(kaeng)*.

A common style of Chinese cafe is the boiled rice shop *(raan khao tom)*, which specializes in both thick rice soups and food ordered from a menu *(aahaan taam sang)*. These Chinese-Thai cafes prepare almost every dish common to Thailand and often stay open very late or around the clock.

Night Markets

A favorite venue for economical meals is the night market *(talaat toh rung)*, found in most villages and towns in Thailand. Essentially an organized collection of street vendors, night markets provide all possible varieties of cuisines, from Chinese stir-frys to noodle soups and blended fruit drinks.

Night markets in popular tourist venues such as Chiang Mai tend to be more expensive than ordinary foodstalls, but are often the only dining opportunity in many smaller villages. Some unique creations have surfaced from night market dining, such as the "flying vegetable" dishes in Phitsanulok and the transvestite cafes in Chiang Mai.

Food Centers

An excellent place to get an idea of the scope of Thai dishes is one of the upscale food centers located in many of the larger towns and cities. Food centers are hygienic self-serve operations where the customer purchases coupons from a central booth, then wanders around to select dishes from various food vendors. Seating is communal and unused coupons can be refunded or saved for another night.

The most popular food centers in Bangkok are at the Ambassador Hotel on Sukumvit Road and in Mahboonkrong Shopping Complex near Siam Square. Food centers are also located on the top floors of shopping centers in smaller towns, often the most dependable and comfortable places to dine off the tourist trail.

Seafood Supermarkets

An outgrowth of Chinese seafood centers originally popularized in Hong Kong and Singapore, seafood supermarkets have been copied throughout most of Southeast Asia. The typical operation features a dazzling display of all types of seafood and shellfish near the front door to lure in hungry customers. Customers select the fish and sauce, then the method of cooking: barbecued, sautéed, boiled, etc. A 100-150B cooking charge is added to the bill.

Dining at seafood supermarkets can be surprisingly expensive; seafood is priced according to weight per 100 grams and many Westerners fail to calculate the final tab until the bill is presented at the end of the meal.

Restaurants with Classical Dance

Many restaurants in Bangkok and Chiang Mai stage classical dance performances accompanied by a set menu often arranged around local specialties. An example is the *khan toke* dinners in the north. Diners typically sit on padded seats in recessed alcoves and are presented a buffet of dishes that can vary in quality depending on the particular restaurant. The food can be bland and insipid, but the performance may compensate for the unimaginative offerings.

Royal Thai Cuisine

The final word in upscale dining is intimate restaurants that serve the style of cuisine once prepared only by palace chefs. In terms of presentation, Royal Thai cuisine is ranked alongside French and Japanese for its finesse and superb attention to detail. Fruits and vegetables are carved into exquisite shapes, carefully matched to create an edible work of art. Prices, as you might expect, reflect the quality of the food and sumptuous surroundings of the restaurant.

DRINKS

Water

Thais don't drink water directly from the tap; most purchase purified water *(nam deum khuat)* bottled in plastic containers.

Many cafes and restaurants serve free glasses along with unsealed bottles of boiled water *(nam tom),* drinking water *(nam deum),* or plain water *(nam plao).* All are safe to drink even if served at room temperature or having a pale straw color. Most are tinted with a weak infusion of tea leaves to signify the water has been boiled. Drinking water provided in cafes and restaurants will not make you sick, and it's more economical than bottled water, which generally costs 5-15B.

Larger cafes and restaurants keep their containers of boiled water, soft drinks, and fruit juices refrigerated, but smaller cafes add ice *(nam khaeng)* to glasses and takeaway containers, i.e., plastic bags. All ice in Thailand is produced in government-licensed factories inspected to guarantee hygienic and potable ice. However, problems sometimes arise in transportation, so ice served in remote locations is best avoided.

Fruit Juices

Fresh-squeezed fruit juices such as *nam som* (orange juice) and *nam manao* (lemon juice) are often served with a little salt or sugar. If you prefer straight juice, no salt, add the words *mai sai kleua* (without salt).

Fruit juices blended or squeezed may be called either *nam khan* (squeezed juice) or *nam pon* (mixed juice) as in *nam malakan pon* (papaya shake or smoothie).

The most widespread fruit juice is sugarcane juice *(nam awy).* It's served year-round no matter what particular fruit may be in season.

Coffee

Thais consider Nescafé and other instant coffees superior to freshly ground coffee, perhaps because of the foreign association or the convenience factor. But decent coffee beans are grown in the north and south and brewed by filtration in many local cafes.

Thais use condensed milk in coffee rather than the plain milk used in the West. Although overly sweet to some Western palates, this authentic coffee can be ordered in morning markets by asking for *kafae thung* (big coffee). To enjoy a steaming cup of black coffee, ask for *kafae dam* (black coffee) followed by *mai sai nam tan* (without sugar).

Another caffeinated treat is iced coffee *(kafae yen)* made from freshly brewed black coffee laced with condensed milk.

Beer

The perfect complement to a Thai dinner is an ice-cold bottle of locally produced beer. Thai beer is strong and tasty, brewed according to German recipes. Beer is the fastest growing beverage in Thailand according to government statistics, which show consumption soaring from 98 million liters in 1987 to almost 400 million liters in recent years.

Thai beer is excellent, though not exactly an inexpensive drink. High excise taxes imposed by the government make beer one of the few consumer products almost as costly as it is in the West. Excise taxes run 30B per large bottle of beer, or 50% of the total price for most alcoholic beverages in the country. A large beer (630 ml) costs 50-60B in Bangkok—about half the minimum wage of a local worker.

Singha Beer: The oldest and most popular beer in Thailand is the Singha brand produced by Boon Rawd Brewery. Boon Rawd was founded in August 1933 by nobleman Phya Bhirom Bhakdi after he realized that the arrival of bridges would quickly ruin his ferryboat transportation business. Bhakdi went to Germany, learned the skills necessary to brew European-style beer, and returned to uncork his first bottle of Singha in 1934. Today, Boon Rawd Brewery is one of the kingdom's most successful companies boasting extensive holdings in farms, bottled water, manufacturing plants, brewpubs, restaurants, and a golf course.

The current success is credited to Bhakdi's son, Prachuab, who served his brewmaster apprenticeship in Munich and took over the helm of Boon Rawd upon the death of his father in the 1950s. The present-day brewery, near the Chao Praya River in Bangkok, uses barley grown on farms near Chiang Mai and imported German hops which cannot survive in the heat of Thailand. Singha beer has an alcohol content of 6.0%, a heady punch much appreciated by the average Thai beer drinker, while the lighter Singha Gold weighs in at a reasonable 4.6%.

Carlsberg: Singha holds almost 65% of the domestic beer market. Second place goes to Carlsberg, jointly owned by Thai and Danish interests and heavily backed by the makers of Mekong whiskey and an energy drink called Krating Daeng. Since its launch in 1993, Carlsberg has seized almost 20% of the domestic beer market by using the distribution system established by the makers of Mekong, and by raising the alcohol content to match that of Singha. Carlsberg, a sweeter beer than the more bitter Singha and Kloster brews, is priced midway between Singha and Kloster.

Kloster and Amarit: Thai Amarit Brewery, in third place with only seven percent of the market share, produces Kloster (the name is leased from a German company) and Amarit NB. Kloster is an upscale beer generally enjoyed by expatriates and wealthy Thais who like the bitter kick and exclusive image.

Heineken: Thai beer drinkers were given another choice in 1995 with the second arrival of Heineken into the Thai market. Heineken's first attempt to penetrate the market in 1990-91 was abandoned due to poor distribution, but the current partnership includes the national distributor of Coca-Cola. For the first time since Boon Rawd opened in 1933, Singha has some real competition in the national beer market.

Whiskey

Approach with extreme caution the whiskeys of Thailand; the 70-proof molasses-based spirits pack an abnormal, almost psychotropic wallop—the tequila of Thailand.

Whiskey has long been one of the country's leading moneymakers, contributing more than five percent of the national budget through excise taxes and license fees. The leading brand is

Mekong, manufactured by the Suramaharas group, which has thrived under a 15-year production contract tied to generous concessions to the government. Suramaharas also produces the less-expensive **Kwangthong** brand. Whiskeys made by the Suramaharas group are sold in liters *(klom)* for about 120B, half-liters *(baen),* and quarter liters *(kok).*

Spirited competition is provided by the Surathip Group and their line of 12 **Hong** (swan) brands. Labels carry variations on the word Hong—Hong Thong, Hong Ngoen, Hong Yok, Hong Tho. Hong whiskeys are somewhat cheaper than Suramaharas brands and generally found in rural rather than urban areas.

The two liquor consortiums waged a bloody war of price cuts and foolish discounting until they were forced into an uneasy merger in the late 1980s. The merger helped recharge government revenues by allowing the quasi-independent companies to raise prices, equalize distribution, and escape many of the onerous production quotas imposed by the government.

Premium whiskeys designed to compete with prestigious imports such as Johnnie Walker, Seagrams, and Chivas Regal are being introduced into Thailand. New arrivals packaged in fancy boxes complete with labels in English include VO Royal Thai whiskey and Golden Cat VO from United Winery Company. The chief problems are government taxes that have been jacked up to unrealistic and perhaps unsustainable levels.

The result of sharply rising taxes has been increased popularity of budget liquors. One beneficiary has been Pramuanphon Distillery (United Winery Company) in Nakhon Pathom and its line of budget whiskeys called Maew Thong (Gold Cat), Sing Chao Praya (Chao Praya Lion), and Singharat (The Lion King).

Other Liquors

Imbibers who can't handle the powerful kick of Mekong or the overwhelming aromas of moonshine might try Sang Thip, a distilled rum made from sugarcane. It's slightly more expensive but much more palatable than moonshine or regional whiskeys.

Perhaps the biggest effect of skyrocketing liquor taxes has been the illegal distillation of moonshine whiskey and various types of white liquors. White liquor, or *lao khao,* is generally made from sticky rice and carries an odor that rises above even the heaviest of dilutions.

Lao khao and other homemade brews can easily undercut the price of legal whiskeys, giving rise to the following joke. What are the only two households in each village that don't produce moonshine? Answer: the government excise office and the Buddhist *wat.* Some even have doubts about the *wat.*

DINING TIPS AND ETIQUETTE

Ordering a Meal

Ordering a meal outside a tourist area can often be challenging since few restaurants offer English menus or employ waiters who speak English. One solution is to point to a dish being served to other patrons; another is to memorize the names of a few Thai dishes served throughout the country. In many smaller cafes and restaurants, customers often wander into the kitchen and point to the pots of food that look promising.

You could also surrender yourself to the waiter and say, *"Mee arai phe set?"* "What's special?" Many upcountry restaurants feature regional specialties—only found by trusting the proprietor.

The typical Thai meal includes dishes that complement each other and provide a range of flavors. Such a selection may include a spicy curry entree with meat or chicken, a stir-fried rice dish, a salad of vegetables flavored with lime and chili, a hot-and-sour soup of the *yam* type, noodles, and a variety of pepper sauces and pastes that show the genius of Thai cooking in its purest form.

The assemblage of dishes is placed on the table and each customer is presented with a plate of rice as the centerpiece. Dishes are eaten in no particular order.

Dining Etiquette

Thais still respect the visitor who uses proper etiquette and understands the correct use of utensils and dining procedures.

Do not allow food to spill on the table, and avoid loud and flamboyant behavior when dining with well-bred Thais. Customs dictate that a spoonful of plain rice be consumed first to acknowledge the importance of rice as the central ingredient of Thai cuisine. Also, to indicate restraint, only one or two spoonfuls of food should be taken from the common platter when dining with guests.

At formal meals, it is considered polite to allow the host to first serve himself or offer the opportunity to a guest. Do not dive into a meal without first acknowledging the generosity and rights of the host.

Utensils

Westerners befuddled by chopsticks will happily note that Thais eat all meals with forks and spoons except for a limited number of Chinese noodle dishes which are handled by chopsticks. The main instrument is a large spoon *(chawn)* held by the right hand, which is filled by a fork *(sawm)* held in the left hand. Food should be pushed in a direction away

PHOTOGRAPHY

*T*hailand is an endlessly photogenic country blessed with lush landscapes, colorful markets, glittering temples, friendly people, and phantasmagoric festivals guaranteed to provide an abundance of photographic possibilities. But to enhance your photographic experience and ensure the highest-quality results, some advance preparation and photographic skills are necessary.

Dragging around camera equipment adds weight and bulk to your pack, the paranoia factor rises since you become a target for thieves, and you will inevitably offend a few people by taking their photo. On the other hand, photography can be an exciting and creative hobby that sharpens visual senses while you search for the perfect photo. Plus, travel memories are forever saved to be shared with friends and family.

Equipment

Serious photographers should consider a high-quality 35mm single-lens-reflex (SLR) camera with two or three interchangeable lenses. Popular choices, such as the Canon EOS A2E, Nikon 8008s, and Minolta Maxxum 9xi, offer all the necessary features including manual and automatic focus, variable film advance speeds, and high-quality interchangeable lenses deemed necessary for professional results. Three lenses will suffice.

Your 28-mm wide angle and 80-250 zoom will probably handle about 90% of your photographic needs, but your 50mm lens is essential when using fast film without a flash in a low-light situation, such as sunsets and the darkened interiors of Buddhist temples.

Pocket Cameras

Travelers ambivalent about photography or fearful of full-sized cameras can substitute a small, lightweight, but high-quality auto-focus camera such as

those made by Canon, Minolta, and Pentax. These rather sophisticated point-and-shoot cameras take excellent photos and cost just US$150-350. Newer models are even fitted with some amazing telephoto lenses. Check out the Pentax IAZoom 928 with its 28-90mm lens, a very sensible zoom range, or the Minolta Freedom Zoom 135EX with its 38-135mm lens.

Polaroid cameras are great for taking instant photographic gifts, especially for children and hilltribe people. Since panoramic film can now be processed at many photo labs in Thailand, you may want to pack along a small disposable panoramic camera as a novelty item.

Film and Processing

Average photographers who shoot judiciously should figure on using two or three rolls of film per week. Active photographers will probably burn up five or more rolls each week. Bring enough film for the first few weeks and then purchase additional film on the road. Film prices and processing fees are comparable to those back home.

Fuji is the most popular 35mm brand of film sold in Thailand, available everywhere in a full range of ASA/DIN ratings. Film choices include Fujicolor and Fuji Super G for prints, Fujichrome and Velvia for color transparencies, Sensia and Provia for professional applications. Fuji films can be processed at one-hour photo stores around the country.

Kodak seems to have surrendered the Asian market to the Japanese. Kodak print and transparency films are more expensive than Fuji and are poorly distributed. Kodachrome is almost impossible to find outside of Bangkok and must be mailed to Australia from Thailand for processing.

To save your film from potential damage by airport x-ray machines, pack it in a film-shield pouch or Ziploc plastic bags and then give the film to the airport

from the body onto the spoon, then lifted into the mouth.

Thais consider it bizarre to eat any type of food with a fork and believe, like the Chinese, that knives *(mid)* belong in the kitchen, not in the dining room.

When finished with the meal, place utensils face down together on the plate or in a 4:20 clockface position to signal that you're finished.

Any other configuration indicates additional food will be consumed and that the waiter should not clear the plates.

Condiments

Tables are generally set with a variety of condiments.

A fermented fish sauce made from anchovies or shrimp paste, *nam pla* is rich in B vitamins

---

security staff for a visual inspection. Airport x-ray machines in some parts of Asia are said to have unpredictable dosage levels that can fog unprocessed film, especially film with ASA ratings of 400 and beyond. Fortunately, the x-ray machines in Thailand appear properly calibrated and customs officials are very cooperative about requests for visual inspections of camera bags and film pouches.

Photo Tips

Photography in tropical countries demands a few guidelines unique to the region. Overexposure, a very common problem, is due to the stronger light diffusion and somewhat different wavelengths found in countries located near the equator. The results are flattened, washed out, and overexposed photographs, especially in the middle of the day when intense sunlight fools the automatic exposure systems of most camera systems. By deliberately underexposing your shots by a half or full f-stop, and by using a polarizing filter, you can increase the vibrancy of your midday photos, put wispy clouds back into the sky, and uncover details often buried in deep shadows.

But the most effective way to produce rich, warm colors and sharply defined forms and textures is to do most of your photography early in the morning or late in the day.

Get close. The single biggest problem with most photographers is they stand too far away from their subject. Sweeping long shots establish the location and provide an overall view, but tightly cropped photos reveal the beauty of form and richness of texture in even the most ordinary of objects. Close-up shots reveal a tactile quality, giving the viewer the feeling he or she can reach into the picture and almost touch the object.

People Photography

Professional travel photographers know people pictures are the universal favorites of almost every-

one; they capture the universality of the human race and confirm the emotional links that form the basic truths of life.

But photographing strangers in a foreign country isn't the easiest task. People may not enjoy the invasion of their personal space or having a camera rudely stuck into their faces. Yet most people enjoy having their photograph taken if they feel they are being admired and respected rather than treated as an exotic trophy.

First introduce yourself and then communicate in a sincere way you want to take a few photographs. Once you make the connection—whether through a few words of the local language or a simple smile—make the best of the moment and take enough photos to really convey the special qualities of your subject. Start with overall shots to put the person at ease and then move in for details of face, hands, clothing, and whatever else makes him or her unique. Some prefer to take photographs in natural and uncontrived settings of subjects unaware of the presence of the photographer. Taking photos without first asking permission requires both boldness and a willingness to possibly ruffle a few feathers. Candid photography is actually less intimidating than commonly presumed, since most Asians may not really mind quick and unobtrusive photos taken with a degree of discretion and sensitivity. The secret is to be *quick*. You should know your camera so well you never need to fiddle with exposure or focus controls.

Subjects will sometimes sense your presence and look in your direction. Don't feel guilty or panic or flee the scene. If the subject firmly declines a photograph, lower your camera and consider this an opportunity to walk up with a greeting. After communicating your sincere interest, ask permission to take a few posed and candid shots. You'll be surprised at how many people will agree to your request.

and protein and is a substitute for salt and pepper in most Thai recipes. Made from salted and fermented fish or shrimp, the translucent brown liquid comes in small bottles or in Chinese sauce dishes filled with chopped chilies *(nam pla prik)* and a squeeze of lime. When combined with additional ingredients, *nam pla* becomes *nam prik*. Fish sauce is to Thai cuisine what soy sauce is to Japanese and Chinese dishes.

Nam som is a vinegar-green chili extract mixed with orange juice to make "sour water." A hot and pungent pepper sauce, *nam prik,* is made from fresh chilies, salt, sugar, vinegar, and any number of optional ingredients. *Thua* can consist of dried beans, peas, or peanuts.

Tipping
Traditional Thai customs do not include tipping, but a smile signals appreciation of the restaurant staff. Good service *(borikan dee)* is considered a given ingredient, though a small tip of 10-20B is appreciated by the underpaid staff. Larger hotels and restaurants that cater to tourists often include a 10-15% tip on the final bill.

SHOPPING

The Tourist Authority of Thailand strongly suggests that all visitors to Thailand shop with great care. Far too many tourists are overcharged and sold fraudulent merchandise with worthless guarantees.

Bargaining
Bargaining is absolutely necessary except in the large department stores. It's challenging and fun—*if* you keep your sense of humor. Haggle with a smile; let the shopkeeper laugh at your ridiculous offer while smiling back at his absurd asking price. Bargaining is a game, not a life-or-death struggle. Expect a discount of 20-30%. As elsewhere in Asia, knowing a few numbers and key phrases will send prices plunging.

Refunds, Receipts, and Guarantees
As a general rule, goods once purchased cannot be exchanged or returned. Deposits are also nonrefundable. Carefully examine all merchandise since receipts and guarantees issued by local retailers are of dubious value after you have returned home.

Touts and Fakes
Touts are paid commissions for rounding up customers. All expenses, including taxi rides and lunches, are added to your bill. Avoid them.

Thailand enjoys a reputation as the Counterfeit Capital of Asia. Most fakes, such as ersatz Lacoste shirts and Cartier watches, are advertised and sold as fakes. More dangerous to your pocketbook is colored glass being peddled as rubies, and newly manufactured Buddhas sold as genuine antiques. Experts at Bangkok's National Museum estimate that 90% of the items sold at the city's antique stores are counterfeit! Unless you are an expert or are prepared to gamble large sums of money, a sound policy is to shun expensive jewelry and pricey antiques.

BEST BUYS

Silk
Thai silk is world famous for both its high quality and beautiful designs. Be cautious, however, of silk fabric being sold at extraordinarily good prices. Cheap silk is often just rayon or rough silk cleverly interwoven with synthetics. A yard of high-quality silk, hand-woven and dyed with modern, colorfast German dyes, should sell for about 500-800B per meter. Check for variations in the size of the silk thread, which gives Thai silk its distinctive uneven texture. Or burn a small piece: synthetics turn to ash but real silk forms little sweatlike beads and does not disintegrate.

Precious Stones
Thailand, once one of the world's primary sources of precious stones, has now almost completely exhausted its domestic supply. Last year Thailand was forced to import over 80% of the gemstones cut in the country, including a worthless milk-white rock called a geuda (corundum) which is found in great quantities in Sri Lanka. When heated to temperatures between 2,912 and 3,272°, this nondescript stone becomes a "sapphire." This scientific process helps

explain the flood of inexpensive sapphires in Bangkok! That's not all. Several years ago it was revealed that Miss Thailand wore a tiara of artificial stones, and letters in the *Bangkok Post* regularly complain about stones being sold at five times their fair value from *government-backed* lapidaries. Little help is offered by the TAT.

The jewelry racket is pushed by friendly, clean-cut students and *tuk tuk* drivers who take you anywhere for just 10B. All are crooks and should be avoided.

The bottom line: if you intend to make a sizable purchase of precious stones in Thailand, ask the jeweler to accompany you to a facility for an independent appraisal. The Tourist Police are completely helpless. The Asian Institute of Gemological Sciences on Silom Road can determine the nature of the stone, but will not offer a monetary valuation. Gem receipts should always be marked "Subject to identification and appraisal by a registered gemologist." Some shops will offer 50% refunds to unhappy customers, but require you to sign a declaration that removes them from all further legal prosecution. You could also pay with a credit card and cancel payments if you have been defrauded.

Antiques

As mentioned before, most Thai wooden antiques are actually clever fakes produced by "instant antique" factories where hundreds of wooden images are carved, treated with special chemicals, and aged under the sun. All antiques, regardless of type or age, can only be exported with written permission from the Antique Art Business Division (tel. 02-224-1370) of the Fine Arts Department in Bangkok. Obtain registration and permission by taking the piece to the Fine Arts Department on Na Prathat Road across from Sanam Luang, together with two six- by nine-cm photographs of the object. An export fee of 50-300B may be charged depending on the piece. This permit must be obtained at least five days in advance of departure. Store owners can often obtain this permit for a nominal fee. Confirm that the shop can handle this process; once the sale has been completed, some shops find little motivation to follow through with the procedure.

Fake antiques do not require export permits. However, since airport customs officials are not antique experts, they often confuse fakes with authentic antiques and block export as you try to get on the plane.

Buddha Images

Thai laws prohibit the export of *all* Buddha images and images of other deities dating from before the 18th century. The only exceptions to this rule are Buddhist amulets. The problem has apparently been misguided tourists who have converted their Buddha images into lamps and doorstops, a sacrilegious act that infuriates Thais. Buddha images can be exported for reasons of

Buddha for sale

religious homage, educational purposes, and cultural exchange programs. Letters of certification issued by your organization must be submitted to the Fine Arts Department in Bangkok.

As a result of government pressure, most Buddhas sold in Bangkok (whether real or fake) are exclusively Burmese images, which are exempt from the law. Rather than worrying about exporting a Buddha, many shoppers opt for images of kneeling monks and female deities.

Hilltribe Handicrafts

Thai hilltribes are well known for their elaborate jewelry, colorful textiles, and esoteric items such as opium pipes and bamboo flutes. All are best purchased in Chiang Mai. Consider your purchases carefully; hilltribe souvenirs which seem exotic in Thailand quickly lose their charm back home. Practical items such as wearable clothing and high-quality handicrafts generally make more sense than a trunkload of cheap and junky oddities.

Other Goods

Bronzeware cutlery sets siliconized to prevent tarnishing are excellent buys in Thailand. Another popular gift is nielloware, a special type of silver inlaid with black enamel designs and crafted into lighters, ashtrays, and bracelets. Celadon pottery, a cottage industry centered in Chiang Mai, attempts to reproduce the sublime glazes of Sawankalok prototypes. Thai lacquerware, similar to Burmese models, is also produced in Chiang Mai.

HEALTH

Thailand is a healthy place and it's unlikely you will lose even a single day to sickness. The secret to healthy travel is adequate preparation, watching your health during your travels, and understanding how to find adequate medical attention in an emergency.

The following information summarizes the possible risks to help you prepare for your trip.

BEFORE YOU GO

U.S. Government Health Advice

Current health recommendations from the United States government can be checked by calling the **Centers for Disease Control** (CDC) in Atlanta, Georgia, at (404) 332-4559 for general information and a printout of fax services, and (404) 639-1610 for malaria tips. The annual CDC publication, *Health Information for International Travel,* is available from the U.S. Government Printing Office at (202) 783-3238.

A handy new service is the **CDC Fax Information Service,** which sends country-specific information to your fax machine in a few minutes. Call (404) 332-4565 and follow the voice prompts for instant advice on disease risk and prevention by region, diarrhea, disease outbreak bulletins, prescription drugs recommended for malaria, the biweekly *Blue Sheets,* and updates on AIDS.

Armed with this information, you'll feel reassured about the situation in Thailand and less willing to purchase unnecessary pills and shots from doctors burdened with yacht payments.

Medical Kit

A small medical kit may be useful for simple problems. Most of the following supplies are available from pharmacies in Thailand but may be difficult to locate in remote villages. Which supplies to carry will depend on the length of your vacation, how remote the regions on your itinerary, and the time of year. Travelers generally need only the following:

• bandages, Band-Aid adhesive bandages, scissors, tweezers
• insect repellent, sunscreen, Chap Stick, foot powder
• Pepto-Bismol tablets
• antiseptic for cuts and grazes
• antihistamine for allergies and colds
• antibiotics as prescribed by your doctor
• malaria pills (if necessary)

Vaccinations

Contact a doctor who specializes in travel medicine for a general health checkup, necessary shots, and perhaps the International Certificate of Vaccination, a small yellow booklet which records your immunizations. Occasionally immigration officials demand this card from visitors arriving from an area infected with yellow fever. The CDC does not recommended a yellow fever vaccination, unless you intend to travel to or from a country in Africa or South America.

Cholera and smallpox vaccination requirements for Thailand have been dropped, though the normal "childhood" vaccinations should be up to date: tetanus, diphtheria, typhoid, measles, mumps, rubella (MMR vaccine), pertussis (DTP vaccine), and polio. Obtain booster shots, if necessary, from your doctor.

A vaccination clinic operated by the Thai Red Cross Society (tel. 02-252-0161) is located in Bangkok at the corner of Rama IV and Henri Dunant Roads.

International Health Certificate

Under the International Health Regulations adopted by the World Health Organization (WHO), a country, under certain conditions, may require from travelers an International Certificate of Vaccination against yellow fever. However, the WHO has recently eliminated the special page for cholera vaccinations, and visitors no longer need an international certificate for entry into Thailand.

INSURANCE

Travel insurance is something many travelers overlook until they face hospitalization abroad or emergency evacuation to medical facilities back home. It may seem unnecessary and overpriced, but a freak accident or serious illness suddenly makes insurance seem like a wise idea.

Finding the right policy at the right price can be tricky. First, review your existing personal insurance policy to find out whether it covers medical treatments and emergency evacuations while traveling overseas. Don't rely on homeowner's insurance, which generally only covers thefts to US$500. Credit cards are limited to flight insurance.

Types of Insurance

Several types of insurance can be purchased from insurance agents, travel agents, student travel agencies, and many tour operators.

Health and Accident Insurance: As mentioned above, check your existing policy for medical coverage overseas. Some policies automatically enroll you with specialized medical-assistance programs described below.

Flight Insurance: Flight insurance sold from machines in airports pays a lump sum to designated beneficiaries if you die on your upcoming flight. Flight insurance is expensive and often unnecessary, and carries worse odds than slot machines in Las Vegas. Flight insurance up to specific limits is automatically provided by all airlines, and tickets purchased with a major credit card also often provide this type of coverage. Save your money for Thailand.

Baggage Insurance: Airline liability is limited to US$20 per kg for checked baggage and US$400 per passenger for unchecked baggage. Additional insurance can be bought directly from the airline at the airport check-in counter, but many expensive items are excluded from their extensive disclaimer policy on the back of your ticket.

Trip Cancellation Insurance: These policies protect you if you are unable to undertake or complete your trip due to personal or medical problems. Read the fine print carefully, especially the sections on family members and denials for preexisting medical conditions.

Default and Bankruptcy Insurance: This insurance covers you in the event that your tour company or other travel supplier fails to deliver the promised services. To avoid problems, purchase tours packaged from a member of the United States Tour Operators Association (USTOA), which provides an insurance policy of US$1 million to reimburse clients in the case of default or bankruptcy. Call the USTOA at (212) 750-7317 for a member list and their brochure on the pros and cons of independent versus organized travel.

Comprehensive Insurance: Several companies sell comprehensive policies with some or all of the coverages described above.

Exclusions, Exclusions, Exclusions

If none of your existing policies cover medical emergencies abroad, ask your agent for additional coverage or request information from another company. Be sure to carefully read the fine print for exclusions and disclaimers designed to protect the financial interests of the insurer, not the policyholder. Some common areas of exclusion include:

Destination Coverage: Some policies exclude remote destinations or regions considered high-risk by the U.S. government. Thailand isn't a problem but Myanmar, Laos, Cambodia, and Vietnam are excluded by some insurance companies.

Emergency Evacuation: The emergency evacuation described on the policy should include all expenses to a medical facility back home, not just to the nearest adequate hospital.

Family Coverage: Check on coverage for family members and travel partners. Most policies have additional fees for family members, children, relatives, and travel partners not related to the insured.

Preexisting Conditions: This is the most common complaint about medical travel insurance policies. Read the fine print carefully; some policies exclude any condition which has been treated by a doctor during the previous six months.

Time Limitations: Many policies have time limits for medical evaluation and treatment. Travelers sometimes wait several weeks to see a doctor for a condition which appeared harmless at the outset, only to discover later their insurance policy had expired one week after their return.

Medical Ceilings and Deductibles: All policies carry maximum amounts for specific conditions and deductibles. As with automobile or life insurance, unrealistic limitations often make medical insurance hardly worth the cost of the premium.

Payments: Check to see whether you are required to pay for medical conditions on the spot and seek reimbursement, or whether the policy makes direct payments to doctors and hospitals.

Activity Exclusions: Adventurous types should note that some policies exclude any activity considered dangerous by the insurance company, such as hang gliding, mountaineering, scuba diving, motorcycling, rafting, sailing, and even trekking. Avoid these policies unless you intend to spend your vacation inside a hotel room.

Travel Insurance Companies
Comprehensive and specialized policies are sold by insurance agents, travel agents, student travel agencies, and tour operators. Once again, read the fine print carefully. The following companies offer medial assistance policies:

International SOS . . . (800) 523-8930
Medex . . . . (800) 874-9125
Near Services . . . . (800) 654-6700
Travel Assistance . . . (800) 821-2828

Try the following for comprehensive insurance policies:

Access America . . . (800) 284-8300
American Express . . . .(800) 234-0375
ARM/Carefree . . . . (800) 323-3149
Mutual of Omaha . . . (800) 228-9792
Near . . . . (800) 654-6700
Travel Guard . . . . . (800) 826-1300
Travel Insured . . . . (800) 243-3174
Wallach . . . . (800) 237-6615

COMMON HEALTH PROBLEMS

Diarrhea
The United States Centers for Disease Control reports that the most frequent problem is common traveler's diarrhea, transmitted by bacteria and parasites found in contaminated food or water. Common sense will minimize the risks: eat only thoroughly cooked food, drink bottled water, wear shoes, resist swimming in fresh waters possibly contaminated with schistomiasis flatworms, and avoid contact with insects, particularly mosquitoes.

Two drugs recommended by the National Institutes of Health for mild diarrhea can be purchased over the counter: Pepto-Bismol Diarrhea Control and Imodium A-D. Both contain loperamide, an antidiarrheal not found in regular Pepto-Bismol.

An alternative to loperamide is three days of a single 500mm dosage of the antibiotic ciprofloxacin, approved by the Food and Drug Administration for traveler's diarrhea.

Hepatitis A
The two main varieties of hepatitis, hepatitis A and B, are highly contagious liver diseases marked by debilitating, long-term symptoms such as jaundice and a feeling of malaise.

Hepatitis A ("infectious hepatitis") is spread by contaminated water and food—conditions common in countries with poor standards of hygiene and sanitation. The disease is transmitted through fecal-oral contact and is often spread by infected food handlers who don't wash their hands. Hepatitis A is a widespread problem in Myanmar, India, Nepal, and Indochina, but is rarely contracted in Thailand by travelers who exercise caution with their drink and food. On the other hand, hepatitis A is serious. Statistics show each infected adult in the United States spends US$2,600 in lost wages, US$700 in medical costs, and an additional US$2,800 for hospitalization. About 20% of those infected experience a relapse and an estimated three percent of adults over 49 years will die from hepatitis A.

Until a few years ago, hepatitis A was regarded as an incurable condition without any effective form of prevention or treatment. A dose of gamma globulin (immune serum globulin) is still the only known antibody which reduces the likelihood of contracting the disease. Gamma globulin's effect wears off after one month, declining to near zero after three months, while also possibly reducing the natural immune systems of the body. Antibiotics administered after infection were useless and other drugs only increased liver damage. The only treatment remained rest and liquids; travelers were told to "go home and rest."

Fortunately, in early 1995, the U.S. Food and Drug Administration approved a new vaccine called Havrix, the first vaccine proven effective in the prevention of hepatitis A. Developed by SmithKline Beecham, Havrix requires two injections one month apart with a booster after six months; it should be taken at least three weeks prior to departure. The newly approved drug is somewhat expensive—US$50-60 for each of the two injections—but recommended for its long-term immunity, estimated to be up to 10 or 15 years. Obtain more information from SmithKline Beecham, tel. (800) 437-2829.

Hepatitis B

Hepatitis B, formerly called serum hepatitis, also affects the liver but is passed through sexual conduct and the exchange of body fluids such as blood or semen.

Hepatitis B is a more serious disease and is of particular risk to homosexuals, intravenous drug users, and health workers who handle body fluids. The disease can cause irreparable liver damage or even liver cancer.

Hepatitis B can be prevented by a course of three shots of vaccine (Hepvac B) over a five-month period, with a booster shot every four or five years.

Malaria

After a general checkup, discuss malaria with your doctor.

The nine-page CDC regional profile on Southeast Asia recently stated that the risk of malaria

culinary creativity?

in Thailand throughout the year is low in all parts of the country, except for limited border areas with Cambodia, Myanmar, and Laos. Another danger spot is the newly developed island resort of Ko Chang near the Cambodian border. Visitors who stick to the standard routes have little risk of exposure and should perhaps avoid powerful anti-malarial drugs.

Travelers who plan to get well off the beaten track—explore remote jungles during the rainy season, camp around equatorial lakes—should take malaria pills, remain well covered, wear dark clothing, use mosquito nets, purchase insect repellents which contain DEET (diethylmeta-toluamide), and faithfully follow the recommended regimen of anti-malarial pills.

Malaria Pills

Prescription drugs recommended by the CDC to treat malaria include chloroquine, mefloquine, doxcycline, proguanil, and primaquine. These drugs resist various strains of malaria with different side effects. About 50% of malaria cases in Thailand are due to *plasmodium falciparum,* a parasite which gives flulike malaise and high fever with shakes, and which if not treated can lead to organ disease, anemia, and even death.

As a general rule, visitors who've been in risk areas should consider any fever as a sign of malaria and seek early diagnosis and treatment for an uncomplicated and complete cure. Malaria clinics are located throughout Thailand; free anti-malarials are provided to those found blood-smear positive. Medical care in Thailand is excellent.

The CDC currently recommends the use of **doxcycline** for travelers intending to spend significant time around the borders of Cambodia and Myanmar. Doxycycline is a more effective drug than mefloquine described below, due to mefloquine-resistant malarial mosquitoes found in the border districts.

Common trade names for doxycycline include Vibramycine, Banndoclin, Doxin, Dumoxin, Interdoxin, and Siclidon. The chief disadvantage to doxcycline is that it must be taken every day at an adult dose of 100 milligrams, beginning the day before entering the malarious area and four weeks after departure. One possible side effect is skin photosensitivity that may result in a sunburn.

Travelers should also ask their doctor about the suitability of **mefloquine,** marketed in the U.S. under the trade name Lariam. The adult dosage is 250 milligrams once a week. Mefloquine has been proven effective against the chloroquine- and Fansidar-resistant strain *P. falciparum,* but is no longer recommended as a malaria prophylaxis due to mefloquine-resistant parasites found in the border areas. Mefloquine in low doses also carries side effects such as gastrointestinal disturbances and dizziness.

Chloroquine is a possible choice for travelers who cannot take mefloquine or doxcycline. The adult dosage is 500 milligrams once a week, starting one week before entering a malarious area, then weekly for four weeks after leaving the area. Chloroquine is marketed in the U.S. under the brand name Aralen and elsewhere as Resochin, Avoclor, Nivaguine, and Kalguin.

Because many mosquitoes in the area have developed an immunity, chloroquine is no longer recommended for visitors to Southeast Asia. It is still effective in the Caribbean, South America, and parts of the Middle East.

The CDC recommends that travelers taking chloroquine should simultaneously take **proguanil.** It's not available in the United States but can be purchased overseas under the brand name Paludrine. The dosage is 200 milligrams daily in combination with a weekly dose of chloroquine.

Fansidar, the trade name for sulfadoxine and pyrimethamine, is a powerful and potentially dangerous drug taken only as temporary self treatment. Fansidar is also sold as Maloprim, the trade name on dapsone and pyrimethamin. The CDC advises that Fansidar should be taken to treat a fever only if professional medical assistance is not available within 24 hours.

Health Concerns for Women Travelers

Female visitors to Thailand should be aware that the extreme heat often brings on unwanted yeast infections. Yeast infection medicine can be difficult to locate in the country's more remote regions, so bring along an ample supply for your trip.

Tampons are available in most larger towns but scarce if you intend to get off the beaten track for any amount of time. Once again, bring an adequate supply and remember to stock up when you're in a larger urban center such as Bangkok or Chiang Mai.

AIDS ALERT

Thailand's sex industry has taken an ominous turn since authorities first detected AIDS in 1984. According to a report issued in 1998 by the head of the European Union's AIDS program in Bangkok, more than one million Thais are HIV-positive, a figure slightly higher than the Health Ministry estimate of 800,000. The same study also showed that more than 222,000 Thais had died of the disease since 1985, compared to the 24,667 deaths reported by the Public Health Ministry. An additional 270,000 Thais have full-blown AIDS but have not yet died of the disease—three times more than the official estimate. The World Health Organization estimates that, by the year 2005, over two million Thais could contract the AIDS virus and up to 500,000 may die from it.

In 1999 the *Far Eastern Economic Review* published an article estimating that AIDs now infects 2.6% of the Thai population, or three to five times the per capita infection rate in the Philippines, India, and Indonesia. Recent international conferences have pointed out the epicenters of the epidemic in Asia are still Thailand and India, which has the highest HIV-infection rate of any country in the world.

In Thailand, AIDS is most commonly spread through heterosexual intercourse rather than anal sex or shared needles. Mechai Viravaidya, former head of the government's anti-AIDS program, estimates that up to 50% of the prostitutes in Thailand carry the virus and up to 10% of the male population is infected. The epidemic is most advanced in the provinces of northwestern Thailand, where government surveys estimate over 75% of the prostitutes carry the AIDS virus and up to 20% of young men aged 20-24 are HIV-positive.

The eeriest quality of the raging epidemic is its invisibility. Most people infected with AIDS or who are HIV-positive do not develop symptoms until years after infection and continue to engage in unprotected sex, unwittingly infecting their partners. A disturbing twist has been the discovery of a new and unusual strain of the AIDS virus that occurs almost exclusively in heterosexuals in northern Thailand and resembles the strains believed to have originated in cen-tral Africa. Some theorize this mutation may explain the rapid spread of AIDS within the Thai heterosexual community.

Initially, the Thai government played down the problem, fearing negative publicity would kill the tourist industry and cut into the nation's largest source of foreign capital. The government claim that the AIDS virus was solely a Western disease soon gave way to a scheme to officially certify prostitutes as clean and ready for work. Another measure restricted HIV-positive people to prescribed activities and movements and threatened detention for those who refused to comply with the orders.

The reality of AIDS finally began to enter the national consciousness in the early 1990s. The man responsible for the new thinking was Mechai Viravaidya, who initiated mandatory radio and TV broadcasts of commercials warning against the dangers of AIDS and popularized the use of condoms so much he was dubbed "The Condom King." Mechai even opened a restaurant—Cabbages and Condoms—near his headquarters in Bangkok. Here he stocks condom key chains and other unique souvenirs. Infection rates fell so dramatically that in 1994 Mechai was awarded the prestigious Magsaysay Award for his remarkable campaign.

Mechai forced the government to accept that the human and economic costs of AIDS far outweighed whatever negative publicity could be incurred by a public campaign against the disease. Mechai's education program—free condoms, school seminars, prostitute outreach programs—so sharply reduced the infection rate that cases now double every two years rather than twice a year as in the late 1980s. The so-called projected vulnerability for AIDS is now estimated to be higher in India, Pakistan, and the Philippines than in Thailand.

The problem with success is that statistics can be used to downplay the situation and provide comforting reassurances to potential visitors. Some tourism officials or others with vested interests dislike public discussion of the problem and somehow wish to turn the clock back to the carefree early 1980s. And statistics can be twisted to prove almost any position on the epidemic.

The fact is Thailand still has a serious problem with AIDS, and the epidemic must remain a cause for concern and ongoing action. AIDS is a worldwide phenomenon; discussions about the problem should not be interpreted as a negative reflection on the country or the character of the people. Sexually active Westerners and Thais alike would do well to practice the only form of safe sex: complete abstinence.

SAFETY

THEFT AND FRAUD

Losing your passport, air ticket, traveler's checks, or cash to a thief can be a devastating experience, but with a certain amount of caution you shouldn't have any problem. Theft in Thailand happens usually by stealth rather than force; armed robbery is rare except in isolated situations. I've traveled for almost 20 years around Southeast Asia and have yet to lose anything of great value.

First, minimize your risk by bringing as few valuables as possible. Leave the expensive jewelry, gold necklaces, flashy camera bags, and other ostentatious signs of wealth at home.

Keep your gear in full sight whenever possible while riding trains or buses and be cautious about pickpockets in crowds, on buses, during festivals, and at boat harbors. A common problem in Bangkok is razor-blade artists on public buses; carry your bag directly in front of you and be extra alert whenever somebody presses against you.

To speed up the replacement of valuable documents, keep duplicate copies of all valuable papers separate from the papers themselves. Immediately report any theft to the local police and obtain a written report including traveler's check serial numbers. This helps you collect on insurance claims after you return home.

Finally, try to maintain a balance between paranoia and trust. Most Thais are extraordinarily honest, so don't worry about everybody who wants to show you around or practice English.

Hotel Security

Check the security of your hotel room and ask for a room with a private lock and lockable windows. Valuables should generally be checked in the hotel safe and an accurate receipt obtained from the front desk. This may not always be necessary in better hotels with good security, but be cautious about fellow travelers in dormitories and other shared living situations.

ILLEGAL DRUGS

Knockout Drugs

Many Western visitors are robbed each year by professional con artists who often spend hours, even days, gaining your confidence before administering a powerful sleeping drug. *Never* accept food or drink from a stranger, and be wary of strangers who offer tours of the city or private boat cruises in Bangkok.

Drug Penalties

Thailand is a country with all sorts of illegal drugs, from marijuana and downers to opium and heroin. The current favorite is speed, which has overtaken the old standbys of opium and heroin.

However, unless you care to spend the next 20 years of your life in prison, don't mess with drugs in Thailand. Local law enforcement officials make little distinction between marijuana and heroin, and penalties are harsh. Several hundred foreigners have been incarcerated in Bangkok and Chiang Mai prisons on drug charges—not pleasant places to spend a large portion of your life. Even the smallest quantities bring mandatory sentences; life imprisonment is common for sizable seizures.

Cautious travelers completely free of drugs sometimes find themselves in serious trouble with the authorities. Raids conducted by uniformed police at popular travelers' hotels in Bangkok and Chiang Mai often involve drugs planted by overzealous officers. Taxi and *tuk tuk* drivers sell drugs to travelers and turn them in for the reward and return of the drug. Arrested, booked, and fingerprinted, the frightened Westerner spends a night in jail before posting a sizable bail and passport as collateral. A few embassies will bail their nationals out of jail and get them on the first plane back home; others leave them to the mercy of the Thai legal system.

The obvious message with illegal narcotics in Thailand is *don't*.

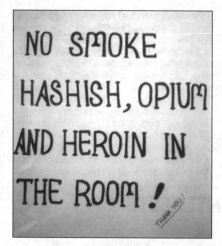

RESOURCES

U.S. Government Travel Warnings
Hear recorded travel warnings 24 hours a day by calling the Citizens Emergency Center of the U.S. State Department at (202) 647-5225. To speak with a human operator, call the Bureau of Consular Affairs at (202) 647-1488 during business hours, 0900-1700 EST. Desk officers (tel. 202-647-2000) may offer additional tips.

However, the most reliable and comprehensive advice is obtained by calling the American embassy in the specific country and asking for the consular section. To obtain these telephone numbers, call the Bureau of Public Affairs at (202) 647-6575 or check the State Department's *Key Officers of Foreign Service Posts* updated three times a year. The booklet costs US$1.75 and is available from Government Printing Office bookstores or by calling the order department at (202) 783-3238.

Legal Aid
Every year 10,000 American travelers are thrown into foreign jails, about one-third on drug charges, the rest for illegal activities such as smuggling or currency violations. Many are unwitting travelers who fail to understand foreign laws or find themselves trapped by corrupt and inefficient legal systems.

Americans arrested abroad have the right to meet with a U.S. embassy official who can make regular jail visits, provide a list of local attorneys, notify friends and family, and relay requests for money and other emergency aid. They can also intercede with local authorities to ensure prisoner's rights are observed. Embassy officials, however, cannot demand an American's release, represent the citizen at trial, give legal counsel, or pay legal fees or fines.

A recent diplomatic initiative created a prisoner-transfer treaty that allows Americans jailed in Thailand to serve their sentences in prisons at home.

Americans arrested abroad should contact their embassy or the Philadelphia-based International Legal Defense Counsel, tel. (215) 977-9982—the only private U.S. organization that specializes in defending Americans arrested in foreign countries. Citizens of the U.K. can contact Prisoners Abroad at 72-82 Rosebury Ave., London EC1R 4RR, tel. (071) 833-3467, fax (071) 833-3467.

WOMEN TRAVELERS

Should women travel alone in Thailand? During my 15 years of traveling around the country, I've talked to countless solo women travelers and most tell me Thailand is one of the safer and more comfortable places for women traveling alone. One reason for this is that Buddhism places great emphasis on respect for females and encourages harmonious relationships between the sexes. Thais are generally shy people who have a deep fear of shame; this discourages much of the sexual harassment common in more religiously fundamentalist countries. Finally, Thailand's crime rate is much lower than that of any Western nation.

However, Thai society has long considered females inferior to beneath men. Thai women are controlled by legal, cultural, and social restrictions. For this reason, many Thai females of the younger generation may be deeply interested in your views on equality and women's rights. It also means that some Thai males will view you as a docile member of a disenfranchised sex. Another viewpoint held by many Thai males is that Western women are morally loose individuals who seek constant sexual satisfaction, an idea created by many pornographic American movies and influential pop idols.

Though Thai males seldom hassle Western females or grope women in public, solo females may experience intimidation and improper behavior by Thai males. The best approach to minimize sexual harassment is to use common sense and follow cultural norms. Attending to your manner of dress is perhaps the first step in preventing unwanted male attention. Dress as conservatively as the location demands; don't show skin except on tourist beaches and Westernized resorts, and remember that modest dress is extremely important in the deep south, where scantily dressed females will find themselves in serious trouble with Muslim authorities.

Women can further minimize sexual harassment by traveling with a Western male; avoiding direct eye contact with Thai men, which is considered an invitation for sex; keeping off lonely streets in the evenings; remaining cool, not flirtatious, with hotel employees and others in the tourism industry; and using humor as a tool to diffuse potentially dangerous situations. Finally, when harassed, groped in public, or verbally abused, yell loudly at the offender. This alerts bystanders and publicly embarrasses the male, who will most likely flee the scene. Don't feel apologetic or worry about being rude—it's your vacation and offensive males should not be allowed to ruin it.

SPECIAL INTERESTS

STUDYING IN THAILAND

International Studies Organizations
Council on International Educational Exchange: America's foremost organization concerned with international education and student travel, CIEE and their travel subsidiary, Council Travel, are excellent sources of information. Ask for *Work, Study, Travel Abroad* for US$13, *Volunteer* for US$9, and the free booklet *Basic Facts on Study Abroad.* Undergraduate programs on Thai history and culture are given at Khon Kaen University. 205 E. 42nd St., New York, NY 10017, tel. (212) 661-1414.

Institute for International Education: The largest educational-exchange agency in America works closely with the U.S. government, the World Bank, universities, private foundations, and corporations to promote international development. Their reference books are expensive but extremely comprehensive. 809 United Nations Plaza, New York, NY 10017, tel. (212) 883-8200.

World Learning (formerly Experiment in International Living): The oldest organization of its kind in the world promotes world understanding through homestays, language training, and graduate study programs. Semester-abroad programs are given in Bali and Chiang Mai. College Semester Abroad, School for International Training, Kipling Rd., Brattleboro, VT 05302, tel. (800) 451-4465.

Universities in Thailand
Applications can also be made directly to universities in Thailand although the response rate is rather dismal. Try the following: Dr. Mathana Santiwat, Academic Affairs, Bangkok University, 40/4 Rama IV Rd., Bangkok 10110; International Students Program, Mahidol University, Nakhon Pathom 73170; International Studies Program, Khon Kaen University, Khon Kaen.

Most of these universities now have websites which explain their programs and tuition fees.

Thai Cooking Courses
Professionally taught courses on the finer points of Thai cooking are now offered by several hotels and private organizations in Thailand. Classes range from one day to a week, and prices start at US$120 per person, per class, depending on the school.

Oriental Hotel Cooking School: Long recognized for its outstanding restaurants, the Oriental Hotel in Bangkok sponsors weekly cooking courses taught by some of the country's most knowledgeable chefs. Classes are held Mon.-Fri. 0900-1200. Oriental Hotel, 48 Oriental Ave., tel. (02) 437-6211.

Other Schools: Chalie's Cooking Thai, 4/2 Sukumvit 1, Bangkok, tel. (02) 225-4605; UFM Food Centre, 593/29-39 Sukumvit 33/1, Bangkok, tel. (02) 259-0620; Modern Housewife Centre, 45/6-7 Sethsiri Rd., Bangkok, tel. (02) 279-2381; Bussaracum Restaurant, 35 Soi Pipat 2, Convent Rd., Bangkok, tel. (02) 235-8915.

Mastering the Language

Several language schools in Bangkok offer courses for foreigners. Tuition fees average about 300B per hour, and most courses last two to six weeks. The following schools also teach English, and sometimes hire foreigners with TOEFL (Teachers of English as a Foreign Language) certification.

American University Alumni (AUA): AUA offers comprehensive group lessons in both Thai and English, sells language tapes and books, has a cheap cafeteria open to the public, and operates a large library filled with Western books and magazines. AUA is the largest English-language school in Thailand. Another AUA branch is located in Chiang Mai. 179 Rajadamri Rd., Bangkok, tel. (02) 252-8170.

Ecoventures Tours & Travel: Ecoventures arranges six-week Thai language courses at the AUA in Chiang Mai for a basic cost of US$300. This includes 60 hours of formal instruction in two-hour segments twice a day. Airfare to Chiang Mai, accommodations, and meals not included. 924 Westwood Blvd., Suite 810, Los Angeles, CA 90024, tel. (800) 543-1230.

Berlitz: Aimed at the business traveler. Two locations in Bangkok: Silom Complex 22nd floor, Silom Rd., tel. (02) 231-3652; Times Square Bldg., 14th floor, Sukumvit Rd., Bangkok, tel. (02) 250-0590.

Union Language School: A small but highly respected school in the Silom area offers the most rigorous and respected Thai-language course in Bangkok. The emphasis is on practical communication rather than theoretical studies. CCT Bldg., 11th floor, 109 Surawong Rd., Bangkok, tel. (02) 233-4482.

YWCA Siri Pattana Language School: This school teaches Thai in an informal setting and prepares foreigners for the advanced *Baw Hok,* the Grade 6 examination required for all *farangs* seeking employment with the public school system. YWCA, 13 Sathorn Tai Rd., Bangkok, tel. (02) 286-1936.

YMCA Nisa Thai Language School: Nisa offers both introductory Thai and preparation for the *Baw Hok* exam, as with the above YWCA Siri Pattana School. YMCA Collins House, 27 Sathorn Tai Rd., Bangkok, tel. (02) 286-9323.

Inlingua: Professional training from a member of a Swiss-based global network of 200 inter-national language schools. Central Chidlom Tower, 7th floor, Ploenchit Rd., Bangkok 10330, tel. (02) 254-7028, fax (02) 254-7098.

Private Instruction: Most of the formal language schools can arrange private instruction in your home or hotel. Private instructors also advertise in the *Bangkok Post,* or you can contact In-Company Language Service at (02) 234-1624.

Cultural Courses

Chulalongkorn University: Thailand's most prestigious university offers an eight-week "Perspectives on Thailand" course on Thai language, culture, and history on their campus in Bangkok. The program is given once a year July-Aug., meets six days a week 0900-1600, and costs US$2,400 including tuition, accommodations, meals, and field trips. Obtain further information from Perspectives on Thailand, Continuing Education Center, 5th floor, Vidhyabhathan Bldg., Soi Chulalongkorn 12, Chulalongkorn University, Bangkok 10330, tel. (02) 218-3393, fax (02) 214-4515.

Oriental Hotel Cultural Programs: Bangkok's finest hotel offers short courses on the history and culture of Thailand. Lectures conducted by leading authorities cost 1,800B daily or 9,000B weekly, and are presented in the afternoons Mon.-Fri. in their annex across the river from the hotel. Choices include Thai Ways (Monday), Thai Beliefs (Tuesday), Performing Arts (Wednesday), Contemporary Thailand (Thursday), and Architecture (Friday). Additional classes are offered on Thai silk painting, gemology, masked dance, music, flower arrangements, meditation, and private tours of the Grand Palace and National Museum. Call (02) 236-0400, ext. 5, for information.

WORKING AND HOMESTAYS

Working in Thailand

Teaching English: One of the few opportunities for working in Thailand is teaching English in Bangkok, Chiang Mai, or other large towns. Pay is very low (US$3-8 per hour) when compared to Japan or Korea (US$10-25 per hour), but you'll have an opportunity to study the culture, attempt to learn the language, and develop friendships with the people.

Teaching opportunities are limited to universities and teachers' colleges, private English-language schools, and fly-by-night operations run from somebody's house. Universities throughout the country pay about US$400 per month plus a small housing allowance. Private English-language schools such as the American University (AUA) and YMCA pay well but the competition is keen. Fly-by-night language schools which advertise in the guesthouses on Khao San Road offer the lowest-paying jobs.

WorldTeach: WorldTeach is a nonprofit social-service program that places volunteer teachers in countries such as China, Costa Rica, Kenya, and Thailand, where over 40 teachers work together with the Population and Community Development Association and Thai Ministry of Education. Programs require a bachelor's degree but previous teaching experience and Thai language skills are not required. Harvard Institute for International Development, One Eliot St., Cambridge, MA 02138, tel. (617) 495-5527, fax (617) 495-1239.

Homestay Programs

Servas: The world's largest homestay program is designed for thoughtful travelers who wish to build world peace and international understanding through person-to-person contacts. Traveler's fees are US$45 annually while hosts contribute US$15 per year. Servas has thousands of host families in Europe and America but only a handful in Asia. 11 John St., Room 706, New York, NY 10038, tel. (212) 267-0252.

Hospitality Exchange: A small but spirited homestay group prominent in America and western Europe, with limited but useful contacts in Thailand. Hosts tend to be college-educated professionals in their mid-forties perhaps acting on cooperative values fostered in the sixties. Membership is only US$15, but you must be willing to be both a host and a traveler. 4908 E. Culver #2, Phoenix, AZ 85008, tel. (602) 267-8600.

The Friendship Force: Founded in 1977 by President Jimmy Carter, this private, nonprofit organization matches travelers and overseas families. For an all-inclusive program fee, including transportation, travelers can live with the families for a week or two and share their lives. Members can also act as hosts for overseas visitors. Membership costs US$18 a year. Call (800) 688-6777 for more information.

VISAS AND OFFICIALDOM

PASSPORTS

American Passports
Essential travel documents include a valid passport and the necessary visa. Passports should be valid for at least six months from the day of entry, though visitors intending to stay longer should ensure their passports are valid for at least one year.

American passports are issued by U.S. Passport Agency offices in 13 cities:

- Boston . . . . (617) 565-6990
- Chicago . . . . . . (312) 353-7155
- Dallas . . . . (214) 653-7691
- Honolulu . . . . . . (808) 522-8283
- Los Angeles . . . . (310) 235-7070
- Miami . . . . (305) 536-4681
- New Orleans . . . . (504) 589-6161
- New York . . . . . . (212) 399-5290
- Philadelphia . . . . (215) 597-7480
- San Francisco . . . (415) 744-4010
- Seattle . . . . (206) 220-7777
- Washington . . . . (202) 647-0518

Passports are also available from some post offices and court houses. Passports are valid for 10 years and cost US$65, renewals US$50. Allow at least five weeks for processing, especially during the busy spring and summer months.

Call the U.S. Passport Information office at (202) 647-0518 for their 24-hour recording about fees, documentation, and other requirements. You can request the brochures, *Passports: Applying For Them the Easy Way* and *Foreign Entry Requirements,* from the Consumer Information Center in Pueblo, CO 81009.

Canadian Passports
Canadians can apply for passports at 28 regional offices as well as post offices and some travel agencies. Passports are valid for five

years; processing usually takes about three weeks. For information on fees, documentation, and other requirements in English and French, call their 24-hour recording at (819) 994-3500 or (800) 567-6868.

Safeguard Your Documents
Losing your passport and other important documents can be a nightmare. Passports can be replaced at overseas embassies and consulates with proof of citizenship, but replacement takes from two days to two weeks depending on circumstances and your nationality. In an emergency, request an immediate temporary traveling permit that allows quick return to your country.

The following precautions will reduce hassles and speed up replacement of important documents. Before you depart, photocopy your passport, airline tickets, identification cards, insurance policies, and credit cards. Leave this information with someone you trust and can contact quickly in an emergency.

While on the road, carry another set of photocopies separate from the original documents to speed replacement after loss. Remember to stash some money in a secret compartment to avoid poverty in the event of a robbery.

VISAS AND ENTRY PERMITS

Visas are stamps placed in your passport by foreign governments that permit you to visit that country for a limited time and for a specified purpose, such as tourism or business. Visas are issued by embassies and consulates located both at home and in most large Asian cities.

Several different types of visas are available, such as tourist, transit, and nonimmigrant. With these visas, you're not allowed to work in Thailand.

The visa situation in Thailand changed dramatically in July 1996 after the Ministry of the Interior approved new immigration regulations that created a free-entry permit good for 30 days. The package also included other visa regulations that offer new benefits for long-term visitors.

30-Day Entry Permit
Nationals from 56 favored nations, who intend to stay 30 days or less and have sufficient funds

and proof of onward passage, may now enter the country without a visa. Immigration officers at the airports in Bangkok, Chiang Mai, Phuket, and Hat Yai will automatically give the permit on arrival. Permits are also given to those who arrive by bus or train from Malaysia and visitors who arrive by cruise ship. This system is essentially an extension of the former 15-day free-entry permit system, which brought complaints from tour operators and hotel chains selling longer excursions.

Citizens from several lucky countries, such as South Korea and Sweden, can stay up to 90 days without a visa in accordance with bilateral agreements between governments. Nationals of another 76 countries, most of which have no existing Thai consulate or embassy, are given 15-day tourist visas on arrival.

Extensions: The 30-day entry permit can be extended for up to 10 additional days, at the discretion of immigration, for 500B. While this may prove useful, travelers who intend to stay longer than 30 days should obtain a 60-day tourist visa, in advance, from a Thai diplomatic mission.

Overstay Fines: Visitors on a 30-day entry permit are generally fined 100B for each day they overstay the limit, up to a maximum of 20,000B. The fines are collected by immigration officers, who conducted a roaring trade from their small glass office at the airport.

60-Day Tourist Visa
The best option for many visitors is the 60-day tourist visa, which costs US$20 and requires a valid passport and three passport photos. This visa must be utilized within 90 days from the date of issuance; do not apply for a visa earlier than three months before your arrival in Thailand.

Extensions: Tourist visas can be extended once for an additional 30 days at the discretion of the Thai immigration office, for a total stay of 90 days. Applicants should dress well and behave politely or run the risk of having their extension denied. As with most countries in the world, immigration officials consider visiting Thailand a privilege, not a right.

To apply for an extension, take three passport photographs, 500B, three copies of the passport pages that show your personal data, visa, and entry stamps to any Thai immigration office in the country. Applications should be made several days prior to the expiration of your visa.

90-Day Nonimmigrant Visa
A 90-day nonimmigrant visa costs US$40 and is available to visitors with valid reasons for extended stays, such as formal research or language studies. This visa must be applied for in your home country and employment in Thailand is forbidden without a work permit. Nonimmigrant visas are not difficult to obtain with the proper paperwork and an acceptable reason—business, study, family visits, religious studies, or

THAI DIPLOMATIC OFFICES

Australia: 111 Empire Circuit, Canberra, ACT 2600, tel. 273-1149
Exchange Bldg., 56 Pitt St., Sydney
464 Saint Kilda Rd., Melbourne

Canada: 85 Range Rd., #704, Ottawa, Ontario, K1N8J6, tel. (613) 237-0476
250 University Ave., 7th Fl. Toronto 110
1155 Dorchester Blvd., #1005, Montreal 102
700 W. George St., 26th Fl. Vancouver

China: 40 Guang Hua Lu, Beijing, tel. 521903 or 522282

Denmark: Norgesmindevej 1B, 2900 Hellerup, Copenhagen, tel. 01-62-50-10

France: 8 Rue Greuze, Paris 75116, tel. 4704-3222

Germany: Ubierstrasse 65, 53173 Bonn 2, tel. (0228) 355065

Hong Kong: 8 Cotton Tree Dr., 8th Fl. Central, tel. 521-6481

India: 56 Nyaya Marg, Chankyapuri, Delhi 110021, tel. 605679
18-B Mandeville Gardens, Calcutta 7000019, tel. 460836

Italy: Nomentana 132, 00162 Rome, tel. 832-0729

Japan: 14-6 Kami Osaki 3-Chome, Shinagawa-ku, Tokyo, tel. 441-1386

Laos: Thanon Phonkheng, Vientiane Poste 128,
tel. 2508, 2543

Malaysia: 206 Jalan Ampang, 504505 Kuala Lumpur, tel. 488222
1 Jalan Tunkoabdul Rahman, Penang, tel. 23352 4426
Jalan Pengkalan Chepa, Kota Baru, tel. 782545

Myanmar: 91 Pyi Rd., Yangon, tel. 82471, 76555

Netherlands: Buitenrustweg 1, 2517 KD, Den Hague, tel. (070) 345-2088

New Zealand: 2 Cook St., Karori, Wellington 5, tel. 735385

Philippines: 107 Rada St., Makati, Manila, tel. 815-4219

Singapore: 370 Orchard Rd., Singapore 0923, tel. 737-2158

Switzerland: Eigerstrasse 60, 3007 Bern, tel. (031) 462281

United Kingdom: 30 Queens Gate, London SW7 5JB, tel. (01) 589-2834

U.S.A.: 2300 Kalorma Rd. NW, Washington, D.C. 20008, tel. (202) 482-7200
801 N. Labrae Ave., Los Angeles, CA 90038, tel. (213) 937-1894,
53 Park Place #505, New York, NY 10007, tel. (212) 732-8166

Vietnam: So Nha El, Kho Ngoai Giao Doan, Hanoi, tel. 56043

media assignments. An official letter from a Thai sponsor or language school is often necessary for approval.

Extensions: The chief advantage to the non-immigrant visa is that extensions may be granted for a total stay of up to one year. To gain extensions, applicants must first collect a number of signatures from Thai sponsors or legal organizations, then pass a series of interviews with immigration officials. Those who arrive well dressed and behave politely seem to have the best success.

After the interviews, successful applicants receive a provisional extension, which might need to be rechecked by local authorities every 10 days over the next three months. This temporary extension may be revoked without warning at any time during this probationary period. At the end of the probation, immigration officials may grant an official extension or ask the applicant to leave the country.

According to recent reports, the extension process is lengthy, but those who dress well and have a good attitude should have few problems.

Extensions for Seniors: Western visitors over 55 years of age may extend their 90-day nonimmigrant visa one year at a time, rather than the 90-day limit for those under 55. You must bring immigration a copy of your passport, one photo, a 500B extension fee, and either proof of financial status or pension. The financial status and/or pension requirement is an annual 500,000B of income for those aged 55-59, but it falls to 200,000B per year for those over 60 years of age.

One-Year Nonimmigrant Work Visa
Thai immigration recently created a new type of visa to make life somewhat easier for qualified Westerners working in the kingdom. This "non-B" visa allows unlimited entries into Thailand for one year, though the country must be left at least once every 90 days to maintain validity of the visa.

This visa is intended for serious businessmen who can meet minimum requirements such as an investment of 15 million *baht* and a minimum of four Thai employees.

Re-Entry Permits
Visitors intending to exit, then re-enter Thailand—and who want to avoid time-consuming

delays at overseas Thai immigration offices—can obtain a re-entry permit from any Thai embassy or consulate. This is a sensible option for travelers heading to Myanmar and who wish to return without trekking over to the Thai embassy in Yangon.

Re-entry permits cost 500B at the Thai Immigration Department on Soi Suan Plu (tel. 02-286-4231) in Bangkok, just off Sathorn Thai Road.

Tax Clearance Certificates
All visitors who earn an income in Thailand must obtain a tax-clearance certificate from the Revenue Department before permission is granted to leave the country. Revenue departments are located in every provincial capital and in Bangkok (tel. 02-281-5777, 282-9899) on Chakrapongse Road near Democracy Monument.

The previous tax regulation required all visitors who stayed more than 90 days in a cumulative year to obtain an annual tax clearance certificate. This decree forced many expatriates on annual pilgrimages to neighboring destinations such as Vientiane or Penang to straighten out their paperwork. The government finally scrapped the regulation in 1991 and replaced it with more realistic policies.

Long-Term Residency
Many expatriates in Thailand remain afloat only with the constant juggling of permits and papers. Visitors who consider jumping ship should be aware that the Thai government officially issues visas and permits for extended stays over 90 days only for a limited number of reasons.

Approved reasons for extended stays up to one year are concentrated in the fields of work or study, religious work, science, skilled labor, and other "approved investments." The bureaucratic process to obtain permission for extended residency is often tedious and confusing for hopeful *farangs,* though the number of approved professions and industries expanded dramatically in 1998.

Work permits necessary for residency are tough to get in most cases. The procedure requires almost 20 applications and statements including a description of the company business, a list of alien workers and their valid work permits, employment contracts, letters of guarantee for commercial registration, trade agreements, company shareholders, supporting letters from public enterprises, business verification, export receipts, legal documents, and financial statements for the previous three years.

Teaching permits require the submission of a work permit, employment contract, and job description, plus letters of guarantees from personal references, the school, and governing committees of the local community.

Marriage, the final hope for some, isn't as easy as you might imagine. Nonresidents married to Thai citizens must produce spousal house papers *(tabeun bahn)*, identification cards, the marriage certificate and marriage registration in Thai translation, photocopies of all pages in each passport plus photocopies of all arrival cards, bank statements with authentic stamps, bank guarantees ensuring a minimum balance of 250,000B, and letters from national embassies certifying adequate financial status.

Residency in Thailand is only for the brave and determined.

Permanent Residency

Westerners who hold nonimmigrant visas and have resided in Thailand for three continuous years may apply for permanent residency at the immigration office in Bangkok. Those who are granted this special application must carry, at all times, an alien identification card.

CUSTOMS AND CURRENCY CONTROLS

Customs upon Arrival

Thailand prohibits the import of drugs, guns, pornography, and harpoons for underwater fishing. Otherwise, customs officials allow you to bring in a reasonable amount of clothes, toiletries, photographic equipment and five rolls of film, business equipment such as laptops and power drills, a carton of cigarettes, and a liter of your favorite booze. These are duty free, but valuable merchandise should be declared to avoid problems on departure.

Customs officials sometimes question visitors carrying expensive gadgets which could be profitably resold in the country. Those bringing in a single stereo or digital assistant are usually allowed to pass, though a refundable deposit may be required from suspicious types. Expensive merchandise imported in large quantities (a dozen Rolexes, six Nikons) will be confiscated and held until your departure.

Exchange Controls

All visitors to Thailand are legally required to bring a minimum amount of currency as determined by their visa category. Visitors who arrive without a visa and receive the 30-day entry permit are required to bring at least US$250 in cash, traveler's checks, bank draft, or letter of credit. The same sum is required for visitors with a 60-day tourist visa. This formality is rarely enforced and immigration officers only check backpackers who arrive with one-way tickets and appear to be potential basketcases. As with all officialdom in Thailand, clean dress and a pleasant demeanor make the wheels of travel turn smoothly.

Thailand specifies no legal limit on the amount of Thai or foreign currency brought into or exported from the country, but amounts over US$10,000 or 50,000B must be declared with customs officials.

Customs upon Departure

Thailand has few restrictions on exported items except for images of Buddha and other religious deities. The purpose is to prevent Buddhas from ending up as lamp fixtures or garden decorations in some *farang's* home. The only exception is small Buddha images worn around the neck as amulets.

Buddha images may also be exported by worshipping Buddhists and those involved with cultural exchanges and academic pursuits. To legally export a Buddha or fragment of a religious deity, a license must be obtained from the Fine Arts Department of the Bangkok National Museum, the Chiang Mai National Museum, or the Songkhla National Museum. The application requires sending two postcard-sized photos of the frontal view of the Buddha image, and a photocopy of your passport to the Fine Arts Department. Allow five days to complete the application process.

Judging from the number of Thai Buddhas in art shops around the world, regulations against their exportation appear less than effective. Some claim Thai art dealers, in tandem with government officials, falsify documents for quick and easy export to foreign collectors around the world.

The same regulations regarding Buddhas also apply to anything considered an "antique" in Thailand. All antiques—whether of Ban Chiang vintage or produced last week in somebody's backyard—must be duly registered with the Fine Arts Department of the National Museum to obtain an export license. The problem is that customs officials at the Bangkok Airport are less than fully trained in recognizing antiques and often confiscate anything that appears of great value or great antiquity.

U.S. Government Customs
Residents of the United States, including each member of the family regardless of age, may bring home US$400 worth of foreign goods duty-free. Goods may be pooled among family members to maximize the legal exemption. A flat 10% duty applies to the next US$1,000 worth of goods; above US$1,400 the rate varies according to the merchandise. In addition, travelers may bring back duty-free one liter of alcohol, 100 non-Cuban cigars, 200 cigarettes, and antiques and works of art more than 100 years old.

Canadian Customs
Canadians may bring back C$300 worth of goods duty-free provided you have been out of the country more than seven days. Canadians should check on other rules regarding time limits and exemptions by contacting the Revenue Canada Customs, Excise and Taxation Department, 2265 St. Laurent Blvd. S, Ottawa, Ontario, K1G 4K3, tel. (613) 957-0275. Ask for the free brochure, *I Declare*.

OTHER USEFUL DOCUMENTS

International Student Identity Card (ISIC)
The green-and-white ISIC card brings very few airline or hotel discounts in Southeast Asia, but is very useful in Europe and the United States. The card, however, can be recommended for the insurance policies which cover up to US$3,000 in total medical expenses as well as US$100 per day in a hospital. The annual fee for the card is US$16.

Students 12-25 years of age can apply at any of the 43 offices of Council Travel Services (tel. 212-661-1450), STA Travel (tel. 800-777-0112), Let's Go Travel (tel. 800-553-8746), and the Canadian student travel agency, Travel CUTS (tel. 416-798-CUTS). The ISIC Association Head Office (tel. 45-33-93-9393) is P.O. Box 9045, 1000 Copenhagen, Denmark.

International Drivers License
An international drivers license is required to rent cars and motorcycles in Thailand. International car rental agencies such as Avis and Hertz follow the rules, but motorcycles can generally be rented without the license. International permits are available from any office of the Canadian or American Automobile Association (AAA).

International Youth Hostel Card
Though invaluable in Europe and expensive in Asian countries such as Japan, the IYHF card is of very limited use in Thailand, which only has a handful of hostels. Youth hostel offices throughout the world sell membership cards and their *International Youth Hostel Handbook* to Africa, America, Asia, and Australasia.

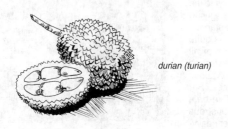

durian (turian)

MONEY

Smart travelers bring a combination of cash, traveler's checks, credit cards, and a bank ATM (Automatic Teller Machine) card. Each has its own advantages and drawbacks depending on the circumstances.

Cash is useful in emergencies, so stash a few U.S. twenties in your pack, well removed from your main money supply. Traveler's checks remain the favorite form of money despite the growing popularity of bank cards. Credit and debit cards used for withdrawals from bank ATMs are slowly becoming a feasible alternative to traveler's checks, though a few kinks need to be worked out before traveler's checks can be completely discarded. Finally, visitors staying longer should consider opening a bank account in Thailand to earn interest on their traveler's checks and provide easy access to instant cash.

The secret to successful money management is to keep your money working in interest-bearing accounts, minimize fees for transfers of funds, demand commission-free traveler's checks, and bring along a credit or debit card.

THAI CURRENCY

Thailand's basic unit of currency is the *baht* (B) divided into 100 *stang*. Coins are issued in one, two, five, and ten *baht* denominations. The 25 and 50 *stang* coins are rarely seen due to their low value and general scarcity. Shopkeepers compensate by routinely rounding prices off to the nearest *baht* or giving sweets in lieu of *stang*.

Thai coinage is quite confusing. Coins of all values have been issued over the years in various shapes and sizes. For example, the five-*baht* coin, once a monstrous nickel-and-copper heavyweight, is down to the size of an American quarter. The one-*baht* coin has gone from the size of an American quarter to the size of an American dime. And 10-*baht* coins are smaller but more valuable than one-*baht* coins.

To further confuse matters, old coins stamped with Thai script continue to circulate amid new coins stamped with both Thai and English script.

The results can be bizarre. A fistful of change might include two sizes of copper 25 and 50 *stang* coins, three sizes of silver one-*baht* coins (only the middle size works in public phones), three completely different five-*baht* coins (one has nine edges, one a copper rim, and the other is all silver), and a copper-and-silver 10-*baht* coin designed with a small brass center encircled by a silver ring.

Fortunately, paper currency bears Arabic numerals and is printed in different colors and different sizes. Denominations include 10B (brown), 20B (green), 50B (blue), 100B (red), 500B (purple), and 1,000B (beige). Currency should not be defaced, crumpled up, or otherwise mistreated in public since all notes feature images of the king and denigration of the royal family is among the greatest of all cultural taboos.

Exchange Rates

The Thai *baht* once was pegged to a basket of currencies heavily weighted toward the dollar. It remained extremely stable, vis-à-vis the dollar, until the currency crisis of 1997-98. The eco-

nomic meltdown of Thailand and the remainder of Southeast Asia forced the Bank of Thailand to finally abandon its monetary defense of the *baht* and accept new exchange levels as set by international forces.

The *baht* fell from its long-standing exchange rate of 25 per dollar to as low as 57 per dollar in early 1998. By late 1998, an improving economy and stabilizing measures introduced by the government of Chuan Leekpai had improved the exchange rate, at least from the standpoint of Thai citizens.

The rate stood at around 38 Thai *baht* per U.S. dollar in early 1999, though daily and ongoing fluctuations mean you will find a different rate on your arrival.

There is no black market for *baht* and therefore no reason to bring in large amounts of Thai currency.

Maximizing your Rate

The subject of exchange rates is popular for almost all visitors, whether student backpackers or wealthy clients attached to an escorted tour.

Traveler's checks bring slightly higher rates than cash, and larger-denomination checks bring higher rates than lower denominations. Note that all currency exchanges are subject to the same 20B commission fee. Exchange rates are higher in Bangkok than in smaller towns, and higher in Thailand than outside the country.

Banks and legal moneychangers post higher rates than hotels, guesthouses, rail and bus stations, shopping centers, and the corner liquor store. Bank rates vary slightly depending on the bank. Exactly which banking system offers the highest rate is subject to debate, though some financial sleuths claim higher rates are consistently given at Thai Farmers Bank and Bangkok Bank. Actually, it varies from town to town and probably depends more on local economies than on a unified banking policy.

You'll get a slightly higher rate inside a bank building than from mobile exchange offices located outside on the front lawn or sidewalk. Other currency booths, however, are conveniently located in the most unlikely spots—remote piers, next to the beach, at festivals and parades—and often stay open until 2100 or 2200, perfect hours for that late-night bowl of *tom yam gai*.

A popular misconception is that exchange rates at the Bangkok airport must be grossly unreasonable. Actually, rates at the airport are excellent and, aside from convenience, there's little reason to bring bushels of *baht* from home. On arrival, exchange enough at the airport to cover your ride into town and your first few days of basic expenses.

Value-Added Tax

Several years ago, Thailand introduced a seven percent value-added tax (VAT) to the *retailer's* cost of certain goods and services. The measure was designed to replace the nine percent graduated business tax and to reduce net prices for consumers.

Few merchants understood the tax and many shops immediately tacked a seven percent tax onto the *consumer's* price of goods, creating confusion and anger among shoppers who resented the price gouging. Most merchants now understand the law but some continue to illegally add VAT surcharges to the bills of unwary customers. Shoppers should point out that VAT surcharges are illegal and report uncooperative shop owners to the TAT police.

The government also has a VAT refund plan for tourists, so if you intend to spend a great deal of money in the country, inquire with your hotel or the tourist office for details.

TRAVELER'S CHECKS

Most of your currency will probably be in traveler's checks, the familiar standby that provides a degree of safety and fairly quick refunds when lost or stolen. The most widely recognized brands are American Express, Bank of America, Citicorp, Thomas Cook, Visa, and MasterCard. Most of your checks should be in larger denominations, such as US$50s and US$100s, to minimize paperwork and garner the slightly higher exchange rates given over smaller denominations. Bring a few smaller checks to cash when exchange rates are dismal and to minimize the aggravation of excess currency at the end of your trip.

Keep a list of serial numbers and an accurate record of each exchange. This provides a running balance of your finances and helps speed up the refund process in the event of loss.

Fees

Traveler's checks are safe and convenient but they certainly aren't free. Most banks and commercial issuers charge one to three percent for purchase, then keep all accrued interest until the checks are cashed. Banks make far more profit using your float than whatever sales fees they might collect. These fees can be minimized by purchasing only commission-free checks and keeping your funds in interest-bearing accounts until the moment of transfer.

MONEY TRANSFERS

Money can be transferred from banks, private companies, and stock brokerage firms at home to financial institutions in Thailand. Be sure to open an account prior to departure and request a list of their international affiliates. Ask about all transfer fees and for suggestions on more economical methods of receiving money abroad.

Bank Transfers

Bank transfers by telex are safe and fast but quite expensive due to mandatory service charges, US$20 per transaction; telex fees, US$20 each way; commissions on traveler's checks, one to three percent; and currency spreads between the buy and sell rates. Bank fees for wire transfers average 6-10% or US$60-100 per US$1,000.

Transfers by mail take two or three weeks but eliminate the need for expensive telexes.

American Express

American Express MoneyGrams can be sent and received from any participating AMEX Travel Office. You don't need to be a cardholder. The first US$1,000 may be paid by credit card but additional amounts must be paid in cash. MoneyGrams take about 30 minutes, and funds can be picked up in either local currency or U.S. dollar traveler's checks.

MoneyGram service fees of 4-10% are based on the amount of funds transferred, the final destination, and method of payment. This means you'll pay US$40-100 per US$1,000, or about the same rate as bank transfers by telex.

AMEX cardholders can withdraw funds directly from their home account up to a limit of

US$1,000 per week. This can be an economical alternative to MoneyGrams or wire transfers through banks. For more information and overseas AMEX locations, call (800) 926-9400 in the U.S. and (800) 933-3278 in Canada.

Western Union

Money can also be wired from Western Union to representative offices in Thailand. To wire money, take cash or a cashier's check to the nearest office of Western Union. Transfers take about 30 minutes. You can also use your Visa or MasterCard by calling (800) 325-6000 in the U.S. or (800) 321-2923 in Canada. Service fees range 4-10% depending on the amount transferred and method of payment.

Brokerage Firms

Another option is to open a managed account at a large investment firm such as Merrill Lynch and use their international transfer services. Many travelers claim this is the fastest and most economical way to transfer funds.

International Money Orders

The Thai postal service has reciprocal agreements with 27 countries abroad, including the U.S., Canada, Great Britain, and Australia. Transfers take one day from your post office back home to a major destination such as Bangkok or Chiang Mai. Allow three or four days to post offices in smaller towns.

U.S. Embassies

Emergency funds *only* can be sent abroad through U.S. embassies or consulates. Fees are US$15-40 per US$1,000. More details are provided in the U.S. government brochure, *Sending Money to Overseas Citizens Abroad.* Call (202) 647-5225 or fax (202) 647-3000.

CREDIT CARDS

Smart travelers carry credit cards for several reasons. First, they're invaluable for major purchases such as airline tickets and electronic equipment since you don't need to haul around buckets of cash or a suitcase packed with traveler's checks. Credit cards provide interest-free loans until the bill arrives back home. Just be sure to make arrangements to have a friend or family member pay the bill if you're staying an extended amount of time.

Credit cards are also useful for instant cash advances from banks in Thailand. For example, you can walk into any branch of Thai Farmers Bank, present your credit card to the clerk, fill out a short form, and quickly pocket up to US$500 in *baht.* Another advantage is that funds are normally converted into *baht* at the favorable interbank foreign exchange rate, the wholesale benchmark used by international banks.

Cash advances have some drawbacks. Advances are considered loans—not lines of credit—and interest charges accrue from the moment of transaction.

This biggest possible danger is that cash advances completed overseas often carry much higher transactions fees than similar services in the West. *Always inquire about the transaction fee!* If the fee is more than two or three percent of the total transaction, move to another bank.

Credit Card Guarantees

Warning: purchase protection is less than most travelers would assume.

Perhaps the blame lies with the aggressive marketing campaigns of the card companies or the general naivete of the public, but anyone contemplating large overseas purchases by credit card should read the fine print, very carefully. United States law states that credit card companies must provide a degree of protection against defective, switched, unauthentic, and inferior goods, but only on items purchased in your home state or within 100 miles of your home address. Did you notice this caveat on your credit card application?

On overseas purchases, credit cards only help with items that never arrive. There are no legal protections against defective, switched, and unauthentic merchandise purchased overseas with a credit card.

In most cases, the customer pays by credit card and agrees to let the merchant ship the items back home. Upon arrival (if it arrives at all), the customer discovers the item to be either defective, broken, or switched with an inferior replacement. The cardholder then turns to the credit card company for help. The card company attempts to resolve the issue by con-

tacting the merchant by mail or phone, but companies are helpless if the merchant quibbles or fails to respond to their inquiries. The cardholder is not only stuck with the merchandise, but also legally obligated to pay the bill.

The most straightforward solution is to hand-carry all purchases back home. Otherwise, ask for an itemized invoice that details exactly what you bought, the date of purchase, and all shipping and insurance costs. Take several photographs of the store owner and yourself standing next the item. Write down the merchant's name, address, and phone number, and all other verbal guarantees. Detailed paperwork often helps settle problems with recalcitrant merchants.

Credit Card Fraud

American Express reports that Thailand has the highest ratio of fraudulent-to-legitimate cards of all its markets, second only in total monetary value to the United States.

Hotel Scams: Far too many visitors return home to discover that large bills have been run up by dishonest hotel employees who remove cards from stored luggage or hotel safes, then go on shopping sprees with the cooperation of unscrupulous merchants. You return home to find that you somehow purchased 20 color TVs and 16 stereo systems during your brief visit to Thailand.

Credit cards should be carefully guarded and carried on your person at all times. Whenever cards are checked with baggage handlers or in hotel safes, be sure to tightly seal all financial documents in theft-proof compartments and obtain a complete receipt of valuables, including credit cards and the serial numbers of all traveler's checks. Carefully inspect the contents of your package when you reclaim your valuables from the front desk or baggage storage room.

Duplicate Receipts: Fraud is also practiced by dishonest merchants who surreptitiously run cards through machines several times to produce multiple copies. The merchant then fills out the extra copies, forges your signature, and submits the receipts to a bank for collection.

The best prevention is to keep an eye on your credit card during purchases. Don't let the merchant disappear into a back room, and do remember to destroy all carbons after the transaction.

Illegal Surcharges: Merchants sometimes add illegal surcharges to credit card purchases, such as value-added taxes (VAT) and merchant fees from three to five percent collected by the credit card company. Both practices are against Thai law and violate the legal agreements signed between the merchant and credit card company.

Customers charged such fees should immediately object and demand that all surcharges be eliminated from the bill. If the merchant refuses but you still want the item, ask for an itemized receipt that clearly states the cost of the product and the amount of surcharge. After your return home, submit photocopies of these receipts to your credit card company for a refund.

Lost Cards: Travelers who lose credit cards issued by Western or Thai banks should immediately contact the appropriate representative in Bangkok. Some major companies include: American Express, tel. (02) 273-0022 or 273-3660; Diners Club, tel. (02) 238-3660 or 236-7455; Visa and MasterCard, tel. (02) 246-0300; Thai Farmers Bank, tel. (02) 271-0234 or 273-1199; Siam Commercial Bank, tel. (02) 256-1361.

ATM WITHDRAWALS

A sensible alternative to carrying around wads of cash is to withdraw funds from ATM machines with a credit or debit card issued by a domestic or foreign bank. ATMs dispense cash 24 hours a day, seven days a week, then charge your credit card or debit your bank account. Debit cards are more widely honored than credit cards at Thai ATMs.

Debit cards are issued by banks in conjunction with either the Cirrus system owned by Visa or the PLUS system owned by MasterCard. Your MasterCard/Cirrus card will work at over 160 ATM machines located in airports, major hotels, and branches of Bangkok Bank and Siam Commercial Bank. The Visa/PLUS debit card works at regional ATMs and branches of Thai Farmers Bank. To obtain an international ATM directory, call MasterCard/Cirrus at (800) 424-7787 or Visa/PLUS at (800) 843-7587.

The most versatile and widely honored cards are those issued by either Thai Farmers Bank or Bangkok Bank. Both banks' ATM cards work at the ATMs of 15 other banks connected to a national system of interlocking networks. The two major ATM systems in Thailand—Siam Net and Bank Net—link over 1,500 ATMs across the country. Visitors spending a month or so in Thailand should seriously consider opening a local bank account and obtaining a debit card.

Daily withdrawal limits are predetermined by your bank, but usually range US$100-200 per day. Many machines have instructions in English on the screen or posted nearby. Thai *baht* is given but your account is debited in your national currency at favorable exchange rates.

Ghosts in the Machine
A few problems exist with automatic teller machines. Many ATMs in Asia do not have the ability to ask whether you want the money withdrawn from your checking or savings account, but will automatically try the primary (usually checking) account. Contact your institution prior to departure to ensure that sufficient funds are in your primary account and that your card withdraws from the correct account. It can be an unpleasant surprise to discover that your card is programmed to withdraw funds from your checking account when all your money is in your savings account.

Another consideration: overseas ATMs often do not accept PIN numbers longer than four digits. Travelers with six-digit PINs should ask their bank to reprogram their card with a four-digit number.

Finally, consider the fees. ATM withdrawals carry transaction fees, either flat fees demanded by the institution that issued the card, or transaction fees based on the amount of withdrawal. Visa and MasterCard fees are determined by the issuing bank, American Express charges a minimum of two percent or US$2 per transaction, Diners Club charges three to four percent.

THAI BANK ACCOUNTS

Visitors who intend to stay a substantial time in Thailand should open a bank account and obtain a debit card with either Thai Farmers Bank or Bangkok Bank. Both banks have branches with ATMs in every possible town and village. As noted above, cards issued by these banks also work at the ATMs of 15 other banks affiliated with the interlocking networks of Siam Net and Bank Net. Bank cards eliminate the paranoia associated with carrying huge amounts of traveler's checks and reduce the hassle of constantly depositing valuables into hotel safes.

Bank accounts can be opened in less than 15 minutes by depositing cash or traveler's checks and providing a permanent address such as an apartment number or other local contact. Room numbers in guesthouses and hotels are not considered permanent addresses.

MEASUREMENTS AND COMMUNICATIONS

MAIL

Thailand has a fairly efficient postal service when compared to those of many other countries in Southeast Asia. However, several expatriates have complained that mail service has deteriorated to the point where a sizable percentage of letters now fail to reach their destinations. To improve the odds, all letters mailed from Thailand should be sent as registered mail. The registration fee is only 20B, a small price to pay for peace of mind.

Mail can be sent to any town or city in Thailand, where postal agents at the central station hold mail for customer pickup. Airmail takes 7-10 days to Bangkok and somewhat longer to outlying destinations.

Letters should be marked "hold" and addressed to poste restante, the French term for general delivery. Since Thais write their last name first and their first names last, postal clerks sometimes misfile letters under your first name rather than your last name. To ensure proper delivery, last names should be both capitalized and underlined on the outside of the envelope. In the event you are missing anticipated mail, ask the postal clerk to check the letter section for your first name.

An example of a proper address: Carl PARKES, Poste Restante, GPO, Bangkok, Thailand. Zip codes are rarely used in Thailand.

When picking up mail, bring your passport or other legal identification to the poste restante counter. The service fee is 1B for each piece of mail, 2B per parcel. Letters held over three months are returned to the sender.

Mail can also be sent to hotels for safekeeping and to guesthouses, which tack the envelope up on bulletin boards. Most embassies and consulates refuse to accept mail except in emergency situations. Travelers with an American Express credit card or using American Express traveler's checks can receive mail at the AMEX office (tel. 02-251-4862) in Siam Center, Suite 414, 965 Rama I Rd., Bangkok. A complete list of AMEX offices is available from AMEX (tel. 800-528-4800) in their booklet, *Travelers Companion*.

Postal Hours
The Bangkok GPO is open weekdays 0800-1800, weekends and holidays 0900-1300. The address for the Bangkok General Post Office is GPO, Charoen Krung Road, Bangkok, Thailand. Provincial post offices elsewhere in Thailand are open weekdays 0830-1630 and Saturday 0900-1200.

Postal Rates

Airmail from Thailand takes 10-14 days, mail by sea requires three or four months. All mail should be registered and receipts retained to trace missing parcels. All valuable parcels should also be insured at t he rate of 10B per 2,000B value of goods.

Rates for parcels over one kg are determined by weight in one-kg increments, by country of destination, and by method of delivery (airmail or surface). Maximum weight is 20 kg. Postal rates to the United States and Europe are almost identical.

POSTAL RATES
All rates in *baht*

ZONE	POSTCARD	FIVE-GRAM LETTERS	10-GRAM LETTERS
Asia	7.00	9.50	10.50
Oceania	8.00	10.50	12.50
Europe	8.00	11.00	13.50
Africa	8.50	11.50	14.50
North America	9.00	11.50	14.50
South America	9.50	12.00	15.50

Parcel Post

All packages must be officially boxed and sealed at special counters inside the main post office or at nearby private agencies. Don't pack a box and expect to just drop it at the post office.

Bring all goods to the post office for inspection. Assuming you aren't smuggling drugs or rare antiques, you may then purchase a cardboard box and string, pack your goods, weigh the contents, purchase stamps, and deliver your assembled masterpiece to the appropriate window.

Packing services situated inside larger post offices do all the work for a reasonable fee. Private packing agencies located nearby can help with the packing and shipping of parcels that weigh over 20 kg.

Packages that require overseas delivery within four days can go via the Express Mail Service (EMS) offered at major post offices. The cost is 320B per 250 grams, or US$22 per pound.

Shipping Services

From the United States, Federal Express delivers to 10 cities in Thailand and DHL delivers to almost 20 destinations. To find out more details about commercial shippers before you go, in the United States call DHL, tel. (800) 225-5345; Federal Express, tel. (800) 463-3339; or UPS, tel. (800) 742-5877.

Overseas delivery services are also offered by commercial shippers such as DHL and Federal Express. Deliveries are fast and dependable but somewhat more expensive than deliveries by government postal services. The average shipping charge from Thailand costs US$24-28 per pound, but worldwide delivery is guaranteed within three or four days, pending customs delays.

The following companies in Bangkok provide guaranteed deliveries to both domestic and international destinations: DHL, tel. (02) 286-7209, 207-0600; Federal Express, tel. (02) 235-8602, 367-3222; TNT Express, tel. (02) 249-5702, 249-0242; UPS, tel. (02) 285-4422; GDM, tel. (02) 285-3512.

TELEPHONE

The Telephone Organization of Thailand (TOT) under the authority of a government agency appropriately called the Communications Authority of Thailand (CAT) operates the phone system. Telephones are fairly reliable except during floods and thunderstorms when connections can be cut for periods of a few hours to several days.

International telephone offices, located in the GPOs of major provincial capitals, are open daily 0700-2300. Phone offices in smaller towns are open daily 0800-2000 or 0800-2200. The Bangkok CAT Telecom Center at the GPO on Charoen Krung Road is open every day, around the clock.

A few idiosyncrasies surround the telephone system in Thailand. Thai telephone area codes always begin with a zero. For example, the area code for Bangkok is 02 and the code for Chiang Mai is 053. This zero is used for calls inside the country but *dropped for international calls or faxes to the country.* For example, to reach Bangkok from the United States you first dial 011 (the international access code), 66 (Thailand's country code), and 2 (city code). Don't dial 02. This is why hotels in Bangkok always list their phone number with a 662 prefix rather than 6602.

Another confusing fact: telephone numbers often have several different final digits to handle multiple incoming calls. Therefore you'll often see strange phone numbers such as 233-4501-09 or 233-4401/09. Advanced multiline systems are still considered an exotic technology in Thailand.

Another vexing problem is that telephone numbers seem to change with the seasons, a horrible curse cast upon society by the TOT. Not only do numbers change quickly, telephone directories list people by their first names rather than their family names.

Finally, travelers attempting to make hotel reservations or contact a business in Thailand will have better luck sending a fax or e-mail rather than attempting a phone call. Faxes eliminate language barrier difficulties and produce a hard copy that hotel receptionists can decipher in their free time. E-mail is even better since it's free and a guaranteed way to find out if your message was received.

International Calls to Thailand

International calls to Thailand from the United States are placed by dialing the international access code for calls from America (011), the country code for Thailand (66), the area code for the particular city (drop the zero), and finally, the local number. To make an operator-assisted call including person-to-person, collect, or calling card, dial the international access code for operator-assisted calls (01) and give the country code for Thailand (66), the area code, and local telephone number.

Before calling Thailand and waking your friends or business partners at some hellish hour, you might consider the time differential. For more information, refer to the section on "Time" in this chapter.

International Calls from Thailand

International calls from Thailand are made by dialing the international access code for Thailand (001), followed by country code, area code, and finally the local number.

The cheapest international calls are made through discount calling plans offered by AT&T, MCI, and Sprint. Phone calls made from CAT Telecom Centers are the next cheapest option, followed by private telephone booths and public phones.

Phone calls made from hotels are generally the most expensive option due to heavy surcharges and stiff connection fees. To avoid surcharges on multiple calls, press the pound key (#) after your first call and you usually won't have to rekey your card number or pay another surcharge.

INTERNATIONAL DIRECT DIAL CODES

From Thailand, dial 001 followed by the country code:

WESTERN NATIONS

Australia	61
Canada	1
France	33
Germany	49
Ireland	353
Netherlands	31
New Zealand	64
United Kingdom	44
U.S.A.	1

SOUTHEAST ASIA

Brunei	673
Myanmar	95
Cambodia	855
Hong Kong	852
Indonesia	62
Laos	856
Macau	853
Malaysia	60
Philippines	63
Singapore	65
Thailand	66
Vietnam	84

Discount Calling Plans
International telephone calls at the lowest possible prices are available from discount calling plans offered by AT&T USA Direct, MCI Call USA, and Sprint Global Fone. These programs allow travelers to dial a toll-free access number from their hotel room and most public phones and speak directly with an operator in their home country. This eliminates language problems, minimizes hotel surcharges, and allows phone bills to be charged to either your telephone calling card or major credit card.

AT&T estimates their program cuts 20-60% off the direct dial rates imposed by hotels. As you might expect, many hotels block access to these discount programs or impose stiff surcharges on permitted calls. Be sure to inquire about all charges prior to making lengthy phone calls from your hotel room.

Anyone can use these calling plans. You don't need to have a calling card or subscribe to their services back home. For more information on these services, call: AT&T USA Direct, tel. (800) 331-1140; MCI Call USA, tel.

TELEPHONE AREA CODES WITHIN THAILAND

BANGKOK

02: Bangkok, Thonburi, Nonthaburi, Prathum Thani, Samut Prakan

BANGKOK VICINITY

034: Kanchanaburi, Nakhon Pathom, Samut Sakhon, Samut Songkhram
035: Ang Thong, Ayuthaya, Suphanburi
036: Lopburi, Saraburi, Singburi

EAST COAST

038: Chachoengsao, Chonburi, Pattaya, Rayong, Si Racha
039: Chantaburi, Trat

CENTRAL THAILAND

055: Kamphang Phet, Phitsanulok, Sukothai, Tak, Mae Sot, Uttaradit
056: Nakhon Sawan, Petchabun, Phichit, Uthai Thani

NORTHERN THAILAND

053: Chiang Mai, Chiang Rai, Lamphun, Mae Hong Son
054: Lampang, Nan, Phayao, Phrae

NORTHEASTERN THAILAND

037: Nakhon Nayok, Prachinburi, Aranyaprathet
042: Loei, Chiang Khan, Mukdahan, Nakhon Phanom, Nong Khai, Sakon Nakhon, Udon Thani
043: Kalasin, Khon Kaen, Mahasarakham, Roi Et
044: Buriram, Chaiyaphum, Nakhon Ratchasima (Korat)
045: Si Saket, Surin, Ubon Racthathani (Ubon), Yasothon

SOUTHERN THAILAND

032: Phetburi, Cha-Am, Prachuap Khiri Khan, Pranburi, Ratchburi
073: Narathiwat, Sungai Kolok, Pattani, Yala
074: Hat Yai, Phattalung, Satun, Songkhla
075: Krabi, Nakhon Si Thammarat, Trang
076: Phang Nga, Phuket
077: Chaiya, Chumphon, Ko Samui, Ranong, Surat Thani

(800) 444-3333; Sprint Global Fone, tel. (800) 767-4625.

Customers without a telephone calling card can also use these discount plans with their credit card. Although only collect calls are permitted with credit cards, rates are still lower than for overseas calls made from CAT Telecom Centers.

The discount programs can be accessed from any public phone that accepts both 1B and 5B coins. To reach an operator from one of the following companies from hotels and public phones, call: 001-999-1111-1 for AT&T USA Direct, 001-999-1200-1 for MCI Call USA, and 001-999-1387-1 for Sprint Global Fone.

ISD International Calls

The Communications Authority of Thailand (CAT) provides international telephone service through their International Subscriber Dialing (ISD) and International Operator Direct Connection, often called "Home Direct."

ISD calls can be made from all CAT Telecom Centers and from most private phones. Home Direct calls can be made *only* from CAT Telecom Centers and from a limited number of private phones.

CAT Telecom Centers are located near central post offices and are open daily 0800-2200. To make an international call, fill out the bilingual form with your name and telephone details, pay a deposit to cover the estimated cost, and find an empty phone booth to make your call. Larger CAT Telecoms permit you to dial the number but smaller offices require the assistance of an operator. Operators are also required for all collect calls, person-to-person calls, and station-to-station calls, and to use your international calling card. Operator assistance is 100.

INTERNATIONAL CLOCK FOR THAILAND

San Francisco	-14
New York	-12
Honolulu	-17
London	-7
Paris	-6
Sydney	+3
Bonn	-6
Tokyo	+2

TRADITIONAL THAI MEASUREMENTS

LAND MEASUREMENTS

waa: 4 sq. meters (100 sq. *waa*)

ngaan: 400 sq. meters

rai: 1600 sq. meters (4 *ngaan*)

WEIGHT

baht: 15.2 grams

taleung: 60 grams (4 *baht*)

chang: 1.2 kg (20 *taleung*)

haap: 60 kg (50 *chang*)

DISTANCE

niu: 2.2 cm

kheup: 25 cm (12 *niu*)

sawk: 50 cm (2 *kheup*)

waa: 2 meters (4 *sawk*)

sen: 40 meters (20 *waa*)

yoht: 16 km (400 *sen*)

Home Direct Calls

Home Direct phones at the CAT Telecom Offices offer one-button connection with international operators in over 20 countries. Home Direct calls from telecom offices are billed as collect calls: the person you call must agree to pay the charges. Home Direct calls can also be made from most public phones by dialing the access number for Home Direct (001-999), followed by the country code and the final access code (usually 1000). You then follow the voice prompts or wait for operator assistance.

Direct ISD calls, made without the help of an operator, cost about US$3 per minute to the United States and Europe between the hours of 0700-2100. ISD calls between 2100-2400 and 0500-0700 receive 20% discounts, calls from 2400-0500 receive 30% discounts; calls from hotels are surcharged 10-30% around the clock.

CAT Telecom Offices in larger towns accept cash and major credit cards. Charges for collect calls are deducted from your deposit except for the nonrefundable 30B service charge required for all phone services.

Home Direct access numbers for several countries follow.

Call 0001-999 followed by the access number:

Australia	61-1000
Canada	15-1000
Denmark	45-1000
Germany	49-1000
Hawaii	44141
Hong Kong	852-1086
Indonesia	62-1000
Italy	39-1000
Japan	81-0051
Korea	82-1000
Netherlands	31-1035
New Zealand	64-1066
Norway	47-1000
Philippines	63-1000
Singapore	351-1000
Taiwan	886-1000
UK	44-1066
USA (AT&T)	11111
USA (MCI)	12001
USA (Sprint)	13871

Pay Phones

Pay phones in Thailand are easy to understand and plentiful in larger towns and tourist zones. Smaller towns with few public phones rely on private phones inside shops and restaurants. Pay phones are differentiated by distinct colors and often marked with a blue triangle.

Phone booths bearing red roofs and red horizontal stripes are for local calls, which cost 1B for three minutes. Note that only the medium-sized 1B coin fits the slot. Warning beeps signal the end of the three-minute period, but additional coins will keep the line open. The remaining time is noted by a small display inside the booth.

Local calls can also be made from small pay phones located inside restaurants, hotels, and shops. Most are painted a bright red or pale blue and cost 5B for three minutes.

Pay phones are often crowded since few people have private lines, which take around three years to obtain from the public phone company. The latest fashions are cellular phones, which cost about 50,000B; and paging systems, which cost 300-800B per month in service charges.

Phone booths painted with blue roofs and metallic stripes are for calling long distance within Thailand. These phones accept 1B, 5B and 10B coins; they are rarely seen outside Bangkok and busy tourist zones.

Local and domestic long distance calls can also be made from card phones located in supermarkets, financial centers, and hotel districts. Card phones have green stripes and only accept payment by telephone card. Markets and shops such as 7-11 sell phone cards in 100B denominations.

Card phone calls 0700-1900 cost 30B per minute. Evening calls 1900-2200 are discounted 50% (15B per minute); night-owl calls 2200-0700 are discounted 66% (10B per minute).

Fax Services

CAT Telecom Offices at GPOs throughout the country also offer fax, telegraph, and telex services. International faxes cost 100-150B for the first page and 65-100B for each additional page depending on the destination and amount of transmission time.

TIME

Thailand is seven hours ahead of Greenwich mean time (GMT+7).

During winter months, Thailand is 15 hours ahead of San Francisco and Los Angeles, 13 hours ahead of Chicago, 12 hours ahead of New York, seven hours ahead of London, and three hours behind Sydney. Daylight saving time will add one hour to these figures.

From another perspective, Bangkok at noon is San Francisco at 2100 (the previous day), Chicago and New Orleans at 2300, New York at midnight, Auckland at 1700, Sydney at 1500, Perth at 1300, London at 0500, and Paris at 0600.

Business Hours

Government offices and private businesses keep similar hours to businesses in foreign countries. National museums and major GPOs have special opening hours and days. Most **government offices** are open Mon.-Fri. 0830-1200 and 1300-1630. **National museums** are open Wed.-Sun. 0830-1200 and 1300-1630; closed on Monday, Tuesday, and national holidays. **Post offices** operate Mon.-Fri. 0830-1630, Saturday 0900-1200, closed Sunday and holidays. GPOs in Bangkok and Chiang Mai stay open until 2200.

You can frequent **tourist offices** daily except holidays 0830-1630. **Banks** are open Mon.-Fri. 0830-1530. Foreign exchange offices adjacent to banks in Bangkok and other tourist destinations are open daily 0830-2200. Most **shopping cen-**

ters are open daily 0830-1700; smaller shops stay open until around 2200.

MEASUREMENTS

Electricity
Electric current is 220 V, 50 cycles. The standard wall outlets accept electrical appliances with two round poles. Some outlets accept flat two-bladed plugs while others accept both round and flat. Electrical adapters and voltage convertors are available from travel supply shops in your home country, from better hotels in Thailand, and at all electrical stores in Thailand.

Weights and Measures
Temperature is expressed in degrees Celsius.

The metric system serves as the national standard of measurement except for a few items still measured according to the traditional Thai system.

THAI TIME

The Buddhist Calendar
The Western Gregorian calendar, introduced to Thailand in 1899, is used for all national and social events, but Thais also consult the Buddhist calendar for some religious events and life cycle ceremonies. Buddhist calendars and the Buddhist Era (B.E.) date from 543 B.C., the year Buddha attained enlightenment and entered nirvana. Thus, A.D. 1998 equals 2541 B.E. in the Buddhist Era.

To add to the chronological confusion, the Buddhist Era in Thailand is one year behind that of Myanmar, Sri Lanka, and India. The situation is similar to that experienced by the Christian world, which took many moons to decide on the exact year of the birth of Christ. It was, of course, Pope Gregory XIII, who finally settled the issue in 1592 by imposing his system and namesake on our Western calendar.

The Lunar Calendar
The Thais also use the lunar calendar to set the dates of many religious ceremonies. The lunar calendar comes from Chinese astrologers who calculated that a complete cycle of the moon takes about 29.5 days. Lunar calendars probably worked well until somebody decided that the lunar year should somehow correspond to the Western calendar.

The problem is that the Western year is divided into 12 months with a total of 365 days (except for leap years), while the lunar year is 12 months with only 354 days. Over a period of years, the difference of 11 days causes the lunar year to gradually creep ahead of the Western calendar. In an attempt to realign the two systems, an extra eighth lunar month is shoved into the lunar year every two or three years.

The Thais also celebrate some lunar-based holidays on days unconnected with the lunar calendar. For example, the Thai New Year (Songkram) takes place each year on 13 April, though the lunar new year generally falls in either February or March.

The Thai Day
Another curious twist on time concerns the division of the day.

While urban Thai citizens observe a 24-hour day divided into two 12-hour segments (midnight to noon and noon to midnight), they also divide the day into four periods of six hours, each given a different term.

This system is the legacy of earlier days when village watchmen used wooden drums and clackers to signal the hour and assure everyone that all was well within the neighborhood. Villagers slept peacefully unless signaled by unexpected drumming or disturbed by the eerie absence of the hourly clack.

Today, the six-hour shifts of the night watchman are reflected in the terminology of time. *Chao* refers to the period between 0600 and 1100, *klung wun* is midday, *bai mong* is 1300, and *bai song* means 1400. Evening hours after 1800 are *yen* with another number to indicate the exact hour, while *keun* replaces *yen* after 2200.

To further complicate the issue, Thais also divide the day into four base hours plus the familiar periods of noon and midnight. *Dee neung* is 0100 in Western time, *neung muang chao* is "one in the morning" (0700 in Western time), *bai muang* is "one in the afternoon" (1300 to Westerners), *thum neung* is "one in the evening" (1900 for foreigners).

Thais also name the days after the planets, in much the same way that Westerners name the days after planetary names of Greek origin. Each day is associated with a particular color. For example, Sunday is associated with red while the lucky color for Wednesday is pink or lilac.

Whew. As you might expect, this refusal to compartmentalize the day according to Western thought should be considered when someone invites you to breakfast at "three in the morning." That's breakfast at 0900.

Land, for example, is parceled into *waa, ngaan,* and *rai.* Gold is measured in a unit of weight confusingly called the *baht,* which is approximately 15.2 grams. *Baht*—rather than ounces or grams—will be quoted when you buy gold jewelry anywhere in the country.

Most of the older measurement terms listed in the chart "Traditional Thai Measurements" have been abandoned except by a few carpenters, traditional boat builders, and hilltribe merchants when speaking about their crops (i.e., opium).

THE MEDIA

NEWSPAPERS AND MAGAZINES

Newspapers

Compared with other newspapers in Southeast Asia, the Thai press has a relatively trouble-free existence and a surprising amount of freedom to cover most political and social issues. The only exceptions are stories and articles that criticize the monarchy and members of the royal family; Thailand has strong laws regarding lese majesty.

Aside from periods of unrest, the Thai government rarely interferes with the press or shuts down newspapers that write about touchy domestic issues. Journalists routinely protect their identities by writing under pseudonyms, but are otherwise free to serve as effective watchdogs against official misconduct. However, many laws and decrees have been enacted over the last 40 years that allow the police to revoke licenses and close down newspapers in the name of national security. These decrees can also be invoked against newspapers that offend public morals, defame government ministries, promote communism, or otherwise degrade the image of Thailand. For this reason, a "free" Thai press is basically a masquerade.

To cite a few recent cases, the Thai-language newspaper *Khaosod* was closed in 1987 for offending the monarchy, the *Asian Wall Street Journal* was shut down in 1989 on charges of insulting the national religion, and *Naew Na,* another Thai newspaper, had its license revoked in 1990 after publishing a story that embarrassed the government.

The fear of closure has forced newspaper editors to use amusing and highly creative strategies to stay in business. Many newspapers protect their franchise by keeping additional publishing licenses stashed in the back room to quickly reopen the paper under a new name.

Newspapers will also resort to self-imposed censorship in times of crisis, such as publishing blank pages in the *Bangkok Post* following the military coup of 1991.

English-Language Newspapers

Two major English-language papers are published in Bangkok, the morning *Bangkok Post* and *The Nation* in the afternoon. Both newspapers cover domestic political stories and international news with contributions from the Associated Press, United Press International, and Reuters wire services.

Circulation figures are about equal but the two papers differ in tone and coverage. *The Nation* is staffed almost exclusively by Thai nationals who focus primarily on domestic issues from a Thai perspective, while the *Bangkok Post* employs both Thai and Western journalists who cover domestic and worldwide events from an international perspective. Both newspapers list current information on cultural performances, national festivals, English-language cinema schedules, social events, and international sporting results.

Bangkok Post: Thailand's first English-language daily (established 1947) is considered one of the best newspapers in the region. Among the leading features are the society page, featuring events, workshops, seminars, art exhibitions, and Siam Society tours; reader letters—quirky opinions from disgruntled *farangs;* Dateline Bangkok, offering news summaries from Thai-language papers; Around the World, providing extracts from international newspapers; Horizons, the travel page; Bangkok Bylines, for shopping tips; and the Juke Page's music reviews. Popular columnists include Trink (nightlife and scandal), Ung Aang Talay (restaurant reviews), and Maew Mong (humor and politics).

The Nation: Once the poor stepsister to the *Post*, *The Nation* now effectively competes through insightful coverage of national news and bolder discussions of political events. Their willingness to challenge the government was apparent the morning following the military coup of 1991. The *Bangkok Post* retreated into the shell of self-censorship while *The Nation* strongly objected to military involvement in the overthrow of the democratic government.

The Friday edition of *The Nation* includes a useful tourist supplement called *Saen Sanuk*.

Thai Newspapers

Many Thais read the English-language papers for current events but turn to the Thai-language newspapers for their daily dose of murder, mayhem, and gossip. Dozens of local newspapers and magazines are published on a daily or weekly basis; the widest readership is enjoyed by the sensationalist tabloid, *Thai Rath* ("Thai State"). According to media surveys, over 25% of the adult population reads *Thai Rath* daily for lurid stories about perverse crimes and grisly disasters, and political articles that zero in on everyone from top to bottom.

The closest competitor is the somewhat more restrained and intelligent *Siam Rath* ("Siam State"), which is read daily by about 12% of the adult population. The *Matichon* may have a far smaller circulation but pundits regard it as the leading Thai-language newspaper for serious and reliable analysis of political events.

Lead stories from all three papers are summarized each day in the *Bangkok Post*.

Magazines

Far Eastern Economic Review, Asiaweek, Time, Newsweek, The Economist, and other publications are sold in bookstores and newsstands in international hotels. *Far Eastern Economic Review* concentrates on political and economic events, while *Asiaweek* tends to run more stories on personalities and social issues.

English-language magazines published in Bangkok are great resources for travel tips and nightlife reviews, though most don't seem to survive more than a few seasons. *Caravan,* a trendy and well-designed monthly, specializes in "flabbergasting films, anarchic art, melodious music, political power plays, and scandalous scoops."

The MetroMania section in the *Bangkok Metro* features valuable information on nightclubs, restaurants, and sporting events.

Magazines oriented toward tourism include *Asia Travel Trade* and *Frequent Traveller* (both published in Singapore), *Business Traveller Asia-Pacific* from Hong Kong, and *PATA Travel News,* the official magazine of the Pacific Asia Travel Association.

Asian Art News and *Arts of Asia* are Hong Kong-based magazines that cover Asian antiques, auctions, and news about contemporary artists.

Airline inflight magazines—*Sawasdee, Discovery, Silver Kris, Mabuhay,* and *Garuda*—feature stories on regional travel destinations. Back issues of inflight magazines and hotel publications such as *Mandarin Oriental* and *The Regent* cost 10B at the Weekend Market in Bangkok.

TELEVISION

In contrast to the freedom given newspapers and magazines, television and radio have until quite recently been considered property of the government and strictly supervised by the military. In 1993, the broadcasting industry was liberalized after public outrage over the lack of coverage of the events of May 1992, a situation that fulfilled the prophecy of the American musician/poet Gil Scott-Heron who wrote, "The revolution will not be televised."

Today, about 75% of the households in Thailand have televisions, which receive broadcasts from five government-owned TV networks. Three are managed by the Mass Communications Organization of Thailand (MOT) and two are military controlled but leased to private firms. Households with parabolic dishes can pick up satellite services broadcast from Hong Kong and Australia. All stations must air daily 30-minute segments on the activities of the Royal Family.

Television Networks

All channels originate in Bangkok and are transmitted via relay substations to most provincial towns. English-language programs are listed in the entertainment sections of *The Nation* and *Bangkok Post*.

Channel 3: A government-owned station leased to Bangkok Entertainment, a privately owned company that broadcasts movies, soap operas, and cartoons. The news program at 1900 is simulcast in English on FM 105.5. Channel 3 operates daily 0900-midnight.

Channel 5: A military network that broadcasts variety shows, documentaries, ABC and CNN segments, and English-subtitled programs at noon, 1900, and 2330. The station's programming runs daily 0900-midnight.

Channel 7: A military network leased to Bangkok Broadcasting that appeals to stock market players who receive market updates during the day along with movies, soap operas, and documentaries. The English-language news program at 1900 is simulcast on FM 103.5. Daily noon-midnight.

Channel 9: Thailand's national public television network specializes in educational programs, news, and variety shows imported from Europe and the United States. The English-language program weekdays at 1900 is simulcast on FM 107. Channel 9 operates daily 0600-midnight.

Channel 11: A nonprofit and commercial-free educational station run by the Ministry of Education. The station specializes in documentaries and correspondence classes produced by Ramkamhaeng and Thammasart open universities. The English-language news program at 2000 is simulcast on FM 88. Operations are daily 0530-midnight.

Satellite TV

The era of borderless television has arrived in Asia, bringing citizens nonstop images of rock stars clad in leather and lace, second-rate movies and sitcoms, and political news beyond the control of government censors. Second-generation satellites—AsiaSat II and Orbx 2—due for launch in the next few years will emit signals powerful enough to be picked up by small 50-cm wide dishes rather than the bulky parabolic dishes currently required to receive satellite broadcasts.

Foreign ministries attempt to control their national airwaves with heavy censorship and a variety of legal measures such as outlawing parabolic dishes, but efforts at enforcement are crumbling and the globalization of Asia airwaves appears to be a foregone conclusion. Four major networks broadcast by satellite.

Star TV: The electromagnetic web of Star TV (Satellite Television Asian Region) from Hong Kong is beamed across Asia via AsiaSat 1. Broadcasts include several pay channels and five free channels: MTV Asia, BBC World News, Prime Sports, a Chinese-language movie channel, and The Entertainment Network with American movies and Western soap operas.

IBC TV: The IBC (International Broadcasting Corporation) network is beamed by Indonesia's Palapa satellite over the more southeasternly sections of Asia, from central India to the eastern tip of Papua New Guinea. IBC has five channels: CNN, ESPN, HBO, and two entertainment channels—one Thai and one American. Note: CNN news broadcasts in Asia are quite different from Western versions—highly abbreviated, politically cautious, and interminably repetitious.

Thai Sky: Thailand recently joined the satellite revolution by launching their ThaiSat 1 in association with AsiaSat. Thai Sky has five channels: BBC World News, MTV Asia, Thai MTV, Thai News, and Thai Variety.

ATVI: Australian Television features wildlife documentaries from Down Under and news about political developments in Asia.

Video Formats

Thailand's videotapes and machines are formatted in PAL, the system used in Australia and most of Europe. PAL videotapes will not work in NTSC-format video machines, those used in the United States and Japan. Many video stores sell tapes in both formats, plus tapes in the SECAM format used in France. Shoppers should check on the format or expect to pay tape conversion charges after returning home.

RADIO

FM Broadcasts

Thailand has over 150 radio stations that broadcast on AM, FM, and shortwave frequencies. AM stations broadcast exclusively in Thai, but many FM stations in Bangkok offer English-language programs around the clock. Radio stations elsewhere generally have daily English-language news shows at 0900, 1200, and 1900.

Bangkok FM stations seem to prefer easy-listening and light jazz to rap or heavy metal rock. Radio schedules are listed in the entertainment sections of the *Bangkok Post* and *Bangkok Metro* magazine.

Gold FM 95.5: An easy-listening station with special worthwhile programs: Night Train (jazz and soul) weekdays 2200-0200; Dixieland and big band music Sunday 2200-0200; and Nation Radio every hour on the hour featuring excellent coverage of local news events.

Radio Thailand 97 FM: Thailand's principal national public radio station, owned and operated by the Public Relations Department, broadcasts public service announcements and news summaries throughout the day, plus daily news bulletins at 0700-0800, 1230-1300, and 1900-1930. The news bulletins are simulcast in English on 95.5 Gold FM, Smooth 105 FM, and Smile Radio 107 FM.

Chulalongkorn 101.5 FM: Radio Chulalongkorn University broadcasts classical music nightly 2130-2400. See the *Bangkok Post* for program schedules.

Smooth 105 FM: Bangkok's most popular easy-listening station features international news at the top of the hour and a Travel Thailand program that relates upcoming festivals and cultural events daily 2000-2030.

Smile Radio 107 FM: Thailand's alternative national public radio station is also Bangkok's only bilingual station aimed at a young and hip audience. DJs play a mixture of tunes during the day, including new rock, phone-in requests, and Thai pop numbers. Smile Radioactive on Saturday night 2030-0430 features cutting-edge releases such as British alternative bands and ambient house music.

BBC and the Voice of America

Although vacations usually imply getting away from it all, many travelers want some contact with the world they have temporarily left behind. Even in the middle of a tropical rainforest, some find it necessary to know about events abroad or the latest sports results.

News-hungry travelers can satisfy their urges by tuning to the BBC World News Service, Voice of America, Radio Australia, and Radio Canada with the use of portable shortwave receivers. The best reception seems to be late at night from the roof of your hotel, using a digital receiver such as the palm-sized Sony ICF-SWIS, Sangean ATS808, or Panasonic RF-45B.

Locating the exact frequency can be tricky since frequencies change at regular intervals or seem to float around the dial. Daily programs and current frequencies are listed in the *Bangkok Post*. Radio fans without shortwave receivers can listen to the Voice of America on 95.5 FM and BBC World Service on 105 FM midnight-0600.

A useful publication is the annually updated *Passport to World Band Radio* from Gilfer Shortwave (tel. 800-445-3371). The BBC magazine, *London Calling,* provides program listings and detailed frequency charts. To order 12 monthly issues, send US$15 to BBC, 630 5th Ave., Suite 2153, New York, NY 10111.

SOURCES OF TRAVEL INFORMATION

The following section will help you obtain background details and travel information before you leave for Thailand.

First visit your public library for titles on Thai history, culture, people, traditions, political developments, and artistic heritage. Unless you live in a major city, libraries rarely carry much on Thailand aside from musty copies of *The King and I* and dated guidebooks such as *Nagel's Encyclopedia Guide to Thailand*. Ask your librarian to order several copies of *Thailand Handbook* and *Southeast Asia Handbook* from Moon Publications.

A list of recommended readings is located in the back of this guidebook. I've indicated my personal favorites and best choices for travelers with limited reading time. The more you learn about Thailand beforehand, the more you will appreciate your travel experience.

Travel agents experienced with Thailand are a godsend, but rare as whale's teeth. Student travel agencies listed in this chapter can sometimes offer reliable travel advice.

The Internet is also an amazing source of information about Thailand.

Best of all, seek out and talk with travelers who have been to Thailand or other areas in Southeast Asia. Throughout the world, an amazing number of people have traveled the region and love to relate their travel experiences.

GOVERNMENT AGENCIES

U.S. Government Information
Current travel conditions and safety advisories on worldwide destinations can be obtained from the new Consular Information Program, which replaced an outmoded and highly criticized system of travel advisories.

Two categories of information exist: travel warnings to avoid certain destinations, and consular information sheets to every country in the world. Both can be heard on tape 24 hours a day by calling the Citizens Emergency Center of the U.S. State Department at (202) 647-5225. Follow the taped recording of menu options. To avoid

voice mail and speak with a human operator, call the Bureau of Consular Affairs at (202) 647-1488 during normal business hours. Desk officers at (202) 647-2000 may offer additional tips.

The same information can be obtained by fax, (202) 647-3000.

The Consular Affairs Bulletin Board (CABB) can accessed using your computer modem via their website. This convenient service allows you to review warnings, information sheets, tips for travelers, medical information, and daily updates of the *Overseas Security Advisory Council Reports.*

Tourist Authority of Thailand
The Tourist Authority of Thailand (TAT) can help you with general travel information such as glossy brochures and lists of upcoming festivals. Tourism employees are friendly, and the department is well funded compared to other government tourist offices in Southeast Asia.

The TAT head office is at 372 Bamrung Muang Rd., Bangkok 10100, Thailand, tel. (662) 226-0060, fax (662) 224-6221. They also have offices at the former headquarters on Rajadamnoen Ave., at the airport, and at Chatuchak Weekend Market.

The TAT has used their additional funding to open new regional offices in Ayuthaya, Lopburi, Rayong, Chiang Rai, Ubon Ratchathani, Khon Kaen, Nakhon Phanon, Udon Thani, and Nakhon Si Thammarat. Phone numbers and addresses of these offices are listed below. TAT offices are open daily except Sunday 0830-1630.

Domestic Offices
Ayuthaya: Si Samphet Rd., Ayuthaya 13000, tel. (036) 442768, fax (036) 422769

Bangkok: 372 Bamrung Muang Rd., Bangkok 10100, tel. (02) 226-0060, fax (02) 224-6221

Cha Am: 500/51 Petchkasem Highway, Petchburi 76000, tel. (032) 471005, fax (032) 471502

Chiang Mai: 105 Chiang Mai-Lamphun Rd., Chiang Mai 57000, tel. (053) 248604, fax (053) 248605

Chiang Rai: 448/16 Singhalkla Rd., Chiang Rai 57000, tel. (053) 717433, fax (053) 717434

Hat Yai: 1 Soi 2, Niphat Uthit 3 Rd., Hat Yai 90110, tel. (074) 243747, fax (074) 245986

Kanchanaburi: Saengchuto Rd., Kanchaburi 71000, tel. (034) 511200, fax (034) 511200

Khon Kaen: 15/5 Prachasamosorn Rd., Khon Kaen 40000, tel. (043) 244498, fax (043) 244487

Lopburi: Provincial Hall, Narai Maharat Rd., Lopburi 15000, tel. (036) 422768, fax (036) 422769

Nakhon Phanom: Provincial Hall, Abhibanbancha Rd., Nakhon Phanom 48000, tel. (042) 513490, fax (042) 513492

Nakhon Ratchasima: 2102 Mittraphab Rd., Nakhon Ratchasima 30000, tel. (044) 213666, fax (044) 213667

Nakhon Si Thammarat: Ratchadamnern Klang Rd., Nakhon Si Thammarat 8000, tel. (075) 346515, fax (075) 346517

Pattaya: 382/1 Chai Hat Rd., Pattaya 210000, tel. (038) 428750, fax (038) 429113

Phitsanulok: 209/7 Boromatrailokanat Rd., Phitsanulok 65000, tel. (055) 252743, fax (055) 252742

Phuket: 73 Phuket Rd., Phuket 83000, tel. (076) 212213, fax (076) 213582

Rayong: 300/77 Liang Muang Rd., Rayong 21000, tel. (038) 611228, fax (038) 611228

Surat Thani: 5 Talat Mai Rd., Surat Thani 84000, tel. (077) 282828, fax (077) 282828

Ubon Ratchathani: 264/1 Khuan Thani Rd., Ubon Ratchathani 34000, tel. (045) 243770, fax (045) 243771

Udon Thani: Provincial Hall, Phosi Rd., Udon Thani 41000, tel. (042) 241968, fax (042) 241968

Overseas Offices

Australia: TAT, Royal Exchange Bldg., Seventh Fl., 56 Pitt St., Sydney, NSW 2000, tel. (02) 247-7549, fax (02) 251-2465

France: TAT, 90 Ave. de la Champs Elysees, 75008 Paris, tel. (01) 4562-8656, fax (01) 4563-7888

Germany: TAT, Bethmannstrasse 58, 60311 Frankfurt/Main, tel. (069) 295704, fax (069) 281468

Hong Kong: TAT, Fairmount House, Room 401, 8 Cotton Tree Drive, Central, tel. (852) 868-0732, fax (852) 868-4585

Italy: TAT, Via Barberini 50, 00187 Rome, tel. (06) 487-3479, fax (06) 487-3500

Japan: TAT, Hibiya Mitsui Bldg., 1-2 Yurakucho 1-chome, Chiyoda-ku, Tokyo 100, tel. (03) 3580-6776, fax (03) 3580-7808

TAT, Hiranomachi Yachiyo Bldg., 5th floor, 1-8-14 Hiranomachi, Chuo-ku, Osaka 541, tel. (06) 231-4434, fax (06) 231-4337

Korea: TAT, Coryo Daeyungek Center Bldg., Room 2003, Chungmu-Ro, Chung-Ku, Seoul 100-706, tel. (02) 779-5417, fax (02) 779-5419

Malaysia: Royal Thai Embassy, 206 Jalan Ampang, 504505 Kuala Lumpur, tel. (093) 248-0958, fax (093) 241-3002

Singapore: Royal Thai Embassy, 370 Orchard Rd., Singapore 0923, tel. (65) 235-7694, fax (65) 733-5653

Taiwan: Thai Trade & Economic Office, 2B Central Commercial Bldg., 16-18 Nanking East Rd., Taipei 105, tel. (02) 778-2735, fax (02) 741-9914

United Kingdom: TAT, 49 Albemarle St., London WIX 3FE, tel. (0171) 499-7679, fax (0171) 629-5519

USA: TAT, 5 World Trade Center, Suite 3443, New York, NY 10048, tel. (212) 432-0433, fax (212) 912-0920

TAT, 3440 Wilshire Blvd., Suite 1101, Los Angeles, CA 90010, tel. (213) 382-2353, fax (213) 389-7544

TAT, 303 East Wacker Drive, Suite 400, Chicago, IL 60602, tel. (312) 819-3990, fax (312) 565-0359

MAPS

The best available maps are the Lonely Planet *Thailand Travel Atlas,* Nelles *Map of Thailand,* Nancy Chandler's *Map of Bangkok* and *Map of Chiang Mai,* and regional maps from Prannok Witthaya and Bangkok Guides. Maps are sold in luxury hotels, Asia Books, and D.K. Books around the country. Lonely Planet and Nelles are available worldwide.

Thailand Travel Atlas: This Lonely Planet creation features place-names in both English and Thai, attractive topographic shadings, and travel tips from the author.

Nelles Map of Thailand: A useful but somewhat outdated map from the publishers of maps to Southeast Asia. Nelles Verlag once ruled the cartographic world but has failed to update its maps.

Nancy Chandler Maps: The *Map of Bangkok* and *Map of Chiang Mai* are useful if quirky maps from artist Chandler, a former Bangkok resident who offers tips on markets, restaurants, and attractions. Nancy lives in San Francisco but conducts regular update trips to Thailand.

Bangkok Guides: Bangkok Guides did a great job a few years ago with the release of the *Guide Map of Chiang Rai* (a godsend for motorcyclists), *Guide Map of Southern Thailand, Guide Map of Krabi,* and *Guide Map of Ko Samui.* You'll find these maps around Thailand. Bangkok Guides, 40/6 Moo 8, Soi Onnuch, Suan Luang, Phrakhanong, Bangkok 10250, tel. (02) 311-1439.

Prannok Witthaya Maps: These maps are confusing but include regions missed by Bangkok Guides. *Map of Chiang Mai & Around* is absolutely vital for motorcycle touring west of Chiang Mai. Other well-researched maps to Pattaya, Ko Samui, Phuket, and Krabi are available. Prannok Witthaya, 823/32 Prannok Rd., Bangkok 10700, tel. (02) 411-2954.

National Highways Department Maps: Four sectional maps of Thailand are published by the Highways Department. Helpful to a limited degree since smaller towns are only shown in Thai script. The Bangkok TAT office sells these maps.

Latest Tour Guide to Bangkok and Thailand: Major bus routes in Bangkok—absolutely necessary for bus riders in the big city.

United States Geological Survey Maps: Topographic maps produced by the U.S. government are sold at D.K. Books branches around Thailand. Somewhat useful but less timely than comparative maps from Lonely Planet, Prannok Witthaya, and Bangkok Guides.

Association of Siamese Architects Maps: Four stylish maps to Bangkok, Grand Palace, canals of Thonburi, and Ayuthaya. Far too artsy, vague, and overpriced to be recommended, except the map to temples in Thonburi.

THE INTERNET

The Internet is a great way to find travel tips on every nook and cranny of the planet. With enough time you can retrieve:

- A 40-page country report on Thailand from the U.S. government
- CIA assessments including concise and detailed advise for the traveler
- Current travel advisories issued by the U.S. State Department
- Thousands of visitor comments from usenet groups
- Satellite photos of current weather patterns
* Political and economic news from wire services
- Currency exchange rates
- Tips from travel writers
- Advice from local residents
- Hotel prices from tourist offices and private firms
- The latest issues of the *Bangkok Post* and *Nation.*

You then print the whole thing out and return your copy of *Thailand Handbook* for a refund.

Internet Access
The easiest way to get started is with an online service such as America Online and tap its proprietary travel forums, e-mail, chat lines, and access to the Web—that vast hypertext network of networks.

More knowledgeable types can connect directly to the Web via an Internet provider such as Worldnet, Earthlink, or Netcom and then browse the Web with either Netscape Navigator or Internet Explorer. Once hooked up, you're part of an electronic community consisting of over 100 million individuals and a million databases covering every possible field of human endeavor.

The biggest problem is navigating the murky waters of cyberspace. Start with a search engine such as Yahoo, which categorizes over a million sites including Web pages, gophers, FTPs, and usenet newsgroups. For more specific inquires, try Alta Vista, Excite, InfoSeek, and Lycos, which spit out lists of websites that match your search criteria. Mega-search engines such as MetaCrawler and LinkSearch allow you to use several search engines at the same time.

An amazing amount of information is found under the "usenet" or "newsgroups." "Soc" groups discuss social and political issues while "rec" groups are geared toward recreation and travel. "Listserv" e-mail groups on many travel topics can be found at www.onelist.com.

Internet Cafes in Thailand
Several dozen Internet cafes now provide Internet access in all the major destinations including Bangkok (mostly in Banglampoo), Chiang Mai, Phuket, and Ko Samui. Internet connections cost about 2B per minute in tourist-oriented venues but only 1B per minutes in cafes serving primarily a Thai clientele.

The best way to check your e-mail is to set up an account with a free e-mail service (Hotmail, Yahoo, etc.) and then check your Hotmail account from an Internet cafe in Thailand. Most services allow you to pull e-mail messages directly off your chief Internet Service Provider (ISP) by checking your POP account.

Moon Sites:
• Moon Publications: www.moon.com
• Carl Parkes e-mail: cparkes@moon.com

Academic Organizations (Southeast Asia):
• Australia National University: coombs.anu.edu.au/WWWVL-AsianStudies
• Cornell: www.arts.cornell.edu/seasia
• Northern Illinois University: www.niu.edu/acad/cseas
• UC Berkeley: violet.berkeley.edu/~csasweb
• UC Berkeley: garnet.berkeley.edu:4252/seascalinfo
• University of Michigan: www.umich.edu:80/~iinet/csseas

Adventure Travel:
• Adventure Travel Society: www.adventure-travel.com
• *Asian Dive Magazine:* www.asian-diver.com
• Earthwatch: www.earthwatch.org
• Mountain Travel Sobek: www.mtsobek.com
• See & Sea Dive: www.batnet.com/see&sea
• Journeys International: www.journeys-intl.com
• Asian-Transpacific Journeys: www.southeast-asia.com
• Sea Canoes: www.seacanoe.com

• Siam Divers: www.siamdivers.com
Asian Magazines and Newspapers:
• *Asia Inc:* www.asia-inc.com/index.html
• *Asiaweek:* pathfinder.com/@@G4FHi2Eq9gl
  AQG4B/Asiaweek
• *Bangkok Post:* www.bangkokpost.net
• *Business Traveler:* www.biztravel.com
• *Far Eastern Economic Review:* www.feer.com

Environmental and Human Rights Groups:
• Amnesty International: www.amnesty.org
• Human Rights Watch: www.traveller.com/~hrweb/hrw/hrw.html
• Rainforest Action Network: www.ran.org/ran
• US State Department Human Rights Reports: www.gdn.org/ftp/US_State_Department/Human_Rights_Report_1998

General Travel:
• Asiaville: www.asiaville.com
• City Net: www.city.net
• Dr. Memory: www.access.digex.net/~drmemory/cyber_travel.html
• No Shitting: www.magna.com.au/~travdude/index
• Rec Travel: www.nectec.or.th/rec-travel
• TEN-IO Travel: www.ten-io.com
• Microsoft Expedia: expedia.msn.com
• U.S. State Department Travel Warnings: www.stolaf.edu/network/travel-advisories
• American Institute of Foreign Studies: www.aifs.org
• CIEE: www.ciee.org
• International Honors Program: world.std.com/~ihp/ihp.html
• Youth Hostels: www.hostels.com/hostels

Travel Media:
• Speciality Travel Index: www.spectrav.com
• Travel Channel: www.travelchannel.com
• Lonely Planet: www.lonelyplanet.com.au/lp.htm
• Travelocity: www.travelocity.com
• Amazon Books: www.amazon.com
• *Condé Nast Traveler:* travel.epicurious.com
• Book Passage: www.bookpassage.com
• *Outside:* www.starwave.com/outside

Health:
• Stanford Medical Center: www-leland.stanford.edu/~naked/stms
• WHO Tropical Disease Center: www.who.ch/programmes/ctd/ctd_home
• Wisconsin Health Clinic: www.intmed.mcw.edu/travel
• Center for Disease Control: www.cdc.gov/cdc.htm

Thailand Sites:
• Asia Online: www.asia-online.com
• Bangkok Airways: www.bkkair.co.th
• *Bangkok Metro Magazine:* www.bkkmetro.com
• *Chiang Mai News:* www.chiangmainews.com
• *Chaing Mai* and *Chiang Rai Magazine:* www.infothai.com/wtcmcr
• Coalition Against Prostitution: www.capcat.ksc.net
• Diethelm Tours: www.asiatour.com
• Issan Guide: www.thaiguide.com
• Ko Phangan: www.kohphangan.com
• Ko Samui: www.sawadee.com
• Loxley ISP: www.loxinfo.co.th
• Ministry of Foreign Affairs: www.mfa.go.th
• Pattaya: www.pattaya.com
• Phuket Info: www.phuket.com
• *Phuket Gazette:* www.phuketgazette.net
• Siam Net: www.siam.net
• TAT: www.tat.or.th
• TAT: www.tourismthailand.org
• Thai Embassy U.S.A.: www.thaiembdc.org
• Thai Embassy Bangkok: www.inet.co.th/org/usis/embindex.htm
• Thai Airways: www.thaiair.com
• Thai Focus: www.thaifocus.com
• Thai Index: wwww.thaiindex.com

BOOKSTORES AND PUBLISHERS

American Travel Bookstores
Bookstores in larger U.S. cities carry a mind-boggling selection of travel guides, maps, accessories, and literature. For rare, out-of-print editions contact **Cellar Books,** Oriental Book Company (no catalog) at 1713 East Colorado Boulevard, Pasadena, CA 91106, tel. (626) 577-2413; and **Oxus Books** at 121 Astonville St., London SW185AQ, tel. (01) 870-3854.

Contact the following for catalogs: Book Passage, tel. (800) 321-9785; Easy Going, tel. (800) 233-3533; Phileas Fogg, tel. (800) 233-FOGG; Cellar Books, tel. (248) 357-1776; Compleat Traveller, tel. (212) 685-9007; Back Door Press, tel. (206) 771-8308; Travel Books, tel. (301) 951-8533; Globe Corner, tel. (800) 358-6013; Forsyth Travel, tel. (800) 367-7984; Literate Traveler, tel. (301) 398-8781.

Publishers in Southeast Asia
Many of the best books on Thailand and Southeast Asia are published overseas and rarely distributed in the West. Companies in Thailand offer the best selection of books on Thailand; contact Asia Books, D.K. Books, and White Lotus for rare editions. Oxford Press publishes reprints of old classics, Times Editions is strong on Singapore titles, Ian Lloyd offers superb photography editions, the academic Institute of Southeast Asian Studies is good for politics and economics.

The following overseas publishers will send their latest catalogs upon request.

Thailand: Asia Books, 5 Sukumvit Rd. Soi 61, Bangkok 10112; **D.K. Books,** 90/21-25 Rajaprarob, Makkasan, GPO 2916, Bangkok 10400; **White Lotus Press,** GPO Box 1141, Bangkok 10501.

Hong Kong: Oxford Press, 18th floor, Warwick House, Taikoo Trading Estate, 28 Tong Chong St., Quarry Bay, Hong Kong.

Singapore: Times Editions, Times Centre, 1 New Industrial Rd., Singapore 1953; **Graham Brash,** 36 C Prinsep St., Singapore 0718; **Ian Lloyd Productions,** 18A Tanjong Pagar Rd., Singapore 0208; **Select Books,** 19 Tanglin Rd. #03-15, Tanglin Shopping Center, Singapore 1024; **Institute of Southeast Asian Studies,** Heng Mui Keng Terrace, Pasir Panjang, Singapore 0511.

GETTING THERE

BY AIR

Thailand is centrally located in the heart of Southeast Asia and is served by over 50 international airlines from all major world capitals. Most international airlines fly to Bangkok's Don Muang International Airport, though direct flights are also available to international airports in Penang, Hat Yai, and Chiang Mai. Travel times to Bangkok are 16-20 hours from San Francisco, Los Angeles, and Seattle; 20-24 hours from Chicago; and 22-26 hours from New York via the West Coast.

Some airlines provide complimentary overnight accommodations in Tokyo, Seoul, Taipei, or Hong Kong—a good way to break up the long and tiring journey. The following tips may save you time and money while you search for the perfect airline ticket.

International Airports in Thailand

Thailand currently has international airports in Bangkok, Chiang Mai, Phuket, Hat Yai, Chiang Rai, and Sukothai, though the latter two airports have never received international flights.

Fares

All major airlines in North America conform to the price guidelines issued by the International Air Transport Association (IATA). Roundtrip advance-purchase weekday fares from the U.S. West Coast are currently US$1,124 (low season) and US$1,231 (high season). Roundtrip is US$1,440 from New York.

Tickets purchased directly from the airlines cost more than tickets purchased from budget agencies and consolidators, but often carry fewer restrictions and cancellation penalties. Special promotional fares offered by the airlines may even match the discounters, such as roundtrips during the winter months priced US$880-940.

Thailand can be reached on dozens of airlines with a variety of tickets sold at all possible prices. Read the travel section of your Sunday newspaper for advertised bargains, then call airlines, student travel agencies, and discount wholesalers for their prices and ticket restrictions. Determined travelers can plan itineraries and discover obscure air routes by studying the *Official Airline Guide* at the library.

Ticket prices vary enormously depending on dozens of factors, including type of ticket, season, choice of airline, your flexibility, and experience of the travel agent. It's confusing, but since airfare comprises a major portion of total travel expenses, no amount of time getting it right is wasted. The rule of thumb is that price and restrictions are inversely related; the cheaper the ticket the more hassles such as penalties, odd departure hours, layovers, and risk of last-minute cancellations.

First Class and Business Tickets: First class (coded F) and business class (coded J) are designed for travelers who need maximum flexibility and comfort, and are willing to pay the price.

Economy Tickets: Economy class tickets (coded Y) are cheaper than first and business classes, plus they often lack the advance-purchase requirements and cancellation charges.

Advance-purchase excursion (APEX) Tickets: APEX tickets—the airlines' main method for deep discounts—are about 25% less than economy class tickets but often come loaded with restrictions which require advance payment, dictate your length of stay, and carry heavy penalties for cancellations or amendments.

Super-APEX: Super-APEX tickets, somewhat cheaper than regular APEX, are limited in quantity and often sell out quickly. APEX and Super-APEX tickets are recommended for visitors with limited time who need guaranteed air reservations.

Mileage Tickets: These permit the traveler to pay the fare from A to B and make unlimited stops en route. For example, the ticket from San Francisco to Bangkok costs US$1,361 and permits 9,559 miles. One possible routing is San Francisco-Tokyo-Seoul-Taipei-Hong Kong-Manila-Bangkok. Mileage tickets are generally good for one year and a mileage surcharge is tacked on for travel beyond the allotted distance. Many airlines have phased out mileage tickets.

Circle-Pacific Tickets: Scheduled on major international airlines, these tickets allow you to circle the North Pacific, Southeast Asia, and the South Pacific for about US$2,400 in economy class. Restrictions are a problem: the ticket limits you to four stopovers, costs US$50 per extra stop, demands 14 days' advance purchase, carries cancellation penalties, has a six-month expiration, and costs US$50 for each reissuance. Worse yet, only those cities served by the principal carrier and partner are possible stopovers. This eliminates most of the smaller but vitally important connections such as Singapore-Jakarta.

Round-the-World-Tickets: Another variation of APEX is the RTW tickets sold by several international carriers. Currently, no single carrier offers round-the-world service, but all major U.S. airlines offer round-the-world routes in conjunction with foreign airlines. RTW tickets cost US$2,570 in economy class on the north Pacific route through Tokyo, Seoul, and Hong Kong; and US$3,217 in economy class on the south Pacific route through Australia and New Zealand. Most airlines allow unlimited stopovers but you can only stop in those cities served by the airlines. Tickets are good for either six months or one year depending on the airline. Other sample round-the-world fares include:

USA-London-Bangkok-Hong Kong-USA:
   US$1,399
USA-Hawaii-Bali-Bangkok-Kathmandu-Delhi-
   Amsterdam-USA: US$1,599
USA-Tahiti-New Zealand-Noumea-Sydney-
   Jakarta-Singapore-Amman-Vienna-USA:
   US$1,799
USA-Tahiti-Cook Islands-Fiji-New Zealand-Aus-
   tralia-Bali-Bangkok-Kathmandu-Delhi-Vien-
   na-USA: US$2,199
USA-Dublin-Amsterdam-Athens-Cairo-Nairobi-
   Bombay-Delhi-Kathmandu-Bangkok-Singa-
   pore-Jakarta-Bali-Hawaii-USA: US$2,299

The major difference among airlines is ticketing procedure. Some, like Delta, have an open ticket policy—you only have to reserve the first international segment and remaining dates are left unspecified, allowing for last-minute alterations.

One Way or Roundtrip?

Travelers on a holiday under three weeks should purchase roundtrip tickets from their homeland to ensure reserved seats. Consider a package tour or adventure travel package, which often includes discounted hotels and internal flights to popular destinations.

Travelers with open schedules should skip roundtrip tickets and purchase a one-way ticket to Bangkok. All future travel arrangements can then be made in Thailand, an option which adds flexibility and saves money since Thai travel agents sell some of the world's cheapest airline tickets. This option also avoids IATA regulations, which dictate that one-way fares priced in U.S. dollars be doubled to arrive at a full-fare roundtrip price.

Low and High Seasons

All airlines and discount agencies price their tickets according to the season.

Airlines in North America and Europe consider the low season the winter months Oct.-April and the high season the summer months May-September. The holiday period Dec.-Jan. is also considered a high season. An intermediate or "shoulder season" is often wedged between the high and low seasons.

The high season for airlines in Australia and New Zealand runs December to 15 January, school holiday periods are shoulder seasons, and the low season is the rest of the year.

Sold-Out Flights

The holiday season Dec.-Jan. can be a difficult time to obtain tickets. Not only are prices about 20% higher, the shortage of seats makes confirmed reservations on specific days a real chore.

This exasperating situation was created by the reluctance of Thai Airways International (THAI) to allow additional flights into the capital by other international carriers. As with other Asian-based airlines, THAI feels they're at an unfair disadvantage against U.S. airlines that have huge domestic networks to feed their transpacific routes. Airlines in the U.S. also benefit from fifth-freedom rights, which allow them to pick up passengers and fly on to a third country in Asia. THAI further argues that U.S. carriers can now fly direct to more Asian destinations with new long-haul aircraft, but won't because of higher yields on intra-Asian routes.

Travelers are advised to make reservations several months in advance to ensure reserved seats on the most convenient dates. After arrival in Bangkok, be sure to reconfirm departure dates to avoid losing your reservation.

Passengers are required to reconfirm all flights at least 72 hours prior to departure. **Reconfirmation** is not necessary on the first flight of your itinerary or on flights with a layover of less than 72 hours. Passengers who fail to reconfirm their flights may have their seats automatically canceled and given to other passengers. Some passengers even reconfirm their reconfirmations!

Nonstop, Direct, Connecting?

Airline terminology is almost as confusing as its ticketing policies. Flights are either nonstop, direct, or connecting. A nonstop flight requires no change of planes and makes no stops. A direct flight stops at least once and may involve a change of planes. The flight number remains the same and the second plane must wait for any delayed arrivals. A connecting flight involves different planes and different flight numbers. Connecting planes are not required to wait for delayed flights on the first leg.

No airline flies nonstop from North America to Thailand. All direct flights require a stop for refueling and possible change of planes in either Tokyo, Seoul, Taipei, Manila, or Hong Kong. A stop in Honolulu is often included.

Getting Bumped

Bumping is another problem encountered by an increasing number of passengers heading off to Southeast Asia. The situation has been created by airline executives who routinely overbook flights to maximize their profits and meet yield management goals. Who gets bumped is often based on check-in time: those who checked in last are the first to be bumped. Passengers denied boarding against their will are entitled to compensation, provided they have fulfilled certain requirements, such as confirming their reservation and checking in before the deadline.

Airline managers know that compensation for bumped passengers is a small price to pay to maximize aircraft capacity. The compensation depends on the price of the ticket and the length of delay until the next available flight. Compensation can be free domestic tickets, cash up to US$400, discount coupons for other destinations, or complimentary hotels and meals. Be-

lieve it or not, some passengers actually attempt to get bumped to pick up these benefits.

Proof of Onward Passage

Some countries in Asia require incoming travelers to show proof of onward passage. Proof of onward passage can be a plane ticket to some foreign destination or a miscellaneous charge order (MCO). Fortunately, Thai immigration rarely checks for onward tickets unless they dislike your appearance.

If you're concerned about not having proof of onward passage, you could purchase the cheapest outbound ticket (Hat Yai to Phuket for example) and request a refund after you've passed through immigration in Bangkok. Be sure to buy this ticket with cash or traveler's checks from a major airline carrier. Requesting a refund for an unused ticket with an obscure airline can be a Kafkaesque experience.

Ticket Tips

Bargain tickets sold by major airlines and discount travel agencies often carry heavy restrictions to prevent passengers from changing their minds and thereby saddling the airline with empty seats. Travelers should read the fine print and understand the restrictions, which aren't always spelled out in airline advertisements. Most airlines only give cash refunds in the event of death—not for a sudden change of plans, marriage, birth of a child, traffic delays, or nervous breakdown at the check-in counter. Passengers who need to cancel their flights may, depending on the type of ticket, be able to have the value applied toward the purchase of another nonrefundable ticket for up to one year after the first was issued. Other tickets are partially refundable but penalties can be 25-75% of the ticket value.

Tickets issued by travel agents will be marked either "OK," "RQ," or "on request." The OK stamp next to the destination indicates the travel agent has checked with the airline and the seat has been reserved in your name. An RQ or "on request" stamp means your seat has not been confirmed by your agent and you are going to be on standby. This is a big problem with many travel agencies in Bangkok. Be sure your ticket is marked "OK" before payment.

Airline tickets cannot be legally transferred from one passenger to another, despite the advertisements placed in newspapers and on bulletin boards in youth hostels and guesthouses. International departures are usually checked by matching the name on the ticket with the name on the passport.

Tickets purchased from mileage brokers are prohibited by airlines and subject to seizure at the airport. In other words, mileage certificates obtained from frequent flyer programs and sold to the public at steep discounts are nontransferable.

Tour conductor tickets given to travel agents as a reward for selling seats on group tours cannot be legally sold or transferred but may be given away as presents. Always check your bargain ticket to see if it's marked "no fare" or "no miles," two terms given by discount operators to denote budget tickets without fare guarantees or mileage benefits.

For passengers, air travel is getting worse. The number of passengers angry enough to complain to the Department of Transportation has risen to record levels in recent years. A few tips may help reduce the aggravation.

Try to avoid flying on weekends or holidays when airport congestion is bad and flight cancellations and delays are most common. Avoid rush hours in the early mornings and evenings. Request your boarding pass when you make your reservation or take advantage of the new "ticketless" travel options offered by many airlines.

Don't check additional baggage; carry everything possible onto the plane. Ask your travel agent about legal limits and pack accordingly. Remove old airport destination tags and write your permanent business address and phone number at your destination on your luggage tag. File claims for lost baggage before you leave the airport.

Know your legal rights. Contact the U.S. Department of Transportation's Office of Consumer Affairs (tel. 202-366-2220) for a copy of *Fly Rights: A Guide to Air Travel in the U.S.*

Resources for Budget Tickets

The cheapest tickets to Asia are sold by wholesalers who take advantage of special rates for group tours by purchasing large blocks of unsold seats. Once an airline concludes it can't sell all of its seats, **consolidators** are offered a whopping 20-40% commission to do the job. They then use most of the commission to offer clients reduced ticket prices.

The drawbacks are these companies rarely provide travel counseling, they keep you guessing about which airline you'll fly, tickets often carry penalties, and routings can be slow and byzantine. Try to get the cheapest ticket, on the best airline, with the fewest unnecessary stops. Consolidators sell tickets through student bureaus, independent travel agents, and travel clubs. In fact, you can buy consolidator tickets from almost everyone except the consolidators themselves and the airlines.

Roundtrip prices currently average US$500-600 from the U.S. West Coast cities to Tokyo, US$550/650 low season/high season to Hong Kong, and US$750-950 to Bangkok, Singapore, and Manila. East Coast departures add US$150-200. Current fares are advertised in the Sunday travel sections of major newspapers such as the *New York Times, Los Angeles Times,* and *San Francisco Chronicle-Examiner.* Advance planning is essential since the best deals often sell out months in advance.

The following penalties and restrictions may apply to consolidator tickets: Peak fares in effect June-Aug. mean an extra US$50-100; tickets purchased less than 90 days in advance are subject to an additional US$50-150; flight cancellations or changes before the ticket issue usually cost US$50; and cancellations within 30 days of departure or any time after the ticket has been issued cost you up to 25% of the fare.

Travel Clubs: These clearinghouses sell leftover space on airlines, cruises, and tours at a 15-50% discount. Many specialize in cruise discounts and all charge an annual membership fee of US$20-50. **Warning:** Most are honest, but some travel clubs are fraudulent scams. Proceed with caution.

Contact the following companies for more details: Cruise Line, tel. (800) 327-3021; Cruises Inc., tel. (800) 854-0500; Entertainment Travel, tel. (800) 445-4137; Great American Traveler, tel. (800) 548-2812; Privilege Card, tel. (800) 236-9732; Traveler's Advantage, tel. (800) 548-1116; Vacations To Go, tel. (800) 338-4962.

Couriers: Aside from working as a travel agent or hijacking a plane, the cheapest way to reach Southeast Asia is to carry urgent mail for a courier company. Anyone can do this, and it's perfectly legal—no drugs or guns are carried, just stock certificates and registered mail. However, you're generally limited to carry-on luggage, and length of stay averages two to four weeks.

The best source of accurate information on courier flights is an extremely helpful monthly newsletter from **Travel Unlimited**, P.O. Box 1058, Allston, MA 02134. Editor Tom Lantos charges US$25 for 12 monthly issues; a great deal since you'll save hundreds on your first flight, whether heading to Asia, Europe, or South America.

Standby Couriers: Absolutely the cheapest way to reach Thailand is as a standby courier. Call any of the courier companies listed in the chart "Courier Phone Numbers" and tell them you can replace passengers who cancel their reservations at the last moment. Courier companies welcome standby volunteers. Companies are legally allowed to confiscate the nonrefundable deposit paid by the client, in many cases the full value of the ticket.

Standby prices decline as the departure approaches. For example, a flight leaving in five days may be discounted only US$100-150, since the courier company has plenty of time to find a replacement. Flights departing in under two days force the company to offer ridiculous fares, such as US$100 roundtrip to Bangkok.

BY AIR FROM NORTH AMERICA

Planning Your Route

By now you've studied the historical, geographical, and cultural background of the country, decided where to go and your motivations for travel, decided what activities carry the strongest appeal, determined your allotted time and monetary limits, and formed a general itinerary for your adventure. You've taken care of legal documents, checked your health, surfed the Internet, and packed your bag. You've also learned about types of tickets, pitfalls, and cheaper travel options from couriers and consolidators.

One last task before purchasing a ticket and hopping on a plane is to plan your route. Of course, if time is limited, you can just fly directly to Bangkok. However, if you have extra time and are flexible about deadlines, you might visit

a few other countries, whether starting from the United States, Australia, or Europe.

Americans can reach Thailand direct from the U.S. West Coast via the northern loop through Japan and Hong Kong, or across the South Pacific.

Northern Loop: The north Pacific loop includes optional stops in Japan, Korea, Taiwan, and Hong Kong before continuing into China or down to Bangkok. This one-way ticket—often on an airline such as Korean Air or China Air—costs under US$900 from budget travel agencies in San Francisco and Los Angeles.

South Pacific Loop: The southern loop includes stops in the South Pacific, New Zealand, and Australia before arriving in Bali and continuing up to Thailand. This ticket—often standby on various carriers—costs around US$1,200-1,400 to Bali from student agencies.

Roundtrip: Another popular and relatively inexpensive itinerary begins with the northern Pacific loop, travels through Thailand and Southeast Asia, routes across the South Pacific, then returns to the United States. This journey covers most of Asia for about US$2,000 in total airfare—a once-in-a-lifetime experience.

Major Airlines in North America

U.S. East Coast travelers can use the North American airlines listed below or a European airline such as Swissair (17 hours, change in Zurich) or Finnair (18 hours, change in Helsinki).

Northwest Airlines (NWA): Northwest Airlines has the most gateways to Bangkok, with flights from Los Angeles, San Francisco, Seattle, Chicago, Dallas, Detroit, Washington, D.C., and New York. The airline also offers the fastest flights with a stop and change of planes in Tokyo. Fares are identical to those of other major airlines. Daily service from Toronto via Detroit or Los Angeles costs US$1,566.

United Airlines (UA): United Airlines flies daily to Bangkok from Canada (Toronto and Vancouver) and from major U.S. cities via Tokyo, Taipei, or Seoul. United offers low-priced promotional fares during the winter. Contact their travel division (tel. 800-328-6877) for information on organized tours.

Canadian Airlines International (CP): Canadian Airlines flies daily from Toronto and Montreal via Vancouver to Bangkok. Promotional fares are available during the winter months, but rates

AIRLINE TOLL-FREE NUMBERS

Cathay Pacific	(800) 233-2742
China Airlines	(800) 227-5118
Delta	(800) 241-4141
Finnair	(800) 950-5000
Garuda	(800) 342-7832
Japan	(800) 525-3663
KLM	(800) 347-7747
Malaysian	(800) 421-8641
Northwest	(800) 447-4747
Philippines	(800) 435-9725
Silk Air	(800) 745-5247
Singapore	(800) 742-3333
Swiss Air	(800) 221-4750
Thai	(800) 426-5204
United	(800) 538-2929

on U.S. carriers departing from the United States are generally much lower.

Asian Airlines
Asian carriers are considered some of the finest in the world in terms of safety records, service, and food.

Thai Airways International (THAI): THAI flies daily from Los Angeles, three times weekly from Seattle, and twice weekly from Toronto. All flights stop in either Tokyo or Taipei; the fastest route is Los Angeles to Bangkok via Seoul.

THAI's frequent flyer program shares benefits with the Mileage Plus Program from United Airlines. Members of either program can now accrue miles and redeem awards on a reciprocal basis. THAI also sells package tours that include transportation, accommodations, and sightseeing.

On the downside, THAI has problems with overbooked flights during the busy holiday season Dec.-Feb. when the airline may bump passengers, delay flights, and change schedules without prior notification.

Other Airlines: Singapore Airlines, Malaysian Airlines, Philippine Airlines, Korean Air, China Air, Japan Airlines, Cathay Pacific, and other Asian-based airlines offer super-APEX flights from U.S. West Coast cities to Bangkok for US$900-1100.

Budget Travel Agencies in North America
Some of the best advice on airline ticketing can be found at agencies which specialize in the youth and student markets.

Student Travel Australia: STA serves not only students and youths, but also nonstudents and tour groups. In the United States call (800) 777-0112 for the nearest office.

Hostelling International (HI): The former International Youth Hostel Federation (IYH) and their associated American Youth Hostels (AYH) provide budget travel information and confirmed reservations at any of almost 200 hostels in the U.S. and abroad. HI-AYH, 733 15th St. NW, Suite 840, Washington, D.C. 20005, tel. (202) 783-6161.

Air Brokers International: A dependable discount agency with many years of experience in the Asian market. Air Brokers sells discount tickets and can help with circle-Pacific and round-the-world airfares. Air Brokers International, 323 Geary St., Suite 411, San Francisco, CA 94102, tel. (800) 883-3273, fax (415) 397-4767.

Council Travel: This excellent travel organization, a division of the Council on International Educational Exchange, has 37 offices in the U.S. and representatives in Europe and Australia. Prices are low and service reliable since they deal only with reputable airlines to minimize travel problems. Best of all, Council Travel sales agents are experienced travelers who often have firsthand knowledge of Southeast Asia.

Council Travel also sells the Youth Hostel Association Card, International Student Identity Card (ISIC), Youth International Educational Exchange Card (for nonstudents under 26), plus travel and health insurance. Larger offices in some major cities include: San Francisco, tel. (415) 421-3473; Los Angeles, tel. (213) 208-3551; Seattle, tel. (206) 632-2448; Chicago, tel. (312) 951-0585; Boston, tel. (617) 266-1926; New York, tel. (212) 661-1450.

BY AIR FROM SOUTHEAST ASIA

Thailand can also be reached by air from nearby Asian destinations. Useful flights include Malaysian Airlines from Sumatra to Phuket via Penang, Cathay Pacific from Hong Kong to Bangkok, and Garuda Indonesia from Bali to

Bangkok. Travelers can fly from Penang to Phuket, from Penang to Hat Yai, or from Kuala Lumpur to either destination. Flights around Southeast Asia are quick, are reasonably priced, and reduce the ordeals of overland travel.

Discount Tickets
Flights within Southeast Asia are approximately equivalent to flights within Europe and Australia; that is to say, overpriced.

Don't be alarmed. Discount tickets are sold in most major Southeast Asian cities from student and budget travel agencies, though finding the budget outlet in some cities—Manila, for example—can be frustrating. Your best source of information will probably be guesthouses and other travelers. Be sure to check prices with several agencies and carefully examine ticket restrictions before handing over your money.

ASEAN Promotional Airfares allow travelers to fly between any of the destinations listed in the chart "Airfares Around Southeast Asia"—no need to start with Bangkok. Longer itineraries to more cities are also available.

The Cheapest Ticket in Asia?
One of the favorite topics of travelers is the exact location of the cheapest tickets in Asia. One week it's Bangkok, the next it's Hong Kong, then Singapore, and finally the shoeshine boy in Macau. My experience is that tickets are cheapest in the city of origin. In other words, buy your ticket from Jakarta to Bangkok from an agent in Jakarta, not some shop in Hong Kong or Singapore.

Routes Leaving Thailand
After Thailand, many travelers continue to Myanmar, Hong Kong, Malaysia, the Philippines, and Indonesia.

Myanmar can be a roundtrip journey from Bangkok, a separate stop en route to India, or reached by air from Chiang Mai. Within a few years, land access will probably be possible through Three Pagodas Pass (west of Kanchanaburi) and from Mae Sot in west-central Thailand. Travelers can now pass from Mae Sai in northern Thailand into the Shan States but this will remain a side trip until connections are made to Yunnan Province in southern China or connecting flights are started between Kengtung and other destinations in Myanmar.

The Philippines can be reached directly from Bangkok or from Kota Kinabalu in Sabah on Borneo. Approaching from Kota Kinabalu is a useful backdoor approach which puts you on the doorstep to Mindanao, the Visayas, and Palawan.

Indonesia is usually considered a separate journey starting from Singapore rather than a side trip or direct connection from Thailand. A popular option for visitors with limited time is a roundtrip ticket between Bangkok and Bali.

Another option is to head west from Thailand to the Indian subcontinent, north to Japan, or eastward through the South Pacific. Favorite routes include a flight to India or Nepal via Myanmar, a flight to Japan via Hong Kong, and the flight to Bali followed by an overland journey across Nusatenggara to Timor. From Timor, you can fly to Darwin or return to Singapore with stopovers in Sulawesi or Kalimantan. No matter what the route, it's a grand adventure through one of the world's most fascinating regions.

BY SEA

From Malaysia
Looking for something unusual? A large ship departs daily from the Malaysian island of Langkawi and arrives several hours later at Satun in southern Thailand, an excellent connection that avoids backtracking and the hassles of public trains and buses. Longtail boats from Kuala Perlis also reach Satun. Few Western travelers arrive by sea transportation and immigration officials rarely wait at the point to welcome your arrival. Therefore, be sure to visit the Thai immigration department and have your passport stamped.

Buses continue from Satun to Hat Yai and points north.

OVERLAND FROM MALAYSIA

There are no direct trains between Thailand and Malaysia. On the west coast, you must get off the Kereta Api Tanah Melayu (KTM) train at the border and transfer to a train operated by the State Railway of Thailand (SRT). On the east coast of peninsular Malaysia, take a bus or taxi from

THE EASTERN & ORIENTAL EXPRESS

*T*he *Eastern & Oriental Express* (E & O) started service in 1993 as a joint venture between Malaysia's YTL Corporation; Orchid Lodge, an Italian-Thai hotel chain; Landmark Holdings, a Malaysian hotel investment consortium; the State Railways of Thailand; the Kereta Api Tanah Melayu (KTM) of Malaysia; the Eastern & Oriental Express Company, based in Singapore; and Orient Express Hotels, the company that restored the famous service between London and Venice.

Patterned after the Venice Simplon-Orient Express, which takes passengers from London's Victoria Station on a trans-European adventure through France, Switzerland, Austria, and Italy to Venice, the Asian offshoot now carries 132 passengers on the 1,943-km journey between Singapore and Bangkok in rather toney style.

The luxury train service has been quite successful, despite a story in *The New York Times* which panned the train for its disappointing menu and shaking cars, and an article in the *Bangkok Post* complaining about the price and limited amount of travel during daylight hours: 16 hours of daylight travel and the remainder of the journey in darkness. In fact, the E & O has been running at over 80% occupancy with about 40% of the passengers coming from the United States and large numbers of honeymooners from Japan.

The E & O takes 41 hours to complete the journey, including a two-hour Butterworth stopover and tour of Penang. Fares for one-way travel begin at US$1,200 for a standard double compartment, and rise to US$3,500 for the presidential suite. Departures are Sunday at 1600 from Singapore and Wednesday at 2030 from Bangkok.

The train can be booked from most travel agencies in the United States such as Japan & Orient Tours (tel. 800-377-1080), Orient Flexi-Pax (tel. 800-377-1080), Pacific Bestour (tel. 800-688-3288), and TBI Tours (tel. 800-223-0266). You can also make reservations by calling the following numbers:

Australia	(02) 232-7499
France	(1) 45-62-0069
Germany	(211) 16-21-06
New Zealand	(9) 379-3708
Singapore	(65) 227-2068
Switzerland	(22) 366-4222
Thailand	(02) 251-4862
United Kingdom	(71) 928-6000
USA	(800) 524-2420

Kota Baru to the border and then continue by bus or train to Hat Yai.

Buses and share taxis operate between Penang and Hat Yai—probably the easiest way to get from Malaysia to Thailand.

Trains
Ordinary trains do not run between Malaysia and Thailand. Diesels from Butterworth terminate at the border town of Padang Besar, from where you can catch the train to Hat Yai.

An **express train** departs Singapore every morning and arrives in Kuala Lumpur by nightfall. Visitors may overnight in the Malaysian capital or continue north by night train to Butterworth, the terminus for Penang.

The International Express departs Butterworth the following day at 1340 and terminates at the Thai border a few hours later. A Thai train meets this train and takes passengers north to Hat Yai (1640 arrival) and Bangkok (0835 arrival the next day).

The express train connection, however, rarely works. Express trains coming from Malaysia are often late, and Thai trains won't wait for the late trains. The upshot is confusion. To minimize problems, check schedules in Singapore and Kuala Lumpur and take your chances with a train departure from Butterworth, not Kuala Lumpur.

The express train is limited to first and second classes and is somewhat expensive because of supplemental charges for a/c, superior classes, and sleeping berths. Singapore to Bangkok costs US$100 in first-class coach with sleeper and takes 41 hours, including a 10-hour layover in Kuala Lumpur. The second-class fare is US$50 with sleeper and express surcharges.

While the 1,943-km journey from Singapore to Bangkok has romantic appeal—and is far cheaper than the *Eastern & Oriental Express*—it's a long and exhausting journey best experienced in shorter segments.

Bus

Buses and taxis can be taken from the west or east coasts of peninsular Malaysia to destinations within Thailand.

West Coast: Crossing the Thai border by public bus from the west coast can be tricky. Buses on the main highway terminate at Changlun, a small and isolated Malaysian town some 20 km from the border. From Changlun, you must hitchhike the distance to Sadao in southern Thailand—not an easy task.

Travelers going overland can also take a bus or train to Padang Besar, where buses and taxis continue to Hat Yai. You'll need to walk over the railway bridge into Thailand, ignore the unofficial taxis and motorcycle taxis at the end of the span, and continue walking until you reach the "official" taxis a few hundred meters beyond the end of the bridge. Official taxis carry a posted government permit near the meter. These taxis will take you to Hat Yai with a brief stop for border formalities at Thai immigration.

Problems with land connections via Changlun/Sadao and Padang Besar make direct buses a good idea for most travelers. Direct buses can be booked through travel agents in Penang or picked up at terminals in Penang, Butterworth, and Hat Yai.

East Coast: Public transport on the east coast of peninsular Malaysia is fairly straightforward. Bus 29 departs each hour on the hour from the main bus terminal in Kota Baru and 20 minutes later reaches the Malaysian border town of Rantau Panjang. You then walk across, conduct border formalities with Thai immigration, and catch a *tuk tuk* for 10B to the train or bus station in Sungai Golok.

Taxi

Shared taxis are fast, comfortable, and cheap; you won't get stranded at the border waiting for buses or trains. Share taxis—usually a lumbering old Mercedes or antiquated Chevy—wait in Penang at the waterfront taxi stand and in Georgetown downstairs from the bus terminal. Travel agents in Penang can book share taxis, and budget hotels in Penang will arrange pickup directly from your hotel.

Share taxis also leave from the central taxi stand in Kota Baru and reach the border in about 20 minutes. You then walk across to Thai immigration and catch a *tuk tuk* into beautiful downtown Sungai Golok.

NEW ROUTES

Thailand and Laos

Laos finally creaked open to the outside world a few years ago.

The Friendship Bridge: After years of delays, the Friendship Bridge between Nong Khai and Laos opened in April 1994 to provide the first land access from northern Thailand to Vientiane. Financed by the Australian government to encourage commerce and tourism between the two countries, the bridge can be crossed by travelers with the proper visa and travel permits.

River Crossings: River crossings are legal from Nong Khai to Tha Naleng, Nakhon Phanom to Tha Khaek, Chiang Khong to Ban Huay Sai, and Mukdahan to Savannakhet. River crossings can also be made from Chong Mek near Ubon Ratchathani to Pakse in southern Laos. The highway from Pakse heads south to Champassak, north to Vientiane, and east to Vietnam.

A New Bridge: The Thai government is now constructing a second bridge across the Mekong near Mukdahan to a village which leads to Sawannakhet. The bridge will be completed in 2001. More details in the Northeastern Thailand chapter.

Several tour companies now operate boats from Thailand to Vientiane and up the Mekong to China. For more information on this amazing travel opportunity, see the Mae Sai, Chiang Saen, and Chiang Khong sections under "The Far North and Golden Triangle" in the Northern Thailand chapter.

Thailand and Myanmar

These two countries are connected by several roads, though the only legal crossing for Western visitors is via the northern Thai town of Mae Sai.

Mae Sai to Taichilek: Land entry is permitted between Mae Sai and Taichilek in the Shan States. No visa is necessary. Visitors can have their passports stamped by Thai immigration, enter Myanmar for a nominal entrance fee of just US$5, and then spend up to 24 hours in the dusty town. You will be given a 30-day entry permit upon return to Thailand—an excellent way to quickly and inexpensively pick up an additional stay in the kingdom.

Closed Land Routes: Other entry points, such as Three Pagodas Pass and Mae Sot, remain closed, though these crossings may open in the next few years. After all, the Burmese government has extended visa permits from one week to one month, opened up dozens of new destinations, and signed agreements with Western investors for new hotels and cruise ships up the Ayeyarwady River from Mandalay to Bagan. Not to mention high-speed boats up the Mekong.

Thailand and Cambodia

Visitors can fly from Bangkok or take a long bus journey to Siem Reap and then continue down to the Cambodian capital.

By Air: Thai Airways International and Royal Air Cambodge fly between Bangkok and Phnom Phen daily, while weekly service is offered between Bangkok and Siem Reap, near Angkor Wat.

By Road: The road from Bangkok to Siem Reap is now open and Western visitors can make the crossing in less than a single day. Direct buses now leave from Banglampoo and head to Siem Reap via the border crossing at Aranyaprathet. This route is only recommended when the political situation is relatively quiet in Cambodia.

Thailand and China

By Air: Several airlines now fly between the two countries, a convenient connection that allows travelers to avoid a backtrack to Beijing or long detour via Hong Kong. Flights between Kunming and Bangkok are on Yunnan Airways and China Southwest Airlines. Thai Airways flies between Chiang Mai and Beijing and Chiang Mai and Kunming twice weekly. Plans have been announced to start flights from Bangkok and Chiang Mai to more Chinese destinations such as Jinghong, Kunming, Shenzhen, and Hainan.

Mae Sai to Kengtung and Yunnan: The latest wrinkle in offbeat travel is the overland route from Mae Sai to Yunnan in southern China, via Kengtung in the Burmese Shan States. Kengtung was opened a few years ago but closes periodically depending on the political situation.

The seven-hour trip to Kengtung follows a twisting 164-km road across regions closed to the outside world since the beginning of WW II. Kengtung has hotels and guesthouses plus trekking and temples. The road from Kengtung to the Chinese border is under reconstruction and will be open within a few years. See "Mae Sai" under "The Far North and Golden Triangle" in the Northern Thailand chapters for more details.

Chiang Khong to Yunnan: Several travel agencies are reportedly offering group tours from Chiang Khong across the river to Ban Huay Sai, then overland to Sipsongbanna District in southern Yunnan, returning to Huay Sai by boat down the Mekong River. Prior to this, the only way to reach Sipsongbanna was to fly from Chiang Mai to Kunming and then take a plane, bus, or train south to Jinghong in Sipsongbanna.

Sop Ruak to Yunnan: Another Chiang Mai agency has renovated old boats that take groups from Sop Ruak in the Golden Triangle to Sipsongbanna and back. The 320-km, five-day journey costs 14,500B, excluding visa fees for Laos and China. See the Northern Thailand chapter for more details.

GETTING AROUND

BY AIR

Thai Airways International

Domestic flights are chiefly provided by Thai Airways International (THAI) which merged with the domestic carrier, Thai Airways Company, several years ago. The consolidation benefits international travelers, who can now purchase all necessary tickets in one package to ensure a worry-free trip with guaranteed connections and seats.

Thailand's Civil Aviation Board has approved the start of two new airlines—Bangkok Airways and Orient Express Air—a decision that effectively breaks the monopoly enjoyed by flag carrier Thai International, 92% of which is owned by the Finance Ministry (no wonder it took so long). The new airlines are permitted to operate on the same routes as Thai, including international and domestic routes. Bangkok Airways has been up and running for several years, but Orient Express is still seeking funding and may never come into existence.

THAI serves 23 domestic airports and several nearby countries with a variety of aircraft, including Airbus 300s and Boeing 737s to larger destinations, and Avro 748s and Shorts 330s to smaller airports. Fares on routes served by both large and small craft will be higher with the larger planes.

Internal flights are fairly expensive when compared to rail or bus travel, but are recommended for those routes not served by train or only reached by long and grinding bus journeys. For example, the flight from Chiang Mai to Mae Hong Song takes only 30 minutes and costs 380B; the bone-crushing bus ride takes at least 12 hours and costs 140B. Another recommended flight is from Ubon Ratchathani to Phuket, a three-hour flight instead of two days of hard travel by bus and train. The 90-minute flight from Chiang Mai to Phuket is also a godsend.

THAI Air Passes: Thai Airways sells a Discover Thailand Air Pass for US$240 that includes four coupons good for four flights anywhere in the country. Additional coupons up to a total of eight can be purchased for an additional US$50 each. The first leg must start in Bangkok and sectors cannot be repeated. Full payment and reservation for the first sector must be made outside Thailand prior to arrival in the country. The air pass is sold at all Thai Airways offices outside the country.

The ticket is only worthwhile for carefully planned journeys that involve travel from the far north to the deep south. The limitation on sector repeats also makes it difficult to maximize any possible savings.

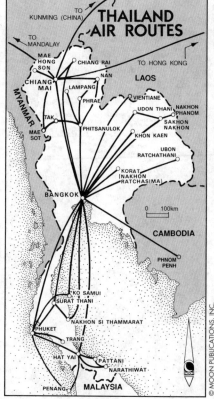

Bangkok Airways

Bangkok Airways, Thailand's only domestic air-line, launched service in 1991 after the Ministry of Transportation decreed that private carriers could operate on routes not served from Bangkok by Thai Airways. Bangkok Airways was formed to take advantage of lower overhead, which allows the airline to turn a profit even on less profitable routes to smaller destinations within Thailand.

Thai Airways seems to tolerate the competition but also may be attempting to steal away any profitable routes with their subsidiary airlines. In 1995, THAI announced plans to pull their Cam-bodia International Airlines out of Cambodia and rename the airline Orient Express Air. The first planned route was from Chiang Mai to cities in northeastern Thailand, though as of this writing the airline has never flown a single route. Coin-cidentally, Bangkok Airways' most profitable route has reportedly been their service from Bangkok to Phnom Penh in Cambodia.

The primary route of Bangkok Airways is from Bangkok to Ko Samui. Additional destinations from Bangkok include Phuket via Ko Samui and Chiang Mai via Sukothai. Flights also run be-tween Ko Samui and Phuket—a useful connec-tion for serious island hoppers.

Sukothai is intended to be a primary airport stop for many Bangkok Airways flights. Desti-nations planned include Sukothai to Chiang Rai, Udon Thani, Kunming in southern China, and Mandalay in Myanmar. From Ko Samui, they plan to offer flights to Hua Hin, U-Tapao near Pattaya, Hat Yai in the south, and Medan in Sumatra. Anticipated flights from Bangkok in-clude Loei, Krabi, and Ranong.

Bangkok Airways also provides international service from Bangkok to Phnom Penh and Siem Reap.

Bangkok Airways' head office (tel. 02-229-3434, fax 02-229-3450) is located in Queen Sirik-it National Convention Centre, New Ratchadaphisek Rd., Klong Toey, Bangkok 10110. Bangkok Airways branch offices are lo-cated in Hua Hin, Pattaya, Phuket, and Ko Samui near the boat landing.

THAILAND TRAIN ROUTES

BY TRAIN

Trains are the best form of transportation in Thai-land. Operated by the State Railway of Thailand (SRT), trains are clean and comfortable, fares are inexpensive, and there is no more pleasant or scenic way to enjoy the countryside. Much safer than buses, trains provide an excellent way to meet other travelers and the Thai people.

Train service is normally quite punctual, and many of the coaches have attached restaurant cars where you order a meal and enjoy a drink before slipping back into your a/c sleeping berth.

Perhaps the chief advantage is that train rides get you off the crowded highways and carry you through countryside unblemished by factories, housing tracts, and other signs of progress. Unlike a bus where you are pinned to your seat, you can wander around the coach or throw open the window to enjoy the passing views. You'll arrive at your destination refreshed and relaxed rather than feeling like a twisted pretzel after a long bus ride. Photographers can snap away without peering through a wall of dirty glass and subjects will probably be ricefields and small villages rather than mundane roadside attractions.

Trains are somewhat slower than buses and don't reach every corner of the kingdom, but they compensate by being safer and more comfortable.

Rail Routes

There are four main train routes in Thailand, along with a few minor side extensions kept open to serve local villagers. Bangkok is the hub for the rail system, which radiates off to the major regions within the country.

Northern Line: This line starts at the Hualampong train station in Bangkok and passes through Ayuthaya, Lopburi, Nakhon Sawan, Phitsanulok, Uttaradit, and Lampang before terminating in Chiang Mai. A spur from Den Chai, a town between Uttaradit and Lampang, up to Chiang Rai is under construction and planned for completion in 1997.

Northeastern Line: This service also begins at Hualampong train station in Bangkok, then heads up to Ayuthaya and Saraburi before reaching the junction at Kaeng Khoi, where it splits into two separate lines. One spur continues to Nakhon Ratchasima (Korat), then goes due east to Buriram, Surin, Sisaket, and Ubon Ratchathani near the Laotian border. The other spur detours north to Khon Kaen and Udon Thani until it ends at Nong Khai on the banks of the Mekong and just opposite Laos.

Eastern Line: The rarely used line leaves Bangkok for Chachoengsao and Prachinburi before terminating at Aranyaprathet on the Cambodian border. Discussions have taken place about reopening the line from Aranyaprathet to Poipet, Battambang, and Phnom Penh in Cambodia, but no one expects much action for the next few years. However, buses now go from Aranyaprathet to Siem Reap, so this train route may gain some popularity in the near future as tourism increases to Cambodia.

Southern Line: This immensely popular line also leaves from Hualampong train station and first heads west to Nakhon Pathom before changing directions and heading south to Petchburi, Hau Hin, Prachuap Khiri Khan, Chumphon, Surat Thani, Phattalung, and Hat Yai. The southern line splits at Hat Yai, one spur going through Yala to Sungai Golok on the border with the east coast of Malaysia, the other continuing due south to Padang Besar on the western border of peninsular Malaysia. This is the train route which continues south to Kuala Lumpur and Singapore.

Probably the most useful spur is the route from Nakhon Pathom through Kanchanaburi to Nam Tok in the direction of Three Pagodas Pass and the Burmese border. Tourists often board the train in Kanchanaburi and ride the rolling coaches along the former "Death Railway," immortalized in the film *The Bridge on the River Kwai*. The State Railways of Thailand has discussed renovating the rail line from Nam Tok to the Burmese border to encourage tourism and, more importantly, complete the rail link from Bangkok to Yangon.

A second spur with great potential is the line from Phumpin near Surat Thani, to Khiri Rattanikhom near Chieo Lan reservoir. The SRT has discussed extending this line down to Phuket, thereby providing direct rail connections between Bangkok and Thailand's most popular resort island.

An extension from Bangkok to Pattaya opened several years ago to provide an alternative to the congested highway that connects the capital with the beach community. The line has been underutilized and service may be discontinued in the near future. Another side route connects Thung Song, near Nakhon Si Thammarat in southern Thailand, with Trang and Kantang on the west coast of peninsular Thailand.

Train Types

Three different types of train are operated by the State Railways of Thailand. Note that the comfort zone of each type of train varies widely depending on whether you are traveling in first, second, or third class compartments.

Ordinary Trains: Diesel railcars and ordinary trains offer the cheapest fares and most basic services but also stop at every single station and town along the way. Languishing ordinary trains are rolling bargains but very, very slow—best avoided except on short journeys during the day.

Rapid Trains: Rapid trains *(rot raew)* haul only second- and third-class cars. Rapids provide better cabins and are slightly faster than ordinary trains since they aren't required to stop at every possible town. Rapid trains, however, are hardly "rapid" since they do stop at approximately every second or third town, a tiring ritual on longer journeys. The chief advantage to rapid trains is experienced on long overnight journeys—having a sleeper makes the trip relatively inexpensive, comfortable, and tolerable since you sleep through most of it.

Express Trains: Express trains *(rot duan)* haul only second- and first-class cars. Express service is faster than rapid; trains only stop at major destinations and can therefore pick up some serious speed between stations. The fastest express services are dubbed special express trains *(rot duan phiset)*.

Train Classes

Trains are divided into three classes that vary in terms of comfort and amenities depending on the type of train. Not all classes are available on all types of trains. For example, ordinary trains often haul only third-class coaches, while first-class coaches exclusively are generally hooked to express and special express trains. Train fares and schedules are listed in the back of this book.

Third Class: Third-class seats are quite cheap but can only be recommended on shorter journeys of under three or four hours. Most coaches have two rows of facing wooden benches designed for three passengers. The padded third-class seats on rapid trains are almost tolerable on longer trips. All seats are nonreserved and coaches are often packed to the gunwales. Sleeping space is on the floor with discarded peanut shells and abandoned bottles of Mekong. Third class costs about the same as an ordinary bus.

Second Class: Depending on the type of train, second class offers a choice of padded seats that often recline enough for sleeping, a/c carriages fitted with individualized reclining seats, and fan-cooled sleepers recommended for overnight travel.

Regular coach cars become sleeping compartments when ordinary seats are folded down into bunk beds by the train attendants. The clever transformation takes place shortly after dinner has been cleared and the bills settled by the porters. Sleeping berths are quite comfortable, with clean sheets; sliding curtains provide a degree of privacy. Choose lower berths if possible since they have more legroom and are removed from the bright ceiling lights that shine throughout the night.

Second class costs about twice third class, or the equivalent of a private bus with air-conditioning. Second-class trains with sleepers are more expensive than night buses, but are far safer and infinitely more comfortable—the best way to cover long distances at a reasonable cost with minimal discomfort.

First Class: Traveling first class guarantees a private compartment with individually controlled air-conditioning, an electric fan, fold-down wash-basins with mirror and towels, and either one or two berths that convert into sleepers. First-class coaches are only available on express and special express trains. First-class rail travel is a delightful experience that costs double the second-class fare or about the same as airfare.

Supplemental Charges

Supplementary charges are placed on all trains except diesels and ordinary services. To compute the total cost, you must add the supplemental charges for superior types of train (rapid, express, special express), charges for a/c, and various charges for sleeping berths. For example, a lower sleeping berth in second class with a/c on an express train costs the basic fare, plus extra charges for express service (60B), sleeper (220B), and a/c (70-120B).

Other supplemental charges include:

• rapid trains	40B
• express trains	60B
• special express trains	80B
• a/c (with catering)	120B
• a/c (no catering)	70B
• sleeper (2nd fan upper)	100-130B
• sleeper (2nd fan lower)	150-200B
• sleeper (2nd a/c upper)	220B
• sleeper (2nd a/c lower)	270B
• sleeper (1st a/c cabin)	520B
• Malaysia crossing (express)	200B
* Malaysia crossing (all a/c trains)	250B

Timetables

Train schedules are available free of charge from the Rail Travel Aids counter in Bangkok's Hualampong station—handy resources for anyone riding the trains in Thailand.

Several types of schedules are available. The condensed English-language timetables include fares and schedules for selected trains on the four primary trunk lines. You can also obtain condensed Thai-language schedules, as well as unabridged Thai-language timetables that include fares and schedules for all trains on all lines.

English-language schedules come in two colors: red brochures with condensed timetables for the southern line, and green brochures that detail the northern, northeastern, and eastern lines. Rules on refunds, breaks in journeys, ticket alterations, and validity of return tickets are included with each brochure.

To obtain further information, contact the Hualampong Information Counter, tel. (02) 223-7010 or 223-7020.

Train Tips

Ticket Validity: Tickets are valid only for the date and train as specified on the ticket.

Ticket Expiration: Roundtrip tickets expire 30-60 days after the initial departure date depending on the length of journey.

Change of Departure Date: Passengers may change their journey to a later or earlier date for a fee of 10B. Departures can be postponed twice up to a total of seven days. Postponement must be made within three hours after departure.

Break of Journey: Passengers who break their journey are not entitled to refunds or further use of the ticket.

Refunds: Passengers may apply for refunds on unused tickets at the point of purchase not more than three hours after departure of the train. Cancellation fees vary 10-40% according to the time of notification and face value of the ticket.

Children's Fares: Children under three years of age can travel free provided they do not require separate seats. Children 3-12 years of age are accepted at half the adult fare.

Luggage Allowance: Passengers are allowed to carry personal luggage free of charge up to 30 kg in third class, 40 kg in second class, and 50 kg in first class.

Seat Selection: To avoid sunstroke, reserve or grab a seat on north-south lines on the side of the carriage away from the sun.

Cautions: Train travel is quite safe but you should not accept offers of free food or drink from strangers, since there is a chance of drugging and robbery. Beware of pickpockets and thieves; sleep with a money belt and padlock your gear to an immobile object such as a luggage rack.

Meals

Meal service is provided in dining cars attached to express trains and to passengers in their seats in second- and first-class coaches. Prices are reasonable and the quality of the Thai fare is fairly high, but some Western dishes, such as breakfast items, are less than inspiring. Vendors also walk the aisles hawking soft drinks, beer, Thai whiskey, and comic books loaned for a small rental fee. Passengers can bring along their own meals and drinks.

Be wary of train staff and independent entrepreneurs handing out what appear to be complimentary face wipes or bags of peanuts. In most cases, the attendant will return later to collect fees from anyone who used the product. You should also confirm the price of meals before ordering and carefully check your bill for overcharges and lousy math.

Station Facilities

All train stations have baggage storage rooms that cost 10-20B per day depending on the size of the luggage. Most cloakrooms are open daily 0700-1800, longer hours in major stations.

All stations have a small cafe or kiosk selling basic food supplies and bottled water. The Bangkok station has a small post office, information booth in the center of the main floor, travel agency, advance-booking service in the rear, showers, and money-exchange facilities operated by the Bangkok Bank. The station in Hat Yai even has a hotel on the premises.

Thailand Rail Pass

Two types of *Visit Thailand Rail Passes* are available to holders of international passports at the Advance Booking Office in the Hualampong train station. Both passes can be used to make advance reservations or to take trains on the day of departure.

Blue Pass: The Blue Pass permits 20 days of unlimited second- and third-class travel for 1,100B adult, 550B children ages 4-12. Supplemental charges for superior trains and sleepers are *not* included.

Red Pass: The Red Pass allows 20 days of unlimited second- and third-class travel for 2,000B adult, 1,100B children ages 4-12. This pass includes all supplemental charges.

Both passes offer some degree of convenience but only provide significant savings for visitors doing a great deal of rail travel in the kingdom. The chief advantage will be realized by someone traveling from Bangkok to Chiang Mai, back to Bangkok and up to Nong Khai, then south to Ko Samui or Hat Yai in less than 20 days.

Advance Bookings

Train reservations can be made 90 days in advance at the Hualampong train station in Bangkok and at terminus train stations elsewhere in the country.

Reservations are essential during holidays, on weekends, and on popular routes such as Bangkok to Chiang Mai or Bangkok to Hat Yai. These busy seasons and routes should be booked at least one or two weeks prior to departure, especially if you intend to reserve a sleeping berth. Most trains to the northeast still have room even a few days in advance.

Roundtrip reservations do not guarantee a seat on the return journey. You should reserve your seat at the station upon arrival at your destination—an important consideration at the train stations in Chiang Mai and Surat Thani.

Reservations are impossible from most stations located midway on a trunk line, an inconvenience which limits you to third-class coaches from places such as Nakhon Ratchasima and Sukothai.

Booking Procedure: Reservations can be made Mon.-Fri. 0830-1600 and weekends and holidays 0830-1200 at the Advance Booking Office (tel. 02-223-3762 or 223-7788) in the back-right corner of Hualampong station. Ticket windows on the left side of the station are for same-day purchases. To make a reservation, take a queue number and wait for it to appear on one of the electronic boards, then report to the proper desk for your particular line—southern or north and northeastern.

Travel Agencies: Reservations can also be made through authorized travel agencies in Bangkok for an additional service charge of 50-100B. Be wary of unauthorized agencies that sometimes take the money but fail to deliver the tickets.

Special Excursions

The State Railways of Thailand offers a variety of organized excursions on weekends and holidays to popular tourist destinations such as national parks and historical monuments. A selection of the more popular programs would include Erawan National Park near Kanchanaburi (one day; 350B), the floating market at Damnern Saduak (one day; 380B), and Phimai Historical Park near Nakhon Ratchasima (two days; 1,600B).

The SRT also sells convenient transportation packages to Kanchanaburi and Ko Samui. The Ko Samui package includes your train from Bangkok to the Phumpin station, bus transportation to Surat Thani, and the boat ride across to Ko Samui—the easiest way to reach the island at minimal cost. These one-day excursions, weekend getaways, and special transportation packages can be booked through the Advance Booking Office at Hualampong train station in Bangkok.

GOVERNMENT BUS

Bus transport in Thailand is fast, clean, and reasonably comfortable on shorter journeys, and serves every settlement from big cities to small villages. In many cases, unless you have the luxury of private transportation, buses are the only way to reach a given locale.

Bus services are provided by the government and by a host of private companies; both offer regular and air-conditioned coaches. Superior types of buses provide reclining airline-style seats and video movies plus smiling hostesses who crank up the air-conditioning and serve icy drinks to their frozen customers.

Perhaps the best choice are buses operated by the government transport company called **Baw Kaw Saw** (BKS) or **Bor Kor Sor,** an abbreviation of Borisat Khon Song—"The Transportation Company."

The cheapest and slowest BKS buses are the orange ordinary buses *(rot mai thamada);* these cover every short route and reach every possible hamlet in the country. Each bus is staffed by a driver, fare collector, and optional attendant who yells "stop" and "go" to make sure all hand-wavers are picked up on the road.

Ordinary buses are fine for shorter journeys but are often packed beyond comprehension since drivers and attendants work on salary plus commission. This incentive program also inspires drivers to hang around the bus terminal for interminable periods in the hopes of finding a few more passengers.

Your best bet for bus transportation in Thailand are the air-conditioned government buses called either *rot air* (air bus), *rot prap akata* (special service bus), *rot mai duann* (express bus), or *rot tour* (tour bus). Whatever *rot* you ride, all will be fast and reasonably comfortable, and will often cost substantially less than private buses with similar amenities. Departures are less frequent than ordinary buses and not all towns are served, but whenever possible, a/c buses operated by the BKS generally offer the best combination of value and comfort.

On longer routes, Baw Kaw Saw also operates two or three superior versions of a/c buses. Regular a/c models *(chan song)* have about 44 seats that may be too tightly arranged for long-legged Westerners. First-class buses *(chan nung)* have the same number of seats but include toilets in the rear. VIP buses, a relatively new creation, have been altered to hold 34 seats instead of the standard 44 seats. This seating arrangement provides additional legroom for leggy *farangs*.

The latest word in spaciousness is the so-called "Super-VIP" bus or "sleeper" *(rot nawn),* which cuts the seat count down to just 24 passengers. Although more expensive, super-VIP coaches allow the seats to recline to near-horizontal positions.

Bus Terminals
Baw Kaw Saw terminals are located in every town in Thailand, often on the outskirts to minimize bus traffic zooming through the city center. BKS terminals in smaller towns will often be conveniently located within walking distance of guesthouses and hotels; in larger cities you may require public transportation to reach the BKS terminal.

Air-conditioned and ordinary buses may depart from different terminals in the same city. In some cities, these terminals are adjacent to each other but elsewhere may be situated on opposite sides of town.

Departures and Tickets
Ordinary buses leave throughout the day without any apparent departure schedule. For short or medium-length journeys, you can show up at any hour and simply board the next available bus heading to your destination. Long-distance buses often depart in clusters in the early morning hours 0500-0900 and in the evenings 1700-2100.

Purchase tickets on the more popular routes a day in advance or, for evening departures, arrive by 1700 to locate the next available seat. Ordinary bus tickets are sold on the bus.

Few buses display their destination in Roman script, but Western travelers are invariably offered assistance from a concerned Thai. If not, check with the ticket office or repeat your intended destination to one of the bus drivers or attendants.

Meals
Most overnight buses operated by the government and by privately owned companies stop for a complimentary meal in the middle of the night, often in the middle of nowhere at what appears to be a cafe owned by the second cousin of the bus driver.

Budget companies often stop at horrifically illuminated restaurants that serve little more than a bowl of vegetable soup or fried rice, while more expensive lines stop for buffet meals and seafood specialties cooked to surprisingly high standards.

In any event, hang onto your BKS bus ticket to provide proof of purchase to the restaurant crew.

PRIVATE BUS

Several dozen private bus companies provide services between most major tourist destinations such as Bangkok, Chiang Mai, Ko Samui, and Phuket. Smaller destinations, including Ko Samet, Ko Chang, and Krabi, are often served by minibuses rather than full-sized coaches.

As with superior BKS buses operated by the Thai government, privately owned bus companies allot reserved seats to their customers and provide a/c, blankets, pillows, snacks, drinks, and, more ominously, videos during the longer journeys. All buses are fitted with window curtains that allow you to ignore the outside world racing by at the speed of light.

Private companies operate several different types of bus priced according to the seat arrangement and levels of service. The most popular services are the VIP buses designed to hold 34 passengers instead of the standard 44 sardines, and "Super VIP" buses (sleepers) which reduce the count to just 24 seats.

Although more expensive, VIP and Super-VIP coaches provide essential legroom for tall *farangs* and, on the Super VIPs, permit seats to recline to near-horizontal positions.

Also note that private companies often misleadingly call their coaches "tour buses" and themselves "tour companies," although no tours are offered and real "tour buses" are identical to buses operated by the government.

Bookings

Tickets can be purchased through most hotels, guesthouses, and travel agencies, and from the head office of the bus company. Note that some budget agencies collect money, then fail to deliver the proper ticket; it's best to purchase tickets from a reputable company or directly from the bus office to avoid complications.

Selecting the Company

Recommending a particular bus company is difficult since companies rise and fall with the seasons, and the quality of service is unpredictable. All bus companies in Thailand are theoretically licensed by the government and required to depart from private bus terminals located adjacent to the Baw Kaw Saw terminal. Some do and some don't, but the private companies that do leave from government terminals are generally more dependable and honest than companies that hustle customers from guesthouses and hotels.

Although getting out to the Baw Kaw Saw terminal can be a hassle in larger cities—especially Bangkok—the reward is that you can choose from an economical government bus or a private bus that will probably be safer and less dishonest than freelance operators.

Safety

Safety, ah, safety. An entire book could be written on the wonders of bus travel in Thailand. Thais pay for speedy service and expect their bus drivers to reach the destination in record-breaking time, often fueled by prodigious amounts of amphetamines and a hell-bent-for-leather attitude.

Traffic accidents kill over 15,000 Thais per year, a chilling statistic recently put forth by the Land Transport Department, which also pointed out that traffic accidents are now the biggest killer of young people in the country. The Ministry of Public Health claims that half the deaths are the result of drunken driving.

Read the *Bangkok Post* for any length of time and you'll soon have your own file of classic collisions and other rolling disasters. One week the featured crash involves a tour bus driver who decides to race the train to the train crossing but misses the mark by a few precious seconds; 60 people dead. Next week the paper reports that one bus loaded with passengers attempts to pass another bus on a blind mountain pass only to slam into a pair of gravel trucks playing the same mad game from the opposite direction. Small wonder the bus drivers plaster their windows with jasmine garlands, Buddha images, and magical amulets for good luck.

Read the newspaper long enough and you'll come across the classic story about the bus stewardess who serves all the passengers complimentary Cokes heavily laced with sleep-inducing drugs. After the riders have miraculously nodded off, the stewardess and bus driver calmly relieve the entire entourage of their wallets, jewelry, and cameras before hightailing it back to their provincial hideaway. Of course, one rider wisely declined the beverage, but then had to play dead while his pockets were rifled and his Rolex cut from his wrist.

What can you do to avoid making the obituary column of the *Bangkok Post*? First, never accept food or drink from strangers. Buses operated by Baw Kaw Saw tend to have less accidents than buses from private companies, and private buses that depart from Baw Kaw Saw terminals tend to be safer than independent operators who depart from cafes and street corners.

Select a safe seat. Although seats at the front of the bus have additional legroom and guarantee great views out the front window, front-row passengers are also the first to die in head-on crashes.

Government or Private Bus?
Private buses on popular routes such as Bangkok-Chiang Mai will cost about the same as government buses, but services and meals will be probably be less comprehensive than those on government buses.

Most other routes served by private companies tend to be more expensive than government buses. For example, Bangkok-Surat Thani fares are 30-70% more expensive on private lines. Services are identical. One advantage could be that private companies often provide pickup from your hotel or guesthouse.

But pickup services are sporadic and undependable. You might wait an extra 30 minutes at your hotel, then be shuttled to some strange neighborhood where you're dumped in a cafe and told to wait for the main bus. Two hours later, another minibus shuttles you to another location where you're once again told to wait for the bus. When the bus finally arrives and accepts passengers, it leaves for another cafe to pick up three more travelers shuttled over from another part of town. At this point, the pickup service seems a twisted joke invented for torture rather than convenience.

The complimentary pickup service offered by private bus companies is often more stressful and a sheer waste of time; you're better off taking local transportation over to the government bus terminal.

YACHTS AND CRUISE SHIPS

A handful of luxury cruises and private yachts can be booked through companies based in the United States and Thailand.

Siam Cruises: *Andaman Princess,* the finest luxury cruise ship in Thailand, conducts three- to five-day sails in the Gulf of Thailand May-Sept., and five-day excursions through the Andaman Sea from Phuket Oct.-April. Onboard facilities include lounges, saunas, and fitness rooms. 33/10-11 Sukumvit Soi 11, Bangkok 10110, tel. (02) 255-4563, fax (02) 255-8961.

Seatran Travel: A Thai company with two luxurious ocean liners departing from Phuket. The *Seatran Queen* heads east of Phuket to the Similan Islands, and down to Hat Yai. The more luxurious *Seatran Princess* reaches Ranong, Ko Phi Phi, Tarutao, and Penang. 1091/157 Metro Shopping Center, New Petchburi Rd., Bangkok 10400, tel. (02) 253-5307, fax (02) 254-3187.

Ocean Voyages: Ocean Voyages arranges charters for individuals and groups on every type of vessel from sleek yachts to superb classic sailing ships. Possibilities include high-performance yachting onboard the *Omni,* excursions with a husband-wife writer team on the *Endymion,* and luxury cruises on the famous 72-foot *Storm Vogel.* All yachts are captained by professionals who have spent years sailing and studying anchorages, local histories, anthropology, and marine ecology. Director Mary Crowley can also help with scuba diving, racing events such as the King's Regatta in Phuket, and charters in the South Pacific, the Caribbean, and the Mediterranean. 1709 Bridgeway, Sausalito, CA 94965, tel. (415) 332-4681.

Asia Voyages: Private yachts for cruising, scuba diving, and big-game fishing, plus larger ships to beach resorts and remote islands. Charn Issara Tower, 942 Rama IV Rd., Bangkok 10500, tel. (02) 235-4100, fax (02) 236-8094.

Southeast Asia Yacht Charter: Owner Dave Owens manages five yachts from Phuket, including the 45-foot *Tonga Queen,* 48-foot sloop *Buccabu,* French-skippered *Celestius,* Aussie-skippered *Wanderlust,* and American-sailed *Quilter II.* 89-71 Thaweewong Rd., Phuket 83121, tel. (076) 321292.

Sea Canoes Thailand: Since 1989, "Caveman" John Gray has organized sea canoe explorations of the coves and caves of Phangnga Bay near Phuket in southern Thailand. Packages range from three-hour coastal departures to one-week expeditions with all camping supplies, food, and professional guide service. Reservations and information from Sea Canoe Thailand, 100 Pine St., Suite 2715, San Francisco, CA 94111, tel. (800) 822-8438, fax (415) 391-2888. In Thailand, contact Sea Canoes Thailand, P.O. Box 276, Phuket 83000, tel./fax (076) 212172.

RULES OF THE ROAD

*P*ublished rules state everyone must drive on the left and observe legal speed limits of 60 kph within city limits and 80 kph on highways. But five minutes on the road proves Thailand operates under a set of road rules quite different from those back home.

The ruling law is bigger vehicles *always* have the right of way over smaller vehicles. Don't get hung up about polite behavior or expect pity for your precious little rental: diesel trucks and thundering buses expect smaller craft to scramble for safety.

Another rule is animals, dogs, people, water buffalo, and elephants are entitled to wander freely down the highways, and vehicles are expected to dodge these living hazards with great care and respect. Buddhism deplores the slaughter of animals; foreigners are expected to share this love for creatures.

Foreigners involved in accidents are always the guilty party and must immediately settle claims or expect to be hauled over to the police station for further negotiations.

Another curious, but entirely sensible habit, is vehicles in front often help drivers to their rear with passing decisions. When trailing a truck or bus, left-turn signals indicate approaching traffic and dangerous passing conditions; right-turn signals indicates the truck driver believes enough space exists for safe passage. You may, however, wish to take his recommendation with a grain of salt before racing around that blind mountain pass.

All these warnings and horror stories may sound discouraging, but after two decades of driving in Thailand, this travel writer would say travel by rented vehicle is both an enlightening and feasible experience for most foreigners. Driving conditions are unique, but after a few weeks you may start to enjoy the spontaneous nature of driving in Thailand.

CAR RENTALS

Thailand is an outstanding country to tour by rented car or motorcycle. Contrary to some dire warnings, traffic is moderate and manageable throughout the country—the notable exception being Bangkok. Highways are kept in excellent condition, and most directional signs are labeled in both Thai and English. Aside from Bangkok, most town streets are laid out in straightforward grid patterns that make navigation relatively easy.

A rental vehicle allows you to explore those unspoilt nooks and crannies usually missed, and to escape the floods of tourists that now wash over most of the country. Best of all, travel by rental vehicle forces you to learn about the culture and meet people while asking for directions to that next temple. For more information on driving in the kingdom, see the special topic **Rules of the Road.**

National Road System

Thailand has over 175,000 km of roadways, including over 16,000 km of two-and four-lane national highway. Principal highways and many secondary roads are maintained in excellent condition for commerce as well as easy navigation for unexpected emergencies. In fact, some of the best roads are those following the national borders of Myanmar, Laos, and Cambodia; incursions from neighboring countries make the maintenance of border roads a matter of national security.

The principal roads heading north from Bangkok are Highway 1, which connects Bangkok with Mae Sai on the Burmese border, and Highway 11, which connects Singburi with Chiang Mai via Phitsanulok and Lampang.

Highway 2, the so-called "Friendship Highway" constructed by the American government during the Vietnam conflict, serves as the principal route from Bangkok to Nong Khai in the northeast. Highway 212 circumnavigates most of the Mekong River, while Highway 24 links Nakhon Ratchasima to Ubon Ratchathani.

The eastern seaboard of Thailand is traced by Highway 3—also called Sukumvit Road—which stretches from Bangkok all the way to the Cambodian border near Trat.

To the south, Highway 4 reaches Phuket, Trang, and Hat Yai, while Highway 41 covers the eastern coastline from Chumphon to Phattalung via Surat Thani.

Toll roads geared to commercial vehicles and tour buses are now under construction from Bangkok to Chiang Mai and from Bangkok down to Hat Yai. Travelers may also notice odd signs marked "Asian Highway," such as "Asia 1" from Mae Sot to the Burmese border and "Asia 12" from Nakhon Ratchasima to the border of Laos. These optimistic signposts anticipate an era of open highways that may link all of Asia in a network of superhighways.

Rental Agencies
Cars, jeeps, and vans can be rented from local outfits and familiar agencies such as Avis and Hertz in major cities, including Bangkok, Chiang Mai, and Phuket. Rental prices are 800-1200B per day for a small jeep (Suzuki Caribian) or compact car (Toyota Corolla), 1200-1500B per day for mid-sized sedans (Toyota Camry), and 1500-1800B per day for larger cars (Nissan Maxima) and minivans (Toyota Hi-Ace and Nissan Urvan).

Visitors intimidated by Asian driving habits might consider hiring a driver for an additional fee of 250-300B per day. The additional cost is small, and probably worth the peace of mind.

Local agencies are less expensive, plus they offer reduced monthly rates that include insurance and unlimited mileage. Monthly rentals split by four people can be an economical and flexible way to tour the country.

Licenses
An International Drivers License is legally required for anyone not holding a current driver's license written in the English language. Few agencies check for a license aside from a handful of international rental outlets in major tourist destinations. Your main risk will be entrepreneurial police who sometimes stop unlicensed Westerners and ask for voluntary donations; savvy bargaining along with smiles and apologies will set you free at minimal cost.

An International Drivers License can be obtained from any local office of the American Automobile Association (AAA) or the Canadian Automobile Association (CAA).

International Driver's Permits can also be obtained in Thailand from any office of the Police Registration Division (PRD), located in Bangkok and most other provincial capitals. A written test may be required.

Foreigners who live in Thailand more than six months must obtain a Thai or International Drivers License from the PRD. Requirements include photocopies of your proof of residency, passport, visa, arrival card, medical certificate, two passport-size photos, and current valid driver's license.

Insurance
Insurance is not only mandatory but a sensible idea since foreigners involved in automobile accidents are likely to be judged guilty—no matter who was actually at fault. As in many countries around the world, unwritten rules state that outsiders are always to blame and that damages should be paid without calling the police.

Major rental agencies such as Avis and Hertz will generally include comprehensive insurance with each vehicle. Smaller local agencies often include nonexistent or inferior insurance policies. A sensible precaution with smaller agencies is to verify insurance coverage prior to signing the rental contract by asking to inspect the official insurance contract. No contract means no insurance, no matter the claims of the rental agent.

Your car insurance policy back home or major credit card may include standard insurance coverage on rentals in Thailand, but this should be confirmed prior to departure. If you qualify, ask your agent or credit card company for an International Insurance Certificate to prove coverage to rental agencies and other foreign officials in Thailand.

Car rental complaints involving the Collision Damage Waiver (CDW) often involve the type of vehicle (four-wheel drive and luxury vehicles are often exempt), limited coverage (tires and undercarriage), restricted countries (inquire), additional drivers, foreign language problems, and problems with final inspection and audits (take photographs).

Gasoline
Gasoline stations are located in almost every possible city and provincial town in Thailand. Remote locations will have mom-and-pop cafes selling *benzin* (gasoline) or *nam man rot yohn* (water travel vehicle) from hand-operated pumps or liter-sized liquor bottles. Local merchants usually charge an additional fee for their service, but government rates should be about 10B per liter. Fuel is sold by the liter and the indicators on the pumps display the amount due in *baht*.

Rental cars require premium *(priset)* while motorcycles are usually fine on regular *(thammada)* gasoline.

MOTORCYCLES

Motorcycle touring is one of the best ways to get off the beaten track and reach isolated sites relatively unaffected by mass tourism. Despite the irrational driving habits of the Thais, and the inherent dangers of two-wheel travel, growing numbers of Western tourists are now exploring every nook and cranny of Thailand by motorcycle.

Rental Locations

Bikes can be rented near the Malaysia Hotel in Bangkok, and in Pattaya, Kanchanaburi, Sukothai, Chiang Mai, Mae Hong Son, Chiang Rai, Mae Sai, Nong Khai, Korat, Hua Hin, Ko Samui, Phuket, Krabi, and Hat Yai—almost everywhere that Westerners want independent transportation in Thailand.

Larger towns such as Chiang Mai and Sukothai have motorcycle rental shops stocked with a variety of bikes, but rentals in smaller towns are often from guesthouses and private owners who loan their bikes for extra pocket money.

Types of Bike

Motorcycles are available in a variety of sizes and conditions. Companies import parts from Japan and assemble bikes at small plants around the country. Thailand currently has over seven million registered motorcycles as opposed to under three million cars. Over 70% of the cars are registered in Bangkok, while motorcycles are distributed evenly around the country.

Most motorcycles assembled in Thailand carry inefficient two-stroke engines that badly pollute the air since the mixing of the fuel and lubrication systems prevents complete combustion of the heavier lubricant. Unburned oil is thus expelled through the exhaust along with the fuel-air mixture. Regulations under consideration by the Thai government will ban the use of two-stroke engines and force all manufacturers to assemble bikes with four-stroke engines.

The legal maximum displacement is currently just 150cc; larger bikes are subject to a 600% import tax to discourage the use of gas guzzlers.

Big bikes in the 600-1000cc range can be rented in Pattaya, Phuket, and Chiang Mai, but these bikes were imported by foreigners and resold on the aftermarket or illegally imported as a basket of parts, then reassembled and relicensed by local dealers. Insurance can be a problem with these larger bikes.

Most visitors will find the smaller 80-100cc scooters perfectly adequate for local touring and reaching destinations within a few days' journey. Many of these economical step-through models have automatic transmissions and sufficient power to climb up steep hills to isolated temples. Scooters cost 80-120B per day depending on the model, condition of the bike, and length of rental. Larger 125-150cc motorcycles cost 150-250B per day.

Japanese dirt bikes, such as the 250cc AX-1 and the Honda XL 250, can be useful for off-road travel but these bikes are also very loud, are unsteady at high speeds, and consume twice the fuel of smaller bikes with four-stroke engines. For example, the 125cc Honda Wing gets about 300 km per tank of gas while a Honda MTX of similar displacement runs dry in about 150 km.

Before You Go

Consider the following guidelines prior to signing a contract and paying for the rental:

Carefully inspect the bike and make note of any problems such as dangling rearview mirrors and loose chains. Check the tire tread and look under the engine for obvious signs of oil leakage. Squeeze the brakes and then point out any problems to the rental shop. An itemized list of deficiencies may help prevent misunderstandings since customers are held responsible for any problems that pop up after rental.

Motorcycles in the best condition are rented first, so shop early for vehicles with the lowest mileage and least amount of potential problems.

Purchase insurance. Most rental agencies will have you sign a contract that includes some type of insurance policy but smaller agencies often lack arrangements with local insurance companies. Read the contract to check on limitations, coverage for theft and damage, repair services outside a limited geographical boundary, and exclusions on third-party liability. Many policies cover repairs made outside their shops but only with proper receipts.

Ask about the replacement value of the bike. Without adequate insurance, you may be held responsible for the full value of the bike in the event of theft or serious accident. Some agencies demand full replacement based on the value of a new bike, not the real value of the clunker. A written estimate that reflects the real value of the bike should be obtained to prevent misunderstandings; take photographs if necessary.

Wear a helmet with visor for protection against minor collisions, windburn, dirt, and insects. Thai laws now require helmets in most urban areas but helmets remain optional outside city limits. Ask for a solid helmet rather than the useless plastic shells that may comply with the law but provide minimal protection in the event of an accident.

Wear a long shirt, long trousers, and hard shoes. Gloves will protect your hands and stop blisters from forming during longer journeys. All this protective gear is invaluable for spills and slides on gravel roads, probably the most common type of motorcycle accident in Thailand.

Exchange enough money to finance longer journeys. Most shops require your passport as a security deposit to cover claims for damage or theft, and exchanging money without a passport is often an impossible task. Some shops rent bikes with photocopies of your passport, a good idea if you intend to be touring for an extended period.

On the Road
A few sensible suggestions for a safe journey:

Always give way to larger vehicles and drive at safe and reasonable speeds. Rules of the road dictate motorcycles outrank people but are far below the pecking order of cars, buses, and trucks. Westerners with their arms and legs wrapped in plaster casts are a depressingly common sight in beach resorts such as Phuket and Ko Samui.

Be extra cautious on dirt and gravel roads. Hitting an unexpected patch of gravel is almost as dangerous as dealing with the bizarre driving habits of the average Thai citizen.

Use your rear brake rather than the front to slow your bike. Front brakes often lock up wheels and throw bikes into sudden slides on roads with less than perfectly clean surfaces—the most common mistake made by beginning motorcy-

clists. Avoid riding at night and around sunset when bugs swarm and smack you in the face.

Oil levels should be checked daily. Motorcycles with two-stroke engines tend to burn oil at prodigious rates since both the fuel and oil are burned through the carburetor. Carry extra two-stroke engine oil for longer trips. Also keep the chain well oiled and adjusted to the proper tension.

Bikes should be locked inside the compound of your guesthouse or hotel each night. Motorcycle theft is relatively rare but sensible precautions may save you the 25,000B replacement fee demanded for lost bikes.

Avoid major highways. The finest rides are on the smaller roads which wind through the hills and along the remote borders, not the congested highways ruled by thundering trucks and enormous buses.

BICYCLES

Most Thais will think you mad, but a surprising number of Westerners now tour sections of Thailand by rented bicycle or one brought from home.

Bicycle rides on small country lanes slow you down and give you complete freedom from bus and train schedules. From a bicycle you enjoy unsurpassed closeness to nature and meet people outside the circuit of mass tourism. Bicycles can be carried on almost every form of transport from minivans to tour buses, and even flown around the country on Thai Airways.

Rentals
Bicycles can be rented for 20-30B per day from rental shops and guesthouses in nearly every town frequented by Western tourists. Mountain bikes cost 50-60B per day. Some visitors purchase bikes in Thailand, then resell the bike prior to departure, a fine idea except that most bikes rented and assembled in Thailand are inferior two-wheeled clunkers fitted with terrible seats and without reflectors, bell, lights, or working brakes.

Ardent cyclists should consider bringing along their own bikes. Airlines often have lenient policies about accepting bicycles as luggage, especially bikes that can be disassembled and carried in a bag. Bicycles brought to Thailand should conform to accepted international specifications to simplify the replacement of wheels, spokes, and gear systems. Avoid delicate racing bikes with skinny tires and be sure to bring along a comprehensive tool kit, pump, and heavy-duty steel cable lock for security.

Suggested Routes

The principal downside to bicycle touring is the general condition of most larger roads: crowded with trucks, plagued with pollution, and often lacking any sort of shoulder or bike path to escape the approaching traffic.

Small roads, however, are rarely used by commercial vehicles and generally deserted except for a few motorcyclists and private cars. The most popular routes are those in northern Thailand starting from Chiang Mai. Bicyclists can put their bike on the top of a bus and head off to a remote location such as Pai or Chiang Saen before tackling the roads; riding from Chiang Mai in almost any direction is sheer madness.

Rides through the northern hills can be scenic but also exhausting; the road system follows every rise and fall of the topography. A more pleasant option is those country roads that skirt the Mekong River, such as the winding stretch from Mae Sai to Chiang Saen and Chiang Khong. When you've reached the limits of your endurance, flag down a bus and throw the bike on the roof for the remaining distance to the next town.

Bicyclists will also enjoy the flatter rides from Sukothai in central Thailand to the nearby historic sites of Si Satchanalai and Kamphang Phet. Another excellent spot for scenery without sweat is the road from Nong Khai to Chiang Khan in northeastern Thailand. This quiet little ribbon of asphalt is relatively flat, offers sweeping views over the Mekong River, and is dotted at convenient intervals with small towns for overnight stops.

Few bicyclists attempt the crowded highways in southern Thailand, though less congested back roads are plentiful around Phuket, Krabi, and Trang.

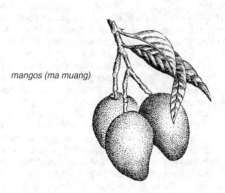

mangos (ma muang)

DAVID HURST

BANGKOK
INTRODUCTION

Thailand's sprawling, dynamic, and frustrating capital offers more variety, sights, and wonders than any other destination in Asia. Far too many visitors, hearing of the horrendous traffic jams and searing pollution, stop only long enough to glimpse a few temples and pick up a cheap air ticket before departing for more idyllic environs. To some degree this is understandable. Packed into these sweltering plains of the lower Chao Praya River are some 10 million residents, 80% of the country's automobiles, and most of the nation's commercial headquarters—a city strangled by uncontrolled development. Without any semblance of a city center or urban planning, traffic grinds to a standstill during rush hours and dissolves into a swamp after summer monsoons. Worse yet is the monotonous sprawl of Chinese shophouses and faceless concrete towers that more closely resemble a Western labyrinth than anything remotely Eastern. It's an unnerving place.

To appreciate the charms and fascinations of Bangkok, focus instead on the positive: dozens of magnificent temples that form one of Asia's great spectacles, countless restaurants with superb yet inexpensive food, legendary nightlife to satisfy all possible tastes, excellent shopping, and some of the friendliest people in the world. Few enjoy the heat, humidity, or traffic jams, but with patience and a sense of *mai pen rai,* Bangkok will cast an irresistible spell.

History
Unless a Thai is condescending to foreign ignorance, he or she will never call the capital city Bangkok ("City of Wild Plums"), but Krung Thep, "City of Angels." Krung Thep actually begins the string of honorariums which comprise the official name, a mammoth tongue twister which, according to Guinness, forms the longest place-name in the world.

Bangkok sprang from a small village or *bang* filled with wild olive and plum trees called *kok.* At first little more than a trading suburb to Thonburi ("Money Town"), Bangkok rose to prominence after Burmese forces destroyed Ayuthaya in 1767 and General Taksin moved his armies south. Taksin soon went insane (claiming to be the final Buddha) and was dispatched to Buddhist nirvana in time-honored fashion—a sharp blow to the back of the neck.

With General Taksin out of the way, Rama I, Taksin's chief military commander, was recalled from Cambodia to found the dynasty which rules to the present day. Fearing further Burmese attacks, Rama I moved the city across the river and relocated the Chinese merchants south to Sampeng, today's Chinatown. Bangkok was formally established on 21 April 1782, with the consecration of the city's foundation pillar at Lak Muang. Rama I constructed his capital to rival once-glorious Ayuthaya: palaces were erected with brick salvaged from Ayuthaya, temples were filled with Ayuthayan Buddhas, and concentric canals were dug to emulate the watery kingdom. The city was then renamed Krung Thep, a title rather ignominiously ignored by Western cartographers, who continued to call it Bangkok.

Bangkok was first centered at the Royal Palace and Wat Pra Keo, a royal chapel constructed in 1785 to enshrine the statue of the Emerald Buddha. Modernization was slow until the coronation of King Mongkut (Rama IV) in 1851. Mongkut expanded the city limits, entered into treaties with the U.S. and several European powers, and, in 1862, ordered the construction of the first road over an old elephant trail which connected the Royal Palace with Chinatown. In the same year, Anna Leonowens arrived in Bangkok to become the governess of Mongkut's children and would later misrepresent them in her published reminiscences, *The English Governess at the Siamese Court.* This misleading yarn eventually inspired the stage and film musical, *The King and I.*

Chulalongkorn (King Rama V) ascended the throne in 1868 and introduced far-reaching reforms and Westernization. By 1908 Bangkok had a grand total of just 300 automobiles. After the death of Chulalongkorn in 1910, Bangkok was ruled by several more kings until a bloodless coup in 1932 changed the system of govern-

REQUIEM FOR A CITY

*O*nce known as the Venice of the East, modern Bangkok is a City in Crisis. Economic boom times have transformed the once-charming town into an environmental horror show where street-level pollution has long since passed international danger levels, waterways not filled with concrete are clogged with garbage, and rush-hour traffic grinds to a complete standstill. One out of five residents lives in illegal slums with no piped water or electricity. Residential pollution, the unregulated dumping of dangerous chemicals and fertilizers, and a complete lack of oxygen have killed the Chao Praya River. Each day, Bangkok produces 5,400 tons of garbage but only 4,200 tons are collected; the remainder is dumped on street corners or in the waterways. Construction of artesian wells and high-rise buildings on soft soil is sinking the low-lying city under sea level, a horrifying prospect that may become reality.

But it is the horrendous traffic that typifies what is most frightening in the City of Angels. Bangkok's traffic crisis—almost certainly the worst in the world—is the result of government inaction and unwillingness to make tough decisions. The problem is that most cities throughout the world use 20-25% of their surface area for streets, but in Bangkok it's only six percent. Additionally, the number of cars doubles about every seven years, but the area of road surface increases much more slowly. The gridwork of roads found in all other major international cities has never been constructed in Bangkok. Instead, city authorities have let Bangkok grow without any form of urban planning, allowing the self-interest of private investors to undermine the controlling force of government policy.

The result is world-class traffic jams. According to the Traffic Committee, the average speed during rush hours has dropped to under four km per hour; people *walk* at five km per hour. The remainder of the day, traffic moves at just seven km per hour. When Dr. Sumet Jumsai, the nation's foremost authority on architecture and urban planning, was asked about Bangkok, he said, "It's irreversible destruction. The city is dying."

ment from an absolute to a constitutional monarchy. A series of 18 military coups occurred from 1932 to the final takeover in 1991, while Bangkok's population soared from 1.5 million in 1960 to a present settlement of over 10 million.

GETTING YOUR BEARINGS

Bangkok isn't a compact or easily understandable city such as San Francisco, but a vast and octopuslike metropolis spread haphazardly across 1,500 square km. Similar in many respects to Los Angeles (heat, smog, and traffic), Bangkok should be visualized as a multiplicity of neighborhoods with distinctive attractions, ethnic populations, variations of nightlife, and styles of hotels and restaurants that appeal to different types of travelers. The quickest way to orient yourself is to study Nancy Chandler's outstanding map of Bangkok and divide the city into the following neighborhoods. (For information on how to obtain this map, see **Maps** in the Introduction.)

Old Royal City
The old royal city around the Grand Palace has the largest concentration of sightseeing attractions such as the Grand Palace, Wat Pra Keo, Wat Po, and the National Museum. Hotels and noteworthy restaurants are relatively rare in this neighborhood, though this is one of Bangkok's few precincts that can be recommended for a walking tour (see below).

Banglampoo
Adjacent to the Old Royal City and the central parade grounds of Sanam Luang is Banglampoo, a traditional Thai neighborhood which has become Bangkok's leading stopover for budget travelers. Banglampoo lacks great nightlife or shopping but compensates with a superb location near great temples and the Chao Praya River. Anyone looking for guesthouses under US$10 should head directly for its principal thoroughfare, Khao San Road.

New Royal City
Most of the important government offices and royal residences were moved here prior to WW II. Top draws are Chitralada Palace (the home of the present king), Vimanmek Palace, the out-

standing Marble Temple, Parliament, and Dusit Zoo. No hotels.

Chinatown
Wedged between the Old Royal City and Silom Road is one of Southeast Asia's great Chinese neighborhoods and the single finest place to experience a sensory overload of Asia. A map and suggested walking tour are provided in the following pages. Chinatown hotels cater primarily to wealthy Chinese businesspeople, but a handful of inexpensive guesthouses are located in adjacent Little India. Travelers searching for a strong and completely authentic encounter might consider staying here rather than in Banglampoo.

Silom
Bangkok's financial center and original tourist enclave is located along a major boulevard known as Silom Road. Sightseeing attractions are minimal and the congestion is unnerving, but Silom offers dozens of moderate to super-luxury hotels, exclusive restaurants, high-end shopping boutiques, great sidewalk shopping, and the infamous nightlife area of Patpong Road. Riverside hotels such as the Oriental and Shangri La are world famous for their extremely high levels of service.

Malaysia Hotel Area
This was once the budget travelers' center for Bangkok. However, hotels and guesthouses along Soi Ngam Duphli have sadly declined in recent years.

Siam Square
Bangkok's alternative to Silom Road is a relatively low-density neighborhood with ultra-elegant hotels and modern shopping centers. The lack of sightseeing attractions is balanced by the vast gardens which surround many of the hotels and the enormous shopping complexes which guarantee some of the best shopping in all of Asia. Hotels are generally expensive, although a few clean guesthouses are located near the house of Jim Thompson.

Sukumvit Road
Once considered on the outer fringes of Bangkok, Sukumvit has developed into the leading area for moderate-budget tourists. The biggest dis-

CHEAP FUN IN BANGKOK

*B*angkok no longer ranks as the bargain center of the East, but visitors with limited funds can still enjoy themselves for a handful of *baht*. The secret is to find activities popular with Thais rather than with wealthy *farangs* on a two-week holiday. Here are a few suggestions:

Chao Praya Express River Cruise—For less than one U.S. dollar, you can enjoy one of the finest river trips in Asia. A 75-minute journey from the Oriental Hotel up to Nonthaburi in the north costs just 10B. Such a deal.

Wat Po Massage—Bangkok is filled with expensive emporiums offering both therapeutic and sexual massages for over 300B per hour. For an authentic rub in a safe environment, try the Wat Po Massage School where an hour's rub costs 150B.

Free Thai Dance—Colorful if somewhat amateurish Thai dance can be enjoyed at both the Lak Muang Shrine near the Grand Palace and the Erawan Shrine at the Erawan Grand Hyatt Hotel. Better performances, at the same reasonable price, can be seen on Sunday afternoons on the grassy courtyard at the National Theater.

Weekend Market—Bangkok's largest and most colorful market is held on weekends in Chatuchak Park. Operated largely by the Issan from the northeast, Chatuchak has everything imaginable at rock-bottom prices.

Meditation Classes—Free meditation instruction is given weekly at the International Buddhist Center at Sukumvit Soi 3, and inside the international hall at Wat Mahathat. Upcoming lectures are listed in the *Bangkok Post.*

Motorcycle Mania—Enjoy death-defying motorcycle stunts? Thanks to the ingenuity of Thai teenagers, you can now hire motorcycle taxis that weave through traffic with wild abandon. Hold onto your seat.

Tai Chi in the Park—Get up early and watch the old men go through their slow-motion paces in Lumpini Park. Then jog along the par course, feed the ducks, and paddle a boat around the small pond.

National Museum Tour:—Best bets for an inexpensive culture fix are the free 0930 tours given at the National Museum. Admission is but 20B.

Golden Sunsets—Sunsets are best enjoyed on top of the Golden Mountain near Wat Saket, and from the luxurious Tiara Restaurant of the Dusit Thani Hotel. Somewhat different crowds, but the same great sunset.

Bus It—A cheap way to explore Bangkok is by public bus from city center to the end of the line. Stay on the bus and you'll return without fuss. Avoid all buses during rush-hour traffic.

Go Fly a Kite—From February to April, kite aficionados gather for aerial warfare at Sanam Luang. Watch the action; buy a kite and try your luck.

Street Dining—Foodstalls provide a wonderful opportunity to rest your aching feet while burning the roof of your mouth. Watch for Issan specialties: fried crickets and roasted grasshoppers.

Thai Movies—Whether kung fu from Hong Kong, sappy love stories with supernatural overtones, or slapstick comedy, Thai cinema is worth the experience. Tickets are cheap and most theaters are air-conditioned.

Say it with Flowers—Thai orchids are among the cheapest in the world. So surprise your partner with bouquets for under 30B.

Get High—Legal highs can be enjoyed at the top of rainbow-colored Baiyoke Towers, Bangkok's tallest building. Ride the elevator to the fourth floor and transfer to the express lift up to the Sky Lounge on the 43rd floor. If the smog god has smiled on you, enjoy the panoramic views and a soft drink.

---

advantage is the enormous distance from Sukumvit to important temples and government services such as the General Post Office and the tourist office. However, Sukumvit has a great selection of hotels in the US$25-50 price range, many of the finest Thai restaurants in the country, wonderful sidewalk shopping including countless boutiques, and the mind-boggling nightlife of Nana Entertainment Plaza (NEP) and Soi Cowboy. Despite the relatively remote location and

problems with noise and pollution, Sukumvit is recommended for midlevel-income travelers and anyone intrigued by the nightlife possibilities.

ADDRESSES

Sprawling Bangkok can be a difficult place to find an address, though a few tips might help in your search.

Street Names

The transliteration problem with turning Thai into English led to a series of different names for the same street, such as Ratchadamri Road also spelled as Rajadamri, Rajdamri, and Rat'dami roads. Another example is Petchburi Road, which can also be spelled Phetburi, Petburi, or Phetchaburi. Si Ayutthaya is the same as Sri Ayudhya.

Another problem is that some streets have two names—a Thai version and an English version—such as Charoen Krung Road, which is also know by its old English title of New Road, and Withaya Road, which is commonly known in English terminology as Wireless Road.

A final challenge is that pronunciation varies and a Thai person may not recognize your feeble attempts at proper intonation. The "th" sound is pronounced like a "t," so that Thanon, Thonburi, Sathron, and Nonthaburi are actually pronounced Tanon, Tonburi, Satom, and Nontaburi.

Street Types

The Thai word *thanon* translates to road, street, or avenue, and always means a major thoroughfare.

Moving down a few notches is a *soi,* a small street or lane, which generally leads off from a larger *thanon. Sois* are sometimes enlarged and widened until they more closely resemble a major road, such as Soi Asoke, which now ranks as a major highway through the Sukumvit district.

The smallest of all roads is a *trok,* which refers to a very small alley generally running off a slightly larger *soi.*

Finding an Address

Principal arteries help determine the location of an address, such as Silom, Khao San, or Sukumvit roads. Cross streets—generally called *sois*—are very useful, since they help pinpoint the exact location in a more precise fashion than the formal street address. For example, finding an address on Sukumvit Road is most easily accomplished by locating the corresponding *soi;* an address such as Sukumvit Soi 18 is much easier to find rather than 268 Sukumvit.

An address can be either simple or complex, depending on how it has been treated over the years by government agencies and local devel-

opers. Many locations are denoted by a series of numbers divided by slashes and hyphens, which indicate increasing degrees of exactness.

88/4-8 Soi 9, Sukumvit Road, involves a series of geographical symbols. The easiest way to find this address is to go to Sukumvit Road, proceed on to Soi 9, and then search out a sign or ask a local shopkeeper.

The 88/4-8 Soi 9 Sukumvit can also be written as 88/4-8 Sukumvit Soi 9 or simply just as 88-4-8 Sukumvit 9. Many times you'll just find the address listed as Sukumvit Soi 9.

What do all those numbers mean? The 88 refers to the original lot number which was assigned to the plot of land several decades ago; it may or may not refer to anything sensible since Bangkok (and most of Thailand) has been developed in an extremely haphazard fashion. The 4 after the slash refers to a building number or perhaps a block of buildings. Generally, you can find a small number 4 tacked onto the lower corner of the building, or you might have to ask around. The 8 is a more precise building number, which generally points out a specific structure within a block of buildings.

Mismatched Sois

Finally, city planning being what it is in Thailand, you'll find that sois on opposite sides of the road often don't match. Note that sois are usually even-numbered on one side of the road, odd-numbered on the other. You would expect Soi 8 to be opposite Soi 9 on Sukumvit Road, but don't hold your breath. As you move down Sukumvit, the disparity between opposite sois increases until you finally find that Soi 41 is opposite Soi 26, and Soi 55 is opposite Soi 38.

SUGGESTED WALKING TOURS

Finding your way around Bangkok can be difficult since street names are rarely marked and the numbering system for addresses is often baffling. Bear in mind that the larger thoroughfares *(thanon)* are intersected by smaller streets *(sois)* that often end in cul-de-sacs. Public transportation—whether in an ordinary bus or an a/c taxi—can be extremely time-consuming, especially during morning and evening rush hours when traffic grinds to a dead stop.

Faced with such obstacles, visitors often think that Bangkok is best experienced on an organized tour rather than a self-guided walking tour. Not true! While organized tours are convenient and relatively inexpensive, reasons to avoid them are plentiful: tour buses get stuck in traffic, visits to major monuments are frustratingly brief, shopping traps designed to extract kickbacks are commonplace, and only the most common (and hence touristy) sights are included in your tour. Worse yet, tours rarely allow an opportunity to freely wander around an ordinary Thai neighborhood and experience the charm and friendliness of the local residents.

Bangkok actually has several compact neighborhoods that can be easily enjoyed on self-guided walking tours by almost anybody with a good map and sense of adventure. A few tips: always get an early start to avoid the midday heat, bring along Nancy Chandler's map of Bangkok, and whenever possible use riverboats to reach your starting point.

First Day—Old Royal City

Temples within the Old Royal City and near the Royal Palace can be toured on foot in a single day. Only a slightly crazed tourist would attempt a single-day walking tour of *all* the temples within the Old Royal City; a leisurely two-day walking tour is needed for the remaining sights such as Wat Suthat and the Golden Mountain.

Visitors staying in Banglampoo can easily walk over to the Grand Palace or National Museum to begin the tour. Visitors staying near Silom Road should take a public riverboat to the Tha Chang boat stop. From Sukumvit Road or Siam Square, take a taxi or public bus to the Grand Palace.

Begin your tour promptly at 0830 with the Grand Palace or enjoy a guided tour of the National Museum Tues.-Thurs. at 0930. Afterward, wander around the Sanam Luang, visit the amulet market near Wat Mahathat, enjoy some dancing at Lak Muang, and then tour Wat Po to see the Reclining Buddha. Finally, take a river shuttle across the Chao Praya River to Wat Arun. This concentration of temples will probably suffice for most visitors with only a casual interest in Thai religious architecture.

Second Day—Old Royal City

Your walking tour on the second day begins at the Royal Palace and heads away from the river toward Democracy Monument. A short visit can be made to Wat Rajapradit and the more impressive Wat Rajabopit before arriving at Wat Suthat, one of the most majestic temples in the old city. Adjacent to Wat Suthat stands the Giant Swing and a small but intriguing Brahman temple.

Nearby sights include a wonderful Chinese temple on Tanao Road and shops selling religious supplies and immense bronze Buddhas on Bamrung Muang Road. The tour ends with a visit to the amulet market at Wat Rajananda and the curious Lohaprasat before climbing to the summit of the Golden Mountain. Fast walkers can accomplish this tour in about four hours.

Third Day—Chinatown

Rather than tour the limited attractions in the New Royal City, spend your third day walking around Chinatown, Little India, and the adjoining riverside markets. The famous Golden Buddha is also located in this neighborhood. Best of all, strolling through Chinatown provides a welcome relief from the endless procession of temples, and gives you an opportunity to discover Chinese culture. An early start is essential to avoid the midday heat.

Fourth Day—New Royal City

Begin your day with a river trip on the Chao Praya from Tha Orienten (Oriental Hotel boat stop) in the south to Tha Pra Arthit (Banglampoo) pier in the north. First, walk through the backpackers' enclave along Khao San Road and briefly visit Wat Bowonivet before heading up Rajadamnern Avenue to the tourist office and the magnificent Marble Temple. Farther on are the Vimanmek Palace and the Dusit Zoo—a long hike best aided with public transportation.

Fifth Day—Sukumvit to Siam Square

The best remaining walking tour is from Sukumvit Road to Siam Square, an easy-to-follow excursion which includes conventional tourist attractions such as Kamthieng and Jim Thompson's House, great sidewalk shopping along Sukumvit Road, comfortable air-conditioned shopping in-

ADMISSION FEES AND CAUTIONS

The Grand Palace/Wat Pra Keo complex will probably be your first experience with the notorious two-tier fee system for selected temples, museums, and historical sites in Thailand. In late 1985 the Fine Arts Department began charging foreigners significantly higher admission fees than Thais. For example, entrance to the Grand Palace is 125B for foreigners but free for Thais. Major monuments in Ayuthaya and Sukothai now charge Westerners 20B admission to each temple but Thais only 5B. Although rarely noticed by tourists (lower entrance fees for locals are posted only in Thai script), this double standard has proven contentious for some travelers, who resent the gouge-the-rich-tourist mentality.

Tragically, this attitude—as propagated and approved by the Fine Arts Department and Thai government—has spread throughout Thailand. Many Thais consider tourists fair game for overcharging on everything from ice cream cones to antique Buddhas. There is no reason to play along with this game. Although there is little you can do about temple admissions, travelers who wish to avoid being ripped off on other purchases should learn the correct prices and refuse to pay any type of surcharge. Complaints about the double-pricing standard should be directed to museum directors, tour operators, editors of local newspapers, and upstairs at the Bangkok TAT office.

Cautions

Touts and con artists are plentiful around the Grand Palace; be extra cautious about free boat rides, invitations to lunch, or suspicious money-making schemes.

By far the most common scam is the free boat ride offered by a well-dressed young man who spends several hours gaining your confidence before inviting you on a boat tour of the Chao Praya and adjoining canals. At some point you will be forced to contribute an enormous amount of money for fuel, or risk being stranded in a remote location. Never get into a boat alone, no matter how honest or sincere your host may appear.

Almost as common and just as costly are the college students who offer unbelievable deals on Thai gems. These smooth-talking fellows will promise fabulous profits on gems purchased from reputable government-supervised stores. This is an absolute fraud: *never buy gems from a street tout.*

Dress Regulations

Please remember that foreign visitors to Buddhist temples must be properly dressed. *Shorts are never appropriate in temples.* Long pants or long dresses should be worn instead. Women should be well covered. Visitors wearing dirty jeans, T-shirts, or halter tops will be refused admittance. All visitors must wear shoes with closed heels and toes; those wearing sandals or rubber slippers will be refused entrance to all major temples, including Wat Pra Keo and the Royal Palace. Photographers should ask permission before taking flash photos inside temples.

---

side the Central and Zen centers, and plenty of great little restaurants and pubs for cold drinks. And not a temple in sight!

Begin your tour from Sukumvit Soi 21 (Siam Society and Soi Cowboy), and walk west past bookstores, local markets, sidewalk shops, tailors, and cafes to the expressway overpass where Sukumvit changes name to Ploenchit Road. Continue west to Central Department Store, the fascinating Erawan Shrine, newish World Trade Center (actually just a shopping complex), and Siam Square Shopping Center where Ploenchit—logically enough—becomes Rama I Road. Farther on is the immense Tokyu Shopping Center and finally, Jim Thompson's House, tucked away on a quiet side street.

Sixth Day—River Journeys

A full day can be enjoyed on the Chao Praya River and canals which circumscribe the city. For suggested itineraries see "River and Canal Tours" later in this chapter.

ATTRACTIONS

THE OLD ROYAL CITY

Wat Pra Keo

First stop for most visitors is the Grand Palace and its adjoining temple complex, Wat Pra Keo (Temple of the Emerald Buddha). Taken together, these brilliant and almost unbelievable monuments form one of the greatest spectacles in all of Southeast Asia. The following description follows a clockwise route corresponding to the map and legend.

Entrance (1): Entrance to both the temple complex and the Grand Palace is on Na Pralan Road opposite the Sanam Luang parade grounds. Walk past the government buildings and turn left down the narrow corridor.

Coin Museum (2): Your entry ticket includes admission to both the Coin Museum on the right and the Vimanmek Palace in northern Bangkok. Through the narrow gateway is a scene of almost unbelievable brilliance: golden spires and wonderfully ornate pavilions guarded by strange mythological creatures.

Ramakien Murals (3): The interior cloister murals depict tales from the Ramakien, the Thai version of the Ramayana. Originally painted during the reign of King Mongkut (1825-50), they have since been restored seven times including such occasions as the Rattanakosin bicentennial in 1982 and the king's 60th birthday celebration in 1987. The story begins by the north gate with the discovery of Sita, and advances through various adventures of her consort Rama and his assistant, the white monkey-god Hanuman. Much of the original artistic merit has been lost to the repeated restorations, though each mural still offers delightful depictions of ordinary Thai life: laughing children, demure concubines, grinning gamblers, and emaciated opium smokers. Marble tablets opposite each fresco provide explanatory texts composed by King Chulalongkorn.

Golden Chedi (4): This dazzling wonder was erected by King Mongkut and modeled after Ayuthaya's Pra Sri Ratana Chedi.

Mondop (5): Just beyond is a richly carved library with a solid-silver floor and interior set with a mother-of-pearl chest filled with sacred texts. Gracing the four interior corners are exquisite Buddha statues carved in a 14th-century Javanese style and miniature sacred white elephants, symbols of royal power. Normally closed to the public.

Angkor Wat Model (6): This miniature model of the famous Khmer temple was constructed by Rama IV when Cambodia was a vassal state of the Thai empire. If you're unable to visit Angkor, this fine model provides a convenient overview. Photographers can get an intriguing aerial view by standing on the railing.

Gabled *Viharn* (7): The Pra Viharn Yot, decorated with ceramics and porcelain, once held the historic Manangasila stone, which served as the throne for King Ramkamheng of Sukothai. Discovered by King Mongkut in the ruins of Sukothai during his monkhood, the stone has since been brought here.

Royal Mausoleum (8): The Pra Naga in the northwest corner of the complex holds urns containing the ashes of royal family members. Closed to the public.

Library (9): The west facade of the Montien Dharma, second library of the temple complex, is considered the finest of its kind in Thailand. As with other temple libraries, this building was constructed to protect sacred texts and copies of the Tripitaka, the holy Buddhist scripture.

Royal Pantheon (10): Ground plan of Prasat Pra Thepbidon is a Greek cross capped by a yellow *prang*. Standing inside are life-sized statues of the first seven kings of the Chakri dynasty. Open annually on 6 April.

Mythological Animals: Surrounding the magnificent Royal Pantheon are bizarre mythological animals such as the *kinaree*, a half-human, half-bird creature of Himalayan origins; and glaring guardian lions known as *norasinghs*. Flanking the main entrance are slender *chedis* supported by a frieze of mythical *garuda* birds—important since the *garuda* is Vishnu's animal and Rama is the reincarnation of Vishnu.

Prangs **(11):** Covered with glazed ceramic tiles, eight Khmer *prangs* (spires) erected by Rama I symbolize the eight planets. Each color corresponds to a different celestial body. Two are located inside the palace walls; another six stand outside the grounds along the east gallery.

Chapel of the Emerald Buddha (12): Bangkok's Royal Temple is Thailand's most important and sacred *wat*. Constructed at the end of the 18th century by King Rama I, this splendid example of Thai aesthetics and religious architecture houses the Emerald Buddha, Thailand's most venerated image. So small and distant that it can hardly be seen, the green jasper (*not* jade or emerald) image symbolizes the independence, strength, and good fortune of the country. Thais believe this religious talisman holds the magical power of the king, who thrice annually changes the holy garments from a golden tunic studded with diamonds during the hot season to a gilded monk's robe for the rainy season. A solid gold robe is placed over the image during the cool season. Shoes must be removed and photography is prohibited. Extreme respect should be shown in this chapel.

Interior walls are painted with superb frescoes. A few moments studying these murals will prove rewarding, since most Thai temples follow similar conventions as to mural placement. For example, murals between the window frames generally depict Jataka scenes from the life of Buddha. The universe is portrayed in Buddhist astrological representation on the back wall be-

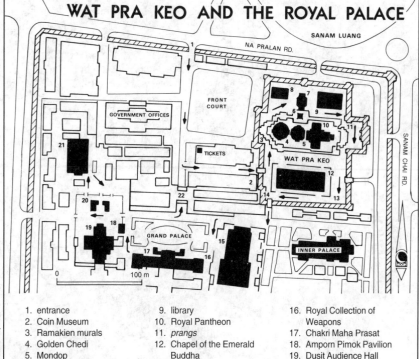

WAT PRA KEO AND THE ROYAL PALACE

1. entrance
2. Coin Museum
3. Ramakien murals
4. Golden Chedi
5. Mondop
6. Angkor Wat model
7. Gabled Viharn
8. Royal Mausoleum
9. library
10. Royal Pantheon
11. *prangs*
12. Chapel of the Emerald Buddha
13. bell tower
14. *yaks*
15. Amarinda Audience Hall
16. Royal Collection of Weapons
17. Chakri Maha Prasat
18. Amporn Pimok Pavilion
19. Dusit Audience Hall
20. courtyard doorways
21. Wat Pra Keo Museum
22. Double Gates

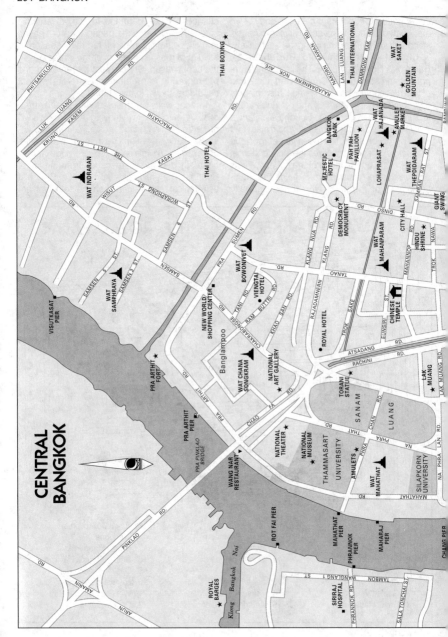

CENTRAL BANGKOK

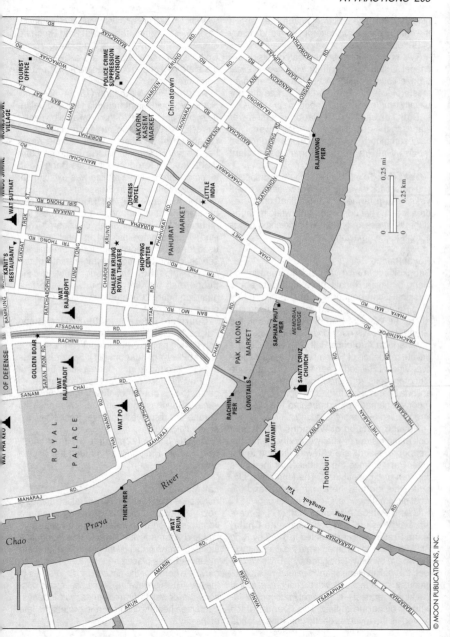

© MOON PUBLICATIONS, INC.

hind the altar. The wall fronting the altar (above the entrance) relates the temptation and victory of Buddha over Mara.

Two points of interest are located outside the chapel. Guarding the entrance are two mythical bronze lions, considered by art historians as masterpieces of Khmer art. Also note the unusually ornate *bai sema* or boundary stones.

Bell Tower (13): An elaborate bell tower stands in the opposite corner. Bell towers typically summon monks for sermons and meals, though Wat Pra Keo no longer has resident monks.

Yaks (14): To exit the Wat Pra Keo compound you must pass towering manlike creatures called *yaks,* sharp-fanged mythological creatures dressed in Thai costumes and wielding huge clubs. *Kinarees* and *garudas* brandishing *nagas* complete the amazing scene.

Royal Palace
Bangkok's former royal palace, an intriguing blend of Italian Renaissance architecture and classical Thai roofing, was begun in 1783 by King Rama I and improved upon by subsequent rulers. As Wat Pra Keo evokes the East, the Grand Palace will remind you of Europe.

Amarinda Audience Hall (15): Originally the private residence of Rama I and the Hall of Justice, Vinchai Hall today serves as a royal venue for coronations and ceremonial state events. An antique boat-shaped throne on which early kings received homage stands behind the Western throne used by the present king.

Royal Collection of Weapons (16): A brief look at the history of Thai weaponry. Left of the weapon museum is a gateway leading to the Inner Palace, once the residence of the king's children and concubines. The king now celebrates his birthday here with friends and the local diplomatic corps. Closed to the public.

Grand Palace Audience Hall (17): Eccentric, half Western and half Asian, the **Chakri Maha Prasat** was constructed in 1882 by King Chulalongkorn to commemorate the centenary of the Chakri dynasty. Designed by a British architect, this Italian Renaissance palace was incongruously superimposed with a Thai *prasat* roof at the king's request—a strangely successful fusion of disparate styles. The Grand Palace served as the royal residence until King Ananda

was shot in bed under mysterious circumstances in 1946. His brother, the current King Rama IX, subsequently moved out to the more spacious Chitralada Palace. Visitors are allowed inside the state reception room decorated with European furnishings.

Amporn Pimok Pavilion (18): At one time, Rama IV would alight from his elevated palanquin, present himself to the crowd below, enter this delicate little pavilion, remove his ceremonial hat and gown, and then proceed into the throne hall. So quintessentially Thai is the architecture that Rama V reproduced it at his Bang Pa In summer retreat, and a replica was exhibited at the 1892 World's Fair in Brussels.

Dusit Audience Hall (19): Mounted on a marble platform in the shape of a Latin cross, this magnificent building is widely considered Thailand's finest example of royal architecture. Once used for outdoor receptions, today the building serves for the ceremonial lying-in-state of deceased kings. Note the interior paintings, the throne built by King Mongkut, and the four guardian figures donated by wealthy Chinese businesspeople.

Courtyard Doorways (20): Exit the Grand Palace through these wooden doors delightfully carved and painted with colorful sentries.

Wat Pra Keo Museum (21): Features inside this fine little museum include a scale model of the Royal Palace and Wat Pra Keo complex—useful to sort out the confusing labyrinths. Javanese Buddhas and the famous Manangasila Throne are displayed upstairs. Best of all, it's air-conditioned!

Double Gates (22): Exit to the front courtyard and Na Pralan Road through the double gates.

Lak Muang
Across the road from the Royal Palace stands a newly renovated marble pavilion housing a lingam-shaped monument covered with gold leaf and adorned with flowers. This foundation stone, from which all distances in Thailand are measured, was placed here by King Rama I to provide a home for the unseen landlord-spirits of the city. Thais believe these magical spirits possess the power to grant wishes, win lotteries, guarantee healthy children, and protect the fate of the city.

Thai classical dance performances sponsored in the rear pavilion by satisfied supplicants include Ramakien routines, the most popular version being an Eastern *Swan Lake* called the Manora. Sponsors pay the dancers 100B for a short *ram tawai* (thanksgiving dance) while wealthy patrons ante up 1,000B for a longer drama. Early morning and late afternoon are the busiest and best times to watch the dancing—extra busy two or three days before a lottery.

National Museum

This museum—the largest and most comprehensive in Southeast Asia—serves as an excellent introduction to the arts of Thailand and the religious iconography of Buddhism.

Collections are open Wed.-Sun. 0900-1600. Admission is 20B. Tickets can be purchased and bags checked at the front entrance. Photography is prohibited. The bulletin board adjacent to the ticket counter often has notices on upcoming cultural and festival tours sponsored by the National Museum and the Siam Society—excellent tours at extremely good prices. Detailed information on the extensive holdings is provided in the *Guide to the National Museum Bangkok* sold at the front desk.

Orientation: The National Museum is comprised of a half dozen buildings. The Sivamokhapiman Hall holds the ticket office and Thai History rooms. Scattered on the outside grounds are the Royal Chariot Pavilion, Wat Buddhaisawan, and Red Pavilion, three excellent examples of traditional 18th-century architecture. To the rear is the Central Wing. Once used by the king's brother, these old royal structures have been subdivided into almost 20 rooms filled with everything from stuffed elephants to golden amulets. The two-storied South Wing, constructed in 1967, features early Thai statuary and artifacts from the Srivijaya, Dvaravati, and Lopburi Periods. The North Wing includes later artwork from the Sukothai, Ayuthaya, and Bangkok Periods.

The following highlights take three or four hours to cover. Visitors with limited time will probably best enjoy Wat Buddhaisawan, funeral chariots in the hall to the right, the Lopburi sculpture in the South Wing to the left, and the Sukothai Buddhas on the second floor of the North Wing.

Free Tours: To quickly sort through the artifacts, which range from Neolithic discoveries of Ban Chiang to contemporary Bangkok pieces, museum volunteers conduct free guided tours starting at 0930 from the ticket desk. These tours are highly recommended. Without a tour, the bewildering collections often confuse and frustrate Western visitors who lack any formal background in the basics of Asian art. English-language tours are given Tues.-Thurs. morning at 0930. French tours are given on Wednesday, German on Thursday, and Japanese on Tuesday. Special tours in Chinese and Spanish can also be arranged. Tours change frequently; call (02) 215-8173 for further information.

Sivamokhapiman Hall (2-4): The ticket office and bookstore are in the front, public restrooms to the rear.

Gallery of Thai History (3): Galleries to the rear of the admission counter are somewhat gloomy and confusing, but nevertheless help you sort through Thai epochs from Sukothai to the modern era. The prize exhibit is the famous Sukothai stele of King Ramkamheng, a stone slab which has generated a great deal of controversy regarding its authenticity. Also of interest are exhibits on possible origins of the Thai peoples, and dioramas of important events in Thai history.

Gallery of Pre-Thai History (4): Highlights include Paleolithic artifacts from Ban Kao near Kanchanaburi, and world-famous pottery and bronze ornaments from Ban Chiang in Udon Thani Province.

Wat Buddhaisawan (6): Finest among the assorted historic buildings on the museum grounds is this superb chapel, widely considered one of the best surviving examples of early Bangkok monastic architecture. Wat Buddhaisawan was constructed in 1787 to house a greatly revered Buddha image (Pra Buddha Sing) which, according to legend, was fashioned in Sri Lanka. However, two identical images are also found in Chiang Mai and Nakhon Si Thammarat, and, as you might expect, residents in those communities are convinced that they possess the original Buddha. For the average visitor, it is the soaring interior roofline, shiny wooden floors, light streaming in through the open windows, and magnificent murals that remain the great attraction.

Chariot Hall (9): Stored inside this large shed are immense ceremonial carriages still used for royal open-air cremations in nearby Sanam

Luang. The largest prototype weighs over 20 tons and requires the physical manpower of several hundred men outfitted in traditional palace uniforms. Also displayed is a replica of the royal cremation pavilion used by the late King Rama VI.

Red Pavilion (10): Once the home of Rama I's sister, the Tamnak Daeng (Red House) provides a quick look at the atmosphere and furnishings of a royal residence, circa 1782-1809. The Tamnak Daeng is constructed of prefabricated walls which allowed it to be moved several times before being placed on the museum grounds.

Audience Hall (12): Formerly the hall of the surrogate monarch (a deputy ruler appointed to succeed the ruling king), the Issaravinitchai Hall now houses special exhibits such as recent archaeological discoveries and shows that have returned from international tours.

Treasure Room (13): Includes golden jewelry and precious gems from U Thong and Nakhon Pathom, and a stunning collection of objects discovered at Wat Rajaburana in Ayuthaya.

Palanquins (14): Funeral palanquins and elephant howdahs used in royal processions are displayed in the Phimuk Monthain gallery. Finest

NATIONAL MUSEUM

© MOON PUBLICATIONS, INC.

piece is the exquisite ivory howdah presented to King Chulalongkorn by a Chiang Mai prince.

Shadow Puppets (15): Stage properties, *khon* masks worn by dignitaries of the court of Rama VI, Chinese marionettes, Siamese polo sticks, and a rare collection of giant shadow puppets make this one of the more intriguing rooms in the central museum.

Ceramics (17): Highlights of this room include 19th-century Bencharong ware, Sawankalok pottery, and Japanese and Chinese porcelains. Beautifully crafted mother-of-pearl screens are exhibited in the upstairs room.

Ivory (20): The sacred role of white elephants is noted here with carved ivory tusks and sculpted elephant armor incised with religious talismans.

Antique Weaponry (21): A life-sized elephant mounted by a Thai warrior and covered with battle regalia dominates a room filled with antique firearms and 18th-century swords.

Royal Regalia (22): The central room features thrones, a small royal pavilion, coronation regalia, and examples of the five traditional emblems of Thai royalty: *chatras* (tiered umbrellas), crowns, golden swords, fly whisks, and small golden shoes.

Woodcarvings (23): Extravagant teakwood carvings include circular monastery pulpits, Khmer *prangs,* mythological creatures such as *kinarees,* and a pair of doors salvaged from the Wat Suthat fire of 1959.

Steles (24): Resembling an ancient graveyard, this room displays teetering stones inscribed in Sanskrit, Pali, Khmer, and Thai.

Costumes and Textiles (27): A rare collection of Cambodian *ikats,* Indian brocades, Chinese silks, painted *phanung* garments, and Thai weavings executed with great skill. The upstairs room is devoted to religious artifacts and a monk's sole possessions: a begging bowl, three orange robes, a razor, a water sieve to filter out living creatures, a sash, and a small sewing pouch.

Musical Instruments (29): Thai and other Southeast Asian instruments (Javanese *gamelans,* etc.) are displayed on an elevated veranda. Note the Thai *phipat* orchestra, comprised of xylophones, metallophones, gongs, cymbals, and flutes.

South Wing—Ground Floor (30-34):

Asian Art (30): This room demonstrates the overwhelming power and influence of Indian culture on early Thai art. Indian merchants, philosophers, and holy men reached Thailand shortly after the beginning of the Christian era, bringing with them Indian languages (Pali and Sanskrit), art, and religions which still influence modern Thai society. Among the highlights are 5th-century Sarnath Buddhas, 7th-century Gupta Buddhas, and 10th-century Pali-style steles. Also displayed are images from Sri Lanka, Myanmar, Tibet, China, and Japan.

1. entrance	19. stamps and coins	**SOUTH WING—UPPER FLOOR**
2. ticket office and bookstore	20. ivory	35. Dvaravati
3. Gallery of Thai History	21. antique weaponry	36. Javanese images
4. Gallery of Pre-Thai History	22. royal regalia	37. Srivijaya
5. King Vijiravudh Pavilion	23. woodcarvings	
6. Wat Buddhaisawan	24. steles	**NORTH WING—GROUND FLOOR**
7. Heir to the Throne Pavilion	25. model boats	38. coin gallery
8. Sala	26. curiosities	39. Buddha images
9. Chariot Hall	27. costumes and textiles	40. textiles
10. Red Pavilion	28. flags	41. decorative arts
11. King Rama IV Pavilion	29. musical instruments	42. Bangkok
12. Audience Hall		43. photographs
13. treasure room	**SOUTH WING—GROUND FLOOR**	
14. palanquins	30. Asian art	**NORTH WING—UPPER FLOOR**
15. shadow puppets	31. museum office	44. Lanna and Chiang Saen
16. royal gifts	32. Khmer and Lopburi	45. Sukothai
17. ceramics	33. Hindu sculpture	46. Ayuthaya
18. models	34. Lopburi	47. Bangkok

Khmer and Lopburi (32 and 34): Khmer culture and political power extended across Thailand from the 8th to 13th centuries, reaching an apex in the northeast and at the small administrative outpost of Lopburi. This room, and the room beyond the director's office, illustrate both pure Khmer styles (Kompong Prae, Baphuon, and Bayon) and Khmer/Thai fusions called Lopburi, named after the town where the two styles were successfully blended.

Hindu Sculpture (33): Brahmanical devotional objects dating from the 3rd to 5th centuries have been discovered at two major sites in Thailand: Si Thep in Petchabun and the southern peninsula near Chaiya and Surat Thani. This room features a 7th-century stone Vishnu image found in southern Thailand near Takua Pa, considered the most impressive Hindu sculpture uncovered in Thailand.

South Wing—Upper Floor (35-37)

Dvaravati (35): The pre-Thai artistic period was dominated by Mon culture (6th-11th centuries). The Mon were a racial group who created empires at Nakhon Pathom near Bangkok and Haripunchai (modern-day Lamphun) in the north. Influenced by Indian post-Gupta styles and Amaravati traditions from South India and Sri Lanka, Mon art chiefly excelled in magnificent Buddhist sculpture with distinctive facial modelings. Displayed in these rooms are terra-cotta images in bas relief, stone Wheels of the Law which retell Buddha's first sermon at Sarnath, and extremely delicate busts which convey the inner calm of the enlightened Buddha.

Java (36): This small but worthwhile collection of images from central Java (Borobudur and Prambanan) and east Java (Singosari and Malang) was donated by the Dutch colonialists to King Chulalongkorn during a state visit in 1896. The more important pieces were returned in the 1920s.

Srivijaya (37): The kingdom of Srivijaya, with its center either in Sumatra or at Chaiya in peninsular Thailand, dominated much of Southeast Asia during its heyday from the 7th to 9th centuries. As an entrepot for trade between India, Indonesia, and China, the resulting art style blends various schools such as Mon, Indian, Indo-Javanese, Khmer, and Chinese. Bodhisattvas and eight-armed goddesses surround a marvelously sinuous Bodhisattva Avalokitesvara from Chaiya.

North Wing—Ground Floor (38-43)

Coin Gallery (38): Numismatists will enjoy the coin gallery collection of Chinese porcelain counters, 17th-century Cambodian coinage, bullet coins from the Sukothai era, and blocks of beaten metal which served as currency until the 19th century.

Buddha Images (39): Rather than a unified collection, this collection includes statues from various epochs. Dominating the enclosure is a colossal quartzite Buddha carved in Dvaravati style and seated in the so-called European fashion.

Textiles (40): Brocades, embroideries, cotton prints, and silks from the Bangkok Period.

Decorative Arts (41): Minor arts of the 19th and 20th centuries, such as lacquerware, ceramics, nielloware, silverwork, mother-of-pearl inlay, and illustrated manuscripts made of palm leaves and paper.

Bangkok (42): The Bangkok Period, also known as Rattanakosin, includes Thai art created since the founding of Bangkok in 1782. Early images imitated the styles of Ayuthaya with richly ornamented headdresses and impassive faces.

North Wing—Upper Floor (44-47)

Lanna (44): Lanna and Chiang Saen were art styles which flourished in Northern Thailand from the 13th to 16th centuries. Buddha images tend to be small but carefully cast with great attention.

Sukothai—(45): The following two rooms contain the supreme art of Thailand, and one of the great movements of Southeast Asian art. Sukothai was an enlightened empire which ruled much of Thailand from the 13th to 15th centuries. Highlights of the first room include a pair of magnificent bronze statues: a four-armed Vishnu with a strangely flaired robe, and an eight-armed Harihara with hands formed in various mudras. The following room features more Buddhas, including a black bronze walking Buddha cast in an androgynous style. Although the long hike through the museum has exhausted you, this room deserves a close and careful inspection.

Ayuthaya (46): Ayuthaya served as the Thai capital between the fall of Sukothai and the establishment of Bangkok. Buddhas created during this period continued the traditions of Sukothai with a gradual embellishment of the headpieces and robes. Bejewelled Buddhas in a pose of subduing Mara are particularly fine.

Bangkok (47): Final stop covers modern Thai Buddhas and the minor arts from the Bangkok (Rattanakosin) Period. The collection seems rather lifeless and formalized after the exquisite pieces in the Sukothai and Ayuthaya rooms.

Wat Mahathat

The "Temple of the Great Relic" was constructed during the reign of King Rama I and houses Mahachulalongkorn University, one of the two highest seats of Buddhist learning in the country. It also serves as national headquarters for the Mahanikaya sect practiced by over 90% of the Buddhist population.

Wat Mahathat has little of great architectural value, but it functions as an important center for the study of *vipassana* (insight) meditation. Westerners can obtain information on introductory seminars (given weekly in English, usually on Friday afternoon) and monthly meditation retreats from the International Buddhist Meditation Center, Dhamma Vicaya Hall, tel. (02) 511-0439, in the rear center of the temple complex. Weekly lecture times and subjects are often listed in the *Bangkok Post*.

Weekends and *wan pra* (Buddhist holy days) are excellent times to visit the lively outdoor market which runs right through the temple grounds. With such great religious importance, it is hardly surprising that the temple serves as a major market for Buddhist amulets. Sales booths are found on Prachan Road near the Sanam Luang, and in a small *soi* (alley) which crosses Maharat Road and opens onto the riverside plaza. Located here are numerous shops filled with amulets, freshly cast Buddha images, and monk accessories such as begging bowls and orange robes.

National Art Gallery

The modern art museum opposite the National Theater exhibits traditional and contemporary works by both Thai and Western artists. Current shows are listed in the *Bangkok Post*. The gallery is open daily except Monday and Friday 0900-1600. Admission is 10B.

Earth Goddess Statue

Just opposite the Royal Hotel stands a small white pavilion and female statue erected by King Chulalongkorn as a public water fountain. This small monument merits a careful study since it illustrates one of the most beloved tales of Buddhist folklore, a story retold endlessly in murals and statues throughout Thailand.

According to legend, Buddha, in the throes of meditation, was repeatedly tempted by the evil goddess Mara and her sensual dancing ladies. Rather than submitting to temptation, the Buddha continued his meditation under the watchful gaze of the Earth Goddess Torani. So impressed was Torani with his courage, compassion, and moral willpower that she wrung her long hair, setting loose a tidal wave which swept away Mara and her evil armies.

Wat Po

Bangkok's oldest and largest temple complex, Wat Po was founded in the 16th century, when Ayuthaya was the capital, and radically remodeled between 1781 and 1801 by Rama I, who renamed the complex Wat Pra Chetupon. The area was extended in the 1830s by Rama III in his quest to establish an open-air university. This educational wonderland included inscriptions on traditional sciences, extracts from the Jatakas, marble tablets that taught the rules of traditional Thai massage, litanies of the reincarnations of Vishnu, treatises on astrology and palmistry, illustrations on world geography, and *rishi* figures contorted to demonstrate control over the physical body. In 1832 Rama III constructed an immense chapel on these grounds to house the statue of the Reclining Buddha; Wat Po is often called the Temple of the Reclining Buddha.

Wat Po today is one of the more fascinating temple complexes in Bangkok because of both its mystique and artistic achievement. Crammed into the courtyards is a bewildering number of chapels, rock gardens, bizarre statuary, educational tablets, bell towers, and small *chedis*. The complex has two major highlights: the superb *bot* to the right of the entrance, and the gigantic reclining Buddha in the rear courtyard. Guides

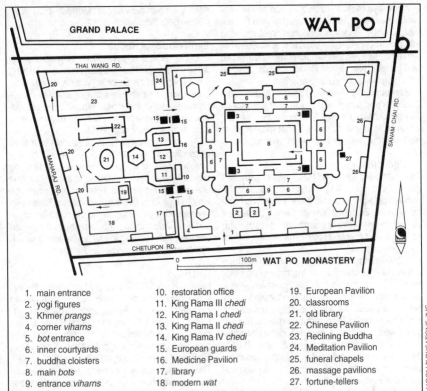

WAT PO

GRAND PALACE

WAT PO MONASTERY

1. main entrance
2. yogi figures
3. Khmer *prangs*
4. corner *viharns*
5. *bot* entrance
6. inner courtyards
7. buddha cloisters
8. main *bots*
9. entrance *viharns*
10. restoration office
11. King Rama III *chedi*
12. King Rama I *chedi*
13. King Rama II *chedi*
14. King Rama IV *chedi*
15. European guards
16. Medicine Pavilion
17. library
18. modern *wat*
19. European Pavilion
20. classrooms
21. old library
22. Chinese Pavilion
23. Reclining Buddha
24. Meditation Pavilion
25. funeral chapels
26. massage pavilions
27. fortune-tellers

are available at the front entrance on Soi Chetupon, though their services are hardly necessary. Guides charge 150B for one visitor, 200B for two, and 300B for three. Air-conditioned buses 6,8, and 12 all stop near Wat Po, or you can take a river boat to Tha Tien Pier.

Wat Po is open daily 0800-1700. Admission is 10B. Visitors can wander around the yards past closing hour but the Reclining Buddha is locked up firmly at 1700. Several travelers have recommended a visit on Sundays, when the temple school teaches young students Thai classical dance and how to play traditional Thai musical instruments.

The following walking tour follows a clockwise route.

Entrance (1): The principal entrance (in the back alley) is flanked by a pair of menacing Chinese guards wearing heavy armor and sporting sculpted beards. Other guardians scattered throughout the complex smoke cigars and wear European top hats! All of these humorous figures were cut from stone blocks taken from ship ballast on the Thailand-to-China trade route.

Yogi Figures (2): After purchasing your ticket and declining the services of a guide, you'll see several miniature mountains covered with figurines of holy men in contorted positions of meditation and massage. The fragile plaster-cast figures are periodically replaced.

Main *Bot* (8): The main temple at Wat Po is widely considered among the most elegant in all of Thailand and a masterpiece of Thai religious architecture. Note the remarkable proportions, elegant rooflines, and exquisite ornamental design on the doors and interiors. Entrance (5) to the *bot* central courtyard passes through an unusual double gallery (6 and 7) which features almost 400 gilded Ayuthaya-style Buddhas throughout and around the outer and inner chambers. All have recently been encased behind glass, a disturbing development. Each corner of the inner courtyard has a white-marble Khmer *prang* (3), and each of the four directional *viharns* (9) features an image of the Buddha. The most remarkable stands in the east *viharn* where the Buddha Lakanard dispenses blessings to the faithful.

Before entering the main *bot,* note the 16 fine bronze lions which guard the eight stairways, and the famous bas-reliefs which surround each base. These tablets relate the story of the Ramakien, the Thai version of the Hindu Ramayana. Rubbings of woodcut copies (not the original stones) can be purchased at the souvenir shop. Also see the Chinese landscapes, *farangs* on horseback, and black-faced Moorish traders on the exquisite mother-of-pearl doorways.

The main doorway to the *bot* is to the east, away from the river. The interior features a high nave flanked by twin rows of thick square columns painted with floral patterns and hung with drawings of old Bangkok. Beware the loudspeaker system! Directly ahead is a well-illuminated Buddha magnificently elevated on a gilded wooden pedestal, an inspiring and extremely powerful image removed from Wat Sala Sina in Thonburi. Interior side wall murals have been badly damaged from water seepage, but murals above the entrance remain in excellent condition; look for depictions of ordinary Thai life such as children in swings, bathing women, beggars, *klong* life, and wandering hermits.

Chedi Quartet (11-14): After touring the main *bot,* exit through the front entrance and walk past the main entrance and restoration committee headquarters to the quartet of Disneyesque-colored *chedis.* All have been recently redone with brilliant porcelains and rededicated to the first four kings of Thailand. The or-ange-and-brown *chedi* (11) on the left honors King Rama III, the central green *chedi* (12) is for Rama I, and the yellow-and-brown *chedi* (13) on the right honors Rama II. To the rear is a blue *chedi* (14) with red and white roses and green foliage, a monument constructed by Rama IV and dedicated to his wife, Queen Suriyothai, who was killed in battle defending the life of her husband. Great views can be enjoyed from the summit. Surrounding the *chedi* cloister are hundreds of standing Buddhas in the double-blessing pose.

West Courtyard Buildings (17-22): This courtyard features a half dozen halls of marginal interest. To the immediate left of the entrance is a new **Buddhist library** (17) and a modern *wat* (18) constructed with little style or imagination. The so-called **European Pavilion** (19)—more Chinese than Western—fronts a small pond flanked with monkey statues and a model of the *chedi* at Nakhon Pathom—a good place to relax and mix with the resident monks. Other buildings include **classrooms** (20); a display of traditional Thai musical instruments; an **old library** (21) restored with decorative flowers, green tiles, and small *nagas* at each corner; and the **Chinese Pavilion** (22) with its centerpiece bodhi tree.

Reclining Buddha (23): Certainly the most famous sight at Wat Po is the gigantic Reclining Buddha housed under a claustrophobic shed in the western courtyard. The 46- by 15-meter image, constructed of plaster over a brick core, represents the Buddha passing into nirvana. Thailand's largest reclining Buddha is difficult to appreciate in such tight settings, but special attention should be paid to the intricate mother-of-pearl designs on the footsoles which depict the 108 signs of the true Lord Buddha.

Massage Pavilions (26): As intriguing as the giant Buddha image is the College of Traditional Medicine in the eastern courtyard. This royal-sponsored mini-university of massage, herbal medicine, and Chinese acupuncture offers inexpensive, traditional Thai rubs: 80B for 30 minutes, 150B for one hour. Thirty hours of professional instruction spread over 10 days (three hours daily) or 15 days (two hours daily) costs 3,000B. **Fortune-tellers** (27) ply their trade in the adjacent courtyard.

MORE OF THE OLD ROYAL CITY

More temples and monuments lie east of the river. Time permitting after visiting the sights listed below, continue down Rajadamnern Avenue to Banglampoo and the Pra Arthit pier, or take a taxi to the Marble Temple in the New Royal City.

Wat Rajapradit

Constructed in 1864 by King Mongkut to complete the holy triumvirate of Ayuthayan temples, this picturesque but minor *wat* is noted for its widely diverse collection of architectural styles. This Thai-style *bot* is raised on a stone platform and surrounded by gray marble columns incised in an unusual checkerboard design. Interior murals offer clear views of Bangkok during the 1860s and royal ceremonies held 12 months a year. Resident monks can unlock the door. To the left is an Ayuthayan-style *prang* superbly carved with images of four-faced Brahma, while a Bayon-style *prang* stands to the right. To the rear of the *bot* is a Sinhalese-style *stupa* wedged between construction clutter and sleeping attendants.

Wat Rajapradit is open daily 0800-1900 and can be easily visited on the walk from the Grand Palace to Wat Suthat. No admission charge.

Before crossing the canal to Wat Rajabopit, you'll see a strange bronze pig near the banks. This funny little porcine monument commemorates the birth year of Queen Saowapha, a consort of King Chulalongkorn.

Wat Rajabopit

One of the more unusual temples in Bangkok, Wat Rajabopit was constructed in 1863 by King Chulalongkorn on the plan of the famous *stupa* at Nakhon Pathom. Entrance is made through doorways carved and painted with whimsical figures of European guards. Surrounding the *chedi* is a circular cloister decorated with ceramic tiles and interrupted at cardinal points by three *viharns* and the principal *bot* on the north. The *bot* displays familiar Thai rooflines on the exterior, but surprises you with its interior: a miniature Italian Gothic chapel inspired by Western models. Special note should be made of the Chinese Bencharong tiles which cover the exterior walls and blend beautifully with the darker golds and blues of the glazed roof tiles. Another glory of

Wat Rajabopit is the symmetrical mother-of-pearl inlays in the 10 doors and 28 windows, some of the finest inlay work in all of Thailand.

To the west of the *chedi* courtyard is a royal cemetery constructed by Rama V to honor his parents and relatives. Tombs have been styled after Indian *chedis,* Cambodian *prangs,* and miniature Gothic cathedrals. The garden even includes a walkway reconstructed in Cambodian fashion with dancing *asparas* and roofline *nagas.*

Wat Rajabopit is open daily 0800-1700. No admission charge.

Wat Suthat

The massive *viharn* and *bot* of Wat Suthat form one of the most powerful and elegant monuments in Bangkok. The complex was initiated by Rama I in the early 19th century and completed by his two successors over the next three decades.

Wat Suthat is open daily 0800-1700. No admission charge. For the best effect, enter from Bamruang Road (opposite the Giant Swing) rather than from the side doors on Triphet Road.

Courtyard: The spacious and well-proportioned courtyard serves as an open museum filled with stone figurines, outstanding bronzework, and Buddha images in various poses. Surrounding the *viharn* balustrade are 28 hexagonal Chinese pagodas and eight genuine masterpieces: absolutely superb bronze horses that flank the four corners of the *viharn.* All have assumed a sheen of fine green patina; several retain their original red eyes. Chinese statuary of American sailors and Chinese warlords strategically stand near connecting doorways.

Viharn: The magnificent *viharn* of Wat Suthat—noted for its exceptional height and powerful proportions—exudes a monumental effect rarely witnessed in Thai religious architecture. The entire sanctuary is elevated on two ascending platforms and bordered by four Chinese stone pagodas which house Buddhas in various poses. Entrance to the central chapel is made through a grandiose portico which frames three massive wooden doors, carved under the direction of Rama III to depict the mythical forest of Himavada. Shoes must be checked outside.

The immense gathering hall houses an eight-meter 14th-century bronze Sakyamuni Buddha previously resident in Sukothai's Wat Mahathat. Widely considered one of the great masterpieces of Thai sculpture, the Pra Sakyamuni Buddha richly deserves the veneration accorded by pilgrims and the sumptuous setting created for it by Rama I and II. Other interior elements include partially restored frescoes that illustrate the lives of various bodhisattvas, eight square marble pillars which support the soaring roof, and an enormous carved wooden pedestal which buttresses the central image. A room with great power.

Bot: Looming beyond the wall which separates the anterior and posterior courtyards is an enormous whitewashed *bot,* constructed between 1839 and 1843 by King Rama III. The surrounding courtyard features elaborate *bai sema* boundary stones protected inside stone chambers, and various oddities such as stone European soldiers and sculpted trees. Entrance into the *bot* can be extremely tricky to find; try all possible gateways, including the small gate at the southwest corner.

Dominating the interior is a life-sized black Buddha figure donated by Rama III and a school of 80 kneeling disciples who listen to the master with backs turned to the entrance. But it is the interior murals—regarded as among the finest in Thailand—that are the chief draw in the *bot.* Dating from the reign of King Rama II (1809-1824) and painted in flat tints, these murals employ primitive perspectives which predate Western techniques. The 24 window panels retell the Jataka tales of previous incarnations of the Buddha, shutters illustrate the celestial city of Indra, and the front wall depicts Buddha overcoming the evil temptations of Mara.

A restoration committee headed by the Fine Arts Department has been charged with returning the badly damaged murals to original condition. After the remaining stucco has been resealed against the wall, the missing sections are sketched in and painted anew with special watercolors. Distinctive brush techniques are used to differentiate restorations from the original artwork.

Giant Swing

Opposite Wat Suthat tower a pair of red teak pillars once used for the Brahmanic Ceremony of the Swing, an annual festival which honored the earthly return of the Hindu god Shiva. Until being halted in 1935, teams of young Hindu priests would swing a full arch of 180 degrees and attempt to snatch a bag of gold coins between their teeth. Some bit the gold, others bit the dust.

Hindu Shrine

Though Brahmanism has been an integral part of Thai royal life since the 14th century, few temples in Bangkok exclusively honor the Hindu triumvirate of Brahma, Shiva, and Vishnu. These three small chapels, situated near the Giant Swing, pay homage with displays of an Ayuthayan-style Vishnu, dancing Nataraja Shivas, and four-headed Brahmas. A replica of the giant swing complete with golden chariot and mythical *kinaree* bird stands in front. Side chapels used for Brahmanic wedding ceremonies display other exquisite Hindu images. The rear alley serves as a production center for enormous bronze Buddhas.

A small Brahmanic Vishnu shrine is located on Mahachai Road adjacent to Wat Suthat.

red-eyed beauty in the courtyard of Wat Suthat

Religious Supplies

Streets adjoining Wat Suthat specialize in religious paraphernalia such as bright orange robes, image stands, alms bowls, fans, and attractive umbrellas. Dozens of shops sell monstrous bronze images that eventually grace many of the temples in Thailand.

Baan Baht—the so-called "Monks' Bowl Village"—is a tiny corner of Bangkok where the forging of alms bowls clings tenuously to the old traditions. Much of this traditional craft has been lost to modern manufacturing methods.

Chinese Temple

Two blocks west of City Hall is a lively Chinese temple called San Chao Pah Sua. Unlike the sedate Buddhist *wat,* Chinese temples are a continual beehive of activity as worshippers arrive to burn incense and have their fortunes told with sticks and kidney-shaped blocks of wood. Caged birds at the front can be purchased and set free to improve your karma.

Wat Rajanada and the Amulet Market

Erected in 1846 by Rama III, the main sanctuary of Wat Rajanada features remarkable wall paintings of paradise and hell above the entrance, and side walls decorated with angels and celestial symbols. Entrance is made from a gate on the right side. The small *viharn* on the left is noted for its unusual design and the Rattanakosin-style Buddhas displayed on the central altar.

Wat Rajanada is chiefly noted for its popular amulet market at the far left end of the courtyard. Much of the informal street trade in amulets once conducted at Wat Mahathat has been moved into more permanent stalls on these grounds. Buddhist amulets may be legally taken out of the country without an official permit.

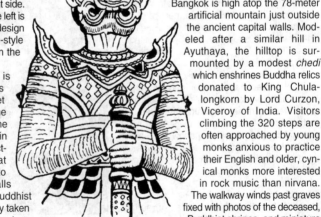

yaksha (demon)

Lohaprasat

To the rear of Wat Rajanada stands a curious pink building which resembles, more than anything else, an ornate wedding cake festooned with 37 candle-spires. Lohaprasat was designed to resemble ancient temples in Sri Lanka and India which, according to legend, served as mansions for the Buddha and his disciples. The first thousand-room structure was erected in India by a rich disciple named Visakha, the second in Anaradapura by a Sri Lankan king who decorated the roof with precious stones and ivory. Both prototypes have long since disappeared, leaving Bangkok's structure the world's only surviving example of this unique style. Lohaprasat is now closed and no longer an active *wat,* but local groundskeepers can provide a key.

Pah Fah Pavilion

In a rare case of civic improvement, the recent destruction of an old eyesore on Rajadamnern Avenue and the subsequent erection of the Pah Fah Pavilion have created an attractive tableau of royal *salas,* Wat Rajanada, and the Lohaprasat.

Golden Mountain

One of the few places from which to peer (smog permitting) over sprawling Bangkok is high atop the 78-meter artificial mountain just outside the ancient capital walls. Modeled after a similar hill in Ayuthaya, the hilltop is surmounted by a modest *chedi* which enshrines Buddha relics donated to King Chulalongkorn by Lord Curzon, Viceroy of India. Visitors climbing the 320 steps are often approached by young monks anxious to practice their English and older, cynical monks more interested in rock music than nirvana. The walkway winds past graves fixed with photos of the deceased, Buddhist shrines, and miniature mountains. Summit views

KAREN McKINLEY

MAGICAL MEDALLIONS

*T*hais believe that protection against malevolent spirits, reckless *phis*, and black magic can be guaranteed with amulets—small talismanic icons worn around the neck or waist. Extraordinarily powerful amulets derive their magic from having been blessed by Buddhist monks or issued by powerful organizations such as the military or monarchy. For example, those recognized by the king and distributed to policemen have acquired considerable renown for their protective powers. Small votive tablets found buried inside the relic chambers of ancient *stupas* are also deemed extra powerful. Amulet collection is big business in Thailand; over a dozen publications are devoted exclusively to their histories and personal accounts of their powers.

Each profession favors a certain style: taxi drivers wear amulets to protect against accidents, thieves to protect against the police. Even American soldiers during the Vietnam War became fascinated with their miraculous powers. Color is also important: white amulets arouse feelings of love, green protects against ghosts and wild animals, yellow promotes successful business deals, red offers protection against criminals. But black is the most powerful color— it provides *complete* invincibility.

Among the more bizarre amulets are those fashioned after the phallus *(palad khik)* and realistically carved from rare woods, ivory, or horn. Related to the Hindu lingam, *palad khik* are attached to cords and worn around the waist. A great way for travelers to make friends and influence people is to proudly wear an amulet of the king or queen.

sweep across the Royal Palace, Wat Arun in Thonburi, and modern edifices such as the multihued Baiyoke Towers.

Wat Saket, at the foot of the mount, sponsors Bangkok's liveliest temple festival each November. Once used as a dumping ground for victims of plague, the *wat* is undistinguished aside from its late-Ayuthayan lacquered windows and the International Central Library of Buddhist Literature to the right of the main walkway. Admission is 5B to reach the top.

THE NEW ROYAL CITY

This area in northern Bangkok consists of a modern administrative center blessed with traditional temples, an old royal palace, and pleasant neighborhoods almost completely untouched by mass tourism. Also known as the Dusit or New Royal City, the region was established around the turn of the century by King Chulalongkorn to escape the cramped conditions in his riverside Royal Palace.

Various walking tours are possible depending on your time and interest. One option is a boat ride to the Pra Arthit pier in Banglampoo, followed by a quick look at Pra Arthit Fort and a stroll through the backpackers' center of Khao San Road. Wat Bowonivet and shopping in the New World Center are also recommended. The famous Wat Benjamabopit (Marble Temple) can be reached by taxi or by long hike along Rajadamnern Nok Avenue or through the neighborhoods which flank the Chao Praya River. Vimanmek Palace and the Dusit Zoo would complete the tour. Visitors short on time: don't miss the Marble Palace.

Pra Arthit Fort

Also known as Pra Sumane, this octagonal fort was constructed by King Rama I to defend the northern extremity of his young capital against Burmese and Cambodian invasion. The present reconstruction dates from 1982 and is based on old drawings and photographs.

Khao San Road

A walk through the neighborhood of Banglampoo is highly recommended for both travelers searching for inexpensive accomodations and tourists exploring the back streets of Bangkok. Khao San Road is not only one of the liveliest travelers' scenes between Kuta and Kathmandu, but also an excellent place for cheap plane tickets, inexpensive clothing, and delicious fruit smoothies. Shopping opportunities include several used bookstores with hard-to-find travel guides, sidewalk cassette emporiums, and a great selection of Thai handicrafts. Travel agents on Khao San Road sell the cheapest airline tickets in town, plus the most economical tours of Bangkok and outlying districts. The local notice boards hold information on upcoming Buddhist retreats, employment opportunities teaching English, and local merchants who pay cash for used Levis, Walkmans, and wives.

A few blocks north is a popular shopping district dominated by the New World Shopping Center; daily bargains are on the main floor and better-quality merchandise on the upper seven floors. Adjacent streets are filled with inexpensive clothing and foodstalls.

Wat Bowonivet

Wat Bowonivet is an architecturally modest but spiritually important temple where many of Thailand's kings and princes have traditionally served their monkhood. The temple was constructed in the early 19th century by King Rama III, but gained great fame when Prince Mongkut (of *The King and I* fame) founded the Thammayut sect of Thai Buddhism and served as chief abbot during a portion of his 27-year monkhood. Today, the complex serves as home to the Supreme Patriarch and as the national headquarters of the Thammayut monastic sect, an order which follows a stricter discipline than that of the traditional Mahanikaya. Because of its royal origin and highly disciplined form of Buddhism, Wat Bowonivet enjoys an elevated reputation among the Thai people.

Courtyard: Several small but noteworthy images are displayed in the courtyard off Pra Sumen Road. The overall plan revolves around a central gilded *chedi* with two symmetrical chapels to the north and south. To the right of the central *bot* is a Buddha's footprint, a walking Buddha in the Sukothai style, two small Buddhas in the Lopburi style, and, on a raised niche, a Javanese Buddha perhaps imported from Borobudur. To the left is a Dvaravati Buddha. A beautiful reclining Buddha is located at the rear wall.

Bot: Though the *wat* lacks many of the graceful attributes so characteristic of other leading monasteries, a few special features make this temple worth a brief visit. The building is constructed in an unusual T-shape with its head facing north. Of special merit inside the *bot* is a bronze Sukothai Buddha, cast in 1257 to commemorate the country's liberation from Khmer rule and considered one of the finest of the pe-

riod. Another Buddha image, finely bathed in diffused half-light, sits to the rear. Flanking these two Buddhas are standing images which represent Buddha's chief disciples, Mokkanlana and Saribut. The top tier of the gorgeously decorated gilt altar features a small image known as Pra Nirantaraj, one of 18 statues distributed among the monasteries of the Thammayut sect by King Mongkut.

The walls are blanketed with extraordinary murals. Far removed from the traditional concept of Thai art, these dark and mysterious frescoes are the highly personalized work of a Thai artist named Kru Ing Khong. Khong revolutionized classic Thai artwork with his original use of three-dimensional perspective, moody shading, and fascinating use of Western subjects: Englishmen at the horse races, American ships arriving with missionaries, colonial buildings, and Dutch windmills.

Murals between the windows depict various religious ceremonies, while high above the windows are 16 tableaux symbolic of the Buddhist Trinity: the Buddha, his Dharma, and the Sangha. Column murals relate the spiritual transformation of humanity, progressing from the dark and gloomy colors on the bottom to the lighter and more exalted hues near the ceiling. As a unified ensemble, the murals are unique in the history of Thai painting.

Chedi: Centerpiece of Wat Bowonivet is the great golden *chedi* which enshrines sacred relics and ashes of Thai royalty.

Viharns: Behind the *bot* and *chedi* are two *viharns,* normally closed to the public. The larger structure contains two famous statues brought from Sukothai and Phitsanulok; the smaller hall offers wall paintings depicting episodes from the famous Chinese story of Sam Kok.

Along with Wat Mahathat near the Grand Palace, Wat Bowonivet is a popular temple for meditation instruction. English-speaking visitors can inquire at the international section.

Wat Indraram

On the way to the Marble Temple, a brief diversion can be made to the 33-meter Buddha image at Wat Indraram. Constructed in 1830 of brick and plaster, this absolutely hideous Buddha redeems itself with great views from the tower to the rear of his head. A short taxi ride or long hike through traditional neighborhoods is required from Banglampoo to the Marble Temple in the New Royal City. The most direct route is down Rajadamnern Avenue, past Democracy Monument, but a more relaxing option is to cross the canal from the New World Shopping Center and head north through the winding alleys that skirt the Chao Praya River.

Wat Benjamabopit (Marble Temple)

The most famous attraction in the Dusit area, and one of the finest examples of modern Thai architecture, the Marble Temple is on Sri Ayuthaya Road near the Chitralada Palace.

Wat Benjamabopit was erected by Rama V at the turn of the century to replace an older temple torn down to expand the Dusit Palace. Designed by the half-brother of the king, the elegant complex is largely constructed of white Carrara marble imported from Italy, hence the popular nickname Marble Temple.

Wat Benjamabopit is open daily from sunrise until 1700. Admission is 10B. The wat is best visited in the early morning hours when resident monks gather to collect alms and chant in the chapel. Services are also held in the late afternoon.

Bot: Beyond the unusual ornamental railing which encircles the complex is a central hall with overlapping multiple roofs, and two small pavilions containing a bronze Buddha seated under a naga and a white alabaster image imported from Myanmar. The four directional gables are elaborately carved with Vishnu riding a garuda (east), the three-headed elephant Erawan (north), an unalom which represents the curl of the Buddha's forehair (west), and a Wheel of the Law (south). Guarding the bot are two mythical marble lions seated in the Burmese position. Considered as a unified ensemble, Wat Benjamabopit is a masterpiece of superb harmony and pleasing symmetry.

Dominating the interior is a large gold statue of Pra Buddha Chinarat, an excellent copy of the highly venerated image in Phitsanulok. An urn under the altar holds the ashes of King Chulalongkorn, while wall niches around the central image, transept, and nave contain murals of famous prangs and chedis from Sawankalok, Ayuthaya, Nakhon Pathom, Nakhon Si Thammarat, Lamphun, Nakhon Phanom, and Lop-

buri. Also note the vibrant and distinctive stained-glass windows designed by Siamese artists but crafted in Florence, Italy.

Gallery Statues: Perhaps the most famous sight at the Marble Temple is the outstanding collection of 53 Buddha statues displayed in the rear cloisters. To present a complete iconography to his subjects, King Chulalongkorn gathered together in one spot the finest examples—both originals and copies—of bronze Buddhas in the world. Taken together, they provide an amazing opportunity to study the artistic development and range of styles from Thailand, India, Sri Lanka, China, and Japan. Each has been carefully labeled with the country of origin and period—better than art school! Notable masterpieces include a Starving Buddha cast from an original in Lahore, two standing Buddhas of the Sukothai Period, Burmese images from Bagan, copies of Japanese and Chinese Buddhas, plus rare stone Dvaravati images protected against theft by iron grilles.

Vimanmek Palace

Vimanmek is a beautiful and gracious L-shaped palace believed to be one of the world's largest golden teakwood structures. The palace was designed by a German architect named Sandreczki and constructed in 1893 by King Rama V on Si Chang Island in the Gulf of Siam. Chulalongkorn's fascination with Western architecture was reflected in the Victorian style and gingerbread fretwork which allowed the sun to make lacy patterns on the walls. In 1901 the king ordered the unfinished palace disassembled and moved to his new royal enclave of Suan Dusit in Bangkok. Vimanmek ("Castle in the Clouds") served as a royal residence for Rama V and his family (92 wives and 77 children) until abandoned for larger quarters in 1908. The palace fell into disrepair until being completely renovated by Queen Sirikit and Princess Sirindorn in 1982, the year of the Bangkok Bicentennial.

Vimanmek today is a three-story, 81-room museum displaying a rich collection of royal regalia and the eclectic assemblage of King Chulalongkorn: period furniture, the country's first shower with a hidden water tank manually filled by royal pages, and a photograph of Thomas Edison inscribed "to the King and Queen of Siam."

The palace is open daily 0930-1630. Admission is 50B at the door, but free with your ticket stub from the Grand Palace. Complimentary guided tours are given hourly until 1500.

Dusit Zoo

Opposite Chitralada Palace, Thailand's largest zoo offers a modest collection of Asian animals such as elephants, rhinos, and monkeys. Also on the grounds is an artificial lake where pedalboats and rowboats can be rented. Though hardly spectacular, the zoo provides a welcome escape from the heat and congestion of Bangkok. Dusit Zoo is open daily 0800-1800. Admission is 20B.

CHINATOWN

Chinatown is one of the most exotic and stimulating ethnic enclaves in Southeast Asia, and the extraordinary showcase of Old Bangkok. Bounded by the Chao Praya River on the west and Charoen Krung Road on the east, this seething, frenetic, jam-packed neighborhood offers visitors a chance to escape the temple rut and experience the old East of Maugham and Conrad. Although the main boulevards have now assumed the monotonous veneer of modernity, behind the facade lies the *real* Chinatown: smoky temples filled with robed Taoist monks, pharmacies selling antelope horn and cobra venom, rattan vendors, innumerable shops where Chinese merchants demonstrate their legendary commercial talents, jewelry emporiums piled high with gold chains and necklaces, and countless street peddlers who add to the perpetual spectacle.

Chinatown came about in the late 18th century after King Rama I asked Chinese merchants to vacate the land intended for his Grand Palace. Early Teochew (Chiu Chow) entrepreneurs built their thriving businesses along Sampeng Lane, a narrow and claustrophobic alley which served as a commercial center by day, but became an untamed district of brothels, gambling dens, and opium parlors at night. By the early 20th century, Soi Sampeng had been dubbed the Green Light District, since local brothels hung green rather than red lanterns over their doorways. Today, Chinatown has traded its notorious reputation for the complacency of commerce, but

enough exotic culture remains to make this one of the best places to explore in Bangkok.

Walking Tour: The scattered attractions and kaleidoscopic sense of disorder make an organized walking tour of Chinatown rather difficult. The following tour is simply meant to steer you in the right direction and help you find the more fascinating side streets and shopping districts. Visitors short on time should concentrate on Sampeng Lane, Wat Leng Nee Yee, the shopping alley of Soi 16, and the Pahurat Cloth Market.

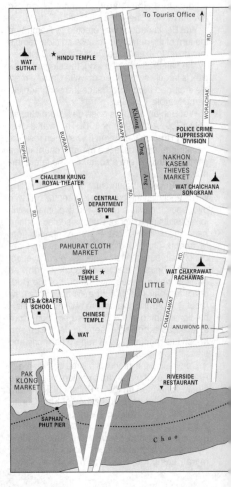

Rajawong Pier

Begin with a boat ride from Silom Road or Banglampoo to Tha Rajawong (Rajawongse Pier) and walk up Rajawong (Ratchawong) Road past several banks and a lovely green trading firm constructed in a Moorish-German style. Turn left on Anuwong Road and then right on Krai Alley to the first sight.

Boonsamakan Vegetarian Hall

Bangkok's finest Chinese woodcarvings are displayed in this lovely yellow century-old vegetarian hall nestled away in a quiet back alley. Exterior details along the front porch include Chinese dragons and mythical phoenixes, miniature wooden tableaux of Chinese opera scenes protected behind glass cases, plus three-dimensional painted tilework of Chinese legends. All have been carved with great care by master craftspeople. Inside are three elaborately carved altars adorned with gilded masterpieces and eight-sided doors which lead into anterior chambers.

Chinese vegetarian halls are only crowded during the annual Vegetarian Festival, which

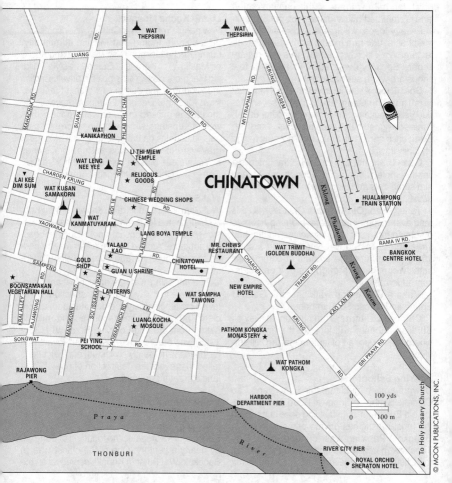

honors the nine deities enshrined here on the main altar. Otherwise, this beautiful hall remains quiet and peaceful, unlike most Chinese shrines and temples which typically teem with worshippers. Just opposite is a stage used for Chinese opera troupes who perform during the Vegetarian Festival, held in the ninth month of the Chinese calendar.

Sampeng Lane

Soi Sampeng, or Soi Wainit 1, epitomizes what is most alluring and memorable about Chinatown. Much too narrow for cars, this canvas-roofed lane is crammed with shopkeepers, porters hauling heavy loads, wholesale and retail clothing merchants, and rare examples of prewar architecture. Walk slowly to enjoy the extraordinary scene. Sensory overload at its finest! A few shops are worth special attention.

Gold Shop: At the intersection of Soi Mangkorn is **Tang Toh Gang,** a remarkable seven-storied yellow building with an imposing tier of balconies designed by a Dutch architect. Tang Toh Gang once served as the central gold exchange for Chinatown.

Guan U Shrine: Left on Soi Issaranuparp is a small temple with a large wooden horse; feed him some oats and then ring the bell around his neck.

Talaad Kao (Old Market): Chinese visit this medieval market in the early morning hours to purchase fresh seafood as well as poultry and vegetables. Talaad Kao winds down around 1000, but an amazing amount of commercial activity continues through the day on Soi Issaranuparp.

Make a U-turn and walk past the Guan U Shrine and across Soi Sampeng.

Chinese Lanterns: Turn right on an alley off Soi Issaranuparp and look for the tiny shops where the ancient art of lantern making still survives.

Pei Ying School

Down the alley, hidden behind Lao Peng Tao Chinese Shrine on Songwat Road, is an imposing old European-style building once considered the most prestigious private primary school in Bangkok. Pei Ying was founded in 1916 by Teochew merchants to encourage the study of the Chinese language and customs. King Rama VII visited the school in 1927 and lectured the audience about his Chinese bloodline. However, since WW II the Thai government has limited the role of Chinese schools; today only five hours per week can be used for the study of Chinese at Pei Ying School.

Return to Soi Sampeng, walk south past the wholesale clothing outlets, and turn right on Yaowapanich Road. This street leads to Songwad Road, where you can view historic old mercantile buildings with fine doorway plasterwork of durians, mangosteens, and mangos.

Luang Kocha Mosque

Few people realize that Chinatown encompasses a sizable Indian and Muslim community. Luang Kocha Mosque (also Masjid Luang Kocha or Masjid Wat Koh) is a European-style building that more closely resembles a private English mansion than the center of worship for Chinatown Muslims. Deserted during the week, the mosque is packed on Friday afternoons; men worship upstairs while women discreetly pray behind curtains on the ground floor. The derelict graveyard to the rear has ancient tombstones of Yunnanese Muslim soldiers of the 93rd Division of the Chinese Nationalist Army.

Wat Sampha Tawong

Wat Sampha Tawong, also known as Wat Koh, is chiefly noted for its grand and imposing three-story *bot,* a highly unusual if not altogether beautiful structure. Around the perimeter stand wooden monks' quarters and other auxiliary buildings.

The imposing *wat* has an unpleasant history. To pave the way for the construction of this lavish building some three decades ago, an ancient 18th-century *bot* decorated with murals dating from the reign of King Rama VI (1881-1925) was ordered demolished. Art lovers and historians vehemently protested, but their efforts failed to prevent the destruction of one of Thailand's great art treasures.

Wat Pathom Kongka

This unassuming temple, once known as Wat Sampeng, was constructed during the Ayuthaya Period and so predates the founding of Bangkok by nearly a century. One of the oldest *wats* in Bangkok, Wat Pathom Kongka served as an ex-

FLOATING SLEEVES AND PAINTED FACES

*C*hinese opera, a sometimes bewildering combination of high-pitched singing, clashing music, and stunning costumes, is an artistic expression with no real counterpart in the West. That alone makes it worth watching at least once. To compensate for the stark simplicity of the staging, costumes are brilliant and unbelievably elaborate—heavily embroidered gowns, superb makeup, and amazing sleeves that float expressively without support.

Although the dissonant music irritates some listeners, it can at times be ravishingly melodic and completely haunting. Stories taken from ancient Chinese folklore are told with symbolic gestures but few props. Role identification is linked to makeup, which ranges from the heavy paint worn in Peking-style opera (derived from older masked drama) to the lighter shades favored by the Cantonese. The more complicated a character the more complex the makeup: a red face indicates a courageous character, black a warrior's face, blue cruelty, white an evil personality, purple a barbarian warlords, yellow an emperor.

Costumes and movements are also highly stylized. The more important characters wear larger headdresses and express themselves with over 50 different hand and face movements. Cantonese opera is the most common genre, followed by highly refined Peking opera, considered the classic version. Soochow opera, with its lovely and soft melodies, is rarely performed.

Chinese opera is a dying art in Thailand, performed only in the lone theater in Bangkok's Chinatown.

Chinese opera star

ecution ground for nobles convicted of state crimes. Today, you're more likely to find traditional Chinese funerals in the open pavilions outside the cloistered courtyard.

The temple compound is split by Songwat Road. The main chapel with its *bai sema* stones enclosed in Cambodian-style huts and *viharn* surrounded by cement *stupas* lie close to the Chao Praya River. The monks' quarters and religious schools are on the other side of the road.

Golden Buddha

Wat Traimit, better known as the "Temple of the Golden Buddha," is one of Bangkok's most popular attractions and home of the world's largest golden Buddha. The gleaming Buddha deserves a brief look, but be forewarned: the image itself has little (if any) artistic value, and the entire complex has sadly disintegrated into a tawdry tourist trap, filled with pleading touts and barking escorts who herd around busloads of camera-toting tourists.

However, the history of the Buddha is worth recounting. According to local accounts, the three-meter statue once sat neglected and unloved in Wat Chotinaram, a disused temple in the business quarter of Bangkok. No one realized its true value since the Sukothai-era image had long been sealed in stucco to protect it from Burmese invaders. In 1953 the East Asiatic Company purchased the land and took over the premises. The Buddha was first moved to a temporary building, and later transferred in 1955 to Wat Traimit. During the process, workers dropped it from a crane and cracked its plaster skin. A heavy rainstorm that night further weakened the covering. The following morning, a resident abbot noticed a metallic glow emanating from the crack and ordered the protective shell peeled back. Underneath the stucco facade lay a 5.5-ton golden image.

Local abbots claim the Buddha is 75% pure gold, though scientific measurements have never been made. To the left of the statue is a piece of original stucco covering.

Wat Traimit is open daily 0830-1700. Admission is 10B.

Yaowaraj Road

This is the main boulevard which cuts through Chinatown. Stroll down this street to appreciate the spectacle: dazzling gold stores with mirrored interiors and richly carved wooden chairs, traditional calligraphers working on the sidewalk, herbal stores filled with antler horn and strange roots, cacophonous restaurants, and deafening noise from the people and traffic—sensory overload to rival anything in Asia.

Mr. Chew's Shark Fin Restaurant: Completely exhausted, you need to relax and enjoy a cold drink in this Yaowaraj Road establishment, which is famous for—what else—shark's-fin soup and other expensive delicacies made from birds' nests and rhino horn. More luxurious settings are found in the air-conditioned Waikiki Cafe, on the ground level of the Chinatown Hotel.

Gold Shops: Chinese love gold, and nowhere else in Bangkok will you find so many gold shops packed together. Filled with every possible form of gold, the shops are themselves artistic creations with their glass facades, upswept ceilings, vermilion lacquer counters, gaudy red walls, glowing neon lights, carved wooden chairs, and legions of anxious salespeople.

Foreigners should note, however, that the unit weight used nationwide is the *baht* system, not the international metric system. One *baht* (no relation to the monetary unit) of ornamental gold equals 15.16 grams, while one *baht* of bullion gold is equal to 15.244 grams. Ornamental gold is only 96.7% pure, no matter what the salesperson claims.

Chinese Opera: Chalermrat Theater and its resident Tai Dong Chinese Opera Troupe are the last of five opera houses which existed before the onslaught of Chinese cinemas and home videos. Today, the opera company must alternate seasons with movies, but lucky visitors might stop in to experience the last of a dying breed. Performances are given Sunday afternoon and daily except Monday at 1900; admission is 100-400B.

Wedding Shops

From Yaowaraj Road, walk east along Plaeng Nam Road and then left on Charoen Krung Road, formerly New Road—King Rama V's name for the first formal road in Bangkok. To the left along Charoen Krung are small shops specializing in items for Chinese weddings, such as elaborately embroidered pink pillows, wedding invitations, delicate tea sets, and pink mattresses. Calligraphers on the street paint gold letters over a red background, auspicious colors for any occasion.

Soi 16 Market

This narrow covered alley, also known as Soi Issaranuparp, is a shorter version of Soi Sampeng with emphasis on food products rather than clothing and plastics. Ignore the filthy floor and enjoy the displays of Chinese snacks, fresh chickens, and exotic fruits. On the left is Lang Boya, a small Chinese temple marked with a sign proclaiming that "Tourists Are Welcome To Visit And Take Photographs Inside The Temple." Unlike many other groups in Asia, Chinese welcome discreet photographers inside their temples; a small donation is appropriate.

Wat Leng Nee Yee

Also called Wat Leng Noi Yi and Wat Mangkon Malawat, this "Dragon Flower Temple" is the most spectacular temple in Chinatown. It was founded in 1871 and has since become one of the most venerated sites for the Chinese of Thailand.

Above the imposing gateway is a nine-story tower which serves as a Museum of Religious Artifacts, not yet open to the public. Inside the spacious courtyard stands an old vegetarian hall and a traditional medicine shop where cures are prescribed by the Chinese god of medicine.

The central complex is divided into several *viharns*. The dominating hall features three gilded Buddhas draped with saffron robes and flanked by gilded statues of the 18 *arahats*. Also located in the central chamber is a fat Maitreya Buddha (the final Buddha before the destruction of the world), six Dharmapala figures found in every large Chinese temple, and the Four Heavenly Kings, Hindu deities converted to Buddhism. To the right is another hall with images of Taoist Star Deities who heal all illnesses; to the left are statues of Taoist patriarchs and the founder-abbot of the temple. The extreme left has a small but beautiful garden and vegetarian hall filled with elaborately carved furniture.

Services are held daily at 1600.

Alley of Religious Goods

Immediately to the south of Wat Leng Nee Yee is a narrow alley crammed with red and gold religious items: incense sticks, paper offerings shaped like gold bars, elaborate shrines for gods of the earth, and brilliantly colored attire for Chinese deities.

Wat Kanikaphon

Soi 16 continues up to a bright orange *wat* constructed by a former brothel madam to atone for her sins. Kanikaphon translates to "Women who sold women"! Attached to the temple is a Chinese *sanjao* (shrine) where devotees perform the *kong tek,* a ceremony in which paper goods fashioned after automobiles and yachts are burned to send to departed relatives. Never has it been so easy to please dead ancestors and ensure that they don't haunt the living.

Wat Kanmatuyaram

Tucked away in a small alley opposite Cathay Department Store is this small Buddhist temple built in 1864. Duck through the small iron doorway to see a striking, whitewashed, Sri Lankan-style *chedi* and a small *bot* graced with some of Thailand's most important murals. Executed in the reign of King Rama IV, these unretouched murals illustrate the lives of Bangkokians in the mid-18th century, and the various incarnations of the Buddha. Admittance is by official authorization only.

Wat Kusan Samakorn

This quaint Vietnamese temple features a seven-tiered Chinese pagoda on the left, and a small central chapel with a large robed Buddha. The original temple was built in 1854 by two Vietnamese monks, but reconstructed after a fire in 1913. Chinese paintings on the wall recount popular stories of 24 children who demonstrated gratitude toward their parents, an important trait in Chinese culture.

Wat Chaichana Songkram

Wat Chaichana Songkram ("Having Won the War") was constructed in the mid-18th century on land donated by a victorious army leader who served under King Rama III. Much of the complex is modern, but to the rear stand a pair of old bell-shaped *chedis,* a Khmer *prang,* and a two-story library filled with religious artifacts.

Nakhon Kasem Market

Once Bangkok's antique center, most of the dealers in the so-called "Thieves Market" have since moved to shopping centers near the tourist centers. A few dusty stores hold on, surrounded by hardware shops and copper merchants. Merchandise runs the gamut from imitation antiques to vintage clocks and Chinese porcelains.

Wat Chakrawat Rachawas

Though not a temple of great architectural merit, this sprawling complex satisfies curious travelers and allows visitors to witness the Chinese funerals held on a near-daily basis. The principal oddities are the crocodiles that sleep in the small pond off the central courtyard. The original croc was a one-eyed monster named Ai Bord; he now sits stuffed after losing a fight with a younger pondmate.

The *mondop* on the artificial hill which overlooks the pond houses a replica of a Buddha's footprint. To the rear is a grotto with statues of a supernatural Buddha shadow and a fat disciple who stuffed himself into obesity to end his sexual passions. Inside the nearby *bot* and *viharn,* both now under reconstruction, are excellent murals that feature life-sized angels and Jataka murals from the reign of King Rama V. All have been totally retouched.

Pahurat Cloth Market
Sampeng Lane terminates at the old cloth market where Sikh and Chinese merchants peddle Indian saris, Malaysian batiks, and Thai silks from enormous open-air tables. Also of interest are the Hindu wedding stores and shops selling accessories for Thai classical dancers.

Little India
Sikh Temple: Up a narrow alley off Chakrapet Road towers a seven-story white temple dedicated to the Sikh community of Thailand. A health clinic and maternity ward are located on the upper floors.

Indian Restaurants: Adjoining alleys all along Chakrapet are filled with travel agencies, which serve the Indian trade, and inexpensive *masala dosa* restaurants. A comfortable if somewhat expensive choice is the **Royal India Restaurant,** where you can dine in air-conditioned surroundings. Less expensive cafes include the **Moon Restaurant** in the rear alley adjacent to the canal, and the popular **Cha Cha Restaurant** on Chakrapet Road. All offer good food in earthy surroundings.

Pak Klong Market
Pak Klong Talaad, at the foot of the Memorial Bridge, is the city's largest wholesale fruit and vegetable market. The action begins at dawn as boats laden with foods arrive to unload their wares. By early afternoon the merchants have packed up and swept out the aisles, though this fascinating market at any hour offers an overpowering sense of medieval commerce.

River taxis back to Silom Road and Banglampoo leave from Saphan Phut dock at the terminus of Triphet Road, and from Rachini Pier just across the canal from Pak Klong.

THONBURI

Thonburi, on the west bank of the Chao Praya River, briefly served as the capital of Thailand after the fall of Ayuthaya until Rama I moved his court to the opposite shore. Temples located near the river can be toured on foot by wandering through the narrow lanes; interior *wats* can be reached by public boat.

Wat Arun
This monumental 86-meter Khmer-style *prang,* one of Thailand's largest religious monuments, towers above the Chao Praya to form Bangkok's most impressive and famous landmark. Wat Arun was constructed by Rama II on the site of a former royal temple which once held the precious Emerald Buddha. Despite problems of erecting such a massive structure on the city's swampy soil, Rama III finally completed the complex in 1842. Rama IV added the final touch: thousands of multiglazed Chinese porcelains donated by Buddhist devotees. The present king donates new robes to the resident monks on the occasion of the Tod Kathin Festival, a merit-making ceremony formerly done downriver from the Grand Palace in royal barges.

Better known as the Temple of the Dawn, Wat Arun symbolically represents the Buddhist universe, with its trident-capped central tower indicating Mt. Meru and the four smaller towers depicting the four worldly oceans. The central *prang* is intersected by four door niches with the god Indra riding his three-headed white elephant. Other figures include the moon god on his white horse and illustrations of the four most important episodes from the life of Buddha: birth, meditation under a protective *naga,* sermon to the five ascetics, and entry into nirvana. Visitors can make the steep climb up to the midway point for views over the Chao Praya and Thonburi.

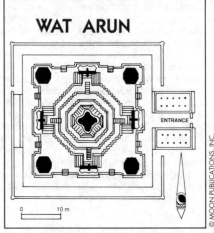

Located on the grounds are several other worthwhile buildings. The *bot* in the northwest corner features four unusual *chedis* and interior murals which depict the life of Buddha. A restored *mondop* between the *bot* and *viharn* contains a Buddha footprint and twin towers used as belfries. The *viharn* behind the primary *chedi* contains a silver and gold Sukothai image brought back from Vientiane by Rama II.

Wat Arun is accessible by shuttle boat from the Tha Tien Pier behind Wat Po. Open daily 0800-1700. Admission is 10B.

Wat Kalayamit

Located near the entrance to Klong Bangkok Yai, this immense temple has dimensions dictated by the huge Buddha image it enshrines. Interior walls of the main *bot* and adjacent chapel are decorated with mural paintings dating from the reign of Rama III. The spacious courtyard is decorated with Chinese gateways and statues, and a bronze bell reputed to be the largest in Thailand. Thais of Chinese origin favor this temple and giant image, which they call Sam Po Gong.

Wat Prayoon

Also constructed during the reign of Rama III, Wat Prayoon consists of two chapels with mother-of-pearl decorations, an artificial hill decorated with *chedis,* frangipani trees, and a pool filled with turtles. According to legend, the hill was modeled after a mound of melted wax formed by a candle of Rama III.

Wat Suwannaram

This extremely well-proportioned and finely decorated *bot* near the Thonburi train station illustrates the transitional architecture of the Ayuthaya and Bangkok Periods. Interior frescoes are attributed to two famous painters from the court of Rama II. Lower murals display scenes from the last 10 Jataka tales of the previous lives of the Buddha, while the entrance wall features the victory of the Buddha over Mara. These 19th-century murals, remarkable for their sensitivity and originality of composition, are considered among the finest in Bangkok.

Wat Dusitaram

Though the primary *bot* is of little architectural interest, Wat Dusitaram, located near the Royal Barges Museum, also features interior murals of great interest. A traditional arrangement is followed. Side walls between the windows show episodes from the life of Buddha, the front fresco masterly renders the Buddhist victory over Mara, while the Buddhist cosmology is depicted on the back wall.

Royal Barges Museum

More than 50 longboats, all carefully restored for Bangkok's 1982 Rattanakosin bicentennial, are dry-docked inside the shed near Klong Bangkok Noi. Crafted in the early part of this century, and only waterborne for very special royal events, these barges are designed after mythical creatures featured in the Ramayana. The principal barge, *Sri Suphannahongse,* is named after the mythical swan which graces the prow. Perhaps the largest dugout in the world, this gilded 45-meter glider weighs over 15 tons and requires the efforts of 54 oarsmen and a rhythm keeper who bangs the beat in time with the chanting of ancient boat poems. Equally impressive is the 44-meter *Anantanagaraj,* with its carved figurehead of a seven-headed *naga.*

The museum is open daily 0800-1700. Admission is 30B.

Bangkok Floating Market

Thonburi's floating market epitomizes what is most crass and callous in the tourist trade. Once an authentic and colorful scene, the market completely died out in the 1960s as modernization forced boat vendors to move into shopping centers. Threatened with the loss of revenue, tour operators came up with a rather awful solution: hire a few Thai women to paddle around and *pretend* to be shopping. Disneyland feels genuine when compared to this outrage, perhaps the most contrived rip-off in the East.

ATTRACTIONS NEAR SIAM SQUARE

Jim Thompson's House

Jim Thompson was the legendary American architect-entrepreneur who settled in Thailand after WW II and almost single-handedly revived the moribund silk industry. No trace was found of Thompson after he disappeared in 1967 while hiking near Cameron Highlands. Jim's maze of seven Thai-style teak houses has since been converted into a small private museum filled with his priceless collection of Asian antiques, pottery, and curiosities. A small gift shop sells fine reproductions of Vessantara Jataka and Brahma Jati horoscopes.

Thompson's house, located off Rama I Road on Soi Kasemsan 2, is open Mon.-Sat. 0900-1600. Admission is 100B; the profits go to Bangkok's School for the Blind. A more comprehensive collection of Thai art is found in the National Museum; the modest layout here disappoints many visitors.

ROMAN-ROBOT FANTASIES

*F*rom Hong Kong to Singapore, economic success has dramatically transformed Asian skylines from low-rise colonial to high-tech Houston. But Bangkok's building boom has unleashed a wave of innovative architecture unrivaled anywhere else in the region. Refusing to clone Western prototypes, the architects of Bangkok have invented some amazing fantasies: corporate headquarters that resemble Roman palaces, condo complexes that fuse art deco facades with Thai rooflines, fast-food emporiums buried inside rocket ships, Mediterranean stucco homes, Bavarian half-timbered cottages—Hollywood holograms in the City of Angels.

This exciting movement is led by an iconoclastic architect named Sumet Jumsai and an innovative design firm called Plan Architect. Sumet's Bank of Asia Robot building near Silom Road—a humorous mixture of an external skeleton fitted with giant nuts and bolts—illustrates the marriage of high-tech themes with cartoon consciousness. The postmodern McDonald's on Ploenchit Road combines gleaming glass walls with Roman columns. Suburban developments include English castles complete with moats, and the new headquarters for *The Nation* newspaper, an 11-story sculpture inspired by the whimsical designs of cubist painter Georges Braque. Bangkok is now more than just Thai temples and nocturnal delights, it's home to some of the most creative modern architecture in the world.

Phallic Shrine

Dedicated to Chao Tuptim, the pomegranate goddess and female animist spirit, this tangled mini-jungle shrine is noted for its hundreds of stylized and realistic phalluses contributed by childbearing devotees. Rather than simply a fertility symbol, the curious memorial also ensures prosperity since the lingam traditionally symbolizes both regeneration and good fortune in Thailand. Devotees of both sexes arrive daily to burn incense and donate brightly painted phalluses in all possible shapes and sizes.

The shrine is on the grounds of the Hilton Hotel at the end of Wireless Road next to Klong Saen Saep. Walk straight through the hotel lobby into the rear gardens, then walk right to the small shrine adjacent to the klong. No admission charge.

Siam Society

Publishers of the scholarly *Journal of the Siam Society*, this group also restores deteriorating murals and maintains a 10,000-volume library of rare and valuable editions. Research facilities are open to members only; write to the Executive Secretary, 131 Soi Asoke (21), Bangkok 10110, Thailand.

Of special interest to foreign visitors is the Society Travel Club (tel. 02-258-3491), which sponsors professionally led excursions to important temples, archaeological digs, and noteworthy festivals. These tours, unquestionably some of the best available in Thailand, are reasonably priced and open to the public. Upcoming tours are listed in the *Bangkok Post*.

Kamthieng House: To the left of the Siam Society headquarters is a restored century-old residence, formerly the home of a prominent family in Chiang Mai until being dismantled and reconstructed on the present site. Kamthieng is chiefly noted for its ethnological artifacts and collection of hilltribe costumes, plus exterior details such as teak lintels serving as magical talismans that hold ancestral spirits and guarantee the virility of the inhabitants.

Kamthieng House is on Soi 21 just off Sukumvit Road. Open Tues.-Sat. 0900-1700 and 1300-1700. Admission is 30B.

Suan Pakkard Palace

Bangkok can be a city of anachronisms. Hidden between the high-rises and construction sites

A RIVERSIDE WALK AND THE ORIENTAL HOTEL

Bangkok's *farang* community once made their commercial and diplomatic headquarters on the banks of the Chao Praya, near New Road (now called Charoen Krung) and the venerable Oriental Hotel. Start this tour at the historic hotel, which consistently ranks as one of the world's finest. Wander into the nostalgic Authors Lounge and perhaps enjoy a cocktail on the riverside veranda. Fine antiques and designer silks are sold in the adjacent Oriental Plaza Shopping Center.

Just opposite the Oriental Hotel is a handsome white building constructed in 1901 to house one of Bangkok's original trading firms. **The East Asiatic Company** was founded by Dutch investors in 1897, and today ranks as one of the world's principal trading conglomerates. A Dutch flag still flies over the central cupola.

Slightly up Oriental Lane and on the right stands Bangkok's principal Catholic church, **Assumption Cathedral.** Constructed in 1910, the interior features a marble altar imported from France and a soaring roofline splashed with Technicolor hues.

Just north of the Oriental, you can stop and admire the **French Embassy.** Built in the mid-19th century, this lovely European-style residence still evokes the atmosphere of old Bangkok with its louvered shutters and spacious verandas.

The **Old Customs House** nearby once housed the head office of the Thai Customs Department. This sadly neglected 19th-century building is one of the finest remaining European structures in Bangkok. Fortunately, the future looks promising. The Treasury Department has registered the building with the Fine Arts Department as a historic site, and private investors intend to renovate and convert it into a Thai cultural hall.

Bangkok's community of Muslims worship in the small **Haroon Mosque** nestled in a narrow alley behind the Old Customs House.

Continue this tour by walking away from the river toward the GPO.

This neighborhood is home to a large community of Indians and Pakistanis who patronize the local cafes. Highly recommended is the **Sallim Restaurant** located in the alley beyond the GPO and past the Woodlands Hotel. Excellent food at rock-bottom prices.

Up from the GPO you'll find the **Portuguese Embassy.** The first Europeans to initiate trade with Siam were the Portuguese, from their maritime empire at Malacca. In 1820 they erected the first embassy in Thailand. Much has been reconstructed though original portions are still visible from the river and over the tall protective wall.

Final stop on your short walking tour is the four-story air-conditioned **River City Shopping Complex** adjoining the Sheraton Royal Orchid Hotel. Special art exhibits are often featured on the ground floor, while the third and fourth floors are devoted entirely to Asian antiques. An auction is held each month; exact dates are listed in the *Bangkok Post*.

---

are several charming homes surrounded by large, peaceful gardens. Suan Pakkard is an old Thai residence complex which was disassembled and brought down from Chiang Mai by Princess Chumbhot, one of Thailand's leading art collectors. The royal quarters were converted into a public museum after the death of Prince Chumbhot and his wife.

Five traditional houses cluster around small lotus ponds and meticulously trimmed lawns. All are filled with an eclectic range of Thai artifacts, from Ban Chiang pottery to Khmer sculpture. House I contains a Gandhara Buddha from Pakistan, an 8th-century Khmer goddess, and valuable celadon from Sawankalok. House II once served as the royal bedroom. House III, the reception area, features a gilded throne and a Chinese cabinet graced with five-colored Bencharong ceramics. The dining room, House IV, was constructed with leg wells for long-legged Western guests.

Suan Pakkard's most impressive structure is the 450-year-old Lacquer Palace to the rear of the gardens. Transferred from Ayuthaya in the face of Burmese invasion, the gold and black lacquer interior panels show the early influences of Westernization on traditional Thai art and chronicle everyday life in 16th-century Ayuthaya.

The semiprivate gardens surrounding the home provide a welcome relief from the dirt and noise of Bangkok. Suan Pakkard is east of Banglampoo on Ayathaya Road and is open Mon.-Sat. 0900-1600. Admission is 150B.

Snake Farm

Also known as the Pasteur or Saowapha Institute, this snake farm is the world's second-oldest snake research facility—established in 1923 to develop antivenins and vaccines for poisonous snakebites. The serpentarium now houses over 1,000 snakes for both educational and medical purposes. Cholera, smallpox, typhoid inoculations, and rabies treatments are available.

The institute puts on a fascinating snake show. The demonstration begins with a 20-minute slide presentation on the work of the institute and dangers of Thailand's poisonous snakes. Afterward, the crowd gathers in the central pit to watch Siamese king cobras milked for their venom. Snake handlers gleefully squeeze the creatures only inches from your camera lens, close enough to watch the milky venom ooze from the fangs. The adjacent museum houses indigenous species such as green pit vipers, banded kraits, and other nonpoisonous snakes.

Near Lumpini Park on Rama IV Road, the Pasteur Institute is open daily 0830-1600. Snake shows are conducted weekdays 1030 and 1330, weekends 1030 only. Admission is 70B.

Erawan Shrine

Thailand's devotion to animist spirits and Hindu deities is best appreciated in the famous shrine on the grounds of the Erawan Grand Hyatt. The memorial was erected after hotel construction was halted by a series of seemingly random disasters: marble destined for the lobby disappeared at sea, workers died under mysterious circumstances, and cost overruns threatened to crush the hotel project. Spirit doctors, desperately summoned for advice, commanded the hotel owners to erect a shrine to Brahma. The mishaps ended and word of the miracle spread throughout Thailand.

Today, the Erawan Shrine hosts a continual circus of devotees bearing incense, flowers, and images of the elephant god Erawan, the three-headed mount of Brahma. Suppliants whose prayers have been fulfilled often sponsor performances of Thai dance. Western visitors are encouraged to make their own offerings; prices for goods are posted at the front entrance. This crazy and magical place amazes even more because of its bizarre location at a major Bangkok intersection, the corner of Ploenchit and Rajadamri Roads.

Lumpini Park

Bangkok's oldest park, Lumpini serves as one of the few green lungs for the congested city. Daytime heat empties the park, but early morning hours are an excellent time to watch the two categories of Lumpini fitness fanatics: traditionalists and modernists. The former, mostly older Thai folk, arrive at sunrise to practice the Chinese art of *tai chi*. Designed to work the muscles in a slow-motion *kung fu*, the ancient dance is now accompanied by portable stereos playing Chinese dirges or modern disco. Competing with the traditionalists are joggers who pound the pavement on a 2.5-km circuit. Kite flyers, soccer players, and bodybuilders fill the park during the afternoon.

This oasis is nestled off Rama IV Road near Chulalongkorn University.

Wat Thamma Mongkol

Completed in 1985 as Bangkok's most modern temple, this 14-story, 95-meter-high blockhouse is capped with a traditional *chedi* which enshrines relics of the Buddha. It combines traditional religion with high-tech conveniences; an elevator whisks visitors to the top for spectacular views. Bangkok's tallest *chedi* is on Sukumvit Road at Soi 101.

RIVER AND CANAL TOURS

UP THE CHAO PRAYA RIVER

A boat cruise along the Chao Praya River is one of the highlights of any visit to Bangkok. River travel offers a rare opportunity to enjoy Bangkok without the hassles of congestion and pollution, plus it opens up fresh vistas impossible to experience from a public bus or taxi. Passengers of other boats seem ready to smile, plus you get an exhilarating sense of speed and a wonderful breeze on your face.

The following sights are included only in the central part of the route from Tha Orienten in the south to Pra Arthit Pier in Banglampoo. Public boats leave from the pier down the alley from the Oriental Hotel. Private tours cost 200-300B per hour, so unless you're looking for an expensive tour, ignore the touts who haunt the pier.

Boat Types

First, you'll need to recognize the three principal types of boats that operate on the Chao Praya.

Longtail Boats: Longtails *(hang yao)* are narrow, high-powered racers that serve the outlying canals.

Shuttle Boats: Shuttles are the squarish, slow boats that make short hauls across the river, useful for quickly crossing to Thonburi and visiting important temples such as Wat Arun.

Express Boats: Express boats *(rua duan)* are long, white boats with red stripes. Operated by the Chao Phya Express Boat Company, these run daily 0600-1800 every 20 minutes from the Krung Thep Bridge in south Bangkok to Nonthaburi, a suburb 18 km north. Note that *express boat service ends at 1800.* The one-way journey includes a total of 36 stops (26 on the Bangkok side and 10 on the Thonburi side) and takes approximately 75 minutes. Government-controlled fares range 5-10B depending on the distance. Rather than linger on the crowded rear landing, walk to the front of the boat where seats are more plentiful.

ORIENTAL HOTEL TO BANGLAMPOO

Holy Rosary Church

Just past the Sheraton Hotel complex, look for the recently restored church, constructed in 1787 by Portuguese Catholics who moved from Thonburi after the destruction of Ayuthaya by Burmese invaders.

Wat Thong Noppakhun and Wat Thammachat

Opposite, on the Thonburi side, are two little-known temples featuring fine proportions in Ayuthaya style, and murals dating from the reigns of Rama III and IV.

Memorial Bridge and Tha Saphan Phut

Boats then glide under the iron-green Memorial Bridge to Tha Saphan Phut. Opened by King Rama VII in 1932, this pier leads to the colorful Pak Klong Market and the Little India neighborhood. Public longtails from this landing stage make inexpensive runs up Thonburi canals.

Wat Prayoon

Across from the Saphan Phut pier stands this temple, constructed during the reign of King Rama III and noted for its mother-of-pearl door decorations and artificial hill decorated with miniature *chedis* and frangipani trees.

Santa Cruz Church

Near Wat Prayoon, you'll see this unmistakable old church, constructed by Portuguese Catholics after the fall of Ayuthaya, but almost completely reconstructed in 1913. Note its distinctive narrow profile and towering cupola.

Wat Kalayamit

Adjacent to the Santa Cruz Church, this immense temple shelters an equally gigantic Buddha. Check out the interior mural dating from the reign of King Rama III.

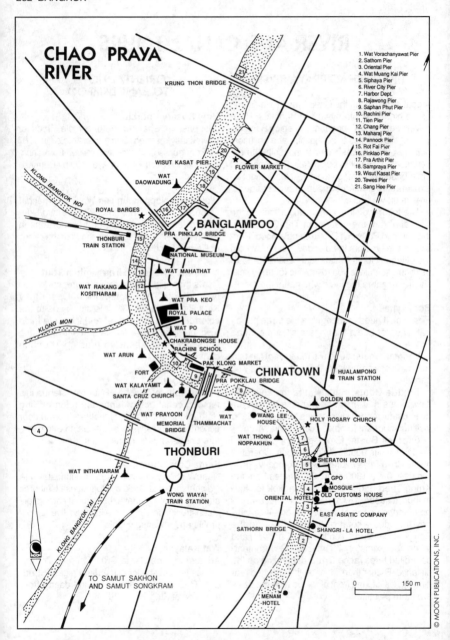

CHAO PRAYA RIVER

1. Wat Vorachanyawat Pier
2. Sathorn Pier
3. Oriental Pier
4. Wat Muang Kai Pier
5. Siphaya Pier
6. River City Pier
7. Harbor Dept.
8. Rajawong Pier
9. Saphan Phut Pier
10. Rachini Pier
11. Tien Pier
12. Chang Pier
13. Maharaj Pier
14. Pannock Pier
15. Rot Fai Pier
16. Pinklao Pier
17. Pra Arthit Pier
18. Sampraya Pier
19. Wisut Kasat Pier
20. Tewes Pier
21. Sang Hee Pier

KRUNG THON BRIDGE

KLONG BANGKOK NOI

WISUT KASAT PIER
WAT DAOWADUNG
FLOWER MARKET

ROYAL BARGES

THONBURI TRAIN STATION

BANGLAMPOO
PRA PINKLAO BRIDGE
NATIONAL MUSEUM
WAT MAHATHAT

WAT RAKANG KOSITHARAM

WAT PRA KEO
ROYAL PALACE
WAT PO

KLONG MON

WAT ARUN
CHAKRABONGSE HOUSE
RACHINI SCHOOL

FORT
PAK KLONG MARKET
WAT KALAYAMIT
SANTA CRUZ CHURCH
PRA POKKLAU BRIDGE

CHINATOWN
HUALAMPONG TRAIN STATION

GOLDEN BUDDHA

WAT PRAYOON
MEMORIAL BRIDGE
WAT THAMMACHAT
WANG LEE HOUSE
HOLY ROSARY CHURCH
WAT THONG NOPPAKHUN

THONBURI

WAT INTHARARAM
SHERATON HOTEL
GPO
MOSQUE
ORIENTAL HOTEL
OLD CUSTOMS HOUSE
WONG WIAYAI TRAIN STATION
EAST ASIATIC COMPANY
SATHORN BRIDGE
SHANGRI - LA HOTEL

KLONG BANGKOK YAI

TO SAMUT SAKHON AND SAMUT SONGKRAM

MENAM HOTEL

0   150 m

© MOON PUBLICATIONS, INC.

Rachini School

A bit upriver on the Bangkok side, behind a low, white wall, stands a beautiful European-style building bearing the insignia of "Royal Seminary." Rachini School was the first school devoted to the education of Thai women and it is still regarded as the finest in Thailand.

Tha Rachini

Adjacent to Pak Klong Market is a busy little pier where shuttle boats cross to the Thonburi attractions of Wat Kalayamit and Santa Cruz Church. Adventurous visitors can enjoy a short walk from the pier through the winding alleys of the old Portuguese quarter.

Chakrabongse House

Past Tha Rachini, hidden behind the thick foliage, is one of the few remaining royal residences which once graced the riverbanks. Chakrabongse House was constructed in 1909 by an Italian architect for the son of King Rama V.

Tha Tien

From the next pier on the river (Tha Tien), travelers can access Wat Po, take a public ferry across to Wat Arun, and explore the canals of Thonburi on any of the waiting public longtails.

Wat Rakang Kositharam

One of the most original temples left from the Rattanakosin Period, this rarely visited structure is noted for its decorated roof supports of unusual size and elegance, retouched interior frescoes, and beautiful three-sectioned library restored several years ago by the Association of Siamese Architects. The opposite shore is dominated by Wat Po, the Grand Palace, and Wat Pra Keo.

Maharaj Pier

Further up the river on the Bangkok side, this distinctive red pier leads to Wat Mahathat, the National Museum, and Thammasart University. Long the hotbed of liberal politics, Thammasart earned worldwide attention in 1973 when a student-led revolution succeeded in overthrowing the military government. In 1976, the university was attacked and hundreds of students murdered after right-wing forces reseized power from the democratically elected government.

After a quick stop at Tha Rot Fai, terminus for the Thonburi Railway Station, express boats pull into Pra Arthit Pier and the backpackers' enclave of Banglampoo.

EXPLORING THE CANALS

Bangkok's waterways offer exceptional sightseeing opportunities and reveal what is most attractive about the city. Three major canals lead off the river: Klong Bangkok Yai in the south, Klong Mon in the center, and Klong Bangkok Noi in the north. All three arteries are intersected by dozens of smaller canals that wind through dense jungle and vine-choked foliage, all flanked with stilted houses and small temples rarely visited by Westerners. Best of all are the children who smile and wave as they cannonball into the murky waters. Miraculously, the pollution and congestion of modern Bangkok seem light years away.

Private chartered longtail boats are somewhat expensive at 200-300B per hour, but hurried visitors who don't mind the rich tourist image may find it worth the cost.

Less pricey and more authentic are ordinary public longtails which race up and down the canals, picking up and dropping off Thai passengers until they finally turn around and return to their starting point. These longtails depart frequently from five piers in central Bangkok: Mahathat, Chang, Tien, Rachini, and Saphan Phut. Which pier to choose hardly matters since the scenery is similar throughout the canal network. Ignore the private operators and instead wait patiently for the next public longtail; fare is 10B in each direction or 20B roundtrip.

You have two options: stay on the boat for the roundtrip or disembark at one end and walk through the plantations to another canal to catch a longtail back to the starting point. Boat operators rarely speak English, but it's almost impossible to get lost. Just sit down, smile, and enjoy the ride.

Canal enthusiasts can purchase *50 Trips Through Siam's Canals* by George Veran or the recently published but rather sketchy *Bangkok's Waterways* by William Warren. The *Thonburi Canal* map by the Association of Architects is also useful.

Warning: Beware of slick professionals who offer free guided tours and then blackmail you for a 1,000B gasoline fare in the middle of the river. Never get into a longtail boat alone.

ORGANIZED RIVER TOURS

*S*everal tour companies offer formal cruises along the Chao Praya and intersecting canals. Tickets can be purchased at the point of departure and from most travel agencies.

Moderate: Each Saturday and Sunday at 0800 a sleek boat leaves Maharaj Pier behind Thammasart University, stops briefly at the Thai Folk Arts and Crafts Center in Bang Sai, and reaches the Royal Summer Palace at Bang Pa In at noon. The return journey visits the fascinating Wat Pailom Stork Sanctuary before arriving back in Bangkok around sunset. This all-day river cruise costs 180-240B. A relaxing day except for the obnoxious loudspeaker. Contact Chao Praya Express Boat Company at (02) 222-5330 or (02) 225-3002.

Mit Chayo Phraya Express Boat Company offers all-day Bangkok Noi canal tours which leave Maharaj Pier daily at 0830 and cost 150B. Call (02) 225-6179 for further information.

Crystal Tour: Three-hour rice-barge tours to Klong Mon, Taling Chan, and Bangkok Noi leave from the Sheraton Royal Orchid Hotel daily at 1500. The 250B fee includes refreshments and soft drinks. Call (02) 251-3758.

World Travel Service: Four-hour longtail and rice-barge tours run up the Chao Praya River to Rama VI Bridge. Tours cost 320B, leave daily at 1400, and include a short visit to the Boonrawd Brewery. Call (02) 233-5900.

Asia Voyages: A teakwood rice barge makes an overnight cruise from Bangkok to Ayuthaya via Bang Pa In. The 3,000B fare includes onboard accommodation, tour guides, and all meals. Asia Voyages (tel. 02-235-4110) is the largest operator of private yachts in Thailand.

Oriental Queen: This air-conditioned cruiser leaves the Oriental Hotel daily at 0800 and returns around 1800. The 1,200B cruise includes a buffet lunch, a visit to Bang Pa In, a guided tour around the historic ruins of Ayuthaya, and splendid sunsets on the return voyage. Call World Travel Service at (02) 233-5900 for more information.

Klong Bangkok Noi

Ordinary longtails that travel up the northern canal of Klong Bangkok Noi depart from three different piers: Tha Tien dock near Wat Po, Tha Chang near Wat Pra Keo, and Tha Maharaj behind Wat Mahathat. Four different *hang yao* routes are possible, but most roar up Klong Bangkok Noi before exploring the smaller and more fascinating canals of Bang Sai, Bang Ramat, Bang Phrom, and Bang Yai. Attractions along these canals include the Royal Barge Museum, Wat Suwannaram, and Wat Suwankhiri. Make a roundtrip journey, or hop off to explore these Thonburi temples.

Klong Mon

Longtails up the central canal of Klong Mon leave from both Tha Chang (left side only) and Tha Tien. If you choose the more convenient pier at Tha Tien, you want the smaller landing to the right. Some longtails race up Klong Mon and then continue up the smaller canal of Bang Chuak Nang. For a longer and more colorful journey, ask for a boat heading for Bang Noi (not Bangkok Noi). The journey passes temples, orchid farms, and leaning coconut trees. Get off at the end when the driver makes his U-turn, wander 45 minutes south through traditional neighborhoods to Wat Chim on Klong Bang Waek, then flag down a longtail back to the Memorial Bridge.

Klong Bangkok Yai

Longtails up this southern canal depart from Tha Rachini, a few blocks south of Wat Po. After following the river for some distance, the longtail veers off and follows the narrow *klongs* of Bang Dan, Phasi Charoen, or Sanam Chai. During perhaps the most colorful route in Thonburi, stops can be made at Wat Sang Krachai, Wat Werurachin, Wat Intararam, Wat Pak Nam, and a snake farm on Klong Sanam Chai.

Klong Tan

This unusual journey originates under the New Petchburi Road Bridge near Pratunam Market, and passes through beautiful residential neighborhoods to Klong Tan. Some boats go left to Bangkapi, while others turn right down Klong Tan to Sukothai Road Bridge at Soi 73. Buses return back to the center of town.

OUTSKIRTS OF BANGKOK

NORTH OF BANGKOK

Wat Thamakai

Located 28 km northeast of the city center near Bangkok Airport in Pathum Thani Province, this rural center was founded 20 years ago to offer instruction in Thamathayard meditation. The central *bot* is a marvel of modern Thai architecture which, unlike that of most Siamese temples, is characterized by pure, simple lines rather than highly ornate decoration. The theme of simplicity continues in the interior, where a black marble floor and plain white walls accent the presiding Buddha image illuminated with a single spotlight.

Wat Thamakai honors the legendary meditation techniques of a Bangkok monk named Pra Mongkol Thepmooni. As taught by the monk from Wat Paknam, meditation involves initial concentration on an imaginary crystal ball, then transferring that focal point to the center of the student's mind. There, the sphere expands to incorporate the universe and ultimately induces Thamakai, the visible Buddha.

Young Thai males come here to enter the monkhood during two-month retreats, held during the summer vacation months March-May. After a month of preparation, the students are ordained at a mass ceremony at the Marble Temple and then return to further their knowledge of Buddhism. Visitors will often find the initiates silently meditating under umbrellas arranged around the pond.

Public Thai-language lectures on meditation and the life of Buddha are given every Sunday 0930-1530. Visitors are requested to dress in white.

Prasart Museum

Notable private collections of Thai art can be viewed at Jim Thompson's House and Suan Pakkard Palace in Bangkok, in the Ancient City, and in the museum of Khun Prasart Vongsakul. Once a successful real estate developer, Prasart has spent the last decade constructing reduced-scale reproductions of historic Thai buildings and filling them with his priceless collection of Sukothai Buddhas, Bencharong porcelains, and paintings in the Thai classical style.

Prasart Museum is past the airport in the Bangkok suburb of Hua Mak. For further information, contact the Prasart Collection, Peninsula Plaza, 153 Rajadamri Rd., Bangkok 10500, tel. (02) 253-9772.

Safari World

Southeast Asia's largest wildlife park includes a wildlife section toured by coaches, a bird park with walk-in aviary, Macaw Island, restaurants, and an amusement park. A friendly American from the San Francisco Bay Area oversees animal care and acquisitions.

Safari World is in Minburi District at Km 9 on Ramintra Road, 10 km northeast of downtown Bangkok. Take bus 26 from Victory Monument to Minburi, then a direct minibus. Open daily 1000-1800; tel. (02) 518-1000. Admission is 400B.

Siam Water Park

Also in the Bangkok suburb of Minburi, the park is popular with families and children who plunge down the longest water slides in Thailand. A small open zoo and botanical gardens are located on the grounds. Take bus 26 or 27 from Victory Monument. Open daily 1000-1800; tel. (02) 517-0075. Admission is 300B.

Nonthaburi

A pleasant day-trip can be made by express riverboat to Nonthaburi, a small town 20 km north of Bangkok. Disembark at the pier near the clock tower and walk left up to the Nonthaburi Prison. The Correctional Staff Training compound on the left has a small museum with displays of torture used to execute prisoners during the Ayuthaya and modern periods. Foreign prisoners convicted of drug crimes can occasionally be visited.

Central Nonthaburi has a floating restaurant and an old wooden provincial hall restored by the Fine Arts Department and converted into a museum of anthropology. Also worth visiting is the modern mosque, several Ayuthaya Period *wats,* and the Singha Brewery, where Thailand's most popular beer is brewed.

A ferry from the Nonthaburi dock leads across the Chao Praya to Wat Salak Dtai and Wat Chalern Pra Kiet, a beautiful temple renowned for its architecture and idyllic location amid breadfruit trees and abandoned buildings.

Organized tours of nearby gardens are organized each weekend by the Suan Tan Noi Tour Company, tel. (02) 583-9279 or (02) 583-7853.

Wat Pailom Bird Sanctuary

Wat Pailom, near Pathum Thani on the Chao Praya River 32 km north of Bangkok, is one of the world's last sanctuaries for rare Indian openbilled storks *(Anastomus oscitans),* which migrate from Bangladesh each Dec.-June. Once a burial ground for execution victims, the bizarre landscape lies covered with denuded trees piled with over 10,000 enormous nests.

Tragically, Wat Pailom, one of the more remarkable nature reserves in Thailand, now seems doomed. Recently constructed upriver dams have choked off the water supply for the dipterocarpus trees, and modern fertilizers have poisoned the apple snail, the storks' primary source of food. The Wildlife Fund of Thailand is attempting to relocate the storks to more suitable colonies at Suphanburi and Ayuthaya.

Wat Pailom is best visited on the weekend river cruises leaving in the mornings from the Maharaj Pier. Contact the Chao Praya Express Boat Company at tel. (02) 222-5330 or (02) 225-3002.

SOUTH OF BANGKOK

Damnern Saduak Floating Market

The floating markets of Thailand are unique wonders. Amid the lowland canals and winding rivers, women in straw hats continue to paddle sampans piled high with vegetables, fruits, and flowers. Despite the popularity of fast-food restaurants and concrete shopping centers, authentic floating markets still serve several communities near Bangkok.

Don't bother visiting the completely artificial Wat Sai Floating Market in Bangkok, one of the worst examples of mercenary tourism in the world. Instead, make the journey to the small town of Damnern Saduak, 109 km southwest of Bangkok, midway between Nakhon Pathom and Samut Sakhon. Though firmly on the tourist route, it remains an authentic experience, but only before the busloads of tourists begin arriving

at 0930. Visitors who arrive before 0900 will have the spectacle to themselves, but arrivals after 0930 will be deluged with thousands of tourists. Either be here early, or skip it.

Damnern Saduak has three floating markets. The principal market at Ton Kem is formed by a narrow canal flanked with foodstalls and souvenir shops. Handicraft bazaars in the rear should be avoided since the merchandise is overpriced and the vendors can be very aggressive. Farther south are the rarely visited markets at Her Kui and Khun Pitak. Photographers at Ton Kem will get their best shots from the bridge which crosses over the canal, and from the produce shed on the right. Chartered sampans cost 50-80B for a short 20-minute look and 250-300B for a one-hour tour, though everything of interest can be seen from the bridge and adjacent walkways.

The best way to experience the floating market at Damnern Saduak is to spend a night in one of the nearby hotels.

Noknoi Hotel: The "Little Bird" hotel in the center of town is conveniently located near the

floating market

bus stop, but is decrepit and only survivable for a single night. Highway 325, tel. (032) 251392, 120-180B fan, 200-250B a/c.

Ban Sukchoke Resort: Your best bet for comfort and atmosphere is this relatively new series of bungalows overlooking the canal. Facilities include a seafood restaurant, meeting rooms, and boat service to the floating market. Take a *tuk tuk* from the bus stop, or make arrangements with a travel agent in Bangkok. 103 M.5 Damnern Saduak, tel. (032) 253044, fax (032) 254301, 250B double bungalow, 400-600B rooms, 700-800B boathouse, 1,200-1,500B suites.

Guesthouse: A cheap but often deserted guesthouse may or may not be open. It's near the coconut factory on the right of the canal. Bare-bones bamboo huts cost 50-80B.

Damnern Saduak has plenty of **restaurants,** but most visitors will opt for the cafes which overhang the market. The coffee shop near the bridge is run by a friendly woman who can't understand why anyone would want Thai noodles for breakfast.

Getting There: Because of the distances involved, most visitors take an organized tour which includes a brief stop at the Nakhon Pathom *chedi* and an afternoon visit to the Rose Garden. Independent travelers can reach Damnern Saduak by public bus 78, leaving every 20 minutes from the Southern Bus Terminal in Thonburi.

To beat the tour buses, catch an early morning bus 0500-0700. The ride takes two hours and terminates in downtown Damnern Saduak. The floating market, located two km up the adjacent canal, can be reached by walking on the path to the right of the canal or by taking a public sampan for 10B at the bridge. You can also take a minibus from downtown or hike along the road south of the bridge just past the information booth.

From the western town of Kanchanaburi, take yellow bus 461 to Bang Pae and then bus 78 to Damnern Saduak. Allow two hours for the journey. Further details are available from Kanchanaburi guesthouses.

Motorcyclists will enjoy the cool, dark ride from Kanchanaburi to the Ratchaburi turnoff, then can follow the large English-language signs which point the way to Damnern Saduak. South of Bang Pae are a snake farm and several beautiful *wats,* including a new complex which resembles a Japanese Zen temple.

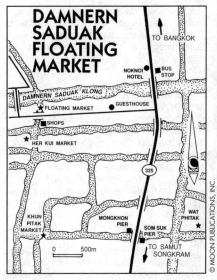

Ancient City

Ancient City, also called Muang Boran, is a 200-acre outdoor park and architectural museum filled with full-sized and reduced-scale replicas of Thailand's 65 most important monuments and temples. Constructed by an art-loving philanthropist and Bangkok's largest Mercedes-Benz dealer, Muang Boran provides an excellent introduction to the country's architecture, including reproductions of buildings which no longer exist, such as the Grand Palace of Ayuthaya. The complex is laid out in the shape of Thailand with monument locations mirroring the actual geography of the country.

Best suited for the visitor with a serious interest in architecture, the vast park is enormous, somewhat neglected, rarely visited, and murderously hot in the summer. Muang Boran publishes a detailed guidebook to their park and a lavish bilingual periodical devoted to Thai art and architecture; old editions are heavily discounted.

Muang Boran is 33 km southeast of Bangkok along the old Sukumvit Highway. Muang Boran group tours (tel. 02-226-1963, 224-1057, or 222-8143) can be booked from travel agents or directly from their office at 78 Rajadamnern Ave. near Democracy Monument.

Independent travelers can take a/c bus 8 or 11 from Sukumvit Road to the clock tower in Samut Prakan, then minibus 38 to the front gate. Muang Boran is open daily 0830-1700. Admission is 150B.

Crocodile Farm

The world's largest reptile farm was founded in 1950 by a former hotel pageboy to save crocodiles from extinction and, parenthetically, turn their hides into wallets, briefcases, and shoes. Today, over 30,000 crocodiles patiently lounge around murky swimming pools waiting for their hourly wrestling matches and frenzied feedings at 1700. After their moment of glory, the beasts are skinned into trendy suitcases and exotic dishes for Chinese restaurants. Also included is a small zoo blessed with oddities such as smoking chimpanzees and dancing elephants. Touristy and strange.

The Crocodile Farm (tel. 02-387-0020) is 33 km southeast of Bangkok in Samut Prakan, six km before Ancient City. Air-conditioned buses 8 and 11 from Sukumvit Road go directly to the entrance. Open daily 0800-1800. Admission is 400B.

WEST OF BANGKOK

Rose Garden

Located on the banks of the Nakorn Chaisri River and set amid beautiful landscaped gardens, this country resort features an eight-acre lake, aviaries with over 300 exotic birds, orchid and rose nurseries, championship 18-hole golf course, and replica of a Thai village where cottage industries such as silk weaving and umbrella painting are demonstrated. Overnight facilities include a resort hotel with 80 first-class rooms overlooking the river. Reservations can be made through travel agencies or by contacting the resort at (02) 259-3261.

The one-hour cultural show, given daily at 1500, is widely considered the finest in Thailand. No matter how contrived or touristy, this show consistently thrills with its nonstop performances of Thai dance, martial arts, a traditional wedding, Buddhist monkhood ordinations, *takraw,* and a demonstration of working elephants.

Rose Garden is 32 km west of Bangkok, on the road to Nakhon Pathom. Most travelers visit the park on a package tour which includes the floating market at Damnern Saduak and the *chedi* at Nakhon Pathom. Luxury hotels in Bangkok provide daily connections, as does Bangkok Sightseeing Travel Agency which charges 280B for a daily roundtrip bus ride at 1300 from the Indra Hotel. The resort can also be reached by public bus from the Southern Bus Terminal in Thonburi.

The Rose Garden is open daily 0800-1800. The 400B admission fee includes the gardens and cultural show.

Thai Human Imagery Museum

Prominent personalities and events in Thai history are examined in a small museum opened near the Rose Garden in 1987. Exhibits include figures of former kings of the Chakri dynasty, 15 great Buddhist monks with descriptions of their achievements, an upstairs hall dedicated to Confucius, and a demonstration room where the fiberglass figures were created. Artists fashioned the 40 figures from fiberglass rather than wax after considering the possible effects of Thailand's intense heat.

The museum is 31 km west of Bangkok. Open daily 0900-1800. Admission is 250B.

Samphran Elephant Park

This 22-acre farm sponsors daily demonstrations of crocodile wrestling, magic shows, an elephant tug-of-war, an elephant roundup, and re-creation of the famous elephant battle between King Naresuan the Great and a Burmese prince.

The park is 31 km west of Bangkok, on the left side of the road just one km before the Rose Garden. Open daily 0900-1800. Admission is 300B. For further information, you can telephone the park at (02) 284-1873.

ACCOMMODATIONS

Bangkok offers a wide range of hotels and guesthouses in all categories and possible price ranges. Budget homestays are plentiful in the Banglampoo District, while some of the finest hotels in the world are found near Siam Square and hugging the banks of the Chao Praya River.

Where to stay depends on your finances, and whether you want to be near the river, sightseeing attractions, nightlife centers, or shopping districts. The following summary will help you decide.

GENERAL INFORMATION

Districts
For quick orientation in Bangkok, think of the city as individual neighborhoods with distinct personalities, hotel price ranges, and styles of restaurants and nightclubs. The city has four major hotel districts (Banglampoo, Silom Road, Siam Square, and Sukumvit Road) and several less-frequented areas such as Chinatown and around the Malaysia Hotel.

Old Royal City: The old royal city around the Grand Palace has the largest concentration of sightseeing attractions but very few hotels or restaurants. Banglampoo is the best choice if you want to stay near the temples in the old royal city.

Banglampoo: Banglampoo has become the backpackers' headquarters, with dozens of budget guesthouses and inexpensive cafes. The area lacks great nightlife or shopping, but compensates with a superb location near great temples and the immensely convenient Chao Praya River. Anyone looking for guesthouses under US$10 should head directly for its principal thoroughfare, Khao San Road.

Chinatown and Little India: Chinatown hotels cater primarily to Chinese businesspeople, but a handful of inexpensive guesthouses are located in adjacent Little India. Travelers searching for a strong and completely authentic encounter with Indian culture might consider staying here rather than in Banglampoo.

Silom Road: Bangkok's original tourist enclave is located near the Chao Praya River and along a major boulevard known as Silom Road. Sightseeing attractions are minimal and the congestion is unnerving, but Silom offers dozens of moderate to super-luxury hotels, exclusive restaurants, high-end shopping boutiques, great sidewalk shopping, and the infamous nightlife area of Patpong Road.

Riverside hotels such as the Oriental and Shangri La are world famous for their extremely high levels of service, though budget accommodations are limited to some older properties and a few grungy Indian hotels near the GPO.

Malaysia Hotel Area: Once the budget travelers' center for Bangkok, hotels and guesthouses along Soi Ngam Duphli have sadly declined in recent years. Although the neighborhood can no longer be recommended, the nearby YMCA represents good value in the lower price range.

Siam Square: Bangkok's most luxurious hotel district is a relatively low-density neighborhood with ultra-elegant hotels and modern shopping centers. The lack of sightseeing attractions is balanced by the vast gardens that surround many of the hotels, and by the enormous shopping complexes that guarantee some of the best shopping in all of Asia. Hotels are expensive, but several low-priced and very clean guesthouses are located near Jim Thompson's House.

Sukumvit Road: Once considered on the outer fringes of Bangkok, Sukumvit has developed into the leading area for tourists seeking moderate-budget accommodations. The only drawback is the enormous distance to important temples and government services, but Sukumvit has the best selection of hotels in the US$25-50 price range.

Other positive notes to this neighborhood include countless excellent restaurants, sidewalk shopping, upscale boutiques, and racy nightlife in the Nana Entertainment Plaza (NEP) and along Soi Cowboy. Despite the remote location and problems with noise and pollution, Sukumvit is highly recommended for anyone motivated by nightlife and shopping.

Prices

Hotel prices and occupancy levels in Bangkok have followed a wild roller-coaster ride of boom-and-bust cycles since the early 1990s.

The economic collapse of 1997-98 effectively halted all hotel construction and stopped the hotel glut that had plagued Bangkok for almost a decade. At the same time, political problems in Indonesia (mostly affecting Bali) and Malaysia (after the freeze of the Malaysian currency) forced many major tour operators to redirect their groups to Thailand where peace and calm prevailed.

The result was that many destinations in Thailand—including Bangkok—are now running at near-capacity levels and a critical shortage of hotel rooms now exists. Visitors can always find a room, though advance reservations may be necessary during the busy winter months, especially December and January. More information below.

Prices cited in the hotel charts are published rack rates, subject to negotiation during periods of low occupancy and the slow season March-November. Most rooms, except for budget guesthouses, carry an additional 10% service charge and 11% government tax. Discounts are often given at the front desk for longer stays (three or more days) and for corporate accounts.

Luxury hotels have recently started to quote their prices in U.S. dollars rather than Thai *baht*, in an effort to stabilize prices and avoid the pitfalls of a wildly fluctuating currency. Those that quote prices in American currency are now substantially more expensive than those properties that continue to quote rates in local currency. Travelers seeking the best value are advised to move down a few notches and stay in smaller, midpriced hotels rather than the top-end properties.

Reservations

Advance reservations for moderate to luxury hotels are essential during the peak season from December to February. Reservations can be made by mail and by phone, though phone reservations are problematic since reservation clerks often have difficulty with English. Fax or Internet reservations are *highly* recommended since the hard-copy printout guarantees fewer mistakes than written or phone requests. Most of the better hotels in Bangkok now have websites where you can quickly and dependably make room reservations.

Fax numbers are listed with most hotel descriptions. The country code for Thailand is 66, and the area code for Bangkok is 02. Since the 0 at the beginning of the area code is dropped when dialing or faxing from overseas, Bangkok can be reached by dialing 662 (not 6602) followed by the seven-digit phone number.

Travelers arriving at the Bangkok airport without reservations can check on vacancies and make reservations at the Thai Hotel Association Reservation Counter in the arrival lounge. Hotels are listed according to price, with the cheapest rooms starting at around 800B. None of the guesthouses in Banglampoo or near the Malaysia Hotel belong to the Thai Hotel Association. Phone calls from the airport to the following guesthouses *might* turn up a vacancy and reservation.

BANGLAMPOO
AND KHAO SAN ROAD

Bangkok's headquarters for backpackers and budget travelers is centered around this friendly little neighborhood just a few blocks from the temples and Chao Praya River. Named after the village *(bang)* where *lampoo* trees once thrived, Banglampoo now serves as a freak street for world travelers who hang out in the guesthouses, cafes, and travel agencies on Khao San Road.

There's a great deal of interest here. Early-morning risers can enjoy an espresso from one of the sidewalk cafes, while late-night strollers will love the sidewalk shopping and general sense of mayhem. People-watching in Banglampoo is excellent and prices on plane tickets, local tours, clothing, and other souvenirs are some of the best in town.

Best of all, Banglampoo is a friendly place with excellent vibes from both travelers and Thais who work the guesthouses and restaurants. Though it's undeniably a travelers' ghetto with all the standard trappings, much of the adjacent neighborhood exudes an authentic Thai atmosphere rarely found in the other tourist areas in Bangkok.

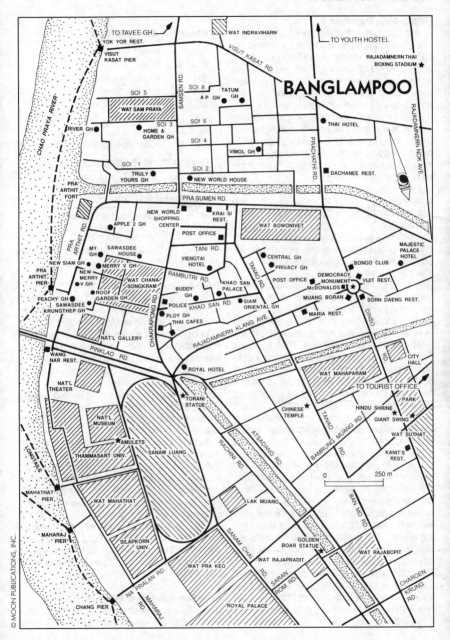

TO TAVEE GH
YOK YOR REST.
WAT INDRAVIHARN
TO YOUTH HOSTEL
VISUT KASAT PIER
VISUT KASAT RD.
RAJADAMNERN THAI
BOXING STADIUM

BANGLAMPOO

CHAO PRAYA RIVER

SOI 5
SAMSEN RD.
SOI 8
TATUM GH
AP GH

WAT SAM PRAYA

RIVER GH
SOI 3
HOME & GARDEN GH
SOI 6
THAI HOTEL

PRACHATIPT RD.

SOI 4
VIMOL GH

SOI 1
SOI 2

TRULY YOURS GH
NEW WORLD HOUSE
DACHANEE REST.

PRA SUMEN RD.

PRA ARTHIT FORT
PRA ARTHIT RD.

NEW WORLD SHOPPING CENTER
KRAI SI REST.
WAT BOWONIVET
MAJESTIC PALACE HOTEL

APPLE 2 GH
POST OFFICE
TANI RD.

MY GH
SAWASDEE HOUSE
VIENGTAI HOTEL
CENTRAL GH
PRIVACY GH
BONGO CLUB

NEW SIAM GH
MERRY V GH
RAMBUTRI RD.
TANAO RD.
POST OFFICE
DEMOCRACY MONUMENT
VIJIT REST.

PRA ARTHIT PIER
NEW MERRY V GH
WAT CHANA SONGKRAM
KHAO SAN PALACE
McDONALDS
SORN DAENG REST.

PEACHY GH
ROOF GARDEN GH
BUDDY GH
KHAO SAN RD.
SIAM ORIENTAL GH
MUANG BORAN

SAWASDEE KRUNGTHEP GH
POLICE
PLOY GH
THAI CAFES
MARIA REST.

CHAKRAPONG RD.
NAT'L GALLERY
RAJADAMNERN KLANG AVE.
DINSO RD.
CITY HALL

WANG NAR REST.
PINKLAO RD.
ROYAL HOTEL
WAT MAHAPARAM
TO TOURIST OFFICE

NAT'L THEATER
TORANI STATUE
CHINESE TEMPLE
HINDU SHRINE
PARK
GIANT SWING
WAT SUTHAT

NAT'L MUSEUM
AMULETS
THAMMASART UNIV.
SANAM LUANG
TANAO
BAMRUNG MUANG RD.
KANIT'S REST.

MAHATHAT PIER
WAT MAHATHAT
RACHINI RD.
ATSADANG RD.
LAK MUANG
BAN MO RD.

MAHARAJ PIER
SILAPKORN UNIV.
SANAM CHAI RD.
GOLDEN BOAR STATUE
WAT RAJAPRADIT
WAT RAJABOPIT
CHAROEN KRUNG RD.

LONGTAILS
CHANG PIER
NA PRALAN RD.
MAHARAJ RD.
WAT PRA KEO
SARAN ROM RD.
ROYAL PALACE

0   250 m

© MOON PUBLICATIONS, INC.

Guesthouse Overview

At last count, Banglampoo had over 70 guest-houses, which charge 60-100B for dorms, 80-300B for single rooms (rooms with one bed), and 120-400B for doubles (two beds). Rooms with private baths cost slightly more those with common baths. Many of the guesthouses also have small air-conditioned rooms in the 400-800B price range. Guesthouses constructed in the last few years often have larger rooms with private baths for 300-900B. The trend appears to be toward better facilities at a slightly higher fee, though low-end rooms still vastly outnumber the more expensive ones.

Most Banglampoo guesthouses are identical in cleanliness and size. There isn't much sense in recommending specific guesthouses, since all will be fully booked simply from word-of-mouth reputation. A small selection of slightly better choices is shown on the map and briefly de-scribed here. Most guesthouses are located near Khao San Road.

Travelers who would like to distance them-selves from the scene should check ones near the river or across the bridge to the north.

Banglampoo does have some drawbacks. Rooms are often small and claustrophobic, fur-nished with only a single bed. Theft can be a problem because of plywood walls and inade-quate locks. Motorcycles which race around late at night can ruin your sleep; find a clean and comfortable room tucked away on a side street rather than directly on Khao San Road. Finally, Banglampoo is a trendy scene (banana pan-cakes, hippie clothes, etc.), which some travelers find unappealing.

Perhaps the worst problem in Banglampoo is that most guesthouses are perpetually filled from morning until night. Finding a room is time-consuming since reservation lists are rarely hon-ored and rooms fill *immediately* after checkout. Room searches are best conducted in the early morning 0700-1100 when travelers depart for the airport and bus stations. Take the first avail-able room, and transfer to another the following day if noise is a problem. Travelers arriving from the airport in the late afternoon or evening should expect a long—but ultimately successful—search. Take a taxi from the airport to Khao San Road, then leave your bags in a sidewalk cafe while you search for an available room. And

RAJADAMNERN AVENUE BUSES	
39, 59	Airport
AC3, AC39	Airport
70	Boxing Stadium
12AC	New Petchburi
39AC	Northern Bus Terminal
45	Rama IV
15, 121	Silom
2, 11AC	Sukumvit, Eastern Bus Terminal

CHAKRABONGSE ROAD BUSES	
3	Weekend Market, Airport

PRA SUMEN ROAD BUSES	
53	Chinatown, Train Station

keep smiling. . . Bangkok is a great place once you find a room!

Transportation from the Airport

From the airport, the easiest way to reach Banglampoo is either by Airport Bus for 70B per person or a metered taxi for 350-450B.

Taxi: Metered taxis leave from the stand out-side to the far left of the exit. You must pay the metered fare, plus a 50B airport surcharge, plus any applicable tolls (30-60B). Ignore the more ex-pensive private taxi services and limousine kiosks inside the terminal—walk outside the ter-minal door and then left about 100 meters. A taxi desk will give you a coupon, which you then turn over to the driver.

Airport Bus: There are three special Airport Buses to go to different sections of Bangkok. The "Route A2" bus goes from the airport down the tollway to Victory Monument, then Democ-racy Monument, and finally stops directly at Khao San Road. It then continues to Sanam Luang before looping back to the airport.

The bus leaves the airport every 30 minutes from 0500-midnight. Apart from the low fares and friendly service, passengers can watch videos prepared by the Tourism Authority of Thailand.

Khao San Road Guesthouses

Several dozen guesthouses are on Khao San Road or tucked away in the small alleys off the main street, though you might find places further afield far more pleasant.

Buddy Guesthouse: Located in the middle of Khao San Road, Buddy Guesthouse is a good place to begin your room search. Though it's perpetually filled, you can drop your bags here and enjoy a quick meal in the comfortable cafe located in the rear. A less-packed restaurant is located upstairs. Buddy Guesthouse, like most other guesthouses in Banglampoo, has a variety of rooms from basic cubicles to small a/c rooms with private bath. 137 Khao San Rd., tel. (02) 282-4351, 80-350B.

Chart Guesthouse: An easy-to-find 20-room guesthouse with a great cafe. All rooms have fans; no a/c. 61 Khao San Rd., tel. (02) 280-3785, 100-300B.

Central and Privacy Guesthouses: Both Central and Privacy Guesthouses to the east of Tanao Road are quiet and somewhat run-down but exude a homey Thai feeling. Alleys branching off Khao San have several more peaceful guesthouses. 69 Tanao Rd., tel. (02) 282-0667, 60-180B.

C.H. Guesthouse: Big and popular place with 27 rooms and a packed video cafe on the ground floor. 216 Khao San Rd., tel. (02) 282-2023, 60-150B fan, 200-420B a/c.

Hello Guesthouse: A 30-room guesthouse with a popular streetside cafe. 63 Khao San Rd., tel. (02) 281-8579, 60-150B fan, 250-450B a/c.

Lek Guesthouse: One of the original guesthouses in Banglampoo. Always filled, but worth checking with Mr. Lek Saranukul. 125 Khao San Rd., tel. (02) 281-2775, 80-240B.

Ploy Guesthouse: A big place with very large rooms with private bath. Entrance is around the corner from Khao San Road. The lobby on the second floor includes a small cafe and the coldest soft drinks in Bangkok. 2 Khao San Rd., tel. (02) 282-1025, 80-300B.

Siam Oriental Guesthouse: Newish spot at the end of the road with large cafe, harried employees at the front desk, and decent rooms in all possible price ranges. 190 Khao San Rd., tel. (02) 629-0312, 350B fan, 400-650B a/c.

Guesthouses behind the Temple

For a slightly Felliniesque experience, walk through the passageways of Wat Chana Songkram (Chanasongkram) to the alleys and guesthouses that surround the temple in all directions. These very popular guesthouses are in a great location and well removed from the hubris of Khao San.

Apple 2 Guesthouse: Apple 2 is a long-running favorite located in a quiet back alley. The big rambling teak house with songbirds and upstairs rooms is also called Mama's. 11 Trok Kai Chae, tel. (02) 281-1219, 70-120B.

Merry V Guesthouse: One of the best guesthouses behind Wat Chana Songkram has clean rooms and a very comfortable restaurant. 33 Soi Chana Songkram, tel. (02) 282-9267, 100-450B.

New Siam Guesthouse: Popular five-story guesthouse with storage lockers and cozy cafe in the alley that connects the temple grounds with Pra Arthit Road. The lobby sign says "Enjoy your Life & Have a Nice Day." 21 Soi Chana Songkram, tel. (02) 282-4554, 200-375B fan, 500-600B a/c.

Roof Garden Guesthouse: Cheap, quiet, and almost completely deserted guesthouse at the far corner of the road behind the temple. Features an outstanding array of junk scattered around the lobby. 62 Soi Chana Songkram, tel. (02)629-0625, 80-180B.

Sawasdee House: Decent rooms, travel agency, Internet connections, and one of the largest open-air cafes in this neck of the woods. Very quiet location back from the busy streets. 147 Soi Rambutree, tel. (02) 281-8138, sawasdeehouse@hotmail.com, 100-450B.

Sawasdee Krungthep Inn: Clean and relatively new spot with small cafe decorated with old Bangkok photos. Superior rooms have a/c, cable TV, and hot showers. 45 Soi Chana Songkram, tel. (02) 629-0072, 250B fan, 350-450B a/c.

Phra Arthit Road Guesthouses

The road that skirts the river just west of Khao San has a half-dozen guesthouses that provide easy walking access to the Pra Arthit Pier.

New Merry V Guesthouse: A popular branch of the nearby guesthouse with a large, open-air restaurant, travel agency, storage lockers, and Internet cafe to check your e-mail. 18-20 Phra Athit Rd., tel. (02) 280-3315, 100-150B fan, 380-400B a/c.

Peachy Guesthouse: Slightly more expensive than Khao San cubicles, but the rooms are clean, spacious, and furnished with writing tables and standing closets. Air-conditioning is available. Perpetually filled, but sign the waiting list. Avoid rooms facing Pra Arthit Road or adjacent to the TV room. 10 Pra Arthit Rd., tel. (02) 281-6471, 120-360B.

Guesthouses North of Khao San Road
Some of Banglampoo's quietest guesthouses are across the bridge north of Khao San Road. All provide an opportunity to experience Thai homestays in a traditional neighborhood.

Samsen 6 Guesthouses: Another idyllic spot far removed from the hype of Banglampoo, near the midpriced Vorapong Guesthouse (250B fan, 300B a/c) and the less inexpensive AP, Tatum, and Vimol Guesthouses. Not a tourist in sight.

Tavee Guest House: To really escape the travelers' scene in Banglampoo, walk north up Chakrabongse Road and turn left on Sri Ayuthaya Road at the National Library. Near the river are three quiet guesthouses including the Shanti, Sawatdee, and Tavee. The latter is at 83 Sri Ayuthaya, tel. (02) 280-1447, 60B dorm, 120-150B private room.

Truly Yours Guesthouse: Samsen 1 Road has Truly Yours and Villa Guesthouse, while Samsen 3 Road has the River, Clean and Calm, and Home and Garden Guesthouses. Worth the walk. All charge 80-150B.

Youth Hostel: Bangkok's only hostel has a fan-cooled building with dorm beds (60B) and private rooms (200B), plus an a/c building with sex-segregated dorms (80B) and private rooms (220-450B). Clean but somewhat isolated. 25/2 Phitsanulok Rd., tel. (02) 281-0361, fax (02) 281-6834. No reservations accepted. Non-members must buy a one-year membership for 300B.

Moderate
Banglampoo isn't exclusively for budget travelers. Bridging the gap between the inexpensive guesthouses and the upscale hotels are several midpriced hotels and guesthouses that offer both fan and a/c rooms. During the fiery summer months March-June, paying extra for air-conditioning is worth it.

Khao San Palace Hotel: The dark and small rooms, probably the cheapest a/c rooms in Bangkok, come equipped with private baths, warm water, and horizontal mirrors geared to short-time business. 139 Khao San Rd., tel. (02) 282-0578, 360-580B.

Nith Charoen Hotel: Another good midpriced hotel in the heart of Banglampoo. Comfortable lounge with a useful bulletin board. 183 Khao San Rd., tel. (02) 281-9872, 300-340B fan, 420-560B a/c.

New World House: A large, modern apartment complex with luxury features at a bargain price. All rooms are a/c, with private bath, telephone, laundry service, and views over Banglampoo. Recommended for anyone who intends to stay a week or longer. Located just across the canal. Soi 2 Samsen, tel. (02) 281-5596, fax (02) 281-5597, 500B daily, 2,500-3,000B weekly, 8,000-12,000B monthly.

Luxury
Luxury is a relative term in Banglampoo. None of the following hotels compare with the Oriental or Shangri La, but all provide adequate facilities for travelers who want the location, with a touch of luxury.

Royal Hotel: This well-priced hotel is within easy walking distance of Bangkok's attractions—an excellent place in a great location. Reservations at this historic hotel (several people's revolutions have taken place inside this art deco building) can be made from the hotel counter at the airport. Budget travelers and overheated travel writers often spend their mornings in the a/c coffee shop reading the *Bangkok Post*. 2 Rajadamnern, tel. (02) 222-9111, fax (02) 224-2083, 1,000-1,800B.

Viengtai Hotel: Banglampoo's longtime favorite has sharply raised prices and failed to make any improvements; not recommended. 42 Rambutri Rd., tel. (02) 281-5788, fax (02) 281-8153, 1,400-1,800B.

Majestic Hotel: The best hotel in Banglampoo may be somewhat overpriced but compensates with an excellent restaurant and great location near the temples and tourist office. 97 Rajadamnern, tel. (02) 281-5610, fax (02) 280-0965, 1,800-3,200B.

Thai: Another mid-range possibility but not in the best of locations. 78 Prachatipati, tel. (02) 282-2833, fax (02) 282-1299, 1,200-1,600B.

MALAYSIA HOTEL AREA

Surrounding the Malaysia Hotel are about a dozen budget guesthouses and several mid-priced hotels which comprise Bangkok's original travelers' center. From the late 1960s to the early 1980s this neighborhood—also known as Soi Ngam Duphli after the main boulevard—was a hotbed of budget guesthouses, discount travel agencies, and banana-pancake cafes. Travelers on the Kathmandu-to-Bali trail made their home at the Malaysia, a near-legendary hotel that offered comfortable rooms at rock-bottom prices.

Unfortunately, the Malaysia Hotel raised its room rates and moved into the sex trade as trav-

elers abandoned the neighborhood and moved over to Banglampoo to enjoy the far superior atmosphere and great location of Khao San Road. Today, the sex orientation has faded somewhat though the lobby of the Malaysia Hotel attracts legions of prostitutes after the bars close on Patong.

Soi Ngam Duphli today continues to offer some of the same kinds of services (guesthouses, budget travel agencies, etc.) or earlier days, but suffers from being noisier, more polluted, and far seedier than Banglampoo. Hard drugs and prostitutes (many gay) are now commonplace and yet the neighborhood survives with first-time visitors who haven't heard about Banglampoo, and those seeking inexpensive accommodations centrally located between the nightlife areas of Silom Road and Sukumvit.

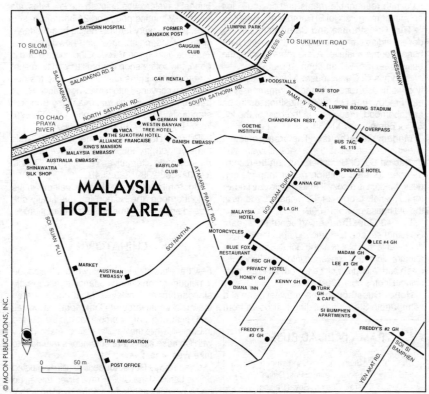

From the airport take the Airport Bus in the direction of Silom Road or a direct taxi for about 350B including all tolls and airport surcharge.

Budget

Several of the budget guesthouses in this neighborhood are fairly comfortable and worth consideration despite the noise and pollution.

Anna Guesthouse: Dismal rooms though the downstairs travel agency may prove useful. 17 Soi Ngam Duphli, tel. (02) 679-6214, 100-180B.

L.A. Guesthouse: Another simple operation with fairly clean rooms but unfriendly manager. 27 Soi Ngam Duphli, tel. (02) 286-8556, 140-200B.

Kenny Guesthouse: Comfortable outdoor cafe with reasonable meals and tiny cubicles only fit for midgets. Soi Si Bamphen, 150-200B.

Turk Guesthouse and Cafe: A surprisingly decent Indian cafe on the ground floor and bare bones rooms upstairs. Avoid rooms facing the busy street. Soi Si Bamphen. 150-200B.

Freddy's #2 Guesthouse: A clean and friendly guesthouse recommended by many travelers. Freddy runs two other guesthouses in the neighborhood, though #2 is the best of the lot. Soi Si Bamphen, 100-150B.

Madam Guesthouse: The area's quietest guesthouses are located in a back alley and cul-de-sac off Soi Si Bamphen. All can be recommended for their solitude rather than cleanliness. Madam is a cozy if rustic homestay known for its friendly proprietor. Ramshackle rooms in the old house go from 100B.

Lee #3 Guesthouse: Adjacent to Madam Guesthouse, and far removed from the horrendous traffic that blasts along Soi Si Samphen, is another old house converted into a backpackers' crash pad. A popular place to nod out in the sunshine. Rooms cost 100-150B.

Honey Guesthouse: A somewhat clean and comfortable 35-room building just down from the Malaysia Hotel. Rooms are available with common or private bath, with fan or a/c. Hefty discounts are given for monthly residents. The adjacent **Diana Inn** (Greco-Roman style) is also recommended. 35 Soi Ngam Duphli, tel. (02) 286-3460, 180-200B inside rooms, 220-300B with balcony.

Moderate

Midpriced hotels in this neighborhood have sadly declined in recent years, but the nearby YMCA and King's Mansion are excellent value. These latter are located midway between the Malaysia Hotel and Silom Road. For more information, see "Silom Road" below.

Malaysia Hotel: A decade ago, the legendary Malaysia was the favored gathering place for budget travelers who enjoyed the low rates, a/c rooms, swimming pool, and 24-hour room service. A large, very famous notice board offered tips on visas, crash pads, and how to see the world on a shoestring. Today, the notice board is gone, the coffee shop doubles as a pickup spot for prostitutes in the late evening, and the pub has been converted into a massage parlor. Rates have risen but are still reasonable by Bangkok standards. 54 Soi Ngam Duphli, tel. (02) 679-7127, fax (02) 287-1457, 620-900B.

Privacy Hotel: If the scene at the Malaysia turns you off, try this less-expensive but very run-down a/c alternative. 31 Soi Ngam Duphli, tel. (02) 286-2339, 320-364B.

Boston Inn: Once the best-value hotel in the neighborhood, the Boston Inn has finally collapsed and now seems beyond redemption.

CHINATOWN

Few travelers stay in Chinatown, but the chaotic neighborhood offers a chance to escape the standard tourist enclaves. Most hotels are on the main boulevards of Chakrapet, Yaowaraj, and Rajawong. Larger properties are signposted in English, while the smaller places, marked only with Chinese signs, are sometimes reluctant to take Westerners.

Chao Phaya Guesthouse: Beautifully situated on the banks of the Chao Praya River, this aging place is easily spotted from the river taxis that cruise between the Old Royal City and Silom

RAMA IV ROAD BUSES

5	Siam Square, Banglampoo
115	Silom, General Post Office
7AC	Train Station, Royal Palace

Road. It's not in the best of condition, though Bangkok could use more waterfront guesthouses like this one. 1128 Songwad Rd., two blocks south of Rajawong Rd., tel. (02) 222-6344, 300-600B.

Riverview Guesthouse: Another riverside choice located north of the Royal Orchid Sheraton. The eight-floor hotel has both fan and a/c rooms and a restaurant with great views on the top floor. Somewhat funky but a great location. Reservations are recommended and call from the River City complex for free pick-up. 768 Soi Panurangsri, Songwad Rd., tel. (02) 234-5429, fax (02) 236-6199, 450-800B.

New Empire Hotel: Located near Wat Traimit, the New Empire is noisy and somewhat decrepit, but compensates with large rooms and a decent swimming pool in the handy location in the center of Chinatown. 572 Yaowaraj Rd., tel. (02) 234-6990, 450-900B a/c.

Chinatown Hotel: The largest and finest hotel in Chinatown is often filled with Chinese business travelers and tour groups. All rooms come with private bath, color TV, telephone, and minibars. 526 Yaowaraj Rd., tel. (02) 225-0203, fax (02) 226-1295, 1,200-1,500B.

TRAIN STATION AREA

The neighborhood around Hualampong train station is hectic and riddled with pickpockets, but it's a handy location near the restaurants and nightlife on Silom Road.

TT 2 Guesthouse: A popular place with decent rooms and spotless communal bathrooms, plus friendly management and a restaurant with good meals and homemade yogurt. It's somewhat tricky to find, hidden away in a quiet residential neighborhood about 10 minutes from Hualampong. From the station, walk left down Rama IV Road, right on Mahanakhon, left at the first alley (Soi Kaew Fa), then walk straight for five minutes to Soi Sawang. 516-518 Soi Sawang, Si Phraya Rd., tel. (02) 236-2946, fax (02) 236-3054. 180-280B.

TT 1 Guesthouse: Only 10 minutes from the train station. Turn left down Rama IV Road, and take a right on Mahanakhon. From here, follow the signs posted on every available telephone pole. Both TT 1 and TT 2 Guesthouses enforce a midnight curfew and have strict rules against

drugs and prostitutes. 138 Soi Wat Mahaphuttharam, Mahanankhon Rd., tel. (02) 236-3053, 160-200B.

LITTLE INDIA

Over a dozen inexpensive Indian-owned hotels in the 150-300B price range are located in the alleys behind Pahurat Market. The clientele is almost exclusively Indian or Pakistani, and room conditions are extremely basic, but nobody cares how many people you pack into the cubicles. On the other hand, this neighborhood has excellent authentic Indian cafes and enough atmosphere to transport you back to India itself. Best of all, not a tourist in sight.

Champ Guesthouse: Located in the heart of Little India and slightly better than most of the adjacent dives. Nearby guesthouses handle the overflow, plus several tasty and very inexpensive Indian cafes are within walking distance. Chakrapet Rd., 150-200B fan, 300-400B a/c.

Asia Guesthouse: Another option to consider is this small guesthouse tucked away in a quiet alley. Chakrapet Rd., 150-180 fan, 250-350B a/c.

Sunny Guesthouse: Just beyond the popular Cha Cha Restaurant is another fairly clean guesthouse that cheerfully accepts Westerners. Formerly called the Rani Guesthouse. Chakrapet Road, 120-250B.

Golden Bangkok Guesthouse: Probably the best hotel in Little India, but only recommended for the seasoned traveler. Chakrapet Rd., 350-500B a/c.

SILOM ROAD

Silom Road, from the Chao Praya River to Rama IV Road, is both Bangkok's financial district and original tourist enclave. Once a luxurious residential neighborhood for wealthy merchants, today it has some of the city's finest luxury hotels and a large number of midpriced properties. The area also offers leading department stores, antique and jewelry shops, and the sleazy nightlife that thrives along notorious Patpong Road. Silom is exciting and vibrant, but also noisy and crowded with high-rises; an inner-city experience.

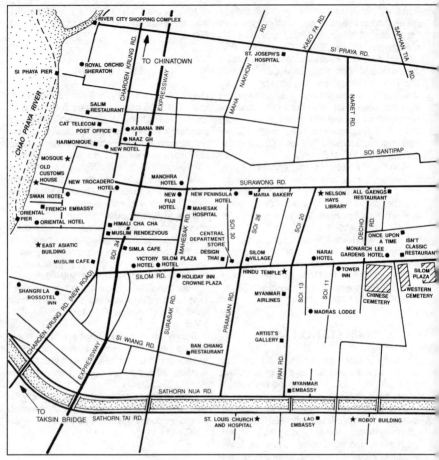

Budget

Silom accommodations are mostly in the mid-price to upper price range, though a few inexpensive guesthouses and hotels priced under 1,000B are found in the side streets. Most of the low-end hotels are operated by Indians and Pakistanis.

Kabana Inn: Opposite the GPO and river taxis, the Kabana is another Indian-operated hotel with relatively clean rooms at bargain rates. All rooms are a/c with telephone and hot showers. 114 Charoen Krung Rd. (former New Rd.), tel. (02) 233-4652, 1,200-1,500B.

King's Mansion: Though constantly filled with long-term residents, this aging property is one of the better bargains in the Silom Road area. King's Mansion is located near many embassies, near Thai Immigration, and only 10 minutes from Silom and Patpong. Air-conditioned rooms with private bath cost under 8,000B per month. 31 South Sathorn (Sathorn Tai) Rd., tel. (02) 286-0940, 700-900B a/c with refrigerator and TV.

Madras Lodge: Better hotels that cater to the Indian community are on several alleys off Silom Road. Madras Lodge and Cafe is a newer three-story hotel about 200 meters down Vaithi Lane,

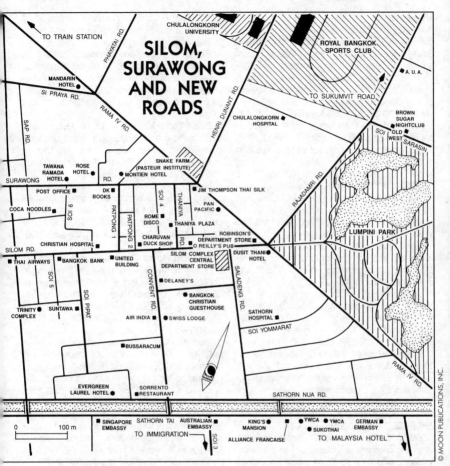

SILOM, SURAWONG AND NEW ROADS

two blocks east of the Hindu Temple. An exceptionally quiet location. Silom Soi 13, tel. (02) 235-6761, 280-350B fan, 450-600B a/c.

Naaz Guesthouse: Indians patronize several of the small and very inexpensive guesthouses on New Road near the GPO. Conditions are extremely rough, but if you want a cheap crash pad and don't mind the atmosphere, then the Naaz might be adequate. Similar spots are around the corner on Soi Puttaosod and to the rear on Nares Road. Several good Indian restaurants are nearby. 1159 Charoen Krung Rd., tel. (02) 235-9718, 350-500B a/c.

Swan Hotel: This inexpensive little hotel is ideally located within walking distance of the GPO, inexpensive Indian restaurants, and river taxis behind the Oriental. All rooms include private bath and telephone, plus there's a small pool and adequate coffee shop. The Swan needs some obvious improvement, but it remains an excellent value for budget travelers. Reservations are accepted for a/c rooms only, and flight number and arrival time are required. Credit cards and traveler's checks are not accepted. Charoen Krung Rd., Soi 31, tel. (02) 233-9060, 500-650B fan, 750-900B a/c.

Moderate

Bossotel Inn: Tucked away in the same alley as the Shangri-La is this small hotel that caters to businessmen on a budget and tourists who enjoy the neighborhood but don't want to break the bank. Rooms are basic but fairly clean and include a/c and private bath with hot showers. 55/8-9 Soi Charoendrung, tel. (02) 630-6120, fax (02) 237-3225, 1,000-1,600B.

New Rotel: A fairly new hotel with modern a/c rooms furnished with color TV, small refrigerator, and telephone. American breakfast is included. A fine place with friendly management. 1216 Charoen Krung Rd., tel. (02) 237-1094, fax (02) 237-1102, 1,100-1,400B.

Niagra Hotel: An old favorite in a quiet location off Silom Road with clean a/c rooms and hot showers. Soi Suksavitthaya, tel. (02) 233-5783, 600-900B.

Rose Hotel: Older property in need of renovation but in a convenient location for gay-oriented night owls prowling around Patpong. 118 Suriwongse Rd., tel. (02) 226-8268, 800-1,000B.

Suriwong Hotel: Another older hotel in decent condition that fills its rooms with solo males seeking action in nearby Patpong. Ask for a room on the upper floors. 31 Suriwongse Rd., tel. (02) 266-8257, fax (02) 266-8261, 700-1,000B.

Swissotel: Formerly the Swiss Guesthouse under the direction of Andy Ponnaz, this recently renovated and reconstructed Swiss-managed hotel has 57 a/c rooms with all the amenities. Good location, with swimming pool and restaurant. 3 Convent Rd., tel. (02) 233-5345, fax (02) 236-9425, 3,200-3,800B.

YMCA Collins House: This modern, spotless, and comfortable hotel is one of the better hotel bargains in Bangkok. All rooms are a/c with private bath and mini refrigerator. There's also a pool and health club. Reservations require one night's deposit. 27 South Sathorn Rd., tel. (02) 287-1900, fax (02) 287-1996, 1,400-2,000B.

YWCA: The McFarland wing is less luxurious but also less expensive than the newer YMCA Collins House. Unfortunately, the swimming pool is perpetually filled with children. 13 South Sathorn Rd., tel. (02) 286-1936, 500-700B.

Luxury

Luxury hotels are the strong suit of this neighborhood. First choice are the fabulous hotels that face the Chao Praya River followed by newer properties both along the river and closer to Patpong.

Some hotels continue to quote prices in local currency and are now about 30% cheaper than several years ago (before the devaluation of 1997-98), while others have changed to a dollar basis and collect top fares no matter the current exchange rate.

Dusit Thani Hotel: One of the most historic hotels in the country with a magnificent lobby, superb restaurants, and rooms in a variety of price categories. Rama IV Rd., tel. (02) 236-0450, fax (02) 236-6400, US$228-284.

Holiday Inn Crowne Plaza: Not the most inspiring exterior architecture but an excellent location between the river and Patong, plus spacious rooms decorated with Asian and European accents. 981 Silom Rd., tel. (02) 238-4300, fax (02) 283-5289, US$120-150.

Marriott Royal Garden Riverside Hotel: South of Silom Road and across the river in Thonburi is this welcome escape from the horrors of Bangkok with resorty amenities and an amazing array of activities. 257 Charoen Nakorn Rd., Thonburi, tel. (02) 476-0021, fax (02) 476-1120, US$177-222.

Monarch Lee Gardens: A decent midrange hotel in a coveted location near popular entertainment and business districts with European touches in the elegant lobby and equally impressive rooms. 188 Silom Rd., tel. (02) 238-1991, fax (02) 238-1999, US$100-125.

Montien Hotel: This locally owned and operated hotel has a strong French flair and is considerably less pretentious than most other luxury hotels in Bangkok. 54 Surawong Rd., tel. (02) 234-8060, fax (02) 236-5219, 2,500-3,800B.

Oriental Hotel: Since it first opened in 1876, this award-winning hotel on the banks of the Chao Praya has remained the undisputed grande dame of Bangkok. Much of the Oriental's fame comes from the authors who have stayed here: Somerset Maugham, Graham Greene, Noel Coward, and even (gasp) Barbara Cartland. Even if you can't afford to stay, take a look at the Writers' Bar, try the Siamese buffet lunch, or enjoy an evening cocktail on the terrace. The Oriental has a 100-million *baht* health spa and Thai herbal-treatment center. Some of the old charm has given way to modernization, but the Oriental remains among the best hotels in the world. 48 Oriental Ave., tel. (02) 236-0400, fax (02) 236-1939, US$250-400.

Royal Orchid Sheraton Hotel: This hotel upriver from the Oriental has 700 rooms with uninterrupted views of the river. The adjacent River City Shopping Complex features two floors devoted to antiques. 2 Captain Bush Lane, tel. (02) 266-0123, fax (02) 237-2152, US$220-276.

Shangri La Hotel: This multimillion dollar hotel boasts 650 beautiful rooms facing the river and overlooking a stunning swimming pool. Facilities include a health club, business center, and spectacular glass-enclosed lobby with seven-meter-high windows. The central tower is supplemented by a newer 15-story wing. Many consider the Shangri La just as impressive than the Oriental. 89 Soi Wat Suan Plu, tel. (02) 236-7777, fax (02) 236-8579, US$180-280.

The Sukothai: Thailand's first capital serves as the inspiration for one of the newer luxury hotels in the Silom district. A good location away from the traffic and surrounded by greenery. 13 South Sathorn Rd., tel. (02) 287-0222, fax (02) 287-4980, US$210-275.

SIAM SQUARE

Named after the Siam Square Shopping Center on Rama I Road, but also known as Pratunam (after the Pratunam Canal and shopping center), this centrally located neighborhood is the city's premier shopping district and home to many of Bangkok's most exclusive hotels. Shopping opportunities include numerous air-conditioned complexes such as Central and Zen (both in the misnamed World Trade Centre), Tokyu, and Narayana Phand for Thai handicrafts, plus the colorful flea market known as Pratunam.

This area is also an entertainment center with dozens of cinemas and coffee shops patronized by trendy Thais. Finally, the Siam/Pratunam neighborhood lies conveniently between the nightlife centers of Sukumvit and the cultural attractions in the Old Royal City.

Budget to Moderate

Though mainly known as an upscale hotel district, several good-value guesthouses and hotels with rooms under 600B are found in an alley (Soi Kasemsan 1) opposite the National Stadium on

Rama I Road. The following hotels are bunched together and can be quickly inspected.

Bed and Breakfast Guesthouse: A small and clean guesthouse with a/c rooms, hot showers, and telephone. Continental breakfast is included. 36/42 Soi Kasemsan 1, Rama 1 Rd., tel. (02) 215-3004, fax (02) 215-2493, 400-550B.

A-One Inn: Another relatively new and very clean guesthouse with friendly management and a/c room complete with private bath and telephone. Quiet, safe, and excellent value. 25/13 Soi Kasemsan 1, Rama 1 Rd., tel. (02) 216-3029, fax (02) 216-4771, 450-600B.

Muangphol Lodging Department: Somewhat ragged but recommended if other nearby spots are filled. All rooms are a/c with private bath. 931 Rama 1 Rd., tel. (02) 215-0033, fax (02) 216-8053, 450-550B.

Pranee Building: An older hotel operated by a motorcycle collector; don't miss his fine collection of Triumphs and antique cars in the front display room. Inexpensive monthly rentals. 931/12 Soi Kasemsan 1, tel. (02) 280-0033, fax (02) 216-8053, 350B small room with cold shower, 450-550B large room with hot shower.

Krit Thai Mansion: This clean and modern hotel is entered through the lobby restaurant and coffee shop. Easy to find since it faces Rama I Road. 931 Rama I Rd., tel. (02) 215-3042, fax (02) 216-2241, 900-1,200B.

Luxury

Like Silom Road, the Siam Square area excels in the expensive category. The following hotels are surrounded by immense grounds, a refreshing change from most properties hemmed in by concrete towers and noisy construction zones. Most hotels now quote their rooms prices in U.S. dollars rather than Thai *baht*.

Grand Hyatt Erawan: The venerable hotel with the famous religious shrine on its grounds was reconstructed several years ago in an amazing pseudo-Roman style; another first-class architectural monument for modern Bangkok. 494 Rajadamri Rd., tel. (02) 254-1234, fax (02) 253-5856, US$240-270.

Hilton International Hotel: Tucked away on the nine-acre Nai Lert Park and surrounded by gardens and bougainvilleas, Bangkok's Hilton is another tropical oasis in the middle of the noisy, polluted city. While somewhat distant from

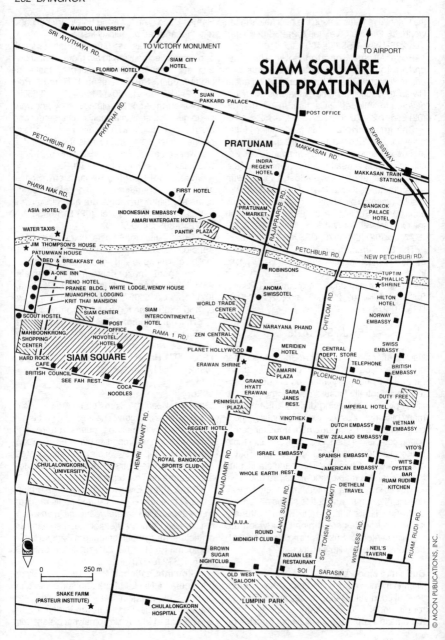

SIAM SQUARE AND PRATUNAM

MAHIDOL UNIVERSITY

SRI AYUTHAYA RD.

TO VICTORY MONUMENT

TO AIRPORT

FLORIDA HOTEL

SIAM CITY HOTEL

SUAN PAKKARD PALACE

POST OFFICE

EXPRESSWAY

PETCHBURI RD.

PHYATHAI RD.

PRATUNAM

MAKKASAN RD.

INDRA REGENT HOTEL

MAKKASAN TRAIN STATION

PHAYA NAK RD.

FIRST HOTEL

ASIA HOTEL

RAJAPRAROB RD.

BANGKOK PALACE HOTEL

WATER TAXIS

INDONESIAN EMBASSY

AMARI WATERGATE HOTEL

PRATUNAM MARKET

PETCHBURI RD.

NEW PETCHBURI RD.

PANTIP PLAZA

JIM THOMPSON'S HOUSE

PATUMWAN HOUSE

BED & BREAKFAST GH

A-ONE INN

RENO HOTEL

PRANEE BLDG., WHITE LODGE, WENDY HOUSE

MUANGPHOL LODGING

KRIT THAI MANSION

SCOUT HOSTEL

ROBINSONS

TUPTIM PHALLIC SHRINE

ANOMA SWISSOTEL

HILTON HOTEL

NORWAY EMBASSY

CHITLOM RD.

WORLD TRADE CENTER

SIAM CENTER

SIAM INTERCONTINENTAL HOTEL

POST OFFICE

RAMA 1 RD.

ZEN CENTRAL

NARAYANA PHAND

SWISS EMBASSY

NOVOTEL HOTEL

MAHBOONKRONG SHOPPING CENTER

PLANET HOLLYWOOD

MERIDIEN HOTEL

CENTRAL DEPT. STORE

TELEPHONE

BRITISH EMBASSY

HARD ROCK CAFE

SIAM SQUARE

ERAWAN SHRINE

PLOENCHIT RD.

BRITISH COUNCIL

SEE FAH REST.

AMARIN PLAZA

COCA NOODLES

GRAND HYATT ERAWAN

SARA JANES REST.

DUTY FREE

IMPERIAL HOTEL

HENRI DUNANT RD.

PENINSULA PLAZA

VINOTHEK

DUTCH EMBASSY

VIETNAM EMBASSY

REGENT HOTEL

DUX BAR

NEW ZEALAND EMBASSY

VITO'S

CHULALONGKORN UNIVERSITY

ROYAL BANGKOK SPORTS CLUB

RAJADAMRI RD.

ISRAEL EMBASSY

SPANISH EMBASSY

AMERICAN EMBASSY

WIT'S OYSTER BAR

RUAM RUDI KITCHEN

WHOLE EARTH REST.

DIETHELM TRAVEL

WIRELESS RD.

RUAM RUDI RD.

A.U.A.

LANG SUAN RD.

SOI TONSIN (SOI SOMKIT)

ROUND MIDNIGHT CLUB

NEIL'S TAVERN

BROWN SUGAR NIGHTCLUB

NGUAN LEE RESTAURANT

OLD WEST SALOON

SOI SARASIN

LUMPINI PARK

0   250 m

SNAKE FARM (PASTEUR INSTITUTE)

CHULALONGKORN HOSPITAL

© MOON PUBLICATIONS, INC.

Silom Road and the temples in the old city, it's convenient for shopping, conducting business at the nearby embassies, and enjoying the nightlife along Sukumvit Road. Popular with business travelers. 2 Wireless (Withaya) Rd., tel. (02) 253-0123, fax (02) 253-6509, US$180-240.

Regent Hotel: Formerly known as the Bangkok Peninsula, this stately structure overlooking the Royal Bangkok Sports Club is considered one of the city's finest hotels. Inside the enormous lobby is a grand staircase and hand-painted silk murals, which relate the colorful history of Bangkok. Actor and kickboxer Jean Claude Van Damme married Darry Lapier here in 1994. The afternoon high-tea ritual is worth experiencing. 155 Rajadamri Rd., tel. (02) 251-6127, fax (02) 253-9195, US$225-275.

Siam Intercontinental Hotel: Built on 26 acres of tropical gardens next to the Srapatum Palace, this oasis of tranquillity is far removed from the noise and grime of the city. Included in the tariff is a sensational array of sports facilities such as a mini-golf course and jogging trail. 967 Rama 1 Rd., tel. (02) 253-0355, fax (02) 253-2275, US$140-250.

SUKUMVIT ROAD

Thailand's longest road (it stretches all the way to Cambodia!) serves as the midpriced tourist center of Bangkok. Though very distant from the temples, Sukumvit offers dozens of good-value hotels in the moderate range, great sidewalk shopping, popular yet inexpensive restaurants, cozy English pubs, great bookstores, numerous tailor and shoe shops, and discount travel agencies. The racy nightlife scenes at Nana Entertainment Plaza (NEP) and Soi Cowboy are now far superior to the mess around Patpong.

Hotels on Sukumvit are available in all prices, but the neighborhood's claim to fame is the midpriced lodgings (600-1,200B) that flank Sukumvit from Soi 1 and Soi 63. Many of these are exceptional values with comfortable a/c rooms, swimming pools, travel services, taxis at the front door, and fine restaurants. Deluxe hotels above 3,000B are starting to appear, though it will be years before the neighborhood can compete with the five-star wonders on Silom Road and around Siam Square.

The best area to stay for shopping and entertainment is along Sukumvit between Soi 2 and Soi 13; hotels further afield are either a long walk or a very trick taxi ride. Best bet are the midpriced hotels near Soi 4 and the Nana Entertainment Plaza.

Visitors looking for long-term rentals and sublets should check the Villa Market bulletin board at Soi 33. Also listed are ads for used cars and motorcycles, plus furniture and miscellaneous goods being sold by departing expatriates.

Budget

Budget accommodations include over a dozen hotels with rooms for 600-900B. Many were constructed in the 1960s in Motel 6-style to serve the American military trade from Vietnam. Though extremely basic and in need of improvement, rooms are air-conditioned, and a small pool and restaurant are often included. Also described below are simple guesthouses constructed in the last few years; these won't have pools but the rooms will be cleaner. Budget travelers who spend more time sightseeing than lounging in their rooms will probably find all the following places suitable for a short stay.

Uncle Rey's Guesthouse: A clean but cramped high-rise with fully furnished, small a/c rooms, the guesthouse features private baths and hot showers. Tucked away in an alley near the Nana Hotel. No pool, no yard. Sukumvit Soi 4, tel. (02) 258-0318, fax (02) 258-4438, 600-900B.

Happy Inn: A small and very simple hotel with clean rooms and a good location near the nightlife and shopping centers. Sukumvit Soi 4, tel. (02) 252-6508, 500-600B.

Atlanta Hotel: An old travelers' favorite has clean rooms, a cheery little cafe, and a surprisingly good pool in the backyard. Proprietor Dr. Charles Henn, son of the German immigrant who founded the Atlanta in 1952, has recently renovated the property with attention to the increasingly rare 1950s decor. The cheapest hotel in the Sukumvit neighborhood. Highly recommended. Sukumvit Soi 2, tel. (02) 252-1650, fax (02) 255-2151, 300-400B fan, 450-700B a/c.

Miami Hotel: An old hotel offers dozens of decent rooms overlooking the courtyard swimming pool. Fan rooms are very basic, but all a/c rooms

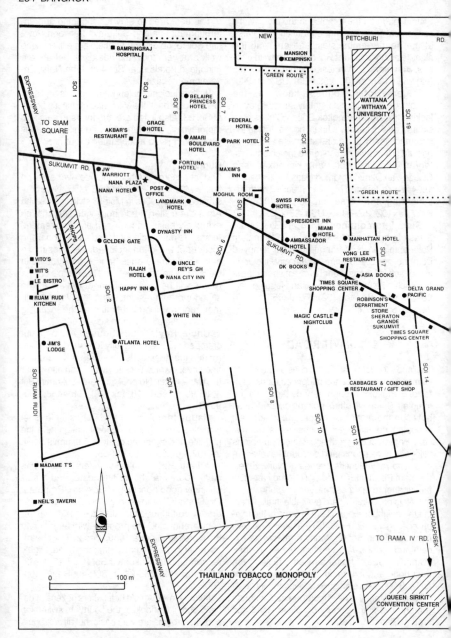

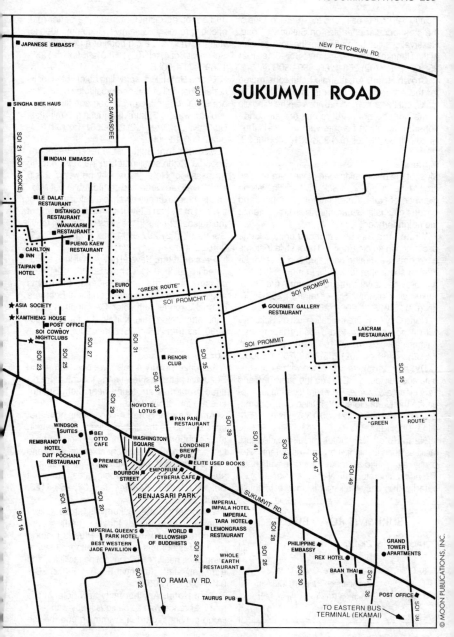

SUKUMVIT ROAD

JAPANESE EMBASSY

NEW PETCHBURI RD.

SOI 39

SINGHA BIER HAUS

SOI SAWASDEE

SOI 21 (SOI ASOKE)

INDIAN EMBASSY

LE DALAT RESTAURANT
BISTANGO RESTAURANT
WANAKARM RESTAURANT
PUENG KAEW RESTAURANT

CARLTON INN

TAIPAN HOTEL

EURO INN

"GREEN ROUTE"

SOI PROMCHIT

SOI PROMSRI

GOURMET GALLERY RESTAURANT

ASIA SOCIETY

KAMTHIENG HOUSE

POST OFFICE

SOI COWBOY NIGHTCLUBS

LAICRAM RESTAURANT

SOI 23

SOI 25

SOI 27

SOI 31

SOI PROMMIT

SOI 29

SOI 33

SOI 35

SOI 55

RENOIR CLUB

PIMAN THAI

NOVOTEL LOTUS

"GREEN ROUTE"

PAN PAN RESTAURANT

WINDSOR SUITES

BEI OTTO CAFE

WASHINGTON SQUARE

LONDONER BREW PUB

SOI 39

SOI 41

SOI 43

SOI 47

SOI 49

REMBRANDT HOTEL
DJIT POCHANA RESTAURANT

PREMIER INN

BOURBON STREET

EMPORIUM

CYBERIA CAFE

ELITE USED BOOKS

BENJASARI PARK

SOI 18

SOI 20

IMPERIAL IMPALA HOTEL
IMPERIAL TARA HOTEL
LEMONGRASS RESTAURANT

SOI 28

PHILIPPINE EMBASSY

REX HOTEL

GRAND TOWER APARTMENTS

SOI 16

IMPERIAL QUEEN'S PARK HOTEL
BEST WESTERN JADE PAVILLION

WORLD FELLOWSHIP OF BUDDHISTS

SOI 24

WHOLE EARTH RESTAURANT

SOI 26

SOI 30

BAAN THAI

SOI 36

POST OFFICE

SOI 38

SUKUMVIT RD.

SOI 22

TO RAMA IV RD.

TAURUS PUB

TO EASTERN BUS TERMINAL (EKAMAI)

© MOON PUBLICATIONS, INC.

include TV, private bath, and maid service. One of the most popular cheapies on Sukumvit Road. Reservations can be made from the hotel counter at the Bangkok airport. Sukumvit Soi 13, tel. (02) 253-0369, fax (02) 253-1266, 550-650B a/c.

Crown Hotel: Another old hotel constructed for the American GI trade in the 1960s. Very funky, but the small pool provides a refreshing dip in the hot afternoon. All rooms are air-conditioned; a longtime favorite with many visitors. Sukumvit Soi 29, tel. (02) 258-0318, 450-650B.

Moderate

Most of the better midpriced places are packed around the lower end of Sukumvit, within walking distance of Nana Entertainment Complex and dozens of small restaurants which characterize the neighborhood.

White Inn: This beautiful and unique lodge decorated in an old English-Tudor style features a/c rooms, swimming pool, and sun terrace. Although somewhat funky, it's in a quiet location and provides a welcome respite from the hell of Sukumvit. Sukumvit Soi 4, tel. (02) 252-7090, fax (02) 254-8865, 900-1,200B.

Nana City Inn: Great location just off Sukumvit with a popular café and decent if somewhat unimaginative rooms. 23/164 Sukumvit Soi 4, tel. (02) 253-4468, fax (02) 255-2449, 750-1,000B.

Dynasty Inn: Fine little place with a comfortable cocktail lounge, CNN on the cable TV, and very clean a/c rooms. Excellent location just opposite the Nana Hotel; often filled by noontime. Sukumvit Soi 4, tel. (02) 250-1397, fax (02) 255-4111, 900-1,200B.

Nana Hotel: A big hotel with all the standard facilities such as nightclubs and restaurants. Recently refurbished a/c rooms include private bath, TV, and refrigerator. The Nana is conveniently located within easy walking distance of nightlife

and shopping districts; one of the better midpriced spreads on Sukumvit. Recommended for visitors who want a big hotel at a decent price. Sukumvit Soi 4, tel. (02) 252-0121, fax (02) 255-1769, 900-1,600B.

Grace Hotel: Big, sprawling hotel noted for its coffee shop full of low-end prostitutes but rooms are spacious and kept in good condition, plus you can walk to Sukumvit in just a few minutes. Sukumvit Soi 3, tel. (02) 253-0651, fax (02) 254-9020, 800-1,200B.

Maxim's Inn: Sukumvit in recent years has added a dozen small hotels in the *sois* near the Ambassador Hotel, especially between *sois* 9 and 13. All are clean and comfortable, but Maxim's is more luxurious and has a better location at the end of a short alley. If it's filled, check any of the adjacent hotels in the price range. Sukumvit Soi 9, tel. (02) 252-9911, fax (02) 253-5329, 900-1,200B.

President Inn: Several new, small inns are located in the short alleys near Soi 11. Most were constructed in the early 1990s, so the rooms and lobbies remain in good condition. Features clean a/c rooms with color TV, telephone, and mini-refrigerator. Sukumvit Soi 11, tel. (02) 255-4230, fax (02) 255-4235, 800-1,200B.

Luxury

A half-dozen luxury hotels have opened around Sukumvit in the last few years, though more refined properties are found near Siam Square and around Silom Road.

Ambassador Hotel: An enormous hotel that once served as the first and finest of its kind in the neighborhood, but has now fallen on hard times and chiefly attracts cheap group tours and a smattering of backpackers who want comfortable if funky rooms at bargain rates. Sukumvit Soi 11, tel. (02) 254-0444, fax (02) 253-4123, 2,200-2,800B.

Landmark Hotel: Sukumvit's largest luxury hotel enjoys a superb location near shops, restaurants, and nightclubs. Pluses include rooftop restaurants on the 31st floor, a swimming pool, health club, convention facilities, and a friendly staff. Sukumvit Soi 6, tel. (02) 254-0404, 3,800-5,000B.

Tara Hotel: Another fairly new hotel in the four-star range with a spacious lobby with teakwood carvings, garden swimming pool on the

---

SUKUMVIT ROAD BUSES

1AC	Chinatown, Wat Po
2	Banglampoo
8AC	Siam Square, Grand Palace
11AC	Banglampoo, National Museum
13AC	Northern Bus Terminal, Airport

eighth floor, and a skyview cocktail lounge on the 22nd floor. Nice place but somewhat removed from the action. Sukumvit Soi 26, tel. (02) 259-0053, fax (02) 259-2896, 3,600-4,200B.

Swiss Park Hotel: A centrally located 108-room hotel with rooftop swimming pool, cafe on the seventh floor, and business center. Sukumvit Soi 11, tel. (02) 254-0228, fax (02) 254-0378, 3,000-3,600B.

AIRPORT AREA

Although there's no sights of interest out near the Bangkok Airport, a late arrival or early departure may necessitate an overnight stay in one of the nearby hotels. All hotels near the airport are overpriced and should only be used as a last resort.

Amari Airport Hotel: Expensive but very convenient—just walk from the airport on the 160-meter air-conditioned passageway which crosses the highway and leads directly to the hotel. Several travelers recommend the "three-hour

special:" unlimited use of a room, the pool, the health club, and other facilities for just 600B. 333 Chert Vudtakas Rd., Don Muang, tel. (02) 566-1020, fax (02) 566-1941, 4,200-5,600B.

Rama Gardens Hotel: Five minutes by taxi from the airport. Another somewhat overpriced hotel that mainly caters to business travelers and conventioneers. 9/9 Vibhavadi Rangsit Rd., Bangkhen, tel. (02) 561-0022, fax (02) 561-1025. 4,600-5,400B.

Central Plaza Hotel: Another convention hotel about 20 minutes from the airport, 20 minutes from city center, and five minutes from the Chatuchak Weekend Market. 1695 Phaholyothin Rd., Chatuchak, tel. (02) 541-1234, fax (02) 541-1087, 4,800-6,400B.

Comfort Inn Airport: A well-priced hotel about five minutes south of the airport by taxi. Facilities include a restaurant, swimming pool, health club, and large air-conditioned rooms with color TV and mini-fridge. Call for free pickup from the airport. Room prices are negotiable. 88/117 Vibhavadi Rangsit Rd., Don Muang, tel. (02) 552-8929, fax (02) 552-8920, 2,400-3,000B.

FOOD

Bangkok richly deserves its reputation as one of the world's great culinary destinations. Spread across the city are some 30,000 registered restaurants and countless streetstalls that produce some of the tastiest food in the East. Whether you try heart-pounding curries or aromatically smooth soups, it's almost impossible to go wrong in the City of Angels.

Gourmets with a serious interest in the restaurants of Thailand will find further information and a discount dining program in *The Restaurant Guide of Thailand* published annually by The Siam Dinner Club. *Bangkok Restaurant Guide* published in 1988 (the first and only edition) by Asia Books is dated, but is still recommended for the neighborhood maps and detailed descriptions of restaurant specialties. Gault Millau's *The Best of Thailand* attempts to "distinguish the truly superlative from the merely overrated" restaurants in Bangkok. Also check the restaurant listings in the *Bangkok Post* and local tourist magazines.

Most of the following summaries describe popular restaurants which have been in busi-

ness for an extended period, or newer cafes that show great potential. The listings range from cheap sidewalk cafes, where you'll find some of the best food in Bangkok, to expensive Thai restaurants that specialize in regional and royal cuisines.

Specific restaurant recommendations are difficult for several reasons. Many establishments tend to change ownership and location with the seasons. Leading chefs often move to other restaurants, or open their own operations to exploit their culinary reputations. And, as elsewhere in the world, successful restaurants often rest on their laurels and eventually go into decline, raising prices and letting food quality suffer. For these reasons, take suggestions from fellow travelers and Bangkok residents.

BANGLAMPOO

Alfresco dining along Khao San Road is a pleasant way to meet other travelers and exchange in-

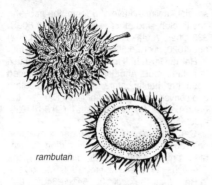

rambutan

formation, though none of the cafes will win any awards for great cuisine or elaborate atmosphere. Banglampoo's other problem, besides the mediocre food, is the noisy video cafes that prohibit good conversation. Try to patronize video-free restaurants.

Inexpensive
Buddy Cafe: One of the more elegant cafes on Khao San Road is tucked away behind the Buddy Guesthouse. The food is bland but safe, a good introduction for first-time visitors fearful of chilies. The upstairs restaurant provides a pleasant escape from the mayhem of Khao San Road.

Streetstalls: If the cafes on Khao San seem overpriced and unimaginative, try the sidewalk stalls just north of Khao San on Rambutri and Tani roads. For half the price of Khao San cafes you can enjoy an authentic Thai meal and soak up an atmosphere a million times more authentic than back in the travelers ghetto. Tani Road has over a dozen sidewalk stalls completely accustomed to the antics of travelers and prepared to offer great meals at rock-bottom prices.

Thai Cafes: Several unpretentious cafes around the corner from Khao San on Chakrabongse (Chakraphong or Chakrapong) Road offer a good selection of unusual dishes. They are best in the morning when the food is freshest; very inexpensive. The no-name cafe at 8 Chakrabongse specializes in southern Thai dishes, #22 has good Chinese noodle dishes, and #28 spicy Thai curries.

Night Foodstalls: Authentic Thai food is found nightly in the foodstalls at the west end of Khao San Road and a few blocks north toward the New World Shopping Center.

New World Shopping Center: Nearly every shopping center in Thailand has a food complex on the top floor where the prices are rock bottom, the quality is good, and the service is near instantaneous. Try the numerous outlets on the eighth floor.

Chabad House: Simple cafe with Jewish kosher meals and a Hebrew message board near the front door. Meetings are held upstairs. 108/1 Rambutri Rd., tel. (02) 282-6388.

Chochana: Another Israeli cafe often packed out with Jewish backpackers and somewhat cheaper than the nearby Chabad House. 86 Chakrabongse Rd., tel. (02) 282-9948.

May Kaidee: Vegetarian cafe with streetside tables and small menu with tasty brown rice, tofu curry, fresh spring rolls, and *som tam jeh.* Open daily until 2100. 117 Tanao Rd., no phone.

Moderate
Krai Si: Small, clean, and very chilly restaurant with Japanese sushi, sashimi, tempura, and Western specialties. Look for the sidewalk sushi man. Pra Sumen Road.

Royal Hotel Coffee Shop: An excellent place to relax in the morning, enjoy a good cup of coffee, and read the *Bangkok Post.* 2 Rajadamnern Avenue.

Yok Yor: Also on the banks of the Chao Praya, Yok Yor serves Thai, Chinese, and Japanese dishes in a rather wild atmosphere: waitresses are dressed in sailor outfits and passengers disembarking from the river taxi saunter right through the restaurant! The restaurant offers dinner cruises for 60B plus meal; the boat leaves nightly at 2000. Try *hoh mok,* duck curry, and *noi na* ice cream for dessert. Yok Yor is on Wisut Kaset Rd., down from the National Bank, a very pleasant 30-minute walk through back alleys which skirt the river. 4 Visutkaset Rd., tel. (02) 280-1418.

Hemlock: One of the first trendy cafes in this neighborhood and still frequented for its well-prepared Thai dishes served without fuss. Nonsmoking section upstairs. 56 Pra Arthit Rd., tel. (02) 282-7507.

Apostrophe's Restaurant: The newest arty enclave serves up tasty Thai dishes in a very small but almost stylish setting. Pra Arthit Rd., tel. (02) 282-7040.

Maria Restaurant: Rajadamnern Avenue serves as an administrative center during the day and as restaurant row in the evening. Scattered along the broad avenue are a several moderately priced restaurants popular with Thai civil servants and businesspeople. Maria's is a large, air-conditioned place with both Chinese and Thai specialties.

Vijit's: Several old favorites are also located around Democracy Monument on Rajadamnern Avenue. All are patronized by Thais who seek a semi-luxurious yet casual restaurant. Vijit's resembles an old American diner from the 1950s, and serves both Asian and Western dishes. Both indoor and patio dining are offered. **Sorn Daeng Restaurant,** just across the circle, is another popular restaurant with a 1950s atmosphere. 77 Rajadamnern Ave., tel. (02) 282-0958.

Dachanee: A long-running Thai restaurant recommended by many tourist guides. The heavy decor is rather gloomy, but the traditionally prepared dishes and skillful presentation provide compensation. Prachathi Road, tel. (02) 281-9332, open daily 1000-1900.

Kanit's: Both French specialties and Italian pizzas are served in very elegant surroundings. Considered the best European restaurant in this section of town. Owned by a friendly Thai woman and her German husband. 68 Ti Thong Rd., near the Giant Swing and Wat Suthat, tel. (02) 222-1020.

MALAYSIA HOTEL AREA

This neighborhood has few decent restaurants, but a string of inexpensive cafes with standard fare lines Soi Si Bamphen. The overpriced restaurant inside the Malaysia Hotel provides a welcome escape from the noxious fumes and noise that plague this area.

Inexpensive
Blue Fox: A quiet little spot of eccentric Thais and lonesome travelers escaping the searing heat with acceptable Western food, bland Thai dishes, and a pickup atmosphere in the evening. Soi Si Bamphen.

Foodstalls: Get tasty, authentic Thai food at the large collection of foodstalls just across Rama IV near the Lumpini Boxing Stadium. Point to a neighbor's dish or look inside the pots. More foodstalls are a few blocks south.

Moderate
Chandrapen: Large and fairly luxurious restaurant on Rama IV Road features Thai and Chinese specialties. The only upscale place within easy walking distance of the Malaysia Hotel.

Pinnacle Hotel: Comfortable a/c cafe with fairly good dishes in this moderately priced hotel just off the main drag. Soi Ngam Duphli.

Kiaow Tra Wang Chun: Popular Chinese cafe opposite the Chandrapen with decent Cantonese dishes but a surly staff. 5/4 Soi Ngam Duphli, tel. (02) 679-7019.

Ratsstube: German home cooking featuring stuffed sausages, sauerkraut, fried potatoes, and traditional desserts including *karamel koepfchen.* The large selection of imported German beers and kitchsy interior decor keeps this place busy with a largely Thai clientele. Goethe Institute, 101 Soi Ngam Duphli, tel. (02) 286-4258.

SILOM ROAD

Silom and Surawong Roads are gourmet ghettos, with dozens of great restaurants and hundreds of cheap cafes and streetstalls. The following suggestions include both classic joints in the high-price range and small spots rarely visited by Westerners.

Inexpensive
Charuvan Duck Shop: Around the corner from Patpong is an old travelers' favorite with, what

jackfruit

KAREN McKINLEY

else, duck specialties over rice and inexpensive curries. The food has unfortunately gone downhill and duck dishes are mostly rice with duck skin. An air-conditioned room is located behind the open-air cafe. Silom Soi 4, tel. (02) 234-2206.

Robinson's Department Store: For a quick bite at bargain prices, try the fast food outlets on the main floor or the well-stocked grocery store downstairs. Silom at Rama IV Rd.

Soi 20 Nightmarket: The few street vendors on this narrow alley during the day are joined by dozens of others after the sun sets. Try a *kuay teow* dish or the trusty point-and-order method.

Maria Bakery: A longtime favorite among local and foreign residents with an extensive selection of Vietnamese, Thai, and Western dishes, along with pizza, baked goods, and hearty breakfasts, served in a simple but air-conditioned dining room. 311/234 Surawong Rd., tel. (02) 234-6362.

Silom Village Trade Center: A very touristy shopping complex but with several decent restaurants at reasonable prices, including a seafood outlet in a patio environment, a popular coffee bar, a cozy Indian outlet for baked crab and spicy beef salad, and an upscale Thai restaurant for a pricey but first-rate dinner-dance show. 286 Silom Rd., tel. (02) 235-8760.

Central Department Store: Department stores often serve excellent food at rock-bottom prices in a clean but inevitably sterile environment. Once again, the coupon system; most dishes cost only 20-40B. Silom Plaza at Mahesak Rd., 5th floor.

Silom Plaza Hotel: Try the wonderful lunch buffet in the fifth-floor dining room with great views, air-conditioned comfort, and all-you-can-eat Thai, Korean, and Japanese dishes. Salad lovers will be in heaven. Open daily 1100-1400. 320 Silom Rd., tel. (02) 236-0333.

Coca Noodles: This palatial Chinese emporium specializes in Thai-style sukiyaki prepared at your table. It also features inexpensive noodle dishes and pricier seafood specialties. Eat noodles and avoid the more exotic offerings—such as shark's fin soup—and you'll walk away without draining the wallet. Surawong, 8 Soi Tantawan, tel. (02) 236-0107.

The Mango Tree: A place with great food, friendly service, and live Thai classical music, plus both indoor and outdoor seating. This popular spot is housed in an old residence with antique cameras displayed in the foyer. 37 Soi Tantawan, Suriwong Rd., tel. (02) 236-2820.

Tom's Quik Pizza: Vegetarians rejoice. When it's three in the morning and you're desperate for a veggie pizza, Tom's Quik Pizza comes to the rescue in under 15 minutes. However, beware of the transvestite heroin dealers upstairs. Patpong 1 Rd., tel. (02) 234-5460.

Anna's Cafe: New place but extremely popular and always packed out for its Thai dishes with a *farang* twist and vice versa. Named after the infamous Anna Leonowens, be sure to try the Anna's Salad and make reservations well in advance. 114 Soi Saladaeng, tel. (02) 632-0620.

Eat Me!: Not the most refined name for a restaurant, though this elegant L-shaped place serves up excellent Mediterranean dishes to local trendsetters and curious tourists alike. 1/6 Piphat Soi 2, off Convent Rd., tel. (02) 238-0931.

Indian Cafes

The Silom Road district has such a large range of Indian and Muslim cafes that it deserves its own category.

Budget Indian Cafes: Cheap open-air Muslim cafes on Charoen Krung Road serve delicious *murtabaks* and *parathas,* but noxious fumes blowing in from the road could kill you. A filling lunch or dinner costs under 50B per person. Indian street vendors sometimes gather opposite the Narai Hotel near the small Hindu temple.

The Indian restaurant next to the Manohra Hotel, has great food served under a video screen blasting out wild Hindu films, while the cafe in the Madras Lodge is recommended for its authentic atmosphere and South Indian specialties. Perhaps the best choices for excellent Indian and Malay food at rock-bottom prices are the simple, open-air cafes in the alleys near the GPO.

Woodlands Inn: Decent accommodations plus a small cafe with Indian, vegetarian, and nonvegetarian specialties and *halal* offerings. 1158 Charoen Krung Rd., tel. (02) 235-3894.

Bismi Restaurant: The alleys near the G.P.O are filled with numerous small cafes and a few somewhat upscale offerings including this relatively new spot that serves both north and south *halal* Indian dishes in a/c comfort. 1133 Charoen Krung Rd, tel. (02) 639-4469.

Tamil Nadu: Small and unpretentious cafe with outstanding samosas and dal plus a range of south Indian vegetarian dishes. Silom Soi 11, tel. (02) 235-6336.

Deen Muslim Restaurant: Another basic Indian cafe just opposite Silom Village known for its fried fish with chili, hot goat's milk, and rich, creamy lassi. 761 Silom Rd., tel. (02) 635-0441.

Simla Cafe: The less-expensive Simla Cafe, located off Silom Road in a small alley behind the Victory Hotel, is another popular choice for Indian and Pakistani dishes. 382 Soi Tat Mai, tel. (02) 234-6225.

Himali Cha Cha: The long-running Himali Cha Cha, up a small alley off New Road near the GPO, is known for its tasty curries, *kormas,* fruit-flavored *lassis,* tandoori-baked breads, and North Indian specialties served in an informal setting. Cha Cha, owner and head chef at Himali, was once Nehru's private chef. 1229 Charoen Krung Rd., tel. (02) 235-1569.

Indian Hut: Cozy cafe with north Indian dishes served in a/c comfort just opposite the Monohra Hotel. 311/2 Suriwong Rd., tel. (02) 237-8812.

Moderate

Most of the following restaurants are near Patpong Road or clustered around Charoen Krung Road near the river.

Bobby Arms: Almost a dozen excellent restaurants are located on Patpong Road, such as this English pub where expatriates gather on Sunday evenings for drinks and Dixieland music. Patpong 2 Road.

Trattoria d'Roberto: Known for its Italian specialties such as veal dishes and chocolate desserts. Patpong 2 Rd.

The Australian Club: A comfortable air-conditioned lounge with imported beers from Down Under, plus helpful literature on local nightlife spots. Patpong 1 Rd.

El Gordo's Cantina: Mexican tavern with south-of-the-border dishes plus live music nightly until midnight. Silom Soi 8, tel. (02) 237-1415.

Cairns Stonegrill Restaurant: An upmarket Aussie barbie where patrons grill their own selections on a heated slab of stone. 167 Surawong Rd., tel. (02) 634-3031.

Bua Garden: Rowdy and fun spot popular with large groups in celebration and the odd *farang* who wanders into this popular party enclave just off Silom Road near Patpong. 1 Soi Convent, tel. (02) 237-6640.

Via Convent: Mediterranean outlet run by Philippe Sdrigotti known for its pumpkin soup with blue cheese, pork scaloppine with balsamic vinegar, and grilled swordfish with capers. 1 Convent Rd., tel. (02) 266-7162.

Sun Far Myanmar Food Centre: One of Bangkok's few Burmese restaurants is predictably located near the Myanmar Embassy and serves regional dishes including the famous and highly recommended Burmese tea leaf salad. Closed daily at 2000. 107/1 Pan Rd., tel. (02) 266-8787.

Once Upon A Time: A wonderful romantic restaurant with outdoor dining under little twinkling lights. Nicely located in a quiet back alley, but within walking distance of most hotels. Decho Rd., Soi 1.

All Gaengs: Unlike most Thai restaurants, All Gaengs has been stylishly decorated with art deco touches and a shiny baby grand piano. Along with the jazz, enjoy shrimp curry, *yam* dishes, and *nuea daed dio,* a beef dish served with a spicy dipping sauce. 173/8-9 Surawong Rd., tel. (02) 233-3301.

Ban Chiang: Wonderful atmosphere in this old house (owned by a Thai movie star) converted into a restaurant; it's decorated with turn-of-the-century memorabilia such as vintage photos, grandfather clocks, and Thai antiques. Try the roast duck curry, minced chicken in coconut milk, or freshwater crab baked au natural. Quite popular with Thai gourmands and local expatriates. 14 Sriviang Rd., tel. (02) 236-7045.

Isn't Classic: An oddly named restaurant that serves fiery "Isn't" food from the Issan area of Thailand. Try something on the English-language menu or Issan specialities such as spicy grilled chicken *(kai yang),* chopped meat salad *(laap, larb),* fiery papaya salad *(som tam),* or more exotic concoctions made from obscure animal parts—classic Issan from Isn't. 154/9 Silom Rd., tel. (02) 235-1087.

Thai Room: One of the stranger joints in town, this American-style, greasy spoon, highly honored time capsule has remained unchanged since it first opened during the Vietnam War. Glance around the room and you might see some wizened old veteran quietly reminiscing about whatever happened here in 1968, Peace Corp volunteers, or curious tourists perusing the English-language menu which lists over 400 items. Thai, Western, Mexican, Italian, and Thai/Mex/Italian dishes. Open until midnight or later. 30/37 Patpong 2 Rd., tel. (02) 233-7920.

Expensive

Sala Rim Nam: Alfresco dining on the banks of the Chao Praya is a memorable if expensive experience. This particular choice may be touristy but it's a beautiful restaurant with excellent Thai salads and traditional dance; use the free boat service from the Oriental Hotel. The set menu includes a classical Thai dance.

Salathip: The Shangri-La Hotel does an excellent Sunday brunch on the veranda overlooking the river.

River City Barbecue: On the rooftop of the River City Shopping Center, this self-service Mongolian barbecue cafe has excellent views from the tables at the edge of the roof. Adjacent to the Sheraton Royal Orchid Hotel.

Normandie Grill: A world-famous French restaurant located in pseudo-dining cars on the roof of the Oriental Hotel. One of the few restaurants in Bangkok that still strictly enforces the jacket and tie rule.

Bussaracum: Restaurants found in luxury hotels generally cater to the foreign palate and temper the degree of garlic and chilies used in their dishes. For something more authentic, try this elegant dining establishment featuring pungent dishes whose recipes stem from the royal palace. *Saengwa* (grilled prawns), *phat benjarong* (vegetables with meats), and *gang kari gai hang* (chicken curry) are recommended. Chef Boonchho has been selected one of the top 10 chefs in the world. 35 Soi Phipat 2, tel. (02) 235-5160. Bussaracum 2, a newer and more modern extension, is wedged inside the Trinity Complex. 425 Soi Phipat 2, tel. (02) 235-8915; very expensive.

Rueng Pueng: Traditional Thai dishes from all regions of the country plus outstanding salads are served in a converted Thai house—a common sight in Bangkok these days. 37 Soi 2, Saladeng Rd.

La Rotonde Grill: Wonderful views of Bangkok can be enjoyed from this revolving restaurant on top of Narai Hotel

Tiara Restaurant: Another restaurant with spectacular views on the 22nd floor of the Dusit Thani Hotel.

SIAM SQUARE

Many of the best restaurants in this neighborhood are located in luxury hotels, while inexpensive cafes and foodstalls are found in the air-conditioned shopping complexes.

Inexpensive

Shopping centers are your best bet for quick, inexpensive Thai and Western dishes. Many operate on the coupon system and are packed with teenagers high on the urban eating experience. For more information on the coupon system see **Other Dining Venues** in the On The Road chapter.

MBK Shopping Center: Mahboonkrong (MBK) is an enormous complex with a food center on the ground floor and a wonderland of stalls on the seventh floor that stretches for half a block. Menu boards are listed in Thai but you can practice the point-and-choose method favored by tourists from Kathmandu to Kuta. Other floors have midpriced restaurants serving steak, pizza, pasta, fried chicken, Filipino dishes, and all variations of Chinese cuisine. Rama 1 Rd.

Beer Garden: Afterwards, head up to the beer garden on the seventh floor for a brew and great views over the holocaust below. Open daily 0930-2200. Rama 1 Rd., tel. (02) 217-9491.

tamarind

Siam Center: If you can't find anything to eat in MBK, don't despair. The Siam Center, just opposite Siam Square, has over a dozen cafes with Thai, Chinese, Japanese, and European dishes that average just 40-60B per dish. Many attempt to cash in on the nostalgic craze for pseudo-1950s American grub, but you'll do better by sticking to Thai or Chinese dishes. Ploenchit Rd.

Oldies Goldies: However, for an insight as to why America's leading export is modern culture—Elvis, Disney, Madonna—wander into Oldies Goldies on the fourth floor, where Thai teenagers embrace nostalgia, bobby socks, and other icons from *American Graffiti*. Rama 1 Rd.

See Fah Restaurant: In operation since 1936, this cozy cafe/ice-cream parlor/patisserie is famed for its seafood specialties pictured on laminated English-language menus. See Fah is tucked away behind the fire house near the Novotel Hotel, tel. (02) 251-5517.

Inter Restaurant: Basic cafe with hearty Issan dishes popular with Chula students and office workers on break. Siam Square Soi 9, tel. (02) 255-4689.

New Light Coffee House: Another longtime favorite known for its Western and Asian dishes served in an unpretentious air-conditioned environment. 426/1-4 Siam Square, next to the Hard Rock Cafe, tel. (02) 251-9591.

World Trade Centre: The two food emporiums on the seventh floor of this massive shopping complex are comfortable places to dine and watch the crowds without busting your budget. Rama 1 at Rajadamri Rds.

Vegeta: A large upmarket cafe with a wide selection of meat-free interpretations of Thai national dishes, plus Chinese cuisine using mock duck, bean curd, and gelatin dishes, plus vegetarian fish—almost indistinguishable from the real thing. Check out their all-you-can-eat weekend buffet lunch. World Trade Centre, tel. (02) 255-9569.

Sarah Jane's: A strange name for a small cafe that specializes in Issan dishes, not the home-style cooking you might expect from Ms. Sarah. 130 Wireless Rd., Sindhorn Tower, tel. (02) 650-9992.

Moderate

Coca Noodles: A colossal, noisy place packed with Chinese families and groups of hungry teenagers chowing down on a plethora of inexpensive noodle dishes, along with chicken, fish, and seafood specialties. Self-cook Mongolian barbecues and sukiyakis are the most popular dishes. 416/3-8 Siam Square, tel. (02) 251-6337.

Baan Khun Phor: An opportunity to dine among the owner's eccentric collection of Victorian and Thai artifacts, served by waitresses attired in traditional garb. Somewhat pricey but the food is decent, especially the spicy crab soup. 458/7-9 Siam Square Soi 8, tel. (02) 250-1733.

La Fontana: A sharp neo-Mediterranean cafe serving authentic pastas and Tuscan dishes, plus cakes, ice cream, and coffees. A Filipino singer croons your favorites after 1800. Open daily 1000-2330. World Trade Center, 1st Floor, tel. (02) 255-9534.

Koreana: As the name suggests, a Korean restaurant with a variety of popular set menus plus Japanese dishes illustrated by photos on the menu. 446-450 Rama 1 Rd., Siam Square, tel. (02) 252-9398.

Siam Intercontinental: Some of Bangkok's least expensive splurges are the all-you-can-eat luncheon buffets served at the Siam Intercontinental and at other nearby hotels. diners must be well attired; no shorts or sandals. Rama 1 Rd.

Expensive

Thanying Princess: The original restaurant—located in a converted private house and owned by a Thai movie star—has been joined by a second branch in the World Trade Center, an upgraded version with a more elegant setting. Thanying is famed for Royal Thai cuisine, served with refined presentation and offering unusual selections such as fragrant chilled rice and marinated whole sea bass. World Trade Center, 6th floor, tel. (02) 255-9838.

Gianni's: An upscale Italian restaurant owned and operated by the president of the local Italian Chef's Organization, with reasonably priced set lunches and more expensive dinners in a fine location just off Ploenchit Road. Considered one of the best in town. 51/5 Soi Tonson, tel. (02) 252-1619.

Amarin Plaza: Upscale Japanese and Thai restaurants are located on the lower floor. Note the wild Greco-Roman-Thai architecture of the adjacent McDonald's for some insight into the Thai penchant for extravagant indulgence. Ploenchit Rd.

Soi Lang Suan

This road which runs from Lumpini Park to Central Department Store on Ploenchit Road has over a dozen very popular cafes and restaurants filled with both expats and locals plus a few curious tourists.

Pan Pan: One of Bangkok's favorite Italian trattorias provides a comfortable environment to try their wood-fired pizzas, linguine with salmon and vodka, the superbly decadent Chicken Godfather, and the thickest gelato in all of Thailand. The newer branch at Sukumvit Soi 33 offers a buffet-style antipasti spread and a large selection of rich desserts. Some local residents abhor the food here, but tourists seem to come away satisfied with the experience. 45 Soi Lang Suan, tel. (02) 252-7104.

Airplane: A cheery Italian restaurant done with an airplane theme and set with simple tables and chairs. 65/9 Lang Suan Soi 3, tel. (02) 255-9940.

Nguan Lee Lang Suan: The south end of Soi Lang Suan at Lumpini Park features simple open-air dining patronized by expats, Thai families, and chefs from some of the best hotels in Bangkok. All arrive to try the huge selection of fresh seafood, plates of fresh vegetables, or chicken steamed in Chinese herbs (kai tun yaa jiin). 101/25-26 Soi Lang Suan (at Soi Sarasin), tel. (02) 250-0936.

Dux Bar & Grill: You like ducks? This is your place. Duck motifs adorn everything from drinking glasses to menu selection, in an old house restored to great condition. 72/2 Soi Lang Suan, tel. (02) 252-5646.

Whole Earth Restaurant: Specializing in creative vegetarian dishes, the menu also features Thai and Indian selections that substitute tofu for meat and include garnishes such as fried mushrooms, cashew nuts, and pickled vegetables. Dine upstairs on traditional floor cushions rather than the conventional Western seating on the first floor. 93/3 Soi Lang Suan, tel. (02) 252-5574.

Le Moulin De Sommai: French restaurant with a homey brasserie atmosphere and decent continental food at reasonable prices. A fine place for an afternoon meal in the sunny front section. 93/3 Soi Lang Suan, tel. (02) 652-2513.

Soi Ruam Rudi (Rudee)

Another road just a few blocks from Soi Lang Suan with plenty of cafes and a selection of nightclubs.

Bali Restaurant: Situated in a relaxed old house with garden seating and known for its mildly spiced Indonesian dishes and variations on local Thai cuisine. 15/3 Soi Ruam Rudi, tel. (02) 250-0711.

Vito's Restaurant: Ruam Rudi Village, just a few steps down from Ploenchit Road, features several upscale restaurants popular with embassy employees and local business people. Chef Gianni Favro serves up all forms of antipasti plus northern Italian dishes such as scallopini and frutta di mare. 20/2-3 Soi Ruam Rudi, tel. (02) 251-9455. Moderate.

Wit's Oyster Bar: The English food served here—baked oysters, Yorkshire puddings, seafood dishes—is favored by the fashionable set in Bangkok. 20/10 Soi Ruam Rudi, tel. (02) 251-9455.

Ruam Rudi Kitchen: One of the few Thai restaurants on the street and a comfortable spot which serves unusual Thai dishes such as nam prik kai poo (crab eggs in chili sauce). 48/10 Soi Ruam Rudi, tel. (02) 256-6253.

SUKUMVIT ROAD

Sukumvit Road and adjacent side roads offer the best selection of restaurants in Bangkok. Inexpensive streetstalls and midpriced restaurants are most plentiful along Sukumvit between the freeway and Soi Asoke. High-end restaurants are concentrated on the backstreets which run parallel to and north of Sukumvit. Three excellent neighborhoods to explore include Soi 23, the Green Route, and Soi 55. Specific restaurants in these popular enclaves are described below.

Inner Sukumvit Restaurants

Most visitors to this section of Bangkok stay at one of the numerous hotels (and flophouses) between the Expressway at Soi 1 and Soi 21 (Soi Asoke) that marks the outer limits of inner Sukumvit. Sois off Sukumvit are rather oddly numbered, but sois 1 to 21 are on the north side of the street, while sois 2 to 14 are on the south. And they don't exactly match up as you might expect: Soi 19 on the north side of Sukumvit is just opposite Soi 14 on the south side. Go figure.

In any event, if you are staying at an inner Sukumvit hotel, these will be your closest restaurants and all are within a reasonable walking distance—a big consideration in the hell that is Sukumvit.

Night Foodstalls: Some of the best food in Bangkok is found in the foodstalls along Sukumvit where most dishes are precooked and displayed in covered pots. Try *som tam,* a spicy salad made from shredded raw papaya and palm sugar; fried chicken with sticky rice; or *pad thai,* sautéed bean sprouts with chicken and peanuts. Delicious!

Foodstalls are near the Grace Hotel, near the infamously seedy Thermae Coffee Shop, at both ends of Soi Cowboy, at the Washington Square pub center, and on Sukumvit at Soi 38. Wonderful food and a great way to mix with the locals.

BH Vietnamese Restaurant: Wide selection of local dishes at very affordable prices. 70/1 Sukumvit Soi 1, tel. (02) 251-8933.

Atlanta Hotel: This historic old hotel has a fine little cafe with variations of Thai cuisine plus an expansive vegetarian menu that claims to offer the widest selection in Thailand. Most dishes drop the meat and substitute either tofu or "quorm," a vegetable protein mix which can be cooked in a bewildering variety of ways. Among the hits are *phaneng jay* (thick coconut curry with a pork substitute), *khaw muu yaang* (spicy pineapple curry), and *kaeng massaman* (mild Indian curry with quorm). The Atlanta Hotel, Sukumvit Soi 2, tel. (02) 252-6069.

Riley's Pub Cafe: Steaks, sandwiches, roasts, and oysters in this newer cafe just below Clouds Disco provides a welcome alternative to the Arabic cafes that dominate this neighborhood near the Grace Hotel. Sukumvit Soi 3, tel. (02) 626-4332.

Nasir Al-Masri: Perhaps the best Middle Eastern restaurant in a neighborhood chock-a-block with similar offerings. Also serves a range of Indian and Thai dishes under the direction of the Egyptian owner. Sukumvit Soi 3, tel. (02) 253-5582.

Akbar's: A top-quality Indian restaurant over 20 years in the same spot offering a wide choice of dishes from both north and south India. The Navrattan curry, chicken *korma,* mutton *marsala,* and *dahls* are recommended. Sukumvit Soi 3, tel. (02) 253-3479.

Restaurant Heidelberg: Chef Franco Vanoli provides three kinds of fondue—Swiss, French, and Chinese—in a pub-like setting near all the craziness of the Nana Entertainment Plaza. Open daily until midnight. Sukumvit Soi 4, tel. (02) 252-3584.

Dhaba Indian Cafe: Indian dishes plus live tabla music at dinnertime, then a very unique Hindi karaoke scene in the later hours. Hindi karaoke? Sukumvit Soi 10, tel. (02) 251-5404.

Cheap Charlie's: Where is the most popular expat gathering spot in Thailand? Believe it or not, this open-air and completely funky cafe may be the place. The place is cheap, packed, popular, and the flavor of the month since it lacks chairs, tables, and anything else that might be misconstrued as shop fixtures. Once again, go figure. Sukumvit Soi 11, tel. (02) 253-4648.

Ambassador Food Center: A few simple cafes hang on in this largely deserted corridor which once led to the entrance to this once-great hotel, now in steep decline. However, the remaining cafes and foodstalls are still worth checking out for their low prices and reasonably decent grub. The adjacent streetside cafe at Soi 11 is a good place to escape the midday heat and enjoy a very cheap luncheon buffet. Sukumvit Soi 11.

Moghul Room: Another popular Indian restaurant with all the standard items. Sukumvit Soi 11.

Bankeo Ruenkwan: This old and partially renovated house serves up top-quality seafood in a/c comfort. Sukumvit Soi 12, tel. (02) 251-8229.

Lum Gai Yia: Another inexpensive and simple cafe where the tables are just old oil drums topped by welded steel tables and just two dining options: a large wok full of soup of a self-serve barbecue where you do your own cooking on a small personal hotplate. Sukumvit Soi 12, tel. (02) 252-4279.

Cabbages and Condoms: Established over a decade ago by Mechai Viravaidhya, "Condom King" and former director of the national birth control center (next door), the restaurant features excellent food in air-conditioned comfort plus some truly strange items at the front desk—

condom key chains and T-shirts you won't find back home. The place benefits the adjacent Population Development Association (PDA). Highly recommended. Sukumvit Soi 12, tel. (02) 252-7349.

Yong Lee Restaurant: A very funky cafe popular with budget travelers and local *farangs* who rave about the Thai and Chinese specialties. Sukumvit Soi 15.

Robinson's Department Store: Cheap eats in this pricey emporium include McDonald's on the main floor, and a downstairs Food Court with several self-service cafes that serve Thai and Japanese dishes. Sukumvit Soi 19.

Middle Sukumvit Road Restaurants

The middle of Sukumvit could possibly be defined as anything between Bangkok and Pattaya (the road runs all the way to Cambodia), but we'll call this section the area from Soi 21 (Soi Asoke on the north side and Ratchadapisek on the south) to just past Washington Square. These restaurants are too far to walk from hotels near Nana Entertainment Plaza, but taxis are plentiful and cheap and fairly quick after the evening traffic dies down.

Sally's Kitchenette: A Filipino place with regional dishes often served in small portions so you can experiment on a budget. The cheese ice cream is something unique. Sukumvit Soi 16, tel. (02) 261-3205.

The Cafe: This hotel coffee shop is superior to most others in town, and worth visiting for the lunch buffet when reservations are recommended. Dinners are served until 0200. Rembrandt Hotel, Sukumvit Soi 18, tel. (02) 261-7100.

Thong Lee Restaurant: A very popular and simple shophouse with good food at low prices. Try the *muu phad kapi* (spicy pork in shrimp paste), and the *yam hed sot* (fiery mushroom salad). Sukumvit Soi 20.

Djit Pochana: One of the most successful restaurant chains in Thailand with three outlets in Bangkok that serve authentic Thai dishes without compromise to Western palates, including an excellent-value luncheon buffet. Sukumvit Soi 20, tel. (02) 258-1605.

Singha Bier Haus: An imitation German chalet owned and operated by the Singha Beer Company where German and international dishes are served with musical entertainment ranging from polkas to Barbra Streisand imitators. Sukumvit Soi 21, tel. (02) 258-3951.

Alfredo: Pizzas, pastas, and other Italian dishes served in an old restored house under the watchful eye of a former champion pizza tosser. Sukumvit Soi 21, Asoke Tower, tel. (02) 258-3909.

Bourbon Street: Several very popular pubs and cafes are located in an old business complex know as Washington Square. This American-style bar and grill serves hearty breakfasts, spicy Cajun food, and local dishes plus a weekly Mexican buffet. Sukumvit Soi 22, tel. (02) 259-0328.

Larry's Dive Shop: Perhaps the only dive shop in the world that also provides a bar and grill with Western and Asian dishes. Another Washington Square hangout. 8/3 Sukumvit Soi 22, tel. (02) 663-4563.

Khing Klao: A cozy little cafe just past Washington Square with Northern Thai specialties including various dishes made from Chiang Mai sausages and great *khao saoi* served amid a riot of clocks of every shape and size. Sukumvit Soi 22, tel. (02) 259-5623.

Lemongrass Restaurant: Embellished with antiques in both the interior dining room and exterior courtyard, Lemongrass offers atmosphere and regional dishes from all parts of Thailand such as the hot fish curry, barbecued chicken, *larb pla duk yang* (smoked catfish in northeastern style), and *nam takrai,* a cool sweetish drink brewed from lemongrass. Sukumvit Soi 24, tel. (02) 258-8637.

Tangerine's: Chinese emporium in the Capitol Club complex along with Paulaner Brauhaus serves Cantonese and Mandarin dishes along with decent ale and tangerine specialties. Even the air smells suspiciously like a lemon. Sukumvit Soi 24, tel. (02) 661-1210.

Seafood Market Restaurant: This expensive seafood restaurant (once located back on Soi Asoke) is worth a look even if the prices cause heart failure. Don't miss the enormous Phuket lobsters and giant prawns in a place that claims, "If it Swims, We Have It." Sukumvit Soi 24, tel. (02) 261-2071.

Whole Earth Restaurant: Somewhat upscale vegetarian dining venue serving fresh fruit smoothies, lassis, seafood dishes, and a range of brewed coffees along with new age music and floor cushions on the upper deck just off an alley near the Four Wing Hotel. Sukumvit Soi 26, tel. (02) 258-4900.

Joe's Place: One of the few Filipino cafes in town with all the standards including crispy *pata*, *adobo*, and *sinigang*. Packed on Sundays when Filipino families arrive after Church services. Sukumvit Soi 31, tel. (02) 259-8164.

Café Deco: Thai, Italian, and Mexican dishes but chiefly know for its "Thaitalian" creations that throw together two of the most famous cooking styles in the world. Sukumvit Soi 39, tel. (02) 258-8336.

Soi 23 Restaurants

Almost a dozen popular restaurants are scattered along Soi 23, a few blocks off Sukumvit Road.

Ruen Pak: An excellent-value cafe located in a renovated wooden house.

Thong U Rai: Traditional Thai dishes served in a pub atmosphere with live music.

Cue: A relatively expensive Swiss inn that serves French and European cuisine.

Le Dalat: A private, intimate house and very classy Vietnamese restaurant known for its *naem neuang*, a tasty version of Vietnamese eggrolls.

Wanakarm: For over two decades, this place has served Thais and *farangs* traditional dishes in air-conditioned dining rooms and in the romantic garden.

Pueng Kaew: Experimental Thai-Western dishes listed on both the Thai and English-language menus.

September: European cuisine in an Art Deco 1930s atmosphere.

Bistango: Western-style steakhouse with meat, chicken, and seafood specialties.

Black Scene: Trendy place with live jazz nightly at 2100.

Baan Kanitha: One of the most famous restaurants in Bangkok, known for its memorable decor, fine service, and classic Thai dishes created from both traditional and rare ingredients.

Club Tacoco: Mexican and Thai restaurant combo on the top floor of Prasarnmit Plaza with an outdoor terrace with fine views and live combo music in the evenings. Sukumvit Soi 23, tel. (02) 664-1217.

Thong U-Rai Chicken: Fairly grungy exterior but popular with locals for its unusual dishes

such as deep-fried salted beef, Chiang Mai sausage, and Vietnamese oddities. Sukumvit Soi 23, tel. (02) 258-2777.

Soi 49 Restaurants (The Green Route)

Several of Bangkok's finest restaurants are located on the so-called "Green Route," a street that runs between Sois 39 and 63, midway between Sukumvit and New Petchburi Roads. All are tucked away off Sukumvit on or near Soi 49.

Gourmet Gallery: An elegant setting with creative cuisine and classical music.

The Library: An upscale restaurant owned by a Thai singer who invites in local celebrities and jazz-fusion musicians.

Laicram: Well-known Thai restaurant with royal dishes.

Piman: Features nightly performances of Thai classical dance.

Soi 55 Restaurants (Soi Thonglor)

Another concentration of fine restaurants is on Soi 55 (Soi Thonglor) between Sukumvit and the Green Route.

Art House: First-class Chinese restaurant set in a country house surrounded by formal gardens and a pleasant pond.

Barley House: A funky bohemian cafe, features nightly jazz and country bands.

L'Hexagone: Bangkok's finest French restaurant might be this place with its pastel interiors and wildly decorated bathrooms.

Sanuk Nuek: Much less formal is this simple cafe with live folk music.

Witch's Tavern: Victorian decor and English pub grub.

Singapore Chicken Rice: The name says it all as this cozy cafe serves up what is considered the best version of the classic Singaporean dish in the city. Also has the shortest menu in town with just two dishes: Hainanese chicken rice (of course) and a smaller dipper sampler. Sukumvit Soi 55, tel. (02) 392-4247.

Duke's: American steakhouse with an unusual decor centered around an interior waterfall and casino theme with imported steaks and venison dishes. Sukumvit Soi 55, tel. (02) 392-5096.

Outer Sukumvit Restaurants

Well, they aren't really as remote as they sound and these two offerings are among the most unique dining venues in Bangkok, but figure on a lengthy taxi ride.

Tum Nak Thai: For many years, Tum Nak held the world's record as the largest restaurant with 10 acres of land, a capacity of 3,000 seats, over 100 professional chefs, and 1,000 servers decked out in national costumes. Some waiters use roller skates to speed up service! A classical dance show is given nightly at 2000. 131 Ratchadapisek Rd., tel. (02) 277-8833.

Mang Gorn Luang: Several years ago, Tum Nak Thai recently lost its crown as the world's largest restaurant to the "Royal Dragon Seafood Restaurant" located at the base of the Bangna Trad Expressway in the southwest section of town. Leaving nothing to chance, this monstrous place boasts 5,000 seats, 1,200 roller-skating waiters, a 400-item menu, moored "happy boats" perfect for couples, soundproof karaoke pavilions for private parties, and a seven-story pagoda from which servers rocket down with heaping platters of steaming seafood. Has Hunter S. Thompson seen this place? Bangna Trad Expressway, tel. (02) 398-0037.

ENTERTAINMENT

Mention entertainment in Bangkok and many visitors will immediately think of the brothels and massage parlors that have made Thai nightlife a world-famous phenomenon, but the city also offers a limited range of classical entertainment, from traditional dance to elaborate dramas. Culture vultures should take advantage of the opportunities in Bangkok, since Thai performing arts are almost exclusively found in the capital and, to a lesser degree, in Chiang Mai.

The three basic venues for cultural entertainment include free Thai dance at various locations, high-end spectacles at the National Theater and the Thailand Cultural Centre, and the familiar dinner-dance shows sponsored nightly by a dozen restaurants in Bangkok.

CULTURAL PERFORMANCES

Free Thai Dance
While professional performances of Thai dance-drama are both infrequent and pricey, travelers can easily enjoy the following free shows.

Lak Muang Shrine: Amateurish but authentic *likay* is sponsored around the clock by various donors in the pavilion to the rear of the City Pillar shrine, near the Grand Palace. Have a quick look, but don't expect a masterful performance from the young girls and tired grandmothers who slowly go through the paces.

Erawan Hotel Shrine: The famous shrine in the courtyard of the Grand Hyatt Erawan Hotel is among the more intriguing scenes in Bangkok. No matter what the hour, a steady stream of devotees arrives to offer flowers and wooden elephants, burn an unbelievable amount of incense, and hire the somewhat unenthusiastic dancers as gratitude for granted wishes.

Visitors are welcome to photograph the dancers and improve their karma by making offerings to four-faced Brahma, the Hindu deity associated with the shrine. Prices for incense and the small wooden elephants are posted at the entrance. Another sign gives prices to hire the dancers: four girls for 15 minutes costs 360B. Erawan Shrine, an amazing place, is most active in the early evening hours and just before the weekly lottery. Grand Hyatt Erawan Hotel, Ploenchit at Rajadamri roads.

Classical Dance and Drama
Considering the size and economic dominance of Bangkok, you would expect to find an overwhelming selection of dance, drama, music, art, and other cultural activities. Surprisingly, cultural events are limited to infrequent performances at the National Theater, smaller cultural centers, diplomatic centers, and local universities. A fairly complete listing of upcoming events is found in the *Bangkok Post* and in the Cultural Activities Programme published bimonthly by the Thailand Cultural Centre, available from the TAT office.

National Theater: Full-length *khon* performances are sponsored by the Fine Arts Department several times yearly in the National Theater. Though a somewhat expensive experience, these majestic pageants should not be missed if you are fortunate enough to be in Bangkok on the lucky weekend.

The National Theater also sponsors less elaborate cultural events on Saturday and Sunday at 1000 and 1400. Performances range from Thai variety shows to presentations of the *manora*. Special presentations are given on the last Friday of each month at 1730. Shows cost 40-100B and include a Thai-language commentary.

Perhaps the best option is the free student shows given Sunday afternoon on the front lawn. Schedules are sometimes listed in the *Bangkok Post,* but it's more dependable to simply wander by the National Theater on a Sunday morning and see if a crowd is gathering. Stageside spots can be reserved by leaving a blanket on the lawn. Local food vendors sell inexpensive snacks from the adjacent stalls.

Thailand Cultural Centre: Many of Bangkok's finest cultural performances take place in the newish cultural center on Ratchadphisek Rd., a few blocks north of New Petchburi Road en route to the airport. Opened by the king in 1987, the cultural center features a 200-seat main auditorium graced with outstanding Ramayana murals, a smaller 500-seat performance hall, and a library where fine-art exhibitions are held. Recent shows have included Thai classical music, folk puppet theater, demonstrations of *khon* drama, chamber orchestras, German vocal music, piano recitals, and opportunities to meet leading Thai artists. Pick up a complete schedule at the tourist office, or call (02) 245-7711 or (02) 247-0013 for more information.

Chalerm Krung Royal Theater: The performing arts were given a major boost in 1994 with the opening of this high-tech *khon* center inside the historic Chalerm Krung theater in Pahurat, four blocks from the Royal Palace. Opened in 1993 as Thailand's largest and most sophisticated movie theater, Sala Chalerm Krung was also the first cinema to feature air-conditioning and was the scene of many important premiers such as *Ben Hur* and *Tea House of the August Moon.* After it fell on hard times and was closed for over a decade, financial support from private industry and a donation from King Rama VIII helped renovate and reopen the grand structure.

Today, the troupe of 170 dancers are complemented by a sophisticated light show, an 80,000-watt audio system, and other technological wonders that never distract from the sumptuous costumes and elaborate choreography. *Khon* and other Thai performances are held at 2000 several times weekly. 66 Charoen Krung Rd., tel. (02) 222-0437, 400-1,000B.

Dinner Dance Shows

First-time visitors who wish an overview of Thai dance can attend performances in almost a dozen air-conditioned Thai restaurants listed in

BANGKOK RESTAURANTS WITH THAI CLASSICAL DANCE

RESTAURANT	ADDRESS	AREA	PHONE
Baan Thai	Sukumvit Soi 32	Sukumvit	258-5403
Maneeya's Lotus Room	Ploenchit Rd.	Siam Square	252-6312
Chao Phraya	451 Arun Amrin Rd.	Thonburi	424-2389
Oriental Hotel	48 Oriental Ave.	Silom	236-0400
Piman	Sukumvit Soi 49	Sukumvit	258-7866
Ruen Thep	Silom Village	Silom	233-9447
Indra Regent Hotel	Rajaprarop Rd.	Siam Square	251-1111
Sawasdee	66 Soi Phipat	Silom	237-6310
Siam Intercontinental	967 Rama 1 Rd.	Siam Square	253-0355
Suwanahong	Sri Ayuthaya Rd.	Siam Square	245-4448
Tun Nak Thai	131 Rajadapisek	Sukumvit	277-3828

the accompanying chart. While these highly abbreviated performances are somewhat artificial and resented by visitors who dislike the "instant culture" mentality, the performances are usually of a high standard, plus the glittering costumes and elegant dance styles are always impressive.

Dinner dance shows follow a standard arrangement. A northern Thai *khon toke*-style dinner is followed by brief demonstrations of *khon, lakhon,* and *likay* folk dancing, Thai martial arts, puppetry, and sword fighting. Dinner is usually served around 1900, and the show begins 60-90 minutes later. Photographers should arrive early and request a seat near the stage.

Prices for the dinner with show range 300-800B; some restaurants offer the show without a meal for 300-400B. Transportation from the hotel to the restaurant is often included with the ticket. Performance times and prices can be double-checked by calling the restaurant or inquiring with the TAT.

Dinner dance shows can be seen at several luxury hotels and at private restaurants in renovated homes. Purchase tickets from most travel agents or get the lowest prices from the bucket shops in Banglampoo and near the Malaysia Hotel.

Baan Thai: Like most Thai restaurants with dance performances, Baan Thai re-creates a traditional Thai house with polished teakwood floors, elegant furnishings, and tropical gardens. Nightly shows from 1900. 7 Sukumvit Soi 32, tel. (02) 258-5403.

Piman: One of Bangkok's more elegant and expensive shows takes place inside this beautiful reproduction of a Sukothai-era house. 46 Sukumvit Soi 49, tel. (02) 258-7866.

Chao Phraya Restaurant: Travelers staying in the guesthouses of Banglampoo often attend the cultural show across the Pinklau Bridge in Thonburi. Packages sold by travel agents include transportation, dinner, show, and possibly a cocktail in the adjacent Paradise Music Hall.

Hotel Shows: Dance performances are also given at the **Sala Rim Nam Restaurant** across the river from the Oriental Hotel (free boat service), and at the **Sala Thai Restaurant** on the rooftop of the Indra Regent.

NIGHTLIFE

Bangkok's nightlife is perhaps the most notorious in the world. Bars, brothels, live sex shows, massage parlors, gay nightclubs, roving transvestites, sex cabarets, all-night coffee shops thick with call girls, child prostitutes, and barbershops that provide more than just haircuts—the range of sexual services is simply amazing. Bangkok alone has an estimated 100,000 prostitutes, and it's said that almost one-fifth of all visitors to Thailand come for sex. Despite the devastating effect of AIDS, local opposition, and the conservative moral attitudes of the Thai people, Thailand's roaring sex industry seems destined to remain a major attraction.

It all begins at the Bangkok Airport, where male visitors are sometimes propositioned by transvestites who boldly drag their unsuspecting prey into terminal bathrooms. Airport taxi drivers often negotiate the fare, then offer up girls in all ages and prices. Many Bangkok hotels—from low-end to prestigious—also serve as "knock-knock" emporiums, where spare girls are sold by the employees or sent uninvited up to rooms at night.

The scene continues throughout the city. Over on Patpong, street touts thrust out Polaroids of young women and well-worn scraps of cardboard that list their sexual talents. Teams of transvestites cruise the tourist enclaves. Local publications such as *This Week in Bangkok* advertise escort services, marriage agencies, gay nightclubs, barbershops, and go-go bars wedged between brief descriptions of temples and upcoming Rotary Club functions.

First-time visitors often assume that prostitution in Thailand is a hangover from the Vietnam War era when American servicemen took their R&R in Bangkok and Pattaya. Actually, Thai society has long been tolerant of prostitution; brothels were commonplace in Chinatown and in the Pratunam *klongs* before the arrival of mass tourism. Today, even the smallest of Thai towns have long-established houses frequented exclusively by local men; *farangs* are often refused admittance in the belief that AIDS is a foreign disease.

Visitors are also surprised to learn that prostitution is illegal in Thailand. For that matter, even topless dancing is prohibited, not to mention the other services available in the massage parlors and darkened nightclubs. Proposals have been made to legalize prostitution to control AIDS, but most Thais prefer to keep the business as private as possible. Police periodically raid brothels and go-go bars, but this formality is done more to ensure a steady stream of payoffs than to stop the flesh trade.

The Bangkok Scene

Nightclubs and girlie bars that cater to foreigners are concentrated in several neighborhoods. The most notorious area is Patpong Road between Silom and Surawong Roads. To briefly experience the mayhem you could spend a few hours wandering through the clubs, but the insistent hawkers and surprisingly aggressive nature of the shopkeepers is a complete turn off.

The second-largest number of clubs is located on Soi Cowboy, a short street near the intersection of Sukumvit Road and Soi 21.

But the best area for this type of entertainment is the roaring Nana Entertainment Plaza (NEP), also called Nana Plaza, just off Sukumvit Road on Soi 4. Serious party animals generally find a hotel in this neighborhood and spend the rest of their vacation haunting the bars and nightclubs on both sides of Sukumvit, spending their early evenings in NEP and later hours at the disco inside the nearby Nana Hotel or down the street at the Thermae.

Washington Square on Sukumvit near Soi 22 is another nightlife center but very quiet and more geared to simple meals and cocktails than the girlie bar scene.

Tidbits and gossip about the bar scene in Bangkok can be culled from Bernard Trink's column in the Friday *Bangkok Post*. Trink does a good job describing what's happening and offers dependable tips. His column is posted on the *Bangkok Post* website.

Patpong

Bangkok's most notorious red-light district is on Patpong 1 and 2 between Silom and Surawong Roads. Once owned by the Patpong family and made popular by American soldiers on leave from Vietnam, this infamous collection of go-go bars, cocktail lounges, live shows, street vendors, pushy touts, and preteen hustlers forms a scene straight from Dante's *Inferno*.

During the day Patpong is almost deserted except for a pair of excellent bookstores and several cozy pubs which screen the latest videos in air-conditioned comfort. Between 1800 and 2000 the bars spring to life with smaller crowds and happy-hour prices. A lively but completely obnoxious night market now takes place along Patpong 1 and on the sidewalks of Silom and Surawong Roads. After 2000, some 30-50 go-go bars and live-show nightclubs operate at full tilt.

Single males, Western females, and even families are welcome to enter a club, watch a show, and perhaps attempt a conversation with the unexpectedly friendly ladies. Surprisingly, *farang* women are often the center of attention and soon become the conversation centerpiece for the entire bar.

Patpong 1: The best strategy for selecting a club is to walk the entire street and quickly peek inside the flashier establishments. Better clubs on Patpong 1 include those owned by the King's Group such as **King's Castle, Queen's Castle,** and the **Mississippi Club,** where scenes from *The Deer Hunter* were filmed. Patpong also served as Saigon's Tu Do Street for Robin Williams's *Good Morning Vietnam*. The **Kangaroo Club** on the north end is an Australian-run pub that provides an air-conditioned escape. **Napoleon Lounge** is an old favorite that serves as a daytime restaurant and nighttime jazz club.

Patpong 2: This narrow alley provides an easy alternative to the madness on Patpong 1. **Bobby's Arms** has a Sunday evening music fest of straight-ahead mainstream jazz performed by both Western and Thai artists. The open-air beer bars (also called bar beers!) on Patpong 2 are less intimidating options where you can relax and watch the passing crowd. Women in the north-end watering holes are friendly and under less pressure to push drinks than their counterparts on Patpong 1. Several of the bars allows patrons to go-go dance with the women.

Live Sex Shows: The most irritating activity on Patpong is the hordes of overly aggressive barkers who accost Westerners with offers of private shows featuring young girls whose special talents are explicitly listed on calling cards. After performing their bizarre biological feats, the girls are joined by a young Thai male who tests his endurance, perhaps knocking over your drink in the process.

Very few visitors enjoy these shows, but if you must, be sure to establish the total cover charge and price for drinks *before* going upstairs for the show—misunderstandings are common. Tourists who are presented with extortionate bills should pay up, then contact the tourist police on the Surawong Road end of Patpong 1, or the larger police station at the intersection of Silom and Rama IV Roads. The tourist police will collect your refund and correct the situation for the next visitor.

Patpong 3 (Silom Soi 4): This dead-end alley off Silom Road is home to several gay clubs that feature transvestites *(gatoeis)* in hilarious follies revues. Solo women and mixed couples are welcome to have a drink and enjoy the show. Also on this alley are several small restaurants such as the **Telephone Cafe** and the wildly popular **Rome Club** disco, where trendy gays and visiting *farangs* come to enjoy the superb sound and lighting system.

Soi Taniya: Japan comes to Bangkok. Taniya Road, three short blocks east of Patpong, more closely resembles a nightlife district in Tokyo than Bangkok. Just for an odd experience, walk past the private gate (the Japanese have apparently purchased the entire street) and pseudo-art-deco Thaniya Plaza building to glance at the Japanese nightclubs, laser karaoke bars, and sushi joints all marked with Japanese script. Most are private clubs which bar admittance to Westerners unless accompanied by a member.

Nana Entertainment Plaza (NEP)

Bangkok's greatest go-go bar scene features three floors of clubs, cafes, and rock 'n' roll cabarets with outstanding sound systems.

Ground floor of the U-shaped complex has a few open-air beer bars for drinks without hassles, especially during happy hours from 1800-2000. The better clubs are all on the second floor. **Asian Intrigue** sponsors rather campy music revues nightly at 2000 and 2300 that run the gamut from Thai classical dancers to simulated love scenes; popular with single males and mixed couples. **Woodstock** is a dark and smoky lounge that features disco tunes, girls, and some of the better rock bands in Bangkok. Other bars on the second floor include the **Farang Connection, Blackout, Hog's Breath Saloon** ("better than no breath at all"), **Sexy Night,** and **Three Roses.**

Nana Entertainment Complex is on Soi 4, directly across from the Nana Hotel.

Soi Cowboy

Bangkok's second-most-active bar area is off Sukumvit Road between Sois 21 and 23. The area gets its name from a black American nicknamed "Cowboy" who owned one of the first bars on the street. Crowds tend to be smaller and made up of Western expatriates rather than locals and tourists. Soi Cowboy is also a good place to meet Western residents and pick up inside tips and anecdotes about the nightlife scene in Bangkok. Set with terrific foodstalls and friendly pubs, Soi Cowboy is the slow and sleazy counterpoint to the flash and glitter of Patpong.

Bars tend to change name and ownership with the seasons, but the current favorites include **Midnight** featuring a dance show around midnight, a country-western pub with live bands sensibly called **Country Road,** brightly illuminated **Tilac,** and the very popular **Five Star,** also with live music. Smaller bars and pubs include the *Apache* with wooden Indians posted above the entrance, *New Klymaxx, New Crazy Cats, Rawhide, Shadow, Long Gun, Toy Bar, Black & White, New Loretta, Dandy Bar, Cowboy Two,* and *After Skool* with, what else, a schoolgirl theme.

The far end of the street is chock-a-block with small bars and cozy nightclubs worth checking out such as *Cowboy One, Big Blue, New Hare & Hound, Suzi Wong, D.L. Irish Pub, Pam's, Our Place, Bluebird* ("Three Floors of Fun"), *Tony's, Moonshine Joint,* and *Virgo.*

Several of these clubs have been enlarged by knocking down the walls between two smaller bars.

Adjacent Soi 23 offers several good British pubs that serve bangers and mash along with the latest videos. Top choices include **The Old Dutch Cafe** right on the corner, the **B.H. International Restaurant & Beer House** just across Soi 23, the **Ship Inn** (a British pub), and the **Old Siam** for Thai fare in a cozy setting.

Washington Square

Another low-key nightlife scene is located on the south side of Sukumvit Road between Sois 22 and 24. Behind the Washington Cinema, which dominates the square, you'll find a small cluster of cheap foodstalls and nightclubs that evoke an American atmosphere. Darts, snooker, videos, and Sunday afternoon barbecues are the main attractions rather than go-go girls and sex shows.

The liveliest spot is the popular **Bourbon Street,** which features Cajun creole cuisine and live Dixieland and other jazz on weekends by the Bourbon Street Ramblers. Other American West saloons include the **Texas Lone Star Saloon** with "Food, Wimmin & Likker," the well-named **No Probl'm Cocktail Lounge,** the *Prince of Wales Pub, Happy Pub, Square One Pub,* and the **Silver Dollar Bar** ("No Weapons Allowed").

Denny's Corner is another cowboy-style bar and restaurant with American grub and inexpensive brew.

Late Night Clubs & Coffee Shops

Moving sharply downscale several notches is a handful of coffee shops which allow freelance prostitutes to ply their trade. Most are rather deserted until about midnight when the bars on Patpong and Soi Cowboy close their doors. Bar girls who haven't found a date then grab a *tuk tuk* to the Grace or Thermae and hang out until sunrise.

Angels: By far the most popular and inviting late-night spot for music, dance, and girls is the almost chic nightclub on the ground floor of the Nana Hotel, just opposite Nana Plaza. Although the club is almost completely deserted until 2200, almost every table fills in the next 30 minutes, so arrive at exact the right moment to grab a table near the dance floor. Nana Hotel, Sukumvit Soi 2.

Grace Hotel Coffeeshop: Bangkok's formerly great late-night hangout has lost much of its sheen and now is favored by a heavily Arab clientele, but this longtime classic may be worth a quick visit to see what floats the surface in the early morning hours. Sukumvit Soi 3.

Thermae Coffeeshop: The famous old rendezvous closed down at its former location several years ago but has reopened in a somewhat more upscale setting with all the familiar trappings—hordes of freelance ladies who pack the cozy club after the other nightclubs close around 0200. Sukumvit Soi 15, under the Ruam Chitt Plaza building.

Massage Parlors

Countless massage parlors, Turkish baths, and steam baths are found throughout Bangkok. Large numbers have cropped up on lower Sukumvit and along New Petchburi Road, north of Sukumvit. Massage parlors come in two varieties: legitimate places which offer traditional "ancient massage" for 200-400B per hour, and sex houses filled with numbered women waiting in viewing rooms. These giant pleasure palaces are equipped with one-way mirrors through which customers watch up to 250 masseuses file their nails and zone out on TV while waiting for a customer.

THAI KICKBOXING

*T*hai boxing is the street fighter's dream of Western boxing mixed with karate and a bit of *tae kwon do.* Barefoot pugilists prior to WW II wrapped their hands in hemp mixed with ground glass; the fight went on for as long as anyone could stand, or had any blood left. Today the boxers wear lightly padded gloves and a few rules have been introduced to control the carnage.

An interesting ritual takes place before the match begins. Wailing music from a small orchestra of Javanese pipe, two drums, and cymbal sets the mood. Often fixed with colored cords and protective amulets, the two contestants enter the ring, kneel and pray to the spirits for victory, then begin a surrealistic slow-motion dance designed to show off their talents while emulating their teachers' movements. Spectators make their bets as the boxers pound and kick each other with ever-increasing frenzy. The drama is heightened by the cacophonous musical accompaniment. At the end of five three-minute rounds, or the merciful intervention of the referee, the fight ends and a winner is declared by the judges.

Thai kickboxing can be experienced at the Lumpini Stadium on Rama IV Road (near the Malaysia Hotel) every Tuesday and Friday at 1800, and Saturday at 1800 and 1330. Superior boxers meet at Rajadamnern Stadium (near the TAT office) every Monday, Wednesday, and Thursday at 1800, and on Sunday at 1700 and 2000. Admission is 50-200B. This spectacle is best watched from ringside rather than with the rabble up in the circular gallery.

male Monroes

It's a flesh market of the most curious type. Customers make their selection by picking a woman and giving her number to the parlor manager. The chosen number is called out, the style of massage is decided, and the bill is paid at the cashier's counter.

Transvestite Revues
"Boys Will Be Girls" is a familiar theme here in the Land of Smiles. For several decades, female-impersonator revues have been a popular form of entertainment in the seaside resort of Pattaya, but today these revues take place in Bangkok and Patong Beach on Phuket. The small gay clubs around Silom Soi 4 put on minor revues in intimate surroundings, but tourists generally favor the more elaborate and professional shows held at the following two clubs.

Calypso Cabaret: The one-hour performance includes dancing sailoresses, comedy skits with audience participation, leather queens, Thai and Chinese dancers in stunning costumes, and above all, a delightful sense of humor and good cheer. Photographers are welcome but arrive early to secure a good seat in this uncomfortably small auditorium. Shows nightly at 2015 and 2145, 600B includes one drink. Asia Hotel, 296 Phayathai Rd., tel. (02) 261-6355.

Mambo: Formed from Calypso's former touring company, this equally professional troupe is now the only choice on Sukumvit after Calypso left the Ambassador Hotel several years ago. Reservations are recommended for either of the twice nightly shows. Shows nightly at 2000 and 2145, 600B includes one drink. Sukumvit Soi 31, tel. (02) 662-0441.

DISCOS, NIGHTCLUBS, AND BARS

The nightlife scene in Bangkok is unrivaled, even by the hedonist pleasures of Manila or Hong Kong. Within easy walking distance or a short cab ride from most hotels are pubs, nightclubs, discos, and cabarets offering everything from country-western tunes to all-night rave scenes packed with trendy Thais and the curious *farang*.

Nightclubs and bars in luxury hotels are okay, but don't compare with the local venues that offer live music and entertainment from about 2100 to the early morning hours. Cover charges at clubs with bands or DJ services run 50-150B during the week and 120-300B on weekends, but a complimentary drink or two is often included in the cover charge. The larger and newer venues feature DJs, private karaoke lounges, restaurants and bars, and "videotheques" where music is backed by laser rock videos.

The following section is arranged by neighborhood.

Banglampoo
The backpackers' enclave near Khao San Road remains an entertainment dry zone though a handful of small spots are worth checking out

before heading off to the brighter lights elsewhere in the city.

Gulliver's Traveller's Tavern: After years of suffering through cheap cafes and dismal clubs, Khao San finally has a professionally designed and operated venue where upmarket backpackers can escape the heat and enjoy a decent meal along with pub games and live music. Khao San at Chakraphonse Rd., tel. (02) 629-1988.

Hemlock: Small but sophisticated cafe and pub with trendy decor and sophisticated music just opposite the express boat pier. 56 Pra Arthit Rd., tel. (02) 282-7507.

Joy Luck Club: A longtime favorite just around the corner from the Hemlock with reasonably priced meals and light music. Open daily noon to 0200. 8 Pra Sumen, Pra Arthid Rd., tel. (02) 280-3307.

Song Muai: Popular and very crowded two-storey pub cafe with inexpensive food and drink and loud music to keep the place jumping. 169 Tanao Rd., tel. (02) 622-1205.

Silom Soi 4

While nearby Patpong Road is mostly go-go bars with dancing girls, the adjacent streets offer dozens of clubs and discos that cater to all sorts of musical tastes and sexual persuasions. Silom Soi 4 has the largest concentration of clubs.

Cactus Club: Owner Brian Sullivan operates a colorful, Spanish-style nightclub with dance floor, long bar, and uncharacteristically high ceiling for a small club on this alley. The place is easily spotted by its distinct green neon light which draws in the loyal mix of Thais and expats. 114/15 Silom Soi 4, tel. (02) 233-8821.

Molly's Jump: An American-style theme bar based on the career of a famed Australian music promoter decorated with photos of Ian "Molly" Meldrun with his singer and musician friends. Downstairs is the dance floor while upstairs is a pool table, satellite TV, and cocktail lounge. 86-8 Silom Soi 4, tel. (02) 235-5891.

Milk Bar: A near-legendary hangout for the artistic Thai set (singers, actors, designers, wannabees) who fill the rafters of the small, 1950s-style interior. Popular spot for a drink before moving on to Deeper, Sphinx, or the D.J. Station. 114/10 Silom Soi 4, no phone, no credit.

Film Mix: A movie-themed cafe with dance music that attracts the spillover from nearby Kool Spot. 114/5 Silom Soi 4, tel. (02) 235-3877.

Kool Spot: Another addition to the crazy alley near Patpong. This music-and-dance bar is set with stone flagging and curvy mirrors facing a long enamel bartop fashioned in the shape of a snake; you'll see the dragon eyes flashing after a few pitchers of Kamikazes. 114/6 Silom Soi 4, tel. (02) 266-4820.

Speed: DJ dance music and themed Saturday hip-hop nights make this about the most crowded and interesting club in the neighborhood. 80 Silom Soi 4.

Hyper: A longtime favorite with a trendy people-watching crowd and laid-back music for the dance inclined. Open nightly 2100-0200. 114/14 Silom Soi 4, tel. (02) 238-5257.

Silom Road Area

Several other pubs and nightclubs are around Silom but not tucked away in lively Soi 4.

Delaney's: Clean and comfortable Irish pub with Guiness and Kilkeeny's plus Irish food and live bands most nights with an emphasis on folk

---

LIVE THAI ROCK 'N' ROLL

*U*nlike Manila in the Philippines, most of the clubs in Bangkok feature recorded music rather than live entertainment. The scene, however, has improved with the arrival of *dontree pher cheevit,* a fresh musical force that has traded the traditional love themes for issues of social injustice.

Early efforts at political consciousness by a group named Caravan proved too radical for public airing, but Carabao in the late 1980s caused a major sensation with their song "Made in Thailand." The hit both ridiculed Thai obsession with foreign-made goods and inadvertently promoted the government's Buy-Thai program! Other Carabao songs have described the plight of Bangkok's prostitutes and poor rural farmers. Instead of simply plagiarizing Western pop melodies to back up Thai lyrics, Carabao has successfully fused American country rock with traditional Thai music. Remember the 1986 disco hit "One Night in Bangkok"? Banned in Thailand.

ZUZU ★ ปะการังไปใต

music and jazz combos. Just across the street from Patpong. 1/5 Convent Rd., tel. (02) 266-7160.

O'Reillys Irish Pub: Another safe escape from the madness of Patpong with dependable grub and drinks without the hassle of hostesses or grubby merchants. 62/1 Silom at Thaniya Rd., tel. (02) 632-7515.

FM 228: An entertainment complex that combines live music, a karaoke lounge, an American restaurant, and a videotheque hall—perfect for the occasional rave party. 323 Silom Rd., United Centre Bldg., 5th floor, tel. (02) 231-1228.

Radio City: Formerly Mars and then Smile but still a dependable choice for DJs spinning oldies and live bands on weekends. 76/1-3 Patpong Soi 1, tel. (02) 234-6902.

Barbican: Not on Patpong or one of its nearby alleys but a trendy nightclub stuck directly in the heart of Japanese Patpong with an upstairs restaurant, international newspapers on the ground floor, and a small disco which welcomes all visitors and rocks until dawn. 9/4 Soi Thaniya, Silom Rd., tel. (02) 234-3590.

Silom Gay Clubs
Almost a dozen gay clubs are scattered around Patpong, often in Soi 4.

Rome Club: A relatively large number of fashionably dressed gays, trendy art-club types, *farang* visitors, and *gatoeis* hang out in the upstairs annex despite the disco's ban against their gay clientele. The scene peaks around midnight and winds down around 3 a.m., but this once-famed club has lost much of its glamour as the trendsetters have moved on to greener lawns. 90 Silom Soi 4, tel. (02) 233-8836.

Deeper: A slow but steady decline at the Rome Club has sent patrons—both gay and straight—to other, nearby clubs. Deeper is popular with trendsetters and creative *farangs* who party and dance until dawn. Be sure to visit the adjacent Deep Bar and try a jug of their lethal Kamikaze (250B) that glows in the ultraviolet lights in the bar's dark recesses. 82 Silom Soi 4, tel. (02) 233-2930.

Telephone: The eight-year-old bar/restaurant has survived the onslaught of newer clubs and continues to draw a regular clientele. However, few folks use the table phones in this era of cellular madness. Have you ever seen so many people packing "handphones?" 114/11-13 Silom Soi 4, tel. (02) 234-3279.

Sphinx: A predominantly gay bar with terraced seating on two spacious floors, creamy Egyptian decor, dance rooms on the upper floors, and a balcony for watching the lip-synching drag shows nightly at midnight or later. Excellent food, too. 98-104 Silom Soi 4, tel. (02) 234-7249.

The Balcony: An offshoot of the Telephone Club with fan-cooled open frontage and breezy balconies for people watching. 86-8 Silom Soi 4, tel. (02) 235-5891.

Bank Studio: Techno dance club with third floor karaoke plus amusing cabaret show around midnight. Mostly a Thai clientele but *farang* and women are welcome. Silom Soi 6, tel. (02) 236-6385.

Disco Disco (DD): Small but packed-out place with two bars and nonstop dance music provided by young Thai DJs. Open nightly 2100-0200. Silom Soi 2, tel. (02) 234-6151.

DJ Station: Gay disco with an unpretentious atmosphere and campy cabaret show nightly around midnight. 8/6-8 Silom Soi 2, tel. (02) 266-4029.

JJ Park: An old favorite known for its tasty Thai food, friendly clientele, and great sounds like live bands, plus attractive setting fixed up with snazzy copper panels. Also, a late-night cabaret show with performers drawn from nearby clubs. 8/3 Silom Soi 2, tel. (02) 233-3247.

Sarasin Road

For many years, Bangkok had few bars in the traditional sense since cafes could legally sell beer and spirits, and Thais generally preferred to socialize with friends at home rather than in public. But over the last few years Bangkok has exploded with dozens of new clubs that cater to both foreigners and locals with rock, country-western, jazz, and other forms of popular music.

The scene started in the late 1980s with the launching of several clubs on Soi Sarasin, just off Rajadamnern Road near Lumpini Park, where clubs modeled themselves after European bistros and cater to an older and more professional crowd rather than the teenybopper set that frequents the Silom Road discos.

Brown Sugar: Arguably the city's best choice for adult contemporary and jazz music featuring three bands per night, ranging from Manop Varonitipas on sax to local pop master Tewan Sapsanyokorn, who plays saxophone, Thai flute, and electric violin with his group Tewan Novel-Jazz. The place has become expensive (drinks run 120-180B) but the good vibes and excellent music have attracted folks such as Willem Dafoe, Gregory Hines, and Spyro Gyra. Cover charge runs 150-300B. 231/19 Sarasin Rd., tel. (02) 250-0103.

Old West Saloon: A longtime favorite that re-creates the American Wild West in a down-to-earth atmosphere. Two bands play country-western nightly, there's no cover, and the place is filled with all kinds of kitsch such as cattle skulls, American Indian photos, and other cowboy memorabilia. 231/17 Sarasin Rd., tel. (02) 250-0103.

Blue's Bar: A two-floor fashionable music club that features alternative and classic rock, plus decent food for the designer set. The place has dropped their former 1980s music in favor of more hip rap but still remains among the better clubs in this neck of the woods. 231/16 Sarasin Rd., tel. (02) 252-7335.

Hi Park: Lively hangout for young and trendy Thais who are well dressed and have money to burn. The downstairs area gets overly boisterous, though a quieter balcony is just upstairs. 231/18 Sarasin Rd., tel. (02) 250-0090.

Soi Lang Suan

Around the corner from Soi Sarasin is another street with a good selection of pubs favored by local expats and upscale Thais.

Round Midnight: The club caters to jazzophiles and lovers of salsa and samba but also features bands playing rock classics and easy listening during the week. Packed on weekends. No cover. 106/12 Soi Lang Suan, tel. (02) 251-0652.

Bee'z: Small and cozy spot with nightly entertainment, mostly folk but also flamenco guitarists and other low-key forms that allow conversation. 63/10 Soi Lang Suan, tel. (02) 252-4630.

Ad Makers: A Western bar with plenty of rough wood and live bands that play your requests, plus a full menu and food served until 0200. 51/51 Soi Lang Suan, tel. (02) 652-0168.

Siam Square

This rather conservative neighborhood will never win any awards for Bangkok party central, though a few places might be worth a quick look.

Hard Rock Cafe: Have you picked up your T-shirt yet? The standard array of rock memorabilia plus live bands most nights starting around 2200. Siam Square Soi 1, tel. (02) 251-0792.

Planet Hollywood: Another American-themed restaurant and nightclub with movie stuff and some of the worst food in the city. Business has been disappointing since this place opened several years ago and this outlet may close in the near future. Ploenchit Rd., Gaysorn Plaza, tel. (02) 656-1358.

Hartmannsdorfer Bauhaus: German microbrewery in an elegant setting with fresh brew and beer hall food at reasonable prices. Rama 1 Rd., Discovery Center, tel. (02) 658-0223.

Sukumvit

The wilder and raunchier spots are near the upper end of Sukumvit, while the classier spots with jazz and otherwise are farther down and tucked away in the side alleys. The following are described starting from inner Sukumvit all the way out to Ekamai at Soi 63.

Woodstock: Entertainment in this funky club alternates between live rock 'n' roll bands on weekends and recorded music during the week. It's oriented toward cruising males but a great place for live music to suit all persuasions. Check the overwhelming collection of *Far Side* cartoons in the men's room. Nana Entertainment Plaza, Sukumvit Soi 4, tel. (02) 258-2565.

Jool's: A longtime favorite for those in the know, Jool's is the Sukumvit counterpart to Bobby's Arms on Patpong. But here you don't have to hassle with the bar touts and other promoters of sleaze to enjoy the British pub food, imported beers, and good conversation from local denizens. Prices are low, but don't ring the bell unless you intend to buy drinks for everyone. 21/3 Soi 4 Sukumvit Rd., tel. (02) 252-6413.

Grace Hotel Streetstalls: Not really a pub, disco, or nightclub in any sense of the word, but the streetstall vendors near the Grace Hotel provide tasty food at rock-bottom prices, plus their honest chatter is an authentic form of Thai entertainment. Soi 1 and Soi 3.

Huntsman Pub: Somewhat sedate but an excellent place to escape the nearby madness and enjoy a drink or meal along with the talented bands that play nightly until 0100. A comfortable venue for those not interested in the girlie bar scene which dominates this area. Landmark Plaza, Sukumvit Soi 6, tel. (02) 254-0404.

Victoria Bar & Pub: An old favorite in operation for over 15 years with imported brews and unique versions of Swiss fondue. 9/1 Sukumvit Soi 7, tel. (02) 484-9717.

Discovery: Large disco with massive dance floor, balconied pub, and open-air porch for escaping the crowds that frequent the retro nights and gay events held weekly. Sukumvit Soi 12, tel. (02) 653-0246.

Isaan 19: Unique Isaan Lao disco with *mor lam* music in a cramped setting just above the Country Road nightclub. Sukumvit Soi 19.

Imageries By The Glass: Strange name but an impressive place with decent food and a nonstop array of bands performing from early evening until closing at 0200. Sukumvit Soi 24, tel. (02) 258-7010.

Taurus Brew House: Upmarket and trendy disco, featuring Latin and funk sounds, both recorded and live. Few Westerners in sight, but a venue that has survived and thrived over the last few years for its attention to detail and outstanding selection of live bands. A very dressy place with a 500B minimum (two drinks included) but among the better places in town. Sukumvit Soi 26, tel. (02) 661-3535.

The Bull's Head: British pub with grub, brew, and a variety of theme nights such as a quiz program on Tuesday and an oldies music session on Fridays. Sukumvit Soi 33, tel. (02) 259-4444.

Londoner Brew House: Another popular English-style pub with homemade bitters and nightly music from retro disco to live bands playing golden oldies. Sukumvit Soi 33, UBC Bldg., tel. (02) 261-0238.

Sukumvit Soi 33: Several cozy clubs—curiously named after European painters—are tucked away in a quiet alley. All offer happy hour drink specials and are popular with Western expatriates who live nearby. Two standards are **Vincent Van Gogh** and the **Renoir Club.**

Axil Cafe: Fashionable boutique with heavy attitude favored by hip young Thais on an early evening bender before moving on to more raucous digs. Sukumvit Soi 39, tel. (02) 261-6232.

Blues Jazz: Classy pub with excellent entertainment and decent food at decent prices, though the remote location holds tourist visits down to a minimum. Sukumvit Soi 53, tel. (02) 258-7747.

Witch's Tavern: Enormous pub with a long bar and music lounge worked by Filipino and Hong Kong bands specializing in jazz, soul, and easy-listening classics. Reasonable prices for beer and spirits. Sukumvit Soi 55, tel. (02) 390-2646.

Barley Castle Pub: Impressive nightclub with pop and jazz band performing nightly until 0100 or 0200 depending on their mood. Sukumvit Soi 55, tel. (02) 390-2646.

Harmonics: Cozy little cafe with reasonably priced food and wafting guitar music, then livelier three-piece bands until the closing hours. Sukumvit Soi 55, tel. (02)390-4484.

Cafe 50: Trendy and very hip cafe with downstairs cafe and upstairs bar with folk music evenings, plus appearances by Thai movie and soap opera idols. Sukumvit Soi 61, tel. (02) 381-1773.

Major Bowl Pub & Restaurant: A flashy newer bowling rink with dance music and designer restaurant serving Thai and Western dishes to the late-night crowd. 122/39 Sukumvit Soi 63 (Ekamai), tel. (02) 714-2849.

Washington Square

This assortment of simple pubs and nightclubs has long been the favorite watering hole for many Western expats living in the nearby apartments and condominium complexes. The "Square" at Sukumvit Soi 22 is rather tame when compared to Patong or Soi Cowboy; the food is familiar and you won't have to hassle with teeny-boppers or Thai trendsetters of questionable sexual persuasion. This is not a place for people who prefer videotheques and flashing lights.

Bourbon Street: A local hangout for a cheap breakfast, leisurely Sunday brunch, Creole cuisine, a Mexican buffet on Tuesday evenings, and entertainment provided by local expats who enjoy meeting the tourist and traveler. 29/4-6 Washington Square, Sukumvit 22, tel. (02) 259-0328.

Denny's Corner: An alfresco bar and restaurant on the edge of the square that guarantees a good place to nurse a beer and watch the passing parade. No entertainment or music, but a pleasant spot to hang out for a few hours. 13 Washington Square, Sukumvit 22, tel. (02) 259-5684.

The Prince of Wales: Another old favorite known for its inexpensive food, cold beer, and shaggy carpets that have been nailed to the walls for unknown reasons. 37 Washington Square, Sukumvit 22, tel. (02) 258-4204.

Silver Dollar: Another expat watering hole with homey vibes and an excellent barbecue on Sunday from noon to late afternoon. Modeled after the American Old West, it now resembles something from the *Gunsmoke* era. 550 Washington Square, Sukumvit 22, tel. (02) 258-2033.

Bangkapi

Bangkapi is in eastern Bangkok near Ramkamheng University, about 15 km northeast of Silom Road or 10 km from the beginning of Sukumvit Road. A taxi from Sukumvit should cost about 150B.

NASA Spacedrome: Bangkok's flashiest disco is a multimillion-dollar dance emporium that packs in over 2,000 sweating bodies every weekend. At midnight, a spaceship descends to the floor amid smoke, flashing lights, and the theme song from *2001: A Space Odyssey*. For sheer spectacle, nothing else compares in Thailand. Afterwards, the house Gypsy Band plays until 3 a.m. 999 Ramkamheng Rd., 100 meters north of New Petchburi Rd., tel. (02) 314-6530.

Thonburi

Travelers in Banglampoo will find the following disco easy to reach and a convenient spot to experience modern Thai culture.

Paradise Music Hall: Another gigantic dance emporium with the standard amenities of flashing lights, laser videos, and booming disco music, it's a very wild place on weekends. The Paradise is on Arun Amarin Road in Thonburi, just across the bridge from Banglampoo; a good choice for travelers staying on Khao San Road. Taxis from Khao San Road cost 50-80B.

SHOPPING

Bangkok enjoys a well-deserved reputation as the shopping capital of Southeast Asia with its range of products from Thai silks, gemstones, tailor-made suits and dresses, to inexpensive shoes, bronzeware, and traditional handicrafts. Even the imported items such as electronics, watches, and cameras are much cheaper than in the so-called "duty-free" ports of Hong Kong or Singapore. It's impossible to beat the deals in Bangkok.

Prices are fairly uniform across town, but selection varies slightly between neighborhoods: Chinatown is best for gold chains and photography equipment, Silom Road for silks and antiques, Sukumvit for leather goods and tailors, shopping centers near Siam Square for high fashion, Pratunan for cheap clothing, Banglampoo for handicrafts and tribal artifacts.

Serious shoppers should purchase Nancy Chandler's outstanding *Market Map of Bangkok* and *Shopping in Exotic Thailand,* published by Impact Publications.

WHERE TO SHOP

Merchants recommended by the Tourism Authority of Thailand are listed in the TAT publication, the *Official Shopping Guide,* and denoted on shop windows by a decal of a female vendor seated with a pair of baskets. Unfortunately, this regulation means very little in Bangkok, so conduct your shopping with extreme caution.

Silk
Thai silk is heavy and coarse and not enjoyed by everyone, though you might want to investigate the product at any of the following shops.

Jim Thompson Silk: Thailand's most famed outlet for traditional Thai silk is expensive though the quality is considered the world's finest. Thompson has outlets all over Southeast Asia including four in Bangkok on Surawong Road near Rama 4 Road, in the Oriental Hotel (of course), in Isetan at the World Trade Center, and at the Grand Hyatt Erawan Hotel.

Shinawatra Silk: Another respected silk outlet with shops on South Sathorn Road near Silom and at Sukumvit Soi 23.

Kanitha: This well-known boutique has been producing world-famous designer fashions made from silk and other fabrics for over 20 years. Silom Rd.

Design Thai: Small but worthwhile shop with decades of experience. 304 Silom Rd.

Antiques
Authentic antiques are extremely rare in Thailand—and cost a fortune—but hundreds of shops sell "instant antiques" that are so convincing that only an expert could tell the difference. Most shopkeepers are very honest about this situation, but shop around as prices vary enormously.

River City Shopping Complex: Bangkok's best selection of antiques and fake antiques is inside this four-story complex right on the river adjacent to the Sheraton Royal Orchid Hotel. A major antique auction is held here on the first Saturday of each month.

Silom and Charoen Krung roads are other good sources of antiques, with antique and pseudoantique shops as far as the eye can see.

Elephant House: Burmese antiques, teak furniture, and decorative artwork in a famous old shop in an alley just off Sathorn Tai Road. This place has been around for several decades and has quite the reputation. 67/12 Soi Pra Phinit, tel. (02) 286-2780.

Krishna's Antiques: Four floors of exquisite crafts and rare collectibles. Sukumvit Soi 6.

L'Arcadia: A small shop that specializes in Burmese antiques and reproductions; ask to see their upstairs showcase. Sukumvit Soi 23.

Rasi Sayam: Another small but high-quality shop operated by Honathan Hayssen, a Stanford MBA graduate. Most of the items are instant antiques but of unusually high quality. Sukumvit Soi 23.

Handicrafts
Most handicrafts are best purchased in Chiang Mai, on the highway that runs between Chiang

Mai and Sankamphang, though the following shops sell good quality merchandise at fair prices.

Narayana Phand: Supported by the Thai government but actually a private enterprise, this sprawling store (the largest of its kind in Thailand) has every possible handicraft at fixed prices— Thai silk, cotton, bronzeware, ceramics, lacquerware, Thai dolls, teak wood products, antique reproductions, and other indigenous handicrafts. This is a good place to get an initial idea of prices before setting off to other shops scattered around town. Rajadamri Rd., tel. (02) 252-4670.

Chitralada: Another handicraft emporium, under the support of the Royal Family, that aims to encourage and promote native handicrafts, and provide employment to the handicapped who create many of the items for sale. Chitralada now has 12 outlets in Thailand, including seven in Bangkok at the Oriental Hotel shopping complex, Grand Palace, Vimanmek Mansion, Amporn Palace, Thaniya Plaza on Silom Road, Amari Watergate Hotel, and the Marriott Royal Garden Riverside Hotel.

Once again, prices are fixed and very reasonable, making this a good place to learn something about the quality and price levels of local handicrafts.

Central Bangkok Shopping Centers
Service and selection are unrivaled at the immense shopping complexes throughout Bangkok, many of which are located in the Siam Square-Ploenchit-Rama 1 Road area.

World Trade Center: Probably the largest and most interesting shopping complex in Bangkok provides eight floors of shops, anchored on one end by the midpriced Zen Central shopping center and the more upscale Isetan at the other flank. Almost everything imaginable is sold here, plus there's plenty of budget cafes and better restaurants on the upper floors. Some of the more familiar outlets are Asia Books, Tower Records, and a new Duty Free outlet. Bad name though—this place has absolutely nothing to do with "world trade." Rama 1 at Rajadamri Rd.

Mahboonkrong (MBK) Center: Bangkok's first large indoor shopping mall includes endless arcades full of trinkets, restaurants, six cin-

emas, a concert hall, and the upscale Japanese-owned Tokyu Department Store. The place is now somewhat outdated and sells more schlock than quality, but don't miss the wonderful food emporiums on the ground floor and an older food center on the seventh. Rama 1 at Phyathai Rd.

Siam Square: Bangkok's original shopping complex (an open-air affair), opened in the 1960s, looks fairly forlorn these days after a fire gutted many of the centrally located shops, though renovation is in progress and this old favorite may return to favor in a few years. Today, there's a handful of small and utilitarian shops and several popular restaurants in the rear section of the complex. Rama 1 at Phyathai Rd.

Gaysorn Plaza: A new and very stylish shopping center with trendy boutiques and several upscale Thai handicraft shops on the second floor. Planet Hollywood occupies much of the ground floor while Narayana Phand, another famous handicraft outlet, is right next door. Ploenchit at Rajadamri Rd.

Siam Center: Just opposite Siam Square is a small but reasonably priced shopping complex with clothing and shoe stores catering mostly to teenagers. Rama 1 Rd.

Siam Discovery Center: Adjacent to the Siam Center is a rather quiet shopping complex catering primarily to children and young adults. Rama 1 at Phyathai Rd.

Amarin Plaza: Prices are atmospheric but some of the highest-quality goods are sold in the Romanesque complex on Ploenchit Road. Sogo—the main department store anchor—has expanded into a building adjacent to the Erawan Grand Hyatt Hotel. Ploenchit at Rajadamri Rd.

Peninsula Plaza: Over 70 small boutiques and a comprehensive branch of Asia Books are located in the small but almost dazzling shopping center on Rajadamri Road near the Regent Hotel. Rajadamri Rd. just south of Ploenchit.

Central Chidlom: A very large and relatively new branch of the largest chain of department stores in Thailand, with reasonably priced goods and handicrafts, especially when compared to Japanese-based chains such as Isetan, Sogo, and Tokyu. Ploenchit at Chidlom Rd.

Duty Free Shop: Much to the dismay of local merchants, the Tourism Authority of Thailand operates a duty-free shop on Ploenchit Road where the liquor and tobacco sections offer great bargains, though better prices on other goods are available elsewhere. Another outlet is in the nearby World Trade Center.

Panthip Plaza: A few blocks from the World Trade Center is a small shopping complex chiefly visited for its dozen-plus computer stores. Pirated software has been illegal for several years now, though some shops still sell discs under the counter to familiar faces. Phetburi Road near the Amari Watergate Hotel.

Sukumvit Road Shopping Centers
Sukumvit isn't a shopper's paradise, though a few shopping centers have opened in recent years.

Ploenchit Center: Small but useful shopping complex right at the beginning of Sukumvit near the Expressway and JW Marriott Hotel.

The Emporium: Bangkok's newest shopping center is almost exclusively comprised of pricey boutiques, far beyond the means of most Thais and many visiting *farangs,* for that matter. The place is largely deserted but provides a welcome escape from the heat if you're actually walking down this messed-up road. Sukumvit Soi 24.

Silom Road Shopping Centers
Shopping around Silom Road and Charoen Krung Road (New Road) tends to be somewhat expensive, as most shops are geared to tourists staying in the nearby upscale hotels.

Central: Thailand's original department store chain has branches on Silom Road (the smallest and least useful outlet), a much better store on Ploenchit Road, a new addition in the Zen Complex, and an immense emporium in the Lard Prao neighborhood. All stores have an upstairs handicraft market and a mind-boggling selection of quality clothes at reasonable prices.

Oriental Place: Top-end shops offering mostly arts, antiques, expensive handicrafts, and fine clothing in the European Renaissance shopping complex near the Oriental Hotel.

River City Shopping Complex: Thailand's largest and most distinguished venue for fine arts and antiques, with four floors of amazing shops plus a handful of smaller spots for inexpensive trinkets. River City holds a monthly antique auction and often has fairly good art and

handicraft shows on the main floor. Several good, reasonably priced restaurants, plus a barbecue cafe on the top floor with outstanding views over the river and Thonburi.

Silom Village: Small shopping center with a handful of antique and handicraft shops where prices are lower than in the exclusive places mentioned above, but much higher than you will find in Chiang Mai or in the government-sponsored stores mentioned above under Handicrafts.

Chatuchak Weekend Market
The granddaddy of all Thai flea markets is Chatuchak's monstrous affair out near the airport on Paholyothin Road. Once located on the Sanam Luang near the Royal Palace, Chatuchak now sprawls over 35 acres with hundreds of booths selling everything imaginable at rock-bottom prices. An attempt has been made to sectionalize areas selling one kind of product, but most visitors are content to simply wander around and see what they discover.

Items for sale include used books and magazines (including back issues of *Sawasdee*), real and fake antiques, textiles and hilltribe artifacts, used Levis 501s, fruit, Siamese fighting fish, and endangered birds and other prohibited species. Afterwards, eat at the famous Djit Pochana Restaurant down Paholyothin Road toward the airport; their inexpensive luncheon buffet is highly recommended.

To reach the market, take a bus and watch for the large carnival tent on the left. Open weekends 0900-1800 and Friday evenings 1800-2300.

Street and Produce Markets
Shopping in Bangkok can be roughly divided into air-conditioned shopping malls and traditional markets where Thai housewives pick up their vegetables. The following local venues are great for photographs and a glimpse of old Bangkok, a slice of life that is rapidly disappearing from modern Thailand. Best choices are the aforementioned Chatuchak Market for general shopping, Pratunam for clothing, and Pak Klong for authentic atmosphere.

Pratunam Market: A sprawling rabbit warren of hygienic foodstalls, vegetable wholesalers, and shoe merchants is located at the intersection of Petchburi and Rajaprarop Roads, slightly north of Siam Square. Pratunam is famous as the best place in Bangkok to shop for inexpensive clothing. Open 24 hours; don't get lost!

Pak Klong Market: Thailand's most colorful and smelly vegetable/fruit market hangs over the riverbanks near the Memorial Bridge. Bangkok's answer to London's Covent Garden is a fascinating experience, a hive of ceaseless activity where porters wheel about stacks of crates while old ladies peddle enormous piles of fragrant orchids. Bring your camera and nose plugs.

Banglampoo Market: Conveniently located near the budget guesthouses on Khao San Road are several alleys packed with inexpensive clothing and backpackers' supplies. The adjacent New World Department Store has great bargains on the main floor and an inexpensive self-serve cafeteria on top.

Teves Flower Market: A permanent sidewalk market with plants and (occasionally) flowers flanks a canal one km north of Banglampoo, near the National Library.

Thieves' Market: Touted in many tourist books as an antique shopping district, the only antiques and thieves located here are the shopkeepers. Best buys include brassware, imitation antiques, old furniture, Chinese porcelains, and industrial supplies. Located near Chinatown and correctly called Nakhon Kasem. Most of the better merchants have abandoned the area and moved into posher digs along Silom and Sukumvit Roads. Bargaining is *de rigueur.*

INFORMATION AND SERVICES

TOURIST INFORMATION

Tourism Authority of Thailand (TAT)
The national tourism organization offers up a fairly good selection of information, though you'll need to request specific topics as most handouts are kept well hidden. The TAT has several offices around town.

TAT Headquarters: The head TAT office has the best supply of brochures and photocopied sheets with travel tips about the entire country. A bulletin board lists upcoming festivals, dance performances, and warnings about safety and rip-offs. 372 Bamrung Muang Rd., tel. (02) 226-0060. Open daily 0830-1630.

Airport TAT: Not as much information but useful for free tourist magazines and last-second tips on transportation into town. Their kiosk is in the arrival area. Open daily 0800-midnight.

Wat Pra Keo TAT: A small tourist outlet is just opposite the royal temple on Na Pra Lan Road. Open daily 0830-1930.

Chatuchak TAT: A final and often deserted TAT kiosk operates weekends at the famous flea market on the outskirts of town near the Northern Bus Terminal. Open daily 0830-1930.

Tourist Assistance Center (TAC)
Complaints about theft, fraud, and unfair business practices can be directed to the tourist police subdivision of the Tourism Authority of Thailand. They are powerless to help if you have only been overcharged, but sometimes are effective when you have purchased fragments of colored glass that you thought were precious gems. You can also contact the Tourist Police for additional help on more serious crimes. Tourist Assistance Center, 372 Bamrung Muang Rd., tel. (02) 282-8129.

Tourist Police
Serious crimes beyond the scope of the TAC are handled by this division of the National Police Department. First take your problems to the TAC office on Bamrung Muang Road and if you are unsatisfied with their results, move up the ladder to National Police Department. You can contact them at their head office or seek out any of the 500 police officers who station themselves at police kiosks in popular tourist venues. 29/1 Soi Lang Suan, Poenchit Rd., tel. (02) 255-2964.

VISAS AND IMMIGRATION

Thai Immigration
Visa applications and extensions are granted at the immigration department off Sathorn Tai Road a few blocks south of Silom Road. Visa extensions require your passport, two photos, and in most cases a payment of 500B. Arrive well dressed and behave politely or expect problems!

Immigration Department, Soi Suan Phlu, tel. (02) 287-1774. Open weekdays from 0830-1630 and Saturdays 0830-1200. Skeleton staff during lunch hours so it's best to arrive early in the morning and allow about two hours to complete the application.

Visas
Bangkok is a popular place to pick up visas for onward travel. Most nations maintain diplomatic relations with Thailand and have embassies in Bangkok. Embassies are generally open Mon.-Fri., but accept visa applications only 0900-1200. Some issue visas within two hours, while others require your passport be left overnight.

Embassies are spread out all over town and can be *extremely* time-consuming to reach with public transportation. It's often easier to let a travel agency obtain your visa for a nominal fee. Addresses, phone numbers, and operating hours of diplomatic missions are listed in most tourist magazines and booklets.

For most Western tourists, visas are unnecessary for travel to Malaysia (up to 30 days), Singapore (two weeks), Hong Kong (one month), the Philippines (21 days), and Indonesia (two months). These enlightened governments stamp an entry permit in your passport on arrival at immigration.

Visas are necessary for most Western visitors to Vietnam, Laos, Cambodia, Nepal, and India. Nepalese visas are issued on the spot and must be used within 30 days. Philippine visas should be obtained before arriving to avoid the byzantine procedures at Manila's immigration department. The Indian Embassy is a disorganized mess with hordes of impatient people getting their first taste of Indian bureaucracy.

Visas for Vietnam, Laos, and Cambodia are generally obtained by travel agents though the exact requirements for these countries seems to change with the seasons. As of this writing, Laos grants visas on arrival for visitors who fly into Vientiane, while Cambodia and Vietnam plan to start this procedure in the near future. Travel agents in Bangkok have the latest details.

MAPS

Sprawling and confusing Bangkok requires a good map. Two essential ones are Nancy Chandler's map and a bus route map if you intend to spend much time in Bangkok. Buy both to quickly understand the layout of Bangkok. Maps can be purchased at most bookstores and from many guesthouses and hotels.

Nancy Chandler's *Map of Bangkok:* Nancy's map has been the best tourist map of the city for over a decade, sensibly drawn with color codes and sectional details, plus inside tips on restaurants and popular shopping districts. Somewhat expensive, but highly recommended for all visitors to Bangkok.

Bangkok Bus Map: Most of the bus routes in Bangkok are shown on this map published by the Bangkok Guide Company. This useful if somewhat outdated resource also includes tidbits on markets, guesthouses, bookshops, river and canal tours, embassies, and airline offices. The same company also produces a small booklet with greater detail on the myriad bus routes, although most visitors will not need to dig this deep into the transportation permutations of this bewildering city.

Groovy Map & Guide of Bangkok: A relatively new map researched by a local expat with sightseeing and shopping tips, plus a full-page map of the core city with a limited number of bus routes. Although somewhat basic, the clean and colorful layout makes this the most understandable map of the city and is probably quite adequate for most first-time visitors.

Association of Siamese Architects: The Fine Arts Department publishes four colorful hand-drawn cultural maps with details on Bangkok and the canals of Thonburi. The map of Thonburi is somewhat useful, but the other maps are too vague and sketchy.

BOOKSTORES AND LIBRARIES

Bookstores
Bangkok's bookstores are probably the best in all of Southeast Asia, although the largest and most complete bookstore is now Tower Books in Singapore. Thailand has two major publishers and book distributors.

Asia Books: The largest selection of English-language books in Bangkok is found in Asia Books, a large chain especially strong on bestsellers, modern literature, business, art, travel, Thailand, and reference works. All the following

Asia Books outlets are open daily 1000-2100. The Landmark Z branch specializes in art and architecture.

Stores around Bangkok include: Main Store, 221 Sukumvit Soi 15, tel. (02) 252-7277; Central City, 309 Bangna Rd., tel. (02) 361-0743; Landmark Plaza, Sukumvit Soi 3, tel. (02) 253-5839; Peninsula Plaza, Rajadamri Rd., tel. (02) 253-9786; Thaniya Plaza, Silom Rd., tel. (02) 231-2106; Times Square, Sukumvit Soi 12, tel. (02) 250-0162; World Trade Center, Rajadamri Rd., tel. (02) 255-6209.

D.K. (Duang Kamol) Books: Khun Suk Soongsang, founder and chair of Duang Kamol, opened his first bookstore at Siam Square in 1970, which he named after a book written by a close friend. Today, D.K. is Thailand's largest book distributor with over 60 stores nationwide, including 23 in Bangkok alone.

They also run the biggest bookshop in Thailand at Seacon Square in the suburb of Bangkapi. This superstore, the size of a football field, displays almost one million books, plus puts on publishing seminars, writing workshops, book signings, and special exhibitions. The store also includes a restaurant and "vinotech" offering quality wines personally selected by Khun Suk, a well-known wine connoisseur.

A few D.K. outlets include: Mahboonkrong Centre, Rama 1 Rd., tel. (02) 217-9301; Pratunam, 90/21 Ratchaprarob Rd., tel. (02) 245-5586; Seacon Square, Srinakarin Rd., tel. (02) 393-8040; Siam Square, Rama 1 Rd. Soi 2, tel. (02) 251-1467; Sukumvit Centre, Sukumvit Soi 8, tel. (02) 252-6261.

Independent Bookstores
A handful of both small and large bookstores are scattered around town.

Kinokuniya: Just about the largest selection of English-language books in town with everything from glossy, coffee table tomes to classics and regional guides. Emporium Shopping Center, Sukumvit Soi 24, tel. (02) 664-8554.

The Bookseller: Excellent selection of English-language books and foreign magazines, plus discount tables for bargains. 81 Patpong Rd., tel. (02) 233-1717.

Book Gallery: Limited number of books but Bangkok's best selection of international magazines. 12/1 Sukumvit Soi 33, tel. (02) 260-6215.

Fine Arts Gift Shop: Specializes in art, music, and Asian culture in a logical location just opposite the Royal Palace near Silapkorn University. Naprathat Rd.

White Lotus: For new and rare books on Asia, plus old maps and prints, order their catalog at GPO Box 1141, Bangkok 10501. White Lotus was relocating as of this writing.

Used Books
Used English-language books are carried at the following bookstores and markets.

Chatuchak Weekend Market: Visit sections 22 and 25 to plough through enormous stacks of used antiquarian books and magazines, including back issues of *Sawasdee* magazine. Paholyothin Rd. Weekends 0900-1800.

Elite Used Books: An old favorite that stocks titles on subjects from fiction and travel to politics and history. This is where most of the expats in Bangkok trade their books for newer titles. 593/5 Sukumvit Soi 33, tel. (02) 258-0221.

Khao San Road: All sorts of backpacker books, including ragged copies of Moon Publications' *Southeast Asia Handbook*. Shops here sell everything used from modern and classic literature to popular fiction, new age novels, used travel guides, and foreign-language novels.

Libraries
Libraries in Bangkok are good places to escape the heat and conduct some background research on the country.

National Library: One of the few libraries in the country, the National Library north of Banglampoo has a small number of English-language books but an extensive selection of Thai manuscripts. The air-conditioned periodicals room has a good stock of English-language magazines. Samsen Rd., tel. (02) 281-5212. Open daily 0930-1930.

Chulalongkorn University: Thailand's premier institution of higher education has an extensive range of books which can be read in an air-conditioned environment. Visitors can purchase a one-day membership pass which allows use of computers equipped with CD-ROM and Internet access. Phayathai Rd., tel. (02) 215-4100. Open daily except Sunday 0900-2100.

American University Alumni (AUA): Features a decent library sponsored by the U.S. Information Service, plus a good selection of American magazines and background reading on Thai history and culture. Visitors can borrow books and use the photocopy machine. 179 Rajadamri Rd., tel. (02) 252-8953. Open weekdays 0800-1700.

Neilson Hays Library: Constructed in 1922 by Dr. Hays to commemorate his wife (Jennie Neilson Hays) and her devotion to the Bangkok Ladies Library Association, this historic structure offers over 20,000 hardbacks, a magazine section, used paperbacks for sale, and a Rotunda Gallery that sponsors monthly art exhibitions and sales. Visitors can browse but membership is required to check out books. 195 Suriwong Rd. near the British Club, tel. (02) 233-1731. Open daily 0930-1600.

Siam Society: The scholarly collection of books at the Siam Society attracts a continual stream of visitors conducting research on the arts, culture, customs, and history of Thailand. Now holding over 10,000 volumes, the library preserves many rare and valuable works, some photocopied and rebound or microfilmed for permanent storage. Informative brochures and booklets are sold at the front desk, but only members are allowed to enter the research facilities. Sukumvit Soi 21, tel. (02) 258-3491. Open Tues.-Sat. 0900-1600.

HEALTH

Medical Care

All of the following hospitals have English-speaking doctors; many are foreign trained and familiar with Western medicine. All provide 24-hour emergency service, ambulances, and a full range of medical and surgical work.

Treatment prices vary depending on the hospital and the patient's needs, but standard private rooms with meals average 1,500-3,500B per day, extra for VIP rooms. Rooms are modern, clean, and luxuriously furnished with color TV, stocked fridge, bathroom with amenities, sofa, coffee table, and balcony.

A deposit of 20,000B is generally required on arrival and all major credit cards are accepted. For longer stays, health insurance can be obtained from Blue Cross (tel. 02-235-5832) and South East Insurance (tel. 02-233-7080).

Recommended hospitals include: **Bangkok Christian Hospital,** 124 Silom Rd., tel. (02) 233-6981; **Bangkok General Hospital,** Soi Soonvijai (Soi 47), New Petchburi Rd., tel. (02) 318-0066, fax (02) 318-1546; **Bangkok Adventist Mission Hospital,** 430 Phitsanulok Rd., tel. (02) 281-1422; **Bumrungrad Hospital,** 33 Soi 3, Sukumvit Rd., tel. (02) 253-0250; **Phayathai Hospital,** 364/1 Sri Ayudhaya Rd., tel. (02) 245-2620; **Samitivej Hospital,** 133 Soi 49, Sukumvit Rd., tel. (02) 392-0011.

Dental Facilities

Hospitals with dental facilities include Bangkok Adventist Mission, Bangkok General, Bumrungrad, and Samitivej. The following clinics have English-speaking dentists. Call for an appointment.

Dental Polyclinic, 211/3 New Petchburi Rd., tel. (02) 314-5070; **Dental Hospital,** 88 Soi 49, Sukumvit Rd., tel. (02) 260-5000; **Orthodontic Centre,** 542/1 Ploenchit Rd., tel. (02) 251-7613; **Ploenchit Clinic,** Maneeya Bldg., Ploenchit Rd., tel. (02) 251-1567; **Siam Dental Clinic,** 412/11 Soi 6, Siam Square, tel. (02) 251-6315.

MAIL

The Bangkok General Post Office (GPO) on Charoen Krung Road is open weekdays 0800-1800 and weekends and holidays 0900-1300. The GPO is a five-minute walk from the Tha Muang stop of the Chao Praya River Express.

Postal branch offices with overseas telephone services are located in several neighborhoods: Banglampoo, Trok Mayom Rd.; Silom, 113/6 Suriwong Center Rd.; Sukumvit, Sukumvit Soi 4; Sukumvit, Sukumvit Soi 23.

Mail Pickup

When retrieving mail, bring your passport or other legal identification to the poste restante counter. The service fee is 1B for each piece of mail, 2B per parcel. Letters held over three months are returned to sender.

Letters sent to you should be marked "hold" and directed to poste restante, the French term for general delivery. Since Thais write their last name first and their first names last, postal clerks sometimes misfile letters under the first name ("given" name) rather than the surname ("family"

ประเทศไทย THAILAND

name). To ensure proper delivery, family names should be both capitalized and underlined on the outside of the envelope. If missing anticipated mail, ask the postal clerk to check under your first name.

Mail intended for the Bangkok GPO should be addressed: NAME, Poste Restante, General Post Office, Charoen Krung Rd., Bangkok, Thailand 10500.

All mail should be registered and receipts retained to trace missing parcels. It's a good idea to insure valuable parcels at the rate of 10B per 2,000B value of goods.

Travelers with an American Express credit card or using American Express traveler's checks can receive mail at the AMEX office at Sea Tours, tel. (02) 251-4862, in Siam Center, Suite 414, 965 Rama I Rd., Bangkok. A complete list of AMEX offices is available from AMEX (tel. 800-528-4800) in their booklet, *Travelers Companion*.

Packing Procedures

All packages must be officially boxed and sealed at special counters inside the main post office or at nearby private agencies. Don't pack a box and expect to just drop it at the post office. You must bring all goods to the post office for inspection, purchase a cardboard box and string, pack your goods, weigh the contents, purchase stamps, then deliver your assembled masterpiece to the appropriate window.

Packing services inside the Bangkok GPO do all the work for a reasonable fee. Private packing agencies located nearby can help with the packing and shipping of parcels over 20 kg.

Express Delivery Services

Packages requiring overseas delivery within four days can be sent via Express Mail Service (EMS)

from the Bangkok GPO. The cost is 320B per 250 grams, or US$22 per pound.

Fast delivery services are also offered by commercial shippers such as DHL, Federal Express, UPS, and TNT Express.

PHONE

International Calls

International calls from Thailand are made by dialing the international access code for Thailand (001), followed by the country code (listed in the On the Road chapter), the area code, and finally the local number. Calls can be made from hotels, businesses, most post offices, and CAT Telecom Centers.

International calls at the lowest possible prices are available with discount calling plans offered by AT&T USA Direct, MCI Call USA, and Sprint Global Fone. These programs allow travelers to dial a toll-free access number (listed below) and speak

USEFUL BANGKOK PHONE NUMBERS
(Bangkok area code is 02)

Airport (Arrivals)	535-1301
Airport (Departures)	535-1385
Airport (Domestic)	535-1253
Airport (International)	535-1111
Eastern Bus Terminal (a/c)	391-9829
Eastern Bus Terminal (Ordinary)	391-2504
Fire	199
General Post Office	233-1050
Hualampong Train Station (Info.)	223-7010
Hualampong Train Station (Advanced Booking)	223-3762
Immigration	286-9176
International Calls	100
Northern Bus Terminal (a/c)	279-4484
Northern Bus Terminal (Ordinary)	271-0101
Phone Information	13
Southern Bus Terminal (a/c)	391-9829
Southern Bus Terminal (Ordinary)	434-5558
Tourist Police	1699
Crime Suppression Div.	225-0085
Train Station	223-7010

directly with an operator in their home country. For more information on these programs, see **Telephone** under in the On the Road chapter.

Discount calls through AT&T, MCI, and Sprint can also be made on special "Home Direct" phones at CAT Telecom Centers. To make an international call, fill out the bilingual form with your name and telephone details, pay a deposit to cover the estimated cost, and find an empty phone booth to make your call. Larger CAT Telecoms permit you to dial the number, but smaller offices require the assistance of an operator.

Operators are required for collect calls, for person-to-person calls, for station-to-station calls, and to use your international calling card. Operator assistance is 100.

CAT Telecom Centers with Home Direct Phones are located at the GPO on Charoen Krung Road (open 24 hours), the airport post office, the Wall Street Building on Suriwong Road, the Queen Sirikit National Convention Centre, the World Trade Center, Sogo Department Store, the Thaniya Building on Silom Road, and the Banglampoo and Hualampong post offices.

To use the Home Direct service, call 0001-999 followed by the access number. Access numbers for several countries include:

Australia:	61-1000	
Canada:	15-1000	
Germany:	49-1000	
Netherlands:	31-1035	
New Zealand:	64-1066	
UK:	44-1066	
USA:	............AT&T	11111
	MCI	12001
	Sprint	13871

Local Telephone Calls

Pay phones in Bangkok are painted distinct colors and often marked with a blue triangle. Phone booths painted with red roofs and red horizontal stripes are for local calls only, which cost 1B for three minutes. Note that only the medium-sized 1B coin fits the slot. Warning beeps signal the end of the three-minute period, but additional coins will keep the line open. The remaining time is noted by a small display inside the booth.

Local calls can also be made from small pay phones inside restaurants, hotels, and shops. Most are painted a bright red or pale blue and cost 5B for three minutes.

Domestic Long-Distance Calls

The phone booths painted with blue roofs and metallic stripes are for long-distance calls within Thailand. These phones accept 1B, 5B, and 10B coins but are rarely seen outside Bangkok and busy tourist zones.

Local and domestic long-distance calls can also be made from "card phones" located in supermarkets, financial districts, and hotel districts. Card phones are painted with green stripes and only accept payment by telephone cards. Markets and shops such as 7-Eleven sell phone cards in 100B denominations.

Domestic long-distance phone calls are made by dialing the area code followed by the local phone number. Area codes for Thailand are listed in the chart "Telephone Area Codes within Thailand" in the On the Road chapter.

TRANSPORTATION

AIRPORT ARRIVAL

Bangkok International Airport
Bangkok's **Don Muang International Airport,** 25 km north of the city, is a busy, modern place with all the standard facilities.

After arrival, you first pass through immigration control to have your visa stamped or to obtain a 30-day Permit to Stay, which is stamped on your immigration card, not in your passport. Custom formalities is fastest through the green lanes marked "Nothing to Declare."

Passengers connecting directly to domestic flights to Chiang Mai, Phuket, Ko Samui, and Hat Yai can take the free shuttle bus to the domestic terminal.

After immigration and customs, you enter the arrival lounge filled with irritating taxi touts who direct you toward expensive private coaches and limousines; give these guys a miss unless you want to pay double the ordinary rate.

The arrival lounge has a post office, left-luggage facilities that charge 20B per day per item, an emergency medical clinic staffed 24 hours a day, and international and local phones. Two restaurants, including an inexpensive self-service cafe and a deluxe joint, are located on the fourth floor. Baggage trolleys are free.

Tourist Office: First stop should be the Tourism Authority of Thailand counter for maps, weekly magazines, and other free information. Current prices for transportation into town are posted here.

Thai Hotel Association: Hotel reservations at member hotels can be made at the adjacent THA counter. They will also call and check on room vacancies, but the cheapest listing (the Miami Hotel) starts at 800B per night. For information on accommodations near the airport, see the **Airport Area** accommodations earlier in this chapter.

Airport Bank: While some airports in Asia offer poor exchange rates, rates are very good at the Thai Military Bank inside the arrival lounge.

Taxi into Bangkok
Bangkok's hotels are 30-90 minutes from the airport depending on traffic. A variety of transportation is available, but ordinary taxis and minibuses are the most popular choices.

Metered taxis are the best option for groups of travelers and solo travelers who want to quickly reach their hotel. A few private taxi companies have offices inside the arrival terminal, but these services are more expensive than the ordinary metered taxis outside.

Finding the taxi booth outside is somewhat tricky since there are few signs pointing the way. Go out the front door then walk left about 100 meters until you see the taxi booth on the sidewalk. You pick up a ticket from one of the girls working the counter and then give this ticket to the next available taxi driver. This coupon system is intended to discourage cheating by the taxi drivers.

When you get in your taxi, be sure the driver turns on his meter. Your fare will be the meter total, plus another 50B airport surcharge, plus whatever tolls are collected on the way. It's best to pay your toll directly rather than let the driver pay for you.

Some hotels only require that you drive on a single tollway, while more distant hotels such as those near Silom Road require travel on two tollways. As of this writing, each tollway costs 30B and the average taxi fare is 200-300B. To reach an Silom Road hotel such as the Oriental would therefore cost 250B taxi fare, plus 50B airport surcharge, plus 60B for two tollways, giving a total of 360B to this particular hotel.

Airport Bus
Several years ago, the Bangkok Mass Transit Authority (BMTA) started running three buses from the airport to various neighborhoods in Bangkok. The fare is 70B per passenger.

The airport bus counter is about 200 m to the left of the arrival lounge. Walk out the door then turn left and walk past the taxi counter to the bus area. Ignore all touts.

Airport Bus A1: This bus heads down the tollway and exits near Victory Monument and then continues down Rajadamri Road to Lumpini Park and Silom Road. This bus reaches the hotels near Pratunam (Indra Regent, Baiyoke Tower, Amari Watergate), Siam Square (Le Meridien President, Grand Hyatt Erawan, Siam Intercontinental, Novotel Siam Square, The Regent), and finally the hotels near Silom Road (Dusit Thani, Pan Pacific, Tawana Ramada, Holiday Inn Crowne Plaza, Oriental, Shangri-La). It can also drop you fairly close to the Malaysia Hotel and guesthouses near Soi Ngam Duphli.

Airport Bus A2: This is the bus for guesthouses and hotels in Banglampoo and along Khao San Road. The bus takes the Don Muang Expressway to Victory Monument to Payathai and Petchaburi roads before heading past Democracy Monument to Banglampoo, where it stops at Tanao Road and drops off all the backpackers heading for Khao San Road. The bus then continues around Banglampoo and terminates at Sanam Luang near the Grand Palace.

Airport Bus A3: This is the bus for hotels on Sukumvit Road. After taking the first expressway to the Din Daeng exit it gets on a second expressway until it makes another exit right at Sukumvit Road. The bus continues down Sukumvit past Soi Asoke (Sukumvit Soi 23) to Ekamai (Soi 53) until it reaches the Eastern Bus Terminal and finally terminates at the Tonglor Police Station.

GETTING AROUND

Bangkok is a hot, bewildering metropolis without any recognizable city center—a place where only the certified insane attempt to walk any great distance. Aside from roaming the neighborhood near your hotel, a taxi, *tuk tuk,* or bus will be necessary. The good news is that public transportation is very cheap; the bad news is that traffic and air pollution are among the world's worst. Avoid rush hours, 0800-1000 and 1500-1800, when the entire city comes to a complete standstill.

Taxis
In 1993, the Thai government passed a law requiring all taxis in Bangkok to install and use meters. In one bold move, the government finally ended one of Thailand's longest nightmares. No more haggling with drivers over the proper fare. No more bailing out of cabs after the driver suddenly doubles the fare en route to your destination. No more bizarre, late-night,

completely baffling routes on a short journey that winds up taking over an hour.

Meter Rates: Metered taxis charge 35B at the outset for the first two km, and 2B for each extra kilometer. Freeway tolls must also be paid by the passenger. Bangkok—the Gridlock Capital of the World—protects the cabdriver by including a surcharge of 1B per minute when the traffic slows to under 5 kph. When you're stuck at a traffic light for 20 minutes or crawling down Sukumvit Road at a speed slower than the average pedestrian (most people *walk* at 5 kph), expect surcharges, then try to relax.

Metered taxis can be ordered by calling (02) 319-9911 24 hours a day.

Taxi Types: Any taxi with the sign "Taxi Meter" will have an installed meter, but the level of service varies between companies. The green-and-yellow taxis are driven by the owners and generally tend to be cleaner and driven with more care. Pink, blue, or red taxis are rented from various cooperatives and drivers seem to have less regard for the value of human life or the general appearance of their vehicle. Taxis with signs proclaiming "Taxi Taxi" are hoping that confused tourists will mistake them for a metered taxi. Taxis with black-and-white license plates are illegal; these often overcharge passengers and intimidate tourists with thinly veiled threats.

Problems: A few problems exist with the new system. Some drivers refuse to use meters and will only take passengers at set fares. Other drivers shut down their meters during long traffic jams, then attempt to negotiate a fixed fare. Meters are sometimes altered to run at higher speeds or the driver forgets to reset the meter for the new passenger. You should always check the meter before setting off and refuse to pay any additional surcharges during the journey.

Tuk Tuks
Affectionately named after their obnoxious sounds that resemble chainsaws on acid, these motorized *samlors* are noisy three-wheelers that race around at terrifying speeds, take corners on two wheels, and scream through seemingly impossible gaps. *Tuk tuks* are the cheapest form of private transportation in Bangkok and generally cost 10-20% less than taxis. However, you must bargain hard and settle all fares in advance. Few drivers speak English or understand maps, so

be sure to have your destination written down in Thai or know how to pronounce it properly.

Negotiation is usually done by raising a few fingers to indicate your offer: two for 20B, three for 30. Smile and grin during price negotiation. If the driver won't come down to a reasonable price then do the taxi ballet—walk away shaking your head until he pulls up and waves you inside. Then hold onto your seat.

Buses

The public bus system in Bangkok is operated by the Bangkok Metropolitan Transit Authority (BMTA). Several private bus companies also operate in the city.

Two maps with reasonably complete bus routes include the *Bangkok Bus Map* published by Bangkok Guide, and *Bangkok Thailand Tour'n Guide Map* by Thaveephol Charoen. The *Bangkok & Central Thailand Travel Map* from Periplus Editions also includes a fairly good summary of the bus routes. The English-language BMTA website at www.bmta.motc.go.th/mainframe-services-e.html is also very helpful for current schedules and fares.

Before setting off, study your bus map and write down all possible bus numbers that go to your destination. Service is haphazard and some buses only pass once per hour.

Hours: Ordinary buses run daily 0500-midnight. Visitors unfamiliar with the bus system will find taxis more useful at night. Buses are quite sensible during rush hours when they speed along specially marked lanes.

Types: BMTA buses come in three colors. Light blue-and-white buses have no fan or air conditioning; these are being phased out. Red-and-cream buses have rotating fans to cool off passengers. Dark blue-and-white buses are air-conditioned coaches that can prove surprisingly comfortable.

Fares: Light blue-and-white buses charge 3B for journeys under 10 km and 4B for journeys over 10 km. Red-and-cream buses cost 3.5B for the first 10 km and 5B for longer journeys. The a/c dark blue-and-white buses charge 6B for the first 8 km and up to 16B for the longest distances, such as from the airport to Banglampoo.

The dark-blue a/c buses are relatively plentiful and worth every single extra *baht* over the crowded and hot non-a/c buses.

Minibuses

The BMTA also operates orange and green minibuses that race around town on unpublished routes. Unless you are positive about the destination, avoid these minibuses. Many have the same numbers as the larger buses but go to completely different sections of town.

The latest addition are red-and-gray air-conditioned "microbuses" that guarantee seats for every passenger and provide amenities such as newspapers, video programs, and mobile phones. Microbuses cost 15B and payment must be with exact change, a coupon, or a "smart card." There are 35 routes. All buses display the beginning point and terminus (Bang Khun Thien-Samrong, Siam Park-Silom, for example), but few visitors will be able to use these buses effectively until a route map is published.

Riverboats

The **Chao Phaya Express Boat** is hands-down the best way to move between any locations on the river—especially useful between Banglampoo and the General Post Office. These open-air boats are fast, cheap, exciting, and a refreshing escape from the horrors of land transportation. Boats operate daily 0600-1800 and charge 3-15B depending on the distance.

Two other types of boats work the Chao Praya River. Short and stubby ferries called *reua kham fak* shuttle across the river. These cross-river barges charge 1B per crossing.

The other are noisy longtail boats called *hang yaos,* which roar along several canals in central Bangkok and charge 5-15B depending on their final destination. The longtail service on Pratunam Canal from Pratunam Market to Democracy Monument is quite useful.

TOURS

Budget Travel Agencies

Bangkok has hundreds of budget and full-service travel agencies offering everything from nightclub tours to excursions to Angkor Wat. Most hotels have attached agencies, but check prices carefully before handing over your money. Rates vary widely around town. For example, a one-day tour of the Damnern Saduak floating market costs 700B from travel agents on Silom

Road, but only 300B from discount shops in Banglampoo.

Travelers should also be aware that agencies often fail to deliver the proper ticket or make extravagant promises simply to make the sale. Double check all restrictions and limitations before making any sizable purchase. A few of the larger and more trustworthy travel agencies are listed below.

Student Travel Australia (STA), the world's largest student travel organization, is somewhat more expensive than bucket shops, but you won't need to worry about fraudulent activities. The Head Office is in the Wall Street Tower, 33 Surawong Rd., tel. (02) 233-2633; STA also has an office in Banglampoo: Thai Hotel, 78 Prachatipatai Rd., tel. (02) 281-5314.

ETC Travel is an agency recommended by readers. They staff the following offices: Head Office, Royal Hotel, 2 Rajadamnern Ave., tel. (02) 224-0023; Banglampoo, 180 Khao San Rd., tel. (02) 249-4414; Malaysia Hotel, 5/3 Soi Ngam Duphli, tel. (02) 356-7781.

Other Travel Agencies

Fully escorted tour packages to Vietnam, Cambodia, and Laos can be booked through the following agencies: Diethelm Travels, 140 Wireless Rd., tel. (02) 255-9150, fax (02) 256-0248; Exotissimo Travel, 21/17 Soi 4 Sukumvit, tel. (02) 253-5250, fax (02) 254-7683; SEA Tours, Siam Centre, Rama 1 Rd., Suite 414, tel. (02) 251-4862, fax (02) 253-2960; World Travel, 1053 Charoen Krung Rd., tel. (02) 233-5900, fax (02) 236-7169.

Most travel agencies will also make train reservations and pick up the tickets for you for an additional 100B surcharge. The following four agencies are licensed to make bookings and issue tickets without the surcharge. Airland Travels, 866 Ploenchit Rd., tel. (02) 251-9495; SEA Tours, Siam Centre, Rama 1 Rd., Suite 414, tel. (02) 251-4862; Songserm Travel, 172 Khao San Rd., tel. (02) 282-8080; Songserm Travel, 121 Soi Chalerm, Phayathai Rd., tel. (02) 255-8790; Viang Travels, Viengtai Hotel, 42 Rambutri Rd., tel. (02) 280-1385.

Educational Tours

Travel agents sell the standard assortment of Thailand tours, but many visitors prefer the educational tours sponsored by public and private organizations in Bangkok. Led by archaeologists, art historians, and other experts in their fields, these well-priced tours are highly recommended for all visitors.

Siam Society: Bangkok's leading private cultural organization sponsors monthly group tours to important historical and archaeological sites in Thailand. They also take groups to major festivals and conduct environmental surveys in national parks through their natural history section. Upcoming tours in Thailand and to Myanmar, Angkor, and China are listed in the *Bangkok Post.* For further information, call the Siam Society office in Bangkok or write and request a copy of their monthly newsletter, which lists upcoming lectures and group tours. Yearly membership at 1,500B includes access to their 20,000-volume library, subscriptions to the *Siam Society Newsletter* and *Journal of the Siam Society,* free admission to most lectures, and discounts on Society books and study trips. Siam Society, 131 Sukumvit 21, Soi Asoke (Soi 21), Bangkok 10110, tel. (02) 258-3491 or (02) 258-3494.

National Museum: The National Museum occasionally sponsors tours similar to the Siam Society's. Check the bulletin board in the museum ticket office for upcoming tours.

Volunteer Guide Group: Unique and personalized tours of Bangkok temples, plus overnight visits to nearby villagers, can be arranged through a small student-run group in Bangkok. Each visitor is accompanied by a student guide who will explain local customs and traditions. Public transportation is used and the tour is free except for a membership fee of 100B and travel expenses for your guide. Volunteer Guide Group, Box 24-1013, Ramkamheng Rd., Bangkok 10241.

GETTING AWAY

By Air

Metered taxis to the airport cost 250-350B including tollway surcharges and take 30-90 minutes depending on traffic. Excess *baht* can be reexchanged into foreign currency at the Thai Military Bank, and last-minute international phone calls can be made from the phone booth in the arrival lounge. The fourth floor features an inexpensive food mall and a semi-luxurious restaurant operated by Thai International.

Airport departure tax is 500B for international flights and 100B for domestic flights.

By Train

Trains are the best form of transportation when leaving Bangkok. Operated by the State Railway of Thailand (SRT), trains are clean and comfortable, fares are inexpensive, and there is no more pleasant or scenic way to enjoy the countryside. Trains are also much safer than buses and provide an excellent way to meet other travelers and the Thai people. Many of the coaches have attached restaurant cars where you order a meal and enjoy a beer before slipping back into your a/c sleeping berth.

Perhaps the chief advantage is that train routes get you off the crowded highways and carry you through countryside unblemished by factories, housing tracts, and other signs of progress. Unlike a bus where you are pinned to your seat, a train lets you wander around the coach or throw open the window to enjoy the passing views.

See "By Train" under "Getting Around" in the On the Road chapter for more information on train types, classes, fares, and sleeping berths.

Hualampong Train Station: Bangkok has two train stations. Hualampong, tel. (02) 223-7010, on Rama IV Rd. is the main station from where most trains arrive and depart.

Bangkok Noi Train Station: This station, tel. (02) 411-3102, on Arun Amarin Rd. in Thonburi, is used by local trains to Hua Hin and Kanchanaburi.

Schedules: Train schedules are available free of charge from the Rail Travel Aids counter in Bangkok's Hualampong station—handy resources for anyone riding the trains in Thailand.

Several types of schedules are available. The condensed English-language timetables include fares and schedules for selected trains on the four primary trunk lines. Condensed Thai-language schedules are also available, as are unabridged Thai-language timetables that include fares and schedules for all trains on all lines.

To obtain further information, contact the Hualampong Information Counter at (02) 223-7010 or (02) 223-7020.

Advance Bookings: Train reservations can be made 90 days in advance at Bangkok's Hualampong train station. Be sure to reserve a seat at least one week in advance during holidays, during weekends, and on popular routes such as Bangkok to Chiang Mai or Hat Yai.

Reservations can be made Mon.-Fri. 0830-1600 and weekends and holidays 0830-noon at the Advance Booking Office (tel. 02-223-3762 or 223-7788) in the back-right corner of Hualampong station. Ticket windows on the left side of the station are for same-day purchases. To make a reservation, take a queue number and wait for your number to appear on one of the electronic boards, then report to the proper desk for your particular line—southern or north and northeastern.

Travel Agencies: Reservations can also be made through travel agencies in Bangkok. Authorized agents who can make reservations and deliver tickets without a service charge are listed in the preceding section on Tours. All other agencies will generally charge around 200-400B to collect the ticket.

By Bus

Provinces throughout Thailand can easily be reached with public and private buses. Bangkok has three public bus terminals which serve different sections of the country. Each station has different departments for ordinary and air-conditioned buses. All are well organized and have English-language signs over most ticket windows. Visitors are often approached by employees who direct them to the appropriate bus. Departures are frequent for most destinations throughout Thailand; the most difficult task is reaching the terminal!

Northern/Northeastern Bus Terminal: Destinations in the north and northeast are served by two sprawling, adjacent terminals on Paholyothin Road, on the highway toward the airport near Chatuchak Market. This terminal is often called Moh Chit station. Take any bus going toward the airport; some numbers include 2AC, 3AC, 9AC, 10AC, 13AC, 29AC, and 39AC. Look for the modern complex on the right side of the highway. The Northern Terminal is divided into two wings. The first section on the right is for air-conditioned coaches (tel. 02-279-4484), the second for ordinary buses (tel. 02-271-0101).

BUSES FROM BANGKOK: ROUTES AND FARES

DESTINATION	KM	HOURS	ORDINARY	A/C	VIP
EAST COAST					
Pattaya	136	2	35B	65B	80B
Chanthaburi	240	6	50B	100B	40B
Trat	320	8	80B	150B	200B
NORTH					
Ayuthaya	75	1.5	25B	36B	50B
Phitsanulok	365	5.5	95B	165B	240B
Lampang	610	9.5	150B	270B	330B
Nan	680	11	170B	290B	340B
Chiang Mai	715	10	160B	300B	480B
Chiang Rai	850	12	190B	360B	530B
NORTHEAST					
Korat	250	5	65B	120B	200B
Khon Kaen	445	7	110B	200B	300B
Nong Khai	615	9	150B	280B	420B
Ubon Ratchathani	679	10	160B	300B	440B
SOUTH					
Kanchanaburi	100	2	25B	50B	60B
Hua Hin	205	4	70B	100B	130B
Surat Thani	670	11	160B	285B	360B
Trang	865	14	195B	370B	400B
Krabi	870	14	195B	380B	420B
Phuket	890	14	200B	380B	450B
Hat Yai	990	16	240B	430B	500B

Southern Bus Terminal: All buses to southern Thailand depart from the new terminal on Nakhon Chaisri Road in Thonburi. To reach the terminal, try buses 7AC, 11AC, 124, or 127. Tickets are sold from the windows near the main road. Call (02) 391-9827 (a/c) and (02) 434-5558 (ordinary) for further information.

Eastern Bus Terminal: The Eastern Bus Terminal on Sukumvit Road near Soi 63 serves east coast resorts such as Pattaya, Rayong, Ko Samet, and Ko Chang. This terminal is often called Ekamai. Take any bus going down Sukumvit and watch for the small terminal on the right. Call (02) 391-9829 or 392-9227 for information on a/c services, and (02) 391-2504 for regular buses.

Private Buses: In addition to these three government-run terminals, a dozen-plus small, independent bus companies operate from private terminals located throughout the city. Private buses are 30-50% more expensive than government buses, but complimentary meals and hotel pickup are often provided, an important consideration in Bangkok. Private buses can be booked through travel agents, but compare prices carefully as they vary enormously.

EAST COAST

With over 2,600 km of coastline along the Gulf of Thailand and Andaman Sea, Thailand offers a wide selection of beaches and resorts with everything from first-class resorts to perfect tranquility on unspoiled islands. While most of the better beaches and island resorts are located down south, the east coast between Bangkok and Cambodia is blessed with good beaches and pristine islands that can be reached in less than a day from Bangkok with public transportation.

But the east coast is more than just beaches and offshore islands. It is an area rich in natural resources where Thailand's future has been laid. Government officials and economic planners have chosen the eastern seaboard as the new economic growth zone for the 21st century. Discoveries of immense deposits of natural gas and the urgent need for an alternative deepwater port to Bangkok have brought massive development on an unparalleled scale. City planners envision a megalopolis of cities stretching from Bangkok to Rayong, forming a gigantic economic engine which would rival the eastern seaboard of the United States and the Tokyo-Osaka region.

Pattaya—the original beach resort in Thailand—is now flanked by the deepwater port at Laem Chabang to the north and massive oil refineries to the south. Entire cities, soon to be home to over a million Thai citizens, are under construction at breakneck speed. More than any other region, the east coast represents the future of Thailand.

Sightseeing Highlights
The twin attributes of beach resorts and economic development have given the east coast a schizoid personality that combines pleasure with business. The end result of all this development is that the best tourist destinations are being pushed farther east toward Cambodia as travelers seek out the more idyllic beaches and islands. Visitors with sufficient time may enjoy a leisurely journey, stopping at each of the following destinations, but hurried travelers should head directly to the beach or island that has the strongest appeal. Distances from Bangkok appear after each destination.

Bang Saen (103 km): Although rarely visited by Western visitors, Bang Saen is a pleasant

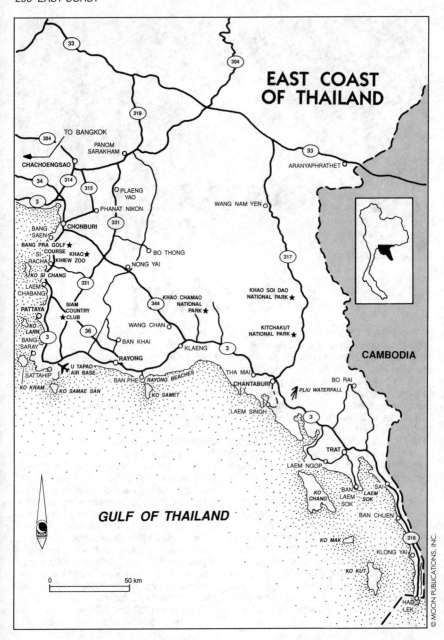

EAST COAST OF THAILAND

beach with an authentic Thai flavor where locals come to picnic and relax on beach chairs. The beach is surprisingly clean and relatively deserted during the week. Day-trippers might consider a quick visit to Bang Saen rather than fight the traffic farther south to Pattaya.

Si Racha and Ko Si Chang (118 km): The busy little fishing town of Si Racha chiefly serves as departure point for the long, narrow island of Ko Si Chang. The southern tip of the island holds the remains of an old royal summer palace used by King Chulalongkorn in the late 19th century. Though a very modest historical monument, Ko Si Chang can easily be visited en route to Pattaya.

Pattaya (137 km): After two decades of uncontrolled growth, Thailand's original beach resort is trying to restore its image with an aggressive and highly publicized improvement campaign. The resort's personality is split between upscale hotels catering to families and group tours, and a raucous nightlife suited to bachelors and sailors. Pattaya's mediocre beach compensates with all types of recreation from parasailing to scuba diving.

Rayong (185 km): Rayong town is an uninspiring place but the southern coastline offers fairly good sand and accommodations from budget bungalows to mid-range hotels.

Ko Samet (210 km): Discovered by budget travelers a decade ago, Ko Samet is now favored by Thai families and group tourists rushing down from Pattaya. The island offers some of the cleanest and finest sand in Thailand, though its popularity and easy accessibility have brought problems of overdevelopment and pollution. Budget travelers have largely abandoned Ko Samet for the more remote island of Ko Chang.

Chanthaburi (320 km): The large town of Chanthaburi lies in an area famed for rubber, rubies, and tropical fruits such as rambutan and durian. Chanthaburi is a rather ordinary town aside from its gem industry and nearby natural attractions such as waterfalls and national parks.

Trat (315 km): Thailand's southeasternmost province and town is the jumping-off point for the islands scattered along the Thai-Cambodian border. Most travelers head directly to Laem Ngop, 15 km southeast, where boats leave throughout the day for Ko Chang and other tropical islands.

Ko Chang (360 km): Thailand's second-largest island after Phuket was officially opened to tourism in 1990 after a series of travel articles publicized its wonderful beaches and unspoiled topography. Following the development cycle of Phuket and Ko Samui, Ko Chang will unquestionably be Thailand's next major island resort as sun-lovers relentlessly march eastward in search of the perfect beach. Over a dozen islands are located farther south, perhaps the final island escapes in Thailand.

Getting There

All of the east coast beaches are located along the Sukumvit Highway (Route 3), which stretches almost 400 km from central Bangkok to the Cambodian border. Buses from Bangkok's Eastern Bus Terminal (Ekamai) on Sukumvit Road depart every 15-30 minutes throughout the day for all possible destinations on the eastern seaboard. Buses to distant destinations such as Chanthaburi and Trat leave mornings only, 0600-noon.

Private bus and tour operators offer similar services in small air-conditioned minivans to major destinations such as Pattaya, Ko Samet, and Ko Chang. Private minibuses are convenient since pickup is made from your hotel in Bangkok, though public buses from the Eastern Bus Terminal are cheaper, safer, just as fast, and much more comfortable for the long haul.

BANGKOK TO PATTAYA

BANG SAEN

Southeast of Bangkok, six km past the commercial city of Chonburi, lies the beach resort of Bang Saen. Once the premier weekend escape for Bangkokians, Bang Saen was replaced by Pattaya after the arrival of better highways and faster buses. Today it caters to economy-minded Thai families and groups of teenagers, who rest under umbrellas or stroll along the two-km-long beach lined with coconut palms and casuarina trees.

Buses from Bangkok stop just beyond the Bang Saen intersection. Minitrucks continue four km down the road to the beach.

Attractions

Bang Saen is only average as a beach resort, though the lack of high-powered development gives it a degree of charm and a refreshingly laid-back atmosphere. A small information office is located adjacent to Ocean World.

The Beach: The beach itself is clean and relatively uncrowded on weekdays, but solidly

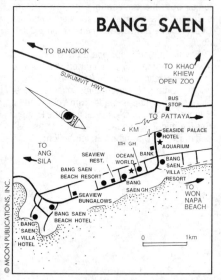

packed on weekends and holidays. The water varies from a nice marine blue to muddy shallows at low tide. Beachside vendors rent multicolored umbrellas, chairs, and inner tubes, and sell snacks and beverages. Being a novelty at the Bang Saen beach, Westerners often find themselves invited to join locals for food and endless rounds of Mekong.

Ocean World: Popular with Thai parents and their children, this water amusement park has several swimming pools, slides, and a small roller coaster. Open daily 0930-1800.

University Aquarium: The medium-sized aquarium, on the road between the highway and the beach, was presented in 1982 to Srinakharinwirot University by the Japanese government. Tropical marine life from the Gulf of Thailand is featured.

Monkey Cliff: A community of wild monkeys inhabits the hill and Chinese shrine at the north end of Bang Saen beach. The small temple honors the goddess spirit of a wife whose fisherman husband never returned from a fishing expedition. Chinese ascribe magical powers to the site and come to fly kites to honor the faithful wife.

Khao Khiew Open Zoo: Tour groups often visit this open-air zoo located 18 km from Bang Saen up a side road off Sukumvit Highway. The zoo was opened in 1973 to provide overflow for the cramped Dusit Zoo in Bangkok.

Bang Pra Golf Course: Located midway up the road to the zoo, the 18-hole, 7,249-yard course has a 54-room motel, lodge, and swimming pool. Tambon Bang Pra, Bangkok reservation tel. (02) 240-9170, 1,500-2,300B.

Accommodations

Bang Saen Villa Resort: The only hotel on the beach; it has a swimming pool, airy restaurant, and small banquet room. 140-16 Mu 14 Tambon Saensuk, Chonburi 20130, tel. (038) 381772, fax (038) 383221, 680-980B.

Bang Saen Beach Resort: A 40-acre landscaped resort with swimming pool, "gathering terrace," and accommodations in the 29-room hotel complex and 102 individual bungalows. The resort is operated by the TAT as a training site for their nearby College of Tourism. 55-150 Tambon Saensuk, Chonburi 20130, Bangkok tel. (02) 428-3262, local tel. (038) 381675, 550-750B fan bungalows, 800-1,200B a/c.

Guesthouses: Several inexpensive guesthouses in the 300-500B range are located on the beachfront road near Ocean World. Try the Seaside Palace, Seaview Bungalows, Picnic, and Sansabai Bungalows.

SI RACHA

The next place of interest on Sukumvit Highway is the busy fishing village of Si Racha, best known as the production center for a pungent sweet fish sauce called *nam prik si racha*. Si Racha has won awards as the cleanest town in the kingdom. Facilities include several banks, postal center, and immigration office.

Attractions
Temples: Surasak 2 Singha Road has the small Wat Sri Maha Racha on the north side, and a larger Chinese temple in a back alley to the south. The market is worth a wander, as are the stilted houses flanking the nearby pier.

Ko Loi: For a quick trip, ask the *samlor* driver to take you to a famous offshore island linked to the mainland by a 1.5-km bridge. Here you can visit the Ko Loi Temple featuring a *chedi, viharn,* and lifelike wax statue of a monk known for his miraculous healing powers. In 1959 the monk disappeared for good, allegedly with all the donations, but superstitious Thais continue to visit his shrine. The causeway is flanked with colorful fishing boats laden with arrow-shaped fish traps constructed from nipa palm. Fare is 10B each direction.

Accommodations
Few visitors spend the night in Si Racha, though several inexpensive hotels are located along the waterfront and on the roads which connect the highway with the seashore. All have breezy open-air restaurants where you can enjoy the local seafood specialties.

Samchai Hotel: Located on the rickety pier across from Surasak 1 Road, the Samchai has both fan-cooled and a/c rooms. 3 Chomchonpon Rd., tel. (038) 311134, 140-200B fan, 350B a/c.

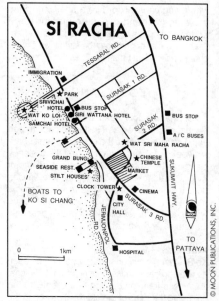

Siri Wattana Hotel: Another seaside hotel offering rooms with or without private bath, plus views over the ocean; probably the best budget choice in town. 35 Chomchonpon Rd., tel. (038) 311307, 140-160B.

Grand Bungalows: Better rooms are found in the hotel on the southern pier. 9 Chomchonpon Rd., tel. (038) 311079, 400-1,000B.

Restaurants
Seafood Restaurants: Lining the seafront are several seafood restaurants serving local specialties such as sautéed oysters and shellfish. One popular restaurant is located at the end of the pier past the houses on stilts. Few have English menus or list prices, so check carefully before ordering.

Central Market: The most economical spot for meals is the market near the clock tower and opposite city hall.

Home & Garden Restaurant: On Jermjonpol Road near the Sukumvit Highway is a more luxurious if less atmospheric restaurant.

Transportation
Buses from Bangkok's Eastern Bus Terminal take about 60 minutes to reach Si Racha, from

where you can walk or hire a *samlor* down to the waterfront and departure pier for Ko Si Chang. Hail buses to Bangkok and Pattaya from the highway or depart from the station on Chomchonpon Road just past the Srivichai Hotel.

KO SI CHANG

Ko Si Chang, about 12 km off the coast from Si Racha, once served as Thailand's custom port and was listed among the country's most popular weekend destinations. Today it's a sleepy place chiefly visited for the decaying palace of King Chulalongkorn and its highly revered Chinese temple. The long and narrow island has a small fishing village with several guesthouses and an arid climate suitable for prickly pear cactus and other desert plants.

Attractions

Ko Si Chang's two principal sights can be seen as you approach on the boat ride from Si Racha: a Chinese temple standing prominently to the right, and the ruins of the old royal palace to the left. Si Chang is very compact and both sites are within walking distance from the arrival pier. Alternatively, hire a *samlor* for a three-hour, 80B tour that includes the Chinese temple, the old royal place, a tiny beach on the north coast, mango plantations, and a Buddhist cave in the center of the island.

Chinese Temple: It's a hot climb up to San Chao Por Khao Yai, but you're rewarded with outstanding marbled floors inside the shrine, a cool natural grotto with Buddha images, plus a Buddha's footprint and excellent views from the 268-meter summit. This temple is much revered by the Chinese, who visit the shrine in great numbers at Chinese New Year.

Chulalongkorn's Summer Palace: The ruins of King Rama V's old summer retreat are one km left of town at the end of a roadway too narrow for cars. Construction began in 1889 after Rama's physician recommended Si Chang as a place of rest and recuperation for his royal consort and her son. Among the early buildings were the two-story Wattana Palace, the octagonal-shaped Phongsri on a nearby hill, and the Aphirom with front and rear porches. A well was dug to supply water, a lighthouse erected to provide

safe passage for passing ships, and 26 roads constructed to link the scattered residences.

In 1892 the king erected a royal compound with four throne halls, 14 royal domiciles, and a royal hillside *chedi* to honor the birth of his new son. Constructed entirely of teakwood, one of the four throne halls was later disassembled and transferred to Bangkok, where it was restored and reopened as the Vimanmek Palace. The final visit to Ko Si Chang of King Chulalongkorn in 1893 was cut short when French gunships, in a territorial dispute, attacked the Thai Navy and occupied the island from 1893 until 1907.

The remaining buildings were deserted and largely disassembled for firewood over time until 1978, when Chulalongkorn University established a marine science research center on the island. In 1991 the Thai government in conjunction with the Fine Arts Department announced an ambitious restoration project.

The surviving foundations, crumbling staircases, beautiful flowering trees, and eerie reservoir blanketed with dead leaves form a pleasant if somewhat unspectacular sight. The Bell

WEIRD WHEELS

*T*he most amazing sidelight to Si Racha is its bizarre but strangely elegant *samlors*, three-wheeled motorbike-rickshaws elongated to outrageous lengths and fitted with huge car or smaller motorcycle engines. Originally constructed from Harley Davidson bikes, these contraptions roamed the streets of Bangkok before being banished to Si Racha since they were not equipped with reverse gears. All have numbers painted on the side, which serve as license plates. Local drivers include Thongkam Sonri, who parks his tricycle near the Savings Bank; Somsak Parnsomboon, who hails from Lopburi; and Urai Chantawat, one of the few female drivers in Si Racha. All can provide sightseeing tours at about 60B per hour.

Unfortunately, their days are numbered since new licenses are no longer issued. The original 499 vehicles now number under 100, and the remaining permits command up to 10,000B each. Motorcycle enthusiasts will love these contraptions!

Rock near the top of the hill rings nicely when struck with a stick. It's hard to locate: look for Thai script in yellow paint. The Asdangnimitr Temple, farther up the hill, once served as the king's meditation chambers but is now locked to protect Rama's portrait and a Buddha image cursed with ungainly large ears.

Budget Accommodations
A few basic guesthouses are located near the dock, but it's more pleasant to stay outside town on a beach.

Camping: Camping is permitted anywhere on the island, including all the beaches and even the grounds of the old royal palace.

Tiew Pai Guesthouse: The most accessible and among the more popular choices is the simple guesthouse with clean rooms at the south end of town. The management offers half-day boat trips around the island that stop at Hin Klom (Round Stone Beach) and small Tawang Beach for swimming and snorkeling. Scuba divers can explore underwater wrecks during the dive season Nov.-February. Atsadang Rd., tel. (038) 216048, 60B dorm, 150-200B fan, 400-600B air-conditioned.

Benz Bungalow: A crazy and creative place unlike the cookie-cutter molds of most Thai hotels. The owner has formed eccentric bungalows from local stone rather than the standard cinder block, and added fans or air-conditioning for his clientele. Benz is located on the road to Tha Wong Beach, just before the entrance to the Aquatic Resources Research Institute, or about one km south of the ferry pier. Hire a *tuk tuk* if your pack is overloaded. Hat Tha Wong Rd., tel. (038) 216091, 400B fan, 600B a/c.

Green House: Travelers happy to stay near the rather rustic town might try the simple but clean guesthouse toward the Chinese temple on the edge of town. Atsadang Rd., tel. (038) 216024, 100-140B.

Sri Pitsanuk Bungalow: A more remote spot but a great location on the edge of a cliff overlooking Hat Tham Beach. It's a one-km walk past the Tiew Pai Guesthouse up the narrow road heading to the tiny beach. Hat Tham Beach, tel. (038) 216024, 300-880B.

Top Bungalows: Just before Sri Pitsanuk is another set of bungalows owned and operated by a local taxi driver, but the rooms lack a view and are generally deserted during the day. Hat Tham Beach, tel. (038) 216001, 200-650B.

Moderate Accommodations
Sichang View Resort: One of the rare upscale resorts with better facilities geared to wealthier clients from Bangkok. Also located toward the Chinese temple. Atsadang Rd., tel. (038) 216210, 800-1,200B.

Sichang Palace: A three-story 65-room hotel in the middle of town with swimming pool, restaurant, and all a/c rooms with private baths. Atsadang Rd., tel. (038) 216276, 1,000-1,600B.

Practical Information
All of the following facilities are located in the main town.

Thai Farmers Bank: Currency exchange at reasonable rates. 9 Atsadang Rd., tel. (038) 216132, open Mon.-Fri. 0830-1530.

Post Office: Atsadang Rd., tel. (038) 216227. Standard services but important parcels should be mailed from Bangkok or Pattaya.

Motorcycle Rentals: Motorcycles can be rented at 150B per day at the Tiew Pai Guesthouse from the owner, who also provides advice on hidden beaches and rather obscure destinations.

Transportation
Ko Si Chang can be reached with small fishing boats which depart hourly from the Si Racha pier on Soi 14, between the seafood restaurants. The shuttle sputters past Russian ocean liners, a large naval station, and cargo ships before docking at the island's nondescript Chinese fishing village.

The last boat back to Si Racha departs at 1700.

PATTAYA

Once a sleepy fishing village popular with harried Bangkokians and American GIs on R&R, Pattaya has since mushroomed into a major beach resort smothered with high-rise hotels, roaring discos, fine restaurants, throbbing go-go bars, and lively nightclubs. Those seeking peace and solitude on a deserted beach should forget Pattaya and head south or east to the less commercialized beaches. Visitors who seek out nonstop entertainment and a honky-tonk environment will love Pattaya, one of the most convoluted and schizophrenic destinations in the world.

Today, this low-powered Riviera of Southeast Asia is undergoing an image crisis as it transforms from a bachelor's paradise to a sophisticated retreat catering to middle-aged couples and families. Pattaya's image problem stems from inadequate sewage facilities, flooding, uncontrolled commercial sprawl, drugs, prostitution, a mysterious series of murders, and water pollution so severe that tourist officials strongly discourage swimming anywhere along South Pattaya Beach. The *Far Eastern Economic Review* once cited Pattaya's problems as a classic lesson for other Asian countries of the dangers of unplanned tourism development.

Criticism from travel agents, tour operators, and local hotel owners has finally pushed local authorities into action. Several new water-treatment plants are under construction, and south Pattaya will soon be renovated with a landfill project, a new beachfront road, a pedestrian promenade, piers for excursion boats, parks, and a concert hall. The main road was still torn up for a new sewer system as of this writing, though most of these projects should be completed by 2000.

Both despised and loved, Pattaya may yet prove itself the first Asian resort destroyed by tourism but saved by government intervention.

Although it's still fashionable to condemn Pattaya as superficial, overbuilt, unplanned, congested, polluted, tawdry, and having nothing to do with the *real* Thailand (all true), most of the three million annual visitors seem to come away satisfied with its wide range of hedonistic offerings.

Recent Transformations

Pattaya is also undergoing a transformation from holiday resort town to a major commercial city due to the economic growth of the entire eastern seaboard. The new deepwater port at Laem Chabang, 20 km north, has necessitated the construction of several new towns to house the estimated 100,000 Thais involved in the massive project. Another major construction project at Map Taphut, south of Pattaya near Rayong, is now attracting dozens of large international companies such as Michelin and Mitsubishi, which have established giant manufacturing complexes and brought in hundreds of expats to keep the gears of the machinery running smoothly.

All this growth has brought in new hotels, new housing estates, expanded highways, modern shopping centers, four international hospitals, five international schools, and a real estate boom that seems to accelerate with each passing year. And, in a sign of the times, Father Brennan at the local orphanage recently was ordered to quit farming pigs as the city limits are no longer considered fit for rural activities.

ATTRACTIONS AROUND TOWN

Big Buddha Hill (Khao Pra Yai)

Fine views over Pattaya can be enjoyed from two small hills in south Pattaya. The closer hill is capped with a microwave station operated by Naval Broadcasting, while Pattaya Hill to the south features a large seated Buddha image surrounded by seven mini-Buddhas representing the seven days of the week.

Mini Siam

Over 100 miniature reproductions of Siamese temples and palaces are located on Sukumvit Road, about three km northeast from central Pattaya. Recent additions include the Eiffel Tower, Big Ben, and a Thai cultural show given at 1600. 387 Moo 6 Sukumvit Rd., tel. (038) 421628, 300B. Open daily 0800-2200.

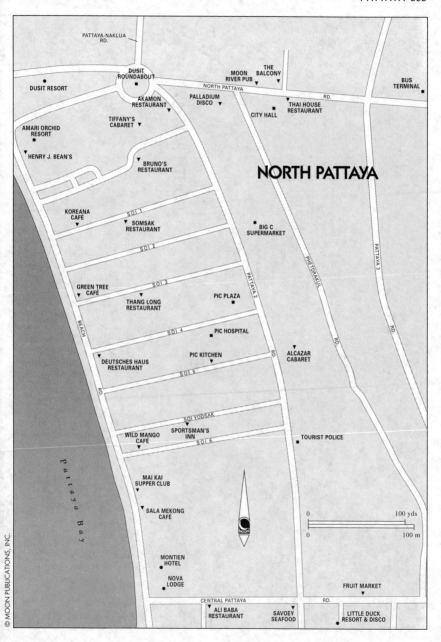

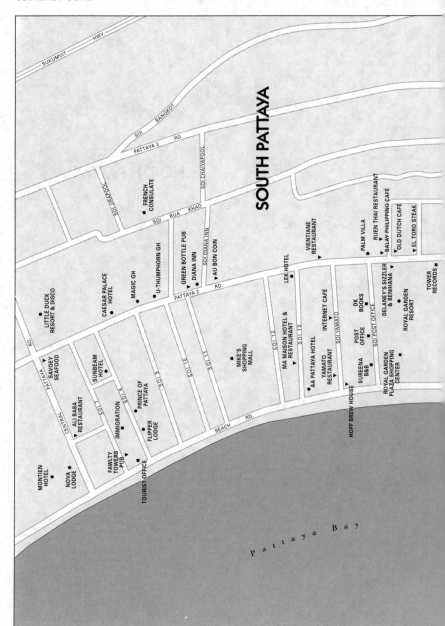

SOUTH PATTAYA

ROYAL CLIFF
BEACH RESORT

MON AMI PIERROT CAFÉ ▶

NANG NUAL RESTAURANT ▶

SIMON CABARET ▶

FOOD FAIR ▶

MARINE DISCO ▶

NEW PIER

ANZAC HOTEL

BLUE PARROT
▶ TEX-MEX

MIKE'S
DEPARTMENT
STORE & HOTEL ■

BAMBOO BAR
& NIGHTCLUB ▶

▶ SWISS FOOD

LOBSTER POT ▶

19TH CAFÉ ▶

BARS & NIGHTCLUBS

MOTI'A
MAHAL ▶

SOI DIAMOND (FOOT TRAFFIC ONLY)
BARS & NIGHTCLUBS

SOI 72 (WALKWAY)

SOI 73 (WALKWAY)

SOI SAENSUKNAN

SOI 6

PATTAYALAND SOI 1

PATTAYALAND SOI 2

PATTAYALAND SOI 3

SOUTH

SOI 14

SOI 15

BEACH RD.

WANMUANG

ATHAJLINDA DR.

PRATUMNOK RD.

PRATUMNOK RD.

PATTAYA

SOI 11

SOI 17

PATTAYA 3

RD.

JOMTIEN RD.

100 yds
100 m

© MOON PUBLICATIONS, INC.

ATTRACTIONS OUTSIDE PATTAYA

Many of the most popular attractions are located in the countryside outside Pattaya. All can be reached with rented car or motorcycle, though travel agents sell tickets that include free roundtrip transportation from your hotel.

Nong Nooch Tropical Gardens
A 600-acre tourist resort—by far the best attraction in the Pattaya region—features landscaped gardens, a mini zoo and aviary, an orchid garden, a man-made lake for rowing, and two restaurants—one Thai and one Western. The highlight to this park is the cultural show with its elephant performances and Thai classical dances, held daily at 1000, 1500, and 1545. This very impressive show features over 100 participants decked out in full Thai regalia.

Visitors can visit the village with their own rented vehicle or join one of the half-day tours that depart Pattaya daily at 0900 and 1300. Sukumvit Rd., Km 163, tel. (038) 429321, 350-400B.

Pattaya Elephant Village
Pachyderms haul logs and play soccer at the elephant *kraal* five km from town on the road to the Siam Country Club. Demonstrations are given by the mahouts and the featured elephant show involves dozens of participants. A two-hour elephant trek into nearby bush country can be arranged with advance notice. Elephants now lead the unemployed list after teak logging was banned in Thailand several years ago. Siam Country Club Rd., tel. (038) 249853, 300B admission, 700B for elephant treks.

Crocodile Farm and Million Year Stone Park
Yet another Thai crocodile farm but with a difference—the petrified trees at this park are over a million years old. Along with the crocodile show is a small zoo with elephants, camels, lions, bears, and tigers. Siam Country Club Rd., tel. (038) 249347, 300B.

Wat Yansangwararam
Seven architecturally unique pavilions and temples in Thai, Chinese, Japanese, Indian, and Western styles are located in a 360-*rai* park 15 km south of Pattaya. Also on the grounds is a primary temple constructed in modern Thai style and a magnificent Chinese museum noted for its fine examples of Chinese painting and scrolls, ancient bronzes, carved granite wall reliefs, and a small scale replica of the excavated tomb from Xian province. Sukumvit Rd., three km north of Nong Nooch Tropical Gardens. Open daily 0600-1800.

Bang Saray
A small, relatively undisturbed fishing village known for game fishing and seafood restaurants lies some 20 km south of Pattaya. Fisherman's Lodge, headquarters for the Thailand Game Fishing Association, sponsors fishing trips and has 16 standard a/c rooms from 800B. The lodge also features a swimming pool and marina.

ISLANDS NEAR PATTAYA

Ko Larn
Islands near Pattaya offer better sand and diving than the mainland beaches. The only island with schedule boat service is Ko Larn, about 45 minutes by boat from Pattaya.

Tours usually include Ko Rin or Ko Pai before stopping at Ko Larn ("Coral Island"), a highly developed resort fixed with several upscale hotels, pricey restaurants, golf course, and dive shops. Coral Island is a fanciful rendition of its rather prosaic name (true translation: Bald Island). Pack food and drinks if you're counting your *baht*.

Beaches: Ta Waen Beach on the northwest coast is the most impressive stretch of sand but also the most commercialized and best avoided on weekends when hordes of Thai tourists flood the island. Daeng Beach around the northern cape is smaller and less crowded but often bothered with jet boats that buzz just offshore. Thien Beach on the southwest side of the island provides a long expanse of white sand but lacks the scenic appeal of Ta Waen. Samae Beach and Nual Beach to the south of Thien Beach are fairly remote and provide more privacy but can be somewhat tricky to reach unless you hire a motorcycle from either Thien or Ta Waen beaches.

Transportation: Converted fishing trawlers leave from the south Pattaya pier daily at 0800 and 1000 and cost 50-100B roundtrip. These boats return at 1200, 1400, and 1700.

Several travel agencies also arrange more expensive excursions, while glass-bottom boat trips are also available. Prices vary depending on quality of meals, diving equipment, and number of islands visited.

Islands near Ko Larn

Ko Larn may be uncomfortably commercialized and probably not worth visiting on weekends, though several nearby islands provide a welcome escape from the crowds.

Ko Sak and Ko Krok: These two small and relatively unspoiled islands with good diving can be reached by chartered boat from Ko Larn.

Ko Pai: Ko Pai and its nearby islands—Ko Luam, Ko Klung Badan, and Ko Manvichai—are under the supervision of the Royal Thai Navy and kept in far more pristine condition than all other islands in the Pattaya region. Travel time is about two hours and these islands can only be reached by private boat charter or with any of the dive companies which make regular excursions to these remote outposts. No accommodations or restaurants so remember to bring along food and water.

WATER ACTIVITIES

Named after the southwestern monsoon wind that sweeps the east coast during the summer months, Pattaya is a beach resort dedicated to the pursuit of pleasure and love of *sanuk*. The range of activities is nothing short of amazing—sunbathing, parasailing, skin diving, golf, game-fishing, zoos, night markets, and the world-famous nightlife.

Traditional culture is not much in evidence within the city limits. But to remind visitors that Pattaya is located in exotic Thailand rather than Miami Beach or Waikiki, outlying attractions include an elephant camp, Buddhist temples, and an orchid farm with Thai dancers.

Beaches

Pattaya's biggest disappointments are the narrow and brownish four-km beach, vastly inferior to the crystalline shores of Phuket or Samui, and the polluted waters that are declared a hazardous zone by a government-sponsored study on environmental pollution. Better sand and cleaner waters can be found at Jomtien Beach, south of Pattaya, and Wong Amat Beach, north of Pattaya in the suburb of Naklua. Wong Amat is recommended as the best option to central Pattaya.

Water Sports

Pattaya offers a wide range of water sports. Most are now found on Jomtien Beach since Pattaya Bay is crowded with powerboats and fishing trawlers. Prices are negotiable, subject to change, and higher on weekends and holidays. For a general guide to current prices, check local publications such as *Pattaya This Week* and *Explore Pattaya*. Check fuel supplies and condition of equipment, and never sign papers that promise liability. Fleecing ignorant tourists is big business here in Pattaya.

Scuba

Pattaya has almost a dozen scuba diving shops that sponsor PADI and NAUI certification courses, and multi-day dive expeditions for licensed divers. A single-day two-dive excursion to nearby islands with all equipment, boat rental, and instruction starts at 2,500B per day. Two days of instruction and three dive days cost 5,500B, while full PADI certification runs 9,000B. Deep wreck, photography, and rescue courses are also offered.

Scuba diving is centered on the offshore Ko Lan archipelago, though farther islands such as Ko Pai, Ko Luam, and Ko Rim offer better opportunities since they are managed by the Royal Thai Navy. The best dive spots with underwater wrecks are located south of Pattaya near the naval base at Sattahip. These diveable wrecks include the *Hardeep* at Samaesan (20 meters) and the *Bremen* near Sattahip (30 meters).

Dave's Divers' Den: Among the oldest and more reliable dive operators in the region. 190/11 Central Pattaya Rd., tel. (038) 429387.

Dolphin Diving Centre: Another reputable company owned and operated by professional divers who provide instruction in English, German, and French. 183/29 Soi Post Office, tel. (01) 944-0992.

Seafari: Bill and Pat Burbridge also provide top-notch instruction and arrange daily dive trips around the Pattaya waters. 359/2 Soi 5, tel. (038) 429060, fax (038) 424708.

Mermaid Dive School: Pattaya's only dive shop with compressor, tanks, and oxygen on board their private boat. 75/124 Moo 12, Soi Mermaid, Jomtien, tel. (038) 232219, fax (038) 232221.

Windsurfing

Visitors undeterred by the pollution can rent sailboards at Jomtien Beach. Pattaya Beach is simply too crowded and dangerous for windsurfing. October to June are considered the best months, though the summer monsoon months can kick up some intimidating surf for the inexperienced. International windsurfing tournaments take place in early December, while the Siam World Cup—a national competition—is held in either April or May.

Yacht and Boat Rentals

All types of boats can be rented by the hour at Jomtien Beach, including Lasers, 16-foot catamarans, and Hobie Cat sailboats. Yacht and sailboat charters by the day, weekend, or longer periods are available from several specialized agencies in Pattaya and south down in Sattahip.

Bamroong Sailing & Paramotor Centre Resort: Five km south of town is Chak Nok Lake where a sailing school offers windsurfing and sailing instruction on waters far more dependable than you would find in the open ocean. They also provide archery lessons, off-road jeep terrain, and training courses in microlight aviation. Facilities include a restaurant and limited bungalow accommodations. Chak Nok Lake, Sukumvit Rd., tel. (01) 946-7859.

Ocean Marina Yacht Club: Large international marina with spacious clubhouse, bar, several restaurants, and facilities for yachters and sailors including pontoon moorings, slip rentals, dry storage, and repairs through the nearby Concord Boatyard. This club also provides boat sales, rentals, and charters. Sukumvit Km 157, just past Ambassador Hotel, Jomtien, tel. (038) 237300.

Royal Varuna Yacht Club: A private club on a fine, unspoiled beach with rack storage, boat repairs, chandlery, large swimming pool, terrace restaurant, and short and long-term accommodations. Although there are no formal boat rentals, club members frequently seek crew for day trips and longer excursions around the islands off the east coast of Thailand. Races are

organized most weekends. The resort is a few minutes south of Pattaya near the Cosy Beach Hotel and Island View Hotel. Royal Varuna Yacht Club, tel. (038) 250115.

Fishing Trips

Big-game fishing at 1,000-1,500B per day can be arranged at most travel agencies and directly at several bars in South Pattaya.

Deutsches Haus: Arranges fishing expeditions for a minimum party of four passengers and will, of course, cook your catch right on the boat. Beach Road at Soi 4, tel. (038) 428725.

Bang Saray Fishing Club: This place in Bang Saray, 20 km east of Pattaya, also arranges multi-day fishing excursions for big game such as marlin, king mackerel, shark, and barracuda.

Panarak Park: Freshwater fishing plus restaurant and play area for the kids. Siam Country Club Rd., tel. (038) 249156.

Pattaya Tower and Water Park

An enormous beachfront park with water slides, swimming pools, and restaurants—a perfect place for families to swim in clean, clear waters. The park is located between Pattaya and Jomtien Beach.

Towering over the water park is an enormous seaside hotel block capped by a soaring concrete pinnacle with revolving restaurant. Great views from the top of the 240-meter high structure. After lunch, you can ride the elevator back down to the ground floor or leap out of the window and return to earth on an absurdly perilous "sky shuttle." This contraption hooks you into a small chair which is released from the tower and follows metal guidelines down to the ground.

Pattaya Park Beach Resort: This relatively new hotel complex has 730 rooms and suites with all the standard resort amenities. 345 Jomtien Beach, tel. (038) 251210, fax (038) 251209, 800-1,800B.

SPORTS

Golf

Pattaya is one of the golfing centers of Thailand with almost 20 golf courses in Pattaya or within a one hour drive.

Golf fees: Greens fees on weekends range from 450B to 1,000B, while weekday rates are heavily discounted. Special rates are given to holders of Pattaya Sports Club or Pattaya Golf Association cards. Pattaya Sport Club cards are sold at Kronborg Hotel on Soi Diana off Pattaya 2 Road, while Pattaya Golf Association cards are available at Siam Golf and Country Club and the Greenway Driving Range.

Tours and Tournaments: Golf tours and tournaments are organized through several clubs on Pattaya Beach Road, easily found by looking for the bags of clubs piled behind the pool table.

Siam Golf and Country Club: One of Thailand's finest course is 20 minutes from downtown Pattaya through the archway on Sukumvit Road just opposite Central Pattaya Road. The 7,016-yard course is one of the oldest in the country with plenty of old trees and tight fairways. 50 Tambol Poeng, Siam Country Club Rd., tel. (038) 249381.

Royal Thai Navy Course: Phu Ta Luang Golf Course, 35 minutes south near the naval town of Sattahip, also ranks among the oldest courses in the country with 27 very challenging holes of golf, plus a fine clubhouse with all possible amenities. Sukumvit Rd., Ban Chang, tel. (038) 431189.

Bang Phra International Golf Club: A long 18-hole professional golf course with driving range and large clubhouse complete with hotel, restaurant, and even Japanese-style bath tubs in the luxurious locker rooms. 45 Moo 6 Tambon, Bang Phra, tel. (038) 341149.

Great Lake Golf Course: A Nick Faldo-designed course with a tricky layout and loads of bunkers. 77 Moo 5, Rayong, tel. (01) 321-1913.

Horseback Riding
Several horseback riding centers are outside town, generally up in the mountains.

Horse Sports Center Pattaya: Willi Netzer and his crew lead organized rides through the countryside and jungle in the Kao Camin hills just east of Pattaya. Rides cost about 700B per hour. Instruction also is provided for beginners and intermediates, and monthly discounted memberships are available. Rayong Highway, tel. (038) 251984.

Thai Boxing Instruction
The latest wrinkle to activities in Pattaya seems to be the various Thai boxing schools that have opened in recent years. The gyms are hardly luxurious but the instruction is professional and rates are reasonable.

Universe Gym: Fitness center with weekly Thai boxing instruction. Soi 2, tel. (038) 421027.

World Class Gym: One of the better operations in town with daily aerobic classes, dance instruction, weight training, and Thai boxing classes for beginners and intermediates. Visitors can use the day rates or sign up for a short-term membership. Pattaya 2nd Rd. Soi 12, tel. (038) 411116.

Sityodthong International School of Boxing: The only facility in Pattaya dedicated strictly to the sport of Thai boxing, located about three km north of town. 90 Moo 6, Nongprue, Sukumvit Rd., tel. (038) 429018.

Mountain Bikes
As with horseback riding centers, most of Pattaya's mountain bike centers are outside town at the edge of the mountains.

Mountain Bike Club Challenger: The largest facility on the east coast with hourly mountain bike rentals and escorted rides through the nearby jungles. Laem Chabang Country Club, tel. (01) 239-5615.

Go-carts
Several surprisingly elaborate go-cart venues have opened in recent years and appear to be doing quite well with the thrill-seeking crowd.

K.R. International Kart Circuit: The biggest and best operation of its kind in the Pattaya area with professional instruction and weekend races with specially modified carts. A pair of Englishmen run this outfit. 62/125 Moo 2 Thep Prasit Rd., tel. (038) 300349.

Pattaya Kart Speedway: The original go-cart place with two tracks (one for beginners and one for advanced drivers) and dual carts for parent-and-kid teams. Thep Prasit Rd., tel. (038) 422044.

Mini Siam: The amusement park at the north end of town has a single cart track only suitable for experienced drivers. 387 Sukumvit Rd., tel. (038) 421628.

Bira Circuit
Named after Prince Bira, one of Thailand's best-known racing enthusiasts, this 2.4-km racetrack has international events and a popular race school managed by Pacemakers AG, a Euro-

pean-based company involved in the racing-tire business. Rentals cost 600-900B per hour and include go-carts, Formula 3 models, and Ford 2000s. Highway 36, Km 14.

ACCOMMODATIONS

Hotel Districts
Pattaya is divided into several districts.

North Pattaya and Wong Amat Beach have swankier deluxe hotels, fine restaurants, and low-key nightlife suitable for families with children. Wong Amat Beach is recommended for its fairly luxurious hotels tucked away in a semi-rural setting on the best beach in the area. North Pattaya is a fairly classy and clean area but it's too far to walk to the nightclubs in south Pattaya and you'll need to flag down a baht bus to go just about anywhere.

Central Pattaya is the place for families or couples who wish to be within walking distance of the nightclubs in south Pattaya, but removed enough to escape the solo males who fill most of the guesthouses and hotels in that particular neighborhood. For many visitors, this is the best part of town.

South Pattaya has budget hotels and restaurants, plus notorious nightlife that ranges from go-go bars to transvestite cabarets that rage until dawn. This area is best left to the single male traveler.

Jomtien Beach to the south is a family resort region with luxurious hotels, soaring condo complexes, and the best selection of water sports in the region.

Hotel Prices
Some 280 guesthouses, hotels, and condominiums are estimated to be operating in and around Pattaya, with a total of over 35,000 rooms.

Tariffs vary according to day and season. Weekdays are cheaper than weekends, and rates are cut about 40% during the slow season May-Oct. Business has been booming in recent years with high occupancy levels provided by the political and economic problems of neighboring Malaysia and Indonesia. And yet rates remain at extremely reasonable levels and there appears to be little pressure to raise prices.

Contrary to popular belief, Pattaya has a good selection of fan-cooled hotels in the 150-300B price range and a/c rooms in the 400-600B range. The cheapest places are just basic cubicles but come equipped with adequate furniture and private bath, and are perfectly acceptable for short stays.

Pattaya's cheapest hotels are located in south Pattaya on Soi Post Office, Soi Yamato, and Soi 13. These places are recommended for single males rather than couples or families.

The following hotel descriptions start from the south end of Pattaya—near the nightclubs and restaurants—and move north to the quieter areas in central and northern Pattaya.

Budget—Soi Post Office
Soi Post Office (Post Office Alley)—a very utilitarian street—has several travel agencies, the well-stocked D.K. Books, real estate agencies with photos of available properties in the front windows, translation and general business services, a dive shop, overseas call outlets, Internet cafes, a used book exchange, a wine shop, and almost every other service you may need.

Several budget-priced guesthouse are also on this street, with decent fan rooms for 200-250B and a/c rooms for just 300-350B, such as **Sureena Bed and Breakfast** and, at the far end of the street, the French-owned **Riviera Beach Hotel** where a/c rooms start from 400B.

Malibu Bar, at the end of the road, puts on a rankly amateurish nightclub show with transvestites and Thai dancers.

Budget—Soi Yamato
Named after a well-known Japanese restaurant just off Beach Road, this rather claustrophobic alley has eight hotels in the 200-450B price range. **Siam Guesthouse** and the adjacent **Porn Hotel** at the eastern end of the road have a/c rooms from 350B and several fan rooms for just 200B. **Sailor Inn** a few steps down is a Norwegian Bar with a few inexpensive rooms upstairs. German-operated **Eiger Bar** has fan rooms from 220-300B.

Hotel Norge is, as you might imagine, a Norwegian haunt with a/c rooms from 350B. **Nipa Guesthouse** and **The Rising Sun Hotel** in the middle of the block also have both fan-cooled and a/c rooms at bargain rates. **Texxan Inn** is owned by a retired USAF officer who serves enormous breakfasts and has nightly CNN broadcasts 1900-2000. **Europa Inn, Joiles Momei Hotel,** and **PS Guesthouse** at the western end of the street are other low-priced choices.

Once again, this street is best suited to single males rather than couples or families.

Budget—Soi 13

This is the northernmost street in south Pattaya which isn't strictly aimed at solo males travelers, but still isn't quite mainstream enough to attract the average visitor. It's also a strangely deserted street with wide stretches of open land between the limited number of guesthouses and hotels.

Starting from Beach Road, you'll first find the large and relatively decent **AA Pattaya Hotel** with 82 rooms priced from 850-1,200B. Heading east along the alley you then reach **Ma Maison Hotel and Restaurant** followed by the **Chris Guesthouse,** where rooms start at 250B. The clean and comfortable **Inn of the Golden Crab,** with a small swimming pool, provides short-term rentals but not rooms by the night (weekly rentals only).

Sportsman Grill, just opposite the **Inn of the Golden Crab,** provides the best dining on the street. The final two accommodations on this very quiet street are **The White House,** almost to the end of the road, and **Lek Hotel** at the corner of Pattaya 2 Road. Both have rooms in the 350-500B price range.

Budget—Soi 8

This narrow street in Central Pattaya just south of Central Pattaya Road is an excellent choice for couples who wish to be near the nightlife action but don't want to descend into the hardcore bachelor enclaves to the south. Quite a number of small clubs and beer bars are scattered along this road, but the atmosphere is fairly friendly and couples and female travelers will find this neighborhood perfectly acceptable for a few nights. Places here tend to be in the mid-market level with a/c rooms and private baths.

Starting from Pattaya 2 Road to the west, you first come across the **Elephant & Castle Pub, Rovers Return Hotel, Top House,** and **Mongkol Guesthouse** at the southern corner of the intersection. These are the least expensive choices on the street with small rooms from 300B.

Just opposite this budget hive is the rather nondescript **Highfive Hotel** with motel-like rooms at bargain rates. Heading west toward the beach is the popular if somewhat sterile **Sunbeam Hotel** surrounded by dozens of beer bars and a few struggling go-go bars. The **Sunshine Hotel** across the street also has rooms in the 350-750B price range.

A few steps to the west is the very large and fairly new hotel complex modestly known as the **Prince of Pattaya Beach Hotel** with several levels of clean and comfortable rooms from 450-1,200B. The outdoor cafes directly in front of this hotel and just across the street are some of the most comfortable places to relax at night and watch the passing parade of Western drunks and local transvestites.

Eastiny Inn & Minimart across the street is small but has decent rooms from 450B while the older **Flipper Lodge Hotel,** adjacent to the **Prince of Pattaya,** provides acceptable rooms in the same price range.

Budget—Pattaya 2 Road

Along with the budget spots mentioned above, almost a dozen inexpensive guesthouses and hotels are located back on Pattaya 2 Road just opposite Soi 6, 10, 11, and 12. Many have posted signs which announce their special room deals, which range from 150-450B. The low-end places are just simple guesthouses with barely survivable cubicles, but you'll also find plenty of decent hotels with small pools and cozy cafes with a/c rooms priced from just 250B. You can walk to the beach in about two minutes.

Hotel names and special promotions seem to change with the seasons, so it's best to just wander down the street and inspect a few places before checking in.

Magic Guesthouse: A French-owned and operated guesthouse with small but clean rooms in a handy location. Pattaya 2 Rd., Soi 9, tel. (038) 720211, 150-400B.

U-Thumphorn: Basic but very inexpensive guesthouse with simple fan-cooled rooms. Pattaya 2 Rd., Soi 10, tel. (038) 421350, 150-250B.

Apex Hotel: A large and reasonably modern hotel with near-spacious rooms at bargain rates. Also has a small pool and good deals on breakfast buffets. You may need to bargain at the front desk, though this hotel seems to perpetually post prices for special discount rooms just outside the front door. 216/2 Pattaya 2 Rd., Soi 11, tel. (038) 429233, 250-500B.

Diana Inn: Simple rooms and a good pool make this a popular spot for budget travelers who want basic frills at low cost. Pattaya 2 Rd., Soi 11, tel. (038) 429675, fax (038) 424566, 450-600B.

Palm Villa: Pattaya's venerable budget hotel has all a/c rooms, an attractive swimming pool, and is within easy walking distance of the bars. Pattaya 2 Rd., Soi 13, tel. (038) 428153, 400-600B.

Moderate—South Pattaya

Most Pattaya hotels priced in the 600-1,500B price range include a/c rooms with private bath, a restaurant, and a small swimming pool. Some charge an additional 20% for tax and service.

Honey Lodge: A clean, quiet, and well-located hotel with a spacious swimming pool and discounts for long-term visitors. 529 Soi 10, Pattaya 2 Rd., tel. (038) 421543, fax (038) 421946, 350-700B.

Lek Hotel: A relatively new hotel with large swimming pool, billiards hall, and rooftop terrace. All rooms furnished with TV, refrigerator, and hot showers. Pattaya 2 Rd., Soi 13, tel. (038) 425550 fax (038) 426629, 800-1,000B.

Caesar Palace Hotel: Las Vegas comes to Pattaya in this pseudo-Romanesque 200-room hotel. The compound includes a large pool and tennis courts. Pattaya 2 Rd., Soi 10, tel. (038) 428607, fax (038) 422140, 900-1,400B.

Luxury

Four luxury hotels are located in Pattaya between Jomtien Beach to the south and Naklua to the north.

Royal Garden Resort: Superb location and wonderful views from rooms facing the beach make this the ideal location for upscale visitors to Pattaya who wish to be near the action and shopping venues in the adjacent complex. The resort lies in a garden setting with swimming pool, health club, and a variety of restaurants from Benihana's to their Saturday night seafood buffet artfully arranged around a series of ponds. South Pattaya Beach Rd., tel. (038) 428122, fax (038) 429926, US$100-180.

Amari Orchid Resort: Tucked away at the north end of town with some of the finest gardens in the region and a vaguely European feel to the property. Popular with tour groups and others drawn to the personality of this large Thai hotel chain. North Pattaya Beach Rd., tel. (038) 428161, fax (038) 428165, 1,800-3,600B.

Montien Pattaya: Considered one of the best in the region with beautiful rooms and all possible amenities in a handy location near the center of town. Central Pattaya Beach Rd., tel. (038) 428155, fax (038) 423155, 2,500-3,500B.

Dusit Resort Hotel: Situated on 15 acres of lovely gardens with great views, two swimming pools, three tennis courts, sauna, billiards, and a health club. Best hotel in north Pattaya, but far removed from the nightclubs and restaurants in the southern part of town—attracts mostly a Thai clientele. North Pattaya Beach Rd., North Pattaya, tel. (038) 425611, fax (038) 428239, 2,600-4,500B.

Naklua Hotels

Naklua is the residential neighborhood just north of Pattaya where many locals live and several intimate midpriced resorts are located near some of the finest beaches in the region.

Wong Amat: Far from the madding crowd, this low-rise bungalow, nicely set on the best beach in Pattaya, may not be the most spectacular place in town, but it remains popular with discriminating Europeans who wish to escape the southern crowds. Wong Amat Beach, tel. (038) 426990, fax (038) 428599, 1,800-3,000B.

Jomtien Beach

Jomtien Beach—a few kilometers south of Pattaya—is somewhat less expensive than staying directly in Pattaya but offers almost no nightlife, and restaurants tend to be unimaginative. On the other hand, Jomtien provides a great beach and the best selection of water sports activities on the entire east coast, and is the preferred destination for many families.

The Icon: Situated between Pattaya and Jomtien is the first so-called "boutique" hotel in the region with 24 finely furnished rooms plus trendy restaurant and swimming pool. 146/8 Thappraya Rd., tel. (038) 250300, fax (038) 250838, 1,200-1,800B.

Mermaid's Beach Resort: European escape with 100 well-designed rooms, private dive boats, and swimming pool just 100 meters from the sandy beach. Jomtien Beach Rd., tel. (038) 232210, fax (038) 231908, 850-1,400B.

Ambassador Jomtien: Thailand's largest hotel has international restaurants, an amoeba-shaped swimming pool, and 5,000 rooms with views over the Gulf of Thailand. Monstrous in conception. Jomtien Beach Rd., tel. (038) 255501, fax (038) 255731, 1,200-3,000B.

Royal Cliff Hotel: Midway between Pattaya and Jomtien Beach, Pattaya's most expensive and exclusive hotel offers four individual hotels with 86 executive suites in their Royal Wing, private butlers, several beautiful pools, and elevators down to the private beach. Cliff Rd., tel. (038) 250421, fax (038) 250511, 4,500-8,000B.

FOOD

Pattaya's dining choices include everything from Arabic and French to Scottish and Japanese—Thai food is an endangered species here. Seafood is the emphasis due to the town's location on the Gulf of Thailand. Many of the best Thai restaurants are not located on Beach Road, but on the side roads leading up to Sukumvit Highway.

Streetstalls
The most inexpensive dining in Pattaya is at the dozens of simple foodstalls which open nightly at dusk at several locations around town.

Soi Diamond: Good cheap alfresco dining, popular with hookers, transvestites, and sailors, can be enjoyed along Soi Diamond, Soi Post Office, Soi Yamato, and Soi Pattayaland 1 and 2. Look for the stalls that sell Thai herbal wines at 10B per shot.

Thai
As you might expect, Pattaya is a place where it can be difficult to find decent Thai food but you always pick up a Swiss fondue or German sausage at any hour of the day.

PIC Kitchen: Classical Thai cooking in a lovely setting accompanied by jazz musicians and traditional Thai dancers on Wednesday evening.

Great atmosphere. Pattaya 2 Rd., Soi 5, tel. (038) 428374.

Ruen Thai: Open-air restaurant with traditional Thai dancing nightly at 1930. 485/3 Pattaya 2 Road opposite Royal Garden Hotel in south Pattaya, tel. (038) 425911.

Thai House: An upscale restaurant with traditional Thai dishes and nightly Thai dancing and music starting around 2000. Somewhat isolated near City Hall in the north of town. 171 Pattaya North Rd., tel. (038) 370579.

Sugar Hut: Certainly doesn't sound even vaguely Thai, but this extremely elegant spot decorated in Ayuthaya style specializes in authentic Thai dishes such as roast duck in curry and seafood with coconut sauces. A very beautiful place and well worth the splurge. Pattaya-Jomtien Rd., tel. (038) 251686.

Sala Maekong: Simple, beachfront, open-air cafe with good food at rock-bottom prices. Beach Rd., Soi 6, North Pattaya, tel. (038) 428645.

Somsak: Another traditional open-air Thai cafe with casual atmosphere and decent food. Beach Rd., 436/24 Soi 1, South Pattaya, tel. (038) 410485.

Wild Mango: Fine name for an inexpensive spot which serves delicious food at very reasonable prices. The managers are friendly and many of the staff speak decent English. Beach Rd., 437/93 Soi 6, Central Pattaya, tel. (038) 361363.

Japanese
Thai and Chinese predominate in the Asian cuisine department, though you can also find restaurants which serve many other Asian styles of cooking, including Japanese, Korean, Indian, Polynesian, and Indonesian.

Benihana: The classic Japanese restaurant with tasty food and amusing jokes from the chef. Beach Rd., Royal Garden Plaza, tel. (038) 425029.

Akamon: Another popular Japanese venue with sushi and tempura in an inconvenient location near the Tiffany Cabaret. Pattaya 2 Rd., North Pattaya, tel. (038) 423727.

Yamato: Such an old-time favorite that the adjacent alley is often just called "Soi Yamato." Japanese favorites, sushi, and sashimi served at dinner only. 219/51 Soi Yamato, South Pattaya, tel. (038) 429685.

Vietnamese and Lao

Thang Long: Vietnamese and Thai dishes in a small cafe at very reasonable prices. Beach Rd., Soi 3, South Pattaya, tel. (038) 425487.

Vientiane: Perhaps the only place in town with Lao dishes along with a large selection of Thai and Chinese specialties as noted on their extensive menu. Moderately priced but service is good and the atmosphere is somewhat unique. 185 Pattaya 2 Rd., near Palm Villa Hotel.

Indian

Indian restaurants tend to be somewhat overpriced but the food provides a welcome change from a steady diet of Thai rice dishes or American fast food.

Ali Baba: Indian restaurant known for its vegetarian dishes and Tandoori cuisine. Open for both lunch and dinner. 14 Central Pattaya Rd., tel. (038) 429262.

Motta Mahal: Somewhat hectic atmosphere near the Marine Plaza Hotel but a wide selection of Indian, Arabic, Pakistani, Bengali, and even Thai dishes. 323/26 Soi Saen Samran, South Pattaya, tel. (038) 429630.

Korean

Krung Seoul: The best Korean food in town served in a spotless little cafe just opposite the Royal Garden Plaza shopping complex. 215/46 Pattaya 2 Rd., tel. (038) 426248.

Koreana: A surprisingly large restaurant (seats over 300) near many of the seedy hotels in South Pattaya. The place is clean, however, and serves all the classic Korean dishes from kim chi to beef bulgogi. 436 Beach Rd., Soi 1, tel. (038) 429635.

More Asian

Filipino, Indonesia, and even Polynesian food can be enjoyed in this multicultural beach resort.

Bahay Philipino: The only Filipino cafe in town is just across the road from the Royal Garden Hotel. Pattaya 2 Rd., tel. (038) 426191.

Mai Kai Supper Club: The only Polynesian restaurant in town is located near the Hotel Tropicana. Also serves a wide selection of seafood dishes plus offers live band entertainment in the evenings. Beach Rd., North Pattaya, tel. (038) 428645.

Dolf Riks: Indonesian dishes and Thai specialties prepared by an Indonesian-born food critic and artist. 116/8 Pattaya-Naklua Rd., tel. (038) 367585.

English and Irish

Most expatriates here are of European extraction so expect an inordinate number of Swiss, German, and Italian cafes. English and Irish places tend to be pubs rather than formal restaurants.

Delaney's Irish Pub: A very large and popular place with Guinness, Killkenny, and Carlsberg on draft, plus a variety of Irish and English pub food. Happy hours daily from 1100-1300 and 1700-1900. Beach Rd., tel. (038) 710641.

Anzac: Typical English pub food plus Thai dishes, pool table, and TV with weekly sporting events. A popular place with expat families and Europeans on short vacations. Open daily from 0700-0300. 325/22 Soi Pattayaland 1, tel. (038) 427822.

Fawlty Towers: Traditional English pub and cafe with British food, snacks, and football games on the telly. Beach Rd., Soi 7, tel. (038) 420853.

Greg's Kitchen: The English chef does a mean job with roasts, traditional pies, and hearty breakfasts. 370/21 Pattaya 2 Rd., tel. (038) 361227.

Sportsman's Inn: Another English cafe/pub with respectable breakfasts and traditional roasts. 437/124 Soi Yodsak, North Pattaya, tel. (038) 429152.

Dutch

Old Dutch: Cozy spot with Dutch decorations and Thai plus Continental cuisine. Open around the clock and popular for breakfasts. 215/62 Pattaya 2 Rd., opposite Royal Garden Plaza, South Pattaya, tel. (038) 723177.

German

Zeppelin: German cafe with traditional fare and not a Led Zeppelin CD in sight. Beach Rd., just north of Central Rd., Nova Lodge Hotel, Central Pattaya, tel. (038) 420016.

Deutsches Haus: German, Thai, and international cuisine served in a comfortable a/c environment. This place also operates a deep-sea fishing yacht, which you can charter and then catch your own seafood. Beach Rd., Soi 4, tel. (038) 428725.

Swiss

Swiss Food: Not the most creative name but a popular and centrally located cafe with traditional Swiss fare, in the heart of the action. The three-course daily set menu is a good deal. 29 Soi Diamond, tel. (038) 423991.

Chalet Swiss: Swiss, International, and Thai cuisine served in the heart of South Pattaya. 220 Beach Rd., tel. (038) 429255.

French

Mon Ami Pierrot: French restaurant supervised by a French chef who prepared at least four set menus each day. Open for dinner only. 220/3 Beach Rd., South Pattaya, tel. (038) 429792.

Bruno's Restaurant and Wine Bar: An elegant French-Thai restaurant with second-floor wine bar with almost 200 different wines; also serves international dishes at reasonable prices. 463/77 Sri Nakorn Centre, North Pattaya, tel. (038) 361073.

Ma Maison: French and Continental dishes plus steaks and pastries in a casual open-air atmosphere adjacent to a small swimming pool. Beach Rd., Soi 13, South Pattaya, tel. (038) 429318.

Le Cafe Royale: A piano bar and sophisticated restaurant in a very seedy district surrounded by gay clubs and low-end strip joints— that must be the appeal. 325/102 Pattayaland Soi 3, South Pattaya, tel. (038) 423515.

Au Bon Coin: Small European cafe with steaks, continental entrees, and daily specials at reasonable cost. 216/59 Pattaya 2 Rd., tel. (038) 421978.

The Balcony: French, Thai, and Western dishes plus a great assortment of pastries. Soi Ananthakul, North Pattaya just beyond Thai Garden Resort, tel. (038) 411429.

19th Hole: Certainly doesn't sound French, but this large bar complex serves French cuisine along with juices from the juice bar, ice creams, and diversions from 10 snooker tables to backgammon and other pub games. Beach Rd., Sophon Plaza, 2nd floor, tel. (038) 429152.

Italian

La Gritta: An old favorite with Italian cuisine and nightly piano entertainment. Pasta with clams and other seafood dishes are recommended. Amari Orchid Hotel, Beach Rd., North Pattaya, tel. (038) 428161.

Borsolino: Another cozy cafe in the heart of the nightlife district with both Thai and Italian ala carte dishes plus bargain-priced set menus which change daily. Soi Diamond, tel. (038) 424450.

American

American-style pubs and steak houses have been gaining in popularity in recent years and now seem almost as common as Swiss fondue joints and German sausage cafes.

Hopf Brew House: Unquestionably the most successful new restaurant, brewpub, and entertainment venue in Pattaya with upscale atmosphere, excellent food, and the healthiest looking crowd in town. Great for families, Western couples, and even bachelors who wish to escape the seediness of South Pattaya for a few hours. The place is huge—takes up an entire city block— but can be absolutely packed on weekends. Live bands most nights (the best in town) plus beer brewed on the premises, not to mention excellent Western and European food. 219 Beach Rd., Soi Post Office, South Pattaya, tel. (038) 710650.

Henry J. Bean's Bar & Grill: Great spot in a finely restored old building with decent Western grub, beers on tap, and live bands nightly except Monday starting around 2030. Amari Orchid Resort, Beach Rd., North Pattaya, tel. (038) 334881.

Sizzler: Some of the best steaks in town, plus chicken, seafood platters, pasta dishes, and a remarkable salad bar—probably the best reason to visit this American chain. Prices are reasonable and the adjoining shopping complex is a delight to explore (it's a/c). Royal Garden Plaza, Beach Rd., tel. (038) 428128.

Captain's Corner Steak House: Just south of Pattaya on the road to Jomtien is this attractive garden restaurant known for its nightly all-you-can-eat "Texas Style Bar-B-Q." Pattaya-Jomtien Rd., tel. (038) 364318.

Maxwell's American Diner: Nostalgia lives on with period music ('50s to '70s only) and basic American grub from shakes and burgers to steaks and cakes. 217/14 Pattaya 2 Rd., Soi 8, South Pattaya, tel. (038) 361247.

El Toro Steak House: As the name implies, a place for steaks in all shapes and fashions from flambe and pepper to Diane and tartare. 215/31 Pattaya 2 Rd., opposite Royal Garden Hotel, tel. (028) 426238.

Green Bottle: Combination entertainment venue (pool table, darts, nightly vocalist) and restaurant which serves steaks, duck, and plenty of fresh seafood dishes. 216/9 Pattaya 2 Rd., opposite Mike Shopping Mall, tel. (03) 429675.

Green Tree: Despite the Western name, this a/c spot serves up Thai, Chinese, and Western dishes along with live musical entertainment most evenings. Beach Rd., Soi 3, North Pattaya, tel. (038) 428586.

Moon River Pub: Cozy little spot near the Thai Garden Resort known for its Saturday evening buffets and live entertainment most evenings. The atmosphere is American Country & Western. North Pattaya Rd., tel. (038) 370614.

American Fast Food Chains: If it's American and fast, then Pattaya's got it: Burger King, Dunkin Donuts, Swensen's, Bud's Ice Cream, A&W, KFC, McDonald's, Pizza Hut, and whatever else you can imagine.

Tex-Mex

The latest food craze to sweep Pattaya is the Tex-Mex food of the American Southwest.

Blue Parrot: The best Tex-Mex food in Pattaya, including fajitas, enchiladas, and nachos. Margaritas are popular, plus there's more sleaze outside the door that you could swing a stick at. 325/151 Soi Pattayaland 2, tel. (038) 424885.

Moonshine: Another Tex-Mex outlet with pool tables, darts, and live music in a raunchy, sleazy part of town. Beach Rd., Soi Diamond, South Pattaya, tel. (038) 411820.

Rancho Tejas: An open-air, family sort of place popular with expats, packed for the Sunday brunches, Thursday buffets, and weekend barbecues. The house band plays Thursday to Sunday starting nightly at 1900. Pattaya-Naklua Rd., Soi Potisan, Naklua, tel. (038) 428787.

Wild Chicken: Tex-Mex plus a variety of chicken specialties in a lively bar setting and a pair of TV blasting away with sporting events. Soi Post Office at Pattaya 2 Rd., tel. (038) 424006.

Seafood

Seafood is a big item here in Pattaya where almost a dozen decidedly upscale restaurants provide absolutely fresh seafood at rather startling prices.

Food Fair: Seafood restaurants at the south end of Beach Road let you personally select your entree, cooking styles, and accompanying sauce, but it's advisable to avoid well-dressed touts and to double-check cooking charges before ordering. Beach Rd., South Pattaya.

Nang Nual: Another longtime favorite with expensive if completely fresh seafood. Beach Rd., South Pattaya, opposite Soi 14, tel. (038) 428708.

Lobster Pot: Another pricey but fun seafood emporium with interior dining spaces and an outdoor terrace restaurant, perfect for sunsets. The restaurant is open daily from 1000 until well after midnight. 228 Beach Rd., South Pattaya, tel. (038) 426083.

Savoey Seafood: One of the few seafood restaurants in town not located on Beach Road, but with an extensive menu at cheaper prices than down by the sea. Somewhat noisy due to its location at a major intersection but quite an authentic dining experience. 164 Central Pattaya Rd., at the corner of Pattaya 2 Rd., tel. (038) 428580.

Restaurants with a View

Several restaurants around town provide decent views of Pattaya and the beach, but one place deserves a special mention for its outrageous panoramic views.

The Pinnacle Revolving Restaurant: A few kilometers south of Pattaya and just slightly north of Jomtien Beach is an amazing tower with revolving restaurants situated on the 52nd and 53rd floors. The views are spectacular. Visitors can just pay for the elevator ride to the top and enjoy the vistas or try the reasonably priced international buffet lunch or more expensive dinner option. Dinners are recommended for the sunsets. Pattaya Water Park, 345 Jomtien Beach Rd., tel. (038) 251201.

NIGHTLIFE

South Pattaya between Soi 13 and Soi 16 is a nonstop barrage of heady go-go bars, seedy nightclubs, high-tech discos, and outrageous live shows that cater to every possible sexual persuasion. It's an amazing experience to wander down Pattaya Beach Road past mud wrestlers, Thai kickboxers, open-air cinemas, touts, transvestite clubs, and whatever new gimmick sweeps the night scene. Much of the action revolves around open-air beer bars in South Pattaya, where friendly women hail customers from the street.

Soi Diamond

A good place to start is Soi Diamond, a small and totally crazy lane a short walk beyond South Pattaya Road. Lively women working the narrow alley drag reluctant customers up to the bar stools and push them into the better bars such as **Caligula** (live shows), **Blackout** (better furnishings), **Baby A Go-Go** (best club on Soi Diamond), and **Limmatquai** (inexpensive drinks). Before you leave the lower section of this surrealistic alley, ride the circular **Chiquita Bar** that revolves like a carousel; Hunter S. Thompson on acid would love this place.

Other nightclubs near the main road worth a look (and then perhaps a drink) include Blue Hawaii, Vixens, Super Girl, and Paris Go-Go.

Heading deeper up Soi Diamond, you then pass the **Diamond Beach Hotel** on the right and then the road narrows and the mid-alley beer bars completely disappear. **Starlights** on the left is a transvestite bar (so beware), followed by the **Jungle Pub, Mama Restaurant,** the delightfully named **Lassi Beer Bar (lassis and beer?), Casa Italia Restaurant,** and finally the **Lucky Corner Bar** almost where Soi Diamond reaches Pattaya 2 Road.

Soi BJ & Golden Mile Plaza

Another large concentration of nightclubs and go-go bars is located about five minutes south of Soi Diamond, on another narrow lane that has been mysteriously nicknamed Soi BJ, though the large sign over the entertainment complex calls the place the Golden Mile Plaza.

In any event, this alley isn't as much fun as Soi Diamond, though it does provide the aimless visitor with another dozen beer bars to explore and the lively **Happy A Go-Go** at the end of the alley.

Pattayaland

Pattaya has several dozen gay clubs, mostly located on Pattayaland Sois 1, 2 and 3 in South Pattaya. The neighborhood isn't strictly gay and

transvestite follies

offers plenty for straight travelers such as British pubs, a French piano bar, inexpensive Thai cafes, guesthouses, several budget hotels, go-go bars with lovely girls, and mundane services such as travel agencies and dive shops.

Pattayaland Soi 1: Just one block south of Royal Garden Plaza shopping complex is this busy alley packed with all manners of pubs, bars, nightclubs, crash pads, and other assorted things. Starting from Beach Road, you'll first pass the Aquanauts Diving Center, Papillon Go-Go Bar, Why Not Cabaret? (a boys show), followed by the Whooters & Pool (I assume this place is straight), the Sugar Shack, and then Dave's G.B. Bar.

On the left in the middle of the block is Tai Boys Boys Club (this place calls itself "the Funny Bar"), then the Gentleman Boy's Club, Winner's Boys, Billion Beer Bar (nice name), and finally the Winner Guesthouse. Spots to explore on the right side of this road include City Boys Club, Dey Mosquetos Beer Bar, Tatoo by Big, and Charlie Boys.

Pattayaland Soi 2: More fun and games on this busy street that connects Beach Road with Pattaya 2 Road. The west end of the road near the ocean has the Bubbles Club, Cheers Pub, Viking Beachcomber Cafe, the very popular Palmers Cafe, the Blue Parrot Cafe mentioned above in the Restaurant section, and Bobby Joe's Guesthouse and Bar. Most of these places are aimed at the straight rather than gay crowd.

Pattayaland Soi 3: This half-block long lane features a mixture of straight go-go nightclubs and a scattering of gay spots for those so inclined. Among the more prominent pubs and nightclubs are the Shamrock Bar, the very lively Misty's Go-Go, Lipstick A Go-Go (also popular), Miss Din's Beer Bar, the cleverly named Classroom Fun A Go-Go Sports Bar, Cats Go-Go Fun Bar, and the A-Bomb Boys Club.

The road curves around this concentration of nightclubs and continues down to Pattaya 2 Road, flanked with another nonstop collection of clubs, restaurants, and places to crash such as Amor Restaurant, Cocobanana Pub, Hotel Serene, Ambiance Hotel, and a Thai porcelain shop (quite out of place).

At the end of this street is the Le Cafe Royale Hotel & Piano Bar, Toy Boys Nightclub, and La Bodega Restaurant. If you need more diversion, walk across Pattaya 2 Road to the Boat Bakery, Simpatico Italian Restaurant, and a towering Russian karaoke palace that opened just a few years ago. Whew!

Transvestite Shows

Pattaya's best entertainment options are the hilarious transvestite shows that take place nightly in two extravagant cabarets in the north end of Pattaya on Pattaya 2 Road. Cheaper and far less professional transvestite shows are given in the larger nightclubs in South Pattaya, an area known as "The Strip."

Alcazar Cabaret: Professional shows of world-class caliber are given here every night of the year, by a company of almost 100 *gatoeis* who perform three times nightly in their 800-seat theater. . . the largest transvestite show troupe on earth. 78/14 Pattaya 2 Rd., tel. (038) 428746. 300-500B includes your first drink. The price varies depending on where you buy your ticket— directly at the cabaret or from a street vendor (or travel agency) that may tack on a hefty commission.

Tiffany's: Tiffany's is an 850-seat theater with over 65 performers who pose for photo sessions after the three nightly shows. Pattaya 2 Rd., tel. (038) 429642. 300-500B includes your first drink.

Simon Cabaret: Inside this enormous nightclub, somewhat seedy and filled with freelancers, you'll find a rather amateurish yet humorous nightly transvestite show, plus other entertainment oddities such as Thai boxing between local professionals and drunken tourists. The place was very quiet at last inspection and may have finally closed after a very long run. Beach Rd., South Pattaya, "The Strip." If this enormous open-air brothel remains in business, expect a modest cover charge of 50-100B depending on where you sit.

Marine Bar: Another monstrous open-air nightclub catering to "girls, guys, and in-betweens." This legendary nightclub also appears to be in financial trouble and may be closed on your arrival. If not, enjoy yourself.

If you haven't noticed by now, transvestites *(gatoeis)* are plentiful here in Pattaya. Since most Westerners have a difficult time distinguishing between women and *gatoeis,* proceed with caution unless you seek a wild war story.

Nightclubs and Discos

Pattaya has several large dance clubs filled with Thai teenagers, cruising call girls, and Western tourists.

Disco Duck: A long-time favorite with large video screens, live band, light shows and entertainment alternatives such as pool tables in the outside hall. Mostly for young Thais rather than Western tourists. Little Duck Pattaya Resort Hotel, Central Pattaya Rd., tel. (038) 428782.

Pattaya Palladium: An enormous place that bills itself as the largest disco in Thailand if not all of Southeast Asia; the claimed capacity is 5000 souls. This place has DJs on weekdays and live bands on weekends. Pattaya 2 Rd., tel. (038) 424933. The 200-300B entrance fee includes two drinks.

Moon River Pub: Popular country and western nightclub with live bands, line dancing, and an abundance of local expats rather than tourists. North Pattaya Rd., tel. (038) 370614.

Bamboo Bar: An excellent place to hear outstanding Thai rock bands and soak up the authentic atmosphere. No cover charge and there's plenty of seating among the tropical decor. Attracts an older and more sophisticated crowd for its quality rock bands and occasional visits by jazz groups down from Bangkok. South Pattaya Rd., between Beach Road and Pattaya 2 Rd., tel. 421361.

INFORMATION AND SERVICES

Tourist Office
The TAT office doles out maps and hotel lists, and can help with upcoming festivals and sporting events. They also have information on other east coast destinations such as Rayong, Chanthaburi, Trat, and Ko Chang. 382 Beach Rd., tel. (038) 428750.

Tourist Police
Contact this group for emergency help. Pattaya 2 Rd., tel. (038) 429371.

Maps
The TAT office distributes a decent free map. The *Pattaya/Eastern Part* map published by Prannok Witthaya has a larger-scale version of Pattaya plus an excellent map of the entire eastern seaboard, but this map is out of print and now very difficult to find.

The best map of Pattaya is the one that comes with *A Guide to Living in Pattaya & Rayong* compiled by the Pattaya International Ladies Club. You can also buy the map separate from the book, which you don't really need unless you intend to move to Pattaya.

Tourist Magazines
The latest word on hotels, restaurants, and nightlife can be culled from free magazines such as *Explore Pattaya* and *Pattaya This Week.* Trink's gossipy column in the *Bangkok Post* is also worth checking for bar and restaurant promotions. English-language local newspapers such as the *Pattaya Mail* cover real estate investments and advertise bankrupt nightclubs for sale.

Books
Duang Kamol Bookstore (D.K. Books) on Soi Post Office offers novels, literature, and magazines, and has a decent selection of travel guides. As of this writing, there are no current and/or comprehensive English-language guides to Pattaya and the east coast of Thailand.

The best collection of books and magazines is found in Bookazine in the Royal Garden Plaza shopping complex. The first floor has maps and books about Thailand and Asia, while the second floor is the place for international newspapers and magazines

Visas
Visas may be quickly extended at the Chonburi Immigration office on Soi 8 just off Beach Road. Visa photos and the necessary copies can be made at the small office just outside their front gate.

Telephone
International calls can be made 24 hours daily from all major hotels, from the exchange service in south Pattaya, and from dozens of public phones scattered around town. The telephone area code for Pattaya is (038).

Post Office
The Pattaya Post Office (tel. 038-429341) is located, sensibly enough, on Soi Post Office between Sois 13 and 14.

Travel Agencies
Budget travel agencies are most plentiful on Soi Post Office and Soi Yamato. Day tours offered include Ko Samet, Chonburi temples and museums, Chanthaburi gem mines, Bangkok, Damnern Saduak Floating Market, Ayuthaya, and River Kwai. The Chonburi and Chanthaburi tours are worthwhile, but the other excursions are far too time-consuming as one-day options. Prices for tours and international travel vary widely, so shop around before signing those traveler's checks.

Cautions
Pattaya police urge visitors not to carry too much money, never to accept drinks or food from strangers (knockout drugs are common), to keep off motorcycles unless you're an experienced driver, and to check prices before buying *anything.*

TRANSPORTATION

Getting There
Pattaya is 147 km southeast of Bangkok.

Train: The State Railways of Thailand has daily service at 0700 from Hualamphong sta-

tion. The three-hour journey passes attractive scenery and is a wonderful alternative to the buses.

Bus: Ordinary and a/c buses depart every 30 minutes 0630-2100 from Bangkok's Eastern Bus Terminal on Sukumvit Road Soi 63 and from the Northern Bus Terminal. These government-franchised buses cost 85-100B a/c and take about three hours to reach the small, very poorly marked *bor kor sor* (government) bus station on North Pattaya Road near the Sukumvit Highway.

The beach and most hotels are about four km down the road. You can hire a private *songtao* to your hotel for about 60B, or take a public *songtao* and pay 10-20B per person.

Private bus companies operate daily a/c buses from major Bangkok hotels direct to your hotel in Pattaya. These buses cost double the a/c government buses but avoid the hassle of getting to the government bus station on Sukumvit Road.

From Bangkok Airport: Buses depart from Bangkok Airport daily at 0600, 1400, and 1830. Tickets cost 200-240B and are sold at the transportation desk in the arrival lounge.

Getting Around

Pattaya is a relatively small town that can be easily explored on foot or with public transportation.

Songtaos: Compact Pattaya is served by *songtaos* that cruise the main roads and—with-

in the city limits—should charge a flat fee of just 5B. In reality, this never happens, since all *songtao* drivers are thieves who will charge whatever they think they can get from unsuspecting tourists.

Fleecing Western visitors is a big business in this town. Just get on a vehicle, get off at your destination, hand the driver five *baht* and walk away. Don't look back. Ignore his pleas and threats. The man is a thief.

Motorcycles: An excellent way to avoid obnoxious minitruck drivers and reach outlying attractions is rented motorcycle. All bikes should be checked carefully for damage before depositing your passport with the rental agency and taking off. International Drivers Licenses are rarely checked.

Small bikes under 150cc cost 150-200B per day and are perfectly adequate for local rides. Larger bikes fitted with an amazing variety of illegal modifications are available from vendors on Pattaya Beach Road. All of these monster bikes are imported as disassembled parts from Japan and reconstructed by local motorcycle enthusiasts. Most are for sale at very low prices (50,000B for a late-model Ninja 750), but few are legally registered with the Thai government.

No matter what size you select, be very careful riding around town; a frightening number of tourists end their vacations on the streets of Pattaya.

Cars and Jeeps: Both self- and chauffeur-driven cars can be hired from **Avis** at the Dusit Resort in north Pattaya, the Royal Garden Hotel in central Pattaya, and the Royal Cliff Hotel towards Jomtien Beach. **Hertz** has closed down. Jeeps can be rented from vendors on Beach Road but be advised that insurance is rarely available and visitors are held responsible for any damage or injury caused in an accident.

Leaving Pattaya

To Bangkok (Eastern Bus Terminal): Ordinary and a/c government buses depart every 30 minutes 0600-2100 from the government bus terminal on North Pattaya Road near the Sukumvit Highway. These buses terminate in Bangkok at the Eastern Bus Terminal (Ekamai) on Sukumvit Road Soi 63, from where city buses continue into town.

Private bus companies provide pickup at Pattaya hotels and drop-off at major hotels in Bangkok. A very popular service; tickets should be purchased several days in advance.

To Bangkok (Northern Bus Terminal): Visitors heading from Pattaya north to Chiang Mai should take a bus direct from Pattaya's bus terminal on North Pattaya Road to Bangkok's Northern Bus Terminal (Morchit). This connection saves precious hours and avoids the traffic snarls that plague Bangkok. This bus leaves every 30 minutes.

To Bangkok Airport: Buses from the terminal on North Pattaya Road to Bangkok Airport cost 200-240B and depart every two hours 0700-1700. Figure on around three hours to reach the airport.

To North and Northeast Thailand: Destinations in the north, such as Chiang Mai and Mae Sai, and northeastern towns such as Korat and Ubon, can be reached directly by buses departing from a private bus terminal located on Sukumvit Highway near Central Pattaya Road. Buses to Chiang Mai depart at 1330 and 1645, to Korat and Khon Kaen every 15 minutes 2100-2330.

These departures should be confirmed with the tourist office in Pattaya.

Train to Bangkok: One train leaves Pattaya daily at 1450 and takes almost three hours to reach Hualamphong train station.

To Rayong and Ko Samet: Orange public buses to Rayong can be hailed on the main highway. Minibuses continue from Rayong down to Ban Phe, the departure point for boats to Ko Samet. Private minibus service is available from Pattaya to Ban Phe, though you'll pay three times the ordinary rate for the convenience.

RAYONG TO CAMBODIA

RAYONG TOWN

The town of Rayong is a rather nondescript provincial capital, 220 km on the old Sukumvit Highway (Route 3) or 185 km on the newer Route 36 from Bangkok. Rayong Province is a fruit-growing center, famous for its durian, pineapple, fish sauce *(nam pla)*, and fish paste *(kapi)*. Rayong chiefly serves as a transit point for excursions to Ko Samet via the nearby port town of Ban Phe, though miles of unspoiled beaches are located to the east between Ban Phe and Laem Mae Phim.

A TAT office (tel. 038-655420, fax 038-85422) has opened at 153 Sukumvit Rd. a few kilometers east of the city center. This office is responsible for tourism efforts in Rayong, Ko Samet, Chanthaburi, Trat, and Ko Chang. However, **Rayong Travel** (tel. 038-653143) on Sukumvit Road is a more convenient location for maps and tourist information.

Attractions

Sights in Rayong are limited to a few temples and historical shrines that commemorate the liberation of Thailand from Burmese occupation.

Wat Papradu: Located in the center of town a few blocks east of the bus terminal, this Ayuthaya Period temple enshrines a large 12-meter reclining Buddha that lies on its left rather than traditional right side. The entrance alleyway is adjacent to the Asia Hotel.

King Taksin Shrine: Two blocks south of Sukumvit Highway, on the grounds of Wat Lum Mahachai Chumphon, is a shrine which honors the early Siamese king who rallied his army and freed the country from Burmese forces.

Pra Buddha Angkarot: The principal Buddhist image in Rayong is located in Sri Muang Park near City Hall. The 70-*rai* park provides a welcome escape from the concrete blandness of Rayong.

Klong Nam Chedi: A 10-meter white *chedi* of indeterminate age lies on an islet at the mouth of the Rayong River, about two km southwest of town. An annual festival with boat races and folk plays is held here in November.

Fish Sauce: Rayong and Ban Phe are both famous for their production of pungent sauces and thick pastes made from small silver fish. The fish are allowed to decompose in the open air for about seven months, then are crushed, filtered, and bottled on the spot.

Accommodations

Hotels in Rayong are concentrated along Sukumvit Highway and around the bus terminal.

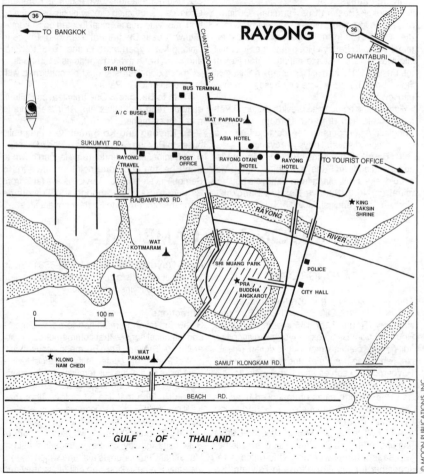

Rayong Hotel: Budget spot with adequate rooms on the south side of the road, about four blocks east of the bus terminal. 65/3 Sukumvit Rd., tel. (038) 611073. 150-350B.

Rayong Otani: Another budget choice very near the Rayong Hotel with similar rooms. 69 Sukumvit Rd., tel. (038) 611112, 200-700B.

Asia Hotel: On the north side of the road with 60 rooms, fan or a/c. 84 Sukumvit Rd., tel. (038) 611022. 200-500B.

Star Hotel: Top-end choice is the 240-room Star Hotel behind the bus terminal. Facilities include a swimming pool, Japanese restaurant, sauna, and nightclub. 109 Rayong Trade Centre Rd., tel. (038) 614901, fax (038) 614608, 1,000-1,800B.

RAYONG BEACH

Most visitors travel directly from Bangkok or Pattaya to Ko Samet, skipping the long and clean beach which stretches almost 15 km southwest from Ban Phe to the craggy cape at Laem Mae Phim. Much of the region lies within the Ban Phe Forest Preserve and has escaped the crass commercialism of Pattaya and Ko Samet. The narrow, casuarina-lined beach is rather ordinary near Ban Phe, but quite white and clean farther south toward Laem Mae Phim. The Thai government has designated the Rayong coastline a tourist development area to divert travelers away from congested Bangkok.

Accommodations

The entire beach is dotted with over 30 mid-priced bungalows and a few upscale hotels and resorts which cater to wealthy Bangkokians and Chinese who arrive during the summer months to enjoy the famous fruits. A good map of the beach with accurate locations of bungalows can be obtained from the TAT office in Pattaya.

Most places charge 500-800B for individual bungalows with fan and 900-1,800B for a/c chalets.

Rayong Resort: Features 45 fairly decent rooms set on Laem Tarn Cape, three km northwest of Ban Phe. 1,400-1,800B.

Rung Napa Lodge: 14 km southeast of Ban Phe with 13 clean lodges in an attractive set-

ting. 800-1,200B.

Wang Kaew Resort: 17 km southwest of Ban Phe with camping tents and cozy bungalows. 900-1,350B.

Palmeraire Beach Hotel: Three km past Wang Kaew Resort is a midlevel hotel with swimming pool, tennis courts, Chinese restaurant, and 60 rooms. Beaches near the Palmeraire and beyond are almost completely deserted. 1,000-1,550B.

BAN PHE

The small fishing town of Ban Phe, 15 km from Rayong, is the jumping-off point for Ko Samet. The town has some fine old wooden architecture and a colorful fish market at the pier. Located just south of the pier is Sobha Gardens, a small botanical enclave with three classical Thai houses furnished with traditional fixtures.

Accommodations

Most visitors go directly to Ko Samet, but inexpensive guesthouses and hotels are available if you miss the last boat, which leaves around 1700. **T.N. House,** two blocks north, is a fairly new and somewhat clean guesthouse with rooms from 200B. **Nuannapa Hotel,** two blocks back from the pier, is an older property offering fan rooms from 150B and a/c rooms from 350B. Top-end choice is the **Pine Beach Hotel,** 300 meters south of town, where a/c rooms cost from 550B.

Transportation

Ban Phe can be reached directly with ordinary and a/c buses from Bangkok's Eastern Bus Terminal on Sukumvit Road. Malibu Travel in Pattaya offers direct minibus service. The Pattaya TAT can help with public buses from Pattaya. From Rayong, take a minibus from the bus terminal to Ban Phe.

Malibu Travel, in the alley opposite the pier, has hourly minibuses to Pattaya. Nearby **SK Travel** has similar services. **DD Tours** on the waterfront sells ordinary and a/c bus tickets to Bangkok. Non-a/c buses for Pattaya and Bangkok depart hourly just south of the pier. The cheapest way to Chanthaburi and Trat is by motorcycle taxi to the main highway for 40B, from where you can flag down ordinary buses heading east.

KO SAMET

This hot and dry island, 6.5 km offshore from Bang Phe, is blessed with extremely fine white beaches and clear blue waters sandwiched between craggy headlands. Thais know Samet as the island where Sunthorn Phu, Thailand's greatest poet, based his most famous work, *Pra Apaimanee*. Ko Samet's great appeal is its easy accessibility to Bangkok and crystalline sands that remain among the purest and finest in all of Thailand.

Haphazard Development

The island was first discovered in the mid-1970s by young Thai weekenders seeking a quick escape from Bangkok. In October 1981 the island was declared a national park and put under the administration of the Forestry Department to prevent overdevelopment and avoid the curses of high-rise hotels, noisy discos, traffic jams, prostitutes, and other problems common to Pattaya and Phuket.

But developers continued to build without permits and local officials did nothing to stop the encroachment. By the late 1980s the island was overrun with bungalows that dumped raw sewage into the ocean and suffered from a complete lack of sanitation and basic infrastructure. Ko Samet became the latest environmental disaster in Thailand.

On 23 May 1990, a special task force of Thai police launched a blitzkrieg, closing down dozens of bungalows and rounding up unlicensed operators. The island was declared off-limits for 48 hours and tourists were restricted to day visits. The crackdown quickly failed after intense political and economic pressure was applied by corrupt forestry officials and influential business interests. The significance of the Samet crackdown lay more in its symbolism than substance, though it helped raise a national outcry about overdevelopment of once-unspoiled havens.

The Future of Samet

What will happen to Ko Samet? The government is caught in a quandary about separating encroachers who hold back-dated titles and those who hold genuine land titles issued before the island was declared a national park.

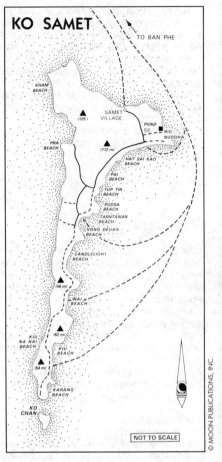

KO SAMET

TO BAN PHE

KHAM BEACH

SAMET VILLAGE

(125)

POND

BIG BUDDHA

PRA BEACH

(112 m)

HAT SAI KAO BEACH

PAI BEACH

TUP TIN BEACH

PUDSA BEACH

TARNTAWAN BEACH

VONG DEUAN BEACH

CANDLELIGHT BEACH

(56 m)

WAI BEACH

(62 m)

KIU NA NAI BEACH

KIU BEACH

(54 m)

KARANG BEACH

KO CHAN

NOT TO SCALE

© MOON PUBLICATIONS, INC.

Park rangers are always there to collect the 50B national parks admission fee, yet decent roads and an adequate sewage system still seem years away. In the 1970s there was virtually nothing on the island, but today there are dozens of hotels that push windsurfing, jet skis, motorboats, motorbikes, and videos during the evening meal. Trash piles up on the beach while offshore coral reefs suffer from overfishing and pollution.

Though the squeaky sand is about the finest in Thailand and the beautifully shaped coves remain inviting, Ko Samet desperately needs attention before it will begin to approach the comfort and attractiveness of Ko Samui or Phuket. Unless the Thai government takes immediate action, the future of Ko Samet—along with other islands such as Ko Phi Phi and Ko Chang—seems extremely bleak.

At Last, Freshwater
Progress of sorts finally took place in early 1999 with the opening of a new 150,000 cubic meter reservoir that now provides freshwater for tourists, resort owners, and local residents. While this may sound positive, the construction of this freshwater reservoir by the Irrigation Department also lends credence to the argument made by resort owners that state agencies have actively supported the tourism business and therefore the 43 "illegal" resorts on the island are actually legal units—and the eviction demands of the Forestry Department initiated in 1990 should be dropped.

Accommodations and Beaches
Ko Samet's eastern coastline is partitioned into beaches and coves filled with bungalows in all possible price ranges. Those on the northern and central beaches are the most developed and expensive. Southern beaches offer less expensive bungalows and primitive bamboo huts badly overpriced at 150-350B per person. Prices rise sharply during weekends and holidays when Thai teenagers, hippies, and folk musicians pack the island.

Ko Samet is, technically speaking, a national park where camping is legal and free anywhere on the island despite signs to the contrary posted by unscrupulous bungalow operators.

Ko Samet is extremely dry except for a short rainy season May-July. The island is parched like Death Valley, USA, during the high season Nov.-Feb., when water shortages—despite the new reservoir—might mean additional charges for showers and drinking water.

Beaches below are described starting from Hat Sai Kao at the northern end to Ao Kiu at the southern tip.

Hat Sai Kao
"Diamond Sand," Ko Samet's longest and most impressive beach, is popular with families with children and tourists down from Pattaya. Located 10 minutes by foot from Na Dan ferry landing,

Sai Kao Beach offers over a dozen moderately priced bungalows with restaurants and watersport facilities that face the broad beach. As with nearly all places on Ko Samet, most bungalow operations have old huts constructed a decade ago and new bungalows erected just last month. All charge 250-500B for simple huts with common bath, and 400-900B for individual bungalows. Off-season rates, with hard bargaining, can be as low as 150B.

Water sports include windsurfing, boat trips around the island, and snorkeling expeditions to nearby islands. A concrete mermaid and phallic shrine have been erected at the southern end of the beach. Magnificent sunsets can be enjoyed from the promontory above the white Buddha.

The following is a sampling of moderately priced bungalows:

Diamond:	450-1,200B
Ploy Talay:	350-800B
Sai Kaew Villa:	250-2,500B
Seaview:	300-700B
Toy:	300-700B
VK Villa:	250-700B
White Sand:	350-900B

Pai Beach
Pai, or Paradise, Beach is a small cove with several bungalows, travel offices such as Citizen Travel, and a small post office with post restante facilities.

Naga's Bungalows: Justifiably one of the most popular gathering spots on Samet, Naga's (tel. 01-321-0732) serves freshly baked goods and decent fish specialties, and keeps a sprawling library of yellowing paperbacks. Try the lemon meringue pie, fudge brownies, and piña colada sundae. Snorkeling equipment, surfboards, and sailboats can be rented here and at nearby **Odd's Little Huts** (formerly Nui's Bungalows). Glass-bottom boat tours of the nearby coral beds cost 150B. Rooms at Naga's and Odd's cost 250-500B.

Samed Villa: Good restaurant with bamboo furniture, plus varnished bamboo bungalows with electricity 300-800B. Recommended.

Sea Breeze Bungalows: Popular but cluttered and noisy from nightly videos. Rooms from 250B.

Ao Pai Huts: Over 70 rooms with basic huts from 250B and individual bungalows for

800B. Boat trips to Ko Kudi and Ko Thalu cost 280B and include snorkeling equipment, lunch, and a complimentary barbecue at Nop's Restaurant.

Nop's Restaurant: Four levels of dining terraces with blinking lights, Buddhas, woodcarvings, Balinese music, and lovely views. A great place to dine.

Tub Tin and Pudsa Beaches

Several sets of bungalows are located over the craggy headlands behind these beaches.

Tub Tin Bungalows: A very popular place on a good beach blessed with hanging palms. A large, well-decorated restaurant displays fresh seafood on ice; there's a bar and patio adjacent. Tub Tin has simple bungalows from 150B and new chalets from 500B. Recommended.

From Tub Tin Bungalow, the road veers right to cross the island and dead-end at Ao Pra (Paradise Beach), where a pair of bungalows stand on Samet's only west coast beach. Excellent sunsets.

Tarntawan Beach

"Sunflower Beach" is dominated by the expansive Tarntawan Bungalows, which maintain huts in all possible price ranges 250-800B. Despite the gaudy concrete sculpture of kangaroos and horses and the mysterious tomb of Franz Merklebach, Tarntawan Beach retains a hippie atmosphere.

Vong Deuan Beach

Ko Samet's second most popular beach (after Hat Sai Kao) is located on a beautifully arched bay bisected by a rickety pier. After the island seizure of 1990, local park officials erected a sign which stated "no overnight stay on visit to Samed Island. Accommodations have been seized as legal evidence for forest encroachment."

Vong Deuan (also translated Wong Deurn or Deuan) is a yuppie destination filled with tourists from Pattaya and Europeans on package holidays. **Sea Horse Travel,** in the middle of the beach, changes traveler's checks, has a mobile telephone, and sells tickets to Ko Chang and Bangkok. Swiss-managed **Delfimarin Diwa Diving Center** not only arranges scuba dives to nearby coral beds and shipwrecks and longer multi-day journeys to islands near Ko Chang, but will sell you bus or airplane tickets.

Vong Deuan can be reached directly from the Ban Phe Pier, but you'll need to inquire about the correct boat. Boats back to Ban Phe depart daily at 1130, 1530, and 1830. The beach has several midpriced to expensive bungalows.

Tents: Tents can be rented from the shop at the north end of the beach from a beautiful woman named Pia; 60B for small tents and 180B for large 10-man tents.

Malibu Garden Resort: All-white A-frame huts with private bath and electricity for 500-950B. Tel. (01) 321-0345.

Sea Horse: The cheapest place on Vong Deuan Beach, simple bamboo huts cost 180B, midsized wooden huts facing the water 250B, and larger huts to the rear 450B. All are overpriced when compared to Ko Samui or Ko Chang.

Vong Deuan Resort: A relatively luxurious place (tel. 02-391-9065, fax 02-391-9571) featuring standard bungalows from 700B and seaview chalets from 950B.

Vong Deuan Villa: Located at the southern end of the beach, Vong Deuan Villa (tel. 01-321-0789 or in Rayong 038-652300) has a miniature golf course and billiard tables, and charges 700B for small fan-cooled bungalows, 1,800B for a/c rooms, and 3,500B for VIP chalets. Although an incredible rip-off, the restaurant has good food with great views from the terrace.

Candlelight Beach

Also called Ao Thian, this long and rocky beach has two sets of primitive bungalows that offer an escape from the commercialism of other beaches.

Candlelight Bungalows: A variety of bamboo and brick huts for 200-450B. Find the office in the octagonal building above the open-air restaurant.

Lung Dam Bungalows: Adjacent to the collapsing pier are bungalows priced from 200B.

Wai Beach

A fairly nice beach dominated by the upscale Samet Ville Resort. Fan-cooled rooms cost 800B per person and include three meals, drinks, and the boat ride from Ban Phe. For information and reservations, call (01) 321-1284.

Kiu Beach

Ko Samet's most attractive beach, Kiu Beach is clean, quiet, and graced with a beautiful row of swaying palm trees. Sunsets can be enjoyed from the western beach and from the hillside viewpoint. Ao Kiu is a very long walk from Hat Sai Kao Beach, but well worth the trouble if you're looking for peace and solitude.

Kiu Coral Beach Bungalows: Old bamboo bungalows with common bath cost 150B, 250B with private bath, and 400-700B in better chalets; tel. (01) 312-1231. Their restaurant has a 13-page menu with seafood and Wild Boar Curry. The *Thep Chomlatee* boat departs daily from Ban Phe at 0830.

Transportation

Air-conditioned buses leave every hour for Ban Phe from the Eastern Bus Terminal in Bangkok. Alternatively, hourly buses go to Rayong from where minibuses continue to Ban Phe.

Travel agencies on Khao San Road in Bangkok can arrange direct minibuses to Ban Phe including boat trip to Ko Samet for about 280B, an expensive if convenient alternative to public transportation.

Boats to Ko Samet leave Ban Phe regularly 0800-1700. Be careful climbing onto these converted fishing boats—mishaps are common. Boats dock at Na Dan (Samet Village) on the north end, Hat Sai Kao, Vong Deuan, and other beaches. Unless you enjoy long and dusty hikes, ask around and take a local boat direct to the specific beach.

Minibuses travel from Ban Phe back to Rayong until sunset. Don't believe taxi driver scare tactics like "Last bus already go." See the Ban Phe section above for more information.

CHANTHABURI

Chanthaburi (Chantaburi), a busy commercial city 330 km from Bangkok, is famous for its gem industry, durian plantations, and Vietnamese-Christian population, which fled religious persecution in Vietnam during the late 19th century. Because of its proximity to Cambodia, Chanthaburi ("City of the Moon") has figured prominently in Thai history as the site of border skirmishes between the Thais and the French who once occupied the city from 1893 to 1904.

Contemporary Chanthaburi shows strong Chinese influence in its temples, shrines, restaurants, and script. The downtown section is a hopeless, confusing network of streets, but the riverside area and adjacent parks are relaxing places to wander and watch the local people.

Attractions

Few Westerners visit Chanthaburi, though the town has enough charm and attractions to merit a quick trip.

Riverside Walk: Begin your walk on Sukapiban Road (also called Rim Nam Road) at the bridge behind the Kasem Sarn I Hotel. This narrow road features old-style houses with intricate woodcarvings and elaborate wooden altars that evoke a timeless atmosphere. Watch for religious-supply stores, Chinese funeral shops selling paper cars and cardboard yachts, 19th-century Chinese medicine halls, and old buildings fixed with French-colonial shutters and filigree plasterwork.

Church of the Immaculate Conception: Chanthaburi's great historic structure was constructed in French style between 1906 and 1909 by Vietnamese-Chinese Catholics persecuted by Emperor Gia Long. Inside the Gothic interior are 26 Moorish-style arches and pediments painted pale green, wooden pews, stained-glass windows imported from Europe, and a semicircular teak roof with three shellwork chandeliers.

Gem Dealers: Much of the jewelry sold in Thailand contains gemstones dug from the open-pit mines near Chanthaburi. Chinese gem dealers operate from sidewalk stalls and in elaborate Greco-Roman showrooms just off Sukapiban Road near the bridge. Business is liveliest on weekends; only recognized customers are allowed into the larger gem shops.

King Taksin Park: A large public park with an artificial lake and statue of King Taksin west of the river provides an escape from the traffic. The nearby foodstalls and Versailles Coffee Pub are great places to eat and mingle in the evening.

Central Market: Wedged between a confusing network of streets and alleys is the lively market filled with local fruits and handicraft specialties, such as famous reed mats from the nearby village of San Hin.

Attractions outside Chanthaburi

Chanthaburi travel agents can arrange tours to the following sights. Local buses leave from the terminal on Saritdet Road.

Wat Bot: Sited on a promontory overlooking the river, Wat Bot offers some chipping murals dating from the reign of King Rama IV that depict the 10 previous lives of the Buddha.

Gem Mines: Over 70% of Thai gemstones come from the region near Chanthaburi, Trat, and Sisaket on the Cambodian border. Tours to nearby mines such as Khao Ploi Wan (Sap-

phire Ring Mountain), 11 km southwest of Chanthaburi, can be arranged through local agencies. A Sri Lankan-style *chedi* constructed during the reign of King Mongkut caps the small hill at Khao Ploi Wan. Blue sapphires, garnets, zircons, and highly prized Siamese rubies are also mined east of Chanthaburi near Ban Nong Bon and Bo Rai.

Laem Singh: The struggle between Thai and French forces is commemorated by two buildings constructed by the French in 1893 on Singh Cape, 31 km south of town. Tuk Daeng ("Red

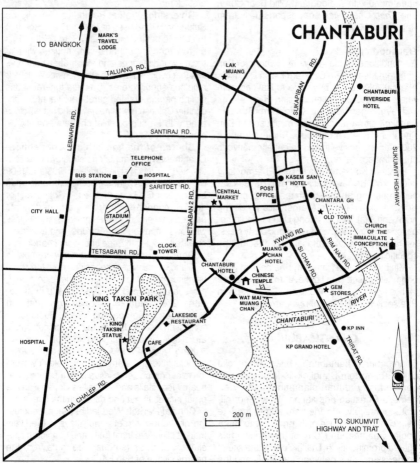

House") once served as an officers' mess hall and administrative headquarters, while the leaning brick Khok Khi Kai ("Chicken Shit Prison") held prisoners below the chicken coop.

Pliu Waterfall: A small waterfall is located in Khao Sabap National Park, 17 km southeast of Chanthaburi. Facing the falls is a stone pyramid dedicated to a consort of King Rama V who tragically drowned at Bang Pa In while her attendants watched; to touch royalty meant a mandatory death sentence.

North of Chanthaburi, Wat Kao Sukim is a spacious temple with beautifully carved furniture in the kingly banquet hall and enormous porcelain vases on the top floor. Take H3 north and turn on H33322. Also north of town, the 50-meter **Krating Waterfall** and several caves can be found in Kitchakut National Park. The 28-km journey passes orchards of rambutan and durian.

Nature lovers can overnight in the government bungalows in **Khao Soi Dao National Park,** 70 km north of Chanthaburi.

Accommodations

Inexpensive and quiet hotels cluster down near the river, a 20-minute walk from the bus station. Hotels in the middle of town are very noisy but convenient for gem dealers.

Kasem Sarn I Hotel: An excellent hotel with very large and clean rooms, all with private bath and decent furniture, plus towels and maid service. A simple cafe is located outside to the right. The hotel is outside the main traffic circles and therefore very quiet. From the bus terminal, turn left and walk down Saritdet Road toward the Chanthaburi River. 98/1 Benchama Rachutit Rd., tel. (039) 312340, 150-200B fan, 300-350B a/c.

Chantara Guesthouse: Offering less expensive rooms on the riverfront road just behind the Kasem Sarn I Hotel, the Chantara is marked only in Thai script. Look for a green two-story building with balconies. 248 Sukapiban Rd., tel. (039) 312310, 100-120B common bath, 1,500-2,000B private bath. Request a room with a view.

Chanthaburi Hotel: A busy and noisy place centrally located near the markets and King Taksin Park. 42/6 Tachalab Rd., tel. (039) 311300, 300-500B a/c.

Mark's Travel Lodge: Top-end choice is the curiously named hotel on the western edge of town. This 220-room hotel is popular with businesspeople and gem dealers. 14 Raksak Chamun Rd., tel. (039) 311531, 350-800B a/c.

KP Grand Hotel: A booming economy has brought several new upscale hotels to Chanthaburi. Across the river but conveniently located near the gem dealers, the Grand opened in 1994 and appears the first choice of jewelry dealers. 35/200 Trirat Rd., tel. (039) 323201, fax (039) 323214, 1,300-2,500B.

Chanthaburi Riverside Hotel: The top-end choice includes individual chalets spread around landscaped gardens, tennis courts, a swimming pool, several restaurants, and facilities for gemology conventions. Chanthaimit Rd., tel. (039) 311726, Bangkok tel. (02) 513-8190, fax (02) 512-5726, 2,200-4,200B.

Restaurants

Chanthaburi is known for its fresh seafood and thick rice noodles, exported throughout the world. As described by a local tourist publication, the noodles are famous for their "toothsomeness."

Lakeside Restaurants: Best place for dinner are the foodstalls and outdoor cafes which surround the north side of King Taksin Park. A very large place on Tha Chalep Road across the street from the Versailles Coffee Pub displays almost 20 sample dishes, including clams sautéed in black bean sauce and crunchy sweet-and-sour fish. Highly recommended.

Central Market: Dozens of streetstalls serve Thai and Chinese dishes every night at the market on Ampawa Road.

TRAT

Trat, 312 km from Bangkok, is the provincial capital and leading commercial center of southeastern Thailand. After the fall of Ayuthaya in 1767, Trat served as the launching point for King Taksin's counterattack against the Burmese invaders. Trat and nearby islands were ceded to France in 1894 for Chanthaburi, but were returned to Thai control in 1906 in exchange for French control over western Cambodia.

As the last major town before the Cambodian border, Trat remained almost completely off the tourist trail until the discovery of Ko Chang in the early 1990s. Trat now chiefly serves as a transit point for visitors heading to Ko Chang

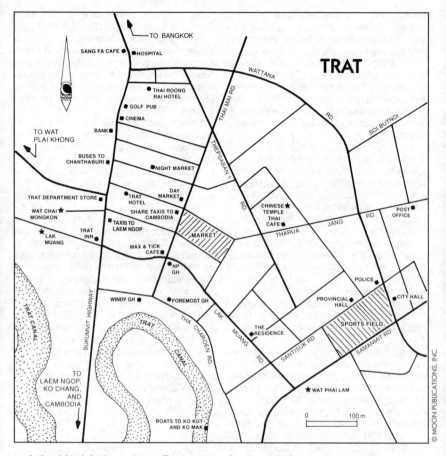

and other islands in the southeast. Trat is an ordinary town with an extraordinary future; you can almost feel the heady air of prosperity.

Attractions

Trat Province is just starting to attract visitors to its gem-mining towns, remote beaches, and modest historical sights.

Wat Bupparam: Two km southwest of town, Wat Pai Klong is an old temple constructed in 1652 during the reign of King Thong of Ayuthaya. The temple consists of a *bot* surrounded by small *chedis* and three *mondops* which contain footprints of the Buddha.

Accommodations

Most travelers head directly to Ko Chang, but a few guesthouses east of the main road offer rooms and information on distant islands. The small tourist information office in the bus terminal can be surprisingly helpful, depending on who is staffing the counter.

Max and Tick's Guesthouse: This old favorite has closed down after a run of almost a decade.

Foremost Guesthouse: Foremost has been recommended by many travelers for the friendly Thai owners who help with travel tips, hot showers, and congenial vibes. 49 Tha Charoen

Rd., tel. (039) 511923, 120-150B private rooms with common bath.

Windy Guesthouse: Same owners as Foremost; they also rent motorcycle and canoes. 37 Tha Charoen Rd., tel. (039) 511923, 40B dorm, 120-150B private rooms.

NP Guesthouse: Friendly little spot one block off the main road with traveler information and helpful managers. The place is adjacent to the former Max and Tick's GH. 10 Soi Luang Ao, tel. (039) 512564, 60-80B dorm, 120-180B private room.

Trad Hotel: The Trad (also called the Meuang Trat) is your best choice for better rooms; the small but decent coffee shop faces the morning market. 4 Sukumvit Rd., tel. (039) 511091, 250-350B fan, 450-8B
50 a/c.

Restaurants
Modern Market: The new market on Sukumvit Road is the best place for cheap eats in a clean environment, as well as shopping for basic supplies. Check the impressive fish market in the rear. Inexpensive foodstalls are located on the ground floor. **Top Star Cafe** on the third floor is a semi-luxurious option.

Golf Pub & Coffee Shop: Western decor, records mounted on the walls, live music in the evening, and a good selection of Thai and Western dishes make this a popular *farang* hangout. The Thai owner once lived in the U.S. You'll find it on Sukumvit Road past the cinema. Inexpensive.

Transportation
Ordinary buses from Bangkok's Eastern Bus Terminal on Sukumvit Road depart in the mornings until 0900, cost 120-150B, and take about eight hours to reach Trat. Air-conditioned buses cost 220-250B, but do the journey in six hours.

Exchange services are available from the Bangkok Bank minitruck parked in the lot adjacent to the pier. Traveler's checks can be cashed at several resorts on Ko Chang, but only at very poor rates. Extra food supplies and drinking water should be picked up from the nearby shops and restaurants. A large sign behind the parking lot commemorates a sea battle between the Thai and French navies in 1941.

Accommodations
Laem Ngop has several small guesthouses that cater to backpackers and travelers who miss the last boat to Ko Chang in the late afternoon.

Chut Kaew Guesthouse and **Laem Ngop Inn** are up on the right side of the highway away from the pier. A few steps further you'll find the **Nong Aye** and the newish **PI Guesthouse.** All have rooms for 100-150B.

Transportation
Travel agencies on Khao San Road in Bangkok have small minibuses direct to Laem Ngop. Services are provided by both Sea Horse and S.T. Travel. Minibuses are convenient, but the air-conditioning rarely works and they travel at frightening speeds. Both services will attempt to put you on private boats that take you to remote beaches where you become a captive audience. Skip this scam and take another boat to the beach of your choice.

Public buses from Bangkok's Eastern Bus Terminal to Trat are both safer and more comfortable for the full-day journey. Minibuses from the main road in Trat continue the 17 km south to Laem Ngop and charge just 20-30B per passenger.

Ordinary and a/c buses depart throughout the day for Pattaya and Bangkok. The Sea Horse minibus departs daily for Bangkok at 1145.

LAEM NGOP

Laem Ngop, 17 km south of Trat, is the departure point for boats to Ko Chang and other remote islands. *Laem* means cape; *ngop* is the traditional Khmer rice farmer's hat. Most of the activity is centered around the pier where dozens of backpackers wait for the next boat to Ko Chang.

KO CHANG

Ko Chang ("Elephant Island") is, after Phuket, Thailand's second-largest island, some 30 km in length and eight km broad at its widest point. Also called Elephant Island, Ko Chang is covered with dense jungle and bisected by a steep wall of mountains.

KO CHANG

The Arrival of Tourism

Ko Chang remained almost completely untouched until an article published in 1989 by *Abenteuer & Reisen,* a German travel magazine, proclaimed the island the next paradise in Thailand. Guidebook coverage the following year by brought worldwide attention to the entire archipelago.

By early 1990 the island had achieved fame as Thailand's next major resort destination. Speculators and land developers quickly arrived to construct bungalows and hotels to take advantage of the expected tourism boom. Land prices soared to astronomical heights as local residents hopelessly fought to retain control of their island. Fishermen abandoned their traditional occupations and converted their trawlers into shuttle ferries.

Local authorities soon jumped on the tourism bandwagon. The Thai government constructed a large pier on the east side of Ko Chang and then began blasting a concrete road which now encircles the northern side of the island, connecting the commercial east coast with the tourist beaches on the western side. Ko Chang quickly resembled the early stages of Ko Samui: a tropical island firmly mesmerized by the promise of mass tourism.

Ko Chang Today

Despite all the construction and development, Ko Chang remains among the more beautiful and relatively untouched islands in Thailand. Most accommodations remain simple bamboo bungalows rather than concrete hotels filled with package tourists, and a majority of Chang's 6,000 residents still make their living from fishing rather than tourism. Few locals speak much English and most residents seem relatively uninterested in catering to foreigners.

When I first visited Ko Chang a decade ago, the island had only one Land Rover and three bicycles for rent (one was broken). Today the island has a plentiful supply of jeeps that serve as taxis over the northern loop, and sufficient motorcycles for rent, yet Ko Chang remains relatively peaceful. Discos, nightly videos, noisy motorcycles, and beer bars are still several years away—a wonderfully refreshing change from the hustle of Samui and Phuket.

Recent government statistics indicate that over 300,000 Thais and some 50,000 foreigners now visit the island each year, and that the island now has almost 75 bungalow operations on a half-dozen beaches.

Several recent visitors have written to complain about soaring prices for guesthouses and the get-rich-quick mentality that seems to be taking over the island. Paying 600B for an airless concrete cubicle with a solitary window and barely functioning fan is not good value, and travelers may need to skip the more commercialized beaches on the northwestern coast (White Beach in particular) in favor of the less developed beaches along the southwestern side of the island.

East Coast Attractions

Most visitors are content to simply relax on one of the west coast beaches, such as White Sand Beach, Klong Prao Beach, or Kai Bae Beach. Ko Chang, however, is a spectacular island blessed with thick tropical jungle, small waterfalls, and narrow trails which follow the deep interior valleys.

Dan Mai: The only sizable village on the east coast has a small market, fishing pier, and surprisingly large villa owned by the local mayor. Mayom Pier, four km to the south, will probably become an important embarkation point upon completion of the road to the west coast. The largest town on Ko Chang is Salak Pet, a somnolent fishing village in a protected cove on the south coast.

Visitors Center: Local authorities have erected a small visitors center near Mayom Waterfall on the east coast. Inside the deserted structure is a three-dimensional model of Ko Chang with English labels, a map of Thailand's national parks, and aerial photos of local beaches marked in Thai script. Adjacent concrete bungalows with private bathrooms cost 400-600B per night and can be hired from local park officials.

Mayom Waterfall: A few kilometers south of Dan Mai is a six-level waterfall and swimming pond 500 meters off the primitive road. The falls have been visited by several Thai kings, including Chulalongkorn, who carved his initials on several rocks. English-language signs point the way. Tham Mayom Huts, about 50 meters north, are five simple bungalows priced from 300B.

Don Keo Waterfall: An unmarked path just north of the broken wooden bridge leads through rubber plantations to these modest falls on the east coast, about 10 minutes south of Saithong Guesthouse.

West Coast Beaches

Ko Chang's best beaches are all on the west coast. Some accommodations remain simple bamboo bungalows with mattresses on the floors, illuminated by oil lamps, although many bungalows now receive electricity from the myriad power lines constructed around the island. Open-air showers and common bathrooms are located to the rear. Restaurants are funky places with good food but rudimentary service; you'll probably be ignored to the point of starvation until you approach the front counter.

Construction of new bungalows is going on at a furious pace as professionals from Bangkok arrive to milk the tourist boom, so expect major changes from the following descriptions. In general, you should take a jeep from the east coast of the island to the beach of your choice and then wander around to inspect a few places. Most bungalows are filled during the high season Oct.-March, but tents can be rented while waiting for vacancies. Ko Chang is, technically speaking, a national park where camping is legal anywhere.

The following beaches on the west coast are described from north to south.

White Sand Beach

Hat Sai Khao, the longest and most popular beach on Ko Chang, is the original escape on the island. The concrete road which skirts the back side of the beach goes south to Klong Prao Beach and cuts through the mountains at the northern end to Klong Son Beach. Alternatively, a poorly marked trail heads north over the ridgetop and brings you to Klong Son in one hour. White Sand Beach is a good place to enjoy the sand and meet other travelers, though prices are on a steep rise and many travelers now prefer the beaches to the south.

Over a dozen bungalows are spread along the beach. Most charge 150-450B for bamboo huts with mattresses on the floor and common bathrooms located back toward the road. Bungalows are almost identical, but restaurants vary from primitive to almost sophisticated. The trend over the last few years has been to tear down the bamboo huts and replace them with far less desirable concrete cubicles that are hot, soulless, and cost 500-800B per unit. If you can't find an airy bamboo hut on this beach, take a jeep south to the less commercialized beaches.

White Sand Beach Resort has 10 rooms tucked under the trailhead to Klong Son Beach. The beach here is relatively deserted due to its isolated location at the far northern end of the island. **Boom Dam** and **Cookie Bungalows,** slightly to the south, are primitive low-end choices. **Sabbai Bungalows,** with a pleasant semicircular restaurant, is a better place located midway down the beach. **Tantawan** and **Bamboo Huts** are nothing special.

Ko Chang huts

Honey Resort, sited near the southern end, has better huts and a nicely elevated restaurant. **Sun Sai Bungalow Resort** at the extreme south features small individual houses connected by pathways fronting a rocky beach.

Klong Prao Beach

The road from White Sand Beach veers inland and skirts the rocky cape at Chai Chet until it approaches the coastline near Klong Prao River. Klong Prao Beach is a long and rapidly developing beach with a limited amount of tracts of property covered with little more than coconut groves and wild vegetation. Klong Prao ("Coconut Canal") offers a finer degree of peace and solitude and is a pleasant change from the more popular backpacker enclaves on White Sand and Kai Bai Beaches.

Attractions: Some great hikes can be made east into the mountains which bisect the island. The path to Klong Prao Waterfall is two km south from the Coconut Beach Bungalows past the small creek, and before the larger Klong Prao River. Turn left on the trail between two houses and hike two km to a cafe, where the trail continues one km upriver to the falls.

Carved Diamond Mountain, Ko Chang's highest peak at 774 meters, is visible from the valley. Guides are absolutely essential for exploring the interior of Ko Chang.

Accommodations: Bungalows are widely scattered along Klong Prao Beach, making bungalow hopping a difficult proposition. Starting from the north end, **Coconut Beach Bungalows** features 12 extremely beautiful bamboo huts for 200-250B set under swaying palm trees, a romantic spot recommended for couples. A lovely restaurant nearby flanks the small canal filled with fishing boats. Unfortunately, the owners of this once fine property have constructed a large number of completely awful concrete cubicles to the rear and ruined much of the former atmosphere. If you can stay in one of the bamboo huts then you are in luck; otherwise, move on. The bamboo bungalows now cost over 400B, while the truly disastrous concrete prison cells cost a more reasonable 300-350B.

Overflow is handled by **Coconut 2 Bungalows** across the river to the north. Boats to Laem Ngop depart daily at 0830 and 1100.

Ko Chang Resort some 200 meters south is the original tourist hotel on Ko Chang. Solid-timber huts and a/c A-frames with hot showers and TV (videos provided) go for 1,500-3,500B. Facilities include an expensive restaurant, cocktail lounge with broken organ, and daily two-hour skin diving tours. Bangkok tel. (02) 276-1233.

The road continues south past the path to Klong Prao Waterfall and across the Klong Prao River. **PSS Bungalows** is beautifully situated on a sandy tip facing the broad mouth of the river. The sand and solitude are superb, with 20 good huts for 200-450B. Boats back to Laem Ngop depart daily at 0730 and 1100.

A long stretch of deserted beach goes south from PSS Bungalows to **Magic Bungalows,** one of the best values on Klong Prao Beach. Magic has over 30 huts, great sand, and a popular restaurant stilted over the clear waters. Adjacent **Good Luck Bungalows** (Chok Dee) faces a rocky beach and is not a good value.

Kai Bae Beach

The last major beach on the west coast has a narrow strip of sand crowded with over a dozen bungalows. **Coral Bungalows** on the rocky promontory has 30 primitive huts and wonderful views from the open-air restaurant. **Nang Naun 2** faces a rocky beach, with huts crowded together except for several bungalows on the rearside lagoon. **Kae Bae** and **Kae Bae Beach Bungalows** are similar, but the beach improves to the south.

Porn Guesthouse, a much better choice, has over 20 huts imaginatively arranged between the hillside and the narrow white-sand beach. **Siam Bay Resort** is the last bungalow on Kai Bae Beach. The cost for each of the above runs 150-400B.

Snorkeling is fairly good at the offshore islands on either local 10-person charters or larger fishing boats.

Kruat Beach

Beyond the rocky promontory are several bays that will soon be developed with beachside and hillside bungalows. Until completion of the road, a narrow path wanders through the jungle and over the mountains to the southern beach at Bang Bao.

South Coast Beaches

The south coast of Ko Chang has several beaches that have been somewhat developed over the last decade (pre-21st century) but still remain somewhat remote and quiet. A limited number of boats from Laem Ngop go direct to both Bang Bao and Long Beaches, plus several of the nearby islands such as Ko Prao, Ko Laoya, Ko Wai, and Ko Ngam.

Bang Bao Beach: A beautiful bay and private pier are located on this primary beach on the south coast of Ko Chang. Most of the beach is dominated by **Bang Bao Resort** and **Sunset Bungalows,** private developments that receive complaints about overcrowding, inadequate water supplies, and decrepit bungalows. Sea Horse Travel often sends their passengers here; resist their generous offer and find a boat heading to White Sand or Klong Prao Beaches.

Long Beach: Perhaps the most spectacular beach and finest waters on Ko Chang are near the southeastern tip. Captain Daniel's Bungalows mysteriously burned down several years ago, but **Long Beach Bungalows** and **Tantawan Guesthouse** have filled the void. The water here is crystal clear and shallow enough for safe swimming. Long Beach is a short boat ride away from the beautiful islands of Ko Prao, Ko Laoya, Ko Ngam, and Ko Wai.

East Coast Beaches

The east coast of Ko Chang is rarely visited because of its brownish sand and mangrove swamps. There are few places to stay aside from homestays following the sad closure of Saithong Bungalows a few years ago.

North Coast Beaches

It's possible to venture up to Klong Son, an almost completely untouched fishing village in a well-protected harbor on the north coast. **Klongson Bungalows** in the village has five bamboo huts facing the bay and a series of connected rooms facing courtyard planks. **Chi Minh Place,** 300 meters behind town in the jungle, has several homestay bungalows with meals included. Klong Son has a small mosque, supply shop, and several seafood restaurants on a rickety fishing pier. Motorcycle taxis reach Klong Son from Saithong Guesthouse, or travelers can hike one hour over the mountains from White Sand Beach.

Transportation

Fishing trawlers converted into ferry boats leave from Laem Ngop daily from 0900 to late afternoon. Prices are fixed at rather unreasonable levels but you can save perhaps 20-40B by purchasing tickets directly from the boat owner rather than the middleman who operates a counter at the pier.

Boats from Ko Chang back to Laem Ngop leave in the mornings until early afternoon. Exact departures are posted at most guesthouses. Guesthouse owners will flag down the boat and provide shuttle services out to the ferry.

Completion of the concrete road around most of the island means that today most boats only shuttle across to Dan Mai Pier on the east coast, from where *songtaos* ("taxis") continue to the beaches on the west coast.

ISLANDS SOUTH OF KO CHANG

The rapid development of Ko Chang has inspired many travelers to explore the islands farther south toward Cambodia. Though most of the islands lie within the boundaries of Ko Chang National Park and should be open to public camping and small-scale bungalow development, many are controlled by private developers, powerful politicians, rich movie stars, Thai royalty, and military officers who have erected expensive resort complexes. A major problem is finding a boat. Reliable information on boats and accommodations should be checked at Foremost Guesthouse before leaving Trat.

Ko Prao

The small island just offshore from Salakpet has 25 luxurious air-conditioned chalets that charge over 1,000B per night.

Ko Ngam

Ko Ngam is a very pretty island bisected by a narrow spit of sand. **Ko Ngam Resort** charges 800-1,200B per night.

Ko Laoya

Owned by a Trat politician, this lovely little island has a beautiful beach, teak bungalows for 1,200-2,000B, and a seafood restaurant popular

*monks on
Ko Chang Beach*

with Thai group tours from Bangkok. Trat tel. (039) 512552, Bangkok tel. (02) 391-1588.

Ko Wai

Ko Wai Resort has several small huts on a small and brownish beach. Local divers recommend the offshore coral beds, but I found the diving rather mediocre.

Ko Mak

Ko Mak Resort (Bangkok tel. 02-319-6714), owned by a Thai movie star, has 10 rooms priced 900-1,200B that cater to Thais rather than *farangs*. Much cleaner is **Lazy Days Resort** (tel. 02-281-3412 in Bangkok) for just 150-250B, in the northwest corner of the island. Boats leave from Laem Ngop and cost 350-500B per person.

Ko Kradat

Owned by a Thai princess, Ko Kradat ("Paper Island") features a seven-km beach and fairly good diving. **Ko Kradat Resort** has 36 bungalows from 1,400B. Also try **Ko Kradat Island** (tel. 02-368-2634) for 700-1,000B. More information on this island is available from Foremost Guesthouse in Trat, or by calling Mr. Chumpon in Bangkok at (02) 311-3668.

Ko Kut

This is the second-largest island in the Ko Chang archipelago and remains a place where backpackers can get off the beaten track without spending a small fortune. Most of the bunga-lows are on the west and northwest coasts. Several rivers with waterfalls run from the central mountain ridge down to the west coast. Klong Chao and Klong Anamkok waterfalls are accessible by boat to Klong Chao and then a short 500-meter hike.

Accommodations: A half dozen inexpensive bungalows have recently opened, including the **First Guesthouse** at Hat Tapho on the western side. Rooms with elevated beds and common bath cost from 100B, plus the restaurant serves surprisingly good food. Check with Foremost Guesthouse in Trat for more information.

Transportation: Ko Kut is a three-hour boat ride from Laem Ngop, from the Chaloemphon pier on the Trat River just east of Trat, or from Ban Nam Chiaw, a small village midway between Trat and Laem Ngop. Several boats make the trip each day despite dire warnings from other operators that "last boat already go." Boats with enough passengers occasionally depart from Klong Yai for Ko Kut.

THE ROAD TO CAMBODIA

Highway 318 continues southeast from Trat down to the Cambodian border. Most of the region remains a military security zone with dozens of checkpoints, though several small towns with excellent beaches seem ripe for discovery. The national elections and surrender of the final Khmer Rouge leaders in late 1998 helped settle the situation, and today there's little danger for most travelers.

You can now take a boat from Ban Hat Lek, at the extreme tip of the Sukumvit Highway across to Pak Kong on Ko Kong (Kong Island) in Cambodia, and another boat to Sihanoukville, a 10-hour trip. From there, taxis are available to Phnom Penh. Cambodian visas *must* be obtained in advance from the Cambodian Embassy in Bangkok.

Ban Chuen and Klong Yai are the two largest towns on Route 318 from Trat to Cambodia. The road ends at Ban Hat Lek, from where Westerners with Cambodian visas can continue to Pak Kong (on Ko Kong) and then Sihanoukville in Cambodia.

Ban Chuen

Sixty km from Trat and 14 km before Klong Yai, Ban Chuen has the best beach in the region. Most of the area is used by the Thai military as an R&R escape from their border patrols. Minitrucks from Trat will drop you at the highway turnoff, from where motorcycle taxis continue for the five-km journey down to the beach. Accommodations in local bungalows cost 150-380B.

Klong Yai

The last major town in southeast Thailand where smuggling operations between Thailand and Cambodia bring in over 10B million per day. Klong Yai has several bungalows and hotels, including Suksamran Hotel on the street that leads to the ocean, Klong Yai Bungalows where

a/c rooms start from 250B, Bang Inn Villa, and Pavinee Hotel. Boats occasionally depart from Klong Yai for Ko Kut.

Ban Hat Lek

It used to be a lonely, somewhat spooky drive down to Ban Hat Lek at the end of the peninsula, but today you need to watch out for speeding Mercedes and tour buses, all of them heading for the once-obscure fishing village that has recently been transformed into a giant parking lot. Ban Hat Lek is the closest spot on the Thai side to the Ko Kong International Casino and Resort, which opened in April 1998. The casino now attracts almost 1,000 daily visitors, a major draw for Thai weekend gambling enthusiasts.

Regulations on border passes and visas to visit the casino remain fuzzy, but it appears to Thais can easily visit the casino without any formal paperwork. Westerners are required to obtain a proper visa from the Cambodian embassy in Bangkok before being allowed to pass across to Ko Kong.

The casino is owned by Cambodian-born Thai businessman Ly Yang Phat, who has close ties with strongman Hun Sen.

Transportation

Trucks to Ban Chuen, Klong Yai, and Ban Hat Lek leave behind the modern shopping complex on Tai Mai Road. Taxis can also be hired for a quick day-trip. The latest information on transportation, hotels, and recommended beaches can be obtained from the Foremost Guesthouse in Trat.

carambola (ma fueng)

VICINITY OF BANGKOK
WEST OF BANGKOK

West of Bangkok lie the three provinces of Nakhon Pathom, Ratchaburi, and Kanchanaburi. Nakhon Pathom and Ratchaburi Provinces are alluvial lowlands once almost entirely covered with ricefields and coconut palms. Today, both are peppered with towns that have transformed themselves from tiny hamlets into thriving industrial estates in less than a generation. Kanchanaburi Province is chiefly known for its bridge over Kwai Yai River and for natural wonders such as lakes, waterfalls, and national parks.

Sightseeing Highlights
The region northwest of Bangkok to the Burmese border offers an outstanding range of attractions, from Buddhist *stupas* and war monuments to Khmer temples and stunning landscapes. Urban sprawl now connects Bangkok with Nakhon Pathom, and Kanchanaburi is firmly on the tourist trail, but the remainder of the region remains largely untouched by mass tourism.

Nakhon Pathom: The world's tallest Buddhist monument is located in this nondescript town about one hour (54 km) west of Bangkok. Nakhon Pathom is generally visited on a day tour from Bangkok, or as an afternoon pause en route to Kanchanaburi.

Ratchaburi: Almost 50 km southwest of Nakhon Pathom, Ratchaburi is a busy commercial town known for several historic *wats* and the production of huge water jars used in households throughout Thailand. Bamboo reed pipes are still handcrafted in the nearby village of Ban Ko Bua.

Kanchanaburi: This town, 122 km west of Bangkok, is one of Thailand's upcoming centers for both domestic and international tourism. Westerners generally visit the famous bridge and cemeteries that commemorate the events of WW II, while domestic tourists use Kanchanaburi as a weekend escape from the horrors of Bangkok. The medium-sized town is beautifully

VICINITY OF BANGKOK

© MOON PUBLICATIONS, INC.

situated on the River Kwai and within easy day-trips to nearby waterfalls and national parks, a combination that often inspires Western visitors to extend their stay from days to weeks.

Kanchanaburi Province: Aside from the historic monuments of Kanchanaburi town, the chief attraction west of Bangkok is the magnificent array of rivers, lakes, and waterfalls between Kanchanaburi town and the Burmese border. Travelers can also visit the border post at Three Pagodas Pass.

Suphanburi: The modern town of Suphanburi is occasionally visited as a short stop between Kanchanaburi and Ayuthaya. A quick three-hour *samlor* tour visits the colossal seated Buddha at Wat Palelai and the ruined *prang* of Wat Mahathat. Southwest of Suphanburi is the Don Chedi Memorial, U Thong National Museum, and a weird Buddhist theme park at Wat Wai Pong Rua.

Transportation

One-day tours to the *chedi* at Nakhon Pathom and Kanchanaburi can be booked from travel agents in Bangkok. A one-day train tour is described in the following Kanchanaburi section. Quickie tours, however, are not recommended in a region so immensely rich with sightseeing attractions.

Public transportation from Bangkok is plentiful and well organized. Buses to Nakhon Pathom and Kanchanaburi depart every 15 minutes 0700-2300 from the Southern Bus Terminal in Thonburi. Discount travel agencies on Khao San Road sell minibus tickets at slightly higher cost.

All trains heading south stop in Nakhon Pathom. Departures from Hualampong station are daily at 0900, 1235, 1400, 1515, 1600, 1730, 1830, 1920, and 2155. Nakhon Pathom takes about 90 minutes to reach by train. Trains to Kanchanaburi leave the train station in Thonburi at 0800 and 1350 and take almost three hours to reach Kanchanaburi. You could, of course, take the train to Nakhon Pathom and continue to Kanchanaburi by bus.

The town of Kanchanaburi is the principal transportation hub in the region. Public buses from Kanchanaburi reach most outlying attractions. Remote sights are served by minitrucks which leave from the smaller towns. Motorcycles can be rented in Kanchanaburi and are a

sensible and immensely convenient way to visit the widely scattered attractions.

NAKHON PATHOM

Nakhon Pathom, 54 km west of Bangkok, is a busy commercial center chiefly visited for its famous *chedi* in the center of town near the train station. The city is regarded as one of the oldest municipalities in Thailand and perhaps the country's first center of Buddhist studies. The surrounding countryside is renowned for its delicious pomelos, fragrant white rice, and thriving wine industry. Skip the sweetish, almost sickening white wines and try the elegant yet unpretentious reds. Thai wines and brandies have vastly improved in recent years.

Nakhon Pathom sponsors a Fruit Festival in September and an immensely popular Temple Festival each November during Loy Kratong. The town's final claim to fame is that it served as Phnom Penh in the Academy Award-winning movie, *The Killing Fields.*

History

According to tradition, the city was founded several centuries before the Christian era as a seaside port for the mythical kingdom of Suwannaphum. During this period, King Asoka the Great (272-232 B.C.) sent two senior monks from India to introduce the principles of Theravada Buddhism. Passing through Three Pagodas Pass, the main land conduit from India to Thailand, Buddhism probably made its first impact at Nakhon Pathom.

Archaeological evidence begins in the 6th century when Nakhon Pathom flourished under the patronage of the Mon people. The Mon built a Dvaravati-Buddhist empire, which thrived in central Thailand in the 6th-10th centuries. Little is known of the history or geographical extent of the Mon, though their presence at Nakhon Pathom is confirmed by local discoveries of several stone inscriptions, small *stupas,* and a coin bearing the inscription "Lord of Dvaravati." The original Pra Pathom Chedi, a pagoda of Sri Lankan style, was probably erected during the Mon Period in the late 10th century.

In the early 11th century, Nakhon Pathom and western Thailand fell to King Suryavarman,

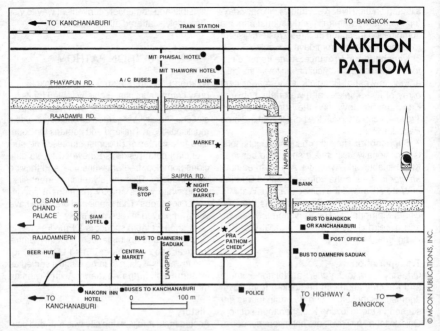

who incorporated Siam into his militaristic Khmer empire. The original Pra Pathom Chedi (a Buddhist structure) was pulled down and rebuilt in the form of a Hindu/Brahman *prang* some 40 meters high. The Khmers held the city until 1057, when it fell to King Anawratha of Bagan. Recognizing the cultural advances of the Mon, the Burmese king soon imported the artistic and religious traditions of the Mon to his powerful capital in central Myanmar.

Nakhon Pathom was abandoned in the 11th century but re-established in the 17th century by King Mahachakraphet as a defensive position against Burmese invasion. In 1860, King Mongkut ordered the restoration of the decaying *chedi,* an ancient Indian-style pagoda which he first spotted during his early years as a monk in the region.

Nakhon Pathom *Chedi*

The massive *chedi* at Nakhon Pathom is staggering. Soaring over 120 meters into hot blue skies, this is the most sacred Buddhist monument in Thailand and the world's largest *chedi,* surpassing even the gilded wonder in Yangon. Although the dome-shaped reliquary lacks the intricate detail of Yangon's Shwedagon, its fairyland of auxiliary *bots,* Buddha images, and curious substructures makes for a fascinating afternoon of exploration. For best impact, approach the *chedi* from the north side facing the train station.

The main *chedi* began as a simple Sri Lankan-style *stupa* constructed by the Mons in the 10th century, replaced by a Hindu-Brahman *prang* erected by the Khmers in the early 11th century. The present enormous cupola was begun in 1860 and completed in the early 20th century during the reign of King Chulalongkorn.

Before climbing into the temple complex, note the dozens of amulet booths, palmists, and foodstalls to the left of the main entrance. The stalls serve iced coffee and bamboo staffs filled with sticky rice laced with coconut milk.

Chedi: The bell-shaped *stupa,* covered with glazed orange tiles imported from China, is believed to contain a Buddha relic of great religious importance. It encases an older *stupa* of hemispherical form with a *prang* superimposed;

a replica can be seen nearby. The innermost *stupa* may hold the original Dvaravati monument, though religious sanctity and inaccessibility prevent excavation. Surmounting the bulbous mound of brickwork is a triple trident (symbol of Shiva), which is in turn capped by the Royal Crown of Thailand.

Ceremonial Halls: Flanking the Grand Staircase are two halls used for ceremonies and ordinations.

Temple Office: A large exterior mural points out the main features of the *chedi*.

North Viharn: This Sukothai-style standing Buddha, known as Pra Ruang Rochanarit, is an object of great veneration to the Thai peoples.

The stone head, hands, and feet were discovered in Sawankalok around 1900, while the bronze body was cast later to match the stone appendages. Buried at the base are the ashes of King Vajiravudh, who completed the restoration initiated by King Mongkut and King Chulalongkorn. An adjacent Public Hall with photographs of expensive reconstruction projects is also used for ordinations of monks.

Bell Chapels: Surrounding the *chedi* are 24 bells rung by pilgrims to witness Buddha's enlightenment. You may do the same with the wooden mallets.

Buddha Poses: Set into the high-walled cloister which separates the circular walkway from

NAKHON PATHOM CHEDI

Labels in map: NUN'S HOUSES, ORIGINAL CHEDI REPLICA, SEATED BUDDHA, NAKHON SI THAMMARAT REPLICA, HOLY TREES, MEDITATION CHAMBERS, MINIATURE MOUNTAIN, DVARAVATI SEATED BUDDHA, SOUTH VIHARN, PREACHING BUDDHA, CHINESE TEMPLE, SEATED BUDDHA EAST VIHARN, RECLINING BUDDHA WEST VIHARN, SALA, BUDDHA STATUES, CHEDI, NORTH VIHARN (PRA RUANG ROCHANARIT), MINIATURE MOUNTAIN, BELL CHAPELS, MUSEUM, PUBLIC HALL, TEMPLE OFFICES, CHAOPO PRASATONG, GRAND STAIRCASES, CHEUN RUTHAI GARDEN, PRAKAN PAKKLOD, CEREMONIAL HALLS

0   25 m

© MOON PUBLICATIONS, INC.

the *chedi* is a remarkable series of bronze Buddhas cast in every possible position of meditation, and labeled in English with confusing translations: "The Buddha look back over one's shoulder." Note the round Chinese-style moon windows with wooden shutters.

Museum: This disorganized museum on the lower platform boasts art treasures such as Dvaravati statuary and Wheels of the Law, plus a great deal of kitsch oddities such as old money and stuffed fish. The Chinese Temple and the Sala Soprong beyond the stairway are used by resting pilgrims.

Dvaravati Seated Buddha: Carved from a piece of white quartzite, this monumental stone image is widely considered one of Thailand's great artistic masterpieces. The solemn, magnificent stone figure is seated in the so-called western style, an unusual pose favored by the Mon, who apparently borrowed the arrangement from Greco-Roman models. Robe contours and Western expression might remind you of Alexander the Great, the world conqueror who led his armies to the edge of Pakistan and whose artistic styles filtered east across India to the Mons of early Thailand. Do not miss this image.

Northeast Courtyard: Down below the circular platform stands the House of Chaopo Prasatong, Prakan Pakklod, and one of many holy trees connected with the life of Buddha.

East *Viharn:* Inside sits an enlightened Buddha under a bodhi tree painted by an artist of King Rama VI, and an important mural which traces the *chedi's* architectural evolution from a white, 11th-century Mon *stupa* to a Khmer *prang* erected after Suryavarman's triumph. Both were covered by the present *chedi* erected in 1860 by King Mongkut. The side walls display portraits of 48 ancient kings and heroic warriors.

naga

Miniature Mountain: Nakhon Pathom's great *chedi* has plenty of oddities designed to impress, edify, and confuse the visitor. Depending on whom you talk to, this artificial grotto represents either monks' meditation chambers, a low-end Disneyland, or Mt. Meru, Buddhist abode of the gods.

South *Viharn:* The central antechamber holds an earth-touching Buddha surrounded by five disciples, and a Khmer Buddha meditating beneath a hooded *naga*. In front are two decorative chimneys used by Chinese worshippers to burn incense and gold paper. The southeast courtyard is filled with decrepit nuns' quarters and sacred bodhi trees.

Southern Courtyard: At the bottom of the staircase is another Buddha seated in the European position—not as impressive as the earlier example, but better for photographs. To the left is a replica of the original *chedi;* to the right a replica of the famous *chedi* at Nakhon Si Thammarat.

West *Viharn:* A much-venerated nine-meter Buddha cast in the reign of Rama IV reclines in the outer chamber, while a smaller image with adoring pilgrims occupies the interior chamber. Note the hilarious sign, "Please take off your shoes and keep them in this chapel before they are invisible." Impressive old wooden buildings used as monks' retreats are located inside the southwest courtyard.

Cheun Ruthai Gardens: The northeast corner of the *chedi* has yellow bodhisattvas and mechanized circulating alms bowls used as surrealistic coin tosses.

Sanam Chand Palace

Another attraction in town is the summer residence built by King Vajiravudh (Rama VI) in an eccentric melange of Thai and English Tudor architectural styles. Some of the buildings are used for private government offices and closed to the public. Most curious is the statue of Yalay, King Vajiravudh's beloved pet dog killed "by some envious people."

Thap Charoen Hall was constructed in 1911 as the residence for the king's entourage. The beautiful gardens and hall were opened to the public in 1990 after several years of restoration by the Fine Arts Department. Today, the lovely white wooden building serves as the Institute of Western Regional Culture under the supervision of Silpakorn University. The culture of western Thailand is recounted with displays of paintings by Petchburi artists, puppets from Samut Songkram, and basketry from the Thai Song tribe.

Sanam Chand Palace is two km west of Pra Pathom Chedi. Open Tues.-Sat. 0900-1700.

Accommodations
Although usually just a stopover en route to Kanchanaburi, good hotels in all price ranges are available.

Mit Thaworn: Two cheap hotels are located near the train station. The Mit Thaworn and adjacent **Mit Phaisal** have rooms acceptable for a short stay. Both are located up a short alley off the busy street market. 305 Rot Fai Rd., tel. (034) 243115, 120-250B.

Siam Hotel: Somewhat better digs a few blocks west of the chedi. Thetsaban Rd., tel. (034) 241754, 150-300B.

Nakorn Inn: Best upscale choice in town is the Nakorn Inn off the main road. This hotel has a coffee shop, convention room, and 70 a/c rooms. 55 Rajwithi Rd., tel. (034) 251152, fax (034) 254998, 500-800B.

Whale Inn: A relatively new place with cleaner rooms at reasonable prices. All rooms are a/c plus there's a restaurant, disco, snooker hall, golf driving range, and sauna facilities. 151/79 Rajwithi Rd., tel. (034) 251020, 500-800B.

Restaurants
Finding a good restaurant in Nakhon Pathom is somewhat difficult. For a quick snack, try the fruit market on the road between the railway station and Pra Pathom Chedi, or the foodstalls on the grounds of the monument. Another option is the central market on Rajavithi Road. Nakhon Pathom is known for its version of *kao lam,* sticky rice and coconut steamed in a bamboo joint.

More formal settings are located in the a/c **Beer Hut** and the **Nakorn Inn,** which features live music in the evenings.

Transportation
Ordinary buses from Bangkok's Southern Bus Terminal in Thonburi depart every 15 minutes and take an hour to reach Nakhon Pathom. Trains depart nine times daily from Bangkok's Hualampong station and twice daily from the train station in Thonburi. Trains from the south also stop in Nakhon Pathom.

To return to Bangkok or continue to Kanchanaburi, take bus 81 from the east side of the *chedi,* next to the canal. The floating market at Damnern Saduak can be reached in one hour with bus 78 from the southeast corner of the *chedi.*

KANCHANABURI

Kanchanaburi, 122 km west of Bangkok, is known for the bridge made famous by Pierre Boulle's celebrated novel of WW II, *The Bridge on the River Kwai,* and the subsequent Academy Award-winning motion picture directed by David Lean. The bridge is rather ordinary, but Kanchanaburi's relaxed atmosphere, historic sights, and nearby waterfalls, caves, and river trips make this one of the *most* enjoyable destinations in Thailand.

Allow plenty of time to explore the town and province. A minimum of three days is needed to visit the sights around town, and a one-day journey up the River Kwai is nice. Several more days are needed to visit the nearby national parks, caves, forests, and waterfalls, and to make an excursion to the Thai/Burmese border at Three Pagodas Pass. Kanchanaburi is an excellent place to discover Thai countryside without having to travel all the way to the far north or extreme south.

Topography is somewhat confusing around the region. Two River Kwais flow through the province: Kwai Yai (Big Kwai) flows from Sri Nakarin Lake, while Kwai Noi (Little Kwai) starts at Krung Kravia Lake near the Burmese border. Both rivers merge near Kanchanaburi to form the Mae Klong River, which flows into the Gulf of Thailand.

History
Located along the road to the strategic Three Pagodas Pass, Kanchanaburi and, more importantly, Kwai Yai Valley, have long been one of the pivotal trade routes and military garrison centers of Thailand. The valley was first inhabited by Neolithic tribes who fashioned pottery and crude utensils over 3,000 years ago. Archaeological evidence of early human habitation is displayed at the Ban Kao Neolithic Museum,

KANCHANABURI

BAMBOO GH

TO BRIDGE (1 km)

323

TRAIN STATION

JOLLY FROG GH

NEW BRIDGE

KWAI

YAI

RIVER

KANCHANABURI WAR CEMETERY

CHINESE CEMETERY

SANGCHUTO RD.

LUXURY HOTEL

P. S. GH

CHURCH

RICK'S LODGE

V. N. GH

RIVER GH

RONG HEEB OIL RD.

MINIBUS TO BRIDGE

BAN NUER RD.

PRASOBSUK HOTEL

RIVER KWAI HOTEL

V. L. GH

NITAYA GH

CHAO KUNEN RD.

THETSABAN BAMRUNG RD.

KRATAI THONG RD.

HIRAN PRASAT RD.

TO SUPHANBURI AND SUKOTHAI

SAM'S PLACE GH

PAK PRAEK RD.

BOVON RD.

TELEPHONE

MARKET

TAXIS

BANK

UTHONG RD.

MARKET

PRASIT RD.

KHUMUANG RD.

NIGHT FOODSTALLS

SPORTS HALL

LAK MUANG RD.

A/C BUSES

BUS TERMINAL

HONDA

SONGKWAI RD.

POST OFFICE

LAK MUANG

TOWN GATE

CITY HALL

TOURIST OFFICE

FERRY

FLOATING RESTAURANTS

SUNIYA RAFT HOUSE

NITA'S RAFT HOUSE

KWAI NOI RIVER

KAMPHANG MUANG RD.

JEATH WAR MUSEUM

VISUTTHARANGSI RD.

MAE KLONG RIVER

SANGCHUTO RD.

THAI SEREE HOTEL

TO POST OFFICE AND BANGKOK

323

TO THREE PAGODAS PASS

CHUNG KAI WAR CEMETERY

STONE GARDEN

KAO POON CAVE

TO WAT THAM MONGKAM

CHUKKADON PIER

FERRY

CHAICHUMPOL RD.

KASEM ISLAND OFFICE

0   200 m

© MOON PUBLICATIONS, INC.

some 40 km west of Kanchanaburi. The region was captured in the 13th century by Khmer commanders who established a military citadel and religious complex at the village of Muang Sing. The ruins of these were restored and reopened to the public in 1987. After the fall of the Khmers, Ayuthayan rulers constructed a garrison town 20 km west of Kanchanaburi. In 1548, the Burmese marched several hundred thousand warriors through Three Pagodas Pass to wage war on Ayuthaya, which fell two centuries later. To monitor Burmese aggression, King Rama I founded Kanchanaburi as a military camp. The town, valley, and jungle pass also played a pivotal role in WW II.

Kanchanaburi received worldwide attention around proposals to construct a massive dam near the Burmese border. Outcries from environmentalists and Britain's Prince Charles, plus a general disenchantment over massive dam projects, led to the cancellation of the proposal. The Nam Choan Dam project was also scrapped to save several species of endangered wildlife and prevent widespread soil erosion. Environmental causes have gained widespread public support in recent times.

JEATH War Museum

First stop should be the JEATH War Museum. JEATH is an acronym for the primary nations which participated in local action: Japan, England, America/Australia, Thailand, Holland. Modeled after POW camps of the period, the simple bamboo structures contain war memorabilia, photographs of emaciated prisoners, personal recollections, and graphic descriptions of tortures committed by the Japanese. The museum is managed by a Thai monk, Maha Tomson Thongproh, who lives in the adjacent Wat Chaichumphon. More than just a museum, JEATH is a simple, immensely moving memorial to the 16,000 Allied POWs and 50,000-100,000 Asians who died from lack of medical attention, starvation, and torture during construction of the 400-km Death Railway.

The museum is open daily 0830-1630 and admission is 20B.

The Bridge over the River Kwai

Kanchanaburi's most famous sight is the simple bridge constructed in just over 16 months by some 60,000 Allied prisoners and 250,000 Asian slave-laborers. The present structure is physically uninspiring—just eight gray, riveted spans on moss-stained concrete pylons—though the historical and emotional elements are fascinating. Best times to visit are 1030, 1430, and 1630 when the Nam Tok train slowly crosses the bridge. The remainder of the day the structure serves as a footbridge across the river to cool picnic grounds on the other bank. Be careful walking across the bridge and watch out for sprinting motorcycles. A popular light-and-sound show is held at the bridge during River Kwai Week in late November or early December.

Misconceptions about the bridge are commonplace, since most visitors only know the movie *The Bridge on the River Kwai*. The iron bridge in Kanchanaburi isn't the original wooden bridge which played a pivotal role in the movie. The old wooden bridge, which once crossed the river about three km south, was abandoned by the Japanese in favor of a sturdier iron structure that was hauled up from Java in pieces. Author Boulle's character, Colonel Nicholson (portrayed by Alec Guinness), was a fictionalized commander who never existed during the construction of the bridge. Colonel Nicholson and other British engineers were portrayed in the movie as instrumental in the design of the bridge; in reality, the Japanese were solely responsible for the project. The movie also overlooked the thousands of Asians who worked on the bridge and died in appalling numbers during construction of the entire railway. Furthermore, the film portrays the escape of Commander Shear (played by William Holden) from camp to reach Allied hands in Sri Lanka and his love affair with a beautiful nurse. Shear then returns to Kanchanaburi to blow up the bridge. In fact, nobody ever escaped from Kanchanaburi and lived to tell the story.

The bridge is five km north of town—too far to walk. Hire a bike or motorcycle, or take a minibus from Chao Kunen Road.

Around the Bridge

Surrounding the bridge are several other stops worth a brief visit, plus an assortment of tourist shops and riverside restaurants. **Solos Restaurant** has good views from the patio terrace, and offers an escape from the tour buses and schoolchildren.

Train Museum: Just opposite the bridge you'll find a steam engine and an ingenious Japanese supply truck that operated on both road and rails.

Art Gallery: Some 30 meters south of the bridge is a big, garish building which features some of the finest modern murals in Thailand. Paintings on the second floor relate ancient battles between the Thais and Burmese, while third-floor murals tell Thai history and provide portraits of prime ministers and other important political figures. This private museum also features Khmer-style woodcarvings, a pair of elaborate Burmese Buddhas, and excellent paintings of Chinese deities.

Japanese War Memorial: Also located slightly south of the bridge is a simple monument erected by the Japanese and dedicated to those who "died through illness during the course of the construction"—a pleasant enough euphemism.

A LIFE FOR EVERY SLEEPER

One of the most famous stories of WW II was the construction of the railway between Kanchanaburi in Thailand and Thanbyuzayat in Myanmar. Construction began on 16 September 1942 after Japanese sea routes were effectively blocked by Allied aircraft and submarine operations near Singapore and in the Straits of Malacca. To provide supplies to their bases in Myanmar, the Japanese conscripted over 50,000 Allied prisoners and 250,000 Asian laborers from Japanese-held countries in Southeast Asia. Initial estimates by engineers that completion of the 415-km railway would take five years were overruled by the Japanese High Command, who ordered the project finished in an incredibly short span of just 12 months.

As progress on the Death Railway fell behind schedule, the Japanese demanded more men who, under the most primitive conditions, worked around the clock and died in frightening numbers from malaria, dysentery, beri-beri, cholera, and starvation—described on death certificates as "Post Dysenteric Inanition." The cost was "a life for every sleeper" (railroad tie) laid over its most difficult sections.

The flimsy wooden bridge which first crossed the River Kwai was abandoned in favor of a stronger iron structure imported from Java. On 16 October 1943 the line was joined at Konkoita as Japanese film crews recorded the event for propaganda purposes. Although an estimated 50,000-100,000 lives were sacrificed, the project was not a success; the bridge was only used *once* before American B-24 bombers from Sri Lanka destroyed the fourth, fifth, and sixth spans in February 1945. The Allies controlled the bridge after the war, but sold the structure for US$2 million to the Thai government a few years later. As war reparations, the Japanese replaced the missing curved girders with two incongruously square beams ironically stamped "Made in Japan."

Kwai River Bridge

5776408 PRIVATE
B. W. BELL
THE ROYAL NORFOLK REGIMENT
25TH SEPTEMBER 1943 AGE 25

WE THINK OF HIM STILL AS THE SAME AND SAY:
"HE IS NOT DEAD, HE IS JUST AWAY"

a life for every sleeper

Kanchanaburi War Cemetery

With its neatly arranged tombstones and poignant messages, this final resting place for 6,982 Allied war prisoners forms one of the most moving tableaux in Southeast Asia. A private foundation in London keeps the cemetery supplied with fresh flowers and supports the Thai gardeners who maintain the lovely grounds. The dead are eulogized on a brass plaque at the entrance, yet not a single grave marker commemorates the estimated 50,000 Asians who perished during construction of the bridge. Among the gravestone messages:

"We think of him still as the same and say: He is not dead, he is just away."

"At the going down of the sun and in the morning, we will remember them."

"Your duty nobly done, my son, sleep on. Mother."

"We shall always remember you smiling, sleep on beloved."

Chinese Cemetery

The adjacent Chinese cemetery is a study in contrasts. Pauper tombs are hidden away against the walls, while tombstones of the wealthy are elevated like Chinese pagodas. Burial sites are arranged according to the principles of *feng shui*, a Taoist belief in divine geomancy, which attempts to balance the ancient principles of yin and yang.

Other Sights

Several other modest attractions are scattered around Kanchanaburi.

Lak Muang: Kanchi's town pillar encloses a Hindu phallic symbol at the original town center, not far from an old town gate and several historic buildings now used as municipal offices. Palmists and fortune-tellers do business across the street from the pillar.

Smashed Car: A curious monument to bad driving sits on Sangchuto Road near the a/c bus terminal. Well worth a photograph.

Old Town: Unlike many of the newer towns in Thailand, Kanchanaburi retains vestiges of its past on several small streets such as Pak Praek Road and near the vegetable market on Chao Kunen Road.

River Trips

A visit to Kanchanaburi would not be complete without a boat trip. Most guesthouses can arrange short evening cruises or full-day expeditions to nearby attractions. Three-hour sunset cruises in longtail boats from Nita's Raft House cost 100B to visit the bridge and Chung Kai War Cemetery. Expensive full-day raft trips can also be arranged through better hotels and conventional travel offices such as DT Tours. River trips with "Thai Water Skiing" and "starring Master Entertainer and Dare Devil Sunya" leave on demand from Sunya Rux's Discotheque Raft.

River trips can also be made at upriver locations. Luxury raft hotels sponsor extended river trips Sept.-March, but not during the dry season when the river is low or during the dangerous rainy season. Alternatively, eight-person long-tails can be chartered at Pak Sang Pier (near Nam Tok some 60 km upriver from Kanchanaburi) to visit upriver caves and waterfalls. Prices from Pak Sang Pier are posted at the train station: to Lawa Caves 300B, Sai Yok Yai Falls 500B, Daow Dung Cave 700B. For more details see **Route 323 to the Burmese Border,** below. Be prepared to bargain with the boat operator.

Tours and Trekking

A wide variety of tours can be arranged through most guesthouses and hotels. Sample tours include: Tham Than Lot National Park, Erawan Waterfall, and sapphire mines; Erawan Falls and the bridge; and Prathat Caves, Erawan Falls, and the bridge. Mr. Pirom Angkudie, civil servant, historian, and amateur archaeologist, can be recommended for his three-hour sunset tours of nearby historical and cultural attractions. You can contact him through most guesthouses in Kanchi.

Trekking near Sangklaburi and the Burmese border is another possibility. **Travelers Trekking** in the V.N. Guesthouse leads a four-day trek that includes visits to Karen villages, an elephant ride, a bamboo river trip, a run through a bat cave, and swimming under waterfalls. Best Tours on Khao San Road in Bangkok can help with reservations.

Budget Accommodations

Local accommodations can be divided between floating guesthouses on the Kwai Yai River and conventional hotels on Sangchuto Road. River-based guesthouses in the center of town are pleasant during the week but incredibly noisy on weekends when Bangkokians flood the region. To escape the all-night parties and blasting disco boats, try the guesthouses north of the park toward the bridge.

The following guesthouses are described starting from central Kanchanaburi and moving toward the bridge.

Nita's Raft House: Several floating crash pads are located along the banks near the city park. Nita's is a popular choice, but can be very noisy at night from the floating discos. Ask for Supachai and Miss Seangthip. 27 Pakprak Rd., tel. (034) 514521, 60B communal floorspace, 100-200B private room.

Sam's Place: One of the better riverside choices in central Kanchanaburi features a beautiful foyer and cozy restaurant (with a *farang* menu), wooden reclining chairs facing a pond filled with ducks, and several detached bamboo bungalows with small porches. American-educated Sam and his staff can help with river trips, motorcycle rentals, and advice on local transportation. Songkwai Rd., tel. (034) 513971, fax (034) 512023, 100-250B fan, 200-400B a/c, 250-300B large bungalow with private bath.

Nitaya Guesthouse: At the north end of the riverside park is an old favorite with over a dozen rickety bamboo bungalows, disco boat, and river tours daily at 1300. Songkwai Rd., tel. (034) 513341, 120-180B.

River Guesthouse: Several guesthouses can be found on Soi 2 to the north of central Kanchanaburi. All are somewhat distant from the discos and fairly quiet. River Guesthouse is a simple place run by Mr. Ek, who also sponsors boat tours. 42 Rongheeboi Rd., Soi 2, tel. (034) 512491, 80-200B.

Rick's Lodge: A friendly place run by a German-speaking Thai from Bangkok, Rick's has several floating bungalows and 12 bilevel rooms senselessly crammed together back from the river. River views are blocked by trees. Try the homemade Farmhouse Bread in the Salad House across the street. 48/5 Rongheeboi Rd., Soi 2, tel. (034) 514831, 220-350B.

P.S. Guesthouse: Excellent views and a cozy restaurant make this a good choice. 54 Rongheeboi Rd., Soi 2, tel. (034) 513039, 60-100B common bath, 140-200B private bath.

Jolly Frog Guesthouse: The largest guesthouse in Kanchanaburi has over 50 rooms facing a central courtyard filled with palms and grass. Rooms inside the two-story thatched buildings are small and ordinary with mattresses placed on the floor. Services include motorcycle rentals, a spacious circular dining hall, German management, and minibuses to Bangkok daily at 1100 and 1430. 28 Maenamwae Rd., tel. (034) 514579, 120-250B.

Bamboo Guesthouse: The most idyllic guesthouse in Kanchanaburi is located at the end of a dirt road about 300 meters before the bridge. It features a big lawn with a small pond, and is often filled but otherwise a fine spot. Call first to check on vacancies. 3-5 Soi Vietnam, tel. (034) 512532, 100-250B bamboo bungalows, 250-700B upstairs rooms in a red brick building.

V.L. Guesthouse: One of the best land-based guesthouses is a modern place opposite the River Kwai Hotel. Rooms are very clean and well furnished, and include a private bath; an excellent deal for anyone who dislikes riverside accommodation. 18/11 Sangchuto Rd., tel. (034) 513546, 150-200B fan, 250-400B a/c.

Moderate Accommodations

Most midpriced rooms in the 400-800B range are located outside of town and described below under "River Kwai Raft Resorts."

Kasem Island Resort: Kanchanaburi's first upscale raft hotel features seven bamboo cottages and 20 houseboats with private baths, patios overlooking the river, and an excellent floating restaurant. Facilities are only adequate but managers are making improvements. Kasem Island head office is located at Chukadon Wharf, 27 Chaichumpol Rd., tel. (034) 513359, Bangkok reservation tel. (02) 255-3603 and fax (02) 255-3604, 750-1,000B.

Luxury Accommodations

The tourist boom finally brought the big boys to Kanchanaburi. Properties that opened over the last decade include a Sheraton, an Imperial, and a hotel operated by the Siam City chain.

River Kwai Hotel: Kanchi's oldest upscale hotel is popular with businesspeople, tour groups, and Japanese visitors. All rooms are a/c and come with private bath, TV, and video. 248 Sangchuto, tel. (034) 511184, 1,200-2,600B.

Felix River Kwai Resort: A luxurious property near the famous bridge. Facilities include two pools, tennis courts, and five restaurants. Tambon Ta Makam, tel. (034) 515061, fax (034) 515086, Bangkok tel. (02) 255-5767, fax (02) 255-5769, 3,600-6,000B.

River Kwai Raft Resorts

Kanchanaburi Province currently lists over 50 registered raft hotels on the upper reaches of the Kwai Yai (near Nam Tok and Sai Yok Falls), at Sri Nakarin Lake, and on Krung Kravia Lake near the Burmese border. The average daily per-person charge of 800B often includes three meals and boat transportation. Some are quite simple and operate without electricity; others have swimming pools and a/c rooms with hot water.

Those most popular are described below. Travel agents in Bangkok make reservations, though these are only necessary on weekends. Most of the following properties provide transportation from downtown Kanchanaburi to the raft hotel. The local tourist office and travel agents near the bus stop can also help with details and phone calls.

Kanchi fish story

Home Phu Toey Resort: Probably the most popular river resort in the Kanchanaburi region. Bungalows include running water and private bath but lack electricity, phones, TVs, and other signs of "civilization." Evening meals are followed by Mon dances accompanied by Burmese gongs and cymbals. Located on the Kwai Noi River, 60 km from Kanchanaburi. Reservations can be made from travel agents in Bangkok. Upper Kwai Noi River near Pak Sang Pier, Bangkok tel. (02) 280-3488, 1,000-1,600B.

River Kwai Village Hotel: A 60-unit lodge composed of a dozen floating rafts and five longhouses subdivided into private chalets. All rooms are a/c with full amenities. Popular with group tours from Bangkok. Upper Kwai Noi River near Pak Sang Pier (70 km from Kanchanaburi), Bangkok tel. (02) 251-7552, 800-1,000B per person including meals.

Restaurants

Kanchanaburi's best restaurants are the half dozen floating cafes tied up at the south end of the fitness park. Most are marked in Thai script only, but all specialize in seafood and highly prized river carp, favored for its fatty and succulent meat. Unfortunately, the giant *pla yi sok* (the Julien carp used for those terrific street signs) has been hunted nearly to extinction, and other species now substitute.

Krua Thien Tong: Arrive for sunset and try deep-fried freshwater catfish or frog legs fried in garlic. Songkwai Rd. Moderate.

Pae Karn: Another floating restaurant known for its *log tong* and country-style Thai dishes such as *tom yam pla* made with river carp. Songkwai Rd. Moderate.

Foodstalls: Cheap meals are found at the outdoor foodstalls on Sangchuto Road near the bus terminal.

Punee Restaurant: The first *farang* bar in Kanchi is owned by Danny and his wife, Punee. Danny does local tours, sells sapphires, rents well-maintained motorcycles, gives fishing advice ("don't bother"), operates a book exchange, and dabbles in real estate while running the bar. Ban Nuer Rd. Inexpensive.

Services

The tourist office (tel. 034-511200) on Sangchuto Road, one of the best TAT branches in Thailand, offers maps and information on river huts, plus tips on local transportation and conditions at the Burmese border. Post offices are located on Sangchuto Road and on Lak Muang Road near the city pillar. Visas can be extended at Thai Immigration, 286 Sangchuto Road. International phone service is available from the Telephone Center on Uthong Road. An excellent map of the Kanchanaburi region is published by Prannok Vidhaya Publisher, though their town details fail to list most of the newer guesthouses.

Getting There from Bangkok

Ordinary and a/c buses to Kanchanaburi leave every 15 minutes and take three hours from the

Southern Bus Terminal in Thonburi. Trains for Kanchanaburi leave twice daily at 0800 and 1350 from Thonburi station.

Weekend Train Tours

Whirlwind tours sponsored by the State Railways are also possible. A special train leaves Bangkok's Hualampong station weekends at 0635, stops at the *chedi* in Nakhon Pathom for 40 minutes (0735-0815), pauses for 30 minutes at the Kanchi bridge (0930-1000), and takes a three-hour lunch break at Nam Tok (1130-1430), enough time to visit the nearby waterfall or go down to the river for a quick look. On the return trip, it stops for 45 minutes at the war cemetery (1605-1650) before arriving back in Bangkok at 1930. Whew! Advanced bookings can be made by calling the State Railways Advance Booking Office at (02) 225-6964.

The State Railways also sponsors other weekend tours of the Kanchanaburi region. The rafting program costs 340B and includes Nakhon Pathom and local sights, plus a short raft trip under the bridge. Another tour for 300B includes Nakhon Pathom, Kanchanaburi, and the Khmer ruins at Prasat Muang Sing. The final option at 280B includes Nakhon Pathom, Kanchanaburi, Sri Nakarin Dam, and Erawan Falls.

Getting Around

Bicycling is the perfect way to get around Kanchanaburi. Old bikes can be rented from most guesthouses for about 20B per day. Motorcycles cost 150-250B per day from the Honda dealer and various guesthouses. Experienced cyclists will find this an excellent way to explore the countryside and visit remote temples and caves. Motorcycle prices and conditions vary widely, so it's best to shop around. Jeep rentals cost 800-1,000B per day; shops near the bus terminal provide the cars.

Slow Train to Nowhere

A slow but romantic way to explore the historic railway is the funky third-class train which leaves Kanchanaburi daily at 0600 and 1030 and arrives in Nam Tok two hours later. The 1030 train allows you three hours to visit the river or a nearby waterfall before catching the 1530 train back to Kanchanaburi. Creaky, hair-raising, and historically poignant, many travelers consider the *Nam Tok Special* the most memorable train ride in Thailand.

Getting Away

Kanchanaburi is connected by road and rail to Bangkok and other neighboring provinces. The chart "Buses from Kanchanaburi" summarizes departing bus services.

Bangkok: Ordinary bus 81 for Bangkok and Nakhon Pathom departs from the main bus terminal. Air-conditioned buses leave every 15 minutes from the office on Sangchuto Road. Share taxis wait at the nearby intersection.

North: Travelers heading north should go direct rather than backtrack to Bangkok. To Ayuthaya, take bus 419 from Uthong Road to Suphanburi (two to three hours), then yellow bus 703 to Ayuthaya (one hour). To Sukothai, take bus 487 to Nakhon Sawan (four hours), then bus 99 to Sukothai (three hours).

South: For Petchburi, take bus 461 to Ratchaburi, then bus 73 to Petchburi. For Hua Hin, take bus 461 to Ratchaburi, then bus 71 to Hua Hin. Bus services are also available from Ratchaburi to Surat Thani and Phuket.

Floating Market: Public transportation is also available to the floating market at Damnern Saduak. An early start is essential to reach the market during prime time, 0700-0900. From the main bus terminal in Kanchanaburi, take yellow bus 461 to Bang Pae intersection, walk down the road, then take bus 78 or the minibus to Damnern Saduak. The market is one km south. Allow two hours for the journey. Alternatively, take bus 81 to Nakhon Pathom and then bus 78 to Damnern Saduak.

SOUTH OF KANCHANABURI

South of Kanchanaburi are several temples such as Wat Tam Mongkam (five km from town), Wat Tam Sua (16 km), and Wat Pra Dong (40 km). None are major architectural triumphs, but all are unique in their sense of kitsch and unbridled commercialism.

Transportation is somewhat difficult to these southern attractions. Wat Tam Mongkam and the Tha Muang temples are easy day journeys with public transportation, but the more distant Wat Pra Dong and the Don Chedi Memorial require private wheels. A few suggestions are given below. Motorcyclists can reach all three sites in a single day. Accommodations are unnecessary in this region since all temples can be visited on day-trips.

Wat Tam Mongkam

The Cave Temple of the Golden Dragon was chiefly known for the 75-year-old Thai nun who, meditating and whistling, floated in a pool of water. The old woman has been replaced with a younger nun who performs only for large crowds on weekends. This neat trick attracts a steady stream of devout Thais, but many *farangs* find the commercialism and zoolike atmosphere rather tawdry.

Aside from the floating meditation routine, the temple complex features nondescript modern *wats* adjacent to the parking lot, and a maze of limestone caves to the rear. The entrance is reached after a long climb up the stairs, which stop near an old Chinese hermit who sits in quiet meditation. The illuminated walkway through a cave leads to viewpoints over Kanchanaburi and the surrounding countryside.

Wat Tam Mongkam is located across the Mae Klong River, some five km south of Kanchanaburi. Visitors with rented bicycles can pedal to the ferry crossing on Chaichumpol Road, cross the river, then continue three km south to the temple. Motorcyclists can use the new bridge

farther south down Sangchuto Road. Public transportation may be available; inquire at the TAT office.

Temples near Tha Muang

Two very impressive but half-completed temples are situated on a limestone hilltop near Tha Muang, 16 km south of Kanchanaburi. Wat Tam Sua, the Chinese-style pagoda to the left, is fronted by a fat, jolly Buddha surrounded by 18 superbly carved figures. To the right is Wat Tam Kao Noi which, perhaps in a show of religious competition, is separated from Wat Tam Sua by a concrete wall. This attractive Thai-style temple offers a worship hall with cool marble floors, mound-shaped tower, and gigantic Buddha complete with automated treadmill to help expedite monetary donations. From the terrace you'll enjoy excellent views over the valley of Kanchanaburi.

To reach the temples, take bus 461 or 81 to the dam near Tha Muang. Motorcycle taxis charge 30-40B for the roundtrip excursion to the temples, four km east.

Wat Pra Dong

This isolated temple, 40 km east of Kanchanaburi, is revered for its immense yellow-frocked stone where, according to Thai tradition, Buddha reclined before ascending to the heavens. A young monk will unlock the main *bot*. A Buddha footprint surmounts the hill to the left.

BUS SERVICE FROM KANCHANABURI

DESTINATION	BUS	HOURS
Bangkok	81	3
Nakhon Pathom	81	1½
Nam Tok	8203	1
Sai Yok Falls	8203	2
Sangklaburi	8203	4
Three Pagodas	8203	6
Ratchaburi	461	2
Suphanburi	411	2
Boploi	325	1½
Erawan Falls	8170	2
Tham Than Rot	325	3

NORTH OF KANCHANABURI— ROUTE 3199

The waterfalls, limestone mountains, caves, and other natural wonders north of Kanchanaburi comprise one of the most beautiful regions in Thailand.

Attractions are mostly natural landscapes rather than historic or religious monuments. The region boasts three immense national parks, dozens of deep caves and plunging waterfalls, and a wildlife conservation park at Khao Salakpra. Highlights include Bophloi (a gem-mining town 50 km from Kanchanaburi), Erawan Falls in Erawan National Park (65 km), Sri Nakarin Dam at the south end of Sri Nakarin Lake (70 km), Pratat

KANCHANABURI REGION

© MOON PUBLICATIONS, INC.

Cave near Sri Nakarin Dam (75 km), Tham Lod Cave in Chalerm Ratanakosin National Park (100 km), and Huay Khamin Falls in Sri Nakarin National Park (102 km).

Erawan Falls is unquestionably the most popular sight because of its superb waterfalls and easy accessibility from Kanchanaburi.

Accommodations

Accommodations abound throughout the region. The TAT in Kanchanaburi has a complete list and can make specific recommendations. Budget hotels are located in the towns of Si Sawat, Nong Prue, and Bophloi, but most visitors head out to stay in a lodge floating on Sri Nakarin Lake.

Kwai Yai River Huts: Fairly decent floating cottages on the lake near Si Sawat, chiefly patronized by Thais with an occasional Western visitor. Tambon Tha Kradan, tel. (02) 252-9337, 750-1,000B.

Romklao Rafts: Very small but certainly upscale place with just 10 luxury floating cottages. 51/5 Moo 2, Tambon Tha Kradan, tel. (034) 516521, 2,500-5,000B.

Erawan Resort: One of the longtime favorites with both budget and midpriced rooms in a fine setting near Khao Salak Pra Wildlife Conservation Park. 140 Moo 4 Kanchanaburi-Erawan Rd., tel. (01) 907-8210, 200-1,000B.

Pailin Rafts: Popular midpriced option with just nine bamboo structures at the edge of the lake. Tambon Tha Kradan, tel. (02) 745-2239, 900-1,000B.

Transportation

Transportation is straightforward. Popular destinations along Route 3199 such as Erawan Falls and Si Sawat can be reached with public bus 8170. Bus 325 reaches the gem mines at Bophloi and Tham Lod Cave west of Nong Prue. Inexpensive group tours to all these attractions can be arranged through most guesthouses and hotels.

Erawan Falls

The 300,000 *rai* of forested area around Erawan Falls were declared a national park in 1967. Its name was changed from Khao Salob to that of the divine elephant whose shape is found in a natural rock formation at the top of the falls. Erawan National Park consists of limestone mountains from which the Erawan Falls crash down through 10 levels before emptying into the Kwai Yai River. The lower falls and swimming pools are perpetually crowded with Thai tourists who rarely make the arduous climb to the far superior falls on the upper sections of the mountain. Keep climbing, and remember to bring along a swimsuit and sneakers for the hike. Unless you enjoy suffocating crowds, do not visit this park on weekends. As with all waterfalls in Southeast Asia, Erawan is best visited during the rainy season July-Nov. when water is most plentiful.

Accommodations are available in the park in a bamboo dormitory for 60-100B and in larger 10-person park chalets for 600B. Ten km south of the park entrance is the popular **Erawan Resort** (tel. 034-513001), where upscale bungalows cost 600-1,200B.

Erawan National Park and falls are 65 km from Kanchanaburi. A full day is necessary to enjoy the falls. Bus 8170 to Erawan departs daily at 0800 from the bus terminal and takes almost two hours to reach the park turnoff, located about one km from the park entrance. Erawan Falls is another two km west of the park entrance. The last bus back to Kanchanaburi departs around 1600.

Sri Nakarin Lake

Sri Nakarin Lake is an immense freshwater lake formed by the Sri Nakarin Dam at the southern end. Accommodations are listed above. The lake offers fishing, luxurious raft hotels, and weekend boat tours aboard the *J.R. Queen*. Prathat Cave is 10 km northwest of the dam on the west side of the lake.

Sri Nakarin National Park

The region's second most popular set of falls, Huay Khamin ("Turmeric Falls"), is located in Sri Nakarin National Park some 25 km north-west of Erawan National Park. Huay Khamin falls are actually larger and more powerful than the falls at Erawan, but the additional travel time minimizes the number of visitors.

Accommodations are available at the park headquarters and in several raft houses on the lake. The Kanchanaburi TAT can help with recommendations and reservations.

The park can be reached by taking bus 8170 to Tha Kradan Pier on the east side of the lake about 24 km north of the dam, followed by a local ferry ride across the lake to the park entrance. Visitors with private transportation can drive directly to the park via the west-side road.

Bophloi

Both blue and star sapphires are mined from open pits that pocket the farmland north and west of Bophloi. Many of the mines have been exhausted, but enough activity remains to make this a worthwhile stop for visitors interested in traditional mining activities. Gem prices are reasonably low from local shops, though many of the stones are either worthless or clever synthetics. Reach Bophloi by motorcycle, jeep, or organized tour.

Chalerm Ratanakosin National Park

This 59-square-km national park, 100 km north of Kanchanaburi, is chiefly visited for its thick jungle, two immense caves of great interest to speleologists, and three waterfalls within easy walking distance of park headquarters. Tham Lod Yai, the largest of the caves with an estimated depth of over 500 meters, is filled with unusual limestone formations capped with miniature temples and images of the Buddha. The three waterfalls are Trai Trang, Than Ngun, and Than Thong.

The park has the usual choice of accommodations. Backpackers can pitch a tent near headquarters for just 20B per night. Accommodations operated by the park service include dormitories for 100B and ten-person chalets from 600B. Reservations should be made in advance through the TAT office in Kanchanaburi.

Chalerm Ratanakosin National Park can be reached with bus 325 to the small town of Nong Prue, from where minitrucks (10B) continue west to the park entrance. One-way travel consumes almost four hours, making this an overnight destination.

ROUTE 323
TO THE BURMESE BORDER

Route 323, the road northwest toward the Burmese border, is the most popular side trip from Kanchanaburi. Dozens of sights are located along the road, which parallels the Kwai Noi River. Many scenes in *The Deer Hunter* (jumping from helicopters into the river, and Russian roulette with the Viet Cong) were filmed near Sai Yok Yai Falls on the Kwai Noi River.

Attractions: Attractions in the area include the Ban Kao Museum (Neolithic remains 38 km from Kanchanaburi), Wat Muang Sing Khmer Temple (43 km), Nam Tok (the railway terminus 60 km from Kanchanaburi), Hellfire Pass Memorial (78 km), Lawa Caves (75 km), Sai Yok Yai Falls (104 km), Hin Da Hot Springs (130 km), Tongpapum (153 km), Sangklaburi (235 km), and the border crossing at Three Pagodas Pass (241 km). No wonder people spend weeks around Kanchanaburi.

Accommodations: Accommodations on Route 323 and along the Upper Kwai Noi River are among the best in the Kanchanaburi region. An excellent way to relax and enjoy the area's great natural appeal is on an upriver raft house. A few are described under **River Kwai Raft Resorts,** above. The Kanchanaburi TAT office can also make recommendations. The TAT has a complete list of over 50 guesthouses and river houses outside Kanchanaburi. River-based accommodations are also available on Krung Kravia Lake near Tongpapum. Land-based hotels and guesthouses are found in Tongpapum, Sangklaburi, and Three Pagodas Pass. More details and specific recommendations are given in the corresponding chapters.

Transportation: Transportation options include group tours, Nam Tok train, public buses, and motorcycle rentals. Inexpensive group tours are arranged by guesthouses, hotels, and travel agencies in Kanchanaburi. Prices vary sharply between low-end guesthouses and expensive travel agencies, making comparison shopping absolutely necessary. The Nam Tok train journey, described in the **Slow Train to Nowhere** section above, is an excellent way to see the countryside and enjoy one of the best train journeys in Thailand. Most visitors take the 1030

train from the central station in Kanchanaburi and return on the 1530 train from Nam Tok.

Most attractions in the Kwai Noi Valley (except for remote spots such as Prasat Muang Sing and Ban Kao Museum) can be reached with bus 8203 departing from the main bus terminal in Kanchanaburi. Bus 8203 plies the highway between Kanchanaburi and Three Pagodas Pass from sunrise until sunset. Service is frequent and buses pick up passengers every 15-30 minutes. Motorcyclists can reach most nearby sights in a single day before returning to Kanchanaburi. Alternatively, you can rent a motorcycle for several days and travel all the way up to the Burmese border at Three Pagodas Pass. Despite the danger of the horrendous driving habits of most Thais, motorcycles provide an unparalleled degree of flexibility and allow you to quickly visit even the most remote destinations.

Chung Kai War Cemetery

This war cemetery, almost identical to its counterpart in town, lies about three km away on the banks of the Kwai Noi River. Chung Kai contains some 1,750 inscribed tombstones set on the former site of the Chung Kai POW camp. The tombstones at Chung Kai and the 6,982 at the Allied War Cemetery in Kanchanaburi account for only half the estimated 16,000 Allied prisoners who died during the railway construction. The missing prisoners were cremated and left unaccounted for by the Japanese.

The cemetery is best reached with rented bicycle or motorcycle taken across the ferry near the floating restaurants on Songkwai Road. Hikers might take the ferry and then attempt to hitch a ride to the cemetery. A long wait can be expected since traffic is very light.

Kao Poon Cave

Limestone caves near Kanchanaburi often serve as Buddhist temples filled with Buddhist and Saivite images illuminated with electric lights. Kao Poon Cave, 6 km from Kanchanaburi, is behind Wat Tham Kao Poon, where friendly monks have erected English-language signs and volunteer as guides through the caves. A small donation is appropriate after the tour.

Stone Gardens

Continue over the hill from Wat Tham Kao Poon and turn right near the Thai Agricultural College, marked in Thai script only. Another left and then right leads to a curious collection of volcanic formations surrounded by poured concrete walkways.

Ban Kao Neolithic Museum

Something good did come from the construction of the Death Railway. In 1943 a Dutch prisoner of war named Van Heekeren stumbled across some Neolithic artifacts while working on the railway near Nam Tok. In 1956 an American anthropologist, Heider, confirmed the importance of Van Heekeren's discoveries. Intrigued by these reports, Thai and Danish archaeologists undertook systematic excavations in 1961 and successfully uncovered evidence that the Kwai Noi Valley had been inhabited by early humans for over 10,000 years. A new chapter in the prehistory of Southeast Asia had been opened.

A small museum housing a modest collection of pottery, ax heads, and jewelry made from animal bone has been constructed beside an open-air burial site. Major artifacts have been transferred to the National Museum in Bangkok.

Ban Kao is on a side road about 10 km off the main highway and is difficult to reach without private transportation. With the opening of Prasat Muang Sing, however, most guesthouses and hotels can now arrange day tours to Ban Kao, Muang Sing, and other nearby sights such as Sai Yok and Nam Tok. Independent travelers can take the train to Ban Kao (Tha Kilen) station, then walk or hitch the remaining two km west to Muang Sing and six km south to Ban Kao. Motorcyclists can easily visit Ban Kao and Muang Sing before continuing north to Sai Yok and Three Pagodas Pass.

Several popular raft houses are located on the Kwai Noi near the Ban Kao Museum. **River Kwai Farm** (Bangkok tel. 02-235-6433), 4 km south from Ban Kao train station, is a well-known raft lodge with rooms including meals from 600B.

Prasat Muang Sing

What were Cambodians doing so far west? This marvelous Khmer temple complex and military outpost, 45 km from Kanchanaburi, was constructed during the Lopburi Period, 1157-1207. It served as a Khmer trading post along the Kwai Noi River and protection against Burmese invasion through Three Pagodas Pass. Now completely restored, Muang Sing ("City of Lions") marks the westernmost advance of Cambodian power and provides elegant testimony to their vast territorial claims. The 460-*rai* park was declared a national historic park under the administration of the Fine Arts Department in 1987.

Muang Sing encompasses four groups of ruins composed of laterite bricks and surrounded by earthern walls arranged to suggest the cosmological symbolism so favored by Angkorian rulers. Entrance is made through reconstructed gates which flank a dusty road that leads to the central compound. A small outdoor museum to the right of the main complex contains sculptures of Mahayana Buddhist deities and stuccowork removed from the interior shrines. Prasat Muang Sing, the principal shrine, faces east toward Angkor. Hemmed in by four laterite walls oriented toward each of the cardinal directions, the interior holds a sculpture of Avalokitesvara, which establishes the sanctuary as a Mahayana Buddhist center.

A pair of Neolithic skeletons are displayed in situ on the riverbanks to the south outside the earthern walls. Other Neolithic remains discovered near Muang Sing have been removed to the museums at Ban Kao and the National Museum in Bangkok.

Idyllic raft houses are plentiful near Prasat Muang Sing and Ban Kao to the south. Within sight of the burial site at Muang Sing are several raft houses where bamboo rooms with three meals cost from 600B per day. North of Muang Sing are the **Yang Thone River Kwai** and **River Kwai Jungle House,** two raft hotels with floating bamboo bungalows from 600B.

Prasat Muang Sing Historical Park is open daily 0800-1600, and entrance is 20B.

Nam Tok

Nam Tok, 60 km from Kanchanaburi, is a nondescript town at the end of the railway line. Most visitors arrive on the 1030 train from Kanchanaburi and leave Nam Tok on the 1530 train.

Public buses back to Kanchanaburi ply the highway until nightfall. A sign posted at the train station lists suggested prices for trips up the nearby Kwai Noi River: Lawa Cave 300B, Sai Yok Yai Falls 500B, Dawa Dung Cave 700B. Be prepared to bargain with the boat operator.

The **Suvatana Hotel** in Nam Tok has basic rooms for 80-100B, while the **Sai Yok Noi Bungalows** 300 meters north along the highway has better rooms for 200-500B.

Kwai Noi River Trip

Several good explorations start from Nam Tok. Visitors short on time might hire a *samlor* or walk three km north to Sai Yok Noi (Kao Phang) Waterfall, an unremarkable and perpetually crowded place surrounded by restaurants and tacky souvenir stalls.

A better option is to take a tricycle from the train station for 10B down to Pak Sang Pier. From here, eight-person longtail boats can be hired for upriver journeys. Boat prices are listed at the train station, but most journeys are prohibitively expensive except for larger groups. A recommended six-hour trip stops at Lawa Caves (biggest cave in the region) and Sai Yok Yai Falls, where the Russian roulette scenes from *The Deer Hunter* were filmed. This tour costs about 1,000B per boatload—not bad for five or six people.

Excellent raft hotels are located around Pak Sang. The River Kwai Village Hotel and Home Phu Toey Resort described in the Kanchanaburi chapter are two beautiful raft lodges which charge 800-1,200B for private room, boat ride from Pak Sang, and three meals. Travel agents in Bangkok and Kanchanaburi can make arrangements.

Hellfire Pass Memorial

A moving memorial to Allied prisoners and Asian conscripts who died while constructing the railway line near Hellfire Pass was erected several years ago by the Australian-Thai Chamber of Commerce. During three months of labor, over 1,000 Australian and British prisoners worked around the clock; only 300 survived the ordeal. The park consists of trails that reach Konyu Cutting, where a memorial plaque has been fastened to the rock; and Hin Tok trestle bridge, which collapsed three times during its construction. The association hopes to restore some of the track and display trains used during the construction.

The memorial is near Hellfire Pass, 80 km from Kanchanaburi and 18 km north of Nam Tok. English signs marking the turnoff are posted on Route 323. Bus travelers should alight at the Royal Thai Army Camp, then hike 500 meters to the trailhead which leads to the Konyu Cutting.

Sai Yok National Park

Tucked away inside 500-square-km Sai Yok National Park are the small but very pretty Sai Yok Yai Falls, which emerge from underground streams and tumble gracefully into the Kwai Noi River. The falls are widely celebrated in Thai poetry and song. Two large caves are located within the park boundaries but across the broad Kwai Noi River. Lawa Cave, the largest in the region, is a wonderland of dripping stalactites and stalagmites. Dawa Dung Cave is northwest of Sai Yok on the west bank of the Kwai Noi River. Other attractions inside the park include some Neolithic remains uncovered by Thai archaeologists, remains of a Japanese military camp, and a small bat cave known for its almost microscopic inhabitants.

The park entrance is about 38 km north of Nam Tok, but the falls and river are hidden three km off the main road. Bus travelers should get off at the national park sign, then flag down a passing car or face a long and dusty walk. Motorcycle taxis may be available.

Camping is permitted inside the park near the hanging bridge which vaguely resembles San Francisco's Golden Gate. The national park has several 10-person bungalows for 600-800B. Within sight of the curious bridge are several beautiful raft hotels where bamboo bungalows cost 450-600B.

Hin Da Hot Springs

Two small and very grubby swimming pools filled with warm water are located 500 meters off Route 323 about 130 km north of Kanchanaburi. Constructed by the Japanese in WW II, the two concrete tanks are now open to both male and female bathers. Not recommended.

TONGPAPUM

The first major town between Kanchanaburi and Three Pagodas Pass is Tongpapum, a cowboy village of twisted, rutted streets, ragged children, and hand-pump gasoline stations. Tongpapum lies at the southern edge of the vast Krung Kravia Lake created by the Khao Lam Dam, a major hydroelectric source for Bangkok and central Thailand. The town essentially serves as a petrol and rest stop en route to Sangklaburi and Three Pagodas Pass.

Accommodations
A few hotels are located on the main road which runs off the highway. **Som Chai Nuk Bungalows** has decent fan rooms with private bath from 150B and a/c rooms from 400-650B. **Si Thong Pha Phum Bungalows** farther down the main road has 28 fan and a/c rooms in the same price range. **S. Bunyong Bungalows** at the end of the street is similar.

Several upscale raft hotels are located on nearby Krung Kravia Lake. **Kao Laem Raft Resort** (Bangkok tel. 02-277-0599) charges 400-600B, while **Thongphaphum Valley** and **Ban Rimdoi** (tel. 034-513218) charge 600-800B for floating bamboo bungalows.

EN ROUTE TO SANGKLABURI

Several natural attractions are located between Tongpapum and Sangklaburi, off the paved road which passes through the rolling hills and limestone canyons that flank Krung Kravia Lake. Some are within walking distance of the highway, while others can only be reached with a motorcycle or jeep. Guesthouses in Sangklaburi can help arrange transportation.

Sunyataram Forest Monastery
This 45-hectare retreat is affiliated with one of the country's most popular living monks, Pra Yantra Ammaro Bhikku, who found himself the center of a national controversy. In 1994, Yantra was accused by his chief rival, Pra Phayom Kallayano, of various sexual transgressions and other unmonklike behavior. Yantra, then 43, aroused national controversy for traveling abroad with large

entourages of women, staying in hotels instead of Buddhist temples, possessing credit cards, and violating his vows of celibacy with at least four women, including a Thai woman who bore him a son in Belgrade, and a Danish harpist who said they had sex in her van.

The end finally came in 1995 after the Supreme Council of Buddhists Monks disbarred Yantra and forced him to surrender his robes in Bangkok at the Royal Temple. Yantra, however, still enjoys great support among the Thai people and with many religious reformers who feel that chastity should not be a basis for passing moral judgment.

Sunyataram Forest Monastery is 32 km north of Tongpapum and 43 km south of Sangklaburi. After all the attention, it's understandable that this monastery is cautious about outside visitors and will welcome only those who can prove their credentials. Permission to visit can be obtained in advance by writing to: Chief Abbot, P.O. Box 20 Tongpapum, Kanchanaburi 71150.

Krung Kravia Falls
Motorcyclists may want to stop at the falls 33 km north of Tongpapum.

Dai Chong Thong Falls
Another set of falls, 35 km north of Tongpapum.

Thung Yai Naresuan National Park
Turn east onto Route 323 to reach the 3,200-square-km national park and Takien Thong Falls. Naturalists claim the park is home to the last remaining wild tigers in Thailand, numbering 200-300. The park is 40 km north of Tongpapum and 34 km south of Sangklaburi. The park can also be reached via the Karen village of Ban San Pong, 15 km north of Sangklaburi.

SANGKLABURI

Sangklaburi is a wonderfully idyllic escape off the standard route and a fascinating region to explore for its historic and natural wonders. The town, situated at the northern edge of Khao Laem Dam, was established in 1982 after the original settlement was submerged by the flooding of the valley and the creation of Khao Laem Reservoir.

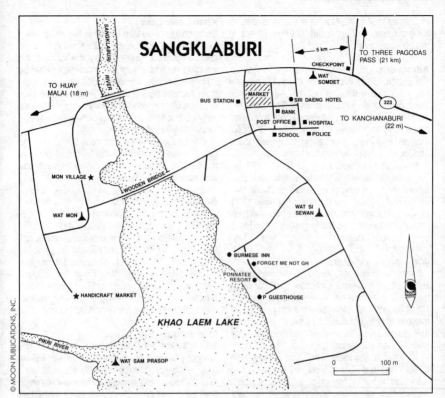

SANGKLABURI

SANGKLABURI RIVER

TO HUAY
MALAI (18 m)

← 5 km →

TO THREE PAGODAS
PASS (21 km)

CHECKPOINT
▲ WAT
SOMDET

BUS STATION ■
MARKET
● SRI DAENG HOTEL

■ BANK
POST OFFICE ■
■ HOSPITAL

TO KANCHANABURI
(22 m) →

323

■ SCHOOL ■ POLICE

MON VILLAGE ★

WOODEN BRIDGE

WAT SI
SEWAN ▲

WAT MON ▲

● BURMESE INN
● FORGET ME NOT GH

PONNATEE
RESORT ●

★ HANDICRAFT MARKET

● P GUESTHOUSE

KHAO LAEM LAKE

0   100 m

PIKRI RIVER

▲ WAT SAM PRASOP

© MOON PUBLICATIONS, INC.

History

Sangklaburi lies just 21 km east of historic Three Pagodas Pass, the pipeline through which much of Thailand history was formed.

Historians believe the earliest visitors to the region were the Mons, who entered present-day Thailand sometime around the beginning of the Christian era and later established Dvaravati settlements from Nakhon Pathom to Haripunchai. The pass continued to serve as the overland trade route between the Gulf of Martaban and the Gulf of Siam—the conduit for the culture, religion, and political institutions of India.

Three Pagodas Pass later figured in many important military invasions. In 1548, Burmese troops under the command of King Tabinshwethi crossed the mountains into Thailand and attacked the kingdom of Ayuthaya. The Burmese returned again in 1592, but were repulsed near Suphanburi

after King Naresuan of Ayuthaya defeated the Burmese prince in a duel on elephantback.

Even today, warfare, political turbulence, and migrations continue to define the ethnic and social landscape of the Sangklaburi region. Many of the Karens, Mons, and Burmese who have settled in the region over the centuries have become political refugees, unable to obtain Thai passports or permits for residence and work. Most remain stateless individual wanderers—shunned by both the Thais and Burmese.

In May 1995, after almost 50 years of struggle against the Burmese government, the Mons signed a cease-fire with the military junta in the southeastern city of Mawlamyine. The treaty allows the Mons to retain their weapons in certain areas. The only major ethnic minority army still fighting the government is the Karen National Union. See "Mae Sariang" under "West of Chiang Mai" in the Northern Thailand chapter for more information about this final phase in the 50-year revolt.

Attractions

Sangklaburi itself is rather ordinary, but several good sights are located nearby. Attractions in the town include Wat Somdet (a Thai temple), Wat Si Sewan (a Karen temple), and a marketplace filled with Mons, Karens, Thais, Chinese, Indians, and Pakistanis selling smuggled goods and locally produced handicrafts.

Guesthouses help arrange tours to Three Pagodas Pass, Mon temples, the lake, and possibly a Mon or Karen refugee camp. These two- or three-day tours are reasonably priced (750-900B) and eliminate the hassle of finding local transportation and possibly getting stranded in some remote location.

Wat Wang Vivangkaram

As with the town itself, Vivangkaram was established after the original settlement was buried by the flooding of the Kwai Noi River at Tongpapum. Often called "Wat Mon" by the local population, the temple is highly revered by the Mons, Karens, and Burmese for its political and religious symbolism, and for its centerpiece, Chedi Luang Phaw Utama. Modeled in the style of the Mahabodhi stupa in Bodgaya, India, the red-tiled *chedi* is topped with about six kg of gold. To the rear is an older *chedi* around 300-400 years old, and across the road is a recently completed temple that reflects the wealth of the goods smuggled through Three Pagodas Pass. Several of the monks speak decent English and are happy to show travelers around the temple and monastery.

The 86-year-old abbot of Wat Mon, Luang Phaw Utama, was responsible for the erection of both temples and continues to be active in the protection of the local Mon peoples. But the recent political rapprochement between the Thai and Burmese governments has put new pressures on the abbot and his followers, who fear repatriation yet remain unrecognized by both governments.

Wat Mon is three km southwest of town toward Khao Laem Lake. A Mon market operates on the east side of the temple, but be forewarned that nearly all gems sold in the region are synthetics imported from Japan.

Khao Laem Lake

Beneath this huge lake lies an entire village once located at the confluence of the Kwai Noi, Ranti, and Sangkhalia Rivers. Today, the spires of the village's primary temple, Wat Sam Prasop ("Three Junction Temple"), can be seen rising from the lake during the wet season. During the dry season, the level of the lake drops dramatically and visitors can walk around the perimeter of the 70-year-old temple.

Canoes can be rented from several of the guesthouses to explore the lake and observe the birdlife, which is most active at daybreak and shortly before sunset.

Bridge and Mon Village

The 400-meter pedestrian and motorcycle wooden bridge that connected Sangklaburi with the Mon village on the other side collapsed a few years ago, but has been rebuilt with less pitch to make it safer. Visitors can walk across the bridge—the longest wooden bridge in Thailand—or take a boat over to the Mon village of Waeng Kha, where refugees scratch out a living by farming, trading, and selling Burmese handicrafts to tourists.

Mon Refugee Camp

Some 30 km from Sangklaburi and about two hours by longtail boat up the Pikri River lies an enormous refugee camp with an estimated 50,000 Mons and Karens. Organized tours to the camp first pass Ayuthaya-era sanctuaries filled with crumbling Buddhas, then approach a pass that marked the Thai/Burmese border until the end of WW II.

Several other refugee camps are hidden away along the border and toward the mining town of Pilok, but access is difficult and many camps have been declared off-limits to outside visitors. Guesthouse owners will know which camps are open and advise you on proper gifts and supplies to bring the political refugees.

Wang Bandan Cave

About two km before Three Pagodas Pass, you'll find a track that leads two km down to a lumber mill and limestone cliffs pocketed with caves and inhabited by local monks. The caves are reached by rickety bamboo ladders that hang against narrow ledges and walkways used by the monks. Guides can be hired to explore the caves but most travelers can wander around alone, then hike back to the road and up the pass.

Accommodations

Sangklaburi has a few excellent guesthouses on the edge of the vast reservoir.

P Guesthouse: The travelers' favorite seems to be this lakeside guesthouse one km from the bus stop—ideally situated for views of the Mon village and wooden bridge. Proprietor Darunee Yenjai and her husband arrange treks; provide information on their bulletin board; rent canoes, bicycles, and motorcycles; help with jungle treks; and organize longtail boats to nearby refugee camps. The guesthouse features a comfortable if somewhat expensive restaurant and bungalows overlooking the lake. 81/1 Tambon Noog Loo, Sangklaburi, tel. (034) 595061, fax (034) 595139, 80-180B.

Burmese Inn: Austrian Armin Hermann and his Thai wife Meo opened this small guesthouse a few years ago and have since expanded to compete successfully with P Guesthouse. Although the location near the stream is less awesome than down by the lake, Armin and Meo compensate with excellent food at reasonable prices and dependable travel tips given in three languages—German, English, and Thai. 52/3 Tambon Nong Loo, Sangklaburi, tel. (034) 595146, 80-180B.

Sri Daeng Hotel: The hotel near the bus stop and central market has clean rooms with hardwood floors but lacks the views of P Guesthouse or the friendly vibes of the Burmese Inn. On the other hand, travelers requiring a/c will find this the only choice in town. 1 Sangklaburi, tel. (034) 595039, 200-250B fan, 350-420Ba/c.

Practicalities

The Siam Commercial Bank three blocks from the bus station changes traveler's checks at reasonable rates. International phone calls can be made from the post office and from most guesthouses for a small service charge. Sangklaburi also has a small hospital across from the post office that can help with malaria, an ongoing problem in most border regions in Thailand. Visitors are advised to take malaria pills and remain covered after nightfall.

Transportation

Sangklaburi is 220 km from Kanchanaburi and 21 km from the Burmese border. Bus 8203 departs Kanchanaburi daily at 0645, 0900, 1045, 1315, and takes about five hours to reach Sangklaburi depending on road conditions.

A minivan leaves hourly from the Asia Sai Yok office on the east side of the Kanchanaburi bus terminal. The van takes under four hours and drops you at the Sri Daeng Hotel or your selected guesthouse, but can be uncomfortable when filled with passengers.

Motorcyclists should allow a full day with stops at Ban Kao Museum, Prasat Muang Sing Khmer ruins, and Nam Tok, and a brief swim at Sai Yok Yai Falls. Gasoline stations are located in Nam Tok, Tongpapum, and Sangklaburi. The stretch from Tongpapum can be tricky and should only be attempted by experienced motorcyclists during the day.

Motorcycle taxis from the central market and bridge provide rides to most nearby destinations for 10-20B. Motorcycles can be rented from the P Guesthouse and Burmese Inn.

THREE PAGODAS PASS

The border crossing into Myanmar at Three Pagodas Pass is named after a trio of historic cone-shaped *chedis* known as Pra Chedi Sam Ong. Centuries ago this was the spot from where marauding Burmese armies marched into Thailand on their traditional invasions. Today the small trading post at the pass is the scene of political struggles between the Burmese government, Mon National Liberation Army (MNLA), Karen National Union (KNU), and the All Myanmar Students Democratic Front (ABSDF), which has set up an opposition government to fight the regime of Ne Win.

Three Pagodas Pass has been in a constant state of flux. During the mid-1980s it thrived as a prosperous trading town dominated by the Karens, who collected a five percent tax on all goods smuggled across the border. Burmese products such as gems, jade, and *longyis* (sarongs) were exchanged for Thai batteries, roofing iron, even television sets. After the political disruptions in 1988, the Burmese government renewed their military offensive against the Karens and Mons by attacking Three Pagodas Pass and burning the town to the ground. The village has since revived itself but remains a staging ground for military and political struggle.

Westerners are now allowed to cross the border for the day by paying the border guards 140B for an entry permit, which is not stamped in your passport. The Burmese border town—Payathonzu—is little more than a dusty market with the standard collection of stalls selling Burmese cheroots, clothes, synthetic gems, questionable jade, *longyis,* blankets, and teak furniture that graphically demonstrates the destruction of the last major teak forests on earth.

The 1995 cease-fire agreement signed between the Mons and the Burmese government will probably end hostilities and someday open the border to Western tourists, who will be able to travel from Three Pagodas Pass to Mawlamyine and Yangon.

Attractions

Locals can point out the few sights around town: the three whitewashed pagodas, the site of the old station that marked the end of the Death Railway, and the track itself which, according to Thai archaeologists, dates back to the earliest human settlement in the region.

Westerners are occasionally allowed to cross the border and visit the adjacent Burmese village where handicrafts, cheroots, and silver jewelry are sold in the local market. A few travelers have reportedly ventured across the border to the Mon outpost of Kreng Thaw and continued by boat down to Kyain Seiggyi and Mawlamyine. Conditions change with the season and should be double-checked with travelers and the TAT office in Kanchanaburi.

Accommodations

Most travelers visit Three Pagodas Pass on a day-trip from Sangklaburi. However, **Three Pagodas Pass Resort** (tel. 034-511079, Bangkok reservations tel. 02-412-4159) has large bungalows from 300B.

Transportation

Three Pagodas Pass is 241 km from Kanchanaburi and 22 km from Sangklaburi along a rough road passable only during the dry season Oct.-June. The road turns off Route 323 about four km before Sangklaburi. Minitrucks to the border leave Sangklaburi each morning and return in the late afternoon.

SUPHANBURI

Suphanburi is an ancient city; one theory holds it may have been the mythical empire of Suwanaphum mentioned in early Buddhist chronicles. The present town was founded in the 15th century as a military outpost against Burmese incursions, although the discovery of Neolithic artifacts and terra-cotta figurines of U-Thong Periods indicate the region has been inhabited since prehistoric times.

Located 107 km northwest of Bangkok and 70 km from Kanchanaburi, modern Suphanburi is a prosperous town with a handful of temples and Buddha images. The town is best visited as a short stop between Kanchanaburi and Ayuthaya. After arrival, hire a *tuk tuk* for 50B and make a two-hour tour of Wat Palalai, Wat Mahathat, the footprint at Wat Pra Rob, and Wat Suwanapum. Ask the driver to drop you at the appropriate bus terminal for onward connections.

Wat Palalai

Suphanburi's most impressive sight is the immense Buddha three km west of town on the road to Kanchanaburi. The whitewashed sanctuary features boat-shaped walls typical of the Ayuthaya Period and a pair of large bronze bells at the entrance. Surrounding the structure are humorous plaster images of an elephant, a monkey, and a camel in the rear courtyard.

The central image, Luang Por Toh ("Giant Buddha"), is one of the most impressive statues in Thailand, not only for its immense proportions but for its unusual, so-called European, position. Cast during the early Ayuthaya Period, the figure sits with both hands on knees and right palm held skyward. The head features a stylized nose, upturned lips, oversized eyelids, and soaring top spires that almost pierce the roof. The ankles and three-meter feet have been almost completely covered with gold leaf. Flanking the massive figure are four seated Buddhas in Ayuthaya style.

Wat Chum Nun Song

On the opposite side of the road and slightly down from Wat Palalai is this restored red-brick *chedi* which dates from the early Ayuthaya Period.

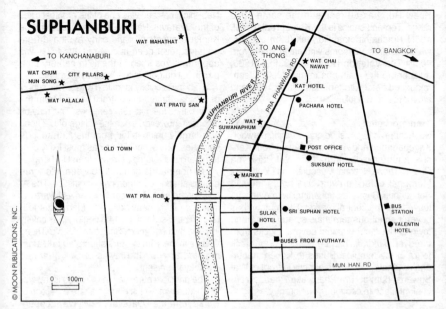

Wat Mahathat

On a side road off Hwy. 321 are the remains of a Khmer-style *prang* which dates from the first period of the Ayuthaya Empire. The front courtyard has a modern *viharn* with Sukothai walking Buddhas mounted in the eaves, and an impressive wooden assembly hall with outstanding portico carvings. To the rear stands the ancient *prang* with a reconstructed concrete spire over corner guardians, *nagas,* and traces of original stucco. A steep staircase leads to the interior crypt, which overlooks several small *salas* filled with seated Buddhas.

Wat Pra Rob

Wat Pra Rob features a large reclining Buddha in the right courtyard and a very rare wooden footprint of the Buddha stored inside the pavilion on the left. The footprint, perhaps the only example of its type in Thailand, is displayed vertically and protected in a case mounted on poles. Also note the back side carved with images of demons, long-haired maidens, and elephants. Resident monks can unlock the building for a modest donation.

Wat Suwanaphum

Situated on the main street in downtown Suphanburi, Wat Suwanaphum was established during the early Ayuthaya Period as Wat Klang. To the right of the central courtyard are several modern buildings, including a school for the study of Pali, and to the rear is a colorful *viharn*. The main attraction of Wat Suwanaphum is Luang Por Pleung Museum, at the back of the courtyard. Inside the museum is a rare collection of local antiques and religious artifacts collected by the late abbot of the temple. Tours are often provided by the local monk and English schoolteacher named Kaliang.

Accommodations

Suphanburi is a prosperous town dominated by Chinese who operate many of the hotels. Most of the hotels, restaurants, and nightclubs are on Pra Phanwasa Road, which parallels the Suphanburi River. The **KAT Hotel,** tel. (035) 521639, 533 Pra Phanwasa Rd., has fan rooms from 150B and a/c rooms from 300B. The hotel is on the main road, two blocks north of the central intersection and just before Wat Chai Nawat. **King Pho Sai Hotel,** tel. (035) 522412, 678 Nen

Kaew Rd., has 80 rooms in the same price range. Top-end choice is the **Kalpapreuk Hotel,** 135/1 Prachathibothai Rd., tel. (035) 522555, which features a/c rooms with private bath from 400B. **The Valentin Hotel,** tel. (035) 521836, adjacent to the main bus terminal, is a clean, midpriced hotel with fan rooms from 150B and a/c rooms from 350B.

Transportation

Suphanburi is best visited on a side trip between Kanchanaburi and Ayuthaya. Buses from Kanchanaburi pass the turnoff for Wat Pai Rong Rua, U-Thong National Museum, and Don Chedi Memorial before arriving two hours later in Suphanburi. Buses to Suphanburi from Ayuthaya leave from the central market. Suphanburi has several small bus terminals scattered around town and a main terminal several blocks from the river. *Tuk tuks* can be chartered for quick tours of the temples. Buses to Kanchanaburi and Ayuthaya also leave directly in front of Wat Suwanaphum on Pra Phanwasa Road, a convenient place to continue your journey.

VICINITY OF SUPHANBURI

Don Chedi

Seven km west of Suphanburi is the turnoff to Don Chedi, site of a famous battle in 1582 during which King Naresuan of Ayuthaya defeated the prince of Myanmar and liberated Thailand from foreign domination. The site is marked by a ruined Sri Lankan-style *chedi* surmounted by a modern monument erected in the same style in 1951. A nearby bronze statue representing the victory of Naresuan is mounted by the king and a mahout who signals the troops with royal symbols.

Don Chedi sponsors a popular festival every January during which the historic battle is re-created with elephant battles and thousands of participants dressed in period costumes. Tours can be arranged through travel agents in Bangkok.

U-Thong

Excavations conducted by Thai and Western archaeologists indicate that U-Thong, 31 km west of Suphanburi, has been inhabited since Neolithic times and was one of the greatest cities of the Dvaravati Period. Though relics from the Khmer occupation or the early Ayuthaya Period have never been uncovered, the town was apparently resettled in the 17th century as a provincial outpost of the Ayuthaya Empire.

U-Thong is chiefly identified with a Thai school of art that thrived in central Thailand from the early 13th to the mid-15th centuries. This may be incorrect, however, since the village of U-Thong was largely uninhabited from the 11th to 17th centuries. The school of art was most likely centered around Ayuthaya rather than U-Thong.

U-Thong art is generally divided into three groups sharing common characteristics. The A-style of the early 13th century shows Dvaravati influence in its heaviness and Mon facial features. The B-style of the 14th century was chiefly inspired by the Khmers. Sculptors of the U-Thong C-style in the 15th century attempted but largely failed to copy the styles of Sukothai and Ayuthayan artisans.

The principal attraction in U-Thong is the National Museum, which houses a rare collection of works from the Dvaravati, Srivijaya, Lopburi, Chaing Saen, and Ayuthaya Periods. Among the highlights are a stone wheel discovered at a nearby *chedi,* beads of the Funan Period, terracotta busts from Ku Bua near Ratchaburi, and some Srivijaya bronzes.

Wat Pai Rong Wua

Buddha might not approve, but 40 km southwest of Suphanburi up a side road from Song Phi Nong, a local abbot has constructed a surrealistic Buddhist theme park more reminiscent of Disney on acid than Buddha in nirvana. Scattered amid the 200-acre park are countless concrete Buddhas, the largest bronze Buddha in Thailand, exotic Indian architecture such as a copy of the Mahabodhi in Bodgaya, and the Land of Hell where grotesquely shaped sinners are tortured for their sins. Buddhist novelty parks, such as Wat Pai Rong Wua and Wat Khaek near Nong Khai, reflect the strong love of macabre kitsch among rural Thais.

Ask the bus driver to drop you at Song Phi Nong; from here *songtaos* continue north up to Wat Pai Rong Rua.

NORTH OF BANGKOK

Nestled between Bangkok and central Thailand are several small towns which have figured closely in Thai history. Bang Pa In is a riverside stop, which once served as a summer retreat for Thai kings. Lopburi, 154 km north of Bangkok, offers both 12th-century Khmer ruins and a royal residence constructed in the 17th century by King Narai. Top draw is the town of Ayuthaya, which served as the second capital of Thailand for over four centuries.

The region owes its prosperity to the rich soil and network of canals and rivers which ensure a bountiful harvest of rice. The Thai people predominate, though large numbers of Thai-Chinese merchants reside in the larger towns. Smaller numbers of Mon and Khmer live in remote villages. Climatic conditions are similar to those of Bangkok, with a rainy season July-Oct., a cool season until February, and the hot season until midsummer when the rains return.

Sightseeing Highlights

While most travelers go directly from Bangkok to Chiang Mai, a more leisurely and informative journey would include short visits to the historical sites of Ayuthaya and Lopburi just north of Bangkok, and the archaeological ruins in central Thailand.

Bang Pa In: Some 60 km north of Bangkok is a small complex of royal shrines and pavilions—once a summer getaway for the kings of Thailand. Generally visited en route to Ayuthaya, Bang Pa In is rather unexceptional, though history and architecture buffs will find it a worthwhile stopover.

Ayuthaya: The city of Ayuthaya, 85 km north of Bangkok, reigned as the political, economic, and cultural center of Thailand from 1350 until conquest by the Burmese in 1767. Set with hundreds of temples and palaces surrounded by rivers and canals, Ayuthaya was described by European traders as among the largest and most prosperous cities in the East. Though it was largely leveled by the Burmese in 1767, large-scale restoration projects have made Ayuthaya one of the most important historical and cultural destinations in Thailand. The surviving monuments are widely scattered and a full day of exploration is necessary to appreciate the magnitude of Ayuthaya. Day tours from Bangkok are not recommended.

Lopburi: One of Thailand's oldest cities, Lopburi served as a Khmer military outpost in the 13th century and as an alternative capital to Ayuthaya in the mid-17th century. Architectural attractions include a fine 12th-century Khmer temple and royal palace dating from the reign of King Narai. The town itself is small, sleepy, and rarely visited by Westerners, yet offers enough historic architecture to merit an overnight stop en route to Sukothai or the northeast.

Pra Buddhabat: Thailand's most famous Buddha footprint is located at Pra Buddhabat, a religious sanctuary near Saraburi.

Transportation

Attractions north of Bangkok can be easily visited en route to central or northern Thailand. One possible plan is to briefly visit Bang Pa In in the morning and continue up to Ayuthaya in the afternoon. A full day is necessary to properly explore Ayuthaya. Lopburi can be reached the following day on an early morning train. Allow about a half day to explore Lopburi, and perhaps make a side trip to Pra Buddhabat. Buses and trains continue north from Lopburi to Phitsanulok and Sukothai.

Ayuthaya and Lopburi—the two most important destinations north of Bangkok—are served by both bus or train. Buses to Bang Pa In and Ayuthaya depart every 15 minutes from Bangkok's Northern Bus Terminal.

Most trains go directly to Ayuthaya. Trains that stop in Bang Pa In depart Hualampong train station daily at 0827 and 0955 only. Trains to Ayuthaya depart daily at 0640, 0705, 0830, 1500, 1800, 1940, 2000, 2200. Whether ordinary, rapid, or express, all trains take about 90 minutes to reach Ayuthaya. Train travel, in general, is a relaxing and scenic way to get around Thailand.

BANG PA IN

Early Chakri kings ignored Bang Pa In as too distant from Bangkok until King Mongkut reestablished the site in the latter half of the 19th century. King Chulalongkorn (1868-1910) erected a half dozen buildings without any great concern for architectural unity and used the retreat as a reception site for distinguished visitors. The complex was abandoned after the tragic death of the king's wife. Queen Sunandakumariratna and her children drowned in the Menam River in 1880 in full view of her royal entourage. None of the entourage attempted to rescue them because, at the time, royal law demanded death for any commoner who dared touch royalty.

Bang Pa In is more odd than amazing, but it's an easy stopover between Bangkok and Ayuthaya or a quick side trip from Ayuthaya, 20 km north. Visitors with limited time should go direct to Ayuthaya and, time permitting, backtrack to Bang Pa In for an afternoon visit.

The outer grounds of the palace, which include most of the important buildings, are open daily 0900-1800. Interior palace buildings are closed on Monday.

Attractions

Bang Pa In today no longer serves as a royal retreat but rather as a tourist site and occasional venue for state ceremonies. The original structures built by King Prasat Thong have disappeared and most of the remaining buildings are the legacy of King Chulalongkorn, who was fascinated by European architecture.

Aisawan Thippaya Pavilion: The highlight of the small park is a delicate water pavilion erected by King Chulalongkorn to replace Prasat Thong's old palace in traditional style. Reconstructed by King Vajiravudh in reinforced concrete, the lovely building has been reproduced for several international expositions and is a favorite subject for photographers. Centerpiece is a life-sized statue of King Chulalongkorn.

Peking Palace: Pra Thinnang Warophat Piman, nicknamed the Peking Palace, was a gift from Chinese Thais who modeled the palace after a Chinese imperial court. A magnificent collection of jade, Ming Period porcelains, Chulalongkorn's intricately carved bed, and lacquer tables are displayed inside the palace. The palace itself was constructed from materials imported from China.

Royal Residence: Warophat Piman Hall, north of the landing stage at the entrance to the palace, is a Western-style palace constructed by King Chulalongkorn to replace King Mongkut's original two-story wooden residence. The building is copied from the pavilion in the Grand Palace where royalty changed regalia before mounting a palanquin. Interior chambers and anterooms are decorated with oil paintings depicting events in Thai history and scenes from Thai literature. Most rooms are closed to the public and open only for state ceremonies.

Gothic Tower: All that remains of the Uthayan Phumi Sathiana Palace (Haw Pra), an old timber structure destroyed by fire in 1938, is a curious six-sided tower in a semi-Gothic style. The hexagonal tower was reconstructed in 1990 as a gingerbread green edifice that now resembles a wedding cake.

Queen's Monument: The white marble memorial across the small bridge honors Chulalongkorn's first queen, who tragically drowned in full view of her entourage. A marble obelisk and cenotaph commemorate the event with Thai and English eulogies composed by King Chulalongkorn.

Wat Nivet Dhammapravat: A fun cable car whizzes across the river to Thailand's only European-style Buddhist temple. Erected by King Chulalongkorn for monks of the Dhammayuttika sect, the incongruous temple features an important image cast by Pradit Varakarn, court sculptor during the reigns of Mongkut and Chulalongkorn.

Transportation

Buses leave from Bangkok's Northern Bus Terminal every 30 minutes and take about one hour to reach the small town of Bang Pa In. Mini-trucks from the market in Ayuthaya take 45 minutes. *Samlors* from the town to the riverside palace cost 10B. You can also take a train from Bangkok for 10B, then a *songtao* for 5B.

An interesting alternative is the Sunday morning boat trip organized by the Chao Praya Express Boat Company. The boat leaves at 0800 from Bangkok's Maharaj Pier, costs 160B, and includes stops at the Wat Pai Lom Stork Sanctuary and the Queen's Folk Arts and Handicraft Center in Bang Sai, before it returns to Bangkok around 1800.

AYUTHAYA

Ayuthaya, 85 km north of Bangkok, served as Thailand's second capital from 1350 to 1767. The city's scattered ruins, colossal Buddhas, decaying *chedis,* and multitude of soaring *wats* restored by the Fine Arts Department provide eloquent testimony to the splendor of this medieval metropolis. Recently declared a national historic park, Ayuthaya has been successfully developed into one of the country's major tourist attractions—a must-see for all visitors to Thailand.

Though Ayuthaya is often visited as a daytrip from Bangkok, it really takes a day or two of leisurely wandering to properly appreciate the sense of history evoked by the far-flung ruins. Travelers who enjoy romantic ruins and have a strong interest in Thai history should allow two full days in *both* Ayuthaya and Sukothai.

History

The first settlements near Ayuthaya were Khmer military and trading camps established in the 11th century as outposts for their distant empire. In 1350 a Thai prince named U-Thong (Ramathibodi) transferred his capital from U-Thong to Ayuthaya to escape a smallpox plague and provide greater military security from Burmese invaders. The site was carefully chosen at the merging of the Lopburi, Prasak, and Chao Praya Rivers where, with the creation of additional canals, the island fortress-city could be easily defended from outside attack. Ramathibodi named his new city after the mythical kingdom of Ayodhya in the Hindu Ramayana epic and constructed royal palaces and temples. Sri Lankan monks soon arrived to reinforce Theravada Buddhism and maintain religious purity in the new Thai kingdom.

Ayuthaya was ruled by a succession of 33 kings of various dynasties who embellished the island capital with magnificent temples and sumptuous palaces. Ayuthayan kings, however, were not the benevolent and understanding Buddhist monarchs of Sukothai, but rather paternalistic Khmer-influenced kings who hid themselves behind walls of ritual, taboo, and sorcery. As incarnations of Shiva, they became focal points for political and religious cults which, in turn, sharply defined all levels of society.

Ayuthaya soon became the most powerful military empire in Southeast Asia. A policy of national military conscription gave Ayuthaya the strength to resist, expand, and then conquer the empires of the Burmese, Cambodians, and Muslims. In 1378, Sukothai was subjugated by King Boromaraja I, the successor of King Ramathibodi, and in 1431 Angkor fell to Ayuthaya after a siege of seven months. By the end of the 15th century, Ayuthaya controlled Southeast Asia from Vientiane in the north to Malacca in the south, and from Angkor in the east to Bago in the west.

A short period of decline in the mid-16th century marked the arrival of one of Ayuthaya's greatest rulers, King Naresuan the Great (1555-1605). As a young man, Naresuan demonstrated great military capabilities against Cambodia and subsequently liberated Ayuthaya from Burmese occupation in 1586. His rare combination of dynamic leadership, personal courage, and force of personality reunited the Thai people, who had suffered from more than a decade of defeat and humiliation at the hands of the Burmese and Cambodians. Naresuan formally became king of Ayuthaya in 1590 and, in 1592, fulfilled his legendary promise to regain Ayuthaya by defeating a Burmese crown prince in a sword duel atop war elephants. For the first time in 30 years, the tables of war turned in favor of the Thais. Naresuan had successfully unified Siam into an ethnic, cultural, and political framework that included the larger international order.

Under the rule of Naresuan and subsequent kings, Ayuthaya also became an important commercial center. First on the scene were the Portuguese, who traded guns and ammunition for rice and gems. Dazzled by the city's gilded opulence and grandeur, emissaries dispatched in 1685 by Louis XIV and other astonished European visitors compared the riverine kingdom to Venice: Ayuthaya was reported to be larger and more magnificent than contemporary London or Paris. Perhaps the most famous Western trader was Constantine Phaulkon, a colorful Greek adventurer who stirred up local resentment by preaching Christianity to a Buddhist monarch named King Narai. When word spread that a dying Narai was close to conversion, xenophobic Thai nobles seized the throne and executed the Greek merchant. Westerners were expelled and Ayuthaya entered into its own Golden Age of arts—an amazing period of vibrant art, literature, and education.

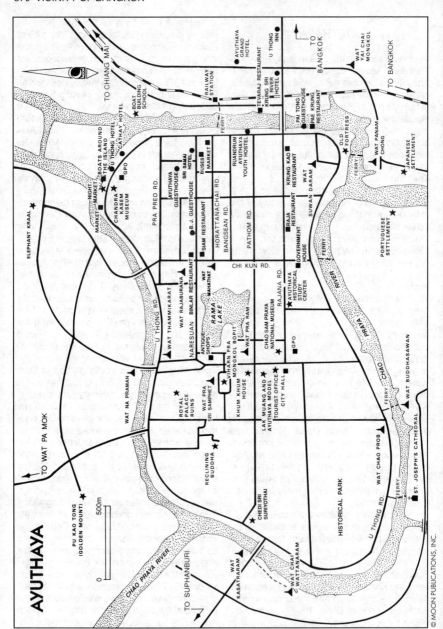

After four centuries of rule, Ayuthaya went into an economic and military decline. In early 1763, an enormous Burmese army overran Chiang Mai and massed for a final assault on Ayuthaya. After two years of siege, the city capitulated and most of the citizens were either murdered or marched off to Myanmar as slave labor. Ayuthaya was burned to the ground. Tremendous art treasures, museums, countless temples, priceless libraries, and historical archives were all destroyed—a horrific act that still profoundly shocks the Thais.

Attractions

A European visitor reported in 1685 that the population of Ayuthaya exceeded one million and that the city boasted over 1,700 temples, 30,000 priests, and more than 4,000 images of Buddha, all of them gold or gilt. Contemporary Ayuthaya has three good museums with dozens of Buddhas and about 30 temples in various stages of reconstruction and renovation. Monuments are widely scattered and only the central temples near the modern town are within walking distance. A few suggestions on bicycle and *tuk tuk* rentals, as well as on boat excursions, are given below under "Getting Around."

Monuments near the city center and within walking distance of guesthouses and hotels include the Chandra Kasem Museum, Wat Rajaburana, Wat Mahathat, Rama Lake, Wat Pra Ram, Sam Praya Museum, Viharn Pra Mongkol Bopit, Wat Pra Sri Samphet, and Wat Na Praman. A full day of walking will cover all these sights, which include the region's most important monuments.

A second set of monuments is located on the banks of the river which encircle the island of Ayuthaya. A convenient if somewhat expensive way to tour these temples and European churches is by rented boat leaving from the quay near the Chandra Kasem Museum. Alternatively, U-Thong Road can be toured by bike or minitrucks that circulate along the road and charge 10B for a ride of any distance. Temples across the river can be reached with local ferries.

Farther afield and outside the city limits is a handful of temples such as the Golden Mount and the elephant *kraal*. A chartered *songtao* is necessary to reach these monuments.

Chandra Kasem Museum

King Thammaraja constructed this 17th-century palace for his son, who subsequently claimed the throne as King Naresuan. Partially destroyed by the Burmese, the palace was reconstructed by King Mongkut and later converted into one of the three museums in Ayuthaya. The Chantura Mukh Pavilion immediately on your left features an impressive standing Buddha flanked by a pair of wooden images, and a finely detailed royal bed. Behind this pavilion stands the Piman Rajaja Pavilion, filled with rare Thai shadow puppets and dozens of Ayuthaya and Sukothai images. Outside to the rear is the startling Pisai Salak Tower, constructed by Narai to study astronomy and follow the eclipses of the moon.

Chandra Kasem is open Wed.-Sun. 0900-1600. Exit the grounds and walk past the public riverside park and Hud Ra Market.

Wat Rajaburana

King Boromaraja II constructed this temple in 1424 to commemorate his two brothers, who died on elephantback fighting for the throne after the death of their father. Boromaraja wisely skipped the battle and, in accordance with royal custom, honored his two brothers with *stupas* erected at their cremation site.

A fascinating history lies behind Wat Rajaburana. The impressive *prang* was erected several years after King Boromaraja had captured Angkor Thom, the capital of Cambodia, and while Khmer influence was still strong in central Thailand. Inside the Khmer-style *prang*, a secret crypt was constructed to guard dozens of 15th-century murals, 200 Lopburi bronzes of Khmer-Bayon style, 300 rare U-Thong Buddhas, 100,000 votive tablets, and a fabulous treasure trove of priceless gold objects.

The crypt was sealed, covered with brick and plaster, and forgotten through the ensuing centuries. Thailand's equivalent of the Tutankhamen treasure lay untouched until 1957, when scavengers broke into the crypt and stumbled on the buried treasure. Much of the booty vanished into international art markets before the government stepped in, stopped the treasure hunters, and placed the remainder in the Ayuthaya National Museum. An unknown number of items vanished and many of the ordinary votives were sold to finance construction of the Ayuthaya Na-

Buddha head in 1980

Buddha head in 1990

tional Museum, but enough relics remained to constitute one of Thailand's greatest archaeological discoveries.

Wat Rajaburana has, unfortunately, been badly restored by the Fine Arts Department with shiny concrete *garudas* and other artificial embellishments that detract from its original state.

Admission to Wat Rajaburana costs 5B for Thais and 20B for Westerners.

Wat Mahathat

King Boromaraja constructed his "Temple of the Great Relic" across the street from Wat Rajaburana in 1374 to honor his dream about a relic of the Buddha. Wat Mahathat architecturally fills the link between Lopburi's 10th-century Khmer *prangs* and the 15th-century-style *prangs* that characterized most monuments in Ayuthaya. The temple once contained murals of the life of the Buddha and a large stone image in the Dvaravati style (A.D. 600-1000) seated in the European manner, perhaps imported from Nakhon

Pathom. The magnificent statue was transferred in 1835 to nearby Wat Na Praman. Valuable artifacts, including a tiny gold casket said to contain Boromaraja's holy relics, were discovered during a 1956 restoration project conducted by the Fine Arts Department. Except for the casket, now displayed in the Ayuthaya National Museum, most treasures have been moved to the National Museum in Bangkok.

Although the temple largely lies in ruin, the monumental floor plans and wildly directed pillars are impressive for what they suggest. One classic sight (in the southeast corner) is a dismembered Buddha head firmly grasped in the clutches of the banyan trees. Take a photo and return 10 years later—it will have grown to a higher level.

Admission is 20B.

Wat Pra Ram

Wat Pra Ram was constructed in 1369 by King Ramasuan as the burial spot for his father, King

Ramathibodi, the founder of Ayuthaya. The elegant Khmer-style *prang* was reconstructed in the 15th century by King Boromatrailokanat, the eighth king of Ayuthaya, and was subsequently altered by the 31st ruler, King Boromakot.

The temple consists of symmetrical sanctuaries which flank a *prang* decorated with miniature *chedis* and stuccowork interspersed with *garudas, nagas,* and walking Buddhas. Although less monumental than Wat Mahathat or Wat Rajaburana, Wat Pra Ram boasts a stunning location. The temple casts a beautiful reflection in the placid lily ponds.

Ayuthaya National Museum

Chao Sam Praya, Thailand's second-largest museum, was constructed in 1959 from sale proceeds of votive tablets recovered from Wat Rajaburana, and was named after Prince Sam Praya (King Boromaraja II), the founder of Wat Rajaburana. The museum consists of a central hall with two floors, and a second building opened in 1970. All major art styles are represented—Dvaravati, Lopburi, U-Thong, Sukothai, and, of course, Ayuthaya. Ayuthayan kings were apparently avid collectors of early Thai art, though the best-represented styles are those of the Lopburi, U-Thong, and Ayuthaya Periods.

The main floor of the central hall holds dozens of statues, votives, lacquer cabinets, decorated palm-leaf manuscripts, and priceless objects discovered inside the left shoulder of the Pra Mongkol Bopit Buddha. Displays are arranged in chronological order and a careful inspection will provide a good overview of the artistic legacy of Thailand. Highlights on the main floor include a colossal bronze Buddha head with square face and broad features typical of the U-Thong Period, and a Dvaravati-style seated Buddha carved from white crystalline stone.

The second floor features a main room filled with lead and terra-cotta votive tablets, palm-leaf manuscript cabinets, and crystal objects found during the restoration of Wat Yai Chai Mongkol in 1980. Highlights of the upper floor are displayed in antechambers to the east and west. The small room on the east side contains dazzling gold objects unearthed in 1956 from the central *prang* of Wat Rajaburana. The western room holds the previously described Buddha relic from Wat Mahathat. Look carefully: it's one-third the size of a rice grain and protected by five bronze stupas inserted one inside the other.

The modern addition to the rear offers a dusty and rather neglected collection of artifacts not native to Ayuthaya.

Chao Sam Praya Museum is open Wed.-Sun. 0900-1600; admission is 20B.

Ayuthaya Historical Study Center

Located on Rajana Road near the Provincial Teachers College is a modern museum designed to relate the history of Ayuthaya. Opened in August 1990, the complex was constructed with a grant from the Japanese government on the site of an old Japanese settlement. Five exhibitions are included: Ayuthaya as the capital, port, seat of government, center of the Thai community, and center of international relations with the Western world. Top sights are a Chinese commercial ship, scale models of old Ayuthaya and the elephant *kraal,* and murals depicting merit-making ceremonies at Pra Buddhabat in Saraburi, an annual event attended by the citizens of Ayuthaya. Other murals illustrate ordination ceremonies, the rice-planting season, an ancient theater, a marriage ceremony, and a Thai funeral.

The Ayuthaya Historical Center is open Wed.-Sun. 0900-1700. Admission is a reasonable 20B for Thais and a stiff 100B for Western tourists.

Lak Muang

Across the street from the National Museum lies Ayuthaya's modern city pillar. It features a scale model of the city which helps with local orientation.

Khum Khum House

Constructed in 1894 as the city jail and now used by the Fine Arts Department, Khum Khum House is an outstanding example of traditional domestic Thai architecture. The compound is surrounded by moats and elevated on teak piles that support a central *sala* roofed with dried palm leaves.

Viharn Pra Mongkol Bopit

One of the largest bronze Buddha images in Thailand is located inside a modern and very claustrophobic *viharn* immediately south of Wat Pra Sri Samphet. Originally erected during the Ayuthaya Period, the old *viharn* and brooding image were badly damaged in 1767 when the roof collapsed and broke off the statue's topknot and right arm. The image was repaired but allowed to remain outdoors until 1951, when the present shelter was erected to protect the enormous statue. Perhaps the Buddha, with its black coating and mysterious mother-of-pearl eyes, should have been left alone—an image of this size and power needs a great deal of room.

Today the statue is an object of great veneration to the Thais. The date of the image is uncertain, though it displays both U-Thong and Sukothai influences and may have been cast in the 15th century.

Adjacent to the *viharn* is a large parking lot and a shopping complex that formerly served as royal cremation grounds. Several of the open-air shops and restaurants sell basketry,

THE ARTS OF AYUTHAYA

*A*yuthaya from the 14th to 18th centuries was among the most powerful and wealthy kingdoms in Southeast Asia. During their four centuries of rule, a series of 33 kings constructed hundreds of glittering temples and supported the arts with lavish royal patronage. Ayuthayan rulers considered themselves heirs to the artistic and religious traditions of Sukothai, Cambodia, and Sri Lanka—a rich mixture manifested in the artistic achievements which survived the Burmese onslaught of 1767.

Some historians consider the art of Ayuthaya decadent when compared to that of earlier periods such as Sukothai and Chiang Saen. However, Ayuthaya chiefly excelled in architecture and city planning rather than sculpture and painting. And yet, a great deal of sensitive work was created before the artistic decline toward the end of the Ayuthaya era.

The Ayuthaya National Museum provides a detailed look at Ayuthaya's art, plus a superb overview of the various epochs of Thai art.

Architecture

Ayuthaya's crowning artistic achievement was its architecture. At its height, Ayuthaya boasted over 600 major monuments and temples that impressed both Asiatic and European visitors with their sheer immensity and grandeur. The majority of these monuments were initiated during the reign of King Ramathibodi, the founder of Ayuthaya, and completed during the first 150 years of the era. Another building frenzy occurred in the early 17th century during the reign of King Prasat Thong, a prolific monument builder who revived the popularity of Khmer-influenced architecture. Tradition demanded that only temples be constructed of stone and brick. Wooden structures such as royal palaces and common residences have all been destroyed by conquering Burmese arsonists.

Ayuthayan architects borrowed the forms and traditions developed by other schools, but modified them according to their own tastes. One of the most important influences was the Khmers, whose corn-cob-shaped *prang* slowly evolved in Ayuthaya from a squat and heavy form into a radically elongated and more elegant superstructure. The best examples are the magnificent *prangs* of Wat Mahathat, Wat Rajaburana, and Wat Pra Ram. Ayuthayan *prangs* were later incorporated into Bangkok religious architecture at Wat Pra Keo, Wat Arun, and Wat Po.

Ayuthayan architects were also influenced by the artistic traditions of Sri Lanka, as shown in the bell-shaped *chedis* adapted from Sri Lankan models. A new elegance emerged as local architects elongated the bulbous Sri Lankan-style *chedi* into soaring, slim spires that seem to defy gravity. Wat Sri Samphet and the memorial to Queen Suriyothai are prime examples.

Ayuthayan architecture evolved through four subperiods until the city was destroyed in 1767. The Lopburi (Khmer-Thai fusion) and U Thong styles of architecture dominated from the founding of Ayuthaya in 1350 to the end of King Boromatrailokanat's reign in 1488. Examples include Wat Pra Ram, Wat Mahathat, and Wat Rajaburana. Sukothai-influenced architecture and the Singhalese type of rounded *stupa* reached Ayuthaya in 1463 after King Boromatrailokanat left to rule the northern town of Phitsanulok. Wat Pra Sri Samphet and Wat Yai Chai Mongkol are the most famous examples. Khmer architecture regained popularity after the conquest of Cambodia by King Prasat Thong in the mid-17th century, as best demonstrated by the Khmer *prang* of Wat Chai Wattanaram.

The final phase of Ayuthayan architecture was a period of restoration of older monasteries and temples which had fallen into disrepair, and the increased popularity of the *stupa* at Wat Pu Kao Tong.

locally produced knives, imitation antiques, cold drinks, and spicy soups such as *tam yam kung.*

Wat Pra Sri Samphet

This famous trio of 15th-century Sri Lankan-style *chedis* is the most important temple complex within the former royal palace compound, similar in function to Wat Pra Keo in Bangkok. The temple was founded in the 15th century by King Boromatrailokanat and expanded by his successors. As with Wat Pra Keo, Wat Pra Sri Samphet served as the private chapel and ceremonial courtyard for the kings of Ayuthaya.

The temple is composed of three famous *chedis* which stand on a long terrace linked by stone *mondops*. In the manner of Khmer monuments at Angkor Wat, all served as royal tombs

---

Late Ayuthayan architecture was also characterized by the use of curved foundations and roofs on *viharns*, column capitals in the form of lotus buds, and the increased use of brick and stone for domestic rather than strictly religious architecture. The surviving structures at Ayuthaya only hint at the magnificence of the former capital.

Sculpture

Ayuthaya is better known for the quality of its architecture than for its achievements in sculpture.

Ayuthayan sculpture is divided into several subperiods. Early sculpture continued the traditions of U Thong, a school of art which predates the establishment of Ayuthaya and demonstrates an indebtedness to Mon and Khmer prototypes. The second period began in 1463 when King Boromatrailokanat went to rule Phitsanulok and local sculpture came under Sukothai influence. Some pieces produced during this period exhibit the sensitive and elegant traditions of Sukothai. But, as time progressed, the spirituality of Sukothai-influenced sculpture gave way to the more ritualistic and powerful images of the third period. These late-Ayuthayan images became increasingly cold and remote as Ayuthayan kings adopted the Khmer notion of *deva raja* (god-king) and hid themselves behind palace walls. The magnificence of the royal court—as reflected by Buddhas covered with princely attire and crowned with elaborate diadems—degenerated into a passion for decoration that obliterated all detail and reduced the images to formless masses of ornamentation. The end result was stereotyped abundance without the sensitivity of earlier eras: a triumph of style over spirituality.

Ayuthayan sculptors, however, were a remarkable creative force. Among their innovations was the depiction of Buddha in a wider variety of poses than those depicted by earlier schools. Buddhas were seated with their feet on the ground in the "European fashion" once used by Dvaravati sculptors, and in the meditating mudra rather than the more common pose of touching-the-earth. Walking Buddhas were shown with alms bowls and with the weight centered on the right rather than left foot. Ayuthayan sculptors were also technical masters of large-scale bronze casting, as demonstrated by the colossal seated Buddha in Viharn Pra Mongkol Bopit. Finally, Ayuthayan sculptors increased the size and magnificence of the pedestal (a tradition carried on during the Bangkok Period) and increased exterior ornamentation to reflect the glory of Ayuthayan kings who, like the Khmer *deva raja,* identified themselves as the Buddha King.

Painting

Ayuthaya's great murals were largely destroyed during the Burmese conquest of 1767, or have disappeared due to shoddy painting techniques which left the frescoes vulnerable to the degenerative effects of rain and heat. Consequently, the best examples of Ayuthayan paintings are outside town in the *wats* of Petchburi, Uttaradit, and Nonthaburi.

The first period of Ayuthayan painting shows Khmer and Singhalese influences and the heavy use of blacks, whites, and reds with dashes of vermilion and gold leaf to ornament the costumes of deities. Crypt murals inside the main *prang* of Wat Rajaburana form the finest surviving example of early Ayuthayan painting. Illustrations from manuscripts and religious documents show the gradual development of Sukothai influence and the increased use of bright colors during the second period. Late Ayuthaya painting is typically Thai, with bright colors, representations of trees and wildlife, and the innovative use of zigzag lines to compartmentalize scenes. Ayuthaya's sole surviving example of late-period painting is in the pavilion at Wat Buddhaisawan, where interior frescoes relate important religious and secular works. Outstanding examples of late-Ayuthayan painting are found in Petchburi at Wat Yai Suwannaram and Wat Ko Keo Suttaram, in Uttaradit at Wat Pra Boromathat, and in Nonthaburi at Wat Po Bang Oh and Wat Prasat.

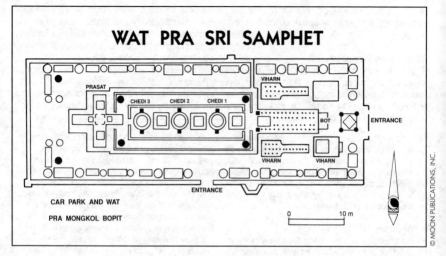

WAT PRA SRI SAMPHET

CAR PARK AND WAT
PRA MONGKOL BOPIT

© MOON PUBLICATIONS, INC.

for Thai monarchs rather than as simple memorials to the Buddha. All once contained secret chambers adorned with frescoes and votive offerings for the dead, and in conformity with classical rules all were constructed on a circular ground plan with elongated cupolas flattened to accommodate a double-layered reliquary plinth. The east *chedi* was erected by King Ramathibodi in 1492 to enshrine the ashes of his father, while the central shrine holds the remains of his elder brother, King Boromaraja III. The westernmost *chedi* was built in 1540 to contain the ashes of King Ramathibodi II.

Their perfect symmetry has made the *chedis* one of the most photographed scenes in Ayuthaya and the very essence of Middle Kingdom architecture. Unfortunately, insensitive restoration projects by the Fine Arts Department and repeated whitewashings have tragically obliterated all architectural detail.

Several famous Buddhas were discovered in the ruins after the destruction of Ayuthaya in 1767. The most famous image, Pra Sri Samphet, is a 16-meter bronze Buddha once covered with gold leaf from which the temple received its name. The image was stripped by the Burmese and subsequently regained by King Rama I, who took it to Wat Po in Bangkok. Pra Buddha Singh, another national treasure, also now resides in Bangkok at the National Museum,

while Pra Buddha Lokanat has been transferred to the west *viharn* of Wat Po.

Admission is 20B, but the *prangs* can be easily seen and photographed from the road. A cluster of small antique shops and restaurants is located just opposite Sri Samphet. Stonecarving is the local specialty. Excellent-quality Cambodian images, Ganeshas, and standing Ayuthayan Buddhas are sold at reasonable prices.

Royal Palace

North of Wat Pra Sri Samphet are some scattered foundations and modest ruins of the old royal palace. The site was chosen by King Boromatrailokanat, who began construction of the palace and Wat Pra Sri Samphet in 1448. The complex was later expanded by several kings, such as Narai, Prasat Thong, and Pra Petracha, who erected reception halls, audience chambers, military review stands, and a royal palace covered with golden tiles.

The palace was burned and completely destroyed by the Burmese in 1767. The remaining brickwork, stucco molding, and Buddhas were removed to Bangkok by early Chakri kings to help rebuild the capital. All that remains today of the royal palace are narrow footpaths and brick foundations which distinguish the ground plans; a great deal of imagination is needed to re-create the palace's former magnificence and lost grandeur.

Wat Na Praman

This tremendous *bot*, across the river from the old royal palace, is one of the most impressive temples in Ayuthaya. The foundation date is unknown, but documents record restoration projects during the reign of King Boromakot (1753-59) and by the governor of Ayuthaya (1824-51) in the Bangkok Period. Wat Na Praman (Wat Pra Meru) was one of the few temples which survived the Burmese destruction of 1767.

Wat Na Praman consists of a large, recently rebuilt *bot* on the left, and a small but very important *viharn* on the right. A long and rather convoluted history of the primary temple is given on the exterior notice board. The main *bot* is an elegant structure elevated on a stepped terrace and covered with varnished tiles over a four-tiered roof. Magnificent examples of classic Ayuthayan architecture are displayed in the monumental entrances, twin facades flanked by smaller porticoes, windows barred with stone colonnades, and beautifully carved pediments over the southern entrance.

The interior is equally remarkable. The centerpiece altar displays a rare gold-leaf, six-meter

COSMIC SYMBOLOGY AND THE ARCHITECTURE OF AYUTHAYA

Thailand's architecture and the temples of Ayuthaya were designed to symbolize aspects of Theravada Buddhism and the powerful belief in Hindu cosmology. Most elements displayed today began as Hindu concepts which filtered through the Khmer Empire and were finally reinterpreted with some degree of originality by Thai architects. A short summary may help you understand the motivations and design considerations of local architects.

As with Angkor Wat in Cambodia, Thai architecture embodies in stone the Hindu concept of cosmology. Hinduism teaches that the world is composed of countless universes which, like their human counterparts, also experience endless cycles of destruction and rebirth. Each universe is dominated by a magical mountain, Mt. Meru, the mythical home of the gods. This colossal mountain is surrounded by seven subordinate mountain ranges and seven seas, beyond which lie the four major continents, one in each cardinal direction. Below Mt. Meru are the four levels of hell inhabited by guardian demons with supernatural powers. The upper levels of Mt. Meru contain the world of angels, guardians of the four cardinal directions, and, at the summit, the city of gods where Indra reigns as king. Above Mt. Meru tower more levels of heaven, inhabited by abstract beings nearing nirvana.

Kings throughout most of Southeast Asia strived to re-create this cosmological order by modeling their royal palaces, temples, and general city plan after the Hindu universe. Ayuthaya, for example, was laid out as the cosmic center of the universe with four important cities in each cardinal direction:

Sukothai to the north (the direction of death), Prapadang to the south (life), Nakhon Nayon to the east (birth), and Suphanburi to the west (dying). The city was constructed as a giant mandala with the royal palace at the center, surrounded by three circles of earthen ramparts and a series of circular moats to represent the great seas.

Hindu cosmology also dictates the shape and arrangement of individual temples. Centerpiece was a massive tower which represented Mt. Meru. The tower was divided into 33 lesser tiers to symbolize the 33 levels of heaven. A row of demon guardian figures was often added just below the seventh tier. *Prangs* were surmounted by a *vajra* or thunderbolt, the heavenly symbol of Indra, while *chedis* were topped by a circular orb which represented the core of nirvana. To the west and east—the axis of purity—were the *bot* (ordination hall) and *viharn* (meeting hall). Moats surrounding the temple complex represent the primordial oceans which separate the world of humans from the abode of gods.

Thai architects reinterpreted Hindu forms in several ways. *Prangs* and *chedis* were subdivided into the familiar 33 tiers, but Thai love of curvature brought along redented corners which added vertical lines, and a bulbous parabolic shape which gave the monument a sense of soaring grace. Thai propensity for asymmetry inspired the use of trapezoidal doors and window frames, tapered columns capped with lotus bud finials, and overlapping roofs which added an effect of soft sensuality. The end result was Hindu cosmology mixed with Thai sensibility: one of the great triumphs of Southeast Asian architecture.

Ayuthaya-style Buddha surrounded by 16 octagonal painted pillars, highly polished floors, and roofs carved with concentric lotus buds. Wat Na Praman is an excellent place to relax and meditate away from the more touristy temples in Ayuthaya.

To the right of the *bot* is a small chapel which guards a green stone Dvaravati Buddha (Pra Kantharat) seated in European fashion with splayed feet resting on a lotus flower and hands curiously placed on the knees. The broad Mon face and firm facial expression exude a meditative serenity rarely experienced in Thai sculpture. Although located in a modest and often neglected setting, this powerful image richly deserves its reputation as one of the masterpieces of Mon Buddhist art.

The combination of striking architecture, stunning sculpture, and pleasant surroundings makes Wat Na Praman one of the finest experiences in Ayuthaya: a refreshing change from the over-restored and dead monuments controlled by the Fine Arts Department.

Admission is 20B.

pre-restoration Wat Chai Wattanaram

Reclining Buddha

Wat Logya Suthat is known for its picturesque 20-meter statue of a reclining Buddha. The image features a very long face and a vertical arm supporting the head which rests on a lotus pillow, a pose characteristic of 16th-century Ayuthaya. The large wooden *viharn* which once covered the image has disappeared, leaving the Buddha exposed to the elements with the contented cows that occasionally graze in nearby grasses. Cokes at the refreshment stand are expensive!

Chedi Sri Suriyothai

The only remaining part of Wat Suan Luang Sopsawan is a rather inelegant and heavily restored *chedi* dedicated to Queen Suriyothai, the wife of King Maha Chakraphet. According to Thai chronicles, the queen sacrificed her life in 1563 by intervening during an elephant duel between King Chakraphet and a Burmese general. Wat Suan Luang Sopsawan was erected at the cremation site of the queen.

Wat Chai Wattanaram

One of the most intriguing monuments in Ayuthaya is located at the southwestern edge of town and across the Chao Praya River. Wat Chai Wattanaram was constructed in 1630 by King Prasat Thong on the site of his mother's palace, and modeled after the Khmer monument at Angkor Wat.

The temple can be approached by crossing the nearby bridge and following the trail to the restored monument. The ruins include a Khmer *prang* surrounded by a square cloister interspersed with well-preserved *chedis* capped with wooden, coffered roofs. Stucco details include additional embellishments of Lanna Thai and Ayuthaya origins.

The overall effect—especially at sunset—is overwhelming: a magnificent temple with headless Buddha torsos being swallowed by creeping vines, cows grazing next to the leaning *prangs*. . . everything you ever imagined about mysterious temples of the East.

St. Joseph's Cathedral

Western architecture in Ayuthaya is the legacy of a period of trade with European powers during the 17th and 18th centuries. European architectural themes introduced to Ayuthaya during the reign of King Narai (1656-1688) include radiating arches, large windows constructed without claustras, and the use of masonry on residential buildings. Windows constructed without claustras remained popular after the death of King Narai, though the other two innovations faded away.

Western capitalists were required to live outside the city limits and could only enter Ayuthaya on official business. The Catholic community was thus served by this 17th-century church built by Monsignor de Beryte during the reign of King Narai. The modest church has been restored several times and still functions as an active house of worship.

A small ferry leaves from the dock at the end of a narrow dirt path off U-Thong Road.

Wat Buddhasawan

Wat Buddhasawan, consecrated in 1353 by the prince of U-Thong (King Ramathibodi), who lived on the site during construction of his new capital, features the most perfect reproduction of a Cambodian *prang* in Ayuthaya. The general layout is derived from Angkor Wat, with a large central *prang,* representing the Buddhist heaven of Mt. Meru, surrounded by six smaller *prangs* which signify the outer heavens. A long series of seated Buddhas fills the open gallery that surrounds the central *prang.* The niche in the northern wall contains a standing Buddha image cast during the reign of King Rama I to replace a statue removed to the Royal Pantheon at Wat Pra Keo in Bangkok.

Adjacent to the *prang* is a large, modern *wat* and a public park which contains a statue of King Ramathibodi flanked by two soldiers.

A small ferry shuttles across the river; the one-way journey costs 5-10B.

Portuguese Settlement

During the reign of King Narai, foreign traders were encouraged to settle and set up residential centers south of Ayuthaya. The Portuguese arrived in 1511 after Viceroy Albuquerque sent a trading mission headed by Duarte Fernandez. Portuguese influence was tempered by the Dutch, who enjoyed a monopoly on the hide trade with Japan, and by the French, who sent Jesuit missionaries to Ayuthaya in 1673. Western influence peaked in the reign of King Narai and then sharply declined under subsequent, more xenophobic rulers.

All of the Western residential enclaves constructed during the 17th and 18th centuries were destroyed in 1767 by the Burmese conquest of Ayuthaya. The former Portuguese community is marked with a memorial plaque.

Japanese Settlement

Soon after the Portuguese established trade agreements with Ayuthaya in 1516, Japanese entrepreneurs arrived to serve as merchants, soldiers, and diplomats. The most famous arrival was a Japanese chief named Nagamasa Yamada, who was later named viceroy of Nakhon Si Thammarat in southern Thailand.

The site of the former Japanese community is marked with a stone inscription, memorial hall, and Japanese-style gate erected by the Thai-Japanese Society.

Wat Panam Chong

One of the oldest and largest temples in Ayuthaya lies on the Chao Praya River southeast of town. According to Thai chronicles, Wat Panam Chong was founded by the prince of U-Thong in 1324, 26 years before the formal establishment of Ayuthaya.

The temple was constructed to house a gigantic Buddha image donated by a Chinese emperor whose daughter had married a local Thai prince. Constructed of brick and stucco covered with gold leaf, Pra Chao Panam measures 19 meters in height and almost 14 meters in breadth—the largest single-cast bronze Buddha in Thailand. The image has been restored several times, but remains a source of great power and inspiration to Thai and Chinese pilgrims who divine their fortunes under the watchful gaze of the great Buddha.

The internal walls feature prayer flags, paper lanterns, and hundreds of small niches filled with votive statues of the Buddha—a rare element in Thai architecture.

Special note should be made of the Sukothai statues inside the small *viharn* to the left of the main *bot.* The 14th-century image on the left was discovered in 1956 when its heavy plaster covering cracked to reveal a statue estimated to be 60% pure gold.

Surrounding the exterior courtyard are dozens of stucco-covered Buddhas and grassy grounds kept neatly trimmed by a small army of devotees.

Wat Yai Chai Mongkol

Dominating the landscape southeast of town is the temple and *chedi* of Wat Yai Chai Mongkol. The monastery was established in 1360 by King Ramathibodi as Wat Chao Praya Thai ("Temple of the Supreme Patriach") for Thai monks who had returned from religious studies in Sri Lanka. The sect, known as Pa Kao, devoted itself to strict meditation, in contrast to other sects which emphasized the study of Buddhist scriptures. The temple now hosts a large community of *mae chi,* Buddhist nuns, who maintain the buildings and keep the lawns in good condition.

The present *wat* derives its name from the towering Chedi Chai Mongkol, located within the fortified temple compound and elevated on a rectangular base bisected by smaller *chedis.* The whitewashed tower was constructed by King Naresuan to commemorate his single-handed slaying of a Burmese crown prince in 1592. The infamous battle was fought on elephantback near Suphanburi and reestablished Thai control of the central Chao Praya plains.

Encircling the massive *chedi* are some 135 Buddhas which once sat in a rectangular cloister marked only by surviving columns. Also within the perimeter wall is a huge reclining Buddha image of the Ayuthaya Period, still highly regarded by local Thais. To the rear is the spirit house of King Naresuan, patronized by Thais who seek counsel from the king's spirit through female mediums.

Wat Suwan Daram

This rarely visited temple is one of the most attractive and fascinating in Ayuthaya. Wat Suwan Daram was constructed by the grandfather of the first king of the Chakri dynasty at the end of the Ayuthaya Period, and was subsequently restored by King Rama II after his accession to the throne.

The curving, concave foundation of the boat-shaped *bot* illustrates mankind's voyage toward nirvana. Elaborate doors and pediments decorated with carved wood complete the exterior detail.

The highlights of the temple are the interior murals in the *bot,* which date from the period of Rama II and rank among the best in Thailand. Painted with great talent, these frescoes depict scenes from the Vessantara and Suvanasama Jatakas with an assembly of divinities in the upper registers. The wall opposite the altar relates the victory of the Buddha over Mara and the spirits of evil. Ayuthaya-style Buddhas fill the central altar.

Also on the temple grounds are a *kambarian, chedi,* and *viharn* completed during the reign of King Chulalongkorn, with modern murals depicting the life of King Naresuan the Great.

Unlike most temples in Ayuthaya, Wat Suwan Daram still serves as an active monastery where religious life continues in traditional fashion. The *bot* is kept locked, but young monks anxious to practice their English can open the building.

Pu Kao Tong ("Golden Mount")

Situated in the open countryside almost five km from town is the gigantic silhouette of Pu Kao Tong, the Golden Mountain of Ayuthaya. The monastery was founded in 1387 by King Ramasuan, but the *chedi* was built by the Burmese to commemorate their conquest of Ayuthaya in 1569 and subsequently remodeled in Thai style by King Boromakot. The Ayuthaya-style *chedi* features four niches which rest on square-stepped platforms reached by monumental staircases.

To commemorate the 2,500th anniversary of Buddha's birthday, the towering *chedi* was capped in 1956 with a 2.5-kg solid-gold orb. Somebody immediately stole it, but views from the top of the 80-meter *chedi* remain outstanding, especially during the rainy season when the surrounding ricefields are flooded. Hire a *tuk tuk* or *samlor* to reach Pu Kao Tong.

Elephant *Kraal*

One of the few surviving elephant *kraals* in Thailand is located on Pu Kao Road, some three km northwest of town. Inside the teak stockade, wild elephants were once herded and battle-trained under the watchful gaze of royalty and spectators. Hunters would gather up to 150 beasts before slowly leading them through the bottleneck opening into the *kraal.* The elephants were then lassoed with rattan cables and selected according to their size and color; white and reddish elephants were favored over gray or mixed-colored animals.

The present structure includes a royal pavilion, elephant gateway, stockade of teak posts, holy *sala* where hunters performed purification ceremonies before the chase, central altar which once held an image of Ganesha, and elephant statue near the spectators' arena. Old-fashioned elephant roundups were re-created here in 1891 for Czar Nicholas II and in 1962 for Danish royalty.

Accommodations—Guesthouses

Several new guesthouses have opened in recent years to provide cheap accommodations for backpackers.

Ayuthaya Guesthouse: Formerly known as B.J. Guesthouse, Ayuthaya's original homestay is 50 meters up a small alley (Chao Phrom Road) running north from Naresuan Road. Mr. Hong Singha Paisal has eight rooms in an old teak house with great atmosphere. Bicycles can be rented from the outdoor patio. 16/2 Naresuan Rd., tel. (035) 251468, 100-150B.

B.J. Guesthouse: The most popular guesthouse in Ayuthaya has 20 rooms in a cinderblock building about 10 minutes west of the market. Banjong, the lady owner, is a good cook and can help with travel tips. They also operate another property a few doors down the street. 19/29 Naresuan Rd., tel. (035) 246046, 60B dorm, 100-120B rooms.

Ruandrum Ayuthaya Youth Hostel: Perhaps the most beautiful lodging in Ayuthaya are these teak houses overlooking the river. The central wing was built by an Ayuthayan aristocrat in the traditional *panya* style found in central Thailand. The owner, Praphan Sukarechit (Kimjeng), has renovated the adjacent homes and refurbished all the rooms with antiques. Curiosities on the grounds include old rowing boats, a kitchen constructed on a floating barge, wooden door frames from the old elephant *kraal,* and other antiques from Kimjeng's antique shop. Rooms are somewhat expensive for a youth hostel, but Kimjeng also intends to open a budget dormitory for backpackers. 48 U-Thong Rd., tel. (035) 241978, 150-200B. The dormitory costs around 100B per person.

Pai Tong Guesthouse: A floating hotel on a reconstructed barge. Rooms are small and the atmosphere dark and dank, but two good restaurants are located nearby. U-Thong Rd., 80-100B.

Accommodations—Hotels

Ayuthaya has a very limited selection of hotels since most tourists visit the town on day-trips from Bangkok.

Sri Samai Hotel: Ayuthaya's central hotel was once a clean and comfortable place with a fairly decent restaurant. Standards, unfortunately, have dropped and the hotel can no longer be recommended aside from its convenient location near the marketplace. 12 Chao Prom Rd., tel. (035) 251104, 300-400B fan, 400-500B a/c.

U-Thong Hotel: A rudimentary hotel for those who want traditional facilities at moderate cost. The U-Thong has rather dirty rooms with fan and common bath, and a few a/c rooms with private bath. Avoid rooms facing the street. The nearby Cathay Hotel is similar in quality and price. 86 U-Thong Rd., tel. (035) 251136, 150-300B.

U Thong Inn: Two km east of Ayuthaya and rather isolated from central Ayuthaya is the first semi-luxurious hotel in town. 210 Rajana Rd., tel. (035) 242236, fax (035) 242235, 800-1,200B a/c.

Krung Sri River Hotel: A new hotel near the train station with an outdoor swimming pool, health club, bowling alley, Pasak coffee shop, and 202 tastefully decorated rooms. 27/2 Rajana Rd., tel. (035) 244333, fax (035) 243777, 1,600-2,200B.

Ayuthaya Grand Hotel: Another recent addition to the luxury hotel market in Ayuthaya. All the standard facilities such as a pool, a snooker hall, and travel services. 55/5 Rajana Rd., tel. (035) 335483, fax (035) 335492, Bangkok tel. (02) 511-1029, 1,200-1,800B.

Restaurants

Most travelers dine in their guesthouses or at the market, though several good restaurants are located along the river and near the monuments on Chi Kun Road.

Night Market: The old night market has been relocated from downtown to a new location on the river across from the Chandra Kasem Museum. A small selection of foodstalls complement the hawkers' emporiums. A comfortable place to spend an evening.

Pae Krung Kao Floating Restaurant: The better of Ayuthaya's two floating restaurants is hardly spectacular, but the atmosphere is relaxed and the food tasty. U-Thong Rd. Moderate.

Krung Kao Restaurant: A small, modern, air-conditioned spot with Thai specialties and an English-language menu. Try the pepper steak or chicken sautéed with garlic. Located on Rajana Rd. near the bridge. Budget.

Youth Hostel: Kimjeng's wife operates a well-appointed restaurant furnished with antiques and knickknacks. The menu includes both Thai and Western dishes. 48 U-Thong Rd. Moderate.

Tevaraj Restaurant: Riverside dining in a large bamboo hall with a small attached floating pavilion. Pictures of cabaret singers are displayed at the front. A big place popular with Thais and tour groups. Railway Station Rd., just over the bridge. Moderate to expensive.

Binlar Restaurant: A large, open-air nightclub with rock music and Thai cabaret singers. Good food at reasonable prices, a popular hangout in the evenings. Naresuan Rd. Budget to moderate.

Siam Restaurant: Just opposite Wat Mahathat is a small a/c restaurant that offers a welcome escape from the heat. Chi Kun Rd. Moderate.

Raja Restaurant: Dine outdoors surrounded by ponds filled with water lilies. Great atmosphere in a very quiet location. Rajana Rd. Moderate.

Getting There

Ayuthaya is 86 km north of Bangkok and can be reached by bus or train.

Bus: Buses leave every half hour from Bangkok's Northern Bus Terminal and take about two hours to reach Ayuthaya. Most buses terminate at the marketplace in the center of town. Stay on the bus until it arrives downtown; get off at the bridge and you are fed to mercenary taxi drivers. Some buses will drop you on the highway about five km east of town. *Tuk tuk* drivers will then yell, "No bus, no bus," but a public bus into town rolls by every 15 minutes. Walk to the intersection and wait at the corner.

Train: Trains leave Bangkok hourly and take about two hours to reach Ayuthaya. From the

station, stroll across the road and walk down to the river, where ferries continue across to town. Bicycles can be rented south of the train station past the Tevaraj Restaurant.

Boat: Public boats no longer operate between Ayuthaya and Bangkok or Bang Pa In. However, one-day luxury excursions to Ayuthaya and Bang Pa In are organized by the Oriental Hotel and Shangri La Hotel. These quickie trips leave daily at 0800 and cost 1,200B with lunch.

Getting Around

Most visitors attempt to see Ayuthaya on a single day-trip from Bangkok—a serious mistake. Ayuthaya is a sprawling place with dozens of great temples that deserve a day or two of exploration. Only the central temples can be reached on foot. Rent either a bicycle, longtail boat, or minitruck for a day tour of all of Ayuthaya. Bicycles can be rented south of the train station past the Tevaraj Restaurant near the temple, and from Bai Thong Guesthouse. Motorcycles are no longer available in Ayuthaya.

Six-person longtail boats chartered from the landing stage opposite Chandra Kasem Museum cost 300-500B for the standard three-hour tour. During the dry season only the lower half of Ayuthaya can be reached due to low waters. Boats can also be hired to Bang Pa In: look for the "Boat Trid Bang Pa In" sign.

Minitrucks cost 250-400B for an afternoon tour which should include the Golden Mount, Wat Chai Wattanaram, St. Joseph's Cathedral, and Wat Panam Chong. Temples on the southern riverbanks are served by small ferries for 5B.

Local *tuk tuks* and minitrucks cost 20-30B for any distance. Ayuthaya, with over 1,100 registered three-wheelers, claims the title of *tuk tuk* capital of Thailand.

Leaving Ayuthaya

Minibuses to Bang Pa In leave from the market on Naresuan Road. To Kanchanaburi, take a yellow bus from the market to Suphanburi, from where buses continue to Kanchanaburi. Buses to Sukothai and Bangkok leave hourly from the market. Trains north to Phitsanulok and Chiang Mai depart eight times daily.

LOPBURI

Lying 150 km north of Bangkok is the pleasant and friendly little town of Lopburi, one of the oldest and most historic sites in Thailand. Lopburi is rarely visited by Westerners and initial impressions are hardly spectacular, though the town offers enough good architecture and historical background to merit an overnight stop.

Local people are friendly, hospitable, and often happy to show visitors around the major sites and point out the better restaurants and

nightclubs. The study of English seems to be a major preoccupation with the population, who will gladly exchange guide services for a few hours of English conversation.

Lopburi is divided between the historic old town near the train station and the new town three km east. The old town has all the temples plus several good budget hotels near the train station. The only reasons to visit the new town are the main bus terminal at the first oversized traffic circle (Sakao Circle) and the nightclubs and swimming pool along the main road towards the second circle. Minibuses shuttle between the old and new town until about 2000.

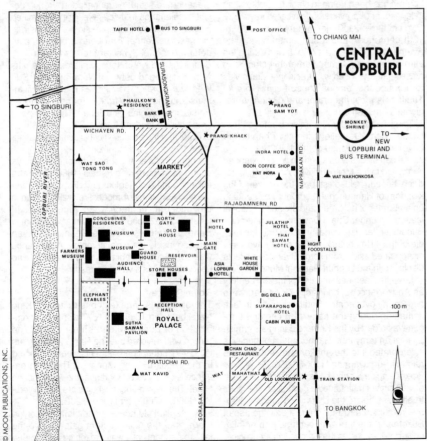

CENTRAL LOPBURI

© MOON PUBLICATIONS, INC.

All major attractions are in the old town near the train station. Hurried visitors can visit the most important sites in about three hours of walking, then continue north by train or bus. Note: the Fine Arts Department now collects a 20B admission fee for most monuments. Although the Royal Palace and Wat Mahathat are worth the cost, other monuments can be easily viewed and photographed from the street.

Lopburi's friendly population, pleasant pace of life, and small selection of historical attractions make it a fine place to break the northward journey.

History

Lopburi has been home to Neolithic settlers, an independent Dvaravati kingdom called Lavo (6th-10th centuries), a Khmer military outpost (10th-13th centuries), and a subcapital during the Ayuthaya Period (1350-1767). It was during the third period that Cambodian architectural and artistic patterns fused with traditional Mon styles to produce the famous Lopburi style—one of Thailand's most important and distinctive regional art movements.

The city has ridden the roller coaster of Thai history. Scholars believe the city (then called Lavo) was established some 1,400 years ago as the capital of a Mon kingdom which extended northward to the Mekong River. According to tradition, Lopburi helped establish the northern Mon kingdom of Haripunchai (Lamphun) by sending up a number of holy men and providing national leadership under Cham Devi, the daughter of a Buddhist ruler. The dynasty lasted until the middle of the 11th century. All traces of Lavo have disappeared aside from some Dvaravati artifacts displayed in the Lopburi National Museum.

Lavo declined near the end of the 9th century as Angkor succeeded in replacing Dvaravati's hegemony over central Southeast Asia. In fact, sometime during the early 11th century, Lopburi was aided by the Khmers during a skirmish against an army from Haripunchai. Lopburi was incorporated into the Angkor empire during the reign of Suryavarman I (1007-1050). As a province of Angkor, Lopburi was ruled by Cambodian governors yet maintained a cultural and religious tradition as heir to the Dvaravati Kingdom. Lopburi remained a Khmer outpost until the rise of Sukothai in the late 13th century. Khmer influence is still evident in the Cambodian architecture of Prang Khaek, San Pra Kan, Wat Mahathat, and Prang Sam Yot, a Hindu shrine which appears on the back of the 500B note.

The city was largely abandoned after the demise of the Khmers until the ascension of King Narai, who ruled Ayuthaya from 1657 to 1688. Lopburi then entered its most brilliant phase, serving as the alternative capital to Ayuthaya after the Gulf of Siam was blockaded by Dutch ships. Even after the gulf reopened to international trade, King Narai continued to spend up to nine months of each year at his palace in Lopburi, nicknamed the "Versailles of Siam." European influences were introduced on an unprecedented scale. Narai called in French Jesuit missionaries to discuss religion and invited French architects to help design and construct his new residence. European architects also helped design his military forts in Ayuthaya, Bangkok, and Nonthaburi, while exquisite gifts were exchanged between Narai and the "Sun King," Louis XIV. The city was filled with diplomats and merchants from all parts of Europe, Persia, India, China, and Japan. The high-powered phase ended in March 1688 after the death of Narai and the execution of his controversial advisor, Constantine Phaulkon.

Lopburi was abandoned in favor of Ayuthaya during the reign of King Petraja (1688-1703) and fell into a state of neglect and dilapidation over the next 150 years. A modest revival occurred in the mid-19th century when King Rama III reestablished Lopburi as an alternative capital to Bangkok and restored the Chantara Phisan Pavilion inside the royal complex. A residence was subsequently built by King Mongkut, who used Lopburi as a vacation resort.

Royal Palace

The enormous complex constructed by King Narai between 1665 and 1677 displays a combination of European and Khmer styles. The palace was restored by King Rama III 150 years later, and further improvements were conducted in the 1860s by King Mongkut. The main entrance is on Sorasak Road near the Asia Lopburi Hotel. The palace and museums are open Wed.-Sun. 0900-1700. Admission is 20B.

A beautiful old house stands immediately to the right of the main eastern gateway. To the left are remnants of a water reservoir and storage houses while straight ahead, through the crenellated walls, are the inner courtyard and central buildings. The middle wall is pocketed with hundreds of small niches which once held glowing oil lamps, doubtless an impressive sight on royal celebrations.

Chantara Phisan Pavilion: The museum on the right was constructed in 1665 as the royal residence of King Narai. French architects designed the palace, which shows European influence in its pointed doorway arches. Restored by King Rama III, today it serves as the Lopburi National Museum with a small but worthwhile collection of Lopburi and Dvaravati images. Impressive statuary is placed on the palace grounds.

Sutha Vinchai Pavilion: Phiman Mongkut Pavilion, on the left, was constructed by King Mongkut and now serves as an extension of the National Museum in Bangkok. The top level of the three-story building holds the private apartment and study of King Mongkut. To the rear is a Farmer's Museum, which exhibits rare tools and farming artifacts, and eight bijou houses which once guarded the king's concubines.

Audience Hall: The Dusit Sawan Thanya Mahaprasat, an eerie hollow shell to the left of the museums, originally served as an audience hall for ambassadors and high-ranking foreign visitors. King Narai hosted guests from the court of King Louis XIV inside the hall once fitted with huge mirrors designed to imitate the Hall of Mirrors in Versailles.

Sutha Sawan Pavilion: Below the central courtyard is another audience hall which served as the final residence of King Narai until his death in 1688. Elephant *kraals* are found beyond the wide gates.

To truly understand the grandeur of the royal court, imagine it laid out with gardens, fountains, and statues surrounded by sumptuously dressed royalty, military leaders, and lovely concubines.

Wat Mahathat

Lopburi's finest architectural treasure and one of Thailand's best examples of Khmer provincial art is located just opposite the train station. The temple was constructed by the Khmers in the 12th century on the ruins of an earlier temple, but was heavily renovated by Siamese kings

during the Ayuthaya and Sukothai Periods. Centerpiece is the Khmer *prang* richly embellished with outstanding stucco lintels lacking the foliage ornamentation popular during the late 12th century. A beautiful and imposing sight, the *prang* architecturally marks the transition from pure Khmer to the Siamese style favored in Ayuthaya.

Also on the grounds is a large brick *viharn* which dates from the reign of King Narai and shows European and Persian influences in its pointed arch window. *Chedis* nearby are later constructions dating from the Sukothai and Ayuthaya Periods. Only traces of the square cloister which once surrounded the central *prang* remain visible.

Admission at the northern entrance is 20B. While some visitors are content to snap a few photos over the wall, this monument is worth the admission fee.

Near the station is a locomotive manufactured in 1919 by North British Locomotive, and a decrepit Khmer temple with odd European statues and racist posters illustrating human evolution.

Wat Nakhonkosa

Bangkok's Fine Arts Department has recently completed restoration on the ruins of this 12th-century Khmer *chedi, viharn,* and small *prang* originally dedicated to Hindu gods. Lopburi and U-Thong images uncovered from the lower *chedi* are now displayed in the Lopburi Museum.

Monkey Shrine

San Pra Khan—the so-called Kala Temple—consists of the ruins of a large 10th-century Khmer *prang,* the dimensions of which indicate its once considerable size, as well as a small later temple noted for its sandstone doorway graced with images of Vishnu and *nagas.* To the rear stands a modern and rather nondescript temple erected in 1953 with statues of Hindu divinities highly revered by the Thai people. The temple is dedicated to, and dominated by, a gold-covered, four-armed image of Kala, the Hindu god of time and death, incongruously capped with the head of Buddha. Behind is an elevated courtyard and giant banyan tree inhabited by aggressive monkeys that snatch purses and cameras from unsuspecting tourists. Hold onto your bags!

Prang Sam Yot

Prang Sam Yot—"Temple of the Three Towers"—is a fairly well-preserved example of Bayon-style Khmer architecture which, together with Wat Mahathat, once served as one of Lopburi's two principal Hindu temples. Archaeologists believe the structure was originally dedicated to Hindu gods and later converted into a Buddhist sanctuary as suggested by the modest interior collection of *nagas,* Hindu images, and life-sized Buddhas in the Lopburi style.

Regarded as the primary landmark in Lopburi, the complex consists of a central corridor which links three laterite towers dedicated to Brahma, Shiva, and Vishnu. This finely balanced trio currently graces the back of Thailand's 500B currency note, though perfect symmetry has been marred by an east *viharn* erected during the reign of King Narai. The floor plan resembles a Greek cross with corbelled-roof porticoes on four sides.

Prang Khaek

The busiest intersection in Lopburi encircles a Hindu shrine erected in the 11th century by the Khmers, and restored in the 17th century by King Narai. The strange location intrigues more than the monument itself.

Wat Sao Tong Tong

Northwest of the Royal Palace stands another temple complex filled with an odd assortment of monuments. The *viharn* (Pra Viharn) to the right of the gaudily painted modern *wat* was originally constructed by King Narai to serve as a Christian chapel for Western diplomats. Though heavily restored in a pseudo-Western style, Pra Viharn shows typical Ayuthayan details such as tall and slightly concave foundations, superimposed roofs, and pilasters decorated with foliage capitals. The elegant structure—now a Buddhist sanctuary—features an immense seated Buddha and recessed wall niches filled with a collection of small but remarkable Lopburi images.

Outside the temple is a modern *sala* which displays a carved wooden pulpit dating from the Ayuthaya Period, monastic buildings constructed by King Narai, and distinctive residences

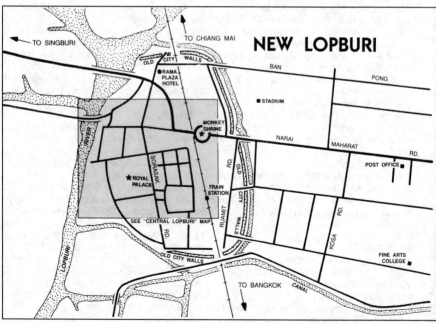

erected for visiting ambassadors and Christian missionaries.

Phaulkon's Residence

This complex displays a broad patchwork of architectural styles in which European predominates, but not to the exclusion of Thai influences. Chao Praya Wichayen was originally constructed by King Narai as a residence for a French ambassador sent from the court of King Louis XIV, but later became the final home to an infamous Greek adventurer named Constantine Phaulkon. Phaulkon's attempts to convert Narai to Christianity resulted in his beheading, the ouster of all Westerners from the royal courts in Lopburi and Ayuthaya, and the near-complete destruction of his residence and all ancillary buildings! (For more about Phaulkon, see the special topic **Phaulkon the Greek.**)

The narrow courtyard to the rear holds a Roman Catholic church, Jesuit residence, and remains of a bell-shaped tower. To the east are residences constructed for members of the 1685 French mission.

The complex has been completely restored, though there's less of interest here than at the Royal Palace and Wat Mahathat.

Accommodations

Hotels in Lopburi are basic but reasonably clean, proprietors friendly, and prices low—a great change from towns dominated by mass tourism.

Asia Lopburi Hotel: Best bet for comfortable lodgings in the center of town is the basic hotel just opposite the Royal Palace. 1 Sorasak, tel. (036) 411892, 140-180B fan, 280-350 a/c.

Naprakan Road Hotels: Several inexpensive hotels are strung along Naprakan Road just opposite the train station. Rooms at the **Suparapong, Thai Sawat, Julathip,** and **Indra** start from 120B fan and 250B a/c. Ask for the cheapest room rather than accept the more expensive options offered by the manager.

Nett Hotel: Tucked away in a quiet alley, this convenient hotel has large, clean rooms and homey decorations. Check this one if the Asia Lopburi is filled. 17/1 Rajadamnern Rd., tel. (036) 411738, 150-300B fan, 300-400B a/c.

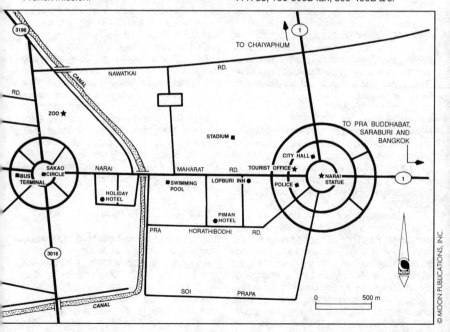

Taipei Hotel: Another decent budget hotel just past the Honda dealership. 29/6 Surasongkram Rd., tel. (036) 411524, 120-180B fan, 200-260B a/c.

Rama Plaza Hotel: A new business traveler's hotel with better rooms than those in the older places in town. 4 Banpong Rd., tel. (036) 411663, 220-320B fan, 320-450B a/c.

Lopburi Inn: Located in New Lopburi on the main road between the two traffic circles, this is the only hotel in town with a/c rooms and modern facilities. 28/9 Narai Maharat Rd., tel. (036) 412300, fax (036) 411917, 600-800B.

Lopburi Inn Resort: Best in town, also located way out in New Lopburi. 144 Tambon Tha Sala, tel. (036) 420777, fax (036) 412010, 2,200-2,800B.

Restaurants

Lopburi offers a limited number of simple restaurants. Snacks are available from the **night market** on Naprakan Road opposite the Julathip and Thai Sawat Hotels. The Chinese restaurant in the **Asia Lopburi Hotel** serves both Chinese and Thai dishes in fairly comfortable surroundings. An escape from the heat is provided by the two branches of a/c **Foremost Restaurant** on Napraka Road and just north of the **Traveler's Drop In.** Other popular restaurants include the **White House Garden** in the center of town, upscale **Chan Chao Restaurant** near Wat Mahathat, and **Boon Coffee Shop** near the Indra Hotel.

Entertainment

Nightclubs and discos are located in New Lopburi near the first traffic circle. The most popular spot is **Chao Praya Nightclub,** where live music is offered during the week and disco on weekends. Back in the old town, **Big Bell Bar** adjacent to the Suparapong Hotel is a popular spot to spend an evening.

Thai classical dance and music can be found at the Nartasin School of Art, where young students from nearby provinces train for professional careers in the performing arts. Mornings around 1000 are the best time to observe the students and take a tour of the facilities. Nartasin (Vithayalia Kalasilpa University) is in New Lopburi, about three km from old town. Take a blue *songtao* from Three Pagodas bus stop to the first traffic circle, walk 10 minutes south, then west along the canal to the Fine Arts College.

Lopburi's municipal **swimming pool** is on the right side of the road in New Lopburi, about one km beyond Sakao Circle. It's open daily 1000-2000 and charges a 25B admission fee.

Transportation

Lopburi, 150 km north of Bangkok and 75 km from Ayuthaya, can be visited as an overnight excursion or as an afternoon trip from Ayuthaya. Rushed travelers can leave their bags at the train station, conduct a three-hour walking tour, and continue by night train to either Phitsanulok or Chiang Mai.

Bus: Buses leave Bangkok's Northern Terminal every 30 minutes 0600-1900 and take about three hours to reach Lopburi. Buses from the central market in Ayuthaya leave every 30 minutes.

Lopburi can also be reached direct from Kanchanaburi, avoiding the nightmare of travel connections in Bangkok. From Kanchanaburi, take a bus to Suphanburi (two hours) where buses continue up to Singburi (three hours) and on to Lopburi (30 minutes). Travelers coming from Korat and the northeast should transfer to a connecting bus in Saraburi. The Lopburi bus station is in the new town about two km east of old town. To reach the station from old town, take any *songtao* going west.

Train: Trains from Bangkok's Hualampong station depart every two hours 0600-2000 and take about three hours to reach Lopburi. The train from Ayuthaya takes an hour and passes through lovely scenery of ricefields and idyllic villages. The express sleeper train from Bangkok to Chiang Mai passes through Lopburi at 2020. Reservations should be made on arrival in Lopburi. The Lopburi station is conveniently located within walking distance of all attractions and the budget hotels in the old town.

SARABURI AND PRA BUDDHABAT

Saraburi is a small provincial town 113 km from Bangkok on the highway to the northeastern town of Korat. Saraburi has little of interest aside from the shrine at Pra Buddhabat and the drug rehabilitation center at Wat Tham Krabok. Most travelers visit the two sites on side trips from Lopburi. For details on Wat Tham Krabok, see the special topic, **Just Say No at Opium Pipe Monastery.**

JUST SAY NO AT OPIUM PIPE MONASTERY

*C*an a radical therapy concocted of strange herbs and rigorous spiritual practice cure hard-core drug addiction? For over 30 years, a Thai monk named Pra Chamroon Parnchand has been saving addicts with an extraordinary 70% success rate. His unorthodox yet highly efficacious treatments won him the prestigious Ramon Magsaysay Award for Public Service in 1975, and his worldwide reputation ensures a steady stream of opium, heroin, cocaine, and crack cocaine addicts.

Although all patients are ensured absolute privacy, visitors over the past two decades have included American lawyers, stockbrokers, corporate presidents, Asian politicians, Italian fashion designers, rock stars, senior Islamic religious authorities, disciples of the Dalai Lama, sons and daughters of the rich and famous, and an African-American Vietnam veteran (Gordon Baltimore from Harlem) who now welcomes nervous arrivals. All share the same quarters and conduct therapy together.

The 15-day rehabilitation course begins with a sacred vow never to use drugs again; the oath is written on rice paper and swallowed. The first five days include detoxifying vomit sessions in which patients drink a potion made from 100 wild plants which grow on the monastery grounds; it "tastes like stale tobacco that burns like fire." Long gulps of holy water are followed by convulsions and violent spasms of vomiting which remove the toxic waste of years of addiction. Afternoons are spent in herbal saunas spiced with lemongrass to purify the blood and morning glory to restore the eyesight. The final 10 days involve working in the fields and helping the resident monks with construction projects. The treatment has been broadened with religious and psychological elements. To date, more than 100,000 drug addicts have taken the treatment, which is completely free aside from voluntary contributions.

Wat Tham Krabok ("Opium Pipe Monastery") is located in a hillside monastery some 125 km north of Bangkok and 25 km from Saraburi, midway between Lopburi and Saraburi. Anyone with a serious drug problem may want to seek out the extraordinary treatments offered by Pra Chamroon Parnchand. Casual visitors are also welcome.

Pra Buddhabat

Pra Buddhabat, 29 km from Saraburi toward Lopburi, is regarded as one of the finest examples of classic architecture in Thailand and is the site of the country's most sacred festival. Along with temples in Doi Suthep, Nakhon Phanom, and Nakhon Si Thammarat, Pra Buddhabat constitutes one of the four most sacred destinations in Thailand. The temple was originally constructed by the kings of Ayuthaya but destroyed by the Burmese in 1765. The present structure was erected by the early kings of Bangkok and improved upon by subsequent rulers.

Entrance is made up a long staircase flanked by a pair of impressive, undulating *nagas* which symbolically transport the visitor from the earthly realm to the heavenly home of the Buddha. The most significant building is an elegant *mondop* that enshrines a two-meter footprint. According to Thai tradition, the footprint was discovered in 1606 by a hunter chasing a deer. Standing on a broad marble platform, the *mondop* features a highly ornate pyramidal roof decorated with a profusion of glass and gold mosaics. Inside the structure is the gold-leaf footprint filled with coins tossed by pilgrims. Also note the elaborate doors inlaid with mother-of-pearl, constructed during the reign of King Rama I.

Pra Buddhabat is considered a powerful place filled with divine magic. Thais believe they can improve their karma by tossing coins into the footprint, ringing the bells with bamboo sticks, and throwing fortune-telling sticks *(siem si)* which now compete with electronic counterparts. Other legends claim you will live a full 93 years if you ring all 93 bells and count them correctly, and that three visits to Pra Buddhabat ensures admittance into heaven.

The temple complex includes several other beautiful and significant buildings. Viharn Luang features a museum filled with religious paraphernalia and donations from pious visitors. Several small *chedis* and *bots* and a temple dedicated to Kala are also located on the temple grounds.

The best time to visit Pra Buddhabat is during the religious festivals held twice yearly in the early spring and late fall. An estimated 800,000 pilgrims arrive to improve their karma and enjoy entertainment provided by Ferris wheels, magicians, beggars, swindlers, and folk shows of *likay* and *khon.* The first festival, held in the third lunar month, is popular with Chinese since it corresponds with the Chinese New Year. The second festival in the fourth lunar month is mainly attended by Thai pilgrims.

While the festivals are still popular events that celebrate the primordial concept of agricultural society, some of the significance has been lost to modernization, which downplays the importance of cyclical festivals.

Accommodations
Pra Buddhabat Hotels: The **Suk Sant** and the larger **Thanin Hotel** on the main road in Pra Buddhabat have fan-cooled rooms for 120-180B.

Saraburi Hotels: Saraburi has six hotels with both fan and a/c rooms. **Kiaw An Hotel** (tel. 036-211656) at 273 Phahonyothin Rd. has fan rooms for 120B and a/c from 260B. Other hotels in the same price range include the **Saen Suk** (tel. 036-211104) at 194 Phahonyothin Rd. and the **Sap Sin** (tel. 036-211047) at 471 Phahonyothin Rd.

Transportation
Buses and *songtaos* to Pra Buddhabat leave from the bus terminal in New Lopburi. Keep your eyes open for the hillside monastery on the right side of the road. Pra Buddhabat and Wat Tham Krabok are also served by buses and *songtaos* leaving from the Saraburi bus terminal on Banthat Road and from the bus stop near the Bank of Asia.

CENTRAL THAILAND

Flanked by mountains to the north, west, and east, the vast plains of central Thailand form the heartland of the Thai nation, both past and present. The region is defined by the provinces of Sukothai, Phitsanulok, Kamphang Phet, Tak, and Petchabun. Watering the fertile region are several major rivers such as the mighty Chao Praya, which flows from the north through the historic heartland before emptying into the Gulf of Thailand. Together with other tributaries such as the Ping and Nan Rivers, central Thailand has been carved into an incredibly complex network of waterways and canals that help produce the rice to sustain the country. Geography and nature have been generous to the region. Unlike in the arid northeast and mountainous north, rainfall here is abundant and the earth is fertile enough to provide a decent living for the people.

Central Thailand, outside the larger towns, has changed remarkably little over the centuries. Most of the population is of pure Thai decent without the mixtures of Chinese, Lao, Khmer, and Malay found throughout the border districts. Although large and modern towns are commonplace, most inhabitants continue to live and work in tiny hamlets where their lives revolve around family, farming, and faith. Rice cultivation remains the chief occupation.

Sightseeing Highlights

As with the rivers that flow through the region, Thai history has moved down through central Thailand and left behind remnants of the past. Most of the archaeological monuments date from the 13th and 14th centuries, when the kingdom at Sukothai controlled central Thailand. Also of interest are several border towns where traditional architecture and simple lifestyles still survive.

Phitsanulok: Located 380 km from Bangkok, this modern city is the hub of commerce and communication for central Thailand. Phitsanulok has few architectural blessings or great sights apart from the Jinaraj Buddha—widely considered the most beautiful image in Thailand—and nearby national parks and wildlife sanctuaries.

Sukothai: An hour west of Phitsanulok, the town served in the 13th and 14th centuries as the first capital of a unified Thailand. Modern Sukothai is rather nondescript, but nearby Sukothai Historical Park offers the finest collec-

CENTRAL THAILAND

© MOON PUBLICATIONS, INC.

tion of historic ruins in the country. Budget guest-houses are plentiful and travel connections can easily be made in all possible directions. Because of its historical and cultural connections, Sukothai is the most important destination in Central Thailand.

Si Satchanalai: Some 55 km north of Sukothai, the small town, which served as a provincial capital and viceroy seat during the Sukothai Period, is modest by Sukothai standards. The ruins inside the historical park have been well restored and provide a genuine sense of timelessness. Si Satchanalai can be visited on a day-trip from Sukothai.

Kamphang Phet: Third part of the Sukothai triumvirate was the garrison town of Kamphang Phet, 85 km southwest of Sukothai. Visitors with

a serious interest in Thai archaeology will enjoy the handful of partially restored temples on the northern edge of town.

Tak: Located on Hwy. 1, which connects Bangkok and Chiang Mai, this modern town serves as the transportation hub for west-central Thailand. Tak lacks any great sights except for the finest collection of old wooden houses left in Thailand. Fans of traditional domestic architecture can spend a few hours exploring the charming neighborhoods before continuing on to Mae Sot or Chiang Mai.

Mae Sot: An intriguing town on the Burmese border. While rarely visited by Westerners, it offers a few temples, a great morning market, and a diverse population of Thais, Chinese, Burmese, and hilltribe minorities. The completion of the road north from Mae Sot to Mae Sariang provides a unique approach to the region west of Chiang Mai.

Transportation

Sukothai is the main destination and tourist hub in central Thailand. Visitors short on time can briefly visit Sukhothai en route to Chiang Mai. A more complete tour would include side trips to Si Satchanalai and Phitsanulok before you head west to Kamphang Phet, Tak, and Mae Sot on the Burmese border. Chiang Mai can be reached by bus from Mae Sot, or via Mae Sariang on a recently completed road, which skirts the Burmese border.

Sukhothai is seven hours by private buses or public coaches leaving from Bangkok's Northern Bus Terminal. Ordinary buses are plentiful from Sukhothai to all other destinations. Motorcycles can also be rented in Sukhothai.

The train line passes through Phitsanulok, from where buses continue west to Sukhothai. Trains from Bangkok to Phitsanulok depart seven times daily at 0640, 0705, 0830, 1500, 1800, 2000, and 2200. Ordinary trains from Bangkok take eight hours and rapid trains take six hours to reach Phitsanulok. The most convenient options are the 0640 rapid train arriving in Phitsanulok at 1230, and the 1500 rapid train arriving at 2115. As noted before, train travel is a very relaxing and scenic way to travel around Thailand.

Thai Airways flies twice daily from Bangkok to Phitsanulok and once daily to Tak.

HISTORIC HEARTLAND

NAKHON SAWAN

North of Bangkok, Nakhon Sawan is an important commercial center located where the Ping, Yom, Wang, and Nan Rivers merge to form the Chao Praya. The city is rarely visited by Westerners except during Chinese New Year, when the predominantly Chinese population sponsors one of the largest festivals in Thailand. Held annually since 1914 as the Dragon and Lion Festival, the colorful and noisy event features a procession of Chinese deities, Thai long-drum troupes, and winners of local beauty pageants.

Attractions

Few traces of local history survive in this modern and rather bland town.

Wat Chom Khiri Nagaprot: Situated on a small hill south of town and across the bridge is a small Chinese temple with splendid views over the river. The central *wat* dates from the Sukhothai Period and holds a fine Ayuthaya-style Buddha. To the rear is a *viharn* with more Ayuthaya Buddhas and a large bronze bell over 100 years old.

Khao Kob Mountain: North of downtown beyond Matuli Road, this mountain features a monastery constructed over 700 years ago by King Lithai of Sukhothai; the monastery contains a footprint of Buddha. Views from the summit include the lake at Bung Boraphet and ricefields spreading west toward the Taunggyi Mountains.

An aquatic bird sanctuary, museum, and small aquarium are located at the large reservoir, **Bung Boraphet,** nine km east of town.

Accommodations

Hotels are mostly in the center of town, near the river, or on busy Suwanwithi Road.

Wang Nakhon Hotel: Excellent location on the river and acceptable rooms with private bath. 42 Sukemok Rd., tel. (056) 222961, 120-180B fan, 250-280B a/c.

Long Lam Noon Singh Hotel: Best bet for bargain rates and well-maintained rooms. Two blocks east of massive Fairy Land Mall. Suwanwithi Rd., tel. (056) 222876, 100-120B fan.

Erawan Hotel: The Erawan also faces the river and has fairly clean fan and a/c rooms with private bath. 1 Matuli Rd., tel. (056) 221899, 150-200B fan, 280-450B a/c.

Pimarn Hotel: An upscale hotel popular with business travelers and Chinese-Thai tourists who flood Nakhon Sawan during the Chinese New Year in late February. Swimming pool, restaurant, and nightclub, plus convenient access to the adjacent Nakhon Sawan shopping center. 605 Asia Rd., tel. (056) 222473, fax (056) 221253, 800-1,200B.

Transportation

Nakhon Sawan is 240 km north of Bangkok and 442 km south of Chiang Mai.

Buses depart every 30 minutes from the Northern Bus Terminal in Bangkok and take four hours to Nakhon Sawan. Buses take seven hours from Chiang Mai. Allow two hours from Lopburi and Kamphang Phet, and three hours from Sukothai. The Nakhon Sawan bus station is west of town on the Asia Highway; take a yellow minitruck to the city center.

The train station is across the river and four km from the city center; take a green minitruck into town.

Orange minitrucks head out to the post office and Khao Kob Mountain.

PHITSANULOK

Straddling the Nan River 380 km north of Bangkok, Phitsanulok is the largest commercial center in central Thailand and transportation hub for the region. The new city possesses a friendly population and a superb location on the banks of the Nan River. Worth a visit are the Pra Buddha Jinaraj (Chinarat) image at Wat Mahathat, an outstanding folklore museum, a Buddha factory,

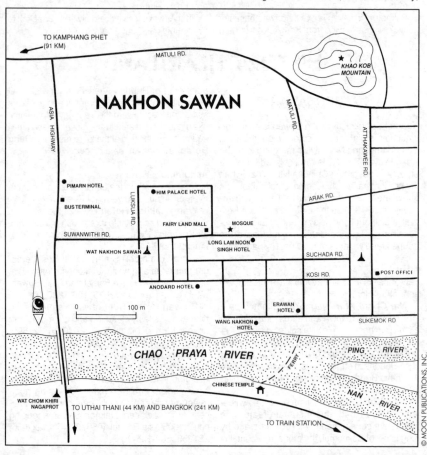

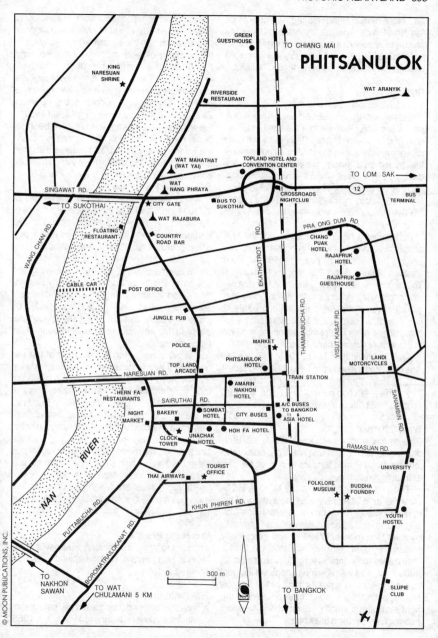

PHITSANULOK

TO CHIANG MAI

GREEN GUESTHOUSE

KING NARESUAN SHRINE

RIVERSIDE RESTAURANT

WAT ARANYIK

WAT MAHATHAT (WAT YAI)

TOPLAND HOTEL AND CONVENTION CENTER

TO LOM SAK

WAT NANG PHRAYA

SINGAWAT RD.

CROSSROADS NIGHTCLUB

12

BUS TERMINAL

TO SUKOTHAI

CITY GATE

BUS TO SUKOTHAI

EKATHOTROT RD.

PRA ONG DUM RD.

WANG CHAN RD.

WAT RAJABURA

CHANG PUAK HOTEL

FLOATING RESTAURANT

COUNTRY ROAD BAR

RAJAPRUK HOTEL

THAMMABUCHA RD.

RAJAPRUK GUESTHOUSE

CABLE CAR

POST OFFICE

VISUT KASAT RD.

JUNGLE PUB

POLICE

MARKET

LANDI MOTORCYCLES

NARESUAN RD.

TOP LAND ARCADE

PHITSANULOK HOTEL

TRAIN STATION

SANAMBIN RD.

HERN FA RESTAURANTS

AMARIN NAKHON HOTEL

SAIRUTHAI RD.

NIGHT MARKET

BAKERY

SOMBAT HOTEL

CITY BUSES

A/C BUSES TO BANGKOK

ASIA HOTEL

RIVER

CLOCK TOWER

UNACHAK HOTEL

HOH FA HOTEL

RAMASUAN RD.

UNIVERSITY

THAI AIRWAYS

TOURIST OFFICE

NAN

FOLKLORE MUSEUM

BUDDHA FOUNDRY

PUTTABUCHA RD.

KHUN PHIREN RD.

YOUTH HOSTEL

BOROMATRAILOKANAT RD.

0   300 m

TO NAKHON SAWAN

TO WAT CHULAMANI 5 KM

TO BANGKOK

SLUPIE CLUB

© MOON PUBLICATIONS, INC.

and night markets and floating restaurants on the Nan River. Another important plus is the complete absence of tourists, making Phitsanulok a refreshing change from the more popular destinations in central and northern Thailand.

History

One of Thailand's oldest and most historic towns, Phitsanulok originally served as a Khmer outpost called Song Kwae before the Kwai Noi River changed its course in the 11th century. Its chief prosperity was during the Sukhothai era, when it functioned as a military bastion, and after the decline of Sukhothai, when it served as the capital of Siam during the reign of King Trailokanat. In the 15th century Phitsanulok was the seat of the Ayuthaya viceroy, who ruled the province of Sukhothai.

Phitsanulok is highly regarded among the Thai people as the birthplace of King Naresuan the Great, who governed the province 1569-84. Then a vassal state of Bago, Phitsanulok and central Thailand were subsequently liberated from foreign rule after Naresuan organized a Thai army that defeated the Burmese in the historic battle at Don Chedi. A memorial to King Naresuan is located on the north side of the river on the grounds of the former Chandahana Palace.

After a devastating fire in 1955, Phitsanulok was relocated five km from the old site and rebuilt in a modern shophouse style (structures with two stories—a shop downstairs, living quarters upstairs) that offers few architectural blessings.

Wat Mahathat

Phitsanulok's major spectacle is the Jinaraj Buddha inside Wat Mahathat (Wat Yai), one of the few Ayuthaya-Period temples to survive the catastrophic fire four decades ago.

The *wat* was erected in 1482 by King Boromatrailokanat of Ayuthaya as the symbol of his domination over Sukhothai and Phitsanulok. The *wat, prang,* and adjacent *viharn* were renovated by King Boromakot (1733-58) and completely restored by the Fine Arts Department in 1991.

Entrance to the temple is made across a broad parking lot filled with souvenir shops selling gold leaf offerings and reproductions of the famous image, palmists and blind fortune-tellers to the right rear, and a small pavilion where students occasionally perform the *khon.*

The *viharn* where the central image is stored is entered through beautifully carved wooden doors after which the splendid doors to Wat Pra Keo in Bangkok were modeled. Architecturally, the structure is a curious mixture of northern and southern styles with a three-level roof and low, sweeping eaves. The particularly fine interior is a stunning triumph of color and proportion. Black columns decorated with gold leaf support the rich red roof. Interior murals have been recently repainted with delightful scenes of a starving Buddha, courtesans, and hunters with their dogs. The lowness of the aisles and dramatic color scheme accentuate the nave and focus attention on the majestic central image.

The central Buddha, Pra Buddha Jinaraj ("Victorious King"), ranks as the great masterpiece of Sukhothai art. Regarded as the most beautiful and sacred image in Thailand, the highly polished bronze statue has been reproduced for the Marble Temple in Bangkok and a Thai temple at Bodgaya, India. Dramatic appeal is furthered by the black backdrop, narrow slit windows, and strong lighting, which add an almost surrealistic effect. The image is surrounded by pilgrims shaking fortune-telling sticks, four elephant tusks, and gold leaf bodhi trees in glass display cases.

The 36-meter *prang* in the center of the *wat* compound was constructed in Khmer style during the Ayuthaya Period. Surrounding the *prang* are long cloisters filled with an amazing array of Sukhothai, U-Thong, and Chiang Saen Buddhas. To the left is a small branch of the national museum with a fine collection of 19th-century wooden seals, mother-of-pearl monks' bowls, pottery, glassware, and figurines from Sawankalok and Si Satchanalai. Other buildings include a *bot* in the southwest corner and an immense *viharn* to the east.

Photographers are welcome but all visitors must be properly dressed; no shorts or immodest tops.

Wat Nang Phraya

Adjacent to Wat Yai is a small *viharn* where the famous Nang Phraya Buddha amulets were discovered in 1901.

Wat Rajabura

Across the road and near the old city gate stands another temple which survived the fire of 1955.

The partially reconstructed Ayuthayan Period *chedi* features a *bot* decorated with Ramayana frescoes painted during the reign of Rama III.

Nan River
A very pleasant walk can be made along the banks of the river dividing the city; floating in the river are dozens of simple homes and restaurants, the only legal houseboats in Thailand since they predate municipal codes banning such establishments. Opposite the General Post Office is a blue cable car crossing the river and providing an up-close glimpse of the houseboats and riverlife.

Clock Tower and Central Phitsanulok
After walking past the Hern Fa Restaurants and riverside bazaar, turn east to the old clock tower on Phayalithai Road and continue through downtown to the railway station and central market. Top Land Arcade is a good place to shop and enjoy a meal in the restaurant on the top floor. The train station is fronted by a 10-wheel locomotive built in 1920 by the North British Locomotive Company. Farther east on Boromatrailokanat Road is the local tourist office.

Folklore Museum
With the finest collection of folkloric artifacts in Thailand, this small museum is a labor of love for Dr. Tawee, a retired major who has amassed an astounding assembly of agricultural and household instruments. Lower level of the front pavilion features Sawankalok ceramics, Thai instruments, and a creative assortment of coconut grinders sculpted in whimsical animal forms. Upstairs are traditional craftspeople's tools, Buddhas, fabrics, and bronzeware collected by the good doctor. To the rear is a lovely home filled with fish traps, old Victrolas, and elephant bells; the building itself is a remarkable structure.

Dr. Tawee's private museum is on Visut Kasat Road two km south of the train station, and is marked by a huge sign. The museum was recently renovated and expanded. Admission is free, but donations are accepted by volunteer guides.

Buddha Foundry
Opposite the folklore museum is a thriving Buddha factory, also owned by Dr. Tawee. Visitors

Chulamani master monk

are welcome to tour the foundry and watch the production of bronze Buddhas cast after prototypes from Sukhothai, Ayuthaya, and the Pra Jinaraj at Wat Yai. Explanation of the lost-wax method is provided by photo exhibits in the front room, while a small souvenir shop in the rear sells bronze images for under 500B. The foundry is a fascinating attraction and one of the few places in Thailand to watch the ancient tradition of bronze casting.

Wat Chulamani
Five km south of town are the ruins of Phitsanulok's oldest historical site, a Khmer-style *prang* constructed during the Sukhothai Period and restored by King Boromatrailokanat of Ayuthaya. The temple is chiefly noted for its ornate plaster designs and stucco friezes decorating the lintels and exterior walls. Nearby are a modern monastery and a ruined *viharn* constructed by King Narai to commemorate the Buddhist ordination of King Boromatrailokanat.

Wat Chulamani can be reached by public bus 5 heading south down Boromatrailokanat Road.

Phitsanulok to Lom Sak Road

Highway 12, which links Phitsanulok with Lom Sak, passes through several mountain ranges that separate the valleys of the Nan and Pasak Rivers. The tourist office in Phitsanulok has a good map which shows the exact location of all waterfalls and national parks in the region. Tours can be arranged through local guesthouses and from travel agents near the Phitsanulok tourist office.

Keangsopa Waterfalls: The falls at Km 72 are recommended as the best in the region, especially during the rainy season and at the end of the monsoon season. The falls, signposted in English, are two km south of Hwy. 12.

Tung Saleng Luang National Park: Located 80 km west of Phitsanulok is a 1,200-square-km park covered by wooded mountains with a variety of flora and fauna. Accommodations in park bungalows can be booked in advance from the Forestry Department (tel. 02-579-0529) in Bangkok.

Phu Hin Rong Kla National Park: From 1967 to 1982, Phu Hin Rong Kla served as the headquarters of the Communist Party of Thailand (CPT) and was the site of numerous battles between the Thai government and communist insurgents. After the surrender in 1982 of the People's Liberation Army of Thailand (PLAT), the region was declared a national park and opened to the public. The park offers a cool climate, hiking trails, waterfalls, scenic views, and remnants of the communist occupation, such as air-raid shelters and military headquarters. Reservations can be made from the Forestry Department office in Bangkok. Large bungalows begin at 600B per night and camping costs 50B. The park is 125 km from Phitsanulok and can be reached by public bus going to the nearby village of Nakhon Thai.

Budget Accommodations

Phitsanulok has two good guesthouses that have opened in the last few years, and several low-end hotels near the train station.

Youth Hostel: Phitsanulok's official youth hostel is somewhat isolated but otherwise an excellent place to stay. The owner, Sapachai

Pitaksakorn, worked in Bangkok as a computer programmer before returning to his hometown and opening the hostel in 1990. The British-designed main house, over 40 years old, has three upstairs rooms containing Burmese antique beds and a small dormitory. The new wing in the back has another dorm plus almost 20 rooms furnished with antique decorations, old boats and oxcart wheels, lanterns, and the remains of teak homes purchased by Sapachai in Tak.

The hostel is two km south of the train station, one km from the airport, and four km from the bus terminal. A *samlor* should cost 10B from the train station or airport, and 25B from the bus terminal. Bus 3 goes from the bus terminal to the hostel. From the train station, catch bus 4 south down Ekathotrot Road. After disembarking, turn left on Ramesaun Road, then right on Sanambin Road. 38 Sanambin Rd., tel. (055) 242060, 50B dorm, 120-300B private room.

Green Guesthouse: Several years ago schoolteachers from Sukhothai opened this small guesthouse in the northern part of town. The lovely teakwood home has a courtyard patio which faces a street made rather noisy by the cars and nearby train line.

The guesthouse is on the left side of Ekathotrot Rd., about two km north of the big traffic circle. Bus 4 from the city bus terminal near the train station goes up Ekathotrot Road and passes the poorly marked guesthouse. However, bus travelers coming from Sukothai should get off after the bridge but before the traffic circle and take a *songtao* going up Ekathotrot Road. 11/12 Ekathotrot Rd., tel. (055) 252803, 100-150B

Sombat Hotel: Inexpensive hotels in the 120-250B range are located near the train station on Sairuthai and Phayalithai Roads. All are conveniently located in the center of town, but none are clean or very quiet. The Sombat is probably the best of a somewhat dismal lot. Overflow is handled by the nearby Unachak, Hoh Fa, and Asia Hotels. 4 Sairuthai Rd., tel. (055) 258179, 120-200B.

Moderate Accommodations

Several hotels in Phitsanulok offer both inexpensive fan rooms and moderately priced a/c rooms.

Phitsanulok Hotel: Slightly better than the low-end hotels is this basic spot on Naresuan

Road just opposite the train station. Rooms are fairly clean but very spartan; ask for a quieter room facing the inner courtyard. Well-located in the center of town at 82 Naresuan Rd., tel. (055) 258425, 140-200B fan, 250-300B a/c.

Chang Puak Hotel: An older 70-room hotel with a restaurant and billiards hall. An okay place though poorly located in the north part of town at 63 Pra Ong Dum Rd., tel. (055) 252822, 150-180B fan, 260-550B a/c.

Rajapruk Guesthouse: Behind the upscale Rajapruk Hotel is a cheaper annex which calls itself a "guesthouse." While the name is just a marketing ploy, the annex has decent rooms for a fair price in an inconvenient location. 99 Pra Ong Dum Rd., tel. (055) 25920, 220-250B fan, 300-340B a/c.

Luxury Accommodations
Phitsanulok has several hotels serving the business and upscale tourist markets.

Rajapruk Hotel An old favorite with 110 a/c rooms, a Thai-Chinese restaurant, a nightclub, car rentals, and a swimming pool. The owner's wife is an American, and English is spoken by some of the staff. The main drawback is the poor location outside town center, across the train tracks. 99 Pra Ong Dum Rd., tel. (055) 258477, fax (055) 251395, 900-1,200B.

Amarin Nakhon Hotel: While not as luxurious as the Rajapruk, this hotel compensates with a great location in the center of town just opposite the train station. Rooms are clean and the coffee shop is a popular spot for U.S. Army personnel from the nearby Thai military base. A very dark disco is located in the basement. 3 Chao Praya Rd., fax (055) 258945, 900-1,200B.

Topland Hotel: Phitsanulok's newest and most luxurious hotel opened in 1995 in the north end of town. The hotel features all the standard amenities, plus a gigantic shopping complex and the only convention facilities in central Thailand. 68/33 Ekathotrot Rd., tel. (055) 247800, fax (055) 247815, Bangkok tel. (02) 215-6108, fax (02) 215-0511, 1,200-1,800B.

Restaurants
Phitsanulok has a wide selection of restaurants, from air-conditioned ones in upscale hotels to alfresco eateries down by the river.

Floating Restaurants: Several popular floating restaurants are tied up just south of the bridge. **Than Tip** has been recommended as the best, followed by **Yardfan Floating Restaurant** and then the **Songkwae Houseboat.** The boats wait for a full house, then serve meals as they slowly sail up and down the Nan River. A small charge is collected for the cruise and no minimum is enforced on food or drink orders. Puttabucha Rd. Moderate.

Hern Fa Restaurants: Perhaps more fun than the floating restaurants are the hilarious food vendors who set up their portable shops each evening on the banks of the Nan River. A brilliant display of cooking and acrobatics is included with every order. First, the cook fires up the wok and sautées a mixture of vegetables and meats. A waiter then climbs to the top of a nearby truck and attempts to catch the mixture flung skyward by the chef. Misses are fairly common, but the best moment is when a drunken visitor agrees to take the role of waiter and catch the flying morning glory. Look for the trucks mounted with ladders, wagons, and even small boats. **Pak Bung, Viroj Pochan,** and **Phakbung** ("The First in the World") are the most popular. Inexpensive.

Night Market: Over a dozen good foodstalls are located on the riverbanks just south of the Hern Fa restaurants. Inexpensive.

Top Land Arcade: A welcome relief from the daytime heat is provided by the a/c restaurant on the top floor of Phitsanulok's largest shopping center. Live music in the evening, a bowling alley up on the sixth floor, and a small coffee shop in the basement. Boromatrailokanat Rd. Inexpensive.

Other Spots: A great little **bakery** is just across from the clock tower. Farther down the road and across from the Hoh Fa Hotel the old-time **Poon Sri Restaurant,** serves good Chinese and Thai dishes. Phayalithai Rd. Inexpensive.

Nightlife
Phitsanulok is a big town with a fair amount of nightlife. Several of the better private clubs are located near the Pailyn Hotel. The **Jungle Pub** and **Country Road Bar** are Thai cowboy joints with both recorded and live music. The **Crossroads Nightclub** near the traffic flyover is simi-

lar. Disco devotees can check the late-night action in the **Pailyn Hotel** and the basement of the **Amarin Nakhon Hotel. Slupie Nightclub** just south of the youth hostel has live rock bands and cabaret shows. Phitsanulok is also a fairly pleasant place for an evening walk.

Services and Information
Tourist Information: Information on nearby attractions and national parks is available from the TAT office (tel. 055-252742) at 209 Boromatrailokanat Rd. near the clock tower. The office is managed by friendly and helpful people, among the most competent in Thailand.

Tours: Travel agencies are located in upscale hotels and near the tourist office. Organized tours and rafting trips on the Yom River are available through the Green Guesthouse and the youth hostel. The tour departs on Saturday morning and includes a three-hour raft trip and overnight camping near Keng Luang Cave before returning Sunday evening.

Shopping: The local produce and fruit market is under the covered shed near the train station. **Tup Tin Handicraft** shop, opposite the clock tower, has a small but high-quality selection of textiles and regional crafts.

Festivals: The Pra Buddha Jinaraj Fair is held on the sixth day of the third lunar month, generally in late February. The six-day fair includes folk performances and homage ceremonies to the Buddha image inside Wat Yai. Boat races are held on the Nan River during the first weekend of October. The Naresuan Festival in January honors the king who liberated Thailand from Burmese rule.

Transportation
Phitsanulok serves as the transportation hub for central Thailand. The city is usually visited on a day-trip from Sukhothai or as an overnight stop between Ayuthaya and Sukhothai. Complete train and bus schedules are available from the TAT office.

Air: Thai Airways flies from Bangkok to Phitsanulok twice daily at 0715 and 1550. Direct flights from Phitsanulok are available to Chiang Mai (daily), Tak (four weekly), Nan (three weekly), and Mae Hong Son (three weekly).

Train: All trains from Bangkok, except the 1940 express service, stop in Phitsanulok. The 0640 and 1500 rapid trains from Bangkok arrive at 1233 and 2115. The 0705 and 0830 ordinary trains from Bangkok arrive at 1440 and 1610. Phitsanulok can also be reached by trains from Ayuthaya and Lopburi, a pleasant alternative to the hot and rather boring bus journey.

The train station is conveniently located in the center of town near the Nan River, but about four km from the government bus terminal. Travelers going direct to Sukhothai can hire a *samlor* from the train station to the bus terminal for about 25-35B. Alternatively, take bus 4 north to the big traffic circle and flag down any bus going west toward Sukothai.

Bus: Ordinary and a/c buses leave hourly from the Northern Bus Terminal in Bangkok and take five hours to reach Phitsanulok. Direct service from Bangkok is also provided by private bus companies such as **Yanyon Tours** (tel. 02-258-941). The government bus terminal is on Hwy. 12 about three km east of downtown. A *samlor* from the terminal to downtown hotels should cost 25-35B. Several city buses circulate around Phitsanulok from the city bus station. Bus 1 goes west to Wat Mahathat (Wat Yai), south along the river, and east along Ramesuan Road, and then returns to the bus station. Bus 7 does the same route in reverse. Bus 3 goes to the airport and Phitsanulok Youth Hostel.

Motorcycles: Motorcycles can be rented from **Landi Motors** (tel. 055-252765) on Pra Ong Dum Road near the Rajapruk Hotel. Cars are available from most large hotels and tour companies on Sithamtraipidok Road near the TAT office.

BUSES FROM PHITSANULOK

TO	DEPARTURES; HOURS
Bangkok	hourly 0700-2300; five hours
Chiang Mai	hourly until 1530; five hours
Sukhothai	hourly until 1800; one hour
Loei	six times daily; four hours
Khon Kaen	hourly 1000-1500; five hours

SI SATCHANALAI

The evocative ruins of old Si Satchanalai rest 56 km north of Sukhothai between Sawankalok and the new town of Si Satchanalai. Although it's less extensive than the ruins at Sukhothai, the superb setting and lonely sense of the past make Si Satchanalai a memorable place.

History

Si Satchanalai was established by the Khmers in the 12th century as a military outpost for their northeastern empire. In 1238, two local Thai chiefs joined forces to free the Thai people from Khmer domination. Although Sukhothai was the seat of Khmer strength, Si Satchanalai was liberated first to serve as the launching pad for an assault on Sukhothai.

Archaeological evidence suggests that many of the surviving temples were constructed by King Indradita, Sukhothai's first ruler, though the city was expanded over the span of many reigns. During the Sukhothai Period, Si Satchanalai served as the residence of the crown prince and enjoyed great importance, as demonstrated by the size of its monastery and other religious ruins.

Si Satchanalai declined in importance during the Ayuthaya Period and was abandoned in the 18th century as a result of the incessant wars with Myanmar.

Attractions

Si Satchanalai consists of three areas along the western bank of the Yom River. The central ruins are enclosed inside an irregular laterite wall that defines the original boundaries. Two km south is Chaliang, which served as the original seat of the Khmer administration. North of the central ruins are dozens of pottery kilns, once producing the famous Sawankalok ceramics.

The present renovation of the monuments was initiated in 1982 by the Fine Arts Department. Today the ruins are connected by a network of paved roads and described by signs providing detailed histories of the individual monuments. Adjacent to the entrance is a small office with a relief model of the city. The central ruins can be easily seen on foot, though a rented bicycle or organized tour is necessary to reach Chaliang and the pottery kilns.

Wat Chang Lom

The most important religious sanctuary in Si Satchanalai is this Sinhalese-style *chedi* constructed in 1285 by King Ramkamheng and possibly modeled after Wat Mahathat at Nakhon Si Thammarat. The monument is enclosed by a beautiful laterite brick wall distinguished by terraced shoulders, ornamental pilasters, and niches penetrated by four gates. Approach is made up a paved laterite walkway leading to a frontal *viharn* and *chedi* to the rear.

Supported by 36 crumbling stucco elephants which give the monument its name, Wat Chang Lom ("Elephant Temple") probably contains Buddha relics brought up from Chaliang by the first ruler of Sukhothai. Deterioration of the elephant images reveals construction techniques of a square brick tower and hollow core covered with stucco. Columns between the standing elephants once supported lanterns. Lining the upper terraces are 20 rare stucco Buddhas in the attitude of subduing Mara. Most of the images have been vandalized by robbers searching for buried treasure.

Wat Khao Phanom Pleung

In the northeastern area of the city is a steep 114-step staircase leading to Satchanalai's hilltop "Temple of the Mountain of Fire." According to the *Northern Chronicles,* a hermit named Satchanalai ordered King Thammaraj of Sukhothai to reserve the hill as a spot for fire worship and the cremation of high dignitaries.

To the right of the landing are stucco-coated octagonal columns and a Buddha poorly restored in 1967. To the left is a collapsed *chedi* which shows Lanna influence and an extremely unusual brick *mondop* that once housed a Buddha image. The *mondop* is known locally as Sala Chao Mae Laong Samli, or "Sacred House of the Goddess Laong Samli."

Views from the hill provide an overview of the architectural layout of Si Satchanalai.

Wat Khao Phanom Khiri

A narrow pathway leads to the well-proportioned Sinhalese-style *chedi* known as the "Temple of the Golden Mountain." Architecturally similar to Wat Chang Lom, the monument is situated in a strategic position from where Thai soldiers once surveyed the movements of enemy troops over

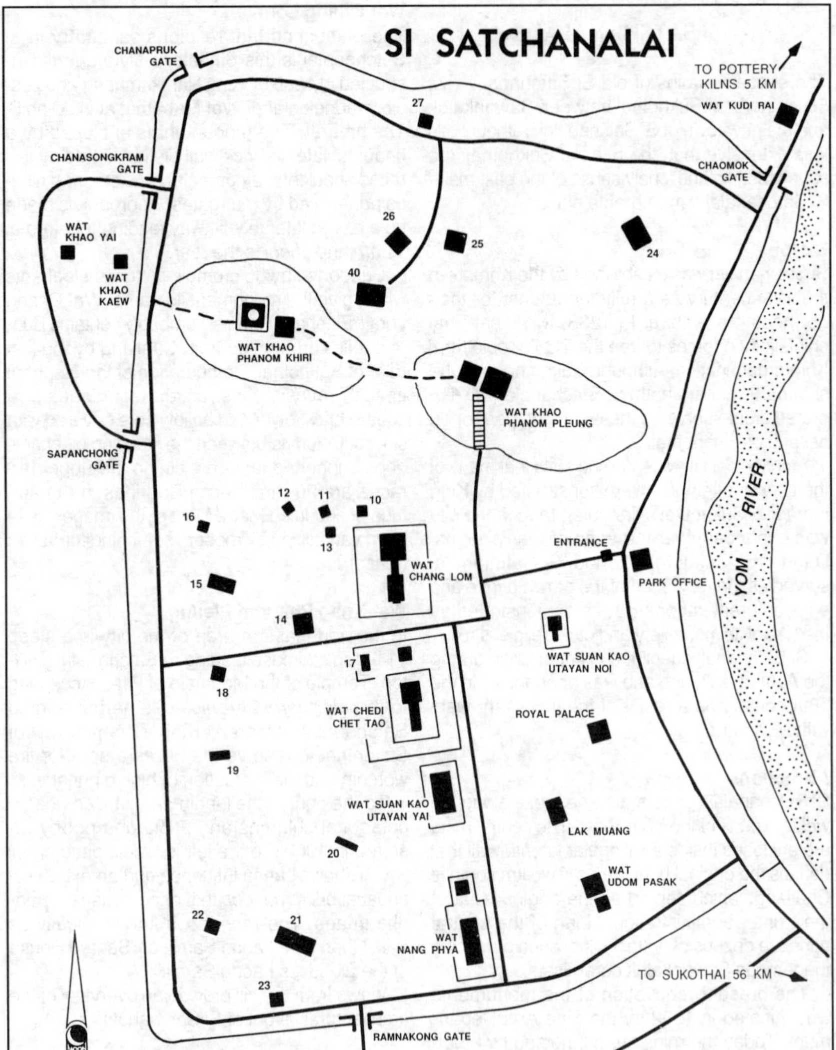

SI SATCHANALAI

CHANAPRUK GATE

CHANASONGKRAM GATE

SAPANCHONG GATE

WAT KHAO YAI

WAT KHAO KAEW

WAT KHAO PHANOM KHIRI

WAT KHAO PHANOM PLEUNG

TO POTTERY KILNS 5 KM

WAT KUDI RAI

CHAOMOK GATE

YOM RIVER

27

26

25

40

24

16

12 11 10

13

15

14

WAT CHANG LOM

ENTRANCE

PARK OFFICE

WAT SUAN KAO UTAYAN NOI

18

17

WAT CHEDI CHET TAO

ROYAL PALACE

19

WAT SUAN KAO UTAYAN YAI

LAK MUANG

20

WAT UDOM PASAK

22 21

WAT NANG PHYA

TO SUKOTHAI 56 KM

23

RAMNAKONG GATE

NUMBERS DENOTE MONUMENTS

0   100 m

© MOON PUBLICATIONS, INC.

the northern plains. A smaller *chedi,* remains of a *viharn,* and old lampposts are also on the grounds.

Across the road to the west are several Buddhist edifices where monks of the *vipassana* sect once meditated in solitude. **Wat Khao Kaew** and **Wat Khao Yai** are enigmatic monuments, but are difficult to reach through the thick underbrush.

Wat Chedi Chet Tao

South of Wat Chang Lom, and on the same axis, is the complex of over 30 *chedis* that provide a gold mine of architectural styles drawn from several regions in Southeast Asia. The main sanctuary, built in the 1340s and modeled after Wat Mahathat in Sukhothai, features an almost Laotian-style *chedi* capped with a distinctive lotus-bud finial. Adjacent to the *chedi* is a *viharn* to the south and a *bot* to the north between the two sets of walls.

To the east of the central monument are seven rows of *stupas* constructed as funerary monuments for members of the royal family. The *stupas* are of great importance because they replicate in stone various shrines once found throughout central Thailand. Some are in Sri Lankan style while others show the influence of Dvaravati and Lanna Kingdoms. Another resembles a wooden *viharn* with a roof capped by a *prasat* and bell-shaped *chedi*. Also of note is the wide variety of doorways and Sukhothai-style walking Buddhas contained in the northern monuments.

From an architectural standpoint, Wat Chedi Chet Tao is the most significant monument in Si Satchanalai.

Wat Suan Kao Utayan Yai

This "Monastery of the Large Precious Garden" features a Sri Lankan-style *chedi* on a square pedestal surmounted by a laterite stairway. Surrounding the ruined *viharn* and restored *chedi* is a laterite wall which has beautifully collapsed into rhythmic shapes.

Wat Nang Phya

Wat Nang Phya, the "Queen's Monastery," is chiefly noted for the remains of a 15th-century *viharn* whose wall is adorned with stucco floral moldings that imitate Ayuthayan woodcarvings. Constructed during the early Ayuthaya Period

and now protected by a sturdy roof, the solitary wall and its embossed motifs are penetrated by twin rows of six tall, very narrow slits in lieu of windows.

Also on the grounds is a circular Sinhalese *chedi* whose interior can be accessed up the eastern staircase.

Wat Suan Kao Utayan Noi

North of the foundations of the old royal palace is a small monument called the "Monastery of the Lesser Precious Garden." Surrounded by a moat and laterite wall, the temple consists of a frontal *viharn* housing a Buddha, and a lotus-bud *stupa* flanked by subsidiary *chedis.*

Wat Kok Singharam

Slit windows of Khmer design and original stucco characterize this ancient sanctuary one km south of old Si Satchanalai. To the rear of the remaining columns are three small *chedis* elevated on a brick pedestal.

Wat Chao Chan

A few hundred meters south of Wat Kok Singharam is a narrow road leading to a laterite Khmer-style *prang* still showing traces of original stucco above the false doorway on the western side. Weathered Buddhas sit inside the *prang* and among the collapsed columns of the old *viharn.*

Wat Chom Cheun

Farther south and marked with a sign is a large *mondop* sanctuary dominated by a crumbling, mysterious image of the Buddha. The statue has a magnificent, surrealistic quality that makes it among the most powerful images in central Thailand. To the rear of the *mondop* is a crumbling *chedi* overgrown with weeds.

Wat Mahathat

No visit to Si Satchanalai would be complete without a stop at this remarkable temple two km south of old Si Satchanalai. Archaeologists believe the temple occupies the site of an ancient Khmer settlement called Chaliang. Sukhothai's Stone Inscription Number 1 relates that in 1285 King Ramkamheng moved sacred relics from the original Khmer monument in Chaliang to a temple in Si Satchanalai, presumably Wat Chang

Lom, and began construction on the shrine. In 1464, the present monument—an Ayuthayan-style *prang* flanked by two ruined temples—was erected by King Boromatrailokanat over the old Khmer sanctuary and small temple erected by King Ramkamheng. The sanctuary and surrounding wall were restored in 1753 by King Boromakot of Ayuthaya.

Surrounding the round-topped *prang* is a laterite wall pierced by doorways aligned on an east-west axis. The extremely unusual doorways are considered among the most important features of Wat Mahathat. Capping the eastern entrance is a carved stone richly embellished with figures of Indo-Khmer inspiration. Beyond the standing pillars of the eastern *viharn* are several Buddhas of varying artistic achievement. The large brick seated Buddha covered with stucco and the standing Buddha half-embedded in the ground are rather ordinary, but special note should be made of the superb Sukhothai-style walking Buddha, considered one of the masterpieces of the period.

The central *prang* features a strong base in the Sukhothai style and an upper tower constructed in the Khmer style which regained popularity during the Ayuthaya Period. Surrounding the *prang* is a restored seated Buddha on the northern side, a bronze Buddha's footprint to the west, and most importantly, a Lopburi-style stone Buddha seated on a beautiful *naga* in the northeast corner of the compound. The climb to the top of the *prang* is dangerous but provides great views over the temple complex and Yom River.

West of the perimeter wall are a Mon *stupa* constructed in the late 14th century and two *viharns* that contain a footprint and large standing image of the Buddha. East of the wall is a small *mondop* which served as a *kuti* (religious dwelling) for monks during the reign of King Ramkamheng. Foodstalls and souvenir stands are across the road on the banks of the Yom River.

Pottery Kilns

Five km north of old Si Satchanalai lies one of the most extensive pottery sites in Southeast Asia. Though largely unknown to the average visitor, the potters of Si Satchanalai produced during the 14th and 15th centuries some of the world's finest glazed ceramics, stoneware, celadon, and decorated vases. The pottery,

known as Sawankalok after an early name for Si Satchanalai, played a major role in Southeast Asian trade and was exported to maritime sites throughout the Indonesian and Philippine islands.

Early scholars theorized the industry was developed by Chinese potters brought to Thailand by King Ramkamheng, but recent research indicates the technology was developed by Thai potters and craftspeople. A joint project funded by the Thai and Australian governments has systematically excavated many of the ancient kilns and opened them as public museums.

Sanghalok Kiln 61 Museum

Opened in 1987 by the Fine Arts Department and Siam Cement, this beautiful museum contains Kiln 61, surrounded by walkways, photographs and diagrams of the excavation, and examples of misfired ceramics uncovered from the site. Pottery shops with "old and new creations" are across the street. Kiln 61 Museum is 4.5 km north of Si Satchanalai on the road through Chaomok Gate.

Kiln 42 and 123 Museum

Some 500 meters farther north is another excavated kiln with pottery displays of smiling elephants, horses, and celadon turtles.

Sawakhalok Museum

A small branch of the National Museum is 37 km north of Sukhothai in the town of Sawakhalok. The museum is open Wed.-Sun. 0900-1630; admission 20B.

Accommodations

Most visitors return to Sukhothai before nightfall, but simple hotels are found in Sawankalok, the new town of Si Satchanalai, and near the ruins.

Wang Yom Resort: About 300 meters south of the park entrance is an upscale development featuring a beautiful restaurant, handicraft village, and comfortable bungalows set in landscaped lawns and tropical gardens. Wang Yom (tel. 055-642244) has 20 a/c cottages for 1,200B and 15 simple country huts for 400B. The adjacent Kang Sak Restaurant caters to tour groups.

Sawakhalok: Simple hotels in Sawakhalok, 20 km south of the ruins, include the **Muang Inn**

on Kasamrat Road and **Sri Sawan Hotel** on Thesaban Damri Road. Both have fan-cooled rooms from 130B and a/c rooms from 220B.

Si Satchanalai: The new town of Si Satchanalai is 12 km north of the ruins. **Kruchang Hotel,** 300 meters north of the Bangkok Bank, has rooms with bath from 120B.

Si Satchanalai is known for a locally woven silk embroidery called *tinchok* available from several shops such as Sathorn Silks at the far end of town. Another attraction is the famous Elephant Ordination Festival, held annually in early April during Buddhist Lent. It differs from other monk-initiation ceremonies in Thailand in that novices wear special *nak* costumes and elaborate *chada* headdresses while parading around town on the backs of elephants.

Transportation

The ruins at old Si Satchanalai are 56 km north of Sukhothai between the towns of Sawankalok and new Si Satchanalai. Buses to the ruins leave from the temple opposite Sukhothai's Chinawat Hotel and take two hours to reach the turnoff. The historical park is a 30-minute walk from the highway. Bicycles can be rented from a small shop near the bus stop. The latest gimmick is elephant rides starting from Wat Chang Lom.

Win Tours in Sukhothai has public buses and organized tours to Si Satchanalai. Tours are a more efficient way to see the ruins than public transportation, which is often slow and sporadic. An excellent option is to rent a motorcycle in Sukhothai and enjoy a great ride through the Thai countryside, though the heat can be overwhelming. Motorcyclists can easily visit in a single day the central ruins, kilns to the north, and southern monuments near Chaliang.

KAMPHANG PHET

Kamphang Phet is an old garrison town on the east bank of the Ping River some 85 km southwest of Sukhothai. Established in 1347 by King Li Thai, the small town served as a regional capital and one of the three primary cities of the Sukhothai Empire. It later operated as a buffer state between Sukhothai and Ayuthaya until 1378, when the final sovereign of Sukhothai surrendered to King Boromaraja.

The modern town of Kamphang Phet is ordinary, but to the north are several intriguing *wats* in various states of repair and restoration, a worthwhile museum, and other *chedis* and sculpture of great historical significance. None of the monuments compare with those in Sukhothai or Si Satchanalai, but visitors with a strong interest in Thai history and archaeology will enjoy exploring the ruins.

Attractions

Kamphang Phet is a long and narrow town with three distinct sections. To the south and along the river is the new town with all the businesses, hotels, and restaurants. The old city with the museum and a few modest ruins is centrally located inside the trapezoid walls. To the north and outside the city walls are the most impressive monuments, constructed by Buddhist monks away from the city to ensure a meditative environment.

Some of the monasteries predate even Sukhothai, but most display post-classical Sukhothai style, as Kamphang Phet served as a regional capital after the demise of Sukhothai and Si Satchanalai. Most of the monuments north of the old city walls were constructed by forest-dwelling monks in a Sinhalese style but were heavily restored during Ayuthayan occupation. Taken together with Sukhothai and Si Satchanalai, Kamphang Phet serves as the third most important historical and archaeological site in central Thailand.

A small tourist information office with handicraft displays, an aerial map of the region, and lacquerware for sale is on Thesa Road in the new town.

National Museum

Located in the old walled city behind Wat Pra Keo, Kamphang Phet National Museum provides a quick historical background and general orientation to the widely scattered monuments. The museum has a small but well-described assortment of artifacts from all periods of Thai art.

Ground Floor: The Khmer Shiva sculpture at the entrance is considered one of the masterpieces of bronzework in Thailand. The life-sized Bayon-style image was cast in 1510 during the reign of King Thammasokaraj, but tragically dismembered in 1886 by a German visitor who

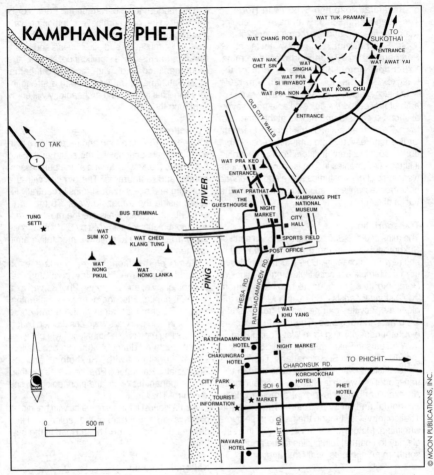

KAMPHANG PHET

intended to give the severed head and hands to the Berlin Museum. Quick actions by King Rama V saved the image, which was skillfully restored and returned in 1971 for the opening of the museum.

Among the other highlights on the ground floor are excellent descriptions of the three major U-Thong schools, Ayuthaya bronzes covered with fine patinas, and the superb U-Thong Buddha flanked by large busts at the right end of the hallway. Also note the five Chiang Saen images, two display windows of Lopburi Buddhas with authoritative explanations, Srivijayan vo-

tive tablets, Dvaravati stucco fragments, and a standing wooden Buddha from Ayuthaya.

Second Floor: Farm implements and handicrafts comprise most of the upper floor. The most significant items are the superb bronze torsos of Vishnu and Lakshmi discovered inside a local Shiva shrine.

The museum is open Wed.-Sun. 0900-1630.

Wat Pra Keo

Little remains of the old royal chapel except scattered foundations, a pair of rebuilt *chedis*, and cantilevered columns which once supported the religious structures. Behind the final northern *chedi* are several weathered Buddhas that have lost their skin and now resemble the abstract sculpture of Giacometti.

Admission to the monuments inside the city walls is 20B. The ticket includes admission to the ruins to the north and a discount for the National Museum.

Wat Prathat

A few hundred meters south of Wat Pra Keo stands the circular *chedi* of Wat Prathat, surrounded by columns and flanked by symmetrical *stupas*. The axial alignment of Wat Prathat and Wat Pra Keo shows the same concern for city planning practiced in Sukhothai and Si Satchanalai.

Encircling Wat Prathat and Wat Pra Keo are ancient moats and crenellated walls forming a trapezoidal shape that names the city: Kamphang ("wall") Phet ("diamond").

Wat Pra Non

Outside the old city walls and to the north, the temple of the reclining Buddha consists of a large *bot* in the foreground, the *mondop* sanctuary of the reclining Buddha in the middle, and a well-preserved *chedi* to the rear. The reclining Buddha has completely disappeared, though small signs scattered in the courtyard indicate locations of the image's neck, head, and feet. More impressive than the vanished Buddha are dozens of immense laterite columns and gigantic bases which once supported the boundary stones of the *bot*.

Wat Pra Si Iriyabot

This nearby sanctuary is dedicated to and named after the four attitudes of the Buddha: standing, walking, seated, and reclining. Wat Pra Si Iriyabot (Si means "Four," and Iriyabot is "Postures") consists of a frontal *viharn* and four-sided *mondop* where colossal images of the Buddha once filled the towering niches. The seated and reclining Buddhas have disappeared, but traces of the other two images can still be distinguished. Dominating the front niche is a Sukhothai-style walking Buddha that has been reduced to a middle torso, thigh sections, upper left arm, and head regions now being picturesquely eaten by weeds. To the rear is a standing Buddha considered one of the masterpieces of Sukhothai

art. The image remains in good condition except for small trees growing out from the shoulders, and chipping stucco revealing the laterite core of the chest.

Wat Singha

The adjacent Wat Singha features a large *chedi* flanked by a quartet of smaller monuments, the pediment of a *bot,* and a pair of *viharns.* Facing the front entrance are three standing Buddhas weathering into beautiful pieces of abstract art. The large Buddha sitting in the *bot* has been strangely restored with a crude nose and enormous right ear supported by a tower of rocks.

Wat Chang Rob

Situated on a hill a few hundred meters northwest with views over the valley is Wat Chang Rob, the "Temple Surrounded by Elephants." Beyond the remains of an old *bot* and *viharn* is one of the most impressive monuments in Kamphang Phet, an enormous *chedi* surrounded and supported by 68 elephants carved in the round. Flanking the elephantine buttresses are stucco figures of demons, divinities, and sacred bodhi trees. The

Giacometti Gautama

Phet parade

quality and elegance of decoration makes Wat Chang Rob a rare example of Sukhothai-style craftsmanship and one of the finest monuments in central Thailand.

Accommodations

Kamphang Phet has an inexpensive Chinese hotel near the bridge, and several midpriced hotels in the new section of town, about four km from the bus terminal. Minibuses from the bus terminal go across the river and down Ratchadamnoen Road to the hotels and information center.

The Guesthouse: A rather straightforward name for a relatively new guesthouse one block north of the roundabout that leads to the bridge. This friendly little spot is owned and operated by a Thai-farang couple who can help with sightseeing advice and bicycle rentals. Thesa Rd., Soi 2, tel. (055) 712295, 80-100B dorm, 140-300B private rooms.

Nittaya Prapa Hotel: The cheapest hotel in town was torn down a few years ago but may be

reconstructed just across the street, near the bridge and old town.

Korchokchai: Another one in the budget category; clean and comfortable. Ratchadamnoen Rd., tel. (055) 711247, 150-180B fan, 200-250B a/c.

Ratchadamnoen Hotel: As with most other hotels in Kamphang Phet, the Ratchadamnoen is an older property with both fan and a/c rooms in a variety of price ranges. Hotel owners assume that all Western travelers are rich and want an expensive a/c room rather than a cheaper fan-cooled room. 114 Ratchadamnoen Rd., tel. (055) 711029, 120-180B fan, 250-380B a/c.

Navarat Hotel: A few blocks south of the new town is a clean and comfortable hotel with 80 a/c rooms. 2 Soi Prapan Thesa Rd., tel. (055) 711106, fax (055) 711961, 350-500B.

Phet Hotel: The best hotel in town has 235 a/c rooms, a coffee shop, a small swimming pool, and Princess nightclub. 99 Vichit Rd., Soi 3, tel. (055) 712810, fax (055) 712917, Bangkok reservations tel. (02) 270-1520, 400-800B.

Chakungrao: Another upscale hotel with restaurant, tennis courts, and all a/c rooms with private bath. 123 Thesa Rd., tel. (055) 711315, fax (055) 711326, 400-1,000B.

Restaurants

Kamphang Phet has two night markets. The most convenient for those staying downtown is on Vichit Road just north of Charonsuk. Foodstalls are also found near the provincial hall and old city walls.

All of the hotels have coffee shops, but more memorable are the restaurants on the Ping River near the bridge.

The local specialty is the small egg banana *(kluay khai),* named after the fruit's short oval shape. A fruit festival held in September features food competitions, cultural performances, and a Miss Banana beauty pageant.

Transportation

Kamphang Phet is 85 km southwest of Sukhothai. Most visitors take a bus from Sukhothai and spend a single night before continuing northwest to Tak and Mae Sot. The bus terminal is inconveniently located three km from town on the west side of the river. Travelers coming from Sukhothai might get off the bus at the ruins and continue into town on a *samlor* or public minibus.

SUKHOTHAI

Thailand's original capital and birthplace of the Thai nation is one of the preeminent archaeological sites in Southeast Asia. Situated 450 km north of Bangkok where the northern mountains intersect the central plains, Sukhothai is to Thailand what Angkor is to Cambodia, Borobudur to Indonesia, and Bagan to Myanmar. Spread out over the 70-square-km national historic park are dozens of magnificently restored temples, palaces, Khmer *prangs,* gigantic Buddha images set with enigmatic smiles, and an outstanding museum safeguarding the grandeur of ancient Sukhothai.

The town also offers good guesthouses, friendly little cafes, and opportunities to become acquainted with the local Thais. Sukhothai is a convenient base for exploring the nearby ruins of Si Satchanalai to the north and Kamphang Phet to the south. It is the best stop between Bangkok and Chiang Mai—don't miss it.

History

Sukhothai was founded in 1238 by two rebellious Thai princes who liberated themselves from Khmer domination by establishing the first independent kingdom in Thailand. Although the city was but one of hundreds of small city-states in the region, it enjoyed a privileged location midway between the ancient empires of the Khmers to the east and Bagan to the west. Preaching a philosophy of political cooperation rather than military might, early kings of Sukhothai ("Dawn of Happiness") successfully united many of the small principalities between Laos and Malaysia to form the most brilliant empire in Thai history, and the only nation in Southeast Asia never to fall under foreign domination.

Under the enlightened leadership of King Ramkamheng (1278-1318), Sukhothai enjoyed a golden age of political, cultural, and religious freedoms. Ramkamheng was a clever warrior and brilliant scholar who devised the modern Thai alphabet from Mon and South Indian scripts, introduced a free-trade economic system, promoted Theravada Buddhism as taught by Sri Lankan monks from Nakhon Si Thammarat, and personally dispensed justice from his Manan-

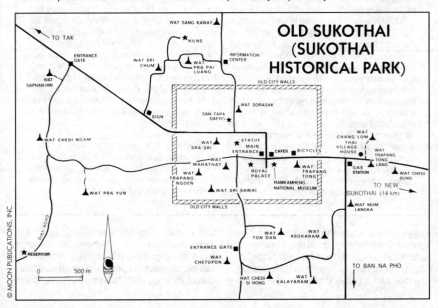

THE ARTS OF SUKOTHAI

Sukothai during the reign of Ramkamheng blossomed into a grand city of palaces, temples, monasteries, and wooden homes protected behind imposing earthen walls. Unlike Ayuthaya, which was destroyed by the Burmese, much of Sukothai's great architecture and art still stands in good condition. The only exceptions are the royal palaces, administrative buildings, and domestic homes which, according to religious protocol, were constructed entirely of wood and have completely disappeared.

Architecture

Sukothai's superb range of religious and secular buildings—from Khmer *prangs* covered with terrifying *nagas* to Sinhalese *chedis* capped with distinctive lotus-bud towers—form the country's most complete ensemble of traditional Thai architecture.

Sukothai architecture is a composite of styles from all regions in Asia. Apparently the rulers of Sukothai wanted to reproduce foreign models that had a reputation for holiness and beauty, and thereby enhance the sanctity of their empire by bringing together the most famous religious monuments of Southeast Asia. Some temples were inspired by octagonal-based Mon monuments constructed in Bagan during the 11th century. Sukothai's heritage as a Khmer outpost is reflected in the Cambodian-style tower-sanctuaries, which soon evolved into distinctive Siamese *prangs.* The most important examples of Khmer architecture are Wat Si Sawai, San Tapa Daeng, and Wat Pra Pai Luang, an ancient sanctuary symbolically surrounded by the primordial oceans favored by Khmer rulers. Another important contribution was made by large, bell-shaped Sri Lankan *stupas* supported by rows of sacred elephants. Constructed of brick and plaster, elephant effigies can be seen ringing the bases of Wat Chedi Si Hong, Wat Chang Rob, and Wat Chang Lom. The variety of religious architecture in Sukothai is nothing short of astounding.

Despite their inspiration from foreign models, the architects of Sukothai managed to vary the ele-

ments and create a fresh style of great originality. The Thai *chedi* is based on the massive *stupas* from Sri Lanka, but is smaller in size with more delicate proportions. Thai *prangs* may imitate Khmer towers, but have added rounded corners, more numerous terraces, and construction from brick and laterite rather than cut stone. Sukothai architects also created new elements such as lotus bud finials on the *chedis* and narrow-slit windows in the *viharns,* which provide an atmosphere of intimate solemnity.

Sculpture

Sukothai's crowning artistic achievement was stuccowork and sculpture—considered by most art historians as the pinnacle of Thai artistic achievement. An astonishing invention, Sukothai sculpture is best represented by the sensual, almost otherworldly walking Buddha who moves with his right foot forward and left hand raised in the gesture of *vitaka* mudra.

Often cast of bronze using the *cire perdu* (lost-wax) method, these graceful Buddha images are typically elongated with a flowing, androgynous body and hand raised in the attitude of calming fears and giving reassurance. The other arm hangs rhythmically and follows the sensual curve of the torso, while the head is shaped like a lotus bud capped by the flame of enlightenment. Perhaps the most intriguing feature is the enigmatic smile, reflecting deep inner contentment and spirituality. The total effect is one of marvelous power and sensitivity; rarely has any religious image so successfully conveyed the unspeakable faith of the creator.

Examples of this walking Buddha can be seen in the national museums in Sukothai and Bangkok, and in Sukothai on the walls of Wat Tuk and Wat Trapang Tong Lang.

Paintings

All paintings in Sukothai have been destroyed by the elements or stolen by art collectors, except for a handful of ornamental designs and stone engravings built into the stairway of Wat Sri Chum.

gasila Throne. According to Siamese traditions, citizens during his reign could ring a bell mounted outside his palace and ask for royal judgment.

Art and architecture reached their apogee in the mid-14th century under the reign of King

Maha Lithai (King Mahatammaraja I). By the end of the 14th century, Sukothai had become one of the largest Buddhist centers in the world. The city continued to prosper through a succession of six kings until losing a power struggle in

1378 with the rising kingdom of Ayuthaya. The last vestige of autonomy was lost in 1438 when the final king abdicated and Sukhothai came under the rule of an Ayuthayan prince.

The city lay abandoned until 1782 when a new line of kings, the Chakri dynasty, came to power in Bangkok. Anxious to legitimize their rule by honoring the past, Rama I gathered together hundreds of Sukhothai statues with which to fill the newly built monasteries in Bangkok; Sukhothai's largest bronze Buddha was installed inside Wat Suthat in Bangkok. Interest in Sukhothai was further revived by Rama IV who, after a visit in 1833, returned with two stone tablets establishing the mythology of Sukhothai.

In 1977 the Thai government, with assistance from UNESCO, began a restoration project that culminated in the completion of the Sukhothai National Historical Park in 1993.

Orientation

Sukhothai is divided into two sections. The unattractive new town has the hotels, restaurants, and transportation facilities. Old Sukhothai with the museum and ruins is 14 km west on the road to Tak. Old Sukothai comprises Sukothai Historical Park. Minibuses to the old city leave from across the bridge about 200 meters on the right side, just beyond the police station.

Ruins in old Sukhothai have been divided into five zones lettered A through E. Each zone now charges a 20B admission fee although the fee can sometimes be avoided by entering through the back roads.

Sukhothai's ruins are widely scattered and difficult to explore on foot except for the central monuments in Zone A. To visit the temples in a single day you must hire a *tuk tuk* at 30-50B per hour, a five-passenger taxi for 500B for a full day, or a bicycle for 20B from the stores just opposite the museum. Determined bicyclists who don't mind working up a sweat can reach all major monuments in a single day, including those to the far west and south. Ruins below are described with English-language signboards and are now safe to visit.

Please remember that all Buddhist images—no matter what their age or condition—are considered sacred objects to the Thais. Visitors should be properly dressed and never touch or climb any image. This is no joke! Several years

ago, a few Western missionaries—dressed only in shorts—posed for photographs on the shoulders of a Buddha. A national scandal erupted after the Bangkok photo lab turned the negatives over to a local newspaper, which then printed them on the front page. The Westerners were thrown in jail and deported from the country.

CENTRAL SUKHOTHAI—ZONE A

Visitors with limited time should first see the monuments in Zone A and Zone B to the north. Minibuses from the new town drop you at the entrance to the National Museum and admission gate into Zone A. Nearby restaurants provide the last chance for refreshment before you reach the foodstalls in the center of the park. Here in the park, try the *som tam* (spicy papaya salad) prepared Thai-style with peanuts and dried shrimp, *bu* with pickled crab, *bla laa* with fermented fish and eggplant, and *mangda* with smashed beetles or in a vegetarian style called *jae.*

Bicycles can be rented from Vitoon Guesthouse at the park entrance.

Remember the last bus back to town leaves at 1800.

Ramkamheng National Museum

Located inside the old city walls and just before the entrance gate to Zone A, Sukhothai's National Museum offers an outstanding introduction to the arts and crafts of Sukhothai and vassal cities of Si Satchanalai and Kamphang Phet. Inside the spacious building are Khmer statues, Sukhothai Buddhas, Sawankalok ceramics, and other archaeological artifacts gathered from central Thailand.

Facing the front entrance stands a bronze walking Buddha, considered the finest example of its kind in the country. Ground-floor highlights include a model of the ancient city (useful for orientation) and a replica of the four-sided pillar inscribed with Thailand's first written script. The original, now displayed in the Bangkok Museum, was reputedly discovered by King Rama IV while on pilgrimage during his monkhood.

Dozens of superb statues are exhibited upstairs. Buddha figures of the Sukhothai style are typically simple and unembellished images fashioned with slim torsos and serene expressions. A

A MYSTERY IN STONE

*C*arefully guarded inside the Sukothai National Museum is a four-sided pillar of dark stone covered with ancient inscriptions traditionally attributed to King Ramkamheng. One section relates that "Sukothai is good. There is fish in the water, rice in the fields, and the king does not levy tax on his subjects. Those who wish to trade are free to trade. The faces of the people shine bright." Identified as Stone Inscription Number 1, the stone also provides information on city planning, Buddhist law and philosophy, and the development of Thai script. Since its discovery in 1833 by King Mongkut during his monkhood, the stone has almost single-handedly created the mythology of Sukothai and the foundation of the Thai nation.

But is it real? Since the early 1990s, Ramkamheng's reputation as the mastermind of Sukothai's cultural development has come under increasing suspicion from both Thai and Western scholars. One skeptic is Dr. Piriya Krairiksh, a history professor from Thammasart University in Bangkok who claims the stone is a fake piece of historical writing created by King Mongkut sometime between 1851 and 1855. Understandably, Thais were very unhappy with the professor's assertion and reluctant to discuss the theory that has rocked the academic world.

Piriya, however, stands by his assertion based on textual analysis: the art and architecture mentioned are not supported by archaeological and historical evidence, the author freely lifted phrases verbatim from writings of later kings, and some inscription phrases are common to late-18th-century Thai literature. On the other hand, Western archaeologists and historians such as Betty Gosling and David Wyatt still feel the puzzling aspects are not sufficient to disprove the authenticity of the inscription. While the controversy remains unresolved, the academic community continues to debate the famous stone, on which rests the fundamental concepts of early Thai history.

small sample of Ayuthaya-style Buddhas are denoted by their regal attire and heavily bejeweled air of haughty arrogance.

Sculpture on the exterior grounds includes a rare phallic shrine of Khmer origins and stucco elephants removed from local shrines.

Ramkamheng National Museum is open Wed.-Sun. 0900-1600. Admission is 20B.

Statue of King Ramkamheng

West of the museum and down the road, Sukothai's great ruler sits on a replica of the historic Manangasila throne, discovered in 1833 by King Rama IV and now protected in the Grand Palace Museum in Bangkok. The original throne was installed in the sugar palm grove of the royal palace, and was charged with such magic and mystical potency as to make it an object of reverence to many Thais. Visitors can summon the ghost and ask for judgment from King Ramkamheng by ringing the bell on the right.

Wat Mahathat

Continuing west, Sukothai's principal monastery and royal temple was constructed by Sukothai's first king, Sri Indradita, but was substantially remodeled in 1345 by Sukothai's fourth ruler, King Lo Thai. The front sanctuary, with two rows of columns and a restored seated Buddha, dates from the Ayuthaya Period. Though largely in ruins, the complex once contained 185 *chedis* filled with funeral ashes of nobility, a dozen *viharns* for public worship, and a central *bot* gilded with stucco surrounded by reflective moats. Most of the stone structures have collapsed and all of the wooden buildings have been destroyed by fire, but large Buddhas and fine stucco remain intact within the royal sanctuary. The monastery reflects both Khmer and Sri Lankan architectural influences, as evidenced by the presence of Hindu sculptures and Buddhist finials.

Towering over the minor *chedis* is a large central tower erected by King Lo Thai to house two important relics—a hair and neckbone from the Buddha—brought back from Sri Lanka by a monk named Sisatta. The monument is chiefly noted for its bulbous, lotus-bud *prang* derived from Singhalese prototypes but copied throughout Thailand as a symbol of Sukothai's magical powers. The large bronze Buddha, which once sat in the principal *viharn* to the rear, was moved by King Rama I to Wat Suthat in Bangkok. Excellent views can be enjoyed from the summit of the central *chedi*.

The Fine Arts Department has extensively restored the monument and recast many of the better stucco friezes. The most artistically significant examples are the disciples walking in ritual procession around the base of the main *chedi,* and the demons, elephants, and lion-riding angels on the southern *chedi.*

Royal Palace

Across from Wat Mahathat lie the foundations of the old royal palace of King Ramkamheng. According to ancient principles, only temples and closely related monuments were built of stone, while royal palaces and domestic architecture were limited to wood which has disintegrated over the centuries. The controversial Stone Inscription 1 Pillar and Manangasila Throne were discovered here in 1833 by King Mongkut.

Wat Sri Sawai

Surrounded by two concentric enclosures and a deep moat, this well-preserved Khmer sanctuary was originally constructed by King Jayavarman VII (1181-1220) but left unfinished when the Khmer withdrew in the 13th century. As suggested by the exterior Hindu images, the temple first served as a Brahmanic sanctuary but was converted to a Buddhist monastery sometime in the 15th century.

The complex consists of a central nave and three brick *prangs* in a modified Angkor style embellished with both original and reconstructed *nagas* and *garudas.* Narrow, vertical windows pierce the walls, while the central tower has been subjected to cement restoration that imparts a hybrid effect and compromises its sense of antiquity. The overall effect remains powerful, though many wish the ruins had been left untouched except for necessary support work.

Wat Trapang Ngoen

Wat Trapang Ngoen ("Silver Lake Monastery") features a *chedi* of exceptional elegance that copies the lotus-bud tower of Wat Mahathat, and the remains of an ancient *viharn* and *bot.* Located on a small island in the center of Silver Lake, this complex serves as the focal point for Sukhothai's annual Loy Kratong Festival.

Wat Sra Sri

Simplicity of design and elegance of location make this one of the most attractive temples in Sukhothai. The central tower, with its bell-shaped dome, square base, and tapering spire, is typical of the Sinhalese style adapted by local Theravadan architects. Overlooking the expanse of still water is a large Buddha image, well restored by the Fine Arts Department. Also on the grounds is a small and very black Buddha in the walking style, an invention which epitomizes the ephemeral achievements of Sukhothai sculpture.

San Tapa Daeng

To the left of the road is a laterite temple characteristic of the Hindu type, with an elevated base and four porticoes which once held figures of the Lopburi school. Khmer statuary and

---

RESTORATION OR RUIN?

*W*hen French archaeologist Lucien Fournerau visited the ruins of the abandoned city of Sukothai in 1890, he was greeted with little more than dense jungle and ancient monuments almost completely buried under the thick foliage. Today, the monuments visited by Fournerau have been restored by the Fine Arts Department and transformed into Sukothai Historical Park.

The project is not without controversy. With little regard for historical tradition or artistic heritage, Thai archaeologists from the Fine Arts Department departed from standard international practice and substantially reconstructed many of the major monuments. Roads and walkways were laid that did not follow the ancient pathways, and an immense concrete plaza complete with reflecting pool and statue of Ramkamheng was erected near the museum. Even more disturbing were stucco details and plaster moldings, which have obliterated much of the historic detail on the surviving Khmer and Sukothai monuments.

Intense criticism also surrounds the restoration of Buddha statues with little, if any, regard for their artistic content. Many of the extremely rare images now sport remodeled, brightly smiling heads—a practice anathema to art historians and archaeologists. The Fine Arts Department— guardian of Thailand's ancient monuments— tragically sacrificed historical accuracy for an idealized version of the past.

Angkor Wat-style divinities uncovered inside the monument date from the reign of King Suryavarman II, in the first half of the 12th century.

Wat Sorasak

The Sri Lankan *chedi* of Wat Sorasak features a square base surrounded by elephant buttresses. A stone inscription dates the *chedi* to 1412. Minor monuments such as Wat Sorasak may seem trivial to the casual visitor, but a careful comparison of *chedi* shapes will reveal an amazing variety of architectural compositions.

NORTH OF THE CITY~ZONE B

Several of the finest monuments in Sukhothai are located in Zone B, just north of the old city walls. Entrance can be made through the gate near the new Information Center, or on the road leading to Wat Sai Chum.

Information Center

Near Wat Pra Pai Luang is a complex of attractive buildings opened by the Fine Arts Department in 1990. The center includes replicas of images now displayed in the national museums of Bangkok and Sukhothai, a small bookstore, a cafe, and an exhibition room with model displays of the old city.

Wat Pra Pai Luang

This 12th-century "Temple of the Great Wind," about one km north of Wat Mahathat, was originally constructed by the Khmers as a Hindu sanctuary in the center of their military stronghold. A fragmented Buddha image in the Khmer style of the reign of King Jayavarman VII, builder of Angkor Thom, was discovered in the *viharn* and moved to the Ramkamhaeng National Museum. Subsequent excavations also brought to light a Shiva lingam dating from the original Hindu temple. Thai kings later converted the complex into a Buddhist monastery second in religious importance only to Wat Mahathat. The monument was tragically pillaged by looters in the 1950s for its valuable collection of Hindu and Buddhist images, but was restored in 1988 with great sensitivity by the Fine Arts Department.

Entrance to the sanctuary passes over the foundations of a *viharn* and *chedi* once decorated with dozens of Buddha images fashioned in the preclassic style of the late 13th century. Most of the images have been vandalized or damaged beyond recognition, aside from the frontal walking image and standing Buddha on the northern wall. Behind the central *viharn* are the collapsed remains of two of the original three Khmer *prangs,* and a restored tower displaying corner *nagas* and a doorway lintel set with praying bodhisattvas and floral motifs.

Pottery Kilns

Archaeologists working near Sukhothai and Si Satchanalai have uncovered hundreds of massive kilns that once produced the most famous celadons in all of Southeast Asia. Traditionally it was believed the kilns were first used around 1300 by experienced Chinese potters brought to Sukhothai by King Ramkamhaeng after his second visit to China. However, recent research by a joint Thai-Australian team uncovered the existence of an indigenous ceramic industry predating the establishment of Sukhothai, making it doubtful the local pottery owes its origins to the Chinese.

Kilns were typically divided into three compartments—the fire area, baking oven, and flue—which produced a wide variety of ceramic goods such as terra-cotta tiles, balustrades, gables, dishes, and bottles fired with the bluish-green glazes that characterize Sawakhalok ceramics. An informative display on these enormous structures can be seen in the Sukhothai Museum. Several of the larger kilns in Si Satchanalai have been fully restored and opened to the public.

Wat Sri Chum

Sukhothai's most impressive Buddha, a monumental 15-meter image seated in the attitude of subduing Mara, dominates the rather dull square *mondop* in the northwest corner of old Sukhothai. The giant Buddha is believed to have been created in the late 14th century after Sukhothai came under the rule of the Ayuthaya Kingdom. A must-see for all visitors, the monument provides a lively scene as Thai pilgrims arrive to pray, make offerings, and burn incense in front of the enormous, superbly modeled hand.

The monument is chiefly noted for the slate slabs engraved with Jataka scenes lining the narrow and claustrophobic passageway leading to the roof. Illuminated only by small windows, these unusual carvings are of the highest artistic and literary value. Unfortunately, in December 1988 the passageway was sealed and closed to the public after a series of falls from the roof, and due to the Buddhist principle no human should elevate himself or herself above the position of the Buddha.

WEST OF THE CITY~ZONE C

Few visitors make the effort to visit the monuments west of the city in Zone C. While most of the temples are rather modest by Sukhothai standards, the region retains the timeless quality and sense of tranquillity lost from the renovated regions of Sukhothai. A bicycle ride along the dirt track leading from Wat Trapang Ngoen to Wat Chedi Ngam is a wonderful experience in the early evening hours. Children wave and suddenly you feel light-years away from the commercialism of historic Sukhothai. The entrance gate with its attendant fee near Wat Saphan Hin can be avoided by backtracking on the dirt road.

Wat Chedi Ngam
The dirt road winds past several modest temples set among rice and sugarcane fields before turning right to Wat Chedi Ngam. Located on a plateau up a short dirt road, this round Sinhalese-style *chedi* has been vandalized by thieves who burrowed a deep hole in the back side.

A left turn at the dusty intersection leads to an ancient reservoir once supplying water for the royal residence and kingdom of Sukhothai. The dam now supplies the modern city of Sukhothai and has been landscaped into a modern park with roving buffaloes and a few noodle stalls. To the right is a deserted modern *wat* and mountain spring reached by a stiff climb up 888 steps.

Wat Saphan Hin
Standing at the summit of Wat Saphan Hin ("Stone Causeway Monastery") is a 12-meter Buddha who overlooks and appears to bless the scattered ruins of ancient Sukhothai. During the reign of King Ramkamheng, the remote monastery once served as the seat of the Bud-

dhist patriarch and site of the annual Tod Kathin Festival. Today the sanctuary consists of a restored *viharn* and colossal image whose raised right hand signifies the mudra of granting peace. The brick-paved floor of the adjoining *chedi* has been raided by temple robbers—a depressing but familiar sight at many of the remote and unprotected temples in Sukhothai.

Wat Saphan Hin is reached by an exhausting climb up a jumble of stone slabs which give the temple its rather odd name. Determined hikers are rewarded with expansive views on clear days.

SOUTH OF THE CITY~ZONE D

Monuments to the south of Sukhothai are the last to be fully restored by the Fine Arts Department. While none of the temples compare to those in the central and northern zones, several monuments boast rare and fine stuccoes from the Sukhothai Period. The region has been left unguarded by the Fine Arts Department and pillage of ancient monuments is a common occurrence.

Entrance to Zone D is through the admissions gate near Wat Chetupon.

Wat Chetupon
Wat Chetupon is chiefly known for its pair of surviving 10-meter stucco Buddhas which capture the sides of the ancient *mondop*. The *mondop* once displayed the holy quartet of Buddha poses—standing, walking, seated, and reclining—but only the walking and standing Buddhas remain intact. The plaster walking image is a masterpiece of Sukhothai sculpture and among the finest stucco creations in Thailand. Adjacent images have been renovated by the Fine Arts Department.

Wat Chedi Si Hong
Chedi Si Hong provides an example of the tragic destruction wrought by artifact collectors throughout Southeast Asia. When I visited the monument in 1987, it was under careful reconstruction and well protected by guards and walls. After being fully restored in 1990, the tomb robbers arrived to strip the *chedi* of its stucco elephants, divinity figures, and well-crafted *garu-*

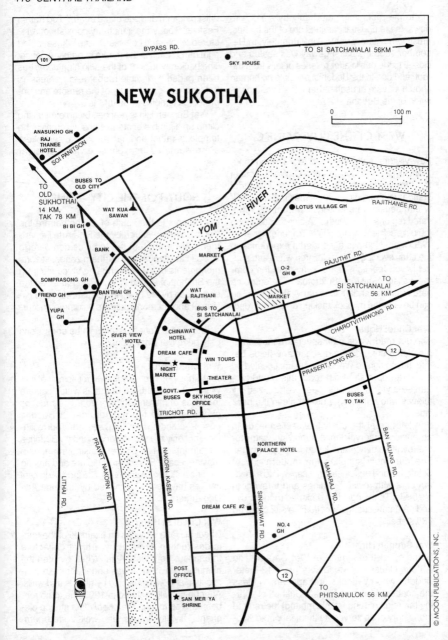

NEW SUKOTHAI

0   100 m

BYPASS RD.

TO SI SATCHANALAI 56KM

101

SKY HOUSE

ANASUKHO GH
RAJ THANEE HOTEL

SOI PANITSON

TO OLD SUKHOTHAI 14 KM, TAK 78 KM

BUSES TO OLD CITY

WAT KUA SAWAN

BI BI GH

BANK

YOM RIVER

LOTUS VILLAGE GH

RAJITHANEE RD.

MARKET

RAJUTHIT RD.

SOMPRASONG GH

FRIEND GH

BAN THAI GH

O-2 GH

MARKET

YUPA GH

WAT RAJTHANI

RIVER VIEW HOTEL

BUS TO SI SATCHANALAI

TO SI SATCHANALAI 56 KM

CHAROTVITHIWONG RD

CHINAWAT HOTEL

12

DREAM CAFE

WIN TOURS

NIGHT MARKET

PRASERT PONG RD.

THEATER

GOVT. BUSES

SKY HOUSE OFFICE

BUSES TO TAK

TRICHOT RD.

NORTHERN PALACE HOTEL

BAN MUANG RD.

DREAM CAFE #2

NAKORN KASEM RD.

SINGHAWAT RD.

NO. 4 GH

MAHARAJ RD.

LITHAI RD.

PRAVET NAKORN RD.

MOON

POST OFFICE

SAN MER YA SHRINE

12

TO PHITSANULOK 56 KM

© MOON PUBLICATIONS, INC.

das. During my most recent visit, the *chedi* lay abandoned, stripped of its artistic heritage, and largely forgotten: a monument to the destructive power of greed.

The dirt track continues past several small temples before intersecting the road north to the city.

EAST OF THE CITY~ZONE E

Monuments east of the historical park are relatively unrestored and rarely visited by foreign tourists. All can be quickly reached by bicyclists.

Wat Trapang Tong Lang

Hidden away among the rice and sugarcane fields is a monastery with four rows of laterite columns and square *mondop* renowned for its remarkable assemblage of stucco decorations. The southern panel shows the descent of Buddha to earth, surrounded by angels and bodhisattvas, to preach his doctrine after a three-month sojourn in the heavenly abodes. Superbly crafted with striking elegance and serenity, the image has traditionally been considered among the crowning masterpieces of Sukhothai art.

Tragically, the stucco relief has deteriorated and lost its artistic appeal through pillage, neglect, and the ebbs of nature. A reproduction is displayed in the national museums of Sukhothai and Bangkok.

Wat Chang Lom

Supported by a ring of 36 sculpted and partially ruined elephants, Wat Chang Lom ("Elephant Temple") features an upper balustrade with 19 Buddha niches filled with miniature figurines. The circular Sinhalese-style *chedi* is accessed by walking through the grounds of the Thai Village House.

Wat Chedi Sung

Easily visible from Wat Trapang Tong Lang, Wat Chedi Sung has been called the finest *chedi* of the Sukhothai Period. The bell-shaped superstructure and stepped platform cap a powerful base which together reflect the cultural minglings of Srivijayan and Sinhalese elements. An adjacent *viharn* is a later design of more classical style and harmonic proportions.

Wat Trapang Tong

Surrounded by a symmetrical pool called the Golden Lake, the *chedi* of Wat Trapang Tong contains an important Buddha footprint honored each year during Loy Kratong Festival. The holy impression was taken from Wat Pra Bat Yai where, according to Buddhist chronicles, King Li Thai discovered the image in 1360. To the west are a modern *bot, mondop,* and ruined laterite *chedi* of Sinhalese type.

Other Attractions

Wat Rajathani: Located in new Sukhothai on the eastern bank of the river is a modern temple and secondary school for boys. Visitors are welcome to wander around and feed the soft-shelled tortoises and giant carp. A popular time to visit is on *wan pra,* Buddhist holy days when pilgrims and Western visitors gather at sunrise to offer food donations to the monks.

San Mer Ya Shrine: King Ramkamheng's mother, now considered the patron saint of Sukhothai, is honored at a small shrine next to the post office. Visitors arriving at 1100 can watch Thais make offerings of pig heads, food, flowers, candles, and gold leaf which is stuck on the shrine.

Wat Thawit: Fifteen minutes by motorcycle from new Sukhothai is a small monastery where a local monk has constructed dozens of plaster images forming a sort of Buddhist Disneyland. Among the weird highlights are a sinner being tortured and a man fitted with a chicken head. The No. 4 Guesthouse has a map.

Ramkamheng National Park: A five-hour hike up a mountain to the southeast reaches a large reclining Buddha and cabins operated by the National Parks Division. The park preserves some of the last remaining rainforest in Central Thailand.

ACCOMMODATIONS

Budget

Most guesthouses and hotels are located in new Sukhothai, a nondescript town of concrete shophouses and streets too wide for the traffic. The great news is Sukhothai's rising popularity has brought almost a dozen new budget guesthouses and cafes. Most guesthouses are tucked away in quiet neighborhoods behind the market and across the river on the west side. All charge 60-100B s and 80-120B d.

Lotus Village: Started by four local schoolteachers and formerly known as the No. 4 Guesthouse (hence the name), this lovely teakwood home is clean, quiet, and immensely popular with budget travelers. Rooms downstairs are somewhat noisy because the plywood walls don't reach the ceiling, but terrific private rooms are located upstairs. Local travel tips are provided on the bulletin board. 170 Rajithanee Rd., tel. (055) 621484, fax (055) 621463, 120-180B.

Ban Thai Guesthouse: A fairly new, clean, friendly, and very popular guesthouse considered by many travelers the best choice in Sukothai. Especially welcome is the open patio and manicured garden overlooking the Yom River, and the dependable travel advice offered by the owners. 38 Pravet Nakorn Rd., tel. (055) 610163, 60-180B.

Friend Guesthouse: Another new guesthouse in the neighborhood across the river.

Sukothai beauty

Amenities include free bicycles, motorcycle rentals, and a small garden and dining area. Good choice if Ban Thai and Yupa are filled—a strong possibility during the high season early December to mid-January. 52/7 Soi Nissan, tel. (055) 610677, 60-140B fan, 220-280B a/c.

Yupa Guesthouse: Sukhothai's original guesthouse recently converted itself into a Thai cultural center and now only admits Thai students into its limited living spaces, though you may want to check out their range of classes, which range from painting and sculpture to lessons on Thai festivals and ceremonial customs. 44 Pravet Nakorn Rd., tel. (055) 612578.

Somprasong Guesthouse: Another new guesthouse has opened across the river near the former Yupa Guesthouse. Somprasong features shiny wooden floors, a large porch on the second floor, rooms separated by short walls and chicken wire, free bicycles, and motorcycles for hire. Once again, this is a traditional homestay where you'll become friends with the family. 32 Pravet Nakorn Rd., tel. (055) 611709, 50-100B.

Ban Thai Guesthouse: Another friendly little budget spot next door to the older Somprasong Guesthouse with the standard range of services and acceptable rooms. 34 Pravet Nakorn Rd., tel. (055) 610163, 60-250B.

Sky House: Though somewhat distant from downtown, Wattana's place is actually a modern townhouse converted into backpackers' quarters after the units failed to sell. Each room has a private bathroom and everyone gets a free bike. Wattana has plenty of motorcycles in excellent condition. The Sky office near the bus terminal provides free transportation and has a few rooms for 60B. 58 Bypass Rd., tel. (055) 612237, fax (055) 611212, 120-200B fan, 300-450B a/c.

Moderate

Several hotels fill the gap between the budget guesthouses and luxury hotels.

Chinawat Hotel: An old and shabby hotel but well located in the center of town near the bus terminals and restaurants. Chinawat serves as Sukhothai's information center, with a wide range of maps, brochures, and travel tips on buses and nearby attractions. The hotel has 40 rooms with private baths, a money-exchange service, overseas-calls facilities, laundry, organized tours, and a popular restaurant serving both Thai and Chinese dishes at reasonable cost. 1 Nakorn Kasem Rd., tel. (055) 611385, 100-180B, fan, 250-450B a/c.

River View: A somewhat luxurious hotel on the banks of the Yom River with clean rooms, a patio restaurant, and a lobby with TV. Pricier than other moderate hotels, but a big improvement in comfort and cleanliness. 92 Nakorn Kasem Rd., tel. (055) 611656, fax (055) 613373, 350-650B a/c.

Luxury
Northern Palace Hotel: The old Kit Mongkol was renovated and renamed several years ago, but looks like nobody has bothered to maintain the old hotel. Facilities in this somewhat overpriced place include a swimming pool, snooker parlor, and coffee shop doubling as a nightclub for evening entertainment. All rooms are a/c with private bath. 43 Singhawat Rd., tel. (055) 611193, 650-900B.

Raj Thanee: Also called the Ratchathani or Rajthanee, this once-great hotel has slipped in recent years though it still offers 86 a/c rooms with private bath and a comfortable coffee shop. 229 Charotvithiwong, tel. (055) 611031, fax (055) 612878, 650-900B.

Accommodations near Old Sukhothai
Most visitors stay in new Sukhothai, though a few guesthouses and hotels have opened recently near the ruins in the historic quarter.

Suwan Guesthouse: Just opposite the entrance to Sukhothai Historical Park are several rudimentary guesthouses with basic cubicles and bicycle rentals. Suwan, however, is an attractive teak guesthouse about 50 meters off the road.

Thai Village House: Sukhothai's old cultural center operates souvenir shops and a small zoo with peacocks and black bears. Wooden bungalows decorated in traditional Thai style are equipped with fan or a/c rooms with private or common baths. Beautiful teakwood dorms are also available at low cost. Thai specialties are served and an entertainment revue is sponsored in their restaurant during the tourist season. Located one km before old Sukhothai on the right side of the road. 214 Charotvithiwong, tel. (055) 612275, fax (055) 612583, 50B dorm, 400-600B private rooms.

Pailyn Sukhothai Hotel: Sukhothai entered the high-end market in early 1992 with the opening of the monstrous 238-room Pailyn Hotel located about four km before the entrance to the Sukhothai Historical Park. The Pailyn has several restaurants, a swimming pool, a disco, a fitness center, and conference facilities. There are no hotel shuttles into town or the ruins, but you can flag down any passing bus on the main highway. Charotvithiwong Rd., tel. (055) 613310, fax (055) 613317, 1,000-2,800B.

FOOD

All of the hotels in Sukhothai have restaurants, but smaller cafes offer a more unique culinary and aesthetic experience.

Night Market: Cheap eats are plentiful at the market which sets up nightly in the alley near Win Tours and the Rainbow Cafe. Popular dishes include *pad thai, gawetio thai nam* (noodle soup with peanuts and greens), *yam nom tok* (spicy beef), and *kanom jinn* (Thai spaghetti). Other choices include mussel omelettes, thick rice soups, ice *kachang,* and *won ton* dishes.

Takeaway Foodstalls: Across the street from the night market are several foodcarts that serve food to go wrapped in plastic bags. Simply point to the more appealing dishes and say *ha baht.* A grand total of 25B will guarantee a delicious and filling meal which you consume back at your guesthouse. Takeaway dishes are often more tasty and varied than stir-fried food from the night market.

Rainbow Cafe: Next to the bus station is a popular open-air restaurant with European fare, Thai noodles, and terrific ice cream. Rainbow is owned by the Chinawat Hotel and has an upstairs a/c dining room.

Dream Cafes: Sukhothai's most eclectic restaurants are the brainchildren of Ms. Chaba Suwatmaykin, who has outfitted her cafes with an amazing collection of memorabilia such as old telephone sets, bottles, and ancient gramophones. The small outlet across from Win Tours is an intimate coffee shop with a sign that reads, "The best coffee is as black as devil, hot as hell, pure as a fairy, fragrant as love."

Dream Cafe 2 at 861 Singhawat Rd. has a menu with over 200 items. Try *kao tang naa tang* (fried rice with pork and rambutan), *muu kam wan kanaa sop* (grilled pork with honey and vegetables), or *laab* (spicy northeastern-style minced pork).

ENTERTAINMENT

Nightlife in Sukhothai is limited to a pair of fan-cooled cinemas and folk entertainment in the Dream Cafe. Sukhothai has three swimming pools, 20B admission fee. Thai Village House on the road to the ruins has a nightly cultural show during the tourist season, including traditional dances and music put on by students from the local dramatic arts college.

A more rewarding cultural exchange is to volunteer to teach English to the wonderfully shy students at the International Friendship Center in Ampur, down the road toward Phitsanulok. As mentioned above, Yupa Guesthouse now sponsors weekly Thai cultural programs at reasonable cost.

SHOPPING

Sukhothai is hardly a shopper's paradise, though the increasing number of Western visitors has helped revive some of the traditional crafts.

Markets: A very picturesque and lively farmers' market operates daily in new Sukhothai near the river and behind the modern temple of Wat Rajathani. The nearby indoor market has a fish section, takeaway foodstalls, and fruit vendors on the northern side. A bullock and buffalo market is held on Friday morning near the Caltex station and Father Ceramics.

Other markets are located outside new Sukhothai. A large public market is held on Thursday in the big wooden building near the Ramkamheng Museum in the old city. Markets are also held on Tuesday in Ban Kwang, Sunday in Ban Gluay, and Monday in Ban Suan.

Teak Carving
Several families in the village near the ruins continue to carve teakwood figures in styles dating back to the days of King Ramkamheng. Walk east from the National Museum and wander up the second street on the left. None of the houses have signs since taxes are collected from signposted businesses. A large collection of teak carvings is sold from the shop at the intersection to Wat Sri Chum.

Ceramics
The best ceramics in Sukhothai are sold at the house of Lung Fang inside the southern wall of the old city. Lung Fang has a small ceramics museum and new creations recognized by the royal family. The Kingdom of Father Ceramics in new Sukhothai is an expensive place patronized by group tours.

TRANSPORTATION

Getting There
Sukhothai is 447 km from Bangkok in the heart of central Thailand.

Air: Bangkok Airways has one daily flight from Bangkok to the new airport at Sukothai, which now serves as their regional hub. You can also fly daily from Chiang Mai. You can take a rather expensive shuttle into town, a taxi, or walk to the highway and flag down a passing bus.

Train: The nearest train terminus is at Phitsanulok, 60 km east of Sukhothai. From the Phitsanulok train station, bus 1 reaches the main bus terminal where buses depart hourly to Sukhothai. Buses can also be hailed in Phitsanulok at the Naresuan Bridge near Wat Mahathat.

Bus: Public buses from Bangkok to Sukhothai depart 10 times daily from the Northern Bus Terminal and take about seven hours. The most convenient departures are early in the morning before 0900, or overnight buses leaving 2200-2300. Companies running a/c coaches include Win Tours (tel. 02-271-2984) and Phitsanulok Yanyon Tour (tel. 02-278-2063). Travel agents in Bangkok sell tickets which include pickup from your hotel.

From Chiang Mai, buses leave hourly from the government bus terminal and take about five hours to reach Sukhothai. Private minibus companies from Chiang Mai often include a brief stop at a temple near Lampang and terminate at the Sky House in Sukhothai.

Getting Away
Three bus companies are located in the center of Sukhothai. Ordinary buses operated by the government transportation company (Bor Kor Sor) leave 12 times daily for Bangkok and eight times daily for Chiang Mai. Eight of the 12 departures to Bangkok are 2100-2350. Their small office is located in the alley near the night market. Bor Kor

Sor buses are much cheaper and almost as fast as private bus companies.

Win Tours has three a/c buses daily for Bangkok and Chiang Mai. Win also sells tickets to Chiang Rai, Si Satchanalai, and Phitsanulok. Seats should be booked well in advance, especially for the overnight buses. Phitsanulok Yanyon Tour in the Chinawat Hotel has five buses daily to Bangkok.

Public buses to most destinations near Sukhothai leave from the government bus terminal. Buses to Si Satchanalai and Sawankalok leave hourly from the corner near Wat Rajathani, just down from the Chinawat Hotel. Buses to Tak leave on Ban Muang Road, four blocks up the main street.

Buses to the ruins in old Sukhothai leave from the dirt yard on the right side of the road, 200 meters across the bridge. Don't get suckered into an expensive *tuk tuk* or taxi ride.

The last bus from old Sukhothai back into town leaves at 1800; otherwise, you'll need to hitch or pay 80B for a *songtao* charter.

WESTERN BORDERLANDS

TAK

Tak is a provincial capital 423 km north of Bangkok on the east bank of the Ping River. The town is at the intersection of Highway 1, which connects Bangkok with Chiang Mai, and the Pan-Asian Highway which, in a more perfect world, would link Singapore with Istanbul.

Tak is laid out in a grid pattern with the central business district wedged between Highway 1 and the Ping River. Business activity is centered along Jompol Road, an absurdly wide boulevard not unlike the oversized road through Mae Sai. Inexpensive hotels and cafes are located on the more cozy lanes of Taksin and Mahathai Bamroong.

Tak is rarely visited by Western tourists, though the town has some outstanding teakwood architecture and is known throughout Thailand as the birthplace of King Taksin. The town also serves as a useful base for excursions to the hilltribe center and waterfalls of Lansang National Park (19 km west), the traditional riverine settlement of Ban Tak (23 km north), and water sports at Bhumibol Dam (65 km north), the largest artificial lake in Southeast Asia.

The TAT office (tel. 055-514341, fax 055-514344) is behind the Provincial Hall by the bus station.

Wooden Architecture

Tak is a western outpost located near the vast teak forests of Myanmar. For several centuries, the town has served as a major teak trade center and conduit for logs harvested and then floated down the Ping River to Bangkok. This abundance of teak has traditionally permitted residents to construct their homes and businesses from the valuable wood.

Today, Thais come to Tak to purchase these rare teak homes, dismantle them, and move them to other regions in the country. Despite the destruction and removal of many homes, Tak still boasts several streets and neighborhoods blessed with old teakwood structures carved and assembled with great skill. Both Mahathai Bamroong and Taksin Roads have fine examples, especially in the northern stretches near Thai Air and Wat Bot Mani Sibunruang. An amazing collection of teak homes is located in the small alleys just south of the town park.

Another location known for traditional teakwood homes is the small village of Ban Tak, 23 km north of Tak on the banks of the Ping River. Ban Tak also has several old *chedis* and monasteries constructed in the Sukhothai Period during the reign of King Ramkamheng.

Wat Bot Mani Sibunruang

Located in the north end of Tak is a gold-topped *chedi* and northern-style chapel containing Pra Buddhamon, an early-Sukhothai image considered among the finest examples of its type.

King Taksin Shrine

Across the road from Wat Bot Mani Sibunruang is a small modern chapel dedicated to the early Chakri king who hailed from Tak. The greatly revered king sits sword in hand, backed by a romantic painting of himself. A celebration in his

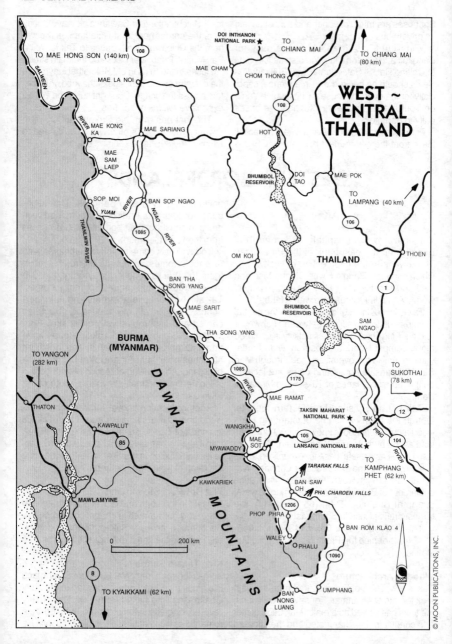

WEST ~ CENTRAL THAILAND

TO MAE HONG SON (140 km)
108
DOI INTHANON NATIONAL PARK ★
TO CHIANG MAI
TO CHIANG MAI (80 km)
MAE LA NOI
MAE CHAM
CHOM THONG
SALWEEN RIVER
MAE KONG KA
MAE SARIANG
108
HOT
MAE SAM LAEP
BHUMIBOL RESERVOIR
DOI TAO
MAE POK
TO LAMPANG (40 km)
SOP MOI
BAN SOP NGAO
YUAM RIVER
NGAO RIVER
1085
106
THANLWIN RIVER
OM KOI
THAILAND
THOEN
1
BAN THA SONG YANG
BHUMIBOL RESERVOIR
MAE SARIT
TO YANGON (282 km)
MOI RIVER
THA SONG YANG
SAM NGAO
BURMA (MYANMAR)
DAWNA
1085
1175
TO SUKOTHAI (78 km)
THATON
MAE RAMAT
TAKSIN MAHARAT NATIONAL PARK ★
TAK
12
KAWPALUT
85
WANGKHA
105
LANSANG NATIONAL PARK ★
PING RIVER
104
MYAWADDY
MAE SOT
TO KAMPHANG PHET (62 km)
KAWKARIEK
TARARAK FALLS
MAWLAMYINE
BAN SAW OH
PHA CHAROEN FALLS
0   200 km
PHOP PHRA
1206
BAN ROM KLAO 4
8
WALEY
PHALU
1090
TO KYAIKKAMI (62 km)
BAN NONG LUANG
UMPHANG
MOUNTAINS

© MOON PUBLICATIONS, INC.

PHAHOLYOTHIN RD.

TAK

★ KING TAKSIN SHRINE

TO CHIANG MAI 252 KM

TO SUKOTHAI 80 KM →

WAT BOT MANI SIBUNRUANG ▲

BUS TERMINAL

CITY HALL AND TOURIST OFFICE ■

TEAK HOUSES ★

TEAK HOUSES ★

■ A/C BUSES

HANGING BRIDGE

PING RIVER

RIMPING RD.

CHOMPOL RD.

TAKSIN RD.

■ Thai Airways

● VIANG TAK 1 HOTEL

LAGOON RESTAURANT

CITY MARKET ★

TAK HOTEL ●

■ THEATER

★ MARKET

● SANGUAN THAI HOTEL

● MAE PING HOTEL

★ LAKE PAVILION

● VIANG TAK 2 HOTEL

■ FF FAST FOOD

MAHATHAI BAMROONG RD.

PARK

HOSPITAL ■

①

MOON

0   100 m

TEAK HOUSES ★

TO BANGKOK 423 KM

← TO MAE SOT 80 KM

© MOON PUBLICATIONS, INC.

honor is held in Tak each year in early January. Pilgrims often come here to burn incense and shake fortune-telling sticks.

Bhumibol Dam

The largest lake in Southeast Asia was created in the early 1960s with the construction of Bhumibol Dam, 65 km north of Tak. The resulting Mae Ping Lake reaches from the dam northward to Lamphun and Chiang Mai, its construction submerging many villages, ancient temples, and tracts of forest which rise eerily from the rib-

bon of water. For 100-250B, visitors can cruise the waters with the Education Tour Center (Bangkok tel. 02-221-5183) or the *Far East Queen* (Bangkok tel. 02-511-1872), a 78-meter ship fitted with observation rooms, restaurant, and 46 a/c cabins. The cruise goes 140 km north from the dam to the self-help settlement at Dai Tao.

Accommodations

Hotels are situated on the three main roads which run parallel to the river.

Tak Hotel: A popular choice for budget travelers with 29 fan-cooled rooms. 18 Mahathai Bamroong Rd., tel. (055) 511234, 150-200B.

Mae Ping Hotel: Down the road is a slightly larger hotel with somewhat cheaper rooms. 231 Mahathai Bamroong Rd., tel. (055) 511807, 120-150B.

Sanguan Thai Hotel: Located near the central market and shopping district. 619 Taksin Rd., tel. (055) 511265, 120-180B fan, 300-350B a/c.

Viang Tak 1 Hotel: Top-end choices are the two branches of the Viang Tak. The original branch has 100 a/c rooms in an older neighborhood. 25 Mahathai Bamroong Rd., tel. (055) 511910, fax (055) 512169, 650-850B.

Viang Tak 2 Hotel: The best hotel in Tak is located on the main drag near the river. Facilities include a comfortable restaurant, small nightclub, and dining veranda overlooking the river. Chompol Rd., tel. (055) 512207, Bangkok reservations tel. (02) 233-2690, 650-850B.

Bantak Youth Hostel: A new and very atmospheric youth hostel recently opened in a traditional Thai village 20 kms north of Tak on the highway to Chiang Mai. Operated by a Thai-farang couple, this cozy little spot (holds only eight visitors) is on the west side of the Ping River, one km from the village center. Take a bus to Bantak, then walk across the bridge and turn right up to the hostel. Bantak, tel. (055) 591286, 125B dorm, 295B private room.

Restaurants

Foodstalls are located in the central market and, in the evenings, across from the Mae Ping Hotel. **Far Far Fastfood,** across from the Viang Tak 2 Hotel, has great dishes in a clean environment. The restaurant inside the **Viang Tak 2** is expensive but the most elegant in town. Tour groups often stop at the **Lagoon Restaurant** surrounded by giant water lilies on Hwy. 1. Across the road is the lagoon with pavilions and gardens.

Transportation

Most visitors reach Tak by bus from Sukhothai or Kamphang Phet. The bus terminal is northeast of town across the ultra-broad Highway 1. *Songtaos* shuttle into town. Air-conditioned buses to Bangkok can be booked from the private bus office off Mahathai Bamroong Road just north of the Viang Tak 1 Hotel.

MAE SOT

Mae Sot is one of the most intriguing towns in the region and a great place to experience Thailand off the beaten track.

The bustling town, 80 km west of Tak and just five km from the border to Myanmar, has found prosperity by trading and smuggling goods between the two countries, augmented by a moderate amount of tourism. Initial impressions are that Mae Sot has little of real interest aside from some dusty Burmese architecture, food, and customs that have spilled over the border. A closer look reveals a complex society composed of Burmese, Thais, Chinese, and tribal minorities such as Karen and Hmong.

Mae Sot also benefits from its isolated location and almost complete absence of Western tourists. As most of Thailand becomes firmly entrenched on the international tourist circuit, visitors who want to understand the original charms of the country must venture further into the more remote regions. Mae Sot fits the bill. A few *farangs* will be encountered at the morning market and busloads of Thai tourists occasionally come to dine and shop, but Mae Sot essentially remains a remote destination rarely visited by outsiders.

The opening of the road from Mae Sot north to Mae Sariang now presents a unique way to reach Chiang Mai from central Thailand. The journey is long and rough but covers some beautiful countryside rarely seen by Western travelers. From Mae Sariang, buses continue to Mae Hong Song, Pai and, finally, Chiang Mai.

Temples

Wats and monasteries in Mae Sot reflect Burmese influence brought across the nearby border.

Wat Chumphon Khiri: The largest *chedi* in town, and visible from the morning market, is covered by brass brickwork and surrounded by 20 smaller plaster *chedis.*

Wat Mae Sot Luang: Adjacent to this minor temple are a small *chedi* and reclining Buddha completely covered with shiny brass plates. The accompanying monastery holds bronze Buddhas and three small alabaster images in display cases to the right.

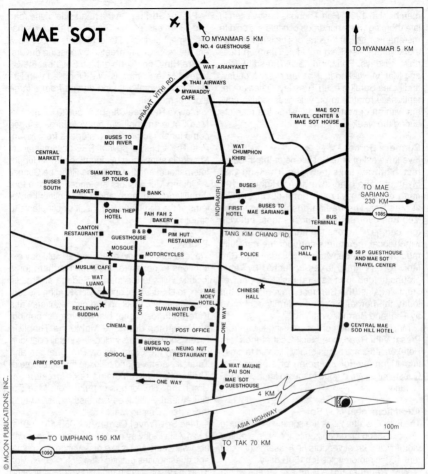

MAE SOT

TO MYANMAR 5 KM
NO. 4 GUESTHOUSE

TO MYANMAR 5 KM

WAT ARANYAKET

PRASAT VITHI RD.

THAI AIRWAYS

MYAWADDY CAFE

MAE SOT TRAVEL CENTER & MAE SOT HOUSE

BUSES TO MOI RIVER

CENTRAL MARKET

WAT CHUMPHON KHIRI

INDRAKIRI RD.

BUSES SOUTH

SIAM HOTEL & SP TOURS

MARKET

BANK

BUSES

TO MAE SARIANG 230 KM

FIRST HOTEL

BUSES TO MAE SARIANG

1085

PORN THEP HOTEL

FAH FAH 2 BAKERY

BUS TERMINAL

CANTON RESTAURANT

B & B GUESTHOUSE

PIM HUT RESTAURANT

TANG KIM CHIANG RD.

MOSQUE

MOTORCYCLES

POLICE

CITY HALL

58 P GUESTHOUSE AND MAE SOT TRAVEL CENTER

MUSLIM CAFE

WAT LUANG

ONE WAY

MAE MOEY HOTEL

CHINESE HALL

RECLINING BUDDHA

SUWANNAVIT HOTEL

ONE WAY

CINEMA

POST OFFICE

CENTRAL MAE SOD HILL HOTEL

BUSES TO UMPHANG

NEUNG NUT RESTAURANT

SCHOOL

ARMY POST

ONE WAY

WAT MAUNE PAI SON

MAE SOT GUESTHOUSE

4 KM

ASIA HIGHWAY

0   100m

TO UMPHANG 150 KM

1090

TO TAK 70 KM

© MOON PUBLICATIONS, INC.

Wat Maune Pai Son: East of the Siam Commercial Bank is another worthwhile temple which features a square building capped with hundreds of small *chedis,* similar to the Lohaprasat in Bangkok.

Markets

One of the chief attractions in Mae Sot is the morning market in the narrow alleys near the Porn Thep Hotel and the central market on the southern road. Both are filled with a gaggle of Thai, Burmese, Chinese, and Muslim traders who compete with the gem vendors who operate from nearby shops. Judging from the license plates of cars, gem buyers arrive from all over Southeast Asia to bargain for blue sapphires from Kanchanaburi, white sapphires from Chanthaburi, and the highly prized light-colored stones smuggled in from Myanmar. Visitors are welcome to wander around, but only professionals should make sizable purchases.

A very colorful cattle market is held one km from Mae Sot at Poe Thong every Wednesday and Sunday morning. Established by a local cow merchant in 1981, Poe Thong is best visited in late morning when hundreds of cattle are sold to merchants from all regions of Thailand. Buffalo markets are also held in Udon Thani on Buddhist holidays, Petchburi each Thursday, Chiang Mai on weekends, Phayao every Monday, and Maha Sarakm each Tuesday. Dates are intentionally rotated to provide prospective buyers with an opportunity to visit all the markets during the week.

Burmese Border

Five km west of Mae Sot is one of the three direct highway links between Thailand and Myanmar, the other two being Highway 106 north of Chiang Mai and north of Chiang Rai at Mae Sai. The trading post is commercialized and overrun with tourist shops, but visitors can gaze across the narrow Moi River to watch local merchants conduct the carefully regulated trade between Myawaddy and Rim Moi. At one time, taxes collected by rebel groups helped fund several resistance movements against the Burmese government, but today the border crossing is firmly controlled by Thai and Burmese officials.

Minibuses to the border crossing leave from Prasat Vithi Road, one block west of the Siam Hotel. Visitors are occasionally allowed to cross into Myanmar for shopping or sightseeing. Guesthouses are a good resource for the current situation.

Attractions near Mae Sot

The following attractions are somewhat difficult to visit except on an organized tour or with a rented motorcycle. Street vendors on Prasat Vithi Road rent 100cc motorcycles for 150B daily.

Wat Wattanaram: A Burmese temple with a large alabaster Buddha is three km west of Mae Sot on the road to the border. The *wat* is marked with an English-language sign.

Wat Prathat Doi Din Kui: Twelve km northwest of town and on a small hill is a forest monastery with a hanging rock shrine similar to the monument in Kyaiktiyo, Myanmar. Motorcyclists should turn right at Ban Mae Tao, four km west of Mae Sot on the road to the border.

Pratat Hin Kiew: Twelve km east of Mae Sot on the road to Tak stands a small hillside shrine with panoramic views over Mae Sot valley.

Pravor Shrine: On the north side of the road and 18 km east of Mae Sot toward Tak is a small monument dedicated to local spirits whose powers are respectfully greeted by passing drivers.

Pra Hin Oon: North of Mae Sot, near the village of Mae Ramat, is Wat Don Keo with Pra Hin Oon, a small Buddha carved from a large block of marble.

Mawka Refugee Camp: About 30 km north of Mae Sot is an unofficial but very large refugee camp inhabited by Karen refugees from Myanmar. The subject of several BBC documentaries, Mawka is supported by donations from Hunger International and the Burmese Refugee Council in Chiang Mai. Visitors are encouraged to tour the village and learn about the political problems of the displaced Karens; it's acceptable to simply walk in.

Tours

Travel agencies now offer several multi-day excursions to nearby attractions. Northern tours include visits to the marble Buddha at Pra Hin Oon, to U Su Cave, and to Mon Krating Resort; elephant rides; trekking and overnight stay at a Karen refugee camp; black-market shopping; and a raft trip down the Moi to the Thanlwin River. Southern tours include a longtail boat journey down the Klong River, Pra Charoen and Tararak waterfalls, and trekking through some of Thailand's last remaining teak forests near Umphang. Trekking is popular from Mae Sot since nearby hilltribes are less exploited than those near Chiang Mai.

Mae Sot Travel Center (tel. 055-531409) at 14/21 Asia Highway next to the radio station can help with tours and make reservations at resorts and guesthouses outside Mae Sot, such as Mon Krating Resort, Umphang Hill Resort, Umphang Guesthouse, Mae Salid Guesthouse, and Sob Moei House. They also run a small guesthouse. Ask for Mr. Asun.

SP Tours: This travel agency is chiefly used by tour groups, but they also assist individual travelers with bus tickets and trekking information. Siam Hotel, 185 Prasat Vithi Rd., tel. (055) 531376.

Mae Sot Conservation Tours: Mr. Wiboon operates a TAT-approved tour company and a small guesthouse a few doors down from the Pim Hut Restaurant. Wiboon specializes in rafting through class 2 and 3 rapids, and

BRIDGE OVER TROUBLED WATERS

*B*ig changes are planned for Mae Sot. In 1988, General Chavalit Yongchiyut proposed constructing a bridge across the Moi River to connect Mae Sot with Myawadday and the road to Mawlamyine and Yangon in Myanmar. The 430-meter concrete bridge is intended to end the black-market racketeering that has long dominated the Mae Sot economy, and to resolve the political conflicts between the Thai government and the military junta in Yangon.

Until 1988, Thai government policy had been to support the ethnic rebels fighting the Burmese government along the border regions. These separatist groups—the Karens, Mons, Shans, and Karenni—formed a political buffer zone that kept the Burmese military occupied with their domestic affairs. The Thai government switched gears in 1988 and announced formal support of Burmese programs against the ethnic rebels, a political decision that culminated in the overthrow of Manerplaw in 1995

(see the special topic **The Fall of Manerplaw**).

The Australians, Japanese, and Americans were all approached by Bangkok to help fund the "Friendship" bridge from Mae Sot to Myanmar. After each country declined, the Thai government decided to fund the US$3.5 million dollars needed for the bridge. The government's decision was warmly greeted by the people of Mae Sot, who had seen their economic fortunes collapse after a 1984 ban ended border trade via Mae Sot. The bridge opened in 1999, although as of this writing, it remains closed to Western travelers. Travelers may cross into Myanmar and visit the dusty trading market at Myawaddy for Burmese handicrafts and wacking great cheroots. Judging from recent actions by the Burmese government, visitors may one day be allowed to continue west to Mawlamyine and on to Yangon. For the first time in history, an Asian highway connecting Singapore with Istanbul appears to be more than a dream.

---

trekking around the Umphang region. B&B Guesthouse, 415/17 Tang Kim Chiang Rd., tel. (055) 532818.

Myawaddy Cafe: Not really a tour agency, but a great source of information from owners Doi and Roger. The cozy shop also sells Burmese lacquerware, trades used books, and serves some of the best Western food (omelettes, burgers, fries, milkshakes, cakes) between Umphang and Mae Sariang. 100/22 Prasat Vithi Rd., tel. (055) 532549.

Budget Accommodations

Mae Sot has a half dozen hotels catering to Thai merchants and a small number of Western visitors.

No. 4 Guesthouse: Backpackers generally stay in this lovely teakwood house west of town in a quiet residential neighborhood. The owners (the four schoolteachers from Sukothai) can help with free maps and information on trekking in nearby provinces. 736 Indrakiri Rd., 40B dorm, 60-90B.

SP Guesthouse: Mae Sot Travel Center operates a small guesthouse on the highway just outside town. 14/21 Asia Hwy., tel. (055) 531409, 40-60B.

Mae Sot Guesthouse: Formerly located in the No. 4 Guesthouse, this original backpackers' place has moved east to a new spot near the unique Wat Maune Pai Son. The Wild West feeling of the region is emphasized by the old wagon wheels embedded around the garden area, and the hospitality of owner Khun Too, who arranges three-day treks to Umphang that include an elephant ride, rafting on bamboo boats, and waterfalls. Figure on 3,000B for the tour. 208/4 Indrakiri Rd., tel. (055) 532745, 100-200B.

B&B Guesthouse: Right near the market and Western-style cafes is a somewhat utilitarian guesthouse owned by the helpful Mr. Wiboon, owner of Pim Hut Cafe and Mae Sot Conservation Tours. The place lacks the character of Mae Sot and No. 4 guesthouses, but rooms are clean and the location is very convenient. 415/17 Tang Kim Chiang Rd., tel. (055) 532818, 150-200B.

West Frontier Guesthouse: A relatively new place in a southern neighborhood with helpful managers who arrange river rafting excursions and extended treks. 18/2 Bua Khun Rd., tel. (055) 532638, 80-150B.

Suwannavit Hotel: The Suwannavit and adjacent Mae Moey Hotels bridge the gap between the Mae Sot Guesthouse and midpriced hotels. 1 Soi Wat Luang, tel. (055) 531162, 100-160B.

Moderate Accommodations

First Hotel: An old favorite opposite the former bus terminal. Rooms are large and clean with private bath. Keys are provided on small piston rods. 444 Indrakiri Rd., tel. (055) 531233, 180-280B fan, 320-400B a/c.

Siam Hotel: The most popular midpriced hotel in Mae Sot has a shopping center, cafe, and outlet for SP Tours. 185 Prasat Vithi Rd., tel. (055) 531376, 180-240B fan, 360-420B a/c.

Luxury Accommodations

Mae Sod Hill Hotel: A luxury hotel complete with swimming pool, two tennis courts, coffee shop, and disco. Each a/c room includes TV, refrigerator, and telephone. 100 Asia Hwy., tel. (055) 532601, fax (055) 532600, Bangkok reservations tel. (02) 541-1234, 1,100-1,600B.

Restaurants

Mae Sot's ethnic community provides a great deal of variety in the various cafes and restaurants around town.

Streetstalls: Several decent stalls are located near the Siam Hotel on Prasat Vithi Road. The night market, surprisingly, is quite disappointing.

Muslim Cafe: A great little cafe filled with local Muslims is just opposite the town mosque. Try the *samosas,* curries, freshly baked breads, steaming milk, and vegetarian specialties. The orthodox Muslims who attend meetings and prayer sessions in the nearby mosque are happy to debate local political and religious issues with you. Inexpensive.

Pim Hut: A comfortable place popular with backpackers and local students. The large English-language menu features pizzas, buffalo steaks, Thai and Chinese specialties, and delicious ice creams. Tang Kim Chiang Rd. Inexpensive.

Fah Fah 2 Bakery: Freshly baked breads, croissants, and desserts, plus Western breakfasts and Thai dishes. Tang Kim Chiang Rd. Inexpensive.

Myawaddy Cafe: One side is a handicraft shop selling Burmese lacquerware, while the remaining space is a popular cafe serving dishes prepared by Ms. Doi and her husband, Roger. Doi's "Magic Jeanie Burger" (bacon cheeseburger), tuna sandwich on wheat toast, and nightly Western dinner enjoys a loyal following among backpackers, foreign volunteer workers, and a few upscale tourists. 100/22 Prasat Vithi Rd. Inexpensive.

Neung Nut Restaurant: A pseudo-Western cafe and nightclub with live music and fiery Thai food. The Christmas lights mounted on the wagon wheels provide a nice touch in the evenings. Indrakiri Rd. Moderate.

Canton Restaurant: The Canton is considered the best restaurant for Cantonese dishes in a reasonably comfortable environment. Moderate.

Transportation

Mae Sot is 80 km west of Tak and 510 km northwest of Bangkok.

Air: Thai Airways flies to Mae Sot from Bangkok four times weekly at 1120, and four times weekly from Chiang Mai. The airport is three km west of town on the Asia Highway. The airport shuttle into town costs 20B. The Thai Airways office (tel. 055-531730) is near the Myawaddy Cafe at 76/1 Prasat Vithi Rd.

Bus: Most travelers reach Mae Sot by bus from Tak or Sukothai, though direct service is available from the Northern Bus Terminal in Bangkok.

There are at least four bus/minitruck stations in town. The government bus station for service to Bangkok, Tak, and Chiang Mai is on the Asia Highway next to the Michelin Man sign.

Minitrucks to Mae Sariang leave from the parking lot behind the First Hotel. Minitrucks to Umphang leave from the southern side of town near the cinema. Orange-and-white minivans to Tak leave hourly from the minivan lot near the First Hotel.

Several private bus companies operate Mae Sot offices. Sukothai Tours opposite the First Hotel, just off Indrakiri Road, has buses to Tak every 30 minutes and service to Phitsanulok daily at 0930. Tranjit Tours in the First Hotel has VIP buses to Bangkok and Chiang Mai, as does Tavorn Frame Tours in the Siam Hotel on Prasat Vithi Road.

WALEY

Few travelers make the side trip to Waley, a small town on the banks of the Moi River just across from the Burmese town of Phalu. Long removed from any form of political control, Waley has traditionally served as a smuggling entrepot and the economic pipeline for the Karen National Union (KNU). The situation changed dramatically in 1989 after Burmese forces crossed the river and drove the KNU from the region, the first in a series of KNU defeats culminating in the fall of Manerplaw in 1995.

Waley today is little more than a sleepy backwater town without the economic or political importance it enjoyed for several decades. Burmese teak keeps the town alive—felled in Myanmar and hauled to Waley where lumberyards cut the enormous trees down to commercial sizes.

Mawker Refugee Camp
This very large refugee camp with perhaps 7,000 Karens lies just off Route 1206 en route to Waley. Visitors are welcome to tour the camp and learn about the political problems of the Karens. Donations of clothes, medicine, or simply a sympathetic ear are always welcome. Some travelers volunteer to teach English in this and other refugee camps near Mae Sot. For more information contact The Myanmar Project, 124 Soi Watthongnopakhun, Somdet Chaophraya Rd., Klongsan, Bangkok 10600, tel. (02) 437-0445, fax (02) 222-5788.

Phalu
Depending on the current political situation south of Waley, travelers are sometimes allowed to cross the river to visit the small trading town of Phalu. Verbal permission must be obtained from the Thai military police at the Moi River bridge.

Accommodations
As of this writing, there are no formal accommodations in Waley, though several trekking agencies in Mae Sot have announced plans to open guesthouses in the near future. In the meantime, your best option is to the north in a small hotel in Phop Phra where rooms cost 50-80B.

Transportation
Songtaos to Waley depart Mae Sot in the mornings until around noon from the stop near the cinema. The minitrucks head south 36 km through the town of Ban Saw Oh, where the road splits and Route 1206 continues another 25 km down to Waley. The road is paved to Phop Phra, but the final 10 km to Waley remains an unpaved dirt road.

UMPHANG

Highway 1090 runs south from Mae Sot through a series of border towns and natural attractions such as waterfalls and national parks, until it reaches the remote village of Umphang. Once a hotbed of guerrillas and Burmese separatist groups, Umphang and vicinity are now safe and starting to attract travelers determined to get off the standard tourist trail.

Umphang, 164 km south of Mae Sot, is worth the journey. Situated at the junction of the Mae Klong and Umphang Rivers, the simple village is surrounded by some of the most impressive scenery in the country. Activities include trekking to hilltribe villages rarely visited by travelers, exploring some of the oldest remaining stands of forest in the country, and joining rafting expeditions down the Mae Klong to enjoy tremendous waterfalls and isolated caves. Umphang is also an ideal place to simply relax, do nothing, and enjoy the lazy pace of life.

En Route to Umphang
The four-hour *songtao* ride from Mae Sot passes through a wonderland of gleaming ricefields, banana groves, chili plantations, and remote villages hemmed in by awe-inspiring mountains.

Tararak Falls: Some 26 km south of Mae Sot is a small waterfall for a quick dip.

Pra Charoen Falls: Another minor but lovely cascade best visited during the rainy season, June-December.

Villages: Many of the villages en route to Umphang are inhabited by Karens, Mons, Lisu, Hmong, Mien, and Lahu, rather than Thais. Midway to Umphang is the village of Ban Rom Klao 4, populated mostly by Hmong and Karen. Thirty km before Umphang is the village of Mae

Klong Kee, where accommodations are sometimes offered in local homes, or you can overnight at the Border Patrol campsites on the Mae Klong. When staying in someone's home, offer them 20-50B for the kindness.

Umphang Town

Umphang is a small town inhabited by perhaps 3,000 citizens—primarily Karens, Mons, and Thais. Pravesphywan Road is the main artery, along with another unnamed street to the west. The post office and pharmacy are on Pravesphywan Road, while the morning market and municipal hospital are found on the paved crossroad.

There are no banks or moneychangers in Umphang. Be sure to change enough money in Mae Sot to last for your entire visit.

The River Journey

Most travelers come to Umphang to make a trip down the Mae Klong River to visit Karen villages, caves, hot springs, and the best waterfall in the region.

The typical tour last three days and costs about 500B per day. Groups are generally very small and custom itineraries are encouraged by putting together a combination of bamboo rafting, elephant rides, caving, and trekking. All tours start with rafting down the Mae Klong to Thilawsu Falls, followed by trekking to the Karen villages of Khotha and Palantha. A jeep makes the 25-km return trip to Umphang.

The faster tour reaches Thilawsu Falls in a single day, then takes a two-day trek to the pickup point. Many travelers prefer to stretch the river journey out to two full days, spending the first night at the hot springs, then slowly floating downriver to the falls.

Organized Tours

Guesthouses can help arrange treks or provide maps for self-guided explorations. An easy and popular trek heads southeast from town to a series of small Karen villages near the Huay Umphang stream. Another trek leads to the unique village of Le Tong Khu, where the Karens continue to follow spiritual customs derived from Hindu traditions.

River trips and trekking expeditions can be arranged at several agencies in Umphang at much lower rates than from tour operators in Mae Sot. For example, river trips average around 500B per day from Umphang operators, but about 2,000B per day from Mae Sot agencies. This higher fee includes roundtrip transportation from Mae Sot, but the convenience may not justify the sharply higher fees.

Trekker Hill: A recommended agency run by the environmentally conscious Mr. Jantawong (Mr. Tee). Khun Tee speaks perfect English (he attended agricultural school in Kansas) and is a gold mine of information on local cultures and the political and economic challenges faced by the Mon people. Trekker Hill is one of the few in Umphang approved by the TAT, and may be found on Pravesphywan Rd., tel. (055) 561090.

BL Tours: Near the Um Phang Guesthouse is another agency with a good reputation. Be sure to compare prices and check the qualifications of your guide. Umphang Rd., tel. (055) 561021.

Accommodations

Guesthouses are springing up like opium poppies as the number of visitors increases each year. At present, Thai visitors vastly outnumber foreign travelers and prices at guesthouses are somewhat higher than elsewhere in the region. Thais with enough money to travel generally demand better facilities than *farang* backpackers and dislike the idea of bare-bones travel.

Trekker Hill: Mr. Tee not only runs the best tour agency in town, he also operates a clean and comfortable guesthouse on the main road just past the power station. Praveshpywan Rd., tel. (055) 561090, 60B dorm, 120-180B bungalows.

Um Phang Guesthouse: Simple rooms in a place just beyond the town *wat*. Nothing special but cheap at just 100-150B per person.

Um Phang House: The local mayor runs a utilitarian set of bare-bones rooms and better bungalows with hot water and fans. His outdoor restaurant is probably the best place in town to try something other than noodles or fried rice. Um Phang House, tel. (055) 561073, 150-350B.

Garden Huts: The riverside location is wonderful and the gardens are delightfully well manicured, but rooms are somewhat overpriced and few of the employees speak English. Rooms vary in price depending on the season, amenities, and location—either around the garden or facing the river. Garden Huts (also called Garden Resort), tel. (055) 561093, 150-500B.

Umphang Hill Resort: Across the Huay Umphang stream are several more "resorts" with bungalows in all price ranges. This one has small huts for backpackers, larger bungalows for couples, and semi-luxurious chalets for upscale visitors. Umphang Hill Resort, tel. (055) 561063, 100-450B.

Ban Huay Nam Yen: About 500 meters downriver from Umphang Hill Resort is another riverside "resort" with bungalows in various price ranges. Somewhat inconvenient, but very quiet and beautifully situated on the banks of the river. No phone, 200-450B.

Gift House: Several guesthouses and "resorts" are located two or three km before you reach Umphang, on the road to Mae Sot. None offer the atmosphere of the riverside venues, but they compensate with lower prices and less congestion. Gift House, Stray Bird, and Umphang Country Huts have simple huts at 60-100B and better bungalows with electricity and private baths at 200-350B.

Transportation
Umphang is 164 km south of Mae Sot. Several *songtaos* leave Mae Sot daily between 0700-0900 from the stop near the cinema, and take about five hours to complete the winding but magnificent journey past ricefields, virgin monsoon forest, and soaring mountains.

Minitrucks usually stop at Ban Rom Klao 4, a Karen village about 80 km south of Mae Sot. After a quick lunch, the truck continues past a few waterfalls and Karen villages to Umphang.

Songtaos back to Mae Sot leave Umphang daily 0700-1000, with an occasional minitruck or van rolling out around noon.

MAE SOT TO MAE SARIANG

One of the most adventurous journeys in Thailand is along the winding road leading north from Mae Sot to Mae Sariang. This unique route reaches the far north, avoiding backtracking to Tak or Phitsanulok. The road skirts the banks of the Moi River, a geographical oddity flowing north through the Dawna Range until it intersects the Thanlwin which, in turn, continues south though the Burmese Shan States. The spectacular scenery includes teakwood forests, waterfalls, villages inhabited by Thais and hilltribes, and refugee camps maintained by the Karen National Liberation Army and other freedom fighters.

A map of the region is available from the Mae Sot Guesthouse.

Accommodations
Several guesthouses and resorts have recently opened on the highway between Mae Sot and Mae Sariang.

Tha Song Yang: Simple bungalows are available in this rather prosperous village composed of teak and concrete houses 83 km north of Mae Sot. U Su Cave is 15 km north of Tha Song Yang. The local mayor can help arrange boats down the Moi River to Ban Tha Song Yang and the village of Mae Sam Riep on the Thanlwin River.

Chao Doi House: One of the most remote but memorable lodges in central Thailand perches on a mountaintop some 15 km east of Mae Sarit. Mr. Narong usually meets the first minitruck each day and takes travelers to his hillside bungalows. Otherwise ask the bus or *songtao* driver to drop you at the police box near Mae Sarit, then hitch a ride up the mountain. The bungalows are operated by Mr. Narong, who charges 300B for an all-inclusive package of rooms, meals, drinks, and escorted tours to Karen refugee camps and hilltribe villages. Chao Doi House has been highly recommended by several travelers.

For more information in Mae Sot, call Khun Narong at (055) 531782 or check with any guesthouse.

Mon Krating Resort: This upscale resort sits on a hilltop east of Mae Sarit and 135 km north of Mae Sot. Most tours overnight here and continue the following day to hilltribe villages and the Moi River. 1421 Asia Hwy., tel. (055) 531409, fax (055) 532279, 750-900B per person including all meals.

Transportation
Route 1085 is now paved all the way from Mae Sot to Mae Sariang, passing through Mae Ramat (30 km), Tha Song Yang (83 km), Mae Sarit (118 km), Ban Tha Song Yang (137 km), and

Ban Sop Ngao (176 km), before reaching Mae Sariang (226 km).

Most travelers spend a night or two in Mae Sarit and then take the morning *songtao* to Mae Sariang, about a three-hour trip. However, direct minitrucks leave Mae Sot four times daily 0700-1200 from the market north of the police station. The 226-km journey takes about seven hours and costs 150B—a very long and tough haul.

A more popular plan is to take a morning *songtao* to Mae Sarit (four hours, 50B) and spend a few nights at the Chai Doi House exploring the region. From Mae Sarit, minitrucks continue north to Ban Tha Song Yang and Mae Sariang. Khun Narong at Chai Doi House might be able to arrange a river trip down the Moi River to Sop Moei or Mae Sam Laep. *Songtaos* go daily from the river to Mae Sariang.

Ban Tha Song Yang: Hwy. 1085 veers east from Ban Tha Song Yang and continues north up to Mae Sariang. Ban Tha Song Yang is 137 km north of Mae Sot and 89 km south of Mae Sariang.

NORTHERN THAILAND

INTRODUCTION

The cool mountainous landscapes, friendly people, unique arts and architecture, dazzling handicrafts, unsurpassed ethnological variety, and superb shopping are the highlights of northern Thailand. Until two decades ago, the north was unknown to all but the most adventurous of travelers. Now, with improved transportation, new hotels, and an unprecedented boom in tourism, more travelers are discovering the exotic charms and romantic appeal of the far north.

Northern Thailand embraces eight provinces bordered by Myanmar to the west and Laos and the Mekong River to the north. The political and geographic center of the region is Chiang Mai, the second-largest city in Thailand and home to over 200,000 citizens. Beyond the valley of Chiang Mai are five regions which can be easily toured. To the west are the thick jungles and remote towns of Mae Sariang, Mae Hong Son, and Pai. South of Chiang Mai lie the historic and cultural centers of Lampang and Lamphun. The third region, to the east, encompasses the rarely visited towns of Phayao, Phrae, and Nan. North of Chiang Mai a series of small towns lead to Thaton on the banks of the Kok River. The fifth region is the so-called Golden Triangle, long associated with the cultivation of opium and battles between warlords for control of the drug trade. Principal towns in the extreme north include Chiang Rai, Mae Sai on the Burmese border, and the historic site of Chiang Saen on the banks of the Mekong River.

Sightseeing Highlights
Most visitors to northern Thailand begin their explorations in the city of Chiang Mai, then make forays to the following destinations depending on their time and interests. The following sketches will help you discover the remote sites where the simple spirit of Thailand still survives.

Chiang Mai: Thailand's second-largest city serves as the hub for local tourism and provides a worthwhile introduction to the charms of the north. Chiang Mai has changed dramatically in

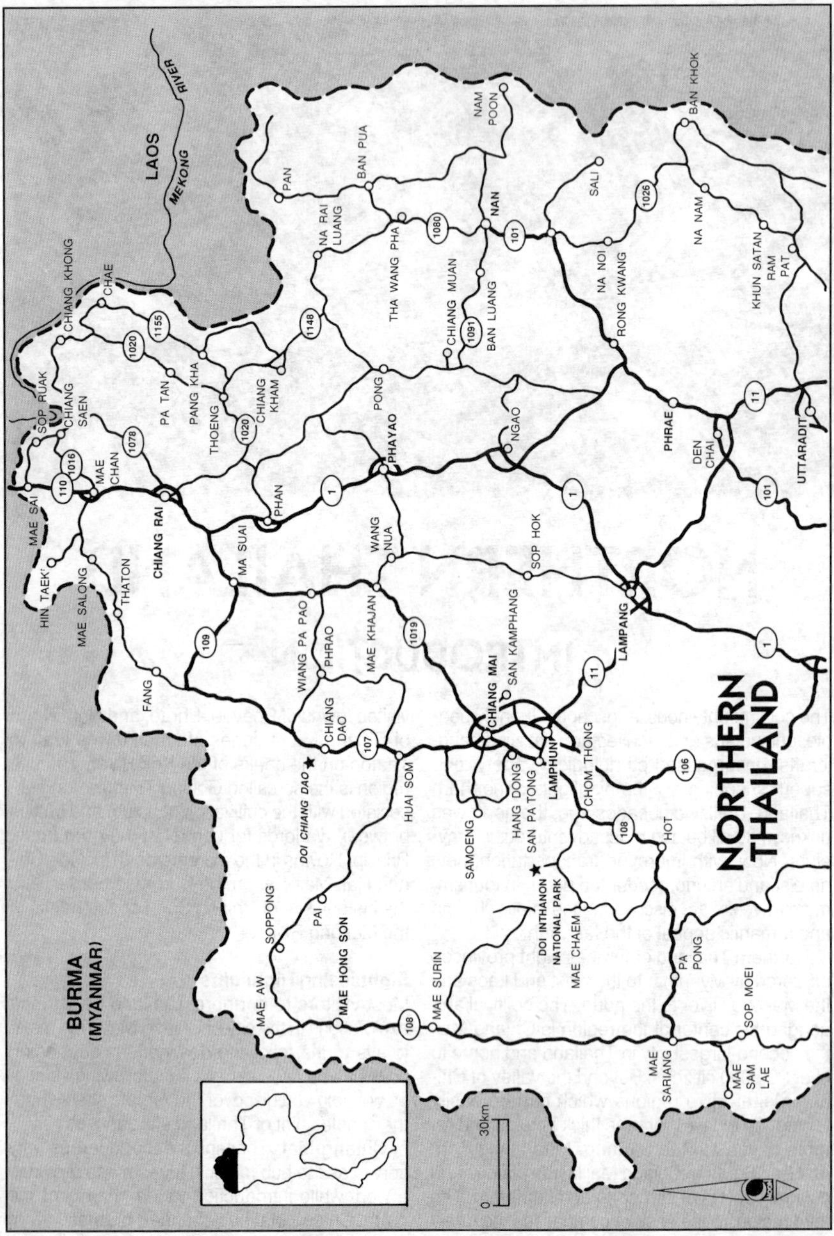

LAOS

MEKONG RIVER

BURMA
(MYANMAR)

NORTHERN
THAILAND

MAE SAI
HIN TAEK
SOP RUAK
CHIANG KHONG
CHAE
CHIANG SAEN
1020
1155
PAN
BAN PUA
NAM POON
BAN KHOK

110
1016
MAE CHAN
1078
PA TAN
PANG KHA
1148
NA RAI LUANG
1080
NAN
101
SALI
1026
NA NAM

MAE SALONG
THATON
CHIANG RAI
THOENG
1020
CHIANG KHAM
PONG
THA WANG PHA
CHIANG MUAN
1091
BAN LUANG
NA NOI
RONG KWANG
KHUN SATAN RAM PAT

109
FANG
MA SUAI
PHAN
1
PHAYAO
NGAO
PHRAE
DEN CHAI
11
UTTARADIT

WIANG PA PAO
PHRAO
MAE KHAJAN
WANG NUA
1019
SAN KAMPHANG
SOP HOK
1
LAMPANG
101
1

CHIANG DAO
107
DOI CHIANG DAO ★
HUAI SOM
CHIANG MAI
11
SAN PA TONG
LAMPHUN
CHOM THONG
106

MAE AW
SOPPONG
PAI
SAMOENG
HANG DONG
DOI INTHANON NATIONAL PARK ★
MAE CHAEM
108
HOT
PA PONG

MAE HONG SON
MAE SURIN
108
MAE SARIANG
MAE SAM LAE
SOP MOEI

30km
0

© MOON PUBLICATIONS, INC.

the last decade. Though it now suffers from traffic gridlock and industrial pollution, the town still offers dozens of superb temples, a great selection of guesthouses and restaurants, and the finest shopping in Thailand. Best of all, the people continue to exude the warmth and hospitality that first popularized the north.

Lamphun: Some 26 km south of Chiang Mai is a small town which served as the capital of an independent Mon kingdom until the 13th century. An easy day-trip, Lamphun features a small museum, a royal monastery with almost a dozen buildings, and an intriguing *chedi* that ranks as the finest surviving example of Dvaravati architecture in Thailand.

Lampang: The busy commercial center of Lampang, 100 km southeast of Chiang Mai, has the best collection of Burmese-style temples in Thailand. Twenty km southwest of Lampang is Wat Prathat Lampang Luang, considered among the finest temple complexes in Thailand.

Mae Hong Son: Tucked away near the Burmese border is the remote village of Mae Hong Son, now being aggressively promoted by the tourist office as the next major tourist destination in the north. Much of the charm has been lost to uncontrolled development, though the region still offers beautiful landscapes, rivers, caves, and tribal villages relatively untouched by mass tourism. Mae Hong Son has several expensive hotels and over a dozen budget guesthouses.

Pai: The finest town west of Chiang Mai isn't Mae Hong Son or Mae Sariang, but the lovely village of Pai. Tucked away in a valley that resembles Chiang Mai two decades ago, the town has a handful of comfortable guesthouses and is an excellent place for tribal trekking and visits to hot springs and remote villages.

Thaton and the Kok River: Four hours north of Chiang Mai is a small village where a steady stream of travelers spend the night before taking a longtail boat down the Kok River to Chiang Rai. En route to Thaton are the lovely valley of Mae Sa, a privately owned elephant camp, Chiang Dao Caves, and the dusty village of Fang.

Chiang Rai: Probably the most overrated destination in northern Thailand is the drab city of Chiang Rai. The town has a few mundane temples and is almost unavoidable for an overnight stay, but a better option is to breeze right through

and proceed directly to other destinations or to one of the lodges described in the following section, "Mountain Lodges."

Mae Sai: Located on the Burmese border is a prosperous but nondescript town where Thai and Burmese citizens are allowed to cross and conduct a bit of shopping. Aside from the border crossing and views from the hillside temple, Mae Sai has little of great interest.

Golden Triangle: Thailand's notorious Golden Triangle is centered at the town of Sop Ruak, a disappointing collection of souvenir stalls, touristy restaurants, pushy merchants, and luxury hotels which have eliminated whatever atmosphere that town once possessed. Sop Ruak is more popular with tour groups than armed terrorists, so forget any fantasies about caravans of drug smugglers.

Chiang Saen: Beautifully situated on the banks of the Mekong is the little town of Chiang Saen, one of Thailand's oldest and most historic sites. The surviving temples are very modest when compared to those at Sukothai or Ayuthaya, but the relaxed atmosphere and lack of tourists make it one of the best untouched destinations in the north.

Chiang Khong: To escape the hordes of tourists in northern Thailand, you'll need to explore the more remote towns such as Chiang Khong and others described below. Chiang Khong features several guesthouses and simple restaurants perched on the edge of the Mekong River.

Phayao: Midway between Lampang and Chiang Rai and nestled on the edge of a beautiful lake, this completely untouched town has a pair of outstanding temples and a modern *viharn* with some of the finest modern murals in Thailand.

Phrae: Another good choice to escape the tourist crowds is the provincial capital of Phrae, known for its Burmese-style architecture and textile industry. As with all other towns in northern Thailand, Phrae has several decent hotels with fan-cooled rooms from 100B per night.

Nan: Some 340 km east of Chiang Mai is a prosperous town that many travelers consider among the most attractive in the north. Nan has a half dozen temples, a branch of the national museum, and a few guesthouses and hotels that cater to the small but steady trickle of international travelers. To the north and east are some of Thailand's most remote and untouched forests. As with Pai and Chiang Saen, Nan has the potential to become one of the leading travel destinations in the next decade.

Routes

Chiang Mai can be reached directly from Bangkok by air, train, or bus, but stopovers in Ayuthaya and Sukothai are highly recommended for visitors interested in history and archaeology. Travelers in Kanchanaburi can avoid backtracking to Bangkok by busing directly to Ayuthaya via Suphanburi. An intriguing alternative approach to Chiang Mai is by bus from Mae Sot up to Mae Sariang, and onward to Chiang Mai via Mae Hong Son and Pai. Several routes are possible from Chiang Mai.

Side Trips: Tribal trekking into the neighboring hills has become somewhat commercialized, but most travelers who undertake a five- to seven-day adventure still seem satisfied. Lampang and Lamphun are the two most popular side trips from Chiang Mai. Lamphun can easily be visited in a single day, but Lampang needs a day or two to visit the temples and markets. One option is to visit Lampang at the end of a loop through the northern towns of Chiang Rai, Nan, and Phrae.

Western Loop: Among the most popular journeys from Chiang Mai is the long and very rugged journey to Mae Sariang, Mae Hong Son, Soppong, and Pai, before returning to Chiang Mai. Bus service is frequent, though travelers with limited time can fly directly to Mae Hong Son and explore the nearby attractions with an organized tour or rented motorcycle.

Golden Triangle: The extreme north of Thailand can either be explored as a short four-day journey through the triangle region, or on a two-week excursion including the more remote towns of Nan and Phrae. The shorter version begins with a four-hour bus ride to Thaton, where longtail boats load up passengers and depart at 1300 for an exciting but deafening five-hour downriver trip to Chiang Rai. Before you return to Chiang Mai, you can spend a few days exploring the villages, hilltribes, and historic ruins in Chiang Saen.

The Grand Adventure: Visitors who want to escape the standard tourist trail can explore all the remote regions of the far north in about two or three weeks. Begin the journey in Chiang Mai and head north to Thaton for the boat ride down the Kok River to Chiang Rai. Venture north to Mae Salong and Mae Sai on the Burmese border. After a brief look at the commercialized town of Sop Ruak, enjoy a few days relaxing in the village of Chiang Saen. Buses continue east to Chiang Khong and then south down to Nan via Chiang Kham. The last leg passes through Phrae and Lampang before returning to Chiang Mai.

Leaving the North: After exploring the north, most travelers head directly back to Bangkok and continue to the islands of southern Thailand. An alternative route is by bus to Phitsanulok and then directly east to Lom Sak, Loei, and other towns in the northeast. Depending on the current political situation, an intriguing option is to visit Laos and run the Mekong River from Luang Prabang to Vientiane. Shades of 1968!

Motorcycle Touring

Transportation around northern Thailand is very simple. Public buses connect all the smaller towns, and private bus companies provide direct connections to major destinations. The problem is getting off the beaten track to reach the isolated mountain lodges and small villages where authentic Thai lifestyles remain unaffected by mass tourism.

The solution is touring northern Thailand on a rented motorcycle. While rough roads and the irrational driving habits of the Thais may seem daunting, an amazing number of Western tourists now explore Thailand by motorcycle.

An excellent pocket guide to motorcycle touring is published by David Unkovich and available at most bookstores in Chiang Mai. Before setting out, read "Motorcycles" under "Getting Around" in the On the Road chapter.

Almost a dozen shops on Moon Muang Road in Chiang Mai rent motorcycles at extremely competitive rates. Small 100cc scooters which cost 100-150B daily are perfectly adequate for local touring and visiting attractions near Chiang Mai. Larger bikes such as 125cc Honda trail bikes cost 180-250B daily and provide enough power to climb the steepest of roads in northern Thailand. Carefully inspect the bike for damage and make note of any problems such as dangling rearview mirrors and loose chains.

You'll be required to leave your passport as a deposit, so exchange enough money to finance your motorcycle tour. Motorcycles in the best condition are rented in the early morning, so shop early for vehicles with the lowest mileage. Oil levels should be checked daily and bikes should be locked inside the compound of your guesthouse each night.

I rented a motorcycle for almost two months and rode nearly all the roads in northern Thailand. The only time I felt in danger was in the larger towns such as Chiang Mai and Chiang Rai. Outside larger towns, the traffic was very light and roads in excellent condition. Gasoline stations were relatively plentiful and bike mechanics could be found in almost every village. The Thai government has put up English-language signs throughout the country and, with a good map, it's almost impossible to get lost. The finest rides traverse the small roads that wind through the hills and parallel the borders of Myanmar and Laos.

Dozens of routes are possible from Chiang Mai, but most motorcyclists begin by riding north up to Thaton and spending a night in a local guesthouse on the banks of the Kok River. From Thaton, continue along the new dirt road through opium country to the village of Mae Salong, where you can spend your second night. Continue down to Chiang Rai and then north to Mae Sai or one of the mountain lodges described in the following section. Continue east from Mae Sai to Sop Ruak and spend a few days relaxing in Chiang Saen.

Motorcyclists short on time can then return to Chiang Mai via Chiang Rai and Phayao. A longer and more fascinating journey is to continue east to Chiang Khong, Chiang Kham, Nan, Phrae, and Lampang before returning to Chiang Mai about a week later. Although the entire journey takes two or three weeks, it remains a world-class ride through some of the most beautiful regions in Thailand.

Mountain Lodges

A wonderful alternative to urban dwelling is the handful of mountain lodges tucked away throughout the region. Travelers who wish to experience rural life at its finest are advised to spend a few nights in one of the following lodges. Unless otherwise noted, all have simple rooms for

60-100B. Many of these mountain lodges change location or close down with the seasons. Please write and let me know about any new discoveries. Be sure to include a business card of the lodge, plus a brief description of facilities, prices, and other amenities.

Pan House: Travelers going to Mae Hong Son via the southern route can stay with Mr. Werapan Tarasan (Mr. Pan) and use his guide services for trekking and elephant excursions. Pan House is on Hwy. 108 at Km 68, 158 km from Chiang Mai and 32 km east of Mae Sariang. Ask the bus driver to drop you at Ban Mae Wan, then hike five km south from the highway.

Cave Lodge: Several popular mountain lodges are located north of Soppong, between Mae Hong Son and Pai, in a district famous for caves and tribal villages. Cave Lodge is the original lodge, operated by an Australian writer, John Spies, and his Thai wife.

Mae Lana Guesthouse: Also near Soppong is a bamboo guesthouse operated by a French woman and her Thai husband. The turnoff is marked by a small sign 56 km from Mae Hong Son and about 20 km west of Soppong. Mae Lana Guesthouse is known for its friendly management, good food, and family atmosphere. Activities include cave explorations, tribal trekking, and relaxing in the natural environment.

Trekker House: Defying all conventional wisdom, several young Thais have constructed a few guesthouses 63 km northeast of Chiang Mai and seven km south of Hwy. 1019. Trekker House is beautifully situated in a forested area that remained completely untouched until Hwy. 1019 was opened as a faster alternative to Hwy. 1. The owners speak some English and conduct guided treks to nearby villages inhabited by Lahu, Lisu, Kuomintang, Meo, Yao, and Karen.

Ban Khum Bungalows: Though rarely visited, Ban Khum Bungalows provides decent accommodations on the slopes of Doi Angkhang. Located in the town of Ban Khum on Hwy. 1249, 137 km north of Chiang Mai and 15 km south of Fang.

Karen Coffeeshop: Probably the oldest mountain lodge in Thailand still operates north of Thaton near the Kok River and small village of Ban Mai. Trekking is popular throughout the region, though tribal villages are now accustomed to Westerners and fairly commercialized. Visitors should be very cautious about interfering with the local opium trade. This region—wedged between the Kok River and Myanmar—is the authentic Golden Triangle through which passes most of the world's opium crop.

Laan Tong Lodge: Several outstanding mountain resorts are located in the foothills north of Chiang Rai and east of Mae Chan. The region is firmly controlled by the Thai government and visitors can safely do self-guided treks to tribal villages. The lodge consists of several bamboo cottages surrounded by landscaped gardens and fruit trees. Facilities are in good condition and the Thai owners specialize in vegetarian dishes and home-baked breads. Laan

Tong Lodge is on Hwy. 1089 near the Mae Chan River, 13 km west of the town of Mae Chan.

Mountain View Bungalows: Located on Hwy. 1207 just 14 km northwest of Chiang Rai is another lodge that arranges tribal trekking, river rafting, and elephant rides. Mountain View Bungalows is just outside the Karen village of Huai Khom and within hiking distance of Akha, Lahu, Lisu, and Meo tribal villages.

Akha Guesthouse: Another longtime favorite is the Akha Guesthouse, located on old Hwy. 1149, 44 km north of Chiang Rai and seven km west of the town of Ban Huai Krai. Views are spectacular from the guesthouses and trails which wind through nearby Akha villages. Motorcyclists can continue up Hwy. 1149 to a temple on Doi Tung and around the back of the mountain range to Mae Sai on the Burmese border.

CHIANG MAI

Chiang Mai, principal city of the north, is the favorite destination for many travelers to Thailand. Situated on the banks of the River Ping and surrounded by green hills and lazing rivers, this thriving city is blessed with a rich history, friendly citizens, and a cool, dry climate—the perfect remedy to the sweltering cities of the south.

Chiang Mai is a world apart. With its unique forms of architecture, dance, music, food, and festivals, Chiang Mai has always been a region both physically and emotionally separated from the remainder of Thailand. The people consider themselves superior to their cousins in Bangkok.

Chiang Mai, however, is also a city in transition. While the so-called Rose of the North still provides a refreshing change from the ordeals of Bangkok, travelers expecting a charming little village of wooden houses and rural lanes are in for a rude surprise. In many ways, the city represents the classic struggle between the national drive for industrialization and the desire to preserve the quality of traditional life.

Sadly, it appears that real estate developers and commercial speculators are winning. Massive projects are routinely approved without regard for land use or zoning considerations. Billboards near the airport and along the superhighway plug the imminent appearance of golf

courses, housing estates, mega-hotels, air-conditioned shopping centers, factories, and other monuments to modern commerce. Chiang Mai also suffers from air pollution, unending noise, and traffic jams in even the smallest of *sois*. In less than a decade, walking in Chiang Mai has gone from a pleasant escape to an ordeal not unlike a stroll in Bangkok.

Is Chiang Mai doomed? An economic report stated that the Board of Investment recently approved a record number of projects in Chiang Mai and northern Thailand: 56 major construction sites worth over US$250 million, 320 factories, 15 new hotels with an additional 5,000 rooms, and construction space up 80% from the previous year. To satisfy local developers, government officials have authorized the construction of a 10,000-seat convention stadium, dozens of new condominium projects, and a twin city in San Kamphang District, 15 km east of the city. Local students and environmental groups have sounded the alarm on uncontrolled development, but the future of Chiang Mai looks grim unless the economic relationship between developers and politicians can be changed.

And yet visitors continue to arrive in record-breaking numbers, and the vast majority leave satisfied with the wonders of Chiang Mai and northern Thailand. The unique ambience and

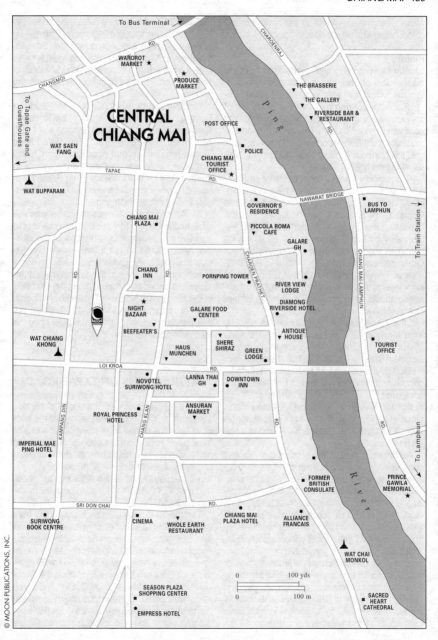

CENTRAL
CHIANG MAI

To Bus Terminal

CHAROENRAJ

WARAROT
MARKET ★

CHANGMOI

PRODUCE
MARKET ★

THE BRASSERIE ■

THE GALLERY ■

RIVERSIDE BAR &
RESTAURANT ▼

Ping

POST OFFICE ■

To Tapae Gate and
Guesthouses

WAT SAEN
FANG ▲

TAPAE

POLICE ■

CHIANG MAI
TOURIST
OFFICE ★

NAWARAT BRIDGE

WAT BUPPARAM ▲

GOVERNOR'S
RESIDENCE ■

BUS TO
LAMPHUN ■

To Train Station

CHIANG MAI
PLAZA ■

PICCOLA ROMA
CAFE ▼

GALARE
GH ●

CHIANG
INN ●

PORNPING TOWER ●

CHARDEN PRATHET

RIVER VIEW
LODGE ●

CHIANG MAI-LAMPHUN

NIGHT
BAZAAR ★

GALARE FOOD
CENTER ▼

DIAMOND
RIVERSIDE HOTEL ●

BEEFEATER'S ▼

WAT CHIANG
KHONG ▲

HAUS
MUNCHEN ▼

SHERE
SHIRAZ ▼

ANTIQUE
HOUSE ▼

GREEN
LODGE ▼

TOURIST
OFFICE ■

LOI KROA

RD.

NOVOTEL
SURIWONG HOTEL ●

LANNA THAI
GH ●

DOWNTOWN
INN ●

To Lamphun

KAMPANG DIN

ROYAL PRINCESS
HOTEL ●

CHIANG KLAN

ANSURAN
MARKET ▼

River

IMPERIAL MAE
PING HOTEL ●

FORMER
BRITISH
CONSULATE ●

PRINCE
GAWILA
MEMORIAL ★

SRI DON CHAI

RD.

SURIWONG
BOOK CENTRE ●

CINEMA ●

WHOLE EARTH
RESTAURANT ▼

CHIANG MAI
PLAZA HOTEL ●

ALLIANCE
FRANCAIS ●

WAT CHAI
MONKOL ▲

SEASON PLAZA
SHOPPING CENTER ●

EMPRESS HOTEL ●

SACRED
HEART
CATHEDRAL ●

0   100 yds

0   100 m

© MOON PUBLICATIONS, INC.

warm welcome extended by the residents still give Chiang Mai an irresistible appeal.

History

Chiang Mai has long been separated from the mainstream of Thai history. Isolated by mountainous terrain and vast jungles, the region developed independently under the influence of the Burmese and Tai peoples who migrated from southern China. Northern Thailand remained almost completely independent from lower Siam until the Northern Railway reached the Ping Valley in the early 20th century.

The region's original inhabitants were Paleolithic settlers who domesticated plants and animals quite independently of the Indians and Chinese. The second known residents were the Lawas, a primitive tribe later forced from the fertile valley by Mons who established a thriving empire at Haripunchai in present-day Lamphun. Other centers of civilization included the kingdom of Phayao, which traded with Pala rulers in India, and Khmer chieftains who operated military outposts ruled from the Cambodian empire at Angkor Wat.

Chiang Mai was formally founded in 1292 by King Mengrai, a Thai-Laotian prince from the Mekong River District. Mengrai had previously founded Chiang Rai in 1261 and established himself as the paramount power in the north by conquering Haripunchai in 1281. After discovering that his military headquarters at Wiang Kung Kam was poorly sited and subject to floods, Mengrai began searching for a new capital for his powerful Lanna Thai Empire, the "Land of a Million Ricefields."

According to legend, the present-day site was chosen after his entourage spotted three lucky omens: two white barking deer, two white sambar deers, and a white mouse. Mengrai immediately ordered the construction of a royal city, regal palace, and Buddhist temples protected by earthenwork walls and 10-meter moats. Mengrai ruled for 21 years and successfully established a dynasty which dominated northern Thailand for over two centuries. Legends also claim that Mengrai dramatically died when struck by lightning at the intersection of Rajadamnern and Pra Poklao Roads in Chiang Mai. The unlucky spot is now marked by a modest spirit temple dedicated to the ambitious king.

Some 20 Thai monarchs ruled the Lanna Thai Kingdom during the next 240 years. Chiang Mai enjoyed its own golden age during the 15th-century reign of King Tilokaraja, a beloved ruler who organized the Eighth Buddhist World Council in 1477 and constructed many of the present-day temples.

But warfare between Chiang Mai and the Burmese undermined the vitality of the kingdom. Northern Thailand fell to the Burmese in 1556, who ruled the region until 1774, when King Taksin regained formal possession of Chiang Mai. After Taksin was declared insane and put to death in 1781, his successor, King Rama I, appointed a governor-prince who revived the hereditary line of rulers of Chiang Mai.

An American Presbyterian mission was established in Chiang Mai in 1867. Its goal was to improve the health and education of the people, rather than attempt a large-scale conversion to Christianity. Evidence of Western occupation can still be seen in the colonial-style mansions and enclosed compounds on the east side of the Ping River. Northern Thailand remained a semi-autonomous state until 1939, when the final prince of Chiang Mai fell from power and the Bangkok administration took full control of the region.

ATTRACTIONS ON TAPAE ROAD

Since the establishment of the city in the late 13th century, Chiang Mai has remained the principal religious center in northern Thailand and focal point for the construction of temples and monasteries. As a result, there are 36 temples within the ancient city walls, 80 officially registered religious sites in the metropolitan area, and over 1,000 *wats* scattered throughout northern Thailand.

Temples in Chiang Mai range stylistically from early Mon and Sukothai prototypes to Ayuthayan and Burmese-style monuments. Northern architects characteristically favored large multi-layered roofs which swoop down lower than those of Bangkok temples, and muted exterior colors; you'll see less of the brazen reds, yellows, and blues found on southern temples. Northern architecture is also noted for flamboyant decoration and woodcarving such as filigree umbrellas and long-necked lions, which reflect its two centuries of Burmese occupation.

Some of the following temples stand in original condition, while others have been heavily restored in unrepresentative styles. Older temples have largely disappeared except for their crumbling *chedis* which often predate by several centuries the primary *bot* and *viharn*.

The following section describes temples on Tapae Road, followed by those inside the old city walls. All can be reached on foot or by rented motorcycle or a chartered *tuk tuk* at about 50B per hour. Monuments outside the city walls are described in the section "Attractions Near Chiang Mai" below and can be reached with public transportation or rented motorcycle.

Chiang Mai has a staggering number of temples, but the best monuments for rushed visitors are Wat Pra Singh, Wat Chedi Luang, Wat Chiang Man, Wat Chet Yot, Wat Suan Dok, and the temple on Doi Suthep.

Wat Saen Fang

Four temples of varying architectural interest are located on Tapae Road between the shopping district and Tapae Gate. All provide a welcome respite from the heat, noise, and carbon monoxide fumes generated by the ceaseless traffic.

Wat Saen Fang is approached up an undulating *naga*-flanked lane that parallels new construction and the crumbling remains of an old city wall. As with all other temples in Chiang Mai, Wat Saen Fang is composed of several distinctive buildings designed for specific purposes. The Burmese-style *chedi* is decorated with four corner cannons, whitewashed *singha* lions, parasols, and golden tortoises on the second tier. To the rear is a Burmese-style building used as a monks' residence and a brightly painted *viharn* fronted by modernistic, abstract *nagas*. The interior ceiling has been embellished with carved leather animal figures and a swinging chandelier.

singha

Wat Bupparam

Just opposite Wat Saen Fang is another temple compound with three *viharns* that illustrate the past, present, and future of Thai religious architecture.

To the left is a soaring, garish, and ostentatious monument to bad taste. It displays every gimmick used in modern Thai architecture: gaudy colors, ferroconcrete instead of wood, slapdash workmanship on the window eaves and pillared supports, and strange mythological animals that resemble Disney worm-dragons rather than traditional Thai creatures. Outside the front entrance a sign aggressively solicits donations from Western visitors, who can then gaze at the interior cartoon murals which depict the life of the Buddha.

Two other buildings in the *wat* compound make a better impression. The large *viharn* in the rear is rather ordinary aside from the unusual carvings of hellish scenes to the right of the entrance.

The chief fame of Wat Bupparam is the tiny, three-centuries-old wooden *viharn* to the right. Exquisitely decorated with stucco on wood and modeled with superb proportions, the ancient structure features unusual horizontal windows set with old wooden pegs and a mysterious interior filled with dozens of Buddha images.

Wat Mataram

Farther west toward Tapae Gate is a temple complex with both Burmese and Lanna Thai influences. The Burmese-style *viharn* is distinguished by an entrance doorway beautifully carved with Buddha preaching to the animals, and by small tinkling bells that dangle from roof *nagas*. Adjacent buildings include a Burmese-style *chedi* girded with monumental lions, a *bot* constructed in typical northern Lanna style, and monks' quarters to the rear which feature excellent filigree work on the wooden facade.

Don't get killed crossing Tapae Road to the next temple.

Wat Chettawan

Just opposite Wat Mataram is another small complex distinguished by three *chedis* with financial donors carefully noted in English script, and a lovely *viharn* with a finely carved gable depicting the eternal struggle between good and evil. The sanctuary attains great charm from its secluded location and broad lawns that support a family of hens and roosters. Note the moral tagged to the trees: "If everything is gotten dreamily, it will go away dreamily too."

The adjacent **Croissant Cafe** is an excellent spot for coffee, conversation, and, what else, croissants.

ATTRACTIONS IN THE WALLED CITY

Tapae Gate

After establishing Chiang Mai in 1292, King Mengrai ordered the construction of a fortified city measuring 1,500 meters on each side. Today, all that remains of the original enclosure are the 10-meter moats and modern reconstructions of the ancient walls and gates.

Superb views and decent grub can be enjoyed from the rooftop restaurant of the **MEI Guesthouse** overlooking Tapae Gate. **Daret's Guesthouse and Cafe,** just north of Tapae Gate, is the most popular travelers' hangout in Chiang Mai and a friendly place to kill a few hours over beer and buffalo steaks. Or walk through the gate and dine in the upscale **JJ Restaurant,** which serves great food in comfortable surroundings.

The following temples in the old walled city can all be reached on foot or quickly toured with a rented motorcycle or hired *tuk tuk*. Chartered *tuk tuks* charge 50B per hour. It takes about three hours to see the interior temples.

The sights below run from Tapae Gate north up Chaiyapoon Road, then west along the moat before returning inside the walled city for visits to the major temples of Wat Chiang Man and Wat Pra Singh. Visitors with limited time should go directly to Wat Chiang Man and Wat Pra Singh, the two most impressive temples inside the old walled city.

Wat Chai Sri Phum

Located on the northeastern corner of the old moat, Wat Chai Sri Phum features an elegant little *bot,* a large *viharn* with well-carved doors, and an unusual *chedi* decorated with Romanesque columns and four gilded Buddhas set into wall niches.

Wat Pa Pao

This collapsing Shan-style temple complex exudes a romantic and poetic charm due to its abandoned state and deserted silence. The unmarked temple is up the alley adjacent to the immense Toshiba sign. The compound features a small *chedi* with attractive blue tilework on the steps and teetering entrance gates to the north and east. To the left is a large Shan monastery with richly carved display cases below a coffered ceiling whose teak pillars have been profusely embedded with colored glass.

Wat Chiang Yuen

The *wat* is rather ordinary except for the massive white *stupa* in the rear courtyard and an unusual octagonal Chinese pavilion near the street. The *stupa* is decorated with yellow flowers and four cartoon characters painted with blue ears and eyebrows. More intriguing is the old wooden pavilion whose triple roofline and fine woodwork can be seen through the dimly lit interior.

Wat Chiang Man

According to legend, Wat Chiang Man was constructed by King Mengrai in 1296 as his royal residence during the construction of Chiang Mai. However, all of the present structures, aside from the ancient *chedi* in the rear, are reconstructions which date from the 19th and 20th centuries.

Central *Viharn:* Directly through the entrance gates stands an older *viharn* with an elaborate gable featuring richly carved images of Erawan, the three-headed elephant that now serves as the symbol of royal patronage.

Modern *Viharn:* To the right of the central *viharn* is an architecturally insignificant building chiefly known for its pair of sacred images protected behind glass doors and two iron gates. To the left is the Crystal Buddha, Pra Setang Khamani, an image miraculously endowed with rainmaking powers and the centerpiece for the annual Songkran Festival. The Marble Buddha on the right, Pra Sila, is an Indian bas-relief image carved in the Pala style of the 8th century. Both are highly venerated and considered the most powerful images in northern Thailand. Interior murals are numbered and explained in English on a free guide wrapped in plastic.

Bot: To the left of the central *viharn* is a small modern chapel and an old *bot* surrounded by flowering plants and a brilliantly green lawn. The 19th-century Lanna-style *bot* contains a fine collection of Lanna and U-Thong bronzes, plus a stone slab carved in ancient hieroglyphics which remain undeciphered.

Library: Between the old *bot* and the rearside *chedi* stands an elevated *ho trai* (library), considered a masterpiece of woodcarving and lacquer decoration, despite a recent repainting in gaudy colors.

Chedi: Behind the modern *viharn* towers one of the more interesting buildings in the complex, a 15th-century square *chedi* supported on the backs of 15 life-sized stucco elephants. The use of elephant buttresses reflects Sri Lankan influences, filtered through the Thai empires at Sukothai and Kamphang Phet.

Wat Duang Di

Tucked away in a circular alley and marked only with a small sign is a minor temple chiefly noted for its fine wooden pediments on the east side of the central *viharn,* as well as the elaborate plasterwork on the rear pavilion capped by four ascending roofs. The baroque pediments are regarded the finest in Chiang Mai.

The old provincial office across the street is worth a quick loook.

Monument to King Mengrai

The founder of Chiang Mai is honored with a small monument erected in 1975 to replace an older shrine "not suitably located for the public."

Wat Pan Tao

Adjacent to Wat Chedi Luang and marked only in Thai script, Wat Pan Tao features a large *viharn* that ranks among the masterpieces of Lanna woodcarving. Note the traditional construction techniques of wooden columns supporting the roof and freestanding walls made entirely of carved wooden panels.

Wat Chedi Luang

Named after the massive but ruined *chedi* behind the modern *viharn,* this famous monument was erected in 1401 by King Sam Feng Ken and

raised to 90 meters by his son, King Tilokaraja. An earthquake in 1546 partially destroyed the *chedi* and reduced its size to 42 meters, though the well-preserved foundations still give a strong impression of its architectural magnitude. Restoration work has been underway for several years and re-creations of the elephant buttresses and *naga*-lined staircases will soon be in place.

Other nearby buildings are less significant, though the triple-roofed *viharn* once held the famous Emerald Buddha during its travels between Lamphun, Luang Prabang, and Bangkok. Today the sanctuary displays 32 Jataka panels and a bronze standing Buddha cast in 1441. Each diorama includes English-language captions explicating the history and teachings of the Buddha.

Also in the courtyard is a remarkably large gum tree that shades the Lak Muang shrine of Chiang Mai.

Wat Mengrai

A small blue sign on Soi 6 marks the entrance to a minor chapel noted for the 4.5-meter bronze Buddha which, some claim, is a life-sized model of King Mengrai himself. More intriguing is the gilded ceremonial gate set with *devas, kinarees, nagas,* and other mythological creatures.

Wat Pra Singh

Wat Pra Singh ("Monastery of the Lion Lord") was founded in the 14th century to house the ashes of King Kham Fu and serve as the principal religious center of the Lanna Kingdom. The complex is composed of several buildings of varying architectural and artistic merit that form the most famous *wat* in Chiang Mai.

Central *Viharn:* Directly facing the street is a modern yet stately *viharn* constructed in 1925 and restored several years ago. The Lanna-style structure features a balustrade with a *naga* grasping a *makara* in its mouth, and a starkly plain interior with an indifferent collection of Buddhas.

Library: A registered historical monument, the *ho trai* of Wat Pra Singh features outstanding stucco *devas* and scrollwork around the concrete foundation supporting the delicate wooden building. The divinities were inspired by those of Wat Chet Yot, while the upper structure of teak paneling has been lacquered in red with

Wat Pra Singh

gilt trim. To the right is another modern *viharn* that serves the large community of monks at Wat Pra Singh.

Bot: Directly behind the central *viharn* stands a Lanna-style *bot* constructed entirely of wood with an impressive entrance of stucco and gold leaf. Strangely constructed with its axis perpendicular to the other *viharns,* the building is kept locked to guard the elaborate altar in the form of a *ku.*

Chedi: To the rear of the *bot* stands a circular *stupa* erected in the 14th century to house the ashes of King Kham Fu. According to architectural traditions borrowed from Sri Lanka, the bulbous reliquary is mounted on sacred elephants constructed from brick and plaster.

Viharn Laikam: The most famous and beautiful structure at Wat Pra Singh—and among the most elegant structures in all of northern Thailand—is the small chapel in the southwest corner of the *wat* compound. Viharn Laikam was built in 1811 in Lanna-style architecture before the influences of Bangkok began to dominate the north.

The exterior is a remarkable melange of fine proportions and delicate woodcarvings in the window frames and ancient doorways. Interior murals, though dimly lit, remain the best preserved in Chiang Mai and provide a glimpse of the religious and civil traditions of 19th-century Siam. Among the vignettes are children riding water buffaloes, men gambling in a circle, and topless maidens collecting fruit.

More significant than the murals is the central Buddha image, the mysterious and ultra-powerful Pra Buddha Singh, cast in northern Thailand during the late 15th century. Exact copies of the highly venerated image are also enshrined in Wat Buddhaisawan in Bangkok and Wat Mahathat in Nakhon Si Thammarat.

Two good restaurants are located near Wat Pra Singh. Sri Phen on Rajadamnern Road is known for its varieties of *som tam,* while Ta Krite has decent Thai food in a comfortable old building.

Wat Pra Pong

Adjacent to Wat Pra Singh is a tiny temple with beautifully carved teakwood windows and doors, depicting strange themes such as sinking ships, charioteers, battle scenes, mythological serpents, and giant *yaksas* ripping apart their victims.

Wat Muang Yakon

South on Samlan Road is an old wooden Lanna edifice, badly restored several years ago. The once-significant *viharn* was ruined when the original wooden walls were covered with thick black paint and bright orange embellishments. Worse yet, the old wooden roof was ripped off and replaced with bright orange tiles that completely ruined whatever architectural integrity the temple once possessed.

Wat Puak Hong

Fortunately, the circular *chedi* at Wat Puak Hong has wisely been declared a national registered ruin and, therefore, protected against insensitive restoration efforts by local monks. Displaying Chinese influence, the 17th-century brick *chedi* features patches of original stucco on the upper nine terraces, and 10 Buddhas tucked away in elevated niches.

ATTRACTIONS NEAR CHIANG MAI

The following temples, monasteries, and museums are just outside Chiang Mai and can be reached with public minitrucks, though a rented motorcycle or chartered *tuk tuk* will save a great deal of time.

Chiang Mai National Museum
Located on the superhighway near Wat Chet Yot, the National Museum provides an overview of both Lanna and other art styles of Thailand.

Main Floor: Centerpiece on the main floor is a gigantic Chiang Saen-style Buddha head over three meters tall. Discovered at Wat Chedi Luang and still believed to possess magical powers, the complete image must have been one of the largest bronzes ever cast in Thailand. Other schools of Thai art are represented on the ground floor by prehistoric pottery from Kanchanaburi, Srivijayan votives, Lopburi bronzes, an outstanding collection of Chiang Saen images, and Haripunchai terra-cotta figurines.

Upper Floor: Displays here are oriented more toward handicrafts and household goods than Buddha images. Among the better pieces are examples of northern Thai regalia, betel nut sets, giant drums mounted on carts, an extremely fine old rice cart, a royal bed complete with mosquito netting, 19th-century coffin covers, hilltribe displays, and a special room devoted to Burmese-Shan arts.

The Chiang Mai National Museum is open Wed.-Sun. 0900-1600. Admission is 10B.

Chiang Mai Contemporary Art Museum
This recently opened modern art museum opposite the Chiang Mai University auditorium and very near Gaad Payom Market may appear a soulless concrete block from the exterior, but an impressive array of modern Thai art awaits the visitor. Nimmanhemin Rd., tel. (053) 211724. Open Wednesday to Sunday from 0900 to 1630. Free admission.

Warbirds Museum
Military aircraft buffs will enjoy a visit to the three storage hangers supervised by members of the Royal Thai Air Classics Association. Among the classic planes are a Douglas Dakota DC 3, Cessna Dragonfly A-37, T-28 Trojan, Canadian-built Chipmunks, and Cessna Bird Dog trainers. The informal museum is located in the military section of the Chiang Mai Airport. Admission is free but you must leave your passport at the front gate.

Wat Chet Yot
From both historical and architectural standpoints, Wat Chet Yot ("Monastery of the Seven Spires") is considered the most important monument in Chiang Mai. The rather unique structure was constructed by King Tiloka in 1455 and vaguely modeled after the Mahabodhi Temple in Bodgaya, India, where the Buddha attained enlightenment. According to legendary chronicles, King Tiloka convened the Eighth Buddhist Council here in 1477 to commemorate the 2,000th anniversary of the Buddhist era. Wat Chet Yot continued to serve as a monastery and center of Lanna Thai Buddhism for several centuries. Subsequent kings covered the temple with a profusion of gold ornamentation, but this was tragically stripped by the Burmese in 1556.

The principal structure is a seven-spired *chedi*, which gives the temple its name, erected on a rectangular laterite base. Mounted on the walls are the chief glory of Wat Chet Yot: 12 stucco figures of seated divinities framed by standing celestial deities. Some have been defaced by vandals and art collectors, though as a unified ensemble the remaining images comprise the finest stuccoes in Thailand.

Wat Suan Dok
Established in 1383 to enshrine a relic of the Buddha, Wat Suan Dok ("Monastery of the Flowers") is now dominated by an extremely large *viharn* erected in 1932 by the same monk who built the road up Doi Suthep. The massive concrete and steel shed—the largest religious structure in Chiang Mai—is fashioned as an open-air *sala* and filled with painted columns, cool hardwood floors, and a large collection of Buddhas including the famous Pra Chao Kao Tue, a 500-year-old image.

In the courtyard to the west is a vast garden of white *chedis* and cenotaphs which contain the ashes of Chiang Mai nobles. A type of royal graveyard, the largest *chedi* contains a legendary relic which figured in the establishment of both Wat Suan Dok and Wat Doi Suthep. The forest of *chedis* is incredibly hot during the day, but a wonderful place for sunsets.

Wat Suan Dok is also known as a massage center where old women offer authentic Thai massage at bargain prices.

Wat Umong

Wat Umong, the oldest forest monastery in the region, was constructed around 1380 as a series of underground cells used by forest monks for silent meditation. Interior walls were painted with birds and flowers in styles similar to Chinese counterparts. A relic chamber and *chedi* were constructed above the caves in the early 15th century, but the present *chedi* dates from the early 16th century.

Wat Umong was abandoned until 1948 when local monks returned to clear out the caves and

MOTORCYCLE RIDES IN CHIANG MAI

*E*xtended rides to Mae Hong Son or the Golden Triangle may seem daunting, but short rides around Chiang Mai are a great way to briefly explore the countryside. A small 100cc step-through motorcycle is adequate for the following journeys.

Doi Suthep: The most popular motorcycle ride near Chiang Mai is up to Doi Suthep to visit the temple, Phuping Royal Palace, and Doi Pui hilltribe village. Go in the early morning for best visibility, and allow about four hours for the roundtrip journey. On the return, visit the zoo, hilltribe center at Chiang Mai University, and Pub Restaurant for drinks and grub in an old-English atmosphere.

East of the Ping River: Another popular ride begins across the Ping River near the American Baptist Mission in a neighborhood long populated with missionary groups, foreign medical associations, and Western expatriates. The beautiful enclave of narrow alleys, elaborate teakwood homes, and old commercial buildings is surrounded by gardens and landscaped lawns.

Then ride south down Highway 106 (the old Chiang Mai-Lamphun Road) to the Gymkhana Club, Mengrai Kilns, and the big tree festooned with offering scarves and miniature shrines. Continue south another kilometer, cross the Mengrai Bridge, and ride north along Charoen Prathet Road past the Sacred Heart Cathedral and the former British Consulate back to town.

Umbrellas and Silk: Everyone with an interest in traditional Thai handicrafts should spend a full day exploring the shops and factories which line the highway between Chiang Mai and the village of San Kamphang, 16 km east of town. Bicyclists will find the road too busy, and group tours are shuttled

through the shops too quickly. The perfect solution is a motorcycle shopping tour.

Mae Sa Valley Loop: Try this four-hour ride to see some backcountry almost completely untouched by tourism. Ride north 16 km up Highway 107 and turn left at the busy town of Mae Rim. Highway 1096 continues through lovely Mae Sa Valley until it finally encircles the entire mountain range and returns to Hang Dong, south of Chiang Mai. The road is in excellent condition and it's impossible to get lost, but keep your gas tank filled and watch for aggressive truck drivers. Views from the back side of the mountain range are simply spectacular.

Lamphun Loop: The following motorcycle tour involves several hours of riding on busy highways, and can only be recommended to experienced motorcyclists. Drive south down Highway 108 and at the pottery village of Meang Koong, the basket shops at Hang Dong, and the woodcarvers' village of Ban Tawrai before turning left at San Patong and following Highway 1015 to the historic town of Lamphun. After lunch and a look at the temples, return to Chiang Mai via Highway 106. Get an early start to avoid the heat and traffic, which both peak around sunset.

Doi Inthanon Loop: This very long ride of 220 km passes through a national park and some of the last remaining rainforests near Chiang Mai. Leave Chiang Mai on Highway 108, visit the beautiful *chedi* in Chom Thong, and head up Highway 1009 through Doi Inthanon National Park. Continue down to Mae Chan and along the newly paved road back to the main highway at Ob Luang Gorge, extravagantly billed as "Thailand's Grand Canyon." Fill the gas tank in Hot and continue north some 90 km to Chiang Mai. Accommodations are available in Mae Chan and Hot.

reestablish the old forest monastery. Today, a large community of both Thai and Western monks live in simple meditation huts located in the forests near the lake to the west. A large map at the entrance describes the general layout and somewhat bizarre highlights like the "Spiritual Mural Painting Hall" and "Herb's Garden." Equally amusing are the dog posters carefully labeled with religious admonitions, and trees thoughtfully tagged with amusing proverbs such as "Those with good eyes are inclined to fall into wells."

Wat Umong is five km west of Chiang Mai, at the end of a long and winding road, and only recommended to visitors with hired transportation.

Wat Ku Tao

Constructed during the 17th century to contain the ashes of a Burmese ruler of Chiang Mai, the completely bizarre Chinese-style *chedi* of Wat Ku Tao resembles five hemispherical balls arranged in descending order of size. The strange, rather than elegant, structure has been variously described as piles of pumpkins, begging bowls, or onions.

One of the most unusual *chedis* in Thailand, Wat Ku Tao is located on Soi 6 off Chotana Road, a few hundred meters north of White Elephant Gate.

Tribal Research Center

Chiang Mai University maintains a small museum and research library with information on local hilltribes. Most of the reading material in the library is in Thai, but some books in English are available.

The Tribal Research Center is in Building 15 at the far western edge of campus, and is difficult to find and reach without private transportation. The center is open Mon.-Fri. 0830-1700.

Hilltribe Museum

Most of the displays from the old Tribal Research Center have been moved to a new building, where you can now get a good look at local cultures before setting out on your trek. Ratchamangkla Park, Chotana Rd., tel. (053) 210872. Open weekdays 0900-1600.

Chiang Mai Zoo

Thailand's second-largest zoo, arboretum, and open-air bird sanctuary was founded by a Westerner who donated hundreds of endangered animals to the local government. A sketchy map is available from the entrance kiosk. The zoo has a large collection of monkeys, reptiles, barking deer, and an Asiatic elephant with a single tusk.

The Chiang Mai Zoo is on the road up to Doi Suthep, and can be a convenient stop on the return journey. The zoo is open daily 0800-1700. Admission is 10B.

ACCOMMODATIONS

Budget Accommodations

Chiang Mai's 100-plus guesthouses comprise one of the finest accommodation scenes in all of Asia. Guesthouses, ideally, are teak houses owned and operated by local families with fewer than a dozen rooms that face a courtyard filled with flowers, books, and lounge chairs. A perfect guesthouse is not only a wonderful experience but a source of trekking services, bike rentals, and advice on sightseeing, restaurants, and shopping. Genuine guesthouses—a marvelous experience for everyone—have become so popular that many of Chiang Mai's conventional hotels now call themselves "guesthouses."

Guesthouses and hotels are located in four areas of town. Those on the east bank of the Ping River are comfortable and quiet, but a bicycle (often provided free) is necessary to get around. Between the Ping River and Moon Muang Road are midpriced guesthouses and hotels ideally located within walking distance of the night market and shopping centers. Inside the old city walls is the largest concentration of guesthouses, especially in the northeast corner. West of town, in the direction of Doi Suthep, are the upscale hotels which are quiet and luxurious, but far removed from the temples and restaurants.

Guesthouse prices are fairly uniform throughout Chiang Mai. Budget choices charge 100-150B for simple rooms with fan and common bath, or 150-220B with fan and private bath. The emerging trend appears to be better guesthouses with a/c rooms and private bathrooms in the 350-600B range, described below under "Moderate Accommodations."

Choosing a guesthouse is a difficult task: ask a dozen travelers and you'll get a dozen different

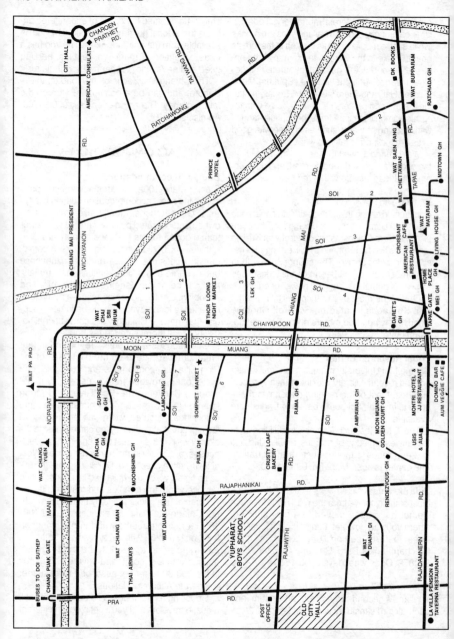

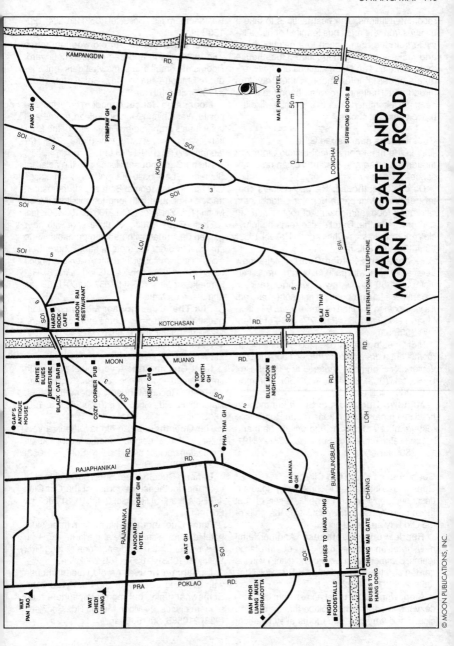

recommendations. The best tactic is to take a minibus from the main bus terminal or hire a tricycle from the train station to a neighborhood and make a walking inspection. Guesthouse touts at the bus and train stations are fairly reliable sources of information. Other travelers throughout Thailand are often happy to make personal recommendations, and these will often prove your best choice.

Guesthouses near Tapae Gate

This is the most convenient location in town, though the noise and road traffic can be a nuisance.

Daret's Guesthouse: The backpackers' center in Chiang Mai has a popular outdoor cafe with good food, and dozens of rooms with fan and private baths. Daret's also rents motorcycles and sells treks. 4 Chaiyapoon Rd., tel. (053) 235440, 100-180B fan.

Moon Muang Golden Court: A fairly new three-story hotel with patio restaurant, travel services, and 30 rooms in various price ranges. Cleanliness has dropped in recent years but it's well located near the center of town. 95 Moon Muang Rd., tel. (053) 212779, 160-260B fan, 280-360B a/c.

MEI Guesthouse: An old place with mediocre rooms, but a great cafe on the top floor and convenient location near Tapae Gate. Tapae Rd., Soi 6, tel. (053) 282448, 100-150B common bath, 280-340B a/c.

Midtown Guesthouse: Small but modern hotel in a great location near Tapae Road. Nice restaurant. All rooms include private bath and hot showers. Tapae Rd., Soi 4, tel. (053) 273191, 160-250B fan.

Guesthouses in the Old City

Guesthouse located on Moon Muang Road are described above in the Tapae Gate section, but those guesthouse to the east inside the walls of the Old City are listed here.

Rendezvous Guesthouse: Another fairly new hotel on a quiet back street with large rooms, common hot showers, and giant TV in the garden courtyard. Rajadamnern Rd., Soi 5, tel. (053) 248737, 140-220B.

Ampawan House: Just across from the Rendezvous is another new place that is modern, clean, and very quiet due to its alley location.

Rajadamnern Rd., Soi 5, tel. (053) 210584, 120-180B fan.

Pata Guesthouse: An old wooden house with rustic charm and tree-covered courtyard. Rooms are small and somewhat dark, but adequate. Moon Muang Rd., Soi 6, tel. (053) 213625, 80-140B fan.

Moonshine House: A modern hotel just opposite Wat Chiang Man with clean rooms and tasty meals prepared by Duan, wife of the English owner. A very friendly place. 212 Rajaphanikai Rd., 100-180B fan.

Racha Guesthouse: Racha and the adjacent Supreme Guesthouse are modern, clean places with good-value rooms. Both are off the beaten track and popular with long-term visitors. Moon Muang Rd., Soi 9, tel. (053) 210625, 100-150B fan.

Rose Guesthouse: Popular spot with beer garden decorated with hanging parasols, cane chairs, and other attempts at atmosphere. Services include motorcycle rentals, overseas phone calls, and trekking services. Good value. 87 Rajamanka Rd., tel. (053) 276574, 100-160B fan and common bath.

Pha Thai Guesthouse: Modern 15-room guesthouse with clean rooms and hot showers. 48/1 Rajaphanikai Rd., tel. (053) 213013, 150-180B low season, 180-240B high season (Nov.-March).

Kent Guesthouse: A very quiet place with small garden and trekking services. English management. Recommended by many travelers. Rajamanka Rd., Soi 1, tel. (053) 278578, 100-180B fan.

Nat Guesthouse: An old favorite in a very quiet residential neighborhood a few blocks off the beaten track. Pra Poklao Rd., Soi 6, tel. (053) 212878, 100-150B.

Banana Guesthouse: Small but decent spot near the southeastern corner of the Old City. 4/9 Rajaphanikai Rd., Soi 2, tel. (053) 206285, 60-140B.

Rama Guesthouse: This modern three-story hotel features a small cafe and a large yard with a swing set for the children. Moon Muang Rd., Soi 5, tel. (053) 216354, 150-200B fan.

Lamchang House: An old wooden house with swaying trees over the courtyard cafe. Somewhat funky, but more atmosphere than modern places. 24 Moon Muang Rd., Soi 7, tel. (053) 210586, 80-150B fan.

Guesthouses East of the Ping River

Several guesthouses are located east of the Ping River in a very quiet neighborhood but only a short bicycle ride into city center. There are also several popular nightclubs out here as well as some excellent cafes and restaurants.

Je t'Aime: One of the oldest guesthouses in Chiang Mai provides a relaxing atmosphere and decent rooms at bargain prices. The owner and staff are somewhat jaded about their Western visitors, though the place continues to attract a steady stream of world travelers. 247 Charoenraj Rd., tel. (053) 241912, 80-150B.

Cowboy Guesthouse: Somewhat closer to town than the venerable Je t'Aime is a newer guesthouse with equally bucolic surroundings and a friendlier staff. 233 Charoenraj Rd., tel. (053) 241314, 70-120B.

The rePlace: Strange spelling but a very quiet guesthouse in an old Lanna-style housing compound adjacent to Wat Chetuphon, just across the street from Je t'Aime. Owned and operated by a Thai-Swiss couple who sponsor weekly Thai massage workshops. 1 Chetuphon Rd., tel. (053) 80-180B common bath, 250-300B private bath.

Pun Pun Guesthouse: Somewhat more distant than the guesthouses mentioned above, but a total escape if you don't mind the longer commute into town. Rooms are in somewhat better condition that other places out here. 321 Charoenraj Rd., tel. (053) 243362, 140-260B.

Hollandia Montri Guesthouse: The most distant of all guesthouses in this neighborhood but a clean and superior choice to the simpler spots closer to town. A rented motorcycle is almost a necessity unless you care to figure out the public transportation in Chiang Mai. 365 Charoenraj Rd., tel. (053) 242450, 180-280B.

Mee Guesthouse: Primitive facilities and plenty of noise from the busy road, but a handy location just a block north of the Riverside Bar and Restaurant. It's also a fairly quick walk into town across the footbridge which crosses the Ping River. 193/1 Charoenraj Rd., tel. (053) 243881, 70-100B.

Moderate near Tapae Gate

Most of the newer guesthouses that have recently opened in Chiang Mai are charging 150-250B for a clean room with fan and private bath, and 250-500B for an a/c room. While they're somewhat more expensive than the budget guesthouses listed above, the improved cleanliness and touch of luxury make these guesthouses an outstanding value.

Lai Thai Guesthouse: A very large 90-room guesthouse that faces the old city and ancient moat. Rooms are clean and the restaurant is a popular hangout for travelers. Highly recommended. 111 Kotchasan Rd., tel. (053) 271725, fax (053) 272724, 300-350B fan, 400-650B a/c.

Gap's Antique House: One of the finest guesthouses in Chiang Mai offers antique decor with modern amenities, plus a memorable cafe filled with artwork and teakwood carvings. Rajadamnern Rd., Soi 4, tel. (053) 278140, 280-550B a/c.

Fang Guesthouse: Beautiful four-story hotel with small garden, open-air dining room, and outstanding rooms with private bath. 46 Kampangdin Rd., Soi 1, tel. (053) 282940, 220-260B fan, 340-480B a/c.

Home Place Guesthouse: This place lacks a coffee shop but is clean, modern, and in a good location near shops and restaurants. 9 Tapae Rd., Soi 6, tel. (053) 273493, 220-250B fan, 350-450B a/c.

Living House: Another modern and very clean guesthouse in a convenient location near Tapae Gate. Friendly manager and a small restaurant. Tapae Rd., Soi 5, tel. (053) 275370, 240-280B fan, 300-350B a/c.

Moderate Elsewhere

The following places are outside city center and a rented motorcycle or car will make life much easier.

Baan Kaew Guesthouse: Tucked away in an alley just south of Alliance Française (southeast of downtown), this beautiful and quiet guesthouse has spacious gardens and a comfortable restaurant—a real escape from the hustle and bustle. 142 Charoen Prathet Rd., tel. (053) 271606, 320-350B fan, 400-580B a/c.

Pension La Villa: The somewhat isolated location is compensated for by the lovely teakwood house and elevated dining room serving some of the best Italian food in Chiang Mai. 145 Rajadamnern Rd., tel. (053) 215403, 220-280B fan, 300-350B a/c.

The Red Hibiscus Guesthouse: The wife of a expat Diethelm Travel employee operates this spotless 3-storey Lanna-style guesthouse, located in the northwestern corner of the old walled city. 1 Arak Rd., Soi 2, tel./fax (053) 217631, 750-900B a/c.

YMCA: The Chiang Mai Y has a swimming pool, restaurant, convention facilities, and over 200 clean and comfortable rooms. Unfortunately, the location can be a problem since it's outside the city center and isolated from shops and the night market. 11 Mengrai Rasmi Rd., tel. (053) 221819, fax (053) 215523, 100-200B a/c dorm, 340-650B a/c rooms with private bath.

Riverside Guesthouses

All of the guesthouses which hug the west bank of the Ping River offer either fan or a/c rooms with private baths, comfortable restaurants, and delightful views over the river. As with all other guesthouses and hotels in Chiang Mai, vacancies are scarce during the busy season Nov.-March and advance reservations are strongly recommended. Reservations by fax are much better than phone calls or regular mail.

River View Lodge: The lodge is nicely decorated with Thai furnishings and traditional woodcarvings, and has a wonderful restaurant. The helpful and courteous owner speaks flawless English. An excellent upscale addition to the Ping River guesthouses. 25 Charoen Prathet Rd., tel. (053) 271109, fax (053) 279019, 1,000-1,800B.

Galare Guesthouse: A modern Thai-style guesthouse with both fan and a/c rooms with private baths. None of the rooms have river views, but Galare remains a good choice in a great location. 7 Charoen Prathet Rd., tel. (053) 293885, fax (053) 279088, 550-650B fan, 700-900B a/c.

Chumpol Guesthouse: Like many other guesthouses in the center of town, the Chumpol has lost much of its atmosphere to noise and traffic jams. Neither the Chumpol nor the adjacent, and extremely dumpy, "New" Chiang Mai Guesthouse can be recommended. 89 Charoen Prathet Rd., tel. (053) 234526, 280-480B.

Once Upon A Time River Ping Palace: A few kilometers south of Chiang Mai on the banks of the Ping River is a 12-room resort constructed in traditional Lanna style with teakwood bungalows and riverside restaurant. Tons of atmosphere. 385 Charon Prathet Rd., tel. (053) 274932, 850-1,800B.

Luxury Accommodations—Downtown

Most upscale hotels in Chiang Mai are conveniently located downtown near the night market or away from town toward Doi Suthep. Discounts of 30-50% are offered during the hot summer months April-June, and during the rainy season July-Oct. All hotels charge an additional 11% government tax and 10% service charge.

Suriwong Zenith Hotel: Central location and primarily patronized by group tours and business travelers. Not in the best condition. 110 Changklan Rd., tel. (053) 236789, fax (053) 271604, 2,000-2,800B.

Royal Princess Chiang Mai: In the heart of town stands this refurbished hotel with two restaurants, poolside bar, and popular nightclub. Formerly the Dusit Inn. 112 Changklan Rd., tel. (053) 281033, fax (053) 281044, 2,800-3,200B.

Chiang Inn Hotel: Another well-located hotel that caters to tour groups. The Chiang Inn is an older hotel; upper-floor rooms are large and quiet. 100 Changklan Rd., tel. (053) 270070, fax (053) 274499, 2,100-2,800B.

Imperial Mae Ping Hotel: Downtown Chiang Mai is dominated by this immense 374-room hotel that opened in late 1989 but has never seemed to attract a large following, although its affiliation with the Imperial hotel group from Bangkok has helped somewhat. Amenities include two restaurants, swimming pool, meeting rooms, and great views from the top floor. 153 Sri Donchai Rd., tel. (053) 270160, fax (053) 270181, 1,600-2,200B.

The Park Hotel Chiang Mai: A newer Lanna-style hotel a few blocks south of city center with restaurant, rooftop swimming pool, and 176 rooms and suites. 444 Changklan Rd., tel. (053) 281997, fax (053) 279979, 1,500-2,500B.

Luxury Accommodations—Northwest

A string of upscale hotels are located northwest of the old walled city, along Huay Kaeo Road enroute to the university and Doi Suthep.

Chiang Mai Orchid: Chiang Mai's original four-star hotel has maintained a good reputation despite the opening of newer and more luxurious properties. The principal drawback is the location outside town. 100 Huay Kaeo Rd., tel. (053) 222099, fax (053) 221625, Bangkok reservations tel. (02) 245-3973, 2,800-3,500B.

Amari Rincome Hotel: One of the best hotels in town continues to thrive under the strong management of this homegrown chain. 391 Huay Kaew Rd., tel. (053) 221044, fax (053) 221915, 2,800-3,600B.

Amity Green Hills Chiang Mai: The former Holiday Inn remains in good condition though the odd location on an isolated stretch of highway makes this a less-than-ideal choice for most visitors. 24 Chiang Mai-Lampang Super Highway, tel. (053) 220010, fax (053) 221602, 2,400-2,800B.

Chiangmai Hills Hotel: An overpriced luxury hotel that badly need renovation to compete in the local market, but still popular with large groups and conventioneers on a budget. 18 Huay Kaew Rd., tel. (053) 210030, fax (053) 210035, 1,800-2,200B.

Luxury Accommodations—Southeast
Several expensive hotels have opened south of city center in the business districts just west of the Ping River.

Empress Hotel: Chiang Mai's first luxury hotel with convention center opened in 1991 just south of city center. The 17-story landmark features various function rooms, restaurants, and the most exclusive disco in town. 199 Changklan Rd., tel. (053) 270240, fax (053) 272467, 1,600-2,800B.

Westin Chiangmai: Chiang Mai's newest and most luxurious hotel has all possible facilities, including a pool, business center, nightclub, health center, and terrace restaurant facing the Ping River. As with the first-class hotels out on Huay Kaeo Road, the chief disadvantage is the location—about five km south of town near the Mengrai Bridge. 318/1 Chiang Mai-Lamphun Rd., tel. (053) 275300, fax (053) 275299, Bangkok tel. (02) 254-1713, fax (02) 254-1716, 3,800-6,500B.

FOOD

Chiang Mai offers a wide range of dining experiences, from northern Thai dishes to European and Asian specialties. Prices are very low, and dining environments run the gamut from simple streetstalls to elaborate teakwood homes. Dining in Chiang Mai is also made pleasant by the rel-atively small size of the town and the presence of the Ping River, which provides for riverside cafes and nightclubs.

Restaurants near Tapae Gate
Restaurants and cafes here in Chiang Mai are chiefly located near Tapae Gate or downtown near the Night Market, though some of the best places are on the east side of the Ping River.

Daret's Restaurant: Chiang Mai's most popular travelers' hangout serves fairly good food, plus outstanding fruit shakes and smoothies in a friendly atmosphere. Daret's is also a great place to meet other travelers and swap information. 4 Chaiyapoon Rd. Inexpensive.

J.J.'s Restaurant: A modern, clean, air-conditioned cafe with bakery, espresso, ice cream, and Thai and American dishes. Great spot for breakfast and the *Bangkok Post*. Montri Hotel. Moon Muang at Rajadamnern Rd. Inexpensive.

Croissant Cafe: Walking tours of Chiang Mai might start with breakfast at either JJ Restaurant, Times Square, or this small a/c cafe near the Tapae Road temples. Not much atmosphere but decent food and a good escape from the traffic and noise. 318 Tapae Rd. Inexpensive.

MEI Guesthouse Roof Garden: Great views and thick coffee can be enjoyed from the rooftop cafe near Tapae Gate. Enter through the dark lobby of the guesthouse and climb the back steps to the roof. Best at breakfast. Tapae Rd., Soi 6. Inexpensive.

AUM Vegetarian Food Cafe: Among the excellent dishes are vegetarian spring rolls, tofu specialties, and meatless entrees drawn from the traditions of the north and northeast. Great food at rock-bottom prices served by followers of the Indian guru, Satya Sai Baba. 65 Moon Muang Rd. just south of Rajadamnern. Inexpensive.

Aroon Rai: Some of the city's best northern Thai dishes are served in this simple cafe near Tapae Gate. An English-language menu is available. Specialties under the native dishes section include *gang hang ley* (pork curry), *nam prik* (spicy salsa), and *kao neow* (sticky rice). Be sure to try the unlisted regional favorite *laab*, a dish of diced pork mixed with chilies, basil, and sautéed onions. Other selections include *tabong* (fried bamboo shoots) and *sai owa* (sausage stuffed with pork and herbs). Brave souls can feast on *jing kung* (roasted crickets) and other exotic specialties. 45 Kotchasan Rd. Moderate.

Lek Steakhouse: Charcoal-grilled buffalo steaks with baked potatoes and veggies are immensely popular dishes in Chiang Mai. Few prepare better steaks than Yves, the French chef who operates this popular cafe. Yves also serves strawberry crepes, homemade yogurts, and vegetarian specialties. 22 Chaiyapoon Rd., tel. (053) 252686. Moderate.

The Wok: A fairly new cafe operated by the owners of the Chiang Mai Thai Cookery School in a lovely teak house plus quiet garden setting. 44 Rajamanka Rd., tel. (053) 208207. Inexpensive.

Bierstube: Ask a local where to dine and the answer will often be this cozy restaurant in the center of Chiang Mai. Though the German and American dishes are popular, Bierstube cooks some of the best Thai dishes in town. Friendly management and wait staff. 33 Moon Muang Rd., tel. (053) 278869. Moderate.

American Internet Cafe: Tony Moon of Salt Lake City, Utah, U.S.A., has turned this cozy spot into one of the favorite hangouts for expatriates and anyone else needing food, drink, and good conversation. While checking your Hotmail account, try the Mexican dishes or Thai and International offerings. 402 Tapae Rd., tel. (053) 252190. Inexpensive.

Bacco: Italian meals at bargain prices in the middle of Chiang Mai adjacent to the Mae Kha canal. 158 Tapae Rd., tel. (053) 251389. Moderate.

The Irish Pub & Crusty Loaf Bakery: Another popular spot for breakfast dishes, sandwiches, excellent coffee, and delicious breads freshly baked by the Irish-Thai owners. They also have darts, chess, and sports on the TV. 24/24 Rajawithi Rd., tel. (053) 214554. Inexpensive.

Restaurants Downtown

The following places are all within walking distance of the Night Market. Most serve European food rather than the Thai dishes you find around Tapae Gate.

Whole Earth Restaurant: Thai, vegetarian, and Pakistani dishes served in a beautiful Thai building surrounded by lovely gardens. Nightly entertainment at 1900 ranges from Indian sitar to Thai folk guitar. No shoes in this very elegant restaurant. 88 Sri Donchai Rd. Moderate.

Shere Shiraz: A downtown cafe with Indian, Pakistani, and Arabic dishes. Fixed meals cost 60-100B in the best cafe of its type in Chiang Mai. 23-25 Chareon Prathet, Soi 6, tel. (053) 276132. Moderate.

Piccola Roma: A very upscale Italian restaurant with meals prepared by an Italian chef. 3/2 Charoen Prathet Rd., tel. (053) 271256. Expensive.

German Hofbrauhaus: German dishes served in an open-air cafe just opposite the Night Market. 115/1 Loi Kroa Rd., tel. (053) 276989. Moderate.

Haus Munchen: Established in 1979 as among the first Western restaurants in Chiang Mai and still the place for German meals and imported German beers. 115/3 Loi Kroa Rd., tel. (053) 274027.

The Red Lion: A traditional English pub with Guinness and Kilkenny along with live sports events on their satellite TV. 123 Loi Kroa Rd., tel. (053) 818847.

Hard Rock Cafe: If you need your fix of Americana. . . 66/3 Loi Kroa Rd., tel. (053) 206103. Moderate.

Cesar Pub: Darts, chess, ping-pong, piped-in music, and Belgian cuisine just opposite the Traveller Inn and Hetty Bar. 59/5 Loi Kroa Rd., tel. (053) 206773. Moderate.

Restaurants East of the Ping River

Some of the best restaurants are located across the river in the old neighborhood once favored by foreign missionaries and diplomats.

Riverside Bar and Restaurants: Probably the most popular *farang* hangout in Chiang Mai offers relaxed dining on riverside terraces. Go for the Thai entrees, then stay for the live music which ranges from light folk to heavy rock. 9 Charoenraj Rd., tel. (053) 243239. Moderate.

Gallery Restaurant: This outstanding place combines an art gallery with a beautiful garden in a renovated Chinese shophouse. Superb atmosphere with pleasant views across the river. Highly recommended. 25 Charoenraj Rd., tel. (053) 248601. Moderate.

The Good View: A few doors from the Riverside is another popular restaurant with open-air dining and views across the Ping

River. 13 Charoenraj Rd., tel. (053) 241866. Moderate.

Ratana's Kitchen: Lovely teak building and stylish surroundings for Northern Thai specialties including their popular *khao soi*. This restaurant is somewhat distant but an easy taxi ride, adjacent to the Indian Consulate. 350/4 Charoenraj Rd., tel. (053) 262629. Moderate.

New Lamduon Faham: A simple cafe famous for its curried noodle soup dish called *khao soi* served with either chicken, beef, or pork. Very rudimentary but popular with Thais and the occasional Westerner. 352 Charoenraj Rd. near the Rama IX Bridge. Inexpensive.

Nang Nual Seafood Restaurant: The largest and certainly the most ostentatious restaurant in Chiang Mai offers seafood dishes in a riverside environment five km south of town. 27 Koalklang Rd., tel. (053) 281955. Moderate.

Restaurants Elsewhere

The following restaurants will require some form of transportation to reach from most guesthouses and hotels.

Pension La Villa: The best Italian restaurant in Chiang Mai is known for its pastas, veal dishes, and pizzas cooked inside the wood-fired oven. Pension La Villa also rents a few rooms in the rear. Italian management. 145 Rajadamnern Rd., tel. (053) 277403. Moderate.

Ta Krite Cafe: Near Wat Pra Singh is a small joint known for Thai dishes and transvestite servers called *pai.* The nearby **Sri Phen** specializes in a wide variety of spicy *som tam* salads, though they aren't listed on their English menu. 17/1 Samlam Rd., one block south of Wat Pra Singh. Inexpensive.

The Pub: Superb English and French meals served in a homey place considered one of the most genial gathering spots in town. The Pub is decorated in English decor with darts, old beer signs, a collection of cigarette packs, and a roaring fireplace in the winter months. Located outside town but worth the *tuk tuk* ride. 88 Huay Kaeo Rd. near the Rincome Hotel, tel. (053) 211550. Moderate.

Galae Restaurant: A few kilometers outside town at the base of Doi Suthep and wonderfully hugging the banks of a large reservoir. 65 Suthep Rd., tel. (053) 278655. Moderate.

Buffets

Several of Chiang Mai's large hotels offer luncheon buffets with northern Thai specialties for about 100-250B—a welcome relief from steaming cafes and chaotic night markets. La Gritta in the Amari Rincome, the Western Grill in Chiang Inn, the Chao Nang Coffee Shop in the Empress, and the River Terrace Restaurant in the Westin Chiangmai all do excellent, low-priced luncheon buffets. Several hotels also offer dinner buffets; check the local tourist publications for recent listings.

Markets

Chiang Mai has one major night market and several small spots popular with Thais and budget travelers.

Ansuran Night Market: Chiang Mai's most lively and authentic dining experience is the food market which operates nightly on Ansuran Road between Changklan and Charoen Prathet Roads, just around the corner from the night bazaar. Dozens of stalls prepare a wide range of inexpensive dishes. Try rich mussel omelettes from the sidewalk showman, steamed crabs large enough for two people, and grilled fish served with a choice of sauces. Other possibilities include honey chicken roasted over an open fire, fried noodles with shrimp and bean sprouts, and the spectacle of "flying morning glory." English-language menus are often available, though the point-at-the-pot method of ordering is more direct. Ansuran Rd. Inexpensive.

Thor Loong Market: Budget travelers staying in the guesthouses near Tapae Gate often frequent the streetstalls and cafes of Thor Loong. Chaiyapoon Rd. Inexpensive.

Somphet Market: Actually in operation only during the day, Somphet is an open-air fruit market with a wide variety of fruits and fresh produce. Moon Muang Rd., Soi 7. Inexpensive.

Dinner Dance Shows

Chiang Mai's classic dining experience is *khantoke,* a traditional northern buffet accompanied by a brief demonstration of Thai dance. It's rather touristy but also fun, reasonably priced, and a rare opportunity to see traditional dance. *Khantokes* cost 200-350B and reservations should be made in advance. Photographers can request a spot in the front row, center stage.

A typical *khantoke* dinner includes: *kao neo,* glutinous rice pinched into bite-sized pieces and dipped into a variety of sweet and spicy sauces; *sai oua,* spicy Chiang Mai sausage roasted over a fire fueled with coconut husks; *naem,* pickled pork sausage; *nam prik ong,* minced pork cooked with chilies and shrimp paste; *gang hang lay,* Burmese curried pork mixed with tamarind or *kathorn;* and *larb,* a northeastern dish of minced meat mixed with fresh mint leaves.

Old Chiang Mai Cultural Center: Since 1971, the complex south of downtown has been presenting meals and dance shows in their teakwood compound. After a very mild but unlimited meal, northern Thai dances are presented in the dining room, followed by hilltribe and folk dances in the adjacent amphitheater. Be sure to try a hand-rolled cigar filled with locally grown tobacco. 185 Wulai Rd., tel. (053) 274093, 300B.

Diamond Riverside Hotel: The most convenient location for *khantoke* is the teakwood mansion behind the Diamond Hotel and near the banks of the Ping River. Unlike the Old Chiang Mai Center, this is an intimate spot where everyone is guaranteed a close look at the dancers. 33 Charoen Prathet Rd., tel. (053) 270081, 400B.

Imperial Mae Ping Hotel: Dinner and cultural shows nightly at 1900. 153 Sridonchai Rd., tel. (053) 270160, 350B.

NIGHTLIFE

Nightlife in Chiang Mai is limited to a few nightclubs and restaurants with live music. The most lively and Western-oriented clubs are located across the Ping River on Charoenraj Road. Pubs and small bars are concentrated along Moon Muang Road near Tapae Gate at the eastern side of the old city. For local low-scale entertainment, try the outdoor garden restaurants along the southern edge of the old city. And for country-western and jazz, the clubs in the northwestern corner of town are your best bet.

Central Chiang Mai

All the major hotels have cocktail lounges or nightclubs with live entertainment, but you'll probably find the independent spots far more lively.

Night Market: Chiang Mai's best nightlife activity is wandering around the night market on Changklan Road and perhaps visiting the small beer bars in the basement of the Central Emporium. More memorable are the free dance shows given nightly 2100-2300 in the rear of the Vieng Ping Market. 100 Changklan Rd.

Nightclubs: Most of the luxury hotels in Chiang Mai have nightclubs (formerly called discos) for local trendsetters—mostly teenagers—and the odd Westerner curious about the local dance scene. Cover charges of 100-200B include the first drink and hors d'oeuvres during happy hour. Music selection varies from hotel to hotel but mostly alternates between recorded music and live bands.

East of the Ping River

Chiang Mai's best nightclubs are across the river, between the Nawarat and Nakorn Ping bridges.

Riverside Bar & Restaurant: The Riverside is regarded by almost everyone as the most congenial and fun spot in town, with entertainment from folk guitar and country-western to fusion and rock 'n' roll. The breezy club can be uncomfortably packed with *farangs,* but remains a great place to meet expats and traveling night owls. Music runs 1900-0200; arrive early to secure a table on the veranda. The Dutch owners have maintained high standards and good vibes. 9 Charoenraj Rd., tel. (053) 243239.

The Brasserie: If the Riverside is packed, walk a few steps away to this club to catch their star attraction, Tuk, a wildly talented guitarist who performs perfect renditions of psychedelic hits by Hendrix, Cream, and Pink Floyd. Showtime at 2300, but arrive early or expect to stand in the back. 37 Charoenraj Rd., tel. (053) 241665.

Near Tapae Gate

Chiang Mai's best bars and beer pubs are located along Moon Muang and Kotchasan Roads, just south of Rajadamnern Road and near the Tapae Gate. Most are quiet, friendly spots perfect for enjoying a brew and easy conversation, while others are low-key girlie bars geared toward the lonely male.

Pinte Blues Pub: Pinte Blues serves a variety of beers and provides pre-recorded blues and jazz as background music. A simple, clean place to kick back for a few hours. 33 Moon Muang Rd., tel. (053) 214040.

The Domino: A few doors away and adjacent to the Top North Guesthouse is another cozy bar suitable for couples and single females. Beer, snacks, videos, and recorded music. Runners note: this is the hangout for members of the local chapter of the Hash House Harriers—those wild and crazy folks who judiciously mix parties with exercise. 47 Moon Muang Rd., tel. (053) 278503.

Black Cat: This rather gloomy spot, adjacent to the Bierstube, features drinks, snacks, and friendly women looking for the kindness of strangers. 25 Moon Muang Rd., tel. (053) 252448.

Cozy Corner: Old-timers remember this place as the old Thai-German Dairy, home to organic foods and fresh dairy products. Today, it's still selling decent food but functions as a low-key brothel disguised by pleasant gardens and a melodic waterfall. 25 Moon Muang Rd., tel. (053) 277964.

South of the Old City

South of the old city are several clubs that cater primarily to a local clientele, providing a refreshing change from the *farang* scenes described above.

Blue Moon Nightclub: A tourist trap that does an amateurish revue by unconvincing transvestites. Forget it. 5 Moon Muang Rd., tel. (053) 278818.

Smiling Monkey Pub: This cleverly named garden restaurant provides excellent food and decent live music—generally light pop or syrupy ballads—under the stars in a quiet neighborhood. The Monkey is just west of the Chiang Mai Gate on the north side of the canal. 40 Bamrungburi Rd., tel. (053) 277538.

The Hill: A rambling, cavernous, multileved music hall that resembles a cross between a bamboo factory and a Tom Sawyer treehouse; quite interesting. Nightly live shows are given by local rock bands or Thai folk singers. The Hill is in the southwest corner of the old city near Buak Hat Park. A small cover charge but no minimum on drinks. 92 Bamrungburi Rd., tel. (053) 277968.

Northwest Chiang Mai

The northwest corner of Chiang Mai has several venues for country music or live jazz.

Old West: As the name implies, this "Wild West" saloon is decorated with wagon wheels and buffalo skulls and features nightly country music bands. Shows 2000-midnight. 323 Mani Noparat Rd., tel. (053) 221494.

The Pub: This well-known English-style inn features imported beers, British snacks, and light jazz or folk musicians most nights. The Pub's enduring claim to fame was their 1986 nomination by *Newsweek* magazine as "one of the world's best bars." Although they have milked this accolade for over a decade, the place glows with comfortable vibes rarely found elsewhere in Thailand. 88 Huay Kaeo Rd., tel. (053) 211550.

SPORTS AND RECREATION

Swimming Pools

Visitors can escape the searing heat of Chiang Mai by plunging into one of the following pools. Several luxury hotels also have swimming pools available without charge to guests and to visitors for fees of 40-80B. Public pools charge a daily rate (10-20B) or offer annual memberships for unlimited entrance (50-200B).

Top North Guesthouse: Handy location in the center of town near Tapae Gate and budget guesthouses. Daily 0900-2000. 15 Moon Muang Rd., tel. (053) 213900, 50B.

Amari Rincome Hotel: An Olympic-sized pool in the northwestern section of town. 301 Huay Kaeo Rd., tel. (053) 221044, 80B, daily 1000-1900.

Suan Dok Hospital: The cheapest pool in town. CMU Faculty of Medicine, Suthep Rd., tel. (053) 221699, 10B, daily except Thursday 0900-2000.

Pongpat: Public pool north of the old city. Daily 0900-1900. 73/22 Chotana Rd., tel. (053) 212812, 15B, 200B annual membership.

Thai Boxing

Organized mayhem breaks out on weekend evenings at 1930 in the boxing arena near the GPO and Chiang Mai train station. Check with the TAT for the latest schedules. Dechanukroh Stadium, Khong Sai Rd., 50-250B.

Running

The Chiang Mai **Hash House Harriers** meet weekly at the Domino Bar to plan their weekend escapades. Visitors are welcome to attend meetings and join the fun on the weekends. Domino Bar, 47 Moon Muang Rd., tel. (053) 278503.

HILLTRIBE TREKKING

One of Thailand's most memorable experiences is visiting and living briefly among the seminomadic hilltribe people of northern Thailand. Most of these agriculturalists migrated here from Laos and southern China via Myanmar over the last century. Today, despite the inroads of Westernization and government programs to encourage their assimilation into mainstream Thai society, these groups have to a surprising degree maintained their distinct languages, animist customs, patterns of dress, and strong sense of ethnoconsciousness.

Although these packaged adventures are called "treks," they more closely resemble long walks and involve several hours of daily hiking over foothills, wading across streams, and tramping under bamboo forests before spending the evening in a village. After a late-afternoon arrival at the village, visitors are welcome to politely wander around, watch the women weave or pound rice, play with the children, and take a few discreet photos. Accommodations are limited to wooden floors in the headman's house, bathrooms are in the distant bushes, and bathing takes place in nearby streams. Dinner is often a simple meal of sticky rice, boiled vegetables, and hot tea. After the plates are cleared, dozens of villagers, children, curious teenagers, and shy young girls fill the lodge for an awkward but fascinating conversation conducted through your interpreter/guide. You can ask about their customs and beliefs, but be prepared to explain yours and perhaps sing a song! Opium is offered after the villagers wander back to their houses and all the children have been put to bed.

Where to Go

Golden Triangle: Hilltribe villages are scattered over most of northern Thailand but the first treks, some 20 years ago, were concentrated in the Golden Triangle area north of the Kok River. Although the hill people continue to live and dress in traditional manner, some of the more accessible villages have been overtrekked and become sadly commercialized. This is, however, one of the only areas to visit Akhas and the easiest place to do some self-guided trekking. Pick up *The Mae Kok River* map from Suriwong

Books in Chiang Mai and then take the bus up to Thaton. Self-guided treks can start here or halfway down the river. Another good spot to start from is Mae Salong, a small Kuomintang village northwest of Chiang Rai. Guesthouses in Chiang Dao, Fang, Thaton, Chiang Rai, Chiang Saen, and Mae Salong can help with details.

North of Chiang Mai: The region around Chiang Dao and Wiang Papao, midway between Chiang Mai and Fang, was the next area opened to explorers. Treks typically begin with a threehour jeep ride to a drop-off point on the Chiang Mai-Fang Highway, then a half day of hiking to reach the first village. Trekking groups occasionally pass each other, and the villagers are now quite accustomed to Westerners.

Mae Hong Son: The early 1980s saw the focus shift west of Chiang Mai toward the isolated town of Mae Hong Son, the newest and leastcommercialized trekking area in Thailand.

Should You Trek?

The question of trekking in northern Thailand has taken on some significance in recent years and should perhaps be considered before you sign up with a local trekking agency.

Those opposed to hilltribe trekking question the underlying motives behind the industry and encourage people to either skip the experience or at least trek with a greater sensitivity to the environment and local cultures. These critics claim that hilltribe villages have become human zoos from the sheer number of trekkers and that the hilltribes faced cultural erosion with their only contact with the outside world coming through a camera lens and a flow of sweets and cigarettes.

Those who see hilltribe trekking in a more positive light believe that the hilltribes benefit from outside contact and remain capable, to some degree, of maintaining their cultural traditions despite the onslaught of Western visitors. They also believe that forces far more powerful than trekking or tourism—government programs, economic needs that encourage assimilation, the unstoppable tide of modernization—are responsible for the declining state of hilltribes rather than the relatively minor impact of trekking on these once remote groups.

General Information

Research: Paul and Elaine Lewis's *Peoples of the Golden Triangle* is the best of recently pub-

PEOPLE OF THE HILLS

The Thai government recognizes six major groups of hilltribes, divided into dozens of subtribes with distinct languages, religious beliefs, customs, costumes, and historical backgrounds. The following descriptions include those tribes most likely to be encountered by trekkers. The Western tribal designation is given first, followed by the local Thai terminology.

Akha

Akha (Ekaw)
Population: 27,000
Origins: Yunnan, China
Locations: Golden Triangle

Considered among the poorest and least sophisticated of all hilltribes, the Akha are also among the most dazzling in costume. Women's dress typically includes a long-sleeved jacket and short skirt woven from homespun cotton dyed dark blue with indigo. The crowning glory is the Akha headdress, an elaborate pile of cloth stretched over a bamboo frame festooned with bird feathers, iridescent wings of beetles, silk tassels, dog fur, squirrel tails, and Indian silver rupees. Leggings are worn to protect against brambles and thorns.

The shy and retiring Akha construct their villages at high elevations to escape neighbors and provide privacy for opium cultivation. Primitive wooden figures flanking the village entrance gates are carved with prominent sex organs to ensure fertility and ward off evil spirits. Don't touch these talisman gates or the bamboo spirit houses scattered throughout the village. Most villages have giant swings used during festivals and a courting ground where young people congregate. Homes are enormous structures divided into separate sleeping quarters for males and females. Like most tribespeople, Akhas are animists who believe that the spirits of nature, departed ancestors, and graveyard-dwelling malevolent ghosts must be appeased with frequent animal sacrifice.

Despite efforts to preserve their traditional lifestyle, Akhas face the challenges of poverty, political impoverishment, deforestation, overpopulation, and discrimination from other tribespeople, who consider them the bottom of the social order because of lack of education and cultural sophistication.

Hmong

Hmong (Meo)
Population: 65,000
Origins: Laos
Locations: Chiang Mai, Laotian border

The Hmong, called Meo by the Thais, are a fiercely independent people who fled Chinese persecution over the last century for the relative peace of northern Thailand. Today the second-largest tribal group in Thailand, Hmongs have become the country's leading opium producers by establishing their villages on mountaintops; higher elevations are considered best for opium cultivation. Thai Hmong are subdivided into White and Blue, color distinctions referring to costume hues rather than linguistic or cultural differences.

continues on next page

PEOPLE OF THE HILLS
(continued)

Despite their isolation, Hmongs are not shy; you will see them in Chiang Mai's night market selling exquisite needlework and chunky silver jewelry. Traditional female costume includes a short jacket of Chinese design, circular silver neck rings, and a thickly pleated dress handwoven from cannabis fiber. Their striking and voluminous hairstyle is made by collecting old hair and braiding it together into a bun. Courting begins during the New Year festivals, when teenagers meet and make arrangements to rendezvous again during rice-planting season. Courting ends when the prospective husband makes a monetary offering of five silver ingots to the girl's parents.

A useful introduction to the Hmong is provided in *The Hmong* by Robert Cooper and published by Artasia Press in Bangkok.

Karens are peaceful, honest, and hardworking; they use sound methods of swidden agriculture to save topsoil and minimize cogon growth. Their women are superb weavers whose multicolored skirts, blouses, and wedding garments have become prized collector's items. Female dress often denotes marital status: young girls wear white cotton shifts while married women wear colored sarongs and overblouses. Multiple strands of beads are popular but most women shun the heavy silver jewelry favored by other tribal groups. Males are often covered with elaborate tattoos that permanently satisfy ancestral spirits and so eliminate expensive spirit ceremonies. Religious beliefs run the gamut from animism and Buddhism to visionary millennial movements that prophesy a future, messianic king. Karen Christians call him the final Christ, Buddhists call him the fifth and final incarnation.

Karen

Karen (Yang, Kariang)
Population: 275,000
Origins: Myanmar
Locations: Thai-Burmese border

Thailand's largest hilltribe is the only group not heavily engaged in opium cultivation. Settlements are so numerous that most trekking groups pass through at least one of several subdivisions. Karens are divided into the Sgaw, who live near Mae Hong Son, and the Pwo to the south of Mae Sariang. Smaller Burmese groups include the Kayahs (Karenni or Red Karens) in Kayah State (just across the border from Mae Hong Son) and the Pao who live in southern Shan State.

Lahu

Lahu (Musser)
Population: 45,000
Origins: Southwestern China
Locations: Chiang Dao, Fang, Golden Triangle

Lahus are one of the most assimilated of all northern tribes. Most belong to the Black (Lahu Na) or Red (Lahu Nyi) linguistic groups, while a minority speak two dialects of the Yellow (Lahu Leh and Shi). Older Lahus, who haven't yet adopted modern costume, dress in black robes richly embroidered with red zigzagged stitching and silver ornaments. Children often wear Chinese beanies sprouting red puff balls.

Lahus are animists who believe their village priests can exorcise evil spirits with black magic and heal the sick with sacred amulets. And like the Karens, they anticipate a messianic movement lead by Guisha, the supreme Lahu god who created the heavens. Their most famous postwar messiah was Maw Naw, the gibbon god who failed in his attempts to restore true Lahu religion and lead his people back into Myanmar. Ceremonial life revolves around the lively New Year festival when, after dancing, top spinning, and other games, males court females by blowing a gourd signal and poking them with sticks through the slats of the bamboo floor. Special pavilions are available for marriage proposals and lovemaking.

blouse and a rakish turban festooned with long strands of multicolored yarn. This dazzling costume is complemented by a cascade of silver buttons and long dangling ornaments which hang over the chest. Lisu religion revolves around the familiar animist spirits, but also weretigers and vampires which might take possession of a person. Lisus practice complicated marriage rituals and a hedonistic New Year festival of endless dancing, drinking, and religious ritual.

Mien

Lisu

Lisu (Lisa)
Population: 20,000
Origins: Myanmar
Locations: Chiang Dao, Fang, Mae Hong Son

Thailand's premier opium cultivators and the most culturally modern of all hilltribes are outgoing, friendly, and economically successful. Lisu villages are often clean and prosperous, loaded with sewing machines, radios, motorcycles, and perhaps a Datsun truck. Terrific salespeople, they enjoy setting up stalls and selling their handicrafts in Chiang Mai's night market.

Their enthusiasm and determination to outshine every other tribal group is reflected in their beautiful and extremely stylish clothing. Females typically wear a brilliant blue skirt topped with an electric red

Mien (Yao)
Population: 35,000
Origins: Southern China
Locations: Chiang Rai Province

Mien are hardworking and materially advanced. Called Yao by the Thai, the Mien originated in southern China as a non-Han group before migrating into Thailand via Laos between 1910 and 1950. Most have dutifully kept their Chinese cultural links such as Chinese script and Taoist religion. Sacred scrolls which function as portable icons (similar to Tibetan *tankas*) are their great artistic creation. When unrolled and hung up, these Taoist tapestries change ordinary rooms into temporary temples. Tragically, most have been sold to Bangkok antique merchants by impoverished Mien.

Mien women wear large black turbans, distinctive red boas around their necks, and loose-fitting pants embroidered with a stunning pastiche of triangle, tie-dye, and snowflake designs.

lished books. Other useful books include the Time-Life publication of Frederic Grunfeld's *Wayfarers of the Thai Forest,* which details Akha lifestyles, as well as *Highlanders of Thailand,* which provides a comprehensive collection of well-edited essays, including a chapter on the effects of tourism. These books are difficult to find in Chiang Mai and should be read in advance. *People of the Hills* by Preecha Chaturabhand is somewhat trashy (detailing the sex lives of the Akhas) but available locally and small enough to be carried on the trek. A few hours of browsing in the Tribal Research Center at Chiang Mai University will also help.

When to Go: Winter months (late October to early February) are the ideal time to enjoy the cool nights and warm days without the threat of rain; it's also the best season to find poppies in full bloom. The rainy months (June-Sept.) can be difficult if not impossible. March-May the climate is unbearably hot.

Group or Independent Tour? Organized treks reduce language difficulties, security problems, and the possibility of getting lost on the winding trails.

Selecting the Trekking Agency: Chiang Mai's 40 registered trekking agencies meet monthly, make reports to the police department, set agreements on rates, and discuss problems. Neither the TAT nor Tribal Research Center makes specific recommendations on trekking agencies, but everyone agrees the most important factor is the qualifications of the guide. Meet with him to determine his age, maturity, trekking experience, knowledge of tribal customs, local dialects spoken, and sensitivity to the hilltribes.

Trek Details: Make a firm agreement on all services the trekking company will provide. How many days will the trek last? Since it takes at least two days to reach the relatively untouched villages, a trek of five to seven days will prove much more rewarding than shorter treks. How big will the group be? Groups of more than six people are large and unwieldy and should be avoided. What areas will be visited? Everybody promises the "newest untrekked area" but exactly how many other trekking groups will be in the region with yours? Crossing tracks with another group is to be expected but should still be held to a minimum. What hilltribes will you visit? Ideally you should visit three or four distinct groups rather than just five Karen groups in five days.

Rates set by the Chiang Mai Trekking Guide Association average 1,500-2,500B for a five-day trek, but special trips with elephant rides and river rafting are much higher. Lodging, food, and transportation are normally included with the package price but check on exclusions. Rucksacks and sleeping bags for cooler winter months may also be provided.

Behavior: Remember that hill people are human beings with customs, values, and emotions just as valid as yours. Visitors should act politely and observe local customs. Your guide can advise you on local taboos such as avoiding villages marked with a bamboo cross or not touching the fertility symbols that guard some villages. Modesty should always be observed. Revealing halter tops on women and nude bathing in the local streams are definitely taboo. Before unpacking the camera, establish some kind of rapport with the villagers. Most tribespeople allow photos when taken discreetly, but it's best to ask permission. Rather than handing out sweets, cigarettes, cheap trinkets, or money, offer food, Band-Aid bandages, disinfectants, soap, toothpaste, and other necessities.

Warning: Should the trekking company or guesthouse offer to keep your valuables, both parties should prepare a complete list of valuables and issue an itemized receipt. Some travelers report that stored valuables, such as traveler's checks or camera equipment, have disappeared during their trek. Even worse, trekkers' credit cards have been surreptitiously used to purchase goods in Bangkok with the cooperation of agreeable shopkeepers—a theft undetected until your bill arrives back home. To prevent this type of fraud (more common than robbery during the trek), make a detailed report and leave all valuables in a locked bag.

SHOPPING

Chiang Mai is Thailand's center of traditional arts and crafts, a veritable bazaar of silverwork, ceramics, antiques, and hilltribe handicrafts—along with tons of mass-produced junk. Take your time, shop selectively, and remember that bargaining is the rule except at leading shops, where prices are fixed.

Chiang Mai has several areas known for their unique shopping venues. The central city offers the night markets, hilltribe handicraft shops along Tapae Road, and large shopping complexes for utilitarian goods and a handful of specialized boutiques.

The Chiang Mai-San Kamphang Road (Hwy. 1006) is the single best area to spend a day exploring almost 100 factories, showrooms, and demonstration sites for almost every possible craft produced in Thailand.

Less familiar to most visitors is the Chiang Mai-Hang Dong Road (Hwy. 108) that has recently emerged to challenge San Kamphang as the hottest area for shopping. Highway 108 heads south from the Airport Plaza past dozens of shops and factories specializing in antiques, ceramics, and woodcarvings. The woodcarving village of Ban Tawai and the ceramics village of Muan Kung are located just off the main highway. Hang Dong is the rattan and wickerware capital of northern Thailand.

Shopping Complexes

Chiang Mai now has almost 20 shopping centers featuring both utilitarian goods and fine antiques, local handicrafts, and other decorative products.

The original shopping center, Tantrapan, now has branches on Tapae Road, at the airport complex, and in the northwestern corner of town near the Chang Puak Gate. Downtown shopping centers include the newish Chiang Inn Plaza across from the Chiang Inn, the Rim Ping Superstore on Chang Puak Road, and Seasons Plaza en route to the Empress Hotel.

Several new shopping centers have also opened in the northwestern section of town, near the luxury hotels and wealthy housing developments popping up like mushrooms at the base of Doi Suthep Mountain. Nantawan Arcade and Tantrapan Shopping Center are convenient places to search for modern clothing, household supplies, and other utilitarian objects.

Kaed Sua Kaew Shopping Complex: The final word in shopping indulgence arrived several years ago with the opening of the massive complex in the northwestern corner of town. Often called the KSK, this five-floor a/c wonderland offers everything from lawn mowers to lingerie, hairdressers to hotels, and cappuccinos to cinemas, plus a lively people-watching scene

geared towards teenagers. KSK also has a Burger King, Pizza Hut, Mister Donut, Swensen's, Kentucky Fried Chicken, Baskin-Robbins, A & W Rootbeer, and four theaters with English-language soundtracks.

Hilltribe Handicrafts

Ethnographic souvenirs such as imitation opium pipes, newly manufactured opium weights, weavings, and chunky jewelry are sold at the night market and from dozens of shops along Tapae Road near the East Gate. Most have already been picked over by Bangkok dealers and the remainder are often shoddy and badly overpriced.

Anongporn: One of the many Tapae Road shops selling both new and old items—from rare textiles made with natural dyes to newly embroidered jackets laced with traditional Hmong designs. A good approach is to visit the shop several times over a few days and form a friendship with the owner before you start bargaining. 208 Tapae Rd., tel. (053) 236654, fax (053) 252899.

Hilltribe Products Foundation: This well-known shop near Wat Suan Dok is a government-run emporium under the patronage of His

Majesty the King, established to promote hilltribe handicrafts and provide an alternative source of income to poppy cultivation. The crafts are of a generally high quality and reasonably priced, and all profits go to worthwhile causes. Open daily 0900-1700. 21/17 Suthep Rd., tel. (053) 277743.

Thai Tribal Crafts: This nonprofit humanitarian foundation near McCormick Hospital is sponsored by Karen and Lahu church organizations to help improve the economic condition of the hilltribes. Handicrafts are well priced and of higher quality and workmanship than those sold in the night market. The shop is somewhat isolated but worth the journey simply to see the beautiful neighborhood and its tree-lined avenues flanked by historic old buildings. Open daily except Sunday 0900-1700. 208 Bumrungaj Rd., tel. (053) 241043, fax (053) 243493.

Golden Triangle People's Art and Handicraft: A British reader has written in to recommend this relatively new shop which sells handicrafts by various hilltribes in an effort to preserve their disappearing arts and crafts. 137/3 Nantharam Rd., tel. (053) 276194.

Chiang Mai Doll Making Center: The largest doll production facility in Thailand also boasts one of the largest doll collections in the world. The center is 23 km south of Chiang Mai on the road to Hot, but worth the effort if you're a doll fanatic. 187/2 Moo 9, Ban Dongkilek, tel. (053) 837229.

Antiques

High-quality and authentic antiques such as Karen frog drums and Kalong ceramics have become, in recent years, both rare and extremely expensive due to an increase in worldwide demand and the collection fever of nouveau riche Asians.

Shops along Tapae Road are difficult to properly categorize since most sell hilltribe handicrafts, new textiles, some silver products, and perhaps a few odd antiques. **Maneesinn Antiques** is one of the few shops that specializes in antiques and avoids the confusing randomness of most retailers. Strong points are handicraft antiques from Myanmar such as baskets, betel nut cutters, and superb lacquerware fashioned into small coffee tables and exquisite boxes. 289 Tapae Rd., tel. (053) 276586.

Silverwork

Chiang Mai's original handicraft was first produced by silversmiths who lived and worked in small shophouses strung along Wualai Road near the southern edge of the old city. Prior to the tourist invasion of the 1970s, visitors could wander around and watch the old guys pound out—under the most primitive conditions—a fascinating array of repoussé rice containers and cigarette boxes ornamented with scenes from the Ramakien. Woodcarving shops featuring items from salad bowls to life-sized elephants were also located in the neighborhood.

After business slowed in the 1980s, many of the craftspeople relocated to larger facilities on the San Kamphang and Hang Dong highways. However, enough businesses remain to make the old neighborhood a fascinating one to explore for a few hours.

Siam Silverware: One of Wualai's oldest and most successful silver shops remains firmly entrenched at the same location it's occupied since the early 1950s. Visitors are welcome to wander around and watch the silversmiths pound away, slowly transforming bare sheets of metal into intricately decorated snuff boxes. Prices are high, but the quality exceeds that of most of the large factories on San Kamphang Road. 5 Wualai Rd., Soi 3, tel. (053) 279013.

Nearby shops include Noparat Silverware (19 Wualai), Hiranyakorn (27 Wualai), Damrong Silver (31 Wualai), Chom Chun (53 Wualai), and Wualai Souvenir (343 Wualai).

Sipsong Panna: One of Chiang Mai's finest silverwork shops is tucked away in the Nantawan Arcade directly across from the Amari Rincome Hotel. Sipsong also sells a high quality selection of rare ornaments created by Thai, Burmese, and Laotian artisans, plus excellent pieces fashioned by the local hilltribes. Nantawan Arcade, 95/19 Nimanhemin Rd., tel. (053) 216096, fax (053) 216022.

Textiles

For collectors of textiles, northern Thailand has always been a wonderfully rich source of both hilltribe and traditional Tai fabrics. The fabrics and patterns created by local ethnic groups— Tai Yuan (the principal Tai group), Tai Lue (recent migrants from Southern China), and Tai Phuan (Laos)—reflect the historical and anthropological origins of the people.

Naenna Textile Studios: Patricia Cheesman Naenna, textile expert and author of *Lanna Textiles* published by Chiang Mai University, operates a sophisticated and varied shop one block south of the Nanatawan Arcade. Patricia sells both older fabrics suitable for textile collectors and original creations chiefly fashioned from silk ikat. Open daily 0900-1700. 188 Soi 9, Nimanhemin Rd., tel. (053) 226041.

The Loom: This lovely old wooden house a few blocks south of Tapae Gate specializes in both antique and modern fabrics from Laos, Cambodia, Myanmar, China, and the various regions of Thailand, including silk ikats from the northeast and woven skirts indigenous to Lanna. 27 Rajamanka Rd., tel. (053) 278892.

Duangjitt House: The Nantawan Arcade in the northwestern section of town features several boutiques offering a wide range of quality antiques and assorted handicrafts gathered from all over Southeast Asia. Duangjitt specializes in antique Thai textiles, Cambodian ikats, traditional artwork, and fine silver jewelry of such workmanship and rarity that collectors include Princess Diana, Elizabeth Taylor, and members of the Thai Royal Family. The owner, Duangjitt Thaveesri, and her daughter, Chitlada, are both gracious and patient hosts who provide export licenses (when necessary) and guarantees of authenticity for all antiques. Nantawan Arcade, 95/10 Nimanhemin Rd., tel. (053) 215167.

Nandakwang: Homespun cotton clothes dyed with varying hues of blue have traditionally been the standard attire for most Thai citizens, including political iconoclast Chamlong Srimuang. From their factory in Lampang, Nandakwang produces some of Thailand's most famous cotton products, which are sold at their branch in Bangkok and from their Chiang Mai location in the Nantawan Arcade. 95/1-2 Nimanhemin Rd., tel. (053) 222261.

Ceramics

Several types of ceramics are produced around Chiang Mai, from simple clay pottery from the village of Muang Kung to elegant celadons considered the final word in Thai ceramics. Celadons are high-fire stonewares fashioned from local clays and then covered with wood-ash composites created thousands of years ago by Chinese craftspeople. Although celadons can be quite expensive, collectors value them for their timeless designs and distinctive green glazes.

Mengrai Kilns: Chiang Mai's most famous celadon factory moved a few years ago from outside town to a new location in the southwestern corner of the old city. For several decades, Mengrai has produced top quality, individually crafted ceramics for connoisseurs and casual collectors. 79/2 Arak Rd., Soi Samlarm 6, tel. (053) 272063.

Ban Phor Liang Muen: Are you in desperate need of a hermit statue, Sukothai-era votive, or snarling gargoyle to impress your friends back home? Or perhaps a Haripunchai mural or a larger-than-life Buddha? Then this unique terracotta shop, in the southeastern corner of the old city, is your kind of place. Well worth a visit if only to enjoy the restored old teak house and lovely gardens just north of the Chiang Mai Gate. 36 Prapoklao Rd., Soi 2, tel. (053) 278187, fax (053) 275895.

Shopping on Chiang Mai-San Kamphang Road

Chiang Mai's most extensive collection of handicraft and arts shops is located along Hwy. 1006 between Chiang Mai and the silk- and cotton-weaving village of San Kamphang. At last count, over 50 stores and factories were selling silverwork, woodcarvings, lacquerware, leather products, dolls, gems, and Thai silk. Together they form the greatest concentration of handicraft industries in Southeast Asia, rivaled only by the artistic centers of Bali.

Perhaps the most fascinating reason to explore Hwy. 1006 are the handicraft demonstrations during which visitors can watch the time-consuming production of silks, silvers, and woodworks. Rarely in Asia can you enjoy such a range of handicrafts and learn first hand the enormous time and skill involved in their production. Whether you buy anything or not, visiting these factory workshops is an experience worth the trip.

Shoppers are strongly advised to spend a full day exploring the showrooms on San Kamphang Road. Group tourists are frantically shuttled from store to store and allowed little time to watch the crafts being made and bargain for discounts. The best strategy is to rent a motorcycle or car and spend an entire day casually visiting the shops. Taxi drivers only charge about 50B per

hour since they receive a commission on your purchases.

Selection is great and prices low for the unhurried traveler. On my last visit, I discovered that many shops will offer discounts of up to 50% to independent travelers not attached to a tour group. All shops can help arrange packing, shipping, and insurance. A few of the better shops are listed below. The kilometers indicate distance from the superhighway.

Jolie Femme Silk (1 km): First stop might be this enormous silk factory on the right side of the road. Behind the modern weaving facilities in the front is a display center where visitors can learn about silk production and watch weavers work the old-fashioned looms.

Thai Shop (2 km): On the left is a large showroom with a superb brassware factory in the rear. A careful inspection of the production techniques shows that brassware remains a cottage industry little changed from generations ago.

Chiang Mai Silver (2.1 km): Most of the silversmiths once located on Wulai Road have reestablished their cooperatives in the enormous showrooms on Hwy. 1006. A very good tour and detailed explanation of silver production are given free of charge at Chiang Mai Silver.

Iyara Art (3.5 km): Inside this beautifully designed building is an outstanding collection of old Burmese furniture and other antiques imported from Myanmar. Iyara Art grants discounts of 35-40% to tourists, and 50% to wholesalers, Thais, and independent travelers.

Borisoothi Antiques (4 km): Chiang Mai's leading antique dealer relocated several years ago from central Chiang Mai to the new showroom on the right side of Hwy. 1006. Products range from Burmese Buddhas and Ming dynasty porcelains to Kalong ceramics and newly manufactured teakwood furniture.

Shinawatra Thai Silk (4.4 km): Thailand's largest manufacturer of silk products operates a large factory in San Kamphang and a more convenient showroom 4.4 km from the superhighway. Prices are somewhat high, but Shinawatra offers the finest quality in the country.

Nakorn Ping Leather (4.4 km): Friendly young women are happy to show the differences in leather quality and explain how elephant hide can be simulated from buffalo leather. Visitors should remember that hides from endangered animals cannot be imported into most Western countries.

Chiang Mai Treasure (5.3 km): This wood-carving showroom sells life-sized elephants and smaller souvenirs to visitors. Since Buddhas cannot be exported from Thailand, most wood-carvers specialize in other images such as animals or cute children.

Arts and Crafts (5.3 km): This immense complex is where most tour buses stop for lunch in the cafe or nearby Sai Thip Restaurant. Arts and Crafts has a good demonstration area.

Borsang Village (6.3 km): Borsang is the center for Thailand's famous umbrellas, made from cotton or *sah* paper stretched over a bamboo frame. Visitors are welcome to wander around Boon Umbrella Center and have a simple drawing quickly painted on their bag or T-shirt.

San Kamphaeng Kilns (8 km): Pottery of all types is fashioned and fired in the large factory on the left side of the road.

Shinawatra Silk Factory (10.9 km): An immense modern factory lies in the town of San Kamphang. The tourist center and demonstration rooms on the left provide every possible detail on silk production.

SERVICES AND INFORMATION

Tourist Information
The tourist office moved several years ago from the convenient location in the middle of town to a remote spot on the opposite side of the Ping River. Free publications include maps, magazines, lists of bus and train departures, hotels, guesthouses, and licensed trekking agencies. Information officers are friendly and speak excellent English, but the location makes this a tiresome journey for most visitors. Open daily 0900-1700. 105/1 Chiang Mai-Lamphun Rd., tel. (053) 248604, fax (053) 248605.

Tourist Police
The Chiang Mai Tourist Police department is adjacent to the TAT office on the east bank of the Ping River. An international Home Phone center is also located in the police station; open daily 0800-midnight. The police offer 24-hour services. 105 Chiang Mai-Lamphun Rd., tel. (053) 248974, fax (053) 240289.

Hospitals
Most hospitals in Chiang Mai have foreign-trained doctors who speak English and provide top-notch service at a reasonable cost. A few doctors are affiliated with a particular hospital but most maintain private clinics and are free to work at the hospital of their choice.

Hospital charges average 1,500-2,000B per day for private rooms. All accept medical insurance plans, and payment can be made with any major credit card.

McCormick Hospital: Expat residents feel that McCormick is the best hospital for Westerners, due to the large staff who all speak English and their long history of treating foreign citizens. Kaew Nawarat Rd., tel. (053) 241107 or (053) 241311, fax (053) 241177.

Chang Puak Hospital: A modern facility with English-speaking doctors and interpreters for many other languages. 1/7 Chang Puak Rd., tel. (053) 220022, fax (053) 218120.

Lanna Hospital: Another private facility recommended by many expatriates. 103 Hwy. 11, tel. (053) 211037, fax (053) 218402.

Specialized Facilities
Medical Specialists: The U.S. Consulate can provide a list of specialists on infectious diseases, internal medicine, parasitology, and orthopedic surgery. 387 Vichayanon Rd., tel. (053) 252629.

Chiang Mai Malaria Center: This government facility provides information on malaria prevention and free blood tests with results in just 30 minutes. 18 Bumrangrit Rd., tel. (053) 221529.

Immigration
Visas can be quickly extended at Thai Immigration (tel. 053-277510) at 71 Sanambin ("Airport") Rd., on the left side of the road some 300 meters before the terminal. Open weekdays 0830-noon and 1300-1600.

Thirty-day extensions to the standard tourist visa cost 500B and require three photos and two copies of your passport photo page, visa page, and arrival/departure card. Take these with you as there are no photocopy facilities at the immigration office. Dress conservatively or expect long delays or denial of visa extension.

Travelers who wish to stay in Thailand beyond 90 days must leave the country to obtain a new visa; Vientiane and Penang are the two popular choices.

Consulates

Chiang Mai has several consulates that grant visas and extend passports. Note the limited visa hours; arrive early to conduct your business.

Australia, 165 Srimungklajan Rd., tel. (053) 221083, fax (053) 219726, weekdays 0900-1200.

China, 111 Changlor Rd., tel. (053) 276125, weekdays 0900-1130.

France, 138 Charoen Prathet Rd., tel. (053) 281466, fax (053) 215719, weekdays 1000-1200.

India, 113 Bamrungraj Rd., tel. (053) 243066, fax (053) 242491, weekdays 1000-1200.

Japan, 90 Mahidol Rd., Suite 104, tel. (053) 203367, weekdays 0830-1630.

Sweden, YMCA, 11 Somsuk Rd., tel. (053) 220844, fax (053) 210877, weekdays 1600-1800.

United Kingdom, 90 Mahidol Rd., Suite 201, tel. (053) 203405, fax (053) 203408, weekdays 0830-1600.

United States, 387 Wichayanon Rd., tel. (053) 252629, fax (053) 252633, weekdays 0800-1130.

Mail

Chiang Mai's main post office (tel. 053-245376) is on Charoen Muang Road just west of the train station. The GPO is open weekdays 0830-1630 and weekends 0900-1200. Take bus 1 or 3 and watch for the train station.

Seven branch postal offices are conveniently located around town.

Mail Boxes Etc.: Prices are somewhat higher than at the post office, but this well-known franchise is dependable and quick and provides a large number of other useful services such as mailbox rentals, domestic courier service, packing, international telephone, and other office necessities. 124 Chang Klan Rd., tel. (053) 818433, fax (053) 818435. Open daily 0900-2300.

Telephone

International calls to Europe and the United States cost about 250B for the first three minutes. To make a call from a private phone, dial 001 (the international access code), followed by the country code, then the area code and local phone number. Dial 100 for an international long distance operator.

Overseas telephone calls can be made from most hotels and guesthouses for a service fee, generally 10-30%. See "Telephone" under "Measurements and Communications" in the On the Road chapter for information on making calls with the help of AT&T and other long-distance phone companies—the least expensive way to make overseas calls.

Home Direct phones that connect you with operators in your home country are located around Chiang Mai. The most convenient spots are the Chiang Inn Plaza near the night market, and Kotchasan Road near Tapae Gate.

Private telecom centers with international phone connections and fax services are also scattered around town. The most convenient locations are the Night Market Overseas in the basement of the night market, P&D Overseas at 278 Tapae Rd., Porn Pas Overseas at 36 Kotchasan Rd., and Micro Overseas at 127 Moon Muang Rd.

Red phones are for local calls. Blue phones are for calls within Thailand. Dial 12 for local directory assistance, 183 for domestic long-distance directory information, and 101 for domestic long-distance service including Malaysia and Laos. Be sure to have a Thai speaker at your side.

Massage

Traditional Thai massage is a unique form of curative techniques designed to reinvigorate your old body and perhaps cure a few of your Western ailments. And Chiang Mai is Thailand's center for this clever combination of shiatsu, reflexology, and osteopathic manipulation. The quality of massage varies, but a few of the more dependable institutions include the following.

Old Chiang Mai Medical Hospital (OMH): Thailand's most vigorous and respected massage school is located in the former city hospital in the southern section of town. Massages cost 150-200B per hour and the average session lasts two or three hours. Soi Sivaraj Komarapaj, opposite the Old Chiang Mai Cultural Center, tel. (053) 275085.

Rinkaew Povech: Also near the former hospital is another large massage school with various services priced from 300B per hour: Thai, Finnish, Western, or Japanese massage plus herbal saunas and facials. A minivan provides transportation from your hotel. 183/4 Wulai Rd., tel. (053) 274565.

School for the Blind: The best massage in Thailand. The masseuses and masseurs have unique insight into the secrets of massage, plus patronizing blind masseuses and masseurs provides important income for the disadvantaged group. Located on the western side of the old city; 150B per hour. Arak Rd., tel. (053) 278009.

Patngarm Hat Wasat: Visitors without the time or inclination to seek out massage schools might try the more commercial yet professional massage centers in luxury hotels. Perhaps the best is the venerable operation in the Diamond Riverside Hotel, a convenient location near the night market and Ping River. Massages cost 350-450B per hour, depending on extras such as herbs and oils. 33 Charoen Prathet Rd., tel. (053) 234153.

Massage Instruction

Chiang Mai is Thailand's center for massage and the best place in the country to study the ancient art form.

Old Chiang Mai Medical Hospital (OMH): Thailand's most vigorous and respected massage school is located in the former city hospital in the southern section of town. This is a serious place, where students take 12-day courses that meet daily 0900-1600 and makes some tough demands on their physical and mental capabilities. Soi Sivaraj Komarapaj, opposite the Old Chiang Mai Cultural Center, tel. (053) 275085.

Suan Samoonprai: A well-respected massage school with three central locations. The seven-day massage course costs 2,500-3,500B. 1/11 Chaiyaphum Rd., Soi 1, tel. (053) 252706; 9/3 Moon Muang Rd., Soi 2; 105 Wangsingkram Rd., tel. (053) 252663.

Chaiyuth Priyasith Massage School: Massage courses are available at the schools operated by Khun Chaiyuth, a former instructor at the Old Chiang Mai Medical Hospital and one of the most famous experts in the country. 52 Soi 3 Tapae Rd.

Thai Language Instruction

Visitors seeking professional lessons in the Thai language will certainly find Chiang Mai a more pleasant place to conduct studies than the big city of Bangkok.

AUA: The language center of the American University Alumni (AUA) offers both group and private lessons taught by native speakers. Private instruction costs 250B per hour, while 60 hours of group lessons over five weeks costs 3,600-4,500B. 24 Rajadamnern Rd., tel. (053) 278407.

Private Instructors: Private instructors often post notices in popular guesthouses, or can be contacted via major schools such as Chiang Mai University.

Cooking Classes

The popularity of cooking classes in Thailand is rising.

Thai Cooking Class: Chef Somphon and his wife, Elizabeth Nabnian, operate this popular cooking school from their home near Tapae Gate. Classes are held daily 1000-1500 and cost 800-1,000B for instruction, copies of recipes, and a five-course luncheon. 101/2 Moon Muang Rd., tel. (053) 490456.

Chiangmai Professional School: Both Thai cooking classes and traditional Thai massage are taught at this school just behind Montri Hotel by, as described on their brochure, "expert mistress Mrs. Malakarn Paungpetch." V.I.P. Bldg., Thapae Gate, Ratchadamnern Rd., Soi 1, tel. (053) 418970.

Compet Thai Cookery School: Another Thai cooking school conveniently located near Tapae Gate. Half-day classes cost 800B while full-day courses go for 1,200B. 1/2 Kotchasarn Rd., tel. (053) 280901.

Meditation

Increasing numbers of travelers are investigating Buddhism and *vipassana* (insight) or *samatha* (calmness) meditation during their visit to Thailand. Chiang Mai is a wonderful place to undertake studies, due to the relaxed atmosphere and reasonable fees, generally just small donations to cover basic expenses such as room and meals.

Visitors intrigued with meditation studies generally arrive on the standard two-month visa, extendible for another 30 days. Students intending to study more than three months might consider obtaining a three-month nonimmigrant visa from a Thai consulate. These student visas can be extended up to 12 months, but only with great difficulty.

The best resource on locations of meditation *wats* is *A Guide to Buddhist Monasteries and Meditation Centres in Thailand* researched and written by Bill Weir, a *vipassana* devotee. Bill's handy 100-page guide is available from the **World Fellowship of Buddhists,** 33 Sukumvit Rd., Bangkok 10110, and from **Insight Meditation West (Spirit Rock),** P.O. Box 909, Woodacre, CA, USA 94973, tel. (415) 488-0164.

Wat Ram Poeng: Twenty six-day *vipassana* courses are given by Thai monks with English interpretation provided by Westerners or bilingual Thais. A popular but tough place to study the intensive *vipassana* based on the Four Foundations of Mindfulness. Students begin practice at 0400 and are encouraged to meditate up to 20 hours a day. The Mahasi Sayadaw system includes walking, bowing, and sitting, with four hours of reclining in the evening. Wat Ram Poeng has about 60 monks and 40-60 laypeople of which half are foreigners. The popularity of this *wat* means that reservations are necessary, preferably in person. Wat Ram Poeng (also called Wat Tapotaram or Northern Insight Meditation Center) is four km west of Chiang Mai near Wat Umong.

Wat Ram Poeng, Tambon Suthep, Amphoe Muang, Chiang Mai 50000, Thailand, tel. (053) 278620.

Wat Umong: *Anapanasati* meditation techniques and dharma talks are given by a German monk named Phra Santitthito (Phra Santi) each Sunday 1500-1800 in the Chinese pavilion near the pond. Phra Santi, a resident of Wat Umong for over 20 years, speaks English, German, and Thai. Westerners who wish to study meditation must write in advance to reserve one of the few *kutis* allotted to novices. Wat Umong is five km west of Chiang Mai at the end of a long and winding road.

Wat Umong, Tambon Suthep, Amphoe Muang, Chiang Mai 5000, Thailand, tel. (053) 277248.

RESOURCES

Bookstores

Chiang Mai has several decent bookstores that carry a large selection of travel guidebooks, background reading, maps, Thai-English dictionaries, and English-language periodicals.

D.K. Book House: Chiang Mai's largest and most complete bookstore also has a much smaller branch at 234 Tapae Rd. 79/1 Kotchasarn Rd., tel. (053) 206995, fax (053) 206999.

Suriwong Book Center: Chiang Mai's second largest bookstore may have a few titles not available at D.K. Book House. The store was recently completely renovated and now rivals its competitor. 54/1 Sri Donchai Rd., tel. (053) 281052, fax (053) 271902.

Maps

For more years than she cares to remember, American Nancy Chandler has been producing her *Map of Chiang Mai,* an illuminating guide to Chiang Mai and environs. Nancy lives near San Francisco, but continues to make annual visits to update her maps and provide readers with accurate tips on restaurants, local transportation, and shopping venues.

The superb *Map of Chiang Mai & Around* from Prannok Witthaya and *Guide Map of Chiang Rai* published by Bangkok Guides are to be out of print, but both remain excellent resources for motorcyclists touring northern Thailand.

Cultural Centers

Several foreign governments maintain cultural centers with reading rooms and exhibition halls for monthly events.

United States Information Service: The USIS office keeps a large selection of relatively current American magazines and newspapers in their a/c reading room. Patrons must show their passports and be well dressed to use the reading room. USIS also sponsors free movies on Saturday at 1900 and periodic cultural exhibitions in the auditorium. Thai language lessons are offered at the AUA Center across the road. Weekdays 1200-1800 and Saturday 0900-1200. 24 Rajadamnern Rd., tel. (053) 278407.

British Council: A small library open to the public, plus free films every Thursday evening at 1900. Weekdays 0900-1700. 198 Bumrungraj Rd., tel. (053) 242103, fax (053) 244781.

Alliance Française: No library but French films are shown every Tuesday at 1630 and Friday at 2000. French conversation classes are held each month. 138 Charoen Prathet Rd., tel. (053) 275277.

TRANSPORTATION

Getting There

Chiang Mai is 700 km north of Bangkok and can be reached by air, train, or bus.

Air: Thai Airways has eight daily flights from Bangkok to Chiang Mai. The one-hour flight costs 1,800B in coach and 2,600B in first class. Thai Airways also flies to Chiang Mai from Phuket, Hat Yai, Surat Thani (Ko Samui), Korat, Taipei, and Hong Kong. Flights are also available on Bangkok Airways. Airport facilities include a TAT information counter, post office, and bank with favorable exchange rates.

The airport is about 10 minutes from downtown Chiang Mai. Taxis to most hotels costs 80B, but minibuses with the Thai Airways logo are half the price. *Songtaos* in front of the airport charge 30-35B per person.

Thai Airways has offices at 240 Pra Poklao Rd. (tel. 053-211541) behind Wat Chang Man and at the airport.

Train: Trains are the best way to reach Chiang Mai, especially overnight second-class coach with sleeper. The only advantage of first class, at twice the price, is two bunks per compartment instead of four. Trains leave Bangkok at 0640 (rapid), 0810 (express), 1500 (rapid), 1800 (express), 1810 (rapid), 1940 (special), 2000 (rapid), and 2200 (rapid). The journey takes 13 hours and costs 540B in second class with lower sleeping berth. As the train from Bangkok to Chiang Mai passes through a flat landscape of ricefields, the best trains to take are the overnight sleepers departing at 1500, 1800, and 1940. Ordinary trains leave throughout the day. Advance reservations are recommended, especially during festivals and the high season.

Tricycles from the train station cost 30-50B to any guesthouse. Most will deliver you to a guesthouse that offers them a small kickback. Cheaper options include bus 3 to Tapae Gate for 3B, or a *songtao* for 5B. Buses and *songtaos* pass along the road in front of the train station.

Bus: Buses to Chiang Mai depart from the Northern Bus Terminal on Paholyothin Road. Air-conditioned buses leave seven times daily 0900-1000 and 10 times daily 2000-2145. Air-conditioned buses cost 320-440B and take 10 or 12 hours via Nakhon Sawan and Ayuthaya. Ordinary buses depart hourly and cost 180-250B. Tickets can be purchased directly at the bus terminal.

Private bus companies in Bangkok offer similar service at slightly higher prices. Surcharges are added for VIP and Super-VIP buses, which

BUS SERVICE FROM CHIANG MAI

DESTINATION	TERMINAL	KM	HRS.	ORDINARY	A/C	DEPARTURES
Bangkok	Arcade	696	10	B150	B250-300	0730-1030, 1800-2100
Chiang Rai	Arcade	180	3	50	70-90	0600-1700
Fang	Chang Puak	151	3	35	60	0530-1900
Khon Kaen	Arcade	720	12	160	220-280	0500-0900, 1700-2000
Lampang	Chang Puak	100	2	25	40-50	0700-1900
Lamphun	Chang Puak	26	½	10	20	0700-1900
Mae Hong Son	Arcade	355	10	100	180-200	0700-1000, 2000-2100
Mae Sai	Arcade	242	5	60	80-100	0700-1500
Mae Sariang	Arcade	191	5	50	70-80	0600-0800, 2000-2100
Nan	Arcade	318	8	70	120-140	0600-1000, 2200-2230
Pai	Arcade	135	4	50	70-80	0700-1400
Phrae	Arcade	225	5	60	80-100	0700-1600
Petchabun	Arcade	580	8	140	140-180	0700-0900, 2000-2100
Phitsanulok	Arcade	265	5	80	120-150	0700-2300
Thaton	Chang Puak	179	4	40	70-80	0530-1900

rickshaw nap

have fewer seats and hence more leg room. Meals, soft drinks, and, most importantly, hotel pickup are included in the price. The bus journey from Bangkok to Chiang Mai is inexpensive and fast, but also cramped, cold, and hair-raising. Trains are recommended over buses.

Buses terminate at the Arcade Bus Terminal in Chiang Mai, located in the northeast section of town near the superhighway. Yellow minibuses 3 and 4 continue to hotels and guesthouses. *Tuk tuk* and *songtao* drivers provide inexpensive rides to guesthouses that give them a kickback.

Getting Around
Chiang Mai is a compact town and all sights in the central section are within walking distance.

Bicycles: To explore the more far-flung destinations, a rented bicycle or motorcycle is recommended. Bicycles cost only 35-50B per day, but traffic conditions may make bicycle touring a dangerous proposition.

Motorcycles: Motorcycles cost 100B daily for small 90cc Honda Dreams, which are perfectly adequate for local destinations; 150B for 125-175cc motorcycles that provide additional power to climb Doi Suthep; and 180-250B for larger bikes for extended tours. Rental is for a 24-hour period and discounts are given for longer periods. Fuel is your responsibility but unlimited mileage is allowed. Passports must be surrendered for the duration of the rental, so change money first. Some of the shops are content with

a photocopy of your passport together with a deposit of 2,000B. Ask about the free use of a helmet and additional charges for insurance, and check the condition of the bike before leaving your passport. Minor problems such as broken mirrors and brake levers are best fixed at local repair shops.

Motorcycles in the best condition are snatched up early in the morning. Several rental shops are located on Moon Muang Road south of Tapae Gate.

Three-wheelers: Pedal trishaws called *samlors* cost 5-10B for short trips. Motorized three-wheel taxis called *tuk tuks* charge according to the distance, starting at 10B for short journeys. Bargain before boarding. *Tuk tuks* around the old city should never cost more than 20B.

Minibuses: Local minibuses called *songtaos* or *seelors* (four wheels) are numbered 1-6 and described on Nancy Chandler's *Map of Chiang Mai*. Chiang Mai has both yellow and red buses which charge 2-5B depending on the distance. Yellow bus 1 runs east and west from the Arcade Bus Terminal to the base of Doi Suthep, stopping at Tapae Gate near the budget guesthouses. Yellow bus 2 runs north and south from Chang Puak Bus Station to the western bank of the Ping River. Yellow bus 3 connects the railway station with guesthouses near Tapae Gate. Red bus 5 runs along the city wall. Red bus 6 circles the city along the superhighway and connects the airport with the Arcade Bus Terminal.

Jeeps and Cars: Cars and jeeps can be rented at several locations. Rates begin at 1,000B per day and mileage is unlimited. Ask for "First Class" insurance, which covers damage to you and other vehicles, minus a 2,000B deductible.

Getting Away
Air: Thai Airways flies from Chiang Mai to most destinations in Thailand. Flights to the south usually include a stopover in Bangkok, except for direct flights to Phuket and Hat Yai. The most useful flight is the twice-daily 30-minute service to Mae Hong Son, which avoids a difficult full-day journey on the bus.

The Thai Airways office on Pra Poklao Road is open 0730-1700. Tickets can be purchased directly at the airport after closing hours. Flights should be booked several days in advance. Thai Airways provides transportation from your hotel to the airport for an additional 40B.

Train: Four very comfortable overnight trains run daily from Chiang Mai to Bangkok. A rapid train departs at 1530 and arrives in Bangkok the next morning at 0530. The *Bangkok Express* leaves at 1640 and arrives at 0625. The *Nakorn Ping Special Express* departs at 1930 and arrives in Bangkok at 0825. A final rapid train departs at 2045 and arrives at Hualampong station at 1040. Second class with a sleeping berth is your best choice, but reservations should be made well in advance.

Bus: Buses to destinations *outside* Chiang Mai Province such as Chiang Rai, Mae Hong Son, Sukothai, and Bangkok leave from the Chiang Mai Arcade Bus Terminal northeast of town. Departures are hourly except for Mae Sai, Khon Kaen, and Korat buses, which leave only in the mornings and evenings. Choices include ordinary, a/c, and VIP buses, which provide additional room for long-legged *farangs.* Air-conditioned fares listed below show the price range from standard a/c to VIP services.

Buses to most destinations *within* Chiang Mai Province such as Fang, Thaton, and Lampang leave from the Chang Puak Bus Terminal north of the city. Lamphun can also be reached by buses from Nawarat Bridge on a longer but more picturesque route that follows the old Chiang Mai-Lamphun Highway.

Buses and minibuses to points south but within Chiang Mai Province such as Chom Thong and Hot leave from the Chiang Mai Gate on the southern edge of the old walled city.

Minibuses to Doi Suthep leave every 15 minutes from the west side of Chang Puak Gate.

custard apple (noi nah)

VICINITY OF CHIANG MAI

Wat Prathat Doi Suthep

The most popular excursion from Chiang Mai is west to the mountain of Doi Suthep, where fresh air and local culture can be enjoyed on a half-day outing. One of northern Thailand's top attractions is the temple and golden 16th-century *stupa* which overlooks Chiang Mai from the summit of Doi Suthep. The architecture is quite modest by Thai standards, but perched on a hilltop at 1,053 meters and nicely situated in a national park, the temple commands a panoramic view of the entire valley and offers a welcome escape from the congestion of Chiang Mai. The full title means temple *(wat)* of the relic *(prathat)* on Mount *(Doi)* Suthep—named after the legendary monk who founded Lamphun, then promptly withdrew into the solitude of the hills.

More importantly to Thai pilgrims, Wat Prathat Doi Suthep is considered among the nation's most sacred places by virtue of its possession of a sacred Buddha relic. The central *stupa* was erected in 1383 after a wandering white elephant carrying the holy relic stopped at the site of the temple, trumpeted three times, and knelt in homage to the Buddha—an auspicious sign to Thais. In 1935, Lamphun abbot Sri Vinchai announced the construction of the winding road up to the remote summit and, with the help of thousands of volunteers, completed the project in just six months. Sri Vinchai is honored with a statue just up from the base of the hill.

Wat Prathat Doi Suthep is approached up a monumental, heart-pounding, 304-step staircase flanked by tremendous mythical *nagas,* which symbolize humanity's progress from earth into nirvana. The present *wat* is composed of several buildings which have been expanded and restored by various rulers since the 16th century. Centerpiece is a golden *stupa* covered with gilded copper plating and flanked by enormous ornamental umbrellas at each corner. *Vihams* on either side feature carved doorways and gilded gables which outrank the interior murals and indifferent collection of Buddhas. The entire complex is usually overrun with camera-clicking tourists who snap away at the monks, views, and oddities such as chicken memorials and signs which warn "Don't push the bell." Go ahead, push the bell.

Wat Prathat Doi Suthep is 20 km west of Chiang Mai. Minibuses leave every 20 minutes from Chang Puak Gate (North Gate) on Manee Noparat Road, and from Tapae Road in front of the Bangkok Bank. The fare is 35B up and 25B down.

Royal Palace

The rose and orchid gardens of Phuping Palace, official winter residence of the royal family, are open Friday, Saturday, Sunday, and holidays 0830-1630. Admission is free, though there's little of interest aside from the rosebushes and fields of snapdragons. The royal residence is down to the left of the central pathway.

Phuping Palace is five km beyond Wat Doi Suthep and can be reached by minitruck from the temple or Chang Puak Gate in Chiang Mai for an additional 20B.

Wat Prathat Doi Suthep

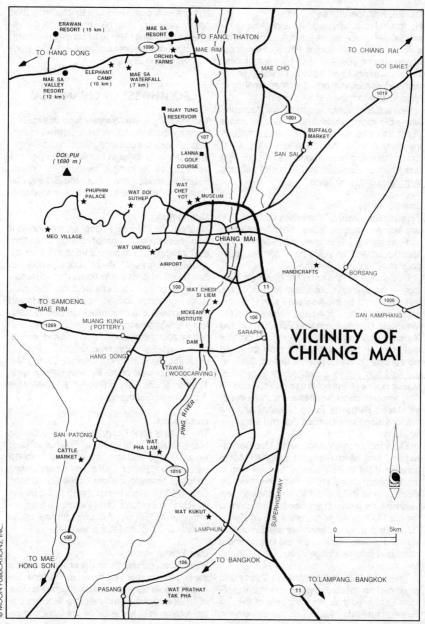

VICINITY OF CHIANG MAI

TO HANG DONG

ERAWAN RESORT (15 km)

MAE SA RESORT

TO FANG, THATON

MAE RIM

ORCHID FARMS

MAE CHO

TO CHIANG RAI

DOI SAKET

1096

MAE SA VALLEY RESORT (12 km)

ELEPHANT CAMP (10 km)

MAE SA WATERFALL (7 km)

HUAY TUNG RESERVOIR

1019

107

1001

BUFFALO MARKET

SAN SAI

DOI PUI (1690 m)

LANNA GOLF COURSE

PHUPHIN PALACE

WAT DOI SUTHEP

WAT CHET YOT

MUSEUM

MEO VILLAGE

WAT UMONG

CHIANG MAI

HANDICRAFTS

BORSANG

AIRPORT

1006

TO SAMOENG, MAE RIM

108

WAT CHEDI SI LIEM

11

106

SAN KAMPHANG

1269

MUANG KUNG (POTTERY)

MCKEAN INSTITUTE

DAM

SARAPHI

HANG DONG

TAWAI (WOODCARVING)

PING RIVER

SAN PATONG

CATTLE MARKET

WAT PHA LAM

1015

SUPERHIGHWAY

0   5km

WAT KUKUT

LAMPHUN

108

106

TO BANGKOK

TO MAE HONG SON

PASANG

WAT PRATHAT TAK PHA

TO LAMPANG, BANGKOK

11

© MOON PUBLICATIONS, INC.

Doi Pui Hilltribe Village

Northern Thailand's saddest and most commercialized hilltribe village is located three km up a dirt road beyond Phuping Palace. Here, costumed Hmong villagers pose for photographs, sell poor-quality handicrafts to busloads of bewildered visitors, and actually charge money to let tourists *watch* them smoke opium.

One amusing attraction is the Opium Museum, where the young curator sells admission tickets (a collector's item), conducts a brief tour through the dimly lit shack, then cheerfully offers a test run on the opium pipe. Above this museum is a tacky hilltribe museum and beautiful gardens with views over the village.

Mae Sa Valley

This beautiful valley, 30 minutes north of Chiang Mai, provides an escape from the city on a half-day outing. The scenery is pleasant but not spectacular, and the valley has a number of decent attractions.

Beginning from the turnoff at Mae Rim (kilometers represent distance from Mae Rim), the first stop might be the **Adisara Farm** (1.4 km), with a small fishing pond and restaurant. Both **Mountain Orchid Farm** and **Sai Nam Orchid Nursery** (2.5 km) provide displays of orchids that many visitors consider the most intriguing sight in Mae Sa Valley. **Mae Sa Resort** (3 km) on the right has individual bungalows from 800B. **Maesa House** (4 km) holds a private collection of Thai antiques inside the all-teakwood villa. Nearby **Maesa Butterfly Farm** (4.2 km) and the **Wang Kulap Rose Garden** (5.5 km) are popular stops.

Every tour seems to include the **Mae Sa Waterfall** (7 km), which plunges through eight sections amid tall trees. Perhaps the best stop is the **Elephant Camp** (10 km) where shows are given daily at 0900 and 1300. Afterwards, the elephants are bathed in the river and marched up the road to their jungle homes. Erawan Resort (15 km) is a major development with European-style bungalows, neatly trimmed lawns, and a simulated hilltribe village called Little Chiang Mai.

The road then climbs Mae Sa Valley and winds past another orchid garden and several resorts until it reaches the back side of the Doi Suthep mountain range. This motorcycle trip guarantees superb views with light traffic. A short break and petrol stop can be taken in the village of Samoeng. The road continues circling counterclockwise until it reconnects with Hwy. 108 near Hang Dong.

SOUTHWEST OF CHIANG MAI

The following towns, temples, and natural features are best visited on an organized tour or with private transportation. Motorcyclists might enjoy the loop through Lamphun, though the traffic can be daunting to inexperienced riders. Public minibuses leave from the Chiang Mai Gate at the southern end of the old walled city.

Muang Kung

Muang Kung ("Meong Koong" on the sign) is a small but well-known pottery village which produces red pots from natural irons or castor oil, and black pots from charcoal. Locally known as Ban Nam Ton for its production of *nam ton* (water jugs), the entire village still produces both giant water jugs and handicraft vessels more admired for their aesthetic than utilitarian beauty. Visitors are welcome to wander around and watch potters shape their clay jars on primitive wheels tucked under elevated houses.

Muang Kung is 10 km south of Chiang Mai and one km west of the highway, where Hwy. 1269 continues west to Samoeng. Look for the sign marked "Samoeng."

Hang Dong

The village of Hang Dong, 13 km south of Chiang Mai, is chiefly known for its bamboo baskets and woodcarvings sold from several stalls two km before town. Better than these disappointing shops is an antique store called Ban Chang Come, 500 meters before Hang Dong on the west side of the road. This place has a great selection of old Thai and Burmese furniture, stored outside and exposed to the elements.

Ban Tawai

Ban Tawai and nearby towns collectively form the largest woodcarving center in Thailand. Situated on both sides of the dusty road are dozens of small workshops and massive factories that produce most of the imitation antiques and immense wooden elephants sold throughout the country. Bargains are plentiful. The larger shops also provide packing and shipping services.

To reach Ban Tawai, turn left at the gas station in Hang Dong and drive 3.5 km past dozens of instant-antique showrooms and shipping companies until you see the English-language sign. Turn right and continue along the dirt road past dozens of small shops and home industries that crank out thousands of Burmese Buddhas, Tibetan masks, and wooden horses. The road continues east to Saraphi Dam and back to Chiang Mai.

San Pa Tong

Two km south of San Pa Tong and located on the right side of the road are dozens of wooden pens which mark the largest cattle market in northern Thailand. Held every Saturday morning, the San Pa Tong cattle fair has recently expanded to include everything from Japanese electronics to used clothing.

Chom Thong

This small junction town is chiefly known for Wat Prathat Sri Chom Tong, a beautiful Lanna- and Burmese-style temple on the left side of the main road. Constructed between 1451 and 1516, this well-maintained temple features a central facade and gilded gables carved with remarkable skill.

Chom Thong is 58 km from Chiang Mai and one km beyond the turnoff to Doi Inthanon.

Doi Inthanon National Park

Doi Inthanon, Thailand's highest mountain at 2,590 meters, offers beautiful scenery, evergreen montane forests, dwarf rhododendron groves, rare birdlife, and impressive waterfalls. Mae Klang Falls, 10 km from the park turnoff, is the official entrance and the site of a tourist center. Beyond the entrance is Wachiratan Falls at Km 20 and Sri Phum Falls at Km 31. Other stops along the winding 47-km road include a Hmong village and experimental farm where hilltribes raise alternative crops, several Karen villages, and the summit where the final king of Chiang Mai is buried. Bring warm clothing and rain gear.

Direct service from Chiang Mai to Mae Klang Falls is sporadic and most visitors must change buses in Chom Thong. Buses to Chom Thong leave regularly from inside Chiang Mai Gate at the southern moat in Chiang Mai. Minitrucks from the temple in Chom Thong go up to the park entrance at Mae Klang Falls, where the park service operates bungalows and an information center. Chartered minitrucks from Chom Thong cost 500-600B per day. *Songtaos* from Mae Klang to the summit of Doi Inthanon leave hourly until late afternoon. Motorcyclists can continue west to Mae Chaem, where simple accommodations and restaurants are found on the main street.

CHIANG MAI TO LAMPHUN

The narrow and very busy road from Chiang Mai to Lamphun runs between twin rows of magnificent tung oil trees planted almost 100 years ago by the princess of Chiang Mai. Most of the trees have been meticulously fitted with wooden pegs which allow the trimmers to climb up and trim the leafy canopy.

While most visitors go directly to Lamphun, several attractions en route are worthwhile visiting.

Wat Chedi Si Liem

Wiang Kum Kam is an ancient town established by King Mengrai six years before he moved his capital to the higher elevations of Chiang Mai. Previously buried under two meters of dirt, several of the remaining temples have recently been restored by the Fine Arts Department. The most important of these are Wat Chedi Si Liem, a stepped pyramid modeled after Wat Ku Kut in Lamphun which exemplifies the oldest *stupa* design in Thailand, and Wat Chang Kham, which features a beautiful Lanna-style *chedi* and a reconstructed *viharn* adjacent to excavations conducted by the Fine Arts Department.

Wiang Kum Kam is 10 km south of Chiang Mai in a privately owned *lamyai* (longan) orchard just west of the Chiang Mai-Lamphun Highway. Motorcyclists should turn right at the sign marked Ban Nong Hoi and continue one km south.

McKean Leper Institute

Founded in 1908 by Presbyterian missionaries to treat sufferers of leprosy, this rehabilitation center has since become an internationally recognized model of a self-contained clinic. Visitors are welcome to tour the facilities, medical clinics, and church, which serve the needs of over 200 patients who live in their own cottages on 160 secluded acres. A useful brochure is available from the administration office.

McKean Institute is four km off the main road on a small island in the middle of the Ping River, open Mon.-Fri. 0900-1700.

LAMPHUN

Lamphun, the old capital of the Haripunchai empire, lies 26 km south of Chiang Mai at the end of the lovely Chiang Mai-Lamphun Highway. In contrast to Chiang Mai, Lamphun remains a sleepy town unaffected by the commercialism and development of northern Thailand. Lamphun is generally visited for its handful of temples, which are of great artistic and historical interest.

History
Lamphun has a long and legendary history. According to the Siamese chronicles, Lamphun (then called Haripunchai) was founded in the 8th century by a wandering hermit named Suthep Reussi, from whom Doi Suthep gets its name. Seeking a resting place for a sacred Buddha relic, Suthep settled on this site and invited Chamdevi, a princess from Lopburi, to reign as the city's first queen. A moat and ramparts were constructed in a slightly deformed oval shape to imitate the conch pattern demanded by Buddhist tradition.

During the next six centuries, Lamphun was ruled by 49 kings and served as capital for an independent Mon kingdom that dominated most of northern Thailand until 1281, when the city fell to King Mengrai and his emerging Lanna Thai Kingdom. Lamphun became an important religious center in 1369 when King Ku Na invited a Sukothai monk to establish the Sinhalese order of Theravada Buddhism. Theravada Buddhism is still favored by Thais today. Lamphun and the Haripunchai Kingdom fell to the Burmese in 1556, but the city returned to Siamese control in 1775 under the rule of King Taksin.

Most of the present temples date from the early 16th century, except for Wat Kukut, which dates from the 12th-century Dvaravati Period.

Lamphun National Museum
A perfect introduction to the arts of Haripunchai is a brief visit to the museum in the center of Lamphun. Inside the small but extremely well-organized museum is a collection of bronzes from Wat Prathat Haripunchai, as well as archaeological discoveries from the Haripunchai Period. Among the better pieces are stucco figurines with the fierce eyes and enigmatic smiles that characterize the early Haripunchai school (8th-10th centuries), and a howdah and gown from the final ruler of Lamphun.

The museum is open Wed.-Sun. 0900-1600. Admission is 20B.

Wat Prathat Haripunchai
The principal attraction in Lamphun was founded in 897 by a Mon king to enshrine a sacred relic of the Buddha, said to be either a fragment of the Buddha's skull or a hair from his head. The present compound was established in 1044 by King Athitayaraj of Haripunchai on the site of the former royal palace. The *wat* consists of almost a dozen buildings erected during the subsequent centuries which display Burmese rather than traditional Thai forms.

Golden Chedi: Dominating the central plaza is a towering 50-meter *chedi* covered with copper plates and surrounded by engraved plaques. The monument owes its present form to a 20th-century reconstruction project initiated when Burmese architecture was popular in northern Thailand. Capping the summit is a nine-tiered umbrella gilded with almost seven kg of pure gold. The potbellied monk who brought the Buddha relics from India is commemorated with a statue in a nearby chamber. Legends claim the monk made himself obese to prevent youthful passion from interfering with his Buddhist meditations.

Temple Museum: Although most of the images have been moved to the nearby National Museum, a spectacular if somewhat dusty collection of rare Lanna-style Buddhas is displayed inside the museum near the entrance. The untouched images have acquired a splendid patina, normally lost when Buddhas are "restored" by resident monks.

Suwana Chedi: Tucked away in the northwest corner is an unusual pyramidal *chedi* with some stucco decoration and niches containing

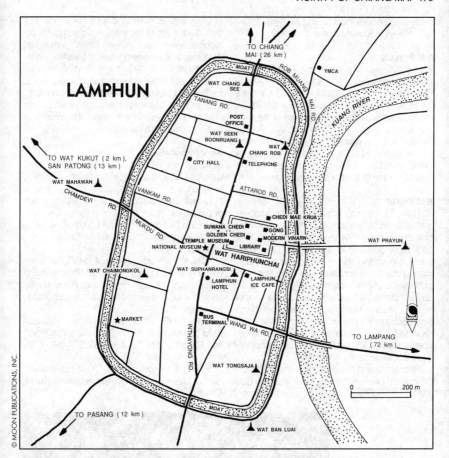

LAMPHUN

TO CHIANG MAI (26 km)

YMCA

MOAT

ROB MUANG

WAT CHANG SEE

TANANG RD.

KUANG RIVER

NAI RD.

POST OFFICE

WAT SEEN BOONRUANG

WAT CHANG ROB

CITY HALL

TELEPHONE

TO WAT KUKUT (2 km), SAN PATONG (13 km)

ATTAROD RD.

WAT MAHAWAN

CHAMDEVI RD.

VANKAM RD.

MUKDU RD.

CHEDI MAE KRUA

SUWANA CHEDI

GONG

GOLDEN CHEDI

MODERN VIHARN

TEMPLE MUSEUM

LIBRARY

WAT PRAYUN

NATIONAL MUSEUM

WAT HARIPHUNCHAI

WAT CHAIMONGKOL

WAT SUPHANRANGSI

LAMPHUN HOTEL

LAMPHUN ICE CAFE

MARKET

BUS TERMINAL

WANG WA RD.

INTHAYONG RD.

TO LAMPANG (72 km)

0   200 m

TO PASANG (12 km)

MOAT

WAT TONGSAJA

WAT BAN LUAI

© MOON PUBLICATIONS, INC.

standing Buddhas. This fine brick Dvaravati-style *stupa* resembles Chedi Si Liem near Chiang Mai and the original prototype of nearby Wat Kukut.

Modern *Viharn*: Behind the golden *chedi* is the principal *viharn*, a fine example of contemporary religious architecture erected in 1925 but completely restored in 1960. Interior murals depict 13 scenes from the life of Buddha. Also note the large Chiang Saen-style bronze image, Pra Chao Thongtip, and the finely carved repositories to the left of the central Buddha.

Big Gong: Cast in 1860 and sheltered in an open pavilion, this immense bronze gong is

among the largest in the world. The reddish building is decorated with images of serpents and gargoyles.

Library: Adjoining the modern *viharn* is a 19th-century Lanna-style *ho trai,* which, according to custom, stands on a high base to protect the manuscripts from termite attacks. Flanking the staircase are Chinese dog-lions and mythological *nagas.* The nearby bell tower shows clear Burmese influence, while the adjacent *bot* contains two bronze Buddha images. The *bot* is kept locked but local monks can provide a key.

Chedi Mae Krua: North of the temple compound in an outside courtyard is a rare Chiang

Saen-style *chedi* (Chedi Chang Yan) influenced by the Srivijayan school of architecture.

Wat Prayun

Across the river and about one km from Lamphun, Wat Prayun was constructed in 1900 as a forest monastery for local monks. The square Burmese-style *chedi* is shaped like a terraced *mondop* with four standing Buddhas at the summit of each symmetrical stairway. Wat Prayun features a great deal of remaining stuccowork and an engraved stele which dates the original *mondop* to 1370. Note the mysterious cat figures at the top of the southern staircase.

Wat Kukut

Wat Kukut, Lamphun's most important monument, is considered by archaeologists the last surviving example of original Dvaravati architecture in Thailand. More properly known as Wat Chamdevi, after the legendary queen of Haripunchai, this intriguing *chedi* was constructed in 1218 and modeled after a similar reliquary in Polonarawa, Sri Lanka. Another theory is that Wat Kukut is a miniature reproduction of the famous Mahabodhi Temple in Bodgaya, India. In any event, Wat Kukut (Suwan Chang Kot formally) means "Topless Chedi," a local nickname given to the monument after vandals stole the golden roof.

By constructing this pyramidal *chedi* with five diminishing tiers graced with 15 diminishing Buddhas, Mon architects created both a monument of great artistic merit and a clever optical illusion. To the left of the walkway is a smaller octagonal stone *chedi* (Ratana Chedi) with Hindu divinities, and a modern *viharn* insensitively constructed between the two historic monuments.

Wat Kukut is two km up the small street next to the National Museum. The entrance is marked by a large blue "Bon Voyage" sign. Visitors can walk to the monument in about 45 minutes or hire a *samlor* from the museum.

Accommodations

Most visitors see Lamphun on a day-trip from Chiang Mai, though a few hotels are scattered around town.

Lamphun Hotel: Simple rooms with common or private baths are available in the yellow building four shops down from the corner. Also called the Notanon Hotel. 51 Inthayong Rd., tel. (053) 511176, 80-150B.

YMCA: The local branch of the YMCA doesn't have any rooms for rent, but American volunteers can sometimes help with accommodations. Visitors are invited to help teach English to the students.

Tareerat Court: A new and almost luxurious hotel one km east of town en route to Wat Kukut. 104 Chamdevi Rd., tel. (053) 560224, 140-160B fan, 350-450B a/c.

Sawat Ari Hotel: Another hotel marked only with a Thai sign and located near Wat Kukut. Chamdevi Rd., 80-120B.

statues at Wat Kukut

Suan Kaeo Bungalows: More luxurious digs are located six km outside town on the road to Lampang. Highway 11 Km 6, 180-300B.

Restaurants

Several simple cafes are located along Inthayong Road and near the market in the southwest corner of town.

Lamphun Ice Cafe: An air-conditioned restaurant that guarantees a welcome relief from the blistering heat of Lamphun. Mukdu Rd.

Khum Ton Kaew: This former residence of a local prince has been converted into a combination handicraft center and open-air restaurant.

Transportation

Lamphun is 26 km south of Chiang Mai and can be reached with blue-and-white buses which leave every 30 minutes from Lamphun Road, about 200 meters south of Nawarat Bridge near the TAT office.

PASANG

Pasang is a one-street town known for its cotton weaving, batik, lamyai fruit, and women, who are considered by many Thais the most beautiful in the country. Cotton production and weaving have left Pasang but survive in smaller villages such as Ban Nong Nguak some eight km southwest of Pasang. The tourist police office has a map to the region.

Several stores in Pasang sell high-quality shirts and sarongs.

Nandakwang Laicum: This spot on the west side of the road has the best selection in Pasang. A batik shirt costs about 250-400B, while dresses run about 350-450B depending on the quality.

Suchada: Across the road, Suchada sells more traditional and less expensive clothing, plus bottles of local honey made from the aromatic *lamyai* blossom.

Pasang is 10 km south of Lamphun on Hwy. 106 and can be reached with *songtaos* from Lamphun and buses from Chiang Mai.

Wat Prathat Tak Pha

Some eight km south of Pasang is the turnoff for a famous Mahanikai *wat* dedicated to a famous northern monk named Luang Pu Phromma and erected on the site where several Buddha footprints were discovered. Wonderfully located on the side of a mountain, the temple is reached up a long tree-lined road that becomes steeper as it gains elevation. This popular pilgrimage spot has several footprint sanctuaries which have been painted with religious artwork and a steep staircase which leads to a golden *chedi* at the top of the mountain. Hikers are rewarded with magnificent views over the Ping River Valley.

LAMPANG

Lampang, 100 km southeast of Chiang Mai on the arterial highway between Bangkok and the north, was once a sleepy town known for its temples and nostalgic horse-drawn carriages. Today it's a busy commercial center of 50,000 residents and contains some of the finest Burmese-style temples in Thailand.

History

Lampang was founded in the 7th century by a son of Queen Chamdevi shortly after the rise of the Haripunchai Kingdom in Lamphun. The town, originally called Kelang Nakorn and located on the east bank of the Wang River, was linked with several fortified settlements, of which only Wat Prathat Lampang Luang still survives.

The city joined the Lanna Kingdom with the rise of King Mengrai, but fell to Burmese invaders in 1556. Two centuries of Burmese rule were reversed in the 18th century with the unification of Thailand under the Chakri dynasty.

By the turn of the 20th century, Lampang had developed into a major teak center populated by Thai, Shan, and English traders who floated massive rafts of logs down the then-majestic Wang River. The rich cosmopolitan mixture of merchants and vast stands of teak brought prosperity and a construction frenzy still reflected in the assortment of Thai, Burmese, and Chinese temples which have survived to the present day.

Old Architecture

Testimony to the long and rich history of Lampang is demonstrated by the well-preserved temples and domestic architecture hidden away in

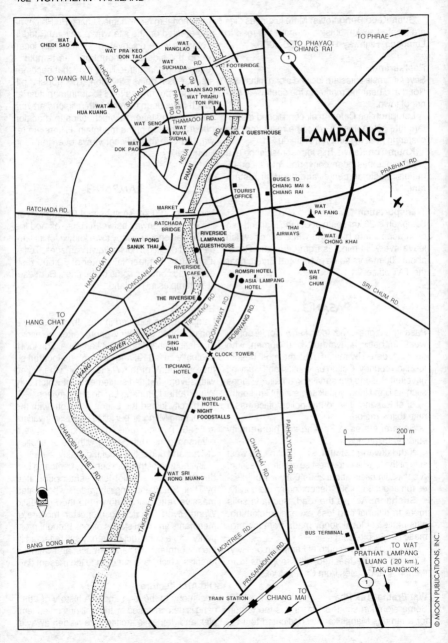

LAMPANG

© MOON PUBLICATIONS, INC.

the smaller streets along the banks of the Wang River. Many of the old mansions and shophouses between the Riverside Cafe and the bridge reflect Western styles favored by Burmese architects during the reign of King Rama V. Most of the old architecture is located on the east banks of the Wang, since Lampang was centered here until several decades ago. Baan Sao Nok, the "House of Many Pillars," is an outstanding example of a teakwood house and rice granary elevated on 116 teak pillars.

Wat Pra Keo Don Tao

This main temple of Lampang is included on every tour of the city. Although located in the middle of a disorienting neighborhood and difficult to find, this Burmese shrine with its massive *chedi,* well-carved Burmese-style chapel, small museum, and Thai-style temple is worth seeking out.

The temple was an important religious center in the 15th century when it briefly housed the Emerald Buddha now enshrined in Bangkok at the Wat Pra Keo. The highlight of the complex is a Burmese-style *mondop* topped with an elaborate pinnacle and decorated with a profusion of ornamental detail. Details include pillars gilded with miniature Buddhas and a coffered ceiling which, reflecting Western influence, is carved with nine small cupids; below the ceiling rests a jeweled Buddha image in classic Mandalay style. Dating from the beginning of the 19th century, this chapel is considered one of the finest examples of Burmese architecture in Thailand.

On the grounds are several other *viharns,* a reclining Buddha, and a fascinating museum filled with Lampang artifacts such as Lanna-style candlesticks and models of *viharns.* Adjacent Wat Suchada is kept locked but note the lintels carved with dragons and flowers.

Baan Sao Nok

Situated in the old city near Wat Pra Keo Don Tao is one of Lampang's most famous sights, the huge teak house often called the "Many Pillars House" for the 116 square teak pillars that support it. The ancestral home of Khunying Walai Leelanuch was constructed in 1896 in Lanna style with Burmese touches favored by local artisans. As with many other houses in northern Thailand, Baan Sao Nok consists of several

sleeping areas and living quarters that span the entire front of the residence.

To the side is a large rice granary raised on 24 pillars, which was moved from a nearby suburb and reconstructed on the grounds several years ago. Rice barns have traditionally served to reflect the wealth and social status of the family as visible proof of the household's extensive field holdings. Both buildings are believed to be protected by resident animist spirits.

The owner of Baan Sao Nok—the female principal of a prominent local school—has furnished the teak mansion with Burmese and Thai antiques and opened the home as a public museum. Baan Sao Nok is open daily 1000-1700; admission 20B.

Wat Hua Kuang

This temple was built in the early 19th century by residents of Chiang Saen after they were forcibly resettled from their home on the banks of the Mekong River. The Lanna-style *viharn* contains Chiang Saen Buddhas and manuscripts relating the history of the displaced people.

Wat Seng

Guarded inside the Chiang Saen-style *viharn* on Thamaoo Road are Buddha images brought from Chiang Saen and painted wooden panels which date from the early 20th century.

Wat Kuya Sudha

Fronting the destroyed monastery is a 15th-century gatehouse decorated with stucco deities, one of the oldest examples of Lanna art in Lampang.

Wat Chedi Sao

Located across the Wang River and outside the city limits, this rather unimpressive temple is saved by its peaceful location among the rice paddies. The temple is chiefly noted for its 20 (*sao*) whitewashed *chedis* in a composite Burmese-Thai style, and collection of humorous statues that lend a circus effect to the modest compound.

Wat Pa Fang

Lampang has several magnificent temples that rank among the finest Burmese structures in the country. Wat Pa Fang, just opposite the Thai Airways office, features a delicate *chedi* surrounded by seven small chapels filled with alabaster Buddhas in Mandalay style that represent the seven days of the week.

Wat Sri Chum

Located on Sri Chum Road opposite a mosque, Wat Sri Chum was once home to an active community of Burmese monks. The temple was constructed in 1893 by Burmese carpenters from Mandalay who melded Burmese woodcarving techniques with traditional Thai motifs. Wat Sri Chum tragically burned to the ground in 1993 but restoration efforts are now underway.

Wat Sri Rong Muang

The most awesome Burmese sanctuary in Lampang dazzles the visitor with its glittering multicolored exterior of carved wood and corrugated iron, superb interior woodcarving, and vast collection of sacred images donated by wealthy patrons.

Budget Accommodations

Lampang has about 20 hotels in all price ranges. Most are located in the downtown district on Boonyawat and Robiwang Rds.

The Riverside: Lampang's best spot for riverside dining also has a few rooms available in the old teak building. Tons of atmosphere and removed from the concrete wonderland of downtown Lampang. 328 Tipchang Rd., tel. (054) 221861, 150-250B.

No. 4 Guesthouse: Outside town but perhaps worth the walk, this guesthouse has 24 simple rooms in an old-style teak house and an attached restaurant with evening entertainment. The owner teaches English at the local school, but the place seems to open and close with the seasons. Check first with the local tourist office or the No. 4 outlets in Sukothai and Mae Sot. 54 Pamai Rd., no phone, 80-140B.

Romsri Hotel: Motel row is packed with perhaps a dozen hotels in various price ranges, but the Romsri is the best choice for inexpensive yet clean rooms. All rooms include hot water and private baths. 142 Boonyawat Rd., tel. (054) 217054, 180-220B fan, 300-350B a/c.

Sri Sangar: Another acceptable low-priced choice on "motel row" with fairly clean rooms with fan and bath. 213-215 Boonyawat Rd., tel. (054) 217070, 120-200B.

Moderate to Luxury Accommodations

Asia Lampang Hotel: Centrally located, the remodeled Asia Lampang has conference facilities, a "Sweety" Room, and the Kumluang Restaurant with "Thai, Chinese and Uropean food by the professional cookers." 229 Boonyawat Rd., tel. (054) 217844, 380-550B a/c rooms.

Lampang Wiengthong Hotel: A large, utilitarian hotel with coffee shop, small swimming pool, banquet facilities, and 235 basic but acceptable rooms at decent rates. 138 Phaholyothin Rd., tel. (054) 225801, fax (054) 225803, 650-900B.

Tipchang Hotel: Lampang's largest hotel features a nightclub, 24-hour coffee shop, swimming pool, and eighth-floor restaurant which overlooks the river and adjacent nine-hole golf course. 54 Takranoi Rd., tel. (054) 226501, fax (054) 225362, 650-850B.

Lampang River Lodge: Sixty beautiful Thai-style bungalows are located six km south of town on the banks of the Wang River. All rooms are a/c with private bath and riverside verandas. 300 Moo 1 Tambol Chompoo, 1,200-1,800B, tel. (054) 226922, Chiang Mai reservations tel. (053) 215072.

Restaurants

Riverside Restaurant: Probably the best place to dine is this teakwood cafe that serves both Thai and Western specialties. The Italian manager and chef puts out some tasty pizzas and lasagnas, plus live folk music is performed most evenings. 328 Tipchang Rd., tel. (054) 221861. Inexpensive.

Ban Chom Wang: Another excellent choice for riverside dining on a multitiered veranda. Thai dishes and seafood items are listed on the English-language menu. 276 Talat Kao Rd., tel. (054) 222845. Moderate.

No. 4 Restaurant: The guesthouse owned and operated by a local schoolteacher wraps around a garden restaurant that attracts many of the local night owls. Entertainment runs from folk to light pop. Open 1000-midnight. 54 Pamai Rd. Moderate.

Tesaban Markets: The foodstalls just off Thakrownoi Road south of the Tipchang Hotel serve all the standard dishes at rock-bottom prices. Inexpensive.

Asia Lampang Hotel: The Kumluang Restaurant inside this hotel has both an open-air dining room which overlooks the street and an a/c section in the rear. 229 Boonyawat Rd., tel. (054) 217844. Moderate.

Information
A small and rather useless tourist office is on Boonyawat Road in front of the provincial hall.

Transportation
Lampang is 100 km southeast of Chiang Mai and 602 km north of Bangkok. The town can be visited as a very long day-trip from Chiang Mai, or as an excellent stopover between Chiang Mai and points south.

Air: Thai Airways flies daily to Lampang from Bangkok via Phitsanulok. The Thai Airways office (tel. 054-217078) is at 314 Sanam Bin Rd. just opposite Wat Pa Fang.

Train: All trains between Bangkok and Chiang Mai stop in Lampang. Local minibuses go from the train station up Chatchai Road to the hotels on Boonyawat Road. Across from the train station is Thap Thim Thong Hotel, where simple rooms cost 80-140B.

Bus: Buses from the Arcade Bus Terminal in Chiang Mai take two hours along one of the best roads in northern Thailand. Direct bus service is also available from Phitsanulok, Sukothai, and Chiang Rai. Private bus companies in downtown Lampang sell tickets to most destinations. Another option is the ordinary buses to Chiang Mai and Chiang Rai which pass regularly on Paholyothin Road near the tourist office and central Lampang.

Minibuses around town are plentiful, but many visitors prefer to hire a horse carriage for a leisurely ride in the early evening hours. Somehow the carriages reflect the confusing state of the local tourist industry, decorated in European style while the drivers are clad in cowboy outfits.

ATTRACTIONS NEAR LAMPANG

Most tours to Lampang include the temples in town and a stop at Wat Prathat Lampang Luang, considered one of the most impressive temples in northern Thailand. Visitors with a motorcycle or car might also visit the nearby temples of Wat Pong Yang Kok and Wat Prathat Chomping.

Wat Pong Yang Kok
Though rarely visited by either Thais or Westerners, this exquisite *viharn* typifies what is most natural and charming about Lanna-style architecture. The open-air *viharn* constructed of aging timbers contains an impressive interior profusely decorated with gold-leaf images of flowering plants, mandalas, golden geese, and famous bodhi tree frescoes behind the central altar. Supporting the brick-tiled roof—a feature rarely seen in modern Thailand—are teak pillars capped with studded crown pediments.

Wat Pong Yang Kok is five km south of Hang Chat on the road which connects Hang Chat with Wat Prathat Lampang Luang. The unmarked turnoff leads 50 meters to the temple, which is surrounded by a yellow wall and framed by a giant bodhi tree.

Wat Prathat Lampang Luang
Northern Thailand's finest monument is the 11th-century walled temple 20 km southwest of Lampang. Artistically, the wealth of its decorative arts and purity of architectural style make Wat Prathat Lampang Luang a singular highlight of Southeast Asian art.

The temple compound was once part of a fortified city founded in the 8th century by the legendary Princess Chamdevi of Lamphun but destroyed by Burmese invaders about 200 years ago. Today the monument is the site of several elaborate festivals such as Songkram and Loy Kratong, when thousands of pilgrims arrive to honor the jasper Buddha (Pra Keo Don Tao) and enjoy a light-and-sound show sponsored by a local preservation society.

Below the steps which lead up to the elevated compound are souvenir stalls and cafes which serve ice-cold drinks.

Main Gate: Entrance is up a flight of stairs guarded by mythological undulating *nagas,* and then through a magnificent 15th-century gateway. The monumental gatehouse has been decorated with delicate stuccowork and painted in brilliant shades of gold. Capping the doorway is a circular lintel, Pratu Kong, in the form of the Buddhist Wheel of the Law. A useful map is posted to the right of the central *viharn.*

Viharn Luang: First stop should be the massive *viharn* which dominates the central courtyard. Originally constructed in 1496 in the shape

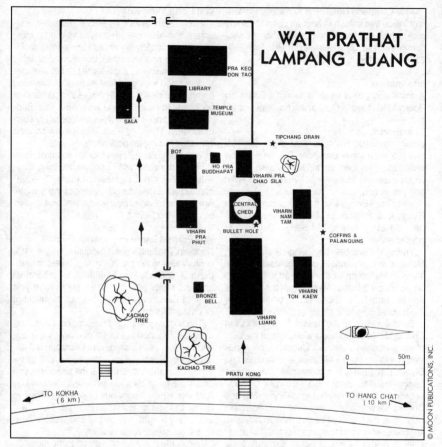

WAT PRATHAT
LAMPANG LUANG

PRA KEO
DON TAO

LIBRARY

TEMPLE
MUSEUM

SALA

TIPCHANG DRAIN

BOT

HO PRA
BUDDHAPAT

VIHARN PRA
CHAO SILA

CENTRAL
CHEDI

VIHARN
NAM TAM

BULLET HOLE

VIHARN
PRA
PHUT

COFFINS &
PALANQUINS

BRONZE
BELL

VIHARN
TON KAEW

KACHAO
TREE

VIHARN
LUANG

KACHAO TREE

PRATU KONG

0   50m

TO KOKHA
(6 km)

TO HANG CHAT
(10 km)

© MOON PUBLICATIONS, INC.

of an open *sala,* Viharn Luang features early 19th-century murals of the Lampang school, and a magnificent *ku* (altar) which enshrines a venerated Buddha image, Pra Chao Lan Thong, cast in 1563. Gracing the half-wall murals are images of big-nosed *farangs,* holy men, Chinese emissaries, scenes of palace life, and personages in Burmese costume.

Viharn Ton Kaew: To the right of Viharn Luang stands a small, open-sided *viharn* tragically restored in 1967 with heavy concrete and whitewash which obliterated whatever artistic appeal it once possessed.

Viharn Nam Tam: Behind Viharn Ton Kaew is another small *viharn* which has blessedly been left unrestored by the local monks. The 16th-century building—possibly the oldest wooden structure in Thailand—houses a seated Buddha, four standing Buddhas, side murals etched in black and white, and a gold-leaf bodhi tree mural behind the Buddha images.

The surrounding compound gallery contains an interesting collection of ancient coffins and royal palanquins decorated with traditional Lanna motifs.

Viharn Pra Phut: To the left of Viharn Luang in the sandy courtyard is a large *kachao* tree, fine bronze bells in an open pavilion, and the so-called Buddha Viharn which dates from 1802. It is ranked among the finest structures in northern Thailand. The carved wooden facade and two-tiered roof complement the proportions of the interior nave. Inside the architectural gem are several Chiang Saen Buddhas and restored murals of doves, *devas,* and gilded flowers.

Central *Chedi:* Directly behind Viharn Luang is an ungilded 45-meter *chedi* with extremely rare carved bronze plaques around the base and a gilded finial at the summit. A small bullet hole in the northwest corner is evidence of the efforts of local hero Tipchang to liberate the town of Lampang. He shot and killed a Burmese general here.

Viharn Pra Chao Sila: Behind the central *chedi* is a *bot* constructed in 1476 but restored in 1924, an elevated sanctuary containing a Buddha footprint, and Viharn Pra Chao Sila, possibly constructed by the father of Queen Chamdevi. To the rear is a small drainage ditch where Tipchang surreptitiously entered the occupied compound to attack the Burmese general.

Kachao Tree: Outside the interior compound is an immense bodhi tree supported by hundreds of sticks donated and signed by pilgrims. The pathway to the right leads to the following attractions.

Temple Museum: Opposite the resting pavilion stands a rather dark museum containing a large bronze Buddha of the Lanna school, stone heads recovered from Phayao, and dozens of dusty manuscript cabinets.

Pra Keo Don Tao: Final stop is the unremarkable building filled with old photos of the royal family, stuffed blowfish, fake deer heads, amulets, fortune-telling sticks, and a highly revered crystal Buddha carefully protected behind two sets of iron gates. According to Buddhist legends, the image was carved from the same block of stone as the Buddha statue in Wat Pra Keo in Bangkok.

Transportation: Wat Prathat Lampang Luang is 20 km south of Lampang and six km west of the small town of Kokha. Minibuses to Kokha leave regularly from the intersection of Paholyothin and Prabhat Roads in Lampang. Motorcycle taxis and *songtaos* continue from Kokha to the monument. Motorcyclists coming from Chiang Mai should turn right at Hang Chat, 10 km west of Lampang.

Elephant School

Thailand's official elephant-training camp recently moved from its old location, 54 km northeast of Lampang, to a new site between Lampang and Chiang Mai in the Tung Kwain Reforestation Center. Here in a beautiful wooded basin, mahouts train young pachyderms each morning, except on Buddhist holidays and during the hot season from March to June.

The elephant industry changed dramatically several years ago when the ban on logging forced local authorities to push the tourist potential of their elephant herds. Once an authentic training camp for wild elephants, the new elephant-preservation center has a small exhibit hall, museum, compound for the elephant show, and several bungalows.

The center is 37 km west of Lampang and 54 km east of Chiang Mai. Take any bus between these two destinations and ask the driver to drop you at the road to the center. The 1000 show is held just 500 meters off the highway during the peak tourist months (December and January), but otherwise at the school's main training grounds.

WEST OF CHIANG MAI

MAE SARIANG

This small town, southwest of Chiang Mai, serves as a good base for treks and river adventures down the Yuam and Thanlwin Rivers which separate Thailand from Myanmar. Progress has arrived slowly to the region, a blessing for the town, which has retained many of its fine old wooden buildings and simple temples constructed in Burmese-Shan style.

Attractions

A quick stroll around compact Mae Sariang turns up a few temples of fairly recent vintage. Wat Jong Sung, a modest temple which dates from 1896, fronts the more impressive Wat Sri Boonruang, constructed by Burmese crafts-people in 1930 in the typical architectural style of the borderlands. Wat Chong Kham down near the bridge is another example of Burmese monastic architecture with multitiered roofs, wooden latticework, and the inevitable corrugated tin roof. Overlooking Mae Sariang and strategically placed on a towering hillside is the concrete Buddha of Prathat Chom Mon, where motorcyclists can enjoy great views from the summit.

Accommodations

Mae Sariang has a handful of simple guest-houses and hotels that cater to the steady trickle of Western tourists.

Riverside Guesthouse: A popular but extremely basic guesthouse overlooking the Yuam River. The breezy restaurant is a great place to relax after a long bus ride or to spend a few hours in the evening planning your river journey. Riverside has only 12 rooms, not in the best condition, and a few thatched bungalows across the river. 85/1 Laeng Phanit Rd., tel. (053) 681188, 80-150B.

Mae Sariang Guesthouse: The Mae Sariang and BR Guesthouses near the bus depot are both dirty and depressing places, only suitable as emergency crash pads when the Riverside is filled. 1 Laeng Phanit Rd., 50-80B.

See View Hotel: A new place which betrays its name and offers concrete cubicles without views of the river or the "See." The modern and clean bungalows come with attached bath and quality furniture. Too bad they don't face the river. 70 Wiang Mai Rd., tel. (053) 681154, 100-210B.

Mitaree Hotel: Mae Sariang's original hotel has seen better days, though the rooms are large and kept fairly clean. Mitaree operates a guesthouse on Wiang Mai Road. Mae Sariang Rd., tel. (053) 681022, 120-250B fan, 350B a/c.

Kamolsorn Hotel: A fairly new and modern three-story hotel with big a/c rooms with private baths. Probably the best in town, though that's not saying much. 83 Mae Sariang Rd., tel. (053) 681204, 350-650B.

Pan House: Travelers going to Mae Hong Son via the southern route can stay with Mr. Werapan Tarasan (Mr. Pan) and use his guide services for trekking and elephant excursions. Pan House is on Hwy. 108 at Km 68, 158 km from Chiang Mai and 32 km east of Mae Sariang. Ask the bus driver to drop you at Ban Mae Wan, then hike five km south from the highway.

Restaurants

Several passable Chinese and Thai restaurants are located along Wiang Mai Road in the center of town.

Intira Restaurant: The most popular dining venue in town seems to be this place which serves chicken with ginger, beef fried in oyster sauce, and fried fish with pepper and garlic.

Renu Restaurant: Across the road from the Intira is another small but jamming cafe with similar food offerings.

Black & White Cafe: Freshly baked goods are available from the shop adjacent to this curiously named cafe.

Puern Prae Restaurant: You can escape the heat and noise at this clean cafe near the entrance to Wat Sri Boonruang, where dining choices include Thai, Chinese, and "General Food" on teakwood tables across from their peaceful garden.

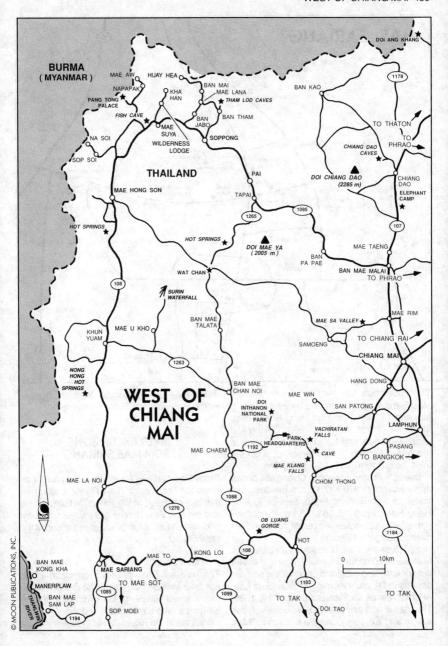

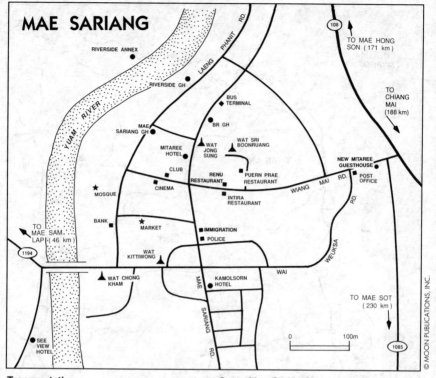

MAE SARIANG

RIVERSIDE ANNEX

RIVERSIDE GH

LAENG PHANIT RD.

108

TO MAE HONG SON (171 km)

TO CHIANG MAI (188 km)

YUAM RIVER

BUS TERMINAL

BR GH

MAE SARIANG GH

MITAREE HOTEL

WAT JONG SUNG

WAT SRI BOONRUANG

NEW MITAREE GUESTHOUSE

CLUB

RENU RESTAURANT

PUERN PRAE RESTAURANT

WIANG MAI RD.

POST OFFICE

MOSQUE

CINEMA

INTIRA RESTAURANT

BANK

MARKET

IMMIGRATION

POLICE

WEUKSA RD.

TO MAE SAM LAP (46 km)

1194

WAT KITTIWONG

MAE SARIANG RD.

KAMOLSORN HOTEL

WAI

TO MAE SOT (230 km)

WAT CHONG KHAM

SEE VIEW HOTEL

0   100m

1085

© MOON PUBLICATIONS, INC.

Transportation

Mae Sariang is 188 km southwest of Chiang Mai and 171 km from Mae Hong Son. Buses leave the Arcade Bus Terminal in Chiang Mai every two hours and take four or five hours to reach Mae Sariang. The same service is offered from the bus terminal in Mae Hong Son.

Buses from Mae Sariang to Chiang Mai depart every two hours 0700-1700 from the dusty terminal on Mae Sariang Road. Service to Mae Hong Son runs 0715-1530. An overnight express bus to Bangkok leaves at 1700 and arrives in Bangkok 13 hours later.

Songtaos and minitrucks from Mae Sariang to Mae Sam Lap on the Thanlwin River and to Tak are sporadic and subject to delays. One *songtao* departs in the early morning for Mae Sam Lap. Another leaves for Mae Sot down Hwy. 1085. The road is now fully paved. More details on this scenic and exciting journey are given in "Mae

Sot to Mae Sariang" under "Western Borderlands" in the Central Thailand chapter.

RIVER EXCURSIONS FROM MAE SARIANG

From Mae Sariang travelers enjoy boat rides down the Thanlwin or Yuam Rivers. Excursions can be organized at the Riverside Guesthouse and the See View Hotel. River journeys are best undertaken Dec.-March, just after the end of the rainy season.

Ban Mae Sam Lap

The Thanlwin River journey begins with a jeep ride from Mae Sariang across the Danwa Range to this small village 46 km southwest of Mae Sariang on the banks of the Thanlwin. Accommodations in the Riverside Huts chalets include verandas which overlook the Thanlwin. A one-day roundtrip longtail boat journey north to Johta costs about 1,500B, but this cost can be shared between eight passengers. Johta is the last town on the Thai border before the Thanlwin veers west into Myanmar.

Boat trips are also possible south from Mae Sam Lap down to the junction of the Thanlwin and Yuam Rivers and the small village of Mae Leh Ta. The longtail boat glides past rudimentary Burmese villages, waterfalls, and logging camps with working elephants.

Mae Kong Kha
Thanlwin River journeys also originate from this Karen village directly west of Mae Sariang. River-side Guesthouse has simple huts on the muddy banks. Across the river is Manerplaw, the Karen outpost that fell to Burmese government forces in 1995.

Other Rivers
A third option is a river journey down the Yuam River, beginning from the town of Sop Moei on Hwy. 1085. Other tributaries of the Thanlwin that can be rafted include the Ngao and Moei Rivers.

MAE HONG SON

Tucked away close to the Burmese border and hemmed in by the mountains which surround the Pai River Valley, Mae Hong Son has recently developed into one of the major destinations in northern Thailand. Before the torturous 369-km road from Chiang Mai was completed in 1965, the town served as a convenient dumping ground for disgraced bureaucrats, who graciously nick-named it the "Siberia of Thailand."

Today, Mae Hong Son is aggressively mar-keted as Thailand's version of Shangri-la—com-plete with lost valleys, tribal trekking, caves, rivers, and waterfalls. While it's not the mystical vision described in tourist literature, the attractive scenery and sense of remoteness make it a wel-come change from the more touristy destina-tions in Thailand.

THE FALL OF MANERPLAW

*S*ince the end of WW II, Thai government policy had been to support the two dozen ethnic rebels fighting the Burmese gov-ernment along the border regions between the two countries. These separatist groups—Karens, Mons, Shans, Karenni, etc.—served as a sort of political buffer zone keeping the Burmese military occupied with domestic affairs and isolating Thailand from the seemingly endless turmoil to the west.

The playing field began to shift in 1988 after the State Law and Order Restoration Council (SLORC) seized power in Yangon and began to attack the ethnic rebels with renewed vigor. The Thai gov-ernment quietly switched allegiances and slowly shifted their support to the Burmese regime. With-out the support of Thailand, the rebels were doomed.

In 1993, five leading Burmese dissidents were barred from entering Thailand to proceed to the United Nations for discussions about Burmese human rights. That same year, the Mons and Karen-nis started formal peace talks with the Burmese government. The Kachin ethnic minority signed a cease-fire agreement with SLORC in 1994, formal-ly ending 32 years of armed rebellion. Members of the Karenni National Progressive Party surrendered later that year, leaving only the Karen National Union (KNU) and much smaller Mon New State Party with-out cease-fire agreements.

In February 1995, Burmese forces overran the Karen National Union headquarters at Manerplaw, just across the Thanlwin River from Mae Sariang. Karen leader Bo Mya disappeared into the jungle and vowed to continue the struggle that had occu-pied his life since 1948.

The fall of Manerplaw was a major victory for SLORC and Thai leaders who were conducting a roaring trade with the Burmese junta. It also bene-fitted the Chinese, who had sold the SLORC regime large amounts of artillery, helicopters, and other advanced weaponry.

But the events at Manerplaw signaled a major defeat to Western countries attempting to isolate the Burmese junta, and for human rights advocates demanding the release of Myanmar's nationally elected leader, Aung San Suu Kyi.

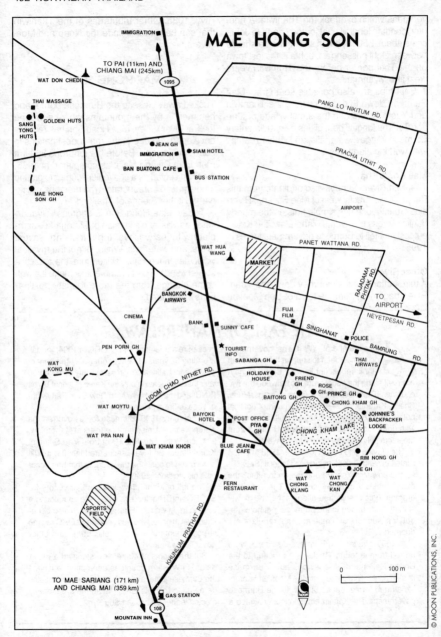

MAE HONG SON

IMMIGRATION

TO PAI (11km) AND
CHIANG MAI (245km)

WAT DON CHEDI

1095

PANG LO NIKITUM RD.

THAI MASSAGE

SANG
TONG
HUTS

GOLDEN HUTS

JEAN GH
IMMIGRATION
BAN BUATONG CAFE

SIAM HOTEL

BUS STATION

PRACHA UTHIT RD.

MAE HONG
SON GH

AIRPORT

WAT HUA
WANG

MARKET

PANET WATTANA RD.

BANGKOK
AIRWAYS

RAJADAMA PHITAK RD.

TO
AIRPORT

CINEMA

BANK

SUNNY CAFE

FUJI
FILM

SINGHANAT

NEYETPESAN RD.

POLICE

BAMRUNG RD.

TOURIST
INFO

PEN PORN GH

SABANGA GH

THAI
AIRWAYS

WAT KONG MU

WAT MOYTU

UDOM CHAO NITHET RD.

HOLIDAY
HOUSE

FRIEND
GH

ROSE
GH

PRINCE GH

BAITONG GH

CHONG KHAM GH

CHONG KHAM LAKE

JOHNNIE'S
BACKPACKER
LODGE

BAIYOKE
HOTEL

WAT PRA NAN

WAT KHAM KHOR

POST OFFICE
PIYA
GH

BLUE JEAN
CAFE

RIM NONG GH

JOE GH

WAT
CHONG
KLANG

WAT
CHONG
KAN

FERN
RESTAURANT

KHUNLUM PRATHAT RD.

SPORTS
FIELD

0   100 m

TO MAE SARIANG (171 km)
AND CHIANG MAI (359 km)

108

GAS STATION

MOUNTAIN INN

© MOON PUBLICATIONS, INC.

Mae Hong Son is also experiencing the problems of rapid and unregulated development. Over the last five years, tourist arrivals have doubled annually to a present influx of over 200,000 visitors. During the high season Oct.-Feb., every flight and guesthouse is fully booked by legions of backpackers and tourists who arrive expecting to discover some quaint and forgotten destination.

Mae Hong Son now has over 30 guesthouses, a post office with phone services, several banks which cash traveler's checks, trekking agencies, a handicraft center, and motorcycle rental shops. Several four-star hotels such as the Holiday Inn and Tara Mae Hong Son now cater to wealthy tourists surprised to discover traffic jams, noise, and commercialization competing with the bucolic charms of the once-neglected village.

Mae Hong Son still has a great deal of charisma, but the future is questionable unless local government authorities take strong measures to manage its growth and somehow preserve its unique heritage.

Chong Kham Lake

This natural lake was once an elephant bathing place where Chao Keun Muang, a Chiang Mai prince, set up a training camp for his newly captured herds in 1831. Several years ago, the municipality converted the area into a fitness park complete with an exercise par course and lush gardens.

More intriguing than the push-up bars is a handful of remaining wooden *sangkasi* houses covered with *tongteung* roofs and bamboo walls. A good example at 1 Singhanat Rd. retains a *tongteung*-leaf roof which must be replaced every three years at a cost of over 2,000B. Although *tongteung* is cooler and certainly more aesthetic, most of the old Tai Yai-style homes have been recovered with corrugated tin roofs for convenience and economics.

Wat Chong Klang

Picturesquely located on the banks of placid Chong Kham Lake are two *wats* in typical Burmese style with tiered roofs and filigree woodwork along the eaves of the two monasteries. Fronting the grounds are a white-and-gold *chedi* and a small Burmese *prasat* that provide outstanding photographs in the misty morning hours.

Chief interest here is the famous collection of 35 wooden figures *(tukatas)* stored inside the small museum in the rear. Inspired by the Buddhist Vessantara Jataka, the images of starving monks and painted horses were brought from Myanmar in 1857. Equally famous but of less artistic appeal are the glass paintings adorning the wall to the left of the central chamber. They also relate the story of the man who became the Buddha in his next reincarnation.

Wat Chong Kan

The large monastery to the east contains an elaborate gilded chair for the head monk, a strange collection of dusty typewriters, hanging Burmese gongs, and the bilingual story of sinners who descend to hell to be devoured by demons. Proper dress is required and shoes must be removed.

To the far east is a chipping building which houses the revered statue of Luang Pho To, a five-meter seated Buddha surrounded by a lovely tiled floor of blue swans and roses painted in art deco patterns.

Wat Kong Mu

The 424-meter peak at the north end of town features great views and two *chedis* constructed in the mid-1800s by Governor Singnatraja, in the same year Mae Hong Son was declared an official Thai settlement. The *wat* also features a small monastery with an extremely beautiful Buddha carved from white alabaster and mounted on a gilded palanquin. Concrete steps lead to the summit, which is also accessible by car on a back road.

Wat Moytu

At the base of Doi Kong Mu are several temples worth exploring. The main sanctuary at Wat Moytu contains a fabulous bronze Mandalay-style Buddha mounted on an enormous palanquin. Note the benevolent yet somewhat sinister expression. To the rear and elevated on a raised platform are four unusual *chedis* embedded with hundreds of small chambers once filled with Buddhist amulets.

Wat Pra Nan

Wat Pra Nan was constructed over a century ago by a Shan ruler to enshrine a large 12-meter

reclining Buddha, now swathed in a sheer orange robe. The image shows typical Burmese
design with its carefully painted, realistic face
that lacks the enigmatic countenance favored
by Thai sculptors. To the left is a small museum
with Mandalay Buddhas, Burmese lacquerware,
eight wall clocks, and, strangely enough, a bar of
Lux soap. Behind the monastery stand a pair of
stone Burmese lions which guard the old footpath
up Doi Kong Mu.

Wat Pra Nan is an active pilgrimage spot that
provides accommodations to Westerners for a
modest donation; a good place to check when all
the hotels and guesthouses are filled.

Wat Kham Khor
Visitors are also invited to spend a night in the
monastery across the road from Wat Pra Nan.
Constructed in 1890, Wat Kham Khor is a delightful wonderland of old religious objects including dozens of Buddhas in various styles,
paintings, photographs, an elevated abbot's corner equipped with telephone and refrigerator,
and a carved 90-year-old peacock throne elevated on the central altar. This place really feels
like Myanmar.

Wat Hua Wang
Several modest temples constructed in Burmese
style with corrugated roofs arranged in diminishing tiers are located in the center of town.
This particular temple, wedged between the
morning market and the bus station, holds a
highly venerated brass Mandalay-style Buddha
that was cast in Myanmar and hauled over the
mountains to Mae Hong Son.

The adjacent market is occasionally visited
by hilltribe women dressed in traditional garb.
Fifty Burmese cheroots cost only 18B.

Trekking
Trekking in Mae Hong Son Province is a popular
activity since the local population is 50% Shan
(Thai Yai), 2% Thai, and 48% hilltribe groups
including Karens, Lawas, Lahus, Lisus, and
Meos. *Farangs* are a common sight, but most vil-
lages are less deluged than those near Chiang
Mai.

Popular stops near Mae Hong Son include
the Shan village of Ban Mai, three km south of
town, and opium fields several kilometers to the

southeast. Farther treks can be arranged to the
border town of Mae Aw and the small village
near Na Soi where some Paduang long-necked
women are held captive and shown to visitors.
Crossing the Burmese border on the Pai River to
visit Karenni army camps is also possible, but illegal and dangerous.

Treks cost 250-600B per day and can be
arranged through guesthouses and trekking
agencies around town. All offer short treks and
longer five-day jaunts all the way to Chiang Mai.

Festivals
Several unique festivals are held each year in
Mae Hong Son.

Poy Sang Long: This March or April mass-or-
dination ceremony for young boys entering the
Buddhist monkhood (also called Buat Luk Kaew)
is a Shan festival featuring dozens of initiates
ritualistically paraded through town on the shoulders of their relatives—one of the most visually
exciting sights in Thailand.

Chong Pala: Another unique celebration, this
October ceremony welcomes the Lord Buddha
as he returns from a visit to his heavenly mother.
The week-long festival includes a candlelight
procession, sword dancing, drum shows, and a
parade of elaborately decorated Chong Pala
floats.

Budget Accommodations
Mae Hong Son's soaring popularity has brought
the town dozens of guesthouses, several midpriced hotels with a/c rooms, and five luxury hotels and countryside resorts. New facilities are
being added each month. Simple rooms with
fan, mattress, and common bath cost 60-120B,
but the trend seems to be better rooms in the
120-280B price range.

Sang Tong Huts: Great views over ricefields
and banana plantations make this somewhat
remote guesthouse one of the best in Mae Hong
Son. Sang Tong offers individual *nipa* huts plus
a comfortable sitting room and small library.
Rooms vary in price according to size, amenities,
and how long you stay. Pracha Uthit Rd., no
phone, 100-200B.

Golden Huts: Adjacent to Sang Tong, *nipa*
huts cling to the hillside amid trees, ferns, and
winding walkways. Huts with hot showers cost
extra. Traditional Thai massage and medicinal

steam baths are available in the adjacent watchtower. Pracha Uthit Rd., tel. (053) 611544, 100-300B.

Mae Hong Son Guesthouse: Also about 15 minutes from town is another popular guesthouse with small huts and nine wooden rooms. A good place to escape the crowds, though a bicycle will be needed for local transportation. Pracha Uthit Rd., tel. (053) 612510, 80-240B.

Garden Guesthouse: Back in town is a quiet spot with solid, dark rooms covered with teak paneling and a great reception area. Khunlum Prathat Rd., no phone, 160-240B.

Sabanga Guesthouse: Centrally located and placed nicely back from the street, Sabanga has a small garden and elevated patio in front of the rooms. Common baths. 14 Udom Chao Nithet Rd., 120-180B.

Johnnie's Backpacker Lodge: Five excellent teak rooms with mosquito nets and mattresses on the floor. Friendly management plus new bicycle rentals and trekking information. Pradit Jongkam Rd., no phone, 60-100B.

Several small places surround wonderful Chong Kham Lake and fitness park in the center of town. Some are rudimentary collections of bamboo huts on the verge of collapse, while other guesthouses are somewhat superior with views over the lake. All cost about 60-150B.

Moderate Accommodations
Piya Guesthouse: A relatively modern motel that faces a central garden. All rooms include fan and attached bathroom but cleanliness can be a problem here. Chong Kham Lake Rd., tel. (053) 611260, fax (053) 612308, 200-250B fan, 300-450B a/c.

Pen Porn Guesthouse: Clean and modern spot up the hill and away from the noise. All wood-decor rooms come with fan, private bath, and hot showers. Doi Kong Mu Rd., tel. (053) 611577, 200-450B.

Hotels
Baiyoke Chalet: Formerly called the Mitniyom, the Baiyoke is an older hotel with a popular a/c restaurant that converts into a disco in the evening. Nothing special, but all rooms are a/c and it's well-located in the center of town. 90 Khumlum Prathat Rd., tel. (053) 611486, fax (053) 611533, 800-1,200B.

Mountain Lodge: Another fairly well-kept hotel a block south of the Baiyoke Chalet with attractive gardens and clean a/c rooms with hot showers. 112 Khumlum Prathat Rd., tel. (053) 612285, fax (053) 612284, 750-950B.

Rooks Resort: Originally intended to be a Holiday Inn, this relatively new addition to the hotel scene is somewhat south of town on the road to Mae Sariang with pool, tennis courts, nightclub, snooker hall, and several restaurants. 114/5 Khumlun Prathat Rd., tel. (053) 611390, fax (053) 611524, 2,400-2,800B.

Resorts Outside Town
Many groups and upscale visitors stay a few kilometers southwest of town on the banks of a river which flows in from Myanmar.

Imperial Tara Mae Hong Son Hotel: Mae Hong Son came of age with the opening of this 104-room four-star hotel operated by the Imperial group of hotels, with convention center, swimming pool, and several restaurants. Highway 108, tel. (053) 611473, fax (053) 611252, 2,400-2,800B.

Mae Hong Son Resort: Six km south on the banks of the Pai River, Mae Hong Son Resort has 30 comfortable bungalows surrounded by manicured lawns, camping facilities, and a good restaurant. 24 Ban Huai Duea, tel. (053) 611404, fax (053) 611504, 1,000-1,200B fan, 1,600-2,000B a/c.

Rim Nam Klang Doi Resort: Four km south of town is another luxury resort with bungalows, campsites, and dormitory for budget travelers. Ban Huai Duea, tel. (053) 612142, fax (053) 612086, 500-750B.

Restaurants
Night Market: A small but lively market sets up nightly in the center of Mae Hong Son near the police box and small tourist information center. Khunlum Prathat Rd. Inexpensive.

Takeaway: Excellent takeaway dishes—some of the best food in Mae Hong Son—can be picked up from the shop near Fuji Photo. Just point to the best dishes and say, *"Ha baht, ha baht"* ("Five *baht,* five *baht*"). Singhanat Rd. Inexpensive.

Fern Restaurant: An upscale cafe with cane furniture and backyard patio that overlooks palm trees and a small guesthouse with a gi-

AIR AMERICA ~ FACT OR FICTION?

Remember that 1990 comedy about a pair of wild and crazy U.S. pilots—played by Mel Gibson and Robert Downey, Jr.—working for Air America, the secret airline operated by the CIA during the Vietnam War? The story revolved around the supposed hilarity of the agency's transport of heroin during the Indochina conflict. The US$40 million film budget included the planting of 250,000 ersatz opium poppies, the demolition of several old planes, and scenes filmed at tiny Mae Hong Son Airport (where shell casings and combat barracks remain in place) and at the Burmese-style temples that surround Chong Kham Lake.

The film crew of 400 spent six weeks at the Rim Nam Klang Doi Resort, six km south of town, drinking beer and exchanging bits of gossip. Among the more sensational rumors was that opium warlord Khun Sa had agreed to refrain from firing on the movie set in exchange for an autographed photo of Mel Gibson.

Was the story of *Air America* fact or fiction? The movie, based on a book by Christopher Robbins, portrayed the pilots as little more than buccaneers who traded guns for opium when not drinking or chasing the local women. But according to the U.S. government and former pilots, the operation existed to deliver military equipment, medical supplies, and food to Laotian guerrillas fighting communism.

The truth remains a matter of speculation, though the history of Air America remains among the more colorful sidebars of the Indochina War. According to Alfred McCoy in *The Politics of Heroin in Southeast Asia,* Turkey supplied most of the world's heroin until poppy cultivation was abolished in the late 1960s. The drug market then passed to the Nationalist Chinese Army (KMT) in northern Thailand, Burmese Shan rebels such as Khun Sa, and Air Laos Commerciale, a Corsican-controlled charter airlines dubbed "Air Opium." The airline was started by French-Corsican war veterans, colonialists, and gangsters who stayed on in Laos after the French military withdrawal in 1954.

According to McCoy, after the escalating conflict forced the airline out of business in 1965, the CIA expanded their counterinsurgency operations by flying Hmong opium out of the hills to Vientiane and to their headquarters at Long Tieng in Laos. Air America later operated the world's largest private airline, ranging from helicopters and small planes to modern jets and giant transports.

Subsequent events are also quite interesting. Air America later resurfaced in Central America as the supply pipeline for Contra rebels attempting to overthrow the Sandinista government of Nicaragua. The airline's chief of operations was none other than Oliver North.

Times have changed and few visitors to Mae Hong Son care about the Vietnam War or the real story behind Air America. But many visitors are still curious about which bungalow housed Mel Gibson at Rim Nam Klang Doi Resort.

---

gantic menu which features over 200 items. 87 Khunlum Prathat Rd., tel. (053) 611374. Inexpensive.

Blue Jean Cafe: Cozy cowboy-style joint decorated with buffalo skulls and rifles and a hangout for Thai hippies and musicians. Chong Kham Lake Rd., tel. (053) 611350. Inexpensive.

Prince Guesthouse: Inside the wild, elevated, semicircular pub is a lakeside restaurant that serves Chinese and Thai dishes. Good views and friendly management. 37 Udom Chao Nithet Rd., tel. (053) 612256. Moderate.

Practicalities
Tourist Information: A small information booth is located on Khunlum Prathat Road near the Sunny Cafe and the night market. The staff is friendly, helpful, and anxious to practice its English. Also try the Tourist Police on Singhanat Bamrung Road.

Police: Adjacent to the tourist office is a police booth which can help with emergencies.

Banks: Several banks which exchange traveler's checks at good rates are located along the main road.

Immigration: The immigration office just north of town can extend tourist visas for an additional 30 days.

Motorcycle Rentals: Motorcycles can be rented from several agencies and guesthouses such as Khun Tu Guesthouse and a small shop near the bus station. Motorcycle rentals cost 150-250B daily and are a great way to explore the countryside near Mae Hong Son.

Transportation

Mae Hong Son is 368 km from Chiang Mai by the southern route through Mae Sariang on Route 108, or 270 km on the northern road through Pai on Route 1095.

Air: The most comfortable way to reach Mae Hong Son is on the three daily flights from Chiang Mai, which take 30 minutes and cost 440B one way. Tickets are heavily booked and should be reserved well in advance. It's best to purchase a roundtrip ticket and confirm return reservations immediately upon arrival in Mae Hong Son. A popular compromise is to fly to Mae Hong Son but return by bus via Soppong and Pai.

Thai Airways (tel. 053-611297) is at 71 Singhanat Bamrung Rd. on the way to the terminal. Motorcycle taxis from the airport to downtown Mae Hong Son cost 25-40B.

Bus: Buses leave the Arcade Terminal in Chiang Mai every two hours 0630-2100 and take 10-12 grueling hours to reach Mae Hong Son via the southern route. An overnight pause in Mae Sariang is a good way to break the ordeal. Public buses along the northern route through Pai are somewhat quicker and pass through better scenery. Pai is an excellent place to break the journey.

Buses from Mae Hong Son to Pai take four hours and depart every two hours 0630-1400. Buses to Mae Sariang also take four hours and depart every two hours 0600-2100.

MAE HONG SON TO SOPPONG

Excursions can be made from Mae Hong Son to several attractions north of town. Most are off the main road and can only be reached with an escorted tour, rented motorcycle, or chartered minitruck.

Na Soi

Twelve km north of Mae Hong Son is a left turn to the Shan village of Na Soi. The dirt road continues west to a border outpost where several long-necked women are held captive for Western tourists who must pay an additional 300B for photography privileges. An experience best avoided.

Pha Sua Waterfall

North of Na Soi, turn left at Km 17 shortly before Huia Pha and continue past Mok Cham Pae and Huai Khan to these modest bathing falls, 11 km off Hwy. 1095. Pha Sua Falls forms one stage of the Sa Nga River, which flows south from Myanmar. The falls are best visited during the rainy season, though the road is often impassable due to floods and landslides.

Mae Aw

North of Pha Sua Falls is a left turn to Pang Tong Royal Palace, where the king retreats every year or two, and several villages inhabited by Shans and Karens.

The road continues up the mountain to Mae Aw, a desolate Hmong village once controlled by renegade forces of the Kuomintang Army. Mae Aw lies directly opposite the former military headquarters of opium warlord Khun Sa, who surrendered to the Myanmar government several years ago and now lives in luxurious digs in Yangon.

This area has been relatively quiet in recent years, though minor skirmishes occasionally break out between Sa and Thai battalions. For obvious reasons, this is a dangerous region best avoided during the opium season Jan.-May. And whatever you do, don't inadvertently ride your motorcycle across the Thai border into Myanmar, as three Western tourists did in 1998 and found themselves in a Burmese jail for almost a month.

A public *songtao* to Mae Aw departs from the bus terminal in Mae Hong Son each morning around 0700 or 0800. Motorcyclists can reach Mae Aw in under two hours.

Fish Cave

Domesticated carp that measure up to one meter in length are fed papaya in Tham Pla, a rock pool 17 km north of Mae Hong Son. The fish are left unharmed since Buddhism teaches reverence for animal life. A one-km-long dry cave is situated across the road and 100 meters south. Just beyond is Huai Pha, the last town between Mae Hong Son and Soppong.

Nam Khong Wilderness Lodge

Ten km beyond Fish Cave and just past Mae Suya is a sign marking the turnoff to a wilderness lodge that offers trekking services and river excursions down the Nam Khong River. Take a bus from Mae Hong Son or Soppong to the Nam

Khong river bridge, walk 300 meters west and follow the path 1.5 km. The lodge is operated by the owners of Cave Lodge near Soppong. The dirt road winds around and continues south to Mae Lana Guesthouse.

Bungalows with common baths cost 60-120B in this wonderfully remote location.

Mae Lana

A Thai signpost, 56 km from Mae Hong Son and 10 km before Soppong, marks the road north to the Black Lahu village of Ban Jabo and Mae Lana, six km from the highway. The turnoff to Mae Lana is labeled by a small sign in English marked Mae Lana Guesthouse.

Mae Lana Guesthouse: Six km off Hwy. 1095 is the village of Mae Lana, where a French woman and her Thai husband operate this excellent guesthouse with inexpensive dormitory and private rooms from 100B per night. The guesthouse is situated in beautiful countryside blessed with thick forests, cool streams, and

---

SMILE FOR THE TOURISTS

*T*he most famous—and exploited—people of the Mae Hong Son region are the so-called "long-necked women" of the tiny Padaung tribe from Myanmar. The Padaung are one of many ethnic minorities of Myanmar, and one of the smallest groups, numbering under 7,000 members who originated primarily in Loikaw, the capital of Kayah State. Yet due to the exceptional ornament favored by their women, the Padaung have achieved fame far greater than their numbers would suggest.

Their eponymous name describes their fate: women lengthen their necks by adding brass rings from about seven years of age to the day of their marriage. The initiation, commonly held at the auspicious time of a full moon, begins a cycle in which the adolescent adds another new ring every two years until her neck is elongated into a giraffesque shape. Once fastened around the neck, the adornment must remain for life; to remove a full stack would cause the collapse of the head and instant suffocation.

In recent times, Padaung women refused to subject themselves to the tortuous tradition. Few modern Padaung were willing to wear 10 kg of brass coils to enhance their beauty or uphold some old legend of questionable origin. In Myanmar, the practice was outlawed as barbaric many years ago and women rejected the coils for over two decades.

But more recently, the tradition, as disfiguring as bound feet, was revived for the sake of tourism. Padaung women are once again donning neck coils, not for cultural tradition or social heritage, but to make money and fuel the tourist organizations that profit from such bizarre traditions.

The Padaung practice began several years ago after thousands of the ethnic tribe fled their homeland

to escape the Burmese army's program of forced labor, slavery designed to help the army defeat the various separatist armies along Myanmar's borders. The Padaung traveled along the Pei River and crossed the border into Thailand where Thai entrepreneurs offered them a relatively lucrative deal. In exchange for living in a subsidized community, wearing neck coils, and being displayed to tourists seven days a week, each Padaung woman would receive a monthly salary and allotment of rice.

Thai tour operators created a village for the women and advertised their sensational attraction to international tour companies around the world, charging US$12 per person to see the women and additional fees for photography and videos. They also invented a cheerful dose of propaganda: the village is typical of Padaung lifestyles, and the long-necks, another of Thailand's endangered minorities, are political refugees supported by the Thai government, not some freak show.

None of this is true. Padaung villages in Thailand are bizarre worlds created by Thai tour operators, and the women receive no official support or legal endorsement from the Thai government. In fact, Padaung are not allowed to farm Thai land, work in Mae Hong Son, or send their children to Thai schools. And they certainly don't represent some sort of altruistic movement motivated by enlightened political goals.

The women themselves take a pragmatic approach to their role in the local tourist industry. Most accept their fate as showcases for the machinery of tourism and quietly sit on their steps while a steady stream of tourists snap photographs—an ethnic minority caught in a web of political intrigue, wretched poverty, powerlessness, and ruthless economic exploitation.

limestone caves. Information from the guesthouse can help with treks to nearby Red and Black Lahu villages, and the trail over to the caves at Tham Lod. Mae Lana is a wonderful place to relax and escape the commercialism of northern Thailand.

Tophill Guesthouse: Just opposite the Mae Lana Guesthouse is another option, although the managers are less adept at helping travelers and the place is often closed during the rainy season.

Huay Hea

The village 12 km northwest of Mae Lana and just one km from the Burmese border has no formal guesthouse, though the local English school teacher can help with an overnight crash and tips on local trekking and cave explorations.

SOPPONG

The small village of Soppong chiefly serves as a departure point for the nearby caves. Soppong is inhabited by Shans and Lisus who largely continue to wear their bright green and blue pantaloons.

Information on trekking is available from Jungle Trekking at the south end of town where a Burmese guide named Sunny claims to be a hilltribe multilinguist, master chef, expert masseuse, comedian, distiller of moonshine whiskey, and teacher of "Hokey Cokey" to local villagers.

Soppong actually comprises the "Old Soppong" village about one km down the road toward Pai and the newer Ban Pangmappa (Pangmappa Village) where the buses now stop. And without scheduled bus service, the original village of Soppong is dying a fast death.

Accommodations

Several guesthouses are located where the buses stop in Pangmappa ("New Soppong").

Central Guesthouse: Behind the Islamic Restaurant is a rough but convenient spot for late-night arrivals. 60-100B.

Kemarin Garden: Better atmosphere is found at this friendly little spot near the bus station, at the east end of town, where you'll find good travel tips and decent food. 60-100B.

Lemon Hill Guesthouse: Just across the road from the bus stop is a very comfortable and convenient alternative to the more idyllic spots outside town. 100-250B.

Jungle Guesthouse: A very popular if simple place with helpful managers and small cafe about one km northwest of town toward Mae Hong Son. 60-100B.

Ten km beyond Soppong toward Pai, in the beautiful Lisu village of Ban Nam Rin, is the popular **Lisu Lodge,** operated by Mr. Tan, who speaks good English. A-frame chalets cost 40-70B.

THAM LOD NATIONAL PARK

Most travelers continue from Soppong eight km north through the Lahu village of Ban Wana and the Shan village of Ban Tham to Tham Lod and other limestone caves, each more than a kilometer long. Tham Lod National Park covers 1,000 hectares.

Guided cave explorations are conducted by all of the guesthouses in the region. Tham Lod National Park rangers also provide guides and lanterns to explore the vast interiors.

Tham Lod

The region's most famous cave is a huge river tunnel called Tham Lod: *tham* (cave), *lod* (through). Formed by the Nam Lang River, the cave is filled with stalactites, deep interior canyons, and prehistoric coffins carved from teak logs that resemble dugout canoes. Locals believe the immense coffins were built by unfriendly *phi* spirits that inhabit the caves, but most likely they were carved by members of the Lawa tribe who lived in the northern hills long before the Thais arrived from the north. Rumor has it that another cave holds a vast amount of gold and archaeological treasures abandoned by the Japanese during their retreat from Myanmar.

Other Caves

Over a dozen other caves are located near Soppong. Twenty km from Tham Lod is Tham Nam Lang, an 8.3-km cave, reputedly one of the longest in Southeast Asia. Professional spelunkers can also explore the Spirit Well—named after its shape and awesome dimensions, 100 meters

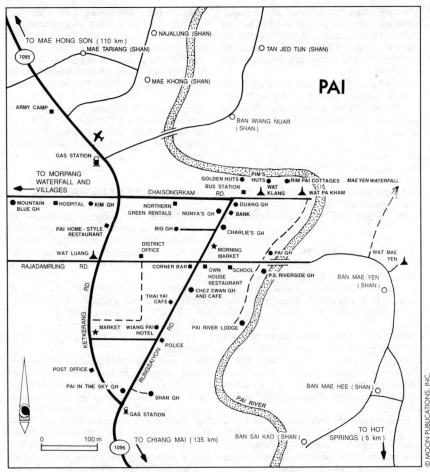

across and almost 200 meters deep. Nearby Spirit Cave is where famed American archaeologist Charles Gorman conducted excavations in the mid-1960s and found evidence of human habitation dating back almost 14,000 years.

Accommodations and Food

Situated in or near Tham Lod National Park are several bungalow operations that provide lodging, meals, guide services, and trekking advice.

Cave Lodge: Operated by Australian John Spies and his Thai wife Diu, Cave Lodge was the first place to take advantage of the caves and surrounding topography. John has authored several articles about trekking and spelunking, and is an invaluable information source on the nearby caves. Diu cooks tasty vegetarian meals and homemade brown bread. Ban Tham Lod, radio phone (66) 536-1171, ext. 822, 50B dorm, 120-280B bungalows.

Tum Lod Guesthouse: A little beyond Cave Lodge is another guesthouse with inexpensive bungalows and a good restaurant that serves communal meals.

National Park Bungalows: The national park has cabins for rent.

Transportation

The road to Ban Tham and Tham Lod National Park leaves from the east end of Soppong. The nine-km hike takes about two hours. A motorcycle taxi costs 40B, public minitrucks 30B (when available), or you can charter a minitruck for 150-200B. Treks from Ban Tham continue six km east to the Karen village of Ban Muang Paem, and 15 km west to Mae Lana. Maps are available from John at Cave Lodge.

PAI

Pai is one of the most beautiful destinations in Thailand. Situated in a broad valley surrounded by mountains and rivers, the idyllic landscape and easygoing pace recall Chiang Mai of several decades ago. This is the kind of place where days lead into weeks and weeks into months.

At first glance, Pai may seem a rather nondescript town with little to offer. A closer inspection uncovers a great deal of superb attractions, from river rafting down the Pai to some of the best hilltribe trekking in northern Thailand. Combined with hot springs, mountains, and an immensely friendly population, Pai ranks as one of the last undiscovered paradises of the north.

Unlike Mae Hong Son, Pai has remained undisturbed because of its somewhat remote location midway between Chiang Mai and Mae Hong Son. Pai is blessedly free of Holiday Inns, fast-food restaurants, or an airport which could haul in planeloads of tourists. The tourist industry remains confined to simple guesthouses and small cafes that serve the needs of budget backpackers—a delightful town that will hopefully remain unspoiled well into the next century. The standard greeting in Pai remains a lazy *"Bai nai?"* ("Where are you going?") to which you might respond, *"Bai tai"* ("Just cruising") or *"Dun lin"* ("Taking a walk").

Most of the attractions in Pai are outside town. Information on treks, river rafting, and hot springs can be obtained from all of the guesthouses. Bicycles are the best way to get around.

Wat Mae Yen

A 30-minute walk east of town past a Shan village is the "Temple on the Hill." Under the patronage of a community of vegetarian monks and situated at the top of a 350-step staircase, the modern temple complex offers great sunset views over Pai Valley and the surrounding mountains.

Waterfalls

Pai has several waterfalls best visited during or shortly after the monsoon season. The most popular is Morpang Falls, seven km west of town on the road past the hospital. En route to the falls are several villages inhabited by Shans, Lisus, and Kuomintang Chinese, plus the temples of Wat Houana and Wat Namhoo. Kim Guesthouse is just beyond the hospital, while Pai Mountain Lodge, with hot showers and campfire, is out near the falls.

Another small series of falls is east of town toward Wat Mae Yen.

Pong Rone Hot Springs

Eleven km southeast of town are several minor hot springs fed by bamboo pipes and located adjacent to a small stream. While hardly spectacular, Pong Rone provides a welcome soak after a long and dusty bike ride. Several of the guesthouses provide nighttime excursions to the baths.

Trekking

Pai is one of the most popular trekking areas in northern Thailand. Most treks head north and make overnight stops in Shan, Black Lahu, and Lisu villages before rafting down the Pai River. An elephant camp is also situated on the banks of the Pai River.

Basic treks without elephant rides or river trips cost 350-600B per day including guide services, accommodations, and all meals. Prices are fixed at the same levels in Chiang Mai. Treks can be arranged through most guesthouses and from independent agencies scattered around town.

The easiest way to avoid crowds is to skip any trek which includes a river trip or elephant ride.

River Trips

The Pai River and a tributary of the Ping near Doi Inthanon National Park are northern Thailand's most popular river-and-trekking destinations. Short day-trips down the Pai River begin north of town near the elephant camp. A longer multiday journey to Mae Hong Son starts at Ban Muang Pang, 26 km south of Pai, and continues downstream to Pang Mu, eight km north of Mae Hong Son. River trips are only offered during and immediately after the rainy season.

Arrangements can be made at Chez Swan, a whitewater rafting company operated by a Frenchman from his restaurant on the main street. The three-day trip begins with a 70-km bus ride to the Nam Khong River, followed by lunch and a raft trip through canyons to an open-pavilion campsite. Day two includes waterfalls, caves, a series of Class 3 rapids, and an evening at a hot springs. Mae Hong Son is reached in the late afternoon of the third day. The rubber raft journey costs 1,800-2,500B per person including food and all transportation from Pai.

Accommodations

Over a dozen modest guesthouses are located in Pai. Most line the main road but the best places are found along the river and on the outskirts of town.

Charlie's Guesthouse: Conveniently located near the bus stop, Charlie's is a clean and comfortable place with friendly management. Guide services are provided by a trilingual Shan-Karen named Seth. The owner can also direct you to Mr. Chan, a Burmese man who offers traditional massage and sauna smoked with special herbs. 9 Rungsaiyon Rd., tel. (053) 699039, 60-120B. Special rooms include Sweet Rooms II and III at 160B and Sweet Room I for 200B.

Chez Swan Guesthouse: Also on the main road is another clean guesthouse with large rooms and private bathrooms with hot showers. Rungsaiyon Rd., tel. (053) 699111, 180-200B.

Nunya's Guesthouse: A two-story hotel with rooms tucked away in the back courtyard. De-cent place but not as clean as Charlie's or Chez Swan. 84 Rungsiyanon Rd., tel. (053) 699051, 50-70B downstairs rooms with common bath, 100-140B upstairs rooms with private bath.

Pai River Lodge: River Lodge has a dozen bamboo huts arranged in a semicircle around the central dining area. The bungalows are fairly run-down, but the place is spacious and has a good location facing the Pai River. Huts cost 70-100B. No phone.

P.S. Riverside Guesthouse: Less inviting than the River Lodge is this place with rudimentary huts crammed together facing a grassy yard and elevated kitchen. Samat, the owner, speaks good English. Huts cost 60-80B. No phone.

Pai in the Sky Guesthouse: Clever name, but little more than an ugly concrete motel with corrugated tin roof and windowless rooms. Rungsiyanon Rd., no phone, 60-100B.

Shan Guesthouse: Perhaps the best guesthouse in Pai is the series of individual wooden huts at the south end of town near some beautiful ricefields. Shan's is run by a Shan who once worked the oilfields in Saudi Arabia and by his Aussie co-owner who printed up business cards which read, "You can check out any time you like . . . but you can never leave." A good slogan for a town like Pai. Rungsiyanon Rd., tel. (053) 699162, 150-200B.

Restaurants

All of the guesthouses in Pai have simple cafes that serve Thai dishes and travelers' food.

Pai paradise

Own House: a.k.a. Own Home, this cafe in the middle of town is a popular spot with comfortable wicker furniture, mellow tapes, and both vegetarian and Thai specialties. Try the exotic dishes like hummus and *samosas*.

Pai Home-Style Restaurant: A cozy but dark cafe with Thai and Burmese dishes, including pork in a mysterious curry. The upstairs section has some antiques and clothing for sale.

Budsaracome Food Garden: Across the river on the right is an outdoor cafe popular with local Mekong whiskey imbibers. Tasty and not oversweet Thai white wine is sold at Northern Green Rentals.

Transportation

Buses from the Arcade Bus Terminal in Chiang Mai depart at 0700, 0830, 1100, and 1400 and take about three hours to cover the 134 km to Pai. Buses from Mae Hong Son to Pai take four hours and leave several times daily 0700-1300. The road from Mae Hong Son is incredibly rugged and winding, but has spectacular views over some of the most isolated regions of Thailand.

Buses from Pai to Chiang Mai depart hourly 0630-1430. An a/c bus departs once daily around 1130. Passengers should arrive early and grab the first available seats. Buses to Soppong and Mae Hong Son depart every two hours 0700-1430.

Motorcycles can be rented from several guesthouses in Pai and from Northern Green Rentals just west of the bus station.

CHIANG MAI TO CHIANG DAO CAVES

Most travelers take an early morning bus from Chiang Mai directly to Thaton and catch the 1300 longtail boat down to Chiang Rai—the most popular river journey in northern Thailand. Visitors with more time might stop at Mae Sa Valley (Km 12), Chiang Dao Elephant Camp (Km 56), and the Chiang Dao Caves (Km 69), before passing through the small town of Fang (Km 149) en route to Thaton (Km 175) on the banks of the Kok River.

Mae Sa Valley is described above in **Vicinity of Chiang Mai.** An overnight stop in Thaton is highly recommended over the rushed journey taken by most travelers. Motorcyclists will pass the following towns and turnoffs en route to the caves at Chiang Dao.

Mae Malai (Km 33)

Mae Malai is a small town which serves as the turnoff for Hwy.1095 to Pai and Mae Hong Son. The Mayura Restaurant on the east side of the road has cold drinks and an English-language menu.

Taeng River (Km 40)

Forty km north of Chiang Mai is a left turn to several villages on the Taeng River used for river journeys by trekking agencies in Chiang Mai.

Traveller Inn Hotel: Visitors heading up to this region for some river rafting may wish to overnight and enjoy the beautiful countryside and perhaps make arrangements for extended treks to the nearby Lisu, Lahu, Karen, and Hmong villages. This particular guesthouse is well maintained and generally filled with groups up from Chiang Mai whose schedules include river rafting and perhaps a day of trekking. 300-450B.

Chiang Dao Elephant Camp (Km 56)

Seen an elephant lately? This privately owned elephant camp on the Ping River sponsors daily shows at 0900 sharp for just 80B. The elephant show begins with a procession of animals up the Ping, followed by log-rolling exhibitions and demonstrations by the mahouts. Afterwards, elephant rides around the grounds cost 50B per person. Boat operators leaving from the open-air restaurant run bamboo rafts 4.5 km down the Ping River to Tha Rua. The quoted price is about 600B but the fare drops quickly after the tour buses have departed. The whole experience is touristy but loads of fun.

The camp is 56 km north of Chiang Mai, under a small patch of jungle on the right side of Hwy. 107. Public buses leave from the Chang Puak Bus Terminal and take about 90 minutes to reach the camp. To make the 0900 show, take the 0700 bus and watch the highway signs to help remind the bus driver.

Hilltribe Center (Km 61)

A signposted track leads west to the Hilltribes Development and Welfare Center, a royal project which provides local hilltribes with medical care, agricultural help, and advice on crop substitution. Reached up a *very* steep and winding seven-km road, the center offers magnificent views and a bracing climate at over 1,000 meters in elevation, but the hilltribes are now modernized and no longer wear traditional clothing. Motorcyclists should attempt this drive only in clear, dry weather.

CHIANG DAO TOWN

Chiang Dao is a dusty little town chiefly known for its nearby caves, mountains, and hilltribes. Travelers arriving by bus can get off in the center of town and walk 100 meters north to the road that leads west to the Chiang Dao Caves.

Doi Chiang Dao
Dominating the landscape to the west of town is the breathtaking outline of Doi Chiang Dao ("Mountain to the Stars"), a moody volcanic cone which, after Doi Inthanon and Doi Phahompok, ranks as Thailand's third-highest mountain at 2,285 meters. Vegetation on the mountain belongs to the temperate class such as Shorea and Dipterocarpaceae, with dense tropical jungle and pine forests over 1,000 meters. Long regarded as the home of magical spirits and animist ghosts which eat the entrails of their victims, Chiang Dao Mountain is now inhabited by hilltribes such as Lisu, Karen, and Musers.

Accommodations and Food
Chiang Dao has a pair of simple hotels on the main road. **Dieng Dao** adjacent to the market and **Santisuk** across the street have rudimentary rooms from 80B.

Our House Restaurant, just beyond the well-marked road to the caves, has an English-language menu and ice cream specialties.

CHIANG DAO CAVES

A large sign at the north end of Chiang Dao town marks the left turn to some of the most famous caves in Thailand. From the highway, the road continues five km west through villages and tobacco fields to the caves, which run into the heart of Chiang Dao Mountain. *Songtaos* go hourly from the highway up to the caves. Otherwise, take a motorcycle taxi for 20B.

Beyond the parking lot and massive tamarind tree is an old Burmese-style *chedi,* a small pool containing tame carp, and a covered stairway that leads into the mouth of the caves. All are filled with Buddhist images left by Shan pilgrims who migrated to northern Thailand from their ancestral homes in Myanmar. Entrance is 10B and a guide with lantern costs 40-60B.

Tham Num: Images inside the main cave are illuminated by floodlights which help the small amount of light spilling in through the natural skylights. Beyond the small reclining Burmese Buddha at the end of the walkway is a darkened extension inhabited by grisly *phi rob* spirits, who dine exclusively on the internal organs of plump *farangs.* Some say the cave continues another 660 meters, others claim over 10 km.

Tham Ma: Immediately to the left of the entrance is a darkened cave that can only be explored with a guide. Inside the 735-meter cave are several Buddhas and terrific rock formations imaginatively named after their shapes, such as Giant Chicken, Baby Elephant, and my favorite, Fried Egg. Guides cost 20B for the 30-minute tour of Tham Ma.

Accommodations
Most visitors spend a few hours exploring the caves and then return to Chiang Mai or continue north to Thaton, though several small guesthouses are tucked away near the caves.

Malee's Nature Lovers Bungalows: Some two km past the caves is a finely isolated guesthouse where the German-Thai owners can help with river trips, treks, and nature explorations. 80-100B dorm, 250-450B private chalet.

Mountain Motorcycle Loop
Shortly before the entrance to the caves, a right turn leads northwest to the back side of Doi Chiang Dao. After crossing cotton fields and passing through a military checkpoint, the steep and winding road continues 12 km to the left turn for the Lisu village of Ban Na La Mai. The road continues another 20 km west to the Karen village of Muang Khong on the banks of the Mae Taeng River. Magnificent views of Doi Chiang Dao are guaranteed, but the dirt road should only be attempted in good weather. Allow one hour to Ban Na La Mai and two hours to Muang Khong.

Rather than turn left to Ban Na La Mai, you can continue north to Thung Khao Phuang and Muang Na near the Burmese border. Once again, this route should only be attempted in good weather and with a full tank of gas.

THE FAR NORTH AND GOLDEN TRIANGLE

The infamous Golden Triangle—located on the Mekong where Myanmar, Laos, and Thailand intersect—is the mysterious and untamed land where powerful opium warlords, remnants of Chiang Kai Shek's Kuomintang army, and communist insurgency groups once fought for control of Southeast Asia's immensely lucrative opium traffic. The Wild West image attracts large numbers of curious travelers who arrive searching for caravans of mules hauling tons of high-grade opium.

The reality is different. Smuggling continues to some degree, but visitors should also prepare themselves for modern towns, lines of tour buses, and a countryside completely in touch with the 20th century. Don't be discouraged by the commercialization—the varied scenery and sense of remoteness still make the Golden Triangle and the idyllic towns along the Mekong River an enjoyable destination.

Routes

Several different routes are possible through the far north depending on your time and interests. Visitors with only a few days should head directly for Chiang Rai and quickly see the border town of Mae Sai and the riverine towns of Sop Ruak (the actual Golden Triangle) and Chiang Saen, before returning to Chiang Mai.

Travelers with a week can explore the smaller towns and escape the tourist trail that now covers all the major spots in the north. The most popular leisurely route is an early morning bus up to Thaton (four hours north), then the 1300 boat ride down the Kok River to Chiang Rai. After a night in Chiang Rai, head north to Mae Sai, then east to Sop Ruak and Chiang Saen. Several mountain lodges north of Chiang Rai provide great atmosphere and are excellent alternatives to city hotels. Villages such as Mae Salong are also worth visiting. Trekking north of the Kok River and river rafting are other popular activities.

Travelers with two or more weeks can continue exploring the very remote areas of the north. Buses from Chiang Saen head east to Chiang Khong, then southeast down to Chiang Kham and Nan, an isolated town that receives rave reviews from most visitors. Heading back toward Chiang Mai, it's easy to visit the medium-sized towns of Phayao, Phrae, and Lampang.

Motorcycle touring—described at the beginning of the Northern Thailand chapter—is an excellent way to get off the beaten track and discover what is most attractive about the north.

TUBTAO CAVES AND HOT SPRINGS

Three km west of Hwy. 107, and marked with a signpost at Km 117, are several caves which have served as pilgrimage centers for several centuries. Beyond the parking lot and small meditation huts are two staircases which lead to Tham Pha Kha ("Light Cave") on the right, and Tham Phan Jak ("Dark Cave") on the left. Light Cave guards a large seated Buddha and a 10-meter reclining image surrounded by statues of kneeling devotees. Guides with lanterns must be hired to explore the recesses of Dark Cave.

Eight km west of the caves is a town called Ban Mai Nong Por, established over a century ago by Chinese migrants from Yunnan Province. The town still retains some of the flavor, customs, and cultures of China, in a fashion similar to the Chinese village of Mae Salong north of Chiang Rai. Tucked away at the east end of town are several small hot springs that offer both communal and private baths.

Doi Angkhang

Motorcyclists might also enjoy the steep and winding 26-km road up to the summit of Doi Angkhang on Route 1248, which leaves Hwy. 107 at Km 134. One of the most spectacular motorcycle rides in northern Thailand, this dirt and gravel road offers great scenery and magnificent views over Fang River Valley. En route to the summit is a small Lahu hilltribe village where a government research station raises temperate fruits and sponsors reforestation projects.

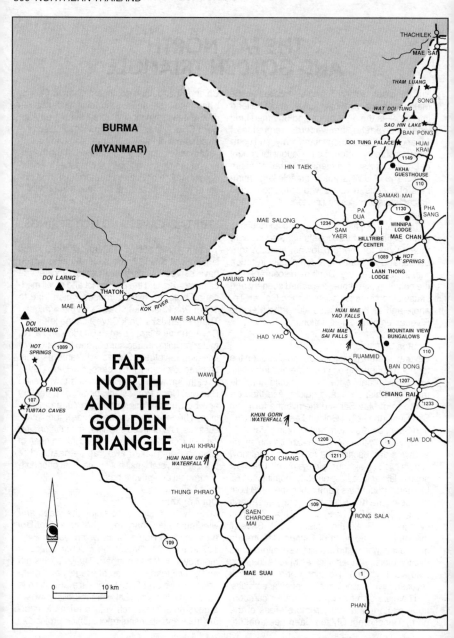

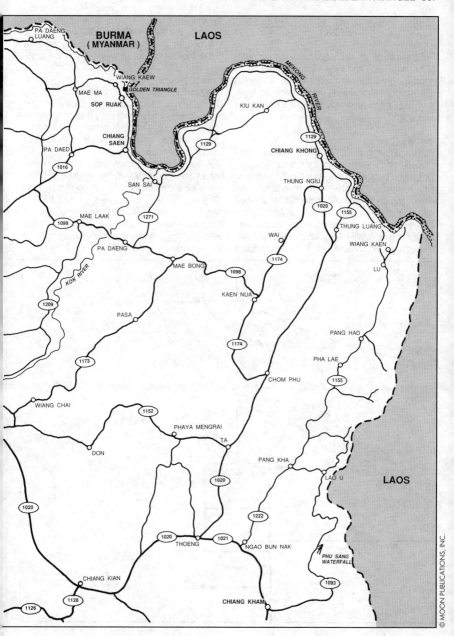

FANG

Fang is a small, rarely visited town 151 km north of Chiang Mai. The region produces rice and a good-quality Virginia tobacco which is dried in striking brick kilns, easily visible from the highway. Top draws are trekking and the nearby hot springs.

History

Fang was founded in 1268 by King Mengrai as an important trading center for the Lanna Kingdom. Destroyed by the Burmese in the early 18th century, Fang recently served as an important opium-smuggling center until the government allowed remnants of Chiang Kai Shek's Kuomintang Army to settle in the region and act as an independent border patrol. A Wild West atmosphere characterized the town until the mid-1970s, when opium warlord Khun Sa was finally driven from the region into the thick forests of Myanmar. Today, this modern town is firmly under the supervision of the Thai military and government officers.

Attractions

Fang is visited most often by travelers who hire guides and conduct treks in the foothills to the west. The region is essentially free of opium pirates, though the security situation should be checked before setting out. Guides can be hired from most of the guesthouses.

A signposted turnoff opposite the police station marks the road to the Fang Horticultural Station, where coffee and apples are grown by local hilltribes. The road continues another 2.6 km to Ban Nam Rawn sulfur springs, where some of the boiling springs have been capped for geothermal energy. A small geyser on the right side of the road erupts every 30 minutes.

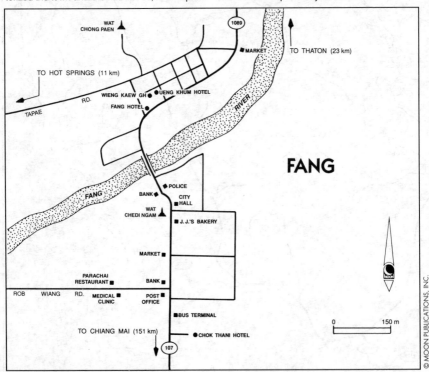

Motorcyclists can make a scenic diversion west from Mae Ai at Km 165, some 17 km north of Fang. The road goes 5.6 km west toward Doi Larng, once the home of Khun Sa, then turns north to a new road which backtracks to Thaton.

Accommodations

Fang is divided into the new town near the bus station in the south, and an older residential and business district in the north past the curve.

New Wieng Kaew Guesthouse: Hotels in Fang are in the northern section where the road curves right and continues up to Thaton. Wieng Kaew, Tapae Rd., tel. (053) 451101, 100-140B, has trekking information.

Ueng Khum Hotel: Down the road from the Wieng Kaew is a better set of bungalows with clean rooms facing a pleasant courtyard. 227 Tapae Rd., tel. (053) 451268, 140-180B.

Chok Thani Hotel: The only semi-luxurious hotel in Fang is on the highway near the municipal administration building. 425 Chotana Rd., tel. (053) 451252, 200-240B fan, 300-350B a/c.

Restaurants

Fang Restaurant: The small cafe adjacent to the hotel of the same name has an English-language menu and is the best choice in the northern section of town. Tapae Rd., Soi 3. Inexpensive.

J.J.'s Bakery: Western dishes, hot fudge sundaes, and hamburgers are served in the bakery across from Wat Chedi Ngam. Chotana Rd., tel. (053) 451282.

Parachai Restaurant: A clean cafe popular with Chiang Mai residents for its steaming *khao soi* with chicken or beef. The doctor in the medical clinic (tel. 053-451234) across the road can help with rooms if you want to avoid the dreary city center. Rob Wiang Rd., tel. (053) 451227. Inexpensive.

Transportation

Buses depart Chiang Mai's Chang Puak bus terminal every 30 minutes and take about three hours to reach Fang.

To Thaton: A limited number of buses leave Chiang Mai and continue through Fang to Thaton. Otherwise, *songtaos* and infrequent buses depart from the Fang bus terminal hourly and take 40 minutes to Thaton. *Songtaos* can be also be flagged down on the main highway near the Fang Hotel.

From Pai: Travelers coming from Pai can bypass Chiang Mai by getting off the bus in Ban Mae Malai on Hwy. 107, and taking any bus heading north to Fang.

THATON

This picturesque town on the banks of the Kok River chiefly serves as the launching point for downriver trips to Chiang Rai. Thaton is a very pleasant place to spend an evening and gather information for the river trip and hikes through the Golden Triangle region.

Wat Thaton

An imposing white Buddha, who seems to be contemplating the steady stream of Western travelers, dominates the town from the hillside to the west. A huge golden Buddha has been erected further up the hill. Excellent views over the valley can be enjoyed by hiking the staircase from the main road or the pathway behind Thip's Guesthouse.

Trekking

Self-guided treks to nearby villages are easy but less than pristine since this region has been trekked for over 20 years. Caution should be exercised since robberies remain a nagging problem despite the presence of the Thai police. Many of the villages can now be reached by public *songtaos* or hiked from stops along the Kok River.

The single best resource is the *Guide Map of Chiang Rai* published by Bangkok Guides and available from bookstores in Chiang Mai.

Budget Accommodations

Several inexpensive guesthouses are located along the Kok River.

Thip's Guesthouse: Near the bridge is the best guesthouse in Thaton, operated by a talkative Thai woman named Thip who once worked with American GIs during the Vietnam War. Kok River Rd., tel. (053) 245538, simple bamboo bungalows cost 60-120B.

Thaton House: Across the river is a quiet guesthouse with 12 rooms facing a courtyard

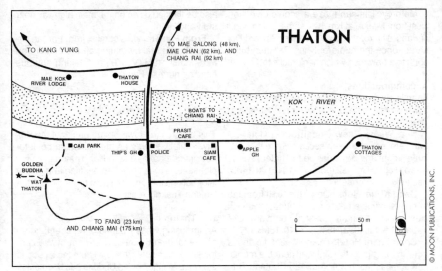

garden. All rooms include private bath and fan for 120-160B.

Apple Guesthouse: Directly opposite the boat launch is an old favorite with rudimentary rooms and a popular cafe.

Thaton Cottages: An upscale and clean operation with individual cottages and private baths. Located about 300 meters south of the main road. Bungalows cost 250-400B.

Moderate Accommodations
Several places have opened in recent years to cater to the more upscale visitors to the region.

Mae Kok River Lodge: This amazing resort complex is wonderfully located on the banks of the river amid lychees and coconut palms, with Thai-style chalets and a great restaurant over the river. Amenities include a small swimming pool, animal sanctuary, and Track of the Tiger tour agency. Mae Kok River Lodge is owned and operated by Irishman Shane Beary. Budget travelers staying at Thip's often congregate here in the evenings for drinks and conversation. P.O. Box 3, Mai Ai, Chiang Mai 50280, tel. (053) 459189 or radio phone 01-5-100-805, 350-400B basic, 800-900B luxury.

Thaton River View Hotel: More resort than hotel, this relatively new place features gorgeous rooms and an outstanding restaurant consid-

ered among the finest in Northern Thailand. The resort is located directly on the river a few hundred meters from the center of Thaton. Bangkok tel. (02) 287-0123, fax (02) 287-3420, 1,000-1,450B.

Transportation
Buses to Fang and Thaton depart from the Chang Puak Bus Terminal north of the White Elephant Gate in Chiang Mai at 0600, 0720, 0800, and 1130, but only the first three departures reach Thaton in time for the boat ride to Chiang Rai. Minitrucks continue from Fang to Thaton. Direct bus service is now available from Thaton to Mae Salong, Mae Chan, Mae Sai, and Chiang Rai.

Thaton to Mae Salong
A great alternative Kok River journey (see "Kok River Journeys" below) is the new paved road which connects Thaton with the Chinese village of Mae Salong, 48 km to the northeast. Minitrucks leave in the early morning from Thaton, but a better alternative is rented motorcycle. Stops along the winding, well-maintained road include mountain lodges operated by various hilltribes, and the Chinese Kuomintang village of Hua Maung Ngam where a small shop has drinks and meals. Hilltribe touts hawking goods

for sale and rooms for rent often wave frantically at passing motorcyclists.

The road is relatively flat until the final section, which climbs steeply through the mountains until it reaches the isolated village of Mae Salong, more formally called Ban Santikhiri.

Unlike Fang and the Golden Triangle town of Sop Ruak, this region remains under the control of opium cartels, which move tons of narcotics from Myanmar down to Chiang Mai and Bangkok. Although travelers who proceed directly through the region are rarely hassled, it's wise to avoid wandering around or acting curious about the heavily laden trucks. Keep your camera well hidden.

KOK RIVER JOURNEYS

The main reason to visit Thaton is the river journey down to Chiang Rai. Longtail boats leave Thaton around 1230, cost 160B per person, and take four or five hours down the Mae Kok to Chiang Rai. Brief stops are made at Mae Salak for police registration and photos of the hanging bridge, and at the Highland Forestry Development Project for cold drinks. The trip is best undertaken while the waters run high from Oct.-Jan.

Early stages of the journey are relatively uncommercialized, but lower sections toward Chiang Rai are plagued with refreshment stalls, souvenir shops, TV antennas, and tacky signs announcing "Lahu Village." Longtail boat rides are exciting and provide a glimpse of the countryside, but not everyone is thrilled with the speed, noise, and cramped quarters.

Bamboo houseboats, constructed per order from Thip's Guesthouse in Thaton, are an excellent alternative to a frenzied longtail ride. Six-person bamboo rafts with cabin and primitive lavatories cost 2,500B per boat and take three relaxing days to Chiang Mai. . . if they don't capsize on the rocks during the dry season Feb.-June. The boats are then resold to other travelers who continue downriver to Chiang Saen.

Guesthouses
Several guesthouses are located on or near the Kok River between Thaton and Chiang Rai. **Ban Mai Guesthouse**, on the north side of the river just opposite Mae Salak, has trekking information and simple bungalows from 40B. The oldest operation in the region is the infamous **Karen Coffee Shop** (also called Phanga's House) between the river and the Chinese Kuomintang village of Ban Maung Ngam on the Thaton-Mae Salong road. Karen Coffee Shop has information on treks, elephant rides, and ways to idle away weeks without purpose. Farther downriver and shortly before Chiang Rai are the **Prasert Guesthouse, Ruammit Resort** for elephant rides, and the **Iam Sam Ang** on the south side of the river. All charge 50-80B.

Trekking from the Kok River

Treks starting from the Kok River are another alternative. Hikes can be made from a dozen different drop-off points such as Ban Mai and Mae Salak, but bring along food, seasonally appropriate clothes, small change, gifts, and caution. Robberies are still a problem, so leave your valuables in Chiang Mai.

The most popular trek begins from the Lahu village of Mae Salak, about one hour downriver from Thaton, and heads south to Wawi where more than 13 different tribes live in a large village on the Mae Nam Wawi. Pickup service is available from Wawi to Fang, Mae Salak, and Mae Suai. The trek continues south from Wawi to the Lisu villages of Huai Khrai and Doi Chang, and through the enormous Akha village of Ban Saen Charoen Mai to Mae Suai on Hwy. 1019. The *Guide Map of Chiang Rai* by Bangkok Guides has an excellent detail map of the region.

CHIANG RAI

Chiang Rai is a drab, medium-sized city without the hustle—or the great sights—of Chiang Mai. Despite the concrete monotony of the architecture and lack of major attractions, tourism is on a sharp rise, as indicated by the crowds and the amazing hotel developments being laid on the bewildered town. Without charm or character, Chiang Rai is best considered a brief stop en route to the more idyllic towns farther to the north and east.

History

The city was founded in 1262 by King Mengrai as the nation's first independent kingdom, but the fickle king later moved his forces south to Lamphun and finally to Chiang Mai. Chiang Rai served as a trading center and focal point for struggles between Siam and Myanmar until 1786, when it was incorporated into the Thai Kingdom.

Wat Pra Keo

Chiang Rai's monuments are modest structures lacking the architectural or historic interest of temples in Chiang Mai. This gaudily restored temple is chiefly noted for its *chedi* where, according to legend, the Emerald Buddha was discovered in 1436 and later moved to Wat Pra Keo in Bangkok. In front of the *chedi* stands a wooden Lanna-style *bot* constructed in 1890 and now filled with several bronze images including an early Chiang-Saen statue, perhaps the largest example of its type in Thailand.

A replica of the famous Emerald Buddha was installed at Wat Pra Keo in late 1991. The image was carved in Beijing from a block of high-quality Canadian jade in honor of the 90th birthday of the princess mother.

Wat Pra Singh

Originally constructed from 1345 to 1400 by King Mahaproma, Wat Pra Singh contains a reproduction of the Pra Buddha Singh now displayed in the temple of the same name in Chiang Mai. The modern *wat* also features a fine pair of doors carved by Thawan Duchanee, a local artist who has achieved great fame in Thailand and among international collectors for his paintings and carvings. Also note the temple guardians' penises: one shaped after a serpent, the other an elephant's head.

Wat Ngam Muang

West of Wat Pra Singh on Ngam Muang Road, you'll find Wat Ngam Muang. Situated up a short flight of *naga*-flanked stairs, the temple features an ancient brick *chedi* constructed in 1318 as a reliquary for the ashes of King Mengrai.

Wat Doi Thong

This recently rebuilt temple atop a hill on the northwest side of town offers superb views of the Mae Kok Valley. Tradition claims this is the spot where King Mengrai first surveyed the site which became his capital for the Lanna Kingdom. Better views can be enjoyed from the nearby Town Hall.

Wat Chet Yot

South of city center is a small temple constructed with a seven-pointed *chedi* which names the complex.

Hor Kham Mae Fah Luang Museum

Opened in 1990 under the patronage of the princess mother, this Lanna-style two-story teakwood museum contains a small but impressive collection of local handicrafts and religious arti-

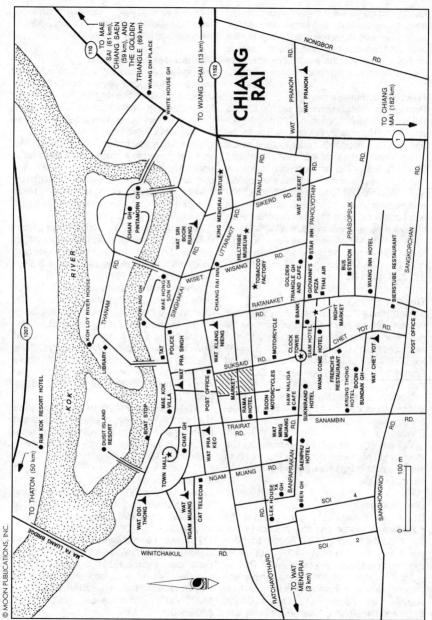

facts. Chief draws are the wooden Buddha images, candelabras used in Lanna ceremonies, and carved wooden screens that represent the best of Lanna craftsmanship. The museum is on Rajyotha Road (the western extension of Tanalai Road) four km west of city center.

PDA Hilltribe Museum

Perhaps the most fascinating sight in Chiang Rai is this museum opened in 1990 by the Population and Community Development Association (PDA), a nongovernmental organization that works with the local hilltribes. The ground floor is staffed by Thai and American volunteers who provide genuine insight into the political and economic problems of the hilltribes. The second floor serves as a handicraft showroom and bookstore, while the third floor has been converted into a superb museum with displays of costumes, baskets, farming implements, and a slide show in an air-conditioned room in the rear. The PDA Museum (tel. 053-713410) is at 620/25 Tanalai Rd.

Trekking

Chiang Rai is a good base for exploring the Golden Triangle and initiating journeys on the Kok River. Over a dozen trekking agencies offer organized tours in the hills around Doi Tung (35 km northwest) or the remote regions around Chiang Khong (65 km northwest). Culturally sensitive tours to hilltribe villages are best booked through the PDA office described above. Budget treks can be booked through most guesthouses, including Chat, Ben, and Boon Bundan.

Self-guided trekking is easiest from Mae Salong, 67 km northwest of Chiang Rai, and from the mountain lodges such as Laan Thong and Mountain View.

River Journeys

Boats from Chiang Rai head both west up the Kok River to Thaton and downriver to Chiang Saen and the Mekong River. Regular longtails depart each morning around 1000 from the city pier and take about six hours to reach Thaton.

Most guesthouses and travel agencies can help with downriver journeys, including the four-day river journey down the Kok River to Chiang Saen and the Mekong River. Prices vary dramatically, so shop around for the best deal and avoid the expensive agencies in luxury hotels. A good average price runs 150-300B.

Guesthouses near the River

Chiang Rai has exploded with dozens of new guesthouses in recent years. Older facilities are uniformly run-down and dirty, but many have refurbished themselves into better haunts. Operators are always on hand at the bus station and to greet boat arrivals from Thaton.

Chat Guesthouse: Several years ago the old Chat moved to a much nicer location in a small alley near the boat landing. Chat has a cozy cafe, laundry services, and information on trekking. Trairat Rd., Soi 1, tel. (053) 711481, 50-80B, 100-180B for luxurious doubles with hot showers. Recommended.

Mae Kok Villa: Like most other former hostels in Thailand, the branch in Chiang Rai has lost its accreditation and has since been poorly run, poorly maintained, and best avoided. 445 Singhakai Rd., tel. (053) 771786, 140-220B.

Bowling Guesthouse: Cozy little family-owned guesthouse with just six rooms in a quiet location near the river. 399 Soi Nanging, Singhakllai Rd., tel. (053) 712704, 80-140B.

Mae Hong Son Guesthouse: A very odd name for a guesthouse in Chiang Rai, though the helpful owners and calm setting in a friendly neighborhood near the river make this a popular choice for many travelers. 126 Singhaklai Rd., tel. (053) 715367, 80-140B.

White House Guesthouse: A couple of blocks back from the river and fairly isolated at the east side of town but with modern, fairly clean rooms at bargain prices. 789/7 Phahonyothin Rd., tel. (053) 744051, 80-280B.

Guesthouses on the Island

Guesthouses on the island just north of Chiang Rai are somewhat distant from downtown but acceptable if you hire a bicycle or motorcycle for your stay.

Pintamorn Guesthouse: Operated by some Germans and a Hawaiian named Bob Watson, Pintamorn compensates for its isolated location with clean rooms, good food, and some of the best-condition motorcycles in Chiang Rai. 199/1 Mu 21 Soi Wat Sriboonruang, tel. (053) 714161, 100-280B.

Chian House: A modern hotel with solid walls, clean rooms with Western toilets and hot showers, and a small pool. The manager, Kiti Kumdee, is friendly and speaks good English. 172 Sriboonruang Rd., tel. (053) 713388, 80-140B small rooms, 100-220B large rooms.

Koh Loy River House: An acceptable place on the river behind the old YMCA, with spacious grounds and a pleasant restaurant overlooking a tributary of the Kok River. All rooms include private bath with hot showers. 485 Thanam Rd., tel. (053) 715084, 150-400B.

Budget Downtown

Guesthouses and cheap hotels near the center of town can sometimes be noisy but the location is handy to quickly reach the restaurants and nightlife of city center.

Ben House: Once the Lek Guesthouse, then Ya Guesthouse, Ben House is a funky, cramped, but popular place with communal rooms and five bamboo bungalows in the rear courtyard. The friendly owners conduct treks and provide free bicycles to their guests. 351/10 Sanghonghoi Rd., tel. (053) 716775, 80-180B.

Lek House: Among the oldest guesthouses in town but actually a simple wooden home divided into compartments. As with most other places in Chiang Rai, the friendly managers rent motorcycles and can help with treks. 95 Thanalai Rd., tel. (053) 713337, 80-120B.

Ya Guesthouse: Another venerable guesthouse in a somewhat ramshackle old home with a variety of small but acceptable rooms plus decent garden and helpful owners. 163/1 Banprapakan Rd., tel. (053) 717090, 80-120B.

Moderate Accommodations

Chiang Rai has several midpriced hotels that bridge the gap between budget guesthouses and luxury hotels. Most of the following are just south of city center.

Boon Bundan Guesthouse: This popular spot has 36 new rooms centrally situated near the bus station and clock tower. All rooms are clean, modern, and include private bath with hot showers. Boon Bundan also has a decent restaurant, trekking services, and rental motorcycles. 1005/13 Chet Yod Rd., tel. (053) 717040, fax (053) 712914, 100-300B fan, 300-450B a/c.

Golden Triangle Inn: Right in the heart of Chiang Rai is this small hotel that blends modern amenities with traditional touches such as thatched walls, teakwood furniture, and Thai paintings. The owners also operate a terrace cafe and popular touring company. 590 Paholyothin Rd., tel. (053) 711339, fax (053) 713963, 700-900B.

Suknirand: Well-located and fairly clean rooms, though the property obviously lacks any semblance of personality. 424/1 Banpaprakan Rd., tel. (053) 711055, fax (053) 714701, 200-250B fan, 300-350B a/c.

Siam Hotel: Budget travelers who seek out a hotel rather than a guesthouse might consider this older yet acceptable property in the center of town, just a block east of the clock tower. All rooms come with fan rather than a/c. 531/6 Banprapakan Rd., tel. (053) 711077, 200-280B.

Krung Thong Hotel: Another rather inexpensive hotel with older but decent rooms, located just one block south of the main road. 412 Sanambin Rd., tel. (053) 711033, fax (053) 711848, 200-260B fan, 340-400B a/c.

Chiang Rai Inn: A few blocks from city center is an attractive and reasonably successful attempt to create a resort with the urban core. All rooms are large, fairly clean, and equipped with a/c and hot showers. Prices are negotiable during the slower summer months. 661 Uttarakit Rd., tel. (053) 712673, fax (053) 711483, 800-1,200B.

Wiang Din Place: Another almost upscale choice in an odd location in the northeastern corner of town with Thai-style a/c bungalows with all standard amenities. 341 Khae Wai Rd., tel. (053) 13363, fax (053) 716790, 800-1,200B.

Luxury Accommodations

Three fairly luxurious properties are near city center, while monstrous and very top-end resort hotels are outside town to the north.

Saenphu Hotel: When I researched Chiang Rai for my *Southeast Asia Handbook,* Country Guesthouse—on the site of the Saenphu—was a wonderful homestay with clean rooms at fair prices. When I returned to research *Thailand Handbook,* the guesthouse had been abandoned and replaced with a large seven-story hotel called Saenphu that overshadows the old residential guesthouse. All this happened in less than 18 months. This, however, is a very well priced semiluxury hotel and probably the best deal in town. 389 Banpaprakan Rd., tel. (053) 717300, fax (053) 711308, 650-900B.

Wiang Inn: Top choice in the center of town is the three-star Wiang Inn Hotel with swimming pool, several restaurants, disco, and traditional massage parlor. Popular with tour groups and well located near the bus station and night market. 893 Paholyothin Rd., tel. (053) 711533, fax (053) 711877, 1,400-1,800B.

Wang Come Hotel: A big hotel with all the standard amenities including a circular pool, lively coffee shop, convention facilities, and "luxurious massage parlor with 50 pretty, fully qualified masseuses" (not traditional massage). Rooms are small but well appointed with Lanna-style furnishings. 869 Pemawiphata Rd., tel. (053) 711800, fax (053) 712972, 1,500-2,000B.

Rim Kok Resort: Although inconveniently located across the river, the Rim Kok offers striking views, great restaurants, and a wonderful pool shaped like an amoeba. The lack of customers has kept rates low and open to negotiation. 6 Moo 4 Tatorn Rd., tel. (053) 716445, fax (053) 715859, Bangkok reservations tel. (02) 279-0102, 1,800-2,400B.

Dusit Island Resort: The splashiest addition to Chiang Rai's expanding tourist scene has been erected on a large delta island in the Kok River. A taxi is necessary to shuttle between town and this enormous hotel. 1129 Kraisorasit Rd., tel. (053) 715777, fax (053) 715801, Bangkok reservations tel. (02) 238-7904, 2,500-2,800B.

Restaurants

Most of the restaurants in town are located in the alleys near the Wang Come Hotel.

Night Market: Though it pales in comparison to the grand affair in Chiang Mai, a small but lively night market with foodstalls operates on Trairat and Tanari Roads near the Wang Come Hotel. Nearby are several small go-go bars, Thai cafes, Turkish massage parlors, trekking agencies, and souvenir shops.

La Cantina: The L-shaped alley at the southeastern corner of the clock tower has evolved into a *farang* wonderland of pizza parlors, coffee shops, and nightclubs. Cantina puts on a great breakfast buffet with all the over-caloric standards from an Omaha diner, plus tasty Italian dinners prepared by Gabriel Vallicelli. Open daily 1000-1400 and 1800-0200. 528/20-21 Banpaprakan Rd., tel. (053) 716808.

Lobo 1 & 2: The flyer reads: "For a real night of enjoyment, A-go-go and No. 1 entertainment, 18 attractive and shapely girls, surprise, very prompt service, party time every night." Sapsin Plaza, just a few doors down from La Cantina. 528/20-25 Banpaprakan Rd., tel. (053) 711042. Moderate.

Bar Nice and Easy: After a mess of prawns at La Cantina and observing the wildlife in Lobo 1, revive your spirits with an espresso in this nice little cafe just two doors south of La Cantina. 528/18-19 Banpaprakan Rd., tel. (053) 712762. Moderate.

Bierstube: Karl Leinz from Mainz runs a small cafe that serves Thai dishes prepared by his wife, and German specialties from sauerkraut to weisswurst. A popular spot for local expatriates. Karl also runs a trekking agency and has motorcycles for rent. 897 Paholyothin Rd., tel. (053) 714195. Moderate.

French's: Big buffalo steaks and cold beer are served in this cozy cafe located on restaurant row. If you can't find French's look for "Cafe de Paris" or some other Francophile name. Chet Yot Rd. Moderate.

Baitong Cafe: Australians Ken Jones and Ray Sawyer operate the popular restaurant just opposite the Wang Come Hotel. 869 Pemawipat Rd. Moderate.

Giovanni's Pizza: The best Italian dishes and pizzas in Chiang Rai are served in the expatriate favorite just up from the night market. 595 Paholyothin Rd. Moderate.

Boat Stop Cafe: A riverside setting and decent Thai food make this funky cafe worth a visit at sunset. Kok River boat landing. Inexpensive.

Shopping

Chiang Rai Handicraft Center: The largest collection of hilltribe shops in Chiang Rai is located four km north of town on the highway to Mae Sai. The center sells ceramics, celadon, textiles, carved woodwork, and jewelry; an adjoining factory produces much of the pottery and cotton goods.

Chiang Saem Antiques: Across from the Wang Come Hotel is an upscale shop with a fine collection of hilltribe handicrafts and designer silk clothing. 869 Pemawipat Rd., tel. (053) 712090.

AIM Department Store: South of town is a shopping mall with several stores that specialize in northern Thai handicrafts. Highway 1 near the Little Duck Hotel, four km south of town.

Ban Du: *Sa* paper is still produced with traditional methods in the village of Ban Du, a few kilometers north of Chiang Rai at Km 834. A small sign points the way to the paper demonstration house.

Practicalities

Tourist Information: The TAT has a small office near the river which, though convenient for travelers at Chat House, is far removed from the better hotels in the center of town. Open daily 0830-1630. 448 Singhakai Rd., tel. (053) 717433, fax (053) 717434.

Motorcycle Rentals: Several shops and guesthouses rent motorcycles, but most bikes have been badly trashed and are unsafe for exploring the hills of northern Thailand. Bikes in better condition are available from the Bierstube Restaurant and Pintamorn Guesthouse. Soon Motorcycles on Trairat Road is the largest rental agency in town. Daily rates are about 150-200B for a 100cc or 125cc motocross, or 250-300B for a large 250cc model.

Festivals: Each February the city sponsors a week of traditional northern culture during the colorful Wai Sa Mae Fah Luang Festival. Activities include the re-creation of an old northern market, an afternoon parade with participants from 73 provinces, Shan folkloric plays, and a theatrical sound-and-light show based on a legendary king who predates the founding of Chiang Rai. A Lychee Festival is held in May.

Transportation

Chiang Rai is 844 km north of Bangkok and 180 km northeast of Chiang Mai.

Air: Thai Airways flies five time daily from Bangkok (one hour and 20 minutes) and three times daily from Chiang Mai (30 minutes).

The new Chiang Rai International Airport (tel. 053-793048) is nine km north of town off Hwy. 110 to Mae Sai. The airport has a bank exchange open daily 0900-1700, gift shops, and a small tourist information counter open at sporadic hours. Taxis outside the main gate cost 100-150B to city center, 300-450B to Mae Sai, and 500-750B to Chiang Saen.

The runway can accommodate wide-bodied jets, and flights are planned from Chiang Rai to Hong Kong, Kunming, and other destinations in southern China.

Thai Airways has offices at 870 Paholyothin Rd. (tel. 053-793058) and at the Chiang Mai Airport (tel. 053-711179). Both offices are open daily 0800-1700.

Bus: Buses from Chiang Mai's Arcade Bus Terminal depart every 30 minutes for the four-hour ride to Chiang Rai via Hwy. 1019 which passes through Doi Saket and Wiang Papao. This is a great drive across rolling landscapes and virgin countryside almost completely untouched by modern times.

A few buses each day take the older and much slower route through Lamphun and Lampang, a boring trip along a modern highway that chews up seven hours of your precious time. Check on the route or estimated time before hopping on a bus in Chiang Mai.

Departures to Chiang Mai happen hourly 0600-1800 and take about two hours on the shorter route. Buses to Bangkok depart hourly and take 14 hours. Overnight sleepers leave 1800-2200 and arrive in Bangkok a few hours after sunrise. Ask the driver to drop you at the neighborhood of your choice or expect to be abandoned at the terminal in some odd neck of the woods.

Buses to other towns leave at various hours; check with your guesthouse owner or hotel concierge, or wander down to the Chiang Rai Bus Terminal (tel. 053-711224) on Prasopsuk Road near the night market and ask about current schedules. Approximate travel times by bus are: Chiang Saen (1.5 hours), Chiang Khong (three hours), Khon Kaen (12 hours), Mae Sai (two hours), Nan (six hours), Phayao (two hours), Phitsanulok (five hours), and Phrae (four hours). In the land of *mai pen rai,* departure schedules vary with the seasons, but as elsewhere in Thailand, you can probably find a bus to any destination at any sensible hour.

Boat: Most travelers arrive in Chiang Rai after taking the boat down the Kok River from Thaton, but boats also make the upriver journey each day departing 0700-1200. The pier is in the northwestern corner of town at the end of Trairat Road. Boats to Thaton cost 180B and take five or six hours, stopping at Ban Ruammit (one hour), Had Yao (two hours), Kok Noi (three hours), and Mae Salak (four hours).

Hikers can get off at the Karen village of Ban Ruammit and walk to a series of villages that provide simple rooms for 50-80B, or alight at Mae Salak and walk south in the direction of Wawi and Khuai Khrai, before continuing through Thung Phrao to Mae Suai. Mae Suai is a major town with frequent bus service to Chiang Rai and Chiang Mai.

Vicinity of Chiang Rai

Highway 110 leaves Chiang Rai and heads north up to Mae Sai and the Burmese border. Several mountain lodges are located between Chiang Rai and Mae Chan, along and just north of the Kok River. Excellent detail maps of the Kok River

and Mae Chan District are provided on the *Guide Map of Chiang Rai* published by Bangkok Guides.

Highway 1207: About one km beyond the Kok River Bridge is the paved highway which leads west and skirts the Kok River. First stop on the south side of the highway is the enormous Rim Kok Resort Hotel. A dirt path one km farther leads down to Bank & Boom's Guesthouse on the river, where bamboo bungalows cost 100-150B.

Highway 1207 continues five km west to Ban Dong, where a dirt track heads south down to a beach, a small cave called Tham Pra, and an old bamboo bridge which crosses the Kok River to Pattaya Noi Beach. The dirt road also continues west along the river to eventually reach the Ruam Mit Resort and Prasert Guesthouse, where bamboo bungalows cost 40-70B. Motorcyclists can continue on the dirt road all the way to Thaton.

THE LOST ARMY: THE KMT

*M*ae Salong is a precariously situated Chinese village populated by descendants of the Kuomintang Nationalist Army (KMT) who fled China in 1949 after their defeat by the communist forces of Mao Tse-tung.

Nationalist troops under the command of Chiang Kai-Shek headed across the Formosa Strait to Taiwan, where they established the Republic of Taiwan and planned their return to mainland China. Nationalist armies abandoned in Yunnan Province were forced to either join the Red Army or flee the country. Most refused to join the communists and headed south into Myanmar and Thailand.

Remnants of the 93rd Regiment, the 26th Army, and the 8th Army, under the command of General Li Mi, marched south into Myanmar in early 1950 where they occupied territory at Mong Moa in northern Myanmar. Others settled between Kengtung and Taichilek. In 1951, KMT forces began receiving financial support and military equipment from the CIA in an attempt to block further communist expansion into Southeast Asia. With new supplies and Western advisors, the KMT underwent a period of vigorous expansion and reorganization. The army launched several invasions into Yunnan, but all failed to make any headway against the People's Liberation Army.

Early Drug Connections

The KMT entered the drug business by seizing control of the Myanmar-Chinese border and collecting taxes on opium exported between the two countries. Their timing was impeccable. China had shut down their opium market in 1950. Turkey and the so-called "French Connection" served as the next drug center until officials banned cultivation in 1959. Thailand also finally ended opium cultivation in 1959 after it was revealed that General Phao, commander of the Thai police, headed the largest opium-trafficking syndicate in Thailand.

Control over the worldwide opium business then passed to the Kuomintang who, in cooperation with local police and regional military agencies, carried hundreds of tons of opium on mule caravans from Myanmar to processing labs in Chiang Mai. The finished product was then exported via Bangkok and Hong Kong to the West. By 1967, almost 90% of opium hauled into Thailand was controlled by the Kuomintang. The anticommunist, CIA-supported "lost army" of Chiang Kai-Shek had become the world's leading drug cartel.

From Ban Dong, Hwy. 1207, now a dirt track under construction, continues west to Huai Mae Sai Waterfall, where treks originate to nearby hilltribe villages. One popular trek heads 18 km north through several Lahu villages to the Laan Tong Lodge on Hwy. 1089. Elephant rides are possible from Suan Plan Forest Park near the falls.

Mountain View Bungalows: On Hwy. 1207 and just 14 km northwest of Chiang Rai is a popular lodge that arranges tribal trekking, river rafting, and elephant rides. Mountain View Bungalows is just outside the Karen village of Huai Khom and within hiking distance of Akha, Lahu, Lisu, and Hmong tribal villages. Rooms cost 50-100B.

Pon Phat Bat Falls: Six km from the Kok River Bridge is a good asphalt road that leads eight km west to a small and disappointing set of falls.

AROUND MAE CHAN

Mae Chan Town
Mae Chan is a dull market town from where minitrucks head west up Hwy. 1089 to Laan Thong Lodge and up Hwy. 1130 to Mae Salong.

A small guesthouse/brothel is located north of town where the road splits to Mae Sai and Chiang Saen.

Transportation: *Songtaos* leave from the center of town near the main temple and police station. Minitrucks to Laan Thong Lodge leave hourly 0900-1700. To reach Mae Salong, take a minitruck two km north to Pha Sang, from where *songtaos* head up to Mae Salong.

Highway 1089
Highway 1089 heads west from Mae Chan to several mountain lodges and tribal villages where

Escape to Thailand
The drug industry moved from Myanmar to Thailand in 1961 after Burmese forces attacked KMT positions, forcing the Chinese cartel out of the country. Several thousand went to Laos where the CIA hired them to strengthen the rightist position in the area. The 5th Division set up its hub at Mae Salong, near Chiang Rai, under the command of General Tuan Shi-Wen. The 3rd Division, led by General Lee Wen Huan, a notorious drug trafficker, settled in Tam Ngop with outposts in Chiang Mai and Mae Hong Son Provinces.

The lost armies were initially welcomed by the Thai government as protective forces against the Myanmar Communist Party (BCP) and Burmese warlord aggression. KMT forces assisted Thai army regulars as well as road construction crews in the north and northeast. KMT troops later joined the Thai army to fight communist insurgents in exchange for Thai citizenship.

The 1967 Opium War
The KMT monopoly was finally challenged in 1967 by a powerful Shan warlord named Khun Sa, who was moving 16 tons of raw opium on a 300-mule caravan from Myanmar to Laos. The destination was a heroin factory controlled by General Ouane Rattikone, commander-in-chief of the Laotian Army.

By the time the convoy reached Kengtung, the column of 500 men stretched several miles along the ridgelines.

KMT generals Tuan and Lee—normally feuding competitors—formed a combined army to challenge Khun Sa and protect their 15-year dominance of the regional opium industry. An expeditionary KMT force attacked Khun Sa near Kengtung, but the Shan leader escaped and reached Ban Kwan at the Golden Triangle. KMT forces attacked Khun Sa once more, but General Ouane caught both armies off guard. He attacked both the KMT and the Shans, defending his nation's territorial integrity with a squadron of T-28 fighters sent from Luang Prabang.

After several days of repeated bombings, Khun Sa retreated across the Mekong into Myanmar and the KMT fled north into a Laotian ambush. General Ouane gathered up the 16 tons of raw opium and sent the bonanza to his refineries situated between Ban Kwan and Ban Houy Sai. In three short days, Ouane had captured an enormous quantity of opium, disgraced Khun Sa, and preserved KMT control over the opium trade in northern Thailand. Over the next two decades, however, most of the remaining KMT regiments in northern Thailand forsake the opium business and began to move into legitimate forms of business.

visitors can safely trek without fear of bandits. Nine km west are some hot springs on the left side of the road near the Mae Chan River. Dear House Lodge near the hot springs has bamboo bungalows from 250B.

Laan Thong Lodge: One of the finest mountain lodges in northern Thailand, Laan Thong Lodge consists of several bamboo cottages surrounded by landscaped gardens and fruit trees. Facilities are in good condition and the Thai owners specialize in vegetarian dishes and home-baked breads. The lodge is 13 km west of Mae Chan. Reservations at Mae Salong Tours (tel. 053-612515) near the Wiang Inn in Chiang Rai. Laan Thong Lodge, 50 Moo 13 Patueng, Mae Chan tel. (053) 772049, fax (053) 772050, 200-500B. Take a bus to Mae Chan, then a *songtao* to Laan Thong.

Treks: Treks from Laan Thong Lodge head either south to Chiang Rai, west to Karen Coffee Shop on the banks of the Kok, or north up to Mae Salong through Yao, Lahu, Lisu, and Akha villages. Independent treks are relatively easy, though guides can be hired at Laan Thong.

Highway 1130 to Mae Salong

The road to Mae Salong is in excellent condition, with superb mountain views and hilltribe villages. Tragically, most of the forest cover has been stripped by hilltribes who use slash-and-burn cultivation to plant their opium poppies. The Royal Forestry Department now provides cassia, bamboo, and pine saplings to help reforest the region.

Winnipa Lodge: Four km west of Pha Sang, on a hillside overlooking the road, is a mountain lodge with 16 individual bungalows priced from 130B.

Hilltribe Center: Twelve km from Hwy. 110 is a rudimentary village with handicraft shops and costumed kids who pose for photos. Donations can be deposited in the wooden box. The rough and challenging dirt road north from the Hilltribe Center continues through several Akha villages to the Akha Guesthouse and Doi Tung.

Pa Dua: Eighteen km from Hwy. 110 is a small Yao village visited by tour groups.

Hin Taek: Sam Yaek, an Akha village 24 km west of the main highway, is the turnoff for Hin Taek, now renamed Thoed Thai, where Khun Sa maintained his opium empire until 1982. The 13-km dirt route is steep and winding, and should only be attempted by groups of experienced motorcyclists.

MAE SALONG (SANTIKHIRI)

Mae Salong has changed dramatically in recent years. The Chinese-language school—reputed for its high teaching standards and once popular with Sino-Thai families from Bangkok—has been closed and converted into a Thai school with a national curriculum. Concurrently, financial and

technical assistance from Taipei ended. Roads now push into the more remote regions, as property speculators and farsighted Chinese purchase the fertile land from displaced hilltribes. The isolation and innocence of Mae Salong are quickly coming to an end.

Mae Salong is a sleepy—and often cold—place where Mandarin is still spoken by the older residents and homes remain guarded by ancient protective talismans.

Attractions

Mausoleum: The most striking landmark in Mae Salong is the mausoleum of General Duan Xi Wen, the former chief of staff of China's 93rd who led 2,000 Chinese Kuomintang soldiers and their families from China into Thailand. The leader lies buried in a marble mansion on the south side of the mountain.

Around Town: Village architecture consists of modern structures and old wooden houses reminiscent of the Yunnan style. A small tea factory is down the road toward the police station.

Morning Market: A lively hilltribe market is held at the west end of town past the school every morning 0500-0800. Hilltribe villagers are often extremely reluctant to have their photographs snapped.

Road to Thaton: A wonderful dirt road winds past the school and morning market and continues 48 km down to Thaton on the banks of the Kok River. Great views and several hilltribe villages, but do not attempt this road in the rainy season.

Cherry Blossom Festival: A festival honoring the pink *sakura* flower is held in early January. Activities include a floral procession attended by contingents of local hilltribes, exhibits which illustrate the colorful history of Mae Salong, agricultural displays, and the crowning of Miss Cherry Blossom.

Trekking

Mae Salong is an excellent place to begin self-guided treks to nearby hilltribe villages. Rough but adequate maps of the region can be picked up from Rainbow and Mae Salong Guesthouses. Shin Shane Guesthouse has a useful trekking map on their wall.

Shopping

Best buys in town include home-brewed medicinal wine, preserved fruits, Chinese herbs, Burmese cheroots, and locally grown Taiwanese tea called Mei Qing, Mei Long, and Qing Qing. Small shops also sell a smuggled Chinese whiskey called *senji* flavored with bizarre roots and centipedes.

Accommodations

Several guesthouses and midpriced hotels are located in Mae Salong. All have cafes which serve Thai and Yunnanese specialties such as rice noodles topped with spicy chicken curry, steamed pork buns, and pickled vegetables.

Mae Salong Guesthouse: Up the hill and on the left is a small guesthouse (tel. 053-765102) with trekking information, a fading but useful map posted on the wall, and horseback tours to nearby villages. Rooms cost 80-120B with hot showers outside the compound.

Shin Shane Guesthouse: Another bare-bones guesthouse is located just off the main road in an old wooden Chinese home. The friendly owners run a small cafe and can help with trekking information. Rooms cost 60-100B. Hot showers run an additional 10B. No phone.

Rainbow Guesthouse: A rudimentary spot with views from the cafe and a solitary room with three beds. 60-80B.

Mae Salong Villa: Two km down the road is a medium-quality place with an elevated restaurant and comfortable rooms equipped with hot showers. Highway 1234, tel. (053) 765114, fax (053) 765039, 450-700B.

Mae Salong Resort: The best hotel in town is wonderfully located up a steep road with views over the entire valley. The adjacent flower park and cherry blossom orchards are popular with visiting Chinese and Thais. Mae Chan, tel. (053) 765014, fax (053) 765135, 450-700B.

Transportation

Mae Salong lies 36 km west of Pha Sang on top of Doi Mae Salong, 1,418 meters above sea level. From Chiang Rai, hire a motorcycle or take the green bus to Pha Sang, three km beyond Mae Chan, from where minibuses continue up the winding road to Mae Salong. Minitrucks from Pha Sang run 0800-1700 and cost 40B up, 30B down.

MAE CHAN TO MAE SAI

Between Mae Chan and Mae Sai are several lodges, temples, and natural attractions accessible by public minitruck and rented motorcycle.

Ban Huai Krai

The small town of Huai Krai, 13 km north of Mae Chan and 19 km south of Mae Sai, marks the junction of Hwy. 1149, which leads west to the Akha Guesthouse and Wat Doi Tung. The turnoff is located before the town and signposted with directions to Akha Guesthouse. Minitrucks leave from the intersection every 30 minutes.

Akha Guesthouse

A longtime favorite is the Akha Guesthouse, located on old Hwy. 1149, 44 km north of Chiang Rai and seven km west of Ban Huai Krai. The lodge offers spectacular views and trails winding through nearby tribal villages. Rooms cost 60-100B.

Motorcyclists should note that the guesthouse is on old Hwy. 1149, on a side road that veers left off the newer bypass at the village of Ban Paka. Watch carefully or you'll miss the turnoff.

Doi Tung Palace

Some 13 km from Ban Huai Krai is a Swiss chalet which serves as home to her majesty the queen mother, whose foundation (Mae Fa Luang) conducts reforestation projects and helps hilltribes grow crops such as macadamia trees and temperate vegetables. Her presence also accounts for the excellent roads and prosperous hilltribe communities.

Wat Doi Tung

Eighteen km from the highway and 2,000 meters above sea level, this 10th-century monastery is considered one of the most venerated shrines in northern Thailand. The complex features a pair of *chedis* which encase relics of the Buddha, and an impressive bronze image seated under a *naga*. All note the jolly fat Buddha with an immense navel!

Wat Doi Tung isn't very impressive, but the views are terrific on clear days. Motorcyclists can continue along a dirt road to the rear of Doi Tung and reach Mae Sai on the Burmese border.

The unmarked dirt road heads left from the main road, several kilometers before Doi Tung. Very tricky to find.

A Lake and Four Caves

Hwy. 110 continues north from Ban Huai Krai past a strangely disfigured mountain called Khun Nam Nang Non ("Sleeping Lady"), named after the anatomically recognizable face but hopelessly contorted body. Several caves are located west of Ban Pong at Km 877, or 13 km south of Mae Sai. Sao Hin, Pla, and Kaeo Caves are all sited around large Soa Hin Lake. A rather strange Khmer temple stands near the entrance of one flooded cave, which can be explored with flashlights.

Ban Tham, a village you must pass to reach the lake and caves, is inhabited by Muslim Chinese Haw from Yunnan Province in Southern China. They are responsible for the Chinese gardens, fishponds, and pavilions which surround the lake.

The road west from Km 878 leads to Tham Phum and the Akha village of Ban San Pasak.

Tham Luang

The Tham Luang ("Great Cave") of Mae Sai is west of Hwy. 110 at Km 884. Beyond the first cavern is a narrow passageway which leads into other chambers thick with dripping formations of fantastic shapes. A narrow path leads south from Tham Luang to Saitong Caves and the hot springs of Khun Nam Nang Non. The hot springs can also be reached by turning left at Ban Jong at Km 882, eight km south of Mae Sai.

MAE SAI

Mae Sai, the newest gateway into the once isolated country of Myanmar, enjoys an image of a frontier town populated by opium smugglers and gangs of renegade bandits. On the surface, the reality is somewhat different. Mae Sai, 891 km north of Bangkok, physically resembles nothing more than a modern, nondescript town choked with concrete shophouses, video stores, souvenir shops, and gaudy restaurants, and bisected by a road enormous enough to land Boeing 747s.

Mae Sai may not be aesthetic or romantic, but the town serves as an excellent base from which to venture into Myanmar or explore the nearby caves, lakes, and mountains described above in **Mae Chan to Mae Sai.** For many visitors, Mae Sai is simply a relaxing place to idle away a few days in a riverside guesthouse reading books.

Mae Sai Bridge

The scene at the bridge is a strange collision of cultures—blond-haired Westerners facing off grim Burmese guards, aggressive Indian hustlers pushing cheap handicrafts such as dusty pendants and opium weights ("very old, very old"), and cute Thai girls posing for donations in brightly colored tribal costumes. En route to the checkpoint, a gauntlet of "gem" sellers offer special deals on 20-carat, eye-clean, cut "rubies" for just US$100. The only thing these rocks have in common with genuine rubies are the color red.

Several years ago, the sign at the bridge entrance marked The Northernmost Point in Thailand was removed after somebody pointed out that the Mae Sai River winds further north as it flows to the east. Mae Sai, however, indeed remains the northernmost *city* in the country and tourism officials will probably erect another sign in the near future.

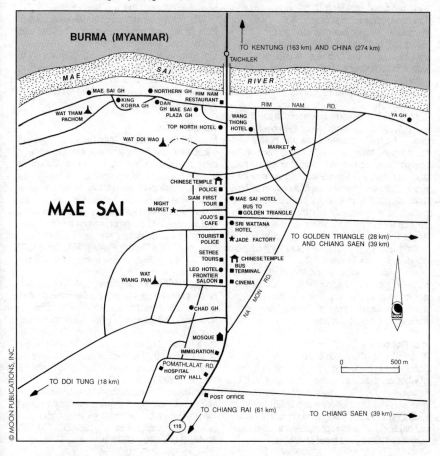

The border crossing into Myanmar provides Thai and Western visitors with easy access to the Chinese goods, sweet orange wine, and Burmese cheroots sold in Taichilek, and allows Burmese citizens to enter Thailand on shopping sprees for shaving blades, pens, and other Western goods.

But that's only the overt side. The bridge also serves as an international smuggling pipeline for teak and timber, opium, stolen antiques, precious jade, and sparkling rubies flowing into Thailand, and for kilos of gold, expensive automobiles, and military equipment moving north into the Shan States.

The border crossing to the dusty town of Taichilek, long a legal crossing for Thais and Burmese citizens, opened to Western visitors in October 1992 but has opened and closed several times since then. Foreigners can sometimes walk into Myanmar and spend the day exploring Taichilek, or travel 167 km to the town of Kentung and perhaps onward to Yunnan Province in Southern China.

Most visitors spend a few hours at the bridge and may climb the hill for views, then overnight at one of the many guesthouses and hotels scattered around Mae Sai. The following morning, arrive at the bridge at the earliest possible hour and pay your fee before walking across for a day in Taichilek. Day visitors must return to Thailand by 1800 or risk some undefined form of punishment—probably a hefty fine or involuntary servitude in the service of the Burmese Army. Plans have been announced to extend visiting hours until 2200 or midnight if political conditions remain calm.

After visiting Myanmar and shopping for gems, travelers generally head east to the Golden Triangle tourist trap of Sop Ruak, or the idyllic and uncommercialized town of Chiang Saen on the banks of the mighty Mekong.

Wat Doi Wao

A long flight of over 200 steps and a *naga*-flanked balustrade lead up a small hill with views of white pagodas, a Chinese cemetery, and the tin roofs of Taichilek inside Myanmar. The *wat* and whitewashed *chedi* were constructed by King Ong Wao of Chiang Saen to enshrine hair of Lord Buddha, but the complex was completely rebuilt in 1953 by the local abbot.

Tours and Trekking

Treks originating from Mae Sai head south and explore many of the same regions as those arranged by trekking agencies in Chiang Rai. The Doi Tung area is a popular and relatively safe destination.

Several tour companies can help arrange visits to Kengtung and other Burmese locales.

Motorcycle Touring

Far and away, the best way to explore the region is with a rented motorcycle from one of the motorcycle rental spots on Sairomjoi Road, about 200 meters west of the bridge, or an outlet on Paholyothin Rd. near the Top North Hotel.

Mae Sai's best source of information on motorcycle touring around northern Thailand and to Kengtung in Myanmar is Chad Guesthouse, tucked away in a residential neighborhood south of city center. Chad has been cruising for years and can provide maps and advice on road conditions, while you enjoy a meal in his homestay compound.

Guesthouses

Mae Sai Guesthouse: Mae Sai's best place to escape the concrete drabness of downtown and relax in a riverside setting. Located at the end of the road, about one km west of the bridge. It's worth the walk but if you'd rather, hire a *samlor* or motorcycle taxi for 20B. Facilities include a small restaurant, trekking information, motorcycle rental and storage, and a sign posted on the front lawn denoting the division between Thailand and Myanmar. 688 Wiang Pakam Rd., tel. (053) 732021, 80-150B common bath, 180-260B private bath.

Mae Sai Plaza Guesthouse: A decent place closer to the bridge but without the relaxed vibes of Mae Sai Guesthouse. An unbelievable assortment of bamboo-and-wood bungalows hang precariously from a cliff which rises sharply from the left side of the road. Wander in and enjoy a bowl of spicy Burmese-style *pad thai* from their large and well-elevated restaurant. 386 Sairomjoi Rd., tel. (053) 732230, 80-280B.

Northern Guesthouse: Another riverside option with simple but adequate rooms and good views across the river from their landscaped gardens. 402 Tumphanjum Rd., tel. (053) 731537, 80-180B fan, 280-450B a/c.

RUBY FEVER IN MAE SAI

*M*ae Sai may appear to be little more than a misplaced freeway flanked by cinder-block shophouses, but beneath the surface lies one of Southeast Asia's hottest economic miracles—the fabulous trade in stones from the Mong Hsu mines of northern Myanmar. Unfashionable Mae Sai is currently where most of the world's finest rubies enter Thailand, before undergoing the cutting and polishing process that makes them such a priceless commodity.

Rubies—among the world's most coveted stones—are chiefly found in Southeast Asian countries such as Thailand, Cambodia, Vietnam, and Myanmar, which has dominated the international market for fine rubies for over seven centuries.

Ruby mining began in earnest after the British took over the country and awarded control of the gem trade to the British-Myanmar Ruby Mines Ltd. The best stones were found in the legendary Mogok Valley, 70 km northeast of Mandalay, acknowledged by experts as the most abundant source of superior rubies in the world.

Mogok dominated the worldwide market until 1969 when Thai gemologists in Chanthaburi, near the Cambodian border, developed a technique of treating low-quality rubies and sapphires with high-intensity heat in specially designed ovens. After years of practice with tons of cheap raw materials—primarily dark sapphires from New South Wales and Queensland—the scientists discovered how to transform pale and inferior colored stones into expensive gems that commanded top prices from Paris to New York. And they had the market all to themselves. Their discovery proved so successful that today over 90% of the world's rubies and sapphires undergo some form of heat treatment for color enhancement, a process now accepted and endorsed by the international gem trade industry.

By the mid-1970s, Thai attention had shifted to Sri Lanka and the worthless, pale-colored gueda sap-

phire. Sri Lankan dealers failed to understand for many years that their cheap rocks were being transformed with Thai technology into expensive gems via sophisticated heat treatments.

Vietnam was the hot spot in the late 1980s, as new mines in the Luc Yen and Nghe An Provinces started to produce impressive rubies, including a 17-carat monster, heat-treated in Bangkok before being marketed to a movie star in the United States. Vietnamese production slowed significantly in the early 1990s after attention shifted to Cambodian mines under the control of the murderous Khmer Rouge.

Mong Hsu rubies first appeared on the world's market in 1992. The impact was overwhelming. According to the International Gemstone Association, within a few months of their discovery, over US$1 million worth of Mong Hsu rubies were passing through Mae Sai *every single day*. Bangkok dealers commonly spent US$2-4 million per month on stones, competing with an estimated 200 Chanthaburi gem traders who poured into the bewildered little town.

Mae Sai's mineral markets can be seen in several spots around town. Soi Phak Maa (Dog's Mouth Lane) is a rowdy, open-air ruby market packed with buyers and sellers who pay 4,000B per month for a rudimentary table perched on the roadside. Negotiations are openly conducted without any apparent concern that millions of *baht* are spread around like piles of Monopoly money. More traders operate out of the upscale Mae Sai Gems Center and its 30 hastily constructed shops.

The most refined venue is on the first to third floors of the Wang Thong Hotel ("Golden Palace"), where Burmese gem brokers purchase 300B memberships to the so-called "gem dealers club" to prowl the hallways, knocking on doors day and night searching for buyers flush with cash. Travelers are always assigned to the top floors with the finest views, never understanding the true nature of business in the concrete city of Mae Sai.

Chad Guesthouse: An old favorite of motorcyclists, who can pick up maps and other advice from the Thai-Shan family of owner Khun Chad. His home-cum-guesthouse is in a quiet neighborhood well removed from the tourist activity near the bridge. Chad occasionally leads motorcycle tours to the more remote regions of northern Thailand and perhaps up to Kengtung.

52/1 Paholyothin Rd., Soi Wiang Pan, no phone, 80-160B.

Hotels

Top North Hotel: A 32-room hotel conveniently situated just 100 meters from the bridge. All rooms have private baths with hot showers. A popular midlevel choice. 306 Paholyothin Rd., tel.

(053) 731955, fax (053) 732331, 300-350B fan, 450-650B a/c.

Leo Hotel: A new structure in the southern part of town near the bus terminal and shopping arcades. Rooms are spacious and clean and include hot shower, color TV, and minibar. Perhaps the best value in the price range. 145 Paholyothin Rd., tel. (053) 732064, 500-850B.

Wang Thong Hotel: Mae Sai signaled its arrival on the international tourism scene with the opening of this modern 150-room edifice, one block from the river and the bridge. Most of the clientele are Thai businesspeople negotiating contracts in spacious rooms overlooking the Mae Sai River. The hotel has a swimming pool, pub, coffee shop, restaurant with Chinese and Western dishes, and the only disco in town. 299 Paholyothin Rd., tel. (053) 733388, fax (053) 733399, Bangkok tel. (02) 225-9298, fax (02) 225-1927, 1,500-2,400B.

Restaurants

Rim Nam Restaurant: Short on atmosphere and somewhat overpriced, but a pleasant place to enjoy a beer and watch the passing parade. Open daily 0800-2200. Situated just below the bridge on the west side. 632 Sairomjoi Rd., tel. (053) 731207.

Golden Dragon: Another dining option near the bridge, but with cleaner facilities and less hassle from begging children and sellers of synthetic stones. The somewhat utilitarian "Chinese and Suki" restaurant on the second floor offers great views over the river, plus there's a patio cafe on the ground floor. Open daily 0600-midnight. Rim Nam Rd., tel. (053) 731617.

Jo Jo's Cafe: One of the few restaurants with a touch of class in the interior decoration department, plus excellent Thai curries, vegetarian specialties, and Western dishes such as sandwiches and desserts. Open daily 0600-2000. Paholyothin Rd., tel. (053) 731662.

Transportation

Buses: Buses depart Chiang Rai every 30 minutes and take about 90 minutes to reach the Mae Sai bus terminal one km south of the bridge. Buses from Chiang Mai leave every hour 0630-1600 and take five hours to Mae Sai.

Direct bus service is now available from Thaton via the newly paved road that passes through Mae Salong and Mae Chan.

Transport to Chiang Saen: Buses and *songtaos* to Sop Ruak in the Golden Triangle and the riverside town of Chiang Saen depart from the bus terminal adjacent to the Thai Farmers Bank and the Mae Sai Hotel. You can also flag down these buses on the road heading east from the Sri Wattana Hotel.

As shown on the map of Mae Sai, two roads from Mae Sai go to the Golden Triangle and Chiang Saen. The northernmost road is in somewhat better condition and follows a scenic route through Ban Rong and Ban Sanna to the junction town of Ban Mae Ma. The southern road passes through Ban San Thanon and Ban Thung Klang before reaching Ban Mae Ma.

From Ban Me Ma, take the eastern fork to the intersection and head north to the Golden Triangle, a fabulous motorcycle ride through lovely landscape that finally skirts the muddy Mekong. The southern route from Ban Mae Ma eventually reaches Chiang Saen, but the journey is tiresome and completely bypasses the Disneyland at the Golden Triangle.

Buses to Bangkok: Public buses to Bangkok depart hourly from the Mae Sai bus terminal and take 16-18 painful hours to reach the City of Angels. Most travelers prefer the private a/c coaches that leave daily at 1800 and reach Bangkok in under 13 hours.

The major bus operators are Chumnai Transport (tel. 053-731481) on Paholyothin Road near the Government Savings Bank, Sethee Tours near the Leo Hotel, and Siam First Tours just opposite the Mae Sai Hotel. All provide sleeper coaches and smiling hostesses dispensing tiny cups of icy drinks.

Practical Information

Mae Sai has blossomed into a major tourist center with all the required facilities for separating tourists from their greenbacks.

Immigration: Thai immigration (tel. 053-731288) on Paholyothin Road in the south end of town can extend visas and help with other legal requirements for holders of work and student visas.

Banks: Over 10 banks now provide currency exchange facilities and instant cash with credit cards issued by Visa and MasterCard. They can also dispense the American currency needed to pay the cover charge for visits to Myanmar—*baht* is shunned by the SLORC (State Law and Order Restoration Council) economists in Yangon.

Telephone: International calls can be made from most guesthouses and hotels, and from private telephone exchanges such as the outlet just under the Mae Sai bridge. A small service charge is collected, but the fee is worth skipping the two-km walk south to the Mae Sai post office and telecommunications center.

THE ROAD TO MYANMAR

Myanmar's Shan States opened their doors to the outside world in 1992 after 45 years of self-enforced isolation. Security conditions permitting, Western visitors are now allowed to cross the border from Mae Sai and wander around Taichilek on day excursions, or make longer journeys to the attractive Buddhist enclave of Kengtung. Onward travel to the Chinese border will probably start after the road is improved and political stability is established between Kengtung and Yunnan Province in southern China.

The stage is now set for the opening of regions not visited by foreigners since WW II due to the surrender in early 1996 of opium king Khun Sa.

Adieu, Opium King?

Although Khun Sa has surrendered and the political landscape dramatically changed in Myanmar, Burmese drug leadership will probably pass to new leaders with improved economic relations with the regime in Yangon.

Kengtung and the Shan States were first closed to contact with the outside world in 1950, after fighting erupted between the Burmese army and Chinese Nationalist soldiers (Kuomintang) driven from China by the advancing Communist armies of Mao Tse-tung. The Burmese government continued to wage four decades of warfare against the Kuomintang and a bewildering collection of secessionist groups, such as the Wa, Kokang, Karen, Shan, Karenni, and Mon.

The situation changed dramatically in 1988 after SLORC seized control of the Burmese government and announced a policy of appeasement with the rebellious groups. An unexpected collapse of the Burmese Communist Party allowed Yangon to start negotiations on cease-fire agreements with many of the insurgency groups, including renegade groups operating throughout the Shan States. Peace accords were signed, and by October 1992, the military leaders felt confident enough to allow foreigners to cross the border and travel up the road to Kengtung, a tranquil town completely undisturbed by mass tourism for over four decades.

The only glitch was Khun Sa and his 30,000 professional soldiers who comprised the Mong Tai Army (MTA). Khun Sa, a Thai-Shan warlord described in the special topic **Opium Warlord Khun Sa,** had controlled Southeast Asia's opium industry for over 30 years with near-complete impunity, aside from periodic incursions that forced him to move his headquarters to new locations. The only significant offensive, a 1982 attack by the Thai military, drove him from Ban Hin Taek in northern Thailand across the border to Ho Mong, a remote village tucked away near Mae Hong Son.

Ho Mong has since grown into a major trading center of well-stocked stores, spacious markets, neatly arranged neighborhoods, a Buddhist monastery and modern hospital, video arcades, two hotels and several karaoke bars, and sophisticated communication centers that provide the 30,000 residents with international phone and fax services.

Khun Sa remained Southeast Asia's undisputed opium king and heroin warlord until the signing of the cease-fire agreements. The Wa, Kokang, and other separatist groups were offered irresistible terms by the SLORC regime: lay down your guns and Yangon will guarantee political autonomy and the freedom to grow poppies without interference from the Burmese government. Some suspect that profit-sharing clauses were included in these peace accords. In any event, opium production soared from 700 tons in 1989 to more than 2,000 tons by the end of 1993.

For the first time since the end of WW II, military warlords from other regions began to effectively challenge Khun Sa for the control of his immensely profitable industry. Khun Sa's position weakened further after Burmese forces surrounded his headquarters and blocked all routes used by the hilltribe farmers and opium traders to reach purchasing agents in Ho Mong. They then began selling their goods to other groups, such as the Wa and Kokang in the Shan States.

OPIUM WARLORD KHUN SA

*T*he Golden Triangle—an isolated area of 75,000 square miles wedged between Myanmar, China, Laos, and Thailand—annually produces an estimated 2,000-2,500 tons of opium and over 70% of the world's illicit heroin supply. Current crop estimates are 2,500 tons from Myanmar, 500 tons from Laos, and under 30 tons from northern Thailand. Most of the product is refined into heroin in sophisticated jungle laboratories inside Myanmar, and then exported through Thailand to Hong Kong and the West. Western narcotics officers in Bangkok lament that less than one percent of the drug haul is now being intercepted before it reaches addicts in the Western world.

The mastermind of the Triangle's opium industry is Khun Sa (a.k.a. Chang Chi Fu), a half-Chinese, half-Shan warlord widely regarded as one of the world's most prolific drug dealers, right up there with the Mafia and the Medellin cartel.

Khun Sa came to the attention of the world's press in 1967 when he launched his Opium Wars to wrestle control of the lucrative trade from the remnants of Chiang Kai-Shek's Nationalist Chinese army. After being captured by Burmese forces and thrown in a Yangon prison, his private army (the Shan States Army or SUA) kidnapped two Soviet doctors as hostages for Khun Sa. Khun Sa was released in 1978, and within a decade he controlled 70-80% of the region's opium trade.

Khun Sa first established his drug headquarters inside Thailand at Ban Hin Taek, north of Chiang Mai near Mae Salong, where his SUA troops worked closely with the Thai Border Patrol Police. This embarrassing situation ended in January 1982, when a major assault drove Khun Sa and his army across the border back into Myanmar. Khun Sa soon reestablished his new headquarters at Ho Mong, a jungle village in Shan State, just 16 km from the Thai border and almost within earshot of Mae Hong Son. Khun Sa lived here without pressure from the Burmese or Thai governments for over a decade. A road constructed by the Thai government, with financial aid provided by the Americans, connects Mae Hong Son with Ho Mong. Visitors report that opium, jade, and logging profits have transformed his once-drab military camp into a thriving boomtown, complete with nine schools that provide free education, a 100-bed hospital, a Buddhist monastery, and hundreds of houses given free to his officers.

Khun Sa's rival for control of the drug industry was another opium warlord named Lo Hsing Han, who, when he isn't playing golf with the Burmese generals in Yangon, spends his time in the town of Lashio. The Burmese government now supports Lo as the next government-approved drug kingpin of Southeast Asia.

Trying to capture Khun Sa was difficult. The U.S. government once offered US$25,000 for his head, but Khun Sa countered by offering payments for the murder of Americans in Chiang Mai. Dozens of concerned citizens were quickly evacuated from Thailand. Despite the 10-count federal drug indictment handed down by the American government in 1990, Khun Sa continued to operate with impunity from his military camp at Ho Mong. Until early 1996 he controlled a well-armed military force of over 15,000 insurgents, and had a de facto peace pact with the Burmese military.

Khun Sa (a local title which means "Prince of Prosperity") was also something of a public relations whiz, having repeatedly offered to sell all his opium to the U.S. government for US$500 million over a six-year period. No American president has taken him up on his bizarre proposal. In 1990, the drug king sent President Bush a video message that invited narcotics agents to visit his camp to see the widespread deforestation being conducted by Thai logging companies with cooperation from the Yangon military regime.

Khun Sa was also a media manipulator who frequently met with the press, including Tom Jarrell and the ABC crew for <I>20/20<P> magazine in 1989. In 1991 new rules for visiting journalists were initiated: journalists actually paid 50,000B and electronic newscasters 250,000B to Khun Sa's representatives in Mae Hong Son before being escorted on good roads to his camp just inside Myanmar, only 20 km from the tourist center of Mae Hong Son.

Khun Sa finally surrendered to the Burmese government in early 1996, ending the career of one of the world's most colorful drug dealers. Khun Sa now lives on his estate in the outskirts of Yangon.

Furious with the traders and farmers, Khun Sa demonstrated the seriousness of his anger by ruthlessly slaughtering an estimated 200 villagers on the Thai-Burmese border in early 1994. Burmese forces responded by closing down Khun Sa's heroin refineries at Mong Gang and Mong Htaw and taking many of his military outposts along the Thai-Burmese border. The opium king was desperate—even the Soviet SAM-7 missiles erected on virtually every major hilltop under his control failed to break the economic stranglehold imposed by the Burmese government.

Khun Sa launched another major counter-offensive in May 1994 with a series of attacks against the Burmese forces occupying his former bases. The conflict quickly spread along the border regions until it reached the tourist zones of Taichilek and Kengtung, where Burmese recruiters seized Burmese citizens to serve as weapons porters in the Opium Wars of 1994.

Tourism halted and borders at Mae Sot and Mae Sai were sealed without advance notice. Hundreds of Thai tourists and a few Western travelers found themselves trapped deep inside Myanmar, including the owner of the Wang Thong Hotel, Mae Sai's most luxurious hotel. In March 1995, Khun Sa raided Taichilek and blasted away at Burmese army troops for several hours, while terrified citizens hid in their homes or fled across the Sai River to the safety of Thailand.

Taichilek and Kengtung are currently closed to visitors though Khun Sa has surrendered to Burmese authorities. Taichilek, Kengtung, and the remainder of the Shan States may reopen sometime in 1996.

SIDETRIP TO TAICHILEK

Visitors crossing from Mae Sai into one of Southeast Asia's final frontiers (Taichilek, Myanmar) will encounter contradictions at almost every turn. Taichilek initially appears to be only the poor stepsister to Mae Sai, but the relentless movement of illegal goods has transformed the small trading post into a mini-boomtown filled with everything from old temples to modern markets.

Few visitors are impressed with the rudimentary shophouses and shoddy goods sold in the central market, but still cannot resist the opportunity to cross the bridge to experience a taste of border town Myanmar.

Entry Formalities

Taichilek can be experienced easily in a single day. The current procedure—subject to change—is to deposit your passport and pay US$10 at the immigration office at the Mae Sai checkpoint. Visa, MasterCard, and Thai currency are not accepted. Thai citizens pay 40B.

Maps can be purchased from the tourist office just over the bridge. Motorcycle taxis charge 20B for most rides but are willing to bargain for full-day excursions. Walk.

Attractions

Taichilek may not be exotic, but the following sights may be worth a brief stop on your day in the "City of Golden Triangle."

Thachilek Market: Thai Yai *samlor* drivers waiting at the far end of the bridge can quickly take you to the Thachilek Market, where you waste your money on fake jade Buddha statues, overpriced lacquerware, enormous bags stuffed with mouse ear mushrooms, sweet orange wine, face powder, wooden dolls fashioned after Burmese hilltribes, leather sandals, teakwood carvings, peacock tails, stuffed armadillos, deer horns, animal feet, tiger hides, and sweet Mandalay cheroots, perhaps the only item worth picking up on your whirlwind excursion.

Wat Prathat Sai Muang: A Thai Yai temple two km north of the market, Sai Muang was constructed 30 years ago around a golden *chedi* lavishly decorated with pieces of broken, colored glass. The primary *viharn* holds ceramics, prayer beads, and rare Chiang Saen Buddha images. Travel beyond this point is prohibited to day visitors.

Wat San Sai: Wat San Sai, a picturesque temple surrounded by ricefields, features a *viharn* and a bizarre collection of bamboo poles under which pilgrims crawl and receive prayers for good luck. Burmese astrological symbols and Buddha images cover the walls and ceiling.

Wat Pra Chao Ra Keng: Taichilek's wealthiest temple offers a modern and spacious *viharn* centered around a Mandalay-style Buddha and five rare images of the faceless Buddha. To the rear is a small hill capped with white Burmese *stupas* and sacred Chinese shrines.

SOP RUAK (GOLDEN TRIANGLE)

Thailand's notorious Golden Triangle is centered at Sop Ruak, where Thailand, Laos, and Myanmar meet at the confluence of the Mekong and Ruak Rivers. Sensationalized fiction and worldwide media attention have cursed the Triangle with a ruinous popularity.

Although the mysterious scenery encourages fantasies about drug smugglers and opium war-lords, you're more likely to find busloads of tourists and gamblers than armed terrorists among the haphazard collection of guesthouses, luxury hotels, and restaurants. A nauseating string of souvenir stalls hugs the banks of the Mekong River. Recent developments have been extremely discouraging, as the once romantic region converts itself into an international playground for wealthy tourists and (perhaps) well-heeled gamblers.

A Casino in Myanmar?

Plans are now in progress to construct a casino on a small Burmese spit of land in the middle of the river. Construction was stalled for almost a decade while permits were secured

THE OPIUM TRAIL

*I*n Homer's *Odyssey,* Helen of Troy mixes an opium-laced potion "to quiet all pain and strife, and bring forgetfulness of every ill." Thomas De Quincey, author of *Confessions of an English Opium Eater,* tells how he experienced "music like perfume and ecstasies of divine enjoyment, living a hundred years in one night."

Papaver somniferum, the opium poppy, has been cultivated as a narcotic since the early Greek empire. Arab traders during the reign of Kublai Khan (1279-1294) introduced the drug to the Chinese, who later used it as a form of currency and method of taxation during the Han dynasty. The so-called Black Mud later dominated British-Chinese trade after the British East India Company discovered that opium sales to Chinese addicts miraculously balanced the trade deficit between China and the company. The Chinese responded by planting vast regions with the poppy to the extent that, by 1875, one-third of the farmland in Yunnan Province was covered with poppies. Hilltribes from the region, who traditionally raised the crop as their primary source of cash, brought their poppies with them when they migrated into Thailand and Laos during the early 20th century.

Opium, and its medicinal derivative morphine, was introduced to the West in 1815 after a German pharmacist isolated the principal alkaloid and named it for Morpheus, the Greek god of dreams. Public usage became commonplace in the early 20th century after Bayer, the pharmaceutical company, promoted diacetyl morphine (heroin) as a miracle cure and packaged the pills in small boxes marked with lions and globes. The Bayer trademark was later used by Laotian traffickers who sold their product under the Double-Globe brand.

Air America

Opium and its derivatives became popular drugs during the Vietnam War era, with a degree of help from the Central Intelligence Agency. The genesis was a CIA-controlled airline called Civil Air Transport (also known as Air America) which first helped supply Chiang Kai-Shek's forces during WW II and later secured a French contract to airlift Catholic refugees from Tonkin to Southern Vietnam during the early days of the Indochina War. Air America later worked with Hmong guerrillas, Khambas from Tibet, and remnants of the Kuomintang army to fight the communist insurgency from Hanoi. Despite denials by the American government, most observers agree that, in addition to carrying out humanitarian efforts, Air America purchased and transported opium to aid their rebel allies in Laos and Vietnam.

A good account of their smuggling operations is retold in Alfred McCoy's classic, *The Politics of Heroin in Southeast Asia.* International drug trafficking is also recounted in the more recent *Drugs, the U.S., and Khun Sa* by Francis Belanger, and in *Myanmar's Golden Triangle* by Andre Bouchaud.

The Opium Trail

The Golden Triangle—the world's largest source of illicit opium—produces an estimated 2,000-2,500 tons annually from Myanmar, Laos and, to a lesser degree, northern Thailand. The opium trail begins in the early spring as farmers scour the countryside

from the Thai and Burmese governments, but it looks like this outrageous project is once again on the drawing boards. The resort will someday include a golf course, a shopping complex, six cruise boats, and a casino with baccarat, craps, poker, slots, and other games of chance.

Approval for the project required some clever footwork since gambling is illegal in Thailand. As a result, tens of thousands of Thais leave the country each year and fly to Macau on weekend junkets, generating a major outflow of capital—a practice unpopular with the Thai government. The businesspeople who proposed the resort successfully argued that the casino would reduce this financial drain on the Thai economy,

and not contravene national prohibitions against gambling since the casino would be located on Burmese soil.

The Burmese rationalized that the 30-year lease removed them from all legal and moral responsibility for the project. A more sinister theory circulating is that the casino will be used by top Burmese leaders and their opium warlord partners to launder huge sums of money generated by the Burmese drug industry. The picture becomes even more intriguing when you look at other recent developments.

Among the largest investors were several wealthy Chinese families and a Macau gambling syndicate anxious to invest abroad prior to the return of the Portuguese enclave to China in

---

looking for the highly alkaline soils best suited for cultivation. Connoisseurs claim the sweeter taste of limestone soil can actually be recognized by the discriminating palate. Fields are cleared of standing trees with a spectacular burn off, and planting begins in September after the tree ash has dissolved into natural fertilizers. The soil is chopped, turned, and strewn with select poppy seeds.

By January, bright red-and-white flowers appear, blossom, and then drop away to reveal an egg-shaped bulb filled with resinous opium. The bulb is scored—like a Vermont maple or Malay rubber tree—with a three-bladed knife; the milky sap then rises to the surface before turning into brownish-black droplets. Tribeswomen return the following morning to scrape the bulb and deposit the residue

into a cup hanging around their necks. The sticky gum is then packed into banana leaves, tied into bundles, and sold to Chinese middlemen who refine it to morphine or heroin and export it to Western countries.

The upward spiral of its value is amazing. One square kilometer of poppy field produces almost 2,000 kg of raw opium. One kg of raw opium, worth only US$35 in Myanmar or US$4,000 as heroin in Chiang Mai, brings US$250,000 as Grade 4 heroin in America. And that's the price *before* being cut six times by street dealers. The final tally: one kg of raw opium eventually brings US$2.5 million, and a single square kilometer of land can yield heroin worth US$50-200 million. Small wonder the hilltribes refuse to grow peanuts.

stoned again

1999. All were concerned about how gamblers would reach the casino from Hong Kong and China. The problem was solved in record time with the approval of several new transportation projects. The most significant was the new Chiang Rai International Airport, which now makes it possible to reach Chiang Rai from Hong Kong and Macau in under 90 minutes. The airport also allows quick access for Chinese gamblers flying down from Kunming and other major cities in the country.

Then, in a remarkable show of international cooperation, the Thai, Burmese, Laotian, and Chinese governments approved the use of passenger ships to connect Jinghang in Yunnan Province with Chiang Saen and the Golden Triangle. This new service allows Chinese visitors to conveniently reach the casino in just a few days and to enjoy spectacular scenery along the Mekong River. Six 102-seat cruise ships, recently purchased by the resort, will someday funnel thousands of gamblers into a region once the domain of opium warlords and renegade armies.

So much for the "romance" of the Golden Triangle.

Attractions

Triangle Monument: The actual intersection of Thailand, Laos, and Myanmar is conveniently framed by a modern signpost—worth a photo for friends back home.

Opium Museum: 212 House of Opium down the road features an excellent collection of opium weights, pipes, headrests, photos of Khun Sa at his rainy camp, and a small hut occupied by a very wasted addict.

Wat Pukao: A hillside temple, located up a winding dirt road to the rear of the temple, offers great views and a small *viharn* with an image that provides miracles to visiting pilgrims. Wishes are granted to anyone who can lift the image.

Wat Sam Mung Maung: On another hill to the rear is a reconstructed temple which once held a large outdoor Buddha before it mysteriously disappeared several years ago.

Boat Rides: Boats down to Chiang Saen and far shorter journeys around the principal island in the Mekong leave from the landing below the Golden Triangle Monument. Fares are steep unless you split the cost with several other travelers.

Accommodations

All budget guesthouses have closed in Sok Ruak and most travelers only make a short day trip from Chiang Saen.

Northern Villa: At the north end of town is a simple but clean place in a fine location overlooking the river with decent cafe and hot water for those chilly nights. 500-750B.

Delta Golden Triangle Resort Hotel: An immense white-elephant hotel wedged between the cliffs and the souvenir stalls on the riverside road. Facilities include an outdoor pool, two restaurants, tennis courts, and nightly classical Thai dances. Sop Ruak, tel. (053) 784001, fax (053) 784006, Bangkok reservations tel. (02) 260-6108, 2,200-3,000B.

Le Meridien Baan Boran Hotel: An amazing hotel, designed and managed by the same group that runs the Phuket Yacht Club, is located a few kilometers west of Sop Ruak on the banks of the Mekong. All 110 rooms overlook the casino and distant Laos. Sop Ruak, tel. (053) 716678, fax (053) 716702, Bangkok tel. (02) 251-4707, fax (02) 254-5365, 2,400-3,600B.

Transportation

Sop Ruak is 28 km southeast of Mae Sai and 11 km west of Chiang Saen, where most travelers spend their nights. Buses and minitrucks to Sop Ruak leave periodically from the intersection just south of the Mai Sai Hotel. From Chiang Saen, it's best to rent a motorcycle or bicycle, though *songtaos* leave in the mornings from the Sala Thai Restaurant.

Boat to China

Several transportation firms are now working on operating boats between the Sop Ruak pier (a few kilometers south of town) and various destinations along the Mekong River, including Luang Prabang, and perhaps as far north as Yunnan Province in China. Several trial runs were successfully completed several years ago but government red tape seems to have delayed all these grandiose projects. For the latest details, check with travel agencies in Chiang Mai, Chiang Rai, Mae Sai, or the hotels in Sop Ruak.

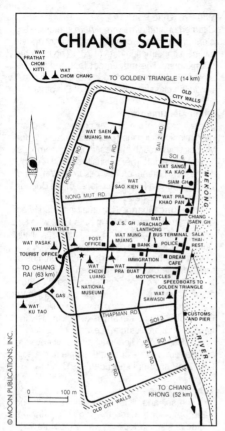

CHIANG SAEN

Chiang Saen is among the most interesting and attractive towns in the far north. Blessed with some minor ruins which attest to its historical legacy, the bucolic village provides a welcome relief from the tourist centers and frantic pace that has seized much of Thailand. Chiang Saen—a sleepy place wonderfully located in a dramatic setting—is highly recommended for its lethargic atmosphere and pastoral charm.

History

Chiang Saen was founded in the 10th century by Thai chieftains as the first independent principality in northern Thailand. The town was later abandoned and perhaps destroyed by Khmer forces but reestablished in 1328 by King Saen Phu, a grandson of King Mengrai. Saen Phu brought with him a group of villagers from Haripunchai (Lamphun). Mengrai's grandson was a devout Buddhist; he constructed many of the *stupas* and *chedis,* which have survived to the present day. King Saen Phu died in 1334, and Chiang Saen was subsequently absorbed into the Lanna Kingdom with the ascendancy of Chiang Mai.

The city and surrounding region were seized by the Burmese in 1558, who ruled until 1804 when King Rama I reconquered and razed the city to prevent foreign occupation. Chiang Saen lay abandoned until 1874 when Chao Inta, a prince of Lamphun, reconstructed the town and brought back descendants of the former population.

Chiang Saen today is a beautiful place overflowing with trees, which complement its idyllic location on the banks of the lazy Mekong River.

Attractions

Chiang Saen offers a great little museum and several restored temples that bear witness to the city's turbulent history. None compare with those in Sukothai or Ayuthaya, but they are worth a quick look to help pass the day. The widely scattered monuments can be quickly toured in a few hours on foot or with a rented bicycle.

Chiang Saen National Museum

The Chiang Saen National Museum, on the main road near the old west gate, provides an excellent introduction to the handicrafts, carvings, and splendid Buddhas of the Chiang Saen Period, considered some of the most beautiful in Thailand.

Front Room: Displayed inside the front room are demon heads and *garudas* recovered from Wat Pasak, and four large seated bronze Buddhas in Lanna style with distinctive topknots. Each is worth a careful inspection. Other artifacts include stone inscriptions that relate the arrival of Buddhism to Lamphun in 1498, and an elegant, mysterious, stone Buddha head carved in Lanna style, Payao school. The collection is small but high quality.

Back Rooms: To the rear are several rooms filled with gongs, bronze kettledrums, Buddhist banners, lacquerware, Burmese tobacco boxes, Akha rattanware, and Lanna-style swords.

Second Floor: Highlights include a useful map of the more important monuments in Chiang Saen, a huge terra-cotta pipe, an elegant bronze Buddha hand from Wat Ton Phung, and humorous divinity figurines discovered at Wat Chedi Luang.

The museum is open Wed.-Sun. 0900-1600.

Wat Chedi Luang

Behind the museum towers an immense 58-meter octagonal *chedi* (the sign reads Wat Jadeeloung) constructed in 1331 by King Saen Phu, and reconstructed in 1551 shortly before the Burmese seized Chiang Saen. The ancient *bot* adjacent to the *chedi* houses a highly venerated Buddha.

Wat Pasak

Beyond the reconstructed walls of ancient Chiang Saen lies the city's oldest surviving *chedi,* constructed in 1295 and modeled after the Mon prototype of Wat Chiang Yan in Lamphun. Erected before the formal foundation of the city in 1328, Wat Pasak testifies to the importance of the valley before the rise of Chiang Mai and the Lanna Kingdom.

The restored, extremely rare stepped pyramid is adorned with niches that once held dozens of Buddha images. Standing Buddhas surrounding the basement have been poorly restored, but excellent stuccowork of *nagas, kalas,* floral motifs, and small elephants still graces the upper levels.

Wat Pasak ("Temple of the Teak Forest") is under the supervision of the Fine Arts Department, which charges *farangs* a 20B admission fee.

Wat Prathat Chom Kitti

Two km northwest of town on a hill overlooking the Mekong River, Wat Chom Kitti and the small ruined *chedi* of Wat Chom Chang are old monuments, which scholars believe also predate the founding of Chiang Saen by King Saen Phu. New copper paneling covers the top half of the central *chedi* and little of the original stuccowork remains on the monument, but note the beatific expressions and wonderful reddish patina of the four standing Buddhas.

Wat Pra Khao Pan

Situated behind a modern *viharn* stands an ancient *chedi* whose concrete stele inaccurately claims a construction date of 761. The real date is unknown. The monument features four restored Buddhas standing in hollowed niches, two in the classic walking style of Sukothai.

Other Monuments

The remainder of the temples of Chiang Saen are quite minor, though they provide an excuse to ride your bicycle through the peaceful neighborhoods.

Wat Pra Buat: The unusually shaped "Temple of the Holy Ordination," across from Wat Chedi Luang, sports a fine stucco torso of the Buddha on the entrance gate.

Wat Mung Muang: This small indented *chedi* dates from the reign of King Kum Phu, who abdicated rule of Chiang Mai in 1334 to rule Chiang Saen after the death of King Saen Phu.

Wat Prachao Lanthong: All that remains of the "Temple of a Million Golden Weights" is a large solid base that once supported the enormous *chedi.* Inside the nearby modern *viharn* sits a large bronze Buddha in the so-called Third Period of Chiang Saen art, as established by the famous Thai art historian Alexander Griswold.

Wat Sao Kien: Hidden away in a weedy yard are the foundations of an old temple and a solitary, seated, completely headless Buddha.

Tobacco Kilns

The rich soil and climatic conditions of Chiang Saen have long made the region a principal source of Virginia tobacco and temperate vegetables such as cabbages and tomatoes. One of the most interesting sights near Chiang Saen are the tobacco kilns northwest of town on the road to the Golden Triangle. Visitors are welcome to wander through the yards and inspect the smoking kilns fired with prodigious amounts of coal. Note the ingenious mechanisms for elevating the leaves, and the pulley systems for controlling the amount of heat and smoke. Workers often sort and bundle piles of green leaves in the front yards.

Wat Prathat Pha Ngao

One of the most awesome and mysterious Buddha images in Thailand is displayed inside a temple 4.2 km south of Chiang Saen on the road to Chiang Khong.

Fronting the complex are two wildly misspelled signs that attempt to relate Buddhist tales with the aid of garish statues. The modern *viharn* to the rear may be an awful portent of popular Thai architecture (precast images, lousy workmanship, trite themes), but inside the gaudy building is a gigantic Buddha torso whose powerful and dramatic shape suggests the ethereal nature of Buddhism with unbelievable clarity.

Outside the complex are some of the Disneyesque Buddhist statues so popular in modern Thai society, and a *chedi* constructed on a large rock, somewhat similar to the hanging rock of Kyaiktiyo in Myanmar.

Accommodations

Chiang Saen offers several basic but relaxing guesthouses on the banks of the Mekong River.

Chiang Saen Guesthouse: Not much atmosphere, though the rooms are fairly clean and manager Chan Chai is friendly. A good location in the center of town near the temples and river. 45 Rimkhong Rd., 80-100B common bath, 120-180B private bath in the new bungalows facing a concrete courtyard. No phone.

Siam Guesthouse: An old and run-down dive with three bungalows crammed together. 294 Rimkhong Rd., 80-150B. No phone.

Gin Guesthouse: Two km north of town is a wonderful place with A-frame chalets facing grassy lawns and an inner orchard filled with lychee and mango trees. Gin's has a small circular cafe surrounded by wagon wheels and marked "Thai Garden Cowboy Restaurant is opened too you're welcome," and dependable rental bicycles for exploring the ruins and pedaling out to the Golden Triangle. A nearby trail leads down to a sandy beach. Small bamboo rooms in the rear cost 80-150B, lovely A-frames with private bath cost 250-350B.

J.S. Guesthouse: Inside the city perimeter and near the museum is another guesthouse that provides an alternative when the places near the river are filled. Clean, comfortable, and managed by a Thai-Swiss couple. Sai 1 Rd., tel. (053) 777060, 100-200B.

Restaurants

Most of the guesthouses provide meals, but travelers often spend their evening hours in the **Sala Thai Restaurant,** which serves mediocre meals but offers great river views. **Streetstalls** set up in the evenings near the Dream Cafe. Several kilometers north of town toward the Golden Triangle is the open-air **Rim Khong Restaurant,** with Thai dishes and caged peacocks. Farther on is the upscale **Meakong Riverbanks Restaurant** with views into Laos. Several midpriced hotels have been constructed in the vicinity.

Yonok Restaurant, outside town near Chiang Saen Lake, is a popular garden restaurant that serves freshwater catfish and northern Thai specialties. Yonok also has several bungalows with private baths and hot showers from 500B.

Practicalities

Siam Commercial Bank near the post office is closed on weekends. Gin's Guesthouse has the best bicycles in town. Motorcycles can be rented in the mornings near the Sala Thai Restaurant.

The new tourist office at the west end of town provides maps and information on the region.

Transportation

Buses from Chiang Rai to Chiang Saen take about an hour and pass through countryside where villagers still harvest rice without mechanized tools. Chiang Saen can also be reached by minitruck from Mae Sai.

Songtao service from Chiang Saen to the Golden Triangle is sporadic and not as reliable as a rented motorcycle or bicycle. Minitrucks to Chiang Khong leave in the mornings from the market along the river.

CHIANG KHONG

Most travelers return to Chiang Rai from Chiang Saen, but an exciting adventure is to continue east to the small town of Chiang Khong, located on the banks of the Mekong River and directly opposite the Laotian town of Ban Huay Sai. Chiang Khong's biggest appeal is its tranquil atmosphere and splendid views of the Mekong and Laos. The Thai Farmers Bank has currency exchange facilities.

History

Chiang Khong was incorporated into the Lanna Kingdom in the early 13th century, taken by the Burmese three centuries later, and returned to

CHIANG KHONG

TO CHIANG SAEN (75 km)
GOLDEN RESORT
KMT CEMETERY
BOATS TO LAOS
PIER
TO BOTEN
HUAY SAI
CHIANG KHONG HOTEL
ANN TOURS
SAI KLANG RD.
BAN TAMILA RIVERSIDE GH.
RUEN THAI HOTEL
SOI 1
WAT PRA KAO
TO THUNG NA NOI
POST OFFICE
SOI 3
WAT LUANG
SOI 5
PIER AND CUSTOMS
MEKONG
LAOS
RIM KHONG CAFE
RIVER
BUSES
POLICE
SOI 13
WAT SRI DONCHAI
MARKET
PLABUK RESORT
BUSES
TO LUANG PRABANG
TO CHIANG KHAM (85 km)
0   200 m
1020
HAT KRAI

© MOON PUBLICATIONS, INC.

and *chedi*. Both were reconstructed after the return of the Siamese in 1881.

KMT Cemetery: The defeat and flight of KMT troops from Mao Tze Dong and his Communist forces led them south into Thailand, where they were offered political refugee status by the Thai government. Many established cultural outposts at Mae Salong and at Chiang Khong, where deceased were buried in a small hilltop cemetery at the north end of town.

Hat Krai: The small village of Ban Hat Krai, one km south of town, remains one of the last places in northern Thailand where giant catfish are occasionally captured by local fishermen. In June 1995, amazed fishermen pulled in a monstrous two-meter, 480-pound catfish that ranks among the largest freshwater fish captured around Chiang Khong in the last decade.

Accommodations

A handful of very sleepy guesthouses and hotels caters to the steady trickle of Western and Thai visitors.

Ban Tamila Riverside Guesthouse: A small Thai-style guesthouse on the main road near Wat Pra Kao, where the owners can help with sightseeing excursions to nearby waterfalls, caves, tribal villages, and the historical sights at Doi Patang. They also organize boat trips down the Mekong and horseback rides through the countryside. The place is somewhat run down but still quite popular. 8/4 Sai Klang Rd., no phone, 100-220B.

Ruen Thai Sophapharn Hotel: A newer spot near the Ban Tamila Riverside with comfortable rooms facing the Mekong. 8/2 Sai Klang Rd., tel. (053) 791234, 100-200B.

Plabuk: Great views and a comfortable cafe make this resort a popular, if somewhat expensive, alternative to the smaller guesthouses. The

the Siamese in 1880. Chiang Khong and most of the left bank of the Mekong was ceded in 1893 to the French, who ruled from Fort Carnot.

Chiang Khong later served as a trading post and smuggling entrepot for Chinese and Laotian goods, and was the last stop on the old Laotian loop frequented by backpackers until it was closed by the widening Vietnam conflict. The new boat service from Chiang Khong to Luang Prabang and Jinghong has somewhat revitalized the somnambulistic town.

Attractions

Wat Luang: While under the suzerainty of the Lanna Kingdom, several temples were constructed in northern Thai style, including this *wat*

owners also organize boat trips down the Mekong, and can help with van and motorcycle rentals. Sai Klang Rd., tel. (053) 791281, Bangkok tel. (02) 258-0423, B 500-650.

Chiang Khong Hotel: Another choice priced midway between the guesthouses and better resorts. Both fan and a/c rooms with hot showers are available. Sai Klang Rd., tel. (053) 791182, 150-320B.

MONSTERS OF THE MEKONG

Restaurants in Chiang Khong occasionally serve *pla buk (Pangasianodon gigas)*, a monstrous type of catfish considered the largest of its kind in the world. *Pla buk*—a term which means "great and powerful fish"—can grow up to three meters in length and weigh over 300 kg, making it the undisputed monster of the Mekong. The fish is praised for its white succulent meat, which tastes like milk-fed veal and guarantees long life to all who eat it. Gourmets also favor the lightly salted eggs, which are reddish in color and nicknamed Laotian caviar by northern residents.

The process of catching *pla buk* begins when local priests invoke dockside prayers to summon the spirits of the legendary fish and to bring good luck to the anglers. The anglers set out in sleek pirogues on 24-hour fishing shifts, only returning after a successful catch. Some drag heavy nylon nets called *maung li* through the narrow channels while others throw stones to drive the *pla buk* into the net. Once snagged, the giant catfish are hauled into the boat and secured with ropes pushed through their mouths and out their gills. A successful expedition is celebrated with bottles of Mekong whiskey and all-night parties; a single catch can pay for a new boat or provide for the children's education.

Sadly, the *pla buk* is an endangered species. Earlier this century, *pla buk* were plentiful and could be captured in lakes from Cambodia to southern China. Overfishing, however, has severely reduced their numbers to the point where just a few dozen are now caught during the April-June spawning season. The Thai Fisheries Department has recently taken steps to save the fish by initiating a strict quota system and conducting an ambitious breeding program at nearby Ban Had Khrai.

Golden Resort: Chiang Khong's most expensive hotel has been constructed in the northern part of town on a hill near the KMT cemetery. Excellent views, a Chinese restaurant, and large a/c rooms with hot showers. Highway 1129, tel. (053) 791350, 650-750B.

Transportation

Chiang Khong is about 75 km east of Chiang Saen. Minitrucks leave in the morning from the riverside market in Chiang Saen. Motorcyclists can use two different routes. Highway 1129 passes through the Hmong villages of Kiu Kan and Huai Yen. A more scenic route is the road that skirts the Mekong River. The turnoff to Chiang Khong is 22 km east of Chiang Saen and marked with a signpost to Suan Dok.

Buses from Chiang Rai take three hours and travel northeast up Hwy. 1020. Direct buses from Bangkok take 14 hours and terminate at the Chiang Khong bus terminal at the south end of town.

MOTORCYCLE JOURNEYS FROM CHIANG KHONG

Some of the most spectacular motorcycling in Thailand can be done south of Chiang Khong, on the roads which lead down to Chiang Kham and Nan. Although in an extremely remote region of Thailand, the roads are well paved and kept in excellent condition by the Thai government. The curious reason for these wonderful roads is an embarrassing defeat of the Thai army by the Laotians in the mid-1980s, after which all perimeter roads were completely repaved to provide an access zone against future border disputes.

Motorcyclists should carry the *Guide Map of Chiang Rai,* published by Bangkok Guides, and a copy of David Unkovich's guide to motorcycle touring in northern Thailand sold in bookstores in Chiang Mai.

The journey from Chiang Khong back to Chiang Mai necessitates overnight stops in Chiang Kham, Nan, and Phrae. A good route is Chiang Khong to Chiang Kham (four hours), Chiang Kham to Nan (five hours), Nan to Phrae (three hours), Phrae to Lampang (two hours), and Lampang to Chiang Mai (two hours).

Hotels are located in all major towns and gasoline is plentiful.

Chiang Khong to Chiang Kham

From Chiang Khong, head south down Hwy. 1020 to the junction with Hwy. 1155. Highway 1020 continues south to Thoeng, but it's a straight and boring road through monotonous ricefields and dusty towns. A much better route is Hwy. 1155 along the Mekong River, then south on the winding, roller-coaster road. Great views and hilltribe villages, including Thai Lue towns with distinctive architecture and unique weavings, are found along the way. Several side roads lead east toward Laos, but the best detour runs from Pang Kha to a road that skirts the border and continues south through Meo Lao U, Huak, Phu Sang Waterfalls, and down Hwy. 1093 to Chiang Kham. Pang Kha to Chiang Kham takes about three hours.

Chiang Kham: Stay at the Chiang Kham Hotel located between the Bangkok Bank and Thai Farmers Bank, opposite the market and police booth. Two blocks northwest is the **Bou Thong Restaurant,** with an English-language menu. Sights around Chiang Kham include Wat Nantarm, some 500 meters from the Chiang Kham Hotel, and Wat Saen Muang Ma behind the Bou Thong Restaurant. Several Laotian refugee camps are nearby, but entry is limited to visitors with official permission.

Chiang Kham to Nan

Motorcyclists with limited time can head directly from Chiang Kham to Phayao and west to Chiang Mai in a single day. A much more leisurely and scenic route goes southeast on Hwy. 1148 to Tha Wang Pha, from where Hwy. 1080 continues south to Nan. The scenery and mountain views are extremely impressive near Sakoen and Pha Lak. Travel time is about five hours, but allow extra time to visit the hilltribe villages and explore the small roads which branch off toward the Laotian border. Possible side roads include the 26-km route up to the summit of Doi Tiu, and east from Tha Wang Phua to Ban Pua and Nam Poon, where a road continues northeast to Luang Prabang.

Nan to Chiang Mai

Two basic routes are possible back to Chiang Mai from Nan. The slower route is down to Phrae on major Hwy. 101 with a possible side trip down Hwy. 1026 to Nan Noi and Khun Satan, the mountain home of a tribal group called "Spirits of the Yellow Leaves." Spend a night in Phrae and continue back to Chiang Mai the following day, spending a few hours exploring the temples in Lampang.

A longer journey heads west on Hwy. 1091 to Ban Luang, followed by 90 km of gravel and asphalt roads to the small town of Ngao. This backroad option avoids the busy highway which connects Nan with Phrae and Lampang. Ngao to Chiang Mai takes three or four hours.

PHAYAO

Phayao is a medium-sized town on Hwy. 1 midway between Lampang and Chiang Rai. Though rarely visited by Westerners, Phayao has several worthwhile temples and a magnificent location on the edge of Phayao Lake.

History

The region is of considerable interest to archaeologists, who believe that settlements have existed on the banks of Phayao Lake since the early Bronze Age. Phayao was abandoned by Bronze Age settlers but reestablished in 1096 as the capital of a small kingdom allied with Chiang Saen and, later, the Lanna Kingdom of King Mengrai. Burmese invasions forced another evacuation in the late 18th century, but the city was reoccupied in 1840 by emigrants from Lampang. Formerly a subdistrict of Chiang Rai Province, Phayao was granted provincial status in 1977, with the lakeside town as its new capital.

Phayao Lake

Phayao lies on the eastern edge of a large freshwater lake, which measures four by six km and supports over 5,000 acres of fish farms. Across the quiet waters looms Doi Bussaracum, a 1,856-meter-high mountain that separates Phayao from the western Wang River Valley. The riverside promenade features several good seafood restaurants, a public park, and a boat launch that rents funny little paddleboats.

Wat Sikhom Kham

The principal temple in Phayao and one of the most significant sanctuaries in northern Thailand, Wat Sikhom Kham is highly regarded by scholars for its 400-year-old Buddha image housed inside the central *viharn*. Named Phra Chao Ton Luang and greatly venerated among the Thais, the gigantic 16-meter brick-and-stucco image impresses with its size, despite the poor restoration conducted by local abbots. Note the variety of Buddha poses displayed on the right side of the *viharn*, and the engraved steles which flank the interior perimeter.

On the grounds to the north is a bizarre collection of the stucco statues so popular in modern Thailand. A sense of humor helps you understand the leap from Lanna art to Lanna kitsch, but it's hard to resist the silly statues of E.T., dinosaurs, and evildoers being boiled in oil or dissected by devils. The sculptures are inspired by Hollywood films and Buddhist legends to serve as both moral guidelines and campy entertainment.

Much more impressive than the garish statues or monster Buddhas are the exquisite murals which grace the modern *viharn* back by the lake. The *viharn* itself is a masterpiece of architectural design, a combination of great symmetry and a wonderful location at the edge of the lake. Inside the dazzling *viharn* are some of the finest modern murals in all of Thailand, designed and painted under the supervision of an extremely talented artist named Angkarn Kalyanaponsga. Angkarn wisely used traditional Lanna motifs but added an almost surrealistic approach that suggests the ethereal nature of inspired Buddhism. Do not miss this temple.

Wat Analayo

A reader wrote in to recommend the temple on the opposite side of the lake from Phayao. The temple was constructed 12 years ago at the top of a hill for a much-revered abbot, who is visited annually by the king. The grounds are filled with religious statuary, including Buddha images from various Thai eras, and representations of Hindu gods such as Vishnu and Shiva. A small *viharn* at the summit holds silver and gold Buddhas presented by the king and decorated with diamonds and emeralds. Four soldiers armed with M-16 rifles guard the *viharn,* which also contains a large elephant encrusted with Ceylonese gems; the elephant was donated by the Sri Lankan government.

Analayo can be reached by *songtao* or a motorcycle rented in Phayao.

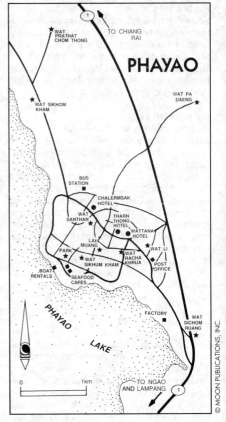

Accommodations

Hotels in Phayao are limited to three places that cater mostly to Thai businesspeople and the occasional *farang.*

Chalermsak Hotel: The cheapest place in town is directly across from the minibus station and very close to the bus terminal. 915 Phahonyothin Rd., tel. (054) 431063, 100-150B fan.

Tharn Thong Hotel: Phayao's largest hotel has 96 rooms with fans or a/c. 55 Donsanam Rd., tel. (054) 431302, 180-220B fan with private bath, 320-460B a/c.

Wattana Hotel: Somewhat less expensive option to the Tharn Thong. 69 Donsanam Rd., tel. (054) 431086, 100-150B fan, 260-300B a/c.

Restaurants

Several good cafes are located in the center of town near the hotels. Sunset dinners are best enjoyed at the seafood restaurants down by the river. **Cabin Restaurant,** just south of the Tharn Thong and near the Lak Muang shrine, is a cozy and somewhat elegant spot that serves Thai, Chinese, and Western dishes.

Transportation

Phayao is 92 km south of Chiang Rai on the old highway that once provided the main link between Chiang Mai and Chiang Rai. Most buses between these two cities now use Hwy. 1019, which cuts through the mountains and passes through Wiang Pa Pao and Mae Suai. Travelers from Chiang Mai must ask for a bus which uses the old route. An easier alternative is to visit Phayao after Chiang Rai, and then return to Chiang Mai or head east to Phrae and Nan.

Motorcyclists can enjoy a wonderful ride west from Phayao on Hwy. 1282, across the towering mountain range, and down to Wang Nua and Hwy. 1019, which returns to Chiang Mai.

PHRAE

Phrae is a modern, provincial capital made prosperous from coal mining and the logging industry. The city served as a Burmese outpost during the Burmese occupation of Thailand, and later hosted a large number of Burmese and Laotian loggers involved in the teak trade. Today Phrae is known for its temples, rattan furniture, and homespun blue farmer's shirts now worn all over Thailand. Phrae temples uniquely combine Burmese and Laotian styles.

Wat Chom Sawan

The Burmese heritage of Phrae is demonstrated by this Shan-style temple constructed some 80 years ago outside the old city walls. The sanctuary features Burmese-tiered roofs with fine coffered ceilings, and a monumental *chedi* gilded with a copper crown.

Wat Sra Bo Kaew

Near the flower gardens on Nam Khue Road stands another Burmese-style temple with a Shan *chedi* and richly decorated altars inside the modern *viharn*.

Wat Prabat Ming

Located near the center of town, Wat Prabat Ming Muang Vora Viharn features a modern *viharn* and an 18th-century *bot* constructed in the Laotian style with sloping columns and a slat-covered roof. Inside the *viharn* is the most significant Buddha image of the province, Pra Buddha Kosa Srichai Maha Sakayamuni.

Wat Luang

West of Wat Prabat Ming, you'll find Wat Luang. Of chief interest here are the Burmese-style *chedi* and decorated wooden beams inside the central *viharn*. A small but worthy museum is also located here.

Down the road, **Wat Pong Sunan** features Laotian influences in the handsome *viharn* graced with carved wooden pediments and gilded reliefs.

Wat Pra Non

Another Laotian-style temple containing a lovely *viharn* carved with fine wooden pediments, and an interior space mysteriously illuminated by narrow vertical slits. The chapel to the left contains a reclining Buddha for which the temple is named and dates from the 18th century.

Ban Prathup Jai Teakwood House

Certainly the most curious sight in Phrae is the old teakwood home in Ban Prathup (also called Ban Sao Roi Tan), about one km west of town. Constructed from an almost unbelievable amount of precious wood, the opulent home and private museum is a testament to the breathtaking beauty of teakwood, and the insatiable lust for the precious commodity. Never again will the world see such lavish use of teakwood.

Wat Prathat Choe Hae

Phrae's most famous temple is eight km east of town, about one km beyond the village of Padang. The temple sits atop a teak-clad hill cut by two stairways flanked by Burmese lions and guardian *nagas*. The right-hand stairway leads to a small shrine, which houses the highly revered Buddha image of Pra Chao Tan Chai, widely believed to have the power to grant wishes and cure sterility. Crammed inside the small grounds of the *wat* stands a 33-meter *chedi* sheathed with gilded copper plates, and a modern *viharn* noted for its unusual cruciform pattern. Wat Prathat Choe Hae derives its name from a type of heavy satin fabric *(choe hae),* which pilgrims often wrap around the *chedi.*

Minitrucks to the temple can be flagged down on Choe Hae Road.

Muang Phi (Ghost City)

Eighteen km from Phrae, off Hwy. 101 on a side road just before Km 143, is an eerie natural wonder created by soil and wind erosion. The resulting geological phenomena resemble surrealistic chimneys, giant mushrooms, or asteroid dwellings—depending on your perspective.

Handicraft Villages

The distinctive *seua ma hawn,* a bluish farmer's shirt worn throughout Thailand as a symbol of proletariat unity, originates from the village of Ban Thung Hong, four km north of Phrae on Hwy. 101. Despite the logging ban initiated several years ago, woodcarving remains a traditional occupation in several villages near Phrae. The best selection is found eight km south of Phrae at Hua Dong Market in the district of Sung Men.

Budget Accommodations

Most of the hotels in Phrae are in the center of town on Rajadamnern and Charoen Muang roads.

Thep Wiman Hotel: Several basic hotels are strung along this busy road including this fairly clean bargain just across the street from the

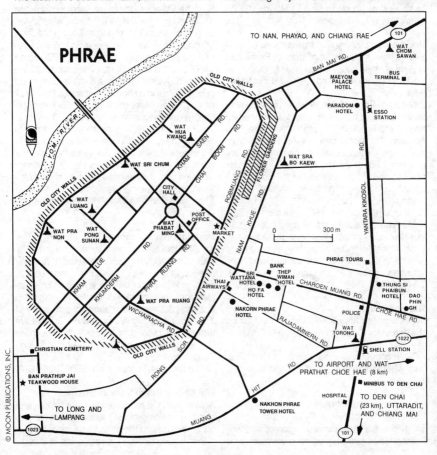

Bangkok Bank. 153 Charoen Muang Rd., tel. (054) 511047, 100-150B.

Ho Fa Hotel: Another inexpensive hotel in the center of town a block down the road from the Thep Wiman. Charoen Muang Rd., tel. (054) 511140, 100-150B.

Siriwattana Hotel: Somewhat cheaper than most other hotels on hotel row but only for the hardy traveler on a super budget. Charoen Muang Rd., tel. (054) 511047, 80-120B.

Dao Phin Guesthouse: The only guesthouse in town owned and operated by the Swiss-Thai couple who can help with sightseeing tips and transportation details to the more remote villages in the province. This place is just off the south end of Charoen Muang Road. 105/29 Chaw Hae Rd., no phone, 80-140B.

Moderate to Luxury Accommodations
Surprisingly, the fairly small town of Phrae has several upscale hotels which cater to the traveling Thai businessman and the occasional Western tourist.

Nakhorn Phrae Hotel: Western travelers who desire a better hotel with standard amenities stay at the Nakhorn Phrae just opposite Thai Airways. The hotel offers tourist information, maps, and guided tours from the *samlor* drivers who hang out at the front door. Their popular cafe has great food and some of the most amusing cabaret singers in northern Thailand. 69 Rajadamnern Rd., tel. (054) 511122, fax (054) 521937, 250-350B fan, 450-750B a/c.

Maeyom Palace Hotel: Phrae's newest and most luxurious hotel is just west of the bus terminal. The six-story hotel has 100 rooms, a large swimming pool, several restaurants, and conference facilities. 181 Yantara Kikosol Rd., tel. (054) 521028, fax (054) 522904, 1,100-2,000B.

Transportation
Buses from the Arcade Bus Terminal in Chiang Mai depart for Phrae hourly until 1900. The journey lasts two hours.

Train commuters should alight at Den Chai, from where minitrucks shuttle continuously up to Phrae.

NAN

Situated in the most remote region of northern Thailand, Nan ranks high among travelers, who regard it as similar to the Chiang Mai of three decades ago. The landscape combines the mountain vistas of Chiang Mai with the bucolic charms of the lazy, brown river which slowly winds to the east.

Nan is a fairly prosperous town with the standard collection of concrete shophouses, but the old temples, idyllic location, and genuine sense of remoteness make it one of the better destinations in northern Thailand.

History
Nan was established in 1368 by migrants from the Mekong River region, who later established formal relations with the emerging Thai Empire at Sukothai. After the demise of Sukothai, Nan was absorbed into the Lanna Kingdom, which ruled most of northern Thailand from Chiang Mai. Nan fell under Burmese sovereignty in 1558 and remained under foreign control until 1786 when the Chakri dynasty of Bangkok liberated northern Thailand. Nan remained a semi-autonomous principality ruled by hereditary princes until 1931 when it came under the full control of Bangkok.

Nan achieved a modest degree of international acclaim in 1927 when the filmmaking team of Schoedsack and Cooper produced *Chang* in the forests outside town. Six years later the pair produced their most famous film, *King Kong,* modeled after their efforts in Nan. More recently, *The Elephant Keeper* was filmed in 1990 near Phrae and Nan by a Thai writer-director named Chatri Yukol.

Nan National Museum
An excellent starting point for an exploration of Nan is the centrally located museum, recently opened in a palace, Ho Kham, constructed in 1903 by Prince Phalida. Inside the small but outstanding museum are informative ethnographic displays, detailed explanations of the history of Thai art, and a highly revered black elephant tusk on the second floor, reputedly brought to Nan some 300 years ago by the king of Chiang Tung.

The museum is open Wed.-Sun. 0900-1630.

Wat Chang Kham Vora Viharn
Across from the museum stands a temple and *chedi* constructed in 1547 with elephant *(chang)* buttresses around the perimeter. One of the two rather unexceptional *viharns* in the *wat* com-

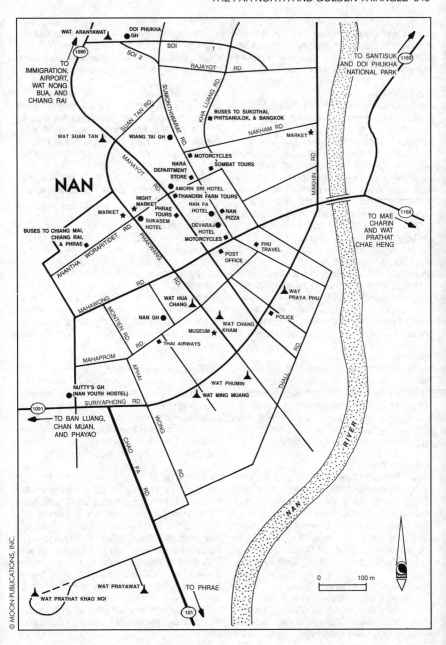

NAN

WAT ARANYAWAT
DOI PHUKHA GH
1080
SOI
SOI 1
RAJAYOT RD.
SOI 2
TO IMMIGRATION, AIRPORT, WAT NONG BUA, AND CHIANG RAI
TO SANTISUK AND DOI PHUKHA NATIONAL PARK
1169

SUAN TAN RD.
SUMONTHIWARAT RD.
KHA LUANG RD.
NAKHAM RD.
MARKET
MAKHIN RD.

WAT SUAN TAN
WIANG TAI GH
BUSES TO SUKOTHAI, PHITSANULOK, & BANGKOK

MOTORCYCLES
NARA DEPARTMENT STORE
SOMBAT TOURS
MAHAYOT RD.

MARKET
NIGHT MARKET
PHRAE TOURS
SUKASEM HOTEL
AMORN SRI HOTEL
THANORN FARN TOURS
NAN FA HOTEL
NAN PIZZA
DEVARAJ HOTEL
MOTORCYCLES
TO MAE CHARIN AND WAT PRATHAT CHAE HENG
1168

BUSES TO CHIANG MAI, CHIANG RAI, & PHRAE

ANANTHA
WORARITIDET RD.
PHAKWANG RD.
POST OFFICE
FHU TRAVEL

MAHAWONG RD.
MONTIEN RD.
NAN GH
WAT HUA CHANG
WAT PRAYA PHU
WAT CHANG KHAM
POLICE

MUSEUM
MAHAPROM RD.
APHAI RD.
THAI AIRWAYS
THAI RD.

NUTTY'S GH (NAN YOUTH HOSTEL)
WAT PHUMIN
WAT MING MUANG
1091
TO BAN LUANG, CHAN MUAN, AND PHAYAO
SURIYAPHONG RD.
WONG RD.

CHAO FA RD.
NAN RIVER

WAT PRATHAT KHAO NOI
WAT PRAYAWAT
TO PHRAE
101

0   100 m

© MOON PUBLICATIONS, INC.

pound contains a 145-cm walking Buddha made of pure gold, discovered by Alexander Griswold in 1955 after the plaster covering the image was broken. The monastery is still actively used to train young novices in the traditions of Buddhism.

Wat Phumin

The finest architectural piece in Nan dates from 1596 with extensive restorations in 1867 and 1991. Unlike most temples in Thailand, the central *viharn* was constructed in a curious cruciform pattern to showcase the four large Sukothai-style Buddhas that face the cardinal points. The superb arrangement of pillars and coffered ceilings make Wat Phumin an excellent example of northern Thai architecture. Also note the carved doors, comparable only to the famous doors of Wat Suthat in Bangkok.

The temple is chiefly noted for its outstanding murals, which depict local society some 100 years ago. Art historians believe the murals were painted by Thai Lue artists who possessed both a fine degree of humor and an amazing attention to detail. Based on the Buddhist Khatan Kumman Jatakas, the murals include a famous scene of a young man courting a thinly clad girl, and a fine portrait of a former governor of the province.

Wat Praya Phu

Enshrined in the undistinguished *bot* are two rare Sukothai-style Buddhas commissioned by a Nan prince named Ngua Phan Sum and cast in 1426. The walking images display slightly different positions with finely varied expressions of great power and sensitivity. Centering the display is an enormous seated Buddha.

Wat Suan Tan

Highlights at Wat Suan Tan include a 40-meter *prang* with a spire of Khmer design, and a 15th-century *viharn* which enshrines an important Buddha image named Pra Chao Thong Tip. According to local chronicles, the four-meter bronze image was cast in 1449 by King Tilokarja of Chiang Mai after his conquest of Nan. The image shows both Sukothai and Chiang Saen influences.

Wat Prathat Chae Heng

Two km southeast of town on Hwy. 1168 lies another impressive temple, constructed six centuries ago on the original site of the city established by King Chao Khun Fong. Leading to the summit of Mt. Phubhiang is a royal staircase guarded by two enormous *naga makara* figures. The elevated courtyard is dominated by a 55-meter golden *chedi* and a marvelous *viharn* capped with a five-level roof of Laotian inspiration.

Wat Prayawat

South of the city stands a strangely shaped *chedi* believed to be the oldest structure in the region. Placed inside the pyramidal *chedi* are niches containing standing Buddhas in the Sinhalese manner. The modern *viharn* contains an altar richly embellished in Laotian style.

Wat Prathat Khao Noi to the rear offers fine views and a pair of Buddha statues in the late Chiang Saen style.

Wat Nongbua

Outside town in the district of Tha Wang Pha is a century-old temple constructed by Thai Lue artists; the temple boasts the finest murals in the region. Unlike the murals of Wat Phumin, these frescoes remain in outstanding condition with bright shades and livelier colors. Perhaps painted by the same artists of Wat Phumin, the stories depict legends from the Candgada Jataka, which once served to encourage ethical behavior among young Thais.

Doi Phukha National Park

A popular day-ride for motorcyclists is 85 km north to Doi Phukha. Take Hwy. 1169 to Santisuk and then Hwy. 1256 east from the town of Pua past waterfalls, caves, and hilltribe villages on one of the most scenic highways in northern Thailand. The return loop can be completed via Pua and Tha Wang Pha down Hwy. 1080.

Mrabi Hill Tribe

Phrae and Nan both serve as launching points for excursions to the Mrabi tribes, called Phi Thong Luang by the Thais and nicknamed the Spirits of the Yellow Leaves from the color of their temporary leaf huts. The Mrabi are elusive nomadic hunters whose very existence remained mythical until their discovery by a jungle expedition several decades ago. Numbering fewer than 150 in the entire country, the Mrabi have been proselytized by American missionaries from Florida and have been the subject of tours organized by international trekking agencies and Fhu Travel.

THE THAI ELEPHANT IN WORLD FILM

*T*he Thai elephant has been the subject of several important and not-so-important films since Ernest Schoedsack and Merian Cooper lensed *Chang* near the town of Nan in 1927.

Chang

Although the filmmaking team of Schoedsack and Cooper will be forever associated with their 1933 classic *King Kong,* this inventive pair accomplished some of their greatest work in 1927 with their depiction of Siamese peasant life near Nan and their relationships with elephants. Filmed on location prior to Nan becoming a province of Thailand, *Chang* ("Elephant") constituted a cinematic blueprint for *King Kong,* complete with roaming jungle cats and marauding herds of elephants.

The pair had previously traveled to Persia to make their first collaboration, *Grass,* a documentary on the migrations of the Bakhtiari tribe. They then decided to make a film about another dissimilar environment—villagers trapped in the overabundance of the Siamese jungle. Nan appeared the perfect setting. The filmmakers then raised US$75,000 from Paramount; half of that sum went to the king of Siam's brother for the use of his private elephants.

Chang—made without trick photography and at tremendous personal risk to both directors—is a marvel of daring and logistics that later inspired the makers of *Tarzan* and other Hollywood adventure films. The only scene not shot in Thailand was a comic-relief shot of a monkey dropping a coconut on an elephant's head. That was made at the Bronx Zoo.

Chang won critical praise and played to sensational box offices, but with the coming of the talkies it was swept aside and confined to the vaults.

In 1988, Milestone Films restored one of the few surviving prints and commissioned Bruce Gaston to provide a new score. Gaston—a former Californian and Thai resident for 23 years—created considerable atmospheric texture by combining drums, oboes, and electronic sounds.

A new 35mm print of the film was released in 1991 at the Rotterdam Film Festival. The film ends with a closing title card, "First there was the jungle. From the beginning until the end of time it stretches." Even the visionary team of Cooper and Schoedsack could not have foreseen the future of the world's rainforests.

The Elephant Keeper

Thailand's greatest director is Prince Chatri Chalerm Yukol (Tan Mui), the great-grandson of King Chulalongkorn and the only Thai director whose films are currently distributed in the West. Tan Mui's father had assisted Cooper and Schoedsack during the 1927 filming of *Chang.* Tan later interned under Cooper in Hollywood. After his return to Thailand, Tan produced more than 30 films dealing with controversial subjects and social realism, including *The Elephant Keeper* (1990), *Salween* (1993), and *Sida* (1995), a brave film focusing on child prostitution and the spread of AIDS.

Tan's 1990 film, set in the doomed tropical forests of Thailand, remains one of the few Thai films ever accepted for screening at international film festivals. A tragic tale of greed and survival, *Khon Liang Chang* ("The Elephant Keeper") conveys the complexities of the logging issue through the eyes of a desperate elephant keeper in a terrible dilemma: the end of the rainforests means the end of elephants and their mahouts. The film also recorded the beauty of the rainforests and emphasized the inherent conflicts between rainforest preservation and economic growth.

Tan Mui's timing was quite remarkable, for it was during filming in the forests of Tak, Phrae, and Lampang that the Thai government formally announced a nationwide ban on logging in a last-ditch effort to save the rainforests.

Dumbo Drop

From the serious to the silly, the Thai elephant continues to star in major Hollywood productions.

This 1995 Walt Disney story about elephants and their mahouts was filmed over a period of two months in Mae Hong Son, Kanchanaburi, Chiang Mai, and Lopburi. The human stars were Ray Liotta and Danny Glover, but the real star was Pathet Thai, an elephant born in Thailand, raised in the United States, and returned to Thailand to assume the lead role as Dumbo.

Director Simon Wincer wisely hired an American named Richard Lair—pachyderm professional, elephant advocate, and former beatnik from San Francisco—to train and supervise the elephants for the film. Lair left the U.S. in the late 1970s to study wild elephants, work for the Thai Association for the Conservation of Wildlife, and eventually write the definitive report on Asian elephants for the United Nations. Today he continues to work in the film industry while working to help protect the last of Thailand's endangered elephants.

Guesthouses

Nan has several guesthouses and hotels in the center of town.

Doi Phukha Guesthouse: Nan's best guesthouse is in a quiet neighborhood inside an old teak house with gardens and a wooden pavilion. Owner Soeren Skibsted is certainly the best source of advice on sightseeing in the province, including caves and waterfalls almost impossible to find without his help. Your interest will be piqued by his collection of photos on the wall, plus the maps and motorcycling insight Soeren can provide. He also rents bicycles and puts together treks in conjunction with Fhu Travel. Take a *samlor* from the northern bus terminal. 94/5 Sumonthiwarat Rd., tel. (054) 771442, 80-120B.

Nan Guesthouse: Nan's first guesthouse was opened several years ago by a Kiwi named Peter who has since departed and turned his cozy operation over to new owners. The old wooden teak house is comfortable and only a 10-minute walk from the western bus terminal. Free bicycle rentals; travel tips are posted on the walls. 57/17 Mahaprom Rd., tel. (054) 771849, 80-120B.

Wiang Tai Guesthouse: A clean and conveniently located choice, though the modern building lacks the memorable atmosphere of Doi Phuka and Nan Guesthouses. Owner Khun Tu provides help with exploring Nan Province. 21/1 Soi Wat Hua Wiang Tai, tel. (054) 710247, 120-180B.

Nutty's Guesthouse: Nan's so-called "youth hostel" seems to change management and names every few years—"No Problem" and "Rob Muang Guesthouse" have been the previous catchy titles—but the place hangs on in the southeast corner of town. Only recommended if the other places are filled during the high season. 3/1 Rob Muang Rd., tel. (054) 772559, 80-100B.

Hotels

Those who prefer more conventional accommodations may want to try one of the following hotels.

Sukasem Hotel: A simple but clean hotel conveniently near the bus terminal and across from the night market. All rooms include private bath with hot showers—a necessity in the winter months. 29 Arantha Woraritidet Rd., tel. (054) 710141, 150-180B fan, 300-360B a/c.

Nan Fa Hotel: Bridging the gap between the basic Sukasem and the midpriced Devaraj is the renovated "wooden hotel" near the Devaraj and just across from the popular Nan Pizza. Some atmosphere in contrast to the other concrete hotels. 438 Sumonthiwarat Rd., tel. (054) 710284, 350-650B a/c.

Devaraj Hotel: Nan's best hotel offers large, clean rooms with hot showers, a popular cafe with cabaret singers in the evening, and a limited amount of tourist information. The hotel lacks character, but compensates with a pleasant courtyard and decent restaurant. 466 Sumon Devaraj Rd., tel. (054) 710094, 300-450B fan, 500-800B a/c.

Restaurants

Guesthouses and hotels provide meals, but the following will offer better fare.

Da Dario Restaurant: Sometimes called the Tip Top (after the former Italian restaurant operated by Paolo and his wife; they went back to Switzerland), this spot in the northern part of town serves up tasty and reasonably priced Thai and Western dishes as prepared by the Swiss-Thai owners. Open daily 0700-2200. 37/4 Rajamunay Rd., tel. (054) 750258.

Night Market: Somewhat disappointing after Chiang Mai, though simple street fare is quick and cheap in the venue across from Sukasem Hotel.

Suan Issan: Nan's best Issan fare is prepared in the popular cafe in the center of town. It's clean and cheap and the English menu helps you decipher the northeastern specialties. Suan Issan is situated in a small alley about 15 meters south of the Amorn Sri Hotel. Open daily 0900-2200. 2/1 Anantha Woraritidet Rd., tel. (054) 710761.

Phin Pub: A refreshing change from nightstalls and street cafes is the first-floor restaurant inside the Nan Fah Hotel. Dishes are well prepared and range from seafood curries to regional specialties. Evening entertainment starts with traditional folk music and later switches gears to Thai pop and Western rock. Prices are very reasonable. Open nightly 0600-midnight. 438 Sumonthiwarat Rd., tel. (054) 772640.

Practicalities

Most of the following services are downtown, near the hotels and restaurants.

Tourist Information: Nan lacks a tourist office, but sketch maps and travel tips can be picked up at Doi Phukha Guesthouse in the northern section of town. Information is also available from Nan Guesthouse, from Mr. Tu at Wiang Tai Guesthouse and, to a lesser degree, from the Devaraj Hotel.

Tours: Fhu Travel, Nan's only travel agency, can help you arrange tours and treks to the neighboring villages, and can advise you on the current visa situation for Laos. The English-speaking manager also rents bikes, mountain bikes, and motorcycles. Fhu Travel, 453/4 Sumonthiwarat Rd., tel. (054) 710636.

Laos Travel: The Laotian government has opened several new entrance points including Ban Huay Kan opposite Muang Ngarn in Laos. The move is intended to promote trade between Thailand and Laos and provide an additional access point for tourists arriving from this section of Thailand. Current details are subject to change though the latest situation can be checked with Nan guesthouses and from Fhu Travel.

Currency Exchange: Thai Farmers and Bangkok Bank on Sumonthiwarat Road are both open Mon.-Fri. 0830-1530. Exchange facilities are closed on weekends but both banks have ATMs for around-the-clock service.

International Telephone: Overseas calls can be made from most hotels and from the CAT Telecom Center at the GPO on Mahawong Road. It's open daily 0700-2200.

Motorcycle Rentals: Far and away the finest way to reach the natural attractions in the Nan region is on a rented motorcycle from Fhu Travel, Overseas Rentals (tel. 054-710258) at 488 Sumonthiwarat Rd. near the Devaraj Hotel, or the shop opposite Wat Hua Wiang on Sumonthiwarat Road, one block north of Nara Department Store. Motorbikes cost 150-200B per day depending on engine size and number of days rented.

Transportation

Nan is 668 km north of Bangkok and 318 km east of Chiang Mai.

Air: Thai Airways flies daily from Bangkok and three times weekly from Chiang Mai, Phitsanulok, and Phrae. Thai Airways (tel. 054-710077) is at 34 Mahaprom Rd. near the National Museum.

Train: The nearest train station to Nan is at Den Chai, 23 km south of Phrae. To reach Den Chai, first take a bus to Phrae (three hours) from the bus terminal on Anatha Woraritidet Road and then take a minibus down to the Den Chai train station (30 minutes). The most convenient train departure leaves Den Chai at 1900 and arrives in Bangkok the following morning at 0700. To make this connection, you must leave Nan by 1400 to reach Phrae by 1700 and make the onward bus down to Den Chai.

Bus: Buses leave Chiang Mai hourly 0700-1100 and take seven hours to reach Nan. Buses from Chiang Rai leave hourly 0700-1000 and also take seven hours. Overnight service may be available from both towns; check with guesthouses or the TAT. Buses also reach Nan from Phrae, Uttaradit, Sukothai, Phitsanulok, and other points south.

Nan has two government bus terminals (Bor Kor Sor) and three private tour agencies that offer VIP a/c bus service to Chiang Mai and Bangkok. The BKS terminal for destinations to the north of Nan is west of town on Anantha Woraritidet Road. The BKS terminal for points south is northeast of city center on Kha Luang Road. Both provide quick and inexpensive services for most destinations in Thailand.

Private bus companies include Phrae Tours one block south of the Amorn Sri Hotel, Thavorn Farn Tours just opposite Amorn Sri Hotel, and Sombat Tours near the Nara Department Store. All sell tickets for direct a/c buses to Bangkok and Chiang Mai, but most travelers feel BKS service is almost as good and far less expensive than private bus companies.

NORTHEASTERN THAILAND

Northeastern Thailand—referred to as the Issan (Ee-saan) by the Thais—is one of the most traditional and least visited regions in the country. In many ways, it is Thailand's heartland, where old Thai customs and lifestyles survive among the friendly and polite population. Few travelers visit the northeast, but promotional efforts of the TAT and the opening of Laos and Cambodia promise to increase the numbers of visitors to the last untouched region in the country.

Issan refers to an old Mon-Khmer kingdom named Isana that once flourished in the region. The term can be loosely translated into either "vastness" or "prosperity," though only the former

seems appropriate.

The Issan spreads over a vast and arid limestone plateau bounded on the north by the Mekong River, which separates Thailand from Laos, to the south by the Dong Rek Mountains, which form the border with Cambodia, and on the west by the Phang Hoei Mountains, which divide the Issan from central Thailand. Comprising some 170,000 square kilometers, this gigantic region sprawls across one-third of the total land acreage in Thailand. The sheer geographic immensity makes it a challenging destination for the visitor with limited time but also helps preserve the region against the onslaught of mass tourism.

INTRODUCTION

The People
Issan inhabitants include Thais, Chinese, and large numbers of Laotians who migrated into the infertile region from their homeland across the Mekong River. Laotian culture and character are readily apparent in the traditional

temple architecture near the Mekong, unique languages which mix standard Thai with Laotian loanwords, and the physiognomy of the people, who can often be recognized by their darker skins, burned by years of toil in the ricefields.

There are also many speakers of Khmer, especially in the Cambodian border districts of Sisaket, Buriram, and Surin Provinces. Less well known are the earlier, pre-Khmer peoples such as the Suay who have traditionally worked as mahouts and hunters of wild elephants.

The Issan has the highest population density, unemployment levels, and rates of poverty in the nation. Consequently, large numbers of Issan people (Khon Issan) migrate to the Middle East where they work the oil fields or to southern Thailand where they take jobs on fishing boats. Most, however, go to Bangkok where they drive *tuk tuks,* operate portable foodstalls, fall into prostitution, or find employment as construction workers on Sukumvit Road.

Despite their poverty, the people of the Issan remain an independent lot who view life with a refreshing blend of fatalism and good humor.

Under the Surface
Nature, unfortunately, has not been kind to the region. Cursed with sandy soils limiting farmers to a single rice crop each year, erratic rainfall bringing famine and floods, a searing hot season, and the country's highest population density, northeastern Thailand ranks as the problem child of Thailand. The Issan is not only its poorest region, but also a land plagued by environmental degradation, peasant landlessness, malnutrition, desertion by the young to the cities, encroachment by farmers into protected forests, and an agriculture based almost exclusively on rice. Newspaper stories relate sad tales of landless farmers forced off their meager plots by well-connected businesspeople, who develop the land into golf courses or industrial estates. Floods, heat waves, drought, and political fights over dams and reforestation programs are other Issan tragedies that fill the newspaper headlines.

Even the spelling of the region seems to be a problem. Over the last few years, tourist and government publications have spelled the territory as Issan, Isarn, I-San, Isan, Isaan, Esarn, E-sarn, Esan, and E-san!

Political and economic solutions have been attempted with varying results. The region now has a good system of highways, and electricity reaches most of the villages. Dozens of dams have successfully been constructed, though large-scale dam construction appears to have ended after the completion of the Pak Moon project near Ubon Ratchathani. Other proposals, such as the ambitious Green Issan project announced with great fanfare several years ago, seem to appear and then disappear with the changing administrations in Bangkok. Despite the rhetoric, critics charge the Issan remains largely ignored except during election campaigns, when politicians arrive to buy votes for 50B per household.

Certainly the most controversial project currently raging in the northeast is the Khor Chor Kor, a reforestation plan sponsored by the Thai army which intends to move some 1.25 million farmers from degraded forest reserves controlled by the Royal Forestry Department onto other lands already inhabited by other farmers. The evacuated land would then be replanted with forest cover such as nonnative eucalyptus gum trees which would, in turn, help expand wildlife habitat and rebuild watersheds. The plan appears well intended, but landless peasants believe it is a camouflage operation designed to convert their farms into corporate pulp and gum plantations for the benefit of privileged Thais.

Sightseeing Highlights
The Thai government has mounted a concerted effort to sell the Issan as a major tourist destination. This is an uphill task. A relative lack of historical and cultural attractions makes the Issan less appealing than other regions, plus the plateau lacks any beaches or tropical islands. Equally discouraging are the vast distances between points of interest, which require frequent flights or long, tough, overland journeys. Although the Issan is unquestionably the most authentic and untouched region in Thailand, tourist arrivals remain at very low levels.

Should you visit the northeast? Issan fans insist the absence of Western visitors is a great change from the rest of Thailand, and recommend the region to those travelers who enjoy getting off the beaten track.

Khao Yai National Park: First stop in the northeast is a large national park four hours from Bangkok. A quick weekend escape for the asphyxiated citizens of Bangkok, Khao Yai provides a lush environment of jungle, waterfalls, some wildlife, and a dozen hiking trails in the most popular national park in Thailand.

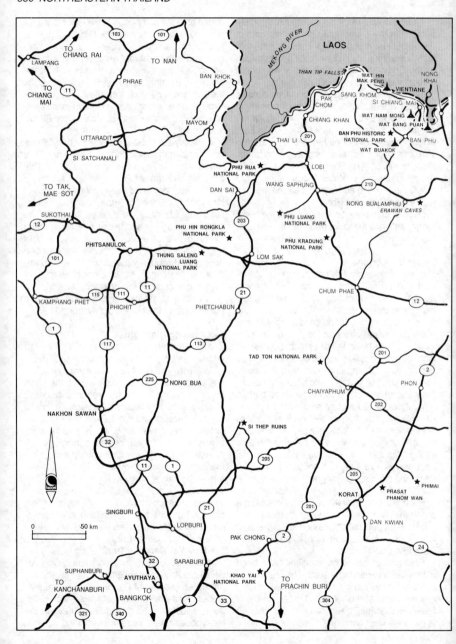

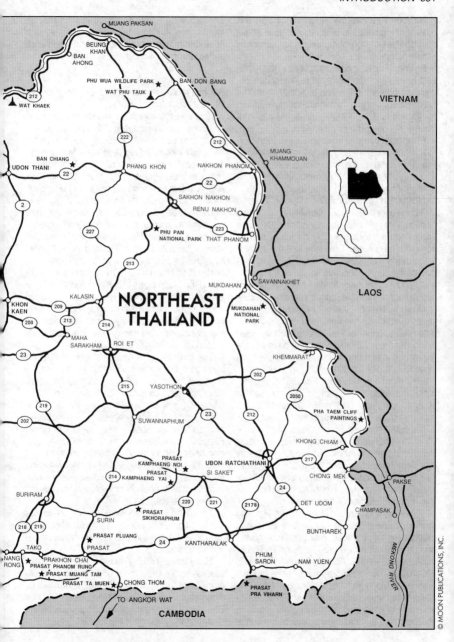

NORTHEAST THAILAND

© MOON PUBLICATIONS, INC.

Nakhon Ratchasima: Also called Korat, this busy town has little to offer except as a transit spot and launching point for visits to the nearby Khmer temples.

Phimai: Top historical attractions in the northeast are the rich collection of restored Cambodian temples which, taken together, form the finest spectrum of Khmer architecture in the world. Prasat Hin Phimai—the stone castle of Phimai—is one hour north of Korat.

Phanom Rung: More impressive than Phimai is the recently restored Khmer temple of Prasat Phanom Rung, three hours east of Korat and slightly south of Buriram. Several other Khmer temples are also near Korat.

Nong Khai: Beautifully situated on the Mekong River, this lovely town is the launching point for visits to Laos. Visitors intending to reach Laos should check carefully on travel restrictions with the Laotian Embassy in Bangkok and with travelers on Khao San Road. Nong Khai is one of the most attractive towns in the northeast, and a great place to start a wonderful journey west along the Mekong to riverside villages.

Mekong River: Some of northeastern Thailand's most idyllic and unspoiled villages are situated on the banks of the Mekong River between Nong Khai and Chiang Khan. All have simple guesthouses and decent cafes offering their services to a steady trickle of Western travelers.

Phu Kradung National Park: The second-most popular national park in the Issan offers spectacular views and thick vegetation on an elevated plateau just south of the town of Loei.

Nakhon Phanom: Few travelers venture beyond the Friendship Highway, which connects Nakhon Ratchasima with Nong Khai, but hardy travelers sometimes visit Nakhon Phanom to see the small, golden, Laotian-style *chedi* of That Phanom, a temple highly venerated by both the Thai and Laotian communities.

Vipassan **Meditation:** Northeastern Thailand has long been the center of Buddhist *vipassana* meditation, as practiced in several forest *wats* near the Laotian border. The famous Thammayut monk named Achaan Man (1870-1949) hailed from Ubon Ratchathani. Three famous *wats* near Ubon Ratchathani include Wat Paa Nanachat ("International Forest Monastery") where most of the monks are English-speaking Westerners; a cave monastery named Wat Tham Saeng Phet also popular with foreign monks; and Wa Non Paa Phong where several American masters including Jack Kornfield once served their monkhood.

Routes

Several routes are possible depending on your interests and time.

Korat and Khmer Monuments: Visitors keen on Khmer architecture but with a limited schedule should use Korat Monument as a base for short side trips to the nearby Khmer Monuments. The finest Cambodian architecture is at Phimai, Phanom Wan, Phanom Rung, and Muang Tam. After a tour of the monuments, return to Bangkok with a stop at Khao Yai National Park. Travelers who need some sun and beach after all the dusty monuments should note that buses now directly connect Korat with Pattaya and other beach resorts on the east coast of Thailand. Allow three to five days for this brief look at the northeast.

Korat to Nong Khai: The most popular journey in the Issan starts with Korat and the Khmer temples described above. Trains and buses head north from Korat to Khon Kaen and Udon Thani, two ordinary towns. Chaiyaphum, however, is a somewhat attractive town providing a worthwhile side trip between Korat and Khon Kaen.

The journey up the Friendship Highway terminates in the lovely town of Nong Khai, on the banks of the Mekong River. You may then continue across to Laos to visit Vientiane and other towns. Otherwise, head west by bus or rented motorcycle to the fine villages that hug the banks of the Mekong. Spend a few nights in either Sang Khom or Pak Chom before reaching Chiang Kham. The road then heads south to Loei and Phu Kradung National Park before returning to Udon Thani or Nong Khai. Alternatively, proceed west from Loei to Lom Sak and Phitsanulok in central Thailand.

This 10-day to two-week excursion covers the highlights of the northeast and avoids the long and exhausting bus ride to the more remote regions.

The Grand Tour: Travelers with over three weeks, and a great deal of patience, can circumnavigate the entire region through Korat, Khon Kaen, Udon Thani, Nong Khai, Nakhon Phanom, Ubon Ratchathani, and Surin before returning to Korat.

EN ROUTE TO THE MONUMENTS

KHAO YAI NATIONAL PARK

Thailand's most popular national park, south of Pak Chong and 200 km northeast of Bangkok, is a world of rich and diverse flora from evergreen and rainforest to *lalang* and rolling hills of tropical grasslands. Established in 1972 as the first national park in Thailand, Khao Yai spreads across four provinces and a variety of ecological zones including marshlands, tropical forests, and the sandstone mountains that form the Dongrak Range. Entry to the park costs 30B.

A small visitors center a few kilometers north of the closed Khao Yai Motorlodge offers some haphazard but informative displays on local wildlife and hiking trails. Adjacent foodstalls provide the cheapest meals in the park. Maps and more details can be picked up from the visitors center.

Problems in the Park

Khao Yai appears a beautiful slice of Thailand, but under the surface the region has problems, ranging from illegal encroachment by condominium and golf course developers, illegal logging, rock mining, and illegal hunting (especially elephants) within the park boundaries.

Several deaths of informants against these activities have resulted, including the 1998 shooting of a villager who had exposed a local politician from nearby Prachin Buri Province. After he encroached on a wide area of the national park to construct a resort, Boonmee Dairerk, alias Uncle Mao, blew the whistle and was murdered in front of his son.

The death of Boonmee Dairerk was protested by six NGOs including the Wildlife Fund Thailand, Green World Foundation, the Khao Yai Protection Assembly, the Environment Assembly of Nakhon Ratchasia, and the Forum of the Poor, but as of this date nothing has been done against the developers and poachers who continue to desecrate the national park.

Waterfalls and Caves

Hiking trails starting from the visitors center lead to several waterfalls and limestone caves. However, the great distances from headquarters to the falls often necessitates a private vehicle or tour organized by the park or a private company such as Jungle Adventures in Pak Chong (tel. 044-31386).

Kong Kao Falls adjacent to the headquarters is small and rather unimpressive except during the rainy season July-November. A narrow trail from the campsite east of the golf course heads to Pha Kluai Mai ("Orchid Falls"), Haew Suwat, Haew Sai, and Haew Pratun waterfalls. These falls can also be reached by walking along the asphalt road that passes through the abandoned golf course, or the eight-km trail that starts at Kong Kao Falls.

Roads west of the motor lodge lead to Manao Falls (7 km), Tatapu Falls (10 km), Tadtakong Falls (14 km), and Nan Rong Falls (20 km), the largest cascade of water in Khao Yai. Tours often include the bat-infested limestone cave at Khao Rub Chang, situated at the periphery of the park.

Hiking Trails

A guidebook distributed at the park headquarters describes 12 hiking trails originally created by wild elephants. Trails near the visitors center are kept in fairly good condition and marked with color-coded trees set 20-30 meters apart. Trails farther into the jungle are often buried under wild vegetation and difficult to follow. Guides can be hired at the lodge.

Trail 1, the most popular hike at Khao Yai, starts behind the visitors center and leads eight km to Haew Suwat Falls, where a paved road leads back to the visitors center. Trail 2 leads six km north from Trail 1 to an elephant salt lick near the main road. Trail 3 heads north from the campsite to the start of trails 1 and 2. Trail 4 heads south from the campsite to Pha Kluai Mai Falls and then back around to the secondary road.

Trail 5 from Haew Sawat Falls cuts through grasslands and emerges onto a spectacular view of Khao Laem Mountain. Trail 6 is a good beginner's trail that goes four km to Nong Phak Chi, a rebuilt wildlife observation tower north-

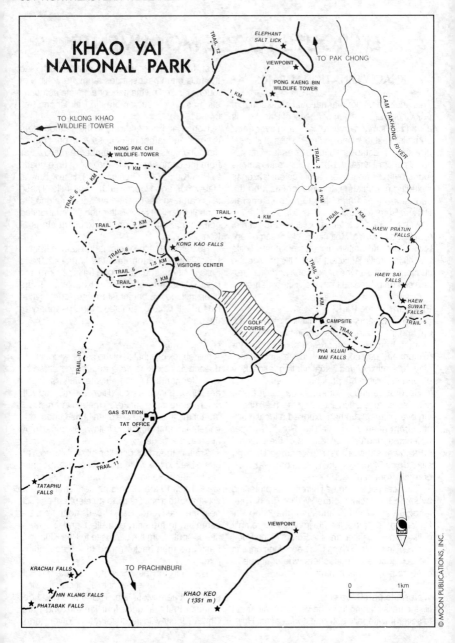

KHAO YAI NATIONAL PARK

ELEPHANT SALT LICK

TO PAK CHONG

VIEWPOINT

TRAIL 12

PONG KAENG BIN WILDLIFE TOWER

1 KM

LAM TAKHONG RIVER

TO KLONG KHAO WILDLIFE TOWER

NONG PAK CHI WILDLIFE TOWER

1 KM

TRAIL 6   5 KM

TRAIL 2   4 KM

TRAIL 7   3 KM

TRAIL 1   4 KM

TRAIL 1   4 KM

HAEW PRATUN FALLS

KONG KAO FALLS

TRAIL 8   1.5 KM

VISITORS CENTER

TRAIL 6   1 KM

TRAIL 9

TRAIL 3   4 KM

HAEW SAI FALLS

HAEW SUWAT FALLS

GOLF COURSE

CAMPSITE

TRAIL 4

TRAIL 5

PHA KLUAI MAI FALLS

TRAIL 10

GAS STATION

TAT OFFICE

TRAIL 11

TATAPHU FALLS

VIEWPOINT

KRACHAI FALLS

TO PRACHINBURI

HIN KLANG FALLS

PHATABAK FALLS

KHAO KEO (1351 m)

0   1km

MOON

© MOON PUBLICATIONS, INC.

west of the visitors center. Visitors are allowed to spend the night on the tower, but bring along all essentials including rain gear, warm clothes, sleeping bags, and flashlights.

Trail 6 starts at the Nong Pak Chi Wildlife Tower and winds south until it reconnects with the main road near the Visitors Center. Trail 7 provides a shortcut from Trail 6 back to the main road in the event you get exhausted during the sometimes tough trek. Trail 8 provides the same function but drops you on the main road closer to the Visitors Center. Trail 9 connects the main road with the intersection of trails 6, 8, and 10.

Trail 10 is a popular hike for visitors staying at the park lodge, while Trail 11 is an eight-km roundtrip hike that visits rivers, caves, and small waterfalls. Trail 12 is the southernmost trail and leads from the main road to a series of waterfalls including Hin Klang and Phatabak.

Wildlife

Wildlife inside the 2,168-square-km park includes wild elephants, a few remaining tigers, and birds such as hornbills and kingfishers. Larger animals such as leopards and Asiatic black bears are extremely shy and rarely seen; the birdlife and fascinating sounds of a tropical rainforest are ample rewards for most visitors.

Although unchecked logging and illegal poaching have sharply reduced indigenous wildlife, elephants and wild deer rummaging through trash dumpsters can sometimes be spotted on "Night Shining" truck drives, which are organized by the motor lodge. Aside from spending a night in a watchtower, night safaris provide the only chance to see wildlife.

Tours

The immensity of Khao Yai and the lack of organized transportation within the park boundaries make an organized tour a sensible idea.

Park Tours: Free day-tours sponsored by park rangers to various waterfalls and viewpoints leave daily around 0900 and 1300 from the visitors center.

Jungle Tours: Several guesthouses in the nearby town of Pak Chong organize both day and evening tours of the park at reasonable cost, though several travelers have written in to complain about the quality of their tours—especially a company known as Jungle Adventures Tours

that operates from the Jungle Guesthouse. Tour companies come and go with the seasons, but the current favorites appear to be Wildlife Safari, Khao Yai Wildlife Tours, and those starting from the Khao Yai Garden Lodge.

Park Accommodations

Within the park, you can camp out with a hired tent or crash on the floor in the park-operated dormitory bungalows.

Camping: Camping within the park boundaries costs 10B per person per night if you bring your own tent. Two-person tents can be rented from the ranger headquarters at 80B per night. Be sure to bring warm bedding such as several blankets or even a sleeping bag, plus be prepared for rainy weather.

Dormitory: Visitors can sleep on the floor inside the park headquarters dormitory for 20B per night. Bedding and blankets are not provided and not available for rent, so visitors must arrive prepared with adequate sleeping materials or face a very cold night.

Food: Simple meals are available from the ranger headquarters building.

Pak Chong Accommodations

Many travelers prefer to overnight in the nearby town of Pak Chong and make day excursions into the park, either as an independent visitor or with an organized tour.

Jungle Guesthouse: This small guesthouse in an alley due south of the stoplight provides decent accommodations, though their park tours should be avoided at all costs. 752/11 Chongwaksin Rd., tel. (044) 313836, 100-200B.

Phubade Hotel: Acceptable hotel with standard rooms in good shape with fan and private bath. 781/1 Thetsaban Rd. 15, tel. (044) 314964, 200-300B fan, 350-450B a/c.

Khao Yai Garden Lodge: Situated some eight km west of town in the direction of the turnoff for Khao Yai Park, this "garden lodge" owned and operated by a Thai-German couple is exactly that, with an amazing garden with hundreds of varieties of exotic orchids, along with budding examples of other local flora. Their organized tours of the park have been recommended by several readers. Take a bus west from Pak Chong or ask your bus driver coming from Bangkok to drop you at the entrance. Pak

Chong, Km 8, tel. (044) 313567, 100-300 basic rooms, 400-1,000B superior garden view.

Getting There

Khao Yai is 200 km northeast of Bangkok on the road to Nakhon Ratchasima.

Buses: Buses from Bangkok's Northern Bus Terminal to Pak Chom take three or four hours on the Friendship Highway, constructed during the Vietnam War by the Americans. Attractions en route include an immense white Buddha and cave complex on the right called Wat Theppitak, Lam Ta Klong Dam, souvenir stalls and experimental projects where Danish experts have established milk farms, a roadside Buddha surrounded by comical figurines, and several expensive hill resorts and golf courses catering to wealthy Thais and Japanese tourists. Khao Yai region has gone from untamed wilderness to condo hell.

The turnoff to Khao Yai is five km before Pak Chom. Since only limited bus service is available from Pak Chom, independent travelers should ask the bus driver to stop at the small Khao Yai signpost on the right side of the road, and then wait for a minitruck or hitchhike up to the park.

The TAT also organizes direct bus service from Bangkok to Khao Yai.

Pak Chom to Khao Yai: Light-blue trucks from Pak Chom to Khao Yai depart when they have enough passengers. Trucks go from the visitors center back to Pak Chom on weekdays at 0800, and weekends at 0800 and 1700. *Songtaos* from Pak Chom to Khao Yai are plentiful on weekends, but scarce during the week.

KORAT (NAKHON RATCHASIMA)

Korat, officially called Nakhon Ratchasima, is the region's largest city and gateway to the northeast. The modern town serves as a handy base from which to explore the nearby Khmer ruins and rest up after a long bus or train ride from Bangkok.

Korat was established during the reign of King Narai after he merged the twin cities of Sema and Khorapura. Evidence of the ancient city is limited to some reconstructed walls and an old moat.

The city enjoyed a brief heyday during the late 1960s and early 1970s when it served as a major base for U.S. forces assigned to the Vietnamese conflict. Legacies of this turbulent era include a handful of retired American veterans who gather for darts and cocktails in the VFW Cafe, massage parlors, nightclubs, and Turkish baths patronized almost exclusively by local Thais.

Suranari Statue

Modern Korat spreads around a statue honoring Thao Suranari, the national heroine who in 1826 convinced Korat women to seduce and then murder invading Laotian soldiers. A two-week festival held in March honors the patron saint of Korat. Her highly revered image—fashioned with a strange but once-chic haircut—is surrounded by stages for performances by itinerant musicians and local dancers.

Korat National Museum

The small Maha Viriwong Museum, in the compound of Wat Suthachinda, offers a very small but somewhat informative display of religious artifacts and archaeological discoveries from northeastern Thailand. Unfortunately, few of the objects are labeled in English, lighting is poor, and most of the pottery is hidden inside dusty glass cases. Among the better pieces are a standing Dvaravati image from Nonthai, Lopburi-style figures, "Buddhas in Abgumentation," and rare statues recovered from Wat Phanom Wan.

The museum is open Wed.-Sun. 0900-1600, admission 20B.

Wat Sala Loi

An unusual modern temple designed in the shape of a Chinese junk is located in the far northeastern end of town along the Lam Tha Khong River. Deviating from the strict geometrical style of traditional temples, Wat Sala Loi has won several modern architectural awards, including a prize from the Thai Architects Guild.

Markets

A great morning market operates in an alley one block west of the Thao Suranari statue. Less lively but worth visiting for cheap cassettes and foodstalls is the small night market on Manat Road just north of the Chomsurang Hotel.

Ban Dan Kwian

Unique pottery fashioned from iron-oxide-rich soil is produced in a small village 15 km south of Korat. Dan Kwian itself is nothing special except for the outstanding collection of antique carts displayed in the rear courtyard of the Village Museum owned by artist Viroj Srisuro, which deserve better treatment in a more accessible location than Dan Kwian.

Bus 1307 to Dan Kwian runs every 20 minutes from the ordinary bus terminal on Burin Lane, and from the south gate bus stop near the intersection of Chainarong and Kamheng Songkram Roads, a few blocks east of the Chomsurang Hotel.

Pak Thong Chai

Several of the most famous silk manufacturers in Thailand operate factories in the Pak Thong Chai, 32 km south of Korat on Hwy. 304. Shops to visit on Sripolratana Road include Srithai Silk and Praneet Thai Silk, though prices are somewhat steep and many of the garments are now produced with varying blends of polyester. A silk museum and cultural center managed by the Silk Weavers Association of Korat opened in 1992.

Bus 1303 to Pak Thong Chai leaves from the ordinary bus terminal on Burin Lane and from the Friendship Highway just opposite the TAT office.

Guesthouses

Korat Doctor's Guesthouse: Dr. Sunan's hostel is Korat's first spot geared for backpackers rather than tourists. The good doctor of Bangkok and his sister Sue (who spent 17 years in Chicago as a nurse) operate one of the friendliest places in the northeast, providing information on tours to nearby Khmer monuments, motorcycle rentals, laundry service, and transportation schedules. Visitors are invited to use their kitchen and crash in either the main house or the teakwood home a few doors away.

Doctor's Guesthouse is one block east of the TAT office and two km west of the train station, on the second lane on the right before the railway tracks. 78 Sueb Siri Rd., Soi 4, tel. (044) 255846, 100-160B fan, 250-350B a/c.

Ratana Guesthouse: Just a few minutes walk south of the doctor's guesthouse is another budget choice with very clean rooms in a two-story home. Soi Suksan 39, Sueb Siri Rd., tel. (044) 255883, 100-180B.

Budget Accommodations

Siri Hotel: Korat's most memorable hotel/pub is constantly filled with budget travelers, Vietnam vets, foreign-service employees, and American GIs doing temporary duty at the nearby Thai airbase. Large clean rooms are furnished with private bath. Notices warn "No lepers, prostitutes or mischievous persons allowed."

The downstairs VFW Restaurant has great Western food, sizzling T-bone steaks, and ice-cold beer—the best place to hang out and throw darts in Korat. 167 Poklang, tel. (044) 242831, 150-200B fan, 300-500B a/c.

Tokyo Hotels: The two hotels are just west of the central bus terminal. Despite the name, there's nothing Japanese about either operation, though the rooms are fairly clean and the location is quite convenient. Tokyo #1 is on the left side and #2 is on the right side about one block to the west. Tokyo #1, 329 Suranani Rd., tel. (044) 242873, fax (044) 257179, 150-250B fan, 300-450B a/c.

Moderate Accommodations

K Star Hotel: Popular with group tours, this old hotel features a nightclub that roars on weekends, and a traditional massage parlor. 191 Atsadang Rd., tel. (044) 242444, 220-280B fan, 350-500B a/c.

Far Thai Hotel: Clean, reasonably priced, and close to city center, but somewhat noisy from street traffic. 35 Poklang, tel. (044) 242533, 250-350B fan, 400-600B a/c.

Phokaphan Hotel: Just opposite the K Star is an older but decent hotel near the massage parlors and the Klang Plaza 1 shopping center. 104 Atsadang Rd., tel. (044) 242454, 220-380B fan, 350-500B a/c.

Chomsurang Hotel: Once the best in Korat, the Chomsurang has faded badly and no longer attracts Western visitors, despite the swimming pool, restaurant, and location near the night market. 547 Mahadthai Rd., tel. (044) 257088, 750-950B a/c.

Luxury Accommodations

Two hotels have opened since the collapse of the six-story Royal Plaza Hotel in August 1993.

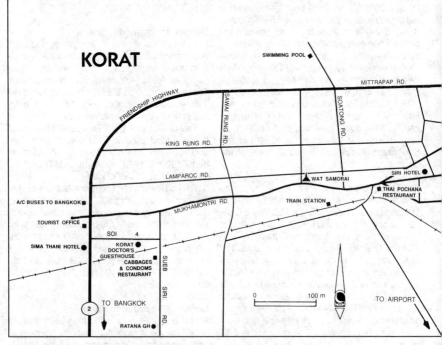

Sima Thani Hotel: Originally a Sheraton franchise but now a Thai-owned hotel, the Sima Thani features a swimming pool, health club, business center, and two restaurants. The inconvenient location, three km west of downtown and near the tourist office, matters little to their main clientele—business travelers and tour groups. Mittrapap Rd., tel. (044) 213100, fax (044) 213121, 2,000-3,200B.

Royal Princess Korat: Korat's newest luxury hotel is somewhat isolated in the northeastern corner of town, but as their brochure points out, "no traffic jam and greenery surrounding." Pool, tennis courts, business center, convention facilities (Korat Motor Show), and trendy Club Korat for disco types. 1137 Suranari Rd., tel. (044) 256629, fax (044) 256601, 2,200-3,500B.

Restaurants
Korat may be lacking in the hotel category, but the town compensates with a decent array of cafes and restaurants.

Night Market: Foodstalls are plentiful in the night market on Manat Road just north of the Chomsurang Hotel, and in the day market just west of the Thao Suranari Statue. Try the fresh fruit shakes and point-and-order foodstalls.

Klang Plaza 2: Western outlets such as Kentucky Fried Chicken and Dunkin Donuts may be found in the shopping complex on Chomsurang Road just south of city center.

VFW Cafe: Certainly the most curious restaurant in the northeast is the small, crowded cafe on the ground floor of the Siri Hotel. As the name implies, the cafe serves as headquarters for the Veterans of Foreign Wars (VFW) and is the gathering point for dozens of American veterans who served in the Vietnam conflict and then retired here in Korat. The air-conditioned cafe resembles an American truck stop and serves good burgers, beer, and T-bone steaks in three sizes. Recommended for a flashback to the sixties. Open daily 0800-2200. 167 Poklang Rd., tel. (044) 256522. Inexpensive.

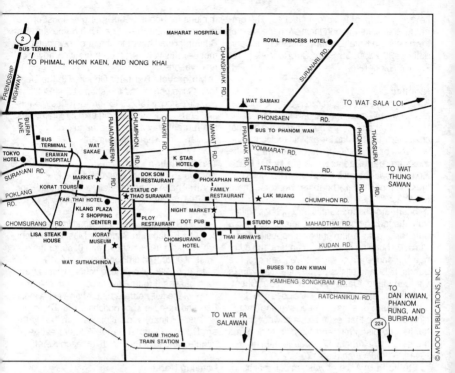

Family Restaurant: A clean and relatively new cafe decorated with artwork and wicker furniture, recommended for its a/c comfort and tasty Thai dishes. Open daily 1100-2300. 157 Chumphon Rd., tel. (044) 246291. Inexpensive.

Ploy Restaurant: Actually an a/c bakery with pastries and cakes plus a small menu for quick meals. Another welcome escape from the searing heat of Korat. Open daily 0800-2100. 220 Chumphon Rd., tel. (044) 242233. Inexpensive.

Dok Som Restaurant: Restaurant Row (Chumphon Road) has several popular places for Issan specialities, including this gaily decorated courtyard cafe complete with bamboo ferns and the ubiquitous Christmas lights. Nearby **Suak Pak** also has an English-language menu, plus Thai, Chinese, and Western dishes. Open daily 1000-midnight. 130 Chumphon Rd., tel. (044) 252020. Inexpensive.

Lisa Steak House: Another collection of restaurants, pubs, and nightclubs is located near the center of town on Chomsurang Road just opposite Klang Plaza 2 shopping center. Lisa is another one of those Thai garden cafes with crawling vines, rock-facade waterfall, and goldfish pond crawling with giant carp. Good food and more atmosphere than other joints in Korat. Open daily 1100-midnight. 199 Chomsurang Rd., tel. (044) 242279. Moderate.

Thai Pochana Restaurant: Heading west from the center of town are several restaurants that draw a steady stream of Thai diners but relatively few **farangs,** despite the low prices and unusual Issan specialities: spicy meat salads, marinated duck curries, and mysterious sauces so hot your eyes will melt for days. Order with caution. Open daily 1100-midnight. 142 Chomsurang Rd., tel. (044) 242557. Moderate.

Cabbages and Condoms: Another branch of the award-winning chain established a decade ago by Chamlong Srimuang and his center for population control. As with other C&C cafes, the place is spotless, and reasonably priced, and has a souvenir counter bursting with condom key rings and other prophylactics. Recommended despite the odd location in the west of town near the Korat Doctors Guesthouse. Open daily 0930-2200. 86 Sueb Siri Rd., tel. (044) 258100. Moderate.

Nightlife

Korat's most dubious attractions are the colossal nightclubs and massage parlors left over from the Vietnam War era. All are now patronized by Thai customers, but provide insight into the continuing world of Thai prostitution. The best of the lot—the massage parlor adjacent to the Royal Plaza Hotel—disappeared in 1993 when the hotel collapsed and killed 130 guests, workers, and a few Western visitors.

Scanners Disco: Korat's hot spot has shifted from the fading hotels in the center of town to a number of pubs and nightclubs opposite Klang Plaza 2 shopping complex. Scanners and other nearby venues are seedy but lively spots for live bands, DJs, and all the psychedelic flashbacks you can stand. Open daily 2000-0200. Chomsurang Rd. The cover charge includes one drink.

Dot Pub: For a less frenetic evening, try the old Thai house that resembles a cowboy bar inhabited by disco hits and blasting rock n' roll bands on weekends. 179 Mahadthai Rd., tel. (044) 251966. Open daily 1700-0200.

Studio Pub: Another western pub that cashes in on the Elvis craze with a nod to Michael Jackson and Liz Phair. Open daily 1800-0200. 66 Mahadthai Rd., tel. (044) 257631.

Thai Dancing: Traditional Thai dancing takes place in the Sima Thani Hotel near the tourist office in the western edge of town. Nightly during the tourist season from 1800-2200. Mittrapap Rd., tel. (044) 213100.

Practicalities

Tourist Information: The TAT office (tel. 044-213666, fax 044-213667) is inconveniently located at 2102 Mittrapap Rd. at the extreme west end of town, three km west of the train station and adjacent to the Sheraton Hotel. Take any bus heading west.

Travel Agencies: The single biggest failure of tourism in Korat is the lack of organized tours to the nearby Khmer monuments. None of the travel agencies offer scheduled tours for solo travelers, unless you are prepared to charter a

minibus for about 1,500B per day. Most of the travel agencies near the TAT office and on Buarong Road near the center of town cater almost exclusively to group tours with advance reservations.

Motorcycle Rentals: Check with the Doctor's Guesthouse and the shop at 554 Poklang Rd. Bikes cost 150-200B for 80-100cc models and 200-300B for 125cc dirt bikes. Motorcycles are a great way to visit the handicraft villages and far-flung Khmer monuments.

Transportation

Korat is 256 km northeast of Bangkok.

Air: Thai Airway flies daily from Bangkok for 650B. Thai Airways (tel. 044-257211) is at 14 Manat Rd.

Train: Thirteen trains a day depart from Hualampong train station in Bangkok. Most convenient are the rapid trains at 0615 and 0650, or the express at 0820. The ordinary diesels at 0910, 1105, 1145, and 2225 take six long hours. However, the train passes through lovely scenery, including views of the golf courses near Khao Yai National Park and the eerie white Buddha at Wat Theppitak.

Bus: Ordinary and a/c buses from the Northern Bus Terminal in Bangkok leave every 15 minutes and take four hours to reach Korat.

Leaving Korat

Train: Trains are the best way to travel around the northeast. A diesel train to Khon Kaen departs at 0807, while an express to Khon Kaen and Udon Thani leaves at 1226, 1515, and 0258. Seven trains a day leave for the eastern towns of Buriram, Surin, and Ubon Ratchathani. The most convenient departures are the 1130 rapid train, 1355 ordinary, and overnight services at 2350, 0155, 0402, and 0530.

Bus: Korat has an ordinary bus terminal in Burin Lane near the First Hotel and Erawan Hospital, and the a/c bus Terminal II on the Friendship Highway (Mittrapap Rd.) about 500 meters north of town.

The ordinary terminal has buses to nearby sights such as Ban Don Kwian and Phimai, plus major towns in the northeast such as Udon Thani and Nong Khai. It also serves Chiang Mai, Chiang Rai and Phitsanulok.

Bus Terminal II on Friendship Highway serves all major towns in the northeast.

BURIRAM

Although Buriram lacks many great attractions within the city boundaries, the town can serve as a base for exploring the numerous Khmer monuments located south along the Cambodian border.

Touring the Temples

Archaeologists have identified over 50 *prasats* in Buriram Province, of which almost a dozen have been restored by the Fine Arts Department. The only problem with touring Khmer architecture in the northeast is transportation. The TAT has attempted for over a decade to encourage tourism in the Issan, but few Westerners are prepared to deal with the challenges of public transportation.

As elsewhere in the world, tourism begins when budget travelers arrive and lay the foundation for group tourism. Budget guesthouses in this section of the northeast are still in their

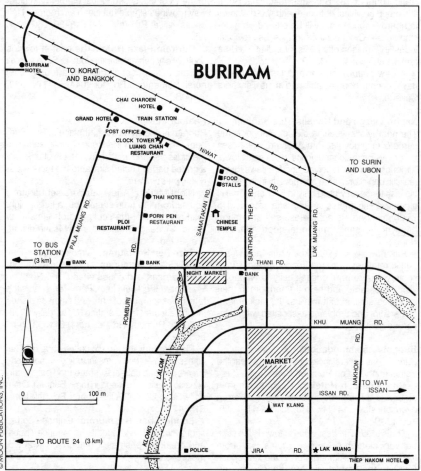

infancy, but it's encouraging to find new guesthouses in a few spots such as the Pirom Guesthouse in Surin.

For the moment, the only options for visiting the widely scattered monuments in the lower Issan are public transportation or the odd tour company that pops up with grandiose plans and then typically disappears after a few short years.

With those cautions in mind, you might check with the Buriram Teachers College, which has established a tour organization called Phanom Rung Tours at 131 Buriram-Prakonchai Rd. If this group survives, both one- and two-day tours to nearby monuments will be offered on a demand basis. Other contacts include the provincial tourist information office Miss Vondi at the Buriram Tour Guides.

A new cultural center and Issan Museum have recently been established at the Teachers College.

Napho Village and Novelist Pira Sudham

The nearby silk-weaving district, Napho, is the hometown of novelist Pira Sudham, who bases his novels on the changing life in the small town. Although Pira has received good reviews for his realistic depictions of life and poverty in the Issan, his insistence on writing only in English—Thai is a passive and imprecise language according to Sudham—and his shameless self promotion have made him a misunderstood native of Napho.

Pira now lives in Bangkok where he owns a public relations firm and heads the local wine society, but returns occasionally to Napho to visit his parents and help the farmers in their struggles against salt miners, the lack of land ownership, and problems associated with widespread gambling.

Budget Accommodations

Buriram has several inexpensive hotels near the train station and on Romburi Road.

Chai Charoen Hotel; Adjacent to the train station is a rough but acceptable spot for an overnight stay. 114 Niwat Rd., tel. (044) 611559, 100-120B.

Thai Hotel: The best value in town is the plain but very clean hotel a few minutes' walk from the train station. Although few of the staff speak English, the employees are friendly and the rooms are kept in spotless condition. 38 Romburi Rd., tel. (044) 611112, fax (044) 612461, 150-190B fan, 350-500B a/c.

Grand Hotel: Good location with reasonably priced but rather simple fan-cooled rooms, though the a/c units have private baths with hot showers. 137 Niwat Rd., tel. (044) 611179, 140-180B fan, 280-380B a/c.

Moderate Accommodations

Buriram Hotel: Buriram's original midlevel hotel to the west of city center just off the main highway provides simple but clean a/c rooms at fair prices. Niwat Rd., tel. (044) 613400, 650-800B a/c.

Buriram Plaza Hotel: The best in town is south of city center near the road to Surin with all the amenities associated with a tourist-level hotel. Suthenthep Rd., tel. (044) 611774, 900-1,400B.

Restaurants

Buriram is known as the birthplace of Pira Sudham—the author of *Monsoon Country* and *People of Issan*—and for its fiery version of *pok pok,* a grated papaya salad similar to the more widely known *som tam.*

Night Market: A few vendors set up stalls across from the train station, but a larger night market occurs at the south end of Samatakan Road. Chinese, Thai, and a few Issan dishes are served.

Porn Pen Restaurant: Almost a dozen Thai and Chinese restaurants, plus a few outdoor beer gardens and coffee shops, line Romburi Road near the Thai Hotel. Porn Pen serves the familiar assortment of Thai and Chinese dishes in a nicely decorated setting. Open daily 0900-2200. 36 Romburi Rd., tel. (044) 611553. Inexpensive.

Ploi Restaurant: An a/c coffee shop for Thai dishes and Western items including hamburgers, ice cream, and cakes. Average food but the air-conditioning is a godsend in torrid Buriram. Open daily 0700-2200. 37/1 Romburi Rd., tel. (044) 613747. Inexpensive.

Luang Chan Restaurant: Chinese coffee shop popular for its noodle dishes, rice soups, and breakfast pastries. Romburi at Niwat Rd. Inexpensive.

Practicalities

Most of the services are near the train station or on Thani Road.

Post Office and International Telephone: The GPO (tel. 044/611142) at 55 Niwat Rd. is open weekdays 0830-1630 and weekends 0900-1200. The overseas phone center on the second floor is open daily 0700-2200.

Banks: Exchange services are provided by Bangkok Bank at the intersection of Thani and Sunthorn Thep Roads, and by Thai Farmers Bank in the center of town.

Buriram Hospital: The city hospital is outside town in the Phuttaisong District. 197 Phuttaisong Rd., tel. (044) 614100, fax (044) 614110.

Shopping: As with many other towns in the northeast, Buriram produces some of Thailand's best silk and cotton products. The industry is centered in the Phuttaisong and Napho Districts.

Transportation

Buriram is 410 km northeast of Bangkok and 151 km east of Korat.

Air: The Buriram airport scheduled to open a few years ago has been delayed and probably won't be completed until Bangkok Airways raises enough capital to finance the project.

Train: Buriram is connected with Bangkok via Saraburi and Korat. Nine trains run daily from Bangkok. An express train with sleepers departs at 2100 and arrives at 0335. Rapid trains without sleepers leave at 0650, 1845, and 2245. Rapid trains leave Korat at 1136 and 2356.

Bus: Buses leave every 15 minutes from Bangkok's northern bus terminal and take seven hours to reach Buriram. Air-conditioned buses leave Bangkok 1900-2130. Buses leave Korat every 30 minutes 0500-1900 and take three hours to reach Buriram.

The Buriram bus terminal is on Thani Road, three km west of city center. Pink *songtaos* head into town and drop you near the Thai Hotel.

SURIN

Most visitors associate Surin with its famed Elephant Fair, held on the third weekend in November. Though the elephant festival is certainly the highlight, Surin is well located near several Khmer temples and serves as a base for visits to an elephant camp, basketry and silk-weaving villages and, with special permission, a Cambodian refugee camp.

Surin is probably the single best northeastern base from which to explore the Khmer monuments scattered along the Cambodian border.

Elephant Festival

Perhaps the most internationally famous festival in Thailand, Surin's annual week-long Elephant Fair is something like the Super Bowl but without the bowl, beer, or football. The madness starts with an elephant roundup and mass procession of over 200 elephants into the Surin Sports Park. Next is a Rocket Festival, followed by a two-hour spectacle of elephants at work, elephants dancing, elephants racing, elephant soccer, elephant war parade, and elephant tug-of-war with 70 men. The elephant always wins. Afterward, the elephants wander around town and give rides to tourists.

Hotel reservations should be made months in advance. Tours with transportation and accommodations can be booked through the TAT and several tour operators in Bangkok.

Tha Klang Elephant Village

City ordinances prohibit Surin citizens from keeping elephants as house pets, so most elephants live outside town where they are trained for exciting careers in log rolling and entertaining wealthy tourists. Several dozen elephants reside in the town of Tha Klang, 58 km north of Surin, where they are trained by descendants of the Suay peoples, Cambodians who have traditionally been elephant hunters since the Ayuthaya Empire.

Avoid visiting Tha Klang during the day, when most of the elephants are out working in the nearby fields and rivers. The only way to learn about the dying art of Thai elephant management is with an overnight homestay arranged by Mr. Pirom at Pirom Guesthouse in Surin.

Silk-weaving Villages

Two villages which specialize in traditional silk production and weaving are located within 20 km of Surin. Khawao Sinarin, north of Surin on Hwy. 214, and Ban Chanron, east of town on Hwy. 2077, both produce and sell hand-woven silks.

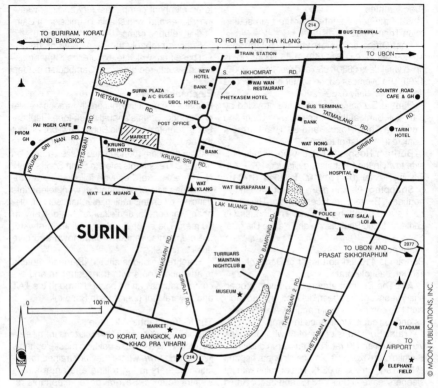

Public transportation is available, or hire a car from Gopchai Rentals on Tesaban I Rd. Rental cars without gas cost 1,200-1,800B daily.

Butom Basket Village
Located 12 km east of Surin and slightly off Hwy. 226, Ban Butom is a small village where many of the residents weave tightly woven baskets adorned with intricate designs. People from Bangkok come to Butom for their baskets, which cost under 100B for even the most extravagant pieces.

Prasat Sikhoraphum
Thirty km east of Surin near the town of Sikhoraphum is an 11th-century Khmer *prasat* recently restored by the Fine Arts Department with mixed results due to the modern cements and mismatched stones that have been inserted into broken segments of the monument.

The sanctuary consists of five brick *prangs* surrounded by moats and studded with lintels carved with scenes from Hindu mythology. Of particular note is the Shiva lintel over the central *prang* and guardian angels and floral patterns surrounding the door jambs and window enclosures.

Prasat Sikhoraphum was erected to honor the Hindu gods of the Khmer dynasties, but was converted in the 16th century into a Lao Buddhist temple, which explains the hybrid architecture and sculptural elements. The original layout still reflects classic Khmer arrangements of massive brick towers enclosed by a protective moat that symbolizes the outer limits of Hindu cosmology. The arrangement is reminiscent of Angkor Wat and smaller monuments in Sukothai and Lopburi.

Buses from Surin take about an hour to reach the signposted road to Prasat Sikhoraphum.

Prasat Pluang

Thirty km south of Surin near the silk-weaving village of Ban Pluang is a well-restored *prasat* raised up on a high laterite base. Constructed in the late 11th century during the reign of King Suriyavoraman, the monument reflects Baphuon style in both the layout and carved decorations.

As with other major Khmer monuments in the Issan, Prasat Pluang stands on the royal road which once connected Angkor with Phimai. The pond, carvings, and remnants of the old moat that surround the sandstone-and-laterite *prang* are Baphuon features repeated from Angkor to their military outposts in modern-day Thailand.

Hindu mythology and traditions are also reflected on the east-facing lintel elegantly carved with Indra riding his elephant Ganesh, and another door overpiece embellished with Krishna lifting a bull by the horns.

Recent excavations by the Fine Arts Department indicate that the Hindu monument was abandoned prior to completion; two unfinished *naga* cornices were uncovered on the grounds.

Prasat Pluang is fairly easy to reach. Take a bus or *songtao* south from Surin down Route 214 to Prasat on Route 24. Another *songtao* continues two more km south to the signposted turnoff to the ruins. The monument is 500 meters off the main road.

Prasat Ta Muan

Three clusters of opened Khmer ruins are located exactly on the Thai-Cambodian border, some 55 km due south of Surin and quite close to the ruins of Muang Tam and Phanom Rung. The border region is still monitored by the Thai military, which operates checkpoints near the towns of Ban Ta Miang and Ban Ampin.

The scale of imagination and wealth of decoration improves as you proceed south along the winding road skirting the Cambodian border.

Prasat Ta Muan: The first site was constructed during the reign of Khmer King Jayavarman VII in the late 12th century as a religious reliquary and resting point for traveling pilgrims. Prasat Ta Muan is a minor monument constructed of laterite blocks forming eight windows and a pair of imposing entrances. Only the lintel over the rear door remains intact; the others have disappeared into rubble or been sold to Western art collectors.

Prasat Ta Muan Toi: The second monument, about 500 meters south of Prasat Ta Muan, was constructed with a square *stupa* and laterite *prang* similar to Prasat Pluang to the north.

Prasat Ta Muan Thom: Also erected during the reign of Jayavarman VII, Prasat Ta Muan Thom is the most impressive monument of the Khmer trio. About 10 km from the preceding *prasats,* the wild and romantic structure features an impressive 30-meter staircase leading down into Cambodian territory, a central sanctuary surrounded by crumbling laterite walls, and minor *prangs* now being swallowed by encroaching banyan trees.

The effect is overwhelming. In a remote and volatile region near the border of Cambodia, these collapsed yet impressive castles convey the power and majesty of ancient Khmer far better than the over-restored and homogenized historical parks at Sukothai and Ayuthaya. As you arrive, Thai soldiers crawl out of their tents armed with automatic weapons and hand grenades. Nobody speaks English, but they carefully guide you through the sites, pointing out landmines that remain buried and uncleared from the region. Banyan vines and creeping tentacles block your path as your slowly step around the decay. Brush fires burn to keep the stones from being completely swallowed by jungle vegetation. Birds cry overhead. Gunfire rings in the distance.

Budget Accommodations

Hotels in Surin are fully booked and charge a 50% premium during the Elephant Fair in late November.

Pirom's Guesthouse: The backpackers' hotel scene in Surin improved dramatically several years ago with the opening of this guesthouse, two blocks west of the market and 500 meters from the bus terminal and train station. Mr. Pirom has converted his six-room teakwood house into a very cozy place with the best travel information in the province. Pirom speaks excellent English and conducts daily excursions to the elephant village and Khmer ruins near the Cambodian border. 272 Krung Sri Rd., tel. (045) 51540, 80-150B.

Country Roads Cafe & Guesthouse (Ron's): Another good retreat is the tiny, three room guesthouse managed by Ron the Texan and his lovely Thai wife. Ron spends most of his time working his cafe/pub across the street, but the guesthouse is perfect for travelers who need a familiar touch in the sometimes dreary northeast. Fan-cooled rooms, hot showers, overseas telephone, fax services, advice, and videos courtesy of Ron's satellite dish. 165/1 Sirirat Rd., tel. (045) 515721, 100-150B.

Moderate Accommodations

Memorial Hotel: A clean and fairly inexpensive hotel well located in the center of town near the temples and restaurants. 186 Lak Muang Rd., tel. (045) 511288, 250-320B fan, 380-550B a/c.

Tarin Hotel: Top hotel in town, a few blocks from the city center, with swimming pool, 24-hour coffee shop and nightclub, snooker hall, and "cosmic atmosphere at Hi-Tech Discotheque, Surin's favorite disco for swingers." 60 Sirirat Rd., tel. (045) 514281, fax (045) 511580, 900-1,400B.

Restaurants

Surin has some simple cafes for great Issan cooking, a night market for quick bites, and a Texan cafe for the homesick American traveler.

Night Markets: Streetstalls set up each evening just opposite the train station and at the municipal market on Krung Sri Nan Road. The latter is larger.

Pai Ngen Cafe: Just 100 meters up the road from Pirom Guesthouse is a simple cafe known for its Thai and Issan specialities such as *laap* and *nua nam doang*. Open daily 1800-midnight. Soi Poi Tanko, Krung Sri Nai Rd., tel. (045) 512151. Inexpensive to moderate.

Country Road Cafe: Ron and his wife (see above) run this attractive open-air cafe serving great burgers, pizzas, and simple Thai dishes to a steady stream of enlightened travelers and local *farang* expatriates. The best place in Surin for an evening of dining and drinking. Open daily 1000-0200. 165/1 Sirirat Rd., tel. (045) 515721. Moderate.

Wai Wan Restaurant: A less satisfying alternative to the Country Road for steaks, pizzas, and burgers in a darkened room decorated with Western artwork. The chief advantage is the air-conditioning. Open daily 1000-2200. 44-46 Santi Nikhomrat Rd., tel. (045) 611614. Moderate.

Turruars Maintain Nightclub: Live bands, bar food, and psychedelic decor in the cowboy pool hall in the south end of town. A madly decorated paean to all forms of kitsch and foreign culture. Open daily 1800-0300; bands start around 2100. 28 Krung Sri Noak Road.

Practicalities

Tourist Information: Khun Pirom, art historian and government social worker, is a gold mine of information on nearby attractions and can help with rural homestays and silk-weaving villages. Ron at Country Road Cafe and Warren Olson, general manager of the Tarin Hotel, can also help with travel advice.

Banks: Bangkok Bank on Thanasarn Road and Siam Commercial Bank on Chao Bamrung Road provide currency exchange weekdays 0830-1530.

Post Office: The post office at the traffic circle provides postal services weekdays 0830-1630 and weekends 0900-1200. International calls can be made from their telecommunications center daily 0700-2200.

Hospital: English-speaking doctors and reliable medical facilities are available at the government-operated Surin Hospital (tel. 045-511006) on Lak Muang Road and the private Ruam Paet Hospital (tel. 045-513192) on Thetsaban 1 Rd.

Swimming Pool: Visitors to Surin are welcome to use the pool at the Tarin Hotel for 30B per day.

Shopping: Surin's newest and largest shopping center, **Surin Plaza** has air-conditioned shops selling imported goods and regional handicrafts, plus several restaurants and coffee shops.

Transportation

Surin is 457 km northeast of Bangkok and 198 km east of Korat.

Train: Surin is connected by rail with Bangkok via Korat and Buriram. Seven trains leave Bangkok daily. An express train with sleepers departs at 2100 and arrives eight hours later in Surin. Rapid trains without sleepers leave at 0650, 1845, and 2245 and take nine hours. Rapid trains leave Korat at 1136 and 2356.

Bus: Buses leave every 15 minutes from the Northern Bus Terminal in Bangkok and take 10 hours to reach Surin. Air-conditioned buses leave Bangkok 1900-2130. Buses leave seven times daily from Korat and take three hours to reach Surin.

KHMER MONUMENTS

PHIMAI

Southeast Asia's finest Khmer *prasats* (stone sanctuaries) outside Cambodia lie scattered across the dry plains near Korat. The Khmers, once a powerful empire which controlled much of Southeast Asia, erected dozens of magnificent temples and military fortresses from the 10th to 13th centuries along a royal highway which once stretched from their capital at Angkor to the borders of Myanmar. Although the Hindu-Buddhist monarchy fell to foreign invaders in 1431, their expansive monuments still bear witness to their artistic vision and primeval sense of grandeur.

Phimai is an easy day-trip from Korat, but the remainder of the monuments in the northeast are widely scattered and difficult to reach without an organized tour or hired transportation. The Siam Society, National Museum, and major tour operators in Bangkok occasionally sponsor group excursions which include transportation and accommodations. Large groups can also contact the travel agents and first-class hotels in Korat.

Prasat Hin Phimai

Thailand's most accessible stone castle is 60 km north of Korat, a short distance off the Friendship Highway. Phimai itself is a very old site where Neolithic artifacts and jewelry have been unearthed by archaeologists. Scholars believe the main sanctuary was constructed during the reign of King Surayavarman I, who ruled the Khmer empire from 1002 to 1050, with later additions by King Jayavarman, who ruled from 1181 to 1220. Contemporary with (and perhaps the model for) Angkor Wat, this vassal outpost and religious enclave was abandoned in the 15th century after the collapse of the Khmer Empire.

In subsequent centuries, Phimai was extensively rebuilt by Thai architects who added Mahayana Buddhist imagery and Buddhist figures over the original Hindu sculpture. The sandstone complex fell into ruin but was magnificently restored several decades ago by the Thai Fine Arts Department and Bernard Groslier, former director of restoration at Angkor, who wisely insisted the stuccowork be left in original condition.

Outside the walls and to the left stand the remains of Klang Ngoen, a royal pavilion once serving as a rest house for important pilgrims. Entrance is across a *naga* balustrade and through a southern *gopura* gateway. Connecting the gateway and gallery is an enclosed passageway which perhaps served as a model for the sanctuaries at Angkor Wat.

Situated in the vast surrounding lawns are five ponds dating from the Ayuthaya Period, and two ancient libraries that once held religious texts and a collection of 30 Buddha images. The central sanctuary is surrounded by another gallery bisected by four arches flanked by stone-barred windows—one of the more distinctive features of Khmer architecture.

Several structures are located inside the central patio. Prang Meru Boromathat on the right was probably constructed by King Jayavarman VII (1181-1220) and features an unfinished lintel depicting Buddha in the preaching pose. To the left is a red stone *prang* and Brahman shrine once used for Hindu religious rites.

Dominating the center of the lawn is a cruciform central sanctuary magnificently carved with elaborate doorways and Ramayana lintels, considered among the finest examples of Khmer stonework in Thailand. The southern pediment shows Shiva dancing to prevent the destruction of the world, while the western carvings depict Krishna lifting Mt. Govadhana and Rama bound by serpentine arrows. The northern pediment shows a battle scene from the *Ramayana* and Vishnu with his conch, lotus, club, and disc in his four hands.

As with other Cambodian prototypes, the central *prang* symbolizes Mt. Meru—the holy mountain and heavenly city of Lord Brahma—while the seven major levels and 33 lesser tiers of the *prangs* represent the levels of perfection necessary for nirvana.

Phimai's perfect symmetry and wealth of sculptural detail make it a must-see for all visitors interested in the ancient monuments of the northeast.

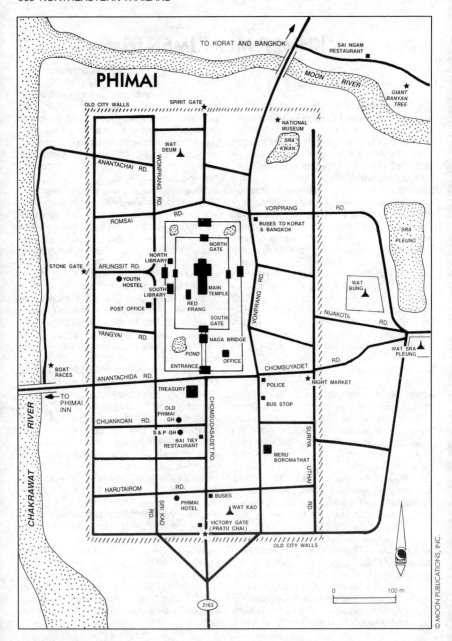

PHIMAI

TO KORAT AND BANGKOK

SAI NGAM RESTAURANT

MOON RIVER

GIANT BANYAN TREE

OLD CITY WALLS

SPIRIT GATE

NATIONAL MUSEUM

SRA KWAN

WAT DEUM

ANANTACHAI RD.

WONPRANG RD.

VORPRANG RD.

ROMSAI RD.

BUSES TO KORAT & BANGKOK

SRA PLEUNG

STONE GATE

ARUNGSIT RD.

NORTH LIBRARY

NORTH GATE

YOUTH HOSTEL

SOUTH LIBRARY

MAIN TEMPLE

WAT BUNG

RED PRANG

POST OFFICE

SOUTH GATE

VONPRANG RD.

NIJAKOTA RD.

YANGYAI RD.

POND

NAGA BRIDGE

OFFICE

WAT SRA PLEUNG

BOAT RACES

ENTRANCE

CHOMSUYADET RD.

ANANTACHIDA RD.

TO PHIMAI INN

TREASURY

POLICE

NIGHT MARKET

PHIMAI RIVER

CHUANKOAN RD.

OLD PHIMAI GH

BUS STOP

S & P GH

BAI TIEY RESTAURANT

CHOMSUDASADET RD.

MERU BOROMATHAT

SURIYA RD.

CHAKRAWAT

HARUTAIROM RD.

UTHAI RD.

PHIMAI HOTEL

BUSES

WAT KAO

SRI KAO RD.

VICTORY GATE (PRATU CHAI)

OLD CITY WALLS

0   100 m

2163

© MOON PUBLICATIONS, INC.

Phimai Museum
An open-air museum at the north end of town safeguards many of the more valuable and well-carved lintels taken from Prasat Phimai and other Khmer temples at Si Saket and Korat. The quality of sculpture makes this an important stop in Phimai. A modern addition, opened in 1995, features the best of northeastern sculpture. Open Wed.-Sun. 0900-1600, admission 20B.

Big Banyan Tree
One kilometer northeast of town, a gigantic banyan tree *(Ficus bengalensis)* spreads its branches. Under the limbs of the largest banyan tree in Thailand are Chinese fortune-tellers, food vendors who prepare a local noodle dish called *mee phimai,* and the Sai Ngam Restaurant, popular with group tours.

Accommodations
Phimai is a fairly pleasant place to spend a night before heading north to Nong Khai.

Old Phimai Guesthouse: Two blocks from the historic monument is a teakwood house with large, clean rooms, hot showers, roof garden, maps, and bicycle rentals. 214 Moo 1 Chomsudasadet Rd., tel. (044) 471918, 80-180B fan, 280-350B a/c.

S & P New Phimai Guesthouse: If the Old Phimai is filled, walk across the street and check their competitor for similar rooms at similar prices. 215 Moo 1 Chomsudasadet Rd., tel. (044) 471992, 80-120B.

Phimai Hotel: South of the ruins is a slightly more upscale but far less useful hotel largely ignored by most visitors to this town. 305 Haruthairom Rd., tel. (044) 471689, fax (044) 471940, 80-180B fan, 220-350B a/c.

Phimai Inn: The best in town is nothing spectacular and somewhat isolated, about two km south of town, but all rooms are a/c and very clean. The hotel has bicycles for guests. Highway 206, tel. (044) 471175, 300-350B fan, 400-550B a/c.

Restaurants
Bai Tiey Restaurant is the most popular restaurant in the center of town. **Issan Restaurant** around the corner and down the alley specializes in local dishes. Out-of-town favorites include the **Rim Moon Restaurant** on the banks of the Moon River, and **Sai Ngam Restaurant** near the giant banyan tree.

Practicalities
Tourist information is available from the Bai Tiey Restaurant just south of the temple entrance. Bicycles can be rented from Old Phimai Guesthouse and Phimai Bikes at the ruins and Bai Tiey Restaurant. The three banks in Phimai change money during standard weekday hours. English-language volunteers are always welcome at Taoruranaree primary school some 200 meters from the main highway.

A popular boat race and a cultural festival are held in late October or early November.

Transportation
Buses to Phimai from Korat leave hourly from the ordinary bus station on Burin Lane behind the Erawan Hospital. The last bus back to Korat departs at 1800.

PRASAT PHANOM WAN

This small but attractive Khmer temple, set in an evocative and tranquil setting 20 km northeast of Korat, can be visited in conjunction with Phimai. Originally built as a Hindu temple by King Suryavarman I, the 10th-century *phanom* (hill) sanctuary follows the standard layout of a courtyard dominated by a central *prang* surrounded by four smaller towers. The temple has a number of Buddha statues still honored by a community of monks, and a finely carved lintel above the north entrance of the main sanctuary. The Fine Arts Department intends to dismantle and reconstruct the decaying complex in the near future.

Hanuman

Prasat Phanom Wan is somewhat difficult to reach, but worth a side trip for visitors seriously interested in Khmer architecture.

Transportation

Direct buses leave at 0700, 1000, and 1200 from Pratu Phonsean, a city gate near Wat Samakkhi in Korat. Alternatively, take a bus bound for Korat and ask the driver to let you off at Ban Long Thong, 11 km from Korat, from where you can walk or hitch a *songtao* ride the remaining six km.

En route to Phanom Wan is the small village of Ban Makam, where craftspeople specialize in the production of handmade knives.

PRASAT PHANOM RUNG

The most spectacular Khmer monument in Thailand is Prasat Phanom Rung, 132 km southeast of Korat and 50 km south of Buriram.

Prasat Phanom Rung ("Temple of the Great Mountain") is splendidly situated on the southern ridge of an extinct volcano that dominates the surrounding countryside and provides views toward Angkor and the Dongrak Mountains, which demarcate the present border between Thailand and Cambodia. Typical of most Khmer architecture and Hindu temple orientation, Phanom Rung faces the east, toward the dawn and the original capital at Angkor.

The political and military significance of Phanom Rung derives from its strategic location just above the Khmer highway that once connected Angkor with Phimai on the Korat Plateau. More importantly, the Hindu traditions of ancient geomancy teach that mountains are ideal sites for religious monuments since they touch the heavens and symbolize Mt. Meru, the highest mountain in Hindu cosmology.

History

Historians believe the hill originally served as a retreat for a community of Hindu *rishis* until the 12th century, when a local Khmer ruler named Prince Narendratitya began construction of the principal sanctuary. Narendratitya was a contemporary and relative of King Suryavarman II (1112-50), the famous Khmer ruler who constructed the complex of Angkor Wat. Local inscriptions suggest Narendratitya was ordained as a yogi after the birth of his son, Hiranya, who continued construction of the sanctuary and added the yogi figures now seen on the temple walls. The sanctuary was never completed, though additions continued into the reign of Jayavarman VII.

Khmer power waned in the 13th century and the empire finally collapsed in 1431 with the sack of Angkor by the Thai. Prasat Phanom Rung was abandoned and fell into ruin until 1972, when the Fine Arts Department initiated a massive reconstruction effort, finally completed on 21 May 1988. The restoration project employed the anastylosis method, in which every building was systematically dismantled and rebuilt on a ferroconcrete base and fashioned around a superstructure of ferroconcrete walls and beams. The massive and difficult project took almost 17 years but resulted in the most impressive singular monument in Thailand.

The Sanctuary

White Elephant Hall: Entrance to the complex begins 400 meters east of the central complex, where three earthen terraces lead up to a large cruciform platform. To the north stands a small, ruined, sandstone-and-laterite structure called the White Elephant Hall, once used for Hindu religious ceremonies.

Royal Promenade: Immediately ahead stretches one of the most remarkable design elements of Phanom Rung, a 160-meter promenade and monumental staircase flanked by ruined *nagas* which symbolically transport the visitor from the earthly realm to the world of the gods.

Naga **Bridges:** Bordered by 68 sandstone pillars carved in early Angkor style, the ceremonial avenue leads down to an extremely unusual *naga* bridge at the foot of the monumental staircase. The cruciform bridge is guarded by 16 five-headed *nagas* carved in Angkor style with Hindu Wheels of the Universe embedded on both sides.

Monumental Staircase: Beyond the *naga* bridge towers a staircase whose massive dimensions reflect the power and drama typical of Khmer design.

East *Gopura:* At the top of the staircase are four rectangular pools arranged symmetrically in front of a second *naga* bridge, and the eastern

Prasat Phanom Rung

TICKETS

EARTHEN TERRACES

PLATFORM

WHITE ELEPHANT HALL

PRASAT PHANOM RUNG

ROYAL PROMENADE

NAGA BRIDGE

MONUMENTAL STAIRCASE

0   50m

POOLS

NAGA BRIDGE

EAST GOPURA

NARAI LINTEL

PRANG

VIHARNS

NORTH GOPURA

MONDOP

SOUTH GOPURA

PRASAT

PRANG NOI

GALLERY

WEST GOPURA

© MOON PUBLICATIONS, INC.

gopura entrance whose perfect alignment characterizes the geometric precision of Angkor architecture. Particular attention should be given to the lintels and pediments elevated over the gopuras at the four cardinal points. Carved above the eastern gopura is an image of Shiva Mahayogi, patron of all ascetics, while other iconography related to both Shiva-ite and Vaishnavite deities can be seen on other gopuras and the curvilinear galleries surrounding the complex. Art historians consider Phanom Rung sculpture and craftsmanship the pinnacle of Khmer artistic achievement, comparable only to the murals and tableaux at Angkor Wat.

Narai Lintel: Immediately through the east gopura is a third naga bridge followed by the most famous piece of sculpture at Phanom Rung—and perhaps the most controversial work of art in Thailand. Elevated above the eastern portico to the central mondop is the infamous Narai Lintel, a stone slab which depicts a reclining Lord Narai (more commonly known as Vishnu) asleep on the Milky Sea of Eternity as represented by a naga snake. Narai is shown elaborately dressed with his right hand supporting his head, while his other hand embraces a baton, conch shell, and discus. Emerging from his navel is a lotus stem that blossoms into many stems, one of which depicts the newborn Brahma and the Hindu creation of the world. Seated at his feet are his consort, Lakshmi, surrounded by Kala, the god of time and death, and other figures of garudas, nagas, parrots, elephants, and monkeys. The Narai Lintel establishes the importance of the Shivaite religion at Phanom Rung, and cosmically represents the Vaishnavite myth of creation.

Directly above the Narai Lintel is a sandstone depiction of Shiva Nataraja, lord of the dance, carved in late Baphuon or early Angkor style. The extremely sensual and smooth-limbed image beautifully illustrates the cosmic dance of Shiva, which sustains but ultimately destroys the universe. The juxtaposition of these two creation myths—Shiva dancing and Vishnu sleeping on the cosmic ocean—is rarely encountered in the Hindu art of Southeast Asia.

Central Prasat: Dominating the center of the temple complex is a towering prasat festooned with ornately carved Shivas, charging elephants, shapely Khmer dancers, and images of Hindu

CONTROVERSY IN STONE

One of the most controversial events in the world of archaeology erupted in the late 1980s over the Narai Lintel, which now graces the top of the east *gopura* at Prasat Phanom Rung. According to local authorities, the sandstone slab was last seen at the temple complex in 1960, when a curator from the Fine Arts Department photographed the broken lintel where it had fallen at the base of the doorway. Art robbers subsequently hauled the lintel to Bangkok, where it was sold on the open market in 1966 to an art collector from New York. In 1967, the 75- by 150-cm carving was purchased by the Chicago-based Alsadorf Foundation, which donated it to the Art Institute of Chicago. In 1976, Professor Diskul of Silpakorn University spotted the lintel in the Art Institute and reported his discovery to the Thai Ministry of Foreign Affairs.

In February 1988 the Thai government demanded the return of the lintel to its rightful place; it had been on display 21 years at the Art Institute of Chicago. Backed by a broad array of politicians, journalists, and residents of Buriram Province, an unprecedented international effort was mounted to recover the stolen artifact. The Fine Arts Department erected a sign at Phanom Rung announcing that the stolen lintel was on display in Chicago. Bangkok newspapers published provocative advertisements which claimed the missing lintel was removed with the use of American military equipment and quickly spirited abroad because of special privileges enjoyed by the U.S. forces. Thai residents and American citizens demonstrated at the Art Institute of Chicago, while the socially conscious Thai rock group Carabao recorded a popular song demanding, "Take back Michael Jackson—Give us back the Pra Narai!" Never before had the government and citizens of Thailand been so united about preserving their artistic and cultural treasures.

The Art Institute of Chicago initially suggested an exchange of a comparable work of equal artistic merit to replace the Narai Lintel. After a series of discussions, a Chicago-based philanthropic group offered to donate comparable Thai artwork to the institute to help resolve the negotiations, which had broken off in July 1988. The campaign failed to restore the lintel in time for the official Phanom Rung opening in May 1988, but did raise the level of artistic consciousness among Thais. The Narai Lintel was restored to its original home in 1989.

Narai Lintel

rishis. Among the highlights are the pediment and lintel at the west portico, which illustrates the battle of Sri Lanka as described in the famous Ramayana epic, a triumphant procession of warriors and elephants on the north and south faces, and motifs of the five yogis on the lintels at the east and south entrances. Interior details include several Khmer statues and a Hindu lingam on which temple priests once poured holy waters and placed offerings of garlands and fruit.

Prang Noi: In the southwest corner of the courtyard is a small square chapel dating from the reign of Suryavarman I and covered with remarkable decoration in the style of Angkor Wat.

Prasat Phanom Rung is open daily 0900-1700, admission 20B.

Transportation

Phanom Rung can be reached from Korat, Surin, and Buriram, though Buriram is the most convenient access point. Nang Rong (see below) is the closest town.

From Korat: Public transportation from Korat takes several hours and an extremely early start is necessary to return before nightfall. Buses leave for Surin from terminal 1 on Burin Lane every 30 minutes starting at 0500. Take bus #274 and ask the driver to let you off at Ban Tako, 15 km east of the larger town of Nang Rong and 12 km north of Phanom Rung. A large sign points the way to both monuments. The 132-km journey from Korat to Ban Tako takes about three hours.

From Ban Tako, you can take a *songtao* or charter a motorcycle taxi to the monuments. Motorcycle jockeys charge 150-200B for the roundtrip tour to both monuments. Pay the driver as each segment is completed, or you might be abandoned by an impatient chauffeur.

A cheaper option is to wait for a *songtao* heading south in the direction of Phanom Rung. *Songtaos* either go the base of Phanom Rung for 15B or continue past the turnoff and continue south to Lahan Sai; be sure to get on a *songtao* going all the way to the monument.

Another option is to bypass Ban Tako and stay on the bus for another km to the larger town of Tapek. Here you can charter a *songtao* or motorcycle from the police station at the three-way intersection.

From Surin: Same routing as from Korat. Take bus 274 and either get off in Tapek or continue another kilometer to the Phanom Rung turnoff at Ban Tako.

From Buriram: First, head out to the Buriram bus terminal on Hani Road at the west end of town, about three km from city center and the train station. Take bus 273 from Platform 11 toward Aranyaprathet and Chanthaburi, and tell the bus driver you are going to Tapek. The bus goes southwest down Hwy. 218 and reaches Nang Rong in about 90 minutes, where it stops and waits to pick up additional passengers. Stay on the bus until it reaches Ba Tako, where you can then take public *songtaos* and motorcycle taxis, or Tapek, where motorcycle taxis and chartered *songtaos* are available to take you the rest of the way.

Tours

The lack of visitors in the northeast makes it difficult for any tour company to offer scheduled tours to the Khmer monuments. Tour companies in Korat can arrange a chartered *songtao,* jeep, or minibus, but prices are stiff unless you can round up enough passengers to split the fare. Khorat Business Corporation at 37 Buarong Rd. does full-day tours of the monuments during the high tourist season for 1,400B.

Nang Rong

A sensible alternative to the long commute from either Korat or Buriram is to spend a night in Nang Rong and leisurely tour the monuments the following day. The Nang Rong bus terminal is south of the main highway.

Honey Inn: A Swiss traveler wrote to recommend this place one block north of the main highway and a few blocks from the bus terminal. Walk up the road from the Nissan building past the reservoir to Ban Nongree, and turn right into the small lane. You can also check with Mrs. Phanna at the Nang Rong School. Mrs. Phanna, who happens to run the Honey Inn, will prepare dinner upon request.

Honey Inn also owns a minibus that provides tours to Phanom Rung and Muang Tam for 300-500B per person depending on the size of the group. Both Mrs. Phanna and her husband, Khun Phaisan, are schoolteachers who welcome Western travelers to visit their schools. 8/1 Soi Srikoon, Ban Nongree, Nang Rong, or contact Mrs. Phanna at Nang Rong School or Khun Phaisan at Prakhonchai Phittayakhom School.

Nang Rong Hotel: If the superior Honey Inn is closed, this basic hovel will suffice for a night before you can tour the ruins and then move on. There's a simple cafe and rooms cost 100-150B.

PRASAT MUANG TAM

A fine contrast to Prasat Phanom Rung is the Khmer temple at Muang Tam ("Lower City"), a 10th-century complex initiated by King Indravarman but completed by Jayavarman V, and therefore older than its more acclaimed neighbor. Although the setting in Ban Chorakae Mak ("Town of Many Crocodiles") is hardly picturesque, the bas-reliefs, intriguing architectural symbolism, and fine state of collapse make it a worthwhile visit for fans of Khmer architecture.

The monument is entered through a thick wall which, like most of the monument, has suffered from ground subsidence and achieved a bizarre state of dilapidation. Despite restoration efforts by the Fine Arts Department with help from German consultants, the perimeter wall has collapsed into a magnificent bulwark that resembles a huge and undulating serpent. Clusters of *nagas* ring the inner ponds, which symbolically represent the primordial oceans of Hindu-Buddhist cosmology. Cows and young monks often wander around the grounds, oblivious to the tour buses parked at the front entrance.

The central sanctuary features five reconstructed brick towers with exquisite sandstone carvings of Krishna killing a *naga* and Shiva mounted on the back of Nandi the bull. Window mullions and delicately carved lintels relate other themes from Hindu mythology. Another unique feature is the three materials used in construction: bricks for the central sanctuaries, sandstone for the sills, and laterite for the walls.

Transportation

Prasat Muang Tam is 10 km southeast of Phanom Rung in the Khmer-speaking village of Chorakae Mak. Public transportation is unavailable to the monument, though motorcycle taxis and *songtaos* can be chartered from Ban Tako and Phanom Rung.

The site is open daily 0900-1700.

OTHER KHMER MONUMENTS

Travelers intrigued with the Cambodian architecture of northeastern Thailand can continue east and visit a half dozen additional monuments. The nearest sanctuary, Prasat Ta Muen, is just 22 km east of Muang Tam on the Thai-Cambodian border.

Khmer *prasats* near Surin include Prasat Pluang and Prasat Sikhoraphum. Further east in the vicinity of Si Saket stand Prasat Kamphaeng Yai and Prasat Kamphaeng Noi. About 100 km south of Si Saket is Prasat Khao Viharn, considered among the most spectacular Khmer monuments in Southeast Asia.

KORAT TO THE MEKONG

KHON KAEN

Khon Kaen, 449 km from Bangkok and strategically located at the intersection of Friendship Highway and National Road 12, is an important crossroads and gateway for visitors arriving from Korat, Phitsanulok, and northern Thailand. Khon Kaen is a bustling city and site of several prestigious establishments, such as Khon Kaen University and Channel 5 Television; visitors can also view the National Museum and take a look at the locally produced silk.

Khon Kaen National Museum

The leading attraction in Khon Kaen offers a small but high-quality collection of arts, with special emphasis on the Dvaravati Period and Ban Chiang artifacts. Engraved steles in the Dvaravati style dating from the 8th and 9th centuries are arranged on the exterior lawns and on the ground floors. Exhibits to the right as you enter concentrate on prehistoric objects discovered at Ban Chiang, and *sema* boundary stones carved with bas-reliefs of Buddha's return to Kapilapasatu.

The second floor features archaeological discoveries from the northeast, such as Lopburi Period images discovered at Nakhon Champasi and a prized 11th-century lintel discovered at Ku Suan Tang in Buriram Province.

The museum is open Tues.-Sun. 0900-1700, admission 20B.

Khon Kaen Silk

The finest silk in Thailand is produced near Korat, Chaiyaphum, and in Chonnabot, a small *mut mee* silk-weaving village 56 km southwest of Khon Kaen.

Several shops in town offer silks and handicrafts, but the best selection is found at the Prathamakant Handicraft Center at 79 Ruen Rom Rd., just one block east of the train station. Prathamakant stocks a wide selection of silks from all regions of the Issan, plus silver jewelry and tribal handicrafts from northern Thailand. The staff speaks English and accepts credit cards.

The lovely Sirinya Wattanasukchai writes to recommend another silk shop called Rin Thai Silk at 412 Na Muang Rd. She was one of the first Thai vendors in the country to send e-mail to this author; therefore, she deserves a mention!

Bung Kaen Lake

This 241-acre freshwater lake provides a quick escape for the citizens of Khon Kaen. Recreational facilities include several seafood restaurants, boat tours, and a fitness park. On the lakeshore is an old *wat* constructed in typical Issan style with Thai and Laotian influences.

Budget Accommodations

Khon Kaen is a major transit and business center in the northeast, with a wide selection of hotels in all price ranges. Hotels are somewhat expensive as there is very little competition for the handful of Western visitors who pass through this town.

Most places are within walking distance or short *songtao* ride from the bus station, though train passengers should take the yellow minitruck which shuttles into town.

Sansumran Hotel: Behind the funky green wooden exterior is a popular and conveniently located hotel with rooms arranged left and right off the central corridor. Manager Montree Saraboon is friendly, and helpful, and speaks excellent English. 55-59 Klang Muang Rd., tel. (043) 239611, 180-250B fan, 320-400B a/c.

Suksawad Hotel: Another old wooden place with rooms in various price ranges, well located in a quiet alley with friendly if somewhat disorganized managers. Ask for the large, clean rooms with private bath in the separate building. 2 Klang Muang Rd., tel. (043) 236472, 120-180B.

Thani Bungalows: Adjacent to the train station is a very decrepit joint with dismal, noisy upstairs rooms and dirty, overpriced bungalows in the rear. Skip the Thani and head into town. 222 Ruen Rom Rd., tel. (043) 221470, 200-280B fan, 350-500B a/c.

Moderate Accommodations

Roma Hotel: The old favorite has been renovated and improved with a new lobby, eleva-

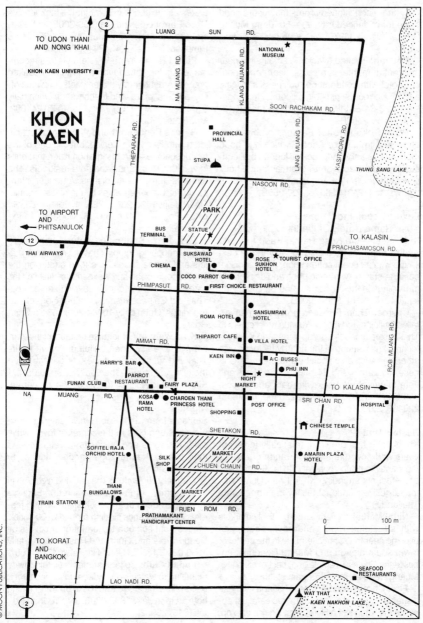

KHON KAEN

TO UDON THANI
AND NONG KHAI

KHON KAEN UNIVERSITY ■

LUANG   SUN   RD.

NA MUANG RD.

KLANG MUANG RD.

NATIONAL ★
MUSEUM

SOON RACHAKAM RD.

LANG MUANG RD.

KASITKORN RD.

THUNG SANG LAKE

THEPARAK RD.

PROVINCIAL ■
HALL

STUPA ■

NASOON RD.

TO AIRPORT
AND
PHITSANULOK

PARK

STATUE ★

TO KALASIN →

PRACHASAMOSON RD.

THAI AIRWAYS ■

BUS ■
TERMINAL

SUKSAWAD
HOTEL ■

ROSE ■ ★ TOURIST OFFICE
SUKHON
HOTEL

CINEMA ■

COCO PARROT GH ■

PHIMPASUT   RD.

■ FIRST CHOICE RESTAURANT

ROMA HOTEL ■

SANSUMRAN ■
HOTEL

AMMAT RD.

THIPAROT CAFE ■   ● VILLA HOTEL

KAEN INN ■   ● A/C BUSES

HARRY'S BAR ◆

PARROT ■
RESTAURANT

FUNAN CLUB ■

FAIRY PLAZA ■

NIGHT ★
MARKET

● PHU INN

ROB MUANG RD.

NA   MUANG   RD.

KOSA ■
RAMA
HOTEL

● CHAROEN THANI
PRINCESS HOTEL

SHOPPING ■

POST OFFICE ■

SRI CHAN RD.

TO KALASIN →

HOSPITAL ■

SOFITEL RAJA
ORCHID HOTEL ●

SHETAKON   RD.

CHINESE TEMPLE

SILK ■
SHOP

MARKET

CHUEN CHAUN   RD.

AMARIN PLAZA
HOTEL ●

THANI ●
BUNGALOWS

MARKET

TRAIN STATION ■

PRATHAMAKANT
HANDICRAFT CENTER

RUEN   ROM   RD.

0   100 m

TO KORAT
AND
BANGKOK

LAO NADI RD.

SEAFOOD
RESTAURANTS

WAT THAT

KAEN NAKHON LAKE

© MOON PUBLICATIONS, INC.

tors, and reconditioned rooms that insure good value for midpriced travelers. 50 Klang Muang Rd., tel. (043) 236276, 240-300B fan, 380-480B a/c.

Phu Inn: Tucked away in a small alley near the central market is a cozy, clean, and modern hotel with coffee shop, business services, and 98 a/c rooms, plus big discounts for longer stays. 26-34 Sathid Juthithum Rd., tel. (043) 243174, 500-750B.

Rose Sukon Hotel: *Farangs* on business often stay in this cozy hotel, which has good rooms and a very dark cocktail lounge but, curiously enough, lacks an English-language hotel sign out front. 1/11 Klang Muang Rd., tel. (043) 238576, fax (043) 238576, 700-950B.

Luxury Accommodations

Kosa Rama Hotel: Of the three big hotels in Khon Kaen—the Kosa Rama, Kaen Inn, and Khon Kaen—the Kosa is probably in the best shape with a decent coffee shop, popular disco, postage-stamp swimming pool, and acceptable furnishings in the a/c rooms. 250 Sri Chan Rd., tel. (043) 225014, 850-1,000B.

Charoen Thani Princess Hotel: Khon Kaen's tallest building and most luxurious hotel caters to Thai businesspeople, group tours, and Western technicians working in the nearby factories with amenities such as a pool, business center, Chinese restaurant and 24-hour coffee shop, and entertainment complex with bars and discos. 260 Sri Chan Rd., tel. (043) 220400, fax (043) 220438, 2,000-2,600B.

Restaurants

Khon Kaen has grown dramatically in recent years and now offers a wide range of restaurants and nightclubs popular with local night owls and students attending Khon Kaen University, the largest educational facility in northeastern Thailand.

Night Market: Several small but lively markets with streetside food vendors appear each evening near the a/c bus terminal in the center of town, south along Lang Muang Road just opposite the Chinese Temple and, best of all, on Na Muang Road en route the train station.

First Choice Restaurant: Thai and Chinese dishes are served in this clean, a/c cafe just opposite the Khon Kaen Hotel. First Choice also op-

erates as the check-in point for the inexpensive Coco Parrot Guesthouse (100-300B) in the arcade to the rear. Open daily 0700-2300. 18/8 Pimpasut Rd., tel. (043) 241283. Moderate.

Parrot Restaurant: Western visitors recommend this longtime favorite for its homebaked breads, American-style breakfasts, brewed coffee, burgers, pizza, and friendly staff. Open daily 0700-2300. 175 Sri Chan Rd., tel. (043) 244692. Moderate.

Harry's Restaurant and Wine Bar: Not affiliated with Harry's in Venice, but still one of the few upscale restaurants in Khon Kaen that pulls in wealthy Thais and expatriate residents. The menu features Italian dishes, American standards, and imported wines by the glass or bottle. Open daily 1030-2300. 229/11 Soi Yimsri, Sri Chan Rd., tel. (043) 239755. Moderate to expensive.

Fairy Plaza Shopping Center: Khon Kaen's largest shopping complex has several pizza outlets and coffee shops. The food center on the fourth floor is clean and inexpensive, while on the same floor the adjacent Mae Ying serves both Thai and Chinese dishes in rather elegant surroundings. Open daily 1000-2200. 185 Sri Chan Rd.

Krua Weh: A Vietnamese restaurant in a partially restored wooden building, known for its Thai and Vietnamese dishes as described on the bilingual menu. Open daily 1100-2200. 1/1 Klang Muang Rd., tel. (043) 239884. Moderate.

Nightlife

Students from Khon Kaen University patronize the clubs and bars in the center of town, while older residents and business travelers spend their *baht* in the massage parlors attached to the larger hotels.

Witchery Nightclub: The pub and nightclub in the basement of Fairy Plaza screens English-language videos during cocktail hours and features live rock bands starting around 2100. Music ranges from soft pop to headbanger covers by Deep Purple and Guns and Roses. Open daily 1800-0200. 185 Sri Chan Rd., tel. (043) 241687.

Funan Club: College students fill this rowdy nightclub to watch MTV videos until a local rock band takes the stage and rocks on until closing hours. Open daily 1800-0200. 3/1 Sri Chan Rd., tel. (043) 239628.

Practicalities

The second largest city in the northeast may lack character, but it offers plenty of services for passing travelers.

Tourist Office: The TAT office east of the park and bus terminal has information on nearby silk-weaving villages, and maps to Khon Kaen, Roi Et, Maha Sarakham, and Kalasin Provinces. Open daily 0830-1630. 15/5 Prachasamoson Rd., tel. (043) 244498, fax (043) 244497.

Tourist Police: The police station adjacent to the TAT office is responsible for Khon Kaen, Udon Thani, Nong Khai, Loei, Sakhon Nakhon, and Nakhon Phanom. An English-speaking officer can help resolve problems faster than police stations elsewhere in the region. Open daily 24 hours. 15/5 Prachasamoson Rd., tel. (053) 236937.

Lao Visas: Several years ago, Laos opened a small consulate that issues Lao visas at official government prices rather than the steep markups expected by travel agencies around town and, more importantly, up at the border town of Nong Khai. Lao visas are now granted on entry to visitors who land by air at Vientiane, but all others are required to obtain a visa in advance. This situation remains in flux but may prove very useful to visitors heading for Laos who wish to save some money from the high rates charged by most travel agencies. 123 Photisan Rd., tel. (053) 223698.

Post Office and International Telephone: The main post office on Klang Muang Road is open weekdays 0830-1630 and weekends from 0900-1200. The attached CAT Telecom Center provides international connections daily 0900-2200.

Hospital: Khon Kaen Hospital in the eastern part of town can help with medical emergencies. Sri Chan Rd., tel. (043) 236005.

Transportation

Khon Kaen is 449 km northeast of Bangkok, 190 km north of Korat, and 115 km south of Udon Thani. The city serves as an important junction for travelers entering the northeast from Phitsanulok in central Thailand.

Air: Thai Airways flies three times daily from Bangkok for 1,300B and three times weekly from Chiang Mai for 1,400B. Thai Airways is located en route to the airport at 183 Mailan Rd., (tel. 043-236523).

Train: Trains are the most comfortable way to travel around the northeast. Five trains leave daily from Bangkok and take seven hours by express or eight hours by rapid train. Trains depart Korat at 0600, 0823, 1145, 1226, and 1515. Departure schedules should be confirmed with the Korat TAT.

Bus: Buses leave hourly from the ordinary bus terminal in Korat and take about three hours to reach Khon Kaen. Air-conditioned buses leave from the terminal on Friendship Highway in the north of Korat.

Buses from Phitsanulok leave hourly and take about five hours to reach Khon Kaen, passing through excellent scenery and several national parks.

CHAIYAPHUM

Chaiyaphum is a medium-sized town that, because of its location well off the main highway, has escaped mass tourism and maintained a relatively untouched atmosphere.

The town was established during the Ayuthaya era as a trading station between Ayuthaya and Vientiane, then a protectorate state of the Thai nation. Local folklore revolves around a citizen named Phya Lae who was executed by Laotian soldiers after he refused to join a rebel movement against authorities in Bangkok. A monument to the hero stands in front of the provincial hall.

Today the region is primarily known for its silk weaving, caves, and migratory birdlife.

Attractions

Chaiyaphum itself has little of great interest, but tours to nearby attractions can be arranged through Yin's Guesthouse.

Silk Weaving: Top draw are the famous silks—reputedly woven from 100% silk and collected by the royal family. Several shops in town provide samples of the various designs, though prices are lowest directly at weaving villages such as Ban Kwiao. Silk bolts from the weavers start at 200B per meter, about half the cost of silk in Bangkok or Chiang Mai.

Wat Prang Ku: Two km east of town in the old section of Chaiyaphum is a Khmer temple constructed on the royal highway that once con-

nected Angkor with Prasat Phanom Rung and Phimai. The central laterite tower houses several images including a seated stone Buddha of the Dvaravati Period and an Ayuthaya-style standing Buddha on the western side.

Tad Ton National Park: A small national park with caves and multilayered waterfalls is located 21 km north of town on the road toward Kaset Sombun. Park bungalows cost from 250B.

Birdlife: Thousands of birds migrate and nest Nov.-April in freshwater Waeng Lake northeast of Chaiyaphum. Waterbirds can also be seen at Lake Laharn some 40 km south of town.

Accommodations

Chaiyaphum has one guesthouse and several midpriced Thai hotels.

Yin's Guesthouse: Five hundred meters north of the main bus station is Chaiyaphum's original guesthouse where the owner, Yin, can help arrange visits to silk-weaving towns and overnight stays in nearby villages. *Samlors* from the bus station cost 10B. 143 Niwetraj Rd., no phone, 60-80B.

Ratanasiri Hotel: Two blocks northwest of the center of town with clean and comfortable fan-cooled and a/c rooms at bargain rates. 73/1 Non Muang Rd., tel. (044) 821258, 200-250B fan, 320-380B a/c.

Paibun Hotel: An older Chinese hotel with simple but clean and very inexpensive rooms. 227 Yititham Rd., tel. (044) 811021, 100-160B.

Lert Nimit Hotel: An upscale hotel with both inexpensive fan rooms and two-story a/c chalets. Located north of the bus station at 447 Niwetraj Rd., tel. (044) 811522, fax (044) 822335, 220-250B fan, 450-500B a/c.

Transportation

Chaiyaphum is 332 km from Bangkok, 118 km north of Korat, and approximately midway between Korat and Khon Kaen on Route 202.

Buses leave hourly from Bangkok's Northern Bus Terminal and from both bus terminals in Korat. Ordinary buses arrive at the main bus terminal on Niwetraj Road near the Lert Nimit Hotel. Air-conditioned buses usually stop at the Air Chaiyaphum office on Non Muang Road, just opposite the Sirichai Hotel, or at the Nakorn Chai Tour office a few blocks south.

Direct bus connections are also available from Phitsanulok, Nakhon Sawan, Chiang Mai, and Chiang Rai.

UDON THANI

This busy commercial center—usually called Udon or Udorn—chiefly serves as a base for visiting the archaeological site at Ban Chiang and the caves and national parks situated in the province.

The city was founded in 1893 by a Laotian general who moved his army from Nong Khai after a dispute with the occupying French forces. Together with Korat and Ubon Ratchathani, Udorn experienced a tremendous boom during the Vietnam conflict after the Americans established a huge military base just outside the city perimeter. The base was closed in 1975 and presented to the Thai government, but the legacy continues with a handful of Western advisers and diplomatic personnel who chose military retirement in Udon. Other reminders include a small American consulate near Nong Prajak Reservoir, the enormous air base that now serves both Thai military and civilian sectors, and a few restaurants where retired servicemen gather to throw darts and complain about their delayed benefits.

Attractions in Town

Udon's few sights are limited to a rather sad little zoo near the sports field, Ban Huay Market (busiest on weekends), and colorful cinema poster shops near the clock tower. The Chinese temple near Kannika Tours features a baroque facade of dragons and mythical birds, plus an unnerving photo collection of people killed in auto accidents on the interior walls. Also note the strange roofless *tuk tuks* constructed with wooden carriages, circular benches, custom wheels, and wild paint jobs.

The remainder of Udon's attractions are outside town and require the service of a tour operator, public transportation, or a motorcycle rented from Kannika Tours, tel. (042) 241378.

Ban Chiang

The region's top draws are the new museum, archaeological excavations, and Bronze-Age artifacts discovered at Ban Chiang, a small hamlet 58 km east of Udon Thani on the Sakhon Nakhon Highway.

The story began in 1966 when a young American sociology student named Steve Young literally stumbled across some pottery shards which were carbon-dated to around 3600 B.C. News of the findings spread and the village became an overnight sensation. Excavations conducted in 1974 and 1975 by the Fine Arts Department of Silapkorn University and Chester Gorman of the University of Pennsylvania led to startling discoveries of ceramic vessels and human skeletons dating back over 5,000 years. Predating the earliest recognized bronze ages, these findings prompted scholars to rethink Southeast Asian history and challenge the traditional notion that civilization originated in the Middle East or China.

Today, Ban Chiang has reverted into a sleepy backwater offering the infrequent visitor an older museum established in 1976 to house early excavations, and a much more impressive modern museum opened in 1986 and funded by the Kennedy Foundation. Installations were designed by the Smithsonian Institution for a worldwide exhibition, which now permanently resides in the modern wing of the Ban Chiang Museum.

Somewhat unimpressive excavation sites are five minutes away within the walls of Wat Pho Si Nai.

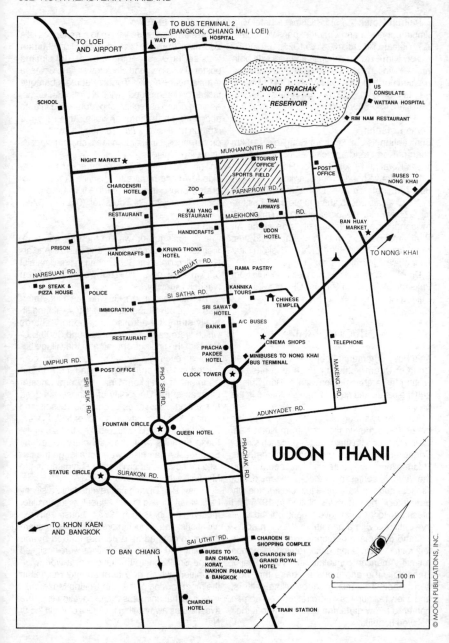

TO BUS TERMINAL 2
(BANGKOK, CHIANG MAI, LOEI)

TO LOEI
AND AIRPORT

WAT PO   HOSPITAL

NONG PRACHAK
RESERVOIR

US
CONSULATE

WATTANA HOSPITAL

RIM NAM RESTAURANT

SCHOOL

MUKHAMONTRI RD.

NIGHT MARKET

TOURIST
OFFICE

SPORTS FIELD

POST
OFFICE

BUSES TO
NONG KHAI

CHAROENSRI
HOTEL

ZOO

PARNPROW RD.

RESTAURANT

KAI YANG
RESTAURANT

THAI
AIRWAYS

MAEKHONG   RD.

BAN HUAY
MARKET

HANDICRAFTS

UDON
HOTEL

TO NONG KHAI

PRISON

HANDICRAFTS

KRUNG THONG
HOTEL

TAMRUAT   RD.

RAMA PASTRY

NARESUAN RD.

SI SATHA RD.

KANNIKA
TOURS

SP STEAK &
PIZZA HOUSE

POLICE

IMMIGRATION

SRI SAWAT
HOTEL

A/C BUSES

CHINESE
TEMPLE

BANK

RESTAURANT

CINEMA SHOPS

TELEPHONE

PRACHA
PAKDEE
HOTEL

MINIBUSES TO NONG KHAI
BUS TERMINAL

UMPHUR RD.

POST OFFICE

CLOCK TOWER

MAKENG RD.

ADUNYADET RD.

FOUNTAIN CIRCLE

QUEEN HOTEL

UDON THANI

SRI SUK RD.

STATUE CIRCLE

SURAKON RD.

PHO SRI RD.

PRACHAK RD.

TO KHON KAEN
AND BANGKOK

SAI UTHIT RD.

CHAROEN SI
SHOPPING COMPLEX

TO BAN CHIANG

BUSES TO
BAN CHIANG,
KORAT,
NAKHON PHANOM
& BANGKOK

CHAROEN SRI
GRAND ROYAL
HOTEL

0   100 m

CHAROEN
HOTEL

TRAIN STATION

© MOON PUBLICATIONS, INC.

The Ban Chiang Museum is open Wed.-Sun. 0900-1600, admission 20B.

To reach Ban Chiang, take a bus or minibus east toward Sakhon Nakhon from the bus stop near the Charoen Hotel. Be sure to get off at Km 50 in the tiny village of Ban Chiang, from where *tuk tuks* continue six km north to the museum and excavation sites.

West of Udon Thani

Highway 210 leads west to Loei and Phu Kradung National Park, one of the most popular parks in Thailand. While most visitors travel north to Nong Khai and then west along the Mekong River to Chiang Khan and Loei, the route could easily be reversed to include the following stops. Motorcyclists will enjoy the flat and lightly trafficked highway.

Wat Tham Klong Phaen: A famous cave temple, once home to a renowned meditation master named Luang Phu Kaeo, is found 40 km west of Udon in the Phuphan Mountain Range.

Erawan Caves: The stalactite caves of Tham Erawan, 50 km west of Udon, are filled with Buddha images illuminated by electric lights. Views over the ricefields are possible after the long climb up 107 steps. Take a bus and look for the sign: THAM ERAWAN.

Budget Accommodations

Most hotels are clustered on Prachak Road and near the clock tower in the center of town.

Sri Sawat Hotel: Budget travelers usually stay in this small hotel just northwest of the clock tower, which is neatly divided into an old and cheap wing on the left and a newer wing on the right. Rooms can get noisy from courtyard reverberation, but the manager is friendly and the rooms are kept fairly clean. 123 Prachak Rd., tel. (042) 243586, 100-180B.

Pracha Pakdee Hotel: Across the street is a clean and modern hotel with good-value rooms. 156/8 Prachak Silpakorn Rd., tel. (042) 221804, 160-240B fan, 280-360B a/c.

Queen Hotel: An older joint that gets the overflow from the Sri Sawat and Pracha Pakdee. 6 Udon Dusadi Rd., tel. (042) 221451, 100-160B fan, 260-360B a/c.

Moderate Accommodations

The best hotels in Udon Thani are geared to traveling Thai businesspeople rather than Western tourists who expect first-class comforts at bargain rates.

Charoen Hotel: Tour groups en route to Ban Chiang usually stay at the Charoen, considered the best in town. Facilities include a swimming pool on the front lawn, tastefully decorated rooms in the new wing, and the excellent Poovieng Restaurant. 549 Pho Sri Rd., tel. (042) 248155, fax (042) 241093, 800-950B in the old wing, 1,200-1,500B in the new wing.

Udon Hotel: An older, unrenovated hotel in a good location near the shops and *kai yang* restaurants on upper Prachak Road. 81 Maekhong Rd., tel. (042) 246529, 600-950B.

Ban Chiang Hotel: Best in town with all possible amenities. 59 Mukhamontri Rd., tel. (042) 221227, 950-1,800B.

Restaurants

Udon Thani is known among Thais for its spicy beef sausages, finely ground pork dishes, crispy fried pork legs and most notably, *kai yang,* succulent sweet chicken barbecued on open fires. The largest collection of *kai yang* cafes is on Prachak Road near the zoo and sports field. Just follow your nose.

Rama Pastry: Ten years of occupation by the American military during the Vietnam conflict left behind a number of chefs who continue to bake some of the best pastries and breads in the country. Rama serves fresh croissants, crusty baguettes, and sweetened desserts in air-conditioned comfort. Open daily 0630-2100. Prachak Rd. Inexpensive.

SP Steak and Pizza House: T-bone steaks, pizzas, and other Western dishes are prepared by a Thai woman who once cooked for American troops stationed at Udon during the Vietnam conflict. Her second branch is on the second floor of the gigantic Charoen Si Complex. Open daily 0700-2200. 63/2 Naresuan Rd., tel. (042) 241058. Moderate.

Rim Nam: Several upscale, open-air restaurants are nicely situated on the edge of Nong Prachak Reservoir in the northwestern corner of town. Thai, Chinese, and Issan specialties are served by cute, smiling waitresses. Open daily 0800-2300. 76/3 Suppha Kitchanya Rd., tel. (042) 242653. Moderate.

TJ's Cafe: For an unusual evening, visit this old favorite near the lake and VFW headquarters.

TJ's is run by an American who serves authentic hamburgers and french fries for the local community of expatriate Americans. Some are retired military, while others work at the new US$200 million Voice of America (VOA) transmitter recently constructed outside town near Ban Duang. Open daily 1700-2300. Nongsamrung Rd. Moderate.

Charoen Si Complex: Issan's largest shopping complex is a world-within-a-world, a monstrous 24,000-square meter wonderland of swimming pools, supermarkets, an amusement park, and dozens of restaurants serving every possible type of food. MD Suki on the ground floor specializes in Thai sukiyaki; the Food Center on the third floor is clean, fast, and inexpensive; SP Steak and Pizza House on the second floor is geared toward carnivores; while Kentucky Fried Chicken and Black Canyon Coffee cover the chicken and caffeine crowds. Open daily 0600-midnight. 660 Prachak Rd.

Practicalities

Udon is one of Issan's larger cities, but most services are in the center of town and within walking distance of your hotel.

Tourist Office: The Udon TAT office can help with maps and transportation advice to the rarely visited caves and waterfalls in the province. They moved a few years ago from the former location in the Provincial Education Office to a more convenient spot on the southern edge of Nong Prachak Reservoir. 16/5 Mukhamontri Rd., tel. (042) 325406. Open daily 0830-1630.

Immigration: The Thai immigration office extends tourist visas for 500B. Open weekdays 0800-1600. Pho Sri Rd., tel. (042) 222889.

Wattana Hospital: Udon's best medical facility is near the lake and U.S. Consulate. 70/7 Suphakit Janya Rd., tel. (042) 241031.

Travel Agencies: Miss Kannika Saetang of Kannika Tours organizes regional tours as well as visas and tours to Laos, Cambodia, and Vietnam. Open daily 0800-1800. 36/9 Si Satha Rd., tel. (042) 241378.

Transportation

Udon Thani is 564 km northeast of Bangkok, 305 km north of Korat, and 51 km south of Nong Khai.

Air: Thai Airways flies once daily from Bangkok and three times weekly from Nakhon Sakhon. Thai Airways (tel. 042-2432220) is at 60 Makkang Rd. The airport is four km southwest of town.

Train: Trains leave Hualampong station in Bangkok daily at 0615, 1900, and 2030, arriving in Udon about 10 hours later. Trains leave Korat at 0807, 1226, 1515, and 0258.

The train station is about two km from the clock tower, and *samlor* drivers ask 25B for the short ride.

Bus: Buses leave hourly from the Northern Bus Terminal in Bangkok and take nine hours to reach Udon Thani. Some buses terminate at bus terminal #1 on Sai Uthit Road, but others go to bus terminal #2 on the northwestern edge of town.

Terminal #1 serves Bangkok, Korat, Sakon Nakhon, Nakhon Phanom, and Ubon Ratchathani.

Terminal #2 serves Loei, Chiang Rai, Chiang Mai, and Bangkok.

Private buses to Bangkok and destinations in the north can be ticketed at the office on Prachak Road near the Sri Sawat Hotel. Ordinary buses to Bangkok leave hourly 0500-2300, while VIP a/c buses leave in the evenings 2030-2130.

Getting Around: Rental cars cost 1,500-1,800B per day depending on the model. Motorcycles are 300B per day. See the following section on the wonderful motorcycle ride west from Nong Khai along the southern banks of the Mekong River. The shortage of motorcycles in Nong Khai makes a rental in Udon a sensible idea. Allow at least four or five days for the complete loop though Nong Khai, Chiang Khan, and Loei. Prada Car Rentals is open daily 0700-1700. 80 Makkang Rd., tel. (042) 248680.

Buses to Nong Khai leave from the bus terminal three km north of town on Udon Dutsadi Road. To reach the terminal, take minibus 3 from the clock tower or hire a *samlor* for about 20B.

Buses to Khon Kaen leave from the halt near the Statue Circle.

MEKONG RIVER REGION

NONG KHAI

Nong Khai rates as the most popular destination in the northeast. Superbly located at the terminus of the Friendship Highway on the banks of the Mekong River, the small and rather sleepy town is chiefly known as an important link with Laos and the national capital of Vientiane. A highly recommended journey west from Nong Khai to Chiang Khan passes through great landscapes, a culturally diverse environment, and charming towns almost completely unaffected by tourism.

Unlike most other towns in Thailand, Nong Khai is endowed with a degree of individuality. French-Laotian influence is reflected in some of the surviving hybrid architecture, and in the bakeries that still produce baguettes and loaves of fresh French bread. Shopping includes a range of goods from Laotian handicrafts to northeastern creations. Best of all, the people are friendly and anxious to help Western visitors enjoy their Issan vacation.

With the completion of the new bridge to Laos and the arrival of several luxury hotels, Nong Khai has changed to some degree, yet it retains the timeless atmosphere that has long made it a great destination. Visitors with limited time in the northeast should see the Khmer monuments near Korat and then head directly to Nong Khai.

Rimkhong Road and Mae Nam Khong

The new bridge has phased out the boat crossing in Nong Khai, but the riverbank trailhead remains a popular spot at which to enjoy a meal from the cantilevered restaurants while gazing across the river to Laos. A humorous note is provided by the trilingual sign describing aliens with hippie characteristics.

A short geographical sidebar should be made about the Mekong River, variously spelled as Mekong, Maekhong, or Mae Nam Khong depending on the source. Thais prefer Mae Nam Khong ("Mother Water Khong"), and not the somewhat redundant Mekong (or Mae Khong) River used by *farangs*.

Wat Po Chai

Tucked away in a back alley east of the bus terminal, Wat Po Chai houses a highly venerated solid-gold statue called Luang Pho Phra Sai, cast in Laos and brought here from Vientiane by General Chakri. Murals in the principal *viharn* relate the legendary casting of the image and miraculous recovery after it was lost in the Mekong River. Also note the well-carved doors, window panels, and outstanding murals of angels, fish, and jungle elephants behind the central altar.

Wat Po Chai is the venue for several important festivals, such as the spectacular Rocket Festival held in April on the full moon, a Candle Festival in late June or early July, and Songkran. You can also view boat races down the Mekong, which capitalize on the end of the rainy seasons.

Wat Prathat Nong Khai

A venerable temple which slid into the river over a century ago is located a few kilometers east of town. Year-round, the top half is still visible.

Wat Khaek

Certainly the most bizarre and memorable temple in northeastern Thailand is the strange Hindu-Buddhist wonderland of Wat Khaek (also called Wat Phuttama Makasamakhom), four km east of town at the end of a dusty side road.

Wat Khaek is the eccentric vision of Luang Pu Bunleuau Surirat, a refugee monk from war-torn Vietnam and Laos who settled in Nong Khai in 1978 to construct his Disneyland of psychedelic statues. Aided by a large community of local devotees, Luang Pu ("Venerable Grandfather") neatly combined his eclectic religious beliefs into a religious theme park that fuses elements of Buddhism, Hinduism, and Eastern shamanism.

Resembling something from the imagination of Hieronymus Bosch, temple ground sculptures feature familiar deities such as the elephant-headed Hindu god Ganesh, Vishnu, and Shiva, nestled alongside huge aquatic creatures, barking cement dogs, and Buddhas cast with Jimmy Durante noses. A rearside courtyard entered

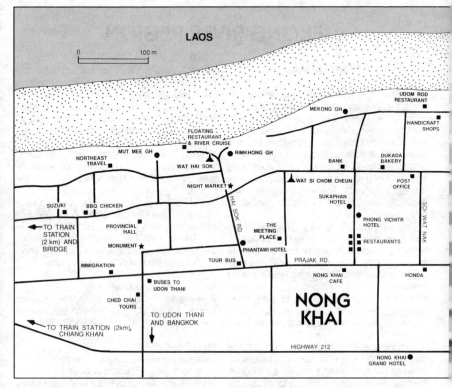

through a demon's mouth includes humorous depictions of model children, the perfect general, and lovers in the flesh and after death. Morality tales continue inside the hall, where followers of Luang Po have realistically cast images of Buddhas, Hindu deities, and other gods of indeterminate origins. The whole affair is mad, amusing, and wildly entertaining.

Goony-Golf Wat Khaek is four km east of town a few hundred meters beyond St. Paul School. Take a *songtao* east and look for the sign marked Sala Kaeoku, from where the dirt road continues 500 meters to the temple parking lot.

Boat Rides

Longtail boat trips on the Mekong can be booked through several guesthouses. A sunset river cruise leaves daily at 1700 from the Floating Restaurant behind Wat Hai Sok.

Budget Accommodations

Nong Khai has several budget guesthouses, almost a half dozen hotels that cater to Thai tourists, and two upscale hotels for international tour groups.

Mut Mee Guesthouse: Probably the most popular guesthouse in town, Mut Mee is favored for its beautiful outdoor restaurant overlooking the Mekong, excellent meals, and reliable information provided by the management. The somewhat run-down bungalows are subdivided into concrete lower floors and better teak rooms on the upper floors. 1111 Kaeworawut Rd., tel. (042) 460717, fax (042) 460717, 80-250B.

Sawasdee Guesthouse: Nong Khai's newest and cleanest guesthouse provides 16 rooms in a convenient location near the center of town. Heavy restoration has removed whatever charm the old building once possessed, but the place is

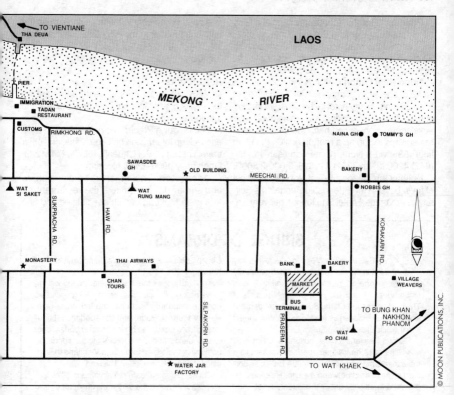

popular with cleanliness freaks and midlevel travelers. Sawasdee has bicycles for rent, hot showers, laundry services, and tourist information from their English-speaking managers. 402 Meechai Rd., tel. (042) 412502, fax (042) 411906, 100-150B fan, 350-450B a/c.

Mekong Guesthouse: Just west of the immigration pier is a centrally located guesthouse with 20 simple but fairly clean rooms that overlook the river. The convenient location compensates for the noisy restaurant doubling as a late-night rendezvous spot for Thais and *farangs*. 519 Rimkhong Rd., tel. (042) 412119, fax (042) 411073, 80-150B.

Espresso Rimkhong Guesthouse: Farther west at the end of the riverside promenade is a newer guesthouse with simple rooms and shared baths. 625 Rimkhong Rd., no phone, 80-140B.

Tommy's Guesthouse: Lovely Niyana fled Nong Khai several years ago to set up operations in That Phanom, leaving behind her old teak homes now leased by a Thai musician and his friends. Very quiet, remote, and funky—a genuine homestay experience. 239 Meechai Rd., no phone, 80-120B.

The Meeting Place: An Australian-owned pub with several small but clean rooms in a handy central location. The owner operates a useful website and can help with Lao visas, plus room reservations in Vientiane. 1117 Soi Chuenjit, tel. (042) 421223, fax (042) 460975, www.palmenterprises.com/mtgplace, 100-150B.

Moderate Accommodations
Nong Khai has over a dozen simple and low-priced Thai hotels, and two luxury properties for upscale visitors heading across the bridge to Laos.

Phantawi Hotel: Probably the best of a fairly dismal lot, the Phantawi is divided into an older wing across the road and a newer addition with 30 clean and comfortable a/c rooms. 1241 Hai Sok Rd., tel. (042) 411568, 350-500B.

Nong Khai Grand Hotel: Nong Khai tourism came of age a few years ago with the opening of this 126-room luxury hotel in the southern section of town. Facilities include a swimming pool, business center, convention hall, disco, and several restaurants including a rooftop grill on the ninth floor. 589 Mu 5 Nong Khai-Poanpisai Rd., tel. (042) 420033, fax (042) 412026, 2,000-2,800B.

Holiday Inn Mekong Royal Nong Khai: West of town beyond the Friendship Bridge, this Holiday Inn-managed hotel is luxurious but very isolated and suited only to those driving across the bridge the following morning. 222 Jommani Rd., tel. (042) 420024, fax (042) 421280, 2,500-3,700B.

Restaurants

Nong Khai's most popular restaurants are on the banks of the Mekong River near the pier and immigration office.

The Meeting Place: The perfect spot to relax and pick up information on Laos, visas, and other travel tips. 1117 Soi Chuenjit, tel. (042) 421223. Open daily 0900-2200. Moderate.

Udom Rod: Though short on atmosphere and somewhat overpriced, the restaurant offers tasty Mekong catfish specialities and fine

BRIDGE OF DREAMS?

A bridge over the Mekong River—the key link in the road network that will eventually connect Singapore with Beijing—was first proposed in the 1950s by the governments of Thailand, Laos, and China. But plans were derailed and finally abandoned as the Indochina War spread into the hills of central Laos.

Despite Thailand's close cultural and linguistic ties with Laos, the visionary bridge remained little more than a pipe dream into the late 1980s, as border clashes flared between the two. Relations improved dramatically under the leadership of Thailand's Prime Minister Chatichai Choonhavan, a business-minded politician who announced plans to "turn battlefields into marketplaces." At the same time, the generals in Vientiane began to loosen their ideological neckties and encourage economic cooperation between the two countries. Private foreign investment was allowed beginning in 1989 and, in 1991, the hammer-and-sickle were removed from the national seal.

After Australia agreed to finance the US$30 million bridge—a gesture designed to expand their diplomatic and commercial roles in Southeast Asia—contracts were signed to begin construction of the first bridge over the lower reaches of the 4,000-km Mekong River. The Friendship (Mittaphab) Bridge opened in April 1994 in ceremonies attended by King Bhumibol and the president of Laos, accompanied by Thailand's Prime Minister Chuan Leekpai and Australia's Prime Minister Paul Keating.

Thailand hopes the 1,174-meter bridge will improve economic conditions across the impoverished northeast and turn Issan into the Indochina gateway for tourism, trade, and transportation. Landlocked Laos needs the bridge as an important door to the outside world, and to end the transportation bottleneck that slows trade from Vientiane to shipping facilities on the Gulf of Thailand.

But deep-seated fears remain among officials in Vientiane. All agree the bridge will encourage trade and tourism as their country gradually converts from communism to a market economy, but many are nervous about moving too fast and opening their mineral-rich country to rapacious Thai and Chinese business interests. Many also worry about the arrival of the ills that plague industrialized Thailand: deforestation, pollution, crime, drugs, and traffic jams. Another concern is that Laos's 4.5 million citizens will be overwhelmed by the flood of products now streaming across the Mekong, and that traditional Lao culture will fade as the country embraces the outside world.

Whether the Friendship Bridge between Thailand and Laos proves to be a bridge of dreams, a bridge over troubled waters, or simply the bridge of sighs, will be determined by diplomatic and commercial ventures initiated by both nations that share the Mekong River.

views across the waters to Laos. Thai and Laotian handicrafts are sold in the attached gift shop. Open daily 0700-2100. 423 Rimkhong Rd., tel. (042) 412561. Open daily 0700-2100. Moderate.

Tadan Restaurant: Almost a Udom Rod clone, but a great place to try the favorites listed on the English-language menu: Vietnamese spring rolls, spicy chicken with basil salad, chicken sautéed in red wine, and small fish prepared in either curry or coconut sauces. Open daily 1000-2200. 403 Rimkhong Rd., tel. (042) 411543. Moderate.

Floating Restaurant: Aside from the food and beer, the novelty here is the one-hour dinner cruise departing daily at 1700 and cruising upriver in the direction of the Friendship Bridge. An average meal with a bottle of Kloster beer costs about 150B. A cruise fee of 40B is added to your bill, whether you eat or simply go along for the ride. Open daily 1000-2200. Rimkhong Rd., tel. (042) 412211.Moderate.

Chor Kun Restaurant: Travelers tired of rudimentary cafes should try the excellent lunch buffet in the Nong Khai Grand Hotel. The 150B buffet includes a wonderful selection of Thai, Chinese, and Italian dishes, plus the only salad bar in town. The rooftop grill is fairly expensive but offers sweeping views from Nong Khai to Vientiane. Open daily 0700-2200. Nong Khai Grand Hotel, tel. (042) 420033. Moderate.

Dukada Bakery: The French influence from Laos has spilled across the border and blessed Nong Khai with several traditional bakeries where fresh breads and croissants are prepared each morning. Dukada also serves pastries, Thai dishes, Western breakfasts, and brewed local coffees. Meechai Rd. Inexpensive.

Mut Mee Guesthouse: Nong Khai's best riverside restaurant is in the guesthouse west of town. Good food and pleasant service in a relaxing atmosphere. Bring a book to read. 1111 Kaeworawut Rd. Inexpensive.

BBQ Chicken: A good escape from the tourist venues is provided by the crowded barbecue cafe west of the provincial hall near the Suzuki dealership. Meechai Rd. Inexpensive.

Restaurant Row: Almost a dozen small cafes serving Thai and Chinese dishes may be found just south of the Phong Vichitr and

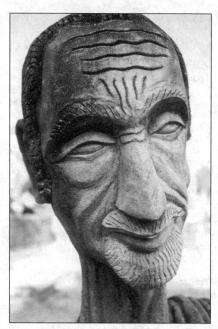

a figure from Wat Khaek

Sukaphan Hotels. The adjacent Nong Khai Cafe is slightly more upscale. Banthoenjit Rd. Inexpensive.

Shopping

Best buys in Nong Khai include Laotian silverwork, locally produced baskets, and traditional cotton and silk weavings.

Rimkhong Road: Handicrafts shops along Rimkhong Road sell inexpensive Laotian silverwork such as bracelets, necklaces, boxes, and tightly woven rattan baskets from Udon Thani. Silverwork is sold by weight rather than quality; the going rate is 8-12B per gram.

Village Weavers Handicraft: The best-quality handicrafts in Nong Khai are found in the charitable foundation established in 1982 by the Good Shepherd Sisters to aid villagers toward self-sufficiency. Excellent quality indigo-dyed cotton ikats and *mut mees* are sold at very reasonable prices, as well as stylish clothes and household items featured in the annual Oxfam gift catalogue. 786 Prajak Rd., Soi Weva, tel. (042) 411236, fax (042) 420333.

Practicalities

Tourist Information: Although the TAT strangely decided to establish a tourist office in the smaller town of Khon Kaen rather than Nong Khai, travel information is readily available from the Sawasdee, Mut Mee, and Tommy's Guesthouses.

Motorcycle Rentals: Motorcycles are an outstanding way to tour the region around Nong Khai and the Mekong River. However, the soaring popularity of motorcycle touring has created a serious shortage of bikes. Availability is best assured by checking the night before with a motorcycle agency. Motorcycles are available from the Honda dealership on Prajak Road, Mekong Guesthouse, and the Suzuki dealership at the west end of town.

Transportation

Nong Khai is 615 km northeast of Bangkok, 356 km north of Korat, 51 km north of Udon Thani, and 20 km southeast of Vientiane.

Air: The nearest airport is in Udon Thani. Reservations can be made at Thai Airways (tel. 042-411530) at 453 Prajak Rd.

Train: Trains from Bangkok depart daily at 0615, 1900, and 2030, and take 10-12 hours. Sleepers are available on the 2030 service.

Trains from Nong Khai to Bangkok depart from the station two km west of town at 1740, 1900, and 0740. The 1900 express train has sleepers.

Bus: Ordinary and a/c buses depart hourly 0530-0800 and 2000-2130 from the Northern Bus Terminal in Bangkok. Trains are much more comfortable than buses.

Government buses depart from the Bor Kor Sor terminal on Praserm Road. Private bus companies with a/c services to Bangkok, Chiang Mai, and other major destinations include Baramee Tours just opposite Prajak Bungalows, Chan Tours on Prajak Road, and Ched Chai Tours on Friendship Highway.

Buses to nearby destinations such as Udon Thani, Pak Chom, and Loei leave from the Friendship Highway.

Laos Transportation

There are several ways to reach Vientiane from Nong Khai. After you have obtained your Lao visa, take a *tuk tuk* to the bridge for 20-30B. You must have Thai immigration give you an exit stamp and will, of course, need to pass through Lao immigration at the other side of the bridge.

Buses make the bridge crossing hourly from the bus halt on the Thai side of the Thai-Lao Friendship Bridge, stopping once for Thai immigration and again for Lao immigration. Minitrucks head from the Lao side of the bridge up to Vientiane and cost 50B per passenger or 100B if you need to charter the entire truck.

A far more comfortable option is to hire one of the a/c taxis which wait on the Lao side.

Lao Visas

Lao visas are now granted on arrival by air at the Vientiane airport and, in some cases, granted directly at the bridge at the "Visa on Arrival" window. This visa-on-arrival policy seems to change with the seasons and it's a wise idea to obtain your Lao visa in advance of your arrival in Nong Khai. Lao visas can be picked up at a Lao embassy or consulate or with the aid of a travel agency.

Visas obtained directly at the bridge cost US$50 and only American dollars are accepted.

Note that the Lao consulate in nearby Khon Kaen now issues Lao visas.

Travelers who arrive in Nong Khai without a Lao visa should visit The Meeting Place on Soi Chuenjit, where Lao visas cost US$50 plus a 300B service charge. The visa application takes just 30 minutes and the managers can make arrangements for transportation to Vientiane. They will also recommend a hotel or guesthouse.

Lao visas are good for 15 days and can be extended in Vientiane, Luang Prabang, and many other towns for US$1-3 per day. Visitors who overstay their Lao visa are generally charged 100B for each day. You can exit Laos at any recognized border crossing. Be sure to obtain a new Thai visa in Vientiane or you will only be granted a 30-day stay on your return to Thailand.

ATTRACTIONS NEAR NONG KHAI

Several Laotian-style temples and geological oddities are located outside Nong Khai. Their isolated locations make them difficult to reach with public transportation, but they are great rides for motorcyclists.

Wat Bang Puan
Eighteen km southwest of Nong Khai is a modern Laotian-style *chedi* built by a ruler from Vientiane and reconstructed in 1978 by the Fine Arts Department. Considered among the most sacred sites in the northeast, Wat Ban Puan is somewhat unimpressive aside from several Buddhas displayed under open tin roofs and a small museum filled with wooden figurines, Dvaravati stone inscriptions, and odd statues of policemen and model *wats.* Photographs of the original *chedi* are posted on the interior walls.

Wat Bang Puan can be reached by a *songtao* to Ban Nong Hong Song and a second minitruck west to the compound.

Wat Prathat Buakok
Far more interesting than Wat Bang Puan is this Laotian stupa and historical park 55 km southwest of Nong Khai.

The principal stupa at Wat Buakok is a modern replica of the famous monument at That Phanom, which is in turn fashioned after the original structure of That Luang in Vientiane. Constructed from 1917 to 1927 to enshrine a footprint of the Buddha, Wat Buakok features exterior friezes of horses, elephants, buffaloes, and monkeys. A billboard points the way to nearby prehistoric wall paintings and abstract designs painted by former monks.

Ban Phu Historic National Park
A dirt road shortly before Wat Buakok leads two km uphill to one of the most curious geological sights in Thailand. An information center at the park entrance shows hiking trails through bizarre rock formations named after Buddhist legends and ancient folk tales. English-speaking guides are usually on hand.

First walk left to several rock formations (Tham Wua and Tham Khon) covered with crude paintings of Dvaravati Buddhas and Hindu gods from the Lopburi Period. The path then circles an upper plateau covered with outlandishly shaped rocks that resemble giant toadstools carved by Martians. A side path leads back to a lookout point called Pha Sadej, and then returns to Wat Luk Koei ("Temple of the Son-in-Law"), recently reconstructed to support the collapsing overhanging rock. The complete hiking loop takes about 90 minutes.

The historical park is 13 km from the town of Ban Phu, which can be reached by *songtao* from either Nong Khai or Si Chiang Mai. A chartered *songtao* will be necessary from Ban Phu, or a chartered *samlor* from Ban Tu.

THA BO

One of the prettiest and least visited regions in Thailand is the northern perimeter of the Issan between Nong Khai and Chiang Khan. The untouched quality of the towns increase with distance from Nong Khai, with the best atmosphere at Pak Chom and Sang Khom, followed by Chiang Khan and Si Chiang Mai.

The road west from Nong Khai first passes through Tha Bo, a town 25 km west of Nong Khai on the banks of the Mekong. Tha Bo lies in a fertile region that produces tomatoes, rice, tobacco, and noodles. The main industry is the production of spring-roll wrappers, as evidenced by the thousands of rice-paper circles drying on crosswork racks. Another unusual product is *kenaf,* which is lowered into shallow ponds to rot until the fiber can be worked into basketry.

Sights west of town include Wat Nam Mong, which contains a highly regarded solid-gold Buddha image (Pra Chao Ong Due) cast in the 17th century, and a public park with strangely sculpted topiary.

The relatively new Huay Mong Dam is also worth a visit.

Accommodations
Isan Orchid Guest Lodge: The best place to stay in town, where Mr. Thom and Don Beckerman run a very clean homestay at the edge of the river. They can arrange tours to nearby temples and the rock formations at Buakok Historical Park. 87/9 Kaew Worawut, tel. (042) 431665, 500-800B.

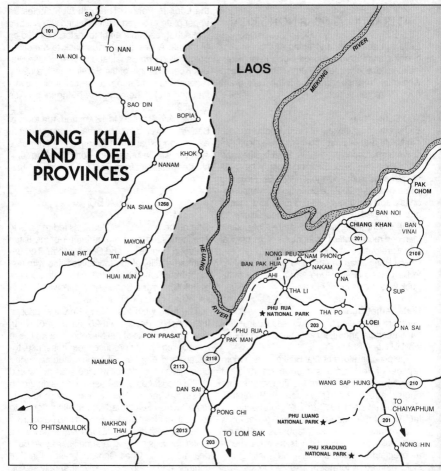

Transportation

Yellow buses to Tha Bo and Si Chiang Mai leave from the street just west of the Suzuki dealership in Nong Khai. Motorcyclists can follow the road skirting the Mekong, or take Hwy. 211 west of Nong Song Hong and visit Wat Bang Puan.

SI CHIANG MAI

Si Chiang Mai is a thriving commercial center 58 km west of Nong Khai and just across the river from Vientiane. First impressions are discourag-

ing since the town has replaced much of its original wooden architecture with the concrete cubicles so typical of contemporary Thailand, but the town has a degree of charm and is a useful point for visits to nearby temples and beaches. Most of the population are Lao and Vietnamese citizens who fled here after the communist takeover of Laos; today they remain stateless peoples without passports or land ownership rights.

Attractions

Lao and Vietnamese refugees in Si Chiang Mai have established a roaring business in the production of spring-roll wrappers, exported to all corners of the planet. Visitors can watch the production of the rice-paper wrappers and visit the bakery on the riverfront road at Soi 30, which still produces fresh French breads daily at 1500. Other sights include a small beach best visited at low tide, a large tomato-canning factory marked Chico-Thai, and Wat Aranyabanpot, about 10 km west of town. Saturday events include cockfights during the dry season and fish fighting during the rainy months.

Wat Hin Mak Peng: Temple fans may also want to visit Wat Hin Mak Peng, west of Si Chiang Mai and 30 km before Sang Khom. This peaceful forest monastery is known for its rigorous precepts followed by a large community of monks and *mae chis*. Residents live in monastic *kutis* constructed among giant boulders elevated over the banks of the Mae Nam Khong.

Than Thong Falls: A small set of falls best visited during the rainy season is located past Wat Hin Mak Peng and 11 km east of Sang Khom.

Accommodations

Hotels: Kusonsuk Hotel at 14 Rimkhong Rd. and Sithisuwan Hotel at 35 Rimkhong Rd. have rooms for 80-100B.

Tim Guesthouse: Several years ago a Swiss citizen named Jean-Daniel Schranz opened a small guesthouse on the riverfront road between Sois 16 and 17. Jean-Daniel and his Thai wife can help with bicycles, motorcycles, boats, car rentals, and information on nearby attractions. Other services include international telephone calls, laundry, hot solar-powered showers, traditional massage, Western and Thai meals, fresh coffee, and home-baked breads, not to mention his collection of over 350 cassette tapes. Rimkhong Rd., Soi 16, tel. (042) 451072, 60-120B.

SANG KHOM

The atmosphere improves considerably in the small town of Sang Khom, 63 km west of Nong Khai. Populated solely by Thais, Sang Khom provides a useful base from which to visit the region's waterfalls, temples, and caves.

Attractions
The only sight in town is Wat Kang Sila, the so-called Leaning Tower of Sang Khom. Maps to attractions outside town can be picked up at the local guesthouses.

Wat Patak Sua: A small temple-monastery with great views is tucked away in the cliffs above Sang Khom. Start from the trailhead four km east of town, and hike one hour through the forest.

Caves: Hikers and bicyclists may also want to visit Padeng Cave and Wat Punakaba, 28 km southeast of town near Ban Dong Tong, and a pair of caves in the hills near Ban Nam Pu.

Than Tip Falls: The best waterfalls in the region are 15 km west of Sang Khom and two km off the main highway. Stop at the sign and hike through rice and tapioca farms to the five-level falls which eventually empty into the Mekong.

Accommodations
Several guesthouses in town provide simple but acceptable digs at bargain rates.

River Huts: No longer located directly on the banks of the river and now tucked away behind town, but still one of the best choices in Sangkhom. The owners provide boat trips down the Mekong, bicycle rentals, rough maps, and "lice removal— one baht each." Rimkhong Rd., 60-100B.

Bouy Guesthouse: The only guesthouse still located directly facing the river with a very popular cafe. Rimkhong Rd., 60-100B.

PAK CHOM

The Lao village of Pak Chom is the prettiest and most laid-back town between Nong Khai and Chiang Khan. Travelers seeking to discover what is most authentic and charming about rural Issan will enjoy a few days gazing at the river and wandering around the surrounding countryside. A wonderful, almost completely untouched destination.

The main activity is simply watching the river and perhaps taking a boat down the Mekong. Gold miners can sometimes be seen working the sandy islands and crumbling riverbanks. Ban Vinai Refugee Center closed in 1992, and the Hmong residents were relocated to a large camp near Chiang Kham in northern Thailand. The Cambodian residents were sent off to a camp near the Kampuchean border.

Accommodations
The sheer beauty of Pak Chom will probably bring more guesthouses, but for the present time the town offers only a few simple bungalows.

Pak Chom Guesthouse: The best place in town has a dozen bamboo bungalows at the end of a dirt trail at the north end of Pak Chom. Started by Niyana from Nong Khai but now managed by a Swiss traveler, the locale and atmosphere of the Maekhong remind you of the Golden Triangle before the arrival of mass tourism. The grounds are surrounded by bamboo forests and a meditation wat with lagoon and beach chairs. Soi 1, tel. (042) 881021. Twin bungalows with no electricity and common bath cost 60-100B. Walk west of town until you reach the small signpost on the right.

Chumpee Guesthouse: The only alternative to the Pak Chom Guesthouse is the rather dismal collection of bamboo huts thoughtlessly crammed together near the river two blocks east of the main intersection. Chumpee sponsors jungle tours at 450B for three people, and has a small cafe with good views over the river. Rooms cost 50-80B.

Restaurants

Pim's Cafe on the main street in the center of town is operated by a very friendly woman who speaks English and serves shots of rice whiskey in addition to Thai dishes listed on the chalkboard menu. A small Thai restaurant is located near the river just one block east of the Chumpee Guesthouse.

CHIANG KHAN

Chiang Khan is a fairly large town 50 km north of Loei on the banks of the Mekong River. Almost entirely constructed of teakwood homes now covered with a fine patina of red dust, Chiang Khan guarantees a refreshing change from other towns in Thailand created from concrete and cinder block. The town is also known for its cotton blankets and excellent bananas.

While it lacks the simplicity and rural charms of Pak Chom, Chiang Khan serves as a useful transit point on a Mekong journey as well as a good spot for boat cruises on the Mekong River.

Temples

Religious architecture in Chiang Khan somewhat reflects the cultural interaction of Thai and French-Lao influences, from the northern-style rooflines to the Lao glasswork and pseudo-French shutters. Examples of local *wats* include Wat Sri Khun Muang with its guardian demons and primitively painted murals, and Wat Pa Klang constructed after Chiang Khan was established by Laotian migrants several centuries ago.

Travelers with motorcycles may want to visit Wat Phu Pha Baen, a small temple and cave complex set with meditation platforms and excellent views, 10 km east of Chiang Khan and one-third the distance up the mountain. Closer temples include Wat Tha Khok, two km east of town, and a forest temple called Wat Si Song Nong near Khaeng Khut Ku. Wat Si Song Nong serves as residence for a highly respected monk named Achaan Mahabun Nak.

Curiosity seekers might visit Ban Kok Lao, 25 km east, where childless women worship huge stone phalluses as fertility symbols.

River Journeys

Guesthouses in Chiang Khan arrange upriver boat trips through sublime scenery to Menam Heuang and the point where the Mekong turns north into Laos. The downriver journey reaches the rapids at Kaeng Khut Ku in about 30 minutes. Fares are 80-200B depending on distances and number of passengers. Most trips include cold drinks and stops for swimming.

Several small companies have announced plans to boat down the Mekong from Chiang Kham to Pak Chom, and perhaps farther east to Sang Khom and Si Chiang Mai. Problems with

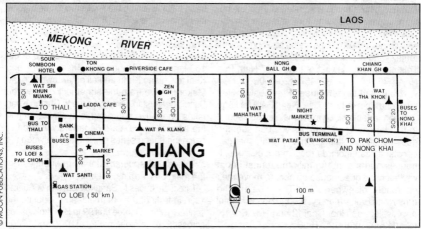

this exciting route include political disputes with Laotian authorities and dangerous rapids on the Mekong.

Festivals

Chiang Khan celebrations include the Miss Banana Beauty Contest in the fall and the Cotton Festival in February. The end of the Buddhist retreat season in late October is celebrated with a week-long festival of boat races, performances of Issan musical comedy, and displays of wax model *prasats* at the local temples.

Kaeng Khut Ku

A large set of rapids and a scenic overlook are located five km east of Chiang Khan at the end of a very long side road. Kaeng Khut Ku is popular with Thai tourists; there you can consume barbecued fish, prawn fritters, and *som tam* in bamboo observation decks elevated over the riverbanks. Accommodations are available at See View Bungalows for 200-350B, and at Coot Cao Resort for 180-280B.

Kaeng Khut Ku can be reached from Chiang Khan by *songtao, tuk tuk,* rented bicycle, or boats chartered from local guesthouses.

Accommodations

Nong Sam Guesthouse: Previously called the Tamarind Guesthouse, the friendliest place in Chiang Khan is operated by a Brit named Rob, his Thai wife Noi, and their two children (Nong and Sam), who have frantic energy levels. Rob, the primary information source for the region, distributes maps and helpful advice to his guests. Other services include boat trips on the Mekong, bicycle rentals, and popular breakfasts in his cozy cafe. This place is southwest of town. 407 Nam Pon Najan Rd., tel. (042) 821457, 120-200B.

Nong Ball Guesthouse: Previously called the Nong Sam Guesthouse, Nong Ball is a large and comfortable place that runs a close second to the current Nong Sam. As you can see, the guesthouse situation in Chiang Khan changes constantly as landlords reclaim popular guesthouses and attempt to milk the tourist boom while forcing guesthouse owners to move their operations elsewhere. The Thai woman who runs Nong Ball is friendly, though not as helpful or articulate as Rob. Chai Khong Rd., Soi 16, tel. (042) 821056, 120-180B.

Chiang Khan Guesthouse: Previously called the Amnatsiri Hotel, but now called a guesthouse to cash in on the travelers' market. A fairly rundown place redeemed by a decent riverside cafe. Chai Khong Rd., Soi 19, tel. (042) 821285, 100-140B.

Souk Somboon Hotel: Previously called the Suksambuh, this is the only hotel worth checking when the guesthouses are filled. All 16 rooms are fan-cooled with common baths down the hall. 243 Chai Khong Rd., Soi 9, tel. (042) 821064, 120-180B.

Restaurants

Nong Sam Guesthouse operates the most popular cafe in town, serving Western breakfasts, Thai dinners, and vegetarian specialties. Favorites in the riverview dining area at the Souk Somboon Hotel include *laab moo, laab gai, ya mut ya* (spicy noodles with sausage), and *pla tot* (fried fish).

Small cafes on Soi 9 include Ladda Cafe for *pad thai,* a *gai yang* stall for fried chicken, and an unnamed duck soup shop across the road. All serve prodigious amounts of Laotian *mao lao* (literally "drunk on liquor"), a grain-alcohol whiskey both cheaper and stronger than Thai Mekong. Shots are thrown down like tequila and washed with beer chasers.

The central market near the cinema and a/c bus terminal has a few foodstalls for morning servings of fried *pla tong goh* (donuts) and steaming cups of *nam ta hu* (sweetened soybean milk). Evening foodstalls are located at the night market near Soi 18.

Transportation

Chiang Khan is 50 km north of Loei and about 160 km west of Nong Khai. Buses from Nong Khai to Chiang Khan and all other towns on the Mekong leave from the street just beyond the Suzuki dealership. Direct service to Chiang Khan takes about five hours but is available only in the early morning. Late departers will need to patch together a series of *songtaos* between the various towns.

Buses and *songtaos* depart frequently from the main bus terminal in Loei.

Direct a/c buses to Bangkok leave at 0800 and 1830 in front of the pharmacy and opposite the central market. Orange bus 99 to Bangkok leaves across from the night market at 0730 and 1730.

Songtaos to Loei leave every 20 minutes from Loei Road opposite the Shell gas station. *Songtaos* to Tha Li occasionally leave from west of town, depending on passenger demand and road conditions.

LOEI

Midway between the north and the northeast on the western edge of the Issan plateau, the provincial capital of Loei serves as an important transit spot for visitors arriving from northern Thailand, and as a useful base for visiting Phu Kradung National Park.

Loei is geographically classified as part of the northeast, though the region more closely resembles northern Thailand with its freezing temperatures and heavy fog in the winter months, searing heat during the hot season, and mountainous topography surrounding the fertile valley. In earlier days, Loei was considered a hardship post for bureaucrats who had fallen out of favor with the government in Bangkok. Perhaps be-

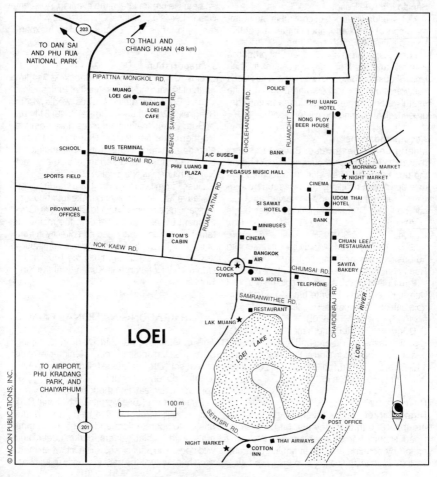

cause of its isolation, Loei and the western valleys have retained some of the traditional flavor lost in the more developed regions of Thailand.

Attractions

The region's principal sights are the three national parks outside town. However, you can enjoy a few hours of wandering around the municipal lake at the south end of town and exploring the small market near the bridge that crosses the narrow Loei River. Adjacent to the lake is a small Lak Muang and a Chinese shrine called Sanjao Por Kud Pong.

Hot-season visitors can cool off in the swimming pool at Loei Land, about three km north of town on the road to Chiang Khan.

Loei is situated in a rich valley that produces minerals and some of the finest cottons in Thailand. Shops on Charoenraj and Ruamchai Roads sell warm cotton blankets and clothing, quite useful when temperatures plunge to zero degrees Celsius during the winter months.

Accommodations

Muang Loei Guesthouse: Budget travelers usually stay in this guesthouse one block north of the bus terminal. The place, now located in a new apartment building, once was run by a retired Thai military officer who served as a liaison between Thai and American forces but is now owned by a local Thai lady. Ruamchai Rd., tel. (042) 812302, 80-100B.

Sarai Thong Hotel: A fairly decent hotel with 56 basic rooms near the center of town. 25/5 Ruamchai Rd., tel. (042) 811582, 120-180B.

Phu Luang Hotel: A good middle-quality hotel with big a/c rooms, private baths, and acceptable cafe. 55 Charoenraj Rd., tel. (042) 811532, fax (042) 812558, 450-650B.

Udom Thai Hotel: Loei's most popular hotel is similar to the Phu Luang and King Hotels, but perhaps in a better location at the center of town. 112 Charoenraj Rd., tel. (042) 811763, 220-300B fan, 350-500B a/c.

Restaurants

Night Market: A small night market sets up around 1800 in the alley just off Charoenraj Road. Rather than sit around, try the takeaway option by pointing at each intriguing dish and saying, *"Ha baht, ha baht"* ("Five *baht,* five *baht").*

Borrow a plate and silverware from your hotel to enjoy the best and cheapest meal in town. A larger night market takes place at the south end of the city lake.

Nong Ploy Beer House: Directly across from the Phu Luang Hotel is a decent restaurant with an English-language menu that lists everything from chicken *laab* to tasty potato soup. 66 Charoenraj Rd. Moderate.

Savita Bakery: Breakfasts are best in this clean cafe serving both Western and Thai specialties. Savita is also a popular place to hang out and eat ice cream late in the evening. Adjacent Chuan Lee is a traditional Chinese cafe with coffee and curries. 137 Charoenraj Rd. Inexpensive.

Transportation

Loei is 520 km northeast of Bangkok, 344 km north of Korat, and 269 km east of Phitsanulok.

Air: Bangkok Air flies twice weekly from Bangkok. 22/13 Chumsai Rd., tel. (042) 811416.

Bus: Buses leave eight times daily from the Northern Bus Terminal in Bangkok. Loei can also be reached by bus from Phitsanulok via Lom Sak. Buses and *songtaos* also connect Nan with Loei via Nam Pat and Dan Sai.

Buses from Loei to Chiang Mai via Phitsanulok leave five times daily and take four hours to Phitsanulok and nine hours to Chiang Mai. Government buses leave from both the main bus terminal on Ruamchai Road and directly in front of the Phu Luang Hotel. Private bus companies with a/c services include Chumprae Tours at the Udom Thai Hotel and Sir Kuarinter at the King Hotel.

PHU KRADUNG NATIONAL PARK

This outstanding park, located on a sloping plateau 82 km south of Loei, is a high-elevation retreat set with pine trees, tall grasses, six waterfalls, dozens of hiking trails, and fields of springtime azaleas and rhododendrons.

Phu Kradung ("Bell Mountain") National Park was established in 1967 to help preserve the unique temperate flora and indigenous mammals such as black bears, barking deer, and wild dogs. The park closes July-Oct. when monsoon rains reduce the trails to muddy quagmires.

Rangers advise visiting the park on weekdays to avoid crowds, and, if possible, during the less popular but very lush months of May and June.

The main trail begins at the base of the mountain at Ban Si Than, where the Parks Division operates an information center with maps, restaurant, and bungalows. Bags can be stored and porters can be hired at the information center. The trail from Si Than climbs steeply for the first kilometer before easing off and finally starting the final ascent. Bamboo ladders and ropes help you through the steeper sections. The trail ultimately emerges onto a sweeping plateau carpeted with grass and covered with wildflowers Feb.-May. The total distance of about nine km takes four or five hours.

Park headquarters at the summit has a small shop with basic provisions, another restaurant with hot meals, bungalows, tent sites, and maps describing the 50 km of trails. Popular hikes include the trail to Liam Phan Nok Aen at the eastern edge of the plateau for views over the Petchabun Mountains, and a southern trail that runs 12 km along the edge of the plateau.

Visitors should bring warm clothes, extra food, flashlight, candles, and insect repellent.

Accommodations
Accommodations include 16 10-person bungalows that cost 500-1,500B. Tents cost 80B per night. Bedding and blankets can be rented. Reservations can be made in Bangkok with the National Parks Division of the Forestry Department (tel. 02-271-3737), or with the Forestry Department in Loei (tel. 042-800776) on the main highway inside the provincial offices.

The Loei Provincial Office also arranges group tours for parties of 10 or more. The three-day, two-night tour costs 800B per person and includes transportation, food, drink, and accommodations in bungalows.

Transportation
Phu Kradung is 74 km south of Loei on Hwy. 201 and then eight km west on Hwy. 2019. Direct minibuses are available on weekends from the main bus terminal. Exact departure schedules can be checked at Muang Loei Guesthouse. Alternatively, take any bus heading south toward Khon Kaen and alight at the park turnoff. Hitchhike or wait for a *songtao*.

PHU LUANG NATIONAL PARK

Phu Luang is an 848-square-km wildlife reserve controlled by the Forestry Department to help protect the remaining wildlife, reputed to include wild tigers and elephants. Similar to Phu Kradung, Phu Luang is situated on a high plateau covered with tropical jungles, deciduous pine forests, and vast stretches of savannah. The park is also known for its variety of rare Paphiopedilum and Sukul orchids, which have been depleted by poachers to the verge of extinction. Trails established by the park rangers lead to Pa Chang Phan ("Elephant Cliff") for sunrises, the wild roses at Pa Somdej, and Pa Talien, where dwarf trees are collected and sold as potted bonsais. Thick jungle and wild orchids are best seen at Khok Prommajan, north of the Forest Reserve Camp, and in Black Forest, where white orchids cling to moss-covered trees.

Accommodations
Accommodations are similar to Phu Kradung's, with group bungalows from 500B and tents on site for 80B. Reservations can be made at the provincial offices in Loei. Bring food, drink, warm clothes, flashlight, and candles.

Transportation
Phu Luang is 26 km south of Loei down Hwy. 201 and then 15 km west from Wang Saphung. Although somewhat closer than Phu Kradung, Phu Luang is more difficult to visit because of its inaccessibility and lack of organized transportation. The easiest option is a tour arranged by the Forestry Department at the Loei Provincial Office. The three-day, two-night tour costs 800B per person and includes transportation, food, drink, and accommodations in park bungalows.

Minitrucks from the bus terminal in Loei go halfway up the mountain, from where a tough trail reaches the summit and park headquarters. Allow three or four hours for the trek.

TOWNS NEAR LOEI

One of the most intriguing travel routes in Thailand is between Loei and northern Thailand, unquestionably one of the most beautiful yet least visited regions in Thailand. Tucked away in the mountains which divide Issan from central and northern Thailand are dozens of small towns and villages that probably receive only a few dozen Western visitors each year. Most towns have small and inexpensive hotels and can be reached by buses and minitrucks.

The most common route is from Loei to Phitsanulok via Lom Sak, past the national parks at Phu Rua, Phu Hin Rongkla, and Thung Salang Luang. A more scenic route is from Loei to Dan Sai, from where the road splits to either Nakhon Thai and Phitsanulok, or north to Nan Pat and eventually Nan. Simple Thai hotels are available on the northern route in Dan Sai, Nam Pat, and Na Noi.

Tha Li

Another lovely town somewhat similar to Pak Chom, Tha Li is eight km south of the Heuang River in a remote valley about 50 km west of Chiang Khan and 45 km north of Loei.

Once under the control of local smugglers who exchanged Thai merchandise for Lao whiskey and other contraband, Tha Li today is firmly guarded by the Thai government to prevent another surprise border incursion by the Laotian army. Roads north of Tha Li head up to a military camp at Ban Pak Hua, the large town of Nong Peu, and the trading village of Ahi (Aharn). All three villages are situated on the Heuang River, a tributary of the Mekong. Longtail boats can be chartered to tour the river and visit some bathing beaches.

Tha Li can be reached by motorcycle and by *songtao* from Loei and occasionally Chiang Khan.

The **O.T.S. Guesthouse** in Ban Pak Hua has rooms for 60-80B, a decent cafe, and bike rentals for exploring the region.

Dan Sai

About 86 km west of Loei is the small town of Dan Sai, an important junction point chiefly known among the Thais for its strange ghostly procession called Pi Ta Khon ("Dance of the Ghosts"). The three-day Bun Luang Festival begins with a masked parade to honor the guardian spirits of a highly revered Buddha image and to kick off the annual rainmaking ceremonies in June. Local residents don bizarre Halloween masks made from coconut husks crowned with a hat formed from glutinous rice steamers. Each ghost carries a phallic-shaped sword in accordance with the fertility rites of Bun Bung Fai (Rocket Festival) and follows the sacred Buddha image from the Moon River to the gates of Wat Por Chai. The festival ends on the third day after the ghosts circumnavigate the principal *bot* three times and fling their masks into the Moon River.

The principal sight in Dan Sai is Wat Prathat Sri Song Rak, on a hill on the west bank of the Moon River about one km from the center of town. The 30-meter brick stupa was constructed in 1560 to commemorate a diplomatic treaty between King Chakrapet of Ayuthaya and King Chaichetha of Vientiane. Sri Song Rak is one of the few temples in Thailand without resident monks, being left to the guardian spirits of Chao Por Kuan and Chao Mae Nan Tiam. Visitors should bring white flowers and avoid wearing red clothing.

A small hotel in Dan Sai has rooms from 80B.

Lom Sak

Lom Sak is a small town in a fertile valley between the Phang Hoei Mountains to the east and the southern extension of the Luang Prabang Range to the west. Lom Sak is a major transit point for visitors traveling between Phitsanulok and Loei and Khon Kaen.

About 175 km south of Lom Sak are the ruins of Muang Si Thep, an important Khmer site which dominated the valley from the 9th to 11th centuries.

Accommodations are available at the Sawang Hotel on Samakichai Road and at the Pen Sin Hotel on Wachi Road.

THE FAR NORTHEAST

BAN AHONG

Travelers heading east from Nong Khai can break the journey in the small village of Ban Ahong, 162 km from Nong Khai and 23 km west of Beung Khan.

Ban Ahong is a collection of traditional houses elevated on pylons and a few simple shops for basic supplies, but the friendly inhabitants and riverside walks provide a refreshing change from larger towns in the region.

Attractions

A small temple lies amid the large boulders lining the southern banks of the Mekong River. A solitary monk, Luang Phra Praeng, resides at the *wat* and spends his days tending his gardens and mixing traditional medicines from herbs and roots.

Swimming is a possibility during the hot season when the Mekong recedes and leaves clear, small ponds hidden among the massive boulders. The owner of the town's only guesthouse can help arrange boat rides out to the islands lying between town and the mountainous banks of Laos.

In the evenings, sit on the banks of the river or wander into town and join the drinking circle at the home of the village mayor.

Accommodations

Hideaway Guesthouse: Provides several simple huts and a pleasant sitting area on the banks of the river. Owner Khun Saksin speaks some English and German, and can help with travel tips about the region. The guesthouse is next to the river and behind the local school. 60-100B.

Transportation

Buses from Nong Khai take about two hours to reach Ban Ahong, a small spot without banks, post offices, police stations, or *tuk tuks*. Be sure to tell the driver to drop you in Ban Ahong, or the bus may roar through the town en route to Beung Khan.

BEUNG KHAN

Highway 212 leaves Nong Khai and continues 135 km east to the small town of Beung Khan, situated on the Mekong River just opposite the Laotian village of Muang Paksan. Beung Khan provides a useful pause or overnight stop for travelers heading down to Nakhon Phanom. Enjoying a drink from a local cafe and watching fishermen maneuver the rapids are the main interests of Beung Khan.

Phu Wua Wildlife Park

A small nature park on Phu Wua Mountain, 45 km southeast of town, features several waterfalls, crumbling cliffs, and a small forest *wat*. Phu Wua can be combined with a visit to Wat Phu Tauk, or get there by taking a bus east on Hwy. 212 to Ban Chayphet, from where *songtaos* continue south down to Ban Noi near Dansanan Falls and Ban Donset near Chetsei Falls.

Wat Phu Tauk

Formally known as Wat Chedi Kiri Viharn, Wat Phu Tauk is one of the most sacred forest temples in the northeast. It is also among the most spectacular in location, being situated on a sandstone mountain which soars vertically from the flat dry plains. The entire outcropping has been fashioned by resident monks into a bewildering maze of stairways and tunnels dissecting the mountain and providing sensational views over the vast expanses.

Wat Phu Tauk is ascended by a series of seven passageways which symbolically represent the seven heavens of the Buddhist universe, and which pass dozens of monastic *kutis* inhabited by friendly monks and *mae chis*. A small headquarters features photographs of the former head monk, Achaan Jun, who studied under a legendary monk named Achaan Man. Issan Thais credit Achaan Man with almost single-handedly revolutionizing *vipassana* practices in northeastern Thailand.

Wat Phu Tauk is 47 km southeast of Beung Khan. Take a bus or minitruck south from Beung

Khan 25 km down to Ban Siwilai, where *song-taos* continue 22 km east on the dirt road to the temple. Visitors can spend the night or continue to Phu Rua Wildlife Park and stay in park bungalows.

Accommodations
The Santisuk, Somanmit, and Neramit hotels on Prasatchai Road in Beung Khan have fan-cooled rooms from 80-200B.

SAKHON NAKHON

Sakhon Nakhon is a provincial center 647 km from Bangkok, on the edge of 32-square-km Nong Han Lake, the largest natural lake in Thailand. Surrounded by lakes and rivers, Sakhon Nakhon Province provides a welcome relief from the dry monotony typical of the Issan.

Sakhon Nakhon was established as a Khmer outpost but was abandoned after a severe drought forced Khmer rulers to relocate to Khotraboon. Prior to the rise of Bangkok, Sakhon Nakhon was controlled by the kingdom of Lanchang. In the 19th century, King Rama III recaptured the city and returned it to Thai control.

Sakhon Nakhon landed firmly on the map of Buddhist pilgrimages several decades ago when a *vipassana* teacher named Achaan Man Bhuidato spent his life propagating insight meditation at Wat Pa Suthawat. After his mysterious disappearance in 1949, Achaan Man was succeeded by his student Achaan Fan Ajaro, who established a cave hermitage at Tham Kham in the Phu Phan Mountains. Pilgrims continue to visit local memorials dedicated to both monks.

A very curious sidelight to Sakhon Nakhon is provided by a gecko shop on Sukkasem Road where live geckos are purchased from villagers, dried, and exported to Taiwan and Hong Kong. Chinese consume the dried lizards with herbal medicines to ensure good health and cure kidney diseases.

Festivals
Sakhon Nakhon sponsors a nationally famous Wax Festival in October, when enormous replicas of *prasat* are paraded through the streets.

Nong Han Lake
Thailand's largest natural lake is a popular place for early-morning joggers and tai chi practitioners. Boats can be hired to reach the interior islands.

Wat Chong Chum
Sakhon Nakhon's major religious monument features a modern whitewashed Laotian *chedi* which encases a 10th-century Khmer *prang*. The adjacent *viharn* contains a large seated Buddha and archaeological remains stored in a back room.

Wat Pa Suthawat
A small temple and modern museum opposite the provincial hall displays the paraphernalia and wax figure of Achaan Man, the fierce meditation master whose intensity is reflected in his lifelike image.

Wat Narai Cheng Weng
Six km northeast of town in the village of Ban Thai stands a Khmer *prang* reputedly constructed in the 10th century by a Khmer princess using only female labor. Also called Wat Prathat Naweng, the sandstone sanctuary features several excellent lintels carved with dancing Shivas and Krishna struggling with mythical lions.

Wat Pa Udom Somphon
Buddhist pilgrims visit this temple to honor and view the religious emblems of Achaan Fan, a *vipassana* master whose life-sized wax image is displayed inside the central *viharn*. The temple is three km outside of town.

Phu Phan National Park
Situated 17 km southwest of town on Hwy. 213, this 645-square-km nature preserve offers hiking trails, three waterfalls, and forest cover over a vast expanse of remote mountains once used by Thai resistance guerrillas in WW II and communist insurgents in the early 1970s. After peace was restored in the late 1970s, the royal family established a palace and research center to help promote the revival of ancient textile weaving.

Accommodations
All of the following hotels are located within a few blocks of the bus terminal on Raj Pattana Road.

Dusit Hotel: Not affiliated with the Dusit hotel chain in Bangkok, this large and somewhat creaky hotel has both fairly clean a/c rooms with private showers. 1782 Yuwa Pattana Rd., tel. (042) 711198, 350-600B a/c.

Araya Hotel: Several hotels are in the center of town near the intersection of Kamchadphai and Premprida Roads. The Araya is about the same quality as the Dusit. 1432 Kamchadphai Rd., tel. (042) 711097, 150-180B fan, 300-350B a/c.

Somkait Hotel: Another inexpensive hotel for an overnight stay, but noisy due to the interior parking lot. 1368 Kamchadphai Rd., tel. (042) 711993, 150-200B fan.

Imperial Hotel: Best hotel in town is nothing special, but it has a decent restaurant and popular nightclub. 1892 Sukkasem Rd., tel. (042) 711119, 300-500B a/c.

Transportation

Sakhon Nakhon is 145 km southeast of Beung Khan, 117 km west of Nakhon Pathom, and 155 km east of Udon Thani.

Air: Thai Airways flies once daily from Bangkok for 1,500B. 1446 Yuwa Pattana Rd., tel. (042) 712259.

Bus: Buses reach Sakhon Nakhon from Ubon Ratchathani, Nakhon Phanon, That Phanon,

Kalasin, Korat, and Bangkok. Travelers coming down from Beung Khan can take a direct bus or patch together a journey along the Mekong with a stop in Nakhon Phanom.

Direct a/c buses back to Bangkok and other towns en route depart several times daily from the Udon Sakon Doen Rot bus office adjacent to the Esso station on Raj Pattana Road.

NAKHON PHANOM

Nakhon Phanom is set along the banks of the Mekong River, across from the small Laotian town of Muang Tha Khaek (Muang Khammouan).

Nakhon Phanom gained fame in the early 16th century when King Phothisarat raised a great reliquary establishing the religious importance of the region, and later promoted trade routes from his Issan capital across the mountain chain to the coast of Vietnam and southward to Phnom Penh.

The town served as a busy American airbase during the Vietnam conflict, but has since returned to a sleepy place populated by Issan farmers, Chinese merchants, Vietnamese refugees, and a modest number of Laotian traders.

Attractions

The capital of Nakhon Phanom Province chiefly serves as an overnight rest stop en route to That Phanom, or the access point to Laos via the trading village of Tha Khaek.

Riverside Promenade: The town's best activity is walking down the landscaped promenade and visiting the souvenir shops for inexpensive silverwork and Laotian handicrafts.

Wat Si Thep: To the south is a small temple complex worth a visit for the paintings inside the *bot* that depict the life of Buddha, and the kings of the Chakri dynasty.

Across to Laos

Visitors holding Lao visas can now take the ferry across the Mekong to Tha Khaek and then continue south to Savannaket and Pakse.

Thai businesspeople have offered to finance a bridge across the Mekong at Nakhon Pathom and improve the road east to facilitate commerce between Thailand and Vietnam. The 240-km highway would provide a direct link between Bangkok and Vinh on the Gulf of Tonkin in central Vietnam. But the new bridge soon to open between Mukdahan and Laos will probably delay any new construction at Nakhon Phanom.

For the present, Tha Khaek remains a lonely outpost with a few French colonial buildings dating from the early 20th century, and a handful of hotels catering to business travelers and the infrequent group tourists.

Festivals

Festivals at the end of the rainy season in late October include the renowned Nakhon Phanom Boat Races and an illuminated boat procession augmented by cultural performances and handicraft fairs.

Accommodations

River Inn Hotel: The only decent place on the river features a terrace restaurant with good food and views into Laos. 137 Sunthon Wichit Rd., tel. (042) 511305, 180-260B fan, 350-450B a/c.

First Hotel: A good alternative to the River Inn is the large hotel across from the clock tower and close to the river. The staff is friendly and the rooms are fairly clean. 370 Si Thep Rd., tel. (042) 511253, 150-200B fan, 280-350B a/c.

Nakhon Phanom Hotel: A midpriced choice is the 58-room hotel located across from the market in the center of town. Facilities include a restaurant and nightclub, swimming pool, and snooker parlor. 403 Aphiban Bancha Rd. (Hwy. 212), tel. (042) 511455, 400-650B a/c.

Mae Khong Grand View Hotel: Nakhon Phanom's newest hotel opened a few years ago on the banks of the Mekong in the southern section of town. The 141-room hotel includes a swimming pool, restaurant, and cocktail lounge with live entertainment. 527 Sunthon Wichit Rd., tel. (042) 513564, fax (042) 511037, 950-1,900B.

Restaurants

Cafes along the river provide spectacular views and tasty food, such as the giant catfish served in curry sauce, with lemongrass and basil, fried with garlic and shallots, or steamed in clay pots and garnished with ginger wedges.

New Suan Mai: Just south of the clock tower is the best spot to try a catfish dinner and enjoy a few beers at sunset. Dishes prepared without the expensive fish cost 50-80B; catfish specialities run 150-200B but portions are large enough to feed several people. Open daily 1000-2200. 271 Sunthon Wichit Rd., tel. (042) 511202. Moderate to expensive.

Golden Giant Catfish Restaurant: Properly called the Plaa Beuk Thong ("Fish Golden Giant"), and adjacent to the New Suan Mai, the restaurant also serves the local speciality and other dishes such as Issan noodles and spicy duck salads. Open daily 0700-2200. 259 Sunthon Wichit Rd., tel. (042) 511218. Moderate to expensive.

Practicalities

Nakhon Phanom is small enough to explore in a single day, but large enough to have all necessary services.

Tourist Office: The TAT office on the river in the northern section of town can provide maps and other information on Nakhon Phanom, Mukdahan, and Sakhon Nakhon. Open daily 0830-1630. 184/1 Sunthon Wichit Rd., tel. (042) 513490, fax (042) 513492.

Post Office and International Telephone: The GPO on Sunthon Wichit Rd. is open weekdays 0830-1630 and weekends 0900-1200. The attached CAT Telecom Center is open daily 0700-2300.

Provincial Hospital: The best hospital in town has English-speaking doctors and emergency evacuation services. 270 Apiban Bancha Rd., tel. (042) 511422.

Transportation

Nakhon Phanom is 740 km northeast of Bangkok, 252 km east of Udon Thani, 303 km southeast of Nong Khai, and 271 km north of Ubon Ratchathani.

Bus: Buses reach Nakhon Phanom from the Northern Bus Terminal in Bangkok, but most travelers arrive by bus from Nong Khai, Sakhon Nakhon, or Ubon Ratchathani. Buses from Nong Khai depart hourly 0700-1500 and take about seven hours via Sakhon Nakhon. Buses also run hourly from both Ubon Ratchathani and Sakhon Nakhon.

THAT PHANOM

That Phanom, a small town on the banks of the Mekong River midway between Nakhon Phanom and Mukdahan, is a major pilgrimage site and home to the most sacred religious monument in the northeast.

A Lao market occurs near the river on Monday and Thursday mornings.

Wat Prathat Phanom

Highly venerated by both Thai and Laotian citizens, the Laotian-style *chedi* of That Phanom forms the talismanic symbol of the Issan people and a source of magical power for the residents of Laos.

The origins of the monument are unknown, though Buddhist legends claim that the original buildings were constructed about 2,500 years ago after a wandering monk named Maha Kasapa brought the breastbone of the Buddha to the region. Folklore relates that five local princes housed the relic in a new *chedi,* which was subsequently renovated in 1614 by the king of Laos and in 1692 by a famous Vientiane monk named Pra Kru Luang Phonsamek.

Disaster struck in 1975 when the principal tower collapsed after heavy rains. Horrified at the plight of the Issan icon, local authorities, aided by the Fine Arts Department, immediately began a reconstruction project which succeeded in erecting a new *chedi* in 1977.

The rebuilt structure features ancient Laotian ornaments and Khmer-style brick reliefs recovered from the original monument. Interior murals depict contemporary social problems such as drug addiction and the communist struggle in Laos.

The full moon of the third lunar month (February or March) is an excellent time to visit, when thousands of devout Buddhists gather for a popular festival.

Renu Phanom

Renu Phanom is a small village renowned for the weaving of cotton and silk fabrics. Several of the weaving homes also produce a rare version of Thai *ikat,* partially dyed before being painstakingly woven into ceremonial robes. A weekly handicraft market is held on Wednesday near Wat Prathat Renu Nakhon, a diminutive copy of the more famous monument in That Phanom.

The turnoff to Renu Phanom is 12 km north of That Phanom and 44 km south of Nakhon Phanom. Direct *songtao* service is available from That Phanom, or take any bus to the turnoff and wait for a *songtao* heading seven km west to the weaving village.

Accommodations

That Phanom is a very small town with a new guesthouse and two hotels located east of the monument and just beyond the Laotian Arch.

Niyana Guesthouse: Lovely and vivacious Niyana operates a popular guesthouse with kitchen facilities, garden, and information on boat trips for travelers. Over the past decade, Niyana has established guesthouses in Pak Chom, Nong Khai, and now, That Phanom. Soi Withi Sarachon, no phone, 80-150B.

Hotels: Chai Von Hotel at Phanom Phanarak Road has 20 fan-cooled rooms costing 100-180B. Saeng Thong Hotel on the same street, but a right turn through the archway, has similar facilities at identical prices. Saeng Thong also has information on nearby attractions such as the ikat-weaving village of Renu Phanom. Comparable rooms are found at the **Lim Charoen Hotel** (tel. 042-541019) on Chayangkun Road, where fan-cooled rooms cost 140-180B.

Transportation

That Phanom is 52 km south of Nakhon Phanom and 225 km north of Ubon Ratchathani. Buses

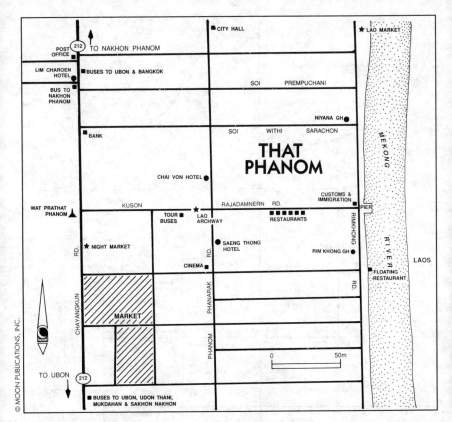

and *songtaos* from the intersection near the Nakhon Phanom Hotel in Nakhon Phanom take about 90 minutes to reach the *chedi* in That Phanom. Buses from the terminal in Ubon Ratchathani to Nakhon Pathom pass through That Phanom.

MUKDAHAN

Mukdahan is the provincial capital of the newest province in the northeast. Situated on the west banks of the wide and sluggish Mekong, Mukdahan has few important sights but offers a degree of atmosphere unique to remote destinations throughout the northeast.

The busy village is directly opposite the Laotian town of Savannakhet ("Golden Fields") and receives a small amount of trading between the two countries.

Market

The daily market, on the waterfront near immigration and customs, offers goods brought over the river from Savannakhet by Lao merchants. The merchandise mostly includes utilitarian products such as machinery and tools, but a few merchants hawk Laotian handicrafts and handwoven textiles rarely seen in other regions of Thailand. The specialty is Laotian sarongs made from cotton or silk and decorated with elephant motifs. Also look for bolsters that substitute for love partners, old baskets, Issan panpipes, and food products such as French bread and fried grasshoppers. Furniture fans will love the intricately carved tables and chairs covered

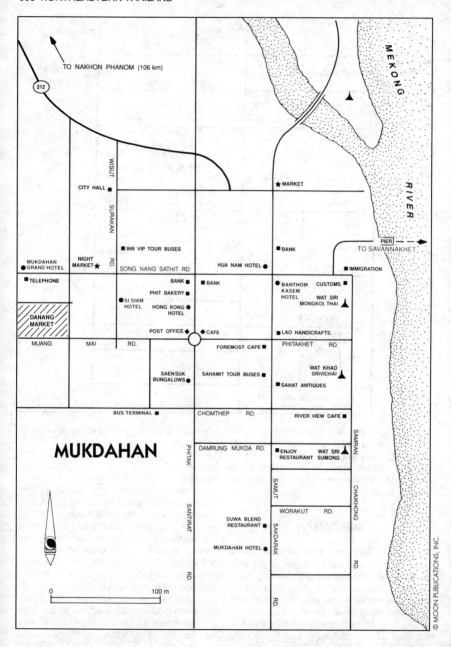

with mother-of-pearl inlays and sold at bargain prices.

Wat Sri Mongkol Thai

This small temple, sited on the riverbanks a few blocks south of city center, was constructed in 1956 by Vietnamese refugees who melded Thai contours, Vietnamese script, and Chinese dragons into an eclectic result. If you wander south down the riverside road, visit the tiny shops and cafes on the banks of the Mekong.

Wat Khao Srivichai

This Laotian-styled monastery and temple complex has the classic lotus bud *chedi* and interior murals depicting Buddha spinning the Wheel of Law.

Wat Sri Sumong

Somewhat unique for its blending of Thai and Lao architectural styles with French colonial elements around the windows and verandas. A distinctive Lao *chedi* is found between the *bot* and modern *viharn*.

Phu Manoram

Excellent views over Mukdahan and the Mekong can be enjoyed from the summit of this 500-meter hill, five km south of town off Samut Sakdarak Road. Rent a motorcycle from Niyana Guesthouse and head two km south on Route 2034, then three km west to Phu Manoram.

Motorcyclists may also want to head 34 km south down Route 212 to Phu Muu ("Pig Hill"), a 353-meter hill popular with Thais for weekend picnics. The spot is named for the wild pigs that once lived in the region.

Across to Laos

Western travelers are now allowed to cross the Mekong from Mukdahan to Savannakhet ("Golden Fields") and continue south to Pakse or east along Route 9 to Dong Ha in central Vietnam. Visitors must have a valid Lao visa.

A new 1.4-km bridge is now under construction with an anticipated completion date of 2001.

Savannakhet is a fairly large trading town serving as a provincial capital and entrepot for goods moving between Thailand and Vietnam.

Visitors can obtain information about Savannakhet

from the tourist office in the Savanbanhao Hotel on Thanon Saenna. The main draws are Wat Sangyangmunkan in the city, Prathat Hin Hang to the north of Savannakhet, and the Ho Chi Minh Trail near Xepon about 160 km east of town on Route 9.

Mukdahan National Park

South of Mukdahan is a small national park known for its strange rock formations resembling giant toadstools and homes of space aliens. The park straddles the geologic division between the northern half of the Issan and the southern half that stretches down to Cambodia. Also known as Phu Pha Thoep National Park, the 52-square-km enclave features dozens of geologic oddities, prehistoric cave paintings, and modest views from the summit of 420-meter Phu Si Chom and Phu Mano near the park entrance.

Mukdahan National Park is 16 km southeast of town on Hwy. 2034, which skirts the Mekong River.

Accommodations

Hotels are the standard collection of unimaginative Chinese joints and old Thai structures that need serious maintenance.

Hua Nam Hotel: A good location in the center of town with fairly clean rooms, hot showers, and a small cafe for basic meals. The central courtyard helps keep noise to a minimum. 36 Samut Sakdarak Rd., tel. (042) 611137, 160-200B fan, 320-380B a/c.

Saensuk Bungalows: Not really what you call bungalows, but another Thai motel with simple but clean and comfortable rooms, plus friendly management. 2 Phitak Santirat Rd., tel. (042) 611214, 140-200B fan, 300-400B a/c.

Hong Kong Hotel: A Chinese-style hotel featuring acceptable rooms with private baths. 161/1 Phitak Santirat Rd., tel. (042) 611123, 150-200B fan, 300-340B a/c.

Mukdahan Hotel: Not much style, but this newer hotel offers better rooms at lower prices than the more centrally located spots near the traffic circle. The four-story hotel has a coffee shop with live music and rooms for budget and midlevel travelers. 8/8 Samut Sakdarak Rd., tel. (042) 611619, 200-360B fan, 380-550B a/c.

Ploy Palace Hotel: Mukdahan's newest hotel is two km south of town on the road to Phu

Manoram and Mukdahan National Park. The hotel has 155 a/c rooms with private baths, restaurant, and small nightclub popular with local night owls. Phitak Phanomkhet Rd., tel. (042) 611075, fax (042) 612574, 1,200-1,800B.

Restaurants

Most visitors spend their single night in Mukdahan exploring the cafes that set up nightly along the banks of the Mekong River. The warm breeze, twinkling lights in the trees, and romantic views across to Laos make this a memorable experience in an otherwise mundane destination.

River View Cafe: A popular place that serves Thai and Lao dishes in a spectacular setting. Issan plates and catfish creations are the local specialties. Open daily 1100-2100. Samran Chaikhong Rd., tel. (042) 611778. Inexpensive to moderate.

Sukawadi Restaurant: Another basic cafe blessed with wonderful views and reasonably priced dishes that take advantage of the river and local cuisines. Open daily 1100-2100. Samran Chaikhong Rd., tel. (042) 611439. Inexpensive to moderate.

Foremost Cafe: This modern and trendy—at least by Mukdahan standards—glass-enclosed cafe serves up tasty Thai and Western dishes in a/c comfort. A welcome change from the relentless heat and monotony of the extreme northeast. Open daily 0700-2300. 74 Samut Sakdarak Rd., tel. (042) 612251. Inexpensive.

Phit Bakery: Menu offerings include freshly brewed coffee, Western breakfasts, basic Thai dishes, and all sorts of desserts from chocolate brownies to durian ice cream. Open daily 0700-2200. 102 Phitak Phanomkhet Rd., tel. (042) 661990. Inexpensive.

Suwa Blend Restaurant: Travelers needing the modern fix might head down to the restaurant and pub adjacent to the Mukdahan Hotel. The downstairs cafe serves Thai and Western dishes accompanied by American music videos, while the karaoke room upstairs provides live forms of aural stimulation. The only place in town open late. 67 Samut Sakdarak Rd., tel. (042) 611555. Open daily 0900-0400. Moderate.

Transportation

Mukdahan is 70 km south of That Phanom and 163 km north of Ubon Ratchathani. As with other towns in the northeast, there are no central bus terminals but various places where buses depart to different destinations.

The government bus terminal is at the west end of town about two km from city center, but travelers often pick up buses from the private companies scattered around town.

The fabulously named 999 VIP Tours, opposite the police station, has ordinary and a/c buses to Bangkok, Nakhon Phanom, and Ubon Ratchathani. The equally creative 927 Tours across from the Lak Muang has similar services to the same destinations. A third option is Sahamit Tours just south of the Foremost Cafe.

YASOTHON

Yasothon is the provincial capital of the province of the same name. The term Yasothon derives from the Sanskrit *Yasodhara* ("Preserver of Glory"), a son of Krishna as related in the Mahabharata. Isolated in the searing hot plains of lower Issan, Yasothon is rarely visited by Westerners except during the Rocket Festival described below.

Rocket Festival

Yasothon is home to the wildly popular Rocket Festival (Soeng Bung Fai) held in mid-May to celebrate the end of the dry season and ensure heavy rains throughout the region. Though fertility-rain festivals are held in most Issan towns, Yasothon receives official support from the TAT and is considered to have the most extravagant production of any northeastern destination.

The festival centers on a procession of floats through the center of town to Wat Si Thai Phum, followed by the launching of enormous rockets from open fields outside the city limits. An enormous fireworks display occurs in the evening. Visitors should book rooms well in advance or join one of the many tours organized by travel agencies in Bangkok.

Accommodations

Yasothon has six small hotels in the center of town on Chang Sanit and Uthai Ramrit Roads. **Surawet Wattana Hotel** (tel. 045-711690) at 128 Chang Sanit Rd. has 30 fan-cooled rooms that cost 120-150B. On the same street you'll find other hotels in the same price range, such as **Suk Niran,** Serm Siri, and Phan Pricha.

Udom Phon Hotel (tel. 045-711564) at 82 Uthai Ramrit Rd. has acceptable fan-cooled rooms from 120B. **Yot Nakhon Hotel** (tel. 045-711662) at 141 Uthai Ramrit Rd. is the largest hotel in town, and the only place with a/c rooms. Fan rooms with private bath cost 140-220B, while a/c doubles with private bath cost 320-460B.

Transportation

Yasothon is 103 km northwest of Ubon Ratchathani, 196 km southeast of Khon Kaen, and 275 km northeast of Korat.

Yasothon is located in a very isolated region that remains well off the beaten track of tourism. One possible route is to visit Yasothon, Roi Et, and Kalasin on a tour from Ubon Ratchathani to Khon Kaen. This shortcut skips Mekong River destinations such as That Phanom and Nakhon Phanom, but it's the most direct connection from Ubon to Nong Khai and the superb towns west along the Mekong.

UBON RATCHATHANI

Ubon Ratchathani—often called Ubon—is a major destination being positioned as the international gateway to Laos, Cambodia, and Vietnam. Ubon lies in the so-called Emerald Triangle due to its proximity to Laos and Cambodia, and firmly on the proposed Asian Highway, a network of road originally planned to link Istanbul with Saigon. Although the road remains a pipe dream, the completion of the proposed eastern extension will allow visitors to reach Angkor Wat and Saigon in less than a single day.

Ubon was established by the Khmers in the 10th century and came under Thai control after the rise of Ayuthaya in the 15th century. Tremendous growth occurred two decades ago when the Americans established an air base just outside Ubon to conduct bombing missions into Indochina. The Americans withdrew in 1975, leaving behind a legacy of deserted hotels, restaurants, and darkened nightclubs. The town quickly slipped back into its old ways, as if the Yanks had never existed.

Since the departure of U.S. troops, Ubon has grown into the major economic center of the

Issan. Recent developments include an international airport designed to serve the expanding economic markets of Indochina, industrial estates with fertilizer and processed-food factories, a new university, and major hotels earmarked for both business and leisure visitors. On the planning boards is the world's first truly international golf course, an 18-hole project overlapping Thailand, Laos, and Cambodia.

National Museum

A good overview of the historical development of the lower Issan and a broad selection of Khmer and Thai artifacts are displayed in the 19th-century building once used as the office of the provincial governor. The museum also offers an ethnographic section with Thai and Laotian handicrafts, costumes, and farm implements.

The museum is on Sri Narong Road and open Wed.-Sat. 0830-1630.

Wat Supatnaram

Financed by King Rama IV as the first Issan temple dedicated to the Thammayut sect of Buddhism, Wat Supatnaram on the Moon River reflects the complex interaction of religious traditions in Southeast Asia. The temple was constructed in 1853 by Vietnamese craftspeople in a fusion of Thai, Western, and Khmer styles to house the highly venerated image of Phra Sapphanya Chao.

The chief wonder is a small open-air museum housing an outstanding collection of rare artifacts. Among the masterpieces are Chinese-style Buddhas, Dvaravati stone boundary markers, 7th-century Khmer lintels, priceless frescoes, carved pillars in Angkor style, and Hindu images of the deity Ganesha. The National Museum in Bangkok has requested the collection be moved to a safer location, the national museum in either Bangkok or Ubon.

Wat Tung Sri Muang

Constructed during the reign of King Rama III (1824-51), this *wat* is renowned for its Tripitaka library elevated in the middle of a small pond, ancient *mondop* housing a Buddha footprint, and erotic wall murals inside the principal *viharn.*

The *wat* is in the center of town just west of Sri Luang Road.

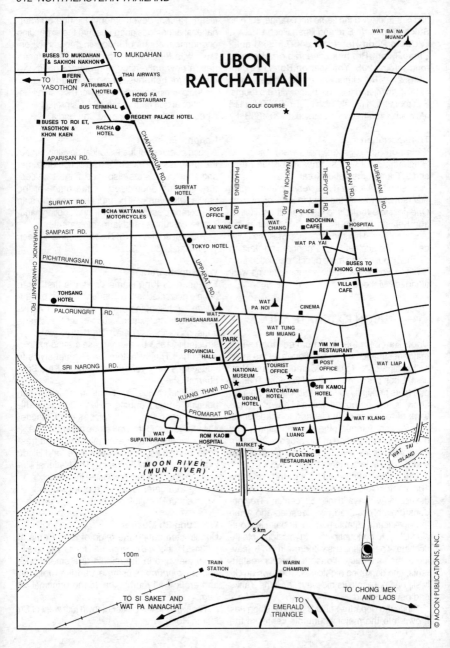

Wat Ba Na Muang

Four km northeast of town on the road past the airport, the latest addition to the *wat* scene is this exotic creation covered with dark red glazed tiles and fronted by a eccentric royal barge filled with dozens of red-tiled boatsmen.

Wat Nong Bua

An impressive copy of the Mahabodhi *chedi* from Bodgaya, India, is located on the outskirts of town on the road to Nakhon Phanom. Nong Bua features a pair of four-sided towers covered with Jataka reliefs and recessed images of Dvaravati Buddhas.

Wat Nong Pa Pong

The region near Ubon offers several *wats* that welcome students of *vipassana* meditation.

Wat Nong Pa Pong was the principal residence of a meditation master named Achaan Cha, a disciple of the famous Achaan Man (1870-1949) who is credited as the inspiration for over 40 forest monasteries throughout the Issan. Achaan Cha furthered the work of Achaan Man by establishing new branches of the strict order, including one in Sussex, England.

A book by Jack Kornfield titled *A Still Forest Pool* provides a useful introduction to the meditation theories of Achaan Cha. Kornfield once studied at Wat Nong Pa Pong under the direction of the master, but now lives in San Rafael, California, where he conducts retreats at Spirit Rock Meditation Center (tel. 415-488-0164). A rather cynical viewpoint is given in *What the Buddha Never Taught* by Tim Ward.

Wat Nong Pa Pong is 15 km southwest of Ubon and can be reached by a Si Saket-bound *songtao* or bus from Ubon.

Wat Pa Nanachat

Travelers interested in Buddhism and *vipassana* meditation are advised to visit the forest monastery across the road from Wat Nong Pa Pong. Wat Pa Nanachat ("Temple of the International Forest") is a Western-oriented temple with a Canadian abbot, Japanese vice-abbot, and several dozen European and American monks who speak English. Laypeople are welcome to stay as guests and conduct a brief study of Buddhism and insight meditation. Discipline is strict and all residents are expected to follow the schedule which involves early-morning meditation and work details on the grounds or in the kitchen. Visitors should arrive in the early morning to avoid interfering with afternoon silent meditations and are expected to make commitments after a stay of three days. A small store at the *wat* distributes free English-language booklets on the teachings of Achaan Cha.

Wat Pa Nanachat is 15 km southwest of Ubon on Hwy. 2193, the road that connects Ubon with Si Saket. From the Ubon bus station, take a bus going south toward Si Saket and watch for the English-language sign on the right side of the road. A *tuk tuk* from Ubon to the temple costs around 60B.

Budget Accommodations

Ubon has over 20 hotels that charge 160-380B for fan-cooled rooms and 400-800B for a/c rooms with private baths. Many of the hotels are sign-posted only in Thai script, and serve the brothel business.

Tokyo Hotel: A clean and popular hotel in the center of town two blocks north of the park. 178 Upparat Rd., tel. (045) 241739, 180-300B fan, 380-450B a/c.

Moderate Accommodations

Racha Hotel: Somewhat north of city center is a moderately priced hotel with both fan and a/c rooms. 149 Chaiyangkun Rd., tel. (045) 254155, 200-280B fan, 320-450B a/c.

Ratchathani Hotel: A very large hotel nicely situated in the center of town across from the tourist office and National Museum. Probably the best midpriced place in Ubon. 229 Kuan Thani Rd., tel. (045) 254599, 300-400B fan with private bath, 480-640B a/c.

Luxury Accommodations

The following hotels are either newly constructed or recently renovated, but most still need maintenance and upgrading to deserve their artificially high rates. Discounts are often given at the front desk; ask.

Sri Kamol Hotel: The central location near the TAT and refurbished rooms with hot showers and TV make this a popular choice for midlevel travelers. Chongmek Travel Agency organizes tours to nearby attractions. 26 Ubonsak Rd., tel. (045) 246088, fax (045) 243792, 1,000-1,650B.

Tohsang Hotel: A new hotel about 15 minutes west of city center with well-appointed rooms and two restaurants. 251 Phalochai Rd., tel. (045) 245531, fax (045) 244814, 1,200-1,800B.

Pathumrat Hotel: A large and reasonably clean hotel that caters to Thai and Western tour groups. Constructed during the Vietnam conflict to meet U.S. military needs, the well-managed seven-story high-rise features a swimming pool, coffee shop, massage parlor, and travel agency. The chief disadvantage is the inconvenient location about 20 minutes north of city center. 173 Chaiyangkun Rd., tel. (045) 241501, fax (045) 243792, 750-1,100B.

Regent Palace Hotel: Another new hotel with all the standard facilities, but also located about 20 minutes north of downtown. Although opened only a few years ago, the hotel is showing signs of decay due to ongoing neglect. 265 Chaiyangkun Rd., tel. (045) 245046, fax (045) 241804, 700-1,200B.

Restaurants

Ubon is highly regarded for its Issan specialties such as *laap phet* (minced duck salad), *yam makheua yao* (fried eggplant), and *gai yang* (grilled chicken). The entire town is packed with streetstalls and cafes serving these dishes and the standard array of Thai and Chinese offerings.

Night Markets: Ubon has several markets that appear in the early evening hours, including the foodstalls on Rajabut Road near the Ratchathani Hotel and down near the river and Wat Luang. A night market also sets up on Chaiyangkun Road across from the bus terminal.

Choikee Cafe: Just opposite the National Museum is a popular spot for Western and Chinese breakfast dishes such as thick rice soup and freshly baked pastries. Open daily 0600-2100. 301 Kuang Thani Rd., tel. (045) 254017. Inexpensive.

Yim Yim Restaurant: Also downtown and across from the post office is an open-air cafe serving Thai standards and Issan specialties. 172 Sri Narong Rd., tel. (045) 255251. Open daily 0700-2100. Inexpensive.

Villa Cafe: Good place for pizza, spaghetti, and other Western favorites in an a/c environment. An easy walk from the center of town.

Open daily 1100-2200. 115 Polpan Rd., tel. (045) 243680. Moderate.

Ko Wat Tai: The small island in the Moon River can be reached on a bamboo footbridge except during the rainy season when the island is closed to the public. Thais come down to dine in the simple cafes or order grilled chicken and picnic in small thatched huts.

Kai Yang Cafe: Grilled chicken is the legendary specialty of this open-air cafe just west of Wat Chang. Other dishes include minced duck salads, sticky rice, and *som tam* made with prodigious amounts of chili. Open daily 1000-0200. Sampasit Rd. Inexpensive.

Indochina Cafe: Walk the other direction from Wat Chang and you'll find this simple Vietnamese cafe and the **Sincere Restaurant** for Thai-French dishes served in a/c comfort. Open daily 0900-2200. Sampasit Rd., tel. (045) 243337. Inexpensive.

Hong Fa Restaurant: Travelers staying in the north end of town at the Regent Palace or Pathumrat Hotels can cross the street to try the excellent Chinese dishes in this sophisticated restaurant. Open daily 0900-2300. Chayangkun Rd., tel. (045) 243558. Open daily 0900-2300. Moderate to expensive.

Fern Hut: A trendy cafe and bakery that serves pastries, cakes, and meals in an a/c environment. Somewhat overpriced, but a welcome change from open-air cafes and crowded nightmarkets. Down the alley just opposite the Ubon Teachers College. Open daily 0700-2100. Rajathani Rd., tel. (045) 244305. Moderate.

Practicalities

Tourist Information: The TAT office in the center of town (surprise!) offers maps with local bus routes, brochures on nearby attractions, and information on Si Saket and Yasothon, two other towns included in their region of responsibility. Open daily 0830-1630. 264 Kuang Thani Rd., tel. (045) 243770, fax (045) 243771.

Tourist Police: An English-speaking officer is on duty 24 hours. Sri Narong and Upparat Rd., tel. (045) 245505, emergency 1699.

Post Office: The downtown GPO is open weekdays 0830-1630 and weekends 0900-1200. Sri Narong Rd., tel. (045) 254000.

International Telephone: Overseas calls can be made from hotels, card phones, and the telephone office attached to the GPO. Open daily 0700-2300. Sri Narong Rd.

Rom Kao Hospital: The best medical facility in the region; English-speaking doctors. 123 Upparat Rd., tel. (045) 244658.

Cho Wattana Tours: Cho Wattana near the Suriyat Hotel rents cars for 1,000B per day and motorcycles for 200-250B. Wattana also arranges tours to outlying regions, day visits to Pakse in Laos, and overnight excursions to Don Khong Island near the Cambodian border. 39/8 Suriyat Rd., tel. (045) 242202.

Transportation
Ubon is 629 km northeast of Bangkok and 370 km east of Korat.

Air: Thai Airways flies once daily from Bangkok to Ubon. Thai Airways (tel. 045-254431) is at 364 Chaiyangkun Rd. The new international airport is on the northern perimeter of town.

Train: Ubon is connected by rail with Bangkok via Korat, Buriram, and Surin. Seven trains leave Bangkok daily. An express train with sleepers departs at 2100 and arrives in Ubon the next morning at 0705. Rapid trains without sleepers leave at 0650, 1845, and 2245. Rapid trains leave Korat at 1136 and 2356.

An express train from Ubon departs at 1700 and takes 10 hours to Bangkok. Rapid trains leave Ubon at 0640, 1650, and 1745.

The train station is five km southwest of town in the suburb of Warin Chamrun. Take a taxi, *tuk tuk*, or bus 2 or 6.

Bus: Buses leave every 15 minutes from the Northern Bus Terminal in Bangkok and take 12 hours to reach Ubon. Air-conditioned buses leave Bangkok 1900-2130. Buses leave seven times daily from Korat and take five hours to Ubon.

The Ubon Bus Terminal is on Chaiyangkun Road about four km north of city center. Take public bus 2 or a *songtao* for 20B. Other bus terminals are shown on the map.

EAST OF UBON RATCHATHANI

Some of the best scenery in northeastern Thailand lies east of Ubon, along the Moon and Mekong Rivers.

Route 217 heads east 42 km to the town of Phibun Mangsahan, and then crosses the Moon River and changes to Route 2222 until it reaches the well-sited town of Khong Chiam, 75 km from Ubon. Several natural attractions are located between Ubon and Khong Chiam.

Ban Kwan Sai
Among the disappearing trades of Thailand are the production of brasswares using the ancient "lost wax" method. Ban Pa Ao, a village some 17 km northwest of Ubon, has a few blacksmiths still fashioning brassware with these traditional methods, but the isolated location makes it difficult to visit without private transportation.

Ban Kwan Sai, 41 km east of Udon on Route 217, is an easy stop for visitors heading east to Khong Chiam and the rock paintings at Pha Taem. This village produces brass and bronze gongs and other musical instruments used in classical Thai orchestras. Methods are elemental—men sit in the dirt and hammer the discs into patterns—but the high-quality results give a brilliant ring after being fired in primitive kilns.

Phibun Mangsahan
Midway between Ubon Ratchathani and Khong Chiam is the riverside town of Phibun Mangsahan, known for its rapids (Kaeng Saphu) one km outside town and adjacent to the Moon River bridge. The rapids are rather tame—especially since the completion of the controversial Moon River Dam—but it's still fun to rent inner tubes and float down the river past the bridge.

Sanamchai Guesthouse: Most travelers press on to Khong Chiam, though the guesthouse in Phibun Mangsahan is clean and is located near several cafes and pubs. Route 217, tel. (045) 441289, 150-180B fan, 350-450B a/c.

Caves and Waterfalls
Several decent caves and falls flank Route 2222 as it continues east to Khong Chiam. Sae Hua Mao Falls at Km 59 is marked by a small sign on the north side of the road. Hao Chai Cave is south of Route 2222 on the same road leading down to Kaeng Tana Rapids.

Kaeng Tana National Park
Kaeng Tana is an 8,000-hectare park gazetted in 1981 and named after the rapids (Kaeng Tana) that are formed shortly before they reach the dam by the Moon River squeezing through a

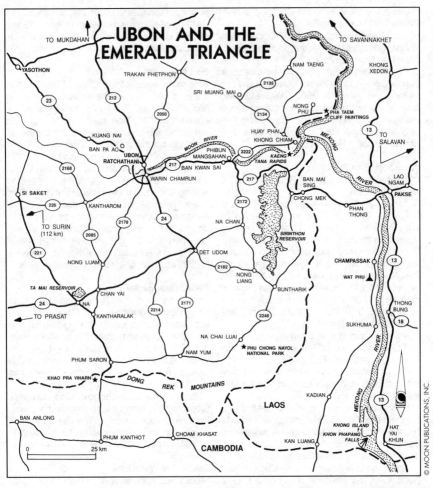

narrow canyon, and then merging with the Mekong.

The park spreads over both sides of the Moon River and includes forested areas, hiking trails, limestone rock formations, and several waterfalls best visited during the rainy season June-November. The park office is south of the river and just off Route 217. However, you can see the rapids by taking the right turn off Route 2222 and continuing two km south to the panoramic overlook. Alternatively, boats can be hired from Khong Chiam to visit the rapids and other features in the park.

Accommodations: National Parks bungalows for up to 10 people cost 500-800B per night. Camping is 50B; check with the TAT in Ubon about tent rentals and other arrangements.

Pha Taem Cliff Paintings

Well-preserved cliff paintings, dating back 2,000-3,000 years, cover a 300-meter section of sandstone cliffs overlooking the Mekong River basin.

Figures possibly related to the Neolithic inhabitants of Ban Chiang include human images, galloping buffalo, gigantic catfish *(pla muk),* and abstract designs that eerily resemble patterns of the American Indians.

A trail leads about one km down from the parking lot to the first level of paintings, many of which are now protected behind unsightly barbed wire. Observation towers provide the best views of the ochre-colored drawings.

Just as rewarding as the artwork are the spectacular vistas extending from the cliffs across the deep gorge cut by the Mekong and into the wilds of Laos.

Sao Chaliang: Two km before the turnoff to Pha Taem are some wonderfully weird rock formations similar to those seen near Mukdahan and Nong Khai. The heavily eroded sandstone formations have assumed curious shapes that resemble birds, bats, and unearthly mushrooms.

Pha TaemTransportation: Pha Taem is 95 km east of Udon and 20 km north of Khong Chiam at the confluence of the Mekong and Moon Rivers. Access is difficult since there is no direct transportation. The easiest method is to rent a motorcycle from a Khong Chiam guesthouse or charter a *tuk tuk* in Khong Chiam for 200-250B roundtrip.

KHONG CHIAM

Khong Chiam, one of the more isolated yet scenic spots in northeast Thailand, is now attracting a few hardy travelers who discover one of the last untouched regions in Thailand. The town offers great views across the river into Laos, and is well sited near the Pha Taem cliff paintings and natural wonders such as waterfalls, caves, and national parks.

Attractions
In addition to Kaeng Tana National Park and other sights described above, visitors can hike to the following or rent a motorcycle from one of the guesthouses in Khong Chiam.

Khong Chiam sits at the confluence of the Moon and Mekong Rivers, at a point where the turbulent waters collide and produce the "Two-Colored River," or *mae nam song si.*

Visitors can rent longtail boats from the land-

ing near the Pak Mun Restaurant to explore the river and visit small, sandy islands. Thai and Laotian officials are considering allowing Western tourists to cross over to Laos and sail down the Mekong to Pakse.

Two km southeast of town is the cave temple, **Wat Tham Hua Sin Chai,** hidden behind a cascading waterfall during the rainy months.

Accommodations
Khong Chiam now has several guesthouses and restaurants overlooking the Moon or Mekong Rivers. Signs posted at the bus station point the way.

Apple Guesthouse: Some 300 meters from the bus station and across from the post office is a clean and well-managed two-story guesthouse with a decent cafe and bicycle and motorcycle rentals. 267 Kaewpradit Rd., tel. (045) 351160, 120-160B fan, 350-400B a/c.

Khong Chiam Guesthouse: Around the corner to the right from the bus terminal is another place with functional if unexciting rooms in a great location near the river. 355 Pukumchai Rd., tel. (045) 351074, 80-120B fan, 300-350B a/c.

Transportation
Khong Chiam is 75 km east of Ubon Ratchathani. Direct buses leave from the Market on Pichit Rungsan Road daily 0900-1300. Check with the TAT to confirm this service and departure schedules.

Alternatively, take a bus from Warin Chamrun to Phibun Mangsahan and get off at the bus stop. Take a different bus heading to Khong Chiam along Route 2222.

Khong Chiam can also be reached by the passenger and vehicle ferry that crosses the Moon River from Route 217 just north of Chong Mek.

CHONG MEK AND THE EMERALD TRIANGLE

Chong Mek is a small border town in the heart of the "Emerald Triangle," the regional intersection of Thailand, Laos, and Cambodia, where developers hope to open the borders and bring economic prosperity to the isolated region.

Chong Mek is a dusty hamlet with a dreary little market open to Laotians, who cross the border to shop for Thai goods.

Across to Laos
Chong Mek, however, enjoys the distinction of being the only legal land crossing between Thailand and Laos, and the access point for exploring the superb topography and natural wonders of southern Laos.

Route 217 passes through Chong Mek to Ban Mai Sing Amphon and continues another 44 km to Pakse on the Mekong River. The highway from Pakse goes east to several hill resorts or south along the banks of the Mekong to the dramatic Khon Phapang Falls, wider than either the Niagara or Victoria Falls. The Dusit hotel group in Bangkok has proposed a US$300 million resort at the falls that would sport two luxurious hotels, a complex of guesthouses and villas, championship golf course, and two casinos.

The crossing at Chong Mek to Laos is open to all foreigners holding a valid Lao visa.

Sirinthon Reservoir
Eight km east of Chong Mek is a massive 30-km-long body of water created after a dam was constructed over a tributary of the Moon River. A small meditation retreat at the northern end of the reservoir, offers some water sports and boat tours in the high season.

Phu Chong Nayol National Park
Forty km south of Chong Mek and straddling the Laos border is a rarely visited national park created in 1987 to protect one of the last remaining major forests in the Issan. The 690-square-km park features the 40-meter Bak Yai Waterfall, four km from park headquarters, and hiking trails past limestone formations to elevated plateaus offering spectacular views.

The TAT in Ubon can help with details on transportation and lodging within the park.

SI SAKET AND KHMER TEMPLES

Si Saket, 63 km west of Ubon Ratchathani, is a convenient starting point for visits to several excellent Khmer temples. The town is also known for its tasty *kai yang* and waterfalls at Huai Chan.

Prasat Kamphaeng Noi
Eight km west of town on the road to Surin are the ruins of a Khmer sanctuary, constructed in the 13th century by King Jayavarman VII. The unrestored *prang* and crumbling laterite foundations are noted for fine carvings, especially the depiction of Hindu mythology on the decorative lintels.

The monument is now under the supervision of the Fine Arts Department, and open daily 0830-1630 with an admission charge of 25B.

Prasat Wat Kamphaeng Yai
The largest Khmer sanctuary near Si Saket has been targeted for restoration by the Fine Arts Department, with an expected completion date of 1995. Kamphaeng Yai was constructed in the mid-11th century and dedicated to the Hindu deity Shiva, but, like many Hindu-Khmer temples in the Issan, it was converted into a Mahayana Buddhist complex by the Thais after the 13th century. Hindu-Khmer influences are still apparent on the northern lintel of Vishnu in slumber, and on the southern lintel engraved with Shiva riding his bull Nandi.

The sanctuary is on Route 2080, about 10 km west of Prasat Kamphaeng Noi.

Accommodations
With the opening of Prasat Pra Viharn, and an increasing curiosity about the more remote destinations of Thailand among independent travelers, Si Saket (SEE-sket) is starting to receive a steady stream of visitors who overnight in the small provincial capital before heading off to explore the nearby ruins.

Guesthouses are probably still several years away, but several basic hotels are located in the center of town on Khun Khun, Si Saket, and Lak Muang Roads.

Phrom Phiman Hotel: A basic but decent hotel on the west side of town near the railway station. Not the cheapest, but reasonably priced with both fan-cooled and a/c rooms. 849/1 Lak Muang Rd., tel. (045) 612677, 280-350B fan, 420-550B a/c.

Thai Soem Thai: Less comfortable than the Phrom Phiman, but acceptable for a single night for *baht* watchers. Si Saket Rd., tel. (045) 611458, 120-200B fan.

Kessiri Hotel: A new, almost-luxurious hotel that opened in 1994 to serve the Prasat Pra Viharn crowd and upscale business travelers. The 11-story tower has a rooftop swimming pool, coffee shop, a/c Thai restaurant, satellite TV, and other surprising facilities for such a small town. 1102 Khun Khun Rd., tel. (045) 614007, fax (045) 612144, 950-1,400B a/c.

Restaurants
Several cafes and foodstalls are located in the center of town near the train station and around the bus terminal to the south near Khun Khun Road. A small cafe adjacent to the Si Saket Hotel serves Issan dishes laced with some of the hottest chilies this side of Hades.

A welcome escape from the heat and dust is provided in the a/c Thai restaurant on the 11th floor of the Kessiri Hotel. Prices are reasonable and the slow service is compensated for by the wonderful views.

Transportation
Si Saket is 571 km from Bangkok and 63 km west of Ubon Ratchathani. Both trains and buses serve Si Saket, though trains provide far more comfort on longer journeys and inevitably pass through more attractive countryside.

Train: The best train departures from Bangkok are the 1105 a/c diesel arriving at 1850, and the rapid no. 51 leaving at 2245 and arriving at 0800. Si Saket can also be reached by several daily trains leaving from Korat, Buriram, Surin, or Ubon Ratchathani.

The train station is in the center of town on Kanrotfai Road.

Bus: VIP a/c buses depart Bangkok's Northern Bus Terminal twice daily at 0900 and 2100 and take about nine hours to reach Si Saket. Buses from Surin take 90 minutes while buses from Ubon Ratchathani take one hour.

The bus terminal is on Khun Khun Road on the south side of town.

Practicalities
Thai Farmers Bank at 1492 Khun Khun Rd. changes traveler's checks and advances funds on credit cards. The nearest tourist office is in Ubon Ratchathani, but information may be available from the Kessiri Hotel.

PRASAT PRA VIHARN

One of the most spectacular but inaccessible jewels of Khmer architecture now welcomes visitors after a span of over three decades.

History
Prasat Pra Viharn crowns a spur of the Dongrak Mountains that mark the frontier between Cambodia and Thailand. The main entrance is on Thai soil in Kantaralak District, Si Saket Province, but the main sanctuary is several hundred meters south in Cambodian territory. The exact location was disputed by the Thai and Cambodian governments in the late 1950s. The territorial claims were submitted to the World Court, which ruled in 1962 that the *prasat* is in Cambodia but the entrance is in Thailand. Neglected and overgrown with weeds, the site was occupied by a handful of young Cambodian soldiers until 1991 when the Cambodian Peace Accord was signed in Paris and the temple finally cleared of land mines and wire fences.

The complex was constructed from the 11th to 13th centuries in a series of courts and *gopuras* connected on different levels by paved stone avenues and imposing stairways. Similar to Prasat Phanom Rung, the complex grows successively larger and more complex with each ascending level. Hindu myths are depicted in the rich craftsmanship on the stairways, lintels, and pediments sited on the three levels. Further information is related in the Siam Society publication, *The Lofty Sanctuary of Khao Phra Viharn,* available at the admission gate.

Prasat Pra Viharn is a superb example of the difficulties of Thai transliteration. Alternate wording for the temple includes Khao Phra Wihaan, Kao Phra Viharn, Prasat Phra Wiharn, Prasat Khao Phra Vihan, and Preah Vihear.

Practicalities
By whatever name, Prasat Pra Viharn opened to the outside world in January 1992 and now remains a fairly safe destination, especially after the surrender in 1999 of the last two Khmer Rouge leaders. However, the current state of affairs should be checked with the TAT in Bangkok or Ubon Ratchathani before making the long journey to the orphaned temple on the Cambodian border.

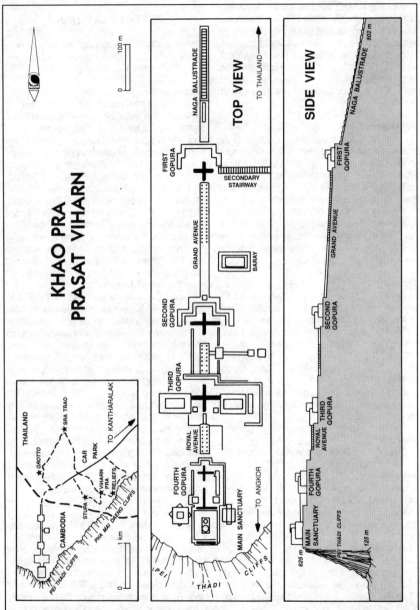

KHAO PRA PRASAT VIHARN

TOP VIEW

SIDE VIEW

© MOON PUBLICATIONS, INC.

Visitors are required to complete an entry form at the Thai army checkpoint and pay an admission fee. The Cambodian army checkpoint may demand additional entrance fees and request the deposit of some form of personal identification.

Follow the designated walkways and don't wander off the path searching for souvenirs or an unusually photographic approach. Most of the land has been laced with minefields and other forms of ordnance that create a serious threat to the casual visitor.

Transportation

Prasat Pra Viharn is 115 km southeast of Si Saket and 158 km southwest of Ubon Ratchathani. The monument is difficult and time consuming to reach from either point.

From Si Saket take a *songtao* in the direction of the temple. On weekends, *songtaos* go all the way to the temple entrance at the Cambodia border. The drawback is hundreds of Thais visit the monument on weekends and holidays, spoiling an otherwise romantic and mysterious destination.

During the week, a few *songtaos* go down Route 211 to the town of Phum Saron, 11 km north of the temple entrance. Alternatively, you can take a *songtao* to Kantharalak and transfer to a final *songtao* for the remaining 25 km to Phum Saron.

Another option is to stay overnight in Kantharalak at the Kwan Yeun Hotel on the main street, where acceptable rooms cost 100-150B, and get an early start the following morning.

Motorcycle taxis from Phum Saron to the complex cost 150-200B roundtrip, including two or three hours of touring.

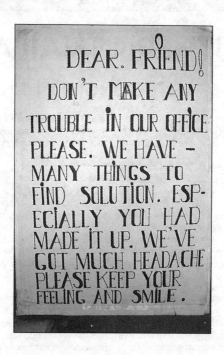

SOUTHERN THAILAND

INTRODUCTION

Stretching 1,250 km from Bangkok to the border of Malaysia, the long and narrow peninsula of southern Thailand encompasses thick jungles, rugged mountains, limestone pinnacles, emerald-blue bays, fishermen and sea gypsies, graceful temples and bulbous mosques, coral reefs, colorful marine life, and some of the most spectacular beaches in Southeast Asia. The south is a fascinating region, not only for its famous beaches and island resorts, but for its ethnic diversity, geography, and long history. Landscapes, religions, languages, and even the people change as you travel deeper into the south: rice paddies give way to rubber plantations, Muslim mosques outnumber Buddhist temples, even the beaches seem to change. . . they get better.

Climate

The climate here varies from the remainder of Thailand's due to the effects of seasonal monsoons, which sweep across the west coast on the Andaman Sea May-Sept. and bring heavy rains to the east coast on the Gulf of Thailand November to late February. Travelers deluged by heavy rains can usually improve their situation by simply moving across the peninsula.

History

The 14 provinces of southern Thailand once comprised the fabled lands of the Golden Chersonese, an ancient region that prior to the 9th century centered on independent city-states at Pahang, Trang, Nakhon Si Thammarat, Takua Pa, and Chaiya. The region was later consolidated into and influenced by the Indonesian culture, in particular the Buddhist Indo-Srivijayan civilization of the 8th-13th centuries.

Following the disintegration of the Srivijayan Empire, Nakhon Si Thammarat became the center of an independent kingdom closely aligned with the Thai kingdom at Sukothai. The southern provinces were brought under the dominion of Ayuthaya in the mid-14th century, though Nakhon Si Thammarat remained the center of

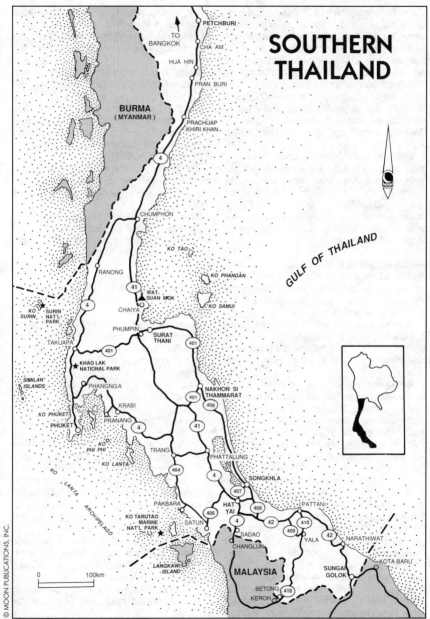

SOUTHERN THAILAND

authority for the entire peninsula. With the fall of Ayuthaya in 1767, the southern provinces came under the control of the Bangkok administration, yet were left semi-independent under the rule of regional governors. Administrative reforms during the rule of King Chulalongkorn included consolidation of the provinces into several regions under the direct control of Bangkok, chiefly to counteract the dangers of Western colonial expansion in Southeast Asia. Nakhon Si Thammarat and Pattani joined the Thai nation in 1906.

Chinese and Muslim influences have long been strong, resulting in a vivacious, polyglot society with intermingled religious and ethnic traditions. Regional differences distinct from those of central Thailand are still evident in the customs, dialects, cultural expressions, cuisine, entertainment, and sports of the *Thai pak tai,* southern Thais.

Sightseeing Highlights
Petchburi: Southern Thailand is chiefly famous for its beaches, but some travelers may want to briefly tour Petchburi, a historic town with the best temples south of Bangkok.

Prachuap Khiri Khan: Although there is little of great interest in this small fishing village, the complete lack of tourists, friendly population, and stunning topography make this beach town an enjoyable destination.

Ko Samui: Ko Samui is a relatively simple and absolutely beautiful island on the east side of the peninsula. Though rapidly approaching saturation, the atmosphere remains much less frantic than on Phuket. Budget travelers, however, have largely abandoned Ko Samui for the less developed islands of Ko Phangan and Ko Tao.

Deserted beaches in southern Thailand are now rather rare, but with nearly 2,000 km of coastline and hundreds of untouched islands, a few gems still await discovery.

Phuket: Southern Thailand's two most popular destinations are the tropical islands of Phuket and Ko Samui. Both have distinct personalities which appeal to different types of travelers. Phuket, the more developed of the two, offers a stunning combination of superb beaches, upscale hotels, outstanding seafood restaurants, sports activities from parasailing to scuba diving, and heady nightlife rivaled only by those in Bangkok and Pattaya. Most of the island is very expensive and highly commercialized, but a few beaches are still pristine—at least for the moment.

Krabi: This bustling fishing town serves as the gateway to several beach destinations such as Ko Phi Phi, Pranang, and Ko Lanta.

Hat Yai: The largest commercial and transportation center in the south provides excellent shopping, restaurants, and nightlife, though few travelers are impressed with the concrete drabness of the city center.

Songkhla: This pleasant and very mellow beach town, one hour outside Hat Yai, is a popular place to soak up local atmosphere without hordes of tourists.

Narathiwat: Visitors who want to experience the traditional side of the Muslim south will enjoy this lovely town almost completely off the standard tourist trail.

GETTING THERE

Routes
Most visitors head directly to Phuket or Samui from Bangkok, but travelers intrigued with Thai architecture and painting should visit Petchburi. Those who prefer a more leisurely approach can also try the family-oriented beach resorts of Hua Hin or Cha Am. One possible route is an early-morning bus to Petchburi for a walking tour, then an afternoon bus to Hua Hin. Prachuap Khiri Khan is a recommended stop prior to Ko Samui.

Ko Samui can be reached by train, bus, or air from Bangkok. Routes from Samui often proceed west over to Phuket or southwest down to Krabi, the access town for Pranang Beach and the islands of Ko Phi Phi and Ko Lanta. South of Krabi are Trang and Satun, near the remote and rarely visited islands near the Malaysian border.

From Hat Yai, the commercial center of the deep south, you can continue southwest to Penang or southeast through the Muslim fishing towns of Pattani and Narathiwat to Sungai Golok, the last stop before crossing to Kota Baru on the east coast of peninsular Malaysia.

For details on getting to Malaysia, see "Departure to Malaysia" under "The Deep South."

Air
Visitors can reach Phuket and Ko Samui directly by air from Bangkok. Thai International connects Phuket and Hat Yai with Bangkok, Penang, and other international gateways. Bangkok Airways flies daily to Ko Samui and between Ko Samui and Phuket.

Train
Train travel is an excellent way to tour the south and see the countryside rather than just the concrete expressways used by bus services. Trains depart nine times daily 0900-2155 from Hualampong station in Bangkok. Services include departures at 0900 (diesel), 1235 (rapid), 1400

(special express), 1515 (special express), 1600 (rapid), 1730 (rapid), 1830 (rapid), 1920 (express), and 2155 (diesel express). Sleepers are available on all trains except the 0900 (diesel) and 2155 (diesel express).

Advance reservations from Bangkok's Hualampong station or a travel agent are *strongly* recommended on all trains going south, especially on weekends and holidays.

Bus
Regular and a/c buses leave frequently from Bangkok's Southern Bus Terminal in Thonburi. Private a/c buses to major destinations such as Ko Samui and Phuket can be booked through most travel agents.

Buses are fast and departures frequent, though you'll arrive in better condition on a train.

BANGKOK TO SURAT THANI

PETCHBURI

Petchburi (also spelled Phetchburi, Petchaburi, Phetburi, and Petburi!), 126 km south of Bangkok, is a charming town with a long history and a half dozen outstanding temples. All can be easily visited on the four-hour walking tour described below.

History
Much of the city's superb art and architecture reflects its long and rich history. Founded as a Mon city that traded with Europe during the Middle Ages, Petchburi remained in the orbit of the Dvaravati Kingdom until the 12th century when it fell to the Khmers. At the end of the 13th century it was absorbed into the emerging Thai nation at Sukothai, and it formed part of the Ayuthaya empire from 1350.

The present township is a treasure house of historical artifacts from nearly all possible eras: Mon sculpture unearthed within the ancient city walls; a small but intriguing Khmer temple in a quiet neighborhood; monastery walls gilded with Thailand's finest Ayuthaya Period murals; Wat Mahathat's 19th-century *prang;* and a hilltop palace of neoclassical inspiration.

Wat Yai Suwannaram
Petchburi's artistic fame is chiefly due to the murals in Wat Yai Suwannaram and Wat Ko Keo Sutharam. Thai murals typically date from the fall of Ayuthaya in 1767 until royal patronage ended about 1910. Ayuthaya Period murals were almost completely destroyed by the Burmese after the destruction of the capital; only Petchburi murals survive to illustrate early Thai painting.

Some of the best are in the small *bot* of Wat Yai Suwannaram. Gracing the interior of the lateral walls and separated by distinct red triangles are rows of 17th-century worshipping divinities that represent Indra, Brahma, and lesser divinities such as *devas* and *yaksas.* Those on the lower registers are chipping and desperately need attention, although the interior door murals are still in good condition. Despite the deterioration, these murals provide fascinating illustrations of naturalistic decorative art and insight into the flora and fauna of 17th-century Thailand.

The adjacent wooden *sala,* supported by wooden pillars, is one of Thailand's few surviving examples of this genre. Also note the nearby *haw trai,* a Buddhist scriptural library filled with copies of the Tripitaka.

Wat Borom
This small but attractive temple, back toward the railway tracks, shows finely plastered roses

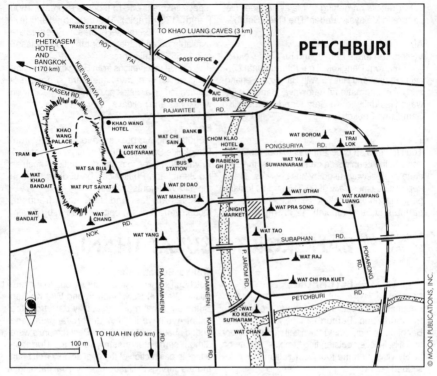

PETCHBURI

around the windows and a whitewashed exterior slowly fading into psychedelic patterns.

Wat Trai Lok

A typical monk's quarters complete with TV antennas, sleeping dogs, and a pet monkey in the tree.

Wat Kampang Luang

This trio of 13th-century Khmer towers comprises the oldest group of structures in Petchburi. Enclosed by an ancient laterite wall, Wat Kampang Luang consists of a central *prang* surrounded by three smaller *prangs* and a *gopura* on the eastern flank. Original stucco can still be seen on the back side of the central *prang*. Buddhist symbology is a later addition to these Hindu monuments. The adjoining *wat* serves as a wildlife refuge for wild turkeys, roosters, and other unidentifiable birds.

Wat Pra Song

Two uniquely circular and rather strange bell towers face the primary *bot*. Although in danger of falling down, the wonderful old monks' quarters to the right remain more appealing than the modern replacements to the rear of the courtyard.

Wat Ko Keo Sutharam

Petchburi's most famous temple is a must-see for all visitors. Inside the small *bot* are some of Thailand's finest, best-preserved, and oldest murals, dated by inscription to 1734. Side walls of dramatic triangles show scenes from the life of the Buddha and comical figures of Arab merchants, a Jesuit wearing the robes of a Buddhist monk, and other big-nosed *farangs*. Facing the Buddha is a wall of Buddhist cosmology—usually placed *behind* the Buddha image—while the posterior wall shows Buddha's victory over the temptations of Mara. Just below the central Buddha image is long-haired Torani, the earth goddess so impressed by Buddha's willpower that she washed away Mara's evil armies by wringing water from her hair. The superb execution, careful attention to detail, and high degree of originality make these murals among the great achievements of Thai art.

Also located in the *wat* compound are several elevated monastic buildings blessed with a linear sobriety rarely seen in modern Thai architecture.

Wat Ko Keo Sutharam is back down a side alley and somewhat difficult to find. Look for the small blue plastic signs, and ask a monk to unlock the door to the *bot* on the left. Watch carefully—it's a strange kind of lock.

Wat Mahathat

The architectural evolution at Petchburi continues at Wat Mahathat ("Monastery of the Great Relic"), an enormous white *prang* that dominates the tiny town like a giant rocket ship resting on a launchpad. Visitors can wander around the cloister filled with Buddha images and studying monks, then climb the late Ayuthayan-style *prang* for views over the town. Near the east entrance is a *viharn* filled with impressive Buddha images and patches of old murals that still display some original flavor.

Khao Wang Palace

Towering over Petchburi and reached by cable car or tough hike up a steep path is Pra Nakhon Khiri ("Holy City Mountain"), a 19th-century neoclassical palace constructed in a delightful mixture of Siamese style and chinoiserie by King Mongkut. The palace comprises a group of *pra thi nang* (throne halls) constructed in different styles. Views are outstanding from several of the buildings, including the astronomical observation tower constructed in 1862 by King Rama IV.

The TAT and local authorities sponsor an annual sound-and-light show on the hill every year in early February. Pra Nakhon Khiri has been declared a national historic park; admission is 20B.

Wat Kao Bandait, another beautiful temple with historical significance, is three km west of town at Bandait hill.

Khao Luang Caves

The cave sanctuary of Khao Luang, five km north of town on Hwy. 3173, is the most fa-mous of Petchburi's dozen caves. Inside the central chamber are dozens of Buddhas donated by pilgrims and King Mongkut, a magnificent array of stalactites, and miniature *chedis* illuminated by sunlight streaming through the roof. The Wagnerian effect is a favorite subject for photographers.

Kaeng Krachan National Park

Thailand's largest national park sits on the rugged Tanaosri mountain range which separates Thailand from Myanmar, 115 km south of Bangkok and some 60 km from Petchburi off Highway 3175.

The immense, 2,915-square-km park is known for its "Swiss Lake," wildlife, thick rainforest, savannah grasslands, impressive waterfalls, and treks starting from park headquarters at Kaeng Krachan Lake. One of the better hikes begins at Km 30 and proceeds uphill to the summit of Mt. Panernthung, some 1,207 meters above sea level. Guides can be hired at park headquarters, three km beyond the dam at the end of the road. Rafting tours on the Petchburi River are also organized by park authorities.

Another highlight is the falls, best experienced during or shortly after the rainy season July-Nov. Pala-U is an 11-tiered falls noted for the distinctive butterflies which claim different levels: blue-green butterflies on the first level, brown ones on the second, golden butterflies near the top falls. The 18-level Ha Thip Falls is five km from Panernthung Peak, while Nam Yod Clif is on the banks of the Petchburi River.

A Karen village is located 13 km from park headquarters.

Accommodations: Campsites are 50-80B per night, large bungalows operated by the parks division are 100B per person. Upscale floating bungalows are called Kaeng Krachan Resorts (Bangkok reservation, tel. 02-513-3238).

Transportation: Kaeng Krachan National Park can be visited from either Petchburi or Hua Hin. The park is served by public minitruck from Tha Yang, about 20 km south of Petchburi. Alternatively, take a minibus from Hua Hin to Ban Kang Krajaren from where motorcycle taxis continue another four km to park headquarters. Tours can also be arranged in Hua Hin and Cha Am.

Accommodations

Day-trippers can store their bags at the train station or in the small office at the bus station. Petchburi, however, is a pleasant place to learn something about local history, art, and contemporary Thai life.

Chom Klao Hotel: On the east bank of the Petchburi River is a small Chinese hotel with adequate rooms and friendly managers. 1 Pongsuriya Rd., tel. (032) 425398, 100-150B.

Rabieng Guesthouse: A very simple teak house with a few rooms at reasonable prices in the center of town on the west side of the river. Phongsuriya Rd., tel. (032) 425668, 120-350B.

Khao Wang Hotel: The best midpriced hotel in town has both fan and a/c rooms in a quiet location at the bottom of Khao Wang. 174 Rajawitee Rd., tel. (032) 425167, 220-350B fan, 350-500B a/c.

Phetkasem Hotel: Although located somewhat outside town on the highway north to Bangkok, this well-maintained hotel represents the best value in town. 86/1 Phetkasem Rd., tel. (032) 425581, 200-260B fan, 300-480B a/c.

Restaurants

The cafe in the Khao Wang Hotel is probably the best spot in town for local seafood. Streetstalls are located along the main street near Wat Mahathat and opposite the clock tower.

Petchburi is known throughout Thailand for its excellent sweets made from local sugars. The primary showcase for specialties such as *khanom mor kang* (baked coconut custard) is a restaurant called **Ban Khanom Thai** ("House of Thai Sweets"), on Petchkasem Highway just outside the city limits. This collection of 13 Thai houses includes displays of sweets, a folk-crafts museum, and a Thai restaurant with classical entertainment in the evenings.

Transportation

Petchburi is 126 km south of Bangkok.

Train: Trains from Hualampong station in Bangkok leave nine times daily 0900-2155.

Samlor drivers charge 10-20B to city center.

Bus: Buses leave every 10 minutes from the Southern Bus Terminal in Thonburi and terminate three hours later in central Petchburi.

CHA AM

A typical Thai beach resort 212 km south of Bangkok and 26 km north of Hua Hin, Cha Am features a narrow beach almost deserted during the week and a long strip of undistinguished bungalows popular on weekends with Thai families and teenagers on holiday. Although Cha Am lacks character, it's an easy escape from Bangkok, and the addition of deluxe hotels between Cha Am and Hua Hin has put the region firmly on the tourist map.

The TAT has a tourist office on the main highway about one km south of the intersection, an illogical location that makes it convenient only to visitors with private transportation.

Attractions

The main road skirts the beach and heads north five km to a small fishing village and Wat Neranchara Rama, one km past the bridge and narrow lagoon. The large Cambodian-style stone temple features a six-armed alabaster Buddha which local monks claim is the largest prototype in the world. Otherwise, relaxing on the sand and trying the local seafood are the main activities.

Accommodations

Most of the midpriced hotels in the 250-500B range are along the beach road some two km east of the bus stop and highway intersection. Inexpensive bungalows under 200B are in short supply, though bargains are available midweek when Cha Am is almost completely deserted. A string of expensive hotels has recently been constructed farther south, midway between Cha Am and Hua Hin. Prices at most properties double on weekends, when thousands of Thais arrive with their guitars and booming radios.

Cha Am Villa: Most of the older bungalows on the beach offer fan rooms for 200-300B and a/c rooms from 400B. Comparison shopping is easy since dozens of bungalows are packed together on both sides of the central intersection. 241 Ruamchit Rd., tel. (032) 471010, 200-300B fan, 400-800B a/c.

Double Dutch: A modern, clean, German-run hotel with a fine restaurant that serves both Thai and European dishes. Located 2.2 km north of the main intersection on a less crowded and cleaner stretch of beach. All rooms are a/c with mini-refrigerator. 223 Ruamchit Rd., tel. (032) 471513, fax (032) 471072, 450-900B.

Cha Am Methavalai Hotel: A five-story terraced hotel with landscaped gardens, swimming pool, sports center, and 115 spacious rooms. Located at the north end of the beach. 220 Ruamchit Rd., tel. (032) 471480, fax (032) 471590, 2,400-2,800B.

Dusit Resort and Polo Club: The name says it all: one of the most prestigious and luxurious resorts in Thailand. Designed for the Thai elite and wealthy tourists, the Dusit features all possible amenities including five restaurants, an enormous pool, mini-golf course, scuba diving, and polo club. 1349 Petchkasem Rd., tel. (032) 520009, fax (032) 520296, 4,000-25,000B.

Transportation
Buses from Petchburi and the Southern Bus Terminal in Bangkok usually stop on the highway at the intersection toward the beach. Motorcycle taxis to most hotels cost 10B; minitrucks can be chartered for 20-30B. A small bus station is also located at the south end of the beach near the Viwanthana and Santisuk bungalows.

HUA HIN

Hua Hin, 238 km south of Bangkok on the sunrise side of the gulf, is a middle-class beach resort favored by Thai families and Western travelers seeking an alternative to Pattaya.

History
The eastern shore of the Gulf of Thailand has long been favored by the royalty of Siam. In 1868, King Mongkut constructed his "Town of the Eclipse" to house hundreds of *farangs* whom the king had invited to witness the August solar eclipse. The next royal discovery took place in 1910 after a hunting party organized by Prince Chakrabongse charged across the lovely beach of Hua Hin. The prince was so impressed that he built a huge summer villa, which still stands in the northern perimeter of town. In 1923, King Vajiravudh erected a long, teakwood palace called Deer Park connected by wooden corridors to the white-sand beach.

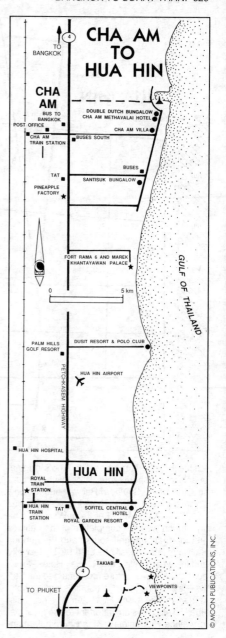

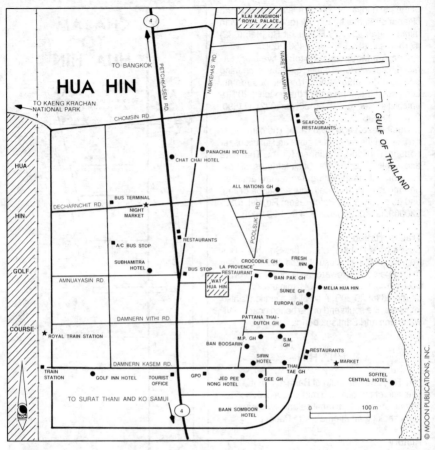

HUA HIN

TO BANGKOK

TO KAENG KRACHAN
NATIONAL PARK

KLAI KANGWON
ROYAL PALACE

PETCHKASEM RD.

NABKEHAS RD.

NARET DAMRI RD.

GULF OF THAILAND

CHOMSIN RD.

SEAFOOD
RESTAURANTS

HUA

PANACHAI HOTEL
CHAT CHAI HOTEL

ALL NATIONS GH

HIN

DECHARNCHIT RD.
BUS TERMINAL
NIGHT
MARKET

POOLSUK RD.

A/C BUS STOP

GOLF

SUBHAMITRA
HOTEL

RESTAURANTS

BUS STOP

CROCODILE GH
LA PROVENCE
RESTAURANT

FRESH
INN

AMNUAYASIN RD.

WAT
HUA HIN

BAN PAK GH

MELIA HUA HIN

SUNEE GH

EUROPA GH

DAMNERN VITHI RD.

PATTANA THAI-
DUTCH GH

COURSE

ROYAL TRAIN STATION

M.P. GH

S.M.
GH

RESTAURANTS

BAN BOOSARIN

DAMNERN KASEM RD.

SIRIN
HOTEL

MARKET

THAI
TAE GH

TRAIN
STATION

GOLF INN HOTEL

TOURIST
OFFICE

GPO

JED PEE
NONG HOTEL

GEE GH

SOFITEL
CENTRAL HOTEL

TO SURAT THANI AND KO SAMUI

BAAN SOMBOON
HOTEL

0   100 m

© MOON PUBLICATIONS, INC.

Hua Hin developed as Thailand's original beach resort shortly after WW I with the construction of the Southern Railway and the new summer palace of King Prajadhipok, which was called Klai Kangwon, "Far From Worries." The final touch was the completion of the nation's first international golf course and the famous Railway Hotel. Initially favored by Thai royalty and the wealthy elite, the Railway Hotel—an elegant Victorian structure now renamed the Sofitel—later stood in as Cambodia's leading hotel in the film *The Killing Fields*. Among the Thais, Hua Hin still plays an important role in royal history since His Majesty, King Bhumibol, maintains a palace and occasionally visits to sail his single- and double-handed boats.

Recently, Hua Hin has witnessed explosive growth that has transformed the once-idyllic seaside resort into a mega-destination that belies her nickname—Queen of Tranquility. The beach is a messy affair of tacky souvenir stalls, plastic bags, water-scooters, and other curses of uncontrolled development. Massive hotels loom over a rather intimate beach. Local authorities are now working to implement some much-needed zoning laws and sort out the problems of pollution, overdevelopment, traffic, and theft that confront Hua Hin.

Hua Hin Beach

The beach at Hua Hin is unspectacular and the modern town undistinguished, but for many visitors, the beautiful bay and picturesque backdrop of green hills make this a fine place to relax for a few days. Early risers can watch fishermen set sail from the northern piers, then walk six km south to a pair of limestone hills for excellent views over the arching bay. Khao Takiab ("Chopstick Hill") can also be reached by motorcycle. Below Khao Takiab is Wat Khao Lad, a Buddhist temple with a 20-meter alabaster Buddha image. Two km west of Khao Takiab lies Khao Krilas ("Spirit Mountain"), a mystical site festooned with over 200 spirit houses, holy relics, and miniature *chedis.*

During the day there's little to do but relax, read a book, wander around the beach, and perhaps visit the quaint burgundy-and-cream building next to the train station which once served as the private waiting room for Thai royalty.

Pilots might investigate the local flying school, which provides English-language training and awards pilot's licenses for about 75,000B.

More information on local attractions, tours, and transportation is available from the municipal tourist office on Damnern Kasem Road.

Marek Khantayawan Palace

Fifteen km north of Hua Hin, on the grounds of the Rama IV Army Base, is a wooden palace constructed in 1924 as a royal retreat for King Rama VI. Entirely made of teak and fashioned in Thai-Victorian style, the Palace of Love and Hope has recently been renovated and opened to the public. Open daily 0800-1600; no entrance fee.

Three Caves

To the west of Hua Hin rises a verdant backdrop of humpbacked mountains. Near the village of Nong Phlab—home to the second-largest pineapple plantation in the world (Dole)—are three ancient caves named Dao, Lablae, and Kailon that show scalloped stalactites and twisting stalagmites. But which is which? Guides with gas lanterns are available to show you around, tell tall tales, and answer questions. Take an escorted tour from Hua Hin, or a local bus opposite Chatchai market. The caves are behind the village police station: Dao Cave is 500 meters distant, Lablae Cave is 2.5 km, and Kailon Cave is 3.5 km.

Budget Accommodations

Hua Hin's dozen-plus guesthouses are tucked away in the alleys one block back from the beach. Rooms during the low season and midweek start from 150B, while weekend, holiday, and high-season rates Oct.-March are 350-500B.

Beach Road Guesthouses: Sriosrapusin, Europa, and **Sunee** guesthouses have simple fan-cooled rooms for 150-350B. Cheaper rooms are found in the private homes down the alley at the **S.M., M.P.,** and **Pattana Thai-Dutch** guesthouses. M.P. Guesthouse features a useful notice board and cozy veranda.

One block north is another narrow alley with several inexpensive guesthouses such as **Crocodile, Phuen,** and **Ban Pak,** where fan-cooled rooms cost 150-300B.

Thai Tae Guesthouse: A newer place in a quiet location slightly back from the street. 6 Damnern Kasem Rd., tel. (032) 511906, 150-250B fan, 350-450B a/c.

Gee Guesthouse: An older wooden place with a busy cafe and nightly videos on Damnern Kasem Rd., 150-250B.

All Nations Guesthouse: English-run guesthouse with clean rooms and ice-cold beer. 10 Decharnchit Rd., 150-300B.

Subhamitra Hotel: An older six-story hotel with a small pool and clean, large rooms. Away from the action, but a good-value choice. Amnuayasin Rd., tel. (032) 511208, 250-350B fan, 400-600B a/c.

Chat Chai: Another reasonably priced guesthouse. 59 Petchkasem, tel. (032) 511034, 150-300B.

Moderate Accommodations

Jed Pee Nong Hotel: Very popular spot with small swimming pool and great outdoor cafe. 13/7 Damnern Kasem Rd., tel. (032) 512381, 450-650B.

Sirin Hotel: An attractive and spotlessly clean cantilevered hotel centrally located near the beach and restaurants with a very luxurious feel about the property. Damnern Kasem Rd., tel. (032) 511150, fax (032) 513571, 950-1,200B.

Fresh Inn: Modern and comfortable hotel under Italian management; try their Lo Stivale

Restaurant for pastas and pizzas. 132 Naret Damri Rd., tel. (032) 511389, 850-1,200B a/c.

Baan Somboon Hotel: An older but very friendly spot with a small garden; room rates include breakfast plus it's tucked away in a less hectic alley, tel. (032) 512079, 750-900B.

Ban Boosarin Hotel: Another cozy hotel with immaculate rooms for "tourists, executive and even the golf gang." All rooms are a/c with refrigerators and TV. 8/8 Poolsuk Rd., tel. (032) 512076, 750-1,100B.

A few more worth a mention are **Golf Inn** on Damnern Kasem, tel. (032) 512473, 650-900B; and **Suphamit,** 19 Petchkasem, tel. (032) 511208, 400-650B.

Luxury Accommodations

Sofitel Central Hotel: Hua Hin's most famous hotel is the grande dame constructed in 1921 by Prince Purachtra. Formerly known as the Railway Hotel, the European-style hotel was completely renovated and redecorated by a French hotel firm several years ago and now features sports facilities, spacious gardens, and a beautiful swimming pool. Damnern Kasem Rd., tel. (032) 512021, fax (032) 511014, Bangkok reservations tel. (02) 233-0974, U.S. reservations tel. (800) 221-4542, 3,400-6,500B.

Melia Hua Hin: A great deal of controversy was caused by the opening of this monstrous hotel property directly on the open beach, effectively shutting out most of Hua Hin from beach views and easy beach access, though the Spanish-owned resort stands as the finest conventional option in town and comes equipped with all possible amenities. Naretdamri Rd., tel. (032) 512879, fax (032) 511135, 3,800-5,600B.

Royal Garden Resort: Hua Hin's most intimate and sophisticated luxury choice, about two km south of town, is a stunning, crescent-shaped, low-rise complex with pool, tennis courts, and sports center outfitted with catamarans, lasers, and windsurfers. Ideally suited for those who seek sports and a beach removed from the clutter of central Hua Hin. 107 Petchkasem Rd., tel. (032) 511881, fax (032) 512422, Bangkok reservations tel. (02) 251-8659, 3,200-5,400B.

Restaurants

Despite ill-conceived development in recent years, Hua Hin has managed to avoid the taw-driness and commercial excesses of other beach resorts like Pattaya and Phuket. Nightlife revolves around seafood dinners and drinks at simple open-air cafes down by the water, and at restaurants in the better hotels.

Night Market: A popular place to dine inexpensively while shopping for socks and cassettes. Streetside specialties include seafoods, Thai sweets, mussel omelettes, and "pigs' bowels."

Beach Road (Naret Damri) Cafes: Several small and inexpensive cafes are located on the beach road near the budget guesthouses.

Fishing Pier: Three basic but lively spots are located at the pier in the north of town. **Sang Thai** provides a good display of fresh seafood packed over ice and a useful photographic menu, but **Charoen Pochana** has a longer pier with better views and finer ambience. **Meek-aruna Seafood** across the street features a snooker club and an upstairs a/c dining room with English-language menus. Good food, too.

European Restaurants: Restaurants rise and fall quickly in Hua Hin, but as of this writing the most popular choices are **La Villa Italian Restaurant** with an Italian chef; **Ban Lan Sao Restaurant** for a curious culinary combination called "Thai-Italian Cuisine"; and beautiful **La Provence Restaurant** in a back-alley courtyard graced with trees and flowers.

Transportation

Hua Hin is 170 km south of Bangkok on the shorter freeway that bypasses Nakhon Pathom and 238 km from Bangkok on the older route through Nakhon Pathom.

Air: Bangkok Airways flies twice daily from Bangkok to Hua Hin for 900B. The airport is five km north of town.

Train: Trains from Hualampong station in Bangkok leave nine times daily 0900-2155. Two trains leave daily from Kanchanaburi.

Advance reservations for train travel south can be made at local agencies, including Western Tours on Damnern Kasem Road. Travelers without reservations will probably need to stand for several hours until seats are vacated by departing passengers.

Bus: Buses from the Southern Bus Terminal in Bangkok leave every 30 minutes and take three or four hours depending on the route and traffic. Buses terminate in the center of town on the main highway or back one block on Sasong Road. Beachside bungalows are a 10-minute walk away.

Travel agencies in Hua Hin can sometimes book direct a/c bus travel south to Ko Samui and Phuket. Ordinary buses can be picked up during the day on Sasong Road and in the evenings near the clock tower on Petchkasem Road.

KHAO SAM ROI YOT NATIONAL PARK

Hua Hin's major attraction is the 98-square-km national park in Prachuap Khiri Khan Province, 65 km south of Hua Hin. Khao Sam Roi Yot ("Three Hundred Peaks") is a geological wonderland of limestone caves, secluded beaches, dozens of strangely disfigured mountains that resemble the angular humps of a sea dragon, and endangered

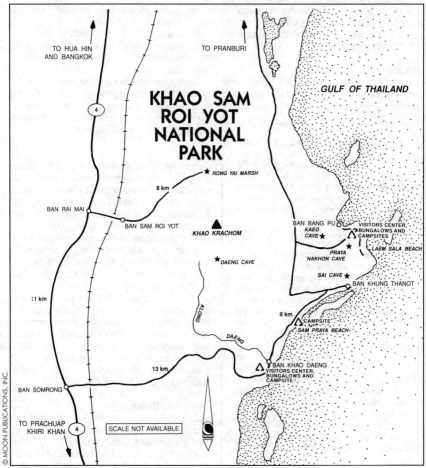

wildlife such as serow mountain goats and crab-eating macaques. Some 237 species of birds have been identified here, best seen during the birdwatching season Nov.-February.

Khao Sam Roi Yot National Park (KSRY) was declared Thailand's first coastal park in June 1966, to protect the environment and bring attention to the magnificent gray limestone mountains that rise dramatically from the Gulf of Thailand to heights above 600 meters. Although the natural surroundings have since made it among the most popular parks in the nation, the chief ecological draws are the freshwater marshes and rich coastal tidewaters that provide an important stopover and breeding grounds for Asia/Pacific birdlife.

Wildlife
The remote location and relatively inaccessible nature of the park has allowed it to support and maintain large numbers of wildlife now driven from most of urban Thailand. Among the more common animals are serow, a blackish goat that can be seen in the early mornings or evenings climbing along the rugged mountain crags.

The park also supports three types of primates: the dusky langur, crab-eating macaque, and the slow loris. Khao Sam Roi Yot is considered one of the best places in Asia to see the dusky langur, easily recognizable by its distinctive eye patches that resemble aviator goggles. Another primate living around park headquarters is the crab-eating macaque, named after its unique ability to pull apart crabs and survive on a diet of shellfish and other sealife. Few visitors see the shy and extremely retiring slow loris, which lives among the trees but can sometimes be spotted late at night with the aid of a strong flashlight.

Other mammals found in the park include the barking deer, Malayan pangolin, fishing cat, common palm civet, Malayan porcupine, Javan mongoose, Siamese hare, and gray-bellied squirrel. Dolphins play in the coastal waters.

PRAWN FARMS IN PARADISE?

*A*ny visitor to the national park will discover not only spectacular landscapes but also one of the more disturbing sights in all of Thailand—the quick destruction of marshlands and mangrove swamps by thousands of illegal shrimp farms.

Legal arrangements between local villagers and the National Parks Division have left behind a patchwork of rules intended to protect the natural environment while insuring the livelihood of local farmers. But wealthy outsiders, funded by regional politicians and powerful merchants, soon moved in with bulldozers and bribes to profit from the industry of black tiger prawn farming. The crisis peaked in 1991 after Klong Khao Daeng, the main outflow for the complex and highly fragile ecological network, was dredged and flooded with highly acidic saltwater, which killed the natural habitats and polluted the marshes. Exposed to the air, the once-fertile marshlands died as bacteria eliminated all the oxygen in the marshes. Within a few years, most of the prawn farms were abandoned due to prawn disease and the destruction of the wetlands that once supported one of Asia's largest collections of migratory birdlife.

Birds
Despite the interesting wildlife, it is birdlife that remains the chief attraction of Khao Sam Roi Yot. Birdwatchers have counted 237 species of birds in this relatively small park, an amazing concentration credited to the park's primary location on the Asian/Australian flyway. About 60% of the bird population are migratory species moving down from Siberia Sept.-Nov., or flying north between March and May, spending several months in the park to feed and rest before continuing their long flight.

The best viewing sites are the freshwater marshes near the village of Rong Jai, one of the few locations in Southeast Asia where the purple heron breeds; and the deciduous woodlands and mangrove swamps near the park headquarters, home to bird species associated with these forms of flora. Visitors can pick up a birdwatching guide at park headquarters.

Laem Sala Beach
Hat Laem Sala is an attractive circular cove surrounded by three limestone hills some 16 km east of park headquarters. Although the formal headquarters is located near Khao Daeng to the south, Laem Sala is a more popular place to

overnight since it's easier to reach from Pranburi and has a larger selection of bungalows.

Transportation: The beach can be reached by either land or sea. Coming down from Hua Hin, first take a public bus to Pranburi. Then take one of the ordinary *songtaos,* which depart hourly, from the Pranburi market to Bang Pu village for 20B.

From Bang Pu, you can walk or hire a 10-person boat to Laem Sala for about 150B return. As you approach from the sea, the beach first appears to be an island set with casuarina trees in the remote corner of the park. A closer look reveals a small restaurant, several sets of bungalows, a campsite, a small visitors center, picnic facilities, and public washrooms.

You can also hike from Bang Pu down a steep but well-constructed trail starting from the seashore village temple. This 20-minute walk provides splendid views over the coastal limestone range and the numerous offshore islands.

Visitors coming up from the south often head first to Khao Daeng and continue on to Laem Sala the following day. From park headquarters near Khao Daeng village, a chartered *songtao* costs about 100B to reach the beach at Laem Sala.

Accommodations: Bungalows on Laem Sala include five cabins that hold 2-20 people and cost 300-1,000B per night. Reservations can be made by calling the Marine National Parks Division in Bangkok at (02) 561-4292, ext. 747.

Although not officially stated, travelers are allowed to stay in the cabins for 100B per person on a space-available basis. Weekends are a bit risky, but bungalows are generally vacant during the week.

A final option is to camp at either Laem Sala, Sam Praya Beach, or park headquarters near Khao Daeng village. Tents are no longer available for rent, but visitors who arrive with their own tents can camp out for just 10B per night.

Praya Nakhon Cave

Another popular stop is the serpentine cavern elevated on a hill high above Laem Sala Beach.

The cave is defined by two large sinkholes whose roofs have collapsed to allow sunlight and rain to reach the floor of the caverns. Tham Praya Nakhon is named after a former ruler who found refuge in the labyrinth some 200 years

ago after violent storms forced his ship in from the churning waters. The cave achieved greater fame on 20 June 1890 after a royal pavilion was constructed inside the chambers to honor the visit of King Rama V. Praya Nakhon was also visited in June 1926 by King Rama VII, who left his signature on the north wall to complement the older signature of King Rama V. The present king of Thailand, Bhumibol Adulyadej, has twice visited the cave to continue the royal tradition.

Praya Nakhon Cave can be reached from Laem Sala Beach via a steep rock trail that winds some 430 meters and rises almost 130 meters before it reaches the magnificently sited cavern. Visitors should wear decent shoes and be prepared for some rather treacherous climbs.

Kaeo Cave

Another cave with less royal trappings but an equally fascinating interior is the dark and mysterious cave in Hup Chan Valley, some two km from the turnoff to Bang Pu village. Guides are necessary since the cave remains in almost total darkness and the hidden ledges and bewildering tunnels can easily confuse the first-time visitor.

Tham Kaeo is entered by descending a ladder and then maneuvering through a series of chambers that connect with various sizes of passageways. After 10 minutes of hiking, you emerge at a large hillside opening after passing limestone formations that glitter like diamonds in the dark. The ancient stalactites and spectacular petrified waterfalls should not be touched, since oils from human skin permanently stop all further lime deposits.

Sai Cave

A final cave worth exploring is the hillside cavern that faces the ocean near the village of Krung Tanot. From the small village, walk 2.3 km along the narrow and sandy road to the cave entrance, where local residents rent lamps for 30B at the small wooden shelter.

With guide and lamp, you then climb the 280-meter trail until you enter the mouth of the cavern and slowly walk around the darkened interior while your guide points out various stalactites and stalagmites named after all types of animals. Tham Sai also features monstrous limestone domes and dangling stone tentacles resembling prehistoric jellyfish.

Sam Praya Beach

Just five km from park headquarters.is a lovely beach sheltered by hills and flanked by casuarina trees. Hat Sam Praya has a simple cafe, washrooms, and campsites situated along the one-km stretch of pure, white sand.

Khao Daeng Viewpoint

Midway between park headquarters and the village of Khao Kaeng is a steep and rocky trail that leads up to the summit of Khao Daeng, 157 meters above the coastal stretches and dramatic limestone mountains that form the natural landscape of Khao Sam Roi Yot. The best time to make the climb is shortly before dawn to enjoy sunrise on one of the more spectacular sites in this section of Thailand.

Khao Daeng Canal

Another popular park activity is to hire a 10-passenger boat in Khao Daeng village and enjoy the 90-minute ride up the canal before returning to the village and the sea. The journey costs 200B for the entire boat, and passes through mangrove swamps rich with species of birds, monkeys, and monitor lizards. Wildlife is most abundant in the early morning hours and shortly before sunset, when the eerie lighting and moody scenery guarantee spectacular photography.

Khao Daeng Visitors Center

The visitors center near the village of Khao Daeng also serves as the park headquarters, with informative exhibits and local rangers who can help with current details about wildlife and sightseeing.

Nature walks from Khao Daeng include the Horseshoe Trail that passes through the habitant of macaques and langur, and the Mangrove Trail that has been signposted with identification markers for mudskippers, crabs, and herons.

Accommodations: The Forestry Department has three bungalows at the Khao Daeng Visitors Center: the eight-person Junpha for 600B, the 10-person Maliwon for 800B, and the 10-person Kalung for 900B.

As stated above, solo travelers and couples are welcome to stay in the bungalows for 100B per night on a space-available basis, or to camp out for just 10B per night.

Transportation

Khao Sam Roi Yot is 63 km south of Hua Hin and 37 km south of Pranburi.

Bus: Take a bus from Hua Hin to Pranburi, 25 km south, and walk over to the *songtao* station at the Pranburi market. *Songtaos* leave from the market every 30 minutes and cost 20B to Bang Pu village, from where you can walk or hire a boat to the bungalows on Laem Sala Beach.

Bang Pu is the final stop for the ordinary *songtao*. To continue on to park headquarters at Khao Daeng, you'll need to charter a *songtao* for about 100B or try hitching.

Pranburi to Headquarters: *Songtaos* cost 250B and motorcycle taxis 150B for the ride to park headquarters near Khao Daeng. Be clear that you want to go to KSRY National Park Headquarters and not the village of Ban Sam Roi Yot.

Tours and Motorcycles: Tours are arranged through travel agencies in Hua Hin and Cha Am. Another idea is to hire a motorcycle in Hua Hin and enjoy complete freedom to explore the park at a more leisurely pace.

PRANBURI

Pranburi is a sleepy seaside resort south of Hua Hin near the entrance to Khao Sam Roi Yot National Park.

Ban Khun Tanot

An intriguing side trip can be made to Ban Khun Tanot, a traditional Thai fishing village that exists where nature refuses to survive. Khun Tanot lies in a bizarre decomposed marsh of sculpted clay, eerie black birds, and thousands of charred trees that stand like forgotten skeletons in a lifeless land. The surrealistic scene may jog your memory: the Killing Fields in the war movie of the same title.

Accommodations

Several moderately priced resorts down at the beach attract a steady stream of visitors discouraged by the commercialism of Hua Hin.

Pransiri Hotel: Right on the highway is a simple but adequate place for a quick overnight. 283 Phetkasem Rd., tel. (032) 621061, 160-320B.

Pranburi Beach Resort: The town's only luxurious resort is popular with upscale Thais but rarely visited by Westerners. Hat Pranburi, tel. (032) 621889, 1,200-1,800B.

PRACHUAP KHIRI KHAN

One of the more delightful and untouristy towns in the northern third of southern Thailand is the unassuming village of Prachuap Khiri Khan, situated on a magnificently arched bay flanked by towering limestone peaks. Prachuap Khiri Khan ("Town Among Mountains") lacks historical monuments and the beach inside the city limits is disappointing, but the genuine Thai feel and nearby geological attractions make it an excellent stop for visitors with extra time.

Attractions
The limestone peaks and arching Prachuap Bay inspired a travel writer to nickname the town the Rio of southern Thailand. While something of an overstatement, it's hard to deny that Prachuap boasts one of the most attractive layouts in the region. A small tourist office behind the night market displays photos of the nearby beaches and can help with transportation details.

Khao Chong Krachok: Looming over the northern end of the bay is a limestone buttress called Mirror Tunnel Mountain after an illuminated arch which appears to reflect the sky. Visitors can climb the stairway to enjoy the panoramic views over the bay and west toward the mountains of Myanmar, feed the hordes of wild monkeys, and visit Wat Thammikaram, established by King Rama VI. The small monastery is shaded by fragrant frangipani trees.

Ao Noi Beach: Fairly clean and white beaches are located both north and south of town. Ao Noi, six km north and reached by minitrucks heading up Chai Thale Road, has several small spots such as Ao Noi Beach Bungalows, where a Thai-German couple rent rooms from 450B, serve both Thai and German meals, and operate a water sports center with windsurfers.

Ao Khan Kradai Beach: Eight km north of Prachuap and within walking distance of Ao Noi is another deserted beach with excellent sand. A

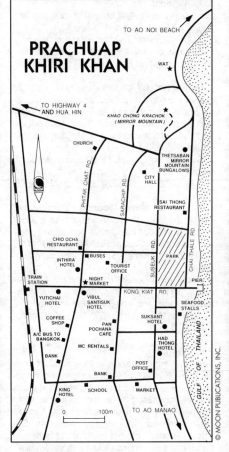

narrow trail to the rear leads up a limestone peak to a modest temple and then to an impressive cave called Tham Khao Khan Kradai. The cave *wat* features excellent views and an immense 16-meter reclining Buddha image illuminated by spilling sunlight.

Manao Bay: South of Prachuap and beyond the limestone peak is an attractive bay and beach under the supervision of the Thai military. Manao was the scene of a battle between the Thai Army and Japanese forces in WW II, an event commemorated each year with a light-and-sound show in early December.

Accommodations

Prachuap has several budget places and one midpriced hotel down by the beach.

Yutichai Hotel: The first hotel near the train station has decent rooms in a convenient location. 35 Kong Kiat Rd., tel. (032) 611055, 120-240B.

Inthira Hotel: Directly across from the night market is a popular spot with inexpensive rooms. No English sign, but look for the car in the lobby and the small hotel desk on the right; avoid the noisy streetside rooms. Phitak Chat Rd., no phone, 120-350B.

Suksant Hotel: An older 80-room hotel painted green with 80 fairly clean rooms. 131 Suseuk Rd., tel. (032) 611145, 220-300B fan, 350-450B a/c.

Thetsaban Mirror Mountain Bungalows: Facing the bay in the north end of town is a collection of seaside bungalows owned and operated by the city. Suseuk Rd., tel. (032) 611150, 350B double rooms, 450-700B individual bungalows.

Had Thong Hotel: The newest hotel in Prachuap features a small swimming pool, comfortable cafe, and well-furnished a/c rooms. 7 Suseuk Rd., tel. (032) 611960, fax (032) 611003, 600-850B.

Restaurants

The small **night market** in the center of town offers the standard collection of quick-cook specialties. Seaside vendors, who set up stalls in the evenings along the waterfront just south of the pier, display fresh seafood that can be cooked to order in a variety of sauces. **Sai Thong Restaurant** just north of the park and the small **Pan Pochana Cafe** are more formal affairs with local specialties such as *haw mok haw* (fish curry and mussels) and *pla samli tae daw* (fried cottonfish with mango salad). Prachuap's most attractive restaurant is located inside the Had Thong Hotel.

Transportation

Prachuap Khiri Khan is 252 km south of Bangkok and 82 km south of Hua Hin.

Train: Trains from Hualampong station in Bangkok leave nine times daily 0900-2155.

Bus: Buses leave regularly from the Southern Bus Terminal in Bangkok and from the bus sta-

tion on Sasong Road in Hua Hin. Buses terminate and depart from the shed just opposite the Inthira Hotel.

PRACHUAP TO CHUMPHON

Several small towns on fairly impressive beaches are located between Prachuap Khiri Khan and Chumphon. Resorts near Bang Saphan Yai are the most popular and attract a small but steady stream of Western travelers.

Thap Sakae

Thap Sakae is a small town with decent beaches both north and south.

Accommodations: Hotels in the city limits include the **Chan Ruan,** the **Chawalit** on the main highway, and the **Suk Kasem** on Sukhaphiban Road. All have acceptable rooms from 150-250B. The Thap Sakae Hotel in the north end of town has superior rooms for 300-400B fan and 450-550B a/c.

Better atmosphere is found at **Talay Inn,** located on a small lake about one km back from the Thap Sakae train station. Proprietor Khun Yo can advise on visits to Huay Yang Waterfall and other recreational activities. The place is somewhat neglected but if still in business will have rustic bamboo bungalows for 80-250B.

Kee Ree Wong Beach

Several beach resorts patronized almost exclusively by Thais are located south of Thap Sakae. Seven km south at Km 372 is an upscale development called **Had Kaeo Beach Resort** (tel. 032-611035) with 30 bungalows in various price ranges starting at 900B.

Two km farther south is the small village of Ban Krut and the turnoff to a long and attractive beach with several inexpensive bungalows such as those at **Tawee Resort** and **Kee Ree Wong Beach Resort.** The latter is operated by a Westerner and his Thai wife, who charge 100-220B for bungalows with private bath and shower. A motorcycle from the Ban Krut train station to Kee Ree Wong Beach costs 20B during the day and 30B at night. Note that only the ordinary diesel trains stop in Thap Sakae, Ban Krut, and Bang Saphan.

Bang Saphan Yai

Bang Saphan Yai, a fishing town 76 km south of Prachuap, also serves as a Thai resort known for its seafood, big-game fishing, and offshore islands such as Ko Thalu.

Accommodations: Several beach hotels and bungalows are located in the small town and along the bay. **B.S. Guesthouse, Had Soom Boon Seaview Hotel, Bang Saphan Resort, Vanveena Bungalows,** and **Sarikar Villa** have fan rooms from 150-350B and a/c rooms at double that price. Fishing boats and tackle can be chartered at Sarikar Villa.

Karol L's Bungalows: Travelers can also hire a motorcycle taxi for 20B and head six km south to a beautiful beach to stay at this fine little spot, owned and operated by a retired American and his Thai wife and an idyllic place almost completely untouched by mass tourism. Karol can help with boat trips and overnight stays on nearby Thalu Island, plus fishing and skin-diving tips. Pickup is arranged in Bang Saphan Yai by calling (032) 691058 and leaving your time and mode of arrival. Wooden bungalows cost 120-180B.

Suan Luang Resort: Another popular choice for Western travelers is this collection of 10 bungalows and a Thai-French restaurant amid coconut groves and local flora and fauna. The resort—very close to Karol L's Bungalows—is set slightly back from the beach and the owners can help you find nearby waterfalls, caves, coves, and lakes, or hire a boat across to Ko Thalu, a beautiful island just off the coast. 13 Mu 1, tel. (01) 212-5687, fax (032) 548177, 300-600B.

CHUMPHON

Almost 500 km south of Bangkok and situated on the Kra Isthmus, Chumphon is an extremely drab provincial capital near several fine beaches on the eastern perimeter. Chumphon is considered the start of southern Thailand and an important crossroads where the highway splits to Phuket on the Indian Ocean side and Ko Samui in the Gulf of Thailand. Chumphon offers beaches and scuba diving—considered among the finest in Thailand.

The main reason people pass through Chumphon is that it serves as a departure point

for boats to Ko Tao, an option which saves heading down to Surat Thani and then backtracking through Samui and Phangan.

Attractions

The beaches and offshore islands near Chumphon are rarely visited by Westerners, who generally head directly to Ko Tao and miss some of the best sand in the south.

The Chumphon region is fortunate to be protected by laws passed soon after a disastrous typhoon in 1989 wiped out most of the coastal area and flooding and landslides killed more than 300 residents. When the disaster was partially blamed on widespread logging which had denuded the protective landcover, the government ended all logging in Thailand and approved environmental codes to protect the coral reefs, fishing grounds, and pristine beaches. Laws also prohibit most commercial development directly on the beach and ban the use of jet skis and other noisy distractions.

The following beaches can be reached with *songtaos* or buses leaving from Pracha Uthit and Paramin Manda Roads.

Thung Wua Laen Beach

Some 12 km north of Chumphon lies a lovely bay almost devoid of tourists, except for small crowds on weekends. The sand is fairly clean and the picturesque combination of mountains and ocean make this an idyllic spot for a day-trip.

Scuba Diving: Many visitors come solely to dive around the half dozen islands just off Ao Thung Wua Laen. Dive sites include Ko Hin Pae, Ko Ngam Yai, a small cavern near Ko Kaloak, and the colorful corals of Ko Ngam Noi. The best corals are found around Ko Ngam Yai, since the island is home to thousands of swiftlets that build the highly prized birds' nests and the island has been declared off-limits to visitors.

Dives can be arranged at the Chumphon Cabana Resort, which has a dive center and over 20 sets of scuba gear. Boat charters cost 2,200-3,800B per day; weekends provide the best opportunity to find other passengers to share the cost.

The islands can also be reached by public boat for just 20B from the Sa Pleu pier.

Seabeach Bungalows: Thung Wua Laen is primarily visited by Thai travelers who prefer to

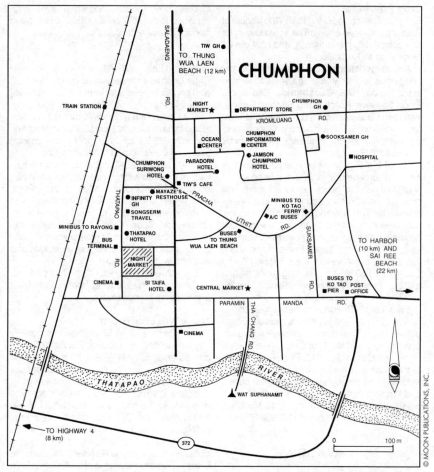

stay in midlevel bungalows. This particular spot features solid brick rooms, a small garden, and a decent seafood restaurant. Thung Wua Laen Beach, 4/2 Mu 8, 350-600B.

View Bungalows: Another modestly priced place with cantilevered bungalows offering great views over the picturesque bay. Thung Wua Laen Beach, 13/2 Mu 8, 350-600B.

Chumphon Cabana Resort: The first resort to open on the beach serves as the local dive center and gathering point for upscale travelers. Bungalows are well furnished, though the fan-cooled rooms can be uncomfortable in the hot season. Facilities include international phone service, dive equipment rentals, and a popular restaurant that serves local crab and other seafood specialties. Thung Wua Laen Beach, Tambon Saphil, tel. (077) 501990, Bangkok tel. (02) 281-1234, 500-800B fan, 950-1,200B a/c.

Sai Ree Beach

Several beaches with decent sand and offshore dive sites are located about 20 km southeast of Chumphon. The road first reaches Chumphon

Harbor at Pak Nam (10 km), then follows the coast to the beaches at Pharadonpap (17 km) and Sai Ree (22 km) before arriving at semi-circular Thung Makham Bay (28 km). Most of the beaches have bungalows, simple cafes, and boat services to the nearby islands.

Boat Monument: A rather strange monument in the shape of a torpedo boat sits on a concrete base near the *songtao* stop in Sai Ree. This geographical oddity is dedicated to the founder of the Royal Thai Navy, who is honored during the Chumphon Marine Festival held in the late spring.

Islands: The chief reason to visit these beaches is to hire a boat and tour the nearby islands, or make arrangements in Chumphon and spend a few days diving the coral reefs. Ko Maprao ("Coconut Island"), better known as Ko Rang Nok ("Bird's Nest Island"), is home to thousands of swiftlets who live in the limestone caves. No visitors are allowed. To the left is Ko Matra, a fairly attractive island with campsites and bungalows. Both Ko Thalu and Ko Samet are surrounded by coral reefs but lack facilities for an overnight visit.

Pornsawan Beach Resort: Seventeen km from Chumphon and one km from the Chumphon estuary is a fairly good beach lined with coconut palms, seafood stalls, and this upscale resort complex with a swimming pool, tennis courts, dive facilities, and 75 a/c bungalows. Pharadonpap Beach, 110 Mu 4, tel. (077) 521031, 900-1,400B.

Sai Ree Lodge: A smaller place with 20 concrete bungalows covered with coconut thatching. Sai Ree Beach, 100 Mu 4, tel. (077) 521212, fax (077) 502479. Rates vary according to the season, but average 350-550B fan and 650-1,400B a/c.

Boats to Ko Tao
Ko Tao is usually reached by boat from Surat Thani, Ko Samui, or Ko Phangan, though an increasing number of travelers prefer to shorten the circuit with a boat from Chumphon.

Slow Boat: A large fishing boat leaves from the Ko Tao boat pier, 10 km from Chumphon, at midnight and takes about six hours to reach Ko Tao. The somewhat rocky journey costs 200-250B. The last *songtao* from Chumphon to the Ko Tao pier departs around 1800. A better option is to take the tourist van, which leaves around

2200 and eliminates the long wait at the pier. Tickets can be purchased at Infinity Travel, Chumphon Information Center, Chumphon Travel Service, and from Tiw's Cafe (from Mr. O).

Fast Boat: A sleek and speedy boat departs daily around 0800 from Tha Yang Pier near the Chumphon harbor. This boat reaches Ko Tao in about two hours and costs 400-450B. Contact the above agencies for more information.

From Bangkok: Various travel agencies near Khao San Road sell combination tickets for 750-900B that include an a/c minivan to Chumphon and the slow boat to Ko Tao. A less expensive option is to take an a/c van from Bangkok for just 300-350B to Chumphon, followed by the slow boat to Ko Tao. Travel agencies in Banglampoo have details and sell tickets.

Budget Accommodations
Travelers generally head down to a beach, though Chumphon has plenty of hotels in all price ranges.

Infinity Travel Service: Opposite the bus terminal is a basic but acceptable place with reliable information on nearby islands and transportation to Ko Tao. 68/2 Thatapao Rd., tel. (077) 501937), 120-160B.

Sooksamer Guesthouse: One of the most popular budget options in town is this attractive wooden house in the northeastern section of town, with a pleasant cafe, basic rooms with shared bathrooms, and large grounds studded with coconut palms. Suksamer is owned by an English-speaking local and his Thai wife, who provide travel tips and decent food in their attached cafe. 118/4 Suksamer Rd., tel. (077) 502430, 120-160B.

Chumphon Guesthouse: Also in the northeastern section of Chumphon and a somewhat lengthy walk from the bus and train station, but another lovely old house converted into a travelers center with small but clean rooms and very helpful managers. The owners can help with local tours, motorcycle rentals, and make sure you make the Ko Tao ferry on time. Krom Luang Chumphon Rd., tel. (077) 501242, 120-160B.

Mayaze's Resthouse: Small but spotless place with just five well-scrubbed rooms all with common bath in a handy location just one block east of the bus terminal. Soi Bangkok Bank, tel. (077) 504452, 150-250B fan, 350-450B a/c.

Si Taifa Hotel: A Chinese hotel with a decent restaurant on the ground floor and balcony views from the 20 fan-cooled rooms upstairs. 74 Saladaeng Rd., tel. (077) 511063, 150-260B.

Moderate to Luxury Accommodations

Chumphon Suriwong Hotel: A Chinese hotel whose lobby and hallway resemble the interior of a tiled bathroom, plus an adjoining restaurant decorated with aquariums and caged singing birds. Worth a look if only for the surrealistic setting. 176 Saladaeng Rd., tel. (077) 511776, 180-200B fan, 350-450B a/c.

Thatapao Hotel: An acceptable midpriced hotel just one block north of the bus station. 66 Thatapao Rd., tel. (077) 511479, fax (077) 502479, 280-350B fan, 480-650B a/c.

Paradorn Hotel: A modern and fairly luxurious hotel with over 100 a/c rooms and a popular nightclub. 180/12 Paradorn Rd., tel. (077) 511598, 430-650B.

Jamson Chumphon Hotel: The best hotel in town opened a decade ago near Ocean Department Center with restaurant on the lobby floor, massage parlor, and disco open until 0200. 188/65 Saladaeng Rd., tel. (077) 502502, fax (077) 821821, 900-1,400B.

Restaurants

Chumphon is known as the town where southern cooking takes hold and the place where Asian fruits start to mature to their most impressive glory. Be sure to try the local durians, rambutans, mangosteens, and *lep mu nang* ("maiden's fingernail bananas") that pack flavor far beyond their modest sizes.

Central Market: Among the more medieval eating and shopping experiences in Thailand is the claustrophobic collection of foodstalls and street vendors in the southern section of town near the Thatapao River. Paramin Manda Rd. Inexpensive.

Night Market: Equally cheap meals are served from the food vendors who set up their stalls at sunset in the northern part of town just a few blocks east of the train station. Kromluang Rd. Inexpensive.

Ocean Shopping Center: Several good and inexpensive restaurants are located on the narrow road which leads to the Jamson Hotel and the upscale shopping center. Try the Japanese restaurant and an unnamed cafe just opposite for point-and-choose dishes in clean surroundings, or the espresso shop behind the shopping center for a somewhat trendy atmosphere. Names change with the seasons, but this neighborhood always guarantees a lively selection of cafes. 588/150 Saladaeng Rd. Inexpensive.

Transportation

Chumphon is 485 km south of Bangkok and 193 km north of Surat Thani.

Train: Trains from Hualampong station in Bangkok leave nine times daily 0900-2155. Luggage can be stored at the train station for 10B per day. Motorcycle taxis into town cost 10B.

Bus: Buses from Bangkok and the deep south terminate at the small bus station on Thatapao Road near the cinema and taxi stand.

THE WEST COAST: RANONG TO PHUKET

The west coast of Thailand from Ranong to Phuket marks the entrance into the tropical wonderland of southern Thailand. Situated on the Andaman Sea and drenched with heavy rains May-Oct., the blazing green mountainous region possesses thick rainforests, plunging waterfalls, majestic limestone mountains, and a translucent sea blessed with magnificent coral reefs and abundant sealife.

Traveling along the coast is a real adventure. Almost 70% of the region is mountainous, while 80% of the land is covered with tropical rainforests. The combination of rugged topography and extraordinary rainfall makes Ranong and Phangnga Provinces the least populated in the country. Rather than pass through the busy towns, dusty plains, and monotonous ricefields that characterize most of the country, you'll enjoy vistas of deserted coastline, wild jungle, and soaring mountains.

The region's chief attractions are several national parks have been established to protect the remaining rainforests and relatively untouched coastline; the parks provide visitors with opportunities to enjoy some of the finest scenery in the country. The other major highlight is scuba diving around the Surin and Similan Islands—offshore archipelagos ringed with the finest coral reefs in Thailand.

Most visitors miss this region in their rush to reach Ko Samui or Phuket, but travelers with a few extra days might pause and enjoy the natural wonders of the Andaman coast.

RANONG

Ranong (pop. 21,000) is the provincial capital and an important trading center for Thai and Burmese merchants.

Ranong was established in the late 18th century by emigrants from Hokkien, China, who discovered tin and named their mining camp *rae* (tin) *nong* (rich). The "tin rich" town was soon populated by hundreds of Chinese who arrived to work the tin mines and create the prosperity that still forms the basis of wealth in the region.

Today, most of the population is of Chinese descent; many of the older homes reflect the architectural traditions of 18th-century China.

Ranong is rather ordinary, though it provides a convenient stopping point for those traveling from Bangkok to Phuket. It also serves as a convenient launching point for visits to nearby rainforests, national parks, and Surin Islands National Park. The region has several hot springs and waterfalls, though nearby beaches tend to be muddy flats or thick mangrove swamps flooded by the heavy rains.

Ranong receives the heaviest rainfall in Thailand—up to 5,000 mm per year—so count yourself lucky if you enjoy more than a few hours of sunlight each day. So heavy are the torrential downpours that local wags have dubbed the town "Rain On."

The Kra Isthmus

Ranong faces the Andaman Sea and borders the southern tip of Myanmar at Victoria Point. The town is also situated on the Kra Isthmus, the narrowest point in peninsular Thailand and the subject of an ongoing debate regarding the construction of a canal that would connect the Andaman Sea with the Gulf of Thailand. At Kra Buri, a small town 58 km north of Ranong, only 22 km separates the Gulf of Thailand from the Chan River, which flows southward into the Andaman Sea.

Ranong Hot Springs

Ranong is locally known for its boiling hot springs one km east of town on the grounds of Wat Tapotharam. The springs have been fashioned into organized ponds surrounded by manicured gardens and tropical forests. Visitors can soak in the public baths and then explore the trails that lead up to the small monastery. Waters bubble up at 70°C—hot enough to cook eggs—but the public baths are cooled down to a more tolerable 40-42°.

Hot springs can also be enjoyed at the Jansom Thara Hotel, which pipes down the waters and charges nonresidents 50B for a dip in their giant jacuzzi.

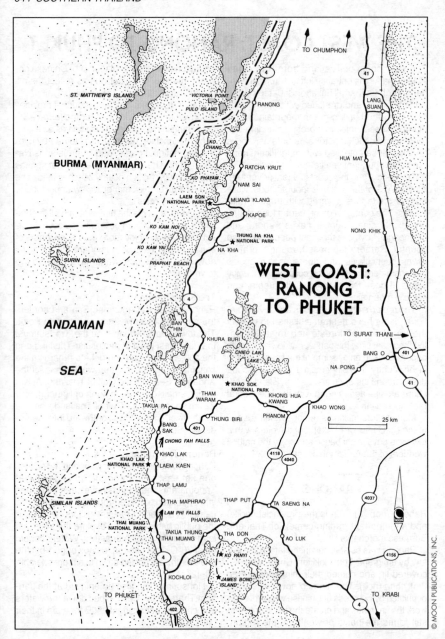

ST. MATTHEW'S ISLAND

BURMA (MYANMAR)

VICTORIA POINT

PULO ISLAND

RANONG

TO CHUMPHON

LANG SUAN

HUA MAT

KO CHANG

RATCHA KRUT

KO PHAYAM

NAM SAI

LAEM SON NATIONAL PARK

MUANG KLANG

KAPOE

NONG KHIK

KO KAM NOI

THUNG NA KHA NATIONAL PARK

KO KAM YAI

NA KHA

SURIN ISLANDS

PRAPHAT BEACH

WEST COAST: RANONG TO PHUKET

ANDAMAN

BAN HIN LAT

KHURA BURI

TO SURAT THANI

CHIEO LAN LAKE

BANG O

SEA

BAN WAN

NA PONG

KHAO SOK NATIONAL PARK

THAM WARAM

KHONG HUA KWANG

KHAO WONG

TAKUA PA

THUNG BIRI

PHANOM

0   25 km

BANG SAK

CHONG FAH FALLS

KHAO LAK

KHAO LAK NATIONAL PARK

LAEM KAEN

THAP LAMU

TA SAENG NA

THA MAPHRAO

THAP PUT

LAM PHI FALLS

PHANGNGA

SIMILAN ISLANDS

THAI MUANG NATIONAL PARK

TAKUA THUNG THAI MUANG

THA DON

AO LUK

KO PANYI

KOCHLOI

JAMES BOND ISLAND

TO PHUKET

TO KRABI

© MOON PUBLICATIONS, INC.

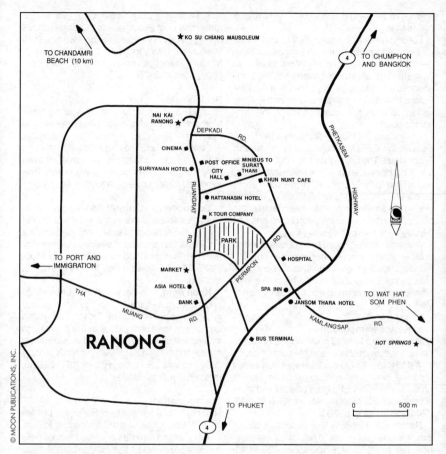

Nai Kai Ranong

Ranong's leading historical figure was a wealthy Fukien Chinese immigrant, Koh Su Chiang, who served as regional tax collector during the reign of King Rama V and was later appointed the first governor of Ranong Province. The Koh family played an important role in the development of the tin industry on Phuket.

The governor's former residence, located on the northern edge of town, honors the Koh family with a collection of mementos and ancestor figurines carved with the names of the deceased.

Koh Su Chiang Mausoleum

The mausoleum and graveyard of the Koh family are three km north of town on Chao Rakathong hill. The primary tomb is approached on a grassy walkway flanked by eight stone sculptures imported from China in the 19th century.

Myanmar and Victoria Point

Just across the broad Chan River estuary lies the southern end of Myanmar and the trading village of Victoria Point, called Kawthaung by the Burmese and Ko Song ("Two Islands") by the Thais for a pair of offshore islands. The passage is also sprinkled with dozens of islands that serve as trading posts for Thai-Burmese commerce.

Foreigners are now permitted to visit Victoria Point and other Burmese islands as independent travelers or with organized tours from Ranong. The Myanmar government has announced plans to construct a road from Victoria Point all the way to Yangon and someday allow visitors to entry the country through this very unique point.

The easiest but most expensive method is on the speedboat *JS Queen* operated by the Jansom Thara Hotel. The full-day tour at 1,000B departs from Chandamri Beach, 10 km northwest of town, and arrives at the Victoria Point market in about 30 minutes. After an hour of shopping and exploring the small Chinese-Burmese temple, the boat continues over to the pearl farms and sea gypsy village on Ko Phayam.

A casino opened here several years ago and another casino is now under construction.

Independent travelers can take ordinary boats over to the immigration point where Myanmar officials collect a nominal entrance fee for a day visit.

Budget Accommodations

Most hotels are located on Ruangrat Road between the main highway and the post office.

Asia Hotel: An old but fairly well maintained hotel with decent fan and private baths. Rooms on the upper floors tend to be brighter and more comfortable. 39 Ruangrat Rd., tel. (077) 811813, 220-260B fan, 450-650B a/c.

Rattanasin Hotel: A less expensive choice than the Asia but be sure to ask for a room away from the street to avoid the noise. 226 Ruangrat Rd., tel. (077) 811242, 180-280B.

Moderate Accommodations

Two hotels can be recommended in this price range, both on the main highway and within walking distance of the bus terminal.

Spa Inn: A popular alternative to the more expensive Jansom Thara, and one of the best values in town, is the recently refurbished hotel just across from the Jansom Thara with well furnished a/c rooms. Phetkasem Rd., tel. (077) 411715, 650-950B.

Jansom Thara Hotel: Ranong's leading hotel offers thermal pools to both residents and visitors, swimming pool, health club, two restaurants, and boat excursions to the Surin Islands during the dry winter and spring seasons. 2/10 Phetkasem Hwy., tel. (077) 811511, fax (077) 821821, Bangkok reservations tel. (02) 448-6098, 1,200-1,800B.

Restaurants

Ranong is famous for its seafood, such as deep-fried soft-shell crabs, barbecued prawns, and steamed white snapper served in coconut sauce.

Central Market: The cheapest eats are found in the municipal market in the center of town near the hotels and banks. Inexpensive Chinese and Muslim cafes are located nearby. Ruangrat Rd.

Somboon Restaurant: Ranong's most famous restaurant serves up a wide selection of Thai and Western dishes as described on their English-language menu. Just across the highway from the Jansom Thara Hotel. Open daily 1100-2300. 2/63 Phetkasem Rd., tel. (077) 822722. Moderate.

Khun Nunt: Don't let the simple surroundings and rudimentary furniture fool you. Khun Nunt is regarded as perhaps the best restaurant in town and one of the finest places in the province to try fried soft-shell crabs and grilled venison during the hunting season Sept.-December. Open daily 0900-midnight. 35/3 Luang Rd., tel. (077) 821910. Inexpensive to moderate.

Transportation

Ranong is 568 km south of Bangkok, 117 km south of Chumphon, and 412 km north of Phuket.

Air: Ranong now has an airport served daily by Bangkok Airways from Bangkok and three times weekly from Phuket. The Bangkok Airways office is two km south of town on the main highway.

Bus: Direct bus service to Ranong is available from Bangkok, Chumphon, Surat Thani, and Phuket. The Ranong bus terminal is on the highway near the Jansom Thara Hotel, though most buses also stop in the center of town on Ruangrat Road near the restaurants and budget hotels.

Direct minibus service to the Jansom Thara Hotel is provided from the Jansom Chumphon Hotel in Chumphon, Muang Thai Hotel in Surat Thani, and Imperial Hotel in Phuket.

Chokeanan Tours and **Mit Tours** on Ruangrat Road have a/c buses departing for Bangkok each day 0630-0830 and 1800-2000.

Motorcycle Rental: Motorcycles can be hired at 250B per day from Soon Chao Phanthip at Soi 2 Tha Muang Rd.

KO CHANG

Not to be confused with the island near the Cambodian border, Ko Chang ("Elephant Island") is a large and beautiful island midway between the provincial capital of Ranong and Laem Son National Park to the south. This island is now the most popular stop in this district, with plenty of inexpensive bungalows.

Accommodations
Almost a dozen simple bungalows now operate on the west side of the island, without electricity or with power from small generators.

Cashew Resort: This old favorite, the largest on the island, was named after the cashew trees that provide the main source of income for the islanders. 120-180B.

Ko Chang Resort: Another original set of bungalows on a lovely stretch of sand, popular with German travelers and other visitors seeking to get off the beaten track. 150-250B.

Rasta Baby: A much newer and clean bungalow operation with friendly and helpful managers owned and operated by an ex-New Yorker and her Thai husband. Huts are well maintained and many consider this the best value on the island. Ranong, tel. (077) 833077, 120-200B.

Ko Chang Contex: Just across the small bay from Rasta Baby is another decent option managed by a Thai couple who serve good meals in their cozy cafe. Ranong, tel. (077) 812730, 120-200B.

Transportation
Take a *songtao* from Ranong south to Saphan Pla and walk down to the pier where longtail boats leave several times daily for Ko Chang. Look for the signs advertising the bungalows on the island.

Boat transport over to the island costs 50-100B per person. Several hotels in Ranong make complete arrangements which includes transport down to Saphan Pla and onward boat travel across to the island.

LAEM SON NATIONAL PARK

Laem Son ("Pine Cape") National Park, 50 km south of Ranong, encompasses over 100 km of coastline and almost two dozen islands inhabited by birds and monkeys and covered with tons of fluffy white sand. The shoreline is mainly dense mangrove swamps popular with crab-eating macaques, interspersed with arching beaches backed by swaying casuarina trees. Laem Son, also called Bang Ben after the principal beach and fishing village, spreads across three districts, two in Ranong and one in Phangnga.

Park Headquarters
The park headquarters, visitors center, restaurant, bungalows, and campsites are located at Bang Ben beach, 12 km off the main highway at the end of a road that winds through a magnificent mangrove swamp.

The visitors center, open daily 0900-1700, provides maps, information on the park, and photos of the gorgeous islands to the west. A new pier is expected to soon provide the quickest passage to the Surin Islands.

Accommodations: As with most national parks in Thailand, camping is permitted anywhere among the trees for just 40B. Park rangers rent tents for 80B. Bungalows that sleep 5-15 visitors cost 350-900B. Visitors are also permitted to stay in unreserved cabins for 100B per person.

Komain Villa: A few hundred meters south of park headquarters is a private guesthouse owned by a pair of schoolteachers. Komain has six clean rooms for 100-150B, a small cafe in the living room, and chess sets and pool tables for evening entertainment.

The food in the park cafe is reasonably priced if somewhat monotonous. Bring extra snacks and a few bottles of Mekong.

Transportation: To reach Bang Ben from Ranong, take any bus or *songtao* to the turnoff 50 km south of Ranong. Motorcycle taxis from the highway to the beach cost 30B and take you past mangrove swamps and wooden racks used to raise oysters in the brackish waters. Hitching is possible, though the lack of traffic makes this a risky proposition on weekdays.

Beaches

Several beaches are located within the park boundaries.

Laem Son: The namesake for the park is three km north past mangrove swamps and small streams. A seaside walk to Laem Son is worthwhile if only to enjoy the strange geological formations and twisted trees that create a surrealistic landscape. Laem Son also insures a welcome escape from the hordes of teenagers who pack the beach on holidays and long weekends.

Praphat Beach: Fifty km south of Bang Ben is another national park with a park office, bungalows, campsites, and small restaurant. Boats can be hired to visit the nearby islands. Look for the large wooden sign that marks the turnoff from the highway.

Nearby Islands

Bang Ben beach is reasonably attractive, but photos in the visitors center will convince you that the nearby islands are the stuff of dreams: powdery sand, crystalline waters, and untouched corals.

Ko Kam Yai: Some 15 km southwest of Bang Ben is a large island set with grassy campgrounds, large bungalows deserted on weekdays, an excellent beach, and fantastic coral and marinelife.

Ko Kam Noi: A few hundred meters from of Ko Kam Yai is another pristine island blessed with aquamarine waters perfect for snorkeling and grassy campgrounds watered by freshwater springs.

Transportation: Park employees can help arrange boat passage to the islands Nov.-June. Monsoons lash the coastline June-Nov. and essentially close down all national parks on the southwestern coast. Weekends are the best time to hook up with other visitors and share the expense of boat charters.

Ko Phayam

This surprisingly large island, 18 km northwest of Bang Ben, is home to several hundred *chao lae* or "sea gypsies" who live nomadic lifestyles and are recognized for their animist religious practices and unique skills as divers and fishermen.

Accommodations: Ko Phayam has several privately owned homestays and higher quality resorts. Payam Island Resort (tel. 077-812297, Bangkok tel. 02-390-2681) features private bungalows on sandy beaches for 500-2,500B. Thawon Resort (tel. 077-811186) is a basic option with bamboo bungalows for 150-300B.

SURIN ISLANDS

Several hours west of the mainland, and just eight km south of the Burmese border, lie five islands which comprise Surin Islands National Park. Blessed with shallow-sea corals, a hypnotizing undersea world, and pristine beaches, Surin guarantees an extraordinary adventure for both amateur snorkelers and experienced scuba divers.

The islands now receive about 25,000 visitors each year, primarily Thai tourists and a handful of Western divers who arrive on dive boats from Phuket and other mainland harbors. The best time to visit is Dec.-April; Surin is often inaccessible during the monsoon season May-Nov.

Dive Sites

Surin National Park is comprised of two large islands—Ko Surin Nua to the north and Ko Surin Tai to the south—plus several other islets surrounded by undisturbed reefs.

The two main islands are hilly and uninhabited aside from a small community of sea gypsies who live on Ko Surin Tai. Visitors can wade across the narrow channel at low tide to explore the reefs and search for the few remaining shells missed by the sea gypsy collectors.

Headquarters Bay: Ko Surin Nua and Ko Surin Tai are divided by a shallow channel—appropriately called HQ or Headquarters Bay—rich with hard corals and a variety of turbinaria. Although commercial fishing has taken larger sealife, divers will still find crustaceans, angelfish, and porcupine pufferfish.

Turtle Ledge: As implied by the name, this shallow ledge off the east side of Ko Surin Tai is known for its turtles and dense schools of baitfish that swarm on the sloping reef. Corals include massive porites, staghorns, and spiny acroporas especially vulnerable to indiscriminate anchorings.

Hin Kong: Just east of Turtle Ledge is a jumble of granite boulders and underwater cliffs pocketed with submarine caves and soaring arches. Gorgonian sea fans and colorful feather anemones cover many of the granite rocks.

Castle Rock: One km north of Ko Surin Nua rises a natural arch which measures 25 meters in width and provides a dive experience past dangerous zebra fish, sea anemones, and perhaps the whale sharks that live in the warm waters of Surin.

Stork Island: Two km north of Ko Surin Nua is a misnamed outcropping—no storks in the region—that compensates with a variety of sea turtles, reef sharks, blue-ringed angelfish, and massive granite boulders perfect for exploring.

Accommodations
The National Parks Division operates bungalows on the southern edge of Ko Surin Nua and campsites across the bay on Ko Surin Tai. Bungalows cost 100B per person or 600B for the entire six-person cabin. Camping costs 40B per night or 80B per two-person tent. Reservations can be made at the national parks office (tel. 076-491378) at the pier in Ban Hin Lat.

The park service operates a supply store and small cafe that offers a three-meal package for 300B per day. Visitors arriving without reservations should bring along extra food and water in the event that supplies are low or the cafe is fully booked.

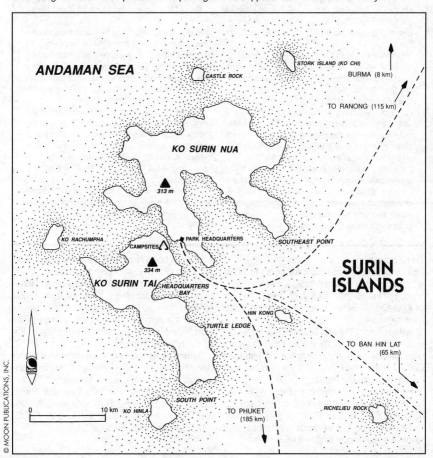

© MOON PUBLICATIONS, INC.

THE LAST OF THE SEA GYPSIES

*A*mong the more unique inhabitants of the Andaman Sea region are the nomadic sea gypsies known by Malays as *chao lay* and by Thais as *chao nam*. These "Peoples of the Sea" prefer to call themselves *moken* to distinguish them from closely related kins such as the *moklen* and *urak lawoi*, two groups that assimilated into modern society several generations ago.

According to French anthropologist Jacques Ivanoff, *mokens* trace their origins back to the Riau archipelago (Indonesia) or the Andaman Islands between India and Myanmar. Several western researchers believe these displaced peoples are related to Austro-Asiatic or Melanesian races who migrated northward from islands in the South Pacific.

Whatever their origins, the seafaring nomads apparently moved to this region hundreds of years ago to resist the arrival of outside religions and follow their animist beliefs and traditional lifestyles. Despite the vicissitudes of the last few decades, many of the elderly *moken* gypsies continue to speak ancient languages unrelated to either Malay or Thai and honor ancestral spirits with mysterious ceremonies such as the boat-floating rituals held on the full moon of the fifth lunar month.

Anthropologists also point out *moken* society has always been remarkably egalitarian and free of omniscient authority from a central leader. Another ethic is that of sharing freely with their neighbors rather than acquiring material possessions that interfere with nomadic lifestyles.

But gypsy life is coming to an end.

Several decades ago, *mokens* on Phuket abandoned their itinerant ways to settle on land-based communities and find work as pearl divers or producers of trinkets for the tourist industry. The more isolated *mokens* of the Surin Islands remained relatively pure until a few years ago when they also discovered that the sale of trinkets and shells provided an easier income than searching for fish in the Andaman Sea.

The problem was most of their shells and coral necklaces were collected from species considered endangered or protected by the Thai Fisheries Department. Government officials quickly ended this lucrative industry.

However, the underlying dilemmas were the decline of fish populations and the ineffectiveness of traditional fishing practices, such as oyster farming and harpooning. Neither oysters nor the use of harpoons insured an adequate supply of food; both practices were banned in the late 1980s, also in an attempt to save endangered sealife.

The *mokens*, banned from shell collection, trinket sales, and traditional fishing, took to fish bombing and the use of water poisons, two highly efficient but horribly destructive activities that destroy fishing habitats and coral reefs. Many *mokens* were arrested and jailed by patrols of the Thai Fisheries Department.

A few hundred *mokens* still survive on the Surin Islands, but many have abandoned their freewheeling lifestyles and found employment on the mainland.

Transportation

The closest departure point for boats to Surin is Ban Hin Lat, a fishing port 90 km south of Ranong, 160 km north of Phuket, or seven km north of Khuraburi. The town is two km west of the main highway.

Independent Travel: The National Parks Division (tel. 076-491378) in Khuraburi provides boat service for 400B during the high season Dec.-March. Boats depart from Ban Hin Lat, seven km north of Khuraburi.

Private boats that hold eight passengers can be chartered for 5,000-6,000B return from the harbor at Ban Hin Lat. Park rangers can help find a reliable boat. Weekends are the best time to join a larger group to share expenses.

Longtail boats hired from park headquarters on Ko Surin Nua cost 400B per four hours.

Buses take 90 minutes from Ranong and three hours from Phuket. Ask to be let off at the turnoff for Ban Hin Lat, then hire a motorcycle taxi or wait for a *songtao*. If stranded, stay at the Hin Lat Port View Hotel overlooking the junction of highway and the road to the pier.

Tours: Boat excursions are organized by the Jansom Thara Hotel in Ranong; Poseidon Bungalows in Khao Lak; and tour operators in Phuket such as Songserm and Asia Voyages. Packages cost 1,500-1,800B for day visits, 2,500-4,000B for two-day excursions, and 4,500-7,000B for three to five days.

SIMILAN ISLANDS

The Similans are considered among the best dive sites in Southeast Asia, comparable to the best of the Maldives and the Red Sea. So spectacular are the coral reefs, massive boulders, profuse sealife, and powdery beaches that *Skin Diver* magazine ranks Similan as one of the world's top 10 dive destinations.

The Similans were declared a national park in the mid-1980s to protect them against dynamite fishing and indiscriminate moorings that were quickly destroying the delicate reefs. The environmental damage is now under control and some say that the Similans are actually improving from the conditions of the previous decade.

The term "Similan" is derived from *sembilan,* which means "nine" in the Malay language. The Thais call the islands Ko Kao or "Nine Islands" in reference to the nine principal islands.

Dive Sites
No one seems to agree on the proper numbering of the islands, but most dive schools name and number the islands from south to north.

Ko Huyong (Island 1): The southernmost island is known for its rugged granite boulders that tumble from the beaches down to the ocean floor and create dramatic ledges, caves, and archways that harbor soft corals and large pelagic fish such as leopard sharks and giant stingrays. Just off the northern coast are the Coral Gardens, covered with massive porites, branching and table acroporas, and gorgonian sea fans.

Ko Payang (Island 2): The best diving is found among the boulders and giant sea fans on the western side of the island.

Ko Payan (Island 3): Ko Payan is barely more than a small rock poking above the surface of the waves, but just east are Hin Phae and Shark Fin Reef, a favorite of dive groups and one of the most impressive granite shelfs in the Similans. Spread over almost two square km, the granite slab provides a perfect environment for mantas, stingrays, and an incredible garden of gigantic sea fans that dwarf the diver.

Ko Miang (Island 4): Overnight visitors not affiliated with a live-aboard dive boat can stay in the bungalows on the northern beach (Bungalow

Bay) operated by the National Parks Division. This is an ideal location since Ko Miang offers three superb dive opportunities. Bird Rock, just off the southern tip, features an undersea ridge that drops sharply to 40 meters and is home to three-meter sea fans, leopard sharks, and a few large turtles migrating between the Andamans and Phuket. Stonehenge Island, another jumble of huge granite boulders off the northern tip, provides habitat to unicorn surgeonfish, snappers, yellowfin, and giant tuna. Finally, corals submerged below Honeymoon Bay, on the eastern side just below the campground, are perhaps the best anywhere in the Similans.

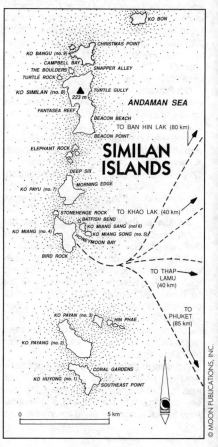

Ko Miang Song (Island 5): Miang No. 2 is a small rockhead known for its Eastern Front strewn with granite boulders that reach the size of small houses.

Ko Miang Sang (Island 6): Miang No. 3 offers the imaginatively named Batfish Bend, where many divers find themselves escorted by inquisitive black-and-white batfish, or perhaps fusiliers and golden damselfish.

Ko Payu (Island 7): Two recommended dive sites are found here. Morning Edge off the eastern side provides spectacular coral heads covered with soft fans, wire corals, and acropora teeming with green chromis, antheus, and iridescent wrasse—a superb combination of coral species and colorful tropical sealife. Deep Six off the northern tip can be a difficult dive due to strong currents but compensates with massive boulders inhabited by larger species of fish, including reef sharks and the occasional sea turtle.

Hin Pouser: An unnumbered island but nevertheless a favorite of Phuket dive companies for its amazing Elephant Pinnacles—three massive boulders that break the surface, plunge over 30 meters to the ocean floor, and create a natural amphitheater that seems to be the world's largest aquarium. Divers can swim through arches and caves while searching for schooling goatfish, yellow snappers, blue-ringed angelfish, and Moorish idols clad in brilliant jackets of yellow and black.

Ko Similan (Island 8): The largest island in the archipelago also has the largest number of dive sites. Off the eastern side are a broad sandy plateau known as Beacon Point, Turtle Gully known for its various species of sea turtles, and a 30-meter cave dubbed Dirk's Decision. Off the north and west sides are Campbell Bay with excellent snorkeling and numerous public moorings, Turtle Rock, and Fantasea Reef, an excellent dive site covered with massive boulders, caves, arches, and garden nooks filled with giant fans and iridescent corals.

Ko Bangu (Island 9): Similan's northernmost island is best visited for drift dives at Christmas Point off the northwestern coast, the massive coral heads in The Mooring, and Snapper Alley for Asian snapper living among the giant rocks.

Accommodations

Bungalows and campsites are located in the center of the archipelago on Ko Miang (Island 4).

Two-person bungalows cost 400B, six- to 10-person bungalows cost 600-1,000B, and dormitory beds cost 100B per person. Two-person tent rentals cost 100B per night. Visitors can also bring a tent or simply sleep on the beach for 40B per night.

Reservations can be made at the national parks office in Bangkok or the office in Thap Lamu at tel. (076) 411913. Note that bungalows and tents are often fully booked during the busy months of December and January and visitors without reservations may be forced to spend a few days on the beach.

The parks division operates a supply store and a simple cafe that charges 250B for three set meals per day. Visitors without reservations should bring extra food and drinking water.

Transportation

Visitors can reach the Similans from Phuket (85 km from the Similans) in three to five hours, Thap Lamu (40 km) in three hours, Khao Lak (40 km) in three hours, or Ban Hin Lak (80 km) in five hours.

Divers generally join an excursion from Phuket, while budget travelers take the park service boat from Thap Lamu or join an organized tour from a guesthouse in Khao Lak.

The dive season runs Nov.-May, though, according to dive companies, rainy months June-Oct. can just as rewarding.

Tour Companies: Seatran, one of the largest cruise companies in Thailand, provides high-speed, Norwegian-built jetfoils that fly to the Similans in under three hours—plenty of time to appreciate the underwater delights. Songserm Travel sells packages from Phuket and less expensive tours from Thap Lamu pier. See "Phuket" later in the chapter for more details.

Boats from Phuket

Almost a dozen tour operators on Phuket organize excursions ranging up to five days. Details on the dive companies and travel agencies mentioned below are listed under "Phuket" later in the chapter.

One-day tours from Patong Beach leave at 0630, return around 2000, and cost US$100-

130 for transportation, food, and snorkeling equipment. Divers pay US$150-200 for the same package plus scuba equipment, three dives, and the services of a divemaster. Three-day tours cost US$350-550; five-day tours US$500-800.

Dive Shops: Siam Diving Center, Phuket's best dive shop, offers live-aboard boats with seven- to 10-day excursions to the Similan and Surin Islands. Fantasea Divers, Phuket's oldest dive center, offers professional instruction and similar programs for the Similan and Surin Islands. Marina Divers, another five-star facility with a full range of services, is also recommended. Southeast Asia Yacht Charter has fast boats and professional escorts on their Similan dives.

Boats from Thap Lamu

A less expensive option are the national parks service boats departing from Thap Lamu, a fishing port 20 km north of Thai Muang, 40 km south of Takua Pa, or 100 km north of Phuket.

Parks Division Boats: Boats operated by the parks division cost 600B one-way, take three hours, and run during the high season Nov.-March. The boat goes directly to the park headquarters, bungalows, and park cafe on Ko Miang. Boats to other islands are rather expensive at 200B per trip.

Charters: An eight-person private boat charter from Thap Lamu should cost 4,000-5,000B return. Weekends are the best times to find other passengers to help share costs. Travelers have reportedly joined Songserm speedboats at lower cost on a space-available basis.

Thai Dive Company: This British-owned dive company offers three- to five-day charters Oct.-May on their 25-meter, live-aboard dive ship. Prices start at 5,000B for snorkelers and 8,000B for divers. Owner Tim Anstee runs a professional operation. Thai Muang Post Office, P.O. Box 2, 10/1 Petchkasem Rd., Thai Muang, Phangnga 82120, tel./fax (076) 571434.

Boats from Khao Lak

The least expensive and most convenient way to reach the Similans is from one of the guesthouses at Khao Lak, 30 km south of Takua Pa, 12 km north of Thap Lamu, 30 km north of Thai Muang, or 110 km north of Phuket. Take any

bus heading along the coast and get off at the guesthouse of your choice; most are signposted with large wooden billboards. Otherwise, take a motorcycle taxi from Thap Lamu for 30B.

Poseidon Dive Center: Poseidon, in conjunction with Poseidon Bungalows, offers several dependable and reasonably priced tours. Their popular three-day cruise for 2,500B visits all the islands and includes food, accommodations, and transportation. More luxurious three-day scuba diving excursions with all equipment and air cost from 6,500B. Other services include one-day trips to offshore coral reefs, equipment rentals, and a four-day PADI certification course for 6,000B. 1/6 Tambon Laem Kaen, Mu 2, Thai Muang, Phangnga, tel. (01) 723-1418.

Khao Lak Bungalows: The northernmost set of bungalows on Khao Lak beach puts together a variety of local tours, including a three-day snorkeling excursion to the Similans for 2,500B. Hat Khao Lak, tel. (01) 723-1197.

TAKUA PA

Takua Pa is an important junction town 170 km south of Ranong, 140 km north of Phuket, and 160 km east of Surat Thani—near the intersection of the coastal Hwy. 4 and mountainous Hwy. 401, which goes east to Surat Thani and Ko Samui.

The town itself has little of interest, though the strategic location makes it a useful spot to change buses for other destinations. Travelers arriving from Phuket or Ko Samui can switch buses and head north to Ban Hin Lat for boats to the Surin Islands. Takua Pa is also a useful place to hire motorcycle taxis for direct service to the guesthouses on Khao Lak beach.

Accommodations

Few travelers stay in Takua Pa, though several acceptable hotels are located near the bus terminal and town center.

Extra Hotel: Just off the main highway with both fan-cooled and a/c rooms with private baths and hot water. 46 Seniraj Rd., tel. (076) 421026, fax (076) 421412, 200-350B.

Amarin Hotel: Comfortable lodgings in the center of town near the night market and cinema. 1/5-8 Montri 2 Rd., tel. (076) 421073, 250-450B.

Transportation

The transportation scene changed after the completion of a new highway between Hwy. 401 and the town of Phangnga. Prior to the opening of Hwy. 4118, all buses between Surat Thani and Phuket passed through Takua Pa and the entrance to Khao Sok National Park. Today, many buses take the shorter route via Phangnga and no longer reach Takua Pa or Khao Sok.

Check that your bus passes through Takua Pa and Khao Lak if you intend to visit these destinations or any other town on Hwy. 4.

KHAO SOK NATIONAL PARK

Khao Sok, a 646-square-km national park one hour east of Takua Pa or two hours west of Surat Thani, makes for a fabulous stop between Ko Samui and Phuket.

Khao Sok is formed by mountain ranges blanketed with tropical and evergreen rainforests inhabited by a variety of wildlife such as monkeys, wild boars, tapirs, giant frogs, and various forms of rare birds and fish. Within the far-flung boundaries are numerous waterfalls, enormous bat caves, the immense Chieo Lan Reservoir, and the Klong Sok River, which winds through thick jungle and past huge limestone cliffs that resemble a misty vision of another world.

Anyone curious about the Asian rainforest will find Khao Sok a marvelous pause on the trail between Ko Samui and Phuket.

Treks

Rough but useful maps of the park can be picked up at the visitors center, three km off the main highway. Several trails follow Klong Sok River, which flows through the park past enormous stands of bamboo and tropical rainforests filled with whooping gibbons and chattering hornbills. The more challenging trail leads 10 km to Ton Sai Waterfall, where the crystal-clear waters ensure a wonderful swim after the rugged hike.

Longer excursions can be arranged through the guesthouses just outside the park entrance. Jeeps can be hired to reach Rajaphraba Lake, 40 km from park headquarters, where bamboo rafthouses provide overnight accommodations.

Accommodations

Visitors can stay inside the park or just outside the entrance in privately owned bungalows.

Park Headquarters: The National Parks Division rents rather unimaginative bungalows for 600-900B and has campsites for 40-80B. Few travelers bother to stay within the park boundaries, since the private guesthouses are far superior in atmosphere and just as well located.

Tree Tops Jungle Guesthouse: Khao Sok's original guesthouse was founded by an American woman, Dwaila Armstrong, who has worked to preserve the park and show visitors the range of natural habitats and wildlife without destroying the environment. Tree Tops consists of five elevated tree houses, two cave lodges, and five raft houses on Rajaphrabha Lake, but unfortunately this property now only accepts package tours from Phuket. Packages cost 4,500-6,000B per day. Contact Vieng Travel in Bangkok, tel. (02) 280-3537, or Greenwood Travel, P.O. Box 463, Phuket 83000, tel. (076) 396425, fax (076) 396426. Tree Tops, P.O. Box 24, Takua Pa, Phangnga 82110.

Art's Riverview Jungle Lodge: A less expensive alternative to Tree Tops conveniently located near the park entrance and hiking trails with huts and tree houses dramatically located between the base of a limestone karst and a wonderful river that winds through the park. Art's, tel. (076) 421155, 300-750B.

Bamboo House: The third choice is just as scenic as the previous two guesthouses but less expensive and just as helpful with information on treks and river rafting. Bungalows cost 150-400B; three set meals 150B per day.

Khao Sok River Huts: Another good choice with a half dozen rooms with private bath and even a tree house. 250-400B.

Khao Sok Rainforest Resort: A somewhat more upscale choice with well-constructed bungalows facing the rainforest, all with private bath and large verandahs. Resort, tel. (01) 464-4362, fax (075) 612914, 350-800B.

Transportation

Khao Sok is 40 km east of Takua Pa, 120 km west of Surat Thani, and 180 km north of Phuket. A new route between Surat Thani and Phuket bypasses the park entrance at Km 108 on Hwy. 401. Travelers coming from Surat Thani should check that their bus follows the old route to Phuket via Takua Pa and Khao Sok, while travelers coming from Phuket will probably need to take a bus heading toward Ranong and change buses in Takua Pa.

KHAO LAK NATIONAL PARK

The shoreline national park, 30 km south of Takua Pa, provides another escape from the familiar tourist trail.

Khao Lak consists of a tiny coastal village; it offers dozens of private coves, waterfalls, caves, and easy access to inexpensive boat excursions to the Similan Islands.

Attractions

The two biggest draws of the Khao Lak coastline are the easy, quick, and relatively inexpensive access to the Similan Islands, and the genuine feeling of remoteness. Beaches are acceptable if somewhat rocky from the pounding waves and monsoons that lash the coastline June-Oct.

A small information stand is located on the beach between Nang Thong Bay Resort and Garden Beach Resort. Volunteers can help you with advice on nearby sights and will book tours to nearby national parks and the Similan Islands.

Waterfalls: Several falls are located near Khao Sok, such as Chong Fah, five km north, and Lam Phi, 20 km south near the town of the same name.

Coral Reef: Visitors without time to visit the Similans can hire a longtail boat to visit the coral gardens about 45 minutes offshore from Khao Lak. Guesthouses charge 300-400B for snorkelers or 1,000-1,200B for scuba divers, including all equipment and two dives.

Turtle Beach: Giant leatherbacks and other species of turtles come ashore Nov.-March on the 20-km stretch of shoreline that forms Thai Muang National Park, 25 km south of Khao Lak and five km north of Thai Muaug. Turtle sightings have become increasingly rare in recent years, though conservation efforts by the Thais appear to have reversed their declining numbers.

Accommodations

Bungalows start about five km south of Khao Lak and are scattered along the coastline north

all the way to Bang Sak beach and beyond toward the town of Takua Pa. Heading from Phuket you'll find Khao Lak Resort (Km 57), Poseidon Bungalows (Km 58), Puppa Bungalows (Km 58), Khao Lak Bungalows (Km 59), Golden Buddha Beach Resort (Km 59), Nang Thong Bay Resort (Km 60), Paradise Cabana (Km 76), Bang Sak Resort (Km 76), Sun Splendor Lodge (Km 77), and finally the town of Takua Pa (Km 86).

Poseidon Bungalows: Five km south of Khao Lak and situated in a sheltered bay surrounded by jungle and rubber plantations is the most popular spot in the region, owned and operated by Olov and his Thai wife, Tukkata. Poseidon organizes trips to the Similans and Surins, plus day excursions to nearby waterfalls and national parks. Rooms range from simple huts with shared baths to private chalets with attached Western baths. 1/6 Tambon Laem Kaen, Mu 2, Amphoe Thai Muang, tel. (01) 723-1418, 150-500B.

Khao Lak Bungalows: The northernmost set of bungalows on Khao Lak beach is operated by a German named Gerhard and his Thai wife, Noi, who organize jungle treks in Khao Lak and boat tours to the Similans at lower cost than Phuket tour operators. Rooms range from simple Thai-style huts with communal bathrooms to luxurious chalets with private facilities and verandas facing the ocean. 158 Sri Takua Pa Rd., Takua Pa, Phangnga 82110, tel. (01) 723-1197, 220-900B.

Nang Thong Bay Resort: A somewhat upscale retreat with an excellent cafe, money exchange facilities, motorcycle and jeep rentals, and minibus services to nearby islands and resorts. The manager, Yoy, and her staff are quite helpful with advice on the region. Hat Nang Thong, Km 60, tel. (01) 723-1181, 250-500B.

Golden Buddha Beach Resort: A new "nature" resort with the best rooms and facilities between Ranong and Phuket. Rooms range from simple bungalows to luxurious chalets with a/c rooms and ocean-view verandas. Same owners as Nang Thong. Hat Nang Thong, Km 59, tel. (76) 421612 or (76) 421155, 350-1,500B.

Khao Lak Resort: The first set of bungalows if you're coming from Phuket faces an attractive shoreline and features panoramic views from an elevated courtyard. Rooms range from bare-bones cubicles to decent A-frames, though the entire place needs maintenance lest it collapse into the sea. 158 Sri Takua Pa Rd., Takua Pa, tel. (076) 421061, 180-400B.

Transportation
"Khao Lak" refers to the coastline between Thap Lamu and Takua Pa. Many buses from Phuket to Surat Thani and Ko Samui now use the new highway via Phangnga and skip the Khao Lak region; be sure to take a bus heading north up Hwy. 4 to Takua Pa or Ranong.

From Krabi and Phangnga, take a bus toward Phuket and change buses in Kochloi. From Surat Thani, buses to Takua Pa pass the entrance to Khao Sok National Park.

All of the guesthouses and bungalows are signposted on the highway, though the easiest method is to get off in Takua Pa and take a motorcycle taxi for 30B to the bungalow of your choice.

EAST COAST: CHAIYA TO KO SAMUI

CHAIYA

Chaiya is a small but historic town on the Gulf of Thailand, 30 minutes north of Surat Thani. Chaiya occupies the site of an ancient empire, which archaeologists believe was connected with the mythical Indonesian empire of Srivijaya. While the exact location of the Srivijayan Empire described in the 7th century by Chinese merchants remains a mystery, Chaiya has provided Thai archaeologists with a bounty of statuary and architectural remnants strongly influenced by Indonesian culture. Among the more important discoveries is the famous Avalokitesvara Bodhisattva, an acclaimed masterpiece of Buddhist art now displayed in the Bangkok National Museum.

Wat Boromothat
The most important Srivijayan monument is south of Chaiya on the road between town and the national highway. Wat Boromothat is chiefly noted for its exposed bases and excavated altars, which show Indonesian influence and closely resemble the *candis* of central Java. Much of the remaining temple has been heavily restored in contemporary patterns. A small museum displays copies of statues discovered at Chaiya but now guarded inside the Bangkok National Museum.

Accommodations
Na Yai Park Guesthouse: Chaiya lacks hotels aside from a solitary hotel down at Phumriang Beach, about four km east of town. Phumriang, a Muslim community settled by fishermen from Pattani, is known for its exquisitely woven fabrics, which are popular among Thai tourists. Na Yai Park has simple huts and bungalows with private baths within walking distance of the beach, village, and old temples. 233 Moo 1 Phumriang, tel. (077) 431387, 80-180B.

Transportation
Chaiya is 54 km north of Surat Thani and four km east of Hwy. 41, which connects Chumphon with Surat Thani. Train travelers coming from the north can get off at the small train station in Chaiya and continue to Suan Mok or Surat Thani by bus. Public buses also connect Surat Thani with Chaiya and Suan Mok.

WAT SUAN MOK

Wat Suan Mokkhablarama—the Garden of Liberation—is a forest monastery near Chaiya dedicated to the study of *dhamma* and *vipassana* meditation. Wat Suan Mok was founded some five decades ago by a highly revered Thai monk named Achaan Buddhadasa, known for his back-to-basics approach that emphasized discipline and rationality over ritual and superstition. Achaan Buddhadasa began his monastic career in 1927 in his home province of Ubon Ratchathani and later studied Buddhism and Pali in Bangkok before establishing an Issan forest monastery near his hometown in the northeast. After moving his headquarters to Chaiya in the 1940s, Buddhadasa was joined by other Buddhist disciples such as Phra Dusadee Methangkuro, Santikaro Bhikku, and Abbot Achaan Poh, who brought his successful meditation retreats from Ko Samui to Suan Mok in 1988. Buddhadasa passed away in 1993 at the age of 87. Today, Wat Suan Mok serves as the most popular temple in Thailand for Westerners to study Buddhism and traditional forms of Thai meditation.

Suan Mok is spread over 80 hectares of forested hillside with dormitories and huts for monks, library and bookstore with literature on Buddhism, a Spiritual Theater decorated with Buddhist murals, and the new International Dharma Heritage Center two km distant near a small mountain and hot springs.

Both novice and experienced practitioners of *vipassana* are invited to join other Westerners during the 10-day meditation retreats held beginning the first day of each month. Instruction is provided in English. The daily program includes a 0400 wake-up and meditation session, vegetarian breakfast, morning lectures on Buddhism, chores around the international center, lunch, private study, afternoon tea, an evening lecture and soak in the mineral baths. Meditation focuses on *anapanasati*, which combines mindfulness with breathing; daily lectures describe the principles of meditation and *dhamma*.

Accommodations
The basic fee of 600B includes dormitory accommodations, vegetarian meals, and all instruction. Visitors are expected to follow local guidelines such as modest dress and periods of silence. Space is limited and reservations should be made by arriving at Suan Mok a few days in advance.

Transportation
Wat Suan Mok is on Hwy. 41, about 50 km north of Surat Thani and four km south of the junction to Chaiya. Buses from the main bus terminal in Surat Thani reach the temple entrance in about 50 minutes. Taxis can be hired from the train station at Phun Phin. Buses and *songtaos* also connect central Chaiya with Suan Mok.

SURAT THANI

Located on the southeastern coast of southern Thailand 644 km from Bangkok, the prosperous port of Surat Thani chiefly serves as a launching point for ferries to Ko Samui, Thailand's third-largest island and one of the leading tourist destinations in Southeast Asia. Surat Thani offers good shopping but otherwise has little of great interest aside from some natural attractions and the historical/religious draws in nearby Chaiya.

The Surat Thani TAT office (tel. 077-281828) is inconveniently located at 5 Talad Mai Rd. at the east end of town. An excellent resource for exploring Surat Thani Province and the nearby islands is the *Map of Koh Samui, Koh Tao & Koh Phangan* published by Prannock Witthaya Publications.

Tickets to Ko Samui can be purchased from the Songserm agents near the harbor and from Samui Tours on Talad Mai Road.

Budget Accommodations
Most visitors head directly to Ko Samui, but late arrivals by train or bus may need to overnight near the train station in Phun Phin or in downtown Surat Thani.

Lipa and Kasem 2 Guesthouses: Adjacent to the bus terminal are several small guesthouses barely acceptable for an overnight crash but with cafes and travel agencies that sell tickets to Ko Samui, Phuket, and Krabi. 150-200B.

Thai Thani Hotel: Also next to the bus terminal is this sprawling old hotel with amazing wooden furniture on the ground floor and reception facilities on the third floor. 442 Talad Mai Rd., tel. (077) 272977, 180-250B fan, 360-500B a/c.

Bandon Hotel: A very clean hotel entered through a Chinese coffee shop. Recommended. 168 Na Muang Rd., tel. (077) 272167, 180-240B.

Moderate Accommodations
Siam Thara Hotel: A popular, older hotel with coffee shop and nightclub located near Samui Tours. 1 Don Nok Rd., tel. (077) 273740, 650-800B.

Wang Tai Hotel: The best hotel in Surat is inconveniently located south of town near the tourist office, but offers a swimming pool, cabaret nightclub, and restaurant overlooking the Tapi River. 1 Talad Mai Rd., tel. (077) 273410, fax (077) 281007, 950-1,400B.

Accommodations in Phun Phin
The train station for Surat Thani is 14 km west in the town of Phun Phin. Except for the very late

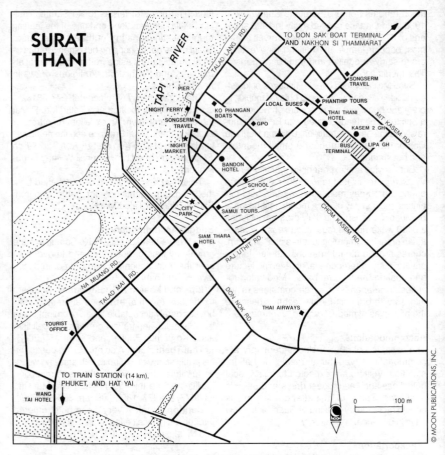

SURAT THANI

TAPI RIVER

TO DON SAK BOAT TERMINAL
AND NAKHON SI THAMMARAT

TALAD LANG RD.

SONGSERM TRAVEL

PIER

NIGHT FERRY

LOCAL BUSES

PHANTHIP TOURS

SONGSERM TRAVEL

KO PHANGAN BOATS

THAI THANI HOTEL

MIT KASEM RD.

NIGHT MARKET

GPO

KASEM 2 GH

BUS TERMINAL

LIPA GH

BANDON HOTEL

SCHOOL

CHOM KASEM RD.

CITY PARK

SAMUI TOURS

SIAM THARA HOTEL

RAJ UTHIT RD.

NA MUANG RD.

TALAD MAI RD.

DON NOK RD.

THAI AIRWAYS

TOURIST OFFICE

TO TRAIN STATION (14 km),
PHUKET, AND HAT YAI

WANG TAI HOTEL

0   100 m

© MOON PUBLICATIONS, INC.

trains, all arrivals are met by buses that connect directly with the boats to Ko Samui. Late-night arrivals can take a taxi into Surat Thani, or stay at one of the guesthouses opposite the train station.

Tai Fah: The Tai Fah and adjacent Sri Thani are basic haunts only survivable for a few short hours; both suffer from their noisy locations and trainyard atmosphere. Phun Phin Rd., tel. (077) 311034, 120-180B.

Queen Hotel: Down the road and removed from the train activity is this somewhat better place. Look for the Singha sign. Phun Phin Rd., tel. (077) 311003, 160-220B fan, 320-350B a/c.

Restaurants

Surat Thani is famous throughout Thailand as home to delicious rambutans known as *ngoh rongrien* and giant tilam oysters grown in Ban Don Bay and Tha Thong Estuary some 30 km south of town. Restaurants here serve the succulent oysters and tasty *kung kuladam* shrimp for as little as 8B each.

Talad Kaset: Kaset Market divides into two sections across Talad Mai Road, with Talad Kaset 1 containing the local bus station (Phun Phin, etc.) and Talad Kaset 2 having the long-distance bus station and dozens of small cafes for a quick bite. Baked chicken and spicy southern curries are popular dishes. Talad Mai Rd. Inexpensive.

Night Market: The market near the Ban Don night ferry pier provides a convenient spot to pick up supplies for the slow boat to Ko Samui. Ban Don Rd. Inexpensive.

Sala Rim Nam Restaurant: Rather than wait for the train on a station bench or in the room of a decrepit hotel, check your bags with left luggage and cross the wooden footbridge over the tracks. Turn right on the main street and walk about 100 meters to the Siam City Bank on your left. The adjacent cafe is a fine place to idle away a few hours in an old-world classic constructed on stilts over the Tapi River.

Sahathai Department Store: A welcome escape from the heat is provided in the a/c food court on the fourth floor. Over 20 foodstalls ladle up Thai, Chinese, and Western dishes at rock-bottom prices. Open daily 0930-2130. Na Muang Rd., tel. (077) 518520. Inexpensive.

J. Home Bakery: Baked goods, fresh coffee, burgers, and Thai fast food are listed on the bilingual menu in this a/c cafe near the Grand City Hotel. Open daily 0730-2300. 428/5 Na Muang Rd., tel. (077) 273942. Inexpensive.

Getting There

Surat Thani is 644 km south of Bangkok, 84 km southwest of Ko Samui, and 290 km northeast of Phuket.

See below under **Ko Samui,** the ultimate destination for most travelers passing through the region, for more information on travel to/from Surat Thani.

Air: Thai Airways (3/27 Karunarat Rd., tel. 077-272610 or 077-273355) flies three times daily from Bangkok, once daily from Phuket, and twice weekly from Chiang Mai (two hours). The airport is 30 km west of town; airport shuttles cost 50B per person. Thai Airways is an alternative to booked-out and more expensive flights to Samui with Bangkok Airways.

Train: Trains depart Bangkok nine times daily and take 11-13 hours to reach the terminal at Phun Phin, 14 km west of Surat Thani. The most convenient departure is the rapid train at 1830, which arrives in Phun Phin at 0600 and allows plenty of time for an early ferry to Ko Samui. Buses from the various ferry companies meet and transfer passengers to the boat and ferry terminals.

MONKEY BUSINESS IN SURAT THANI

*A*t the age of four, Kai Nui earned more than most middle-grade government officials in Bangkok.

Nui wasn't a working girl or real estate magnate, but a highly trained monkey who could pick up to 500 coconuts each day. At the standard rate of 50B per 100 coconuts, Kai Nui raked in almost 10,000B each month; not bad for a stubborn monkey with an evil temperament.

Surat Thani and Ko Samui Provinces are the coconut capitals of Thailand, shipping each month over 3,000 tons—six million coconuts—to the copra factories and export merchants in Bangkok. Collecting all that copra is a difficult and dangerous job since palms in southern Thailand are particularly tall and . . . well, when was the last time you tried to climb a coconut tree?

The solution to this nutty problem is the Macaca nemestrina monkey (pig-tailed macaque), known to the Thais as a ling kiang or ling gep maphrao, the coconut-picking monkey. Although ling kiang can be bred in captivity, seasoned trainers prefer wild creatures because of their higher innate vitality. Trainers also prefer males over females, and avoid "shortsighted" monkeys with white brows, which are considered stubborn lazybones. A knowledge of a monkey's ngow heng (personality) is also drawn from the size of his hands, mouth, lips, thickness of fur, and detail of the fingerprints, which should closely resemble a human print.

Male ling kiang monkeys between one and three years old cost the coconut collector about 3,000B, with an additional 1,000B in training fees at monkey schools. The monkeys are first taught how to distinguish ripe from unripe coconuts, then how to bite and spin the stems to release the fruit. Advanced training includes placing poison on trees to kill rodents, and removing the master's shoes at naptime!

Several monkey-training schools are located near Surat Thani, but the most famous is 13 km southeast in the village of Ban Tha Thong. Established in 1985 with a 100,000B endowment from Princess Sirindhorn, Surat Thani Monkey Training School and trainer Somphorn Saekaew occasionally sponsor public demonstrations. The Surat Thani TAT office can advise on the next scheduled performance.

BUS SERVICE FROM SURAT THANI

DESTINATION	TYPE	FARE (BAHT)	HOURS
Hat Yai	ordinary bus	90	5
	a/c	130	4
	share taxi	150	3
Krabi	ordinary bus	55	4
	a/c	95	3
	share taxi	160	2
Nak Thammarat	ordinary bus	40	3
	a/c	60	2
	share taxi	75	2
Narathiwat	ordinary bus	130	6
	a/c	170	5
Phuket	ordinary bus	85	6
	a/c	150	5
	share taxi	160	4
Ranong	ordinary bus	80	5
	a/c	100	4
	share taxi	160	3
Satun	ordinary bus	80	4
	a/c	120	3
Trang	ordinary bus	60	3
	a/c	90	2
	share taxi	110	2
Yala	ordinary bus	110	6
	a/c	150	5
	share taxi	180	4

cate the situation, some of the travel agencies in Surat Thani and Ko Samui are unreliable, disorganized, or downright dishonest in their dealings with *farangs:* reserved seats never appear and V.I.P. buses are nothing more than tin wagons held together with string and baling wire.

Train and bus reservations should be made at reliable travel agencies such as Phanthip, Songserm, World, and other agencies listed below.

Ordinary buses from Surat Thani to Bangkok take 12 hours and depart five times daily 0700-1230, and every half hour 1700-2100. Buses to Phuket take seven hours and depart eight times daily 0530-1300.

Transportation to Ko Samui
See **Getting There** under **Ko Samui,** below, for full details on transportation from Bangkok and Surat Thani.

Most travelers take all-inclusive train or bus packages that depart Bangkok in the early evening and arrive on Ko Samui the following day around noon. Independent travelers will be

Overnight trains should be reserved several days in advance. Travelers without reservations must often stand for several hours until a seat is vacated.

Bus: Six a/c buses depart from the Southern Bus Terminal in Thonburi daily 0700-0930 and 1800-2100, arriving in 11-13 hours at the Surat Thani bus terminal. Buses meet them and provide transfer to the various ferry piers.

Getting Away
Departure options include buses from the center of town, Thai Airways, or trains from the terminal in Phun Phin, 14 km west of Surat Thani.

Planes and buses are plentiful, but finding a seat on a train can be tricky since most are fully booked from their points of origin and seats are often reserved weeks in advance. To compli-

met at the train and bus terminals by transportation agents who sell tickets on the various ferries across to Ko Samui, Ko Phangan, and Ko Tao.

Boat tickets can also be purchased directly at Songserm Travel on Na Muang Road and near the waterfront, at Samui Tours on Talad Mai Road, and from independent agents near the bus terminal.

Recommended Travel Agencies
Dozens of agencies sell tickets in Surat Thani, but only the following are guaranteed to be safe, reliable, and honest. The first is a travel agency, while the latter two are transportation companies that operate ferries to the islands.

If your schedule is fixed, it may be wise to make train or plane reservations in Surat Thani before departing for Ko Samui.

Phanthip Travel: Phanthip, a travel agency and authorized agent of the State Railways and Thai Airways, charges no "service fees" and provides honest reservations for all modes of transportation. 442/24 Talad Mai Rd., tel. (077) 272230, fax (077) 285127.

Songserm Travel: Songserm, one of the largest transportation companies in Thailand, operates the express ferry from Tha Thong Pier, the night ferry from downtown Surat Thani, and buses

and minibuses between Ko Samui and Phuket. It is also an authorized agent for the national trains and Thai Airways. 30/2 Mu 2 Bangkoong Rd., tel. (077) 286341, fax (077) 285127.

Samui Tours: Samui Tours, the travel subsidiary of Samui Ferry Company, operates the vehicle and passenger ferry from Don Sak to Thong Yang Pier on Ko Samui, plus arranges bus transport to Bangkok and Phuket. 326/12 Talad Mai Rd., tel. (077) 282352.

KO SAMUI

Thailand's third-largest island (247 square km) lies in the warm seas of the gulf some 644 km south of Bangkok. With its long beaches of dazzling white sand, aquamarine waters, and sleepy lagoons fringed with palm trees, this tropical retreat has justifiably become one of Southeast Asia's premier beach resorts.

Ko Samui has, since the mid-18th century, been visited by Chinese merchants trading for coconuts and cotton, the two traditional products of the Chao Samui, the local peoples. The island was opened to tourism in the late 1960s by shoestring travelers who found passage on coconut boats from Bangkok and trickled in to construct their simple thatched huts on deserted beaches. For over a decade, Samui remained an untouched paradise, visited only by backpackers drifting up and down the overland trail between Bali and Kathmandu. This happy state of affairs ended in the early 1980s as the island's reputation attracted Thai and foreign developers who replaced the bamboo huts with midpriced bungalows and luxury hotels geared strictly for well-heeled tourists.

Ko Samui today is a major tourist destination with some 500,000 annual visitors and over 240 hotels and bungalows lining the beaches. For better or for worse, since the opening of the airport in 1989 Samui has gone from backpacker's paradise to an upscale resort with all the glitz, glamour, and problems that plague other Thai beach destinations. Group tourists now vastly outnumber the backpackers, who have largely moved on to more remote destinations. Land prices on Samui are reputedly higher than on Australia's Gold Coast, and many of the simple, smiling coconut pickers have become slick millionaires concerned more with their pocketbooks than with traditional Chao Samui hospitality. The get-rich-quick mentality permeates the entire island: menus list cute dishes such as "fried prawn noodles sautéed in aromatic sauces—80 *baht*," which turns out to be *raht nah*, which sells for 15B elsewhere in Thailand.

Despite all the changes, Ko Samui beaches remain absolutely spectacular, and the interior is still a tangled mess of jungle and coconut. The dazzling island still ranks among the best of Southeast Asia.

Climate
Samui is best visited during the hot and dry season Jan.-June. Rains start in early July and continue to build until the end of the year. Torrential rains often lash the island in November and December; during these months try the islands on the west coast of southern Thailand.

The chief advantages to fall visits are the lack of tourists and the lower prices offered at most hotels and resorts.

NATHON

Nathon—the commercial center and transportation hub for Ko Samui—is a bustling town with a few decent hotels, plenty of cafes and restaurants, travel agencies and banks, souvenir stalls, and government services such as immigration, police, and a small tourist office.

Nathon may be a convenient place to shop, make onward travel arrangements, and take care of legal matters, but it's also a messy hodgepodge that makes a poor introduction to the island. Don't be discouraged; a few kilometers in either direction lie beautiful beaches washed by lovely blue waters.

TO KO PHANGAN

TO KO PHANGAN
(HAT RIN BEACH)

KO SOM   LAEM SUMRONG

CHONG MON BAY

BANG PO BEACH

LAEM NA PRALAN

MAE NAM BEACH

BAN TAI

BAN BANG PO

BAN MAE NAM

BOPHUT BEACH

BIG BUDDHA BEACH

BIG BUDDHA

LAEM YAI

BAN MAKHAM BEACH

BAN BOPHUT

TO KO PHANGAN
(THONG SALA)

NATHON

SAMUI AIRPORT

KO MATLANG

TO SURAT THANI

HIN LAD WATERFALL

KO SAMUI

4169

HOSPITAL

BAN LIPA YAI

SAMUI HIGHLANDS

BAN CHAWENG

NORTH CHAWENG BEACH

CHON KRAM BAY

(545 m)

CHAWENG BEACH

LAEM CHON KHRAM

BAN LIPA NOI

KHAO YAI
(636 m)

SOUTH CHAWENG BEACH

THONG YANG PIER

BAN SAKET

NA MUANG WATERFALL

TO DONSAK AND KHANOM

(565 m)

BAN LAMAI

OVERLAP STONE

4170

4169

LAMAI BEACH

TALING NGAM BEACH

BAN TALING NGAM

BAN THURIAN

BIRD'S NEST ISLANDS HAT YAO

BAN HUA THANON

PHANG KA BAY
(EMERALD BAY)

4173

NA HAI BEACH

BAN PHANGKA

TRIPLE COCONUT TREE

BAN THALE

4170

LAE HINKHOM

BAN THONGKRUT

BANG KAO

LAEM SET

THONG KRUT BEACH

BANGKAO BEACH

CHEDI LAEM SO

LAEM SOR

GULF

OF

THAILAND

KO TAEN

226 m

KO MAT SUM

0   3 km

KO MAT KONG

KO WANG NOK   KO RAP

© MOON PUBLICATIONS, INC.

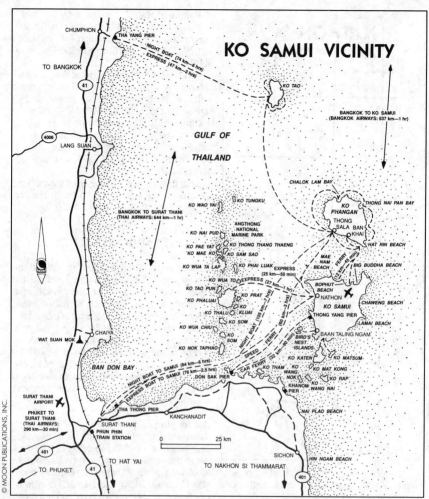

KO SAMUI VICINITY

CHUMPHON
THA YANG PIER
NIGHT BOAT (74 km—6 hrs)
EXPRESS (47 km—3 hrs)

TO BANGKOK

41

4006

LANG SUAN

KO TAO

GULF OF

THAILAND

BANGKOK TO KO SAMUI
(BANGKOK AIRWAYS: 537 km—1 hr)

CHALOK LAM BAY

THONG NAI PAN BAY

KO WAO YAI
KO TUNGKU
KO
PHANGAN
THONG
SALA BAN
KHAI

BANGKOK TO SURAT THANI
(THAI AIRWAYS: 644 km—1 hr)

KO NAI PUD
KO THONG THANG THAENG
ANGTHONG
NATIONAL
MARINE PARK

HAT RIN BEACH

KO PAE YAT
KO MAE KO
KO SAM SAO

KO WUA TA LAP
KO PHA LUAK
EXPRESS (25 km—50 min)

MAE
NAM
BEACH

BIG BUDDHA BEACH

KO WUA TO
EXPRESS (27 km—1 hrs)
KO TAO PUN
KO PRAT
KO PHALUAI
KO
KLUAI
KO THALU
NIGHT BOAT (105 km—7 hrs)
KO SOM
KO WUA CHIU
EXPRESS FERRY (69 km—2 hrs)
KO SOM
KO NOK TAPHAO

BOPHUT
BEACH
NATHON
KO SAMUI
THONG YANG PIER

CHAWENG BEACH

LAMAI BEACH

BAAN TALING NGAM

WAT SUAN MOK
CHAIYA

BIRD'S
NEST
ISLANDS
KO KATEN
KO MATSUM

BAN DON BAY

NIGHT BOAT TO SAMUI (84 km—6 hrs)
EXPRESS BOAT TO SAMUI (78 km—2.5 hrs)

SPEED FERRY (52 km—30 min)
CAR FERRY
DON SAK PIER

KO THAM
KO
WANG
NOK
KHANOM
PIER
KO
WANG NAI

KO MAT KONG
KO RAP

SURAT THANI
AIRPORT

PHUKET TO
SURAT THANI
(THAI AIRWAYS:
290 km—30 min)

THA THONG PIER
KANCHANADIT

NAI PLAO BEACH

SURAT THANI
PHUN PHIN
TRAIN STATION

0   25 km

SICHON

401

TO PHUKET

41

TO HAT YAI

TO NAKHON SI THAMMARAT

HIN NGAM BEACH

401

© MOON PUBLICATIONS, INC.

Arrival

Most visitors arrive at the vehicle and passenger pier at Thong Yang, 10 km south of Nathon, and proceed by *songtao* directly to the beach of their choice.

Travelers on an express or nightboat from Surat Thani will arrive in Nathon, at the new pier in the center of town—probably the most impressive pier in all of Thailand.

Boat arrivals are met by *songtao* drivers yelling, "Chaweng, Chaweng, Chaweng!" or

"Lamai, Lamai, Lamai!" Pick your beach and pay the proper fare, which should be signposted inside the minitruck. Beware of drivers who overcharge unwary passengers.

Important: Tell the driver which beach *and* bungalow you want to be dropped at, or expect to be dumped at an inconvenient location. Travelers unsure of where they'll stay should get off in the middle of the beach, leave their bags at the closest restaurant, and inspect a few bungalows.

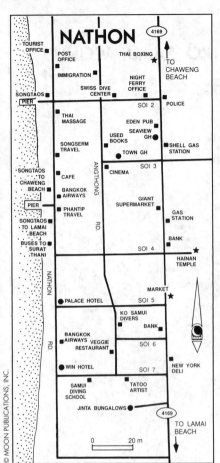

Palace Hotel: A conveniently located if somewhat overpriced hotel with clean rooms and private baths. 152 Nathon Rd., tel. (077) 421079, fax (077) 421080, 300-350B fan, 400-600B a/c.

Win Hotel: Somewhat quieter due to the location in the south end of town. All rooms are a/c with TV, telephone, and hot showers. 285 Nathon Rd., tel. (077) 421500, 440-600B a/c.

Chao Ko Bungalows: North of town, past the post and tourist offices, is a quiet operation with 20 comfortable bungalows facing the sea. 29/4 Tambon Ao Nan, tel. (077) 421157, 300-350B fan, 400-800B a/c.

Jinta Bungalows: Another quiet escape from the cacophony of Nathon. 310 Mu 3, Tambon Angthong, tel. (077) 421323, 200-250B.

KO SAMUI ATTRACTIONS

Samui is about 70 km in circumference and can be easily toured in a single day. The following sights are described in counterclockwise order starting from Chaweng Beach. Samui's splendid scenery is best seen by rented car or motorcycle, but first, a word of caution. Motorcycle touring is deceptively dangerous. Far too many people kill or badly cripple themselves on the two-lane highway that circles the island. Please drive slowly, stay sober, and wear long pants, shoes, and a shirt to prevent sunburn and protect against minor scrapes.

Coconut Industry
Samui's claims to fame are the sandy beaches, clear waters, and thriving coconut industry which forms the traditional occupation of Samui's 45,000 residents. At times it seems the entire island is yanking down coconuts with long swaying sticks or burning huge piles of coconut shells. Watch for trained *ling gaeng* monkeys, which deftly climb the palm trees, spin the coconut until it falls to the ground, and then return for their reward. Nearly every part of the coconut is used: flesh for eating, milk for cooking, and fiber for thatching and bed stuffing. Much of the fruit is converted into a sweet coconut oil, a process that comprises scraping the meat from the shell, drying it for several weeks, and then pressing it with hydraulic machinery.

Travelers can also rent a motorcycle or jeep from one of the agencies in Nathon and return the vehicle on departure.

Accommodations
Few travelers stay in Nathon except to catch an early morning boat or bus back to Surat Thani.

Sea View Guesthouse: The name is a misnomer (there's no view of the sea), but rooms are immaculate and the management can help with travel details in this relatively new establishment. 67/15 Tawirajapakdi Rd., tel. (077) 420052, 150-250B fan, 300-350B a/c.

Almost every type of coconut tree grows on the island, including several two-headed mutants and one rare four-headed specimen near Mae Nam Beach, perhaps the only one in the world since it bears no nut.

Chong Mon Bay

Begin your tour with a motorcycle ride along the dirt road that hugs the coast to the arching bay at Chong Mon—a highly recommended route through fabulous scenery. A decade ago, the beach was lined with magnificent dry-docked fishing boats elegantly carved with gigantic rudders. Then—as it always seems to go in places like Ko Samui—a hotel conglomerate purchased the boats and converted them into private chalets elevated on varnished supports. The bizarre effect detracts from the beach but certainly proves the creativity of Thai hoteliers.

Big Buddha Beach

Ko Samui's famous 12-meter Big Buddha statue, surrounded by meditation huts elevated on stilts, is a few kilometers west of Chong Mon and can be reached on the main road or along the dirt trails that skirt the coastline. Big Buddha Beach—more properly called Ao Bang Rak ("Bang Rak Bay")—is named after the image at Wat Hin Ngu which sits atop Ko Farn ("Barking Deer Island"), a tiny islet surrounded by polychrome Buddhas, the earth-goddess Torani, souvenir shops, and small cafes. Attached to the temple is a meditation center, which offers instruction to Thais and *farangs.*

The road continues west past bungalows and hotels, boat service to Ko Phangan, and the turnoff to Ko Samui Airport and a meditation center tucked away under the mountains. Back on the highway, posterboards nailed to trees advertise upcoming buffalo fights, Thai kickboxing, and nightclubs with everything from reggae to world beat.

Bophut Beach

Bophut Beach has long been the backpacker's choice for its reasonably good sand, isolated location, and magic mushrooms, which grew to mythical sizes and were served by local cafes in soups and omelettes. Now, massive development has almost completely transformed the dusty wooden village into a continuous string of expensive bungalows and luxurious hotels that tower over the narrow beach. Asking for mushroom soup only brings quizzical looks and nostalgic stories about the good old days. . . pre-1987.

Bophut town is still worth a visit for its restaurants with French names, banking facilities, a used bookstore, and boat connections to Ko Phangan. Beyond the dead-end road to the west are several bungalows still untouched by commercial activity.

Mae Nam Beach

Mae Nam Beach is 12 km from the ferry pier, midway between the principal town of Nathon and Chaweng Beach. The beach is long, narrow, somewhat coarse, and relatively untouched by mass tourism because of its isolation and because the main road essentially bypasses its beach. Visitors who want a look should drive up a dirt road to visit one of the bungalows. **Nature, Moon, Lolita, Mae Nam Resort,** and **Shangrila** are good places to stop for a meal and walk on the beach.

Ban Mae Nam, the commercial center, has several restaurants, a clean bakery, laundries, a medical clinic, a gas station with fair prices, and a big monkey tied to the tree on the interior road.

Hin Lad Falls

The small set of waterfalls and bathing pools, two km south of Nathon, can be reached with a half-hour hike up a narrow pathway through thick jungle. Hin Lad is rather disappointing, but it provides the drinking water for Nathon.

Emerald Cove

Phang Ka Bay, a very pretty and isolated cove at the southwest corner of Ko Samui, has several small bungalows in a magnificent setting of limestone peaks and swaying palms. **Pearl Bay** and **Seagull** bungalows provide a welcome escape from the commercialism of Samui.

The nearby beach at Tong Yang lacks the splendid sand of Chaweng and Lamai, but it does offer good corals and blazing sunsets over dragon-spired Angthong National Marine Park.

Thong Krut Beach

Longtail boats can be chartered from Thong Krut Beach to explore the nearby islands of Ko Katen

("No Dog Island") and Ko Mat Sum. Both islands have coral beds on the eastern fringes. Snorkeling is best during low tides Aug.-April. A primitive set of bungalows is located on Ko Katen, also known as Ko Taen.

Wat Laem Sor
An unusual Indian-style *chedi* modeled after Bodgaya is situated on the isolated cape. The dirt road continues east past several modest bungalows to the Muslim fishing village of Ban Bang Kao.

Na Muang Falls
The best falls on Ko Samui are located past Ban Thurian, a village famous for its enormous durian trees, which bear fruit in the hot summer months. Visited by several kings of the Chakri dynasty, the 30-meter falls are best experienced shortly after the rainy season ends in December or January.

Hua Thanon
About 200 meters from this small Chinese fishing village are several coral blocks carved in Buddha images. One km farther is Silangu, with a venerated pagoda reputed to enshrine a bone fragment of the Buddha. Traditional *vipassana* meditation courses geared to Western visitors are occasionally sponsored at Silangu.

Phallic Rocks
Hin Yai and Hin Ta ("Grandfather Rock" and "Grandmother Rock") are geological oddities at the south end of Lamai Beach that closely resemble enormous sexual organs. A large and humorously mislabeled sign Wonderfull Rock shows the way to the curious formations.

Lamai Cultural Hall
Wat Lamai at the north end of Lamai Beach features a small cultural center dedicated to the arts and crafts of the Chao Samui, the local inhabitants who consider themselves different than their northern cousins. The wooden showroom is filled with old lanterns, gramophones, pottery recovered from shipwrecks, *nang talang* (buffalo-hide) puppets, and agricultural implements used in the coconut industry.

Angthong National Marine Park
The beautiful archipelago of Angthong ("Golden Basin") northwest of Ko Samui comprises 40 islands covering 250 square km. Once an experimental training ground for the Royal Thai Navy, Angthong was declared a marine national park in 1980 to protect the coral beds and short-bodied mackerel that spawn in the surrounding waters Feb.-April. The park has dozens of pristine beaches, aquamarine bays, and islands named after whimsical forms such as Broken Stone, Rhinoceros, Camera Head, and Tree Sorrow Island.

Tours from Nathon include stops at various coral reefs for snorkeling before arrival at the main island, where visitors can climb to the top of a 240-meter hill for panoramic views of lakes and islands. The boat continues to a second island with a crystal-green saltwater lake connected to the sea by a subterranean tunnel.

Tour agencies in Nathon and other Samui beaches offer day-trips 0800-1730 to Angthong Park for 350-500B, including soft drinks and snorkeling equipment.

Accommodations are available on Ko Wua Ta Lap ("Sleeping Cow Island") at the national parks headquarters. Two-person tents or dormitory space in 20-person bungalows cost 100-150B per night. Camping elsewhere is free, since the island is under the supervision of the National Parks Division. A small restaurant and freshwater lake are also located on the main island.

RECREATION

Thai Boxing
Boxing matches are held most weekends at the stadium in the northern end of Nathon. Admission is 100-120B to most events.

Sea Kayaking
Sea kayaking is the latest water sport to arrive at Ko Samui, after years of popularity in the bays near Phuket. Several outfits provide beach rentals, professional instruction, day excursions and coastal trips, and overnight excursions to Angthong National Marine Park, Ko Phangan, and Ko Tao. One kayak rental and instruction center is at the Blue Lagoon Hotel on Chaweng Beach.

Scuba Diving

Ko Samui offers great diving and snorkeling for both beginners and experienced divers.

Dive Sites: Coral cover and underwater visibility off the west and northern coasts are rather poor due to sea turbulence and runoff sediment, but reefs off the east and southern coasts remain relatively clear and undisturbed. Dive shops recommend the tiny islands around Angthong National Marine Park and multi-day excursions to Ko Tao for the most spectacular corals and sealife. Ko Tao, a four-hour boat ride from Samui, ranks among the best places in southern Thailand to enjoy year-round diving among submerged granite boulder and coral gardens that support large numbers of reef fish.

Snorkeling: Snorkeling is popular near the small island off the northern end of Chaweng Beach, and around Angthong National Marine Park. Several shops on Chaweng and Lamai Beaches rent snorkeling equipment for 60-80B per day, and organize full-day excursions with longtail boat for 350-600B per person.

Gear Rental: Scuba gear costs 450-600B for beach dives. A day of diving with all equipment, boat, and divemaster costs 1,400-2,200B depending on the destination and dive company. A five-day PADI certification course costs 5,500-8,500B. Excursions to Ko Tao cost 3,500-5,000B for two days and 5,000-7,500B for four-day packages.

Dive Shops

Most of the following dive shops have offices in Nathon and at either Chaweng or Lamai Beaches. Several maintain offices on Ko Phangan and Ko Tao.

Koh Samui Divers: The oldest and most experienced dive shop on the island also operates offices on Ko Phangan and Ko Tao near the Mae Hat Pier. P.O. Box 1, Nathon, tel. (077) 421465, fax (077) 421465.

Swiss International Dive Center: Another reliable company with professional instructors, equipment rentals, and five-day PADI certification courses. Swiss has offices in Nathon and at Lamai Beach. P.O. Box 33, Nathon, tel. (077) 420157 or (077) 422478.

ACCOMMODATIONS

Ko Samui has a half dozen beaches in various stages of development and with distinct personalities. Chaweng Beach and Lamai Beach on the east coast are the most popular beaches for good reasons: best sand, longest uninterrupted terrain, and ideal climate. North coast beaches such as Bophut and Menam are quieter and less expensive, but the sand isn't as white or plentiful. Isolated bungalows are found on the west and south coasts.

Each beach appeals to different types of travelers, depending on their finances and desired ambience. One possible plan of action is to spend your first few days on Chaweng or Lamai, then move to a more isolated beach if you crave solitude and want to escape the beer gardens, discos, and pickup bars.

Ko Samui beaches offer all ranges of accommodations, from cheap shacks under 100B to luxurious hotels with landscaped gardens and swimming pools. Basic wooden huts with electricity, mosquito net, and common bath charge 100-350B. Many of these original huts have been torn down and replaced with better bungalows with tiled rooms, verandas, private baths, and comfortable mattresses. These cost 500-800B during the slow season, and generally double in the high summer months and Christmas holiday. Many of these midpriced bungalows represent extraordinary value when you consider the comfort level and fabulous beach just a few steps away. Air-conditioned bungalows with fancy restaurants and manicured gardens cost 1,200-1,800B, while luxury hotels over 3,000B per night are now commonplace on most beaches.

Samui bungalows have evolved into a veritable patchwork of huts and chalets in various styles and prices. For example, Joy Bungalows—one of the first sets of huts on the island—offers old huts at 200B, duplexes with fans at 600B, large family rooms for 900B, and a/c suites from 1,400B. Another curious phenomenon is that low-end cheapies are often wedged between expensive hotels, such as K John Bungalows for 250B adjacent to Samui Villa Flora for 2,800B.

Recommending a specific hotel is a difficult task, since room quality, price, and overall value vary widely at almost every property. A sensible compromise for budget travelers is to stay at the cheapest room in a moderate-priced hotel. High season can be an extremely difficult time to find a room; expect to take an expensive room until cheaper bungalows are vacated. Reservations are best made by fax rather than phone to avoid miscommunication with reception personnel.

All hotels listed in the following sections, except for inexpensive bungalows, add 11% tax and 10% service charge.

CHAWENG BEACH

Chaweng Beach—Ko Samui's longest and prettiest stretch of sand—is almost completely blanketed with bungalows, hotels, restaurants, dive shops, convenience stores, and nightclubs, yet it has somehow managed to keep a reasonably mellow atmosphere. During the day you can wander the beach without bumping into hordes of people, and nightlife remains limited to a few discos and open-air restaurants that screen the latest videos. Chaweng is now very middle class, but there's no denying the beauty of the beach and brilliance of the water.

The six-km curving beach is divided into three sections: Chaweng Noi (Little Chaweng to the south), Chaweng Yai (Big Chaweng in the center), and North Chaweng Yai (Big Chaweng to the north).

Chaweng has an estimated 300 bamboo huts or bungalows in the 200-500B price range, several dozen midlevel hotels aimed at the average visitor, and an increasing number of luxurious resorts geared to wealthy tourists.

Songtaos from Nathon turn off the highway at the southern end of Chaweng at Km 28 and head north up the beachside road to Samui Cabana or Marine Bungalows on North Chaweng Beach. Travelers should specify a hotel or expect to be dropped at the northern end, a fine spot but removed from the heart of the action.

Visitors without a specific guesthouse might ask to be dropped at Charlies Bungalows, a centrally located guesthouse with over 100 budget rooms and a convenient place to start your bungalow search.

South Chaweng (Chaweng Noi) Beach

Chaweng Noi (Little Chaweng) is a small arching bay at the southern end of Chaweng Beach. Somewhat isolated and less crowded than the central region, Chaweng Noi has both cheap shacks and luxurious hotels, described below from south to north.

Tropicana Beach Resort: A moderately priced hotel elevated on a cliff above the south end of the beach. 4 Mu 3, Chaweng Noi Beach, tel. (077) 422451, 1,200-1,800B.

Chaweng Noi Bungalows: Three sets of cheap bungalows once existed at the southern end of the beach, but today only Chaweng Noi survives to serve the budget traveler. 90/2 Mu 3, Chaweng Noi Beach, 150-200B.

Imperial Samui: Chaweng entered the big leagues with the construction of this enormous Mediterranean-style property in the mid-1980s. Managed by a Thai-owned hotel chain, the Imperial features several restaurants, swimming pools, and workers frantically adding sandbags to save the eroding beachwall. Chaweng Noi Beach, tel. (077) 422020, fax (077) 422396, Bangkok reservations (02) 261-9000, 3,600-6,000B.

President Samui: The former Fair House remains a popular choice in a great location with older huts at bargain rates and better chalets with a/c and private baths. 4/3 Mu 2, Chaweng Noi Beach, tel. (077) 422256, 600-900B fan, 1,200-1,500B a/c.

First Bungalows: Another well-located favorite situated midway between Chaweng Noi and Chaweng Yai; the office and restaurant are on Chaweng Yai, bungalows across the bridge on Chaweng Noi. Chaweng Noi Beach, tel. (077) 421444, 800-1,500B.

Central Chaweng Beach

Central Chaweng—Ko Samui's most impressive stretch of sand—is where hippies first gathered when the lotus-eating life was in full bloom to enjoy the wonderful beach, perfect vistas, and endless supply of mushrooms and grass.

The first arrival on the beach was perhaps an English photographer who landed in 1968 after a long ride on a coconut boat from Bangkok, or perhaps European wanderers moving along the hippie trail from Istanbul to Kuta. Others claim that the first Westerner to learn of Chaweng was

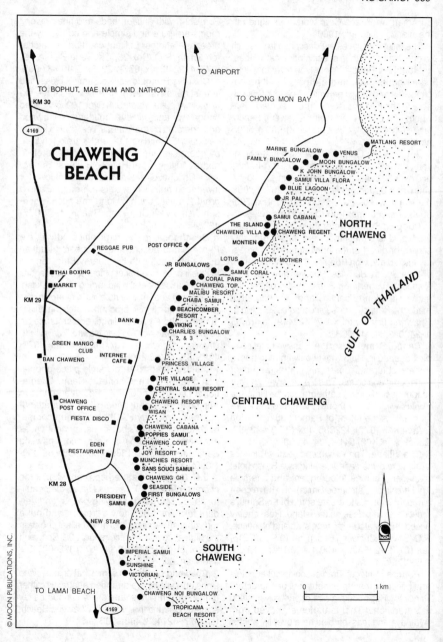

TO BOPHUT, MAE NAM AND NATHON

KM 30

4169

TO AIRPORT

TO CHONG MON BAY

CHAWENG BEACH

MATLANG RESORT

MARINE BUNGALOW • • VENUS
FAMILY BUNGALOW • • MOON BUNGALOW
• K JOHN BUNGALOW
• SAMUI VILLA FLORA
• BLUE LAGOON
• JR PALACE

• SAMUI CABANA
THE ISLAND •
CHAWENG VILLA • • CHAWENG REGENT
MONTIEN •

LOTUS •
• LUCKY MOTHER

REGGAE PUB ■   POST OFFICE ◆

JR BUNGALOWS

SAMUI CORAL
CORAL PARK •
CHAWENG TOP •
MALIBU RESORT •
CHABA SAMUI •
BEACHCOMBER RESORT •
VIKING •
CHARLIES BUNGALOW 1, 2, & 3 •

NORTH CHAWENG

GULF OF THAILAND

■ THAI BOXING
■ MARKET

KM 29

BANK ■

GREEN MANGO CLUB

BAN CHAWENG ■   INTERNET CAFE ■

CHAWENG POST OFFICE
FIESTA DISCO ■

EDEN RESTAURANT ■

KM 28

PRESIDENT SAMUI ■

NEW STAR •

• PRINCESS VILLAGE

• THE VILLAGE
• CENTRAL SAMUI RESORT
• CHAWENG RESORT
• WISAN

• CHAWENG CABANA
• POPPIES SAMUI
• CHAWENG COVE
• JOY RESORT
• MUNCHIES RESORT
• SANS SOUCI SAMUI
• CHAWENG GH
• SEASIDE
• FIRST BUNGALOWS

CENTRAL CHAWENG

• IMPERIAL SAMUI
• SUNSHINE
• VICTORIAN

SOUTH CHAWENG

0   1 km

TO LAMAI BEACH

4169

• CHAWENG NOI BUNGALOW
• TROPICANA BEACH RESORT

© MOON PUBLICATIONS, INC.

an American Peace Corp worker assigned to the island in the early 1960s.

The following places are described from south to north rather than in specific price categories.

Munchies Resort: A longtime favorite whose name harks back to the days of mushroom omelettes and magic brownies—no longer available in their cozy restaurant but served elsewhere as "special breakfasts." Chaweng Beach, tel. (077) 422374, 350-600B fan, 1,000-1,500B a/c chalets.

Joy Resort: One of Chaweng's first operations now offers a collection of rustic A-frames and over 30 comfortable chalets with a/c rooms. Chaweng Beach, tel./fax (077) 422376, 200B old hippie bungalows, 500B fan duplex, 700-900B family rooms, 1,000-1,500B a/c suites.

Poppies Samui: Veterans who experienced the hippie-and-mushroom era in Bali probably stayed or dined at the now legendary homestay tucked away on Poppies Gang in the center of Kuta Beach. Surprise. Poppies now operates a second property on Samui that provides the same attention to service and ambience that made the Kuta original so successful. 28/1 Mu 3, Chaweng Beach, tel. (077) 422419, fax (077) 422420, 2,500-4,000B.

Central Samui Resort: A massive hotel complex opened in 1995 with two swimming pools, three restaurants, six tennis courts, and over 200 rooms and suites. This Vegas-style monster resembles a Roman cathedral airlifted into the tropics without any thought to appropriate design. Is this the future of Samui? 38 Chaweng Beach, tel. (077) 422385, fax (077) 422385, Bangkok tel. (02) 541-1234, 4,000-7,000B.

The Village: The Village and nearby Princess Village are owned and operated by a Swiss hotel manager (Thomas Andereggen) and a female Thai architect (Patcharee Smith) who have combined their talents to create some of Ko Samui's most creative places on the island. Reasonably priced and created with great style and elegance. P.O. Box 25, Chaweng Beach, tel. (077) 422216, fax (077) 422382, 1,400-1,600B fan, 1,700-2,800B a/c.

Princess Village: Tired of cookie-cutter hotels and concrete resorts without soul or character? Princess Village offers a rare opportunity to sleep in a traditional Thai teak home, moved from Ayuthaya and reassembled here over lily ponds.

Furnished with antique beds and fine artwork, rooms are pure and simple and cooled by the breezes—another brilliant creation of Patcharee Smith. P.O. Box 25, Chaweng Beach, tel. (077) 422216, fax (077) 422382, 2,400-3,600B.

Charlies Bungalows: Ko Samui's oldest and largest travelers' center now includes three extremely popular wings with over 100 low-priced bungalows and midlevel cottages, still owned and operated by the famous Teera, also known as "Mama." Charlies 1, 2, and 3 are often filled by noon; sign the waiting list and head off to nearby Viking, Thai House, Suneast Bungalows, Coconut Grove, and Lotus Bungalows for low-priced huts. Charlies is a great place in a great location, but how long can such a godsend survive? Chaweng Beach, tel. (077) 422343, 120-850B.

Beachcomber Resort: Compared with the Princess, the Beachcomber appears utilitarian but its affiliation with the nearby Blue Lagoon makes it one of the better places for water sports (Hobie Cat sailboats, windsurfing, water-skiing, parasailing) and nightlife pursuits in nearby clubs. As counterpoint, their brochure states that this is "a resort where you can linger and embrace life in the company of Mother Nature." 3/5 Mu 2, Chaweng Beach, tel. (077) 422041, fax (077) 422388, 2,000-3,200B.

Malibu Resort: An old-style place popular with dive groups and home to Samui International Diving School that organized dives to Angthong, Phangan, and Ko Tao. After attending their three-day PADI certification course, retire to their upstairs bar for happy-hour prices and views over the gorgeous beach. Chaweng Beach, tel. (077) 421386, 450-600B fan, 850-1,300B a/c.

J.R. Guesthouse: Perhaps named after the character from the TV series *Dallas,* the beautiful shady courtyard, swaying palms, and verdant ferns of J.R.—now a "resort" and not a "guesthouse"—makes this an excellent choice in the budget- to middle-price range. 90/1 Chaweng Beach, tel. (077) 422258, fax (077) 422402, 400-450B fan, 600-1,200B a/c.

Chaweng Garden: A somewhat unique place since bungalows are arranged abstractly rather than in uniform lines, and a few surfboards lay scattered around the grounds. Chaweng Beach, tel. (077) 421403, 450-900B fan.

Lucky Mother: A popular and well-priced set of bungalows that face a beautiful sandy courtyard dotted with swaying palms. Recommended. Chaweng Beach, no phone, 150-600B.

Chaweng Regent: A few steps past the budget huts of Lucky Mother lies the luxurious Regent property with over 150 Thai-style cottages, an amoeba-shaped pool, and natural swimming area behind offshore rock barriers. 155/4 Chaweng Beach, tel. (077) 422008, fax (077) 422222, 2,800-4,500B.

The Island: A popular resort owned by a former attorney from New York who now runs one of the best-value places on Chaweng. Rooms are well priced and kept in good condition. P.O. Box 52, tel. (077) 421288, fax (077) 421178, 450-1,500B.

Louis Bungalows: Decrepit huts (no electricity, no running water, no furniture, no managers), but some of the wildest people and collection of stray dogs on the island. Chaweng Beach, no phone, 60-80B or whatever.

North Chaweng Yai Beach

Chaweng's finest bungalows are tucked along the shallow bay north of the last cape, the most beautiful stretch of sand on Samui and an ideal spot to wade in shallow waters, sailboard, swing from a rope suspended from a leaning coconut tree, or just stare out to Matlang Island. *Songtaos* from Nathon reach the following bungalows by request.

J.R. Palace: Wild architecture, multitiered roofs, and creative interiors are the hallmarks of this sprawling resort. Chaweng Beach, tel. (077) 421402, 950-1,600B.

Blue Lagoon: A luxury resort with beautiful pool, open-air restaurant, water sports center, and 54 superior rooms plus seven deluxe Thai-style bungalows. Also, a pet elephant wanders the grounds. 99 Mu 2, Chaweng Beach, tel. (077) 422037, fax (077) 422401, Bangkok tel. (02) 253-3915, 3,000-4,200B.

K John Bungalows: High marks for the unusual octagonal bungalows, pet monkey, and friendly managers who have kept prices low over the years. 46 Mu 2, Chaweng Beach, tel. (077) 422116, 100-200B fan, 400-650B a/c.

Family Bungalows: Immaculate rooms and large, clean baths make this a good choice for budget travelers. 119 Mu 2, Chaweng Beach, no phone, 100-200B.

Moon Bungalows: A well-named set of bamboo huts and newer bungalows facing a gorgeous stretch of sand. 125 Mu 2, Chaweng Beach, tel. (077) 422167, 200-350B huts, 400-600B bungalows.

Marine Bungalows: Another inexpensive place with clean bungalows, shared and private baths, and nightly videos shown in their breezy restaurant. 134 Mu 2, Chaweng Beach, 250-500B.

Matlang Resort: Tucked away at the far northern tip of the beach are several excellent places removed from the hubris of central Chaweng. 154/1 Mu 2, Chaweng Beach, tel. (077) 422172, 300-500B fan, 500-900B a/c.

LAMAI BEACH

Ko Samui's second most popular beach has been developed in a rather haphazard manner with little thought to traffic patterns or hotel aesthetics. The beach is long and beautiful, and you can visit the fishing village at the north end. However, bungalows in the central region are packed closely together and the nightlife is turning toward noisy discos and bar girls—a bad sign. And with all the tax dollars flowing into local coffers, government authorities can certainly afford to pave the dusty roads and hire a crew to pick up trash from the beach. The get-rich-quick and me-first mentality is quite evident at Lamai.

Dozens of bungalows crowd the center but those isolated on the hills to the east are quieter and more relaxing. Unlike Chaweng Beach, Lamai still has a good supply of inexpensive bungalows in the 150-350B range. Budget travelers should check accommodations on the southern end of the beach (Noi, White Sand, Samui Pearl) and just east of the central beach (Marine Park, My Friend, New Huts, Tapi).

Minitrucks' routes terminate in the center near the restaurants and bars. Lamai has all possible services, including money exchanges, supermarkets, bookstores, motorcycle and jeep rentals, and countless bars and discos that rock until dawn.

South Lamai Beach
South Lamai stretches from the discos and nightclubs in the central section south past the phallic rocks (Hin Tan and Hin Yai) to a handful of small resorts perched at the edge of a small bluff.

Rocky Chalet: A popular and very clean place run by two Germans, Linn and Erwin Werrena, on a private beach that guarantees a welcome escape from the noise of central Lamai. Facilities include a cozy cafe and scuba equipment rentals. Bang Nam Chut Bay, South Lamai Beach, 600-1,400B.

Noi Bungalows: Several very cheap places, such as this spot owned by a Thai-Swiss couple, are situated on either side of the rocky-erotic cape. Noi caters to solo travelers and welcomes couples with small children. Ban Nam Chut Bay, South Lamai Beach, 150-350B.

White Sand Bungalows: For over two decades, White Sand has provided bamboo huts

and basic meals for legions of passing travelers. Quiet, relaxed, and only a 20-minute walk from the nightclubs in central Lamai. South Lamai Beach, 120-250B.

Paradise Bungalows: Perhaps the oldest set of bungalows on Lamai still caters to budget travelers who enjoy the clean grounds, decent cafe, and easy access to a lovely stretch of sand. South Lamai Beach, tel. (077) 424290, 150-250B wooden huts, 450-700B brick bungalows with private bath.

Casanova Resort: The huge rooms elevated on a hillside, lovely restaurant, and stunning pool make Casanova a good choice for midlevel travelers. 124 Mu 2, South Lamai Beach, tel. (077) 424425, 1,400-2,500B.

Central Lamai Beach
Central Lamai may be convenient for transportation and shopping, but avoid guesthouses within earshot of the discos unless you intend to party every night. Be extra way of places near the Mix Pub, a raging disco that opens at 2100 and grinds on until 0430.

Lamai Inn 99: The central location, beautiful grassy grounds, and reasonably priced bungalows make this a good choice near the heart of the beast. Central Lamai Beach, tel. (077) 421427, 450-900B.

Weekender Bungalows: Adjacent to the Weekender Supermarket is another Lamai favorite with a variety of huts and bungalows in various price ranges. Simple and clean but somewhat noisy due to the nearby clubs. Central Lamai Beach, tel. (077) 424427, 350-800B.

Coconut Villa: A big place with over 50 spacious bungalows, all with private baths. 124/4 Mu 3, Central Lamai Beach, tel. (077) 421424, 300-650B.

Mui Bungalows: Mui, Utopia, and Magic are three simple places in a great location: within walking distance of the nightclubs but distant enough to escape the disco noises. The nearby Verandah Restaurant is headed by a former chef from the Oriental Hotel in Bangkok. 123 Mu 3, Central Lamai, tel. (077) 424224, 200-350B huts, 550-900B a/c bungalows.

Pavilion Resort: Central Lamai's most luxurious resort features large octagonal suites, attached rooms in a hotel block, and a beautiful pool facing an attractive stretch of sand. Cen-

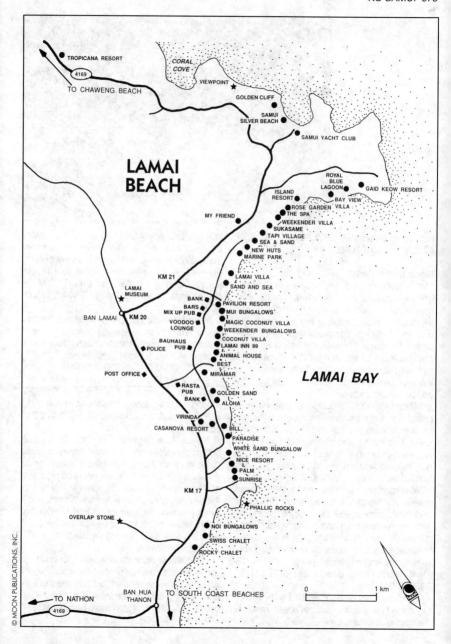

TROPICANA RESORT

4169

TO CHAWENG BEACH

CORAL COVE

VIEWPOINT

GOLDEN CLIFF

SAMUI SILVER BEACH

SAMUI YACHT CLUB

LAMAI BEACH

ROYAL BLUE LAGOON

GAID KEOW RESORT

ISLAND RESORT

BAY VIEW VILLA

ROSE GARDEN VILLA

THE SPA

WEEKENDER VILLA

SUKASAME

MY FRIEND

TAPI VILLAGE

SEA & SAND

NEW HUTS

MARINE PARK

KM 21

LAMAI VILLA

SAND AND SEA

LAMAI MUSEUM

BANK

BARS

MIX UP PUB

PAVILION RESORT

MUI BUNGALOWS

BAN LAMAI   KM 20

VOODOO LOUNGE

MAGIC COCONUT VILLA

WEEKENDER BUNGALOWS

COCONUT VILLA

BAUHAUS PUB

LAMAI INN 99

POLICE

ANIMAL HOUSE

BEST

POST OFFICE

MIRAMAR

LAMAI BAY

RASTA PUB

GOLDEN SAND

BANK

ALOHA

VIRINDA

CASANOVA RESORT

BILL

PARADISE

WHITE SAND BUNGALOW

NICE RESORT

PALM

SUNRISE

KM 17

PHALLIC ROCKS

OVERLAP STONE

NOI BUNGALOWS

SWISS CHALET

ROCKY CHALET

TO NATHON   BAN HUA THANON   TO SOUTH COAST BEACHES

4169

0   1 km

© MOON PUBLICATIONS, INC.

Lamai Beach

tral Lamai Beach, tel. (077) 424420, fax (077) 424030, 2,200-2,800B.

North Lamai Beach

The following resorts are situated in the quiet and peaceful northern section of Lamai. Bungalows are spread over larger grounds and lack the claustrophobic edge of those to the south, plus most offer better value than those elsewhere on Lamai. Although the beach is narrow and rocky, and the remote location makes nightlife access a tricky task, North Lamai more than compensates with its sense of solitude and peaceful surroundings.

Marine Park: North Lamai begins with low-priced huts and bungalows that recall the lifestyles of an earlier era. Marine Park, New Huts, Sea & Sand, Tapi Village, and No Name consist of aging A-frames or bamboo huts, plus simple cafes that play light reggae from morning to midnight. North Lamai Beach, no phone, 150-250B.

Weekender Villa: Weekender Villa, nearby Weekender Resort, and Weekender Bungalows in central Lamai are all owned by a local family who have prospered and grown wealthy from the tourism boom on Samui. All bungalows at the Villa face a beautiful inner courtyard lined with sandy walkways and swaying palms. 184 Mu 4, North Lamai Beach, tel. (077) 421372, 300-650B.

The Spa: Guy Hopkins and his wife, Toi, operate the first and only natural health resort on the island. Unfortunately, Guy has failed to main-

tain this property which has fallen into severe disrepair and can no longer be recommended. This author has received several letters of complaint about this property and the poor reception provided by the management. 171/2 Mu 4, North Lamai Beach, tel./fax (077) 424126, 300-500B.

Island Resort: Bamboo bungalows, friendly management, and carefully tended gardens make this an ideal place for beach hounds on a budget. 142 Mu 4, North Lamai Beach, tel. (077) 424202, 300-450B fan, 500-700B a/c.

Bay View Villa: A stunning restaurant and idyllic location make this low-priced choice among the finer places to relax on this part of the island. North Lamai Beach, tel. (077) 272222, 500-800B.

Royal Blue Lagoon: Peck and family own and operate this upscale hotel complex some three km from the nightclubs of central Lamai. Facilities include an attractive pool and jacuzzi, a seafood restaurant with panoramic views over the bay, money exchange, vehicle rentals, and a private beach for swimming and snorkeling. 108/1 Mu 4, North Lamai Beach, tel./fax (077) 424195, 600-900B fan and private bath, 2,400-2,900B a/c chalets.

Gaid Keow Resort: The final spot on North Lamai features a small pool on the wooden deck and bungalows overlooking a stony beach. Quiet and relaxing but a rented vehicle is almost a necessity. 46/1 Mu 4, North Lamai Beach, tel. (077) 472222, 550-900B.

NORTH COAST BEACHES

Chong Mon Beach

Ko Samui's prettiest bay is a graceful crescent with excellent sand and offshore islands with deserted beaches. Chong Mon was considered well off the beaten track until the 1990 opening of the immense Imperial Chong Mon Resort, which creatively utilized the old fishing boats that once lined the bay. Chong Mon now has regular mini-truck service from Nathon and Chaweng Beach.

Sun Sand Resort: A superb arrangement of 33 individual bungalows, breezy restaurant, and stunning views over Chong Mon Bay make this resort a popular choice with European group tours. Highly recommended. Chong Mon Beach, tel. (077) 425404, fax (077) 421322, 1,200-1,500B.

P.S. Villa: The spotless bungalows, spacious lawns, and bamboo restaurant make this the best bargain on the beach. Chong Mon Beach, tel. (077) 425160, 350-800B.

Chat Kaeo Resort: Small but very pretty bungalows at reasonable cost. 59/4 Chong Mon Beach, no phone, 450-550B fan, 900-1,200B a/c.

Choeng Mon Bungalows: Three classes of bungalows that increase in price as you get closer to the beach. 24/3 Chong Mon Beach, tel. (977) 425372, 200-250B fan, 350-550B a/c.

Imperial Tongsai Bay: A super-exclusive Mediterranean-style hotel with 24 hotel rooms and 48 individual a/c cottages overlooking a private beach just north of Chong Mon Bay. Facilities include a free-form saltwater pool, landscaping tended by an army of gardeners, several restaurants, and all possible water sports. One of the most spectacular resorts in the country. Ban Plailaem, Bophut, tel. (077) 421015, fax (077) 425462, 4,800-8,000B.

Big Buddha Beach

Ao Bang Rak—more commonly called Big Buddha after the nearby image—offers almost a dozen inexpensive to moderate bungalows on an arching beach which is narrow and brownish but generally deserted. Bungalows are clean and comfortable, though beach conditions and noise from highway traffic here make Bophut and Mae Nam Beaches more idyllic locations.

Dive facilities are available at the Champ Villa, where the one-day dives go from 1,800B.

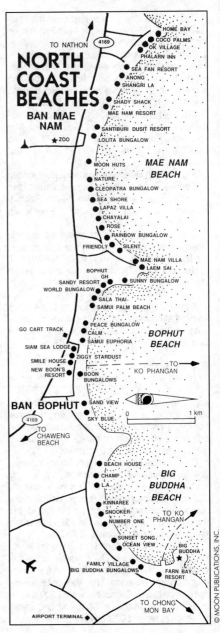

Boats to Ko Phangan depart near the Buddha daily at 1530 and return from Hat Rin on Ko Phangan at 0930.

Farn Bay Resort: An expensive hotel with Thai dance shows on weekends. But, as their brochure claims, "No more hustle-bustles, no more pollution, no more rat-race." Big Buddha Beach, tel. (077) 273920, 1,200-1,600B.

Comfort Resort Garden: An American-operated hotel with renovated rooms, pool, and ambience popular with families. 88 Mu 4, Big Buddha Beach, tel. (077) 421364, 1,600-2,600B.

Big Buddha Bungalows: Large new wooden bungalows and friendly management make this one of the best bargains on the beach. Recommended. 34/1 Mu 4, Big Buddha Beach, tel. (077) 485282, 250-600B.

Sunset Song: Another inexpensive place with clean rooms, big porches, and comfortable cafe. Big Buddha Beach, tel. (077) 421363, 250-400B.

Number One: German management under Dim and Hans. Good value. Big Buddha Beach, tel. (077) 425446, 250-500B.

Kinnaree Bungalows: Large bungalows somewhat crammed together, but the cheapest spot on the beach. 73/2 Mu 4, Big Buddha Beach, tel. (077) 425217, 150-300B.

Bophut Beach

Travelers who want to escape the congestion of Chaweng or Lamai will find Bophut an acceptable alternative. The narrow and coarse beach isn't as impressive as Chaweng or Lamai, but many visitors consider the friendly people and sense of isolation adequate compensation. Bophut also has wonderful sunsets.

Bophut town has a branch of Siam Commercial Bank, Reader Mate Bookstore, and several restaurants with Thai and European dishes. Cafes here once served the most potent hallucinogenic mushroom soups on the island, but the banning of psychedelics in 1989 forced the trade over to Ko Phangan and Ko Tao.

Bophut is a convenient departure point for Ko Phangan. The *Hadrin Queen* departs daily at 0900 and 1300 for Hat Rin Beach on the southeast corner of the island. The "Midnight Express" taxi service leaves Bophut nightly at 2200 and returns from the discos on Chaweng and Lamai Beaches at around 0300-0400.

Basic bungalows and midlevel hotels are situated in the town, but bungalows farther down the beach are quieter and located on better sand. Bophut remains cheaper than Chaweng or Lamai, but bungalows have sharply raised rates in recent years and expensive hotels are arriving in rapid order.

Smile House: At the edge of town is a very clean place with small fan-cooled bungalows and pricier a/c chalets, plus a wonderful pool surrounded by palms. Bophut Beach, tel. (077) 425361, 450-1,250B.

Ziggy Stardust: Beautiful Lanna-style bungalows, a lovely garden, and a popular restaurant make Ziggy's a great choice for midlevel travelers. 99 Mu 1, Bophut Beach, tel. (077) 425410, 250-450B fan, 850-1,200B a/c.

Peace Bungalows: A longtime favorite located away from town on a quieter stretch of sand. Low-end bungalows are dismal, but those in the 250-400B range are clean and comfortable. Large restaurant and friendly management. 178 Mu 1, Bophut Beach, tel. (077) 425357, 250-500B fan, 660-900B a/c.

World Bungalows: One of the most popular and reasonably priced places at Bophut features a small swimming pool, lush gardens, and luxurious restaurant facing the deserted beach. A great place to escape the crowds. 175/1 Mu 1, Bophut Beach, tel. (077) 425355, 150-250B small bungalows, 650-750B large bungalows, 950-1,200B a/c chalets.

Sunny Bungalows: Very popular for its adequate if rudimentary bungalows and isolated location at the end of the beach. Bophut Beach, tel. (077) 425486, 150-350B.

Mae Nam Beach

Mae Nam is an isolated and relatively undeveloped beach midway between Nathon and Chaweng Beach. Over a dozen inexpensive to midlevel bungalows on this beach are signposted on the main highway. Well hidden behind scrub and jungle, most offer quiet rooms facing a deserted beach and a relaxed atmosphere ideal for reading and relaxation. Beaches are narrow, but the solitude and remote location are quite appealing.

The following spots are described from east to west.

Laem Sai and Mae Nam Villa: Both of these inexpensive and very popular guesthouses are located at the end of the cape that forms the extreme southern end of Ao Mae Nam (Mae Nam Bay). Both are difficult to reach without private transportation but well suited to determined escapists and families with children. Mae Nam Beach, no phones, 150-350B.

Rainbow Bungalows: Good-value bungalows constructed with brick and wood. 44/4 Mu 1, Mae Nam Beach, 150-350B.

Cleopatra Bungalows: Friendly and inexpensive spot with older but adequate huts. Mae Nam Beach, tel. (077) 425486, 150-350B.

Moon Huts: Attractive bamboo bungalows, an elevated restaurant with views, and a brilliant stretch of sand make well-named Moon a good choice. Recommended. 67/2 Mae Nam Beach, no phone, 250-350B.

Lolita Bungalows: Lolita boasts an excellent beach with stunning palms, easy access to the town of Ban Mae Nam, and decent bungalows in all possible price ranges. Mae Nam Beach, tel. (077) 425134, 300-900B.

Mae Nam Resort: Beautiful bungalows, comfortable restaurant, and grassy landscapes make this the best midpriced resort at Mae Nam Beach. Highly recommended. Mae Nam Beach, tel. (077) 425116, 350-800B.

Shangrila: Inexpensive bungalows, new restaurant, and safe swimming make Shangrila popular with families. Mae Nam Beach, tel. (077) 425189, 180-400B.

Sea Fan Resort: A fully developed resort complex with luxurious cottages, pool, and sports activities on a remote and almost completely unspoiled beach; the best choice for upscale travelers. Mae Nam Beach, tel. (077) 425204, fax (077) 425350, 500-4,000B.

Coco Palms Village: Escape the crowds at the west end of the beach. Coco Palms is a friendly place with great meals prepared by a Western chef. Good value, plus dazzling aquamarine waters. Mae Nam Beach, no phone, 500-800B.

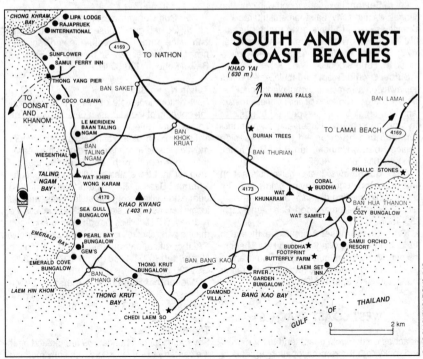

SOUTH AND WEST COAST BEACHES

© MOON PUBLICATIONS, INC.

SOUTH COAST BEACHES

The south and west sides of Ko Samui are characterized by stony landscapes with minimal beaches, but they offer the last possible relief from the crowds that fill the more popular beaches on the west and north shores.

The following bungalows and hotels are listed from west to east, starting with Thong Krut Bay and ending at the town of Ban Hua Thanon.

Thong Krut Bungalows: Nisit and Nu run a decent place with fishing tours, snorkeling boats, and seaside bungalows for 250-400B.

Diamond Villa Bungalows: Small but new huts with volleyball net and snorkeling April-Aug. when the seas are calm and tides low. 180-320B.

River Garden Bungalows: A great place with friendly managers, good beach, and small river with wading fisherwomen. Recommended. Bang Kao Bay, 200-450B.

Laem Set Inn: Luxurious resort with elevated bungalows and surly management. International reviews seem to have gone to their heads. 110 Mu 2, Hua Thanon, Laem Set Beach, tel. (077) 424393, fax (077) 424394, badly over-priced at 3,800-8,000B.

Samui Orchid Resort: A fabulous resort hidden away on a 25-acre coconut plantation. Features two large swimming pools, luxurious restaurant, and small but well-appointed bungalows on a deserted beach. Reservations and transportation can be arranged at their Seaside Palace Hotel in Nathon. Ban Harn Beach, tel. (077) 424017, 850-1,800B.

Cozy Bungalows: Inexpensive huts set on grassy grounds under swaying palms. Well located within walking distance of an interesting fishing village. Recommended. Ban Harn Beach, 250-450B.

Natta Guesthouse: A small guesthouse in the colorful fishing village of Ban Hua Thanon, the only Muslim community on Ko Samui and a good place to experience traditional life rather than a tourist ghetto. 100-280B.

WEST COAST BEACHES

Beaches on the west coast tend to be narrow and rocky, but the remote location appeals to visitors who seek privacy rather than the perfect beach. Another advantage is the easy access to Thong Yang Pier and sunset vistas unavailable at the more popular beach destinations.

The following bungalows and hotels are described from Emerald Cove at the southwestern tip to Cape Yai a few kilometers north of Nathon.

Emerald Bay

Emerald Bay (Pungka or Phangka Beach) is a stunning destination tucked away at the southwestern corner of Ko Samui off an isolated side road rarely explored by visitors. En route to the beach you'll pass the rather mundane Emerald Cove Bungalows and Gem's House.

Pearl Bay Bungalows: The road terminates at several wonderful spots on a sandy beach flanked by striking limestone mountains—the perfect escape for the world-weary traveler. Pearl Bay can help arrange boat trips and canoes to explore the arching cove. Emerald Bay, no phone, 140-500B

Sea Gull Bungalows: Another rustic but superbly located guesthouse tucked away at the end of the winding dirt road. A rented vehicle is necessary to reach these bungalows. Emerald Bay, no phone, 180-500B.

Taling Ngam Bay

Few visitors took note of this remote bay until the opening of the Mandarin Oriental Group resort in early 1994.

Le Meridien Baan Taling Ngam: Ko Samui's most exclusive resort is named after the nearby town burdened with an unpronounceable moniker that translates to "Village by Peaceful Shores." Baan Taling Ngam features seven beachside villas, six Thai-style *salas,* and 42 jungle houses on the steep hillside just across the highway. BTN activities include tours to Angthong marine park, snorkeling at Ko Taen, and four-day PADI certification courses. 295 Mu 3, Taling Ngam, tel. (077) 423019, fax (077) 422220, US$320-650.

Wiesenthal Bungalows: The same beach but at somewhat lower rates. Taling Ngam Bay, no phone, 280-950B.

Thong Yang Pier

Several midpriced bungalows are located near the car ferry to serve visitors with early morning departures, or those who simply want to escape the crowded beaches elsewhere on the island.

Samui Ferry Inn: The closest spot to the pier but rather utilitarian and sterile in design. Thong Yang, tel. (077) 421388, 550-900B.

In Foo Palace and Sunflower Resort: Budget spots just north of the pier past the Samui Ferry Inn and Aran Resort. Thong Yang, no phones, 150-380B.

Coco Cabana Beach Club: A short walk south from the pier is the best-value choice in the area. Friendly, quiet, and clean. Thong Yang, tel. (077) 421465, 450-850B.

Chong Khram Bay

The sweeping and secluded bay between Thong Yang Pier and Nathon may lack great sand but guarantees the best sunsets on the island, plus aquamarine shallows perfect for wading or snorkeling.

Lipa Lodge: The best budget option has over 20 clean bungalows, a decent cafe, and a great location at the north end of the bay. Chong Khram Bay, 140-290B.

International: An alternative choice when Lipa Lodge is filled. Chong Khram Bay, tel. (077) 423366, 250-450B fan, 600-950B a/c.

Rajapruek Samui Resort: The top-end choice is situated between the International and Lipa Lodge across the access road. Swimming pool, restaurant, water sports, and a bit of nightlife in the bar. Chong Khram Bay, tel. (077) 423399, 1,600-3,800B.

INFORMATION AND SERVICES

Tourist Information

The TAT office dispenses a few brochures about Ko Samui and can help with information on Ko Phangan and Ko Tao. Open daily 0830-1630. 126 Mu 3, Tambon Maret, tel. (077) 420504 or (077) 421435.

Travel Agencies

Dozens of agencies sell tickets on Ko Samui, but only the following are guaranteed to be safe, reliable, and honest. The first two are travel agencies, the latter two transportation companies that operate ferries to the islands and also make travel arrangements. Most of the other smaller travel agencies simply act as middlemen and tack their service fees on tickets obtained from the following agencies.

Phanthip Travel: A travel agency and authorized agent of the State Railways and Thai Airways that charges no service fees and provides honest reservations for all modes of transportation. Open daily 0600-1700. 84/1 Nathon Rd., Nathon, tel. (077) 421556, fax (077) 421222.

World Travel: One of Thailand's largest tour operators and a dependable source for transport tickets, airline confirmations, and room reservations at upscale hotels. Open daily 0700-1700. 66 Nathon Rd., Nathon, tel. (077) 421475.

Songserm Travel: Another major transportation agency that operates the express ferry from Tha Thong Pier, the night ferry from downtown Surat Thani, and buses and minibuses between Ko Samui and Phuket. Open daily 0600-1700. 64/1 Nathon Rd., Nathon, tel. (077) 421316, fax (077) 421544.

Samui Tours: The travel subsidiary of Samui Ferry Company operates the vehicle/passenger ferry from Don Sak to Thong Yang Pier on Ko Samui, plus arranges buses to Bangkok, Phuket, and other destinations in the south. Open daily 0600-1700. Thong Yang Pier, tel. (077) 421367.

Tourist Police

The Ko Samui tourist police station is two km south of Nathon just past the road to Hin Lad Temple. The tourist police can be contacted by calling their office or the TAT and requesting radio contact with a roving patrol. Highway 4169, tel. (077) 421281, emergency tel. 1699.

Immigration

Visa extensions at the immigration office in Nathon cost 500B and require two passport photos. Open weekdays 0830-1530. 6/9 Tawirajapakdi Rd., tel. (077) 421226.

Mail

The General Post Office in Nathon handles mail, poste restante, faxes, telegrams, and money transfers. Private mail services at all major beaches charge small commissions for their services. Open weekdays 0830-1630, weekends 0900-1200. Nathon Rd., tel. (077) 421013.

The postal code for Ko Samui is 84140.

International Telephone
The International Telephone Center is located in the GPO in Nathon. Open daily 0700-2200. Nathon Rd., tel. (077) 421013.

Overseas calls can also be made from most guesthouses and hotels for a small service fee.

Banks
Currency can be exchanged at banks in Nathon and at exchange booths at all major beaches. Banks close at 1600 or 1630, but exchange booths remain open until 1800-2000.

Medical Facilities
The Ko Samui Hospital is two km south of Nathon on a side road near the beach. Serious accidents are evacuated to the Ban Don Hospital in Surat Thani. 61 Mu 5, Tambon Anthong, tel. (077) 421232.

Maps
The map produced by the Surat Thani TAT office and available at their post in Nathon has decent coverage of the island, plus Angthong National Marine Park and Surat Thani Province.

Private maps with excellent detail include *Guide Map of Koh Samui* from Hongsombud and the outstanding *Ko Samui and Southern Thailand* from Periplus Editions.

GETTING THERE

Ko Samui is 537 km south of Bangkok and 84 km northeast of Surat Thani. The island can be reached with either an arranged package that combines land and sea transportation, or by patching together the various segments and saving a few *baht*.

The Bangkok-Ko Samui flight is expensive but the only alternative to a long overland journey. Land options include a bus or train to Surat Thani, followed by an express ferry, car ferry, hydrofoil, or night ferry to the island. The overnight train or bus, plus ferry ride, will land you on the beach around noon.

My recommendation is to fly if you can afford the fare (2,400B), or take the overnight train with a ferry package. The all-inclusive fare is 480-560B with a sleeper in second class. Overnight buses are cheaper but just too exhausting.

Air
Bangkok Airways flies from Bangkok eight times daily (70 minutes, 2,400B) and twice daily from Phuket (40 minutes, 1,500B) into Ko Samui Airport.

The airport, at the northeast corner of the island, has a small restaurant, hotel reservation desk, and a/c minibuses to the beaches for 60B. Reservations can be made from travel agents in Bangkok or directly at Bangkok Airways (tel. 02-253-4014) at the airport on Ratchadaphisek Road. Tickets from Samui can also be booked all over the island or at the Bangkok Airways office in Nathon. Bangkok Airways, 72/2 Mu 3 Nathon Rd., Nathon, tel. (077) 273710.

Note: Flights are often completely booked several weeks in advance during the high season periods, Dec.-March and Aug.-September. Reservations should be made well in advance. Visitors on short holidays should ask their travel agent to make reservations several months before departure.

An alternative to Bangkok Airways is **Thai Airways** to the Surat Thani Airport, then a shuttle to the pier and a ferry across to Ko Samui.

Thai Airways flies three times daily from Bangkok to Surat Thani, once daily from Phuket, and twice weekly from Chiang Mai. The airport shuttle to Surat Thani (23 km) costs 50B per person.

Thai Airways, 3/27 Karunarat Rd., Surat Thani, tel. (077) 272610, 273355.

Train and Bus
Visitors can purchase an all-inclusive package that covers all transfers and boat connections.

Overnight Train: By far the most comfortable way to reach Ko Samui is the overnight train to Phun Phin, 14 km west of Surat Thani, followed by a bus to the ferry terminal. The all-inclusive price is 480-550B for a second-class sleeper with fan, or 580-650B for a second-class a/c sleeper. Seats cost 280B in third class and 390B in second class. Fares include boat passage across to Samui.

Tickets should be purchased well in advance at the Hualampong station or from an authorized agent in Bangkok. Train packages cost 30-50B more than patching together your own transportation, a modest surcharge that eliminates the hassle of separate bookings.

Train: Rapid trains depart Bangkok nine times daily and take 13 hours to reach Phun Phin, 14 km west of Surat Thani. The most convenient departure is the rapid train at 1830, which arrives in Phun Phin at 0600 and allows plenty of time to catch an early morning boat to Samui. Buses from the various ferry companies greet arrivals at the train station and provide immediate transport to the boat terminals for Samui.

Overnight trains should be reserved well in advance, especially for weekend and holiday departures.

Government Bus: The a/c bus from the Southern Bus Terminal in Bangkok departs four times daily 1800-2000, costs 360-450B, and includes the ferry across to Ko Samui.

Private Bus: Travel agents around Khao San Road sell bus tickets to Ko Samui for 280-450B, depending on the quality of the bus and ferry. The lower priced packages generally use older buses with less legroom and a slow boat from the mainland, while the more expensive packages use VIP buses with reclining seats and faster ferries from Don Sak.

Bus: Several a/c buses depart from the Southern Bus Terminal in Thonburi 1800-2000 and arrive the next morning at the bus terminal in Surat Thani. Buses there provide transfer to the various ferry piers.

Boat

Several different types of boat go from Surat Thani to Ko Samui. The situation appears confusing since there are two boat companies (Songserm and Samui Ferry), one jetboat company (Island Jet), three piers in Surat Thani (Ban Don, Tha Thong, Don Sak), and two piers on Ko Samui (Thaton, Thong Yang).

The fastest and least expensive option is the ferry from Don Sak, 60 km east of Surat Thani, though this hardly matters since most travelers simply take the first available boat.

The following departure schedules change with the seasons, but independent travelers can simply follow the ferry tout at the train or bus terminal and be escorted directly to the next available ferry.

Vehicle Ferry (Don Sak to Thong Yang): Car and passenger ferries (40B) operated by Samui Ferry depart from Don Sak, one hour east of Surat, five times daily and arrive 90 minutes later at Thong Yang Pier on Ko Samui. This service is quick and relatively inexpensive since Don Sak is the closest mainland departure point for the island. All bus packages from Bangkok use this ferry, as well as many of the all-inclusive train packages.

Buses to Don Sak depart from the Phanthip Tour office on Talad Mai Road at 0650, 0830, 1030, 1230, and 1530. Ferries depart Don Sak one and a half hours later and sail to Thong Yang, where *songtaos* continue to the beaches.

The bus-and-ferry combination ticket can be purchased at Phanthip Travel, at Samui Tours, and from touts hanging around the Phun Phin train station.

Express Boat (Tha Thong to Nathon): An express boat operated by Songserm departs from Tha Thong Pier, six km east of Surat Thani, daily at 0730, 1200, and 1400 Oct.-June, and at 0730 and 1200 during the rainy season June-Oct. The two-level boat takes two and a half hours to reach Nathon and then continues to Ko Phangan.

The fare includes a bus ride to the pier from the Songserm office at 0700, 1130, and 1330.

Jet Boat (Tha Thong to Nathon): The Island Jet departs Tha Thong daily at 0830 and takes one and a half hours to reach Nathon. Tickets can be purchased from Phanthip Travel and the Island Jet office (tel. 077-272230) on Talad Mai Road.

Night Boat (Surat Thani to Nathon): The cheapest option is the night boat, which departs from the Ban Don municipal harbor at 2300 and arrives in Nathon around 0500. Fares are 60-90B on the lower deck with straw cushions, or 100-150B upper deck with mattresses and pillows.

The night boat is somewhat rough but arrives in Samui at daybreak and eliminates an overnight in Surat Thani.

GETTING AWAY

Boat

Bus and ferry departures from Ko Samui tend to change frequently and schedules should be checked at travel agencies in Nathon. Onward tickets should be arranged through one of the travel agencies mentioned above.

Vehicle Ferry (Thong Yang to Don Sak): The car and passenger ferry operated by Samui Tours departs Thong Yang Pier five times daily at 0730, 1000, 1200, 1400, and 1600, and takes one and a half hours to reach Don Sak on the mainland. The fare includes a bus from Nathon to Thong Yang, the ferry to Don Sak, and a final bus to Surat Thani or the train station in Phun Phin.

Express Boat (Nathon to Tha Thong): The Songserm express boat leaves Nathon daily at 0730, 1230, and 1500 Nov.-May, and at 0730 and 1230 May-November. The fare includes transportation to the Surat Thani bus terminal or the Phun Phin train station.

Night Ferry (Nathon to Surat Thani): The night ferry leaves Nathon at 2300 and arrives in Surat Thani the following morning around 0500.

Buses from Nathon
Air-conditioned buses from Nathon are twice the cost of public non-a/c buses from the Surat Thani terminal. Budget travelers can compare the cost of buses from Ko Samui with the bus fares listed under Surat Thani, and decide whether the convenience factor is worth the additional tariff.

NEARBY ISLANDS

The smaller islands just south of Ko Samui offer good snorkeling, private beaches, and simple bungalows on Ko Taen (Ko Katen), known as "No Dog Island" by villagers who believed that animal life was impossible on such an arid piece of land.

The two closest islands—Ko Taen and Ko Matsum—can be reached for 40B each way with longtail boats departing from Thong Krut Bungalows (see "South Coast Beaches" above). Getting to Ko Rap, Ko Mat Kong, Ko Wang Nok, and Ko Mat Daeng requires 10-person chartered longtails at 1,000-1,200B per full day.

Ko Taen
No Dog Island now has three bungalows on the east coast and one set of huts on the west coast.

Tan Village, Ko Taen Resort, and Coral Beach cost 150-250B for accommodations from simple bamboo huts to larger bungalows with private baths. S.S. Cove on the east side is similarly priced but may require a long and tiring hike across the hilly interior.

Ko Matsum
The much smaller island to the east of Ko Taen lacks accommodation, but camping is permitted on any of the excellent beaches that encircle the elongated island. Dive excursions from Thong Krut Bungalows often spend a few hours over the offshore reefs.

Bird's Nest Islands
Four islands highly prized as sources of bird's nest soup are located 20 minutes west of Taling Ngam Bay on the southwestern corner of Samui. Ko Talu, Ko Din, Ko Malengpong, and Ko Mae Tap are privately owned islands guarded by armed watchmen during the collection season.

The islands can be seen from a safe distance on afternoon tea cruises sponsored by the Baan Taling Ngam resort on Samui's west coast.

KO PHANGAN

Phangan Island, 20 km north of Ko Samui, is a wild and primitive place with isolated beaches, tropical jungles, and arching coves accessible only by long hikes or chartered boats. Ko Phangan seems a return to the mid-1970s, with its pockets of gypsyish travelers bedecked with amulets and beads, where during the day there's little to do but relax on the beach and perhaps rent a motorcycle to visit some of the local waterfalls. Nightlife remains limited to a few video shows and meditation classes directed by Buddhist monks and Rajneesh devotees.

Destined for cataclysmic changes, Ko Phangan—like Ko Samui—also faces major challenges. Transportation hassles and the isolated beaches long kept the island relatively

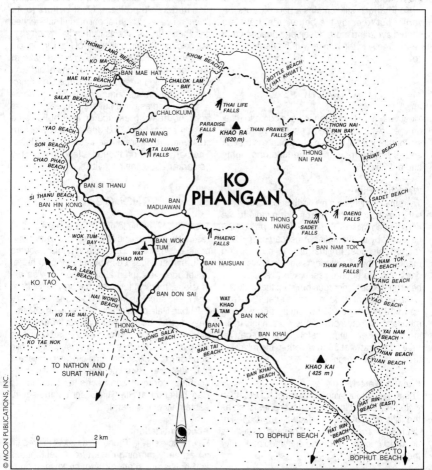

© MOON PUBLICATIONS, INC.

undeveloped, but modern pressures have wrought great changes on the once-pristine island. Phangan now reels under a boom cycle fueled by entrepreneurs who anticipate a Ko Samui-style explosion. Over the last five years, hundreds of bungalows have been constructed with wild abandon and little thought to zoning codes or pollution controls. Without adequate compensation for hotel operators or funding from municipal authorities, trash piles up on beaches and sewage is dumped directly into the waters.

Ko Phangan still remains a backpackers' favorite, but to enjoy the better side, travelers should avoid the more developed beaches and head directly to the remote, off-the-beaten-track coves.

ATTRACTIONS

Most visitors to Ko Phangan have come to relax on the beach and gaze at sunsets while waiting for the next full moon party, though naturalists and explorers may enjoy the following sights and activities.

Wat Khao Tam

The small temple on a hill north of Ban Tai sponsors meditation retreats from the middle to the end of each month. Ten-week *vipassana* courses taught by an Australian-American couple at a reasonable cost for instruction, rooms, and meals. Prospective students should arrive a few days early to secure reservations and should be prepared for a rigorous program that includes wake-up calls at 0430, no meals after 1200, and up to 12 hours per day of sitting and walking meditations. Some practitioners finish this training and proceed immediately to the 10-day retreat offered at Wat Suan Mok from the middle to the end of each month.

Phaeng Waterfalls

The rugged mountainous interior of Ko Phangan includes several impressive cascades such as the falls east of Ban Maduawan up a one-km dirt road. As with all falls in Thailand, cascades are most impressive during or immediately after the rainy season.

Than Sadet Historical Park

Trivia buffs may appreciate learning that the three kings of the Chakri dynasty—Rama V, VII, and IX—hiked up the Sadet River to carve their initials on boulders near the Sadet Falls. The park is best visited on longtail boat tours from Hat Rin or Thong Sala that drop passengers at the headwaters and wait while visitors hike three km up the river to the falls and royal signatures.

Full Moon Party

Too busy for meditation, waterfalls, and historic signatures? No problem. Most visitors to Ko Phangan yearn to learn about natural substances and their curious effects during full moon parties held monthly on both sides of Hat Rin Beach. An estimated 5,000 revelers arrive to gaze at the moon and carry on the traditions of old Goa during the high season around the Christmas holidays and in late summer July-September.

These parties have suffered in recent years from the heavy presence of Thai police who quickly arrest both Thai dealers and Western customers who break the national drug laws. The party rages on though attendants should be careful about their activities.

THONG SALA

Thong Sala—home to half of the island's 10,000 residents—serves as the main port and commercial center of the island, and primary source of tourist services such as money exchange, travel agencies, international phones, visa extensions, medical facilities, motorcycle rentals, and basic supplies from the local market.

Thong Sala consists of the pier, a small business district, and several roads that head off in different directions. Thong Sala Road connects the pier with beaches on the west coast, while another road splits north and crosses the island to Chalok Lam Bay. The other major road veers southeast of town and traces the coastline to Ban Tai and Hat Rin (Rin Beach) at the southeastern tip of the island.

Accommodations

Few visitors stay in Thong Sala except to prepare for an early morning departure. Guesthouses and hotels are scattered around town, though most travelers prefer the beachside bungalows east of city center.

Phangan Central Hotel: The first luxury hotel in Thong Sala opened in 1994 near the pier to serve midlevel tourists curious about the future alternative to Samui. Although the five-story hotel appears overly ambitious, Phangan tourism will someday turn this white elephant into a gold mine for the hotel investors. Thong Sala, tel. (077) 377068, fax (077) 377032, 350-450B fan, 800-950B a/c.

Information and Services
Thong Sala is the best place on the island to find supplies and conduct official business.

Tourist Information: Until the TAT opens an office on the island, travel information is limited to a few brochures from the Phangan Central Hotel and Songserm Travel office on Thong Sala Road.

Banks: Siam City Bank offers excellent exchange rates at their main office (weekdays 0830-1700) near Phangan Central Hotel and from their exchange booth (daily 0830-1730) at the Thong Sala pier. Currency can be changed at larger beaches, but at inferior rates.

Post Office: The GPO near Siam City Bank has poste restante, overseas mail, and other essential services. Also try the small shop across the street for packages and stamps. The postal code is 84280.

Telephone: International calls are expensive from bungalows and private shops but cheaper from authorized agents such as Cafe de la Poste, just opposite the post office. Open daily 0800-2100. 25/1 Thong Sala Rd., tel. (077) 377043.

Medical Services: Medical emergencies require evacuation to Surat Thani or Bangkok, but minor problems can be checked at Thong Sala municipal hospital, three km north of town en route to Ao Chalok Lam, or at the private medical clinic just opposite the post office. Both are open 24 hours. Thong Sala, tel. (077) 377036.

Police: At the Ban Don Sai police station, two km north on the road to Ao Chalok Lam, an English-speaking officer is on duty around the clock. Ban Don Sai, tel. (077) 377114, emergency 191.

Bovy Supermarket: Basic supplies can be picked up at the market near the pier on the road to Hat Rin. Open daily 0830-2100. Thong Sala, 44/25 Mu 1, tel. (077) 377231.

Watana Books is a small bookstore near the pier with both new and used English-language books. Open daily 0900-1800. 145 Mu 1, Tambon Ko Phangan, tel. (077) 377024.

Transportation
Thong Sala is the place for travel reservations, motorcycle rentals, and transport to beaches and coves around the island.

Boat tickets to Samui and Surat can be purchased directly at the pier or on the boat. Train and Thai Airways reservations can be made at the travel agencies just north of the pier.

Motorcycle Rental: Shops near the pier and in town rent standard motorcycles for 150-200B per day or 250-300B for MTX motocross models. Be sure to check the bike for missing parts and other problems before leaving the shop.

Local Transport: Ko Phangan can be tricky since most of the mountainous island is crossed by a limited number of paved roads and dirt tracks washed out during the rainy months. *Songtaos* serve some beaches and proceed toward others until the driver stops and tells you to walk. Longtail fares are posted on stubby masts.

SOUTH COAST BEACHES

Ko Phangan's best beaches are located in the coves and bays on the eastern and northeastern sides of the island. Beaches on the north and west coasts are narrow and brownish flats often filled with mangroves, while south coast beaches range from mediocre to decent depending on the location.

The following beaches are described counterclockwise from Thong Sala.

Accommodations
Ko Phangan has over 100 sets of bungalows concentrated mainly on the southern coast and southeastern tip of the island. Another two dozen bungalows are situated in the coves on the northwestern and northeastern regions. Many of the best beaches remain relatively undeveloped due to the lack of road transport to the isolated bays.

Simple bamboo huts with common baths and basic furniture cost 80-150B, while larger huts or bungalows with private baths and electricity cost 150-350B. A handful of more expensive places in the 500-900B price range are now appearing on a few beaches.

Accommodations during the busy months, Dec.-Feb. and July-Sept., are often booked, though villagers open their homes, and camping on the beach is safe and pleasant. Discounts of 30-50% often can be negotiated during the slower months, especially for travelers staying for an extended period.

Many of the cheaper bungalows make their profit on meals rather than rooms and expect travelers to dine in their cafes on a fairly regular basis. Ask in advance about their dining policy to avoid misunderstandings or an eviction notice.

Thong Sala Beach (Ao Bang Charu)

The beach just east of Thong Sala is somewhat muddy and uninspiring but is a convenient place to overnight to catch boats leaving the following morning. Ao Nai Wok on the other side of Thong Sala is similar in quality but often filled with travelers heading to Ko Tao or Surat Thani the next day.

Bungalows in the 80-180B price range starting from Thong Sala include Petch Cottages, Phangan Villa, Windlight, Nawlin House, Moonlight, Sun Dance, Wieng Thai, Coco, Bamboo Huts, Charm Beach Resort, Chokana Resort, First Villa, First Bay Resort, and Park Resort.

Ban Tai and Ban Khai Beaches

Beaches improve a few kilometers east of Thong Sala, near the small villages of Ban Tai and Ban Khai. Those near Ban Khai and beyond are dotted with impressive granite boulders that provide privacy in the narrow coves, and shallow waters perfect for wading and snorkeling.

The following bungalows can be reached by *songtao* from Thong Sala. Longtails from Ban Khai to Hat Rin cost 50B per person (30B per person for larger groups), though it's a beautiful one-hour walk past narrow coves filled with crystal-clear waters.

From Thong Sala, bungalows in the 80-250B price range include S.P. Resort, Pink's, Triangle Lodge, Wave House, Jup, Sabai, New Heaven, Lee Garden, Free Love, Copa, Pan Beach, Phangan Rainbow, Green Peace, Golden Beach, Sea Side Resort, Banja Beach, Thong Yang, Phangan Island, Booms, and Silver Moon.

HAT RIN

Hat Rin (Had Rin) was the first beach opened on the island and remains the most popular stop for many travelers. Hat Rin splits into two beaches, Hat Rin Nai (West) and Hat Rin Nok (East) connected by a dirt road that passes over a hilly cape.

Visitors come for the white sands and clear waters that provide fine snorkeling and sparkling vistas across to Ko Samui. Many arrive simply for a full moon party before moving off to more idyllic locations.

The problem with Hat Rin is one of overpopularity and a disregard for the environment, which threatens to turn the beachfront into an open garbage pit littered with plastic bags, discarded water bottles, coconut shells, and trash tossed into the ocean by unconcerned bungalow owners. The simple lifestyle of an earlier era has been lost to the present array of shops and restaurants that provide cheap beer, junk food, T-shirts, mind-numbing videos, moped rentals, and mushroom soups to the young backpackers and aging hippies waiting for the next full moon party.

Hat Rin may be perfect for party animals and stoners, but visitors seeking solitude and quiet reflection should avoid this beach and head directly to a more isolated cove.

Hat Rin East

Hat Rin Nok is formed by an arched cove filled with excellent sand and washed by clear waters perfect for swimming and diving. Stormy weather and large waves are common from Oct.-Feb., but conditions are pleasant the remainder of the year.

Accommodations: Hat Rin East has the greatest concentration of bungalows on the island, in all price ranges and conditions. Those near the beach tend to be packed tightly together and suffer from nightclubs that play music until the early hours. Bungalows on the northern end of the beach and back in the hills are quieter and generally less expensive than those in the central area.

Rooms average 100-200B with common bath and 200-300B with private bath. Larger bungalows cost 300-500B, depending on the season. Prices rise 30-50% during the busy months around Christmas and July-Sept. when Europeans flood the island. Room rates also skyrocket at full moons when early arrivals find accommodations; others just party until the following morning and then crash on the beach or catch a boat to a less congested beach.

Hat Rin West

The beaches on the western (or southern) side of Laem Hat Rin are narrow and the water tends to be murky, but the slower lifestyle and cheaper rooms attract many of the long-term visitors to Hat Rin. Hat Rin Nai often has rooms when Hat Rin East is filled and sometimes during full moon periods when both beaches are packed with all forms of wildlife.

Accommodations: Bungalows and huts cost 80-150B in low season and 30-50% higher during the busy months. Travelers seeking solitude and lower prices should walk west along the coast past the impressive granite boulders to a series of isolated coves dotted with inexpensive thatched bungalows priced 80-100B.

Information and Services

Hat Rin now provides many essential services in the small village located between the two beaches.

Currency Exchange: Small booths of Siam City and Krung Thai Bank provide exchange services at slightly lower rates than in Thong Sala. Open daily 0900-1700.

Visa Extension: Phanga Bay Shore Resort extends visas for a modest service charge, plus provides currency exchange at reasonable rates. Open daily 0830-2000. Hat Rin Nok, tel. (077) 725-0430.

Post Office: A licensed postal office handles outgoing mail and intends to provide poste restante services in the near future. The postal code is 84280. Open weekdays 0830-1700, Saturday 0900-1200.

International Telephone: Overseas calls from the post office cost 80-90B per minute. Open daily 0830-2100.

Police: A small booth is located midway between the two beaches near the school and Krung Thai Bank. Patrols are beefed up during the full moon parties.

Medical Services: Phangan Clinic and several other places in the village provide basic ser-

vices and can help with emergency evacuations. Open daily 0800-2200. Hat Rin, tel. (077) 723-0989.

Travel Agents: Phanthip Travel is an authorized agent of the State Railways and makes reliable reservations on Thai and Bangkok Airways. Open daily 0800-1800. Hat Rin, tel. (077) 725-0052.

Diving: Five Stars Dive on Hat Rin East rents snorkeling equipment and organizes dives to reefs around Ko Phangan.

EAST COAST BEACHES

The east coast of Ko Phangan is pocketed by isolated coves blessed with incredible sand and backed by swaying palms that form a picture-perfect paradise. The only problem is that most beaches are inaccessible by land, and few travelers are willing to camp on such remote coves.

A narrow track suitable for hiking (but too rugged for motorcycles) heads north from Hat Rin to wonderful coves at Hat Yuan, Hat Yai Nam, Hat Yao, Hat Yang, and Hat Ban Tok, where the trail veers northwest past Tham Prapat Falls to the town of Ban Nam Tok.

Sadet Beach

Hat Sadet and Thong Reng Bay to the south now have a few bungalows for the adventurous traveler.

A rugged road heads from Ban Thong Nang to Thong Reng Bay but *songtao* service is erratic and the trail is often closed during the rainy months. Most visitors arrive on boats from Hat Rin that depart each morning Sept.-April.

Accommodations: Bungalows on Ao Thong Reng include Than Wang Thong, Pra Thip, Ka Wao, and several places aptly called No Name Bungalows. All cost 80-250B.

Bungalows on Sadet Beach just north of the headlands include Nit's, Mai Pen Rai, No Name, and Sunrise Bungalows with huts 80-120B.

Thong Nai Pan Bay

Ao Thong Nai Pan is a horseshoe-shaped bay separated by rocky headlands that create two fine coves. Thong Nai Pan Yai to the south is the larger of the twin beaches, while smaller Thong Nai Pan Noi to the north features equally wonderful sand and clear waters perfect for swimming and diving.

Thong Nai Pan Yai: The more scenic of the two beaches now features almost a dozen places that cost 80-180B for basic huts and 200-300B for larger bungalows with private baths. Current choices include White Sand, Chanchit Dreamland, Nice Beach, Pingjun Resort, and Pen Bungalows.

Thong Nai Pan Noi: This somewhat smaller but striking half-moon bay (also called Thong Tapan Noi) features turquoise waters and dazzling sands backed by coconut trees shading the seaside bungalows. Buildings are arranged near the ends of the bay or elevated on cliffs overlooking the bay. Budget choices priced 100-200B include Thong Tapan Resort, Star House, Honey Bungalows, and Bio Guesthouse.

The top-end choice is **Panviman Resort** on the hillside, with a circular restaurant and 45 bungalows with ocean views. Hat Thong Nai Pan, tel. (077) 377048, Bangkok tel. (02) 587-8491, fax (02) 587-8493, 500-800B fan, 900-1,500B a/c.

NORTH COAST BEACHES

Bottle Beach (Hat Khuat)

Tucked away on the northeastern corner of Ko Phangan lies an isolated cove blessed with immaculate sands and crystalline waters.

Transportation: Hat Khuat may be the finest beach on the island and the perfect place to escape civilization, but the remote location makes access somewhat tricky for most travelers. The road from Chalok Lam remains closed to motorcycles and *songtaos* due to rivers without bridges. Few visitors attempt the three-km trail that takes two or three hours in the hot sun. Most travelers hire a longtail boat from Chalok Lam or join an organized excursion from Hat Rin.

Accommodations: Several sets of bungalows are open during the busy season but close down when business is slow and few travelers visit the isolated cove. Sea Love, Bottle Beach I, and Rock Beach Bungalows cost 100-350B depending on the season and mood of the owners. Several of the bungalows are constructed over granite boulders and reached by rather shaky bamboo walkways.

Chalok Lam Bay

The northern fishing village of Chalok Lam (Chalok Lum) faces a curving bay and blackened beach ringed with emerald-green mountains soaring in all directions. Chalok Lam is a utilitarian place filled with fishing boats and small cafes that serve local fish and calamari collected during the squid season April-Oct.

Facilities in town include shops with bicycle rentals and snorkeling equipment. Beaches near the center of town are brownish and uninspiring, though better sand is located on both ends of broad Chalok Lam Bay.

Khom Beach: Hat Khom, a semicircular bay midway between Chalok Lam and Bottle Beach, can be reached by longtail from Chalok Lam or via a three-km hike over a very rough trail. Bungalows include (yet another) No Name, Buddy, and Coral Bay with huts from 100B.

Accommodations: Simple bungalows east of town include Thai Life, Fanta, Chalok Lam Resort, Mr. Phol's, and Try Thong Resort with rooms for 100-200B. Choices west of town include Wattana Resort on a superior beach with better huts priced 120-250B.

WEST COAST BEACHES

Mae Hat Beach

West coast beaches are often disappointing places covered with brown sand or muddy mangrove, though the coral reefs, blazing sunsets, and perfect isolation compensate.

Accommodations: Bungalows in this remote corner of Phangan tend to open and close with the seasons, though a few remain in operation as travelers explore the more untouched sections of the island. The following bungalows cost 100-150B for huts with common baths and 100-150B for bungalows with private baths. Mae Hat Bungalows and Mae Hat Villa to the north are basic options, while Mae Hat Bay Resort and Island View Cabana on the southern beach offer newer chalets with private baths for 200-350B.

Ko Ma, a small islet just opposite Ban Mae Hat, has huts under 50B.

Yao Beach

Hat Yao and Hat Salat to the north are difficult to reach over the rugged roads that lead from Ban Si Thanu and prevent *songtaos* from completing the journey. Most visitors arrive on longtails from Thong Sala or Ban Si Thanu or take boats from Ao Chalok Lam.

Accommodations: Bungalows on the bay include Sandy Bay, Ibiza, Hat Yao, Blue Coral Beach, Phong Sak, Benjawan, Dream Hill, Silver Beach, Hat Thian, and several others that rise and fall with the seasons. All cost 100-150B. **Bay View Resort** on the northern stretch costs 250-600B for bungalows with fan and attached bath.

Chao Phao Beach

Chao Phao may have brownish sand dotted with mangroves, but spectacular sunsets and easy access from Thong Sala make this a popular alternative to other, more frequented beaches. A small freshwater lake lies back from the beach.

Accommodations: Bungalows facing the bay include Bovy Resort, Seetanu, Sea Flower, and Great Bay Resort at the northern end. All cost 100-150B with common bath and 180-300B with private bath. **Hat Chao Phao Resort** charges 350-500B for large bungalows with private baths and comfortable verandas.

Si Thanu Beach

South of Laem Son cape and near the town of Ban Si Thanu lies a semicircular bay with decent sand and coral beds perfect for snorkelers and divers. Si Thanu can be reached by *songtao* from Thong Sala in about 30 minutes.

Accommodations: Beachside bungalows include Loy Fah and Nantakan at the southern end of the cape, Ladda Guesthouse and Sea View near Si Thanu, and Laemson on the northern stretches. All have simple huts for 100-150B and better chalets with private baths for 180-350B.

Wok Tum Bay

Ao Wok Tum and beaches near Ban Hin Kong are easy to reach from Thong Sala and acceptable choices for visitors on short stays.

Accommodations: Bungalows on the south end of the bay include Kiat, Porn Sawan, and Tuk. All cost 100-150B depending on facilities and size of the room. The owner of **Kiat Bungalows** arranges dive boats to nearby reefs and offshore islands.

Lipstick Cabana and Hin Kong Bungalows on the northern tip of the horseshoe-shaped bay, properly known as Ao Hin Kong, are priced in the same range and within walking distance of Ban Hin Kong.

Pla Laem Beach

The four-km road heading north from Thong Sala passes several beaches lined with huts and bungalows that provide useful options for travelers heading back to Thong Sala for early morning departures.

Accommodations: A track leading from the main road leads up to Mountain View Resort and Bungtham Bungalows. Beachside choices include Beach, Cookies, Sea Scene, Chuenchit, Porn Sawan, and Darin. All cost 100-120B for basic huts or 180-350B for larger bungalows with fan and private baths.

Nai Wong Beach

Hat Nai Wong is useful for early-morning departures and an entertaining stop thanks to a boxing arena and cockfighting field in nearby Ban Nai Wong.

You can reach Nai Wong by *songtao* or by walking (about 30 minutes) from the Thong Sala pier across the concrete footbridge and then up the dirt road to the following guesthouses and bungalows.

Accommodations: Two km from the center of Thong Sala is a string of bungalows, including Phangan, Charn, Siriphun, and Tranquil Resort, where rooms cost 120-200B.

TRANSPORTATION

Ko Phangan (pronounced Ko PA-gahn, *not* Ko FAN-ghan) is 12 km north of Bophut on Samui, 25 km from Nathon, and 105 km northeast of Surat Thani.

Transportation is easy since the island can be reached from Ko Samui or directly from Surat Thani, a route that skips Ko Samui, once legendary among adventurous world travelers.

Inclusive Transport from Bangkok

The most convenient option from Bangkok is an all-inclusive package that includes all transfers and boat connections.

Overnight Train: The State Railways sells an all-inclusive package that combines an overnight train to the Phun Phin train station, bus to the Surat Thani (Ban Don) pier, and ferry to Thong Sala on Ko Phangan.

Tickets should be purchased well in advance at the Hualampong station or from an authorized agent in Bangkok. Train packages cost 50-80B more than patching together your own transportation, a modest surcharge that eliminates the hassle of separate bookings.

Private Bus: Travel agents around Khao San Road sell bus tickets to Ko Phangan for 280-560B, depending on the quality of the bus and ferry. Buses leave Banglampoo 1800-2000 and reach the island the following day at 1400.

Boats from Surat Thani

Transport options include direct boats from the mainland to Thong Sala on Ko Phangan, and boats that first stop on Ko Samui before continuing across to Phangan.

Departures and prices change with the seasons. Tickets can be purchased and schedules checked at Songserm Travel, Phanthip Tours, and the Phangan Ferry Company in Surat Thani.

Direct Boats: A ferry operated by Phangan Ferry Company departs daily at 0915 from Don Sak pier and arrives on Ko Phangan at 1200. The fare is 120-180B each way. The night train from Bangkok is met by a Phangan Ferry Company bus that picks up passengers and departs Phun Phin at 0700 for the Don Sak pier. Another company bus leaves at 0800 from its office in Surat Thani near the Ban Don pier.

Night Boat: The cheapest direct option is the Songserm night boat which departs from Surat Thani municipal harbor at 2300 and arrives at Ko Phangan at 0600. Fares are 100B lower deck with straw cushions, 140B upper deck with mattresses and pillows.

Boats via Ko Samui: Boats that first stop at Ko Samui include the Songserm express and the Island Jet.

Express Boat: Songserm express boats depart from the Tha Thong pier near Pak Nam, six km northeast of Surat Thani, daily at 0800 and 1430 and take two and a half hours to reach Nathon on Ko Samui. The express unloads passengers and then continues to Ko Phangan, arriving at 1130 and 1800. The 150B fare includes a bus to the pier from the Songserm office at 0730 and 1400.

Island Jet: The Island Jet leaves at 0830 from Tha Thong pier and takes one and a half hours to reach Nathon on Ko Samui. After picking up new passengers, the jet leaves Nathon and reaches Thong Sala on Ko Phangan at 1100. Tickets cost 180-250B and include the

bus ride to the pier from the Island Jet office on Talad Mai Road in Surat Thani.

Boats from Ko Samui

Transport options from Ko Samui include the express and the jet boat from Nathon, and fishing boats from Bophut and Big Buddha Beaches on the north coast.

From Nathon: Songserm express boats leave from the Nathon pier daily at 1000 and 1600 and take 50 minutes to reach Thong Sala on Ko Phangan. The fare is 80-150B one way. Contact Songserm or Phanthip Travel in Nathon for tickets and current departure schedules.

The Island Jet leaves Nathon daily at 1020 and takes just 30 minutes to Ko Phangan. The fare is 80-140B depending on class.

From North Coast Beaches: Converted fishing boats from the northern beaches provide convenient alternatives for travelers staying nearby or coming up from Chaweng Beach.

Fishing trawlers leave Bophut Beach daily at 0930 and 1530 for Hat Rin Beach on the southeastern tip of Ko Phangan. The fare is 80-150B and the crossing takes about 45 minutes. During the high season months Jan.-Sept., boats sometimes continue up the eastern coast to Thong Nai Pan Bay at the northern tip. Passengers can request to be dropped at other beaches such as Yuan, Thian, Yao, Yang, Nam Tok, or Kruat.

Another fishing boat heading to Hat Rin departs from the east end of Bang Rak Beach (Big Buddha) daily at 1030 and 1530 depending on the season and number of passengers.

A fishing boat also departs Mae Nam Beach daily at noon during the high tourist season. Fares are 80B to Hat Rin and 150B to Thong Nai Pan Bay in the north.

Boats from Chumphon

You can make an intriguing back-door approach by boat from Chumphon via the tiny island of Ko Tao. See "Chumphon" in the Southern Thailand Introduction for more information on this alternative route.

Boat from Ko Tao

Boats leave daily depending on weather conditions from Ko Tao and take about three hours to complete the 47-km journey to Thong Sala. The fare is 180-250B during the high season but rises sharply if there are too few passengers.

KO TAO

Tiny Ko Tao is a turtle-shaped island 38 km north of Ko Phangan and 58 km from Ko Samui. Named after its peculiar shape, which resembles a kidney bean or abstract turtle shell, Ko Tao measures just seven km long and three km wide, for a grand total of 21 square km. The population of 750 is occupied with coconuts, fishing, and bungalow operations that attract a steady trickle of world travelers. The island is chiefly known for its outstanding coral beds off nearby Ko Hang Tao and Ko Nang Yuan, and for a half dozen beaches with fairly good sand and crystal-clear waters.

SCUBA DIVING

Dive experts regard Ko Tao as the best dive site in the Gulf of Thailand and almost the equal of the more famous islands north of Phuket near the Burmese border. Due to its isolated location well removed from coastal runoffs, Ko Tao and near-

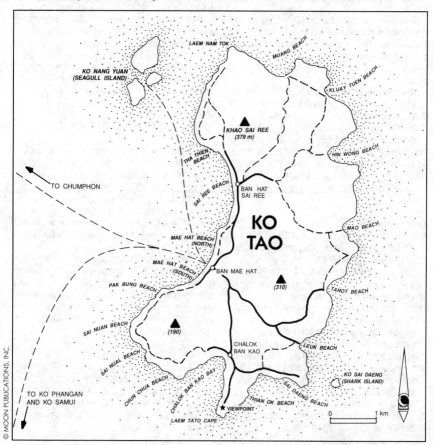

by islets are surrounded by exceptionally clear waters that provide ideal conditions for coral growth and large numbers of reef fish.

Ko Nang Yuan

The three islands off the northwest corner of Ko Tao form a mini-archipelago encircled by a ring of coral and connected by sandbars during low tides.

Ko Nang Yuan ("Seagull Island"), also called Ko Hang Tao, once served as a detention center for political prisoners who remained exiled on the island until royal pardon or death by malaria. One survivor, Phraya Saraphaiphat, described his experiences in the novel *My Nightmare.*

The island provides an ideal setting for dive certification due to its shallow waters and protection from the southwest monsoons that lash the region June-Oct. Hikers can enjoy splendid views from the peak on the southernmost island.

Accommodations: Ko Nang Yuan Bungalows on the southern island is often filled with divers on escorted packages from Ko Samui or Ban Mae Hat. 10/1 Tambon Ko Tao, tel. (01) 726-0085, 300B with common bath, 700B for bungalows with private baths and balconies.

Transportation: Boats leave Mae Hat pier daily at 1000 and 1600; the fare is 20B to the bungalow office and restaurant on the middle island.

Other Dive Sites

Many of the dive sites near Ko Tao have both Thai and English names describing something unique about the destination.

Hin Kaew (White Rock): A few hundred meters southwest of Ko Nang Yuan lies a collection of gigantic submerged boulders covered with corals that appear white when viewed from the surface.

Ko Sai Daeng (Shark Island): Just off the southeastern tip of Ko Tao is a small granite island that vaguely resembles a stony shark fin, surrounded by branching acropora corals, bushy antipatharians, and waving gorgonian fans.

Hin Bai (Sail Rock): Some 10 km southeast of Ko Tao are limestone pinnacles that rise over 30 meters from the bottom of the ocean floor to just over the surface of the water.

Dive Services

Dives can be arranged with dive companies on Ko Samui or the dive shops near the pier on Ko Tao. Among the larger operations are Master Divers, Big Blue, and Dolphin. Another PADI outlet to the left of the pier is Samui International Diving School, Mu 2 Tambon Ko Tao, tel. (01) 725-0828 or (077) 421056. Samui can help with dive packages, equipment rentals, bungalows, and maps of the island. Open daily 0800-2000.

Dive prices are standardized on Ko Tao. Certified divers with equipment pay 350-500B for tanks and boat transport, or 600-800B per dive with equipment rental. A one-day introductory course costs 1,200-1,800B for one dive and 2,200-2,800B for two dives. The four-day certification course including all equipment, transportation, meals, and instruction costs 6,500-8,500B depending on the season.

Snorkel equipment can be rented for 150B per day from the dive shops, which also organize full-day snorkeling tours around the island for an additional 180B per person.

ACCOMMODATIONS

Most bungalows are concentrated on the western and southern coasts, with a few places tucked away in the isolated coves on the eastern shores.

Simple thatched huts with common bath cost 80-150B or 120-250B during the busy months around Christmas and July-September. Larger wood or brick bungalows with private baths and decent furniture cost 200-300B or 400-600B during the peak seasons.

All bungalows have attached cafes that visitors are expected to patronize during their stay, since meals provide the bulk of profits for most bungalow owners. Electricity delivered on power lines or provided by generators operates in the evenings 1800-midnight; bring a flashlight for late-night walks.

Arrival

Rooms are in short supply around Christmas and in late summer when Europeans flood the island. Finding a room in the low season can also be tricky since many bungalows close down, especially those on remote beaches not served by public transportation.

Boat passengers are met at the pier by hotel touts, *songtaos,* and longtail boats. *Songtaos* cost 20B to all accessible beaches such as Chalok Ban Kao, Thianok, Sai Daeng, Luk, Tanot, and Sai Ree and Tha Thien just north of Mae Hat. An entire *songtao* can be chartered for 100B.

Beaches and bays inaccessible due to lousy roads are served by longtail boats that charge 20B to west coast beaches, 30B to Chalok Ban Kao and Ao Sai Daeng, and 50B to beaches on the eastern shores.

A sensible idea—especially during the high season—is to hook up with a bungalow tout and accept his offer of transportation. Travelers can also walk north along the footpath for 10-20 minutes to the bungalows facing beautiful Sai Ree Beach.

BAN MAE HAT

Ban Mae Hat ("Mother Beach Town"), the principal town and arrival point for all passengers, has evolved in less than five years from a backwater village without electricity or telephones to a relatively modern town offering most of the necessary travel services.

Information and Services
All of the following services are within walking distance of the pier and adjacent market.

Currency Exchange: Traveler's checks can be cashed at local moneychangers, but rates will be lower than on Ko Samui or the mainland. Credit cards are accepted by dive companies and most travel agencies.

Post Office: The GPO, just south of the pier, is open daily 0830-1700.

International Telephone: Overseas calls can be made at the post office 0830-1700 and around the clock from private outlets in Mae Hat and Chalok Ban Kao.

Medical Services: A public health center and a private medical clinic are located on a side road just east of the pier. Both are open daily 0830-1700.

Travel Agencies: Nang Yuan Travel Service and several other agencies near the pier sell combination tickets to Bangkok and Phuket, make air and train reservations, and arrange passage to nearby dive destinations.

Motorcycle Rentals: Shops in Mae Hat rent motorcycles for 200B per day, though the road system is primitive and dirt roads often disintegrate into sandy trails almost impassable on motorcycles.

WEST COAST BEACHES

Mae Hat Beach
Several bungalows are just a five- to 10-minute walk north of Mae Hat pier, useful stops for travelers taking boats the following morning.

Bungalows from south to north include Crystal, Dum Bungalows, Queen Resort, and Tommy Resort.

Sai Nuan Beach
Several simple bungalows are just south of the pier on the southern extension of Mae Beach. The trail continues another two km past a series of headlands to Sai Nuan Beach at the southwestern tip of the island.

The first two bungalows are 10 minutes from Ban Mae Hat; the remainder are on Sai Nuan Beach and require transport in a longtail boat.

Bungalows from north to south include Paew Bungalows, Coral Beach, Sai Thong, Siam Cookie, Cha, Tao, Thong Villa.

Sai Ree Beach
Just beyond the cape at the north end of Mae Hat lies the longest beach on the island, backed by coconut palms that lean toward the gently arching bay. The two-km stretch of sand is perfectly set for sunset-gazers and offers decent snorkeling over the shallow coral reefs. The following bungalows are a 10- to 20-minute walk or a 20B *songtao* ride from the pier: A.C. Resort, Ko Tao Cabana, Sai Ree Cottages, Hat Sai Ree Villa, and O Chai.

Tha Thien Beach
Almost a half dozen sets of bungalows are located on the rocky headlands three km north of town, just beyond the final curve of Sai Ree Beach. Some of the places face the water, while others are elevated on the rocky hillside and gaze over the three-pronged beach of Ko Nang Yuan.

Bungalows from south to north are Golden Cape, Silver Cliff, Sun Lodge, Eden Resort, Mahana Bay, and C.F.T. Bungalows.

SOUTH COAST BEACHES

Chalok Ban Kao Bay
Perhaps the prettiest bay on the island is two km southeast of Ban Mae Hat near the village of Chalok Ban Kao. This horseshoe ring of squeaky white sand has sparkling waters so clear they mirror the outline of the surrounding cliffs.

The sheer beauty of the bay makes it among the most popular destinations on the island and keeps the bungalows packed during the high season months and holiday seasons. During these periods, hook up with a bungalow tout at the pier who promises an available room in his place.

Bungalows from west to east include View Point, Taraporn, Black Rock, Laem Klong, Nang Nuan, Sunshine, Buddha View, Carabao, K. See, and Ko Tao Cottages.

Mian Ok and Sai Daeng Beach
Just east of Laem Tato is another large bay followed by the final beach on the south coast.

Bungalows from west to east include Rocky Resort, Khuan Thong, and Kiet.

EAST COAST BEACHES

Several small but picturesque bays pocket the east coast of the island, long the neglected stepsister to the more accessible beaches on the west and south coasts. Each bay now has a few bungalows that remain open during the busy season but may be closed in the slower months.

Many of the dirt paths to the following beaches have been improved and are now wide enough for *songtaos*. At present, Leuk and Tanot beaches are connected via dirt roads, and the remainder of the bays to the north will probably be opened in the next few years.

Visitors seeking to reach these remote coves should find a bungalow tout at the pier who will provide transport in a *songtao* or longtail boat.

The following beaches are listed from south to north.

Leuk and Tanot Beaches
The completion of the dirt road from Ban Mae Hat will encourage bungalow owners to open new spots in these once remote bays.

Bungalows include Ao Leuk Resort, Tanot Bay Resort, Diamond, Sunrise, and Laem Thian.

Mao, Hin Wong, and Muang Bays
Bungalows on these isolated bays have opened and closed with the years, including Sahat Huts on Hin Wong and Mango Bay Resort on Ao Ma Muang (Mango Bay).

Several huts have reopened on Hin Wong Beach, and bungalows on the other bays may open in the near future.

TRANSPORTATION

Ko Tao is midway between Ko Samui and the mainland town of Chumphon. Direct boat service is available from Chumphon, Surat Thani, and Ko Phangan; service from Ko Samui is via Ko Phangan.

From Bangkok
Travel agencies on Khao San Road sell combination tickets for 450-650B that include an a/c minivan to Chumphon and the overnight boat to Ko Tao. Much less expensive is a third-class train to Chumphon and slow boat to the island for around 300B.

From Chumphon
Ko Tao can be reached by boat from Surat Thani, Ko Samui, or Ko Phangan, though some prefer to first visit Ko Tao from Chumphon and then head south to Phangan and Samui.

A large fishing boat leaves from a pier 10 km east of Chumphon at midnight, costs 200-250B, and takes six hours to reach Ko Tao. The pier is served by a final *songtao* at 1800 and by tourist vans that leave around 2200. Tickets are sold at Infinity Travel, Chumphon Information Center, Chumphon Travel Service, and Tiw's Cafe.

A speedboat departs daily at 0800 from the Tha Yang Pier near Chumphon harbor, costs 400-500B, and reaches Ko Tao in under two hours. Chumphon travel agencies can provide more information.

From Surat Thani
Several times each week a boat leaves Tha Thong pier near Surat Thani at 2300 and arrives at Ko Tao the following day around 0600. Tickets

are sold by Songserm, Phanthip Travel, and agencies near the municipal pier in Ban Don.

From Ko Samui
All boats from Ko Samui stop on Ko Phangan before continuing to Ko Tao. The Songserm express boat leaves Nathon at 1030, reaches Ko

Phangan at 1130, and picks up passengers for the final segment of the journey to Ko Tao.

From Ko Phangan
The Songserm express boat leaves Thong Sala at noon and takes three hours to reach Ban Mae Hat on Ko Tao.

SOUTH OF KO SAMUI

NAKHON SI THAMMARAT

One of Thailand's oldest and most historic sites, Nakhon Si Thammarat (Nakhon) is a prosperous city known for its bell-shaped *chedi* at Wat Mahathat and a large collection of Thai art in the National Museum.

The rather undistinguished town is divided into three districts. To the south is the old city with Wat Pra Mahathat, the National Museum, and a few other sights worth a brief visit. North of the old city walls is the hot and dusty new town with the train station, travel agencies, and all the hotels and restaurants. East of town on the highway to Thung Song are the bus terminal and a long string of monotonous concrete buildings that form the newer economic heart of the city.

History
Nakhon first served in the early Christian era as the Hindu capital of the Tambralinga Empire at a city-state called Ligor. Sometime in the 8th century, Ligor fell under the suzerainty of the Srivijaya Empire, which ruled the Malay archipelago from its lost capital in Sumatra. At the end of the 10th century, a Tambralinga king conquered the Mon Kingdom of Lopburi (Lavo) and placed his son, Suryavarman I (1011-1050), on the Khmer throne at Angkor. Ligor became a vassal state of the Khmer Kingdom until a brief spell of independence in 1250 and final incorporation in 1292 into the Sukothai Kingdom.

By the early 13th century, Nakhon Si Thammarat (or Muang Nakhon) had become the leading economic power in the region and an important religious center which promoted the Sri Lankan school of Hinayana Buddhism. Subsequently embraced by the rulers of Sukothai, Hi-

nayana (Theravada Buddhism) remains the official religion of Thailand.

Wat Mahathat
Wat Pra Mahathat Woramahaviharn—the most sanctified and architecturally significant monument in southern Thailand—was constructed over 800 years ago by King Sri Thammasokaraj in conjunction with his founding of Nakhon Si Thammarat. The religious significance of Wat Mahathat is attributed to its former possession of the Pra Buddha Singh, a historical image now kept in a small modern chapel wedged between two administrative buildings near the clock tower.

Chedi: Wat Mahathat (also called Wat Prathat Muang Khon) centers on a towering, bell-shaped *chedi* of Sinhalese style crowned with a solid-gold spire that weighs over 200 kg. Over the centuries, the 77-meter *chedi* has been restored and enlarged by royalty of both the Ayuthaya and Rattanakosin periods, including a massive 1992 project sponsored by Princess Sirindorn.

Surrounding the reconstructed *chedi* is a vast cloister filled with Buddha images and elephant heads derived from Sinhalese inspiration. Two symmetrical chapels hidden deep inside the monument feature standing Sukothai-style Buddhas and a narrow stairway which leads to an inner sanctum.

Viharn Luang: South of the central *chedi* is Viharn Luang with a beautiful red ceiling held aloft by unadorned pillars angled like a trapezium, an architectural canon derived from Ayuthaya but rarely carried to such an extreme. The central image smiles, while 16 Buddhas in various styles are displayed in a rear room.

Temple Museum: North of the *chedi* is another chapel that serves as a museum and repository for donations from pilgrims. Aside from the bric-a-brac and silver trees called *bunga*

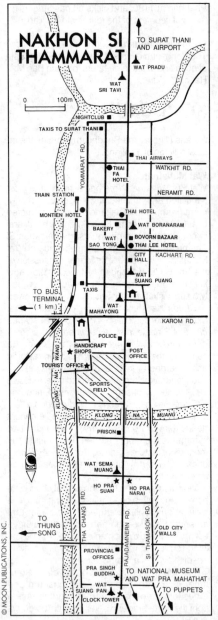

mas in Malaysia, the museum features several worthwhile pieces, including a standing stone Buddha of the Dvaravati Period and a seated Buddha in Srivijaya style.

Wat Mahathat is two km south of the new town center and about 300 meters south of the clock tower shown on the map. Take a *songtao* or make the long hike past several minor temples and remains of the old city walls.

National Museum

One of the most comprehensive arrays of artifacts in the south is displayed in the six rooms of the Nakhon Si Thammarat National Museum. The collections are arranged in chronological order, with the finest pieces shown in the third room on the left.

Front Rooms: The first room is devoted to prehistoric artifacts such as the largest Dong Son kettledrum uncovered in Thailand, and a 5th-century stone Vishnu considered the oldest of its type in the country. Bronze Buddha images in the next room display typical traits of the Nakhon Si Thammarat school: exaggerated eyebrows, bulbous eyelids, distinctive neck folds, and long and narrow torsos.

Rear Room: Displayed in the back room are several extremely fine sculptures, including a centerpiece 9th-century Vishnu stone image in the Pallava style, and two Vishnu attendants and Ganesha images derived from Indian prototypes. Discovered near Takua Pa and once abandoned in a weedy grove, the curious history of the Takua Pa is related with photographs mounted on the wall. Also note the rare silver standing Buddha and Shiva incarnated as Nataraja.

Second Floor: Upstairs rooms are devoted to ceramics from various Thai dynasties and folkcrafts such as shadow puppets, basketry, theater costume ornaments, textiles, and a fascinating display of children's games.

The museum is two and a half km south of the new town center and about 200 meters beyond Wat Mahathat. Minitrucks travel there frequently from the new town.

Wat Suang Puang

Several other temples are located on Rajadamnern Road between the downtown hotels and Wat Mahathat in the old city. Behind a peaceful garden sits an immense Buddha and a modern *chedi* constructed in classic Nakhon style, with tiny trees sprouting from the spire.

Mosque

Beautifully constructed with green cupolas, gray minarets, and elegant balustrades, the small mosque near Na Wang Canal is among the most attractive in southern Thailand.

City Walls

The ancient walls and moats that once surrounded the "City of Priests" are now being reconstructed to the original dimensions of 460 by 2,230 meters. Much of the old brickwork was used to construct the prison near Klong Na Muang.

Ho Pra Suan

Nakhon Si Thammarat originated as a Hindu community that supplied many of Thailand's first Brahman court astrologers, who had considerable influence on contemporary Thai Buddhism. Even today, Brahmans from Nakhon participate in the annual Hindu ploughing ceremony held at Sanam Luang in Bangkok. The Hindu legacy is reflected in the dancing Shiva (Suan), stone lingam, and Ganesha image displayed in the modern shrine of Ho Pra Suan. Also note the miniature Giant Swing in the courtyard, formerly used to honor the Hindu gods.

Ho Pra Narai across the street is another modern Hindu shrine with a life-sized Vishnu identical to the original image displayed in the National Museum.

Pra Singh Buddha

Although of little artistic merit, Pra Singh Buddha is among the most sacred and revered images in all of Thailand. The history of the image is a mystery. According to Buddhist tradition, the statue was cast in Sri Lanka and brought to Sukothai by the king of Ligor (ancient Nakhon) and, after various vicissitudes, moved to Chiang Mai in the 16th century. The most puzzling feature is the existence of three similar images—one in Nakhon Si Thammarat, a second at Wat Pra Singh in Chiang Mai, and a third in the National Museum in Bangkok. The bottom line is that the three images differ in size and style, lack Sinhalese influence, and are probably local works dating from the Srivijaya Period.

Even more intriguing are the adjacent complementary Buddhas fashioned from silver and copper.

Information and Services

Nakhon Si Thammarat ("Glorious City of the Dead") or Nagara Sri Dhammaraja ("City of the Sacred Dharma Kings") is under heavy promotion by tourism officials who have opened an office in the city park a few blocks south of the train station.

Tourist Office: The new TAT office behind the sports field dishes out colorful pamphlets, maps, and useful tips on nearby beaches and national parks. Other areas covered by the office include Phattalung and Trang. Open daily 0830-1630. Sanam Na Muang, Rajadamnern Rd., tel. (075) 346515, fax (075) 346517.

INTO THE SHADOWS

*n*akhon is known for leather puppet plays called *nang talung*. Shadow puppets were introduced to Thailand during the Ayuthaya Period and gained great popularity in both Phattalung and Nakhon Si Thammarat. Several different styles developed over the centuries. *Nang yai* puppets were very large, nonarticulated pieces brightly painted for daytime performances, or transparent versions used for night shows. Smaller *nang talung* images featured articulated arms, legs, and even genitals. Both versions were manipulated by highly talented puppet masters called *nai nang talung* who sang and spoke the dialogue in various voices, and were accompanied by a small ensemble of gongs, drums, cymbals, wooden clappers, *chatri* drums, and a Javanese oboe. Performances began around 1800 and continued until around 0600 the next morning.

Today, *nang yai* puppetry is almost a lost art aside from troupes at Wat Khanom in Ratchaburi Province and Wat Sawang Armon in Singburi. *Nang talung* is almost single-handedly promoted by an old master named Suchat Sapsin, who demonstrates the ancient artform daily in his house in Nakhon Si Thammarat. Performances are occasionally given at Wat Mahathat during temple festivals, and on the grounds of city hall under the patronage of the Southern Artists Association.

Post Office: The GPO is near the tourist office and opposite the police station. Postal code is 80000. Open weekdays 0830-1630 and weekends 0900-1200. Rajadamnern Rd., tel. (075) 356130.

International Telephone: An international phone center is on the second floor of the main post office. Open daily 0800-1800. Rajadamnern Rd., tel. (075) 356015.

Shopping

Nakhon is known throughout Thailand for its nielloware *(krueang tom)*, baskets woven from superfine grass *(yan lipao)*, and leather puppets. Perhaps in an attempt to improve the reputation of Nakhon—once considered the gangster capital of the country—several handicraft centers have recently opened, and leather puppets are now being produced by master craftspeople.

Bovorn Bazaar: A popular collection of handicraft stalls and renovated cafes is located in the center of town near the hotels and cinemas. Open daily 0900-2200. 1106 Rajadamnern Rd.

Handicraft Shops: Another concentration of handicraft shops selling nielloware, colorful baskets, bronze metalware, betel nut boxes, and shadow puppets centers on a street behind the tourist office and the sports field. Check for TAT-approved vendors such as Thai Handicraft Centre, Nabin House, and Manat Crafts. Open daily 0900-1800. Tha Chang Rd.

Leather Puppets: Suchat Sapsin—one of Thailand's most talented puppet masters—welcomes visitors to his modest workshop near Wat Mahathat and the National Museum. His handcrafted puppets are sold at reasonable cost; ask him about upcoming performances or fees for a private demonstration. Open daily 0900-1700. 110/18 Si Thammasok, Soi 3.

Bookstores: English-language guidebooks, magazines, and maps are sold at the store near the train station. Open daily 0800-2000. 1415/2 Neramit Rd., tel. (075) 356172.

The Book Garden: Suan Nang Seu is a nonprofit bookstore that specializes in literature on local history, national politics, fine arts, and religion. The store resides in a southern Thai-style wooden house constructed without nails in 1888 to successively serve as a Chinese medical clinic, opium den, brothel, and now bookstore that sponsors art exhibits and Dhamma lectures. Open daily 1000-2000. 1116 Rajadamnern Rd.

Festivals

Nakhon is the religious capital of the south and therefore an important center for Buddhist festivals, celebrated in the "City of Monks" with awesome enthusiasm.

Hae Pha Khun That: Pilgrims arrive from all over Thailand to pay homage to the relics of the Buddha enshrined at Wat Mahathat and walk around the temple carrying a sacred yellow cloth measuring over 300 meters long. The festival is held in the third lunar month (February or March).

Chak Phra Pak Tai: A southern Thai festival held in Nakhon, Songkhla, and Surat Thani that includes a ritualistic parading of Buddha images to raise funds for temple renovation, and evening performances of *nang talung* and *lakhon*. Chak Phra Pak Tai does not take place on a fixed schedule.

Tambon Duan Sip: A 15-day festival held to placate dead relatives condemned to hell but granted a brief visit back home to haunt the living. These unhappy and potentially dangerous spirits are kept amused with merit-making ceremonies in the temples and nightly performances of shadow puppets, traditional dance, and modern Thai pop. This festival takes place in the 10th lunar month (October or November).

Accommodations

Modern-day Nakhon is built alongside a single road, which makes most temples, hotels, and transportation facilities easy to find. Visitors arriving by train disembark within walking distance of all the following hotels. The bus terminal is one km west of town on Hwy. 4015. Motorcycle taxis to city center cost 15B; *songtaos* cost 5B.

Thai Lee Hotel: A newer budget place with large rooms and clean baths just a few steps away from Bovorn Bazaar. 1130 Rajadamnern Rd., tel. (075) 356948, 140-220B.

Thai Fa Hotel: Unimpressive from the outside, but this older hotel is relatively clean, very cheap, and surrounded by cafes and street vendors. 1751 Charoen Vithi Rd., tel. (075) 356727, 120-180B.

Thai Hotel: Nakhon's largest hotel is divided into an older and cheaper wing to the right of the main lobby and a more expensive section entered just opposite the small bakery. Rooms are large and clean but can be noisy from the nonstop street traffic. Ask for a room facing the inner courtyard or stay on the upper floors. Also, check out the lounge act in their unbelievably dark Thai Cafe. 1373 Rajadamnern Rd., tel. (075) 341515, fax (075) 341512, 350-450B old wing, 350-550B new wing, 450-650B a/c.

Montien Hotel: Adjacent to the train station is a 110-room hotel with comfortable rooms above a rather grim lobby. Look for the sign that reads Mun Tien Hotel. 1509 Yommarat Rd., tel. (075) 341908, fax (075) 345560, 450-650B a/c.

Restaurants

Nakhon compensates somewhat for its dismal collection of hotels with a better range of restaurants that serve regional specialities such as fiery southern curries, Muslim breads *(roti),* and fresh prawns raised in the hundreds of nearby prawn farms.

Sichon (Sinocha) Bakery: Start your day with freshly baked sweets from the cafe just opposite the Thai Hotel. Open daily 0600-1800. Pak Nakhon Rd., tel. (053) 341705. Inexpensive.

Krua Nakhon: This popular spot inside Bovorn Bazaar is one of the few cafes in Nakhon with an Indian rubber tree rising on the grounds beside the rustic pavilion. Excellent atmosphere, decent service, and a wide selection of regional specialities such as southern rice plates *(khao yam),* spicy fish curries dashed with ginger and bamboo *(kaeng tai pla),* curried noodles *(khanom jin)* served with a plate of crispy raw vegetables *(pak ruan),* and several versions of coconut milk custards *(khanom wan).* Note the early closing time. Open daily 0700-1500. Bovorn Bazaar, 1106 Rajadamnern Rd. Inexpensive.

Ban Lakhon: Tucked away in the back of Bovorn Bazaar is an old, renovated house that serves up good Thai dishes on open verandas. Open daily 1100-2200. Bovorn Bazaar, 1106 Rajadamnern Rd. Inexpensive.

Hao Coffee: Another Bovorn Bazaar winner that brews up international coffees, exotic teas, and Hokien-style coffee served with a tea chaser. Open daily 0600-2200. Bovorn Bazaar, 1106 Rajadamnern Rd. Inexpensive.

Rot **Vendors:** After a meal at Krua Nakhon and coffee at Hao's, try one of the splendid *rotis* prepared by the street vendors at the entrance to Bovorn Bazaar. The freshly grilled breads can be filled with your choice of bananas, eggs, southern-style curries, or various types of meats mixed with local vegetables. Open daily 1800-2200. Bovorn Bazaar, 1106 Rajadamnern Rd. Inexpensive.

Transportation

Nakhon Si Thammarat is 780 km south of Bangkok, 125 km south of Surat Thani, and 122 km northeast of Trang.

Train: Nakhon Si Thammarat is connected by a trunk route from the interior town of Khao Chum Thong, 30 km west of Nakhon. Direct trains from Bangkok leave at 0835 and 1730. Otherwise, get off the train at Khao Chum Thong and continue to Nakhon by local bus.

Bus: Buses from Surat Thani, Trang, and Bangkok terminate at the bus station about one km west of the hotels. Motorcycle taxis and minitrucks head to city-center hotels. Bus departures are sporadic in the late afternoon, so most travelers take a share taxi from the taxi station shown on the map.

Share Taxi: Taxis shared by three or four passengers are faster than buses at about a 50% price premium. The share taxi terminal is on Yommarat Road one block north of the mosque.

PHATTALUNG AND VICINITY

Phattalung, better known as Muang Luang among southerners, is a small provincial town situated between verdant ricefields and towering limestone mountains pocked with cave temples and meditation grottoes. Although an uninspiring destination, Phattalung is renowned among Thais as the home of shadow plays, *norah* dance, waterfowl at nearby Thale Noi, and a geological landscape somewhat similar to Phangnga Bay's. The morning market north of the Ho Fah Hotel is one of the best in the south—a photographer's dream since produce merchants display their goods outside the covered enclosure.

Wat Kuhasawan

Located inside the limestone peak west of town and once used by Srivijayan monks, Wat Kuhasawan features a lower cave packed with old votive tablets dating from the 8th-11th centuries and more than 40 highly stylized statues of monks, gurus, and Buddhas. Dozens of monkeys roam the grounds and beg for peanuts near the burial sites carved in the steep terrain.

A hillside trail leads up to another cave filled with seated and reclining statues, offering excellent views over Phattalung and nearby Khao Ok Talu.

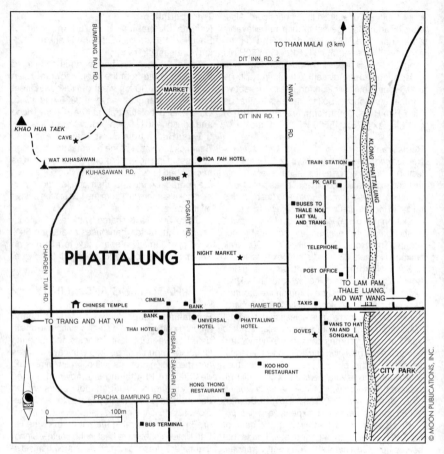

Tham Malai

Wat Tham Malai, three km northeast of Phattalung, features illuminated grottoes filled with stalagmites, and endless views from the Chinese shrines at the peak.

The grotto is flanked by two limestone peaks. Khao Ok Talu ("Broken Chest Mountain") on the right and Khao Hua Taek ("Broken Head Mountain") on the left are named after a legendary struggle between two jealous women over their adulterous lover. Their resulting wounds—a broken chest and broken head—somewhat resemble the geological peculiarities of the limestone peaks.

Wat Wang

Wat Wang, seven km east of Phattalung on the road to Thale Luang, was constructed simultaneously with the establishment of Phattalung during the reign of King Rama III. The temple once served as the venue for an oath ceremony in which local officials drank consecrated water and pledged allegiance to the authorities in Bangkok.

The chief draw of the reconstructed chapel is the outstanding murals painted by Rattanakosin artists in the late 18th century. Considered as precious as those of Wat Pra Keo in

Bangkok, the murals of Wat Wang complement the beautifully carved sermon seat donated by King Rama V and the array of gilded Buddhas on the central altar.

Lam Pam and Thale Luang

A small fishing village called Lam Pam hugs the banks of Thale Luang, a freshwater lagoon that forms the northern end of Songkhla Lake. Vendors at nearby Hat Saen Suk Lumphum ("Lumpum Beach of Happiness") sell freshwater specialties and rent beach chairs for an afternoon of escape. You can hire boats to visit the nearby islands of Ko Si and Ko Ha, where hundreds of swallows create the highly prized nests used in Chinese soups. Accommodations are available in bamboo bungalows at Lumpum Resort.

Lam Pam and Thale Luang, eight km east of Phattalung, can be reached by minitruck from the Phattalung canal.

Thale Noi Waterbird Sanctuary

Top draw among the natural wonders near Phattalung is Thale Noi, Thailand's largest waterfowl park, which hosts some 200 species of birds in the vast lagoon Jan.-April. Though it resembles a swamp in the Everglades, Thale Noi ("Small Sea") is actually a freshwater lake filled with floating lotuses and grasses called *don kok* and *krachood*. Birds use the grasses to construct their nests, while nearby villagers weave the reeds into bags, hats, and brightly colored mats.

Each year Jan.-April, Thale Noi hosts an estimated 100,000 birds, which migrate from Siberia to escape the cold and to breed in the vast and reedy swamp. Among the more common species are the long-legged *nok ikang* and a redheaded duck called *nok pet daeng.*

Visitors can hire longtail boats for about 150B and conduct a two-hour tour of the lake. The birds are liveliest in the early morning 0500-0700, and most plentiful during March and April when the waters recede. An observation platform is located in the middle of the lake.

The 475-square-km park is administered by the Wildlife Conservation Division of the Forestry Department, which maintains four large shelters for visitors.

Thale Noi is 32 km northeast of Phattalung and can be reached in about one hour by local bus.

Accommodations

Phattalung Hotel: The cheapest spot in town is entered through the bird and fish shop on the ground floor though rooms are only tolerable and the owner speaks little English. 43 Ramet Rd., tel. (074) 611078, 100-150B.

Thai Hotel: The best choice in Phattalung has large rooms with private baths, friendly managers, and a small coffee shop with nightly entertainment. Good value. 14 Disara Sakarin Rd., tel. (074) 611636, 160-200B fan, 350-420B a/c.

Hoa Fah Hotel: Another reasonable place, with the popular Diana Cafe located on the ground floor. 28-30 Kuhasawan Rd., tel. (074) 611645, 160-220B fan, 350-420B a/c.

Restaurants

Inexpensive foodstalls are found inside the night market that spreads across both sides of the alley between Posart and Ubon Nusorn Roads. **PK Cafe** is a handy place to snack while waiting for a train. **Diana Cafe** in the Hoa Fah Hotel offers good food and cabaret songbirds decked out in gold lamé and red sequins.

Koo Hoo and **Hong Thong** restaurants are Chinese spots that specialize in seafood caught in the inland sea. Hong Thong is recommended for its spicy crab claws, catfish fried with chili and basil, and freshwater perch steamed with mushrooms and pineapple.

Transportation

Phattalung is 840 km south of Bangkok, 95 km north of Hat Yai, and 57 km east of Trang.

Train: Phattalung is on the principal northside train route that connects Bangkok with Hat Yai and the Malaysian border. Train travel from the north is somewhat difficult unless you happen to be at the Phum Phin train station near Surat Thani, but the train ride north from Hat Yai passes through some of the most spectacular and undisturbed agricultural scenery in southern Thailand. Trains depart Hat Yai four times 1400-1650.

Train schedules are posted on the walls inside the Phattalung station.

Bus: Buses from Trang take one hour, while those from Hat Yai and Nakhon Si Thammarat take about two hours.

PHUKET

The island of Phuket—Thailand's most popular beach resort—is located in the sparkling green Andaman Sea, 885 km south of Bangkok.

Like all other successful beaches in Asia, Phuket was discovered by backpackers searching for an escapist holiday of simple huts and local food. Facilities were limited or nonexistent; early arrivals slept on the sand or lived with locals. The scene was so idyllic that William Duncan wrote in his 1976 guide *Thailand* that "for a few years more, Phuket may be allowed to sleep undisturbed, for this island province is not yet ready to cater to the needs of foreign tourists. There are no first-class hotels or restaurants . . . ."

This author first visited the island in 1979, when the main beach destination of Patong had nothing but a few bamboo bungalows and a solitary lime-green hotel on the largely deserted beach. I rented a motorcycle and started a tour around the island, only to discover my route blocked by a giant sleeping lizard on Patong's main beach road—an amazing sight no matter the state of the island. Phuket then was an uncharted land.

But word of the tropical paradise spread among world travelers and soon a steady trickle of curious visitors tiptoed down to Phuket, hoping to beat the rush and inevitable commercialization. Entrepreneurs spotted the island's potential and started constructing massive resorts at Patong Beach; soon they spread out to other tranquil bays and remote coves. In the remarkably short span of just one decade, the island transformed itself from hippie paradise to yuppie nirvana.

Paradise or Perversion?
Present-day Phuket will disappoint travelers who dislike commercial development and delight those who find perverse pleasure in running down resorts once they become popular. And yet Phuket remains an outstanding holiday destination.

First, few islands in the world can boast of so many excellent beaches in so small an area. Comparisons between Phuket and Ko Samui are almost inevitable, but I'd say that Phuket's beaches are just as beautiful—and certainly more plentiful—than the handful on Ko Samui.

Secondly, Phuket's enormous size has allowed the beaches to absorb a great deal of development without being completely overwhelmed. Beaches such as Patong have suffered from faceless hotels and seedy bars, but other regions on the island have generally been spared the tourist-ghetto fate of Pattaya and other Southeast Asian resorts.

Most of Phuket, the largest island in Thailand, remains unaffected by mass tourism. Tourists generally stay glued to the beach and rarely venture into the interior or up to remote coves, but a 10-minute motorcycle ride away from Patong and Kata-Karon Beaches reveals the secret of Phuket: the remote corners of the island are pristine, unspoiled, and still fabulously beautiful.

In addition, Phuket offers far more geographic and historical diversity than Samui, as well as outstanding scuba diving, a national park with thick rainforest, several waterfalls, tin mines, pearl farms, Buddhist temples, villages of sea gypsies, and a handful of deserted beaches rarely seen by Western visitors.

Don't dismiss Phuket for its overdeveloped tag—the people remain friendly, the weather is perfect, and enough scenic wonders and cultural highlights remain to keep even the most jaded of travelers happy for several weeks.

History
Phuket, surprisingly, actually has some history worth considering.

Little is known about the early history of the island, though archaeologists suggest that the region was first inhabited by Mon-Khmers from Myanmar, who lived in the northern regions, and Chao Lay or sea gypsies, who constructed settlements along the southern coastlines. The Thais reached the island in the 13th century during the reign of King Ramkamheng of Sukothai, settling the region to mine the vast deposits of tin easily extracted from veins near the surface of the earth.

Western explorers arrived in the 16th century to ride out storms in Phuket's calm bays and to

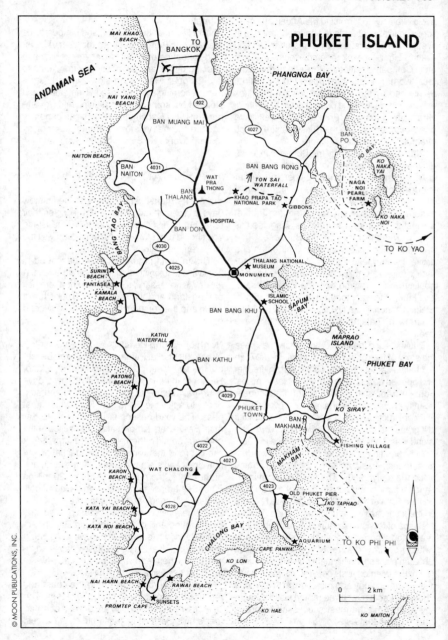

avoid pirates who terrorized the Andaman coast-line. The island later played an important role in Western imperialistic aspirations after Captain Francis Light, an explorer employed by the East India Company, settled in Phuket and married a local woman. Light later bowed to suzerainty demanded by the Thai royal court in Bangkok and moved his fledgling outpost down to Penang. Had Light remained, Phuket might well have been incorporated into the British empire, which eventually moved to Singapore.

Phuket was invaded by the Burmese in 1785, a five-week insurgence that elevated two young sisters to the status of national heroines. After the death of the governor of the northern town of Thalang, his widow Chan and her sister Muk assumed responsibility for defending Phuket against the murderous Burmese. Disguised as male warriors to intimidate the Burmese, Chan and Muk successfully led the Thai forces and drove the Burmese from Phuket. In reward for their bravery, King Rama I conferred titles of nobility on Chan, who became Lady Tepsatri, and Muk, who was honored as Tao Srisuntorn. Statues honoring the two heroines now stand on the road in Thalang near the site of their brave deed.

Phuket, since the early 20th century, has been the story of tin, rubber, and tourism. In 1907, an Australian captain introduced the first tin dredger and opened dozens of fabulously lucrative mines. Foreign traders and Chinese laborers subsequently arrived to work the mines, grow wealthy, and construct the Malacca colonial houses which still grace the side streets of Penang Town. The island was declared an official province in 1933.

Although tin and rubber are still major industries, tourism has dominated the local economy since the early 1980s. The opening of an international airport and construction of a Club Med and the Phuket Yacht Club firmly placed Phuket on the tourist trail in the previous decade. The importance of tourism was forcefully demonstrated years ago when demonstrators set fire to and virtually destroyed a newly built US$44 million tantalum plant on the northern outskirts of Phuket Town. Environmentalists believed the plant would disturb the ecology and ruin tourism. Yet, today Phuket attracts over three million visitors annually—making it the most successful resort island in Southeast Asia.

Climate

Phuket lies near the equator, and temperatures are fairly uniform throughout the year. The island is hot and dry from November to May and affected by the annual monsoons from June to late October. Rains start slowly in early summer, becoming most intense in September and October but sometimes continuing into November and early December. Visitors can generally escape the heavy storms of late summer by moving over to Ko Samui on the east coast.

ATTRACTIONS

Visitors to Phuket generally spend the first few days relaxing on the beach and working on their tans, but to discover the beauty of the island you should rent a motorcycle or car and visit the more remote regions.

The following attractions are described in clockwise fashion starting from Patong Beach. A full day is necessary to explore the northern half of the island and the east coast. Tour Phuket Town and the southern beaches on the second day.

North of Patong Beach

Most tours start at Patong or Kata-Karon Beaches, the two most popular spots on the island. Rather than head inland to Phuket Town, drive north past some outdoor restaurants and stop briefly to enjoy the views from Khao Phanthurat pass. The road descends *very* steeply to Kamala Bay, where simple cafes are nestled at the northern end. To the rear are ricefields and a circular road that winds past residential neighborhoods and a small mosque. At the north end of the bay is the newly opened US$20 million FantaSea amusement park, worth a look if only for its wildly imaginative architecture.

The beachside road then climbs past several small coves and cozy Laem Sing Beach, accessible down a narrow pathway. At Surin Beach, turn left at the police station and head toward the Chedi and Amanpuri resorts, two of the most exclusive digs in Thailand.

The narrow road cuts along the coast and reaches the broad, clean stretches of Bang Tao Beach. Sited on the beach are dozens of fishermen's huts that face Laguna Phuket, the largest resort complex in Southeast Asia. The Banyan Tree in the Laguna Phuket complex is a wonderful place to stop and enjoy a cocktail.

After you reconnect with the main road, continue up to Ban Thalang and visit the following attractions.

Ban Thalang

Thalang Town was the first settlement on Penang and site of the famous battle between two Thai women and Burmese invaders. The following three attractions are all near Ban Thalang.

Wat Pra Na Sang

About 50 meters south of the central intersection stands a 200-year-old *wat* on the right and its modern counterpart on the left. A walking Sukothai-style Buddha stands in the front courtyard. Exterior doors of the modern *bot* feature well-carved guardians on the right, and heroines Chan and Muk on the left; note their tiny feet and enormous eyes. Murals on the interior walls relate the fall of Ayuthaya, King Narusen's famous elephant fight, Chan and Muk defending Phuket against Burmese invaders portrayed as horrid creatures, and the four traditional industries of Phuket—tin, rubber, fishing, and pineapples. What happened to tourism?

To the right is an old, unrestored *bot* whose *bai semas* resemble giant pawns from a monstrous chess set. Although often closed, the *bot* is highly regarded for its ancient metal Dvaravati-style heads and unusual rear doors, which indicate that the temple once served as a site for white magic rites. It is said that Wat Pra Na Sang monks still bless weapons and provide magical incantations to protect devotees against bullets and black forces. The *wat* reputedly contains the longest *lai tong* in the country, an accordionlike religious manuscript covered with maps of buried treasure.

Wat Pra Thong

One of the most bizarre Buddha images in Thailand lies half-buried in the middle of Wat Pra Thong, an otherwise ordinary temple about one km north of Thalang. Once coated with plaster to thwart Burmese invaders, the unaesthetic but immense statue has since been gold-leafed by pilgrims into an unwieldy blob. Of more interest

are the burial vaults embedded in the rear walls, dozens of small images perched near the ceiling, and eight auxiliary Buddhas dedicated to each day of the week plus an additional Buddhist day called Palaelai.

Khao Prapa Tao National Park

Four km east of Thalang is one of the most spectacular scenes on Phuket: an awesome park which provides a rare opportunity to experience the splendor of an endangered rainforest. Rainforests in Southeast Asia are uniformly difficult to visit, since most are well off the beaten track and impossible to reach without long bus rides or arduous treks. Located at the end of a rubber plantation, Prapa National Park might be your *only* chance to see a rainforest—don't miss it.

Khao Prapa Tao was created in 1978 to conserve indigenous vegetation such as the *Karedoxa dolphin,* a silver palm that survives only on Phuket. The park is also home to several species of birds such as the crimson sunbird, scops owl, and paradise flycatcher. At the park entrance are a ranger station, map to nearby Ton Sai Waterfall, refreshment stalls, and bungalows you can rent from park headquarters. Overnighting in the park is highly recommended.

A road passable only with dirt bikes and four-wheel-drive vehicles continues across the park to the east coast. Escorted jeep tours are provided by several companies on Phuket.

Nai Ton Beach

Head north and then west down Hwy. 4031 to the turnoff for Nai Ton Beach. Suddenly, all the tourists are gone and Patong Beach seems like a distant nightmare. Nai Ton is a spectacularly sited stretch of sand with simple cafes, private homes that admit overnighters, and beach chairs for sun worshippers. The road continues south past a beautiful swimming cove before finally disintegrating into an impassable and dangerously rutted mess. Return to Hwy. 4031 and continue north to Nai Yang.

Nai Yang Beach

After driving through a beautiful stretch of rubber trees, turn left into Pearl Village and continue through the back lot to Nai Yang Beach, a narrow stretch of sand under the supervision of Nai Yang National Marine Park. Nai Yang offers seaside restaurants, windsurfing, jet skis, swaying casuarina trees, and elephant rides into the surf. Accommodations are available at the Nai Yang Visitors Center at the north end of the beach.

Continue north around the airport to the next beach.

Mai Khao Beach

Mai Khao is an absolutely deserted beach, eyed covetously in recent years by ambitious developers. The road that parallels the beach passes several Thai villages and fields of grapes, which produce the sweet reds and unpretentious whites of Thailand. Highway 402 terminates at Sarasin Bridge.

Northwest Passage, Pearls, and Gibbons

Highway 4027 heads east from Muang Mai past some enormous old trees that have miraculously escaped the chainsaws and become holy symbols to local residents. A left turn brings you to Po Bay (Ao Po) and a small fishing village where you can get cold drinks.

Ao Po is the departure point for visits to Naga Noi Pearl Farm on Naka Noi Island. Phuket travel agents can arrange tours to the farm, which provide insight into the considerable skills of pearl cultivation. The highly successful operation once created the world's largest cultured pearl, a 30-gram monster now displayed in the Mikimoto Pearl Museum in Japan.

An even more unusual stop can be made at the nearby Gibbon Rehabilitation Project, where former pet gibbons are taught how to survive in the wild. Visitors can observe the gibbons, learn about protection of the rainforest, and trek through the adjacent park.

ENDANGERED PHUKET

*P*huket was once a tropical island, blanketed with jungle inhabited by tigers, lions, and wild elephants. But over the last two decades, most forms of exotic wildlife have been driven off the island, including turtles, gibbons, and backpackers. The prognosis is turtles are a lost cause, but the gibbons stand a chance due to new programs in the northeastern corner of the island.

Turtles

Phuket once served as a nesting ground for thousands of giant turtles that laid their eggs (*kai chalamet*) each winter on the sandy northern beaches of Hat Mai Khao and Hat Nai Yang. In the early 1970s, almost 100 turtles arrived each night to lay their eggs on the remote coastline.

This began to change when natural enemies (sharks and seagulls) were joined by human predators (turtle and egg collectors) who pushed the animal toward extinction in the mistaken belief that turtle eggs were aphrodisiacs and medical rejuvenators. After less than 50 turtles were sighted during the entire nesting season of 1985, legal egg collection concessions were canceled in an effort to reverse the precipitous decline. But even today, poachers continue to wander the beaches in search of eggs that bring princely sums in Phuket markets.

The most ambitious program to save the turtles was the rehabilitation project launched at the Phuket Marine Biology Center on Panwa Cape. The idea was to purchase eggs and infant turtles from licensed collectors for incubation on supervised beaches. The biologists also collected mature ridleys, hawksbills, greenbacks, and loggerheads for scientific research and distribution to other turtle rehabilitation centers. One curious fact learned from the studies was most species survive in captivity except for the large and rare leatherback, which refuses to eat or breed.

After a few months of protected incubation, the mature turtles were released from their cells during the Buddhist festival of Songkram. But problems with insufficient funding and illegal poachers forced the cancellation of the highly publicized event in 1993 and the relocation of the incubation site to a secret destination.

Whether efforts to save the turtles will succeed is an open question, but recent statistics are rather grim: less than a dozen turtles were sighted on the island in 1995.

Gibbons

You sometimes hear the call on a calm morning in the limestone monoliths of Phangnga Bay—the haunting, primeval cry of the gibbon. One of the closest relatives to humans, gibbons display remarkably human characteristics, making them prized pets both in Thailand and around the

Heroines Monument
and Thalang National Museum
Highway 4027 intersects Hwy. 402 at the monument dedicated to the two sisters who successfully defended Phuket against Burmese invaders. A fruit and vegetable market is held here on Monday.

Thalang National Museum, 100 meters east of the monument, is a new attraction with displays on local history, industry, the environment, and a highly prized 9th-century Vishnu image discovered near Takua Pa. The museum is open Tues.-Sat. 0900-1630.

South of the intersection are a striking Islamic school, native handicraft center, Thai performance venue, and Phuket Town.

Ko Siray
Ko Siray is an extremely disappointing fishing village populated by Malay-Burmese pearl divers who prefer to be called "New Thais" rather than sea gypsies. Ko Siray consists largely of dusty roads, rough tin huts, and kids yelling, "Ten *baht*, ten *baht*"—an experience best avoided.

Cape Panwa
Phuket's Marine Biology Research Center and Aquarium on the south coast contains displays of tropical sealife, fishing devices, and facilities to ensure the survival of the endangered ridley sea turtles that once laid their eggs on Nai Yang Beach. Despite the turtle release each year during Songkram, egg hunters and turtle poachers have pushed the ridley toward extinction. The aquarium is open daily 0900-1630.

On the grounds of the Cape Panwa Sheraton Resort stands a classic Sino-Portuguese mansion filled with a quality collection of antique furniture and art objects. The public is invited to tour Panwa House and enjoy high tea on the veranda.

world. The captured gibbons then spend the rest of their lives entertaining customers in bars or, more likely, chained in the backyards of disillusioned owners.

The reality is baby gibbons first appear to be cute and rather docile pets, but later become wild and dangerous adults with aggressive personalities and incredibly sharp canine teeth. Most are abandoned at temples or released into the wild without any of the skills necessary for jungle survival. And, unlike their more celebrated cousin, the orangutan, abandoned gibbons seemed to concern few people.

The situation changed a few years ago when Terrance Dillon Morin, an American zoologist and documentary filmmaker, joined forces with the Thai Royal Forestry Department in the world's first attempt to rehabilitate domesticated gibbons. Terrance and his band of volunteers now accept unwanted gibbons at Bang Phae Wildlife Reserve ("Willie's Halfway House") for several months of reacclimatization. After a period of readjustment and introductions to prospective mates, the gibbons are relocated to Ko Boi off the eastern coast of Phuket in Phangnga Bay. Here, gibbons learn the forest skills necessary for jungle survival on Ko Boi or adjacent Ko Tong. The hope is that the animals will reproduce with other released gibbons and ensure the survival of these magnificent creatures.

The camp is funded by local hotels owned primarily by Western corporations. Volunteers from around the world donate their time. For more information, contact the Gibbon Project, Marine Asia, tel. (076) 381065.

Backpackers? Politicians?
When I first visited Phuket in 1979, Patong had one small hotel painted a sickly shade of green and a few grass shacks facing a magnificent stretch of sand. The beaches were deserted except for a handful of hippies smoking pot and armies of enormous iguanas blocking the road from Kata to Nai Harn. A local fisherman offered to sell me 20 hectares of beachfront property for a ridiculously low sum, but I declined, since most of Phuket appeared far too isolated to ever attract much tourism.

An intriguing situation has arisen over acquisition of land by local politicians. Government investigations conducted in early 1995 revealed that several wealthy families on the island had benefitted from government programs intended to redistribute land to poor farmers. Among the accused was the husband of a parliament leader and several members of the Democratic Party led by Prime Minister Chuan Leekpai. The scandal started slowly, then escalated after Chamlong Srimuang, the leader of a minority faction within the ruling coalition, withdrew his support and forced Leekpai to call fresh elections. Thailand's longest serving elected premier lost the July 1995 contest to Banharn Silpaarcha and his Chart Thai Party.

The moral: Property on Phuket can be bad news for young travel writers and people in high places.

Wat Chalong

Wat Chalong ("Celebration Temple") is the largest and most sacred temple of the 29 monasteries on Phuket. Enshrined in the modern *viharn* are the gilded statues of two monks and herbal doctors—Luang Po Chaem and Luang Po Chuang—who helped quell an 1876 rebellion of warring tin miners.

As with other Buddhist temples in Thailand, Wat Chalong is best visited on *wan pran,* the weekly holy day when monks chant Pali scriptures 0900-1200 before having their final meal at noontime. The date is determined by the lunar calendar but the tourist office and hotel owners can help with schedules.

Seashell Museum

An impressive collection of shells is exhibited in the modern, blue-tiled building on Hwy. 4021 just north of Rawai Beach. Shells sold at the shop include key scallops, variegated sundials, spiny venus murexes, and humpback cowries.

Rawai Beach and Tristan Jones

Situated behind a mediocre stretch of sand is Rawai Beach, a commercialized sea gypsy village often inundated with groups of tourists. Several lackluster cafes are located near the old pier.

A few hundred meters west is the small boat that crossed the Kra Isthmus in 1987 with a crew of disabled sailors, including a blind German and a one-legged Englishman named Tristan Jones. Jones later sailed the craft north up the Chao Praya to Chiang Rai and penned a book about his experiences, but died of complications from a stroke in Phuket in 1995.

Promtep Cape

Promtep Cape and the viewpoint at the south end of Kata Noi Beach are the best spots on Phuket for spectacular sunsets. Promtep is marked with a large parking lot filled with Thai tourists and an elevated shrine of a four-headed Brahma who calmly surveys the fingertipped peninsula. Note the signpost listing approximate sunset times, which vary from 1804 in November to 1850 in July—only a 46-minute differential throughout the year. That's what happens when you live near the equator!

Nai Harn Bay

The road continues north past an experimental but inoperative windmill before dropping down to Nai Harn Bay and the luxurious Le Meridien Phuket Yacht Club. Visitors can drive right through the parking lot of the Le Meridien Phuket Yacht Club and continue past cozy Ao Sane Beach to a wonderful little hideaway called Jungle Beach Resort. Stop for a drink.

Rather than return on the beach road, head west past Nai Harn Beach Bungalows to Crazy Horse Ranch, where escorted rides tour the nearby ricefields and beaches. The beautiful backwoods road continues east to the highway and then north past a viewpoint to Kata and Karon Beaches. This makes a terrific ride for motorcyclists.

SPORTS AND RECREATION

Canoe Tours

The best environmental experiences around Phuket include escorted canoe tours of Phangnga Bay that slip into watery caves and overnight on deserted beaches.

Sea Canoes: Sea kayaking started in 1989 when "Caveman" John Gray led his first canoe group into Phangnga Bay, the limestone-studded backdrop for the movie *The Man With the Golden Gun.* The concept was so successful that Sea Canoes tours are now available in Ko Samui, Halong Bay, Fiji, and the Palawan Islands. Packages cost US$150-250 per day. Sea Canoes, 367/4 Yaowarat Rd., Phuket 83000, tel. (076) 212172, fax (076) 212252.

Several other companies organize canoe tours at far lower costs. Check with travel agencies, dive shops, and Santana Divers on Patong.

Golf

Many of the old tin mines that once scarred the island have turned into gold mines for sports developers and lovers of the links. The Bangkok Wanderers, one of Thailand's largest multinational golf groups, includes Blue Canyon and the Phuket Golf and Country Club in their list of top 20 courses.

Greens fees for the following courses are 1,500-3,000B, but sizable discounts are available from participating hotels and travel agencies.

Phuket Golf and Country Club: The island's first golf course opened in 1989 on an abandoned tin mine between Phuket Town and Patong Beach. Highway 4029, Amphoe Kathu, tel. (076) 321038.

Phuket Century Country Club: Another 18-hole championship course carved out of an old tin mine just off the road to Patong. Highway 4020, Amphoe Kathu, tel. (076) 321997.

Banyan Tree Golf Club: Phuket's finest golf facility faces Ban Tao Bay in the northern part of the island near the Dusit Laguna, Sheraton Grande Laguna, and Banyan Tree Resorts. 393 Mu 2, Tambon Cheong Talay, tel. (076) 324350, fax (076) 324351.

Blue Canyon Country Club: A professional 18-hole course near the Phuket airport, where Tiger Woods won an important tournament several years ago. Highway 402, Ban Muang Mai, tel. (076) 311176.

Running

Hash House Harriers: The running fraternity established by British soldiers in Malaysia sponsors weekly foot races followed by serious fun for party animals. *Warning:* James Eckardt in his *Waylaid by the Bimbos* describes the Hashiers as a "wretched, loutish, bedraggled, nomadic tribe which can be found periodically gallumping half-naked through the jungle, blowing horns and whistles and screeching their barbaric war cries."

Visitors can join the Saturday afternoon foot races; get information at the Expat Bar on Soi Bangla in Patong.

Horseback Riding

Crazy Horse Stables: Tucked away on a beautiful road back from Nai Harn Bay is a friendly spot that provides horseback rides through fabulous countryside. Rides led by Western instructors cost 350-500B per hour.

Bungee Jumping

Tarzan Jungle Bungee Jump: Falling from a platform with only a rubber band around your ankles may not appeal to everyone, but watching the daredevils leap into an abandoned tin lake is almost as fun. Highway 4029, Amphoe Kathu, tel. (076) 231123.

PHUKET TOWN

The capital of Thailand's only island province is worth visiting for its shopping, restaurants, and delightful examples of Indo-Portuguese mansions constructed by Chinese tin and rubber barons. Phuket Town was originally settled about a century ago by Chinese residents of Malaysia who were drawn to the lucrative mineral deposits. Tin and rubber fortunes created by the great rush formed the great Sino-Thai dynasties, which still dominate the economies of southern Thailand.

Most visitors simply pass through town en route to a beach, but if you have some extra time, an informative walking tour can be done in about two hours. Start your tour in the middle of town at the tourist office.

Rasda Road

Rasda Road is the main tourist center, with all types of restaurants and travel services. Asia Voyages and Songserm Travel are located on the U-shaped road to the south. Kanda Bakery to the north is overpriced but a good place to relax for a few minutes. Continue west on Rasda Road through the traffic circle to the central market to the south. A beautiful old colonial house is tucked away behind the nearby offices of Thai Airways. On the left are a pottery shop and bird emporium opposite a Thai temple.

Pu Jao Temple

Pu Jao (the sign says Kwanim Teng) is a Chinese Taoist temple dedicated to Kuan Yin, goddess of mercy. The central chamber contains both plastic and traditional bamboo sticks used to tell fortunes and diagnose illnesses. Visitors can shake the sticks, read the number, and select a matching fortune from the boxes in a room on the left. The red wooden blocks shaped like mangoes simply answer questions with a yes or no.

To the right is another room filled with dozens of small statues, including a monkey god wearing a mock leopard-skin robe. An oven used to burn hell notes is located in the alley to the next temple.

Jui Tui Temple

This much more impressive Chinese Taoist temple honors Kiu Won In, a vegetarian god who

SCUBA DIVING NEAR PHUKET

*T*hailand's finest scuba and skin diving are centered on the islands near Phuket in the Andaman Sea. The warm, clear waters of the Andaman Sea provide excellent conditions for the growth of corals and a rich variety of marine life. Among the most unique draws of the region is the bipolar nature of the underwater geology: massive granite boulders rise from the ocean floors in the northern regions; towering limestone karsts dominate the landforms south of Phuket.

The dive season off the west coast of Thailand is during the dry season, Nov.–June. During the rainy summer months, days tend to alternate between clear and sunny skies and torrential downpours that sharply reduce visibility to less than 10 meters.

Dive Sites near Phuket

Serious divers often head directly north to the Similan and Surin Islands near the Burmese border, or south to the relatively untouched islands west of Trang. But decent coral and undisturbed marine life can also be found around the islands south of Phuket in the direction of Ko Phi Phi.

Coral Island and Ko Maiton: Just 30 minutes from Chalong Bay are two exquisite islands fringed with perfect sand and surrounded by corals undisturbed by dynamite fishing, poisons, or the tin dredging industry that first brought wealth to the region. (More details at the end of the "Phuket" section in the Southern Thailand chapter.)

Ko Racha Yai: This lovely island lies just 20 km south of Phuket and can be explored on a day excursion or a longer visit onboard one of Phuket's many live-aboard dive boats. Dive sites are best along the eastern coastline, where a few simple bungalows are located for overnight guests. Small coves on the northwestern side provide anchorage for dive boats during the busy winter months.

Ko Racha Noi: As you move south, underwater visibility increases and the variety of underwater topography seems to improve. Ko Racha Noi, 25 km south of Phuket, offers pristine coral gardens in shallow waters, and deeply submerged boulders provide a suitable habitat for larger pelagic fish. This island is generally visited on a two-day, one-night package leaving from Phuket.

Ko Dok Mai: About 12 km east of Cape Panwa on the southeastern tip of Phuket lies a tiny island recently declared a protected marine sanctuary. The most impressive features are vertical limestone cliffs that plunge down to the ocean floor and submarine caves filled with larger pelagic fish.

Shark Point: Phuket's most famous dive site has also been declared a marine sanctuary to protect the extensive beds of soft and hard corals, and the abundant marine life that includes harmless bottom-dwelling leopard sharks accustomed to handouts from generous divers. A less welcome sight are the dangerous moray eels who hide in the so-called "Eel Nursery" while waiting for tidbits from uninformed divers.

Anemone Reef: Just two km north of Shark Point is a submerged pinnacle and shallow reef covered with a carpet of anemones and inhabited by moray eels and variations of zebra fish. The reef also has been declared a marine sanctuary and therefore prohibits anchoring by any vessel.

Northern Islands

Dive sites north of Phuket and in the more remote waters off the coast of Ranong are uniformly superior to those near Phuket, since they have escaped two decades of tourism and over a century of tin dredging.

Similan Islands: This archipelago of nine wondrous islands is consistently ranked among the top 10 dive sites in the world, thanks to its crystal-clear waters, impressive range of marine life, unsurpassed corals, and crystalline beaches surrounding the principal islands. The Similans can be visited on multi-day excursions leaving from Phuket and closer west coast towns between Phuket and Ranong.

Surin Islands: The final frontier in Thai dive sites is the scattering of islands just eight km south of the Burmese border. Found here are the last surviving sea gypsies, who appear doomed to lose their traditional lifestyles due to environmental and political factors. See "Surin Islands" under "Ranong to Phuket" in the Southern Thailand chapter for details.

Ko Phi Phi: Two hours southeast of Phuket lie several limestone islands surrounded by magnificent cliffs and washed by crystal-clear waters that guarantee almost unlimited visibility. Ko Phi Phi has been ruined in recent years by unregulated tourism, though the underwater attractions remain among the most impressive in the Andaman Sea.

See "Phangnga Bay and Ko Phi Phi" in the Southern Thailand chapter for more information.

Patong Beach Dive Shops

Phuket, the dive capital of Southeast Asia, has over a dozen professional dive shops providing the full range of courses from PADI Open Water Certification to PADI Five-Star Instructor. Several dive shop professionals own live-aboard boats that guarantee the best possible dive experiences at remote destinations such as the Similan and Surin Islands, plus newer sites such as the Myanmar Banks and Andaman Islands.

Patong is the dive center for Phuket. Several dive shops are also found in the town of Phuket and on Chalong Bay.

Fantasea Divers: Phuket's original dive center provides instruction and certification courses from open water to assistant instructor, and multi-day dive excursions aboard its four live-aboard boats. The most popular choice for the dive center's two-week trips to the Andaman Islands is the MV *Fantasea*, a fully equipped live-aboard with video-viewing rooms and an E-6 photo lab. Fantasea Divers, Holiday Inn, 93/95 Thavewong Rd., Patong Beach, P.O. Box 20, Phuket 83150, tel. (076) 340309, fax (076) 340309.

Southeast Asia Yacht Charter: Although not as large as other dive shops, SAYC provides equally dependable dive excursions to remote destinations both north and south of Phuket. 89/71 Thavewong Rd., Patong Beach, P.O. Box 199, Phuket 83121, tel. (076) 340406, fax (076) 340586.

Some other dive shops are:
Andaman Divers, 83/8 Thavewong Rd., tel. (076) 340322
Holiday Diving Club, Patong Beach Hotel, tel. (076) 311166, fax (076) 340440
Ocean Divers, 61 Thavewong Rd., tel. (076) 340166
PIDC, Amari Coral Beach Hotel, tel. (076) 321106
Poseidon Club, Phuket Island Resort, tel. (076) 215950
Santana, Thavewong Rd., tel. (076) 340360, fax (076) 340360

Kata-Karon Beach Dive Shops
Two of the best shops on Phuket are located on Kata-Karon hill midway between the two beaches.

Siam Diving Center: An excellent operation staffed by professional divers who lead day excursions to nearby islands, longer programs to the Similan and Surin Islands, and exploratory expeditions to the uncharted waters of Myanmar and the Andaman Islands. Siam Diving Center's boats are well-designed and the food is superb. Instruction includes PADI Open Water Certification, Medic, Rescue, Dive Master, and PADI Open Water Instructor; this is one of the few shops accredited as a Five-Star PADI Instructor Development Center

(IDC). Director John Williams also runs a dive center at the luxurious Phi Phi Palm Beach Hotel. Siam Diving is located on Kata-Karon hill just opposite Marina Cottages. Siam Diving, 121/9 Patak Rd., Mu 4, Kata-Karon Beach, Phuket 831001, tel. (076) 333936, fax (076) 330608.

Marina Divers: A five-star facility with a full range of rental equipment, a repair center, and an on-site pool for all possible certifications, from the basic license up to PADI Instructor. Its live-aboard boats are some of the best on Phuket. Marina Divers is located in Marina Cottages on Kata-Karon hill. Marina Divers, Kata-Karon Beach, P.O. Box 143, Phuket 83000, tel. (076) 330625, fax (076) 330516.

Other dive shops in the area are:
PIDC, Coral Beach Hotel, tel. (076) 321106
Southeast Asia Yachts, Le Meridien, tel. (076) 340480, fax (076) 340586

Phuket Town Dive Shops
The following are all sources for equipment and excursions:
Andaman Sea, 54 Phuket Rd., tel. (076) 211752
PFC Dive Center, tel. (076) 215527
Phuket Aquatics, 62 Rasada Rd., tel. (076) 216562, fax (076) 214537
Phuket Divers, 7 Phunphon Rd., tel. (076) 215738

Chalong Bay Dive Shops
The following shops and boat agencies are useful for southern dive sites such as Ko Maiton, Shark Point, and Coral Island. All are located near the Chalong pier.
Reef Explorers, tel. (076) 381957
Marine Asia, tel. (076) 330065
PIDC, tel. (076) 330219
Chalong Bay Boat Centre, tel. (076) 381852
Ao Chalong, tel. (076) 381190

Prices
Prices for equipment, instruction, and organized tours are fairly standard around the island. Scuba equipment rentals cost 600-850B per day. Sample prices:
single dive: 600-800B
two dives: 1,000-1,200B
one-day introduction: 1,000-1,500B
five-day course: 5,000-7,500B
PADI Certification: 6,000-8,000B
PADI Instructor: 15,000B
Raja Islands tour: 1,000-1,200B per day
Phi Phi Islands tour: 2,000-2,500B per day
Similan Islands tour: 3,000-4,000B per day

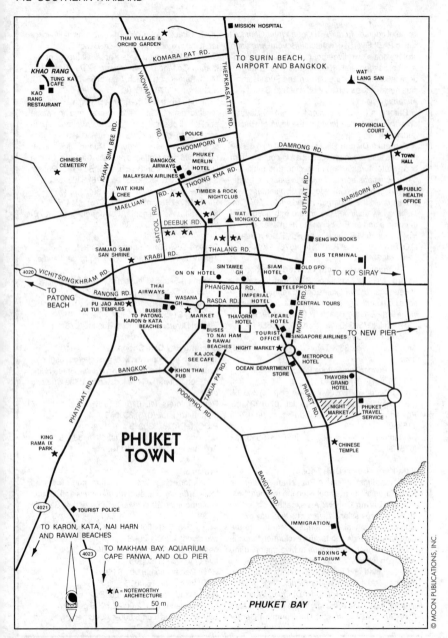

MISSION HOSPITAL

THAI VILLAGE &
ORCHID GARDEN

KOMARA PAT RD.

KHAO RANG
TUNG KA
CAFE

KAO
RANG
RESTAURANT

TO SURIN BEACH,
AIRPORT AND BANGKOK

WAT
LANG SAN

YAOWARAJ

THEPKRASATTRI RD.

POLICE

CHOOMPORN RD.

DAMRONG RD.

PROVINCIAL
COURT

TOWN
HALL

KHAW SIM BEE RD.

CHINESE
CEMETERY

BANGKOK
AIRWAYS

PHUKET
MERLIN
HOTEL

MALAYSIAN AIRLINES

THOONG KHA RD.

SUTHAT RD.

NARISORN RD.

PUBLIC
HEALTH
OFFICE

WAT KHUN
CHEE

MAELUAN

RD. ★ A

★ A

TIMBER & ROCK
NIGHTCLUB

SATOOL RD.

DEEBUK RD.

★ A

WAT
MONGKOL NIMIT

★ A ★ A

A ★ ★ A

SENG HO BOOKS

SAMJAO SAM
SAN SHRINE

KRABI RD.

THALANG RD.

BUS TERMINAL

OLD GPO

4020 VICHITSONGKHRAM RD.

SIN TAWEE
GH

ON ON HOTEL

SIAM
HOTEL

TO KO SIRAY

RANONG RD.

THAI
AIRWAYS

WASANA
GH

PHANGNGA

RD.

IMPERIAL
HOTEL

TELEPHONE

MONTRI RD.

TO PATONG
BEACH

PU JAO AND
JUI TUI TEMPLES

BUSES
TO PATONG,
KARON & KATA
BEACHES

RASDA RD.

MARKET

THAVORN
HOTEL

PEARL
HOTEL

CENTRAL TOURS

SINGAPORE AIRLINES

TO NEW PIER

BUSES
TO NAI HAM
& RAWAI
BEACHES

TOURIST
OFFICE

KA JOK
SEE CAFE

NIGHT MARKET

METROPOLE
HOTEL

KHON THAI
PUB

BANGKOK
RD.

OCEAN DEPARTMENT
STORE

PHUKET RD.

THAVORN
GRAND
HOTEL

POONPHOL RD.

TAKUA PA RD.

NIGHT
MARKET

PHUKET TRAVEL
SERVICE

PHATIPHAT RD.

PHUKET
TOWN

KING
RAMA IX
PARK

CHINESE
TEMPLE

4021

TOURIST POLICE

BANGYAI RD.

TO KARON, KATA, NAI HARN
AND RAWAI BEACHES

IMMIGRATION

4023

TO MAKHAM BAY, AQUARIUM,
CAPE PANWA, AND OLD PIER

★ A = NOTEWORTHY
ARCHITECTURE

0   50 m

BOXING
STADIUM

PHUKET BAY

© MOON PUBLICATIONS, INC.

oversees frantic celebrations during the Vegetarian Festival. Inside the central hall are images of Chinese deities, including Laosia, and small spears with carved heads used in magical Taoist rites. The building also features a red-tile roof with green porcelain dragons and outstanding doors carved with fierce gods.

A smaller room on the right has six life-sized statues of Taoist gods and a small tiger also used in Taoist rites. Over 50 smaller images crowd the altar in the left room, including frightening black-faced gods guaranteed to scare small children. Also note the photographs that show the evolution of the temple from 1911 to the latest reconstruction in 1982.

Samjao Sam San Shrine

Constructed in 1853, Samjao is dedicated to Tien Sang Sung Moo, goddess of the sea and patron saint of Chinese sailors. Ceremonies are held here to bless new ships and ensure the safety of the crew. Note the five-level pagoda and brass Chinese dog with ball in mouth.

Sino-Portuguese Homes

Head north up Satool Road. Though not as impressive as Penang's Malaccan-style terrace houses, Phuket's old homes and estates add charm and atmosphere to an otherwise ordinary city. On the left stands a lovely home behind an ornamental ironwork fence, then a fabulous cream-colored residence constructed in the late 19th century by a wealthy tin baron. At the corner is a large yellow home destined for destruction or conversion into a tourist attraction.

Some of the best Sino-Portuguese homes are located along Deebuk Road. Fortunately, many of the ornately decorated residences are now being restored by wealthy individuals who appreciate the rare beauty of the floral woodcarvings, pastel tilework, and elaborately carved doors. On the left is a wonderful blue two-story building with louvered windows and graceful balconies.

Several more fine structures, including an ornate white home with gingerbread molding, are located up Yaowaraj Road. Return to Deebuk Road and the next attraction.

Wat Mongkol Nimit

A somewhat interesting Thai temple is on Deebuk Road just past a Chinese ancestral hall.

Lucky visitors will be greeted by Mr. Tim Punyaputho, who cheerfully poses for photographs in front of the central Buddha image.

Soi Romanni returns to Thalang Road past old-fashioned barbershops and seedy Chinese shophouses.

Town Hall

The 70-year-old Phuket Town Hall might look familiar—it served as the French Embassy in the film *The Killing Fields*. Visitors can count the 99 doors, then cross the street and peek through the windows of the equally beautiful Phuket Provincial Court.

Khao Rang

Rang Hill is a tough climb but offers great views over Phuket and decent meals in the Kao Rang Restaurant and Tung Ka Cafe. The hill is now a fitness park, popular with Chinese yuppies airing out their lungs.

Budget Accommodations

Few visitors stay in Phuket Town unless they arrive late or need to catch an early bus.

On On Hotel: Established in 1929, the historic On On is the best choice for budget travelers. Overflow is handled by the adjacent P.R. Guesthouse. The On On Cafe is a popular spot to hang out and wait for evening buses. Portions of the 1999 film, *The Beach,* starring Leonardo DiCaprio, take place inside this vintage structure. Leonardo stayed not here, but at the Cape Panwa Hotel. 19 Phangnga Rd., tel. (076) 211154, 100-280B fan, 320-450B a/c.

Wasana Guesthouse: The only other budget spot worth mentioning is located just past the market. A clean place with friendly managers. 159 Ranong Rd., tel. (076) 212936, 150-200B fan, 350-400B a/c.

Thavorn Hotel: A convenient midlevel hotel in the center of town near shops and restaurants. Facilities include a coffee shop, lounge, and swimming pool. All rooms are a/c. 74 Rasda Rd., tel. (076) 211333, 450-750B.

Luxury Accommodations

Metropole: A first-class hotel with over 400 rooms, convention facilities, and a massive lobby overloaded with marble in a central location near the tourist office and Ocean Department Store.

The coffee lounge inside serves native brews, somewhat difficult to find in a country obsessed with Nescafe. 1 Soi Surin, Montri Rd., tel. (076) 215050, fax (076) 215990, 3,000-4,500B.

Phuket Merlin: One of the better hotels in town just north of the Sino-Portuguese homes on Dee-buk Road, offering complimentary shuttle service daily to its sister hotel on Patong Beach. 158/1 Yaowaraj Rd., tel. (076) 212866, 2,200-3,800B.

Restaurants

Phuket has plenty of restaurants in the center of town near the travel agencies and souvenir shops. All serve standard Thai fare, plus southern specialties such as: *khao yam*—rice with fermented shrimp paste, *khao mu daeng*—roast pork over rice, *khao mun gai*—grilled chicken over rice, *khao mok gai*—Muslim chicken with saffron rice, *pla yang*—barbecued fish, *phat phet satah*—bitter lima beans with shrimp or pork, *Khanon chin*—minced beef in a spicy red sauce, *nam prik kung siap*—grilled prawns with chili, *mi sapam*—thick seafood soup, and *gaeng tai pla*—fermented curry sauce over noodles.

Ocean Department Store: Over a dozen clean and inexpensive foodstalls are located on the top floor of the shopping center across from the Metropole Hotel. A good escape from the heat and crowds of downtown. Inexpensive.

Kanda Bakery: A popular cafe and coffee shop in the center of town with familiar surroundings and tasty if somewhat pricey dishes. Rasda Rd. Moderate.

Krua Thai: One of the best Thai cafes in Phuket, Krua Thai serves barbecued fish, prawns topped with coconut sauce, and lemon chicken. 62/7 Rasda Center, tel. (076) 213479. Moderate.

Tung Ka Cafe: This simple cafe atop Rang Hill serves authentic and very fiery dishes. Specialties include seafood marinated in coconut sauce, mixed grill, and dried shrimp fried with peanuts. Excellent views. Rang Hill. Moderate.

Ka Jok See: A surprisingly upscale Thai cafe with tablecloths, elegant decor, and piped-in jazz to accompany the curries and green mango salad. Open only for dinner but one of the best places in town for its food and atmosphere. 26 Takua Pa Rd. Moderate.

Mae Porn Seafood: Popular spot in the center of town with excellent Thai and Chinese dishes, plus awesome coconut shakes. Diners can sit in the open-air cafe or retreat into the a/c enclosure. 50/52 Phangnga Rd., tel. (076) 212106. Inexpensive.

Island View Restaurant: An expensive penthouse restaurant with elegant food and some of the best views on Phuket—you can see as far as Ko Phi Phi on a clear day. Thavorn Grand Plaza Hotel, 40/5 Chana Charoen Rd., tel. (076) 222248. Expensive.

Je t'aime: Popular cafe in the bus station complex serving Thai and Vietnamese specialties in a/c comfort, plus live folk music entertainment nightly after 2100. 183/93 Phangnga Rd. Inexpensive.

Mala: Thai and European meals served in a old-world atmosphere of antiques, cane chairs, and local memorabilia. 5/72 Mae Luan Rd., tel. (076) 218994. Moderate.

Raya Thai Cuisine: An elegant restaurant inside a restored Sino-Portuguese mansion with elevated ceilings, tall windows, and spacious dining rooms overlooking the well-tended gardens. Considered the most exclusive restaurant in Phuket Town. 48/1 New Dibuk Rd., tel. (076) 218155. Expensive.

Sawasdee: A locally renowned chef operates this upscale restaurant which specializes in Royal Thai cuisine, favored by many of the more wealthy residents of the island—known as "Phuketians." 8/5 Maeluan Rd., tel. (076) 215853. Expensive.

Sip Gaeng (Ten Curries): Small cafe which serves only *khanom jin,* rice noodles topped with one of 10 curry sauces along with a supply of fresh and pickled accompaniments. Nothing fancy, but some of the best food in town at super-bargain prices. Yaowaraj Rd. Inexpensive.

Somjit Noodles: Another simple cafe with cheap, outstanding local dishes, including stir-fried noodles with an assortment of sauces and famous Hokkien soup known as *mee nam.* This cafe is diagonally across the traffic circle from the Metropole Hotel. 214/6 Phuket Rd. Inexpensive.

Entertainment

Thai Boxing: Pugilists attempt to kill each other Friday at 2000 inside the Phuket Boxing Stadium, south of Phuket Town in the suburb of Saphan Hin. Tickets cost 80-200B.

Timber & Rock: The most popular live music club in town with excellent Thai bands working on their finest versions of *Hotel California* and other modern Thai classics. It's best to arrive around 2200. Bangkok Rd.

Khon Thai Pub: Another worthwhile club with some of the best bands from Bangkok, along with decent food and ice-cold beers. Bangkok Rd.

Ram Wong Clubs: Nightlife revolves around restaurants, nightclubs with live rock bands, shopping, and Thai boxing, but for something different, visit one of the curious and slightly twisted *ram wong* clubs. Inside the seedy clubs—marked by red and yellow lightbulbs—young Thai girls dressed like girl scouts and innocent schoolgirls taxi dance for *baht* tickets. The club opposite the Metropole Hotel still gives a traditional *wai kru* introductory dance.

Thai Village: The one-hour show includes *nang talung* shadow puppets, *nora* classical dance from southern Thailand, *chak pra* religious procession, wedding ceremony, Thai boxing, and *ram wong:* Instant Thailand. Open daily 1000-2200. Thepkrasattri Rd., tel. (076) 214860, admission 250B.

Massage: Ancient "massage" is available from the 170 women at Pearl Massage in the Pearl Hotel on Montri Road and from Grand Plaza Parlour on Tilok Uthit Road. Sauna, soap, and sex cost about 1,500B. AIDS is rampant, so wear a condom or stay away.

Traditional massage (sans sex) is offered at Daeng Plaza Hotel on Phuket Road.

Information and Services

Most services are in Phuket Town or at larger beaches such as Patong and Karon.

Tourist Information: The Tourism Authority of Thailand office between the bus terminal and city center provides maps, bus schedules, hotel listings from luxury resorts to basic guesthouses, brochures on shopping and food, and correct *songtao* fares from Phuket Town to the various beaches. Open daily 0830-1630. 73-75 Phuket Rd., tel. (076) 212213, fax (076) 213582.

The TAT office at the airport is open daily 0830-1630 and briefly after the arrival of flights later in the evenings.

Tourist Police: Assistance is available at the main police office in the S.T. Plaza Hotel and at substations on Patong and Karon Beaches. 5/39 Sakdidet Rd., tel. (076) 212468, emergency 1699.

Immigration: Visas can be extended at the immigration office in Saphan Hin District. Applicants should arrive well dressed and neatly groomed. Open weekdays 0830-1630. South Phuket Rd., tel. (076) 212108.

Post Office: The General Post Office provides packing and poste restante services. Open weekdays 0830-1630 and weekends 0900-1200. 158 Montri Rd., tel. (076) 211020.

International Telephone: Overseas calls can be made from the Telecom office around the corner from the GPO. Open daily 0800-2400. Phangnga Rd., tel. (076) 261861.

PHUKET'S AMAZING *NGAN KIN JEH*

*P*huket's renowned Vegetarian Festival *(Ngan Kin Jeh)* is held during the first nine days of the Chinese lunar month, generally late September to early October.

The origins of *Ngan Kin Jeh*—a Taoist festival marking the start of a month-long period of purification—are obscure, though several theories have been tossed around over the years. Some claim the event is of mainland Chinese origin and was introduced to the island by Chinese immigrants during the reign of King Rama V. Local residents believe the practice dates from the mid-19th century, when the entire cast of a Chinese opera company, on tour from the mainland, came down with a life-endangering fever (cholera?) that quickly spread across the island. Unable to find a cure and convinced the gods were angered over their neglect of religious rites, the performers did a penance, including a vegetarian diet and other acts of self-purification. The end of the plague firmly established what is now one of Thailand's most celebrated festivals.

The curious fact is that the highlights of Phuket's Vegetarian Festival, such acts of self-mortification as body piercing, flagellation, and walking across hot coals, are not included in records of ancient China. Many assume early participants were influenced by the Hindu festival of Thaipusam, which featured similar rituals and was celebrated annually at Penang and Kuala Lumpur in Malaysia.

Ngan Kin Jeh starts with vegetarian offerings to the gods and a ritualistic cleaning of the five major Chinese temples on the island. Each temple displays an array of knives, swords, axes, and spears to be used by entranced mediums over the next nine days. During the altar-side rituals held around the clock, gods and spirits are invited to take possession of volunteers. The volunteers then use their newly acquired supernatural powers to perform bizarre acts atoning for past transgressions and preventing bad luck in the future: cheeks are pierced with needles and knives, ladders of razor-sharp blades are climbed, and burning coals are walked upon without any visible signs of pain or physical damage.

The festival culminates with an elaborate parade of Chinese deities and temple mediums who honor the Nine Emperor Gods with similar acts of self-mortification. Shortly before midnight, Phuket explodes in a deafening thunder of firecrackers, drums, cymbals, trumpets, and gongs played by thousands of frantic participants. The crowd surges toward three urns of incense covered by yellow parasols and the Supreme Emperor, borne on an ornate sedan chair carved with dragons and Taoist symbols—all surrounded by mediums deep in a state of trance.

As the procession moves toward the beach, Taoist priests chant from the Sutras and pour symbolic libations of tea to purify the heavens and suffuse the earth with a bright, clear light. After arrival at the shore, the incense urns are loaded onto a small boat which is pushed out into the ocean, symbolizing the journey of the gods back to heaven.

Consulates: The French consulate (tel. 076-321199) at 89 Mu 3, Patong Beach, Kathu, and the Italian consulate (tel. 076-391151) at 89/2 Sakdidet Rd. are open weekdays 0900-1600.

Medical Facilities: Phuket Adventist Mission Hospital is considered the best on the island, with English-speaking doctors and emergency clinics at Patong Beach. 4/1 Thepkrasattri Rd., tel. (076) 211173.

Bookstores: The Books near the TAT office has the widest selection of books and maps on Phuket. Open daily 0900-2130. 53-55 Phuket Rd., tel. (076) 211396.

Maps: Recommended maps include *Phuket and Southern Thailand* published by Periplus Editions, followed by *Phuket Island* from Prannok Witthaya, and *Guide Map of Phuket* by Bangkok Guides.

Phuket Internet Resources: For an amazing amount of information about Phuket, visit the island's official website at www.phuket.com, which is updated to a fairly reliable level. Perhaps most importantly, you can visit the home pages of over 50 luxury hotels and make instant reservations before you take off on your vacation.

Newspapers: Phuket has one great English-language newspaper, the *Phuket Gazette* with all the insider tips you can handle, plus information on upcoming events and festivals. Their website at www.phuketgazette.com is a gold mine of information about the island.

Travel Agencies: Agencies in the center of town and at major beaches sell organized tours and bus tickets and make airline reservations. Sea Tours, adjacent to the tourist office, is an authorized agent for AMEX and Thai Airways, and can help with bus reservations and reasonably priced tours around the region. 95/4 Phuket Rd. tel. (076) 216979. Open weekdays 0830-1700, Saturday 0900-1200.

World Travel Service: Another large travel agency with honest and reliable services. Phuket Merlin Hotel, 158/1 Yaowaraj Rd., tel. (076) 212866. Open daily 0900-1700.

Songserm Travel: The largest boat transportation company in Thailand provides passage to Ko Phi Phi and Similan National Marine Park, plus standard services such as reservations for airlines, trains, and hotels. Open daily 0800-2200. Rasda Complex, 64/2 Rasda Rd., tel. (076) 214272, fax (076) 214301.

THE BEACHES

Phuket's best beaches are all on the western coast of the island. Each differs from the others in natural setting and degree of development, but all offer superb sand, warm waters, and endless sports activities.

Hotels are available in all possible price ranges. Budget hotels charge 400-800B for clean, modern rooms, while super-luxurious resorts with all possible amenities cost 1,800-4,000B.

Contrary to popular belief, simple bungalows under 300B are still available at all beaches—even the top-end world of Patong. The largest concentration of inexpensive bungalows is at the junction of Karon and Kata Beaches, appropriately called Karon-Kata. An easy way to locate a budget hotel is to tell your minitruck driver which beach you want, and what price range you can afford.

Phuket's hotels use a two-tiered pricing system. Rates are highest during the high season (Nov.-May), when Europeans flood the island, but discounted 30-50% during the rainy season (May-Oct.), when tropical storms lash the west coast. Luxury hotels add 10% service charge, 11% government room tax, and 8.25% food and beverage tax.

Phuket's most popular beaches are Patong, Karon, and Kata. Patong is the commercialized and tawdry tourist center of Phuket, but the best place for nightlife and water sports. Karon and Kata beaches attract a more sedate crowd who want to avoid the excesses of Patong.

NAI YANG BEACH

Tucked away near the northwest corner of Phuket, Nai Yang National Park encompasses the beach area once known for its annual turtle nestings. The sand is fairly good, and the beach is deserted except on weekends, when Thai families flood the park.

National Park Bungalows: Accommodations from park headquarters include campsites from 60B, bungalows off the beach for 200-300B, and beachside chalets for 500-800B. Nai Yang Beach, tel. (076) 327407.

Pearl Village: Located on the edge of the national park, Pearl Village is probably the most isolated hotel on the west coast of Phuket. The hotel is quiet, friendly, and far removed from the nightlife action of Patong—both a plus and a minus. Nai Yang Beach, Box 93, tel. (076) 327006, fax (076) 327338, 3,000-3,800B.

NAI TON BEACH

Looking for an immaculate yet absolutely deserted beach? Nai Ton fits the bill. Nai Ton lacks hotels, restaurants, beer bars, water-scooters, and parasailing—it's just a place to relax under a beach umbrella and stare into the dazzling waters.

The only drawback is the complete lack of formal accommodations. However, facing the long expanse of untouched beach is a line of private residences that rent rooms to visitors. Check at the cafe at the end of the beach, or with the owner of the blue-and-white cafe in the middle. Homestays in a/c rooms cost 300-500B, depending on length of stay and your bargaining abilities.

BANG TAO BAY

Ao Bang Tao, an arching four-km bay used during the filming of *The Killing Fields,* has long been an untouched corner of Phuket, well removed from the commercialism of other west coast beaches.

The bay's southern section features a handful of moderately priced bungalows for the budget-minded traveler, and the northern portion is covered by the sprawling Laguna Phuket Resort designed for the rich and famous.

Accommodations

Despite the jarring changes to the northern bay, reasonably priced bungalows and inexpensive cafes can still be found near the small fishing village in the south.

Bang Tao Lagoon Bungalows: Travelers seeking to escape the crowds but not break the bank are well served by this quiet place at the end of the bay. Facilities include a restaurant with Thai and European dishes, campsites, and 25 simple but clean bungalows with fan and private bath. Recommended. 72/3 Mu 3, Tambon Cheong Talay, tel. (076) 324260, fax (076) 324268, 250-650B.

Royal Park Travelodge Resort: A cozy yet upscale resort just outside the gargantuan complex to the north. First-class amenities. Moo 2 Tambon Cheong Talay, Amphur Talang, tel. (076) 324022, fax (076) 324023, 2,600-3,800B.

Laguna Phuket Resort

Bang Tao was first developed by tin mining consortiums that dredged the canals and carved out hundreds of enormous pits to extract the valuable ore. After the land was depleted, the mining companies departed and left behind tons of discarded machinery, rows of ramshackle huts, and dozens of enormous tin dredges that clogged the once-lovely lagoon. The soil was so polluted with industrial wastes that a United Nations survey later declared the area unfit for human habitation.

Bang Tao surprised the doomsayers in the mid-1980s when a Singapore-based development company announced plans to invest over US$200 million in Laguna Phuket, a mega-resort complex that would include five super-luxurious resorts arranged around six saltwater lagoons, over 100 privately owned condominiums, a championship 18-hole golf course, and sports facilities open to all guests residing within the complex.

Earth-moving machines were brought in to level the moonscape terrain, fresh topsoil was spread over the polluted grounds, and the un-

sightly tin dredges abandoned in the bay were hauled away and sold as scrap. The project was completed in 1995 with the opening of the final property, the Banyan Tree Resort.

Laguna Phuket may not appeal to everyone, but a quick look at the complex is worthwhile if only to appreciate the staggering transformation of an abandoned tin mine into Thailand's largest and most ambitious beach resort.

Resort Facilities: The five resorts share 25 bars and restaurants, 11 tennis courts, eight swimming pools, three fitness centers, two spas, two PADI-certified dive shops, a sports center with catamaran and sailboard rentals, and the Banyan Tree Golf Club surrounded by three ball-eating lagoons. What, no bungee jump?

Accommodations: Properties include the Dusit Laguna Resort Hotel, Sheraton Grande Laguna Beach , Laguna Beach Club, Allamanda Phuket, and the Banyan Tree Resort. Price ranges are listed below.

Each property has been designed with a unique personality. The Dusit Laguna is an elegant and classic resort directly on the beach, while the Sheraton Grande resembles an aquatic village surrounded on all sides by saltwater lagoons. The Laguna Beach Club follows the all-inclusive Club Med concept, while the Allamanda has 96 condominium apartments that include kitchens and other amenities for longer stays. The Banyan Tree consists of 128 ultra-luxurious villas, some of which include private swimming pool, sauna, and jacuzzi.

Dusit Laguna Resort Hotel: Perhaps the best mainstream resort in this region with several restaurants, pool, three bars, water sports, and spacious guest rooms, often facing the numerous lagoons which surround the property. Bang Tao Beach, tel. (076) 324320, fax (076) 324174, US$280-320.

Sheraton Grande Laguna Beach: An immense and well-equipped operation with lovely grounds bisected by countless lagoons and waterways; it offers seven restaurants, 325 rooms, and all other possible amenities. Bang Tao Beach, tel. (076) 324101, fax (076) 324108, US$200-360

Laguna Beach Club: This once-great property appears to have been mismanaged and has fallen from grace. Bang Tao Beach, tel. (076) 324355, fax (076) 324353, US$220-280

Allamanda: A rather ordinary set of condominiums of little interest to most visitors, aside from businessmen or golfers on extended stays. Bang Tao Beach, tel. (076) 324361, fax (076) 324360, US$180-240.

Banyan Tree Laguna Phuket: The most exclusive property in the resort and among the finest in Thailand, with 128 luxury villas spread over landscaped grounds and surrounding a large lake adjacent to a renowned 18-hole golf course. Request a room near the lobby and restaurant or expect some very long walks. Bang Tao Beach, tel. (076) 324374, fax (076) 324375, US$320-650.

SURIN BEACH

Also known as Pansea Bay, Surin is essentially a series of small coves and private beaches dominated by two super-exclusive resorts. Swimmers should be careful of dangerous undercurrents during the rainy season.

The Chedi: Formerly the Pansea, this upscale property is owned and operated by one of the most prestigious hotel chains in Asia—the same folks who own the Amanpuri. Pansea Beach, tel. (076) 324017, fax (076) 324252, 3,500-5,500B.

Amanpuri Resort: Few resorts in Asia can compare with the almost legendary Amanpuri Resort—a place for the "privileged few" with prices to stop your heart: high-season rates *start* at 8,000B. Pansea Beach, tel. (076) 324333, fax (076) 324100, 8,000-24,000B.

KAMALA BEACH

This almost picture-perfect half-moon bay offers good sand, a friendly Thai fishing village, and few *farangs*.

Budget Bungalows: Several inexpensive bungalows and cafes are tucked away at the north end of the beach and down the path on Laem Sing Beach. Villagers in town also rent rooms at negotiable rates.

Phuket Kamala Resort: Situated on the southern side of the bay is a midpriced resort with swimming pool and dive facilities. 74/8 Mu 3 Kamala Beach, tel. (076) 212901, 1,800-2,400B.

Kamala Beach Estate: Private homes owned by top executives and Western investors are rented to visitors at Estates One and Two; this is an unusual opportunity for homestay rather than hotel accommodations. The manager here is especially friendly and helpful. Kamala Beach, tel. (076) 324111, fax (076) 324115, 4,500-6,000B.

PATONG BEACH

This crowded yet beautiful four-km-long beach is the island's liveliest and most popular, the Pattaya of Phuket. Although it's fashionable to condemn Patong as overdeveloped, raunchy, polluted, expensive, and the worst example of unplanned madness (all true), the beach is outstanding, and daytime activities run the gamut from sailboarding and snorkeling to parasailing and sunbathing. Nightlife revolves around countless bars, discos, massage parlors, and nightclubs strung along the centerpoint of Soi Bangla. Your impression will largely depend on what you expect from Phuket: Patong is a place for parties and good times, not solitude and contemplation!

Patong has all possible facilities: banks, police, post office, tourist police, international phones, travel agencies, car and motorcycle rentals, and scuba diving shops.

Budget Accommodations

Although budget travelers generally avoid Patong and head to Kata-Karon, over a dozen bungalows still survive with rooms for 250-400B. Prices drop to as low as 150B during the slow summer months and are subject to negotiation anytime occupancy rates drop on the island.

The best hunting ground is on Soi San Sabai, the eastern extension of Bangla Road in the central beach area. Soi San Sabai is a good location since it's within walking distance of the beach and Soi Bangla nightclubs, but somewhat removed from the general mayhem.

Several other acceptable spots with rooms under 400B are located on Ratuthit Road north of Soi Bangla. These are quiet but, aside from the spots near Soi Bangla, you'll need public transportation or a motorcycle to reach the beach and nightlife centers.

Patong has, at last count, 126 hotel and bungalow operations with a total of 4653 rooms, so

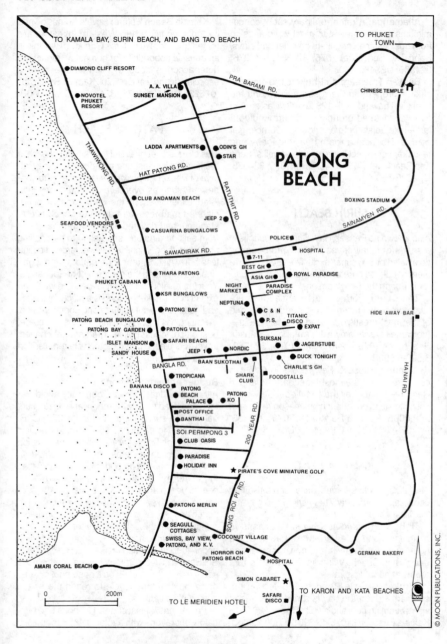

TO KAMALA BAY, SURIN BEACH, AND BANG TAO BEACH

TO PHUKET TOWN

DIAMOND CLIFF RESORT

PRA BARAMI RD.

CHINESE TEMPLE

A. A. VILLA
SUNSET MANSION

NOVOTEL
PHUKET
RESORT

LADDA APARTMENTS
ODIN'S GH
STAR

THAWIWONG RD.

HAT PATONG RD.

RATUTHIT RD.

PATONG BEACH

CLUB ANDAMAN BEACH

BOXING STADIUM

JEEP 2

SAINAMYEN RD.

SEAFOOD VENDORS

CASUARINA BUNGALOWS

POLICE

SAWADIRAK RD.

7-11
HOSPITAL

BEST GH

THARA PATONG

ASIA GH
ROYAL PARADISE

PHUKET CABANA

KSR BUNGALOWS

NIGHT
MARKET

PARADISE
COMPLEX

PATONG BAY

NEPTUNA

K
C & N
TITANIC
DISCO

PATONG BEACH BUNGALOW

P.S.

PATONG BAY GARDEN

PATONG VILLA

EXPAT

ISLET MANSION

SAFARI BEACH

SUKSAN

JAGERSTUBE

SANDY HOUSE

JEEP 1
NORDIC

BANGLA RD.

BAAN SUKOTHAI

DUCK TONIGHT

HIDE AWAY BAR

CHARLIE'S GH

TROPICANA

SHARK
CLUB

FOODSTALLS

BANANA DISCO

PATONG
BEACH
PALACE

PATONG
KO

HA NAI RD.

POST OFFICE
BANTHAI

200 YEAR RD.

SOI PERMPONG 3

CLUB OASIS

PARADISE

HOLIDAY INN

PIRATE'S COVE MINIATURE GOLF

PATONG MERLIN

SONG ROI PI RD.

SEAGULL
COTTAGES

SWISS, BAY VIEW,
PATONG, AND K.V.

COCONUT VILLAGE

HORROR ON
PATONG BEACH

HOSPITAL

GERMAN BAKERY

AMARI CORAL BEACH

0   200m

SIMON CABARET

SAFARI
DISCO

TO LE MERIDIEN HOTEL

TO KARON AND KATA BEACHES

© MOON PUBLICATIONS, INC.

I'll just mention a few that seem clean, quiet, and friendly, or important enough to be included on my map of Patong.

Soi San Sabai: A half dozen inexpensive guesthouses and hotels are tucked away on this quiet extension of Soi Bangla, such as **Suksan Mansion,** a modern four-story hotel with fan rooms from 300B and a/c rooms from 600B. Popular and dependable **Charlies Guesthouse** costs 300-450B for fan-cooled rooms. German-managed **Jagerstube** has a popular restaurant with award-winning breads and large a/c rooms from 700B.

Small alleys just a few steps north of Soi San Sabai are also great places to check for budget guesthouses and low-priced hotels with comfortable a/c rooms.

Soi Bangla (Bangla Road): Soi Bangla is the heart of the beast—a nonstop string of honky-tonk bars, wild nightclubs, pickup joints, raging discos, hordes of transvestite hookers, drunken tourists, and low-life restaurants and pubs where the truly sleazy find nirvana. Hence, bungalows are noisy, but easy to find after consuming a case of Singha. **Jeep 1, Sea Dragon,** and **Nordic Bungalows** cost 300-450B fan and double that for a/c. Although these are hardcore bachelor pads, some travelers may find them acceptable for a few days.

Ratuthit Road: Several inexpensive hotels are located north of Bangla Road. **Expat Hotel** is quiet but has somewhat overpriced a/c rooms from 800B facing a small pool. Big discounts are given to long-term residents; their catapult just outside the entrance is the anti-gravity answer to bungee jumps.

P.S. and **C & N** bungalows cost 300-400B. Farther north are **Jeep 2, Star,** Scandinavian-run **Odin's Guesthouse,** and the spotless **Ladda Apartments** with rooms from 450B.

Asia Guesthouse: A short walk north of the bar zone on Soi Bangla is Paradise Complex, where several budget guesthouses have operated for many years. The units are somewhat sterile but the area is quiet and without the sleaze of central Patong. Asia Guesthouse has 44 rooms, either fan-cooled or a/c, with private baths. Paradise Complex, 70/44 Ratuthit Rd., tel. (076) 340962, 350-650B.

Best Guesthouse: Another popular "guesthouse" in the same area as the Asia Guesthouse, but with just 18 rooms. Paradise Complex, 77/164 Ratuthit Rd., tel. (076) 340958, 350-600B.

Moderate Accommodations

Midpriced hotels in the 800-2,500B range sport a/c rooms, private baths, TVs, restaurants, and perhaps a small swimming pool. Reservations should be made in advance during the high season Nov.-March.

Lower Thawiwong Road: A half dozen small, inexpensive hotels are tucked away at the south end of the beach road, variously spelled Thaweewong, Thaviwong, and Taveewong. The road is also know as "Patong Beach Road," probably the best name for this busy road.

Swiss Hotel costs 1,600-2,200B, **Bay View House** 1,200-1,500B, **Patong Bed & Breakfast** 900-1,400B, and **K.V. House** 900-1,400B. **Seagull Cottages** is a good-value complex with inexpensive fan-cooled bungalows for 900-1,200B and superior seaview chalets for 1,500-2,000B.

Soi Post Office: In the narrow alley adjacent to the post office are several hotels and restaurants such as Shalimar (Indian), Fuji (Japanese), Cowboy (Western), Roma (Italian), and My Way (gay). Bungalow choices include **Palace Inn, Patong Ko,** and **Cowboy Inn** with a/c rooms for 700-1,000B. **Paradise Hotel** is a fine place with fan-cooled bungalows from 600B facing a lovely garden. Nearby **Club Oasis** has older but acceptable rooms in a quiet garden with singing birds.

On the Beach: Several midpriced hotels are located right on the beach. **Sandy House** lacks beach views but has cheap a/c rooms for 900-1,200B. **Islet Mansion** has rooms without views from 800B, and seaside vistas for 1,200-1,800B. **Patong Beach Bungalows** are old and not recommended.

Safari Beach Hotel: Right in the center of Patong and just across the road from the beach with tennis courts, two restaurants, and 35 a/c rooms. 83/12 Thawiwong Rd., tel. (076) 340230, fax (076) 340231, 1,600-2,400B.

Patong Villa: Just a few steps north of Safari Beach is another midpriced hotel with tennis courts, cafe, and 24 a/c rooms. 85/3 Thawiwong Rd., tel. (076) 340132, fax (076) 340133, 1,200-2,400B.

KSR Bungalows: One of the few bargain priced hotels in the center of Patong and very near the beach with 20 small but acceptable a/c rooms. 83/3 Thawiwong Rd., tel. (076) 340938, fax (076) 340322, 900-1,200B.

Casuarina Bungalows: An older hotel on the beach road a few blocks north of Soi Bangla, with basic facilities and somewhat overpriced rooms, but well located in a quiet part of Patong. 77/1 Thawiwong Rd., tel. (076) 341197, fax (076) 340123, 1,800-2,600B.

K Hotel: Beautiful gardens, small pool, and efficient Austrian management make this another good choice, popular with European group tours. Ratuthit Rd., tel. (076) 340832, fax (076) 340124, 800-1,600B.

Neptuna Hotel: A lovely French-owned hotel with sculpted gardens, intimate French cafe, and a small but acceptable pool. 82/49 Ratuthit Rd., tel./fax (076) 340188, 1,400-1,800B.

Sunset Mansion: Good-value rooms at the far north end of Ratuthit Road. The nearby **A.A. Villa** is another modern, clean place. 73/24 Ratuthit Rd., tel. (076) 340516, 300-400B fan, 600-800B a/c.

Coconut Village: Well-priced hotel at the south end of town with swimming pool and 75 clean a/c rooms. Several other hotels on this road provide decent rooms at far better prices than hotels closer to the center of town, and all are just a 10-minute walk to Soi Bangla. 20 Prachanukro Rd., tel. (076) 340146, fax (076) 340144, 800-1,500B.

Luxury Accommodations
Top-end hotels over 3,000B typically include a swimming pool, fitness center, tennis courts, and whatever else the marketing director dreamed up. All can be booked through Bangkok travel agents.

The following hotels are listed in alphabetical order.

Amari Coral Beach: Removed from the clutter of central Patong, Coral Beach is an all-inclusive resort with swimming pool, squash, tennis courts, and fitness club. 104 Mu 4 Patong Beach, tel. (076) 340106, fax (076) 340115, 3,600-4,800B.

Baan Sukothai: Baan Sukothai is something different: an attempt at traditional Thai architecture with pavilions and cottages in a landscaped tropical garden. A welcome change from the concrete cubicle. 95 Ratuthit Rd., tel. (076) 340195, fax (076) 340197, 2,800-3,600B.

Banthai Resort Hotel: Facing the beach a few blocks south of Soi Bangla, Banthai Resort is set in a superb location near the nightlife and restaurants, tucked away along Soi Permpong and Soi Post Office. It offers a swimming pool, two restaurants, and 190 well-maintained rooms. 89/71 Thawiwong Rd., tel. (076) 340850, fax (076) 340330, 2,500-3,600B.

Club Andaman Beach Resort: An older hotel on the north end of the beach with 55 decrepit Thai bungalows and an eight-story building with two wings. The tropical gardens are lovely, but the group tours that predominate here give it a less-than-refined atmosphere. 77/1 Thawiwong Rd., tel. (076) 340530, fax (076) 340527, 2,800-3,800B.

Diamond Cliff Resort: At the far northern end of Patong, clinging to the side of a surprisingly steep cliff, is another favorite of tour groups who almost need to be mountaineers to reach their rooms from the lobby. 61/9 Kalim Beach Rd., tel. (076) 340501, fax (076) 340507, 3,600-4,800B.

Holiday Inn Resort Phuket: Typical Holiday Inn property with cookie-cutter architecture and a small pool, but in an excellent location at the south end of the beach. 86/11 Thawiwong Rd., tel. (076) 340608, fax (076) 340435, 2,800-4,600B.

Novotel Phuket Resort: Somewhat isolated just north of town, but a popular hotel with European group tours and other visitors fond of this famous hotel chain. Kalim Beach Rd., tel. (076) 342777, fax (076) 342168, 2,800-4,400B.

Patong Bay Garden: One of the better hotels located directly on the beach; it features a pool, roof garden terrace, and fine restaurant. 61/13 Thawiwong Rd., tel. (076) 340297, fax (076) 340560, 3,200-4,500B.

Patong Beach Hotel: Gorgeous pool, outstanding views from the top floors, and spacious rooms make this deluxe hotel one of the better bargains on Patong. Bananas Disco inside this massive hotel is one of Patong's most popular. 124 Thawiwong Rd., tel. (076) 340301, fax (076) 340541, 3,200-4,000B.

Patong Merlin: A very large hotel at the south end of Patong, with swimming pool, tennis courts, two restaurants, and 386 a/c rooms. 44 Thawiwong Rd., tel. (076) 340037, fax (076) 340194, 3,200-4,200B.

Phuket Cabana Resort: The best beachfront hotel is somewhat overpriced, and many of the bungalows in the rear are dark and gloomy, but you can't beat the location in the heart of Patong. 41 Thawiwong Rd., tel. (076) 340138, fax (076) 340178, 3,200-3,600B.

Royal Paradise Hotel: It's impossible to ignore the controversial architecture of the tallest hotel on Patong Beach. All rooms have panoramic views and the pool is spectacular, but the hotel is a long walk from the beach. 70 Paradise Complex, tel. (076) 340666, fax (076) 340565, 2,800-4,600B.

Thara Patong Beach Resort: Just a short walk north of central Patong, this 128-room resort spread over a large piece of land has all the standard amenities, from swimming pool and health club to business center and convention facilities. 170 Thawiwong Rd., tel. (076) 340135, fax (076) 340446, 2,800-4,400B.

Bargain Restaurants

Patong is a tourist heaven, where you can find almost every conceivable form of Western food and badly overpriced Thai cuisine; but you could die of starvation if you insist on an inexpensive bowl of noodles.

Foodstalls: A small collection of basic foodstalls set up nightly on Ratuthit Road just south of Soi Bangla, chiefly to serve the local prostitutes and motorcycle taxi drivers who hang out at the nearby intersection. This section of Rathuthit Road is sometimes called "200-year-old Road" for reasons unknown to this author.

Night Market: Another possible spot for inexpensive noodle and rice dishes in the night market on Rathuthit Road about one block north of Soi Bangla. This place has a good selection of food vendors where you can have a full dinner for less than 50 *baht*. Anyone who needs to eat—but not break the bank—should head directly to this night market.

Seafood Vendors: Your final choice for a fairly inexpensive yet authentic meal are the collection of seafood vendors who set up their portable kitchens on the beach each night, just opposite the Club Andaman Beach Resort. Prices are higher than the two places mentioned above, though you might enjoy dining alfresco amid the coconut palms and swaying casuarina trees.

Sabai Beach: Among the assortment of simple bamboo shacks that make up the "Seafood Vendors" above is this slightly more formal spot with excellent food at bargain prices in the shade of casuarina trees. Adjacent Restaurant 7 is also recommended. All these places are right on the beach across from the Club Andaman Beach Resort—a 15-minute walk from Soi Bangla.

Soi Bangla Restaurants

Several dozen cafes and restaurants are located along Soi Bangla or tucked away in the various alleys which branch off this very lively street.

Soi Patong Resort Restaurants: This dead-end alley, in the middle of the block on the south side of Soi Bangla, is packed with decent Western cafes, often a/c and serving acceptable food in the moderate-to-expensive price range. Among the more popular choices are the Rundetarn for Scandanavian food and fondue, The Islander for English and Thai dishes, an Indian cafe called Navrang Mahal, Buffalo Steakhouse for obvious reasons, Italian ice cream and light snacks in Paciuco, more hearty meals plus pool and Internet connections in Waikiki Dive Cafe, and fine Italian cuisine in Gino's Paradiso at the end of the street. Soi Patong also has a few travel agencies and small grocery stores for takeaway beer and basic supplies.

Soi Bangla Square: Just a few steps east of Soi Patong is another short alley packed with convenience shops, souvenir outlets, and several restaurants, such as Le Croissant Cafe, located on the corner for baked goods and Thai food in a/c comfort, Rico's Pizzaria & Steakhouse, Victor Restaurant for Belgian and French meals, and the flashy Viking Grill Garden at the end of the street, where you can dig into unlimited buffets every night of the week.

Soi Eric: Across the street from the two above-mentioned venues are several dead-end alleys filled with outdoor "beer bars," go-go lounges, inexpensive guesthouses, cafes, coffeeshops, and thousands of prostitutes and transvestites hustlers. You may not want to indulge in the sex, but hanging out here for a few hours is certainly among the world's more unique travel experiences.

Ristorante & Pizzeria D'Italia near the end of the alley has good Italian food and provides a safe place to observe the action without having to deal with the hookers and con artists. Flash A-Go Go just above this Italian restaurant is another place to escape the crowds and relax in a/c comfort, while Caffe Le Bistro right at the corner of Soi Eric and Soi Bangla is the ultimate place to watch the action while working on your espresso or cappuccino.

Restaurant Alleys

A half-dozen narrow alleys branch off Thawiwong Road (the beach road) between Soi Bangla and the south end of Patong.

Soi Permpong 3: This busy dead-end street serves as the single most concentrated "restaurant row" in Patong, with such culinary choices as Restaurant Europa for Italian and Thai meals; Zum Schlawiener for Austrian specialties; the very popular Sea Hag for fine atmosphere at steep prices; Bauernstuberl for German and Swiss dishes prepared by a Swiss chef; Shalimar, which claims fame as the oldest Indian restaurant on the island; Viva Mexico for Mexican offerings and margaritas; home-cooked Scandinavian meals at Lisa's; and French cuisine at L'Auberge, located at the end of the alley.

Several of these restaurants also have guesthouses on the upper floors where a/c rooms with either common or private baths cost from 350-700B—at least you won't need to walk far for a meal. Check with Frank's Bauernstuberl or the friendly French guys at L'Auberge.

Soi Post Office: The alley adjacent to the post office has a much smaller number of cafes than Soi Permpong 3, though you might want to check the posted menus at Pizzeria Napoli and other Italian and Thai cafes on the street.

Nightlife—Pubs and Bars

Soi Bangla is obviously the nightlife center of Patong, though a few individual pubs and small bars are worth a special mention.

Kangroo Bar: One of the better drinking holes with an Australian theme and friendly staff, plus fewer bar girls than most other pubs in this neighborhood. Soi Bangla.

Gonzo Bar: One of the largest bars on the strip, this spot always is filled with an odd mixture of local expats, visiting *farangs,* and enough wandering females to keep it all interesting—especially late at night when the whole affair starts to resemble the bar scene from *Star Wars.* Soi Bangla.

Pow Wow Indian Pub: A Wild West nightclub with reasonably priced bar snacks, cold drinks, and nightly live music—often country and western bands—without the hordes of bar girls common to Soi Bangla pubs. This place is a few blocks north of Soi Bangla and attracts an almost exclusively Thai clientele, along with a handful of curious Westerners. 70/179 Paradise Complex, Ratuthit Rd.

Nightclubs and Discos

Disco wars have broken out in Patong with the opening of several new disco cum nightclubs in recent years.

Banana Disco: The oldest disco on Patong attracts a very young and rather unsophisticated crowd that suffers through overpriced drinks and uniformly dismal rock bands. Still, the place is always packed and best visited around midnight. Patong Beach Hotel, Thawiwong Rd.

Shark Club: Banana Disco's chief competitor is this newer nightclub just off Soi Bangla on a less commercialized backstreet, where sporting events are screened during the day and DJs spin tunes nightly after 2100. Corner of Soi Bangla and Soi Ratuthit (called "Soi 200 Year" in this section).

Titanic Star Disco: A smaller and less-successful disco tucked away in an alley just north of Soi Bangla, where bar girls rather than ordinary customers often prevail. Ratuthit Rd., Soi Sunset.

Chicago Fun Pub: A new 20-million *baht* nightclub and restaurant complex just across the road from the Shark Club. Ratuthit Rd.

Safari Club: Patong's best nightclub and disco is a few kilometers south of town on the road to Karon, where a uniquely styled building provides the largest dance floor on the island; entertainment ranges from DJs to live bands, not to mention "special shows" several times weekly at midnight. Safari Club has a bizarre Tarzan motif and sprawling gardens where visitors can escape the disco beat and relax under the stars—the best nightclub on the island. Patong-Karon Rd.

Entertainment Oddities

As if Soi Bangla wasn't strange enough.

Phuket Simon Cabaret: The same folks who brought you the famed transvestite review in Pattaya now operate a similar nightclub at the south end of Patong, where over 70 drag queens sing and dance twice nightly at 1930 and 2130. Patong-Karon Rd.

Horror on Patong Beach: You know that a beach resort has achieved some sort of twisted pinnacle when it boasts not only thousands of prostitutes and transvestite hookers but also Asia's biggest horror house. This landmark to bad taste is south of Patong near the much classier Phuket Simon Cabaret. 24 Patong-Karon Rd. Open daily 1800-0100.

Pirate's Cove Adventure Mini Golf: Practice your putts and enjoy a burger and cold beer at this surprisingly good miniature golf course just behind the Phuket Holiday Inn.

KARON BEACH

Phuket's second-most-popular beach remains beautiful, despite the rising tide of hotel construction and the creeping presence of nightclubs and so-called Bar Beers. As with Kata Beach to the south, Karon seems much less crowded than Patong, and the hotel employees seem a little more willing to smile rather than stretch out their hands. There's little to do at Karon but sailboard, eat Phuket lobster, laze on the beach, and act nutty with the working girls. Surprisingly, an idyllic lagoon lies in the north end, and fishermen still pull in baskets of fish from the ocean.

Karon and Kata are superior beaches to Patong, though there's also far less nightlife and a surprisingly limited selection of restaurants aside from the cookie-cutter offerings in the luxury hotels. Therefore, these two beaches are recommended for families, couples, and other visitors who find the nightlife scene in Patong too raunchy for their taste. If you're looking for amusement and dislike transportation hassles, then you should probably stay over the hill in Patong.

Budget Accommodations—Kata-Karon

Karon is probably 80% upmarket hotels, but a handful of inexpensive bungalows under 350B are spread around the beach, many located at the south end on a hill called Kata-Karon (or Karon-Kata, depending on your geographical perspective). None are great value, but they're cheap enough to allow you to check out Phuket without wrecking your budget.

Kata Tropicana: The largest budget bungalow operation on Phuket is a sprawling complex of over 100 huts on the hill, just up a dirt road off the main highway. The place has a limited number of bungalows for 150-300B, but most cost 300-900B. Amenities include a backpackers' restaurant and an enormous pig that wanders around and poses for pictures. Kata-Karon Hill Rd., tel. (076) 330408, 150-900B.

Happy Huts: Beyond Kata Tropicana and farther up the hill in a small valley with palms is another budget option, with old but acceptable bungalows, a 10-minute walk from the beach. Kata-Karon Hill Rd., tel. (076) 330230, 150-350B.

Fantasy Hill Good location and well priced, but most of the rooms are in an ugly concrete longhouse without charm or character. 112/1 Patak Rd., tel. (076) 330106, 200-400B.

Budget Accommodations—North Karon

North Karon, near the large traffic circle, is taken up largely by a major commercial development with several guesthouses and hotels, a few shops for groceries and other necessities, and a dozen or so cafes for inexpensive meals. This is a great place to stay, since all necessary services are within walking distance and Patong is only a 10-minute taxi ride. Several old guesthouses hang on, along with the midlevel places described below.

Lume & Yai Bungalows: At the extreme north end of Karon Beach, well off the beach and surrounded by enormous luxury resorts, is a friendly and cheap set of bungalows which date from the early days of the hippie invasion. The place has improved itself over the years, but it's difficult to say how much longer this anachronism can hang on in the face of relentless progress. 7/3 Patak Rd., tel. (076) 396096, 300-600B.

My Friend Bungalows: Formerly known by its highly superior name, "Much My Friend Bungalows," this old favorite just south of the traffic circle remains one of the original hippie operations still surviving along this stretch of beach. 36/6 Patak Rd., tel. (076) 396344, 200-450B.

Karon Seaview Bungalows: Nicely isolated between open grounds and the beach, with 70 characterless concrete bungalows and nothing in the distance but luxury hotels. 36/9 Patak Rd., tel. (076) 396912, 300-450B.

Budget Accommodations—Central Karon
Several inexpensive places are located in central Karon on Soi Luang Pho Chuan (also called Soi Bangla) near the raging Club 44 Disco and assorted small cafes

Jor Guesthouse: Small guesthouse with just nine rooms. 102/4 Patak Rd., tel. (076) 396546, fax (076) 396258, 300-750B.

Robin House: Another budget guesthouse, located some 200 meters off the beach road near several cafes, a nightclub, and a handful of other guesthouses, all with decent rooms at reasonable prices. 128/12 Soi Bangla (Soi Luang Pho Chuan), tel. (076) 396496, 350-700B.

Moderate Accommodations—North Karon
Midpriced hotels in Karon average 500-1,000B for an a/c room with private bath and hot showers, though most of the following places also offer fan-cooled rooms with private bath for 300-600B, and superior rooms with extra spacious dimensions and better furniture for 1,200-1,800B.

Karon Cafe Inn: This popular and recently expanded hotel also runs one of the better cafes in the north end of Karon. Manager Eric Conger works hard to please. 33/76 Patak Rd., tel. (076) 396217, fax (076) 396745, 800-1,400B.

Karon Guesthouse: Spotless rooms and friendly management make this a good-value place in north Karon near the modern commercial district, which now makes up the heart and soul of Karon. 92/1 Patak Rd., tel. (076) 396860, fax (076) 396117, 350-750B.

Crystal Beach Hotel: A large, modern, 120-room hotel with restaurant and travel facilities conveniently located in the north Karon commercial enclave. All rooms are a/c with private baths and hot showers. 36/10 Patak Rd., tel. (076) 396580, 350-700B.

Phuket Ocean Resort: North of the commercial district is a moderately priced hotel that's poorly stuck back against the hillside and separated from the beach by a large lagoon. The highway traffic also makes this a less-than-ideal

choice for most visitors. 9/1 Patak Rd., tel. (076) 396599, fax (076) 396470, 1,200-1,800B.

Phuket Golden Sand Inn: A 74-room hotel with basic facilities, just north of the commercial district and within walking distance of the street-stalls which set up nightly just north of the traffic circle. 8/6 Patak Rd., tel. (076) 396493, fax (076) 396117, 850-1,800B.

Moderate Accommodations—Kata-Karon
Kata-Karon Hill—midway between Karon and Kata beaches—now serves as a leisure and recreation center for the two beaches, with several dive shops and other cultural oddities, such as the weird and twisted Dino Park at the top of the hill. Dino Park is, well. . . the Flintstones on acid.

Ruamthep Inn: An older property with just 14 rooms in a wonderful location at the south end of Karon Beach. 120/4 Patak Rd., tel. (076) 330281, 600-800B fan, 1,200-1,500B a/c.

Karon Beach Resort: Just up the hill from Ruamthep Inn with small restaurant, friendly staff, and 81 a/c rooms, many overlooking the ocean. Karon-Kata Hill Rd., tel. (076) 330006, fax (076) 330529, 2,200-3,500B.

Marina Cottages: One of the best midpriced resorts on Phuket, overlooking a private beach and adjacent to the truly strange Dino Park with tropical gardens, coconut groves, and a variety of bungalows in various price ranges depending on particular views. Kata-Karon Hill Rd., tel. (076) 330625, fax (076) 330516, 1,200-2,200B.

Green Valley Bungalows: Visitors with private transportation will enjoy this idyllic spot hidden away in a lush valley behind Hwy. 4028; it offers a small pool, landscaped gardens, and plenty of coconut trees. 66/3 Patak Rd., tel. (076) 381468, 900-1,400B.

Luxury Accommodations
Almost a dozen luxury resorts spread themselves between the northern hills which lead to Patong and the Kata-Karon hillock to the south. Most of these places have been around for many years, though skyrocketing tourism will almost certainly bring new properties in coming years.

Felix Karon Swissotel: Hidden away at the extreme north end of the beach, and hemmed in by the busy highway, is a Swiss-operated hotel with 121 rooms and all the standard services.

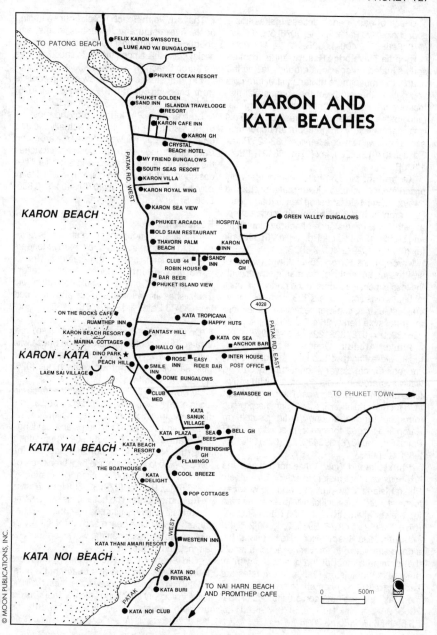

KARON AND KATA BEACHES

TO PATONG BEACH

FELIX KARON SWISSOTEL
LUME AND YAI BUNGALOWS

PHUKET OCEAN RESORT

PHUKET GOLDEN
SAND INN ISLANDIA TRAVELODGE
RESORT

KARON CAFE INN

KARON GH

CRYSTAL
BEACH HOTEL
MY FRIEND BUNGALOWS
SOUTH SEAS RESORT
KARON VILLA
KARON ROYAL WING
KARON SEA VIEW

KARON BEACH

PATAK RD. WEST

PHUKET ARCADIA   HOSPITAL
OLD SIAM RESTAURANT
THAVORN PALM   KARON
BEACH   INN

GREEN VALLEY BUNGALOWS

CLUB 44 SANDY
INN
ROBIN HOUSE
BAR BEER
PHUKET ISLAND VIEW

JOR
GH

4028

ON THE ROCKS CAFE
RUAMTHEP INN

KARON BEACH RESORT
MARINA COTTAGES

KARON - KATA
DINO PARK ★
PEACH HILL

LAEM SAI VILLAGE

KATA TROPICANA
HAPPY HUTS

FANTASY HILL

HALLO GH

KATA ON SEA
ANCHOR BAR

ROSE EASY INTER HOUSE
INN RIDER BAR POST OFFICE
SMILE
INN
DOME BUNGALOWS

PATAK RD. EAST

TO PHUKET TOWN →

CLUB
MED

SAWASDEE GH

KATA
SANUK
VILLAGE

KATA PLAZA SEA
BEES BELL GH

KATA YAI BEACH KATA BEACH
RESORT
FRIENDSHIP
GH
FLAMINGO

THE BOATHOUSE
KATA
DELIGHT COOL BREEZE

POP COTTAGES

PATAK RD. WEST

WESTERN INN

KATA THANI AMARI RESORT

KATA NOI BEACH

KATA NOI
RIVIERA

KATA BURI

PATAK RD.

TO NAI HARN BEACH
AND PROMTHEP CAFE

KATA NOI CLUB

0   500m

© MOON PUBLICATIONS, INC.

The lack of easy beach access makes this a poor choice. 4/8 Patak Rd., tel. (076) 396666, fax (076) 396853, 2,400-3,600B.

Islandia Travelodge Resort: Unlike most resorts situated on spacious grounds facing the beach, this much more utilitarian structure puts you right in the middle of the commercial district of north Karon, but still within walking distance of the beach and many restaurants. This isn't really a luxury property but an upper mid-priced hotel with upscale services. 33/125 Patak Rd., tel. (076) 396200, fax (076) 396491, 1,200-1,800B.

Karon Inn: Modest hotel with moderately priced rooms, just below luxury category tucked away on a quiet sidestreet off beach road in central Karon, with 100 a/c rooms and coffee shop, all within walking distance of nearby nightclubs and beach. 128/4 Patak Rd., tel. (076) 396519, fax (076) 330529, 1,400-2,600B.

Karon Villa & Karon Royal Wing: Two massive resorts under the same management, with the less expensive rooms to the north and more luxurious digs south; offers 323 rooms plus several restaurants, conference facilities, and most other possible perks. 36/4 Patak Rd., tel. (076) 396139, fax (076) 396122, 2,800-4,200B.

Phuket Arcadia: One of the few architecturally interesting resorts on the island, with curvaceous towers cleverly connected by curving walkways around pools decorated with sculptures and Thai spirits houses. The place is huge (475 rooms) and often filled with Japanese group tours, but it ranks among the finer hotels on Karon and a good choice for most visitors. 78/2 Patak Rd., tel. (076) 396433, fax (076) 396136, 2,800-3,800B.

Phuket Island View: While not as large and luxurious as other major resorts on this beach, Phuket Island View provides enough services for most visitors at significantly lower prices than top-drawer alternatives. 127/23 Patak Rd., tel. (076) 396452, fax (076) 396632, 1,600-2,600B.

South Seas Resort: Not quite luxurious, but a good alternative to the very expensive hotels that dominate most of the beach. As with all other luxury hotels on Phuket, room rates are subject to 10% service charge, 11% government tax, and peak-season surcharges of 550-700B. 36/12 Patak Rd., tel. (076) 396611, fax (076) 396618, 2,800-3,800B.

Thavorn Palm Beach Hotel: Four swimming pools, five restaurants, luxurious rooms, and enormous grounds (just try to find the reception desk!) make this among the more varied choices on Karon Beach. The clipped and sculpted topiary in the gardens near the swimming pools is worth checking out. 128/10 Patak Rd., tel. (076) 396090, fax (076) 396555, 4,500-8,500B.

Le Meridien Phuket: One of the most famous resorts on the island is actually located on a private bay midway between Karon and Patong, with an enormous pool that stretches the breadth of the complex and extra facilities designed for families with children in tow. Relax Bay, tel. (076) 340480, fax (076) 340479, 3,800-5,600B.

Restaurants

Karon has few independent restaurants compared to Patong, though a few hardy pioneers are attempting to change the situation.

Karon Cafe Inn: Cozy cafe with excellent American and Continental cuisine, along with Thai dishes at reasonable prices and great service. 33/76 Patak Rd., tel. (076) 396217. Moderate.

On the Rock: An old favorite worth a splurge, located at the southern end of Karon Beach with sweeping views of the beach and some of the best seafood in town. Karon Beach, tel. (076) 330625. Moderate.

Al Dente: An Italian outlet near the traffic circle in north Karon, with expert dishes and a wonderful motto which encourages visitors to "eat oysters and love long, eat clams and last long." 35/7 Patak Rd., tel. (076) 396569. Moderate.

Little Mermaid: Recommended by the *Groovy Map to Phuket* for the best breakfasts on Karon; also called the "backpackers favorite." 36/10 Patak Rd., tel. (076) 396628 Inexpensive.

Ruamthep Cafe: The hotel of the same name operates a uniquely situated cafe that provides superb views of the beach and bay at sunset, as well as the surfers when the waves are up. Ruamthep Inn. Moderate.

Old Siam: Unabashedly among the more touristy restaurants on this beach but a noteworthy combination of pricey buffet tubs, twinkling lights in coconut trees, and graceful Thai dancers dodging tourists as they wander towards the buffet spreads. This is one of the few places on the island that makes an honest attempt to recreate an atmosphere of "Old Siam." Dance routines twice weekly on Wednesdays and Sundays. Thavorn Palm Beach Resort, 128/10 Patak Rd., tel. (076) 396090. Expensive (at least for a buffet).

The Float: Built to resemble an abandoned boat, The Float offers buffets and ala carte entrees served by friendly maidens in nautical gear. Located just north of the Thavorn Palm Beach Resort. 110 Patak Rd., tel. (076) 396552. Moderate.

Dino Kitchen: Totally weird, but perhaps the only place in Thailand to dine under an active volcano on Dinoburgers and Dinobeer before heading off for a round of miniature golf. Kata-Karon Rd., tel. (076) 330625. Moderate.

Sala Thai: Fine hotel restaurant in open-air *salas,* surrounded by lush gardens serving both Thai and Western dishes at reasonable prices. Marina Cottages, tel. (076) 330625. Moderate.

Talay Tai: Hotel outlet with better seafood fare than expected and almost-reasonable prices. Karon Villa, tel. (076) 396038. Expensive.

Rainbow Room: Small cafe overlooking Karon Bay with memorable sunset cocktails and decent food. 9/6 Patak Rd., tel. (076) 286030. Expensive.

Buffalo Steak House: Back from the beach, near the north Karon traffic circle, and serving exclusively vegetarian dishes prepared by a Scandinavian chef. 35/19 Patak Rd., tel. (076) 396824. Moderate.

Restaurant Wiener: A peculiar cafe that only serves food from authorized war zones around the world. 128/81 Patak Rd., tel. (076) 396579.Inexpensive but intellectually confused.

KATA BEACH

Kata's two beaches—Kata Yai in the north and Kata Noi to the south—once served as Phuket's main hippie area until Club Med opened its facilities in 1978. Now, the beaches are blanketed with upscale hotels and expensive restaurants, along with a few budget bungalows that still hang on. Kata Yai is dominated by Club Med, though public access is provided by a beachside road, while Kata Noi is a cozy cove with good sand and several inexpensive places to stay.

Budget Accommodations

Contrary to popular folklore, over a dozen bungalows and small hotels on Kata Beach have rooms for 300-500B, mostly on Kata Noi Beach near the expensive hotels or at the south end of Kata Yai near Kata Plaza. The following guesthouses are described from north to south.

Dome Bungalows: Small spot with 16 fan-cooled and a/c rooms just south of the Karon-Kata commercial district and across the road from Club Med. 116 Patak Rd., tel. (076) 330620, 300-600B.

Rose Inn: Right in the heart of the nightlife in Kata Center, with 16 rooms that can get noisy in the evening as the beer bars crank up the action. Kata Center, 114/23 Patak Rd., tel. (076) 330582, 300-600B.

Sea Bees: A small, 10-room operation a block from the beach, just east of Kata Plaza. Several other cozy guesthouses on this street open and close with the seasons. 13/2 Patak Rd., tel. (076) 330090, 300-550B.

Friendship Bungalows: A longtime favorite in a handy location near the Kata Yai beachhead, with 23 small but acceptable rooms and friendly managers. 6/5 Patak Rd., tel. (076) 330499, 300-650B.

Bell Guesthouse: A 15-minute walk back from the beach but perhaps the least expensive guesthouse in the region, with a handful of super-bargain rooms and larger facilities at higher prices. 1/2 Patak Rd., tel. (076) 320111, 200-450B.

Kata Sanuk Village: Just back from the main road and within easy access to nearby shops, cafes, and beach access, just past the Club Med perimeter road. Features a small pool and comfortable restaurant decorated with European porcelains. 7/7 Patak Rd., tel. (076) 330476, 350-600B.

Cool Breeze Bungalows This place suffers from incessant traffic but offers 16 fairly comfortable rooms just opposite the Boathouse. 5/5 Patak Rd., tel. (076) 330484, 300-650B.

Kata Noi Riviera: The far southern section of Kata Noi once served as the hippie center until several modern resort complexes gobbled up all the beachfront property and forced the bungalow operators out of business. Kata Noi Riviera is one of the few budget spots left down here. 3/21 Kata Noi Beach Rd., tel. (076) 330726, fax (076) 330924, 350-650B.

Moderate Accommodations

Kata also has a good supply of moderately priced hotels in the 500-900B price range, described here from north to south.

Peach Hill Hotel: A clean and modern hotel with Chinese restaurant, snooker hall, and 40 a/c rooms centrally located on Kata-Karon hill near the nightlife, cafes, and dive shops. 113/16 Patak Rd., tel. (076) 330603, fax (076) 330895, 500-900B.

Smile Inn: A larger property with 30 a/c rooms adjacent to Kata Center. 116/10-12 Patak Rd., tel. (076) 330926, fax (076) 330925, 700-950B.

Flamingo: Small, 10-room hotel in the busy commercial center across from the Kata Beach Resort, which blocks out any possible view of the beach. 5/19 Patak Rd., tel. (076) 330776, fax (076) 330814, 450-750B.

Pop Cottages: Large operation with 78 fan-cooled and a/c rooms at the south end of Kata Yai Beach; this spot offers a cafe and small swimming pool. 2/12 Patak Rd., tel. (076) 330181, fax (076) 330794, 450-950B.

Luxury Accommodations

A half-dozen luxury properties complete the hotel scene here at Kata and Kata Noi beaches.

Club Mediterranee: Club Med commands an enormous and highly coveted section of beachfront property on Kata Yai Beach, with all standard amenities such as swimming pool, health club, tennis courts, water sports, and mini-camp for the kids. An article in *Conde Nast Traveler* informed readers that last-minute discounts of 33-50% can be obtained by calling the Club Med Bangkok sales office at (02) 253-0108. 7/3 Patak Rd., tel. (076) 381455, fax (076) 330461, 3,800-4,800B.

Laem Sai Village: An isolated little retreat at the end of a private road that sits right on a cliff overlooking Kata Yai and Club Mediterranee; this place has a very intimate feel, despite poorly maintained rooms. 119/5-21 Patak Rd., tel. (076) 212901, 2,800-3,400B.

Kata Beach Resort: Big but somewhat ugly concrete monster at the south end of Kata Yai, just past the Club Med beach but with private access to its own piece of fine sand. 5/2 Patak Rd., tel. (076) 330530, fax (076) 330128, 3,200-3,800B.

The Boathouse: A lovely smaller property with famed restaurant; public areas and gue-strooms are poorly maintained and facilities are limited to a small pool and open-air cocktail lounge adjacent to the cozy cafe and restaurant. 2/2 Patak Rd., tel. (076) 330557, fax (076) 330561, 3,400-4,200B.

Kata Delight: Just south of The Boathouse, this place has a small cafe, no pool, easy access to the beach, and just 19 acceptable rooms. 3/1 Patak Rd., tel. (076) 330636, fax (076) 330481, 1,400-3,600B.

Kata Thani Amari Resort: The entire length of beach at Kata Noi is now taken up with this huge resort, which extends north to south and even has another building across the road. It boasts all possible facilities—a wonderful pool, over 480 rooms, and lovely landscaped grounds. Worth a visit, even if you're not staying here. The beach here is one of the best on the island. 3/24 Patak Rd., tel. (076) 330417, fax (076) 30426, 3,800-5,200B.

Restaurants

Kata cafes and restaurants are limited to a handful of outlets at the north end of Kata Yai near Kata Center, and the area between the two beaches on the main road just opposite The Boathouse.

Bluefin Tavern: "Restaurant row" on the busy street that cuts east from Kata Center to the rear perimeter road is flanked with almost a dozen Western-owned and operated cafes, including this old favorite known for its American-style burgers, pizza, and Tex-Mex specialties. 111/17 Taina Rd., tel. (076) 330856. Moderate.

Helvetia Restaurant: Another popular cafe, with delicious baked goods and some of the better Thai dishes in the neighborhood. Taina Rd. Moderate.

Anchor Bar and Restaurant: British, American, and Thai food served along with free pool and sporting events on the television, also located along "restaurant row." Taina Rd. Moderate.

Grand Seafood: Thai seafood dishes and Chinese duck entrees as prepared by chef Khun Suthee and served on an open-air terrace. 112/5 Taina Rd., tel. (076) 330717. Moderate.

The Flamingo: Popular pizzeria just across from The Boathouse. Patak Rd. Moderate.

The Gallery Grill at Baan Kata: This expensive, exclusive restaurant in a wonderful hillside location serves California-Asian cuisine. Offers superb views of Kata Noi Beach. Patak Rd., tel. (076) 330975. Expensive.

The Boathouse Wine & Grill: Perhaps one of the most famous restaurants on Phuket, known for its Thai and Continental dishes. The atmosphere has declined in recent years and only lunch at a beachside table can now be recommended. The Boathouse, tel. (076) 330015. Expensive.

NAI HARN BEACH

Phuket's most picturesque lagoon is backed by sweeping hills studded with coconut palms and exotic scrub. Once the haunt of hippies and backpackers, Nai Harn (Nai Han) hit the big time with the 1985 opening of the extravagant Phuket Yacht Club, now under the management of the Le Meridien group. Despite a few changes over the last decade—including a surrealistic windmill that slowly turns over the bay—swimming remains excellent and the sunsets are always spectacular at nearby Promthep Cape.

About the only point of interest aside from sunsets from the cape and a few organized viewpoints is a small monastery—Samnak Song Nai Harn—situated in the middle of the beach, where chief abbot Pra Piksu Wira Achito supervises a small number of monks. The monastery's existence is the chief reason the beach and bay remain largely undeveloped and among the more idyllic spots on the island.

Accommodations

Nai Harn has two inexpensive bungalows, two midpriced hotels, and one super luxurious resort on the north side of the bay.

Ao Sane Bungalows: Most of the cheap huts have disappeared, except for this small collection of rudimentary bungalows just through the driveway of the Phuket Yacht Club. A fairly decent place tucked away on a private cove. 11/12 Ao Sane, tel. (076) 288306, 150-450B.

Jungle Beach Resort: A good-value place about one km beyond the Phuket Yacht Club, at the end of a dirt path surrounded by thick foliage; offers a small pool, funky restaurant, and 40 cantilevered bungalows in various price ranges. 11/3 Ao Sane, tel. (076) 381108, fax (076) 381542, 550-1,200B fan, 1,800-3,000B a/c.

Nai Harn Village: A rather unimaginative motel structure back from the beach but near the lagoons. 14/29 Viset Rd., tel. (076) 381595, fax (076) 381961, 600-950B.

Romsai Bungalows: Another small set of bungalows back from the beach and just across the road from the lagoon. 14/7 Viset Rd., tel. (076) 381338, 300-450B.

Le Meridien Royal Phuket Yacht Club: One of the most exclusive hotels on Phuket, with fitness club, several fine restaurants, and enormous rooms, all offering wonderful views of the bay and the slowly spinning windmill. Nai Harn Beach, tel. (076) 381156, fax (076) 381164, 8,000-18,000B.

RAWAI AND CHALONG BEACHES

The beaches located south and east of Phuket Town once were the original destinations for international tourists, who stayed in town and made daytrips down to the nearby beaches. Unfortunately, south Phuket was damaged long ago by offshore tin mining. The beaches now tend to be muddy and lack the appeal of those found in Patong and Kata-Karon.

However, if you prefer solitude over sand, then Rawai and Chalong Beaches might be acceptable, especially if you are a scuba diver and wish to be near the boat piers on the island's southern side.

The main attractions are the restored colonial structure at Cape Panwa Resort, a quick stop at the Sea Gypsy village for a snack and drink, and the surprisingly large and modern shell museum.

Budget Accommodations

Rawai Garden Resort: Small guesthouse with several large and lovely bungalows overlooking ponds and surrounded by coconut trees. Room rates vary by the season—and how wealthy you appear—but probably run 250-350B.

Rawai Plaza Bungalows: A handful of basic and rather unimpressive bungalows. 147 Viset Rd., tel. (076) 345871, 150-350B.

Porn Mae Bungalows: Simple spot with six decrepit *nipa* huts and newer concrete rooms. 58/1 Viset Rd., tel. (076) 381300, 150-350B.

Rawai Bayshore Resort: Big place with over 80 rooms in every possible price category. 182

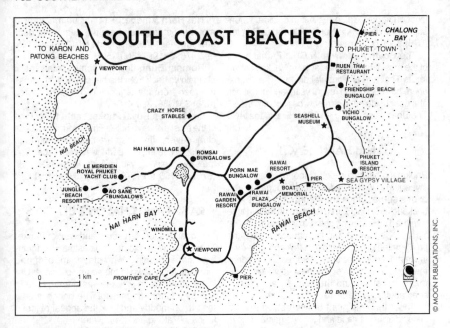

Viset Rd., tel. (076) 381278, fax (076) 381370, 150-850B.

Siam Phuket Resort: Fairly new operation with 21 rooms, cafe, and information about local boat tours and diving expeditions. 11/9 Sakdidej Rd., tel. (076) 391377, 200-850B.

Luxury Accommodations

Phuket Island Resort: Nestled amid 65 acres of palm plantations and landscaped gardens, this old but fully renovated resort has two swimming pools, tennis courts, and every imaginable water sport, including diving expeditions to nearby islands and coral beds. Rawai Beach, tel. (076) 381010, fax (076) 381018, 2,200-3,500B.

Cape Panwa Resort: Formerly a Sheraton property, this 160-room resort on the southeastern tip of the island overlooks a private cove. Dinners are served in the faux-colonial Panwa House and the English-style Lighthouse Grill. The place is so secluded and private that Leonardo DiCaprio stayed here during the 1999 filming of *The Beach.* l27 Mu 8 Sakdidej Rd., tel. (076) 391123, fax (076) 391177, 3,600-5,800B.

ISLANDS NEAR PHUKET

Off the southeast coast of Phuket are a half dozen islands ringed with great beaches and blessed with crystal-clear waters perfect for diving and snorkeling. All have moderately priced resorts associated with travel agencies or tour operators in Phuket Town, who can help with transportation and reservations.

Longtail boats to the following islands can be hired at Rawai Beach, at the pier at Chalong Bay, and in Ban Makham near the old Phuket pier. Roundtrip fares for the entire longtail are 600-1,500B depending on the season and your bargaining skills.

More reliable, but also more expensive, are larger boats hired from professional groups such as Phuket Yacht Services or Thai Marine Leisure on Laem Prao. Boats also can be chartered on Chalong Beach from Marine Asia and Chalong Bay Boat Centre.

Ko Lon

Just a few kilometers from Chalong is the large and easily accessible island of Ko Lon with the small fishing village of Ban Ko Lon on the northern coast. Longtails take about 15 minutes from either Chalong or Rawai.

Lon Pavilion: A 30-room resort on the north shore with 28 a/c bungalows, restaurant, and longtails to reach the more remote beaches. 47/5 Chalong Bay, tel. (076) 381374, fax (076) 213704, 1,600-2,800B.

Ko Hae (Coral Island)

Thirty minutes by boat from Chalong is the beautiful island of Ko Hae, also called Coral Island for the outstanding reefs that encircle the elongated island. Although many of the coral reefs near Phuket have been destroyed by pollution, offshore dredging, or dynamite fishing, those around Ko Hae have somehow survived to complement the island's fine beaches and isolated coves.

Coral Island Resort: The island's only resort has 40 a/c bungalows, restaurant, and dive facilities. Details can be arranged at the resort's office in Chalong. 50/4 Viset Rd., tel. (076) 281060, fax (076) 381957, e-mail: coral.island.resort@phuket.com, 2,000-2,800B.

Ko Maiton

Ko Maiton, another gorgeous island located one hour east of Chalong, proves the maxim that the greater the distance from Phuket, the more outstanding the beaches and underwater world.

Maiton Resort: This expensive resort on Ko Maiton's east coast was established by All Nippon Airways and for many years catered exclusively to wealthy young Japanese on escorted tours. The newly appointed American manager now welcomes both Asian and Western guests to this strangely pseudo-Roman resort. P.O. Box 376, Phuket, tel. (076) 214954, fax (076) 214959, 2,800-3,600B.

Ko Taphao Yai

Several small islands are 10 minutes offshore from Ban Makham.

Taphao Yai Island Resort: A conveniently located place offering a tiered swimming pool, a few small beaches, and a/c bungalows spread over the rocky headlands. Taphao Island, tel. (076) 391217, 1,800-2,400B.

GETTING THERE

Phuket is 885 km south of Bangkok, 287 km southwest of Surat Thani, and 176 km by road northwest of Krabi.

Air

Thai Airways serves Phuket from Bangkok, Hat Yai, Narathiwat, Nakhon Si Thammarat, and Surat Thani.

From Bangkok: Thai Airways flies 12 times daily from Bangkok for 2,200B one-way. The flight takes just over an hour aside from departures, which make a 30-minute stopover in Surat Thani.

From Ko Samui: Bangkok Airways flies twice daily from Ko Samui for 1,400B. The flight takes 45 minutes.

From Malaysia: Thai Airways and MAS fly twice daily from Penang (1,600B, one hour), a quick and relatively inexpensive flight that eliminates a long and exhausting bus ride. Flights are also available from Langkawi (2,400B) and Kuala Lumpur (2,800B).

International Connections: Phuket is served from Europe, Hong Kong, Malaysia, Singapore, Taiwan, and Japan by almost a dozen airlines including Thai, Malaysian, (MAS), Tradewinds, Silk Air, Dragon Air, China, and All Nippon (ANA).

See Phuket Town for the addresses of airlines and recommended travel agencies.

Phuket Airport

The international airport is 32 km north of Phuket Town. Airport facilities include luggage storage service, cafe, Thai reconfirmation desk, currency exchange, travel agencies, car rental, currency exchange booths, and a hotel reservation office, which is open daily 0800-1700. Visitors arriving on late flights should make reservations at the Bangkok airport prior to departure.

Transportation: Luxury hotels provide minivans to the beaches for standard fees, while meterless taxis ask 300B to Phuket Town and 400-500B to various beaches. Taxis can be negotiated down to 150B in the reverse direction.

A private shuttle service from the airport costs 80B to Phuket Town and 120B to Patong, Karon, or Kata beaches.

Train

There is no direct rail service to Phuket. The nearest railway station is in Phun Phin, 14 km west of Surat Thani. Some travelers take an overnight train to Phun Phin, where buses wait to take passengers on the five-hour trip to Phuket.

Bus

Ordinary buses leave every 15 minutes, between 1800-2000, from the Southern Bus Terminal in Bangkok, cost 220-260B, and take 15-17 hours to reach Phuket. First-class a/c (380-420B) and V.I.P. buses (550-600B) leave 1800-1900 from the same terminal. These buses do the journey in 13-14 hours and provide sufficient legroom for most Western travelers.

Private tour buses from Bangkok cost 400-550B one-way or 700-850B return. The fare includes hotel pickup, meals, and videos to distract you during the long and hair-raising trip along the west coast south of Ranong. Most departures are in the evenings 1800-2000.

Buses, a/c minivans, and share taxis connect Phuket with various towns in southern Thailand. Vans are also available from Penang (550B), Kuala Lumpur (650B), and Singapore (750B).

Public buses arrive and depart from the Phuket terminal off Phangnga Road behind the new shopping center. Private tour buses leave from offices in the center of town on Rasda and Phangnga Roads.

Most bus departures for Bangkok leave in the afternoon around 1500.

Bus tickets should be purchased several days in advance from travel agents or directly at the bus terminal in Phuket Town.

GETTING AROUND

From Phuket Town to the Beach

Buses from Bangkok and all other points within Thailand stop at the terminal in Phuket Town, located a few blocks east of the tourist office.

Songtao drivers at the bus terminal ask 100-200B per carload to the beach, but they will drive around until they find you a room at your requested price—a good idea during the busy winter months.

A less expensive option is to walk into town (five minutes), visit the tourist office for a list of current taxi fares, and continue to beaches on public songtaos departing from the halts shown on the Phuket Town map. Public buses to Patong and other west coast beaches cost 15-30B.

Bus and songtao services stop at 1800. Afterwards, songtaos and taxis can be hired at city center and the bus terminal.

Car Rentals

Cars and jeeps can be rented in town and at most beaches—a convenient way to avoid the hassles of public transportation. Roads are in good condition and driving poses few hazards except on small roads in the evenings.

Rates are lowest in Phuket Town and 20-40% higher at the beaches. Hertz and Avis charge 1,200-1,800B for Suzuki Jeeps or Toyota Corollas, including insurance and unlimited mileage. Both agencies have offices at the airport, in Phuket Town, and at most beaches.

Smaller outlets, such as Pure Car Rentals on Rasda Road and Phuket Travel opposite the tourist office, rent cars and jeeps for 800-1,200B per day. Most grant discounts of 10% for weekly rentals and 25-30% during the low-season months Aug.-October.

Motorcycle Rentals

Motorcycles cost 150-200B per day for smaller displacements (under 150cc) and 200-350B per day for larger bikes (150cc). Bikes in superior condition are rented from guesthouse and hotel owners, rather than from rental shops along the beaches.

Remember to carefully check the condition of the bike before signing the rental agreement, and always drive with extreme caution. Ask for a helmet. To minimize damage on minor spills and reduce the threat of serious sunburn, it's essential to wear shoes, long pants, and a long-sleeved shirt.

PHANGNGA BAY AND KO PHI PHI

PHANGNGA BAY

The surrealistic and unforgettable limestone mountains in Phangnga Bay—one of the great natural wonders in Southeast Asia—co-starred with James Bond (if you consider Roger Moore, the *real* James Bond) in the 1973 classic, *The Man with the Golden Gun.* Created by glacial flow some 10 millennia ago, Phangnga (pang-GA) resembles Neolithic skyscapers not unlike the ethereal Chinese landscapes of Guilin; it is a world not to be missed.

Phangnga Bay Tour
The standard tour starts from Tha Don pier, 10 km south of Phangnga, and winds through a mangrove-lined waterway past *nipa* palms and magnificent stands of tropical forest. On quiet mornings, gibbons may be heard calling from this strange, neolithic environment inhabited by ospreys, crab-eating macaques, and the land-walking fish.

Tham Lod: The boat then drifts through Tham Lod ("Great Cave"), not a cave but a 50-meter water tunnel carved on the side of an island and laced with ancient stalactites that slowly drip into an eerie lagoon.

Khao Khian: After exiting the cavern, boats continue along the complex network of river estuaries past Khao Khian ("Writing Mountain") and its prehistoric cave covered with drawings of sharks, crocodiles, dolphins, hornbills, dugongs, and other creatures familiar to local inhabitants 3,000-5,000 years ago. The route skirts the Muslim village of Ko Panyi and enters an open sea studded with sheer limestone monoliths that rise dramatically from the ultraviolet haze.

James Bond Island: The goal, of course, is the celebrated rocky cleft that served as Scaramanga's hideaway in *The Man with the Golden Gun.* Ko Pingan ("Leaning Island") appears smaller than expected and often disappoints visitors as a tourist trap overrun with the standard assortment of persistent hawkers and tacky trinket stalls. Yet the beach remains lovely and wonderful vistas over the hauntingly beautiful bay

can be enjoyed by hiking up the network of trails that lead to spectacular vantage points.

The Man with the Golden Gun not only managed to transform one of the most peaceful settings in Southeast Asia into a cinematic scene of murder and mayhem, it also moved Phangnga Bay to the coast of China and cast Roger Moore as the *real* James Bond. Today, few visitors can recall Roger Moore or even the appearance of James Bond Island, commonly mistaken for nearby Ko Tapu ("Nail Island") which is shaped like a ridiculous, fern-covered nail pounded into the greenish sea. And few visitors receive the same welcome Roger Moore did—a butler in a white coat carrying a tray of martinis.

Perhaps fearing that the precarious, crumbling rock will collapse on his passengers, the boat driver collects his group and races off past other geological oddities before circling around and heading back to Ko Panyi and the pier.

Remote Places: Visitors on privately chartered longtails can ask to visit **Tham Nak** ("Naga Cave"), named after its bizarre stalactites that resemble a serpentine *naga* snake; **Ko Hong** ("Chamber Island"), dubbed for its soaring wall pocketed with condominiumlike caves; **Tham Kao** ("Glass Cave"), reminiscent of Capri's Blue Grotto; and perhaps **Ko Mak Noi,** a large island one hour east that offers spectacular sunsets from deserted beaches.

Ko Panyi: All tours make a final stop at the highly commercialized Muslim fishing village of Panyi, a uniquely sited matchstick village constructed on sturdy mangrove stilts over the water and under the protective umbrella of an immense slab of limestone. Seafood cafes, souvenir shops, a primary school and cemetery, a post office, a health clinic, and a turquoise-green mosque are connected by a maze of wobbling walkways. It's better to wander to the back of the island or visit the simple foods talls around the mosque than waste time in the overpriced seafood cafes and tacky souvenir stalls near the waterfront.

Although Ko Panyi first appears another victim of tourism, residents emerge from their homes after the final boat has departed to resume their

KO PHI PHI AND PHANGNGA BAY

LAMU
TO RANONG
THA MAPHRAO
LAM PHI
HIN LAT
THAI MUANG
KLONG CHON
THAP PUT
TA SAENG NA
4118
4040
TO SURAT THANI
4035
4152
PHANGNGA
THAM SUWAN KHUHA
THA DON
TAKUA THUNG
KHAO KHIAN
THAM NAK
KO PANYI
THAM HUA KRALOK
AO LUK
THAM PHET (DIAMOND CAVE)
THAM BOKARANI PARK
4
4
KO MAK NOI
LAEM SAK PIER
4039
KHOK KLOI
KO TAPU
KO PINGAN (JAMES BOND ISLAND)
LUK BAY
BAN BA KAN
4205
THAM KAO
KO HONG
4
KHAO PHANOM BENCHA NATIONAL PARK
0   10 km

PHANGNGA BAY

KO YAO NOI

SEE "KRABI VICINITY" MAP
SEE "PRABANG CAPE AND AO NANG BEACH" MAP
KRABI
TO TRANG

NAI YANG
BANG TAO
THALANG
402
BAN CHONG LAT
KO NAKA YAI
KO NAKA NOI
KO YAO YAI
SURIN
KO MAPHRAO
KO PODA
KO YAWA
KO HUA KWAN
FERRY TO LANTA (54 km—2 hrs)

PATONG
PHUKET
BAN LIPA YAI
FERRY (42 km—2 hrs)
KARON
PHUKET BAY
EXPRESS BOAT (48 km—2 hrs)
SHARK POINT
KO YUNG
KO MAI PHAI
SEE "KO PHI PHI" MAP
KO JUM (KO PU)
KATA
CHALONG BAY
KO DOK MAI
KO PHI PHI DON
NAI HARN
KO BON
KO MAITON
KO HAE (CORAL ISLAND)
KO KAI
FERRY TO KO LANTA (34 km—5 hrs)
KO KAO YAI
KO PHI PHI LEY

KO RACHA YAI
KO MA
KO HA YAI

ANDAMAN SEA

KO RACHA NOI

© MOON PUBLICATIONS, INC.

daily activities: cooking, chatting with neighbors, complaining about spouses, and visiting the handsome mosque that clings to the face of a limestone cliff. Ko Panyi may appear an over-priced tourist ghetto from dawn to dusk, but overnight visitors will discover a sublime village populated by warm, friendly people.

Escorted Tours

Phangnga can be seen with an organized tour from Phuket or Krabi, or independently by joining a group directly in Phangnga or down at the pier.

Quick-and-easy tours from Phuket and Krabi cost 300-600B for a four-hour whirl around the bay. Buses leave Phuket around 0800 and converge at the harbor at 1000. Passengers are unloaded into a miniature armada of longtail boats, speedcraft, and small yachts that roar off madly toward the infamous haunt of Roger Moore.

Package tours are somewhat more expensive than independent tours, but the main reason to avoid this option is that many of the boats are too large to explore the more interesting areas; also, you'll be trapped in a large flotilla of Nikon-snapping tourists.

Bus arrivals in the evening and early morning are often met by Sayan Tamtopol, a former postman from Ko Panyi who has been leading tours for over a decade. Sayan leads five-hour tours departing at 0730 during the rainy season and similar tours at 0730 and 1400 during the dry months Dec.-June. These half-day excursions with a seafood meal on Ko Panyi cost 150-300B.

A better option is Sayan's overnight tour that costs 400-500B and includes the standard half-day package, an evening sunset cruise around less-explored sites, a seafood dinner on Ko Panyi, accommodations in Sayan's home, and an early morning breakfast before the sunrise boat ride back to the mainland pier. Sayan can be contacted at his office (tel. 076-411521) at the Phangnga bus terminal or at the Thawisuk Hotel (tel. 076-411686) in the center of town.

Independent Tours

The real beauty of Phangnga Bay is at dawn, when the mist rises from the water and the sea turns from purple to rose. Rising from the perfectly quiet lagoons are the magnificent limestone mountains that now resemble mist-borne temples casting silhouettes through the shifting

light. The only way to really experience the grandeur of Phangnga is to spend the night in town and start your tour at the crack of dawn, beating the hordes of tourists racing down from Phuket and Krabi.

Boats are available at the pier throughout the day, so there's no problem finding one on short notice. Most visitors make arrangements with a boat operator for an early departure the following morning.

A final alternative is to take a *songtao* from Phangnga to the pier at Tha Don (10B), then a public ferry to Ko Panyi (25B). Accommodations include dormitories and simple homestays.

Attractions

The whole of Phangnga Province is riddled with limestone caves now converted into Buddhist monasteries. Few visitors visit the following sights, but all can be reached easily with a motorcycle rented from the Fuji photo shop on the main road.

Sanchao Mae: Phangnga has little to offer except for a quick glance inside this 150-year-old Chinese shrine decorated with ink drawings depicting scenes from Chinese legends. The recently restored temple is behind the market on Phetkasem Road.

Tham Reusi Sawan: Sinakarin Park, three km west of town on Route 4, is a pleasant spot containing Reusi Sawan ("Hermit Heaven") cave guarded by an image of the holy hermit.

Tham Phung Chang: Just behind the provincial government offices two km west of town lies "Elephant Belly Cave," with a small spring and minor collection of Buddha images.

Tham Suwan Khuha: More impressive than other nearby grottoes is this pilgrimage cave, 12 km west of town, filled with dozens of reclining and seated Buddhas illuminated by mysterious shafts of light. Find the initials carved on the rocks in 1890 by King Chulalongkorn, then visit the nearby temple and climb up the stairs and explore the network of tunnels that look over the tropical landscape.

Accommodations

Phangnga is a one-street, one-horse, one-night sort of town with most hotels, banks, and cafes near the bus terminal. A semi-luxurious resort hotel is situated down near the pier.

Thawisuk Hotel: The first and still most popular place for budget travelers is the rather ordinary concrete hotel in the center of town a few blocks from the bus terminal. Rooms are large and reasonably clean, plus wonderful sunsets over the Phangnga mountains can be enjoyed from the rooftop cafe. 79 Phetkasem Rd., tel. (076) 411686, 100-150B.

Muang Thong: Visitors who need a/c comfort at bargain rates can find suitable rooms with private baths in the establishment across from the bus terminal and two blocks in the direction of Phuket. 128 Phetkasem Rd., tel. (076) 412132, 120-180B fan, 300-350B a/c.

Phangnga Bay Resort: An upscale hotel with swimming pool, tennis courts, boat hire, decent restaurant, and modern rooms with disappointing views considering the bayside location near an estuary ringed with limestone mountains. The overpriced resort caters to tour groups hauled in from Phuket. 20 Tha Don Rd., tel. (076) 411067, fax (076) 412057, Bangkok reservations tel. (02) 216-2882, 950-1,400B.

Transportation

Phangnga is 90 km northeast of Phuket and 82 km northwest of Krabi.

Buses leave Phuket hourly 0620-1800 and take two hours to reach Phangnga. Buses leave Krabi hourly 0700-1600 and also take two hours to Phangnga.

From the bus terminal, you can check with Sayan at his adjacent office about an upcoming tour, check into a hotel, or take a *songtao* for 10B down to the pier for immediate departure on a longtail boat or the public ferry over to Ko Panyi.

KO PHI PHI

Phi Phi's almost indescribable combination of powdery white sands, brilliant blue waters, soaring limestone cliffs, and colorful corals make it one of the most beautiful islands in all of Asia.

Phi Phi (pronounced "Pee Pee" to the amusement of some visitors) was discovered in the early 1970s by backpackers who hitched rides with fishermen from Krabi and stayed with villagers in the port of Tonsai. The following decade witnessed an incredible amount of change as developers replaced the grass shacks with expensive resorts, and cheap cafes with pricey restaurants. Local authorities did little to control the sprawl, which quickly spread up the mountains and off to the most isolated coves.

Ko Phi Phi is now deluged with over a quarter million annual visitors who completely pack every square centimeter of land and sand. Tonsai is a rather ugly village that has sold its soul to tourism; piles of trash lie uncollected on even the most remote of beaches. In the space of less than a decade, Ko Phi Phi transformed itself from travelers' paradise to an environmental horror show.

Despite the damage, many visitors still regard the island as a wonderful place to laze in the sun, snorkel around the coral beds, and enjoy spectacular views from the limestone peak behind the small village.

The island received worldwide attention in early 1999 when Leonardo DiCaprio arrived to film portions of *The Beach* on Maya Bay and other areas around the Phuket region. Local environmentalists objected to the disturbances and demanded the end of the filming, though the film eventually was completed after a six-week shoot.

Attractions

The primary island of Phi Phi Don is an hourglass-shaped islet with narrow crescent bays wedged between soaring limestone mountains. To appreciate the beauty of the island, take the path from the back side of Tonsai village to the mountain viewpoint where a thatched hut restaurant sells expensive soft drinks. Do the 45-minute hike in the morning, and bring your wide-angle lens.

Hikers can continue along a rudimentary trail to Bakao Beach in the north, or attempt to climb the 498-meter limestone peaks that dominate the island on the east.

Boat Tour and Ko Phi Phi Ley

For most visitors, the highlight of Ko Phi Phi is an all-day boat tour from Tonsai Beach. A typical tour begins with 30 minutes of skin diving at coral beds to the east, followed by a one-hour stop at stunning Bamboo Island. The boat then heads counterclockwise around the north end of Phi Phi Don and crashes through the waters past limestone cliffs to the southern island of Phi Phi Ley.

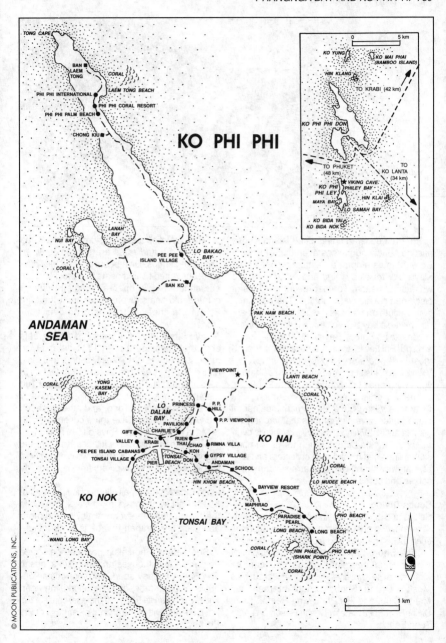

boats at Ko Phi Phi

Phi Phi Ley is an uninhabited island whose pristine beauty surpasses even that of Phi Phi Don. All tours stop at an amazing cove called Maya Bay for skin diving and relaxing on the white-sand beach. Too bad about the piles of discarded plastic water bottles. The boat then heads south and makes a quick detour into another scenic bay before stopping for skin diving in fjordlike Lo Samah Bay at the extreme southern end. Phi Ley is another amazing bay, though most boat operators skip this cove in favor of Viking Cave; insist on a 15-minute cruise here or you'll miss one of the wonders of Phi Phi.

The day cruise ends with an hour-long visit to famous Viking Cave, an immense cathedral named after cave pictographs that vaguely resemble ancient Viking ships. Viking Cave is overrun with tourists but intriguing for its bamboo scaffolding used by bird-nest collectors and rickety gateway strung with a bizarre assortment of cables and cords.

Scuba Diving

Scuba and snorkeling—the first activities to arrive—now compete with more exotic offerings such as sea canoes and big game fishing.

Dive Shops: PADI certification, equipment rentals, and overnight excursions can be arranged at several dive shops in Tonsai such as Moskito Diving, Scuba School International, Manta Club, and Phi Phi Diving Center. Siam Diving is at Phi Phi Palm Beach Resort on Laem Tong Beach.

Dive instruction and excursions cost the same as in Phuket, and rates are similar between competing shops. Dive boats may be fully covered, converted fishing boats that provide room and shade, or just open-air longtails without comfortable seats or protection from the sun. Be sure to check before handing over your money.

Dive Sites: Most dive tours explore the reefs and coral beds near Ko Phi Phi Don and then move south to the more deeply submerged reefs off Ko Phi Phi Ley. The best Phi Phi Don dive sites include Hin Phae (Shark Point) about 100 meters off Long Beach, the shallow corals near Hat Lanti and Laem Tong, and other reefs on the western coasts. Dive tours continue south to Maya and Lo Samah Bays off Phi Phi Ley.

More remote dive sites include Ko Mai Phai (Bamboo Island) and Ko Yung, two islands about five km north that draw divers from both Ko Phi Phi and Krabi.

Ko Bida Nok, a small island one km south of Ko Phi Phi Ley, is considered the best dive site in the region due to superior visibility and more abundant sealife than that of its larger neighbors.

Snorkeling: Snorkeling gear can be rented from most guesthouses and the dive shops in Ton Sai. A full-day snorkeling tour costs 250-350B for boat transportation, snorkeling gear, and dives near Hin Phae, off the east coast of Phi Phi Don, and within the crystal-clear bays of Phi Phi Ley.

Other Sports

Several new sports activities now complement scuba and snorkeling.

Sea Canoes: John Gray and his innovative company organize inflatable kayak tours of the bays around Phangnga, Krabi, and Ko Phi Phi. See "Phuket" above for more information.

Big Game Fishing: Several shops organize Andaman Sea excursions in search of sailfish, blue marlin, barracuda, and shark. A full day of fishing with all equipment, bait, lunch, and drinks costs 1,800-2,000B, one of the better fishing deals in the region.

Accommodations

Phi Phi Don is a fully developed island with a wide range of accommodations, from simple huts from 100B to first-class resorts from 3,000B.

Ko Phi Phi is no longer an inexpensive destination. Prices have escalated sharply since backpackers first arrived in the early 1980s. Bamboo bungalows that cost 40-60B in the mid-1980s now cost 200-500B for the same old decrepit shack, and most of the cheaper places have been torn down and replaced with midlevel bungalows or expensive resorts.

Ko Phi Phi is *not* good value.

Despite the rise in prices, a handful of simple bungalows still offer rooms during the high season for 100-250B. Most of these places are tucked away in small coves along the southeastern coast of the island. The rule of thumb is that prices decline as you move away from the pier.

Ko Phi Phi is often fully booked from mid-December to early February and July-Sept. Room rates double during these periods but return to more reasonable levels after the tourists go home.

Finding a room can be tough during the busy months. Travelers should arrive early in the morning to secure a room or sign a waiting list at the more popular places.

The more expensive resorts should be reserved several months in advance to guarantee rooms during the busy months. Ko Phi Phi lacks direct phone service, but better resorts can be contacted by calling their agents in Krabi (area code 075), Phuket (076), Ko Samui (077), or Bangkok (02). Many resorts can also be contacted via their radio phones (01) or cellular phones (075).

Tonsai Beach

Tonsai Beach may be congested and trashy, but most of the island's travel agencies, dive shops, cafes, and entertainment sites are located in the messy village near the Tonsai pier. All accommodations near the pier are very expensive.

Pee Pee Island Cabanas: A badly overpriced place with unimaginative a/c chalets and an expensive restaurant filled with tour groups. West Tonsai Beach, tel. (02) 255-7600 or (075) 611496, 1,200-2,600B.

Tonsai Village: The best hotel on this side of the island but also overpriced, considering the rooms were constructed in the early 1980s. West Tonsai Beach, tel. (02) 255-7600 or (075) 611496, 1,900-2,800B.

Phi Phi Hotel: A large, 68-room hotel adjacent to the pier with all the standard mod-con amenities. West Tonsai Beach, tel. (01) 712-0138, 200-2,800B.

Chao Kho Phi Phi Lodge: Just beyond Tonsai village are several old-timers with decent rooms that are often noisy and busy with traffic. East Tonsai Beach, 400-600B.

Lo Dalam Bay

The northern bay has a few inexpensive huts on the less attractive western edge, and a half dozen sets of midpriced bungalows in the center and eastern end of the fabulous bay. Lo Dalam is very quiet, scenic, and just five minutes from the pier and Tonsai village.

Gift Bungalows: Rudimentary but survivable huts that are often full; also, the owners are impossible to find. Gift is probably doomed for destruction and may be gone at your arrival. Lo Dalam Bay, 100-150B.

Valley Bungalows: Another rough collection of wooden shacks set back from the beach—perfect for firewood. Lo Dalam Bay, 100-150B.

Krabi Pee Pee Resort: Handles the overflow from Charlie's with 60 fairly clean rooms. Lo Dalam Bay, tel. (075) 611484, 400-800B.

Charlie's: A midpriced place with almost 100 bungalows in fairly good shape but tightly packed together behind the overpriced restaurant. Lo Dalam Bay, tel. (02) 224-2786 or (076) 7230495, 400-800B.

Pee Pee Pavilion Resort: Another well-sited place with 60 rooms facing the lovely beach. Lo

Dalam Bay, tel. (075) 611295, fax (075) 611578, 900-1,800B.

Pee Pee Princess Resort: The final choice on the northern bay has 60 individual bungalows, restaurant, and satellite TV. Lo Dalam Bay, tel. (075) 612188, fax (075) 620615, 1,400-3,200B.

The Interior

Several reasonably priced bungalows have been constructed in the flatlands and the hills facing Lo Dalam Bay or just behind Tonsai Bay. The following are a 10- to 15-minute walk from the pier.

Ruen Thai: Bamboo bungalows near a bizarre collection of Patong-style bars and juke joints. Inexpensive, but Ruen Thai and adjacent bungalows suffer from ghetto vibes and blaring discos. Lo Dalam Bay, 100-300B.

P.P. Viewpoint Resort: Probably the best choice is this cantilevered hillside complex, where over 70 individual bungalows have been cleverly connected with rickety wooden walkways. The beach is about 10 minutes away. Recommended. Lo Dalam Bay, tel. (075) 612193, 900-1,200B.

P.P. Hill: A fairly luxurious set of bungalows constructed over a rocky landscape stripped of vegetation; uncomfortably hot during the summer months. Lo Dalam Bay, tel. (076) 723-0865, 800-1,000B.

Rimna Villa: Quiet and secluded with almost 20 clean and well-spaced bungalows facing a small valley. Recommended. Tonsai Bay, tel. (076) 212901, 500-700B.

Gypsy Village: About 30 bungalows erected in perfectly straight lines—an unimaginative arrangement, but rooms are clean and well priced. Tonsai Bay, tel. (076) 723-0674, 300-400B.

Hin Khom Beach

Just beyond the small cape lies the first in a series of narrow coves and longer bays blessed with perfect sand and crystal-clear waters. Hin Khom, also called Laem Hin, offers several reasonably priced bungalows that improve in quality as you continue east toward Laem Pho.

Phi Phi Don Resort: This "resort" consists of a few primitive shacks and rudimentary bungalows bisected by a beachside trail. Resort? Hin Khom Beach, tel. (01) 722-0083, 600-900B concrete bungalows.

Pee Pee Andaman Resort: A surprisingly large place with over 100 huts in various price ranges; best values are beachside huts numbered 26-45. Tonsai Beach, 100-150B primeval shacks, 200-250B good-value huts with private bath, 400-500B beachside chalets.

Bayview Resort: Tucked away at the secluded eastern end of the beach are some 30 thatched bungalows and 12 a/c chalets, constructed in 1990 and therefore in better condition than older "resorts," but still badly overpriced. Hin Khom Beach, tel. (075) 612964, fax (075) 620559, 1,400-1,800B fan, 2,200-3,200B a/c.

Maphrao Resort: Facing a private cove and a tiny beach is this Thai/Belgian-owned resort with 25 thatched bungalows and a cozy little cafe. Secluded, quiet, and within walking distance of Tonsai village. Hin Khom Beach, 200-450B common bath.

Long Beach

Long Beach (Hat Yao) at the southeastern tip has the best-value places on the island. Bamboo huts and wooden A-frames cost 100-250B, while larger bungalows with private baths cost 300-500B. The sand is clean and the nearby island of Hin Phae offers excellent diving over shallow coral beds. Long Beach is a 30-minute walk or a 20B longtail ride from Tonsai pier.

Viking Village: Basic but acceptable huts constructed near the rocky cape that marks the beginning of Long Beach. A somewhat isolated but very peaceful place. Long Beach, 100-250B.

P.P. Paradise Pearl: A longtime favorite with over 100 bungalows, large restaurant, videos, private boats to Tonsai pier, and daily excursions around the island. Long Beach, tel. (076) 723-0484, 250-900B.

Long Beach Bungalows: The final spot on the beach has bamboo huts, wooden A-frames, and newer bungalows with private baths. A trail continues over the headlands to a small cove and the fishing village of Lo Mudee. Long Beach, 100-400B.

Lo Bakao Bay

One solitary resort lies in the wide bay on the north-central side of the island.

Pee Pee Island Village: This laid-back place has over 75 breezy bungalows facing the horseshoe-shaped bay. Although the beach is beautiful and the resort provides a range of water sports activities, the small, native-style huts are badly overpriced and only patronized by tourists arriving on packaged holidays. Lo Bakao Bay, tel. (02) 277-0704 and (076) 211-1907, 900-1,800B.

Laem Tong Beach

The former home of wandering sea gypsies *(nam chao),* Laem Tong has effectively been purchased by developers who have opened up three luxury resorts on the island's most splendid beach. A small village of *nam chao* is located at the north end of the bay.

A 60-meter concrete pier now under construction will bring direct boat service from Phuket and Krabi, but visitors not on packaged tours that include transport must charter a longtail from Tonsai or attempt to follow the poorly defined trail that winds over the hilly spine of the island.

Phi Phi International Resort: Top-end choice with 85 a/c rooms, international restaurant, water sports, island tours, and glass-bottom boat for reef excursions. Laem Tong Beach, tel. (076) 214272, fax (076) 214301, 2,600-3,200B.

Phi Phi Coral Resort: The midpriced alternative. Laem Tong Beach, tel. (02) 250-3356 or (076) 218884, 1,600-2,400B.

Phi Phi Palm Beach Travelodge Resort: Perhaps the finest luxury resort on Phi Phi with all the standard facilities plus the island's only freshwater swimming pool, two tennis courts, and a refurbished Chinese junk for cruises around the island. Siam Diving Center, one of the best dive companies in the country, is located here and can help with scuba instruction and overnight excursions to the superb dive sites around Ko Phi Phi. Laem Tong Beach, tel. (076) 214654, fax (076) 215090, 3,800-7,600B.

Information and Services

All of the following services are located in town, on the roads that head up to the viewpoint, or east toward Long Beach.

Information: There is no TAT office on the island, but travel agencies and boat companies in Tonsai can help with essential information.

Post Office: Letters can be posted from mailboxes near the pier.

Telephone: There is no direct phone service to Phi Phi, but travel agencies and most resorts have radio phones (area code 01) or cellular phones (area code 075) for hire. Cellular calls to Phuket or Krabi cost about 15B per minute.

Police: A police and marine police station is east of town near Phi Phi Andaman Resort.

Medical: The Phi Phi Medical Clinic is adjacent to the police station near the road that heads north to the viewpoint trail. Nurses can help with minor injuries, but serious problems require evacuation to Phuket.

Banks: Ko Phi Phi's sole bank, on the east side of town near the police station, provides currency exchange services daily 0830-1700. Hotels will cash travelers checks but at lower rates than the bank.

Travel Agencies: The agencies and boat offices in Tonsai provide all the standard services at very competitive rates. Songserm Travel, Phi Phi Marine, and Arida Tours are recommended.

Transportation

Ko Phi Phi is 48 km southeast of Phuket, 42 km southwest of Krabi, and 34 km northwest of Ko Lanta. The island can be reached in two or three hours from all three points.

Boats are less expensive from Krabi than Phuket, though the savings are minimal.

Boats from Phuket: Over a dozen boat companies operate from piers in Phuket, Patong, and south coast beaches such as Rawai and Chalong. The largest company, **Songserm,** shuttles over a dozen boats between Phuket, Phi Phi, and Krabi, ranging from 40-person fishing boats to an enormous 600-passenger catamaran called the *King Cruiser,* which closely resembles a monstrous car ferry—a curious choice in boats since Ko Phi Phi presently lacks both roads and cars.

Tickets for the *Andaman Queen, Silver Queen, Phi Phi Princess* and other ferries can be purchased from agencies on Phuket such as Aloha Tours, CBC Ventures, Phi Phi Hydrocraft, Seatran, and Diamond Travel. Ticket price includes hotel pickup and transportation to the pier.

As with life, the slower the journey the cheaper the fare. Slower boats cost 200-250B and take two hours, express boats cost 250-350B and take 90 minutes, and jet boats or hydrofoils cost 350-500B but fly across the bay in under one hour—almost as fast as seaplanes that charge 1,200B for the 55-minute flight.

Boats from Krabi: Ferries depart Krabi daily at 0900, 1200, and 1500 Oct.-June, and once daily during the rainy months depending on the weather.

Slower boats cost 100-150B and take just over two hours, while express boats with a/c cabins take 90 minutes and cost 150-200B. Several upscale resorts also provide direct boat service from Krabi to their property.

Tickets can be purchased directly at the Jao Fah pier or in advance from Krabi travel agencies such as Grand Travel and Jungle Book Tours.

Boats from Pranang and Ao Nang: Boats also serve Phi Phi from Ao Nang (Nang Bay) and Pranang, two beaches west of Krabi. The fare is 150-175B and the crossing takes two hours.

Boats from Ko Lanta: Ferries depart Ban Sala Dan daily at 1300 Nov.-June, and when conditions permit during the rainy season. The fare is 150-250B and the crossing takes two or three hours.

When service is canceled during the rainy months, travelers must go to Krabi and continue onward with larger boats.

KRABI AND KO LANTA

KRABI

Krabi Province comprises one of the most geologically interesting and scenically stunning landscapes in Thailand, an oceanic wonderland of magnificent limestone outcroppings surrounding white-sand beaches and primeval islands.

Krabi Town is a pleasant place to overnight but has little to offer except for a good selection of guesthouses and transportation connections to nearby destinations such as Ko Phi Phi, Pranang, and Ko Lanta. Visitors should be forewarned that Krabi—once the idyllic counterpart to Phuket and Ko Samui—is now inundated with travelers and tourists; an estimated 300,000 visitors annually pass through town, mostly Europeans on holiday in search of an untouched paradise.

Although the original Thai character has disappeared, the friendly people and well-developed infrastructure make Krabi an acceptable stop en route to nearby beaches.

Wat Tham Sua

Krabi is known for its beaches and islands, though a few cultural sidelights are located near the provincial capital.

Tiger Cave Monastery, seven km northeast of Krabi, is a decade-old retreat set in a natural amphitheater of caves and gigantic trees. Named after a rock formation which resembles a tiger paw, southwestern Thailand's most important forest *wat* was established by Achaan Jumnean Silasetho, a venerable monk from Nakhon Si Thammarat who uses grisly pictures of internal organs to emphasize the transitory nature of life. Each day, an estimated 200 monks and nuns gather before dawn to collect alms in Krabi, then return to the monastery to study Theravada Buddhism and listen to sermons broadcast over loudspeakers mounted in the banyan trees. Afternoons are spent in meditation, or perhaps chatting with the infrequent Western visitor.

Meditation practices at Tiger Cave Monastery emphasize *vipassana,* a yogic system which translates to "insight meditation," and the Buddhist precept of *mehta* (loving kindness). Visitors are welcome to climb up the long staircase at the end of the parking lot and politely wander past the cave sanctuaries and *kuti* huts to a pair of absolutely huge banyan trees with soaring buttresses that would dwarf an elephant. The jungle path continues through some thick foliage before returning to the stairway. Be sure to visit the meditation hall and museum with Buddhist images and photos of Achaan Jumnean. Tiger Cave Monastery is highly recommended for anyone interested in Buddhism or *vipassana* meditation.

Wat Tham Sua can be reached from Krabi by minitruck to Krabi junction at Talat Kao, then any bus heading south to the turnoff to the monastery. The monastery is two km up the

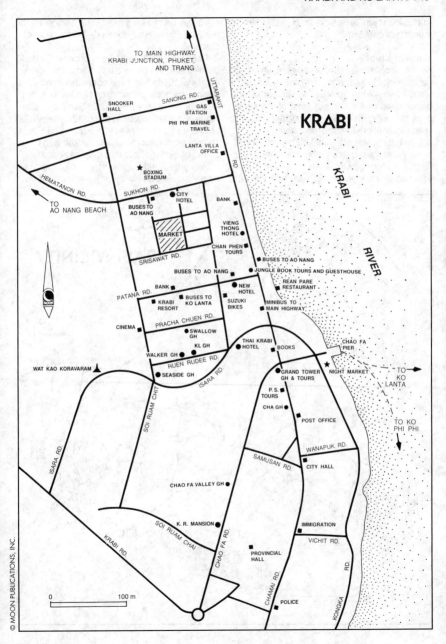

TO MAIN HIGHWAY,
KRABI JUNCTION, PHUKET,
AND TRANG

SANONG RD.

SNOOKER
HALL

GAS
STATION

PHI PHI MARINE
TRAVEL

LANTA VILLA
OFFICE

UTTARAKIT RD.

KRABI

KRABI RIVER

BOXING
STADIUM

SUKHON RD.

HEMATANON RD.

TO
AO NANG BEACH

CITY
HOTEL

BUSES TO
AO NANG

BANK

MARKET

VIENG
THONG
HOTEL

SRISAWAT RD.

CHAN PHEN
TOURS

BUSES TO AO NANG

BUSES TO AO NANG

JUNGLE BOOK TOURS AND GUESTHOUSE

REAN PARE
RESTAURANT

PATANA RD.

BANK

KRABI
RESORT

BUSES TO
KO LANTA

NEW
HOTEL

SUZUKI
BIKES

MINIBUS TO
MAIN HIGHWAY

CINEMA

PRACHA CHUEN RD.

SWALLOW
GH

KL GH

THAI KRABI
HOTEL

BOOKS

CHAO FA
PIER

TO
KO
LANTA

WALKER GH

RUEN RUDEE RD.

SOI RUAM CHIT

ISARA RD.

WAT KAO KORAVARAM

SEASIDE GH

GRAND TOWER
GH & TOURS

NIGHT MARKET

P. S.
TOURS

CHA GH

POST OFFICE

TO KO
PHI PHI

SAMUSAN RD.

WANAPUK RD.

CITY HALL

ISARA RD.

CHAO FA VALLEY GH

KRABI RD.

SOI RUAM CHAI

K. R. MANSION

CHAO FA RD.

IMMIGRATION

VICHIT RD.

PROVINCIAL
HALL

CHAMAI RD.

KONGKA RD.

POLICE

0   100 m

© MOON PUBLICATIONS, INC.

road. Motorcycle taxis from Krabi junction to the monastery cost 5B.

North of Krabi

Several worthwhile caves and waterfalls are situated north of Krabi in the direction of Ao Luk, a small town 42 km up Hwy. 4. Minitrucks and buses head to Ao Luk, but most of the attractions are well off the main highway and difficult to reach without private transportation.

The best option is a rental motorcycle. Traffic is light and most of the sights are marked with English-language signs. An extremely scenic tour can be done in a single day with an early start, but bring along the *Guide Map of Krabi* published by V. Hongsombud—an absolute necessity.

Reclining Buddha: A colorful concrete Buddha lies serenely under a pair of limestone peaks on Hwy. 4034. The road continues southeast down to the shell cemetery and Ao Nang Beach.

Shell Cemetery Beach: Su San Noi is a famous shoreline collection of fossilized seashells at Laem Pho, 19 km west of Krabi. The site is composed of limestone slabs flecked with thousands of oyster shells that date back some 75 million years. Although a rare geological phenomenon, Su San Noi actually resembles a slab

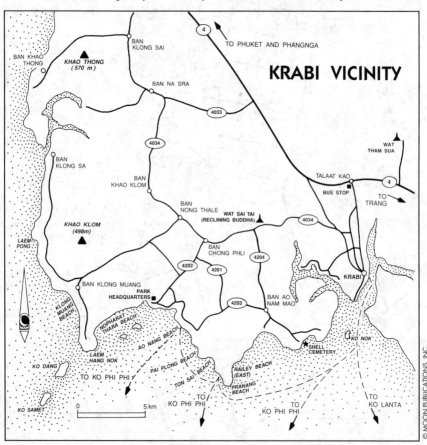

KRABI VICINITY

of parking lot that fell into the ocean: unimpressive and hardly worth the effort unless you arrive at low tide in the early-morning hours.

Ao Nang Beach: Ao Nang is described in more detail in the following section. Have a cold drink and then continue north. Beyond the coconut tree near Ban Khao Klom, the deserted road passes limestone mountains, rubber plantations, and sheets of latex drying in the sun. Take a photo and the kids laugh at you.

Khao Phanom Bencha National Park: Ten km north of Krabi is the turnoff to the 50-square-km national park known for Tham Khao Phung Cave and the three-tiered falls of Huay To. Campsites are at park headquarters.

Diamond Cave: A right turn 40 km north of Krabi and two km south of Ao Luk leads to Tham Phet, one of the largest and most beautiful caves in the region.

Ao Luk: This small town is the junction point for stops to nearby caves and falls. **Ao Luk Bungalows,** about 200 meters west on Hwy. 4039, has private bungalows from 200B.

Tham Bokarani National Park: A small national park with limited trails and some minor falls is located two km west of Ao Leuk Nua. The trail to the left leads to greenish bathing pools that drain through the mixed forests. Nearby **Waterfall Inn** has rooms from 200B fan and 300B a/c.

Dirt roads farther east lead to Than Khao Pra (past the golf course) and the boat dock for Tham Hua Kra Lok, a riverside cave with ancient pictographs.

Budget Accommodations

In recent years, Krabi has exploded with new places to stay after a massive renovation project replaced most of the old wooden shacks with modern shophouses, which have since been converted into guesthouses, cafes, and travel agencies. The best guesthouses are located just south of town or outside city limits in quieter locales.

Seaside Guesthouse: A fairly new, somewhat clean, but quiet spot with both fan and a/c rooms. 105/5 Maharaj Rd., tel. (075) 612351, 100-150B fan, 250-300B a/c.

K.L. Guesthouse: Another good choice with 43 rooms tucked between an a/c cafe and liquor store. 28 Ruen Rudee Rd., tel. (075) 612511, 100-250B.

K.R. Mansion: Slightly outside town is a very comfortable guesthouse with fully furnished rooms, spotless bathrooms, and popular cafe. A recommended escape from downtown Krabi. 52/1 Chao Fa Rd., tel. (075) 612761, fax (075) 612545, 120-250B.

Grand Tower Guesthouse: The former offices of Songserm Travel continue to function as a travel agency on the ground floor; they also rent rooms in the six-story building. The rooms are large and fairly clean and include private baths, except for the dismal hovels on the top floor. 73/1 Uttarakit Rd., tel. (075) 611741, 220-280B.

Swallow Guesthouse: Cozy little spot with clean rooms, all with private baths at bargain rates. Prach Chuen Rd., tel. (075) 611645, 100-140B.

Cha Guesthouse: Small but acceptable place with a few rooms just south of town near the post office. Uttarakit Rd., tel. (075) 611882, 100-120B.

Chao Fa Valley Guesthouse: Rudimentary bamboo and wooden shacks south of town en route to the far superior K.R. Mansion. 50/1 Chao Fa Rd., tel. (075) 612499, 150-300B.

Moderate Accommodations

Krabi's older hotels have been joined by several recent additions that finally give Krabi quality rooms at reasonable prices.

Vieng Thong Hotel: Although completely renovated a few years ago, the rooms once again need fresh paint and interior work to justify the unrealistic rates. 155 Uttarakit Rd., tel. (075) 611188, 650-800B a/c.

Thai Krabi Hotel: A centrally located but deteriorating hotel with overpriced rooms. 7 Isara Rd., tel. (075) 611122, fax (075) 612556, 300-450B fan, 600-900B a/c.

Riverside Hotel: The best midlevel hotel is one km north of town, but rooms are spotless and most offer terrific views over the river. 287/11 Uttarakit Rd., tel. (075) 612128, 240-280B fan, 350-490B a/c.

City Hotel: Another hotel with decent rooms and facilities, located near the morning market a few blocks north of city center. This spot is somewhat more expensive than the Riverside (same owners), but within walking distance of the cafes, travel agencies, and Chao Fa pier. 15/2 Sukhon

Rd., tel. (075) 611961, 250-350B fan, 480-550B a/c.

Krabi Meritime Hotel: Krabi's only luxury hotel is a few kilometers north of town on the way to the main highway. 168-170 Uttarakit Rd., tel. (075) 628028, 2,200-3,600B.

Information and Services

Most travelers blaze straight through Krabi en route to Ao Pranang Beach or Ko Phi Phi, but essential services are available for overnight visitors.

Tourist Information: The TAT office dispenses a few brochures and sketchy maps from their waterfront kiosk, though more reliable information can be picked up from the travel agencies listed below. Open daily 0830-1630. Uttarakit Rd., tel. (075) 612740.

Immigration: Visas can be extended at the immigration office a few blocks south of city center. Uttarakit Rd., tel. (075) 612884. Open weekdays 0830-1630, Saturday 0900-1200.

Post Office: The GPO has poste restante services. Krabi postal code: 81000. 190 Uttarakit Rd., tel. (075) 611944. Open weekdays 0830-1630, Saturday 0900-1200.

International Telephone: Overseas calls can be made from most hotels and guesthouses, travel agencies, and the international phone center at the post office. Open daily 0700-2400. 190 Uttarakit Rd., tel. (075) 611944.

Banks: Bangkok Bank, Siam City, and licensed vendors on the waterfront provide currency exchange services daily 0830-1600. Bangkok Bank has a 24-hour ATM.

Travel Agencies: Krabi has plenty of travel agencies and tour companies that arrange onward bus transport, plane reservations, and bus-and-train packages to Bangkok, Penang, and Singapore. Most sell advance tickets for boats to nearby beaches and islands, a somewhat unnecessary service since few boats have reserved seats and most depart with plenty of empty seats. Perhaps their most useful service is reserving rooms at nearby beaches and islands, a wise idea during the busy months (Dec.-March) when most places are booked out.

Recommending a specific agency can be difficult since many tend to open and close with the seasons. However, the following shops have been open for many years and seem to offer reliable service at reasonable prices.

Chan Phen Tours: The helpful owner, Miss Lee, has provided travel services since the mid-1980s, when Krabi was popular with savvy world travelers. Open daily 0700-2000. 145 Uttarakit Rd., tel. (075) 612404, fax (075) 612629.

Jungle Book Tours: The agency adjacent to Chan Phen Tours has been in business for over 10 years at the same location. Tours, reservations, and photos of Krabi guesthouses are available. Open daily 0700-2000. 141 Uttarakit Rd., tel. (075) 611148.

Grand Tours: This hotel and tour agency is doing remarkable business due to its perfect location in the old Songserm travel center. Open daily 0630-2100. 73/1 Uttarakit Rd., tel. (075) 621456.

Transportation

Krabi is 815 km south of Bangkok, 211 km southwest of Surat Thani, and 282 km northwest of Hat Yai. Krabi is only 54 km due west of Phuket, but buses must travel 176 km on Hwy. 4 around the north end of Phangnga Bay.

The most popular connections are buses from Ko Samui and Surat Thani, ferries from Phuket and Ko Phi Phi, and buses from Trang and Hat Yai. The transportation system is well organized and agents everywhere will help you find the best possible connection.

Air: The nearest airport is on Phuket.

Boats: Fishing boats, longtails, ferries, and speedboats depart Chao Fa pier for Ko Phi Phi, Ko Lanta, Ao Nang, and Pranang Beach.

Boats to Ko Phi Phi leave four times daily Oct.-June and once daily during the rainy months. Ferries cost 100-150B and take about three hours to Tonsai, while speedboats with a/c cabins cost 150-250B and take 90 minutes to the pier at Ko Phi Phi. Several resorts operate private express boats to their properties, notably the expensive resorts on the northeastern beaches.

Purchase tickets directly at the pier or in advance from Krabi travel agencies such as Chan Phen and Jungle Book Tours. Boat passage should not be attempted during poor or uncertain weather conditions, despite the assurances of boat captains and pier attendants. Many smaller boats have been swamped or lost during fierce storms that sweep in suddenly from the Andaman Sea.

Boats depart daily for Ko Lanta at 1030 and 1300 during the dry season and once daily during the rainy months. The fare is 150-200B for the two-hour journey to Ban Sala Dan, where *songtaos* and hotel touts wait for customers.

Fishing boats and longtails leave Chao Fa pier to Pranang and Ao Nang when filled with enough passengers. The scenic trip down the estuary and across the bay costs 40-60B to Pranang and Railey Beaches, and 60-80B to Ao Nang Beach. See "Ao Nang" below for more details.

Bus: Ordinary buses depart during the day from the bus terminal at Talat Ko, four km north of town. Private buses and minivans depart from tour offices and travel agencies such as Chan Phen, Jungle Book, and Grand Tours.

Transportation from Phuket

Krabi can be reached by bus via Phangnga or by boat via Ko Phi Phi.

Bus: Buses leave every half hour during the day from the Phuket bus terminal and take four or five hours to Krabi. Most terminate at the Talat Ko intersection, four km north of Krabi. *Songtaos* cost 10B into town.

Private buses often go directly to Chao Fa pier or tour offices such as Chan Phen and Grand Tours. Guesthouse and boat company touts greet arrivals and provide free transportation to their guesthouse or pier for immediate departure. Unless you arrive late in the day or wish to see the wonders of Krabi, it's best to depart immediately for Pranang or Ko Phi Phi.

Boat: The bus journey from Phuket passes through attractive scenery but is far less memorable than the boat trip across the Andaman Sea.

Fishing boats, ferries, speedboats, and hydrofoils leave Phuket daily from piers in Phuket Town, at Patong Beach, and along the southern coast. Most boats take two hours to Ko Phi Phi, where they drop passengers and then return to Phuket. A limited number continue on to Krabi the same afternoon. Departure schedules and routes can be checked with agents in Phuket.

Transportation from Ko Phi Phi

Boats leave Tonsai pier three times daily during the high season and once daily during the rainy months, subject to delays and cancellations due to weather conditions.

Most boats go to Krabi, but some boats head directly to Ao Nang or Pranang—superior routes that eliminate the need to overnight in Krabi.

Transportation from Ko Lanta

Krabi can be reached by boat from Ban Sala Dan, or with a boat/bus combination from Ban Ko Lanta.

Direct Boat: Boats leave daily during the high season at 0800 and 1500 from Ban Sala Dan on the northern tip of the island and reach Krabi in two hours. One boat leaves daily during the rainy season, subject to weather conditions.

Boat and Bus: When direct boats from Ban Sala Dan are canceled due to weather conditions, visitors must ferry from Ban Ko Lanta on the east coast to the mainland town of Ban Ba Muang, then continue by bus for the final leg to Krabi. This route takes four or five hours from the west coast beaches.

AO NANG

Geographical terminology is somewhat confusing around Krabi. Ao Nang, 17 km northwest of Krabi, is a disappointing stretch of sand that caters mostly to group tours shuttled here by uninformed travel agents. Hat Nopharat Thara is a somewhat better beach to the north. Pranang—also called Ao Phra Nang (Pranang Bay) or Laem Phra Nang (Pranang Cape)—is one of the most stunning destinations in Thailand. Don't miss it.

Ao Nang is cursed with mediocre sand and murky waters, but offers decent accommodations in a dramatic juxtaposition of beach and mountains. Longtail boats to Pranang leave on demand from the waiting shed in the middle of the beach.

Several travel agencies and dive shops run inexpensive snorkeling tours to nearby Poda and Chicken Islands—probably the best reason to stay on Ao Nang.

Ao Nang is best considered an overnight stop en route to Pranang.

Accommodations

Bungalows spring up weekly to serve the ever-increasing crowds. Minitrucks from Krabi pause at the Bank of Siam and the boat launch to

Railey East Beach

Pranang, then continue west past the bungalows facing the beach.

The best spots are **P.S. Cottages** (directly on the beach), **Coconut Garden** with simple huts arranged around a landscaped courtyard, and semi-luxurious **Krabi Resort** for upscale visitors.

Sample prices from south to north: Dum Guesthouse, 60-100B; Jungle Hut, 80-150B; Krabi Seaview, 500-1,000B; Green Park, 150-200B; B.B. Bungalows, 250-400B; Princess Garden, 150-300B; Phra Nang Inn, 1,400-1,800B; Ao Nang Villa, 1,200-2,000B; Peace Laguna, 600-1,000B; Gifts, 250-400B; Coconut Garden, 150-250B; Sea Breeze, 150-250B; Ao Nang Bungalows, 150-250B; P.S. Cottages, 200-500B; Ao Nang Ban Lae, 250-400B; Krabi Resort, 1,500-2,500B; and Ao Nang Thara, 300-600B.

Transportation
Ao Nang can be reached from Krabi in 40 minutes by minitrucks leaving from Uttarakit Road near Chan Phen Tours, or by *songtaos* leaving across from the New Hotel on Patana Road. The fare is 15B.

NOPHARAT THARA BEACH

One km north of Ao Nang and 18 km from Krabi is a broad and clean beach supervised by Phi Phi

Islands National Marine Park. The road from Ao Nang terminates at the parking lot adjacent to park headquarters and several small cafes. Just beyond is a broad estuary that can be waded across, except during and immediately after the monsoon season. The sand is very fine and known for the quality of its seashells, best uncovered at low tide. Nopharat Thara is usually deserted and a fine place to wander around for some solitude.

Accommodations
Bungalows and campsites can be arranged at the park headquarters just behind the parking lot. The remainder of the privately owned bungalows are across the estuary.

Emerald Bungalows has a pleasant restaurant, nightly videos, and bungalows for 150-500B, making this a popular spot. For transportation details, contact Emerald Tours (tel. 075-612258) at 2/1 Kongka Rd., just up from the Krabi pier.

Krabi Andaman Inn is another remote place with dozens of bungalows set amid pine trees. Small huts cost 60-100B, while private bungalows cost 250-350B. The Krabi office (tel. 075-611932) is at 6/1 Patana Rd.

Pine Bungalows is about six km west of Nopharat Thara Beach and around the cape of Ao Siam Beach. Dives can be arranged to nearby Ko Dang and Ko Bileh, and to coral beds just offshore. Pine has small huts for 60-100B and larger bungalows with attached bath for 120-250B. Contact Pine Tours (tel. 075-612192) on Prasak Uthit Road near the Thai Krabi Hotel.

Transportation

Songtaos from Uttarakit Road in Krabi leave frequently for park headquarters. Bungalows across the estuary on Nopharat Thara Beach are served by longtail boats from the parking lot, or with free transportation arranged with travel agents and guesthouse representatives in Krabi.

PRANANG

Pranang is comparable only to the wonders of Ko Phi Phi: an amazing landscape of soaring limestone mountains, aquamarine waters, and squeaky white sand in an outlying corner of paradise. The special grandeur of Pranang comes from the limestone cliffs encrusted with vegetation that resembles an instant designer garden, and pinnacles leached by rains into phantasmagoric shapes not unlike embryonic dollops of dripped wax. Pranang Beach is composed of

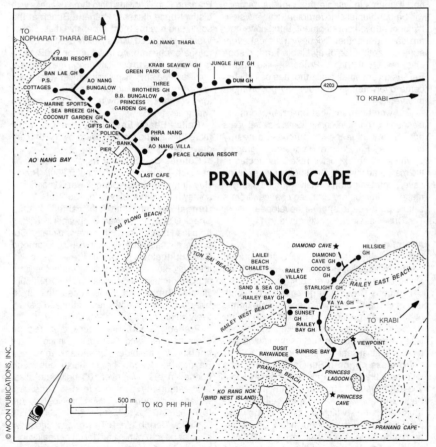

silken sand so white it almost hurts your eyes. Few places in Thailand offer such a stunning combination of water, sand, and land.

Pranang was first discovered in the early 1970s by travelers who whispered to fellow trippers about the unbelievable beauty of the remote cape. As it goes with such places, Pranang was subsequently developed by wealthy speculators into a major tourist destination—with all the benefits and drawbacks of famous resorts.

Compared to Phuket or Ko Samui, Pranang is still somewhat off the beaten track, but the pace of change has accelerated in recent years, and it seems inevitable that serious damage will be done unless government officials stem the uncontrolled development. Bungalows now are packed together, occupying almost every square centimeter of available land; discos blast away until dawn. Pranang—like Ko Phi Phi—is a very small place that has quickly become overwhelmed without any government intervention.

The worst news is that upscale resorts are planned by Thai hotel consortiums. Several years ago, Siam Lodge tried to purchase a nearby cove called Pai Pong and construct Paradise Cove Hotel, an exclusive resort connected to the main road through a 400-meter tunnel. Plans have been temporarily shelved, but it's only a matter of time before Pranang changes from a simple paradise to another developed resort. The Dusit has opened: stay tuned.

Attractions

Lazing on the beach and volleyball at sunset are the main activities, but hikers and divers will also enjoy the natural wonders.

Princess Cave: A large cave at the south end of Pranang Beach derives its name from a mythical sea goddess who gave birth to her earthly lover. Fishermen now place wooden phalluses inside to ensure successful fishing and protect against seasonal monsoons.

Princess Lagoon: Spectacular views and unforgettable photographs are possible when you climb the steep trail up the limestone peak behind Princess Cave. Ropes help with the treacherous trail, which winds left to the viewpoint and then descends down to a gigantic lagoon of seawater. Rock climbers can continue up the mountain for views of the entire cape and the islands of Ko Poda and Ko Hua Kwan.

Diamond Cave: Up the hill behind Diamond Cave Bungalows is a large cave with a short walkway and dripping stalactites. Borrow a flashlight from the caretaker and slide between the iron bars. Local folklore claims this is the grand palace of the mythical sea princess, while Princess Cave is her summer palace.

Ton Sai Beach: The secluded beach just north of Railey Beach can be reached at low tide, but first check the tide charts at Sunset Bungalows or risk a long swim back to Pranang.

Accommodations

Pranang Cape is divided into three beaches with distinct price classes. Pranang Beach at the south end has the most expensive digs, Railey West is midpriced, while Railey East is the last refuge of cheap bungalows under 100B. Bungalows are filled to capacity during the high season Nov.-March, when visitors must sometimes camp out under the coconut trees while waiting for a vacancy. Bungalow reps in Krabi can help with reservations.

Railey Beach East: Railey East is hardly more than a long mudflat overgrown with mangrove trees.

Sunrise Bay Bungalows at the south end has semi-luxurious chalets for 300-600B. **Railey Bay** (formerly Queen Bungalows) has decent if somewhat overpriced huts for 150-250B. **Ya Ya Bungalows,** and the aptly named **Swamp Shack Disco,** are somewhat cheaper but suffer from loud music that might drive you crazy. **Coco's** is a small place with just six huts. **Diamond Cave Bungalows** has a small basketball court, the lively Blue Bar tucked away under the limestone mountain, and bungalows for 100-250B. **Hillside Bungalows,** at the far eastern end, offers good views from the restaurant and distinctively painted huts for 100-180B.

Pranang Beach: The south end of the cape offers the finest sand, the best swimming, yachts bobbing in the blue lagoon, and the Dusit Rayavadee Resort. The ultra-luxurious resort opened in 1994 with over 100 individual villas, two restaurants, pool, two tennis courts, and water sports center. 67 Su San Noi Rd., tel. (075) 620740, fax (075) 620630, US$420-650.

Railey Beach West: The longest and most popular beach, with a half dozen bungalow operations and private homes at the northern edge. Flanked by a pair of towering limestone mountains, this is the place to start your room search.

Sunset Bungalows at the western end is a very pretty place, with 45 bungalows elevated on wooden platforms rather than the ugly concrete bases used elsewhere. Rooms here cost 350-600B. **Railey Bay** and **Starlight Bungalows** to the rear offer ordinary, overpriced bungalows for 200-350B. **Sand & Sea** has the most popular restaurant on the beach, volleyball games at sunset, and average bungalows for 150-300B. **Railey Village** at the eastern end is a better choice, with bungalows for 250-400B facing a grassy courtyard and rows of palms.

The final word in luxury is provided by **Lailei Beach Chalets** (Bangkok tel. 02-278-2676, Krabi tel. 075-611944), a private American development. Luxurious chalets rented from expat homeowners cost 600-2,200B.

Transportation

Pranang is 15 km northwest of Krabi and can only be reached by longtail boat from Krabi or Ao Nang Beach. Don't confuse Ao Nang with Pranang; if you're on a beach with a road, you haven't reached the latter.

Boats from Krabi cost 40B and take about 45 minutes. Boats from Ao Nang cost 20B and take about 15 minutes, passing Pai Plong and Tonsai Beaches.

ISLANDS NEAR KRABI

South of Krabi lies a string of small islands blessed with lovely beaches, clean waters, and shallow reefs perfect for snorkelers. Top draws include Ko Rang Nok just off Pranang; Ko Poda and Ko Hua Kwan, eight km south of the mainland; and Ko Mai Phai and Ko Yung, 22 km south of Pranang and just north of Ko Phi Phi.

Longtails to Poda and other centrally located islands cost 50-75B per person, depending on the number of passengers and mood of the captain. Check with the longtail owners at Pranang and Ao Nang.

Tours

A variety of tours are arranged by travel agencies and bungalows in Krabi, Ao Nang, and Pranang. A five-hour tour including lunch, longtail, and snorkeling gear costs 250-350B. Two-day tours with meals, longtail, and camping under the stars cost 500-700B.

More adventurous types can sign up for three-day "nautical tours" that visit Poda, Hua Kwan, and several other islets in the nearby Yawa archipelago. These camping-and-snorkeling tours also visit Ko Yung and Ko Mai Phai just north of Ko Phi Phi.

The 1,000-1,500B fee includes dive gear, tents, meals, and campfires on completely deserted beaches. Many excursions are led by *chao nam,* wandering sea gypsies intimately familiar with the hidden coves and beaches of Phangnga Bay.

Accommodations

Most islands rest within the boundaries of Ko Phi Phi National Marine Park, so camping is permitted anywhere except directly on the beach. Visitors should bring camping gear and adequate supplies of food and water.

One lonely set of bungalows sits on Ko Poda, despite the island's location within the national park. Ko Hua Kwan may have bungalows within a few years.

Ko Rang Nok (Bird's Nest Island)

Just off Pranang Beach lies Bird's Nest Island and an unnamed rock to the rear. The easily accessible islands are great spots for swimming and sunbathing, as well as havens for snorkelers, who can explore an underwater cave and sunken boat on the south side of the island.

Ko Poda

Ko Poda, eight km south of Pranang, provides an ideal retreat for snorkelers and sunbathers unhappy with the crowded beaches of Pranang and Ao Nang. Poda is also popular with yachters, who anchor in the bay and wade ashore to enjoy the beaches and shallow reefs.

Accommodations: Krabi Resort on Ao Nang Beach manages 20 large bungalows and a small restaurant with decent—if somewhat overpriced—food. Bungalows include private baths and electric lights 1800-2200. Krabi Resort, 53-57 Pattana Rd., Ao Nang, tel. (075) 612121, fax (075) 612160, 350-450B.

Ko Hua Kwan (Chicken Island)

Just south of Poda is Ko Hua Kwan, dubbed Chicken Island for its unusual rock formation at the northern tip. Ko Hua Kwan, also called Ko

Poda Nok and Ko Dam Khwian, features lovely beaches and offshore reefs considered just as impressive as those on Ko Poda.

Camping is permitted anywhere on the island; bungalows may be open by the time of your arrival.

Ko Yung and Ko Mai Phai

Ko Yung (Mosquito Island) and Ko Mai Phai (Bamboo Island) are two small islands about four km north of Ko Phi Phi. Both are chiefly visited by dive groups who arrive on chartered boats from Tonsai, but people on longer excursions from the mainland also arrive after spending time on Poda and Hua Kwan.

Dive sites range from the shallow coral beds that encircle Ko Mai Phai to dramatic limestone walls off Ko Yung that plunge straight down to the sea floor, then slowly spread out in all directions. Hin Klang, a series of submerged rocks between Ko Mai Phai and Laem Tong, also provides dive opportunities for scuba groups coming up from Ko Phi Phi.

KO LANTA

The search for an undiscovered paradise is quickly pushing travelers south from Krabi toward the Malaysian border and dozens of islands near Trang and Satun. Several years ago, Ko Lanta was an offbeat destination inhabited only by Muslim fishermen who couldn't understand why anyone would visit their hot, remote island. Ko Lanta today has over a dozen bungalows stretched along the west coast, from the northern village of Ban Sala Dan down to Ban Sangka U at the southern tip.

Ko Lanta archipelago consists of over 50 islands, but only Ko Lanta Yai (Big Ko Lanta) and a few small islets have formal accommodations. Ko Lanta offers some fairly good beaches almost completely untouched by mass tourism, and a bit of skin diving over offshore coral beds. Another sidelight is the near-complete dominance of Islam on the island, a world where Muslim mosques vastly outnumber Buddhist *wats*.

Ko Lanta has a few drawbacks. The isolated location demands at least two full days of travel from Bangkok or Phuket, though direct boat service is now offered from Krabi and Ko Phi Phi. Secondly, the sand ranges from fairly good crystal to rough volcanic rock depending on the beach. Weather

also can be a problem: the island is murderously hot in the dry season March-June, and as on other islands on the west coast of southern Thailand, monsoons bring heavy downpours June-Oct. Getting around is difficult since transportation along the west coast is sporadic; visitors often find themselves limited to a single beach. Finally, most of the bungalows—constructed from concrete and tin rather than natural materials—are needlessly crammed together to the point of absurdity.

Although the island has drawbacks—and lacks the stunning topography and pristine beaches of Ko Phi Phi and Pranang—visitors searching to escape the crowds and willing to endure some transportation hassles will probably enjoy their discovery.

Ban Sala Dan

The largest village on Ko Lanta is where most boats from Krabi and Ko Phi Phi terminate. Ban Sala Dan is a typical Thai fishing village, with several cafes overlooking the bay and Ko Lanta Noi—new spots like La Creperie, which serves French crepes and sells boat tours. Motorcycle rentals are available from Petchpalin Restaurant and several other cafes in town, though rentals are very expensive. Money-exchange services will probably arrive by the time you visit.

Sahamit Tours at the central intersection sells bus tickets to Bangkok and boat tickets to Krabi and Ko Phi Phi. Seaside Restaurant down the dusty street is a good place for a cold drink.

Kor Kwang Beach

A few bungalows are located west of town on the rocky promontory called Laem Kor Kwang. The beach itself (Kaw Kwang) is nicely curved and absolutely deserted, and has aquamarine waters with a few fishing boats.

Deer Neck Cabanas: A popular spot at the northern edge of the cape with spacious grounds and a pleasant cafe—one of the few places on Ko Lanta from where you can walk into Ban Sala Dan. Bungalows here cost 180-300B with a few upscale cabins from 600B.

Kar Kwang Beach Bungalows: At the southern edge of the bay is another longtime favorite that organizes dive trips to nearby islands. It also has fairly decent bungalows facing a fine sand beach priced from 150-300B, plus a handful of superior bungalows at double the price.

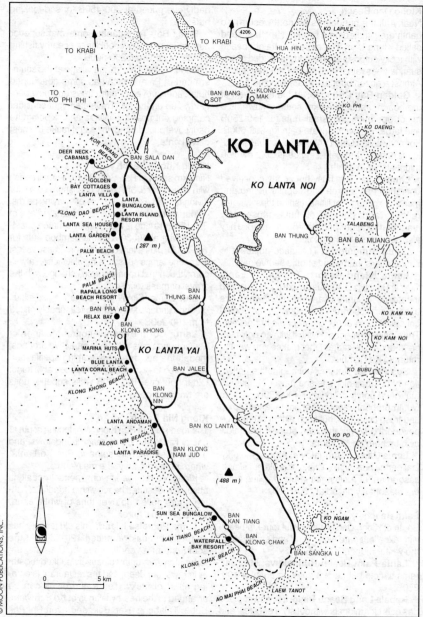

TO KRABI

TO KO PHI PHI

4206
TO KRABI

KO LAPULE

HUA HIN

BAN BANG
SOT

KLONG
MAK

KO PHI

KO DAENG

KOR KWANG BEACH

DEER NECK
CABANAS

BAN SALA DAN

KO LANTA

KO LANTA NOI

GOLDEN
BAY COTTAGES

LANTA VILLA

LANTA
BUNGALOWS

LANTA ISLAND
RESORT

KLONG DAO BEACH

LANTA SEA HOUSE

LANTA GARDEN

PALM BEACH

(287 m)

KO
TALABENG

BAN THUNG

TO BAN BA MUANG

PALM BEACH

RAPALA LONG
BEACH RESORT

BAN PRA AE

RELAX BAY

BAN
THUNG SAN

KO KAM YAI

BAN
KLONG KHONG

KO KAM NOI

MARINA HUTS

KO LANTA YAI

BLUE LANTA

LANTA CORAL BEACH

BAN JALEE

KO BUBU

KLONG KHONG BEACH

BAN
KLONG
NIN

LANTA ANDAMAN

BAN KO LANTA

KLONG NIN BEACH

KO PO

LANTA PARADISE

BAN KLONG
NAM JUD

(488 m)

SUN SEA BUNGALOW

BAN
KAN TIANG

KO NGAM

KAN TIANG BEACH

WATERFALL
BAY RESORT

BAN
KLONG CHAK

BAN SANGKA U

KLONG CHAK BEACH

AO MAI PHAI BEACH

LAEM TANOT

© MOON PUBLICATIONS, INC.

0   5 km

Klong Dao Beach

Nearly all the bungalows on northwestern Ko Lanta are situated on a two-km stretch of sand called Klong Dao. The perfectly straight beach with rocky outposts at both ends is shaded by casuarina trees rather than much-preferred palms. Almost a dozen bungalows are sited here.

Golden Bay Cottages: At the north end of the beach, about three km south of town, is a major operation with small huts for 150-250B and larger digs with private bath for 300-600B. Formerly called Club Lanta, the place has friendly managers, but cafe service is so slow you might starve to death.

Lanta Villa: This busy but poorly conceived operation has a large and popular restaurant, money-exchange facilities, fishing trips, longtail rentals, and dozens of huts senselessly crammed together and priced 200-400B. They also sell tickets to Bangkok.

Lanta Bungalows: The place adjacent to Lanta Villa is trashy and should be avoided.

Lanta Island Resort: The former Lanta Royale Beach has 40-plus deluxe chalets packed together like canned sardines, all of which are badly overpriced from 300-500B for fan-cooled units and up to 800B for larger a/c bungalows. The whole affair goes downhill with an ugly concrete-and-tin restaurant that makes you want to return to Ko Samui.

Sea House: Another unimaginative collection of decrepit old huts and newer bungalows that need porch railings for 400-800B. Visitors would probably appreciate some landscaping and trash collection, but such extras seem to be beyond the comprehension of most bungalow owners here on Ko Lanta.

Lanta Garden Bungalows: Among the original earthy huts on the island, this old but simple assortment of rudimentary huts is falling down but reasonably priced at 100-250B.

Palm Beach

South of Klong Dao is a beautiful four-km beach with excellent pure white sand and small surf in the winter months.

Lanta Palm Beach Bungalows: Mr. "Bat" rents simple but decent bamboo huts for 100-250B.

Rapala Long Beach Resort: A newer place designed for midgets without style or class, and badly overpriced at 200-450B for sad-looking huts.

Relax Bay Tropicana: Somewhat superior huts up on the hill overlooking the nearby fishing village, priced from 200-600B.

Ban Pra Ae: This fishing village at the southern end of Palm Beach has some abandoned huts under groves of palm trees and new bungalows up on the hill. Travelers might consider camping out near this village and skipping the badly overpriced bungalows that make up most of Ko Lanta.

Klong Khong Beach

Nine km south of Ban Sala Dan is a small beach with limited sand, but plenty of offshore corals for diving and an excellent grove of swaying palms.

Marina Huts: Just south of the small village of Ban Klong Khong is a beautifully situated guesthouse with about 30 A-frame bamboo huts for 100-300B, plus a tent campsite on grassy lawns. Kerosene lamps substitute for electricity—a welcome touch that hopefully won't change with the arrival of mass tourism.

Blue Lanta: Simple huts set among spacious grounds under coconut trees, reasonably priced from 100-250B.

Lanta Coral Beach: Another melange of newer bungalows with fairly attractive grounds, though the beach here is nothing special and you'll need to hike north to find acceptable sand. Older huts cost 100-200B while superior units are twice the price.

Klong Nin Beach

The road splits at Ban Klong Nin, forking south to Laem Tanot and other beach bungalows, and east across the hilly spine to Ban Ko Lanta, where boats depart to the mainland.

Klong Nin is a five-km-long, perfectly straight, absolutely deserted beach with a handful of fishing boats pulled up over tons of white sand. Great potential here.

Lanta Paradise Island: This old favorite has about 40 bungalows priced 120-350B at the south end of a very fine beach. The huts, unfortunately, are unimaginatively packed together in rows four deep, and the restaurant is nothing short of tacky. Tours and dives can be arranged to the nearby islands of Ko Son, Jam, Bubu, Talabeng, Hai, Bok, and even Phi Phi.

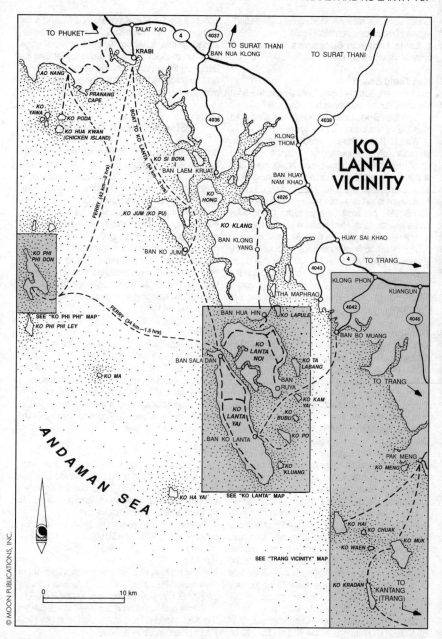

TO PHUKET

TALAT KAO

KRABI

4037

BAN NUA KLONG

TO SURAT THANI

TO SURAT THANI

AO NANG

PRANANG CAPE

KO YAWA

KO PODA

KO HUA KWAN (CHICKEN ISLAND)

4036

KLONG THOM

4038

KO LANTA VICINITY

KO SI BOYA

BAN LAEM KRUAT

KO HONG

BAN HUAY NAM KHAO

4026

FERRY (42 km—2 hrs)

BOAT TO KO LANTA (54 km—3 hrs)

KO JUM (KO PU)

KO KLANG

BAN KLONG YANG

HUAY SAI KHAO

4043

4

TO TRANG

KO PHI PHI DON

BAN KO JUM

SEE "KO PHI PHI" MAP

KO PHI PHI LEY

FERRY (24 km—1.5 hrs)

THA MAPHRAO

KLONG PHON

KUANGUN

4042

4046

BAN BO MUANG

BAN HUA HIN

KO LAPULE

KO LANTA NOI

BAN SALA DAN

KO TA LABANG

BAN RUYA

TO TRANG

KO MA

KO KAM YAI

KO BUBU

KO PO

KO LANTA YAI

BAN KO LANTA

KO KLUANG

A N D A M A N   S E A

KO HA YAI

SEE "KO LANTA" MAP

PAK MENG

KO MENG

SEE "TRANG VICINITY" MAP

KO HAI

KO CHUAK

KO MUK

KO WAEN

0   10 km

KO KRADAN

TO KANTANG (TRANG)

Other services include windsurfing, gamefishing, and motorbike rentals.

Lanta Andaman Bungalows: An ugly dive without views of the beach.

Kan Tiang Beach

Eighteen km south of Ban Sala Dan is the final series of coves and deserted beaches.

Sun Sea Bungalows: This old place on Had Kan Tiang has bamboo huts for 80-180B.

Waterfall Bay Resort: A surprisingly upscale and relatively well-planned resort at the southern tip of the island, with split level bungalows and water sports activities such as local diving, boat excursions, and hikes to the nearby waterfall. This resort is rather expensive—bungalows cost 450-800B—but worth the price for those who can afford the tariff. Reservations can be made at their Krabi office at (075) 612084.

The dirt road continues south to Klong Chak Beach and Ao Mai Phai Beach near the cape of Laem Tanot. The road ends at the cape, but a narrow path continues east around the rocky headlands to the Thai Muslim fishing village of Ban Sangka U.

Transportation

Ko Lanta Yai is 100 km southeast of Krabi, 77 km northwest of Trang, and 12 km from the mainland pier at Ban Bo Muang.

Boat: The most convenient way to reach Ko Lanta is by direct boat from Krabi or Ko Phi Phi. Travel agents sell tickets and can advise you on the latest schedules.

Most boats terminate in the town of Ban Sala Dan at the north end of Ko Lanta Yai. Minitrucks and motorcycle taxis continue south down to the beaches. Bungalow owners are often on hand with photos, personalized recommendations, and private transportation. You can also rent motorcycles in Ban Sala Dan.

Land: Ko Lanta can also be reached with public transportation and by hired motorcycle. Two routes are possible. From the Talat Kao junction (Krabi junction) near Krabi, take a minitruck or bus south to Ban Hua Hin; continue by public ferry to Ko Lanta Noi and finally Ban Sala Dan on Ko Lanta Yai. The entire 100-km journey takes a half day with public transportation, but only three hours with rented motorcycle.

Alternatively, take public transportation to Ban Ba Muang (Bo Muang), at the end of Hwy. 4042, about 88 km south of Krabi. Ban Ba Muang is the primary ferry port for Ko Lanta; large 80-passenger ferries depart for Ko Lanta several times daily, take about one hour, and stop at Ban Ko Lanta on the east side of the island. Minitrucks and motorcycle taxis meet the ferry, then head over the mountains to the west-coast beaches.

ISLANDS NEAR KO LANTA

Several of the small islets near Ko Lanta Yai have been developed into private hideaways. Most of the bungalows have representatives in Krabi who can show you photos of the property and advise you on transportation.

The string of islands continues south to Ko Hai, Ko Muk, and Ko Kradan, before reaching the mainland town of Trang. All islands now have bungalows; islands to the south are described in "Island Near Trang" under "Trang to Satun" below. Adventurous travelers can hire longtail boats on Ko Lanta, motor south, and visit each island before stopping at Trang or Ko Tarutao National Marine Park.

Ko Bubu

Bubu Bungalows is a typical operation with 13 huts priced 200-500B per night.

To reach Ko Bubu, take a minitruck from Krabi to Bo Muang pier on the mainland, followed by a private or chartered boat across to the small island. Transportation can also be arranged in Krabi from Thammachart Tours on Kongka Road near the Chao Pa pier.

Ko Si Boya

Ko Si Boya is a small island north of Ko Lanta with a solitary set of bungalows called Islander Huts that cost 120-350B. Ko Si Boya is deserted except for a few fishermen, and the beach is fairly clean despite murky waters.

Reservations in Krabi are available from Siboya Tours at 246 Uttarakit Rd.

Ko Jum

North of Ko Lanta Yai is another small islet where Jum Island Resort offers basic bamboo huts for 150-200B, and more luxurious chalets for 250-600B.

Transportation can be arranged in Krabi from the Jum Island Resort office, and from the New Krabi Hotel on Patana Road.

TRANG TO SATUN

TRANG

Trang is the gateway to one of the newest tourist regions in Thailand. The town itself is reasonably clean and attractive. Within a day's journey are more than 20 waterfalls located within national parks, several large limestone caves filled with Buddhist images, and wildlife sanctuaries. The highlights of Trang, however, are the broad and deserted beaches on the western coastline,

and a half dozen small islands with pure-white beaches and outstanding diving.

Like Phuket, Trang owes its original prosperity to the Fukien Chinese who settled here in the late 19th and early 20th centuries. Originally located in Kantang at the mouth of the Trang River, the town was moved to its present location (the former Taptieng) by King Mongkut to avoid annual floods and protect against naval invasion. Trang now derives most of its wealth from hundreds of rubber and palm-oil plantations in the outlying countryside.

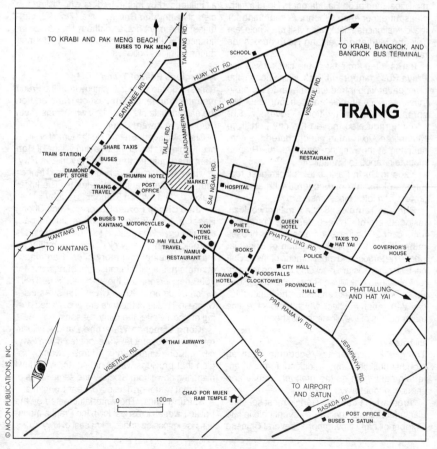

Attractions in Town

Trang itself has a few historic monuments and a pleasant layout over small hills or *khuans.*

City Central: The central clock tower—constructed in an unusual shape with a narrow base and wide top—is a good spot to sample local specialties offered by city street vendors, including roast pork braised in honey. East of the clock tower is the historic governor's house, city hall, and courthouse on a small *khuan* that provides views toward Khao Nong Yuan, where a small temple enshrines a footprint of the Buddha.

Markets: Trang often wins the "Cleanest City in Thailand" award, which makes a visit to its municipal market on Rajadamnern Road a fairly pleasant experience. Shoppers searching for the lowest prices should also visit the wholesale Taklang Market on Taklang Road across the railroad tracks.

Parks: One km east of the clock tower lies **Praya Rusadanupradit Park,** which honors the civic leader who introduced rubber to the province—and Thailand—and encouraged the spread of its cultivation. Governor Rusadanupradit also moved the city port from Khuanthane to Kantang and ordered the construction of the winding road over the Prapha mountain range to Phattalung.

Kapang Surin Park, a few blocks east, features a pleasant pond covered with acres of flowers and lotus blossoms.

Chinese Temples: Since a majority of local residents are of Chinese descent, Trang features over 20 Chinese temples or *joss* houses rather than the typical collection of Buddhist *wats.* The largest and most famous of these Chinese clan houses are Kew Ong Eia and the century-old Chao Por Muen Ram off Visetkul Road Soi 1. Both serve as venues for the famous 10-day Vegetarian Festival, which honors the nine major deities of the Chinese pantheon.

Events

Trang is known for its Vegetarian Festival, monthly bullfights, and traditional forms of entertainment such as the *manohra* dance and shadow puppet plays.

Vegetarian Festival: Trang's most spectacular celebration is the 10-day event held in late October or early November at several Chinese temples. See the special topic **Phuket's Amazing** *Ngan Kin Jeh* for more details.

Bullfights: Residents of Trang seem to wager on just about anything that moves: fighting fish, roosters, and highly prized bulls valued up to one million *baht.* Bullfights are held monthly on selected weekends in Sanam Chon Koe District. The entrance fee is 20B and the event starts around 1100.

Puppets and Dance: Southern-style shadow puppet plays are performed at Chao Por Muen Ram temple during religious festivals, and at Trang municipal hall on civic holidays. *Nang talang* differs from northern styles in the selection of stories, puppet shapes, and styles of music—all influenced by Indian traders who visited the district during the Srivijaya era (7th-12th centuries). The *manohra,* a southern Thai dance influenced by Hindu traditions, is also performed during religious holidays.

Attractions East of Trang

Almost a dozen waterfalls plunge from the Prapa mountain range, 20 km east of Trang and on the eastern side of Hwy. 4125, which runs south from Hwy. 4 toward Satun.

Crafts Villages: En route to the turnoff, visitors might enjoy a stop at the weaving village of **Ban Namunsri,** just north of Ban Nayong on Hwy. 4, where women weave brightly colored fabrics with distinctive, traditional patterns. The knife-making village of Ban Pranpor is nearby.

Khao Chong Forest Reserve: Khao Chong Reserve, just off the Trang-Phattalung Road, contains one of the region's few remaining stands of tropical rainforest, which provides shelter for many species of migratory birds. Park headquarters has a wildlife museum, bungalows for 100B per person, and the so-called "Blue Trail," which leads up to Khao Chong Falls. As elsewhere in Thailand, the falls are best visited during or shortly after the rainy season.

Klong Lamchan Waterbird Park: A wildlife refuge and several falls are located down Hwy. 4125. Klong Lamchan is a large, swampy region that provides winter habitat for waterfowl migrating down from Siberia—the same range of birds that winter on Thale Noi near Songkhla.

Sairung Falls: The waterfall created by the Palian River as it rushes down the Prapha mountains is signposted and four km east of Hwy. 4125.

Praisawan Falls: Five km south is another series of cold plunges popular with Trang residents in the hot summer months.

Tonteh and Tontok Falls: The final pair of falls, 46 km from Trang, are considered the longest and most impressive in the province. Tonteh—an awesome 320-meter cascade—and Tontok Falls can be accessed up a rough three-km dirt road.

Attractions North of Trang

Highway 4 heads north from Trang toward Krabi and Nakhon Si Thammarat, past several magnificent waterfalls and limestone caves filled with pictographs, rare pottery and porcelains, and large Buddha images. Public transportation is limited and most of the sights are on side roads off the main highways; rent a car or motorcycle in Trang.

Wat Su Rajapradit: The cave of Tham Iso, 20 km north of Trang and five km east of the highway, features a modern reclining Buddha facing a courtyard shaded by an enormous iso tree.

Wat Khao Pina: Hwy. 4 heads west at Huay Yot toward this six-leveled limestone cave filled with Buddha images, reached via a maze of concrete staircases.

Wat Khao Phra: Anthropologists remain puzzled about the origins of the mysterious red symbols discovered at the cave temple 15 km north of Huay Yot. Some assume the pictographs were carved by an unknown subculture dating back to the Ligor Empire of Nakhon Si Thammarat. The strange scene at Wat Khao Phra (also called Wat Tham Tra or "Seal Cave Temple") is complemented by the mummified corpse of an abbot that shows few signs of decay.

Wat Tham Phra Phut: Perhaps the most significant of all provincial caves is the limestone cavern 17 km east of Klongpang in northeastern Huay Yot District. When archaeologists rediscovered the cave earlier this century, they were surprised to find a large Ayuthaya-Period Buddha reclining over a collection of royal regalia and upper-class household items, including religious talismans, fine pottery, silverwork, and lacquerware. The collection may have been stashed inside the cave prior to the destruction of Ayuthaya, or moved here in the late 18th century to honor the principal image.

Scuba Diving

Snorkeling tours can be arranged at Trang Travel and resort offices near the train station. A full-day snorkeling tour to several islands plus lunch and gear costs 600-800B.

The solitary dive shop in Trang closed down several years ago, though scuba diving excursions can be organized at Rainbow Divers on Ko Hai by Brigitte Monat and Lothar Gensing, but only from the middle of November until the end of April.

Accommodations

Trang remains well off the tourist trail, and hotels generally cater to Thai visitors rather than *farangs*. Most hotels are centrally located on Pra Rama VI Road near the bus terminal, train station, and clock tower.

Koh Teng Hotel: Trang's backpackers' center offers a very useful bulletin board with maps and bus schedules, photos of nearby beach resorts, and a notebook with firsthand tips on current travel conditions throughout Trang Province. Rooms are spacious and clean, and the manager is extremely helpful. 77/79 Pra Rama VI Rd., tel. (075) 218622, 180-250B.

Phet Hotel: If the Koh Teng (Ko Teng) happens to be closed or bankrupt, this rudimentary hotel has large if somewhat unkempt rooms at bargain prices; located in the center of town, just one block off the main drag. Rajadamnern Rd., tel. (075) 218002, 100-180B.

Queen Hotel: Good-value hotel near several decent restaurants and nightclubs. Visetkul Rd., tel. (075) 218522, 200-250B fan, 350-450B a/c.

Trang Hotel: Refurbished hotel near the clock tower that often grants 30-50% discounts upon request. 134/2 Visetkul Rd., tel. (075) 218944, 450-500B fan, 600-800B a/c.

Thumrin Hotel: Trang's only semi-luxury hotel features a comfortable cafe, convention facilities, and a limited amount of tourist information from the front desk. Pra Rama VI Rd., tel. (075) 211011, fax (075) 218057, 700-1,200B.

Restaurants

Trang owes a great deal of its past prosperity to the Fukien Chinese, who settled down and left behind a rich legacy of Sino-Portuguese architecture in the port of Kantang. Perhaps the most interesting aspect of modern Trang is the cuisine, which combines Chinese styles with regional variations favored in the deep south.

Trang specialties include succulent roast pork *(muu yang)* marinated overnight in honey and then grilled to crispness, Chinese-style donuts *(paa thong kao),* coconut-filled dumplings *(khanom thip),* and *khanom jin,* a spicy curried noodle dish served with cucumbers, pickled cabbage, and mint leaves. Trang's other culinary treat is locally grown Khao Chong coffee, filter-brewed and served at breakfast with plates of *dim sum,* dumplings, and donuts.

Night Markets: All of the above are served by food vendors who appear magically every evening under the clock tower and on Sathanee Road near the Diamond Department Store—perfect spots to dine outdoors and hang with the locals.

Koh Teng Cafe: The coffee shop inside the hotel of the same name cooks up most of the regional specialties, as well as Western dishes for homesick travelers. 77/79 Pra Rama VI Rd., tel. (075) 218622. Open daily 0600-2200. Inexpensive.

Hokkien Coffee Shops: Most of the Hokkien-style coffee shops around Trang are small, dark places filled with elderly Chinese-Thais from dawn to dusk. Recommended cafes include Ko Daeng on Pra Rama VI Road near the Bangkok Bank and Sin Jiao on Kantang Road just off Pra Rama VI Road. Inexpensive.

Sinochai Bakery: The modern alternative to Hokkien digs is the clean and cheerful bakery adjacent to the train station and opposite Diamond Department Store. Open daily 0700-2200. 25/25 Sathanee Rd., tel. (075) 211191. Inexpensive.

Hoa Cafe: Another clean, comfortable, and reasonably priced coffee shop is situated inside Diamond Department Store just opposite the train station. Friendly waitresses. Open daily 0700-2200. 16 Sathanee Rd., tel. (075) 211884. Inexpensive.

Namui Restaurant: The cafe opposite the Koh Teng Hotel serves Chinese seafood dishes in an enclosed a/c dining room and in the open-air garden to the rear. Open daily 1000-2200. Pra Rama VI Rd. Moderate.

Kanok Restaurant: A popular place with a large menu; unfortunately, the restaurant overlooks the badly polluted canal of Klong Huay Yang. Open daily 1100-2200. Visetkul Rd. Moderate.

Queen Hotel: The restaurant inside the Queen Hotel serves decent Western breakfasts and a wide variety of Thai and Chinese dishes at lunch and dinnertime. Open daily 0800-2100. Visetkul Rd., tel. (075) 218229. Moderate.

Shopping

Trang handicrafts include wickerwork baskets and colorful mats woven from the leaves of the pandanus plant. Pandan mats are traditionally given as bridal gifts and cost 100-200B in the Taklang Market. Trang is also known for its distinctive styles of weaving in a variety of patterns, most notably the *lai luk kao* weave once reserved only for members of the wealthy classes. Today, the residents of Ban Namuen Sri weave scarfs, handkerchiefs, headdresses, sashes, and blouse covers *(sabai)* for visitors and private agencies supported by the Royal Family.

Information and Services

Trang is a large town with all necessary services centered near the train station or along Pra Rama VI Road.

Tourist Information: Trang doesn't have a TAT office, but information on nearby beaches, islands, and resorts can be picked up at travel agencies and hotels such as Koh Teng. Koh Teng has been a reliable source of information for over a decade, providing the latest word on transportation and new destinations on a bulletin board in their cafe. Also, check their logbook for personal tips from other travelers. Trang Travel, Trang Tourism Business Association, and resort offices can also help.

Mail and International Telephone: The GPO and overseas phone center is about one km up Pra Rama VI Road. A postal branch is near the train station. Jermpanya Rd., tel. (075) 218521. Open weekdays 0830-1630, Saturday 0900-1200. Postal code: 92000.

The international phone center upstairs is open daily 0800-1800.

Hospital: The Ratchadamnern Hospital is one block from the municipal market. 25 Soi 1, Sai Ngam Rd., tel. (075) 211200. Open 24 hours.

Bookstore: A limited selection of English-language newspapers and magazines is sold at Mit San Books near the clock tower. 130 Visetkul Rd., tel. (075) 218811. Open daily 0800-2130.

Travel Agencies and Resorts: Travel information, resort reservations, and island tours are provided by the following businesses.

Trang Travel, just opposite the Thumrin Hotel, arranges island tours, rents snorkeling gear, sells maps and booklets, and makes reservations for planes, trains, and buses. Open daily 0800-2030. Pra Rama VI Rd., tel. (075) 219598, fax (075) 218057.

Many of the larger resorts on nearby islands have representative offices in Trang for reservations and transportation. Check with the following offices prior to departure, especially during the rainy season when many resorts close: Ko Hai Villa, 112 Pra Rama VI Rd., tel. (075) 210496; Ko Hai Resort, 112 Pra Rama VI Rd., tel. (075) 210496; Ko Libong Resort, 158/1 Kantang Rd., tel. (075) 210013; Ko Muk Resort, 25/36 Sathanee Rd., tel. (075) 211367; Ko Kradan Resort, 25/36 Sathanee Rd., tel. (075) 211391.

Transportation

Trang is 870 km south of Bangkok, 136 km south of Krabi, and 163 km northwest of Hat Yai.

Air: Thai Airways flies three times weekly from Bangkok and Surat Thani, and four times weekly from Phuket. Thai Airways, 199/2 Visetkul Rd., tel. (075) 218066.

The Trang airport is seven km south on Hwy. 404 toward Pailin. Trang Travel runs airport vans.

Train: Trang can be reached on a side track that splits from the north-south railway line at Thung Song in Nakhon Si Thammarat Province. Direct train service from Bangkok is limited to rapid no. 41 from Hualampong at 1830 and express no. 13 at 1700. Trains take 15-16 hours via Surat Thani. Trains leave Thung Song at 0930 and 1530.

Trains to Surat Thani and Bangkok depart Trang at 1330 and 1810.

Bus: Buses, minivans, and share taxis connect Trang with nearby destinations from stations scattered around town but shown on the Trang map. Travelers can check schedules at Trang Travel and the Koh Teng Hotel.

Buses and a/c vans to Krabi, Phuket, Surat Thani, and Hat Yai leave from the bus terminal opposite the train station. Buses to Satun leave from the terminal on Rasada Road. Express and a/c buses to Bangkok depart from the bus terminal northeast of town on Ploenpitak Road. Air-conditioned vans to Hat Yai also leave from the Koh Teng Hotel, while share taxis leave from Phattalung Road near the police station.

Getting Around: Nearby beaches and piers are served by buses and vans leaving from stops near the train station. Buses to Kantang Pier leave from Kantang Road, near the train tracks. Buses to Pak Meng Beach leave from the stop near the tracks on Taklang Road.

Motorcycles: A handy way to quickly tour the region. Bikes can be rented from Koh Teng Hotel, from kids who hang out in the municipal market, and from the motorcycle shop at 44 Pra Rama VI Rd. Small but racy little bikes with low handles and plenty of kick cost 180-200B per day.

BEACHES NEAR TRANG

The star attractions of Trang are the nearby beaches and islands, popular with Thai tourists but rarely visited by Western travelers.

Most of the beaches and offshore islands are within Hat Chao Mai National Park, a 230-square-km park that stretches almost 120 km from south to north and encompasses 47 islands within the Andaman Sea.

Park officials at headquarters on Hat Chang Lang grant permits to the bungalow and resort owners who operate facilities on most of the islands. Park offices are also located on Hat Chao Mai and Hat Yong Ling.

Pak Meng Beach

Ban Pak Meng is a small fishing village 38 km from Trang in the district of Sikao. Pak Meng is the only semi-developed beach on the mainland, but facilities remain limited to a few small cafes and bungalows between the piers at the north and south ends of the beach. Fishing boats and charters depart for Ko Hai and Ko Kradan from both piers, but only from the southern pier during the rainy season.

Pak Meng Beach is composed of off-white sand and shards of coral, and the shallow bay is paved with sharp shells that keep most visitors firmly glued to their beach chairs. The mediocre sand is compensated for by the wonderful panoramic vistas over an azure sea punctuated by dramatic limestone mountains. Reminiscent of

TRANG VICINITY

KLONG PANG

TO BANGKOK, SUKRAT THANI, AND NAKHON SI THAMMARAT

WAT KHAO PHRA

WAT THAM PHRA PHUT

0   10 km

403

TO KRABI AND PHUKET

4

KUANGUN

TONPHO

HUAY YOT

WAT KHAO PINA

NAM PHRA

WAT SU RAJAPRADIT

NAMPUD

WAT PHU KHAO TONG

4123

TO PHATTALUNG

4

SAI CAPE

HUA HIN

SIKAO

TONCHOD

4046

4

NAYONG

NAMUNSRI

TRANG

KHAO CHONG FOREST PRESERVE

KLONG LAMCHAN WATERBIRD PARK

KHAO CHONG FALLS

PAK MENG

KO MENG

PAK MENG BEACH

CHANGLANG

CHANG LANG BEACH

KO HAI

KO MA

KO CHUAK

KO WAN

KUAN TUNGGU

KO MUK

SAN BEACH

EMERALD CAVE

PHANGKA COVE

YONG LING BEACH

KO KRADAN

YAO BEACH

CHAO MAI BEACH

ICHAO MAI

PRA MUANG

TONKE BAY

BAN HIN KHAO

TUNG YAKHA BEACH

BAN LAN KHAO

KO LIBONG

JUHOI CAPE

SAMRAN BEACH

403

404

KANTANG

YAN TAKAO

LAMHAI

4124

SAIRUNG FALLS

PRAISAWAN FALLS

LAMPLOK FALLS

TONTOK FALLS

CHONG BAN PHUT FALLS

TONTEH FALLS

4125

LAEM PO

404

4125

CHAO PHRA FALLS

NANU

BAN LAEM

PALIAN

4072

ANDAMAN SEA

KO LAO LIANG

KO LAO LIANG

KO PETRA

YONG SATA

YONG SATA CAPE

KO SUKORN

TO SATUN

© MOON PUBLICATIONS, INC.

a Chinese landscape painting, the bay is flanked by Ko Meng to the south, said to be riddled with caves, and by a broad central mountain that resembles the shape of a reclining man.

Residents of Trang come here in early November to collect sweet-fleshed *hoi tapao,* oysters that thrive in the rocky but shallow waters of Ao Pak Meng.

Accommodations: Simple accommodations are available with Kit in the first foodstall, and with Joi in the last bungalow on the left. **Pak Meng Resort** (tel. 075-210321), about three km south of the intersection, has a pleasant open-air restaurant and 12 rooms in the rear. Simple bamboo huts cost 100-150B, while cottages with clean baths and fan cost 250-300B. The manager rents motorcycles and arranges eight-passenger longtail tours to Ko Muk (350B), Ko Hai (500B), and Ko Kradan (500B) during the high season.

Pak Meng Restaurant (tel. 075-219271) rents spacious rooms with marble floors and massive bathrooms for 300-400B downstairs and to the rear of the restaurant. A less expensive alternative is **Relax Bay Pak Meng Resort** (tel. 075-218940) with simple thatched bungalows for 100-250B.

Transportation: Direct vans to Pak Meng leave from the yard on Takland Road near the railway tracks, a few blocks north of the train station. You can also get to Pak Meng by taking a *songtao* toward Sikao, and a second *songtao* from the intersection down to the beach.

Chang Lang Beach

Hat Chao Mai National Park headquarters forlornly sits on this long and deserted stretch of sand, 47 km from Trang via Pak Meng or Kantang. The visitors center features a hand-painted map that shows park boundaries, topographic features, and oceanic depths.

The road splits just north of park headquarters. The coastal road ends at a casuarina-lined bay dominated by a limestone karst riddled with small caves. Campsites are plentiful.

The main road veers inland to the turnoff for Kuan Tunggu, a small fishing village with an intriguing charcoal factory and longtails across to nearby Ko Muk.

Accommodations: Park headquarters has campsites on the front lawn—like camping at Mom's—and eight-person bungalows for 600-

800B. Camping is permitted anywhere on the beach, but the bay just south of headquarters seems to be the most popular location.

Yong Ling Beach

The road continues south from Hat Chang Lang to a dirt track that veers west to a narrow but fairly clean beach at the base of a limestone mountain. Yong Ling is often deserted, aside from a few groups of partying Thais, who are amazed at the arrival of a Western visitor.

A narrow track leads north around the twin bays to a series of interconnected caves that provide shelter and barbecue sites for more groups of partying Thais.

Accommodations: Park facilities include a dozen elevated bungalows and several common baths just back from the bay in a tangle of vegetation and wildflowers. The bungalows are free, or you can join the teenagers and camp in the shoreline caves.

Chao Mai Beach

Hat Chao Mai (a.k.a. Hat Yao) is the most attractive and popular mainland beach near Trang.

The five-km beach stretches from the fishing village of Chao Mai around a pair of limestone buttresses north to Yao and Yong Ling Beaches. Tucked away at the base of the principal mountain is a 30-meter cavern, Tham Chao Mai, where thousands of stalactites slowly drip toward the sandy floor and prehistoric skeletal remains occasionally are discovered by amateur spelunkers.

Hat Chao Mai is backed by rows of swaying casuarina trees and faced by an elliptical bay that provides direct views across to Ko Libong—the idyllic counterpart to the beaches of Krabi and Ko Lanta.

Accommodations: Overnight facilities include campsites for 50B, national park bungalows for 100B per person, and bungalows operated by entrepreneurs from Trang. Unhappy park officials are threatening the private bungalows with foreclosure, but as of this writing, two sets of bungalows survive on this wonderful beach.

North of the limestone mountain lies **Mr. Wong's Bungalows,** where bamboo shacks cost 100-150B. The question is, who runs the place—Mr. Wong, his wife, or the ducks?

Back on the main beach is another set of bungalows owned by a gregarious fellow who once served with the Thai Army in Vietnam and later saw action in Florida. Sinchai has longhouse-style rooms from 100B, picnic tables under casuarina trees, and longtail boats to nearby Ko Muk, Kradan, and Libong.

Transportation: Chao Mai, 38 km from Trang, can be difficult to reach due to the lack of scheduled transport. Several routes can be attempted, but details should be sorted out in advance at the Koh Teng Hotel.

The longest route involves a van to Pak Meng and then a chartered *songtao* down the coast to Hat Chao Mai, an expensive option unless you can join a group of Thai passengers at Pak Meng.

A more direct route is the dirt road that splits off Hwy. 403 about five km south of Trang and heads down to park headquarters at Hat Chang Lang. Once again, you'll need to charter a *songtao* or hitchhike for the final leg.

The third option involves a bus from the stop on Kantang Road to the port town of Kantang, followed by a ferry ride across the narrow bay to a small pier. *Songtaos* leave this pier around 1100 for the dusty ride down to Hat Chai Mai. Visitors who miss the *songtao* can either wait for a later departure or hire a motorcycle taxi for about 60B. Hold onto your bags.

ISLANDS NEAR TRANG

The exotic coral islands off Trang lie sprinkled across the Andaman Sea, from Ko Rok Nok in the south to the shores of Ko Lanta Yai. Most of the islands are blessed with dazzling white beaches, fantastic coral gardens, and abundant marine life.

The most popular islands include (from south to north) Ko Sukorn (Sukon or Muu), Ko Libong (Talibong), Ko Kradan, Ko Muk (Mook), and Ko Hai (Ngai).

The central islands—Ko Muk and Ko Kradan—lie within the 231-square-km boundaries of Hat Chao Mai National Park. Ko Sukorn in the south near the town of Palien, and Ko Libong off Chao Mai Beach, are outside the park perimeter. Ko Hai resides within Krabi Province but is best reached from Pak Meng pier in Trang Province.

Climate

The high and dry season Nov.-May is the best time to visit the islands near Trang. Monsoons sweep the coast June-Nov., when boat service often ends and many resorts close for the season.

Visitors during the rainy summer months may be able to enjoy the mainland beaches such as Hat Chao Mai and Hat Yong Ling, both protected from the elements by enormous limestone mountains.

Accommodations

Accommodations are available on the five principal islands, though lodgings are rather expensive for the quality of service and facilities.

Budget travelers favor Ko Muk for its bungalows, which start as low as 100B. The least expensive bungalows on the other islands cost 600B on Ko Sukorn, 300B on Ko Libong, 600B on Ko Kradan, and 250B on Ko Hai.

Camping is possible; several upscale resorts provide tents for 150B per person.

Transportation

The coral-fringed islands of Trang have so far escaped the clutches of mass tourism—good news for divers and nature explorers, but an obstacle to the formation of cheap and easy transportation. The islands are best reached from either Kantang (24 km southwest) or Pak Meng (38 km west).

The southern islands—Ko Sukorn and Ko Libong—are served by fishing boats and longtails from Kantang, but more directly by fishing boats from Yong Sata pier, 10 km south of Palien.

The central islands—Ko Muk and Ko Kradan—are best reached on longtails (ordinary or chartered) departing from Kantang. However, fishing boats from Pak Meng also travel to both islands, though departures are less frequent than from Kantang and subject to cancellation without sufficient passengers.

Reach the northernmost island, Ko Hai, by boat from Pak Meng.

Tours

Travelers on tight schedules may be satisfied with an organized day-trip that includes lunch, snorkeling gear, and visits to Ko Kradan, Ko Muk, and the coral reefs near Ko Chuak and Ko Wan, between the two larger islands.

Trang Travel and several of the resort offices listed above organize island tours for a minimum of four passengers for 500-600B. For an additional fee, they also will drop passengers on the islands and pick them up a few days later.

Ko Hai

Ko Hai (Ngai) lies in the southernmost waters of Krabi Province, but is most easily reached from Pak Meng, 20 km southwest. The five-square-km island is covered with jungle and fringed with dazzling beaches. Flanking the eastern coast and hardly submerged beneath the aquamarine waters is a coral reef that almost scrapes your belly as you paddle along.

For fabulous snorkeling, rent a longtail to explore the shallow bays, partially submerged caverns, and brilliant seven-colored coral reefs that surround Ko Chuak and Ko Wan, two small islands a few kilometers east of Ko Hai. Ko Wan also features a cathedral-shaped cavern filled with giant barracudas, large stingrays, and an occasional shark.

Serious divers often use Ko Hai as the jumping-off point to Ko Rok Nai and Ko Rok Noi, 24 km southwest, and Hin Muang and Hin Daeng, 42 km from Ko Hai. Scuba experts have proclaimed Hin Muang and Hin Daeng among the finest dive sites in Thailand, rivaled only by the brilliance of the Similans.

Two resorts are located on the east side of the island, facing a superb beach and outstanding coral beds. Both operate full-day boat tours to Ko Kradan, Ko Wan, and Emerald Cave on Ko Muk.

Ko Hai Villa: The "villa" on the middle of the beach suffers from a mediocre restaurant, incompetent employees, and 15 primitive and overpriced bamboo huts starting at 300-400B. Ko Hai Villa Travel Agency, 112 Pra Rama VI Rd., tel. (075) 219874, Bangkok tel. (02) 318-3107.

Ko Ngai Resort: A superior choice is tucked away on a fabulous beach in the southeastern corner, near immense boulders that offer the best diving on the island. The small but clean wooden beachside bungalows cost 250-300B. Large hillside chalets with two bedrooms, private baths, and enclosed verandas cost 600-950B. Ko Hai Villa Travel Agency, 112 Pra Rama VI Rd., tel. (075) 210496, Bangkok tel. (02) 316-7916.

Ko Muk

Ko Muk (Mook), the second-largest island in the national park, features lovely Phangka Bay and the fishing village of Ban Hua Laem on the east coast, and a brilliant west-coast beach, Hat Sai Yao, backed by limestone cliffs where swallows nest.

The island is renowned for its miraculous Emerald Cave (Tham Morakot), locally known as Tham Nam (Water Cave), on the northwestern side of the island near Hat Farang.

The cave can only be entered by boat at low tide, passing under a limestone ridge that falls below waterline at high tide. Enveloped in total darkness and complete silence—except for the squeals of flying bats—the boat slowly drifts through an 80-meter tunnel toward the mythical domain of Captain Kurtz. The boat gradually emerges from the heavy darkness into a surrealistic scene: a brilliantly illuminated interior lagoon fringed by powdery white sands and enclosed by towering limestone walls—a translucent emerald world not unlike the final scenes in Jules Verne's classic, *Journey to the Center of the Earth.* Ko Muk—a limestone donut floating in the Andaman Sea.

After lunch and a swim, passengers return to the outside world before rising waters block the western passage.

Ko Muk Resort: Ko Muk has one set of bungalows on the east coast near the village of Ban Hua Laem. Ko Muk Resort faces an uninspiring beach but provides well-designed if tightly packed bungalows for 100-250B. The low-end rooms are inside the longhouse, while more expensive individual bungalows include fan and private bath. Ko Muk Resort, 25/36 Sathanee Rd., tel. (075) 211367, 100-250B.

Ko Kradan

The teardrop-shaped island of Ko Kradan ("Flat" or "Board" Island) lies primarily within the boundaries of the national park; about 20% of the land is covered with privately owned rubber and coconut plantations.

The island has broad beaches and a magnificent coral reef on the east coast, and to the south a pair of sunken Japanese freighters that once supplied occupation forces stationed on Phuket.

Ko Kradan Resort: The privately owned resort on the southeastern coast faces a fine beach and superb coral gardens, but the poorly designed bungalows and concrete villas are overpriced at 600-900B. However, tents cost 150B. Reservations and transportation can be arranged in Trang. Ko Kradan Resort, 25/36 Sathanee Rd., tel. (075) 211391, Bangkok tel. (02) 392-0635.

Ko Libong

Trang's largest island, situated within the southern Petra group, is chiefly visited for its migratory birdlife that winters near Juhoi Cape on the eastern tip of the island, and for the attractive beaches and coral reefs along the southwestern coast.

The eastern third of the island is administered by the Libong Island Wildlife Association as a sanctuary for migratory birds down from their Siberian homelands, and for endangered sealife such as green turtles, dolphins, and the rare manatee. Waterfowl sighted by ornithologists include curlews, redshanks, reef egrets, crab plovers, and rare black-necked storks who search the tidal beds for mollusks, crustaceans, and sweet *hoi chakten* oysters. December and January are the best observation months.

Wildlife rangers also estimate that two dozen endangered manatees *(Manatus senegalensis)* live in the protected waters off Laem Juhoi. Called *dugong dugong* (mermaid, mermaid) in the Melayu dialect, these blubbery, whiskered creatures are associated with the nubile mermaids of Hans Christian Anderson, a connection that for many requires a great leap of the imagination.

Ko Libong (Talibong Island) is inhabited by three villages of Muslim fishermen, including the main town of Ban Hin Kao, where the ferry docks from Kantang docks and motorcycle taxis proceed along dirt tracks to Ban Lan Khao on the southwestern coast. Clean beaches are located near Ban Lan Khao and to the north on Ao Tonke and Hat Tung Yakha near small but pleasant waterfalls.

Libong Beach Resort: On the southwestern beach near Ban Lan Khao are 15 basic A-frame bungalows at 300-400B and a simple restaurant set back inside a coconut grove that faces a sandy beach and decent corals. Note: the conservative nature of the island discourages immodest sunbathing and the open consumption of

alcohol. Ko Libong Resort, 158/1 Kantang Rd., tel. (075) 210013.

Park Bungalows: The Libong Island Wildlife Association maintains free shelters and campsites in the protected sanctuary at Laem Juhoi. The bungalows should be booked in advance and guests should bring adequate supplies of food and water. P.O. Box 5, Kantang, Trang 92110, tel. (075) 251932.

Ko Sukorn

Ko Sukorn (Sukon), Ko Petra, and Ko Lao Liang (Nua and Tai) comprise the Petra Islands group, off Palian and 47 km south of Trang.

Ko Petra and Ko Lao Liang are remote, uninhabited islands of sheer cliffs that provide nesting sites for swiftlets, which produce the highly valued ingredient (saliva) in bird's nest soup.

Ko Sukorn is locally known as Ko Mu (Pig Island), an ironic nickname since the island is inhabited solely by Muslims. The island is visited for its golden sands and coral beds on the east coast, and for its delicious watermelons that mature in the hot months of March and April.

Sukon Island Resort: The former Black Pearl Bay Resort has bungalows and chalets for 450-600B per night. Details and transportation arrangements should be checked at the Koh Teng Hotel in Trang.

SATUN

Satun is the departure point for boats to Kuala Perlis and Langkawi Island in Malaysia, and the jumping-off point for Tarutao National Marine Park.

Satun is nestled in a lovely valley surrounded by limestone karsts and cut by the Bambang River that flows into the Andaman Sea. The sleepy little town was founded in 1813 and named after *satoey,* the Malay term for the santol tree. Satun was awarded to England in 1908 and administered from Penang until 1933, when the town was returned to Thailand.

Satun Province is predominantly Muslim with over 120 mosques that serve 80% of the population.

Attractions

Satun has little of interest, aside from Bambang Mosque near the library and immigration office, and a messy market on the banks of the river.

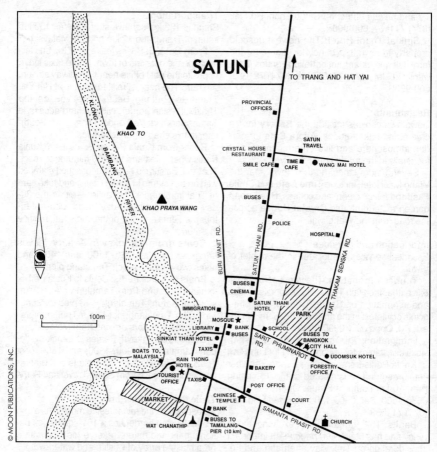

Just north of town rise two limestone peaks—Khao To and Khao Praya Wang—accessed on a trail off Buri Wanit Road. Food vendors prepare dishes on the riverbanks; a rough track leads up to the summit for wonderful views over ricefields and coconut plantations.

Accommodations

Buses coming in from Hat Yai first stop at the north end of town near the Wang Mai Hotel, then continue south to the center depot near the library and Satun Thani Hotel.

Udomsuk Hotel: An older hotel with large and fairly clean rooms, all with private bath. 71 Sari Phuminarot Rd., tel. (074) 711006, 130-180B.

Satun Thani Hotel: While not the cheapest spot, this small hotel has a cozy a/c cafe, friendly management, and very clean rooms with private baths. There's no English sign and their business card says "Satool Thani." 90 Satun Thani Rd., tel. (074) 711010, 200-250B fan, 320-380B a/c.

Rain Thong Hotel: Three doors before the end of the street is a narrow hotel with old but clean rooms and private baths. 4/6 Samanta Prasit Rd., tel. (074) 711036, 120-180B.

Wang Mai Hotel: Satun's original luxury hotel has a coffee shop, disco, and a/c rooms with

TV and private baths. 43 Satun Thani Rd., tel. (074) 711607, 600-900B.

Sinkiat Thani Hotel: The newest upscale property in town in a handy location near the ferry halt and other transportation venues. Buriwanit Rd., tel. (074) 721055, fax (074) 721059, 600-900B.

Restaurants

Downtown choices include the **Bakery** for ice cream and baked goods, **Ajjara Cafe** for garden atmosphere and live entertainment, and foodstalls in the market near the river.

Several more cafes, north of town near the Wang Mai Hotel, include **Time Cafe** and **Smile Fastfood** for ice cream and coffees, **Bua Luong** garden restaurant, and **Crystal House** across the road from the Wang Mai.

Information and Services

Essential services are located in the center of town.

Tourist Information: The very useful tourist office near the Rain Thong Hotel supplies maps and information on Satun, Tarutao, and other points of interest in the province. 4/5 Samanta Prasit Rd. Open daily 0900-2000.

Immigration: The Thai immigration office provides exit stamps for visitors leaving for Langkawi or Kuala Perlis from the pier in Satun. Another immigration office is located at the Tamalang Pier, 10 km south of Satun. Open weekdays 0830-1630, Sat. 0900-1200. Buriwanit Rd., tel. (074) 711989.

Banks: Thai Farmers Bank exchanges currency and has Malaysian *ringgit*—an important consideration on Thursday afternoon and Friday when banks are closed in Malaysia. Open weekdays 0830-1630. 31 Sulakanukul Rd., tel. (074) 721354.

Post Office: The post office has poste restante and international telephone service. The postal code is 91000. Open weekdays 0830-1630, Saturday 0900-1200. The telephone office is open daily 0800-2000. 99 Satun Thani Rd., tel. (074) 711013.

Satun Travel and Ferry: The best place for tours to Tarutao, vans to Krabi and Hat Yai, and ferry tickets to Langkawi and Kuala Perlis. Open daily 0700-2200. 45/16 Satun Thani Rd., tel. (074) 711453, fax (074) 721959.

Transportation

Satun is 123 km southwest of Hat Yai, 152 km south of Trang, and 12 km north of Malaysia.

From Hat Yai: Buses leave from the bus terminal on the outskirts of town. Share taxis leave opposite the post office near the railway station.

Train: The nearest rail terminus is at Hat Yai. Trains to Padang Besar drop you on the Thai/Malaysian border, without land access to Satun. See "Hat Yai" under "The Deep South" later in this chapter for schedules.

Boats from Kuala Perlis: Boats leave Kuala Perlis when filled and take 90 minutes to reach Thailand. Be sure to have your passport stamped with an exit stamp in Kuala Perlis, and take care of Thai immigration formalities—either the 30-day entry permit or 60-day tourist visa—at either the Tamalang pier or the immigration office in Satun.

Boats from Langkawi: A ferry leaves Langkawi daily at 0730, 1100, and 1400, and takes two hours to reach Tamalang pier.

Boats to Kuala Perlis: Boats to Kuala Perlins leave year-round from Tamalang pier, 10 km south of Satun. Tamalang is served by *songtaos*. The Tamalang pier has a Thai immigration office for visitors arriving from Malaysia.

Boats to Langkawi: Ferries to Langkawi depart Tamalang at 0900, 1300, and 1600, cost 150B, and take two hours. Tickets can be purchased in advance from Satun Travel and Ferry.

Thale Ban National Park

Spread across the rain-forested mountains along the Malaysian border lies a 101-square-km national park and nature reserve teeming with a breathtaking array of wildlife and waterfowl.

Thale Ban encompasses a dipterocarp rainforest inhabited by Sundaic mammals such as white-handed gibbons, lemurs, tapirs, serow, wild boars, dusky leaf monkeys, and, perhaps, Malayan sun bears. The white meranti forests also shelter birdlife and migratory waterfowl such as bat hawks, booted eagles, flamed pheasants, argus hornbills, masked finfoots, dusky crag martins, and black baza hawks.

Park headquarters is on the banks of a large lake surrounded by sloping hills. Rangers have maps that indicate trails to caves (Tham Tondin, Tham Puyu), waterfalls (Rani, Ton Pila, Chingrah), and mountains (Khao Chin), but trails are rough and poorly marked; guides may be necessary.

The most spectacular site is considered to be Yaroy Waterfall, six km north of park headquarters and one km east of Hwy. 4184. The well-maintained path follows the stream and leads to nine waterfalls and delightful bathing pools at the uppermost cascades.

Accommodations: Park bungalows that sleep 6-15 people cost 500-800B; solo visitors can share bungalows for 70B per person.

Transportation: Thale Ban is 40 km northeast of Satun and just two km from the Malaysian border. Direct *songtaos* leave in the mornings from Satun and take an hour to Wang Prajan, three km west of the park entrance. On Friday, *songtaos* continue to Ban Khuan Don at the Thai/Malaysian border, where Malaysians arrive each Friday to trade at the roadside market.

You can also take a *songtao* to Ban Khwan Sator, 19 km north of Satun on Hwy. 406, from where *songtaos* make the 20-km journey south to Wang Prajan and park headquarters.

A fairly good road connects Satun to Kuala Perlis, but the crossing remains closed to Westerners until border formalities are worked out between Thailand and Malaysia.

KO TARUTAO NATIONAL MARINE PARK

The 61-island archipelago of Tarutao comprises the final frontier for tourism in Thailand.

Once the haunt of sea pirates and later a penal colony for political dissidents until the end of WW II, Tarutao was declared Thailand's first marine park in 1974 to help protect the fragile environment and its luscious combination of deserted beaches, thick jungle, and blazing coral beds. The remote location at the extreme southwestern corner of Thailand—only five km from the Malaysian island of Langkawi—has served to maintain the pristine nature of Tarutao. It remains a wild and relatively untouched destination blessed with stunning beaches, tranquil bays, and a seemingly endless number of deserted islands.

Tarutao has also enjoyed the support of both Thai and Western volunteers, in particular Khum Boomrung Saison, who have ceaselessly worked to prevent the uncontrolled growth and gaudy commercialism that have ruined other "protected" national parks, such as Ko Samet and Ko Phi Phi. The fight to save Tarutao was boosted several years ago when the islands were nominated as a UNESCO World Heritage Site.

But tourism is on the increase, and forestry officials are under pressure to grant permits for direct boat service from Langkawi and private hotel concessions. Reports indicate that developers have purchased land from sea gypsies and are now drawing up blueprints for the first commercial resorts in the park. Go now and beat the rush.

EN ROUTE TO THE PARK

Pakbara

Pakbara is the departure point for Tarutao. The town is bypassed by most travelers, except for souls who arrive after the final departure or when boat service has been canceled due to inclement weather.

A handful of seedy bungalows attached to juke joints are found near the pier, including filthy Andrew Guesthouse. Somewhat better places are located on an unsightly and polluted beach 500 meters east of the pier, including Marena, Suanson, Pakbara, and Pornrae Guesthouses, with okay bungalows for 120-250B.

Ko Kebang

An infinitely better alternative to loitering around Pakbara is to take a longtail from the Ko Bulon Lae pier for the 15-minute journey (10B) to Ko Kebang, an attractive island separated from the mainland by the narrow Langu River.

The island is locally called Ko Bor Chet Luk ("Seven Wells Island") after an old legend about a villager with seven daughters who demanded seven separate wells. Another story explains the surprising number of elderly residents with crystal-blue eyes: Scandinavian sailors left behind more than just a warm welcome.

Pak Nam Resort: Several facilities are available on Ko Kebang, but most visitors head to peaceful Pak Nam Resort on the western side of

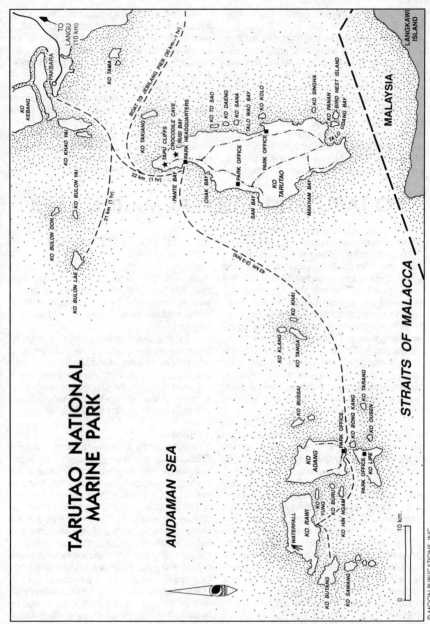

TARUTAO NATIONAL
MARINE PARK

MALAYSIA

LANGKAWI
ISLAND

STRAITS OF MALACCA

ANDAMAN SEA

TO
LANGU
(10 km)

PAKBARA

KO KEBANG

KO KHAO YAI

KO TAMA

BOAT TO JEBILANG PIER (30 km, 1 hr)

KO BULON YAI

KO BULON DON

KO BULON LAE

22 km (1 hr)

21 km (1 hr)

KO TAKIANG

TAPU CLIFFS
CROCODILE CAVE
CRUSI BAY
PARK HEADQUARTERS
PANTE BAY
CHAK BAY
SAN BAY

KO TO SAO
KO DAENG
KO SANA
TALO WAO BAY
KO KOLO

PARK OFFICE

PARK OFFICE

KO TARUTAO

MAKHAM BAY

KO SINGHA
KO PANAN
BIRD NEST ISLAND
TALO
UDANG BAY

43 km (2-3 hrs)

KO KLANG
KO TANGA

KO KHAI

KO BUSSAI

PARK OFFICE
KO BONG KANG
KO TARANG
KO OUSEN
KO LIPE
PARK OFFICE

KO ADANG

WATERFALL

KO RAWI
KO YUNG
KO BURIO
KO HIN NGAM

KO BUTANG
KO SAWANG

10 km.

© MOON PUBLICATIONS, INC.

the island. Pak Nam Resort has a seafood cafe, deck chairs facing the beach, and spacious palm gardens backed by a vibrant green jungle. The manager can arrange longtail charters up the Langu River, past mangrove swamps teeming with otters, dugongs, river turtles, giant lizards, langurs, and macaques. Pak Nam Resort, Ko Kebang, tel. (074) 781129, 150-320B.

Ko Bulon Lae

Ko Bulon Lae and the two adjacent islands of Bulon Don and Bulon Yai are included in the Petra Island National Marine Park, established in 1982 and chiefly located within Trang Province. Although not a member of the Tarutao group, Ko Bulon Lae is best reached from Pakbara rather than Trang.

Residents of these islands have not been forced to leave, including the *chao ley* living on nearby Ko Bulon Don and Ko Bulon Yai, who were recently granted legal permission to reside on the island and given title to their hereditary properties.

Bulon Lae features excellent beaches on the west coast, shallow coral reefs on the northeast side, and bat caves to the south. The pier, the small village of Ban Bulon Lae, and the best beaches are on the northeastern side.

Accommodations: Rawi, Punka, Adang, and Bulon Lae bungalows provide huts for 120-250B.

The island's most popular place is **Pansand Resort,** facing the other islands within the Petra group. Facilities include a cafe, sand lot volleyball courts, water sports, and boats to visit the near-

DEVIL'S ISLAND

*T*he isolated setting of Tarutao perhaps explains its surprisingly varied history and odd assortment of pioneers—pirates, prisoners, and politicians.

Tarutao was first inhabited by nomadic sea gypsies and seafaring pirates who raided passing ships and, perhaps, buried their loot in the island's limestone caves.

The archipelago came to national attention in 1939 after Prime Minister Phibun moved to quell potential opposition to his regime by arresting 40 members of the royal family, old bureaucratic nobles, army rivals, and members of the assembly on charges of plotting coups against the government. After trials of dubious legality, 18 were executed and many others were banished to the most remote corner of the kingdom—Tarutao.

These political prisoners—many of them educated in the West—had resisted the nationalistic, xenophobic policies of Phibun: anti-Chinese laws, the renaming of Siam to Thailand, and the promotion of books and articles that admired authoritarian leaders like Benito Mussolini and Adolf Hitler.

These dissidents were shipped off to Talo Udang on the southern end of the island, where they were charged with the construction of their own prison and assigned to road details. Conditions could have been worse. Many were allowed to pursue intellectual hobbies such as legal matters and the study of foreign languages, and later returned to Bangkok and assumed roles in the Thai government.

Tarutao was also the favored banishment site for high-security criminals—not politicians—who were incarcerated at Talo Wao on the east coast, and forced to construct the 12-km "convict highway" that connected the two penal colonies.

After the Japanese invasion of WW II, when Tarutao found itself cut off from lines of communication and sources of food, prisoners and guards joined forces and turned Tarutao into a Devil's Island. The desperate survivors attacked and terrorized ships moving through the Straits of Malacca—not unlike the pirates of earlier days.

Tarutao remained a wild place until 1947 when British troops, stationed in Malaya, overran the rebels' headquarters and returned the island to Thai peasants, who planted coconut and rubber trees on plantations still seen on the trail from park headquarters to Talo Wao Bay.

The final chapter in the story occurred in 1974 when Tarutao National Marine Park was established and residents were asked to leave the island. Resistance against the central government has continued—for instance, bombings and attacks on sea patrols—but a new war looms on the horizon, the struggle between government officers charged with the preservation of Tarutao and rapacious developers eager to seize the last untouched islands in Thailand.

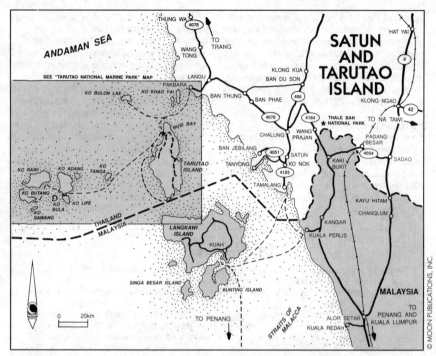

by reefs. Pansand Resort, Ko Bulon Lae, 60B tents, 100-120B shared bath, 200-350B private bath. Get reservations through Andaman Travel, 82/84 Visetkul Rd., Trang, tel. (075) 218035, fax (075) 219513.

Transportation: Boats leave Pakbara pier daily at 1400 Nov.-May and at infrequent intervals the remainder of the year. The crossing takes one hour and costs 80B. Boats return from Ko Bulon Lae around 0900.

INFORMATION AND SERVICES

Park Seasons

Tarutao National Marine Park is officially open Nov.-May and closed the rest of the year, when monsoons lash the island and boat services are shut down. During the rainy season, visitors are permitted to visit Tarutao at their own risk and stay in park bungalows, but food, drink, and other supplies must be brought from the mainland.

Tarutao currently receives over 20,000 annual visitors. The busiest periods are Dec.-Jan. and major holidays such as Chinese New Year, Songkram, and Christmas, when most of the bungalows are fully booked.

Accommodations

Tarutao has limited phone service, few roads and cars, no banks or post offices, and no formal accommodations such as hotels, resorts, or other forms of private housing. Your only choices are campsites and government bungalows on Ko Tarutao and Ko Adang, plus homestays on Ko Adang.

Bungalows: Park facilities include four-bed dormitories in longhouses (280B per room); two-room, four-bed concrete bungalows (400B); and two-room, eight-bed cottages (600B).

Individuals can book single beds for 80B, but must be willing to share the room with other visitors. During the busy season on Ko Tarutao, solo travelers and couples may be asked to pay for the entire room in advance, then wait for late arrivals to help share the cost. Park rangers rarely enforce this rule during the slower months or anytime on Ko Adang.

Campsites: Tents can be pitched at park headquarters and designated beaches on both Ko Tarutao and Ko Adang. Camping costs 10B with your own tent, and 60B for a rented tent. Tents can only be rented at park headquarters on Ko Tarutao. Visitors intending to camp on the more remote and peaceful bays should bring their own tent.

Reservations: Ko Tarutao is governed by the National Parks Division of the Royal Forestry Department in Bang Khen, Bangkok (tel. 02-579-0529) with regional headquarters at the Ko Tarutao Pakbara office (tel. 074-781285 or 074-781383), adjacent to the pier. Both offices makes reservations; Bangkok officials speak better English, but Pakbara rangers have a better understanding of current conditions. Park officials set limits on the number of visitors during peak periods to ensure adequate room and food supplies. Visitors arriving during these periods should check with Pakbara park rangers before setting off to the islands.

TARUTAO ISLAND

Ko Tarutao is the largest, most scenic, and most varied island in the park, a mountainous dragonback-shaped island swathed in tropical rainforest, thick mangrove swamps teeming with wildlife, crashing waterfalls, deep limestone caves, pristine coral gardens, and brilliant beaches that line most of the western coastline.

Pante Bay

Boats from Pakbara dock at Pante Malacca Bay on the northwestern coast, where rangers collect an admission fee (50B), then point you toward park headquarters and the visitors center. The village has two small restaurants, a shop with basic supplies such as T-shirts and maps, the tourist police, emergency services, and a wide range of bungalows and tent sites.

The visitors center features displays on local ecology and efforts to raise endangered hawksbill, green, and Pacific ridley turtles in protected nursing ponds. The adjacent well-stocked library

has exhibits on regional history as well as books on the subject. Be sure to pick up a map and *The Traveler's Adventure Handbook to Tarutao.*

Tapu Cliff: From park headquarters, a steep half-hour climb takes you to the summit of 114-meter Tapu Hill for wonderful views over the island—the perfect spot for sunsets.

Crocodile Cave: A great adventure awaits you on the two-km longtail journey (150B) up Klong Pante to the entrance of Tham Choraka (Crocodile Cave), past mangrove swamps thick with crab-eating macaques, hornbills, and white-bellied egrets. Crocodiles once lived inside the stalagmite-dripping cave, still a largely unexplored one-km cavern that leads toward views over Ao Chak. Bring a flashlight and be prepared to wade through mangrove swamps.

Papillon Cliffs: Pha Papinyong, on the northwestern tip of the island, towers over some of the best reefs on the island. Snorkelers can charter longtails from park headquarters.

Accommodations: The turbulent waters between Ko Tarutao and Adang and the rudimentary boats used for inter-island transportation prevent most visitors from venturing off the main island. As a result, nearly all formal accommodations are on Tarutao—in Pante Bay or on the superb perfect beaches that line the 26-km length of the west coast.

Ao Pante has over 20 standard bungalows, "deluxe" cottages, dormitory rooms in bamboo longhouses, and tents—all around 50-250B.

Food: Pante has two dining choices. The cafe does cheap, simple dishes such as fried rice and curried noodles; open daily 0730-1730. The open-air restaurant has a more varied and expensive menu that includes fresh seafood entrees and traditional Thai dishes; open daily 0900-2200. Both eateries are pricey and serve monotonous meals. Treat your taste buds and bring a supply of food and drink from the mainland.

Chak and Malae Bays

Ko Tarutao's finest beaches are those on the west coast, from Ao Pante to the bay of Makham; the most popular are Ao Chak and Ao San. The trail from Ao Pante follows the beach, filled with an amazing amount of shells and marine life.

Thirty minutes south lies a pair of arching bays filled with fluffy white sand, backed by swaying coconut palms that face a shallow coral reef. To the east rises a magnificent wall of mountains, covered with thick jungle and semi-evergreen rainforest inhabited by langurs, mouse deer, and wild boar. Follow the trail to Taru Cave and then explore other limestone caverns, perhaps the sites of buried pirate booty or treasure buried by the Japanese in the final days of WW II.

Visitors can camp at the south end, near the trail that leads over the promontory to Ao San.

San Bay

Curvaceous Ao San boasts a three-km stretch of dazzling sand and acres of excellent coral. The south end of the bay is covered with a thick mangrove swamp, while the north is bisected by a freshwater stream (Klong Lapo) near the ranger station and a small village. Trails lead into the jungle and up to three waterfalls, two on Klong Yula and another on Klong Lapo, the island's second largest stream after Klong Pante.

Ao San is a four-hour hike from Pante Bay on a well-maintained trail that hugs the coast, then veers inland and snakes through tropical rainforest seething with wildlife and waterfalls. Visitors often hire a 10-person longtail (250B) to Ao San, then hike back along the trail.

Campsites are on the north end of the bay, near the ranger station and facing the delicious beach.

Talo Wao Bay

East coast beaches tend to be windswept and rocky, though their primitive nature and complete isolation will appeal to adventurous travelers.

The 11-km, four-hour hike from Ao Pante passes though old coconut and rubber plantations abandoned after the island was declared a national park in 1982.

Talo Wao is chiefly remembered for its historical role as the Devil's Island of Southeast Asia, though the prison, fermentation tanks, and abode of Captain Kurtz have all returned to the jungle. Thirty minutes west of the pirate's nest is Nakathat Falls near Tham Nakathat, another cave filled with golden swords and precious jewels.

Visitors can camp on the beach or stay in primitive longhouses.

Talo Udang Bay

Tarutao's southernmost bay marks the end of the 12-km trail constructed by high-security criminals and political prisoners incarcerated at Talo Wao. A few penal remnants are still visible: concrete fermentation tanks, charcoal furnaces, and graveyards.

Talo Udang has a ranger station, a small settlement of fishermen, and campsites facing the horseshoe-shaped bay. The sand is fairly good. Almost within spitting distance lie Ko Lotong and Ko Rang Nok (Bird Nest Island), sources of the swiftlet regurgitation so highly prized by Chinese gourmets.

The remote, isolated, and rarely visited bay is an eight-hour hike from Ao Pante and four hours down "pirate's promenade" from Talo Wao. Most visitors hire a longtail from park headquarters, then return on the convict highway, now a narrow path choked with weeds and the skulls of forgotten inmates. Another trail heads west to Makham Bay, an untouched beach with a ranger station and campsites under swaying palms.

KO ADANG

Ko Adang, a thickly forested island that is the third largest in the national park, lies 43 km west of Tarutao and 80 km from Pakbara.

The 30-square-km island is covered with wild, rugged jungles, with narrow beaches on the south coast near the pier and park station at Laem Son. Most of the original *chao ley* have moved across to the more hospitable island of Ko Lipe.

The trail behind the Laem Son ranger station heads up to Shado cliffs, where views sweep over Ko Lipe and small islands to the southeast. Two km west from the park station lies a rocky beach lined with palms and an abandoned customs house, behind which a narrow trail leads up to Thale Mon Falls, once a freshwater source for visiting pirates. Three km east of the ranger station is Rattana falls and then the *chao ley* village of Taloh Puya, facing a fine beach and offshore coral reefs.

Accommodations: The ranger station at Laem Son has four-bed bungalows for 280B or 70B for a single bed. Tent sites cost 10B (bring your own tent). A cafe serves simple if somewhat expensive meals.

Transportation: Boats leave Tarutao on Tuesday, Thursday, and Saturday at 1230 and take two hours to reach Laem Son. Boats often stop at tiny Ko Khai in Mu Ko Klang (Middle Island Group) for snorkeling and lunch on the fine sandy beach. A natural stone archway marks the end of the bay.

Boats back to Tarutao leave Ko Lipe at 0900 on Wednesday, Friday, and Sunday, and pick up passengers at Laem Son before departing for Ao Pante and Pakbara.

KO LIPE

Ko Lipe, a four-square-km island just south of Ko Adang, is the commercial and transportation center in the Adang-Rawi archipelago.

The pancake-flat island is home to some 500 *chao ley* who left nearby islands for the freshwater springs and farmlands on this triangular island. Chinese merchants and businesspeople have arrived in recent years to purchase beachfront land from the gypsies and open a few guesthouses for overnight visitors.

Ko Lipe is covered with coconut plantations and vegetable gardens near the *chao ley* village on the eastern bay. Facilities include a ranger station, pier, school, health center, and some small, Chinese-owned shops with basic supplies.

Accommodations: Visitors can camp near the ranger station or stay in bungalows owned by the sea gypsies and Chinese merchants. Longhouse dorms cost 50B per person, simple huts 100B, and larger bungalows 200-250B. Homestays are available in the fishing village. Laem Son On to the north coast, and Pattaya and Lipe Island Resort on the southern side, one km from town, face lovely expanses of sand and fine offshore reefs.

Transportation: Ko Lipe can be reached with the boat service described above, or with longtails from Laem Son on Ko Adang. Boats back to Tarutao leave Ko Lipe at 0900 on Wednesday, Friday, and Sunday and reach Ao Pante in two hours.

TRANSPORTATION

Tarutao Island is 22 km southwest of Pakbara, 65 km northwest of Satun, and 100 km southwest of Trang.

From Pakbara: You must first travel to Langu (La Ngu), 60 km north of Satun, then take a *songtao* 10 km west to Pakbara pier. Langu has several banks that exchange currency and shops for last-minute supplies; remember to bring enough money and extra stocks of food and drink.

Boats depart Pakbara at 1030 and 1400 Nov.-May, cost 200B roundtrip, and take one hour to reach park headquarters on Ko Tarutao. Boats return from Tarutao at 0900 and 1400. Boats depart Pakbara during the rainy season, but on irregular schedules depending on weather conditions and at the discretion of the captain.

Tour boats operate most weekends around the year and charge 400-600B for roundtrip transportation, meals, sightseeing, and snorkeling gear. A final option is a chartered eight-passenger longtail for 600-800B.

From Krabi: Direct connections are arranged by several travel agencies such as Chan Phen and Jungle Book Tours.

From Trang: Buses, *songtaos,* and share taxis from Trang take two hours to Langu, from where *songtaos* continue down to Pakbara. Trang Travel on Pra Rama VI Road can help with organized transport.

From Satun: Buses direct to Pakbara leave from the terminal on Buri Wanit Road across from the library. Share taxis leave from Buri Wanit Road one block south of the library. You can also take a bus or *songtao* to Chalung, then wait at the dusty intersection for connections to Langu.

From Hat Yai: Buses direct to Langu and Pakbara leave from the Plaza Market on Petchkasem Road daily at 0700, 1100, and 1500. Share taxis leave from the post office near the Utaphao bridge and from the taxi stop behind Siam Nakharin department store.

Travel agents arrange weekend tours that include transportation and accommodations. Finally, take a bus toward Satun and get off in Chalung, from where *songtaos* continue north to Langu.

New Routes

The Thai and Malaysian governments are discussing direct boat connections between Langkawi and Tarutao, a route which would avoid a great deal of backtracking but would quickly flood the island with hordes of tourists.

Boats also can be chartered from Ko Nok pier, four km south of Satun; Tamalang pier, 10 km south of Satun; and Jebilang pier, 13 km west of Satun.

The managing director of Satun Travel and Ferry has announced plans to build a pier on Ko Tanyong, 17 km south of Satun, for direct ferries to Tarutao and Langkawi. The road from Satun to Ko Tanyong was completed a few years ago, and the opening of this pier would make Satun a feasible point in the Andaman Triangle.

THE DEEP SOUTH

HAT YAI

Hat Yai—the dynamic commercial center and transportation hub of Southern Thailand—receives wildly divergent reviews from visitors. Many feel the city is monotonous, oversized, and lacks any compelling reason to stay more than a few hours. Others enjoy the outstanding shopping, lively street markets, and heady

nightlife, and don't mind that Hat Yai is a clean and well-ordered city rather than a romantic fishing village.

Named after a long beach once located on the city's river, Hat Yai mainly serves as a transit point for departures and arrivals to Malaysia, and as the gateway to Songkhla and other seaside towns in southern Thailand. Most visitors are Malaysians who shop for duty-free goods in the department stores and consider Hat Yai a pleasurable escape from the conservative strictures of their fundamentalist nation. Although the town has a rather wild and seedy reputation, the sex trade is kept well hidden. Hat Yai is also one of the safest cities in Thailand, due to high levels of wealth and a relatively honest police force.

Travelers from Malaysia who have little interest in Hat Yai can proceed directly to Songkhla, Krabi, Phuket, or Ko Samui by changing buses, taking the next train, or waiting for a share taxi near the train station. Schedules can be quickly checked with the score of travel agents located near the Cathay Hotel, three blocks east of the train station.

Wat Hat Yai

Hat Yai is known for its shopping and nightlife, not its historical or religious monuments. The only temple of note features a 35-meter reclining Buddha inside a *viharn* on Petchkasem Road, four km southwest of town toward the airport. Visitors often are greeted by friendly monks who conduct tours of their subterranean souvenir shop and encourage the pious to throw coins into a wooden carousel of miniature monks.

Songtaos to the temple leave from the intersection of Niphat Uthit 1 and Petchkasem Roads.

Budget Accommodations

Most of Hat Yai's 60-plus hotels are in the center of town along the three Niphat Uthit Roads, also called Sai Nueng (Road 1), Sai Song (Road 2), and Sai Sam (Road 3). Train arrivals are within easy walking distance of most hotels. Buses from the Malaysia border usually stop at the main bus terminal outside town, from where minitrucks continue to city center. Bus arrivals from Songkhla can walk or take any *songtao* heading south.

Cathay Guesthouse: Hat Yai's traveler center is a friendly and clean place with a popular cafe and a self-serve soda machine. The bulletin board and travelers' logs are gold mines of information on upcoming beaches, new guesthouses, and travel tips on visas and shopping. Their downstairs travel agency can help with onward transportation and hotel bookings. The Cathay needs some paint, and the loud TV needs a quick death, but overall this is the best-value spot in Hat Yai. Arrive early to find a room. 93/1 Niphat Uthit 2 Rd., tel. (074) 243815, 60B dorm, 120-200B common bath, 220-280B private bath.

King's Hotel: An older hotel centrally located near the train station and popular Washington

THE DEEP SOUTH

South

China Sea

410

Sai Buri

Yala

42

Narathiwat

Tak Bai   Tumpat

KOTA BHARU

Bang Lang
Reservoir

Sungai Golok

Pulau
Perhentian
Besar

MALAYSIA

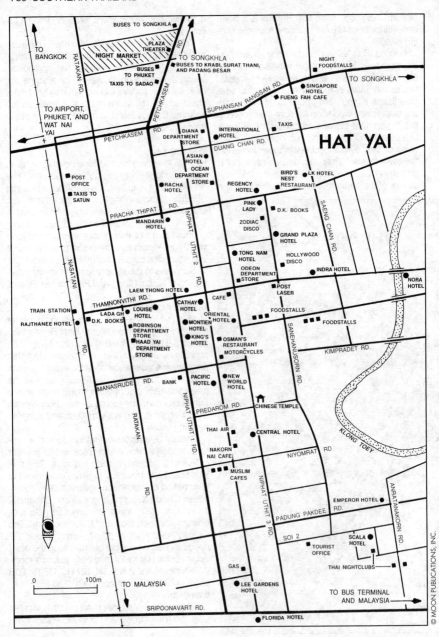

HAT YAI

TO BANGKOK

RATAKAN RD.

BUSES TO SONGKHLA

NIGHT MARKET

PLAZA THEATER

BUSES TO PHUKET

TAXIS TO SADAO

TO SONGKHLA

BUSES TO KRABI, SURAT THANI, AND PADANG BESAR

PETCHKASEM RD.

SUPHANSAN RANGSAN RD.

NIGHT FOODSTALLS

TO SONGKHLA

SINGAPORE HOTEL

FUENG FAH CAFE

TO AIRPORT, PHUKET, AND WAT NAI YAI

PETCHKASEM RD.

DIANA DEPARTMENT STORE

INTERNATIONAL HOTEL

DUANG CHAN RD.

TAXIS

POST OFFICE

TAXIS TO SATUN

PRACHA THIPAT RD.

ASIAN HOTEL

OCEAN DEPARTMENT STORE

RACHA HOTEL

REGENCY HOTEL

BIRD'S NEST RESTAURANT

LK HOTEL

MANDARIN HOTEL

PINK LADY

D.K. BOOKS

ZODIAC DISCO

GRAND PLAZA HOTEL

HOLLYWOOD DISCO

SAENG CHAN RD.

NASATANI RD.

NIPHAT UTHIT 2 RD.

TONG NAM HOTEL

ODEON DEPARTMENT STORE

INDRA HOTEL

LAEM THONG HOTEL

THAMNONVITHI RD.

CAFE

POST

TRAIN STATION

LADA GH

D.K. BOOKS

LOUISE HOTEL

CATHAY HOTEL

ORIENTAL HOTEL

LASER

FOODSTALLS

NORA HOTEL

RAJTHANEE HOTEL

ROBINSON DEPARTMENT STORE

HAAD YAI DEPARTMENT STORE

MONTIEN HOTEL

KING'S HOTEL

OSMAN'S RESTAURANT

MOTORCYCLES

FOODSTALLS

SANEHANUSORN RD.

KIMPRADET RD.

MANASRUDE RD.

BANK

PACIFIC HOTEL

NEW WORLD HOTEL

NIPHAT UTHIT 1 RD.

PREDAROM RD.

CHINESE TEMPLE

RATAKAN RD.

THAI AIR

CENTRAL HOTEL

NAKORN NAI CAFE

NIYOMRAT RD.

KLONG TOEY

MUSLIM CAFES

NIPHAT UTHIT 3 RD.

EMPEROR HOTEL

ANRATANAKORN RD.

PADUNG PAKDEE RD.

0   100m

TO MALAYSIA

SOI 2

TOURIST OFFICE

SCALA HOTEL

THAI NIGHTCLUBS

GAS

LEE GARDENS HOTEL

SRIPOONAVART RD.

TO BUS TERMINAL AND MALAYSIA

FLORIDA HOTEL

© MOON PUBLICATIONS, INC.

Nightclub. 126 Niphat Uthit 1 Rd., tel. (074) 243966, 220-260B fan, 320-380B a/c.

Tong Nam Hotel: Small and clean, the Tong Nam has a good fast-food cafe on the first floor, "ancient massage" in the lobby, and some of the cheapest a/c rooms in Hat Yai. 118-120 Niphat Uthit 3 Rd., tel. (074) 244023, 150-220B fan, 350-480B a/c.

Pacific Hotel: A fairly clean hotel with a pool hall on the ground floor. 149/1 Niphat Uthit 2 Rd., tel. (074) 244062, 200-250B fan, 350-450B a/c.

Louise Hotel: Tucked away in an alley near the train station is a new place with small but spotless a/c rooms. 13-15 Thamnonvithi Rd., tel. (074) 243770, 320-380B. Nearby Laem Thong Hotel is unfriendly and overpriced.

Mandarin Hotel: A relatively inexpensive and older hotel three blocks from the train station. 62-4 Niphat Uthit 1 Rd., tel. (074) 243438, 180-260B fan, 320-380B a/c.

Lada Guesthouse: Another small and relatively new hotel near the train station, with clean, if somewhat cramped, rooms at bargain rates. 13-15 Thamnonvithi Rd., tel. (074) 220233, 180-240B fan, 320-380B a/c.

Laem Thong Hotel: Big, old Chinese hotel in the center of town with comfortable, if somewhat musty, rooms. 44 Thamnonvithi Rd., tel. (074) 352301, 280-340B fan, 360-420B a/c.

Moderate Accommodations

Hat Yai's better hotels (in the 350-600B range) are popular with traveling businesspeople, Malaysians on holiday, and Western visitors who want a/c comfort without breaking the bank.

Montien Hotel: Adjacent to the King's Hotel is a high-rise hotel with sparsely furnished but large and comfortable a/c rooms. Check the back of their hotel brochure to see what is really sold by most Hat Yai hotels. 120 Niphat Uthit 1 Rd., tel. (074) 234386, fax (074) 230043, 340-600B.

Oriental Hotel (O.H.): Not quite a member of the Mandarin Oriental chain of hotels, but an acceptable middle-of-the-road place in the center of town, with large and fairly well-maintained rooms. 35 Niphat Uthit 3 Rd., tel. (074) 230142, 260-300B fan, 420-540B a/c.

Singapore Hotel: At the lower end of the moderately priced hotels in the northeastern cor-

COOING IN CHANA

*T*his lovely and unique experience takes place in the town of Chana, 40 km southeast of Hat Yai. Zebra doves raised primarily by Muslims have long been fashionable throughout southern Thailand, but Chana is the acknowledged cooing capital of the region. Singing competitions are held in open fields on which hundreds of cages are hung from eight-meter metallic poles. The feathered competitors are judged on pitch, melody, volume, and length of tone, plus a special category in which all the tones are judged as a unified ensemble. Bird species include zebra doves and Java mountain doves, which cost 5,000B at birth but could bring over 600,000B after capturing grand prizes. Only the males sing; females serve for breeding.

Competitions are held in Chana on most weekends, with a grand finale in late December or early January.

ner of central Hat Yai, near the foodstalls that set up nightly just across the road. 66 Suphansan Rangsan Rd., tel. (074) 244535, 220-280B fan, 320-450B a/c.

Racha Hotel: An older Chinese hotel with large rooms in good shape and friendly managers. 40-42 Niphat Uthit Rd., tel. (074) 230951, fax (074) 234668, 550-900B.

Grand Plaza Hotel: Hat Yai's "only generous and gentle hotel" features a small pool, coffee shop, and 211 a/c rooms equipped with TV, refrigerator, and international direct dial phones. 24/1 Sanehanusorn Rd., tel. (074) 234340, fax (074) 234428, 750-900B.

Rajthanee Hotel: Train travelers who need to overnight in Hat Yai but don't want to experience the city can stay in this all-a/c hotel, located directly at the train station. 47 Rattakan Rd., tel. (074) 232288, fax (074) 232188, 560-750B.

Luxury Accommodations

Hat Yai Central Hotel: The newest semi-luxury hotel in Hat Yai features several restaurants, karaoke lounge, snooker club, and citywide views from the 12-story complex. 180 Niphat Uthit 3 Rd., tel. (074) 230000, fax (074) 230990, 900-1,500B.

Central Sukontha Hotel: A small swimming pool, the Zodiac disco, and brightly decorated rooms make the Sukontha a popular choice; all rooms come complete with TV, telephone, and refrigerator. Sanehanusorn Rd., tel. (074) 243999, fax (074) 243991, 1,950-2,900B.

New World Hotel: A popular and reasonably priced place a few blocks south of the train station with 133 a/c rooms plus basic amenities. 144-158 Niphat Uthit 2 Rd., tel. (074) 230100, fax (074) 230105, 580-900B.

LK Hotel: One of the finer hotels in town, located in the northeast corner of central Hat Yai but within easy walking distance of the nearby brothels and massage parlors. 150 Saeng Chan Rd., tel. (074) 2325681, fax (074) 238112, 950-1,650B.

Asian Hotel: An older yet still fairly luxurious hotel, situated on the main drag at the north end of town near Ocean Department Store. 55 Niphat Uthit 3 Rd., tel. (074) 353400, fax (074) 234890, 950-1,400B.

Emperor Hotel: A somewhat odd location in the southeast corner of central Hat Yai, but very popular with Malaysian and Chinese visitors for its large, comfortable rooms and extra-curricular activities available in the cocktail lounge. 1 Ranrattanakorn Rd., tel. (074) 235457, fax (074) 234165, 550-1,400B.

JB Hotel: An upscale hotel with all possible facilities, in an inconvenient location well outside town. 99 Chuti Anuson Rd., tel. (074) 234300, fax (074) 243499, 1,850-3,800B.

Regency Hotel: Teakwood lobbies, restaurant-cum-cabaret, and very large rooms make the Regency one of the best accommodations in town. 23 Pracha Thipat Rd., tel. (074) 234400, fax (074) 234515, 1,600-2,000B.

Restaurants

Most of Hat Yai's restaurants are on Niphat Uthit 1 and 2 Roads, within easy walking distance of the hotels.

Foodstalls: A small but lively market sets up nightly in the northeast corner of central Hat Yai on Suphansan Ransan Road. Other foodstalls are located on Sheuthit Road, opposite the Oriental Hotel. Inexpensive.

Fueng Fah Restaurant: A small, clean a/c cafe with buffalo steaks and other Western specialties. Suphansan Rangsan Rd. Moderate.

Bird's Nest Restaurant: Unassuming cafe with shark's fin soup (200-1,800B!) and bird's nest soup listed under the dessert section. Pracha Thipat Rd. Moderate.

Osman's Restaurant: Small Malay cafe with regional specialties such as *soup daging, udang goreng, nasi etek,* and *telor bungkus.* A pleasant change from Thai fare. Niphat Uthit 2 Rd. Inexpensive.

Nakorn Nai Cafe: Clean and modern, this stylish cafe serves rice dishes, salads, and lasagnas. To the south is a curious little shop that sells fresh honey. Niphat Uthit 2 Rd. Inexpensive.

Muslim Cafes: Tasty Muslim and Indian dishes are prepared at three simple cafes at the south side of central Hat Yai. Aberdeen, Sharefa (Ruby's), and Mustafa 2 have English menus offering vegetable *korma,* mutton curry, and fish marsala served with fresh chapatis. An even *better* change from Thai fare. Niyomrat Rd. Inexpensive.

PATA Food Center: Inside the Kosit Hotel is a large food emporium with live music in the evenings. 199 Niphat Uthit 2 Rd. Moderate.

Entertainment

Hat Yai's action is centered on hotels, rather than bars or nightclubs as in Bangkok and Pattaya, with a variety that is amazing: sultry torch singers in cocktail lounges dimmed nearly to the point of absolute darkness; massage parlors packed with wealthy Muslims; live rock 'n' roll clubs; hotels that employ more prostitutes than maids; and Thai cinemas complete with special English-language sound booths.

A quick word about the distinction between "Thai traditional massage" and "ancient massage." The former is strictly massage while the latter belongs to the world's oldest profession.

Massage Emporiums: A typical example of the local sex industry is found in the Pink Lady Complex, where over 200 women work the barbershop and cafe and give traditional, body, and "ancient massage." Pink Lady Hotel, 24/12 Sanehanusorn Rd.

Cabarets: Dinner with warbling songbirds and optional hostesses include the nightclubs inside the Lee Gardens Hotel, Kosit Hotel (see map for exact location), and JB Hotel.

Discos: Video jockeys and live bands play at Hollywood and Zodiac discos in the entertainment district at the north end of Sanehanusorn Road. Bands also play at the nightclub adjacent to King's Hotel. Drinks cost about 100B, but there's little pressure to keep drinking or pay for the services of a hostess.

Post Laser Disk: This Thai nightclub is rarely visited by *farangs,* but it provides good music and no pushy hostesses, along with nightly English-language movies. 82/3 Thamnonvithi Rd., tel. (074) 232302. Open daily 1000-0100. No admission charge.

Sports and Recreation

Bullfights, kickboxing, and snakes—that's the sports lineup for Hat Yai.

Bullfights: Thai-style bullfighting matches, which pit bull against bull in a dramatic shoving match, are held on the first Saturday of each month at the arena near the Nora Hotel on Thamnonvithi Road, and on the second Saturday at the Hat Yai Arena on Hwy. 4 near the airport.

Prior to the match, the bulls are bathed, massaged, and displayed to the audience. Matches last anywhere from a few seconds to a half hour; the contest ends when one of the bulls is knocked down or runs away. The frenzy of the audience is as entertaining as the match itself. The fights take place 1000-1800, with the most important matches in the late afternoon. Admission is 60-100B.

Kickboxing: Boxing fans can enjoy the mayhem on Saturday afternoons at 1400 at the boxing stadium, or relax and watch the pugilists on Channel 10 TV.

Snakes: Not quite sport, but a rather unique sight are the snake sellers on Thanon Nguu (Snake Street), Chaniwat Road Soi 2. Malaysian and Singaporean Chinese arrive to drink snake blood and eat the gall bladder in the belief that such delicacies improve eyesight, lower blood pressure and, most importantly, boost virility.

Once the customer has made his selection—often poisonous cobras or pythons—the snake is strangled with a wire, washed with white whiskey, and deftly sliced open to extract the blood and bladder. The half-glass of blood is diluted with Chinese rice wine, herbal liquor, or Mekong whiskey and immediately consumed. The meat is then chopped and cooked with herbs into a fragrant soup, while the skins are sold to leather factories in Bangkok.

Snakes cost from 200B for small cobras up to 2,000B for giant pythons. All snakes are deadly and must be handled with great caution; many handlers have been paralyzed or killed while showing off to frightened onlookers.

Shopping

Prices are low and selection unlimited in the shops and street stalls on Niphat Uthit 1, 2, and 3 Roads.

Shopping Centers: Among the larger department stores are Ocean, Diana, and Yongdee on Niphat Uthit 3 Road, and World, Odean, and Haad Yai City on Ratakan Road. Robinson Department Store near the train station is also worth a visit.

Batiks and Sarongs: High-quality and reasonably priced Indonesian batiks, shirts, and scarves are sold at SMS Muslim Store at 17 Niphat Uthit 1 Rd., and at Pekalongan and Shah Panich on the north end of Niphat Uthit 2 Road.

D.K. Books: English-language guides, topographic maps, and foreign newspapers; near the train station and opposite Pink Hotel. Open daily 0900-2100. 2/4 Thamnonvithi Rd., tel. (074) 230759.

Information and Services

Hat Yai is a service-oriented city.

Tourist Office: The TAT office provides decent maps of the region and lists of hotels, travel agencies, and transportation schedules. Ask them anything—homestays on Ko Adang, hiking in Thale Ban National Park, ferry departures from Tamaling. Open daily 0830-1630. 1/1 Soi 2 Niphat Uthit 3 Rd., tel. (074) 245986, fax (074) 245986.

Tourist Police: This agency speaks English and helps settle problems with fraudulent merchandise and unscrupulous travel agencies. Open 24 hours. Sripoonavart Rd., tel. (074) 212213.

Immigration: Visa extensions are provided here for tidy applicants. Visas are not necessary for Malaysia. Open weekdays 0830-1430. Ratakan Rd., tel. (074) 243019.

Post Office: The GPO is north of town on Niphat Songkrao 1 Road. A more convenient office is just north of the train station. A private packing service is next door. The postal code is 90110. Open weekdays 0830-1630, Sat. 0900-1200. Ratakan Rd., tel. (074) 244480.

Travel Agencies: Hat Yai has dozens of agencies, but most of the budget places are near Cathay Guesthouse in the center of town. The travel agency downstairs from Cathay Guesthouse makes plane and bus reservations, and organizes quick transport to most destinations in Thailand and Malaysia. Open daily 0700-2000. 93/1 Niphat Uthit 2 Rd., tel. (074) 234535.

Travelers going to Malaysia should beware of travel agents and bus attendants who request your passport and then demand "visa fees." Again, Malaysian visas are *not* required for Westerners, only for visitors from Bangladesh, Myanmar, China, India, Pakistan, South Africa, and Sri Lanka.

Transportation
Hat Yai—an important travel junction used by almost every traveler heading between Malaysia and Thailand—is 1,013 km south of Bangkok, 350 km south of Surat Thani, 60 km north of the Malaysian border at Padang Besar, and 260 km northwest of Kota Baru in Malaysia.

Motorcycles can be rented and purchased at the shop just south of Osman Restaurant.

Air: Thai Airways International flies twice daily from Bangkok via Phuket, and weekly from Pattani and Narathiwat. Thai Airways is at 166/4 Niphat Uthit 2 Rd., while Malaysian Air is in Lee Gardens Hotel on Niphat Uthit 2 Road.

Thai and Malaysian Air fly once daily from Phuket and Kuala Lumpur. The Hat Yai airport, 12 km west of town, is served by inexpensive minitrucks and private limousines.

Train: Trains from Hualampong station in Bangkok to Hat Yai depart at 1400 (special express), 1515 (special express), and 1600 (rapid). The 1515 and 1600 departures are recommended since they arrive at 0704 and 0850. Sleepers are available on all trains.

Advance reservations from the Bangkok station or a travel agent are *strongly* recommended on all trains going south, especially on weekends and holidays.

From Malaysia, the *International Express* leaves Butterworth (the train terminus for Penang) daily at 1340, crosses the Thai border, and arrives in Hat Yai three hours later. The *IE* is limited to first and second class and is some-

what expensive because of supplemental charges for a/c and superior classes. Make reservations with Penang travel agents.

Ordinary trains no longer connect Butterworth with Hat Yai but rather terminate at the Malaysian border town of Padang Besar. Walk across the border, have your passport stamped, and catch a bus to Hat Yai.

From Hat Yai, trains going north to Phattalung, Surat Thani, and Bangkok depart at 1534, 1617, 1814, and 1849. Sleepers are available on all trains. Trains going south to Sungai Golok on the Malaysian border near Kota Baru depart at 0452, 0605, 0810, 1035, and 1322. Trains to Padang Besar and Penang depart once daily at 0704.

Taxi: Share taxis are an important travel component in southern Thailand since they are fast, comfortable, and relatively inexpensive—about the same price as an a/c bus.

Share taxis leave 0600-1000 from the Butterworth station in Malaysia just across the channel from Penang. Share taxis from Kota Baru terminate at the border, from where you have your passport stamped and continue to Sungai Golok by *tuk tuk.*

Hat Yai has several share-taxi stands that specialize in specific destinations. Taxis to Phattalung, Nakhon Si Thammarat, Trang, Narathiwat, and Sungai Golok depart from Suphansan Ransan Road near the night market. Taxis to Surat Thani, Phuket, and Krabi leave one block south on Duang Chan Road. Taxis to Songkhla leave from Petchkasem Road, three blocks south of the President Hotel and within walking distance of the downtown hotels.

Travel agents near the Cathay Hotel organize share taxis to most destinations in Thailand and Malaysia. Taxis to Penang, Kota Baru, Krabi, Phuket, and Ko Samui depart 0900-1200.

Bus: Bus 29 from Kota Baru terminates in the Malaysian border town of Rantau Panjang, where you have your passport stamped and continue on to the Sungai Golok train or bus station by *tuk tuk* or trishaw.

Hat Yai's public bus terminal is in a remote spot in the southeast corner of the town. An easier if somewhat more expensive option is private service arranged through travel agents near the Cathay Hotel. Sample fares: Satun, two hours, 40B; Narathiwat, three hours, 50B; Trang, three hours, 50B; Krabi, four hours, 150B; Surat

Thani, four hours, 160B; Penang, five hours, 220B; Ko Samui, six hours, 220B; Phuket, seven hours, 220B; Kuala Lumpur, 12 hours, 220-280B; Bangkok, 14 hours, 350-450B; Singapore,18 hours, 300-450B.

SONGKHLA

Songkhla is a deceptively sleepy beach resort, picturesquely situated between the Gulf of Thailand and a saltwater sea called Thale Sap ("Inland Sea") or Songkhla Lake. Somewhat off the beaten track, and overshadowed by the economic powerhouse of Hat Yai, Songkhla has largely escaped commercialism and blessedly remained a pleasant town of Sino-Portuguese buildings, bobbing fishing boats, and beaches filled with Thai families rather than Western tourists.

Songkhla National Museum
The regional history of Songkhla and the deep south can be traced in this 19th-century Sino-Portuguese mansion, constructed as a private residence for a wealthy Chinese merchant who later served as governor of Songkhla Province. Inside the elegant teak-beamed, two-story estate is a fabulous collection of Thai and Chinese art treasures gathered primarily from the seven provinces of southern Thailand.

Ground Floor: Immediately to the left of the entrance is a useful topographic map and aerial photos of Songkhla Province. Arranged throughout the rear courtyard are artistic treasures such as a wooden gable from Wat Machimawat and curiosities including giant tortoise shells, old Raleigh bikes dating from WW II, and coconut grinders fashioned like wooden dogs.

Second Floor: Highlights on the upper floor are a pair of leather *nang yai* puppets, beautifully cracked and peeling Ayuthaya-Period Buddhas, Thai furnishings including a teapot made from an ostrich egg, and the bed of King Mongkut—apparently a very small man.

The museum is open Wed.-Sun. 0900-1600. The entrance fee is 20B.

Old Town
Songkhla was established over 300 years ago, though most of the present Sino-Portuguese architecture dates from the early 20th century, when the town served as an important trading port for Thai and Chinese merchants. A fairly interesting walk through the old town can be made in about an hour, starting at the museum and walking south along the waterfront. First, visit the modern fishing boats, which unload their catch on private piers accessed through warehouses on Nakhon Nak Road. The road continues south for views from the rooftop of Lake Inn, then past a mosque before returning north past Wat Machimawat.

View several distinct styles of architecture on Saiburi and Nang Ngam Roads: Peranakan homes with well-carved shutters, Chinese homes capped with long red-tiled roofs that dramatically slope toward the ground, and wooden Thai shophouses.

Wat Machimawat
Wat Machimawat (Wat Klang)—the oldest and most important temple in Songkhla—was established during the reigns of Kings Rama III and IV, when the maritime port served as a provincial outpost of the Bangkok administration.

Central *Bot*: Modeled after Wat Pra Keo in Bangkok, the principal sanctuary of Wat Klang features beautiful murals of 19th-century life in Songkhla and episodes from the Jatakas, and a highly venerated marble Buddha commissioned by King Rama III. The outer verandas are adorned with stone bas-reliefs imported from China, which illustrate a Chinese epic called *Romance of the Three Kingdoms.*

Museum: The small museum north of the *bot* has a minor collection of jasper Buddhas, votive tablets, unlabeled ceramics, and the standard assortment of mechanical oddities.

South *Viharn*: Adjacent to the Buddhist monastery is an unusual *viharn* that incorporates both Chinese and Peranakan architectural styles, with European touches such as Dutch and English hanging lanterns.

Samila Beach
The focal point of Songkhla is the eight-km stretch of sand dotted with seafood restaurants, a municipally owned hotel, and hardly any tourists since Thais leave sunbathing to mad dogs and unenlightened backpackers. The road continues north to several popular cafes such

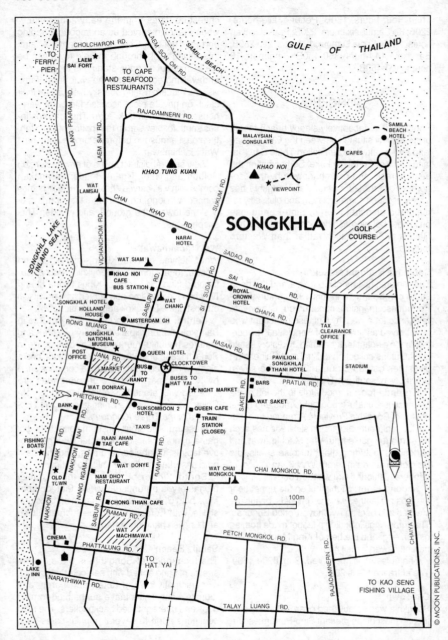

as Seven Sisters, Nongnuch, and Mark's. The offshore humpbacked islands of Ko Maeo ("Cat") and Ko Nu ("Rat") are named after their respective shapes. Excellent views over Songkhla are guaranteed from the deserted park at the top of Khao Noi.

South of the promontory is a long straight beach lined with swaying casuarina pines beneath cobbled promenades. A Thai naval base, three km south, rents sailboards and sailboats, and operates a fairly good cafe with cheap beer. The road continues one more kilometer south to the Muslim fishing village of Kao Seng, known for its roadside market, seafood restaurants, and brightly painted *kolae* boats.

Ko Yo

Yo Island is known for its seafood restaurants, traditional weavings, and Institute of Southern Thai Studies. The thickly wooded island is 12 km from Songkhla and can be reached by bus from the clock tower.

Institute of Southern Thai Studies: The newly opened Folklore Museum features a comprehensive collection of southern artifacts displayed in 17 traditional Thai houses capped with distinctive roof styles—*balano, panya,* and *chua.* Also on the grounds is a cultural park, audiovisual center, and outdoor performance stage, thought to be the largest in Thailand. The museum, open daily 0830-1630, is near Ban Ao Sai at the north end of the island.

Weaving: Cotton weavers on the island produce both traditional cotton fabrics from home looms and spectacularly gaudy fashionwear covered with flamingos, palm trees, and riotous tropical sunsets. Roadside stalls are concentrated in the center of the island.

Food: One of the most popular choices is **Porntip II,** where visitors can select giant bass from the nearby fish pen or try a seafood combination called *ai klang talay hut. . .* passionate sea in sexual heat! Porntip is just across the 700-meter Tinsulanonda Bridge, which connects the southern extension of Songkhla with Ko Yo. **Suan Kaeo Restaurant** at the north end of the island is another popular choice.

Khu Khut Bird Sanctuary

A large 520-square-km wildlife refuge, similar to Thale Noi near Phattalung, is 30 km north of Songkhla near the town of Sathing Phra. Birds are most plentiful in the mornings and late afternoons from December to early January. Boat tours of the inland lake are available at park headquarters. Buses heading north across Ko Yo and up the coastline stop at Sathing Phra, from where motorcycles can continue three km to park headquarters. Sathing Phra is also noted for its numerous Srivijaya-era monuments, such as Wat Sathing Phra, with a pure Srivijaya *chedi;* and Pra Chedi Phratan, known for its reclining Buddha and preserved frescoes.

Sathing Phra Resort, five km short of Sathing Phra, has campsites and beachfront bungalows for 150-280B.

Budget Accommodations

Songkhla is a compact town with most hotels within walking distance of the bus stop near the clock tower.

Narai Hotel: Run by Uncle Wanno and a wonderful woman named Tip, the backpackers' favorite is somewhat isolated but compensates with travel tips, bicycle rentals, laundry service, and decent rooms in the yellow building with a red-tiled roof. 14 Chai Khao Rd., tel. (074) 311078, 100-200B.

Amsterdam Guesthouse: A popular and clean guesthouse run by a friendly Dutch woman. Tidy rooms in a central location. 15/3 Rong Muang Rd., tel. (074) 322788, 160-200B.

Holland House: Not much Dutch flavor, but a cozy cafe, bicycle and motorcycle rentals, downstairs TV, and friendly Thai manager who runs the place in the absence of her Dutch husband, a Songkhla resident. 18/1 Rong Muang Rd., tel. (074) 322738, 200-350B.

Songkhla Hotel: An older hotel, full of character and recently refurbished, with large and clean wooden rooms, common or private bath. 68 Vichanchom Rd., tel. (074) 313505, 150-250B.

Suksomboon 2 Hotel: A split-personality sort of hotel with ordinary fan-cooled rooms in the old wing and spotless, spacious a/c rooms in the new annex. 14 Saiburi Rd., tel. (074) 311149, 160-220B fan, 300-380B a/c.

Moderate Accommodations

Songkhla has a few midlevel hotels in widely scattered locations.

Samila Beach Hotel: Songkhla's faded lady features a small swimming pool, tennis courts, water sports, nine-hole golf course, and 75 frayed but tidy rooms in an unbeatable location facing the sea. Does anybody know what happened to the bronze mermaid? 1 Rajadamnern Rd., tel. (074) 311310, fax (074) 322448, 500-800B.

Royal Crown Hotel: This quiet retreat is favored by British and American oilies working the offshore fields. All rooms are a/c with TV and videos, and bars are nearby. 39 Sai Ngam Rd., tel. (074) 312174, 1,100-1,800B.

Lake Inn: The only hotel that enjoys views over the fishing wharf and beautiful Songkhla Lake, a big plus despite the strange location at the south end of town. 301 Nakhon Nak Rd., tel. (074) 314240, fax (074) 314843, 480-800B.

Haad Kaew Princess Resort: A first-class beachfront hotel, five km north of Songkhla, with pool, restaurant, gardens, and 143 a/c rooms facing Sai Khao Beach. 163/1 Km 5, Ban Sai Khao, tel. (074) 331059, fax (074) 331058, 1,200-1,500B.

Pavilion Songkhla Thani Hotel: Songkhla's newest luxury property has 182 rooms in a nine-story structure three blocks east of the traffic circle in city center. 17 Pratua Rd., tel. (074) 311355, fax (074) 323716, 1,700-2,400B.

Restaurants

Seafood, street stalls, and southern-style curries are the secrets of Songkhla.

Night Markets: A small night market gathers on Saiburi Road near the old city walls and behind the new shopping complex—great for local fruits and takeaway specialties. Another night market materializes east of the clock tower near the train station.

Beach Cafes: Rudimentary shacks near Samila Beach Hotel include Buakeow and Boonriam Cafes, plus a collection of vendors pushing mobile units. Try the curried crab claws, grilled squid, and *khanom tang tok,* a dessert pancake filled with jams and jellies.

Posher digs, north of curvy Samila Beach on straight-laced Hat Son On, include Nong Nok, Lop Mun, Nam Kam, Ying Muk, and several others.

Khao Noi Cafe: Clean, tasty seafood dishes and southern-style curries in one of Songkhla's favorite cafes. Open daily 0730-2000. 14/22 Vichanchom Rd., tel. (074) 311805. Inexpensive.

Ouen Cafe: A breezy cafe near the defunct railway station, with excellent Chinese fare, including Peking duck and *mu shu* pork. Open daily 1100-2200. Sisuda Rd. Moderate.

Raan Ahan Tae: Escape the tour buses at this old-style, rudimentary, hole-in-the-wall in old Songkhla. 85 Nang Ngam Rd. Inexpensive. Other nostalgic favorites include nearby **Nam Dhoy** and **Chong Thian** on Raman Road near Wat Machimawat.

Laguna Terrace: Songkhla, unfortunately, lacks any decent cafes facing Thale Sap, except for this breezy but pricey beer garden on the top floor of Lake Inn. Open daily 1000-2200. 301 Nakhon Nak Rd., tel. (074) 314240. Moderate.

Information and Services

Sleepy Songkhla has a surprising number of services, since Songkhla, not Hat Yai, is the provincial capital.

Thai Immigration: Visa extensions are available here. Open weekdays 0830-1430. 1/65 Lang Praram Rd., tel. (074) 313480.

Malaysian Consulate: Malaysia doesn't require tourist visas, but the consulate can help with business and cultural visas. The American Consulate closed in 1992. Open weekdays 0900-1600. 4 Sukum Rd., tel. (074) 311062.

Post Office: The GPO is open weekdays 0830-1430, Sat. 0900-1200. The upstairs overseas phone center is open daily 0800-2100. Nakhon Nai Rd., tel. (074) 311013. Postal code: 90000.

Hospital: English is spoken at Songkhla Hospital. Open 24 hours. 161 Ramvithi Rd., tel. (074) 321072.

Banks: Thai Farmers Bank has a 24-hour ATM. Open weekdays 0830-1530. 49/1 Nakhon Nai Rd., tel. (074) 321065.

Transportation

Songkhla is 1001 km south of Bangkok and 28 km northeast of Hat Yai.

From Hat Yai: Songkhla can be reached in 30 minutes by a green bus from the Plaza Theater on Petchkasem Road, or by a share taxi from the nearby President Hotel. Otherwise, buses stop at the clock tower and then continue to a bus station on Saiburi Road near Wat Chang.

From Songkhla: Buses back to Hat Yai leave from Rong Muang Road near the museum and

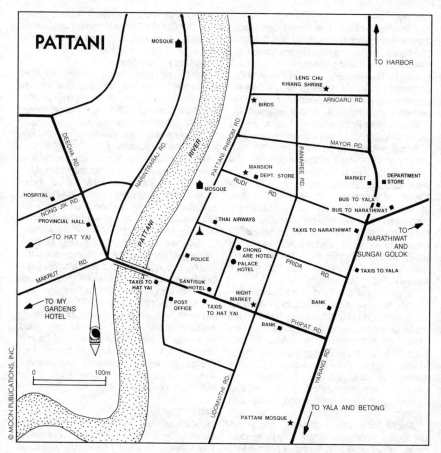

PATTANI

MOSQUE

LENG CHU
KHIANG SHRINE ★

★ BIRDS

ARNOARU RD.

MAYOR RD.

MANSION ★
DEPT. STORE

MARKET ■

DEPARTMENT
■ STORE

MOSQUE

BUS TO YALA ■
BUS TO NARATHIWAT ■

THAI AIRWAYS ■

TAXIS TO NARATHIWAT ■

TO
NARATHIWAT
AND
SUNGAI GOLOK

HOSPITAL ■

NONG JIK RD.

PROVINCIAL HALL ■

TO HAT YAI

POLICE ■

● CHONG
ARE HOTEL
● PALACE
HOTEL

■ TAXIS TO YALA

MAKRUT RD.

TAXIS TO
HAT YAI

SANTISUK
HOTEL ■

NIGHT
MARKET ★

BANK ■

TO MY
GARDENS
HOTEL

POST
OFFICE ■

TAXIS
TO HAT YAI

BANK ■

PHIPAT RD.

TO HARBOR

DEECHA RD.

NARINTRARAJ RD.

RIVER

PATTANI PHIROM RD.

PATTANI

RUDI RD.

PANAREE RD.

PRIDA RD.

YARANG RD.

UDOMVITHI RD.

0   100m

© MOON PUBLICATIONS, INC.

PATTANI MOSQUE ★

TO YALA AND BETONG

from the bus station on Saiburi Road near Wat Chang. Other buses to Ranot and Khu Khut Waterbird Sanctuary leave from Jana Road just east of the clock tower.

Train: The train station has been closed for several years.

PATTANI

Thailand changes dramatically south of Hat Yai. Suddenly, Islamic mosques outnumber Buddhist *wats,* Yawi (a Malay dialect influenced by Arabic) joins Thai as the *lingua franca,* and old men sport Muslim *haji* caps rather than Buddhist robes. The style of domestic architecture changes from Thai to Malay, and women living outside urban areas wear lace veils or brightly colored clothing typical of Muslim housewives.

Farangs are extremely rare in the deep south, aside from a handful of travelers heading from Hat Yai down to Kota Baru in Malaysia. Visitors who need to stay overnight or who have a strong interest in Thai-Malay culture will discover the most pleasant interlude to be the idyllic fishing village of Narathiwat. Pattani, Yala, and Sungai Golok are modern concrete towns with little of great interest except for their political backgrounds, mosques, and women dressed in traditional Muslim garb.

History

Archaeologists believe that Pattani and nearby Yarang were once the mythical Buddhist empire called Langsigia by the Chinese, and Langasuka by the Indians. Recent diggings conducted by Thai students from the Fine Arts Department have uncovered miniature *chedis*, stone Buddha images inscribed in Pali, and Persian pottery destined for Chinese collectors.

Present-day Pattani takes its name from a powerful Malay sultanate under the influence of Malacca that rose to prominence in the 14th century. In 1516, the Portuguese established a post at Pattani, while the Dutch arrived toward the end of the 16th century. By the 17th century, Pattani served as the center of Islamic studies for all of Southeast Asia, and as the leading entrepôt for trade between China and Southeast Asia. Western merchants left records of the wealth and power of its Islamic rulers, and of the marriage alliances that cemented relationships between Pattani and southern Malay empires.

Today, the four provinces of the deep south—Pattani, Narathiwat, Yala, and Satun—form the ideological and political boundary between the Buddhist cultures of northern Thailand and the Muslim world of lower Southeast Asia. Surveys show that almost 75% of the population are of Malay stock and follow the precepts of Islam, a statistic not lost on the rulers in Bangkok who must cope with demands for greater ethnic privileges such as Islamic schools and *shariah* court systems.

Despite some political changes—and a modest degree of self-government—the deep south remains more devoted to the call of Islam than to the culture of Bangkok.

Walking Tour

Pattani is hardly a fascinating destination, though a few pleasant hours can be spent walking through what remains of the old town. Begin your walk by crossing the bridge and heading north along the riverbank past dozens of large and gaily decorated fishing boats. Several brightly painted *kolae* boats sit under the bridge.

Return to city center and walk north along the river past a small mosque and city park. Traces of traditional architecture are still found at the impressive mansion on Rudi Road and in the Chinese shophouses, with their sloped and tiled roofs, scrollwork in the roof eaves, and louvered windows surrounded by glazed tilework.

Leng Chu Khiang Shrine

The legends, history, and traditions of Pattani are preserved at this shrine and at Kreuze Mosque, seven km east of town. Leng Chu Khiang is dedicated to a Chinese goddess named Chao Mae Lim Ko Neo who possesses magical powers and is highly revered throughout Pattani and the deep south.

The legend begins in the mid-16th century, after an immigrant Chinese merchant named Lim To Khiang marries a Pattani Muslim and converts to Islam. Distressed relatives in China send his sister Lim Ko Neo to Pattani to convince Mr. Lim to abandon Islam and return to his homeland. To prove the depth of his newfound faith, Lim begins construction of the Kreuze Mosque, but his sister puts a curse on the monument that dooms its completion. In a final attempt to reform her recalcitrant brother, Lim Ko Neo commits suicide by hanging herself from a cashew tree.

A shrine dedicated to the feisty sister, and a replica of the hanging tree, are displayed inside the Leng Chu Khiang Shrine on Arnoaru Road. An annual fair, held on the full moon of the third lunar month, honors Ms. Lim with a procession of Chinese dragons and religious devotees who walk across red-hot coals and pierce their bodies with swords and spears.

Pattani Mosque

Architectural variety is provided by the Matsayit Klang, a classic mosque constructed in the early 1960s that ranks among the most elegant and striking in Thailand. Flanking the broad sidewalk that approaches the sanctuary are twin minarets from where Islamic prayer calls are electronically broadcast five times each day. The primary hall is characterized by an orange-tiled facade, arched windows set with stained glass, and bulbous domes inlaid with green stone. Well-dressed visitors can watch the Friday afternoon prayer services.

Kreuze Mosque

The legendary companion to Leng Chu Khiang is another highly revered, yet exceedingly controversial, monument. As described above, the rudimentary shell stands half completed after the magical curse cast from Ms. Lim on her turncoat brother. In recent years, the mosque has been the scene of a political struggle by Sunni and Shiite groups who have demanded that the Thai government abrogate the mosque's historical status so that construction can be completed and religious services resumed. Political rallies at the mosque have criticized the government for alleged mistreatment of Muslims, urged the removal of a nearby Chinese shrine, and demanded the establishment of an Islamic state in Pattani Province.

In an effort to appease local Muslims who felt their mosque had been eclipsed by the adjacent Lim Ko Neo Chinese shrine, Kreuze Mosque was recently renovated by the Fine Arts Department. The monument is seven km southeast of town on Hwy. 42 and plainly visible from buses heading down to Narathiwat.

Accommodations

Several small hotels are located in central Pattani, plus a midlevel choice about one km from city center.

Palace Hotel: This five-story hotel, the best deal in central Pattani, is set back in a quiet alley away from noisy Phipat Road. Fairly good meals are served in their Chongar Restaurant. 38 Soi Preeda, tel. (073) 349171, 150-220B fan, 300-350B a/c.

Chong Are Hotel: Another decent choice with rooms offering either common or private bath. The reception is located inside the darkened restaurant and nightclub. 190 Prida Rd., tel. (073) 349039, 160-280B.

Santisuk: The cheapest place in town, with both fan-cooled and a/c rooms in acceptable condition. 29 Phipat Rd., tel. (073) 349122, 120-180B fan, 300-350B a/c.

My Gardens Hotel: The only luxury hotel in Pattani, with large rooms and a narrow nightclub popular with Thai and Chinese residents. The hotel is two km from the bridge, down Makrut Road. 8/23 Charoen Prathet Rd., tel. (073) 331055, fax (073) 348200, 300-380B fan, 480-700B a/c.

Transportation

Pattani is 124 km southeast of Hat Yai, 40 km north of Yala, and 96 km northwest of Narathiwat.

Share taxis from Yala leave from various stops near the train station and take about 30 minutes. Buses from Narathiwat leave from the waiting shed near the clock tower and pass some of the lushest scenery in Thailand.

YALA

Yala Province and its Betong District on the Malaysian border make up the southernmost region of Thailand. Yala itself is a modern commercial center fashioned around a grid of roads with city parks and lakes on the perimeter. Most of the inhabitants are Chinese who dominate the rubber and rice industries, while the surrounding countryside is populated by Thai-Malays who follow the call of Islam and work the fields in the only landlocked province of southern Thailand.

Attractions

Aside from local festivals and cave temples outside town, Yala has little of interest for most visitors. Yala has won several awards for being the cleanest town in Thailand, though the central market in the northeast corner is hardly an example of pristine beauty.

Wat Phutapoom features a large walking Buddha elevated on a concrete pedestal and covered with small golden tiles. South of town at the terminus of Pipat Pakdee Road is Kwan Muang Park, with its city pillar shrine in the nearby traffic circle, and immense artificial lake fixed with small cafes and boat rentals.

Yala Town is also known for its ASEAN Bird Singing Contest held in March in Kwan Muang Park, and Southern Thai Culture Week with parades and beauty pageants held in early August. The Lak Muang Fair occurs in late May.

Wat Kuha Phimok

The chief historical and architectural attraction of Yala is six km west of town on the road toward Hat Yai. Believed to date from the Srivijaya era, the cave complex at Wat Kuha Phimok (also called Wat Na Tham) features a highly venerated reclining Buddha image considered by southern Thais equal in religious stature to Wat Boromothat in Nakhon Si Thammarat and Wat Chaiya in Surat Thani Province.

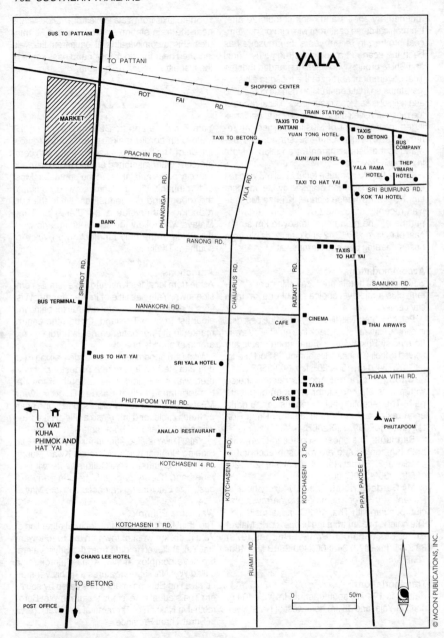

YALA

BUS TO PATTANI

TO PATTANI

ROT FAI RD.

SHOPPING CENTER

MARKET

TRAIN STATION

TAXIS TO PATTANI

TAXI TO BETONG

Yuan Tong Hotel

TAXIS TO BETONG

BUS COMPANY

PRACHIN RD.

AUN AUN HOTEL

YALA RAMA HOTEL

THEP VIMARN HOTEL

PHANGNGA RD.

YALA RD.

TAXI TO HAT YAI

SRI BUMRUNG RD.

KOK TAI HOTEL

BANK

RANONG RD.

TAXIS TO HAT YAI

CHAIARUS RD.

RATAKIT RD.

SAMUKKI RD.

SIRIROT RD.

BUS TERMINAL

NANAKORN RD.

CAFE

CINEMA

THAI AIRWAYS

BUS TO HAT YAI

SRI YALA HOTEL

THANA VITHI RD.

PHUTAPOOM VITHI RD.

TAXIS

CAFES

TO WAT KUHA PHIMOK AND HAT YAI

WAT PHUTAPOOM

ANALAO RESTAURANT

KOTCHASENI 2 RD.

KOTCHASENI 3 RD.

PIPAT PAKDEE RD.

KOTCHASENI 4 RD.

KOTCHASENI 1 RD.

RUAMIT RD.

CHANG LEE HOTEL

TO BETONG

POST OFFICE

0   50m

© MOON PUBLICATIONS, INC.

Wat Tham Silpa, a cave grotto two km west of Wat Kuha Phimok, offers some fading patches of 13th-century cave art, perhaps the only surviving examples of Srivijaya paintings in Thailand. Both caves can be reached by buses leaving from Sirirot Road. Ask the driver to stop at the English-language sign, and follow the path to the limestone sanctuary.

Sakai Village
Ban Sakai is home to some of Thailand's last remaining Sakai tribe peoples, dark-skinned and frizzy-haired descendants of the Proto-Malay race who once populated the entire Malay Peninsula. Most have now integrated into Thai society and found work in local rubber plantations, though about 20 families continue to live in a relatively traditional village 80 km south of Yala.

Visitors interested in anthropology should take a bus south on the road toward Betong and ask to be dropped in Thanto District near the village of Ban Rae. A laterite road continues four km to Ban Sakai, also called Village No. 3.

Betong
Betong is the southernmost district in Thailand, about 140 km south of Yala on the Malaysian border. Betong is popular with Malaysians, who are allowed to cross the border and conduct trade, but rarely visited by Westerners, who prefer the more convenient land crossings at Sadao (the Hat Yai-Penang route) and Sungai Golok (the Hat Yai-Kota Baru route). Betong valley is cool, mountainous, elevated at over 500 meters, and often foggy—a dubious charm that has earned Betong the nickname of "Misty City."

Betong has over a dozen hotels in the 120-250B price range, including the Cathay, Fortuna, Kongka, Khai, Kings, Venus, First, Betong, Rama, and My House.

Accommodations
Budget Hotels: Several inexpensive Chinese hotels are located near the train station and taxi stops. The **Yuan Tong Hotel** in the yellow-and-white wooden building, **Aun Aun Hotel** in the five-story gray concrete tower, and **Kok Tai Hotel** with green shutters, have acceptable if somewhat dreary rooms for 120-160B.

Sri Yala Hotel: A somewhat better hotel with both fan-cooled and a/c rooms at bargain rates.

18-22 Chaijarus Rd., tel. (073) 212815, 180-220B fan, 300-380B a/c.

Thep Vimarn Hotel: Slightly more expensive but a big leap in comfort are the clean rooms in the deserted hotel just beyond the imposing Yala Rama Hotel. 31-37 Sri Bumrung Rd., tel. (073) 212400, 180-250B fan, 350-450B a/c.

Yala Rama: Facilities at Yala's former top-end choice include the Rama Cafe, a nightclub with live music, and 126 rooms in various price ranges. 21 Sri Bumrung Rd., tel. (073) 212563, fax (073) 214532, 320-400B fan, 550-800B a/c.

Chang Lee Hotel: The best in town with swimming pool, two restaurants, business center, and nightclub, in the southwestern corner of town near the post office. Sirirot Rd., tel. (073) 211223, fax (073) 211773, 1,400-2,600B.

Transportation
Yala is 130 km southeast of Hat Yai and 100 km north of the Malaysian border at Sungai Golok.

Train: Trains to Yala leave Hat Yai daily at 0625, 0810, 1035, and 1322.

Bus: Buses to Yala leave from the main bus terminal in Hat Yai, and from the bus halt at the south end of Sungai Golok. Buses from Yala to Hat Yai leave from a small office on Sirirot Road a few blocks south of the central market. The main bus terminal is on Sirirot Road, several blocks south of the post office. A private bus company across from the train station can help with a/c coaches to Phuket, Ko Samui, and Bangkok.

Taxi: Share taxis to Yala leave from the Cathay Hotel in Hat Yai and from the train station in Sungai Golok. Taxis from Yala to various destinations leave from several spots near the train station. Exact locations change frequently, but approximate venues are shown on the Yala map.

NARATHIWAT

This small and sleepy fishing village is the most pleasant stop between Hat Yai and Sungai Golok. The town itself lacks any great monuments or historical sites, but the undisturbed wooden architecture, deserted beaches, and laid-back atmosphere make it a wonderful spot to escape the more congested and touristy towns of southern Thailand.

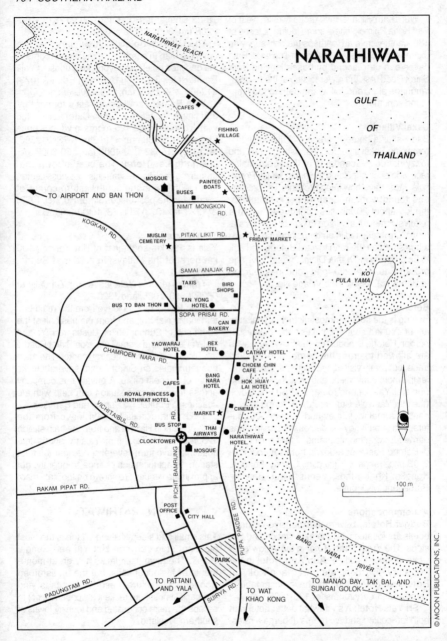

NARATHIWAT

An excellent time to visit is September, when Narathiwat celebrates the temporary residence of the king with parades, displays of local handicrafts, zebra dove cooing contests, and flotillas of handsomely painted *kolae* boats, the traditional craft of Malay fishermen.

Walking Tour

A very agreeable three-hour walking tour can be made starting from the clock tower and heading north along the riverfront road toward the Muslim fishing village and cafes at Narathiwat Beach. Several bird shops on the left display highly prized zebra doves cooing in lovely wicker baskets. A pair of brightly painted *kolae* fishing boats is docked at the north end of Pupa Pakdee Road, followed by the large and modern but rather sterile Narathiwat Mosque. Across the bridge lies a typical Muslim fishing village where kids yell "Hello good morning," and several cafes with English-language menus and beach parasols emblazoned with Coca-Cola logos.

Walking south down Pichit Bamrung Road, you'll pass a large Muslim cemetery before arriving back at the clock tower.

Wat Khao Kong

Six km south of Narathiwat is a small hill called Khao Kong, on which local Buddhists have constructed the largest seated Buddha in Thailand. Known as Pra Buddha Taksin Ming Mongkol (Taksin Buddha), the 25-meter bronze image incongruously dominates a rural setting populated entirely by Muslims.

The image is plainly visible from the road and can be reached with any bus or minitruck heading south down Hwy. 42 toward Sungai Golok.

Taksin Palace and Manao Bay

Sited on a lemon-shaped bay some 12 km south of Narathiwat is a summer palace visited by the royal family each year Aug.-Oct. Closed during the royal visit, which coincides with the Narathiwat *kolae* festival, the modern palace and landscaped gardens are otherwise open to the public daily 0900-1600.

Manao Bay is the first of a series of almost completely deserted white-sand beaches that stretch south from Narathiwat to the Malaysian border.

Wadin Husen Mosque

One of the oldest and most intriguing mosques in Thailand is located in the village of Lubosawo in Bacho District, some 15 km north of Narathiwat and a few kilometers off Hwy. 42. The finely carved and heavily weathered wooden mosque, constructed in 1769, displays both Thai and Muslim architectural styles.

Wat Chonthara Singhe

A temple that changed the course of Thai history is located in the small seaside town of Tak Bai, 34 km south of Narathiwat and 28 km north of Sungai Golok.

Wat Chonthara Singhe was constructed in 1873 by a young monk on land donated by the governor of Kelantan. Embodying a mixture of southern Thai and Chinese influences, the temple became well known for its beauty and idyllic location on the banks of the Tak Bai River. Toward the turn of the century, British colonialists in Malaysia attempted to expand their domain by claiming the four northern Malay states under Thai suzerainty. King Rama V was forced in 1909 to give up the provinces of Trengganu, Kelantan, Kedah, and Perlis, but he argued that the surrender of Wat Chonthara Singhe would represent an irreplaceable cultural and religious loss for Thailand. The British agreed, and today the present boundaries of Thailand and Malaysia are due to the existence of Wat Chonthara Singhe and the clever diplomacy of King Rama V.

Accommodations

Most hotels are near the river on Pupa Pakdee Road, or a block back on Pichit Bamrung Road.

Narathiwat Hotel: The cheapest spot in town is the yellow wooden hotel marked with a small English sign. Rooms fronting the street are noisy, and badly in need of paint and new mattresses, but rooms facing the Bang Nara River are a good value and worth requesting. 341 Phupa Pakdee Rd., tel. (073) 511063, 120-160B.

Bang Nara Hotel: Another budget spot similar to the Narathiwat but without the river-view rooms. **Hok Huay Lai** and **Cathay** Hotels are in the same price range. 174 Phupa Pakdee Rd., tel. (073) 511036, 120-140B.

Rex Hotel: A small step up in quality. 6/1 Chamroen Nara Rd., tel. (073) 511134, fax (073) 511190, 180-220B fan, 350-460B a/c.

Yaowaraj Hotel: Narathiwat's second-largest hotel offers clean rooms with private bath at reasonable prices. 131 Pichit Bamrung Rd., tel. (073) 511148, fax (073) 511320, 140-180B fan, 320-380B a/c.

Tan Yong Hotel: Narathiwat's first upscale hotel features a snooker hall, Ladybird "ancient massage," and a popular restaurant with live cabaret—a surprisingly luxurious hotel for such a small town. 16/1 Sopa Prisai Rd., tel. (073) 511477, fax (073) 511834, 650-800B.

Royal Princess Narathiwat Hotel: The best in town, just north of the clock tower with swimming pool, business center, restaurant, nightclub, and 126 rooms with all possible amenities. Pichit Bamrung Rd., tel. (073) 511027, fax (073) 511882, 1,600-2,400B.

Restaurants

The night market opposite the cinema is small and disappointing. Better atmosphere is found at the funky **Choem Chin Cafe** on the corner, and the row of informal restaurants just north of the clock tower. **Can Bakery** is a clean and comfortable spot popular with young Thais.

Transportation

Narathiwat is 222 km south of Hat Yai and 55 km north of Sungai Golok on the Malaysian border.

Air: Thai Airways flies from Hat Yai to Narathiwat on Monday, Wednesday, and Sunday. Thai Airways (tel. 073-511161) is at 324 Pupa Pakdee Rd.

Train: The nearest train station is at Tanyong Mas, 20 km west of Narathiwat. Trains leave Sungai Golok at 0600, 0840, 1005, 1150, 1335, and 1535. Minitrucks and buses continue to Narathiwat.

Bus: Buses leave every two hours from the halt at the south end of Sungai Golok. Buses from Hat Yai leave from the main bus terminal at the southeastern outskirts of town.

Taxi: Share taxis from Sungai Golok leave from the train station and take about one hour to Narathiwat. Taxis from Hat Yai depart on Niphat Uthit 2 Road near the Cathay Hotel.

SUNGAI GOLOK

Sungai Golok (or Sungai Kolok) is the final town for visitors heading south from Thailand to the east coast of peninsular Malaysia. Aside from its immigration functions, the town serves the sexual desires of Malaysian males who pack the hotels, nightclubs, and massage parlors on weekends. Sungai Golok during the week is almost completely deserted and offers absolutely nothing of interest for Western travelers.

However, a small but useful tourist office is located at the border. Sungai Golok also has several banks, an immigration office, and a Chinese shrine east of the police station. Merchants accept both Thai *baht* and Malaysian *ringgit.* The town is multicultural, as evidenced by the signs in Thai, Malay, and Chinese.

Warning: The Thai border closes nightly sometime between 1700 and 1800, depending on the whim of immigration officials and border guards. Unless you care to spend a night in Sungai Golok—not a pleasant thought—arrive early enough to conduct border formalities and catch a share taxi down to Kota Baru.

Accommodations

The local tourist office claims that Sungai Golok has 44 hotels in all price categories. Most cost 150-200B fan, 300-450B a/c, or 450-650B in better hotels.

Budget Hotels: Travelers arriving late at night can quickly locate an inexpensive hotel on Charoenkhet Road or the parallel avenues to the west. Hotels on Charoenkhet Road with rooms for 150-200B include the **Chiang Mai, Pimarn, Shanghai, Asia** with a tiled lobby and aquariums, and **Savoy** with potted plants in the balcony. The very inexpensive **Thaliang** has rudimentary rooms from 120B and a small coffee shop with caged songbirds.

Merlin Hotel: A very large and centrally located hotel; its brochure shows photos of lovely women taking bubble baths, cutting hair, and sitting in bedrooms dressed in blue party dresses. You get the idea. 40 Charoenkhet, tel. (073) 611003, fax (073) 613325, 420-600B a/c.

Plaza Hotel: Semi-luxury hotel with cabaret in the Bunga Restaurant and the curiously named Cae Sar Disco downstairs. 2 Thespathom Rd., tel. (073) 611875, fax (073) 613402, 400-600B.

Genting Hotel: Best in town, a few blocks from city center and just off the road that heads east to the Malaysian border. Asia 18 Rd., tel. (073) 613231, fax (073) 611259, 650-900B.

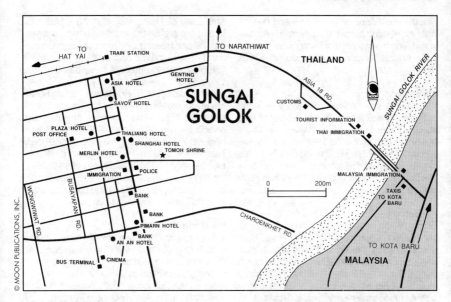

Transportation
Sungai Golok is 1,215 km south of Bangkok and two km north of Malaysia.

Train: Trains in the deep south are slow and limited to destinations shown below, but compensate with landscapes removed from dusty towns and concrete expressways. Train arrivals in Sungai Golok are greeted by trishaw drivers who continue to the border. There is no direct train service between Sungai Golok and Kota Baru.

Bus: Buses from Hat Yai can be arranged through travel agents near the Cathay Hotel, though most services head southwest toward Penang and Kuala Lumpur. Ordinary buses leave from the Hat Yai bus terminal on the outskirts of town.

Buses generally arrive and depart from the train station in Sungai Golok, adjacent to the Valentine Hotel, or from the bus terminal at the south end of town near the cinema and An An Hotel. Air-conditioned buses to Surat Thani and Bangkok leave from the Valentine Hotel at 0800 and 1230. Ordinary buses to Bangkok leave throughout the day until 1630 from the train station and bus terminal.

Taxi: Share taxis are the fastest way to travel in the deep south. Share taxis from Hat Yai, Satun, Pattani, and Narathiwat stop at the train station in Sungai Golok, from where *tuk tuks* and pedicabs continue east to the Malaysian border.

Share taxis to all towns in the deep south leave 0700-1600 from the Sungai Golok train station. Travelers arriving from Malaysia should proceed directly to the train station and find the next available taxi.

DEPARTURE TO MALAYSIA

Via Sungai Golok
The border is about two km from the train station in Sungai Golok. Thai immigration will check your visa expiration date and charge 100B per day for staying beyond the allotted period.

Malaysian authorities across the Sungai Golok River grant free entry permits to most Western visitors on arrival. You then walk into the small Malaysian border town of Rantau Panjang. To the right is a small cafe where you can dine and wait for the next available share taxi to Kota Baru. The cafe manager and taxi drivers accept Thai *baht* at fair exchange rates.

Malaysia comes as a wondrous shock. Signs are marked in English, communication is easy with the multilingual shopkeepers and taxi drivers, vegetation appears more trimmed and controlled, and the standard of living jumps dramatically. And wait until you try the food in the Kota Baru night market.

Via Tak Bai

Tak Bai is a small coastal village 28 km north of Sungai Golok. Buses from Narathiwat take about an hour to reach Tak Bai. Ferries to the Malaysian border town of Pengkalan Kulor depart 0800-1700 from Tak Bai and Ban Taba, another small coastal town about five km south of Tak Bai. Bus 27 continues from Pengkalan Kulor to Kota Baru.

Via Betong

Betong is the southernmost town in Thailand, about 140 km south of Yala on the Malaysian border. Betong is rarely visited by Westerners, who prefer the more convenient land crossings at Sungai Golok and Sadao (the Hat Yai-Penang route), but the winding road from Yala is considered among the most scenic in Thailand.

Remember that Thai immigration and the international border close around 1800. The adjacent Malaysian town is called Keroh.

Via Sadao

A Thai border town 70 km south of Hat Yai, Sadao is on the main highway between Hat Yai and Penang—the transit spot for most buses and taxis traveling between Southern Thailand and the west coast of peninsular Malaysia. Changlun, the nearest Malaysian town, is about 30 km south of Sadao.

The best way to reach Penang from Hat Yai is either by a share taxi leaving near the train station or along Niphat Uthit 2 Road, or by a bus organized from a travel agency near the Cathay Hotel.

Sadao also can be reached by public bus from Hat Yai, though transportation is sporadic and sometimes nonexistent to Changlun. A better option for budget travelers is a bus or train from Hat Yai to Padang Besar; from there, you can walk across the border and continue to Penang with public transportation or private taxi.

Via Padang Besar

Padang Besar is a Malaysian border town 60 km south of Hat Yai and two km south of the Thai town of Thung Mo. Padang Besar and Thung Mo are on the main train line between Hat Yai and Penang, and most visitors take the train between the two countries.

Highway 4—the main highway between Hat Yai and Penang—is the primary route for buses and share taxis, but Thung Mo and Padang Besar are useful crossing points for independent travelers who wish to patch together their itinerary without the use of Hat Yai travel agents. Buses from Hat Yai reach Thung Mo in about one hour. Travelers should have an exit stamp posted in their passport by Thai immigration before walking the one km south to Malaysian immigration officials in Padang Besar. Taxis and buses continue south to Penang and Kuala Lumpur.

Via Wang Prachan

Wang Prachan is a border town 40 km southeast of Satun, in the middle of Thale Ban National Park. Visitors in Satun can reach Wang Prachan by bus, taxi, or motorcycle taxi. After border formalities, taxis continue south to the Malaysian towns of Kangar, Alor Setar, and Penang.

Via Satun

Satun is the southwesternmost town in Thailand, and a useful spot from which to reach Malaysia after a visit to nearby Tarutao National Marine Park.

The land route to Malaysia involves a car or motorcycle taxi to the Thai border town at Wang Prachan, followed by a bus south to Kangar and Penang.

A more intriguing and adventurous option is a boat from Satun to Kuala Perlis in Malaysia. Boats take about 90 minutes and leave from two locations. Longtails depart several times daily from the city pier on Klong Bambang near the Rain Tong Hotel. Larger boats leave from Tammalang Pier in the estuary about 15 km south of Satun. Tammalang Pier can be reached by *tuk tuk* or motorcycle taxi.

More sensible than boat to Kuala Perlis is direct service to Langkawi Island, a well-developed Malaysian resort destination just 90 minutes south of Satun. Boats to Langkawi depart daily at 1600 from Tammalang Pier and return from Langkawi daily at 1300. Tickets cost 150B and can be purchased on the ship or from Charan Tours near the Thai Airways office.

APPENDIX
BANGKOK'S SKYTRAIN

As this book went to press Bangkok's newest form of public transportation finally opened to the public in December 1999, after almost a decade of construction.

Bangkok officials began serious talks about mass transit for the badly congested Thai capital in the 1980s, and early plans called for four independent, privately built, elevated systems that were to crisscross the city but not connect to each other. One of the four systems was to be a "skytrain" built by Canada's SNC-Lavalin, but it fell into political quicksand in the early part of this decade as did two other projects. The existing Skytrain is a US$1.2 billion elevated mass transit train system constructed by Tanayong Co. Ltd. and the Bangkok Mass Transit System Corp.

The 23.5 km elevated train system consists of 35 three-carriage trains which ply the tracks daily from 0600 until midnight on two lines. The Sukumvit Line is 16.5 km long, running from Mor Chit Bus Terminal on Phahon Yothin Road to the end of Sukumvit at Sukumvit 77. It has 17 stations.

The other, the Silom Line with seven stations, starts from Sathorn Bridge and heads up Silom, Rajadamri, and Rama I Roads to the National Stadium. The two lines intersect at the Central Station at Siam Square on Rama I.

A few routes seem quite logical for the average visitor, such as starting on Silom Road and then transferring to Sukumvit Line to head out to the shopping and entertainment venues along Sukumvit. You could also continue along the Sukumvit Line to the Eastern Bus Terminal for bus connections to Pattaya and other destinations along the East Coast. The Skytrain will also prove useful for reaching the Weekend Market and the major shopping centers near Siam Square.

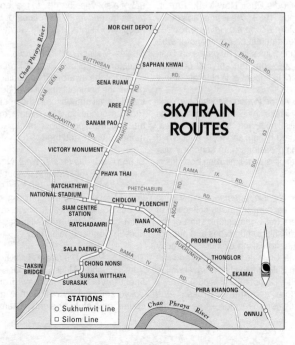

SUGGESTED READING

The following books will help orient you to Southeast Asia and Thailand, discuss the impact of mass tourism on third-world destinations, and fire up your imagination. All books are best read before departure, though *Mai Pen Rai, Culture Shock,* and *Thai Ways*—three highly recommended paperbacks—are available in Bangkok bookstores.

GENERAL TRAVEL LITERATURE

Bloodworth, Dennis. *An Eye For The Dragon.* New York: Farrar, Straus and Giroux, 1970. The former Far East correspondent of *The Observer* incisively examines the comedies and tragedies of Asia, from the fanatic wranglings of Sukarno to racial tensions in Malaysia. Bloodworth makes history and politics—often dry and dull subjects—fascinating and memorable.

Buruma, Ian. *God's Dust.* New York: Farrar, Straus and Giroux, 1989. The former arts editor for the *Far Eastern Economic Review* provides sharp and unsentimental observations of various Asian countries, including 40 pages on Thailand. Buruma questions the survival of Asian cultures against the impact of Westernization.

Fenton, James. *All the Wrong Places.* New York: Atlantic Monthly Press, 1988. In this work, James Fenton—journalist, poet, and critic—is jaundiced, self-indulgent, hard-hitting, and more concerned with personal impressions than scholarly dissertation. The result is a mesmerizing book full of great perceptions.

Iyer, Pico. *Video Night in Kathmandu.* New York: Vintage, 1988. Iyer's incongruous collection of essays uncovers the Coca-colonization of the Far East in a refreshingly humorous and perceptive style. His heartbreaking accounts of decay in the Philippines, brothels in Bangkok, and cultural collisions in Bali form the finest travel writing in the last decade. Do not miss this book.

Nelson, Theodora, and Andrea Gross. *Good Books for the Curious Traveler—Asia and the*

South Pacific. Boulder, CO: Johnson Publishing, 1989. Outstanding in-depth reviews of over 350 books, including almost 50 titles to Southeast Asia. Written with sensitivity and great insight. The authors also run a service that matches books with a traveler's itinerary. Write to Travel Source, 20103 La Roda Court, Cupertino, CA 95014, tel. (408) 446-0600.

Richter, Linda. *The Politics of Tourism in Asia.* Honolulu: University of Hawaii Press, 1989. A scholarly study of the complex political problems which confront the tourist industries in Thailand, the Philippines, and other Asian destinations. Filled with surprising conclusions about the impact of multinational firms and the importance of targeting grass-roots travelers rather than upscale tourists.

Schwartz, Brian. *A World of Villages.* New York: Crown Publishers, 1986. A superbly written journal of a six-year journey to the most remote villages in the world. Rich tales of unforgettable people and lands of infinite variety and beauty.

Shales, Melissa, ed. *The Traveler's Handbook.* Chester, CT: Globe Pequot Press, 1988. Fifth edition of the award-winning guide that puts together the contributions of over 80 experienced travelers, all authorities in their particular fields. Practical suggestions on climate, maps, airfares, internal transportation, backpacking, visas, money, health, and theft.

Simon, Ted. *Jupiter's Travels.* New York: Doubleday, 1980. Fascinating account of a 63,000-km motorcycle journey (500cc Triumph Tiger) from Europe, down the continent of Africa, and across South America, Australia, and India. And what does Ted do now? Raises organic produce in Northern California.

Theroux, Paul. *The Great Railway Bazaar.* New York: Houghton Mifflin, 1975. One of the world's finest travel writers journeys from London to Tokyo and back by rail. Rather than a dry discourse on history or sights, Theroux's masterpiece of observation keeps you riveted with personal encounters of the first order. Highly recommended.

Viviano, Frank. *Dispatches from the Pacific Century.* New York: Addison Wesley, 1993. Frank Viviano, foreign correspondent for the *San Francisco Chronicle,* has reported extensively on Asia. His 18-part narrative focuses on his encounters with ordinary individuals, rather than dry interviews with politicians or businesspeople. Viviano's consistently elegant prose and keen interest in the human element make *Dispatches* the best overview since *An Eye for the Dragon.*

DESCRIPTION AND TRAVEL

APA Insight Guides. *Thailand.* Singapore: APA Publications, 1995. Superb photography and lush text make this a useful introduction to the country. Read before traveling.

Clarac, Achille. *Guide to Thailand.* Malaysia: Oxford University Press, 1981. Published over a decade ago, but still the most comprehensive guide to the architecture of Thailand. Dated travel information but highly recommended for historical background and temple descriptions.

Jones, Tristan. *To Venture Further.* Grafton: Hearst Marine Books, 1988. Amazing true tale of how the author and his crew completed the first crossing of the Isthmus of Kra in a longtail boat; both Jones and his assistants were disabled or amputees. A memorial to the crossing is found on the southern coast of Phuket.

O'Reilly, James, and Larry Habegger. *Travelers' Tales Thailand.* Sebastopol, CA: O'Reilly & Associates, 1993. The first of a new series of travel books designed to deepen and enrich your experience in Thailand. Rather than do another guidebook, O'Reilly & Associates collected the finest descriptive writings of 46 talented writers, such as Pico Iyer, Simon Winchester, Norman Lewis, and John Hoskins. Excellent background reading.

Smithies, Michael. *Old Bangkok.* Singapore: Oxford University Press, 1988. Professor Smithies leads you around modern Bangkok but describes the modern attractions in erudite terms.

Valli, Eric, and Diane Summers. *Nest Gatherers of Tiger Cave.* London: Thames and Hudson, 1992. Large-format photography of birds' nests in Southern Thailand. The authors spent over a year living and working with nest collectors on Ko Phi Phi.

Veran, Geo. *50 Trips through Siam's Canals.* Bangkok: Duang Kamol, 1979. A fascinating but outdated guide to the confusing labyrinth of rivers and canals that stretch across southern Thailand. Included are over 30 maps, Thai prices, and brief descriptions of the temples. Later attempts to describe these canals have been less than successful.

HISTORY

Bock, Carl. *Temples and Elephants.* Singapore: Oxford University Press, 1986. Late 19th-century account of the remarkable expedition of Bock from Bangkok to the Golden Triangle. A valuable record of life in Old Siam as seen through the eyes of a percipient traveler.

Davis, Bonnie. *Postcards of Old Siam.* Singapore: Times Editions, 1987. A fascinating pictorial record of the Siamese kingdom from 1883 to WW II told with reproductions of hand-tinted black-and-white postcards.

Gray, Anthony. *The Bangkok Secret.* London: Pan, 1990. A melodramatic novel based on the mysterious death of King Ananda in 1946. The story draws heavily on Thai exotica—drug smugglers, student activists, hilltribe shamans. Gray's semi-pornographic prose and heavy cribbing from *The Devil's Discus* make the novel just as murky as whatever happened in 1946. For obvious reasons, the book is banned in Thailand.

Kruger, Rayne. *The Devil's Discus.* London: Cassell, 1964. The best historical narrative on the death of King Ananda. Sets the stage for events following the national calamity—the purge of the ruling liberals and rise of right-wing generals who oversaw three decades of repressive government until the democratic revolution of 1976. The book is banned in Thailand.

Leonowens, Anna. *The English Governess at the Siamese Court.* Singapore, Oxford University Press, 1988. The overimaginative yet entertaining memoirs of the 19th-century English governess that inspired *The King and I.* Originally written in 1870 but reprinted by Oxford in Asia.

Vincent, Frank. *The Land of the White Elephant.* New York: Harper & Brothers, 1881. One of the best travelogues of the era recounts the adventures of an observant man with cultivated tastes and catholic interests. Vincent describes his encounter with the king of Siam before tramping across the country to visit Angkor, rediscovered only 13 years prior to the publication of the book. Several of the wonderful illustrations are reproduced in this book.

Warren, William. *The Legendary American.* Boston: Houghton Mifflin, 1970. The remarkable career and strange disappearance of Jim Thompson is retold by one of Thailand's most prolific writers. Thompson almost single-handedly revived the mordant silk weaving industry in Thailand; his mysterious disappearance in the hill resort of Cameron Highlands, Malaysia, remains one of Southeast Asia's great puzzles.

Wyatt, David. *Thailand: A Short History.* New Haven: Yale University Press, 1984. The best available synopsis on Thailand is a scholarly yet catchy read for both serious students and interested laypeople seeking insight into the convolutions of Siamese history.

CURRENT EVENTS

Kulick, Elliott, and Dick Wilson. *Thailand's Turn: Profile of a New Dragon.* New York, Martins Press, 1993. Kulick, an international lawyer, and Wilson, a former editor at the *Far Eastern Economic Review,* combined their talents to produce an excellent 200-page introduction to the state of modern Thailand. It covers the problems of deforestation, landless peasants, industrial pollution, AIDS, soaring crime rates, and loss of Buddhist values. Kulick and Wilson then put forth the reasons why Thailand will meet the challenges of the next century with more success than their authoritarian neighbors. Let's hope these two are prophets in their own time.

Laothamatas, Anek. *Business Associations and the New Political Economy of Thailand.* Boulder, CO: Westview Press, 1993. Is the present government just another periodic break from military rule, or has the military elite really given up the reins of power? Major changes are suggested by the rise of nonbureaucratic institutions within the government and the ability of business interests to affect government policy. This new political model is explained in the work of Anek Laothamatas as well as in *Demi Democracy* by Likhit Dhiravegin.

Wright, Joseph. *The Balancing Act: A History of Modern Thailand.* Bangkok: Asia Books, 1991. Solid analytical framework and careful attention to detail make this a useful guide to modern Thai politics. Wright's assertion that Thailand's political culture will forever be controlled by elites helps us understand the failure of democracy but also undermines recent changes that indicate otherwise.

THE ENVIRONMENT

Boyd, Ashley, and Collin Piprell. *Thailand, The Kingdom Beneath the Sea.* Bangkok: Artasia Press, 1990. Superb photography, detailed descriptions of marinelife, and tips for scuba divers. Reprinted in 1994 by Hippocrene Books as *Diving in Thailand.*

Caufield, Catherine. *In The Rainforest.* Chicago: University of Chicago Press, 1984. Marvelous descriptive writings on tropical forests and their ongoing destruction—a story of corruption, greed, disaster, and murder told in a sympathetic yet impassioned voice.

Gray, Denis, and Collin Piprell. *The National Parks of Thailand.* Bangkok: Communications Resources, 1991. An excellent survey of 30 national parks and wildlife sanctuaries, plus background on problems faced by park rangers working to save the remaining wildlife in the parks.

Lekagul, Boonsong, and Jeffrey McNeely. *Mammals of Thailand.* Bangkok: Association for the Conservation of Wildlife, 1988. The finest overview of wildlife in Thailand is enriched with maps, photos, and sketches by two of the leading environmentalists in the country.

Lekagul, Boonsong, and Philip Round. *The Birds of Thailand.* Bangkok: Sahakarn Bhaet, 1991. A newer publication that updates the original 1974 guide written by Lekagul and Edward Cronin.

McNeely, Jeffrey, and Paul Spencer Wachtel. *Soul of the Tiger: Searching for Nature's Answers in Exotic Southeast Asia.* New York: Doubleday, 1991. This timely and ambitious book argues that the ancient relationships between humanity and nature provide the best hopes for saving the environment.

Rush, James. *The Last Tree: Reclaiming the Environment in Tropical Asia.* New York: The Asia Society, 1992. Rush uses his expertise as an historian to recount how the Asian environment has been plundered, polluted, and wrecked to the point of exhaustion in less than five decades. Rush blames both the Western world and its insatiable need for natural resources, and the Asian power elite who allow the rape to continue. Money, of course, is the motive.

ART AND ARCHITECTURE

Boisselier, Jean. *The Heritage of Thai Sculpture.* Bangkok: Asia Books, 1987. Written by one of the world's leading authorities on the art of Southeast Asia, the original 1974 edition has been reprinted and is now available from Asia Books in Bangkok.

Conway, Susan. *Thai Textiles.* Seattle: University of Washington Press, 1992. A richly illustrated work that traces the evolution of Thai weaving and costumes from early kingdoms to the 20th century.

Gosling, Betty. *Sukothai: Its History, Culture, and Art.* Singapore: Oxford University Press, 1990. Authoritative survey of the ruins of Sukothai and the lives of the kings who commissioned their construction.

Poshyananda, Apinan. *Modern Art in Thailand.* Singapore: Oxford University Press, 1993. The most important and brutally honest survey of modern Thai art is based on the author's doctoral research at Cornell. Apinan shows how Thai modernism traces its genealogy from Western sources, then continues to evolve through court patronage, nationalistic movements, the turbulent 1970s, and the unending military coups. Apinan's insight and brutal honesty about the current state of Thai art make this a rare and remarkable book.

Siribhadra, Smitthi, and Elizabeth Moore. *Palaces of the Gods: Khmer Art and Architecture in Thailand.* Bangkok: River Books, 1991. An expensive large-format book loaded with excellent photos of Cambodian monuments, all graciously described by the art historian from London's School of Oriental and African Studies.

Van Beek, Steve, and Luca Invernizzi Tettoni. *Arts of Thailand.* New York: Thames and Hudson, 1991. The best introductory guidebook to Thai arts in print. Rich text and great photos.

Warren, William, and Luca Invernizzi Tettoni. *Legendary Thailand.* Hong Kong: Travel Publishing Asia Limited, 1986. Outstanding photographs and clean text; a good introduction to the land and people.

Warren, William, and Luca Invernizzi Tettoni. *Thai Style.* Bangkok: Asia Books, 1988. Thai interior design ranks with Japanese as among the most elegant and highly refined in the world. Bill and Luca will convince you of the sensitive creativity of the Thai people.

FOOD AND SHOPPING

Brennan, Jennifer. *Thai Cooking.* London: Futura Publications, 1984. The California author lived in Thailand for almost a decade during the 1960s and returned home to teach her culinary secrets. Her book offers both dependable recipes and superb insight into the authentic styles of regional cooking.

Hoskin, John. *A Buyer's Guide to Thai Gems and Jewellery.* Bangkok: Asia Books, 1988. Essential reading for anyone contemplating a sizable purchase of gems in Thailand. Excellent photography by Michael Freeman.

Kahrs, Kurt. *Thai Cooking*. Bangkok: Asia Books, 1990. The executive chef at the Menan Hotel in Bangkok serves up delicious recipes from the various regions of Thailand. Color photographs help you visualize the final masterpiece.

Piper, Jacqueline. *Fruits of Southeast Asia*. Singapore: Oxford University Press, 1988. Practical background on the use of tropical fruits in cooking, medicine, and rituals accompanied with helpful photos and early botanical illustrations.

Reimer, Joe, and Ronald Krannich. *Shopping in Exotic Thailand*. Manassas, VA: Impact Publications, 1990. Step-by-step guide to the secrets of shopping in Thailand with detailed descriptions of shopping centers, arcades, factory outlets, and exclusive boutiques.

HEALTH

Dawood, Richard, M.D. *Traveller's Health, How to Stay Healthy Abroad*. Oxford University Press, 1994. This guide to healthy travel is very comprehensive and medically authoritative, though highly technical.

Hatt, John. *The Tropical Traveller*. Hippocrene, 1984. A readable book which served as the bible of healthy travel for many years. Remains useful for its clear descriptions of health and related travel issues such as theft, communication, and culture shock.

IAMAT Directory. The International Association for Medical Assistance to Travelers (IAMAT) in Lewiston, New York, publishes a worldwide directory of English-speaking physicians whose qualifications meet IAMAT standards and who have agreed to treat members for a set fee. Membership in IAMAT is free.

Schroeder, Dirk G., ScD, MPH. *Staying Healthy in Asia, Africa, and Latin America*. Moon Publications, 1999. A handy and compact guide that updates the original publication from Volunteers in Asia. The book includes three chapters on the prevention of illness and general health maintenance on the road, while the remainder describes the diagnosis and treatment of illnesses

common to foreign countries. Written for the average traveler in a lively and direct tone.

The Travel Clinic Directory. A free list of physicians specializing in travel medicine in the United States is available from Connaught Laboratories (tel. 717-839-7187) in Swiftwater, Pennsylvania.

Werner, David. *Where There Is No Doctor*. Hesperian Foundation, 1992. A health-care handbook written in nontechnical language with information on children's diseases, pregnancy, use of drugs with recommended dosage, and first aid in third-world countries. Designed for both certified professionals and Peace Corp volunteers intending to work abroad in remote villages.

HUMOR AND PERSONAL TALES

Eckardt, James. *Waylaid by the Bimbos*. Bangkok: Post Publishing, 1991. James Eckardt—writer-in-residence and former dominant guru in Songkhla—finally received worldwide acclaim with his deranged ramblings that resemble a Thai-style Fear and Loathing in the Land of Smiles. A weird and funny work recommended for twisted readers.

Eckardt, James. *Running With the Sharks*. Bangkok: Post Publishing, 1993. An adventure story set in South Thailand filled with assorted characters such as escapist spearfishermen, a heroin smuggler, ex-pirates, and Burmese crewmen armed with M-16s.

Hollinger, Carol. *Mai Pen Rai*. Boston: Houghton Mifflin, 1965. The story of an American housewife's humorous introduction to life in Bangkok. One of the warmest books you will ever read. Highly recommended.

Stephens, Harold. *Asian Portraits*. Hong Kong: Travel Publishing Asia, 1983. Adventurer and free spirit Stephens ran away from his English teaching position in the United States to live out his fantasies in Southeast Asia. The prolific author describes many of the fascinating expatriates he has met over the years.

CULTURE

Cooper, Robert, and Nanthapa. *Culture Shock Thailand.* Singapore: Times Editions, 1993. A humorous paperback that succinctly explains the Thai people, their customs, and hidden rules of social etiquette. Filled with great insight and charm but minimal clichés about the "Land of Smiles." Widely available in Bangkok bookstores; highly recommended.

Cooper, Robert. *Thais Mean Business: The Foreign Businessman's Guide to Doing Business in Thailand.* Singapore: Times Editions, 1993. Cooper, an anthropologist, and his wife Nanthapa forgo ludicrous cultural fantasies to explain cultural idiosyncrasies and prove that cultural awareness is profitable. A serious subject treated with great humor.

Fieg, John Paul. *A Common Core: Thais and Americans.* New York: Intercultural Press, 1989. A fine book explaining with great insight the key similarities and differences between Western and Thai cultures. Highly recommended for any visitor who intends to live or work in Thailand.

Segaller, Denis. *Thai Ways.* Bangkok: Allied Newspapers, 1984. A collection of short essays on Thai ceremonies, festivals, customs, and beliefs. This and the sequel *More Thai Ways* are great books to read while traveling in the country.

Smithies, Michael. *Bight of Bangkok.* Singapore, Heinemann Asia, 1994. The widely published scholar of Asia addresses the forces of modernization in this hard-hitting but realistic look into the underside of a threatened Thai society. His dozen fictional profiles of local residents are based on real stories collected from local newspapers: the mother who trades her two teenage daughters for a red motorcycle; the transvestite hooker with a heart of gold; a three-year-old Buddhist faith healer in the northeast.

HILLTRIBES

Anderson, Edward. *Plants and People of the Golden Triangle: Ethnobotany of the Hill Tribes of Northern Thailand.* Portland, OR: Dioscorides Press, 1994. A botanist at the Desert Botanical Garden in Phoenix, Anderson explores the ethnobotany of the hilltribes and problems associated with the loss of plants used for medicinal purposes, construction, and pleasure.

Campbell, Margaret. *From the Hands of the Hills.* Hong Kong: Media TransAsia, 1978. Lavishly illustrated guide to the handicrafts of the hilltribes.

Grunfeld, Frederic. *Wayfarers of the Thai Forest: The Akha.* New York: Time-Life Books, 1982. Photographic essay on the poorest and most ill-treated of the northern tribes.

Lewis, Paul, and Elaine Lewis. *Peoples of the Golden Triangle.* London: Thames and Hudson, 1984. Paul and Elaine have worked as missionaries in northern Thailand since 1947. This lavishly illustrated book is the best guide available to these intriguing peoples.

Wijeyewardene, Gehen, ed. *Ethnic Groups Across National Boundaries in Southeast Asia.* Singapore: Institute of Southeast Asian Studies, 1990. This collection of essays argues ethnicity is a modern invention, despite the claims of anthropologists who believe ethnicity can be defined by language and historical migrations. The minorities of Thailand threaten government assertions of racial purity and cultural superiority; this sets them on a collision course with the ruling state.

RELIGION

Ross, Nancy. *Three Ways of Asian Wisdom.* New York: Simon and Schuster, 1966. A great and powerful book—beautifully written, well organized, and full of love and understanding. Now considered among the finest books on Asian religions; a superb introduction for the reasonably intelligent reader without prior exposure to Hinduism, Buddhism, and Zen. Highly recommended.

Ward, Timothy. *What the Buddha Never Taught.* Berkeley, CA: Celestial Arts, 1993. Timothy Ward recounts his experiences at a Buddhist monastery in northeastern Thailand (Wat Pa Nanachat) and describes the conflict and disillusion encountered by many Westerners during their initial encounters with Buddhist monastic practices. An amusing but superficial tale told by a young man who stayed only six weeks before reaching his sad and misguided conclusions.

Weir, Bill. *A Guide to Buddhist Monasteries and Meditation Centers in Thailand.* Bangkok: World Fellowship of Buddhists, 1995. The best currently available survey of the meditation retreats of Thailand was meticulously researched and compiled by the author of Moon Publications' guides to Arizona and Utah. Bill's superb tome includes a brief description of Buddhism, advice on living for extended periods in a retreat, and an exhaustive list of all temples that accept Western novices.

Wray, Elizabeth. *Ten Lives of the Buddha.* This beautifully illustrated book describes the final 10 lives of the Buddha from the ancient Jataka tales of the Mahabharta. Filled with rare photos of murals from Wat Suwannaram in Thonburi, Wat Yai Intharam in Chonburi, and Wat Buddhasawan in Ayuthaya.

DRUGS AND PROSTITUTION

Belanger, Francis. *Drugs, the U.S., and Khun Sa.* Bangkok: DK Books, 1989. A brief survey of opium production and profile of drug kingpin Khun Sa. Now badly dated but useful for its hardhitting accusations against almost everyone connected with the drug industry.

Marshall, Jonathan. *Drug Wars—Corruption, Counterinsurgency and Covert Operations in the Third World.* San Francisco: Cohan & Cohen, 1991. A former economics editor at the *San Francisco Chronicle,* Marshall provides further support to the views of Alfred McCoy that America's costly war to stop drugs at their source has been both hypocritical and ineffective.

McCoy, Alfred. *The Politics of Heroin: CIA Complicity in the Global Drug Trade.* New York: Lawrence Hill, 1991. The Wisconsin University history professor updates his 1972 classic with new information on CIA collaboration with Thai heroin smugglers, Panama's Noriega, Afghan *mujahedeen,* the Sandinistas, and the Pakistani military.

Moore, Christopher. *A Killing Smile.* Bangkok: White Lotus, 1991. Moore peers into the rotten world of bars and prostitution. This fictional account of life in Bangkok's Thermae Cafe then becomes a pedantic lecture on morality with an unbalanced mix of honest *farang* and corrupt bargirls. His "Land of Smiles" trilogy continues with *A Bewitching Smile* and *A Haunting Smile.*

Truong, Thanh Dam. *Sex, Money and Morality: Prostitution and Tourism in Southeast Asia.* London: Zed Press, 1994. A critical and highly charged account of the sex industry in Thailand. Zed Press also publishes *Access to Justice: The Struggle for Human Rights in Southeast Asia.*

THAI AUTHORS

Ekachai, Samitsuda. *Behind the Smile: Voices of Thailand.* Bangkok: Post Publishing, 1990. Revealing interviews by a *Bangkok Post* journalist with impoverished Thai peasants in the Northeast. Valuable insight into the effect of unparalleled economic growth on the rural poor of Thailand.

Majupuria, Trilok Chandra. *Erawan Shrine and Brahma Worship in Thailand.* Bangkok: Tepress Press, 1990. Concise introduction to the complexities of Thai religion and animistic practices that overlay contemporary Buddhism.

Pramoj, Kukrit. *Four Reigns.* Bangkok: DK Books, 1953. Historical romance spanning the reigns of Rama V to Rama VIII written by a former prime minister and movie star *(The Ugly American).* Pramoj's novel about a noble family has been remade into films, plays, and TV dramas that feature the central character as the archetypical femme fatale.

Rajadhon, Phya Anuman. *Some Traditions of the Thai.* Bangkok: DK Books, 1993. Detailed essays on traditional society written by one of Thailand's leading scholars.

Sivaraksa, Sulak. *Siam in Crisis.* Bangkok: DK Books, 1986. An unusual analysis of Thai politics from one of Thailand's leading intellectuals and political dissidents. Sivaraksa melds Thai Buddhism with his admiration for individualism into themes of disenfranchisement in a burgeoning economy. Although he was forced to flee the country several years ago after accusations of lese majesty, Sivaraksa has returned to continue his biting criticisms of Thai society.

Sudham, Pira. *People of Esarn.* Bangkok: Siam Media International, 1988. Thailand's most well-known author who writes in the English language brings great insight into the realities of poverty in northeastern Thailand. Sudham also wrote *Siamese Drama* (1983) and *Monsoon Country* (1988), and today enjoys a lifestyle in striking contrast to his impoverished background—successful businessman and former president of the Siam Wine Society.

Good Reading

Conrad, Joseph. *Lord Jim.* London: Penguin, 1900. Conrad's place as one of the greatest writers in the English language was established several years after his visit to Bangkok in 1887 to assume control of a vessel carrying teak to Australia. His three-week visit to Bangkok was spent in the billiards room at the Oriental Hotel (he never stayed there) and on a leisurely excursion to Ayuthaya by two-wheeled gig.

Eames, Andrew. *Crossing the Shadow Line.* London, Hodder and Stoughton, 1986. Eames's account of a two-year odyssey through Southeast Asia speaks of crossing Joseph Conrad's "shadow line" between sanity and madness, youth and maturity. His vivid reporting and personal candor cover the philosophical matters faced by many modern travelers.

Gray, Spaulding. *Swimming to Cambodia.* New York: Theater Group, 1985. Monologist Gray describes his experiences in Thailand during the production of *The Killing Fields* with great insight into the emotional impact of Thailand on a Western visitor. The book later became the movie of the same name.

Maugham, Somerset. *The Gentleman in the Parlour.* London: Heinemann, 1930. A record of the author's journey from Yangon to Haiphong in the early 1920s. Perhaps inspired by a meeting with Joseph Conrad in the spring of 1918, Maugham's subsequent 60 years of creative output eventually shaped many popular conceptions of life in Southeast Asia.

Thompson, Thomas. *Serpentine.* New York: Doubleday, 1979. The true story of Charles Sobhraj, the so-called "bikini killer," who terrorized the continent from India to Thailand until his capture by the Indian police. A compelling, exotic, glamorous, and completely frightening story about psychopaths who wander the backstreets of Southeast Asia.

Young, Gavin. *In Search of Conrad.* London: Hutchinson, 1991. A well-known British writer attempts to retrace the steps of Conrad while interlacing his impressions of the region with quirky opinions about contemporary social issues.

ELECTRONIC SOURCES OF TRAVEL INFORMATION

Surfing the information superhighway is the hottest way to find travel information about every nook and cranny of the planet. With enough hardware and computer expertise you could:

- Retrieve a 40-page country report on Thailand, courtesy of a World Wide Web site
- Add a chapter or two of visitor comments from the Rec.Travel Library at the University of Manitoba in Winnipeg
- Read the CIA's assessment of the country, including concise and detailed advice helpful to the traveler
- Attach a satellite photo of current weather patterns over a map of the country
- Pick up the latest news on political and economic developments from various news services
- Find current travel advisories issued by the U.S. State Department
- Determine the currency exchange rate from Global Network Navigator
- Chat online with a famous travel writer
- Ask for travel advice from an expatriate in Bangkok
- Uncover the newest nightclubs recommended by Worldview Systems
- Check out upcoming adventure tours offered by Mountain Travel Sobek
- Print the whole thing out

• Return your copy of *Thailand Handbook* for a refund

Internet Resources
The easiest way to get started is with a major online service such as America Online (tel. 800-827-6364), CompuServe (tel. 800-848-8199), Prodigy (tel. 800-776-3449), or Delphi (tel. 800-695-4005). All offer special travel forums, e-mail addresses, chat lines, and limited access to the Internet.

You can also get connected directly to the Net through an Internet provider such as Netcom (tel. 800-353-6600). Once hooked up—and familiar with terms like Mosaic, World Wide Web, Gopher, Archie, and Usenet—you're part of an electronic community consisting of over 20 million individuals and 10,000 databases covering every possible field of human endeavor.

The biggest problem is navigating the murky waters of cyberspace. A good place to start is the Traveler's Center from the Global Network Navigator (GNN) Travel Center, a project of O'Reilly & Associates (tel. 800-998-9938) in Northern California. GNN combs the Internet gathering the best travel tips for their readers and dividing it into five sections: Editor's Notes (new communications and editorial advice), Notes from the Road (columns from regional correspondents), Internet Resources (information gathered from websites), Traveler's Marketplace (commercial listings), and Regions in Focus (such as Thailand).

Perhaps the largest travel database is Rec.Travel Library, a nonprofit information service established by the University of Manitoba in Winnipeg with mirror server sites around the world. Rec.Travel is the repository for thousands of travel resources covering every possible topic and worldwide destination. Rec.Travel Library may be reached via tel. (204) 992-2312, fax (204) 831-5583, e-mail: lucas@mbnet.mb.ca, or website www.mbnet.mb.ca/lucas

Two net groups worth checking for online chat are rec.travel.asia (general travel talk) and soc.culture.thailand (political, social issues, etc.).

Travel Publishers and Services
Contact Moon Publications for the current issue of *Travel Matters,* search for health tips, download the Moon booklist, and contact Moon authors. Lonely Planet and other publishers also are online.

Travel Guides and Magazines:
Moon Publications: www.moon.com
Lonely Planet: www.lonelyplanet.com
Condé Nast Traveler: www.cntraveler.com
Destination Vietnam:
  www/well.com/www/gdisf

Tours and Tourism:
Mountain Travel Sobek: www.mtsobek.com
Pacific Area Travel Assoc.:
  www.singapore.com/pata/
Global Travel Village: www.neptune.com
Travel Connection:
  www.kaiwan.com/-travel/agents
TEN IO: www.ten-io.com

General Information:
Adventure Travel Books: www.gorp.com/at-book.htm
Fodor WorldView:
  gnn.com/gnn/bus/wview/index.html
travel library: ftp.cc.umanitoba.ca
exchange rates: gnn.com/cgi-bin/gnn/currency
youth hostels: www.hostels.com/hostels
homestay exchange: hospex.icm.edu.pl
city sites: www.city.net
U.S. govt. maps: www.usgs.gov/
maps: www.lib.utexas.edup

THE THAI LANGUAGE

Far too many travel books have called Thai an impossible language. The truth is that the vocabulary and syntax are not difficult to grasp and dedicated students can learn to speak some Thai within a few weeks. Even a few rudimentary phrases will help you make friends and save money.

Thai is a monosyllabic, tonal language with 44 consonants, 24 vowels, and five tones. Script is written from left to right without separation between words. There are no prefixes or suffixes, genders, articles, plurals, or verb conjugations. If this makes Thai seem a simple language, think again.

Thai is a tonal language in which each syllable cluster can be pronounced with five different tones: low, middle, high, rising, or falling. Each tone completely changes the meaning of the word. *Suay* with a rising tone means "beautiful" but with a falling tone means "bad fortune." Therefore, Thai pronunciation should be checked with a native speaker for the correct inflection.

Thai Script

The principal "letters" you see in Thai script are the consonants; vowels are represented by a series of squiggles written above, below, behind, or in front of the consonants. This complication means that most visitors should first learn to speak a modest vocabulary before attempting to learn any Thai script. Additionally, most signs at tourist destinations and along highways now show both Thai and Western script, so Westerners on shorter vacations will have few problems making sense of the more important signs in the country.

From English to Thai

Translating English into Thai also poses problems. A few years ago, Pepsi-Cola entered the local soft drink market with their familiar slogan, "Come Alive, Join the Pepsi Generation." But the translation came out as "Drink Pepsi and Bring Your Ancestors Back from the Dead." The wording was quickly changed, but humor columnist Job Bob noted that the mistranslated pro-

motion was "the only thing that could make Texans swear off all forms of drinking permanently."

Thai Challenges

Westerners who speak non-tonal languages such as English will find that tones are initially a big challenge since we are not accustomed to listening to or associating tones with words in this way. But this must be done. To speak Thai without including the proper tone will result in confusion and, in many cases, peals of laughter from highly amused Thais who appreciate your efforts but find your tonal mishaps a source of constant fun.

Tonal ignorance is the biggest challenge, but another problem for Western visitors is our tendency to use Western-style inflection in our sentences, such as a rising inflection at the end of any sentence that is a question. "Where did you go today?" is pronounced with a rising "today" to indicate that this is a question and not a statement. We also indicate anger, joy, threats, sexiness and other emotions with our Western tonal inflections. You'll have to break these tendencies—and the urge to express emotions with your tone—to speak Thai properly.

An additional obstacle to speaking and learning Thai is that many consonants, vowels, and diphthongs are completely unique sounds with no equivalents in English or other Western languages and no accepted standardization of spelling. Thus, Thai words can be spelled several different ways—such as the avenue in Bangkok variously rendered as Rajadamnern, Ratchadamnoen, and Rajdamnoen. A town south of Bangkok can be spelled either Petchburi, Petchaburi, or Phetchaburi. In general the transliteration from Thai sounds to Western script is a very imprecise science and what you read may not exactly correlate with the proper Thai pronunciation. Several unique Thai sounds cannot properly be expressed with Roman letters. For example, there are sounds midway between "d" and "t" and others midway between "b" and "p". Fortunately, Thai pronunciation is much more logical and consistent than English. Pity the poor

Thai student studying English when confronted with cough, rough, though, thought, and through!

The best way for Westerners to get around this stumbling block is to listen carefully to Thai speakers and ask for their help with your pronunciation at every possible opportunity. The simplest possible spelling has been used in this book, but it's no more correct than the system used in other travel guidebooks.

Pronunciation

Thai uses five different tones—low, middle, high, falling, and rising—to alter the meaning of each word in five different ways. The individual tones are represented as low tone (`), high tone (´), falling tone (^), and rising tone ( ). No mark is used to indicate middle tones.

The pitch of each tone is determined by average vocal range. Low, middle, and high tones are variations of one's average tonal range, and each tone is pronounced evenly with no vocal inflection. They don't rise or fall but are flat tones spoken at slightly different vocal ranges.

The falling tone is spoken with an obvious drop in pitch, with the loudest part at the beginning of the tone with a quick drop-off into vocal oblivion. The rising tone is quite similar to the Western tone use when asking a question. "Yes?" has the same tonal pattern as the rising tone *"măi."*

The Thai word *mai* is a classic example of the effect of tonal variation which has different meanings depending on the tone. The low-tone *mài* (say it low and soft) means "new," the no-tone (or middle-tone) *mai* means "burn," and the high-tone (say it a little louder and at a higher pitch) *mái* means "question?" The falling-tone *mâi* is a negative indicator, and the rising-tone *măi* means "wood." Therefore, if you say "Mai, mai, mai, mai, mai" with five different inflections, you have said "New wood doesn't burn, does it?" This same principal applies to all other Thai words, which means that you must memorize not only the word but also the proper tone for each particular meaning.

Pronunciation Tips

The various ways to pronounce consonants and vowels are described below, though Thai has a few other common quirks to keep in mind.

B: The Thai "b" is pronounced like the English "p." For example, King Bhumibol is actually pronounced King Pumiphon. The "l" changes to the sound of an "n" (see below).

V: The "v" sound doesn't exist in the Thai language. Any Thai word with a "v" should be pronounced as if written with a "w." Sukumvit Road is actually pronounced "Sukumwit Road."

L and R: These two letters are often used interchangeably in written English and their pronunciation changes to "n" when used at the end of a word. Satul (a fairly rare spelling of a town in southern Thailand) is therefore pronounced "Satun," while *banhar* is pronounced as "banharn."

A and U: These two letters are also used interchangeably in the English transliteration of the Thai language. Therefore, you will find "tam" and "tum" to have the same meaning.

Consonants and Vowels

When you read a Thai word written in English script, you may need to pronounce the word with an original Thai tone. Most of these English transliterations are pronounced the same as in English, though the following letters and combinations of letters have slightly different pronunciations that you might expect.

Once again, the best way to figure out correct pronunciation is to listen to a native Thai speaker or purchase a Thai language cassette or CD-ROM as a learning tool.

Consonants

Most of the 44 Thai consonants are pronounced exactly like English, though the following English-script equivalent of Thai consonants have unique sounds which should be mastered.

th / as a "d" or the "t" in "tea" rather than the "th" in "the"

ph / as the "p" in "put" and never as the "ph" in phone

kh / as the "k" in "keep

k / flat and closer or a "g" than a "k" sound

t / flat and closer to a "d" than a "t" sound

p / flat and closer to a "b" than a "p" sound

ng / as the "ng" at the end of "sing"

r / flat and closer to a "l" than a "r" sound

Vowels

Many Thai vowels carry unique types of sounds somewhat different than in English.

a / short "a" as in "dad"

aa / long "a" as in "father"

ai / long "i" as the "i" in "pipe"

ae / nasal "a" as in "bat"

ao / nasal inflection as in "now"

aw / as in "awe"

ay / long "I" as in "buy"

e / as the "e" in "pen"

ee / as the "ee" in "feet"

eh / as the "a" in "gate"

eu / as the "deux" sound in French

i / as the "i" in "tip"

ia / say "eee" then "yah"

o / as the "o" in "bone"

oe / short "u" sound as in "hut"

oh / as the "o" in "toe"

u / as the "u" in "loot"

uu / as the "oo" in "food"

More Language Tips

Several other important points should be made before launching into a list of words and useful phrases.

Polite Particles: Expressions of politeness are tacked to the end of most sentences, depending on whether the speaker is male or female. Male speakers should add *"kráp"* (with a high and strong tone!) at the end of most statements or questions, while females should add *"kà"* (with a soft and falling tone). Thus, men use the phrase *"sawàsdee kráp"* (a general greeting) while females say *"sawàsdee kà."*

Negatives with Falling Tone *"Mai":* Negatives are indicated by putting a falling tone *"mâi"* before a verb or adjective. For example, *"sabai"* means "well" and *"mâi sabai"* means "not well."

Questions with Rising Tone *"Mǎi":* Questions are created by adding a rising tone *"mǎi"* at the end of a phrase, somewhat similar to tacking on "isn't it?" to an English language statement. Therefore, *"kow dai mǎi"* means "may I come in?" Remember, when asking a question to a Thai, add a *"mǎi"* to the end of the sentence

rather than raising the inflection of the final word (as you normally do in English).

Common Expressions

Here are a few phrases for the first-time visitor.

Mâi pen rai: Roughly translates to "Never mind" or "It doesn't matter." It suggests a state of mind similar to the Buddhist disregard of the unimportant events of life since what happens is inevitable and it doesn't help to get uptight. This rather happy-go-lucky attitude is an essential element of the Thai spirit, although it can irritate the rigid Westerner. Learning to say *mâi pen rai* in the event of a delayed train or lost luggage will help you keep your sanity while on the road.

Sanùk: "Pleasure" or "fun." Thais believe life is meaningless without fun! High value is placed on whether something is pleasurable or not. Food, drink, sex, sports, festivals, and fairs are all great fun. Even a poorly paid job is acceptable if pleasurable. *Tuk tuk* drivers roar around corners on two wheels for the sake of *sanùk*.

Pai tio: To wander aimlessly, hang out, or just waste time. Going *pai tio* is definitely *sanuk*. Strolling aimlessly on a warm evening is the ultimate in *pai tio*. When a Thai asks you where you are going, just respond with a friendly *"pai tio."*

USEFUL TRAVELER'S PHRASES AND VOCABULARY

Greetings

hello / *sawàsdee*

How are you? / *pen yangai?*

I'm fine. / *sabày dit*

Thank you. / *kàwp khun*

Excuse me. / *khǎw thâwt*

Good luck. / *chôck dee*

please / *kor*

Language Difficulties

Do you understand? / *khâw jai mǎi?*

I don't understand. / *mâi khâw jai*

I speak little Thai. / *puût pasǎ Thai nitnòy*

It doesn't matter. / *mâi pen rai*

Questions, Requests, and Answers

Can I take a photo? / *tai ruûp dâi mâi?*
How far? / *kiai taôrai?*
How long? / *nan taôrai?*
How much? / *taô rai?*
How? / *yang rai?*
I don't know. / *mâi róo*
I want . . . /
  dichán tonggam . . . (spoken by female)
I want . . . /
  pŏm tonggam . . . (spoken by male)
What does that mean? /
  maăi kwarm wâa arai?
What is the problem? / *mee punhăa arai?*
What's this called in Thai? /
  née pasă Thai riàk waâ arrai?
When? / *meûa rai?*
Where is . . . ? / *. . . yutînăi?*
Where? / *tinăi?*
Who? / *krai?*
Why? / *tammăi?*
don't have / *mâi mee*
don't want / *mâi aò*
no / *mâi*
no good / *mâi dee*
okay / *oh-kay*
sorry / *kŏr tôwt*
yes / *châi*

Transportation

Where is the bus station? /
  sattăni rót may yutînăi?
How many buses per day? /
  rót may òrk wan la geè tiâo?
When is the first bus? /
  rót may tiâo râck òrk geè mong?
When is the last bus? /
  rót may tiâo sutái òrk geè mong?
When is the next bus? /
  rót may tiâo nâa òrk geè mong
When does the bus arrive? /
  rót may maa tỷ ng geè mong?
Where can I leave my luggage? /
  gapao ao wai têe năi dee?

Can you buy a ticket for me? /
  *chuây sỷ y tŭa hâi dichán (spoken by
  female)*
Can you buy a ticket for me? /
  chuây sỷ y tŭa hâi pŏm (spoken by male)
Please write down the timetable. /
  chuây kiăn
boat / *rya*
boat dock / *tah rya*
boat, longtail / *rya hang yao*
bus, air-conditioned / *rót tooa*
bus, mini / *rót sŏng tăyo*
bus, ordinary / *rót tammada*
bus station / *sattăni rót may*
express / *duan*
ferry / *rya doy sam*
ferry pier / *thaa rya doy sam*
plane / *kryang bin*
seat / *têe nâng*
sleeper / *tôa non*
ticket / *tŭa*
timetable / *tarang welaa*
train / *rót fai*
train station / *sattăni rót fai*

Vehicle Rentals

Where can I rent a bicycle? /
  châo rót jakayarn têe năi?
Where can I rent a car and driver? /
  châo rót próm kon úp daî têe năi?
Where can I rent a motorcycle? /
  châo rót motorsay têe năi?
Where can I hire a boat? /
  châo rya têe năi?
How much per hour? /
  káh châo chuamong la tâorai?
How much for a half-day? / *kryng wan tâorai?*
How much for one day? / *wan nỳing tâorai?*
bicycle / *rót jàkrayan*
driver/guide / *kon kúp rót*
motorcycle / *rót motorsai*
motorcycle taxi / *rót motorsai láp jârng*
taxi / *teksî*

Destinations

airline office / *têe tam ngam saăi kam bin*
airport / *sanăm bin*
bank / *tanakan*
beach / *hàt*
bookshop / *rám kăi nangsyý*
drugstore / *ráhn kaiyăa*
embassy / *sathăn tôot*
gas station / *pam namman*
hospital / *rong payabaan*
market / *talaàt*
museum / *pipitaphan*
police station / *sattăni tamrùat*
post office / *praisinee*
restaurant / *ráan ahăan*
temple / *wàt*
tourist office / *samnakngan karn tong tiâo*

Accommodations

May I see the room? / *doo hôrg dâi măi?*
Can you give me a discount? /
  lòt raakah dâi măi?
bathroom / *hông naám*
bathroom, men's / *hông naám chai*
bathroom, women's / *hong naám ying*
dormitory / *hŏr púck*
guesthouse / *guest how*
hotel / *rong raem*
hotel, budget / *rong raem tùke*
hotel, good / *rong raem dee*
mosquito net / *mûng*
room with air-conditioning / *hông air*
room with bath / *hông têe mee hông naam*
room, double / *hông kôo*
room, single / *hông dêeo*
room, triple / *hông non sărm kon*
sheets / *pâr poo têe non*
shower / *aàp naám duay fárk bua*
shower with hot water / *naám ron*
telephone (noun) / *tora sap*
towel / *pâr chét tua*

Medical

I need a doctor. / *tong hăa mŏr*
I need a dentist. / *tong hăa mŏr fun*
Please help. / *chuây duây*
cold (adj.) / *pen wàt*
diarrhea / *tóng dern*
drugstore / *rárn kai yaa*
emergency / *chúg chĕrn*
fever / *kaî*
headache / *puàt hua*
hospital / *rong payabuarn*
sick / *mâi sabai*
sore throat / *jèp kor*

Shopping

How much is this? / *nee taôrai?*
Do you have? / *mee măi?*
Do you have anything cheaper? /
  toòk gwa née mee măi?
Can you give me a better price? /
  loàt raakah dâi măi?
I will come back. /
  dichán ja giàp maa (spoken by female)
I will come back. /
  pŏm ja giàp maa (spoken by male)
new / *mai*
old / *gaò*
too big / *yài kern pai*
too expensive / *paeng pai*
too small / *lék kern pai*

Personal Questions

What is your name? / *khun chêu arrai?*
My name is . . . /
  dichán chêu . . . (spoken by female)
My name is . . .
  pôm chêu . . . (spoken by male)
Where are you from? / *khun maa jàk năi?*
I come from . . . /
  dichăn maa jàak . . . (spoken by female)
I come from . . .
  phŏm maa jàak . . . (spoken by male)
America/Canada/Australia /
  Ameriga/Kanada/Australia

British/French/Italian / *Angrit/Farangset/Italee*
Where are you going? / *pai nǎi?*
I'm just having fun. / *pai thîaw*
How old are you? / *kun aayú taôrai?*

Family Status

married / *tangngam layo*
single / *pen soàt*
husband / *sǎr mee*
wife / *phanlaya*
mother / *mâre*
father / *pôr*
children / *lûke*
son / *lûke chai*
daughter / *sǎo*
brother / *pêe (older), nóng (younger)*
sister / *chai (older), sǎo (younger)*

Flattery

The food is delicious. / *ahǎan arròi*
The food is excellent. / *arròi maâk*
Cheers! / *chai yo*
I had a great time. /
    dâi ráb kwam sanùk sabai
I love this town. / *myang nêe pǒm chôp mârk
    (spoken by female)*
I love this town. /
    *myang nêe dichán chôp mârk
    (spoken by male)*
beautiful / *suǎy maâk*
excellent / *dee maâk*
good / *dee*
interesting / *nâr son jai maâk*

Directions

How far is it to . . . ? / *pai . . . taôrai?*
How many kilometers? / *gi kilo pai?*
I want to see . . . /
    dichán yùck doo . . . (spoken by female)
I want to see . . . /
    pǒm yùck doo . . . (spoken by male)
I'm going to . . . / *pai . . .*
Let's go. / *pai ler ee*

Stop here. / *yùd tî nêe*
Wait here. / *ror têe nêe*
Where can I get a map? /
    sýy pǎntêe têe nǎi dâi?
fast / *rayo*
slow / *cháa*
slow down / *cha cha noi*
straight ahead / *trong pai*
turn left / *leó sai*
turn right / *leó kwǎ*
east / *tawanòrk*
north / *neua*
south / *tâi*
west / *tawantòk*

Geographical Terminology

bay / *ào*
beach / *hàt*
bridge / *saphan*
canal / *klong*
cape / *laem*
city / *nakhon*
district / *amphoe*
hill / *khâo*
island / *kò*
lane / *soi*
mountain / *doi*
pier / *tha*
province / *changwàt*
river / *mae nám*
street / *thanôn*
town / *muang*
village / *ban*
waterfall / *nám tòk*

Time

What is the time? / *kee mohng láew?*
afternoon / *bai*
day / *wan*
evening / *yen*
month / *deuan*
morning / *ton chaó*

now / *deeo née*	
this evening / *ye née*	
today / *wan née*	
tomorrow / *prung née*	
tonight / *kern née*	
year / *pee*	
yesterday / *mya wan née*	

60	*hòk-sìp*
70	*jèt-sìp*
80	*baàt-sìp*
90	*gôw-sìp*
100	*neùng rói*
500	*hâ rói*
1,000	*neùng pan*
10,000	*mern*
20,000	*sŏng mern*
100,000	*sǎn*
1,000,000	*lárn*

Days of the Week

Sunday / *wan aathit*
Monday / *wan jan*
Tuesday / *wan ang kan*
Wednesday / *wan poót*
Thursday / *wan prýhàrt*
Friday / *wan sòok*
Saturday / *wan sǎo*

Numbers

0	*suun*
1	*neùng*
2	*sŏng*
3	*sǎm*
4	*si*
5	*hâ*
6	*hòk*
7	*jèt*
8	*baàt*
9	*gôw*
10	*sìp*
11	*sìp-èt*
12	*sìp-sŏng*
13	*sìp-sǎm*
14	*sìp-si*
15	*sìp-hâ*
16	*sìp-hòk*
17	*sìp-jèt*
18	*sìp-baàt*
19	*sìp-gôw*
20	*yî-sìp*
30	*sǎm-sìp*
40	*si-sìp*
50	*hâ-sìp*

FOOD PHRASES AND VOCABULARY

General Terms

to eat / *kin*
to drink / *duem*
breakfast / *ahâan cháo*
lunch / *ahâan glang wan*
dinner / *ahâan kam*
snack / *klaem*
classic meal of the north / *khan toke*

Ordering

Please bring me the menu. / *kǒr doo menu*
May I have . . . ? / *kǒr . . . ?*
Let's eat! / *cher tarn ná kâ (spoken by female)*
Let's eat! /
  chern tam ná kráp (spoken by male)
The bill please. / *kǒr check bin*
Have you eaten? / *Kin khâo?*
Do you have . . . ? / *. . . mi mâi?*
I'm a vegetarian. / *kin jeh*
I can't eat beef. / *kin néua mâi dâi*
I can't eat pork. / *kin mu mâi dâi*
I don't like hot or spicy. / *mâi châwp phèt*
I like it hot and spicy. / *châwp phèt*
I can eat Thai food. / *kin ahâan Thai pen*

Places to Eat

cafe / *raan*

cafe, Chinese thick-rice / *ráan khâo tôm*
cafe, curry-and-rice / *ráan khâo kaeng*
garden restaurant / *ráan suan*
market / *talaat*
night market / *talaat toh rung*
noodle shop / *ráan kuay teow*
restaurant / *ráan ahâan*
vegetarian restaurant /
 ráan ahâan mangsâwirát

Adjectives

bitter / *khôm*
cold / *yen*
dry (without soup) / *haeng*
hot (temperature) / *ráwn*
hot and spicy / *châwp phèt*
hot, a little / *phèt nít nòy*
hot, not at all / *mâi phèt*
large, big / *yai*
liquid (as in curry or soup) / *gaeng*
raw, half-cooked / *dip*
salty / *khem*
sour / *brio*
spicy / *phèt*

Basic Ingredients

bread / *khanôm pan*
cake, biscuit / *khanôm*
egg / *khài*
salt / *kleua*
salted egg / *khài khem*
sugar / *nám tan*

Beverages

coffee, iced, black with sugar / *o liang*
ice / *nám khãeng*
lemon juice / *nám manao*
milk / *nom*
orange juice / *nám sõm*
rice liquor / *lâo kão*
rum, made from sugar cane / *sàng sõm*
tea / *nám cha*
water, boiled / *nám tôm*

water, drinking / *nám dèum*
water, plain / *nám plào*
water, purified bottled / *nám dèum khùat*
whiskey, Thai (national brand) / *Mêkõng*

Cooking Methods

baked, toasted / *ping*
barbecued, roasted / *yang*
boiled / *dom*
boiled until jelled / *long*
fried / *pat*
ground, grated / *see*
roasted / *phao*
steamed / *neung*
stir-fried / *taud*
stuffed / *sawd sai*

Fruits

banana / *klûay*
coconut / *máphráo*
custard apple / *náwy naa*
durian / *thúrian*
guava / *faràng*
jackfruit / *khanun*
lime / *mánao*
longan / *lam yài*
mandarin orange / *sôm*
mango / *mámûang*
mangosteen / *mangkút*
papaya / *málákaw*
pineapple / *sàppàrót*
pomelo / *sôm oh*
rambeh / *máfai*
rambutan / *ngáw*
rose apple / *chom phû*
sapodilla / *lamut*
tamarind / *mákhãm*
watermelon / *taeng moh*

Meats

beef / *núa*
bird / *nok*

chicken / *gài*
duck / *pèt*
frog / *kob*
meatball / *luchin nua*
pork / *mú*
poultry / *gài lae pèt*
quail / *nok krataa*
rabbit / *kratai*
spiced minced ground beef / *laab*
spicy sausages / *nem*
tongue / *lin*

Seafood

crab / *pu*
dried fish / *kûng haeng*
fish / *pla*
lobster / *kûng talai*
mussel / *hôi malaeng po*
oyster / *hoi naang rom*
prawn / *kûng foi*
scallop / *hôi shell*
shellfish / *hôi*

Vegetables

bean / *thua phuu*
bean sprouts / *thua ngok*
bitter melon / *márá jeen*
brinjal / *màkhĕua prà*
cabbage / *phàk kà làm*
cauliflower / *dàwk kà làm*
corn / *khâo phôht*
cucumber / *taeng kwa*
eggplant / *màkhĕua mûang*
garlic / *kràtiam*
lettuce / *phàk kàat*
long bean / *thùa fák yao*
mushroom / *hèt*
onion bulb / *hua hăwm*
onion scallions / *tôn hăwm*
peanuts / *tùa lisŏng*
potato / *man faràng*
pumpkin / *fák thawng*
spinach / *pàk kôhm*
taro / *pheùak*
tomato / *màkhĕua thêt*

GLOSSARY

aahan—food
achaan—religious leader; teacher
amphoe—district
amphoe muang—provincial capital
ao—bay
apsara—female celestial being
Avalokitesvara—a principal bodhisattva

ban—village
ba nam ran—hot springs
bang—village along a waterway
bhikku—Buddhist monk
bo—tree under which the Buddha became enlightened
bodhisattva—saint in Mahayana Buddhism; the future Buddha in previous incarnations in Theravada Buddhism; an enlightened being who has returned to help humans
bot—temple building for sermons and services; surrounded by foundation stones
Brahma—four-faced creator in Hindu mythology
bung—lake or swamp
buri—town

changwat—province
chao nam—sea gypsies
chedi—decorative spire containing amulets or religious icons
chiang—town or city
chofa—slender, curved temple decoration adorning the ends of roofline ridges; symbolizes the *garuda*

deva—angel or divine being
devaraja—divine king
dhammachakha—Buddhist Wheel of Law; circular motif used in Dvaravati sculpture
dharma—law and teachings of the Buddha
doi—mountain

Erawan—mythical three-headed white elephant; mount of Indra

farang—foreigner of European descent

Ganesha—elephant-headed Hindu god of literature and success
garuda—mythical animal with bird head and human torso; the mount of Vishnu; half-brother and enemy of the *naga*
gatoei—transvestite
gopura—Khmer ornamental covered gateway

hang yao—longtail boat
Hanuman—mythical monkey warrior who leads the monkey army in the Ramakien epic
hat—beach
hin—stone
ho trai—temple library

Indra—chief Hindu god of heaven; resides at the top of Mt. Meru
Issan—northeastern Thailand

Jatakas—previous life stories of the Buddha
Jiin—Chinese

kaeng—rapids
kambarian—sermon hall
kamphang—wall
kan tuei—carved wood supporting roof eaves
kaw lae—traditional fishing boats of southern Thailand
keo—gem, precious stone, honorific title
khaen—reed instrument common to northeastern Thailand
khao—hill or mountain
khon—masked dance-drama based on Ramakien stories
kinnari—mythical animal with bird and female elements
klawng—Thai drums
klong—canal
ko—island; also *koh*
kuay haeng—Chinese-style work shirt
kuti—small huts used as monk residences

laem—cape or point
lakhon—Thai classical dance-drama
lak muang—city pillar; home to animist spirits

lao khao—white liquor popular in the northeast
likay—Thai folk dance
longyi—Burmese *sarong*
luang—royal

mae chi—Buddhist nuns
mae nam—river
mahathat—honorific term for very sacred temples which contain Buddha relics
Mahayana—one of the two principal Buddhist sects; Zen and Nichiren traditions
mai ku—pan pipe played at Thai kickboxing events
Mara—evil goddess who tempted the Buddha during his meditations
maw hawn—Thai work shirt
maw kwan—triangular-shaped pillow
metta—loving kindness
mondop—temple building erected over a sacred relic, often a footprint of the Buddha
Mt. Meru—mythical mountain abode of the gods; symbolized by the *prang* and *chedi* in Thai and Khmer architecture
muang—small town or city
muay Thai—Thai kickboxing
mudra—symbolic hand gesture of the Buddha
mut mee—tie-dyed silk

naga—mythical animal; the snake which protected the Buddha against rain
nakhon—large town or city; also *nakorn*
nam tok—waterfall
nang—Thai shadow play
ngop—traditional Khmer rice farmer's hat
nirvana—a state of enlightenment
nong—lake or swamp

paknam—estuary*pa tai*—batik
Pak Thai—people of southern Thailand
Pali—scriptural language derived from Sanskrit; language of Thai Theravada texts
pa tai—batik
phanom—hill or mountain
phi pat—Thai classical orchestra
phu—hill or mountain
pong lang—musical instrument made of resonant logs
pra—honorific title given to important Buddhas and temples; also spelled *phra*

prang—solid spire-shaped temple building containing religious icons
pra phum—earth spirits
prasat—royal religious edifice with distinctive rooflines
pratu—decorated door

rai—1,600 square meters
Ramakien—Thai version of the Ramayana epic; recounts the adventures of Rama and Sita and their battles with Totsakan, king of the demons
ram muay—Thai boxing dance
ram wong—traditional Thai dance
reua duan—river express boat
reua kam fak—cross-river boat
rot thammada—ordinary bus
rot thua—tour bus

sala—open-air building used for resting
sala klang—provincial offices
samlor—three-wheeled pedicab
sanam—open grounds
sangha—monastic community
saphan—bridge
sema—sacred boundary stones placed at corners and axis of the *bot*
Shiva—Hindu god of death, destruction, and regeneration
soi—lane
songkran—Thai new year
songtao—small pickup truck used for public transportation
sra—pond
stupa—synonymous with *chedi*
suan—garden
susaan—cemetery

talaat nam—floating market
talat—market
tambon—precinct
tha—pier
thale—sea
tham—cave
thanon—road
that—northeastern religious shrine; reliquary for religious objects
thep—angel or divine being
Theravada—one of the two principal Buddhist sects; the main form of Buddhism in Thai-

land; also called Hinayana or the Lesser
Vehicle

thung—savannah

thu thong—monks who have to take ascetic
vows

tongteung—rattan

Tripitaka—Theravada Buddhist scriptures

tuk tuk—three-wheeled motorized
transportation

ubosot—another term for *bot*

vajra—thunderbolt of Vishnu

viharn—major temple building similar to but
less important than the *bot*

vipassana—Buddhist insight meditation

wai—Thai greeting with palms pressed
together

wang—royal palace

wat—temple complex, not a single building

WATS OF THAILAND

INDEX

BEACHES

NATIONAL PARKS

WATERFALLS

ABOUT THE AUTHOR

Carl Parkes, author of *Thailand Handbook, Southeast Asia Handbook,* and *Bangkok Handbook,* was born into an American Air Force family and spent his childhood in California, Nebraska, Alabama, and Japan, where his love of Asia first began. After graduating from the University of California at Santa Barbara, Carl traveled throughout Europe and later returned to work in Hawaii, Lake Tahoe, Aspen, Salt Lake City, and, finally, San Francisco.

But childhood memories of Asia continued to pull him eastward. After a 12-month journey across Asia, Carl returned to San Francisco to work as a stockbroker and plan his escape from the nine-to-five world. A chance encounter in Singapore with publisher Bill Dalton offered a more intriguing option: research and write a travel guidebook to Southeast Asia—one that addressed more than travel practicalities by exploring the region's rich culture and history.

Carl fervently believes that travel is an immensely rewarding undertaking that affirms the basic truths of life. "Travel is much more than just monuments and ruins. It's an opportunity to reach out and discover what's best about the world. Travel enriches our lives, spreads prosperity, dissolves political barriers, promotes international peace, and brings excitement and change to our lives."

Carl also believes in the importance of political, economic, and environmental issues. "Historical sites and beaches make for wonderful memories, but national agendas such as human rights and rainforest preservation are just as fascinating in their own right. Understanding the contemporary scene enriches travel experiences and opens avenues rarely explored by the visitor."

In addition to his guidebooks for Moon Publications, Carl also writes for Fodor's *Worldview Systems, PATA Travel News America,* and *Pacific Rim News Service.* Carl also has updated portions of *Indonesia Handbook* for Moon Publications, lectured onboard *Pearl Cruises,* and appeared on CNN and the Travel Channel with Arthur Frommer. In 1995, Carl won the Lowell Thomas Award from the Society of American

Travel Writers in the travel guidebook category for his *Southeast Asia Handbook.*

Besides travel writing, Carl enjoys straight-ahead jazz, photography, Anchor Steam beer, opera, art openings, poetry readings, and samba nightclubs in his favorite city of San Francisco. Future plans include more books on his favorite destinations in Southeast Asia.

ABOUT THE ILLUSTRATOR

Terra Muzick, one of America's premier illustrators of children's books, calendars, and toys, started her career with Hallmark Cards soon after graduation from art school in Ohio. In 1980, she moved to San Francisco, where she drew Snoopys before going freelance the following year. Since then, Terra has rafted in Thailand, enjoyed a massage on Kuta Beach, explored Costa Rica and Paris, and kept busy with gallery openings, Cacophony capers, and the Art Deco Society.

READER SURVEY

Knowing a bit about you and your travel experiences will help me improve this book for the next edition. Please take a few minutes to complete this form and share your tips with the next traveler. Remember to send along corrected copies of photocopied maps from this book and business cards collected from your favorite hotels and restaurants. All contributors will be acknowledged in the next edition.

The author also appreciates correspondence from expatriates living in Thailand and other local residents with special insight into travel conditions. Research correspondents are also needed to help update several Moon Handbooks to destinations in Southeast Asia. You may write to Moon Publications at the address below or contact the author directly via e-mail: cparkes@moon.com.

Send the following survey to:
Carl Parkes/Reader Survey
Thailand Handbook
Moon Travel Handbooks
5855 Beaudry St.
Emeryville, CA 94608
USA

Date of Letter: _____

1. Gender: ☐ male ☐ female

2. Age: ☐ under 25 ☐ 25-30 ☐ 31-35 ☐ 36-40
☐ 41-50 ☐ 51+

3. Status: ☐ single ☐ married

4. Income: ☐ $20K ☐ $20-30K ☐ $30-40K ☐ $40-50K
☐ $50K+

5. Occupation: _____

6. Education: ☐ high school ☐ some college ☐ college grad ☐ post grad

7. Travel style: ☐ budget ☐ moderate ☐ luxury

8. Vacations: ☐ once yearly ☐ twice yearly ☐ 3+ yearly

9. Why do you travel? _____

_____

10. What's best about travel? _____

_____

11. What's worst about travel? _____

_____

12. This Journey:
Length of time: _____
  Enough time? _____

Countries visited: _____

Countries planned for next visit: _____

Season: _____
How was the weather? _____

Travel companions? _____

Do you prefer solo travel or with companions? _____

Purpose of Trip?
  a. ☐ Pleasure b. ☐ Study   c. ☐ Work   d. ☐ Volunteer e. ☐ Hanging out

Main Activities?
  a. ☐ Sights   b. ☐ Culture   c. ☐ Beaches and outdoor activities
  d. ☐ Meeting people   e. ☐ Nightlife and entertainment
  f. ☐ Food and shopping

Main regions? Please give specific locations:
  a. ☐ Cities _____

  b. ☐ Smaller towns _____

  c. ☐ Beaches and islands _____

  d. ☐ Mountains _____

Primary modes of transportation? _____

Expenses:
  a. Total: _____
  b. Average daily expenses: _____

c. Average hotel price: _____

d. Average meal price: _____

e. Total airfare: _____

f. Shopping expenses: _____

Unexpected encounters: _____
_____

13. Favorites:

a. Countries: _____
_____
_____

b. Hotels and guesthouses (include address, price, description): _____
_____
_____

c. Restaurants (address, price range, favorite dishes): _____
_____
_____

d. Airline: _____
_____
_____

e. Cuisine: _____
_____
_____

f. Nightspots: _____
_____
_____

g. Cultural events: _____
_____
_____

h. Outdoor adventures: _____
_____
_____

i. Temples or historical sites: _____
_____
_____

j. Beaches: _____
_____

k. People: _____

_____

_____

14. This Book:

Where did you buy this book? _____

Why did you select Moon Publications? _____

What other Moon Handbooks have you used? _____

What other guidebooks have you used? _____

What is your favorite series of guides? _____

How does this book compare with other guides? _____

_____

Your opinion about the following:

   a. Hotel listings (how accurate?) _____

   b. Restaurants _____

   c. Background information _____

   d. Maps _____

   e. Charts _____

   f. Photography _____

   g. Writer's attitude _____

   h. Price of this book _____

   i. Distribution _____

   j. Design and layout _____

How accurate did you find the following information?

    a. Hotel prices _____

    _____

    b. Restaurant recommendations _____

    _____

    c. Maps _____

    _____

    d. Charts _____

    _____

    e. Writer's opinions _____

    _____

Favorite introduction section (history, government, etc., none) _____

_____

Did you use the hotel charts? _____

_____

Weakest points of this book: _____

_____

    Suggestions for improvements: _____

_____

    How does this book compare with the competition? _____

_____

15. Name and Address

_____

_____

_____

_____

Thanks for your help!

LOSE YOURSELF IN THE EXPERIENCE, NOT THE CROWD

For more than 25 years, Moon Travel Handbooks have been the guidebooks of choice for adventurous travelers. Our award-winning Handbook series provides focused, comprehensive coverage of distinct destinations all over the world. Each Handbook is like an entire bookcase of cultural insight and introductory information in one portable volume. Our goal at Moon is to give travelers all the background and practical information they'll need for an extraordinary travel experience.

The following pages include a complete list of Handbooks, covering North America and Hawaii, Mexico, Latin America and the Caribbean, and Asia and the Pacific. Please check our Web site at **www.moon.com** for current prices and editions, or see your local bookseller.

"An in-depth dunk into the land, the people and their history, arts, and politics."
—*Student Travels*

"I consider these books to be superior to Lonely Planet. When Moon produces a book it is more humorous, incisive, and off-beat."
—*Toronto Sun*

"Outdoor enthusiasts gravitate to the well-written Moon Travel Handbooks. In addition to politically correct historic and cultural features, the series focuses on flora, fauna and outdoor recreation. Maps and meticulous directions also are a trademark of Moon guides."
—*Houston Chronicle*

"Moon [Travel Handbooks] . . . bring a healthy respect to the places they investigate. Best of all, they provide a host of odd nuggets that give a place texture and prod the wary traveler from the beaten path. The finest are written with such care and insight they deserve listing as literature."
—*American Geographical Society*

"Moon Travel Handbooks offer in-depth historical essays and useful maps, enhanced by a sense of humor and a neat, compact format."
—*Swing*

"Perfect for the more adventurous, these are long on history, sightseeing and nitty-gritty information and very price-specific."
—*Columbus Dispatch*

"Moon guides manage to be comprehensive and countercultural at the same time . . . Handbooks are packed with maps, photographs, drawings, and sidebars that constitute a college-level introduction to each country's history, culture, people, and crafts."
—*National Geographic Traveler*

"Few travel guides do a better job helping travelers create their own itineraries than the Moon Travel Handbook series. The authors have a knack for homing in on the essentials."
—Colorado Springs *Gazette Telegraph*

MEXICO

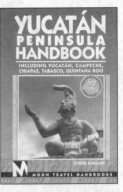

Archaeological Mexico	**$19.95**
Andrew Coe	420 pages, 27 maps
Baja Handbook	**$16.95**
Joe Cummings	540 pages, 46 maps
Cabo Handbook	**$14.95**
Joe Cummings	270 pages, 17 maps
Cancún Handbook	**$14.95**
Chicki Mallan	240 pages, 25 maps
Colonial Mexico	**$18.95**
Chicki Mallan	400 pages, 38 maps
Mexico Handbook	**$21.95**
Joe Cummings and Chicki Mallan	1,200 pages, 201 maps
Northern Mexico Handbook	**$17.95**
Joe Cummings	610 pages, 69 maps
Pacific Mexico Handbook	**$17.95**
Bruce Whipperman	580 pages, 68 maps
Puerto Vallarta Handbook	**$14.95**
Bruce Whipperman	330 pages, 36 maps
Yucatán Handbook	**$16.95**
Chicki Mallan	400 pages, 52 maps

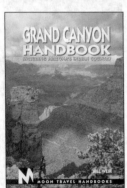

LATIN AMERICA AND THE CARIBBEAN

"Solidly packed with practical information and full of significant cultural asides that will enlighten you on the whys and wherefores of things you might easily see but not easily grasp."

—*Boston Globe*

Belize Handbook	**$15.95**
Chicki Mallan and Patti Lange	390 pages, 45 maps
Caribbean Vacations	**$18.95**
Karl Luntta	910 pages, 64 maps
Costa Rica Handbook	**$19.95**
Christopher P. Baker	780 pages, 73 maps
Cuba Handbook	**$19.95**
Christopher P. Baker	740 pages, 70 maps
Dominican Republic Handbook	**$15.95**
Gaylord Dold	420 pages, 24 maps
Ecuador Handbook	**$16.95**
Julian Smith	450 pages, 43 maps
Honduras Handbook	**$15.95**
Chris Humphrey	330 pages, 40 maps
Jamaica Handbook	**$15.95**
Karl Luntta	330 pages, 17 maps
Virgin Islands Handbook	**$13.95**
Karl Luntta	220 pages, 19 maps

NORTH AMERICA AND HAWAII

"These domestic guides convey the same sense of exoticism that their foreign counterparts do, making home-country travel seem like far-flung adventure."

—*Sierra Magazine*

Alaska-Yukon Handbook	**$17.95**
Deke Castleman and Don Pitcher	530 pages, 92 maps
Alberta and the Northwest Territories Handbook	**$18.95**
Andrew Hempstead	520 pages, 79 maps
Arizona Handbook	**$18.95**
Bill Weir	600 pages, 36 maps
Atlantic Canada Handbook	**$18.95**
Mark Morris	490 pages, 60 maps
Big Island of Hawaii Handbook	**$15.95**
J.D. Bisignani	390 pages, 25 maps
Boston Handbook	**$13.95**
Jeff Perk	200 pages, 20 maps
British Columbia Handbook	**$16.95**
Jane King and Andrew Hempstead	430 pages, 69 maps

Canadian Rockies Handbook	**$14.95**
Andrew Hempstead	220 pages, 22 maps
Colorado Handbook	**$17.95**
Stephen Metzger	480 pages, 46 maps
Georgia Handbook	**$17.95**
Kap Stann	380 pages, 44 maps
Grand Canyon Handbook	**$14.95**
Bill Weir	220 pages, 10 maps
Hawaii Handbook	**$19.95**
J.D. Bisignani	1,030 pages, 88 maps
Honolulu-Waikiki Handbook	**$14.95**
J.D. Bisignani	360 pages, 20 maps
Idaho Handbook	**$18.95**
Don Root	610 pages, 42 maps
Kauai Handbook	**$15.95**
J.D. Bisignani	320 pages, 23 maps
Los Angeles Handbook	**$16.95**
Kim Weir	370 pages, 15 maps
Maine Handbook	**$18.95**
Kathleen M. Brandes	660 pages, 27 maps
Massachusetts Handbook	**$18.95**
Jeff Perk	600 pages, 23 maps
Maui Handbook	**$15.95**
J.D. Bisignani	450 pages, 37 maps
Michigan Handbook	**$15.95**
Tina Lassen	360 pages, 32 maps
Montana Handbook	**$17.95**
Judy Jewell and W.C. McRae	490 pages, 52 maps
Nevada Handbook	**$18.95**
Deke Castleman	530 pages, 40 maps
New Hampshire Handbook	**$18.95**
Steve Lantos	500 pages, 18 maps
New Mexico Handbook	**$15.95**
Stephen Metzger	360 pages, 47 maps
New York Handbook	**$19.95**
Christiane Bird	780 pages, 95 maps
New York City Handbook	**$13.95**
Christiane Bird	300 pages, 20 maps
North Carolina Handbook	**$14.95**
Rob Hirtz and Jenny Daughtry Hirtz	320 pages, 27 maps
Northern California Handbook	**$19.95**
Kim Weir	800 pages, 50 maps
Ohio Handbook	**$15.95**
David K. Wright	340 pages, 18 maps
Oregon Handbook	**$17.95**
Stuart Warren and Ted Long Ishikawa	590 pages, 34 maps

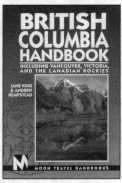

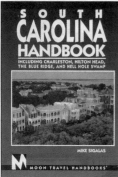

Pennsylvania Handbook	$18.95
Joanne Miller	448 pages, 40 maps
Road Trip USA	**$24.00**
Jamie Jensen	940 pages, 175 maps
Road Trip USA Getaways: Chicago	**$9.95**
	60 pages, 1 map
Road Trip USA Getaways: Seattle	**$9.95**
	60 pages, 1 map
Santa Fe-Taos Handbook	**$13.95**
Stephen Metzger	160 pages, 13 maps
South Carolina Handbook	**$16.95**
Mike Sigalas	400 pages, 20 maps
Southern California Handbook	**$19.95**
Kim Weir	720 pages, 26 maps
Tennessee Handbook	**$17.95**
Jeff Bradley	530 pages, 42 maps
Texas Handbook	**$18.95**
Joe Cummings	690 pages, 70 maps
Utah Handbook	**$17.95**
Bill Weir and W.C. McRae	490 pages, 40 maps
Virginia Handbook	**$15.95**
Julian Smith	410 pages, 37 maps
Washington Handbook	**$19.95**
Don Pitcher	840 pages, 111 maps
Wisconsin Handbook	**$18.95**
Thomas Huhti	590 pages, 69 maps
Wyoming Handbook	**$17.95**
Don Pitcher	610 pages, 80 maps

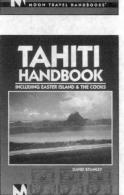

ASIA AND THE PACIFIC

"Scores of maps, detailed practical info down to business hours of small-town libraries. You can't beat the Asian titles for sheer heft. (The) series is sort of an American Lonely Planet, with better writing but fewer titles. (The) individual voice of researchers comes through."

—Travel & Leisure

Australia Handbook	**$21.95**
Marael Johnson, Andrew Hempstead,	
and Nadina Purdon	940 pages, 141 maps
Bali Handbook	**$19.95**
Bill Dalton	750 pages, 54 maps
Fiji Islands Handbook	**$14.95**
David Stanley	350 pages, 42 maps
Hong Kong Handbook	**$16.95**
Kerry Moran	378 pages, 49 maps

Indonesia Handbook	**$25.00**
Bill Dalton	1,380 pages, 249 maps
Micronesia Handbook	**$16.95**
Neil M. Levy	340 pages, 70 maps
Nepal Handbook	**$18.95**
Kerry Moran	490 pages, 51 maps
New Zealand Handbook	**$19.95**
Jane King	620 pages, 81 maps
Outback Australia Handbook	**$18.95**
Marael Johnson	450 pages, 57 maps
Philippines Handbook	**$17.95**
Peter Harper and Laurie Fullerton	670 pages, 116 maps
Singapore Handbook	**$15.95**
Carl Parkes	350 pages, 29 maps
South Korea Handbook	**$19.95**
Robert Nilsen	820 pages, 141 maps
South Pacific Handbook	**$24.00**
David Stanley	920 pages, 147 maps
Southeast Asia Handbook	**$21.95**
Carl Parkes	1,080 pages, 204 maps
Tahiti Handbook	**$15.95**
David Stanley	450 pages, 51 maps
Thailand Handbook	**$19.95**
Carl Parkes	860 pages, 142 maps
Vietnam, Cambodia & Laos Handbook	**$18.95**
Michael Buckley	760 pages, 116 maps

OTHER GREAT TITLES FROM MOON

"For hardy wanderers, few guides come more highly recommended than the Handbooks. They include good maps, steer clear of fluff and flackery, and offer plenty of money-saving tips. They also give you the kind of information that visitors to strange lands—on any budget—need to survive."

—US News & World Report

Moon Handbook	**$10.00**
Carl Koppeschaar	150 pages, 8 maps
The Practical Nomad: How to Travel Around the World	**$17.95**
Edward Hasbrouck	580 pages
Staying Healthy in Asia, Africa, and Latin America	**$11.95**
Dirk Schroeder	230 pages, 4 maps

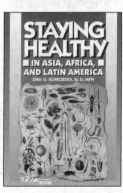

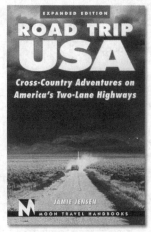

U.S.~METRIC CONVERSION

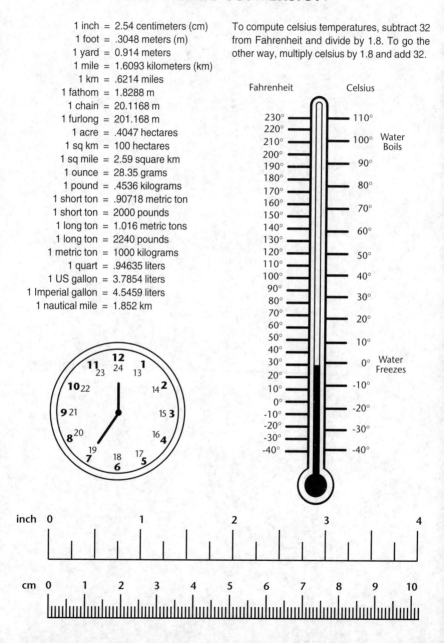

1 inch	=	2.54 centimeters (cm)
1 foot	=	.3048 meters (m)
1 yard	=	0.914 meters
1 mile	=	1.6093 kilometers (km)
1 km	=	.6214 miles
1 fathom	=	1.8288 m
1 chain	=	20.1168 m
1 furlong	=	201.168 m
1 acre	=	.4047 hectares
1 sq km	=	100 hectares
1 sq mile	=	2.59 square km
1 ounce	=	28.35 grams
1 pound	=	.4536 kilograms
1 short ton	=	.90718 metric ton
1 short ton	=	2000 pounds
1 long ton	=	1.016 metric tons
1 long ton	=	2240 pounds
1 metric ton	=	1000 kilograms
1 quart	=	.94635 liters
1 US gallon	=	3.7854 liters
1 Imperial gallon	=	4.5459 liters
1 nautical mile	=	1.852 km

To compute celsius temperatures, subtract 32 from Fahrenheit and divide by 1.8. To go the other way, multiply celsius by 1.8 and add 32.

Fahrenheit   Celsius

230° — 110°
220°
210° — 100°   Water Boils
200°
190° — 90°
180°
170° — 80°
160°
150° — 70°
140° — 60°
130°
120° — 50°
110°
100° — 40°
90°
80° — 30°
70°
60° — 20°
50°
40° — 10°
30° — 0°   Water Freezes
20°
10° — -10°
0°
-10° — -20°
-20° — -30°
-30°
-40° — -40°

inch 0   1   2   3   4

cm 0 1 2 3 4 5 6 7 8 9 10

NOTES